Racial and Ethnic Diversity in Higher Education

Edited by

Caroline Sotello Viernes Turner, Lead Editor
University of Minnesota

Mildred Garcia
Montclair State University

Amaury Nora
University of Illinois at Chicago

Laura I. Rendón
Arizona State University

ASHE READER SERIES
Barbara Townsend, Series Editor

SIMON & SCHUSTER
CUSTOM PUBLISHING

Printed in the United States of America

10 9 8 7 6 5 4 3 2 1

ISBN 0–536–59003-6
BA 0168

SIMON & SCHUSTER CUSTOM PUBLISHING
160 Gould Street/Needham Heights, MA 02194
Simon & Schuster Education Group

COPYRIGHT ACKNOWLEDGMENTS

The ASHE Reader Series

The ASHE Reader Series presents a collection of high quality readers on topics of sweeping interest in today's higher education scene. The books are designed to be used as supplementary text material in courses in the field of higher education or as reference. They reflect the collective ideas of those who teach in particular areas.

NEW TEACHING AND LEARNING IN THE COLLEGE CLASSROOM

Edited by Kenneth A. Feldman and Michael B. Paulsen

A comprehensive review of classic and recent research in the area, TEACHING AND LEARNING IN THE COLLEGE CLASSROOM addresses issues from diverse theoretical and philosophical perspectives. Each section includes quantitative and qualitative research, a separate introductory essay, research reports, literature reviews, theoretical essays, and practitioner-oriented articles. It emphasizes teacher-student and student-student interaction. It considers multicultural and gender issues and contains practical teaching strategies based on research.

Paperbound 704 pages ISBN 0-536-58535-0

NEW ASSESSMENT AND PROGRAM EVALUATION

Edited by Joan S. Stark and Alice Thomas

This reader effectively provides the broad perspective necessary for the study of assessment by consolidating articles from a wide range of sources, some not easily obtained. By addressing such topics as the historical and philosophical context and ethical issues, this volume will help readers develop the necessary assessment skills, attitudes and knowledge to conduct and supervise studies and program reviews or to be informed clients inside or outside the academic environment.

Paperbound 832 pages ISBN 0-536-58586-5

COMMUNITY COLLEGES

Edited by James L. Ratcliff

This updated edition includes new information on the diversity of the student population and features a special focus on community college scholarship and faculty renewal. It will give you and your students a review of the current community college systems in American history, philosophy, and purpose: organization, administration, and finance; programs and services; students; professional staff; and the social role.

Paperbound 503 pages ISBN 0-536-58571-7

QUALITATIVE RESEARCH IN HIGHER EDUCATION:
Experiencing Alternative Perspectives and Approaches

Edited by Clifton E. Conrad, Anna Neuman, Jennifer Grant Haworth, and Patricia Scott

Designed to help students and teachers prepare for, enter into, participate in, reflect on, and give voice to the experience of doing qualitative research. Organized around six topics: Explicating Frames of Reference, Approaching Inquiry, Doing Fieldwork, Interacting with Self and Other, Creating a Text, Reading a Text.

Paperbound 600 pages ISBN 0-536-58417-0

WOMEN IN HIGHER EDUCATION: A Feminist Perspective

Edited by Judith Glazer, Estela Bensimon, and Barbara Townsend

Essays representing the best of feminist scholarship in the field of higher education on four main themes: Theoretical and Research Perspectives, Context Historical, Social, and Professional, Institutional, Women in Academe: As Student, Faculty, Administrators, and Trustees, and The Transformation of Knowledge: Circular Change and Feminist Pedagogy.

Paperbound 600 pages ISBN 0-536-58351-0

FOUNDATIONS OF AMERICAN HIGHER EDUCATION

Edited by James L. Bess

A comprehensive introduction to the basics of American higher education—45 articles by some of today's most respected leaders in the field, in six parts: The Scope of Higher Education in American Society, The Participants, The Conduct of Education and Research, The Management of the College or University, Innovation, Change, and the Future, The Study and Practice of Higher Education Administration.

Paperbound 772 pages ISBN 0-536-58013-8

THE HISTORY OF HIGHER EDUCATION

Edited by Lester E. Goodchild and Harold S. Wechsler

Included are an introductory essay on American higher education historiography; introductory overviews of each of the five chronological periods of higher education; in-depth scholarly analyses from journal articles, book chapters, and essays; and the use of primary readings to capture the flavor and meaning of important issues for each period.

Paperbound 675 pages ISBN 0-536-57566-5

ORGANIZATION AND GOVERNANCE IN HIGHER EDUCATION, Fourth Edition

Edited by Marvin W. Peterson, with Associate Editors Ellen E. Chaffee and Theodore H. White

The selections not only reflect the changing views of colleges and universities as organizations, but also highlight the areas of literature applied to higher education that need to be addressed. The text is divided into three parts: Organization Theory and Models, Governance and Management Processes, and Leadership Perspectives.

Paperbound 475 pages ISBN 0-536-57981-4

FINANCE IN HIGHER EDUCATION

Edited by Dave Breneman, Larry L. Leslie and Richard E. Anderson

Practical and theoretical, the selections look at the financial management of colleges and universities, higher education economies, and federal and state policies, and represent a number of divergent perspectives and opinions.

Paperbound 450 pages ISBN 0-536-58352-8

COLLEGE STUDENTS

Edited by Frances Stage, Guadelupe Anaya, John Bean, Don Hossler, and George D. Kuh

To Order:

To order copies of these titles for your class, please contact your campus bookstore and provide them with the quantity and ISBN. You can receive a complimentary desk copy with an order of 10 or more copies.

To order copies for yourself, simply call Simon & Schuster Custom Publishing at 800-428-4466 (or 617-455-7000 in Massachusetts and Canada) from 8:30 to 5:00 EST.

Contents

PART VI RESEARCH ISSUES

Acknowledgments

Many challenges, both personal and professional, made this project a challenge to complete. For example, this anthology presents several articles which were not readily available to the co-editors or to Simon and Schuster Custom Publishing. Thus, the assistance of the Advisory Board and the support of a very persistent graduate student made this reader a possibility. We extend our appreciation to the Advisory Board for their generosity in sharing syllabi and bibliographies, offering suggestions, and evaluating sections. The following scholars participated in this process

Mary Belgarde	Turtle Mountain Community College
Estela Bensimon	University of Southern California
Alberto Cabrera	State University of New York, Albany
May Chen	Los Angeles Community College District
William Harvey	University of Wisconsin, Milwaukee
Elizabeth Higginbotham	University of Memphis
Sylvia Hurtado	University of Michigan
Berta Vigil Laden	Vanderbilt University
Michael Nettles	University of Michigan
Michael Olivas	University of Houston
Cheryl Presley	Colorado State University
Daryl Smith	The Claremont Graduate School
Patrick Terenzini	The Pennsylvania State University
James Valadez	North Carolina State University
Nancy Walters	Minnesota Higher Education Coordinating Board
Chunsheng Zhang	Bowling Green State University

Special recognition is due to Willie Johnson, a University of Minnesota doctoral candidate and tenured faculty member at Normandale Community College, for his contribution to the preparation and completion of this anthology.

We are indebted to the staff of the University of Minnesota Department of Educational Policy and Administration for providing funding for research assistance and supplies in support of this project.

We are grateful to Daryl Smith, past editor of the ASHE Reader Series, and Barbara Townsend, present editor of the ASHE Reader Series, for their cogent advice and unwavering support throughout the project. Special thanks are also due to Kathy Kourian and Kristen Colman of Simon and Schuster Custom Publishing for their assistance and efforts in this project.

A Note to the Reader

This edition of the *Racial and Ethnic Diversity in Higher Education* is expected to be printed for approximately three academic years, beginning in the Spring of 1996. It is the policy of the *ASHE Reader* series to update the collection of readings included in each *Reader* every two or three years.

A new edition of this *Reader* is anticipated. We would appreciate your comments on the current *Reader* and suggestions for improvement. Specifically, we would like to know which articles, documents and/or book chapters you found particularly helpful, thought-provoking, or informative. We would like to know how you came to use this *Reader* as well, so that future editions can be targeted to your specific needs. Lastly, we ask your help in identifying professional and academic literature which should be included in future editions of this *ASHE Reader*.

Please send your suggestions, comments, and recommendations regarding this *ASHE Reader* to the editor:

Caroline Turner, Associate Professor
Department of Educational Policy and Administration
College of Education and Human Development
330 Wulling Hall
86 Pleasant St. SE
University of Minnesota—
Twin Cities Campus
Minneapolis, MN 55455

Suggestions regarding other topics which could be addressed through the *ASHE Reader* series should be sent to:

Barbara Townsend, Editor
ASHE Reader
Department of Educational Leadership
University of Memphis
Patterson Hall 113,
Memphis, TN 38152

Higher Education's Diverse Racial/Ethnic Populations

Introduction

Caroline Sotello Viernes Turner, Lead Editor
with Mildred Garcia, Amaury Nora, and Laura Rendón

During the past two decades there have been dramatic changes in the face, or more accurately faces, of American college students, faculty, and administrators. For example, figures on nation-wide enrollments indicate the growing diversity of our students. According to these figures, there has been a substantial increase in the numbers of individuals from nonmajority racial and ethnic groups and in the number of women who are enrolled in American colleges and universities. The numbers of students with special needs, including the physically challenged and those with learning disabilities, have grown as society's increasing sensitivity to problems of physical and educational access has been translated into legislation. In addition, older students constitute an ever-increasing percentage of higher education enrollment, reflecting both the aging of the general population and the growing trend of career changes during adulthood. Finally, the increasing availability of financial aid and targeted recruiting have resulted in the enrollment of more individuals from financially disadvantaged families. The students on our campuses are diverse not only in terms of background characteristics they bring with them, but also with respect to membership in student subcultures. Both students and faculty at institutions of higher education who come from different ethnic backgrounds are likely to be culturally different. Furthermore, even students and faculty who share the same ethnic culture may differ subcultur-ally because of differences in their sex, age, physical, financial, or educational status, or their campus peer group memberships. There is much diversity within diversity. Differences between and within each racial/ethnic group abound.

Sociologists have a long tradition of studying individuals and groups that are viewed as "different" from the social norms. There are many definitions of difference or ways to think about difference in American society (Turner and Louis, in press). Difference can be defined as diversity excluded or marginalized. Hill's essay on "Multi-Culturalism: The Crucial Philosophical and Organizational Issues" describes this phenomenon in the context of higher education by stating, for example, that "marginalization ends and conversations of respect begin when the curriculum is reconceived to be unimplementable without the central participation of the currently excluded and marginalized." (p. 45)

Another response to difference is illustrated by the notion that inclusion is costly and "takes away" instead of adding to the educational experiences of others. Duster (1991), in his study of student diversity at the University of California at Berkeley, underscores the importance of physical proximity and collaboration for breaking down stereotypes on a university campus. He states: "Seeing others from a distance and being seen from a distance" allows individuals to maintain stereotypes of each other. (p. 15) From this perspective, diversity is seen as vital for learning and understanding.

Difference can also preserve advantage or status in our society. Thus, difference can be valued by those who are more advantaged or by those who are viewed as the norm against which all else is judged. Duster (1991) expresses the importance of this form of difference as advantage in the following remarks:

> Being culturally competent in the context of Anglo-conformity has always meant being able to participate in a monocultural (Anglo-Saxon) world. For majority group members, this presents fewer problems. Indeed, it can be viewed as an advantage conferred at birth. For members of underrepresented groups, however, the very process of becoming a component in the culture of the dominant group is itself an obstacle, a barrier. (p. 52)

Many of the readings presented here provide further examples of this phenomenon for racial/ethnic minorities in higher education settings. For example, the Cuadraz article describes the importance of having access to "appropriate" cultural capital for Chicana "Scholarship Women." Unequal access to the dominant cultural capital comprises disadvantage.

In the main, studies and essays included here indicate that people of color (whether student, staff, or faculty) do not find a positive level of comfort on college campuses. Individuals within higher education may perceive that they are offering a welcoming environment to those who are new to campus. However, another response to difference has been to treat the "others" as guests and not as a part of the family. Ron Wakabayashi, National Director of the Japanese American Citizens League, expressed this sense of exclusion very well. He said, "We feel that we're a guest in someone else's house, that we can never relax and put our feet up on the table" (quoted be Lee Daniels 1991, p. 5). Daniels points out that guests are not family, whose foibles and mistakes are tolerated. On the contrary, guests must follow the family's wishes without question, keep out of certain rooms in the house, and always be on their best behavior. Like students of color in the university climate, guests have no history in the house they occupy. There are no photographs on the wall that reflect their image. Their paraphernalia, paintings, scents, and sounds do not appear in the house. There are many barriers for students and staff who constantly occupy guest status that keep them from doing their best work. (Turner, p. 356)

There are so many ways in which this reader could be structured to address the topic of racial/ethnic diversity in higher education. Other important topics and issues of diversity in higher education could be added to this volume, but due to time and space constraints the project was limited. Manuscripts in this anthology present ways in which the authors observe and experience racial/ethnic difference in American higher education institutions. Differences are discussed from an historical perspective, providing a context for the many contemporary experiences described in these writings by and about students, staff, and faculty. Authors provide the reader with perspectives from their observations and study of African Americans, Asian Americans, Native Americans, and Latinos within the American higher education context. This collection of readings highlights the work, research perspectives, and theoretical models of many scholars, and includes exemplary articles on diversity in higher education published in mainstream and non-mainstream manuscript outlets.

This text is presented as only one resource on ethnic/racial diversity available for use by faculty, staff, and students in higher education. Administrators and policy makers who are addressing issues of diversity at the level of the individual college or state/national higher education systems may also find the content of these readings helpful in informing their decision-making processes. For example, statistics provide evidence about the underrepresentation of faculty, staff, and students of color in higher education. Why is this the case? What scholars examine in the published higher education literature provides an insight to some of the possible solutions to this situation. Most of the writings presented here focus on the examination of racial and ethnic diversity on predominantly white college campuses. As a result, these perspectives tell us a great deal about past and present situations for faculty, staff, and students of color within these contexts. More writing needs to be done to examine racial/ethnic diversity issues in other institutional contexts such as the tribal college, the historically black college, or the predominantly Hispanic college.

This text is organized in six sections: Racial/Ethnic Diversity in Higher Education History; Curriculum, Teaching and Learning; Students; Faculty; Administration, Leadership, and Governance; and Research Issues. Articles presented under each category are only a sampling of the tremendous work produced by scholars examining issues of race and ethnicity in higher education. Many excellent articles were not included in the final anthology due to space and monetary constraints. Articles included here address the notions of difference as presented in the preceding paragraphs.

Racial/Ethnic Diversity in Higher Education History

Past practices and occurrences provide a context for understanding present situations and provide needed understanding for proceeding into the future. As Steinberg (1989) has written, pluralism in the United States originated from a system of conquest, slavery, and exploitation of foreign labor creating a negative environment for the preservation or appreciation of racial/ ethnic difference. The articles in this section demonstrate how this history, one of exclusion, has influenced past and present outcomes for people of color in higher education.

Curriculum, Teaching, and Learning

In the words of Estela Bensimon (1994), "multiculturalism rejects the notion that there is a single perspective, interpretation . . . there are many bodies of knowledge and different ways of knowing . . . education can come to encompass far more diverse knowledge than it does now." (p. 4)

The implementation of a multicultural curriculum is done in the classroom and is, thus, closely linked to teaching and learning. Adams (1992) challenges the common belief that college classrooms are culturally neutral, stating, "While most faculty and students who have been socialized into the traditional classroom culture are scarcely aware of its existence, those students who have not already been socialized into this culture by previous schooling or a congruent home or community culture often become painfully aware of it . . . their values and beliefs are in conflict with many traditionally sanctioned classroom procedures." (p. 5) Garcia and Smith (in press) note that the process of curriculum transformation must be manifested not only in what is to be taught but who is to teach it and how it is to be taught.

Readings included in this section present a view from the perspective of individuals who have traditionally been excluded in the creation of knowledge presented in the college curriculum. These works examine the curriculum transformation movement, which also recognizes the necessity of the transformed classroom.

Students

A recent report by the Carnegie Foundation for the Advancement of Teaching (1990) notes "alarming signals that racial and ethnic divisions are deepening on the nation's campuses," a problem that has to do with "more than access; it has to do with the lack of support minority students feel once they have enrolled." (p. 26) In summarizing research from the late 1960s through the 1980s on college effects on students, Pascarella and Terenzini (1991) make the following observation:

> It is clear that many of the most important effects of college occur through students' interpersonal experiences with faculty members and other students. It is equally clear that the academic, social, and psychological worlds inhabited by most nonwhite students on predominantly white campuses are substantially different in almost every respect from those of their white peers. (p. 644)

Currently, significant increases in the number of college-going students marked by diversity in race/ethnicity as well as diversity—for example, in student disability, socioeconomic status, immigrant status, and alternative lifestyles—has taken place. These demographic shifts have prompted a challenge to the largely unexamined practices in higher education. Included in this volume are published works by scholars studying higher education processes and practices related to the experiences of students of color. These selections serve to increase the knowledge base about students of color in higher education. They also challenge assumptions which previously affected theory development and practice. Previous theories, for example, treated these students as the "problem" to be fixed. Thus, they were cast in a marginal status and situated as outsiders needing to be acculturated into the formal and informal networks of the academy in order to attain academic success as defined by the dominant culture. College retention programs failed to understand the cultural differences among first-generation students as well as students of color which made it necessary for these students to negotiate two cultures in their efforts to make connections with institutional life. Recent studies, such as those included in this volume, examine the nature of racial/ethnic minority student experiences in college from their perspective. While most manuscripts focus on student experience within a predominantly white two- and four-year college setting, discussion of the role of historically black colleges and tribal colleges in educating students of color is also included.

While the selections presented here represent some of the most substantive and enlightening pieces on students of color, the literature on ethnic/racial minority college students is still emerging. The areas, to name a few, of student retention, the first-year college experience, and the interactive nature of institutional dimensions and the socialization experiences of ethnic/racial minority students continue to be explored. In addition, new theoretical frameworks which examine these concerns will likely be addressed in future work.

Faculty

Overall, the literature examining the situation for faculty of color in academe highlights the socialization and isolation that faculty of color face. Articles included here focus primarily on faculty experience at the four-year college. Two-year college contexts are described by Carter and Ottinger (1992) and Opp and Smith (1992). More work needs to be done on the experience of faculty of color in the two-year college. There are a number of common themes, approaches, and observations that pervade the literature on racial/ethnic minority faculty development. The image of a pipeline is frequently used to describe the linkage between the availability of faculty of color, the training of minority graduate students, the accessibility of undergraduate education for minorities, and the success of minority students at the elementary and secondary school levels. The presence of "leaks" in this pipeline provides one explanation for underrepresentation.

Delving beyond this explanation, however, researchers included here have also identified barriers within academia itself that hinder minority faculty recruitment and retention. Among these obstacles are

1. *Isolation/Lack of mentoring opportunities.* Minority faculty find themselves outside the informal networks of the department. Thus, untenured minority professors find themselves isolated and struggling through the faculty socialization process alone.

2. *Occupational stress.* The existing underrepresentation of minority men and women in academe and the desire of universities to have minority representation on committees combine to place formidable responsibilities on the shoulders of minority faculty.

3. *Institutional Racism.* Minority faculty find that research on minority issues is not considered legitimate work, particularly if articles are published in journals that are not "mainstream."

4. *The "token hire" misconception.* Minority faculty report that colleagues expect them to be less qualified or to be less likely to make contributions in research. Some have noted a pervasive attitude among the faculty of complacency, manifested in the belief that hiring one minority person in a department should be sufficient.

Another obstacle to the employment of racial/ethnic minorities among the tenure track faculty ranks is underemployment. Lomperis (1990) documents this phenomenon for women in academe by pointing to the disproportionate hiring of women for part-time and non–tenure-track faculty positions. Further study of this situation as it relates to racial/ethnic minorities needs to be undertaken.

Administration, Leadership, and Governance

There are more questions than answers that abound when addressing this section. How will administrators organize and lead our colleges and universities in the 21st century? How will campuses prepare our students for a pluralistic and global society? How will campus policies, practices, and structures address the challenges of our fast-changing environment?

According to these and other papers presented in this volume, higher education administration and leadership must address the problem of underrepresentation of racial and ethnic minority group members among faculty, students, and administrators in colleges and universities. Policy responses to eradicate educational disparities and racial inequality are needed. General retrenchment in higher education, budget cutbacks, and the shifting demographics of the college-age population provide a challenging context within which academic leadership must address the improvement of access of persons of all races and ethnic origins to quality higher education opportunities.

A beginning list of specific institutional actions to address the above-stated issues can be found within the articles presented here. For example, Smith (1989) states the importance of creating a campus which emphasizes cooperation, collaboration, and community. She states that this step may challenge the traditional mission and values of higher education, where competition and individualism are entrenched values. Yet it is an important step. Smith asks, "Have we gone too far in encouraging competitive and highly individualistic practices at the expense of concern for the community and at the expense of good learning?" (p. 58) Providing opportunities and incentives for diverse groups of students, faculty, and/or staff to collaborate on various campus endeavors (teaching, research, curriculum design, etc.) is also underscored. In another article, Hill (1991) argues that if a college or university is truly committed to democratic pluralism, then the priorities and the core of the organization must be changed. He states that in such a college, the faculty could not do their everyday teaching and research without being in conversation with the representatives of different cultures.

As in other sections of this text, much more discussion and study of issues brought up here needs to take place. However, these manuscripts provide an initial basis to open such explorations.

Research Issues

Present research in higher education must grapple not only with diverse populations of students and faculty but also with a diverse and complex set of issues. Both the increasing diversity of American college students and faculty and the complexity of issues being studied have implications for research frameworks and methods. For example, the cultural and subcultural diversity of students and faculty calls for the use of methods that allow the researcher to be sensitive to diverse frames of reference, many of which may be quite different from the investigator's own. A standardized questionnaire developed from the researcher's own frame of reference will not adequately capture the experiences and attitudes of students who have diverse racial or ethnic backgrounds or who are subculturally diverse due to peer group affiliation. Rather, the researcher also needs to be able to draw upon the rich research methodology developed by anthropologists and others who have traditionally engaged in cross-cultural research. The researcher needs to ground his or her understanding of what happens to students and faculty in their own understanding of specific events.

The body of literature presented here expands on the issue of diversity by examining different theoretical (or conceptual) frameworks needed to be considered in studying students and faculty in higher education institutions. The different perspectives not only consider the complex student and faculty-related issues that researchers in higher education strive to understand, but also consider different methodological perspectives for the selection of research and assessment methods. Finally, the literature presents some alternative research strategies for examining the experiences of diverse student bodies and faculty relative to complex issues.

Conclusion

Institutions of higher education across the United Stated have yet to provide a welcoming environment for students, faculty, and staff of color. Some steps toward campus transformation are being implemented. Special programs have been established to offer support to students and staff of color, and they are important. Still, change must take another step forward or, rather, a leap forward. Deeply embedded values, the very culture itself, must undergo transformation so the institution comes to belong as much to people of color as to the majority culture.

Higher education institutions must seize the opportunities that the goal of diversity brings to reexamine missions and values. Although strong institutional statements in support of diversity by faculty and administrative leaders are helpful, strong actions that change the "way things are usually done around here" will do more than strong statements to nurture an open and inclusive climate. An inclusiveness is needed that means more than "come on in, but don't change anything." (Martha Minnow in Carnegie Foundation, 1990, p. 35)

An American Indian student interviewed for a study (Turner, Summer 1994, p. 368) said, "There is a desire here to be gainfully employed, to help others, to go on and become a professional. Surely if students are willing to take these risks [navigating an alien environment], higher education should be able to respond." As an African-American staff respondent said, "Too often what occurs is a mending of the exterior, rather than addressing the core issues." Colleges and universities must put their houses in order, not just patching holes and adding rooms, but renovating them from the inside out so that there is space and permission for all students to put their feet up on the table.

Many in the academic community will welcome the dialogue needed for the transformation of our educational institutions as progress or a form of rebirth; others who have invested much of their lives in building these institutions may experience the radical change as a kind of death and a great loss. Such responses are understandable. Nevertheless, there must be a resolution of these differences in order for education to meet the fast-changing needs of our society.

References[1]

Adams, Maurianne. (Spring 1992). "Cultural Inclusion in the American College Classroom," in Laura L.B. Border and Nancy Van Note Chism (Eds.) *New Directions for Teaching and Learning: Teaching for Diversity*, no. 49. San Francisco: Jossey-Bass Publishers, pp. 5–17.

Bensimon, Estela Mara. (1994). "Philosophical Concepts: The Contested Meanings of Multicultural Education" in Estela Bensimon (Ed.) *Multicultural Teaching and Learning: Strategies for Change in Higher Education*. The Pennsylvania State University: National Center on Postsecondary Teaching, Learning, and Assessment.

The Carnegie Foundation for the Advancement of Teaching. (1990). *Campus Life: In Search of Community*. Lawrenceville, New Jersey: Princeton University Press.

Daniels, Lee A. (1991) "Only the Appearance of Diversity: Higher Education and the Pluralistic Ideal in the 1980s and 1990s." *Policy Perspectives*. Philadelphia: The Pew Higher Education Research Program.

---

[1] Does not include references to authors whose selections are part of this anthology.

Duster, Troy. (November, 1991). *The Diversity Project: Final Report*. University of California at Berkeley: Institute for Social Change.

Garcia, Mildred and Daryl Smith. (In press). "Curriculum for the 21st Century in Higher Education: The Process of Transformation," in L. Rendon and R. Hope (Eds.) *Educating A New Majority*. San Francisco: Jossey-Bass.

Lomperis, Ana Maria Turner. (November/December 1990). "Are Women Changing the Nature of the Academic Profession?" *Journal of Higher Education*, vol. 61, no. 6, pp. 643–677.

Pascarella, Ernest T. and Patrick T. Terenzini. (1991). *How College Affects Students*. San Francisco: Jossey-Bass.

Turner, Caroline Sotello Viernes. (Summer 1994). "Guests in Someone Else's House: Students of Color." *Review of Higher Education,* vol. 17, no. 4, pp. 355–370.

Turner, Caroline Sotello Viernes, and Karen Seashore Louis. (In press). "Society's Response to Differences: A Sociological Perspective" Special issue of *Remedial and Special Education*.

PART I
RACIAL/ETHNIC DIVERSITY
IN
HIGHER EDUCATION HISTORY

History of American Indian Community Colleges

W. Larry Belgarde

In 1968, the Navajo Nation of southwestern United States founded the first American Indian community college, Navajo Community College (NCC). Four years later on Columbus Day, October, 1972, NCC joined with five other American Indian community Colleges—Hehaka Sapa College of D-Q University (Davis, CA), Oglala Lakota Community College (Kyle, SD), Sinte Gleska College (Rosebud, SD), Turtle Mountain Community College (Belcourt, ND), and Standing Rock Community College (Fort Yates, ND)—to form the American Indian Higher Education Consortium (AIHEC). These colleges would be joined by others throughout the 1970s and 1980s to comprise the American Indian controlled community college movement, establishing a new genre of higher education institutions.

Early Indian Higher Education Efforts

Until the late twentieth century, colleges had exerted little effort to provide higher education services to American Indians. What efforts they made were sporadic and short-lived. In colonial America, Harvard College stated its intention "to educate English and Indian youth of this country in knowledge and Godliness" (Morison, 1935). But by 1665 the Indian college building at Harvard housed exclusively English scholars and was completely torn down in 1698. Similarly, William and Mary College reflected a total enrollment of 16 Indian youths through 1776 at which time, "The Indian school was abandoned in consequence of the loss of the manor of Brafferton by the Revolution" (Morrison, 1874). Dartmouth abandoned its Indian higher education efforts after enrolling a grand total of 25 Indian students, and only graduating three: Daniel Simons in 1777, Peter Pohquonnopeet in 1780, and Lewis Vincent in 1781 (Chase, 1891).

In post-Revolution America, the responsibility to educate Indians devolved to the federal government. The U.S. Constitution authorized the federal government "To regulate commerce with foreign nations, and among the several states, and with Indian tribes." This clause became broadly interpreted as relieving the states of the responsibility of providing colleges or, indeed, any education services to Indians. Instead, between 1778 and 1871, the United States dealt with Indian nations as quasi-sovereign entities making numerous treaties, most of which included federal educational services responsibilities. Thompson (1978) reported that 97 treaties contained education-related clauses. The underlying themes of federal education services were Christianization, forced acculturation, and assimilation of Indians. To implement these themes, the government supported efforts to remove Indians from their local settings and enroll them in boarding schools—some of which provided postsecondary vocational training as well as elementary and secondary schooling.

By 1842, 37 such schools were in place; increasing to 106 in 1881. Such schools as General Pratt's Indian Industrial Training School in Carlisle, Pennsylvania (the alma mater of famous Sac & Fox athlete Jim Thorpe); Haskell Institute in Lawrence, Kansas; and the Institute of American Indian Arts in Santa Fe, New Mexico, operated as federal institutions for Indians.

Significantly, like the private colonial colleges, these institutions were managed and controlled by non-Indians who, on their own, decided what might be best for Indians. However, as an unanticipated side effect which would not be experienced fully until mid-twentieth century, the schools provided a setting within which Indians of various tribes could exchange ideas and form inter-tribal cooperative networks.

The first Indian controlled schools, including higher education institutions, were founded by the Cherokee Nation of southeastern United States. The Cherokees, one of the Five Civilized Tribes—along with the Choctaws, Chickasaws, Muscogee (Creeks), and Seminoles—were forcibly removed to Indian Territory, now Oklahoma, under the Indian Removal Act of 1830.

By 1851, the Cherokee Nation had established two seminaries—one for males, one for females. The female seminary was modeled on the Mt. Holyoke Female Seminary of South Hadley, Massachusetts. The seminaries flourished. "The progress of the Cherokees was due to the excessive pride in their schools, which were never allowed under the supervision in any way of the educational authorities of the United States and none of their schools were ever visited by officers and agents of the Department of Education at Washington, until after June 30, 1898 (p. 229) (Starr, 1921)." By 1906, the United States government took over the Cherokee school system—including the seminaries. By 1909 the seminaries became co-ed; and on March 10, 1910 the male seminary building burned. The entire educational system shortly thereafter, under government control, went into decline (Fuchs and Havighurst, 1972). Bureau of Indian Affairs rhetoric of the time affirmed the need for Indian self-sufficiency; issuing policy statements in 1901 and 1905 urging termination of government subsidizing of Indian services (Prucha, 1975).

From Termination to Self-Determination

The termination talk continued through mid-century. At the same time alternatives to unilateral termination began to emerge. In 1928, Lewis Meriam and his research group published one of the most influential reports on Indian affairs entitled, *The Problem of Indian Administration*. Among other federal services criticized, the report paid special attention to the poor education services provided through federal supervision. The report recommended that Indians be given a large role in the services being rendered to them. This gave rise to two pieces of legislation which sought to turn over Indian services to the tribes and to the states—the Wheeler-Howard Act (the Indian Reorganization Act or IRA); and the Johnson O'Malley Act (40 Stat. 1458, 25 U.S. C., 452-456). But neither Act significantly increased Indian enrollment in higher education nor Indian participation in the governance of colleges. Rather the Acts appeared to emphasize voluntary rather than forced assimilation of Indians into the larger society. And few Indians chose to voluntarily assimilate. Thus, in the post World War II era unilateral termination again became the philosophy of the federal government (U.S. Senate, 1969).

Flushed with U.S. successes in Europe and Asia during World War II, the subsequent withdrawal of U.S. forces and European rebuilding via the Marshall Plan, the federal government applied the same philosophy to domestic Indian affairs. The Congress apparently saw withdrawal of the U.S. Bureau of Indian Affairs (BIA), and resettlement of the Indians as similar to the WW II situation. Thus, they advanced plans for gradually liquidating the BIA and promoting relocation/training of Indians to integrate them into the larger U.S. society (U.S. Senate, 1969). Any educational support granted Indian individuals would be deducted as offsets against later tribal land claims judgments. Again Indians of various tribes found themselves pursuing common vocational educational trajectories away from their home communities, in Oakland, CA; Cleveland, OH; Chicago, IL; and elsewhere—which fostered intertribal bonds.

The notion that Americanizing Indians was the only foreseeable solution to the "Indian problem" dominated policy thought in the 1950s and early 1960s (Horse, 1982). This federal policy called "termination" became embodied in U.S. House of Representatives Concurrent Resolution

108 which classified Indian tribes regarding their readiness to become free-standing communities terminated from federal assistance. Indian tribes—and various states when they discovered that destitute Indians after termination would need to be supported under state welfare funds—opposed in the implementation of the termination policy but not before the Klamath Tribe of Oregon and the Menominees of Wisconsin had been severed from federal responsibility.

As the 1960s progressed a new concept gained currency—local community action. Applied to Indian country, the Johnson administration's great society philosophy of "grass-roots" empowerment provided Indians (perceived simply as another group of the poor, victimized by society) an alternative to relocation/termination. The Economic Opportunity Act of 1965 funded such programs as Head Start, Upward Bound, Job Corps, VISTA, and Community Action in Indian communities.

Although nested in the demeaning notion of "cultural deprivation," the programs provided immediate leadership opportunities for young Indians as well as "career ladder" options for them to pursue further education to become equipped to take over professional and managerial positions. Most importantly, the success of tribal efforts to address problems long ignored by the top-down efforts of the BIA produced a cadre of energetic, newly educated Indians convinced that Indian self-determination was the appropriate approach to address long-standing social problems of Indian communities.

Many actively promoted self-determination and were instrumental in convincing successive administrations to adopt the approach as official policy. In fact, in 1970 President Nixon specifically declared "Self-determination" by name as the official U.S. policy toward American Indians.

As one of the primary expressions of self-determination, Indians sought to demonstrate that Indian controlled schools are more effective than federally directed services for educating Indian populations. In the mid-1960s Navajos established the first Indian controlled elementary, secondary and postsecondary schools at Rough Rock, Ramah and Many Farms respectively as demonstration projects.

Throughout the seventies, Indians lobbied to include Indian control features in such legislation as the Indian Education Act of 1972 (P.L. 92-318); the Indian Self-Determination and Education Assistance Act of 1975 (P.L. 93-638); the Education Amendments of 1978 (P.L. 95-561); and the Indian Community College Assistance Act of 1978 (P.L. 95-471). By 1973, 12 federal schools had been turned over to Indian school boards. Seven years later, in 1980, the number had grown to 38 schools; currently 65 Indian controlled elementary and secondary schools enrolling 10,553 students are in operation. In addition, today 24 Indian community colleges enroll more than 4,400 students and provide other services to 10,000 Indian individuals (Carnegie, 1989).

The American Indian Controlled Community College Movement

The American Indian controlled college movement arose within community contexts in which many Indian adults had failed to complete elementary school, much less high school. Not surprisingly, many would be skeptical that tribal community colleges were needed or likely to be successful if established. However, like the rest of the U.S. a wave of Indian "baby-boomers" were enrolling in the nation's colleges and universities. Most were finding mainstream colleges uncongenial, stopping out and returning to their Indian communities to regroup—convinced that higher education was useful, but questioning whether the alien culture of mainstream campuses was worth enduring. They found a ready audience in Indians managing student support and assistance programs—Talent Search, Upward Bound, and Special Services (the so-called "trio programs"). As well as assisting Indian students on the various college campuses, trio program managers often arranged for extension courses from state colleges and universities to be offered to elder Indian students in the communities.

In 1972, several Indians involved in trio programs were in Washington, D.C. to attend a national meeting to become informed of the new provisions for FY 1973. Most arrived on Sunday, ready to meet with individual federal officials on Monday prior to the Tuesday meeting. But

Columbus Day fell on Monday and federal offices were closed. Instead, the Indians attended a conference organized by four Indian educators: Patricia Locke of the Western Interstate Commission for Higher Education (WICHE), Gerald One Feather of Oglala Sioux Community College, David Risling of D-Q University, and Helen Schierbeck of the U.S. Office of Education. Trio program administrators became aware that the Higher Education Act of 1965 (HEA)—Title III provided support to "developing institutions," primarily traditionally black colleges and colleges serving impoverished whites. They also learned that USOE administrators were willing to consider including Indians as a group funded under HEA Title III.

The ensuing discussion concerned the formation of a consortium of Indian colleges to pursue funding for mutual development assistance under HEA Title III—tentatively entitled the "American Indian Higher Education Consortium (AIHEC)." In addition, Locke et al. told participants that individual Indian colleges would need to effect bi-lateral Title III relationships with assisting institutions in order to participate in AIHEC. Those participants whose extension course efforts provided a form of community college services, scrambled to identify their efforts as "developing institution" activities. Thus, for example, Turtle Mountain Community College, previously a loose collection of interested people who provided oversight to classes extended to their reservation by several colleges and universities, sought and obtained a formal charter from the tribal council of the Turtle Mountain Band of Chippewa Indians on November 9, 1972. Under the Tribal Resolution No. 678-11-72, the council also approved of the college's membership in the American Indian Higher Education Consortium (Davis, 1987).

One organization influential in shaping the initial form which the AIHEC took was the Coalition of Indian Controlled School Boards (CICSB). CICSB pre-dated the consortium and in the initial time of development shared office space with the AIHEC development office as well as a common political outlook. The coalition had sprung from the network of Indian social activities of the late 1960s whose rising expectations for escaping the barriers of prejudice and discrimination had been fueled by social action programs in Indian communities under the Office of Economic Opportunity (OEO), the Economic Development Administration (EDA), the Small Business Administration (SBA) and other agencies of the Kennedy and Johnson administrations. Of particular impact was the passage of the Indian Education Act of 1972 (P.L. 92-318) which amended the elementary and Secondary Act of 1965 to include services to Indians and which also called for representation in governance by Indian tribes and organizations. Several tribes moved quickly, incorporating Indian school boards to contract for education services formerly performed directly by federal agencies, especially the Bureau of Indian Affairs.

Not surprisingly, the new Indian boards decided to band together as a political group to insure comprehensive implementation of the contracting process, which they perceived as an unprecedented opportunity to regain control of one of the most influential institutions affecting their lives—elementary and secondary schools. They decided to formally incorporate their political coalition as the Coalition of Indian Controlled School Boards—to assist their mutual development. In this sense, AIHEC represented virgin territory. Whereas CICSB represented governing boards whose primary difference from the status quo was legitimation of Indian membership—the schools, in many cases, had operated in the communities for several years and the only real change was the turnover to Indian governance, the consortium represented a new level of aspiration, establishment of an entirely new genre of institutions—built from scratch.

Environmental Factors

Several factors were present in the environment within which the new tribal colleges were established. One such factor was the core of college-experienced Indian people in the community where each new tribal college had its genesis. Although many of these individuals had returned to their reservations and did not complete college, in most cases their experiences with higher education had been predominantly positive. They had some familiarity with the processes common to colleges—registration, classes, academic inquiry, and so on—but were aware of the difficulties they and other Indian students had faced in such institutions. In addition, an Indian Administrator Development Program funded by OEO at the University of Minnesota, Pennsylvania State University and other graduate schools was graduating Indians with masters and doctoral degrees.

Another community factor present in the establishment of Indian controlled community colleges was the tribal political environment. Indian reservation politics (the majority of Indian controlled colleges are located on Indian reservations) are extremely volatile, occasionally devolving to highly polarized groups. This divisiveness made survival extremely difficult for new educational organizations which sought to serve a broad constituency based upon need for services rather than political affiliation. All tribal colleges experienced spirited political debate, and successful ones were able to forge an enduring coalition of support to insulate them from partisan threats to their autonomy.

One new element was the pan-Indian movement which had established inter-tribal networks of Indians. These networks were often not only at odds with representatives of the larger society's institutions—which they perceived as oppressing Indians—but also at times out of step with many conservative Indians on reservations who deplored confrontational tactics (Steiner, 1968). To explain *Indian control* in this context, it is important not to limit its linkage solely to the particular Indian tribe served by each college. On the other hand, the founders of the colleges understood the *tribal* rather than the *Indian* nature of Native American identity, eschewing amorphous "professional Indians" with tenuous connection to particular constituencies and insisting instead upon tribal legitimation requirements of formal charter and all-Indian board.

The development of tribal colleges was a movement which simultaneously supported development of new Indian colleges in several western states. The formal structure initiated by tribal colleges was the American Indian Higher Education Consortium; established in 1972 to support the development of Indian controlled higher education institutions. The consortium (AIHEC) had five charter members who decided that the criteria for membership would include Indian control as exemplified by possession of (1) a formal charter from Indian tribe(s) being served, (2) an all-Indian governing board, (3) a majority Indian student body, and (4) evidence of actively providing educational services. Although the developmental assistance activities of AIHEC were predominantly funded by Title III of the Higher Education Act—Aid to Developing Institutions, none of the criteria were *essential* for receipt of federal funding from that source. Indeed, as time passed AIHEC was persuaded by a variety of groups, including federal officials, to dilute its membership by requiring a "majority Indian membership" rather than an "all-Indian membership" institutional governing board.

Stein (1985) in his history of the colleges describes many similarities among the problems each faced, but also differences dependent upon local tribal political contexts. The experiences of the first six Indian controlled colleges is illustrative. At the Navajo Nation, a group of individuals including a non-Indian, Dr. Robert Roessel, married to a Navajo, actively pursued the founding of Navajo Community College (NCC). But NCC also enjoyed initial widespread support by the Navajo Tribal Council, the leadership of which strongly supported local control of education and was willing to exert leverage with state and federal officials with whom they had dealings.

Also at Navajo, the Office of Economic Opportunity had supported the tribal high school and extended that support to the community college level to help found Navajo Community College (Hannaway, 1989). Significantly, as the largest tribe in the United States, the Navajo were able to persuade Congress to pass the Navajo Community College Assistance Act (P.L. 92-189) on December 15, 1971. By contrast, the ardent supporters of D-Q University, part of an off-reservation inter-tribal and minority movement centered on the University of California-Davis campus, first gained control of a facility, an abandoned U.S. Army Signal Corps base near Davis, California, then sought to legitimate their efforts by declaring the occupancy to be an Indian/Chicano college, D-Q University (Belgarde, 1989). The next four Indian colleges consciously modeled themselves on NCC, but like D-Q University drew support from Indians centered at existing institutions.

Oglala Lakota Community College (Pine Ridge, SD) and Sinte Gleska College (Rosebud, SD) were helped by Indian educators at Black Hills State College. Unlike NCC, local tribal factionalism threatened the Sioux colleges early on as individuals working with the college at Pine Ridge were associated with the American Indian Movement take over at Wounded Knee in 1973 which was strongly opposed by then tribal chairman, Wilson. Similarly, Chairman Robert Burnette of the Rosebud Reservation opposed the Sinte Gleska College supporters which included several of his political opponents on the tribal council (Stein, 1985).

At Turtle Mountain, similar support existed among the tribal council membership but outright vocal opposition from the tribal chairman, James Henry, never materialized. Rather Chairman Henry, who believed that job creation and supporting the intertribal vocational college effort, the United Tribes Educational and Training Center (UTETC), were more important, engaged in a policy of benign neglect. By contrast, Standing Rock Community College enjoyed enthusiastic cooperation from Tribal Chairman Melvin White Eagle and BIA Superintendent Shirley Plume as well as local Indian educators who all shared a mutual vision of a well educated tribal membership for the Standing Rock Sioux.

The Tribally Controlled Colleges (TCCCs)

Stein (1985) designated the tribally controlled colleges as "TCCCs," a convention this article follows. He divided the TCCCs into three groups as follows:

First Wave of TCCCs

1969–   Navajo Community College, Tsaile, AZ
1970–   D-Q University (Hehaka Sapa College), Davis, CA
1971–   Oglala Lakota Community College, Kyle, SD
1971–   Sinte Gleska College, Rosebud, SD
1972–   Turtle Mountain Community College, Belcourt, ND
1972–   Standing Rock Community College, Fort Yates, ND

Second Wave of TCCCs

1973–   American Indian Satellite Community College, Winnebago, NB
1973–   Fort Berthold Community College, New Town, ND
1973–   Sisseton-Wahpeton Community College, Sisseton, SD
1973–   Lummi School of Aquaculture and Fisheries, Lummi, WA
1973–   Cheyenne River Community College, Fort Totten, ND
1975–   Blackfeet Community College, Browning, MT
1975–   Inupiat University of the North, Barrow, AK
1975–   Dull Knife Memorial College, Lame Deer, MT

Third Wave of TCCCs

1977–   Little Big Horn College, Crow Agency, MT
1977–   Salish-Kootenai Community College, Pablo, MT
1977–   College of Ganado, Ganado, AZ
1978–   Fort Peck Community College, Poplar, MT
1978–   Keeweenaw Bay Ojibway Community College, Baraga, MI

Stein's historical account only covered the period up to 1978. Since that time some of the colleges he included have ceased to function and others have come into existence. Those now considered nonfunctional as Indian community colleges include Lummi School of Aquaculture, Inupiat University of the Arctic, College of Ganado, and Keeweenaw Bay Ojibway Community College.

New additions to the list include Bay Mills Community College (Brimley, MI): Crownpoint Institute of Technology (Crownpoint, NM); Fond du Lac Community College (Cloquet, MN); Fort Belknap Community College (Harlem, MT); Lac Courte Oreilles Ojibwa Community College (Hayward, WI); Northwest Indian College (Bellingham, WA); Stone Child College (Box Elder,

MT), which addition brought Montana to the same status of North Dakota—that of having an Indian community college on each of its reservations; and United Tribes Technical College (Bismarck, ND) (Carnegie, 1989).

Common Attributes of TCCCs

All of the tribal colleges share common goals. They seek to promote the culture of the tribe they serve, work to strengthen the economies of their Indian communities and strengthen the social fabric of the tribal community both internally and in conjunction with outside communities through empowering individual Indian people. This contrasts sharply with the BIA colleges which recruit a multi-tribal clientele seeking to enable their students to fill lower social strata in mainstream society. The tribal colleges also differ from Indian programs instituted by many of the western state colleges. In state institutions responding to Indian needs is secondary, usually part of an old priority goal of "pluralism" originally applied to the then unassimilated European immigrants, now dusted off to encompass nonwhite minorities. Tribal college student bodies, governance structures, faculty, and physical facilities display commonalities unique to the genre (Carnegie, 1989).

Students

The colleges are located on Indian reservations. Not surprisingly, the majority of their students reside on or near the reservations of the tribes which chartered these colleges. In this respect, they are similar to majority society community colleges which tend to be nonresidential services. However, tribal college students reside in rural areas—not part of the urban or suburban clientele associated with mainstream community colleges. The tribal colleges tend to enroll students who are considerably older than those in nontribal institutions. In several colleges, the modal student is a woman who is the solo parent of one or more children. Also, the Indian students are frequently members of the first generation of their families to attend college. And they are far below the national average in income.

Tribal colleges act as a bridge between Indian students and the outside world. Often, they help the Indian student who is "stopping-out" from a majority, society college re-enroll by providing emotional, academic and financial support and assistance. Or, the college might provide specific training to equip students for all particular job opportunities becoming available off the reservation, but within commuting distance. For example, the college may train a small cadre of students in particular construction trades for which demands are growing due to economic development activities in the state. Nevertheless, the modal student at TCCCs is one who would generally not be served by existing state higher education institutions.

Governance Structures

Indian college governance structures follow a common model, perhaps due to the early successes of AIHEC colleges in maintaining adequate financial support. The pattern of soliciting a tribal charter to sanction college efforts, establishing and maintaining an all-Indian (or majority Indian) membership governing board and appointing an Indian professional as chief executive dominate Indian colleges. In fact, a number of the college founders visited the campuses of other Indian colleges to view and adopt the governance designs they found at the successful institutions. Certainly not all the colleges initially sought AIHEC membership; for example, the College of Ganado remained aloof until it appeared that substantial funding for Indian colleges was imminent through the Indian Community College Assistance Act of 1978 (P.L. 95-471).

Interestingly, although the Indian colleges sought charters from their tribal governments, the successful ones needed to maintain an arms-length relationship and avoid becoming part of the tribal government bureaucracy. Sinte Gleska survived a critical test when Chairman Burnette sought to dissolve the college's board (Stein, 1985). In addition, Turtle Mountain consciously insulated itself from direct tribal government control by the tribal council and a second board of directors selected by the trustees to oversee the college's day-to-day affairs. Other colleges sought to be controlled by the Indian *society* they served, but eschewed dependence on the Indian *state* as exemplified by particular regimes of the tribal councils.

From the very outset, the Bureau of Indian Affairs colleges—Haskell Indian College, Southwestern Indian Polytechnical Institute, the Institute of American Indian Arts—were defined as different from the AIHEC colleges. In fact, when testifying before Congress, AIHEC used BIA colleges as examples of the top-down federal bureaucracy's waste and ineffectiveness. In addition, AIHEC colleges defined themselves as different from the Indian studies programs at state universities, as well. State colleges and universities relate to Indian individuals rather than their communities, per se. Indian studies programs occupy a peripheral role in state institutions, folded in with other minority programs. In tribal colleges, cultural revitalization is often the central mission of the institution. Indian controlled colleges occupy a narrow niche, characterized by local control and orientation toward development of *particular* American Indian communities. They are neither federal, nor state, nor even tribal governmental adjuncts. They are a socio-cultural product of the Indians they serve (U.S. Senate. 1976).

As part of the focus, leadership including Indian women as well as men significantly define American Indian controlled colleges. For example, today eight of the AIHEC college presidents are women. Carol Davis is proclaimed as the "Founding Mother" of Turtle Mountain Community College. And it should be recalled that two women, Patricia Locke and Helen Schierbeck, (assisted by David Risling and Gerald One Feather) convened the conference which founded AIHEC. It comes as no surprise that American Indian women on some reservations find the institutions so congenial and responsive to their needs that they outnumber the men students at their tribal colleges.

Faculty

Despite their colleges' focus on Indian participation both in the student body and administration, TCCC faculties are generally non-Indian. This is not by choice. Were a sufficient number of American Indian professionals available, most Indian colleges would employ them. Although the number of Indian teachers is growing, the demand at Indian elementary and secondary schools remains high enough to employ most graduating Indian professionals—and these schools offer much more attractive salaries than the financially strapped Indian controlled colleges. A special group of instructors with little formal education are employed by some institutions. These are the Indian culture specialists—Indian elders hired to pass on the native culture traditionally transmitted as an oral rather than written tradition. In addition to lecturing, they authenticate what other younger, and often times non-Indian, instructors provided as content in their courses (Carnegie, 1989). At times this creates tension. The non-Indian faculty holding masters and doctorate degrees sometimes perceive themselves to be less highly valued than the Indian "nonprofessionals"—a status reversal particularly difficult to endure in a setting where salaries already are lower than those of state colleges (Stein, 1985).

Whatever their background, most tribal college faculty members are sensitive to the tribal communities' needs. Some are non-Indian who have resided on or near the reservation for most of their lives. Others arrive from the outside and elect to become permanent residents. More often, faculty turnover is a chronic problem at TCCCs. The reality that TCCC faculty need to assume enormous teaching loads conspires with the unattractiveness of isolated settings to limit the tenure of instructors. It also takes a special sort of faculty member, for example, to accept the challenge to incorporate Indian culture and contemporary concerns into all of their courses—as demanded by at least one tribal college (Carnegie, 1989).

Horse (1982) found that tribal studies programs were being developed and implemented in most of the TCCCs. They varied in terms of their theoretical and normative dimensions, and suffered by comparison to the state of development of the standard academic curricula offered at the same institutions. TCCC tribal studies programs emphasize what he called "Tribal Liberal Arts." The content often included "Indian" as well as "tribal" studies, but accreditation of such courses was an issue. Nevertheless, he perceived the role of tribal studies curriculum in TCCCs as "singular among all higher education institutions" (p. 153).

Facilities

The physical facilities of TCCCs share a common degree of woefulness, although they vary from college to college. At Navajo, a large residential campus with impressive buildings suffers from insufficient funds for maintenance and upgrading since being built in the early seventies. More commonly the deterioration took place long before the local college took over the facility. Some campuses use donated space—sometimes BIA buildings previously condemned and turned over to the tribe. Other colleges construct buildings as money becomes available. Rarely elegant, often these metal frame buildings are nevertheless (barely) sufficient to provide classroom space for growing student bodies (Carnegie, 1989).

The facilities lack has necessitated some cooperative partnerships with other local organizations. Usually the local college, although sometimes perceived as a competitor for professionals, nevertheless is allowed to use high school classrooms for evening classes. Continued contact thus smoothes over some of the resistance against including the college as part of the local educational "establishment." In addition, cooperative links with businesses sometimes grow as colleges use their facilities as training sites for vocational students. Colleges with a geographically scattered clientele sometimes look to the tribal housing authority as a source of abandoned mobile homes which can be converted to temporary classrooms in isolated areas. And occasionally, the state government will construct a building for a special purpose at the college—for example, to house a particular type of vocational training the state seeks to promote. Tribal college administrators joke about being part of an anthropologically interesting "hunting and gathering" culture—in relation to facilities!

Consequences of Common Attributes

The colleges developed very similarly due to the common attribute of their local environments. All see the source of financial support as necessarily coming from outside the communities in which they are located. Perceiving themselves as one of the truest expressions of the tribal will, the colleges see themselves as inheritors of the quasi-sovereign status of their tribes and of the special relationship with the federal government forged in replacement for tribal lands ceded to the United States. But, unlike federal schools for Indians, the colleges consider direct grants, rather than federally directed services, the appropriate means of federal financial support. In any case, whether through successful pursuit of competitive grants or through funding specifically for Indian community colleges, the federal government remains, overwhelmingly, the primary source of financial support for tribal colleges.

Because the colleges' clientele is similar, they tend to offer curricula closely associated with employment available on the reservation—clerical training, health-related occupations, paraprofessional training, education aide training, and the like. These are positions disproportionately filled by females and others coming from a low-income background. Another consequence of their older female clientele is an orientation toward family, traditionally a role responsibility of women. Tribal colleges often address services to the entire family, encouraging grandparents of students to join the core of elders providing Indian studies authentication, or help to obtain services for students' children by serving as ombudsmen.

Stein (1985) tells a touching story of the parent of a child needing special education services who credited Sinte Gleska College with being the only organization willing to help her obtain appropriate services for her child. The incident could just as easily have taken place at any of several Indian colleges. Although student-centeredness may be characteristic of other small colleges, the actual involvement of students' family members as cultural assets is unique to, but common among, Indian community colleges.

Having an Indian board keeps the colleges closely attuned to the demands of the tribe, rather than to other colleges. Often the board members are not college graduates and their focus is upon the local community's developmental needs. On one hand, TCCCs are less likely to adopt a practice simply because it has become popular among other colleges in the state. On the other hand, they are more likely to participate in local trends. They are likely to be seen as a corporate citizen in times of community celebrations. Indian colleges regularly donate to local causes. Of course, the college is also likely to employ Indian, rather than non-Indian staff. However, the professional staff, whether Indian or non-Indian is less likely to be allowed free reign to define the role of the college. Rather, decision-making at the TCCCs is often communal, suited to the egalitarian norms common among Indian societies. Unlike the faculty at research universities, the TCCC faculty do not dominate the activities of the college. The before-mentioned status reversal regarding Indian elders (often not holding college degrees) and non-Indian college faculty (usually younger) inhibits some faculty solidarity needed to make it formidable at the TCCCs. In addition, the high percentage of part-time faculty that continue to be needed also dilutes the impact of the faculty as a whole, some part-timers simply do not get very involved. But probably the simple overwhelming burden of multiple preparations plus struggling for funding leaves little time for political jockeying, creating a low level of faculty dominance at Indian colleges. This does not mean that colleges do not provide high quality instruction. Rather, it means that such high quality is often viewed as institutionally opportune (as an aid to accreditation credibility, for example) rather than appreciated as an end in itself or as a means to enhance the reputations of individual faculty members.

Summary

The tribally controlled community college movement offers an apparently successful alternative means for educating Indians. Although earlier models—federal postsecondary schools for Indians and federal scholarships for Indians to attend mainstream colleges and universities—persist, the tribal college model currently dominates Indian higher education. In addition, the colleges reflect a social, cultural and political force in their communities that is attuned to tribal and intertribal demands, rather than those of mainstream society. A critical attribute of the colleges is their maintenance of important linkages with the outside world—particularly with the academic professional community and with the federal government which supply critical kinds of legitimacy and funding.

References

Belgarde, W. Larry (1989). Interviews with staff at D-Q University: Davis, CA.

Carnegie Foundation for the Advancement of Teaching (1989). *Tribal Colleges: Shaping the Future of Native America*. Princeton University Press: Princeton, NJ.

Chase, Fredrick (1981). *A History of Dartmouth College and the Town of Hanover, New Hampshire*. John Wilson and Son: Cambridge, MA.

Davis, Carol (1987). Interview of TMCC founding board chairperson conducted by Wayne Stein at Turtle Mountain Community College: Belcourt, ND.

Fuchs, Estelle and Robert J. Havighurst (1872). *To Live on this Earth: American Indian Education*. Doubleday & Company: New York.

Hannaway, Jane (1989). Interview regarding her experiences as a program officer for the Office of Economic Opportunity at Washington, D. C. in the late 1960s conducted at Stanford University: Palo Alto, CA.

Horse, Perry (1982). *Tribal Cultural Educational Concepts in American Indian Community College Curricula*. Unpublished dissertation, University of Arizona: Tucson.

Morison, Samuel Eliot (1935). *The Founding of Harvard College.* Harvard University Press: Cambridge, MA.

Morrison, Robert J. and members of the faculty (1874). *The History of the College of William and Mary from its Foundation, 1660, to 1874.* J.W. Randolph & English: Richmond, VA.

Prucha, Francis Paul, Editor (1975). *Documents of United States Indian Policy.* University of Nebraska Press: Lincoln.

Starr, Emmet (1921). *History of the Cherokee Indians.* The Warden Company: Oklahoma City.

Stein, Wayne (1985). *A History of Tribally Controlled Community Colleges.* Unpublished dissertation, Western Washington University: Bellingham.

Steiner, Stan (1968). *The New Indians.* Harper & Row: New York.

Thompson, Thomas, Editor (1978). *The Schooling of Native America.* American Association of Colleges for Teacher Education in Collaboration with The Teacher Corps, United States Office of Education: Washington, D. C.

U.S. Senate (1969). *The Education of American Indians: The Organization Question.* Committee on Labor and Public Welfare, Subcommittee on Indian Education. U.S. Government Printing Office, Washington D.C.

U.S. Senate (1976). *Testimony on S. 2631—A Bill to Provide Financial Assistance to Indian Colleges.* Committee on Labor and Public Welfare, Subcommittee on Indian Education. U.S. Government Printing Office: Washington, D.C.

Bricks Without Straw
Missionary-Sponsored Black Higher Education in the Post-Emancipation Era

JOHNETTA CROSS BRAZZELL

Long before the abolition of slavery, Blacks recognized the importance and power of education. At the same time, slave-owners understood the need to control the slaves' access to literacy and therefore made learning to read a criminal offense. The illegality of learning did not keep some slaves from seizing every opportunity to acquire as much education as was possible. The slaves understood that a thing denied was a thing to be desired. If it were extremely important to their owners that they not know how to read and write, then it was equally important for the slaves to learn to do so. Although only a small percentage of slaves emerged from bondage with any degree of literacy, as a group they exhibited a thirst for education they immediately began to pursue.

One of the groups most closely identified with Black education endeavors during and after the Civil War was the cadre of teachers from the North. They came to the South with their own ideas about what it would take to prepare Blacks for their new roles as freedmen. The individual teachers were, in most instances, recruited and sponsored by missionary aid societies. These societies were quite varied in their ideological intentions. Too often, however, the teachers and their sponsoring societies have been evaluated as a single monolithic entity. Although they shared certain traits and patterns, one cannot fully appreciate the scope and nature of the post-emancipation Black educational work without appreciating the variety among the individual teachers and missionary groups.

Historians have been of several minds as they have interpreted motivations of Northern educators and their impact on Southern Blacks after the war. The prevailing view before the Second World War, as most starkly presented by Wilbur Cash, was of a fanatical, extremely religious, naive, anti-Southern group. Additionally, they were portrayed by Cash as a group determined to upset the equilibrium of Southern society by teaching dangerous and subversive ideas to the ex-slaves. A less derogatory and more reasoned work by Henry Swint served as the prevailing analysis of Northern teachers until the 1960s. Even in Swint's work, however, the portrait of Northern teachers is not particularly flattering. They are portrayed as purveyors of social and political equality for Blacks without regard for the traditions and sensibilities of White Southerners. The teachers are presented as mere extensions of the Republican party, whose prime directive was to control and direct the exercise of voting among the freedmen. While W. E. B. DuBois was generally sympathetic in his portrayal of Northern teachers, Carter G. Woodson in his 1933 work took the missionaries to task for giving Blacks a White-oriented education that was anathema to their needs and that de-emphasized their African heritage and racial pride.

The revisionist literature that emerged during and after the 1960s presents a different but dichotomous rendering of missionary activity. One camp, as represented by Jacqueline Jones and Elizabeth Jacoway, presents such activity in a much more sympathetic and humane light by exploring the missionaries' use of education to promote racial equality, whereas the other, represented by historians such as Ronald Butchard and James McPherson, questions that this was one of their objectives. Both camps challenge the interpretations of Swint.

There are several works that deal with the broader arena of Black education. Among the earlier efforts are Theophilus McKinney's *Higher Education among Negroes*, 1934; Dwight O. W. Holmes' *Evolution of the Negro College*, 1934; Willard Range's *The Rise and Progress of Negro Colleges in Georgia: 1865–1949*, 1951; Jeanne Noble's *The Negro Woman's College Education*, 1956; and Henry Allen Bullock's *A History of Negro Education in the South from 1619 to the Present*, 1967. Of these, Range gives the most comprehensive curriculum information about Black women's education after the Civil War. He focuses on Spelman College and the content of its instruction. Noble's work is really a survey of Black women college graduates in 1956. There is a historical section, which includes a look at Spelman College, but very little about instructional content.

More recent works by some revisionist historians are posing different questions about the nature of Black education. They revisit the debate that dominated Black educational concerns at the turn of the twentieth century—classical education versus industrial education. The most representative works of the revisionists are: James Anderson's *The Education of Blacks in the South, 1860–1935*, 1988; Ronald Butchart's *Northern Schools, Southern Blacks, and Reconstruction: Freedmen's Education, 1862–1875*, 1980; *New Perspectives of Black Educational History*, edited by Vincent Franklin and James Anderson, 1978; and James M. McPherson's *The Abolitionist Legacy from Reconstruction to the NAACP*, 1975. They argue that those individuals and institutions advocating an industrial education curriculum were intent on creating a permanent Black underclass, forever relegated to the lowest economic and political rungs of the Southern social hierarchy. Of the three, Butchart delves more deeply into Black male and female curricular differences. He describes the theme of domesticity and piety that pervaded the curriculum for Black females but does not explore the countermessage sent through that same curriculum—that they were to learn practical skills and become wage earners.

Of interest in this article is the development of missionary-sponsored Black higher education institutions in the post-emancipation era as represented by the creation of Spelman Seminary in Atlanta, Georgia. This school for Black females was established in 1881 under the auspices of the Woman's American Baptist Home Mission Society (WABHMS) located in Boston, Massachusetts. The creative forces behind the development of Spelman were cofounders Sophia B. Packard and Harriet E. Giles, Society members and, respectively, the first and second presidents of Spelman.

Attention will be focused on the founding and founders of Spelman and how the educational process was used to shape and define the roles of the women who were in attendance. By founders is meant not only Packard and Giles but also the organizations to which they were attached and which shared in the responsibility of developing and nurturing the school.

An exploration of the founders' role necessitates an examination of their motives for creating or being affiliated with this school. Embedded in those motivations are the views of the women and/or Blacks that they brought to the affiliation. These views would be critical in defining the kind of social roles envisioned by the founders of the women leaving this school. The philosophical/ideological underpinnings of the founding organizations is another critical part of understanding motivations. Spelman was founded and managed by White Northern female and male Baptists. This distinction shaped not only the motivations and visions of the founders, but also the status and receptivity of the external world to the founding group.

In order to understand the founders and the institution they created it is imperative to understand the milieu within which they existed. This requires an understanding of (1) the status and societal expectations of Southern Black women in the post–Civil War era; (2) the state of elementary/secondary education for Blacks, especially in the State of Georgia; and (3) the role of missionary organizations in the development of Southern education institutions.

The State of the State

Out of the chaos created by the Civil War rose the determination of Black Georgians to celebrate their newly won freedom with the establishment of religious, cultural, political, and educational institutions. This was not to be an easy task given the intransigent posture assumed by some white

Georgians who still viewed the ex-slaves as inferior beings who should never acquire any of the trappings of civilization.

Georgia occupied an important position among the Confederate states. In 1860 it was the largest of the Lower South states in terms of total population, slaves, slave-holders, and non-slaveholders. It acquired a reputation among freedmen's workers after the War as having a particularly unrepentant and violent white population [25, pp. 30, 67].

By 1871 Georgia had been readmitted to the Union and was once again firmly in the hands of the Democratic party. In the interim, Blacks and Northern teachers had moved to establish schools in all sectors of the state. The most intransigent white Georgians viewed these schools as the most prominent feature of the new order of things that threatened their traditional way of life and hegemonic hold over their ex-slaves [25, pp. 26, 81]. They determined to reassert their control through violent attacks and the enactment of laws that relegated the freedmen to positions they had occupied before the war [39, pp. 57, 158–60].

By the early 1880s other changes had occurred that blocked efforts by Blacks to achieve social, economic, and political independence. White Southern control had been strengthened by the complete withdrawal of all Union troops, the Freedmen's Bureau had been disbanded, and the federal government had essentially assumed a hands-off policy toward the ex-Confederate states. Some of the missionary and Freedmen's Aid Societies that had been so active during and after the war had become financially strapped to the point that they could no longer maintain their Southern operations. Additionally, many of the Northern teachers who had come to the South after the war were now disillusioned and chose to return to the North.

The Mission

It was into this environment that the Atlanta Baptist Female Seminary, later to become Spelman Seminary, was created. The specifics of the founding of Spelman should be viewed within the general characteristics shaping other missionary organizations and individuals. By 1866 there were 1,405 teachers affiliated with Northern organizations teaching in 975 Southern schools. When the decade ended, there were more than 2,560 teachers in 2,039 schools. These figures reflected the involvement of 51 missionary organizations in freedmen's education between 1862 and 1875 [9, pp. 5–7].

The involvement of the Northern missionary societies in the development of Black Southern education was very important. Given the nonsupport and outright hostility of many Southern whites to any type of education for Blacks, the missionary schools were quite often the only educational outlets for Blacks. Their elementary schools became the foundation for the Southern public education system for Blacks. Their universities, colleges, academies, and normal schools were responsible for most of the higher education available to Blacks well into the twentieth century [31, p. 143].

By the late 1870s and early 1880s, due in no small degree to the continued persistence of Blacks and the Northern missionary societies, a slight shift in the attitudes of White Southerners had occurred. The beginning of a rudimentary, common school system was being put into place across the South. Those who championed the industrialization of the South were now beginning to view universal education as a way to produce a labor force in harmony with their economic goals. They sought to create an organized, efficient agricultural sector that would complement the emerging industrial sector. To that end, a rudimentary educational system could be used to upgrade Black labor productivity within racially prescribed roles. Education could be used as a form of social control, defining the position of Blacks and Whites in the Southern racial hierarchy. For the Black masses, education would be used to train and socialize them for unskilled and semiskilled positions, such as household managers, share croppers, dressmakers, commercial cooks, chauffeurs, janitors, and laundry women [1, p. 27].

By the 1880s many of the missionary elementary schools had been absorbed into the public education system, and those missionary societies still active in Black Southern education turned their attention and resources to the development of secondary and higher education institutions. By 1900 an elementary education system had been established in all the Southern states. In

Georgia, of the 151,516 Black children between five and nine years of age, 22 percent were attending school. Of those between ten and fourteen years of age, 46 percent were attending school. However, there was such opposition to any form of secondary education for Blacks that as late as 1915 the five largest cities in Georgia, including Atlanta, had no public high schools for Blacks [1, pp. 151,188–92].

Although not the largest of the missionary societies, the Home Mission Society represented the Southern educational endeavors of the Northern Baptist denomination. To understand the type of educational institution created at Spelman, it is necessary to understand not only the philosophical underpinnings of the parent group but its view of Blacks who were the recipients of its largesse. Its members looked upon the experience of slavery as one which had morally, spiritually, and culturally bankrupted Blacks. Many of the missionaries believed Blacks to have emerged from the "dense darkness of ignorance dazed and terrorized by the new responsibilities of freedom" [6, p. 368]. Blacks were often portrayed as child-like creatures, incapable of handling the myriad problems facing them. Thus, the Baptist Missionaries saw Blacks as being greatly in need of the guiding hand and wisdom of dedicated teachers who could show them the way to take their "proper" place in society.

In spite of the paternalistic, and perhaps racist, attitudes of the missionaries, their motivations, upon examination, tend to be complex. This complexity is also characteristic of how they viewed Blacks. First and foremost, the mission of the Society through its educational activities was evangelical in nature. The teacher was viewed as "God's co-worker" whose task it was to mold their Black students into useful, virtuous, Christian, and obedient citizens. Given the "depravity" with which the missionaries viewed Blacks to have emerged from slavery, Blacks had to be "prepared" before they could fully share in American culture [6, p. 368; 9, pp. 15–18].

Contrary to the then conventional belief, many Northern Baptists professed the belief that Blacks were mentally equal to Whites; their growth had simply been stunted by slavery. Education, then, was to be used as a liberating force. It was their assumption that with the proper training Blacks would be able to move into the American mainstream and make life choices limited only by their sense of self-worth and effort. The Woman's American Baptist Home Mission Society in expressing its view of Blacks' capacity to take advantage of educational opportunities states, "The colored pupils are equal in ability to the white, and when we are asked what kind of instruction and instructors we shall give them, our answer should be, the best"[4]. In order to give them the edge necessary to make the transition it was felt that through education they would be taught White middle-class values and behavior patterns that would not only make them competitive but also would make them acceptable to the larger White society [1, pp. 79–80; 9, pp. 21–23].

The Founding

The American Baptist Home Mission Society (ABHMS) had its beginning in 1832. Its purpose was "to promote the teaching of the Gospel in North America." With the outbreak of the Civil War in 1861, the Society felt compelled to expand its mission drastically. At its 29 May 1862 annual meeting, the Society committee itself to the work of "evangelization and Christian education of the colored people of the South." The Society resolved "to take immediate steps to supply with Christian instruction, by means of missionaries and teachers, the emancipated slaves . . . and to inaugurate a system of operation for carrying the Gospel alike to free and bond throughout the whole southern section of our country, so fast and so far as the press of our arms, and the restoration of order and law shall open the way"[3].

As corresponding secretary for the Woman's Society, it was Sophia Packard's responsibility to travel to cities and towns in Massachusetts and adjoining states to garner support and set up affiliated groups. She held this job for two years after the group's beginning. In order to assess conditions in the South and to determine the nature of the work to be done there, WABHMS authorized a trip by Packard. On 24 February 1880 she left Boston and over the next few weeks made stops in Richmond, Nashville, and New Orleans. In Nashville, Packard apparently encountered White resistance to the type of educational endeavor for Freedmen she had in mind. She was warned by a Mrs. Weed that she "had better let the Nigers [sic] alone"[14]. Ignoring this warning, Packard continued to visit Black elementary schools, churches, homes, and even called on Fisk University in Nashville. Due to an illness that overtook her in New Orleans, Packard was joined by her long-time friend, Harriet E. Giles, who attended her and visited Black homes and schools in the area [34, pp. 35–36].

The two women returned to Boston convinced that they could serve the needs of Southern Blacks by opening a school somewhere in the South, for women and girls. Giles, writing in 1895 about what prompted their desire to open such a school, states, "The conviction was profoundly impressed upon them [Packard and Giles] that their should be given to the education and Christianization of those downtrodden people" [34, p. 38].

The official history of WABHMS does not report the intense struggle surrounding the creation of Spelman Seminary. Some WABHMS members were concerned that such an undertaking would financially bankrupt the Society. They cautioned, "There is no money in the treasury; wait until autumn." Others thought the two women were too old to take on such a task. Packard was fifty-six years old and Giles was forty-eight [6, p. 375; 34, p. 36]. The Society's initial refusal to endorse the plans of Packard and Giles served only to fuel their determination to push forward. Apparently in a move both to signal the strength of her intent and to give herself a free rein to solicit funds outside the Society, Packard on 7 February 1881, resigned from her position as corresponding secretary. She approached individuals and churches for donations and raised nearly $200. In the meantime, the Society was still debating whether or not it would support the venture.

The diary entries of both women reflect the emotional roller-coaster they were on for much of 1881. Giles, on 10 March 1881, wrote in her diary, "Board meeting plans laid for our going South to open a school." then the Board reversed itself on 12 March and withheld approval for establishing the school; "Board meeting proceedings of Thursday all upset. Dark days." Another vote on 24 March granted approval, "Board meeting in which we were appointed to go to Atlanta as missionary teachers. Very pleasant" [13].

Although the school was officially launched in April, the WABHMS continued to negotiate with the American Baptist Home Mission Society (ABHMS) in New York to assume the teachers' salaries. ABHMS formally declined to do so in October 1881. It was not until January 1882, that the WABHMS gave official notice of Packard's and Giles's reappointment. They were to be paid $500 each per year, retroactive to December 1881 [13, 14].

Implementing the Vision

Why a school for Black women and girls? Why not a coeducational institution? Or a school for Black males? The latter type of institution had been established by ABHMS in 1867 in the form of the Atlanta Baptist Seminary (later to become Morehouse College). Atlanta University, which had been founded in 1865 by the Congregationalists, was coeducational. Yet, based on their Southern trip and the empathy created from that experience, there was a great need felt by the founders to create a school that exclusively served females. Thus, it became the first school exclusively for Black women.

To understand the evolution of education for women one must have an awareness of how the social roles for women have been perceived and articulated. The kind of instruction developed for women was fully grounded in those perceptions and role definitions.

Thomas Woody, in his 1929 foundational historical work on women's education, used an interesting phrase to describe the role of colonial women. He called it the "sphere of women." Females were prepared for their sphere (the home) in the same manner males were prepared for their spheres—they each served apprenticeships—the girls to their mothers in the home, and boys to their fathers [40, pp. 92–95]. The role for women was very simply defined—they took care of everything in the home. There was, therefore, no need for formal learning. Everything a girl needed to know would be taught to her by her mother. The Puritans were one of the few religious sects to value literacy for women. For them, the ability to read the scriptures was viewed as an appropriate activity for women but it was to be done under the guidance of a male. Even though the education received by Puritan females was rudimentary and inferior to that received by Puritan males, it was superior to that received by other women [11, pp. 1–2; 23, p. 9].

A major change occurred in the late eighteenth and early nineteenth centuries. Between 1787 and 1805, much of the country was held within the grip of the Second Great Awakening. This growth and spread of evangelicalism was characterized by a powerful fusion of official church teachings and the day-to-day lives of individuals. The result was a redefinition of women's roles [19, p. 7]; to be more precise, a redefinition of how women were to fill their roles.

Following the War of Independence, women came to be viewed in a different light. Given the new nation's quasi-democratic impulses, the need for an enlightened White male populace took on a new sense of urgency. Those who were to be the future electorate and representatives of the body politic needed to be trained morally to assume these responsibilities. The rationalizations, then, for redefining the roles of women included reasoning such as: (1) the United States in the 1790s had no national religious organizations that could be responsible for moral instruction; (2) the family unit was, therefore, the only social unit that was capable of providing moral training, and discipline for the children; (3) the children were to be found in the home with the mothers; (4) the new role for women should be that of guardian of moral standards [11, pp. 2–4; 23, p. 10].

If women were now to assume this expanded responsibility they would need to be trained in a more systematic manner than the time-honored apprenticeship method. Women needed to be educated. The woman's sphere had not changed, she simply needed to be better educated to fill it.

The late nineteenth century's evolving notion of women's roles was shaped by their relationship to family, morality, and the undergirding of civilization. Men were to dominate the material world, and women were to be responsible for family and moral development [9, pp. 23–24]. In exerting moral influence over their families, women would be ensuring the development of a nation of happy and stable households. Their first duty as mothers, wives, and daughters was not to themselves but to others around them [25, pp. 39–40].

The work undertaken by Packard and Giles was at once a contradiction and an affirmation of this female credo. They were engaged in wage-earning work in which they were responsible for organizing and directing an enterprise that some might have deemed more suitable for men. They were far from family and friends and had to be the driving force behind the educational, financial, and spiritual essence of this school. On the other hand, the nature of the work in which they were engaged was an affirmation of the credo. They were certainly putting others before themselves. This was a very self-sacrificing activity. In a sense, the school was a home and the students were children to be trained morally and spiritually. This training also included an appreciation for the ideals and precepts of White American culture.

This female credo also had to be balanced with the fact that in the nineteenth century the teaching profession had increasingly become feminized. Four-fifths of the teachers in Georgia after the war were women. This state of affairs was rationalized by stating that women were more peculiarly fitted for this work because it involved the training of the young [25. p. 36]. The practical reason was that men had access to a variety of other occupations and there simply were not enough of them willing to engage in this type of work. But signing on a teachers did afford women a unique opportunity to break out of the conventional social roles they were expected to play without being totally outside the realm of social acceptance and respectability.

The position of Black women in the South before 1865 was defined by their status as slaves. The concept of the domestic mission took a decidedly different twist for Black women, given their prime value as sources of labor. "Femaleness" was not enough to protect Black women from the physical rigors demanded of agricultural work. In pursuit of the most "efficient" use of labor, slaveowners recognized no gender differences when assigning field work. Black women were expected to plow, hoe, pick cotton, and perform all other tasks as men did [26].

However, once the slaves left the field, gender differences came into play. Black women were expected to be responsible for all the tasks thought to be within the purview of women. They were responsible for cooking, housecleaning, sewing, and washing clothes [20, pp. 495–96]. This made for a very long day for female slaves who operated under a dual status—both slave and female. In the field they were "equal" to men. At home, they were women with certain prescribed responsibilities.

This dual status remained after the Civil War and posed a special challenge for those seeking to define Black women's roles. They were, on the one hand, seen to have the same responsibilities as White women as it related to the moral development of the family. But in addition to being responsible for hearth and home, they were also expected to be full participants in that material world dominated by men. They were expected to earn their bread and make it too.

As the teachers defined their mission in shaping the educational procedures to which the Spelman females would be exposed, they were guided by their views of Blacks as having been depraved by the slavery experience. Black women, then, had to be purified and changed before they could be expected to assume their responsibilities in the home. Their femininity, which they had lost during slavery, had to be rediscovered. As White women were the keepers and nurturers of civilization, so too were Black women seen as the force within the Black community that would lead it to respectability.

Thus, the purpose of the training at Spelman was to prepare the women for both of these areas of responsibility—the home and the workplace. This was consistent with one of the main tenets of Baptist missionary doctrine, which viewed collegiate education as the process by which a cadre of Black leaders would be developed to uplift the masses of Black people. Because the missionaries professed not to be operating from a position that doubted the intellectual capability of Blacks, it was quite a logical educational goal [1, pp. 240–42]. The role of Black women was to lead from the home and the classroom.

The 1887–88 Spelman catalog describes the approach used to foster the twin directives of intellectual development and industrial training as

> Our Aim: The Seminary is distinctly Christian as its founders willed it to be, and it welcomes those of every faith to its advantages. The aim is to build character. Christianity and morality are the foundation of all our teaching, for if these are neglected all else is vain. To this end, we train the intellect, store the mind with useful knowledge, induce habits of industry and a desire for general information, inspire a love for the true and beautiful, and prepare the pupils for practical duties of life.

> Industrial Department: This is made a prominent feature in this institution. The results . . . prove beyond a doubt, the desirableness and practicability of industrial training to coincide with other courses of study. For all, especially for those who are to be teachers and mothers, we believe industrial training is essential in making them self-reliant and self-supporting; yea, necessary for the best intellectual and moral discipline of the colored people. Our great aim is to make education practical.

> Every woman should be a good house-keeper, for her own honor and the progress of civilization. Hence, all the boarders are required to learn the art of house-keeping in its various branches [36].

These themes were expanded and refined as the institution matured. The vision and educational goals of the founders were in line with those of their parent organization. Although the WABHMS continued to support Spelman by paying the salaries of its teachers in the academic department, in April 1887 educational and financial management of the school had been transferred to ABHMS in New York [21, p. 17]. Although the two Societies nominally shared responsibility for the school, ABHMS assumed the greater share of the burden for defining its educational directions.

One of the central ABHMS figures involved in the early history of Spelman was General Thomas Jefferson Morgan. He was a graduate of Rochester Theological Seminary, served on the faculty of Chicago Theological Seminary, and was principal of the Postdam Normal School and the State Normal School in Rhode Island. In 1893 he was appointed corresponding secretary of the ABHMS and served until his death in 1902 [34, p. 146]. From his ABHMS position General Morgan spoke and wrote about issues pertaining to Black Southern education. In a speech entitled "What Spelman Seminary Stands For," delivered 19 November 1901, at Spelman, General Morgan outlined his vision for the school and enunciated its reason for being:

Spelman Seminary is aiming to do, as far as practicable, for the Negro woman precisely what is being done for white women by Smith, Vassar, Wellesley, and other institutions of Christian learning, which for decades have been contributing most liberally and patently to their preparation, not only for the homely duties of life, but for the larger sphere of activity to which the age calls them, thus fitting them to add their quota to the great work of human betterment. Spelman aims to be the center and source of good influences, seeking to ennoble and purify the lives of its individual pupils, to reform their homes, to permeate churches and Sunday Schools with a new and uplifting force, to supply the public schools with competent teachers, and to enrich the whole life of the Negro race, industrial, social, religious, political, with higher ideals, improved methods and trained and qualified leaders [7, p. 15].

Clearly, the responsibility to be borne by the women at Spelman was an awesome one. As envisioned by the missionary leaders the women bore the weight of the entire race. If they failed, a whole people failed.

In the same speech, General Morgan enunciated a threefold credo which articulated the philosophical parameters defining the school as follows:

Education as carried on at Spelman has a threefold value.

1. *It is an instrument of livelihood.* The girls under instructions here obtain primarily that knowledge of ordinary household duties that will enable them to earn by their own labor their bread and butter. Whether they do this in their father's house, in their own homes, or in work for others, they are all expected to be able to support themselves, and not be dependent upon others for a livelihood.

2. *Education qualifies its possessor for service.* The highest obligation of life is service. It is the aim of a school like Spelman to fit its students to become skilled workers creating more than they destroy and adding year by year to the increasing wealth of the State.

3. *Education has a culture value.* The school seeks to put its pupils into right relationship with nature, with society, with God. It puts into their hands the key that unlocks the treasures of the universe. The discoveries of science, the creations of art, the triumphs of invention [7, pp. 15–17].

Classical Versus Industrial

One of the most intense struggles in the late nineteenth and first quarter of the twentieth century involved the definition of the "proper" role of education for Southern Blacks. For some, industrial education represented the answer to this dilemma. Any other type of education would simply not prepare Blacks for their "proper" societal roles.

Over time, what was meant by industrial education took on a connotation that was not the way the contemporary participants understood its use. Essentially, industrial education as envisioned by many of its proponents in the late nineteenth century was a moral program. It was designed to instill the virtue of industry, that is, the development of appropriate habits such as thrift, sobriety, self-discipline, and a rejection of secular pleasures. It was believed that such habits, in turn, developed character. Morality was an inextricable part of this equation [24, pp. 2–5; 30, p. 611]. In short, industrial education, as conceived by some, was designed to teach people how to live. The acquisition of vocational skills was secondary. Teaching people how to think and how to conduct their lives was of far greater importance.

For some, the notion of industrial education has become synonymous with a type of education associated with the training of Blacks during the post-emancipation era. It is important to note, however, that there was an industrial education movement in the late nineteenth century that was much broader than Black education. There were essentially three categories of industrial/vocational training. The first was characterized by the type of training being provided by schools of applied science and technology, designed to train engineers, architects, and chemists for professional positions in the emerging technology-based economy. The second type involved trade schools, whose purpose was to train workers for lower-level positions in the industrial sector of the economy. The third type of training involved schools using manual instruction (learning to work with the hands) as a supplement to the traditional academic curriculum. The main intent of this instruction was to inculcate in the students habits of industry, thrift, and moral correctness. The employment of the third type in any number of well-known institutions, such as Mt. Holyoke Seminary for women, Wellesley College, and Oberlin College was a common occurrence in the nineteenth century [1, p. 35].

The employment of this third type of industrial/vocational training seems to characterize Spelman. The founders of Spelman envisioned themselves training leaders; and this could only be accomplished through intellectual training, not industrial training. The proper place of industrial education was reiterated in a treatise written by Dr. George Sale, circa 1907. Sale was first chosen as president of Atlanta Baptist Seminary (Morehouse College) in 1890 and then as superintendent of education of ABHMS in 1906. In his treatise, entitled *Our Part in the Solution of a Great Problem*, Sale explores the relationship between academic training and industrial education:

> Throughout the discussions that have taken place as to the value of industrial education, the Home Mission Society has stoutly maintained its position that industrial education is second in importance to the training of the few for higher service as leaders of thought and action of the Negro race.

> It should always be borne in mind that we are not engaged in the education of the Negro people, but in the education of a few who shall serve as constructive leaders of the race, and for this the higher intellectual training is essential [35, pp. 10–11].

By some educators' choosing the third type of industrial training, a debate was created over who would be the messengers to the masses of Black people and which message they would bring. The nature of the message seemed to be the heart of the struggle surrounding the definition of the type of education to be received by Blacks. Tuskegee Institute was begun in 1881. The message embodied in its creation as carried forth by its founder, Booker T. Washington, and as embraced by its supporters, targeted a select number of Black leaders for training. These black leaders were being trained to carry a specific message to the Black masses.

Some radical revisionist historians have postulated that Washington and like-minded supporters were interested in training indigenous Black educators whose task it would be to mold the masses of Blacks into a nonthreatening, cheap labor force. Those historians contend that the educational policies of Washington and their supporters were aimed at the development of a social and economic order in which Blacks would be content with a racial hierarchy that relegated them to the lowest economic levels [1, pp. 35–38; 2, pp. 61–62].

On the other side of this debate were Black leaders such as W. E. B. DuBois and Northern missionary representatives who saw education as the vehicle by which political and economic independence could be achieved through the training of Black intellectuals who would organize the Black masses. For such individuals, industrial education would be linked pejoratively to a speech delivered by Booker T. Washington at the 1895 Cotton States Exposition in Atlanta, Georgia. In that speech, Washington asked his race to "cast down your bucket where you are. . . . Cast it down in agriculture, in mechanics, in commerce, in domestic service, and in the professions." Again speaking to his Black brethren, he states, "Our greatest danger is that we may overlook the fact that the masses of us are to live by the productions of our hands, and fail to keep in mind that we shall prosper in proportion as we learn to dignify and glorify common labor and put brains and skill into the common occupations of life." To those who were white in the audience, Washington sought to assuage their anxieties by stating, "In all things that are purely social we can be as separate as the fingers, yet one as the hand in all things essential to mutual progress." He sought to further assure them by stating, "The wisest among my race understand that the agitation of questions of social equality is the extreme folly, and that progress in the enjoyment of all the privileges that will come to us must be the result of severe and constant struggle, rather than of artificial forcing" [5, pp. 13–16]. This retreat from social, economic, and political rights was anathema to most Black leaders and Northern missionary educators. To some Southern Whites and Northern philanthropists Washington's proposal was the perfect solution to a difficult problem.

Until the latter part of the nineteenth century, the major philanthropic interest in the work among people of color in the South was exhibited by the missionary societies. They established schools at the elementary, secondary, and college level; recruited, trained and sent teachers to staff the schools; and raised thousands of dollars to support their endeavors. Their motives were guided by evangelical zeal, a commitment to safeguarding the newly won rights of the freedmen, and a genuine desire to improve the plight of Southern Blacks. By the turn of the century, a power vacuum had been created by the complete withdrawal of the federal government and the inability of the societies to sustain financially the Black education institutions they had created. Increasingly in the latter part of the nineteenth century, Northern philanthropists moved in to fill the vacuum. This group included bankers, merchants, railroad entrepreneurs, and other business tycoons.

For Spelman and the Baptist Societies, this necessitated maintaining a delicate balancing act. On the one hand, there was consistent reaffirmation of the commitment to an academically based education. On the other hand, Spelman's need for financial resources to keep its doors open forced the founders to compromise by introducing industrial training. This training was funded by philanthropic entities such as the John F. Slater Fund. The Fund supported the Industrial Department, which offered courses in chamberwork, table-work, dishwashing, cooking, washing, ironing, and plain sewing. As an elective, students could learn printing. Of the 836 students attending Spelman in 1892, 419 are listed in the Industrial Department and 44 in the Printing Department. This represented 55 percent of the total student body [36].

In 1902 Giles appealed to George Foster Peabody for funds to support a nature study. The study was to be housed under the science department and would include subjects such as zoology, botany, and physiology. Students were to engage in such learning activities as understanding the basis for the classification of birds and fishes; field trips to classify flora; the study of muscles and nervous system; and laboratory study of at least one specimen under each of the subdivisions of the animal kingdom. Additionally, the student teachers in the senior class were to be taught how to teach science at the grade-school level. In all, a ten-page proposal was submitted to Peabody outlining the parameters of the nature study. Peabody, in turn, asked Jean Davis, manager of the Nature Study Bureau at Hampton Institute to give her opinion of what was being proposed at Spelman. Davis wrote back that the program lacked purpose, was too detached, was not practical, and seemed identical to a program at Cornell University that had been the subject of serious criticism. Davis suggested that Spelman should, instead, choose a study in agriculture. She suggested:

> Since they have sufficient land at Spelman, it might be well to have a garden where germination and the growth of plants and the study of animals in their relation to plants could be studied in a practical way. It might be helpful to teach the girls how to raise vegetables and small fruits and how to take care of poultry [28, pp. 1–2].

The funding was received from Peabody but substantial curricular changes were made based on the Hampton suggestions. What emerged was an agriculture rubric which in 1904 included courses such as kinds of soil, fertilizers, preparation of soil, gathering, preparation for market, and practical gardening [36]. The acquisition of funds for this program illustrates how the funding sources often dictated curricular content. These sources actively sought to subvert academically based programs in favor of the industrial approach.

By 1907 sixteen percent of Spelman's budget was coming from the John F. Slater Fund for industrial training. Spelman was reputedly the only college in Georgia receiving from the Fund an amount substantial enough to equip an efficient Industrial Education Department [36]. However, by 1912 there was a conscious effort on the part of the Spelman administration to make sure that those students concentrating their efforts in the industrial courses were exposed to literary offerings as well: "The Industrial Courses are as follows: cooking, sewing, dressmaking, millinery, basketry, benchwork, printing, laundering and agriculture. No boarding student can give her whole time to any of these except dressmaking. She must also enter some literary class"[36].

A perusal of Spelman's catalogs from 1887 to 1909 points up a curiosity. Although large numbers of students are shown as being enrolled in industrial education classes, a relatively small number are shown as actual graduates of these areas of study. The overwhelming majority of students graduated from the Normal, Preparatory, Academic, and Collegiate departments (see table 1). Although 50 students were enrolled in dressmaking, only 14 were "majoring" in it. Likewise, 108 students were enrolled in millinery, but only one was a "major."

When Spelman started tracking and reporting on the progress of its graduates, it never included among its alumnae the individuals who were solely graduates of the industrial areas. A distinction is made between those who receive diplomas and those who receive certificates, and subsequently those whom the institution tracked after graduation. The policy was stated as

> *Diplomas and Certificates*: Diplomas are awarded to those who have completed the full courses and passed all the required examinations, provided their deportment and moral character, in connection with their scholarship, shall justify the honor.
>
> Certificates are given to those who complete the courses in the industrial, nurse-training, dress-making, and printing departments.
>
> *Graduates*: We keep a record of the life-work of each graduate, and request that each one will keep us informed of any change in her address or work. One hundred thirty-seven have already received our *diplomas*. A large majority of these have been engaged in teaching [36].

In celebration of Spelman's twenty-fifth anniversary in 1906, President Giles included in her annual report to the Board of Trustees an accounting of the school's graduates from its inception (see table 2).

How then does one account for the numbers cited in the catalogs as being enrolled in industrial training? Apparently all students took some industrial training but few were receiving certificates solely in these areas. Students could and did earn certificates and diplomas, thus accounting for many of the students counted under the certificates column. Additionally, one of the tenets espoused by the missionary society was the need to develop character, industry, thrift, and morality through the training of the hands as well as the heart and mind. For them it was not inconsistent to have all the students take industrial courses. It prepared them for their home and classroom responsibilities. These women, however, were getting their most substantial training in academic topics that prepared them for the leadership roles envisioned by the founders. Appar-

Table 1 Distribution of Students in Majors/Courses

Number of Students Majoring in Units

College Department	2
Missionary Training Department	4
Normal and Training Department	17
College Preparatory Department	6
Academic Department	57
English Preparatory Department	403
Dressmaking only	14
Nurse Training only	17
Millinery only	1
Shorthand	1
Total number of students	522

Number of Students Taking Courses

Nurse Training Department	33
Domestic Arts	12
Dressmaking	50
Millinery	108
Printing	28
Instrumental Music	66
	(36)

Table 2 Diplomas/Degrees/Certificates Granted

Number of diplomas given, teachers, professional, Christian workers, high school, and nurse training department	285
Number of degrees given, college department	6
Number of different persons, alumnae	251
Number of certificates given: total Domestic arts, nurse training, printing, dressmaking, cooking, music	402
	(36)

ently those responsible for the school were able to manipulate the curriculum in such a way as to receive the sorely needed external funds but also keep the curriculum on a steady course that was firmly grounded in the classical/literary education arena.

Could one construe this as duplicitous behavior? Was money accepted from the Slater Fund under false pretenses? This is a difficult question to answer. The Fund had access to all enrollment and graduation records. Perhaps it felt that its purposes were being served by the mere attendance of students in those classes. The school consistently received praise from Atticus G. Haygood, general agent of the Fund. In 1884 he wrote to WABHMS, "My judgment is, no school in proportion to the investment of money in it is doing so much good work" [34, p. 88]. Apparently those responsible for the school were able to balance their act in such a way as to receive the sorely needed funds but also keep the curriculum on a steady course that was firmly grounded in the classical education arena.

The Curriculum

The founders decided from the school's inception to offer a course of study modeled on the type of education they had received and had taught in academies in New England. The first circular of Spelman Seminary (then called the Atlanta Baptist Female Seminary), published in May 1881, outlines a course of study for first, second, and third year students in the Normal Department and first, second, third, and fourth year courses in the Academic Department. The former included such topics as intellectual arithmetic, geography, history of the United States, and composition and recitations. These are the same types of courses offered in the Preparatory Department of the Oread Institute for Young Ladies in Worcester, Massachusetts, in June 1865. That year at Oread, Sophia B. Packard was one of the principals and instructor of metaphysics and literature; and Harriet E. Giles served as instructor of ornamentals and music [34, pp. 19–23].

There is little doubt that the 1881 circular advertising the school was far more ambitious than Packard and Giles were able to deliver in those early years. They had entered a state where minimal formal education was available to Blacks. The students who initially came to them had very little if any educational background.

Even given these obstacles, a slow but steady educational course was set by the founders based on the New England classical liberal curriculum. By 1898 a college course of study had been added to the curriculum. It consisted of such course of study had been added to the curriculum. It consisted of such course work as Latin, Greek, Chemistry, Ethics, Geology, Economics, and Sociology. There was no rush, however, to move students into a course of study before they were prepared to do so. During the 1898–99 year, only 2 students were enrolled in the College Department, while 6 were enrolled in the College Preparatory Department, and 57 in the Academic Department. These latter two were the equivalent of high-school preparation. From here students could enroll in either the College Department or the Normal and Training Department [36].

It was not until 1904 that the Preparatory department was distinctly called a high school and set apart as such within the curriculum. The high school had a four-year program which included an English course and an English-Latin course. Students taking the former could enter the Normal department; students taking the latter were admitted to either the Normal or the College department [36].

Education is not a neutral process. Whenever decisions are made about what is taught and how it is taught, a political statement is made. Although one cannot discern any overt political statements as one looks at Spelman's curriculum over time, by virtue of their choosing the classical curriculum and not emphasizing the industrial curriculum, a political statement was made. A message was conveyed to the women who entered the institution that there were enormous responsibilities being placed on their shoulders and they were being given the skills that were judged to be the best to have to assume those responsibilities.

The Faculty—Who Were They?

Because the work at Spelman was viewed as a missionary effort, the first faculty members were missionary teachers who were either reassigned to Spelman from other sites or who were new missionary workers. Their academic training tended not to be very rigorous. As described by Florence Fleming Corely, the Spelman faculty consisted of "unmarried white women" who were "staunch Baptists" [12, p. 130].

In 1886 Spelman had 20 teachers in all departments. They were all White females (English Annual Report WABHMS, 1886). In 1910 there were 49 teachers at the institution. Of that number, 42 were White females and 7 were Black females. There were no male teachers of either race. That same year Atlanta University had a total of 24 teachers—five White men, 12 White women, 4 Black men, and 3 Black women. Atlanta Baptist College's instructional staff numbered 16, of whom 2 were White males, 4 were White females, 8 were Black males, and 2 were Black females. Clearly, the gender/racial balance at the other institutions was more diverse than at Spelman [15, pp. 23–27].

Conclusions

As one examines the missionary historiography, the portraits painted vary widely. The truth probably lies somewhere in the middle. They were neither the naive, callous, insensitive interlopers presented by Wilbur Cash and Henry Swint, nor were they totally the sympathetic, caring saints portrayed by W. E. B. DuBois and to some degree by Jacqueline Jones. They were sincere in their efforts, had clear views of what they hoped to accomplish, and endured tremendous hardships to see those visions fulfilled.

However, despite their sincerity, the missionaries were often narrow in their thinking and myopic in their view of the world. Their vision was often very narrow when it came to how they saw Black people and how they defined the problems facing them. Too often the issues related to Blacks were treated from the posture that Blacks were the problem. This is called "blame the victim"; how can they (Blacks) be changed to solve the problem. George Sale's treatise was entitled *Our Part in the Solution of a Great Problem*. He states, "It is the Negro of today that makes our problem" [35, p. 5]. The solution was that Blacks had to be educated and trained properly in order for them to assume their places in society. This necessitated change on the part of Blacks and the inculcation of White, middle-class values that would make them acceptable to Whites.

Rarely did the missionaries talk about the disengagement of the federal government in finding a solution to the "problem." There were never any legal challenges to the wholesale political disenfranchisement of Blacks at the end of the nineteenth century. Although General Morgan in his 1901 speech at Spelman condemned the lynching and burning of Blacks that was so prevalent in the South at that time, the Home Mission Society took no active role in lobbying for an end to such barbaric behavior. Morgan's admonition to those who were Black in his audience was "that they must exhibit those qualities of manhood and citizenship which are the essential conditions of the white man's confidence and esteem" [7, p. 14].

Probably the single most pressing issue facing Blacks after being emancipated was the matter of land acquisition. Had there been some program implemented for redistributing land to ex-slaves, the history that flows from the Civil War undoubtedly would have been very different. Yet

ABHMS and WABHMS are strangely silent on this major topic. It was not a part of their agenda. Blacks were then left at the mercy of their former masters without the opportunity to gain economic independence and stability. There was deafening silence from the Society.

One of the stated educational goals of Spelman was to prepare a college-bred Black leadership to uplift the masses. Yet it would appear that this leadership was not to be involved in the institutions created by the Society. Well into the twentieth century, after thousands of Blacks had received the proper credentials, the faculty, administrators, and boards of trustees of Black Northern-sponsored missionary schools remained overwhelmingly White. Spelman was no exception to this state of affairs. To its credit, there were two Black men on the board of trustees from the beginning, but significantly, there were no Black women. Also to its credit, it invited the first two college graduates in 1901 to join the faculty as instructors in the Normal Practice School. It was not until 1987 that Spelman acquired its first Black female president. The legacy of not encouraging Black female leadership within the college was to be handed down for a very long time.

References

1. Anderson, J. D. D. *The Education of Blacks in the South, 1860–1935*. Chapel Hill, N.C.: The University of North Carolina Press, 1988.

2. _____. "The Hampton Model of Normal School Industrial Education, 1868–1900." In *New Perspectives on Black Educational History*, edited by V.P. Franklin and J.D. Anderson. Boston: G.K. Hall, 1978.

3. Annual Reports of the American Baptist Home Mission Society, New York: American Baptist Home Mission Society, 1887, 1892, 1895.

4. Annual Reports of the Woman's American Baptist Home Mission Society, Boston, Mass.: C.H. Simonds and Co., 1886, 1891.

5. Bacon, A.M. *The Negro and the Atlanta Exposition*. Baltimore. The John F. Slater Fund, 1896.

6. *The Baptist Home Mission Monthly*, 17 (October 1895), 368.

7. _____, 24 (January 1902), 15.

8. Bullock, H.A. *A History of Negro Education in the South from 1619 to the Present*. Cambridge, Mass.: Harvard University Press, 1967.

9. Butchart, R. E. *Northern Schools, Southern Blacks, and Reconstruction*: *Freedmen's Education, 1862–1875*. Westport, Conn.: Greenword Press, 1980.

10. Cash, W. J. *The Mind of the South*. New York: Alfred A. Knopf, 1941.

11. Conway, J. "Perspectives on the History of Women's Education in the United States." *History of Education Quarterly*, 14 (Spring 1974).

12. Corley, F. F. "Higher Education for Southern Women: Four Church-Related Women's Colleges in Georgia, 1900–1920." Ph.D. dissertation, Georgia State University, 1985.

13. Diary of Harriet E. Giles, 1881–1909 (Spelman Archives).

14. Diary of Sophia B. Packard, 1881–1891 (Spelman Archives).

15. Dickerson, G. S. (ed). *Reports from Schools to the Trustees of the John F. Slater Fund for the Year Ending June, 1910*.

16. DuBois, W. E. B. *Black Reconstruction in America, 1860–1880*. Cleveland and New York: The World Printing Co., 1964 (reprint).

17. _____. The Souls of Black Folk. New York: Washington Square Press, 1970 (reprint).

18. Franklin, V., and J. Anderson. *New Perspectives on Black Educational History*, 1978.

19. Friedman, J. E. *The Enclosed Garden: Women and Community in the Evangelical South*, 1830–1900. Chapel Hill: University of North Carolina Press, 1985.

20. Genovese, E. D. *Roll, Jordan, Roll*. New York: Pantheon Books, 1972.

21. *Historical Sketch of the Women's American Baptist Home Mission Society*. Boston, Mass.: S. G. Robinson, 1909.

22. Holmes, D. O. W. *Evolution of the Negro College*. New York: AMS Press, 1934 (reprint, 1970).

23. Horowitz, H. L. *Alma Mater: Design and Experience in the Women's Colleges from Their Nineteenth-Century Beginnings to the 1930s*. New York: Alfred A. Knopf, 1984.

24. Jacoway, E. *Yankee Missionaries in the South: The Penn School Experiment*. Louisiana State University Press, 1980.

25. Jones, J. E. *Soldiers of Light and Love: Northern Teachers and Georgia Blacks, 1865–1873*. Chapel Hill: The University of North Carolina Press, 1980.

26. _____. *Labor of Love, Labor of Sorrow: Black Women Work, and the Family from Slavery to the Present*. New York: Basic Books, 1985.

27. _____. "Women Who Were More than Men: Sex and Status in Freedmen's Teaching." *History of Education Quarterly*, 19 (Spring 1979).

28. Letter from Jean Davis to George Foster Peabody, 14 June 1902.

29. McKinney, T. *Higher Education among Negroes*. Charlotte, N.C.: Johnson C. Smith University, 1932.

30. McPherson, J. M. "The New Puritanism: Values and Goals of Freedmen's Education in America." In *The University and Society*, edited by L. Stone. Princeton, N.J.: Princeton University Press, 1974.

31. _____. *The Abolitionist Legacy from Reconstruction to the NAACP*. Princeton, N.J.: Princeton University Press, 1975.

32. Noble, J. *The Negro Woman's College Education*. Chapel Hill: University of North Carolina Press, 1956.

33. Range, W. *The Rise and Progress of Negro Colleges in Georgia, 1868–1949*. Athens: University of Georgia Press, 1951.

34. Read, F. M. *The Story of Spelman College*. Princeton, N.J.: Princeton University Press, 1961.

35. Sale, G. *Our Part in the Solution of a Great Problem*. New York: The American Baptist Home Mission Society, ND.

36. *Spelman Seminary Catalogues*, 1881–1913.

37. Swint, H. L. *The Northern Teacher in the South, 1862–1870*. New York: Octagon Books, Inc., 1907 (reprint, 1941).

38. Woodson, C. G. *The Mis-Education of the Negro*. Washington, D.C.: The Associated Publishers, Inc., 1933.

39. Woodward, C. V. *Origins of the New South: 1877–1913*. Louisiana State University Press, 1951.

40. Woody, T. *A History of Women's Education in the United States. Volume I*. New York: Octagon Books, Inc., 1929 (reprint, 1966).

Ethnicity in American Life: The Historical Perspective

JOHN HOPE FRANKLIN

The United States is unique in the ethnic composition of its population. No other country in the world can point to such a variety of cultural, racial, religious, and national backgrounds in its population. It was one of the salient features in the early history of this country; and it would continue to be so down into the twentieth century. From virtually every corner of the globe they came—some enthusiastically and some quite reluctantly. Britain and every part of the continent of Europe provided prospective Americans by the millions. Africa and Asia gave up great throngs. Other areas of the New World saw inhabitants desert their own lands to seek their fortunes in the colossus to the North. Those who came voluntarily were attracted by the prospect of freedom of religion, freedom from want, and freedom from various forms of oppression. Those who were forced to come were offered the consolation that if they were white they would some day inherit the earth, and if they were black they would some day gather their reward in the Christian heaven.

One of the interesting and significant features of this coming together of peoples of many tongues and races and cultures was that the backgrounds out of which they came would soon be minimized and that the process by which they evolved into Americans would be of paramount importance. Hector St. Jean de Crevecoeur sought to describe this process in 1782 when he answered his own question, "What, then, is the American, this new man?" He said, "He is either an European, or the descendant of an European, hence that strange mixture of blood, which you will find in no other country. . . . He is an American, who, leaving behind him all his ancient prejudices and manners, receives new ones from the new mode of the life he has embraced, the new government he obeys, and the new rank he holds. He becomes an American by being received in the broad lap of our great *Alma Mater*. Here individuals of all nations are melted into a new race of men, whose labours and posterity will one day cause great changes in the world."

This was one of the earliest expressions of the notion that the process of Americanization involved the creation of an entirely new mode of life that would replace the ethnic backgrounds of those who were a part of the process. It contained some imprecisions and inaccuracies that would, in time, become a part of the lore or myth of the vaunted melting pot and would grossly misrepresent the crucial factor of ethnicity in American life. It ignored the tenacity with which the Pennsylvania Dutch held onto their language, religion, and way of life. It overlooked the way in which the Swedes of New Jersey remained Swedes and the manner in which the French Huguenots of New York and Charleston held onto their own past as though it was the source of all light and life. It described a process that in a distant day would gag at the notion that Irish Catholics could be assimilated on the broad lap of Alma Mater or that Asians could be seated on the basis of equality at the table of the Great American Feast.

By suggesting that only Europeans were involved in the process of becoming Americans, Crevecoeur pointedly ruled out three quarters of a million blacks already in the country who, along with their progeny, would be regarded as ineligible to become Americans for at least another two centuries. To be sure, the number of persons of African descent would increase enormously, but the view of their ineligibility for Americanization would be very slow to change. And when such a change occurred, even if it merely granted freedom from bondage, the change would be made most reluctantly and without any suggestion that freedom qualified one for equality on the broad lap of Alma Mater. It was beyond the conception of Crevecoeur, as it was indeed beyond the conception of the founding fathers, that Negroes, slave or free, could become true Americans, enjoying that fellowship in a common enterprise about which Crevecoeur spoke so warmly. It was as though Crevecoeur was arguing that ethnicity, where persons of African descent were concerned, was either so powerful or so unattractive as to make their assimilation entirely impossible or so insignificant as to make it entirely undesirable. In any case Americanization in the late eighteenth century was a precious commodity to be cherished and enjoyed only by a select group of persons of European descent.

One must admit, therefore, that at the time of the birth of the new nation there was no clear-cut disposition to welcome into the American family persons of any and all ethnic backgrounds. Only Europeans were invited to fight for independence. And when the patriots at long last relented and gave persons of African descent a chance to fight, the concession was made with great reluctance and after much equivocation and soul-searching. Only Europeans were regarded as full citizens in the new states and in the new nation. And when the founding fathers wrote the Constitution of the United States, they did not seem troubled by the distinctions on the basis of ethnic differences that the Constitution implied.

If the principle of ethnic exclusiveness was propounded so early and so successfully in the history of the United States, it is not surprising that it would, in time, become the basis for questioning the ethnic backgrounds of large numbers of prospective Americans, even Europeans. Thus, in 1819, a Jewish immigrant was chilled to hear a bystander refer to him and his companion as "more damned emigrants." A decade later there began a most scathing and multifaceted attack on the Catholic Church. On two counts the church was a bad influence. First, its principal recruits were the Irish, the "very dregs" of the Old World social order; and secondly, its doctrine of papal supremacy ran counter to the idea of the political and religious independence of the United States. Roman Catholics, Protestant Americans warned, were engaged in a widespread conspiracy to subvert American institutions, through parochial schools, the Catholic press, immoral convents, and a sinister design to control the West by flooding it with Catholic settlers. The burning of convents and churches and the killing of Catholics themselves were indications of how deeply many Americans felt about religious and cultural differences for which they had a distaste and suspicion that bordered on paranoia.

Soon the distaste for the foreign-born became almost universal, with Roman Catholics themselves sharing in the hostility to those who followed them to the new Republic. Some expressed fear of the poverty and criminality that accompanied each wave of immigrants. Some felt that those newly arrived from abroad were a threat to republican freedom. Some saw in the ethnic differences of the newcomers an immediate danger to the moral standards of Puritan America. Some feared the competition that newcomers posed in the labor market. Some became convinced that the ideal of a national homogeneity would disappear with the influx of so many unassimilable elements. Soon, nativist societies sprang up all across the land, and they found national expression in 1850 in a new organization called the Order of the Star Spangled Banner. With its slogan, "America for Americans," the order, which became the organizational basis for the Know-Nothing party, engendered a fear through its preachments that caused many an American to conclude that his country was being hopelessly subverted by the radical un-Americanism of the great variety of ethnic strains that were present in the United States.

If there was some ambivalence regarding the ethnic diversity of white immigrants before the Civil War, it was dispelled by the view that prevailed regarding immigrants in the post–Civil War years. The "old" immigrants, so the argument went, were at least assimilable and had "entered practically every line of activity in nearly every part of the country." Even those who had been non–English speaking had mingled freely with native Americans and had therefore been quickly assimilated. Not so with the "new" immigrants who came after 1880. They "congregated together in sections apart from native Americans and the older immigrants to such an extent that assimilation had been slow." Small wonder that they were different. Small wonder that they were barely assimilable. They came from Austro-Hungary, Italy, Russia, Greece, Rumania, and Turkey. They dressed differently, spoke in unfamiliar tongues, and clung to strange, if not exotic customs. It did not matter that Bohemians, Moravians, and Finns had lower percentages of illiteracy than had the Irish and Germans or that Jews had a higher percentage of skilled laborers than any group except the Scots. Nor did it matter that, in fact, the process of assimilation for the so-called "new" group was about as rapid as that of the so-called "old" group.

What did matter was that the new nativism was stronger and more virulent than any anti-immigration forces or groups of the early nineteenth century and that these groups were determined either to drive from the shores those who were different or to isolate them so that they could not contaminate American society. Old-stock Americans began to organize to preserve American institutions and the American way of life. Those who had been here for five years or a decade designated themselves as old-stock Americans and joined in the attack on those recently arrived. If the cult of Anglo-Saxon superiority was all but pervasive, those who were not born into the cult regarded themselves as honorary members. Thus, they could celebrate with as much feeling as any the virtues of Anglo-Saxon institutions and could condemn as vehemently as any those ideas and practices that were not stricty Anglo-Saxon. Whenever possible they joined the American Protective Association and the Immigrant Restriction League; and in so doing they sold their own ethnicity for the obscurity that a pseudoassimilation brought. But in the end, they would be less than successful. The arrogance and presumption of the Anglo-Saxon complex was not broad enough to embrace the Jews of eastern Europe or the Bohemians of central Europe or the Turks of the Middle East. The power and drive of the Anglo-Saxon forces would prevail; and those who did not belong would be compelled to console themselves by extolling the virtues of cultural pluralism.

By that time—near the end of the nineteenth century—the United States had articulated quite clearly its exalted standards of ethnicity. They were standards that accepted Anglo-Saxons as the norm, placed other whites on what may be called "ethnic probation," and excluded from serious consideration the Japanese, Chinese, and Negroes. It was not difficult to deal harshly with the Chinese and Japanese when they began to enter the United States in considerable numbers in the post–Civil War years. They simply did not meet the standards that the arbiters of American ethnicity had promulgated. They were different in race, religion, language, and public and private morality. They had to be excluded; and eventually they were.

The presence of persons of African descent, almost from the beginning, had helped whites to define ethnicity and to establish and maintain the conditions by which it could be controlled. If their color and race, their condition of servitude, and their generally degraded position did not set them apart, the laws and customs surrounding them more than accomplished that feat. Whether in Puritan Massachusetts or cosmopolitan New York or Anglican South Carolina, the colonists declared that Negroes, slave or free, did not and could not belong to the society of equal human beings. Thus, the newly arrived Crevecoeur could be as blind to the essential humanity of Negroes as the patriots who tried to keep them out of the Continental Army. They were not a part of America, these new men. And in succeeding years their presence would do more to define ethnicity than the advent of several scores of millions of Europeans.

It was not enough for Americans, already somewhat guilt-ridden for maintaining slavery in a free society, to exclude blacks from American society on the basis of race and condition of servitude. They proceeded from that point to argue that Negroes were inferior morally, intellectually, and physically. Even as he reviewed the remarkable accomplishments of Benjamin Banneker, surveyor, almanacker, mathematician, and clockmaker, Thomas Jefferson had serious doubts about the mental capabilities of Africans, and he expressed these doubts to his European friends. What Jefferson speculated about at the end of the eighteenth century became indisputable dogma within a decade after his death.

In the South every intellectual, legal, and religious resource was employed in the task of describing the condition of Negroes in such a way as to make them the least attractive human beings on the face of the earth. Slavery was not only the natural lot of blacks, the slaveowners argued, but it was in accordance with God's will that they should be kept in slavery. As one sanctimonious divine put it, "We feel that the souls of our slaves are a solemn trust and we shall strive to present them faultless and complete before the presence of God. . . . However the world may judge us in connection with our institution of slavery, we conscientiously believe it to be a great missionary institution—one arranged by God, as He arranges all moral and religious influences of the world so that the good may be brought out of seeming evil, and a blessing wrung out of every form of the curse." It was a difficult task that the owners of slaves set for themselves. Slaves had brought with them only heathenism, immorality, profligacy, and irresponsibility. They possessed neither the mental capacity nor the moral impulse to improve themselves. Only if their sponsors—those to whom were entrusted not only their souls but their bodies—were fully committed to their improvement could they take even the slightest, halting steps toward civilization.

What began as a relatively moderate justification for slavery soon became a vigorous, aggressive defense of the institution. Slavery, to the latter-day defenders, was the cornerstone of the republican edifice. To a governor of South Carolina, it was the greatest of all the great blessings which a kind Providence had bestowed upon the glorious region of the South. It was, indeed, one of the remarkable coincidences of history that such a favored institution had found such a favored creature as the African to give slavery the high value that was placed on it. A childlike race, prone to docility and manageable in every respect, the African was the ideal subject for the slave role. Slaveholders had to work hard to be worthy of this great Providential blessing.

Nothing that Negroes could do or say could change or seriously affect this view. They might graduate from college, as John Russwurm did in 1826, or they might write a most scathing attack against slavery, as David Walker did in 1829. It made no difference. They might teach in an all-white college, as Charles B. Reason did in New York in the 1850s, or publish a newspaper, as Frederick Douglass did during that same decade. Their racial and cultural backgrounds disqualified them from becoming American citizens. They could even argue in favor of their capacities and potentialities, as Henry Highland Garnet did, or they might argue their right to fight for union and freedom, as 186,000 did in the Civil War. Still, it made no sense for white Americans to give serious consideration to their arguments and their actions. They were beyond the veil, as the Jews had been beyond the veil in the barbaric and bigoted communities of eastern Europe.

The views regarding Negroes that had been so carefully developed to justify and defend slavery would not disappear with emancipation. To those who had developed such views and to the vast numbers who subscribed to them, they were much too valid to be discarded simply because the institution of slavery had collapsed. In fact, if Negroes were heathens and barbarians and intellectual imbeciles in slavery, they were hardly qualified to function as equals in a free society. And any effort to impose them on a free society should be vigorously and relentlessly resisted, even if it meant that a new and subordinate place for them had to be created.

When Americans set out to create such a place for the four million freedmen after the Civil War, they found that it was convenient to put their formulation in the context of the ethnic factors that militated against complete assimilation. To do it this way seemed more fitting, perhaps even more palatable, for the white members of a so-called free society. And they had some experience on which to rely. In an earlier day it had been the Irish or the Germans or the free Negroes who presented problems of assimilation. They were different in various ways and did not seem to make desirable citizens. In time the Irish, Germans, and other Europeans made it and were accepted on the broad lap of Alma Mater. But not the free Negroes, who continued to suffer disabilities even in the North in the years just before the Civil War. Was this the key to the solution of the postwar problems? Perhaps it was. After all, Negroes had always been a group apart in Boston, New York, Philadelphia, and other northern cities. They all lived together in one part of the city—especially if they could find no other place to live. They had their own churches—after the whites drove them out of theirs. They had their own schools—after they were excluded from the schools attended by whites. They had their own social organizations—after the whites barred them from theirs.

If Negroes possessed so many ethnic characteristics such as living in the same community, having their own churches, schools, and social clubs, and perhaps other agencies of cohesion, that was all very well. They even seemed "happier with their own kind," some patronizing observers remarked. They were like the Germans or the Irish or the Italians or the Jews. They had so much in common and so much to preserve. There was one significant difference, however. For Europeans, the ethnic factors that brought a particular group together actually eased the task of assimilation and, in many ways, facilitated the process of assimilation, particularly as hostile elements sought to disorient them in their drive toward full citizenship. And, in time, they achieved it.

For Negroes, however, such was not the case. They had been huddled together in northern ghettoes since the eighteenth century. They had had their own churches since 1792 and their own schools since 1800. And this separateness, this ostracism, was supported and enforced by the full majesty of the law, state and federal, just to make certain that Negroes did, indeed, preserve their ethnicity! And as they preserved their ethnicity—all too frequently as they looked down the barrel of a policeman's pistol or a militiaman's shotgun—full citizenship seemed many light years away. They saw other ethnic groups pass them by, one by one, and take their places in the sacred Order of the Star Spangled Banner, the American Protective Association, the Knights of the Ku Klux Klan—not always fully assimilated but vehemently opposed to the assimilation of Negroes. The ethnic grouping that was a way station, a temporary resting place for Europeans as they became Americans, proved to be a terminal point for blacks who found it virtually impossible to become Americans in any real sense.

There was an explanation or at least a justification for this. The federal government and the state governments had tried to force Negroes into full citizenship and had tried to legislate them into equality with the whites. This was not natural and could not possibly succeed. Negroes had not made it because they were not fit, the social Darwinists[1] said. Negroes were beasts, Charles Carroll declared somewhat inelegantly. "Stateways cannot change folkways," William Graham Summer, the distinguished scholar, philosophized. The first forty years of Negro freedom had been a failure, said John R. Commons, one of the nation's leading economists. This so-called failure was widely acknowledged in the country as northerners of every rank and description acquiesced, virtually without a murmur of objection, to the southern settlement of the race problem characterized by disfranchisement, segregation, and discrimination.

Here was a new and exotic form of ethnicity. It was to be seen in the badges of inferiority and the symbols of racial degradation that sprang up in every sector of American life—in the exclusion from the polling places with its specious justification that Negroes were unfit to participate in the sacred rite of voting; the back stairway or the freight elevator to public places; the separate, miserable railway car, the separate and hopelessly inferior school; and even the Jim Crow cemetery. Ethnic considerations had never been so important in the shaping of public policy. They had never before been used by the American government to define the role and place of other groups in American society. The United States had labored hard to create order out of its chaotic and diverse ethnic backgrounds. Having begun by meekly suggesting the difficulty in assimilating all groups into one great society, it had acknowledged failure by ruling out one group altogether, quite categorically, and frequently by law, solely on the basis of race.

It could not achieve this without doing irreparable harm to the early notions of the essential unity of America and Americans. The sentiments that promoted the disfranchisement and segregation of Negroes also encouraged the infinite varieties of discrimination against Jews, Armenians, Turks, Japanese, and Chinese. The conscious effort to degrade a particular ethnic group reflects a corrosive quality that dulls the sensitivities of both the perpetrators and the victims. It calls forth venomous hatreds and crude distinctions in high places as well as low places. It can affect the quality of mind of even the most cultivated scholar and place him in a position scarcely distinguishable from the Klansman or worse. It was nothing out of the ordinary, therefore, that at a dinner in honor of the winner of one of Harvard's most coveted prizes, Professor Barrett Wendell warned that if a Negro or Jew ever won the prize the dinner would have to be canceled.

By the time that the Statue of Liberty was dedicated in 1886 the words of Emma Lazarus on the base of it had a somewhat hollow ring. Could anyone seriously believe that the poor, tired, huddled masses "yearning to breathe free" were really welcome here? This was a land where millions of black human beings whose ancestors had been here for centuries were consistently treated as pariahs and untouchables! What interpretation could anyone place on the sentiments expressed on the statue except that the country had no real interest in or sympathy for the downtrodden unless they were white and preferably Anglo-Saxon? It was a disillusioning experience for some newcomers to discover that their own ethnic background was a barrier to success in their adopted land. It was a searing and shattering experience for Negroes to discover over and over again that three centuries of toil and loyalty were nullified by the misfortune of their own degraded ethnic background.

In the fullness of time—in the twentieth century—the nation would confront the moment of truth regarding ethnicity as a factor in its own historical development. Crevecoeur's words would have no real significance. The words of the Declaration of Independence would have no real meaning. The words of Emma Lazarus would not ring true. All such sentiments would be put to the severe test of public policy and private deeds and would be found wanting. The Ku Klux Klan would challenge the moral and human dignity of Jews, Catholics, and Negroes. The quotas of the new immigration laws would define ethnic values in terms of race and national origin. The restrictive covenants would arrogate to a select group of bigots the power of determining what races or ethnic groups should live in certain houses or whether, indeed, they should have any houses at all in which to live. If some groups finally made it through the escape hatch and arrived at the point of acceptance, it was on the basis of race, now defined with sufficient breadth to include all or most peoples who were not of African descent.

By that time ethnicity in American life would come to have a special, clearly definable meaning. Its meaning would be descriptive of that group of people vaguely defined in the federal census returns as "others" or "non-whites." It would have something in common with that magnificent term "cultural pluralism," the consolation prize for those who were not and could not be assimilated. It would signify the same groping for respectability that describes that group of people who live in what euphemistically called "the inner city." It would represent a rather earnest search for a hidden meaning that would make it seem a bit more palatable and surely more sophisticated than something merely racial. But in 1969 even a little child would know what ethnicity had come to mean.

In its history, ethnicity, in its true sense, has extended and continues to extend beyond race. At times it has meant language, customs, religion, national origin. It has also meant race; and, to some, it has always meant only race. It had already begun to have a racial connotation in the eighteenth century. In the nineteenth century, it had a larger racial component, even as other factors continued to loom large. In the present century, as these other factors have receded in importance, racial considerations have come to have even greater significance. If the history of ethnicity has meant anything at all during the last three centuries, it has meant the gradual but steady retreat from the broad and healthy regard for cultural and racial differences to a narrow, counter-productive concept of differences in terms of whim, intolerance, and racial prejudice. We have come full circle. The really acceptable American is still that person whom Crevecoeur described almost two hundred years ago. But the true American, acceptable or not, is that person who seeks to act out his role in terms of his regard for human qualities irrespective of race. One of the great tragedies of American life at the beginning was that ethnicity was defined too narrowly. One of the great tragedies of today is that this continues to be the case. One can only hope that the nation and its people will all some day soon come to reassess ethnicity in terms of the integrity of the man rather than in terms of the integrity of the race. [1989]

Notes

1. SOCIAL DARWINISM: The theory that applied Darwin's theory of evolution, "survival of the fittest," to society; it assumed that upper classes were naturally superior, and the failure of the lower classes was the result of their natural inferiority, not of social policies and practices.

2. JIM CROW: Laws and practices, especially in the South, that separated blacks and whites and enforced the subordination of blacks.

3. RESTRICTIVE COVENANTS: Codes prohibiting members of some groups—often blacks, Jews, and Asians—from buying real estate in certain areas.

Understanding the Reading

1. Today, why do we today find de Crevecoeur's 1782 definition of "the American, this new man" inadequate or inappropriate?

2. How did the principle of ethnic exclusion that omitted people of African descent affect later immigrant groups in the nineteenth century?

3. What does nativism mean?

4. How was the exclusion of African-Americans from American society justified?

5. How was it maintained?

6. How did the treatment of African-Americans affect other groups in the twentieth century?

Suggestions for Responding

1. According to Franklin, America has not lived up to its ideals. Do you think his pessimistic views are justified? What arguments would you offer to support or refute his analysis?

2. Is the "really acceptable American" today still that person whom de Crevecoeur described, as Franklin claims? Why or why not?

Indian, Chicano, and Puerto Rican Colleges: Status and Issues

Michael A. Olivas

The enormous problems facing Indian, Chicano, and Puerto Rican colleges have not been addressed by legislative efforts aimed at redressing historic exclusion nor by educational assistance designed for colleges in general. In the unique case of Indian colleges, specific legislation and program initiatives have not been effective, in part because of the fragile nature of the colleges themselves and in part because of the organizational difficulties Indian people face daily in their relationship with government agencies. Because there are only three historically Hispanic colleges, efforts to improve access for Hispanic students are not likely to be successful through minority institution initiatives.

National debates over racial inequality have historically centered upon slavery, its abolition, and its vestiges. Historical perspectives of educational inequality arise from the same memory, inevitably framing educational debates in terms of access for blacks into white institutions and school systems. Because majority Americans frequently perceive equality solely in terms of increased minority access into white institutions, adequacy of public resources for minority-controlled institutions is not often acknowledged as a corollary dimension of increased minority access. Yet, the litigation in the *Adams v. Califano* case,[1] leading to "desegregation" of black higher education institutions, has caused educators and policymakers to confront this dimension and to consider the role of black colleges in a society that perceives itself to be integrated.[2]

The Status of Historically Black Colleges

Lorenzo Morris has succinctly summarized the risk for black colleges in a search for racial balance:

> At a fundamental level of the disagreement over the Adams case(s) is a conceptual difference concerning black colleges: What are their goals, and what has been the role they fill in society? On one side, they are viewed as being just like all other colleges and universities, except for their histories of unique service to blacks under conditions in which black students and faculty have had no other educational choices. On the advocates' side, the historical conditions are similarly emphasized, but there is a rarely articulated view that black colleges are a product of the choice of black Americans and not simply a byproduct of a no-choice situation. Some imply that black institutions are an automatic outgrowth of racial inequality. Advocates, however, maintain that black institutions are the willful creations of a people seeking an opportunity that has been restricted everywhere else. Blacks attend and have attended black institutions under great constraints, but ultimately have made the choice to do so because these institutions offer them what they want and

need. Through that free choice, [black colleges] are understood to have developed a special capacity to serve their communities—a capacity which will constitute an essential part of free choice in the education of blacks for a long time to come.[3]

This disagreement has profound implications for the framing of arguments and policy choices. How will white and black institutions co-exist in proximity with each other? How can both recruit a shrinking pool of qualified students? How can both draw upon state and private funds? How can historical funding patterns favoring white institutions be altered to compensate for historical underdevelopment? While no answers are proposed in this article, the questions are not rhetorical, for desegregation plans have been drafted, institutions have merged (e.g., the University of Tennessee at Nashville merged with Tennessee State University[4]), and legislation has been amended to incorporate *Adams* issues. Southern and northern states have submitted *Adams* plans to the courts for approval[5] and the Higher Education Act of 1965 reauthorized by Congress contains language requiring that federal programs comply with *Adams* mandates.[6]

The future of the 106 black colleges, particularly the 43 public black colleges,[7] remains uncertain, although recent events suggest a belated acknowledgment of federal responsibility for the network of historically black institutions. President Carter was aggressive in supporting these institutions. In January 1979, he signed a memorandum for a "Black College Initiative"; in August 1980 he signed Executive Order 12232, directing federal agencies to target money for black institutions; in September 1980 he signed another memorandum to accompany the Executive Order (see Appendix A).[8] A black college "setaside" has been incorporated into Title III of the Higher Education Act, while the College Housing Program targeted 10% of its 1980 monies for black college facilities.[9] Several federal departments have designated staff to monitor the Executive Order and Initiative and the charter of the National Advisory Committee on Black Higher Education and Black Colleges and Universities has been renewed.[10] These formal structures have increased black colleges' share of federal dollars and have provided visibility, portfolio, and support for the Black College Initiative.

The attention paid these institutions, however, has not led to comparable initiatives for other minority institutions. The memory of slavery and its present-day legacy, as well as the existence of a network of historically black colleges, have served to overshadow the more fledgling network of non-black minority institutions. Further, the larger societal perception of "minority" issues as synonymous with black civil rights derives from the larger black presence in the American minority population. Additionally, although the black colleges enroll a smaller percentage of black students than they have in the past when the colleges were the near-exclusive avenues of access (in 1976, the 106 colleges enrolled only 18% of the black students),[11] many black leaders have graduated from these colleges; this alumni network is widespread in black communities and constitutes an important minority constituency.

Non-black minorities lack such an extensive historical network, for the few Indians, Chicanos, and Puerto Ricans who hold college degrees are graduates of majority institutions. No similar network has developed for Indians, Chicanos, and Puerto Ricans, for reasons that are unclear. Although it is incontestable that these minorities have been denied educational access equal to that of majority citizens, the differences in the groups' histories of oppression may account, in part, for the lack of a college network comparable to that of blacks.

Many black colleges have been creations of official governmental segregation policies, precluding blacks from attending white colleges. A recent National Center for Education Statistics study noted of black colleges:

> They were established primarily through the efforts of missionary groups, northern-based philanthropists, and the Freedman's Bureau. More than half . . . were created during the Reconstruction period and prior to 1890. The second Morrill Land Grant Act of 1890 spurred the construction of public [black colleges] with the intention of paralleling the network of land-grant institutions which had already been established for whites, thereby legalizing "separate colleges for whites and coloreds." The remainder . . . were constructed for the most part before the outbreak of World War I, although 10 new [black colleges] emerged in the 2 decades following World War II.[12]

No similar large-scale efforts were mounted or developed for colonized American minorities: Native Americans, the first occupants; Chicanos, *mestizo* descendants of Spaniards and Indians; or Puerto Ricans, whose island was claimed by the United States following the Spanish-American War.[13] Although extensive histories of these groups are beyond the scope of this paper, a brief summary of these histories adds context to the development of non-black minority institutions.

The Development of Indian Colleges

The historical development of higher education for Indians, Chicanos, and Puerto Ricans can be characterized as a record of evangelism, majority dominance, paternalism, and neglect. Although several prestigious colleges founded during colonial times (e.g., Harvard, Dartmouth, Columbia) had missions that included instructing Indians,[14] few Indians were educated in these institutions. Indeed, the founder of Dartmouth perhaps typified the colleges' view of educating Indians when he said of one of his students, "I have taken much Pains to purge all the Indian out of him, but after all a little of it will sometimes appear."[15]

Also typical was the abrogation of education treaties signed between the U.S. government and Indian tribes. While the government issued regulations, created special funds, and sold Indian land to finance Indian education, the most common mechanism to educate Indian children before 1870 was by treaty.[16] Of these treaties, Vine Deloria has noted,

> Treaty records and related correspondence in the nation's archives relate only to a fraction of the nearly 400 treaties negotiated from 1778 to 1871. Many agreements were oral; many records have been lost. Records that do exist show conclusively, however, that Indian nations ceded their hands to the federal government with great reluctance and that they did so in the end largely on the basis of federal promises to educate their children.[17]

Appendix B lists over 100 treaties negotiated between 1804 and 1868 that had educational provisions.

Even though the treaties were patently one-sided, the government did not meet its responsibilities. A recent congressional report noted of education treaties, "Many treaty provisions for education were never effective since Congress failed to appropriate the funds to fulfill those obligations."[18] Moreover, as treaties expired, these sources of income became even less secure. The first treaty provisions for Indian higher education appear to be in a September 1830 treaty with the Choctaw Nation,[19] although the money was not used until 1841 when Indian students were given scholarships to attend white colleges; students also attended Hampton Institute, then a black normal school, under other scholarship provisions.[20]

Sheldon Jackson College was founded for Alaskan Natives in 1878 by the United Presbyterian Church.[21] Indian University was founded by the American Baptist Church in Tahlequah, Creek Nation, in February 1880; it moved in 1885 to Muskogee (later Muskogee, Oklahoma) and became known as Bacone College.[22] In 1887, North Carolina established a normal school for Indian students; it became a college in the 1930s and offered its first degree in 1940; in 1969 it became Pembroke State University, which in 1978 still enrolled over 20% Indian students.[23] No additional efforts were undertaken to establish Indian colleges until the 1960s. What federal efforts were aimed at assisting Indians to attend college consisted of establishing normal schools (including Carlisle and Haskell high schools), providing boarding or reservation schools, arranging special contracts with mission schools or black normal schools (e.g., Hampton Institute), and funding scholarships for the few Indian college students to attend majority institutions.[24]

The hodgepodge nature of support had prompted the federal Superintendent of Indian Schools to report in 1886, "The systematic organization of the educational work of the Indian [is] an impossibility."[25] The federal efforts, meager as they were, were consolidated in the Indian Reorganization Act and Johnson-O'Malley Act of 1934, although Indian affairs continued to be spread over the Bureau of Indian Affairs (BIA) of the Department of the Interior, the Office of Education, and other public agencies and departments whose policies affected Indians. It was not until 1966 that BIA officials began to plan for a federally sponsored Indian college, when studies were begun to extend Haskell Institute's high school program into a junior college, offering the first two years of a college curriculum. This effort took four years, resulting in the accreditation of Haskell Indian Junior College in 1970. Other BIA-administered colleges include the Institute for American Indian Arts, which in 1968 became the postsecondary extension of the Santa Fe Indian School, and the Southwestern Polytechnic Institute, established in Albuquerque in 1973.[26]

In addition to state-established and BIA colleges and religious-affiliated colleges, a fourth category of Indian colleges was established in 1968, when Navajo Nation began Navajo Community College. More than a dozen tribes have since established tribal colleges with Indian community boards of trustees. This has become the most fruitful method of establishing Indian colleges. Although Navajo Community College was begun as an independent tribal institution,[27] the smaller tribes have established a fifth type of institution—affiliating themselves with larger, accredited colleges, either as branch campuses or extension centers of majority institutions.

In this manner, a public institution such as Oglala Sioux Community College evolved from its original affiliated status with Black Hills State College and the University of South Dakota into a preaccredited candidate for formal accreditation on its own. Sinte Gleska College, a private institution, has also moved from its ties to Black Hills and the University of South Dakota to similar preaccredited status.[28] The Lummi tribe has an arrangement with Whatcom Community College in Bellingham, Washington, to offer a degree in aquaculture (fishery management), with technical courses taught on Lummi Island and the certificate awarded by the mainland campus.[29] Through these creative means, Indians have begun to organize and administer tribal colleges and other Indian institutions. However, these schools' relative regency and their dependency upon majority institutions for demographic and political reasons have stifled the development of Indian colleges. Sadly, the status of many of these institutions is uncertain and the list (see Table 1) is fluid. In particular the rural isolation, lack of property tax bases, and benign neglect by government have stunted the growth of Indian colleges.[30]

Historically Chicano Institutions

The development of higher education for Chicanos has had a radically different history from that for Native Americans, although the benign neglect accorded Indian education policy was similarly accorded Hispanic groups living in the Southwest and Puerto Rico once these lands became United States territory. One commentator, writing in 1914, likened Mexican American educational conditions to those of blacks:

> Just so surely as Booker T. Washington is right in saying that Tuskegee and similar institutions are the ultimate solution of the Negro problem, so surely is the same kind of education the necessary basis upon which to build a thorough and complete solution of the Mexican problem. Like the Negro, the Mexicans are a child-race without the generations of civilization and culture back of them which support the people of the United States.[31]

Not only was this commentator surely ignorant of black and Mexican history and culture, but the reference to Booker T. Washington and Tuskegee makes precisely the opposite point intended: Although many whites sought only to relegate blacks to black colleges and to prevent them from attending white institutions, blacks took the development of their own colleges seriously and developed black leadership through these institutions.[32] Chicanos, however, were not relegated to their own institutions, since racism, their economic condition, and the rural characteristics of the Southwest precluded them from completing elementary and secondary school, while no governmental or religious groups founded colleges for Mexican Americans.[33] One education historian has noted, "Mexican American children suffered not only the general inadequacies and discrimination of the rural school and caste-like community social structure but also the additional handicap of migrancy."[34]

Concerning the children of migrants in California, Irving Hendrick has summarized: "Responsibility for formal schooling of migrant children was not being assumed by any agency of local, county, or state government until after 1920."[35] Even with a California state plan for migrant education begun in 1920, local school districts ignored truancy laws and failed to serve these students.[36] Complex problems of poverty, increasing urbanization of Chicano families, immigra-

Table 1
Indian Colleges

College (State) [Affiliated Institution]	Public/ Private 2 yr/4 yr	1979 Accred. Status	BIA/ Tribal Affiliation
Bacone College (OK)	Priv, 2	1	—
Blackfeet Community College (MT) [Flathead Valley CC]	Publ, 2	4	Blackfeet
Cheyenne River Community College (SD) [Northern State C}	Publ, 2	4	Cheyenne River Sioux
College of Ganado (AZ)	Priv, 2	1	Hopi
Dull Knife Memorial College (MT) [Miles C}	Publ, 2	4	Northern Cheyenne
Flaming Rainbow University (OK)	Priv, 2	4†	—
Fort Berthold College Center (ND) [Mary C]	Priv, 2	4	Mandan, Hidatsa, Arikara
Fort Peck Community College (MT)	Publ, 2	4	Assiniboine and Sioux
Haskell Indian Junior College (KS)	Publ, 2	1	BIA
Hehaka Sapa College at D-Q University (CA)	Priv, 2	1	Hoopa Valley, Soboba
Institute of American Indian Arts (NM)	Publ, 2	2	BIA
Inupiat University (AK)	Priv, 4	2	Inupiaq Eskimo
Little Bighorn Community College (MT) [Miles C]	Publ, 2	4	Crow
Little Hoop Community College (ND) [Lake Region JC]	Publ, 2	4	Devil's Lake Sioux
Lummi School of Aquaculture (WA) [Whatcom CC]	Publ, 2	3	Lummi
Native American Educational Services (IL)	Priv, 4	2	—
Navajo Community College (AZ)	Publ, 2	1	Navajo
Navajo Community College Branch (NM) [Navajo CC]	Publ, 2	3	
Nebraska Indian Community College (NE) [Northern Technical C]	Publ, 2	4	Santee Sioux, Omaga, Winnebago
Nebraska Indian Satellite CC (NE) [Nebraska Indian CC]	Publ, 2	3	
Oglala Sioux Community College (SD)	Publ, 2	4†	Oglala Sioux
*Pembroke State University (NC)	Publ, 4	1	—
Salish-Kootenai Community College (MT) [Flathead Valley CC]	Publ, 2	4	Salish, Kootenai
Sheldon Jackson College (AK)	Priv, 4	1	—
Sinte Gleska College (SD)	Priv, 4	2	Rosebud Sioux
Sisseton-Wahpeton Community College (SD)	Publ, 2	4	Sisseton-Wahpeton Sioux
Southwestern Indian Polytechnic Institute (NM)	Publ, 2	1	BIA
Standing Rock Community College (ND)	Priv, 2	2	Standing Rock Sioux
Turtle Mountain Community College (ND) [North Dakota State U at Bottineau]	Publ, 2	2	Turtle Mountain Chippewa

Accreditation Key: (1) Accredited; (2) Preaccredited; (3) Branch or extension campus; (4) Unaccredited.

*Formerly Pembroke State College for Indians.

†Not listed in *Accredited Postsecondary Institutions* (September 1, 1979), but listed as having preaccredited status in *Education Directory* (May 1980).

tion from Mexico, deportation of Mexican-origin Americans, segregation, and English-only instruction characterized Mexican American education and precluded the development of historically Chicano colleges.[37]

In the 1960s, increasing minority political participation led to the development of Chicano Studies programs in majority colleges, the establishment of "Third World colleges" within majority universities (e.g., Oakes College at the University of California at Santa Cruz), and the establishment of alternative Chicano postsecondary institutions: Juárez-Lincoln Center (Austin, Texas); Colegio Jacinto Treviño (Mercedes, Texas); Universidad de Aztlán (Fresno, California); Escuela y Colegio Tlatelolco (Denver, Colorado); Colegio César Chávez (Mt. Angel, Oregon); and Deganawidah-Quetzalcoatl (D-Q) University (Davis, California), begun as a Chicano-Indian college.[38] Of the alternative institutions—all established in the late 1960s and early 1970s—only Colegio César Chávez and the Indian college of D-Q University (Hehaka Sapa) remain in 1980.[39] D-Q University (see Table 1) is accredited by the Western Association of Schools and Colleges (Accrediting Commission for Community and Junior Colleges), and Colegio César Chávez has preaccredited status with the Northwest Association of Schools and Colleges (Commission on Colleges).[40] Both institutions secured their campuses through struggles with the federal government over the land: the Davis land was a federal military base, while the Colegio campus was formerly a Catholic seminary.[41]

Even with the acquisition of its campus, the establishment of a research institute (Instituto Colegial César Chávez), and preaccreditation status, Colegio César Chávez has a difficult future until it increases and stabilizes its enrollment, which in 1978–79 stood at a mere 25 full-time undergraduates in the four-year institution. Its struggles to become established and to secure its campus, its focus to serve older students and migrant farm workers, its rural isolation, and its founding in a time when few institutions are being established all have prevented the Colegio from being recognized and supported by the larger Chicano community. Today it remains virtually unknown outside the Chicano education or alternative college communities.

This is unfortunate, for the Chicano conditions in higher education is not good, and, with the exception of Colegio César Chávez, Chicano students are enrolled in historically majority schools, predominantly two-year colleges. Furthermore, in mid-1981 the status of Colegio César Chávez became even more precarious when it was denied accreditation by the Northwest Association of Schools and Colleges.[42] Without a developed, historically Chicano college, Chicano students have a diminished range of institutions from which to choose, although the demographics of some previously majority schools have changed to enroll predominantly Chicano student bodies.[43] A few of these institutions (e.g., New Mexico Highlands University, East Los Angeles College, Northern New Mexico Community College) have significant Chicano administrative leadership, while others (e.g., California State University at Los Angeles or Pan American University) have

Table 2
Chicano and Puerto Rican Colleges

	Accred. status	Publ.	Priv.	2 yr.	4 yr.	UG FT Enrollment 1978	UG Total 1978
Chicano							
Colegio César Chávez Mt. Angel, Oregon	2		X		X	25	25
Puerto Rican							
Boricua College New York, NY	2		X		X	455	455
Hostos Community College New York, NY	1	X		X		2506	2634

(1) Accredited; (2) Preaccreditation status

never had Chicano presidents.[44] The future of Chicanos in higher education appears to be in penetrating majority institutions, convincing policymakers that minority institution programs will not reach enough Chicano students, strengthening the network of Hispanic community-based organizations to supplement the colleges,[45] and in attracting wider community support for Colegio César Chávez.

Historically Puerto Rican Colleges

Within the Hispanic communities, Puerto Ricans in the 50 states and D.C. are the most educationally disadvantaged subgroup. For instance, although the 1976 high school noncompletion rate for all Hispanic students was 25%, the figure for Puerto Ricans was 31%.[46] This appalling figure means that 3 of 10 Puerto Ricans between the ages of 14 and 30 were not in school and had not completed their high school degree. The figure for male Puerto Ricans was 35%.[47] Moreover, even the seeming progress has been illusory: "From 1950 to 1970 the median school attainment for continental Puerto Ricans advanced nearly two years. But this was due primarily to a shift from elementary school attainment to partial high school, and not to an increase in the high school completion rate, which remained proportionately the same."[48]

The colonization of Puerto Rico by the United States as a result of the Spanish-American War replaced the island's earlier colonization by Spain; in 1899, Puerto Rico came under the jurisdiction of the U.S.[49] A series of laws since that time has not yet given autonomy to Puerto Ricans, who, since 1952, have been residents of the Commonwealth of Puerto Rico.[50] Thus, like Native Americans and Mexican Americans, Puerto Ricans share a colonial heritage. The poor condition of Puerto Rican education is, in part, the legacy of the economic exploitation of Puerto Rico, first by Spain and thereafter by the United States.

While sharing a history of colonialism with other indigenous American minority groups, the demographic and political characteristics of Puerto Ricans have resulted in a different educational history. Migration and reverse migration from the Island to the mainland and back have been major determinants of Puerto Rican educational access, including that to higher education. By 1910, Puerto Ricans in the states and D.C. numbered several thousand; by 1940, the number was approximately 70,000; by 1978, the number had grown to more than 1.8 million.[51] While most Puerto Ricans have settled in the industrial Northeast (notably New York, New Jersey, and Connecticut), large numbers of Puerto Ricans have settled in Hawaii, Florida, and California.[52]

That this massive migration occurred did not mean, however, that Puerto Ricans had increased access to mainland higher education. In 1970, for instance, New York City census data revealed that there were only 3,500 Puerto Rican college graduates in the city, an increase of only 1,000 since the 1960 census.[53] The open admissions policy of the City University of New York (CUNY), begun in 1970, substantially increased Puerto Rican enrollments, although the city's fiscal crisis has since decreased minority access.[54] In 1970, Puerto Ricans comprised 4.8% of CUNY undergraduates; by 1974 this had increased to 7.4%; Puerto Rican first-time freshmen in New York State during the same period went from 7.8% to 13.4%.[55]

It was during this time of drafting plans for an open door policy for the CUNY system that Hostos Community College was established in the South Bronx. Begun in late 1969, Hostos was the first historically Puerto Rican college to be established in the continental United States.[56] Hostos enrolls more than 2,500 students as freshmen or sophomores[57] and is accredited by the Middle States Association of Colleges and Secondary Schools, Commission on Higher Education, making it the only fully accredited Hispanic institution in the continental United States.[58]

Despite its successes, however, Hostos remains a poor relation within the CUNY system. Although it is ten years old, it has no permanent campus. Students attend classes in rooms rented in offices on the Grand Concourse in South Bronx, minutes from the spot where President Carter appeared in a "photo opportunity" to pledge his support for rebuilding the devastated slums. The fiscal crisis in New York City has prevented any construction or substantial long-term support to the college, although the students who attend are drawn from the City's poorest borough.[59] However, the college is expanding its curriculum and its status as a public institution assures a continuing base of government support.

Boricua College, the second historically Puerto Rican college, evolved from Universidad Boricua, which in turn had grown from a community group in Washington, D.C.—the Puerto Rican Research and Resources Center, Inc.[60] Boricua was established in Brooklyn in late 1973 and enrolled its first class in 1974; it opened a second facility in Manhattan in 1976.[61] A distinctive characteristic of Boricua is its network of off-campus classrooms. Its catalog boasts that "lofts, storefronts, and other easily-accessible facilities seem quite as satisfactory as ivy-covered monumental structures."[62]

Boricua's enrollment is 455 freshmen and sophomores. It has attempted to reach an extraordinarily neglected segment of the disadvantaged: older students whose situation in life prevented their having been accorded the access made available to the more traditional college-going population through CUNY's open door policies of the early 1970s. Boricua's bilingual courses and academic credits for life experiences may ameliorate to a small extent the historical exclusion of Puerto Ricans from mainland colleges.[63]

Higher education in Puerto Rico, however, has thrived. Whereas in 1940 there were only 5,000 college students on the island, by 1970 this number had grown to 257,000.[64] By 1978, colleges in Puerto Rico enrolled one quarter of all full-time undergraduate Hispanic students in the United States and awarded over 30% of all the baccalaureate degrees.[65] [See Appendix C for selected characteristics of colleges in Puerto Rico.] In 1975, four percent (4,547) of the Puerto Rican residents enrolled in college attended school in the 50 states or D.C., while 1,300 students from the mainland enrolled in Puerto Rican colleges.[66]

Legal and Legislative Issues

As the initial sections have indicated, the survival status of Indian, Chicano, and Puerto Rican colleges is the major issue confronting these institutions. While majority institutions have serious concerns of survival in difficult economic times and while black institutions continue to face economic and legal peril, non-black minority colleges face far more serious economic futures. Their attempts at development are occurring in a time of retrenchment throughout higher education and at a time when public support of minority issues is less evident than that shown during the enactment of the 1965 Higher Education Act.[67] Moreover, several fundamental issues of a legal and legislative nature uniquely affect Indian, Chicano, and Puerto Rican colleges. Chief among these issues is identification: What is an Indian college? What is an historically Chicano or Puerto Rican college? Although these questions seem rhetorical, government programs and community support issues make the answers important. Much as black college leaders have coined new designations for institutions that serve black students but do not have "historically" or "traditionally" black missions,[68] Indian and Latino educators have insisted upon certain criteria for designation, affiliation, and program eligibility.[69]

For Indians, these criteria include a record of service to Indians or a historical Indian mission, tribal affiliation, majority Indian control or influence, a predominantly Indian student body, or a combination of these factors. Applied strictly, these criteria would include few institutions, particularly since issues of tribal identification and control fluctuate and corollary Indian legislation alters standards and even removes or restores tribal status.[70] A list of Indian institutions such as that in Table 1 necessitates as many footnotes as entries. Pembroke State University, founded for Indians, today enrolls approximately 20% Indians; in this regard, Pembroke resembles three formerly black, now predominantly white, colleges—Bluefield State College, Lincoln State University, and West Virginia State—that have been considered "traditionally black," with an asterisk.[71]

These definitional issues are not mere ethnic nitpicking, for program eligibility and political identification are important factors in minority self-determination and in educational policymaking for minority access. In the 1979 Title III (Strengthening Developing Institutions) awards, for instance, only 7 of the 25 awards to Indian Programs[72] went to the Indian colleges listed in Table 1; four of the majority institutions are affiliated with the Indian colleges in Table 1, and these arrangements had Indian participation. As Indian testimony in the Title III reauthorization noted, however, the bulk of this money designed to strengthen Indian colleges is being administered by majority institutions.[73]

More fundamental definitional issues underlie all of Indian education (indeed, all Indian affairs), and although they are beyond the scope of this article, they deserve mention to show the dilemma inherent in the need for governmental targeting of Indian programs and Indian self-definition and self-determination. Thus, for Census Bureau purposes in the 1970 questionnaire, persons identified themselves as "Indian (American)" and delineated their tribal membership and race.[74] Education eligibility for Indian programs, however, is more specific and draws upon Department of the Interior recognition and the Alaska Native Claims Settlement Act[75] for identification. In the main, these are overlapping definitions[76] incorporated into the Indian Education Act, which consist of tribal membership or enrollment, blood quantum (Indian descendancy in the first or second degree), status as an Eskimo, Aleut, or other Alaska Native, or other evidence of Indian heritage.[77] Of course, these issues have resulted in litigation, which most frequently results in inaccurate or debilitating results for Indians: confusing the Blackfeet and Sioux Blackfoot,[78] ignoring unanimous expert testimony and interpretation of treaties,[79] and deciding that the Wampanoag (Mashpees) were not a tribe and therefore had no standing in a land claim.[80]

Although it has not yet been litigated, the concept of what constitutes an Indian college is a potential conflict area, particularly if more federal programs emerge to direct assistance to minority initiatives and as more majority institutions receive federal money to serve Indian students.[81] Two examples of the ambiguity over Indian institutions or Indian eligibility will serve to illustrate the potential for conflict or confusion: What is an "Indian college" and what is an "institution of higher education"?

Recently published rules and regulations for the Indian Education Act[82] define an "Indian institution" as a "[postsecondary school] that—(1) Is established for the education of Indians; (2) Is controlled by a governing board, the majority of which is Indian; and (3) If located on an Indian reservation, operates with the sanction or by charter of the governing body of that reservation."[83] Under the terms of the Tribally Controlled Community College Assistance Act of 1978 (PL 95-471)[84] stricter definitions are drawn since only tribally controlled community colleges are targeted, except for Navajo Community College, which has its own federal legislation.[85] Any eligible institution[86] is required to be "formally controlled, or . . . formally sanctioned, or chartered, by the governing body of an Indian tribe or tribes, except that no more than one such institution shall be recognized with respect to any such tribe";[87] further, it "must be one which—(1) is governed by a board of directors or board of trustees a majority of which are Indians; (2) demonstrates adherence to stated goals, a philosophy, or a plan of operation which is directed to meet the needs of Indians; and (3) if in operation for more than a year, has students a majority of whom are Indians."[88]

While there may not need to be any clarification of these two definitions, there are curious scenarios that could occur to vitiate the purpose of either act. Taking into account the demographic characteristics of the colleges noted in Table 1, these scenarios are not far-fetched. Under the Indian Education Act, for instance, a predominantly Indian student body is not required for eligibility. It is conceivable that Indians could win election, be appointed to, or otherwise control a majority institution governing board, and by establishing an Indian mission could create an Indian institution—entitling such a non-reservation college to eligibility for a number of adult education programs under the Act.

Several colleges have altered their governance structure and have become tribal institutions. One such college is the College of Ganado, in Ganado, Arizona, on the Navajo Reservation. Previously a private college affiliated with the United Presbyterian Church,[89] the college has become a tribally controlled community college of the Hopi Tribe and is eligible for money from the Tribally Controlled Community College Assistance Act.[90] D-Q University, established as an Indian-Chicano College, is now chartered by the Hoopa Valley and Soboba tribes.[91] In both instances, institutions with predominantly Indian student enrollments reconstituted themselves and secured tribal charters. In both instances, the rural isolation and college characteristics made such transformations possible and economical.

In future cases, however, policymakers would do well to recall the distribution of resources for Indian institutional development, administered by majority institutions. While the eligibility requirements of Title III are not race-specific, many white institutions have taken Indian program initiatives in order to be eligible for Developing Institutions resources without altering their basic governance structures, which rarely include Indians.[92] Indeed, a 1976 survey of all two-year college trustees noted that fewer than .2 of 1% were Indian.[93]

A more important definitional issue than that of "Indian college" may be the definition, seemingly obvious, of "institution of higher education." The Tribally Controlled Community College Assistance Act (PL 95-471) requires that eligible colleges be "institutions of higher education" in the commonly understood and statutory meaning of the terms.[94] However, as with other provisions of law, when applied to special populations—in this case, Indian colleges—the definition becomes less obvious and may prevent the target population from being effectively served. PL 95-471 breaks down at this threshold point, for few tribally controlled community colleges can meet the definitional tests of "institutions," notably in the requirements for accreditation status. In this case, Indian colleges find themselves in a classic catch-22 situation: They are not eligible for Act money because they are not accredited, but they cannot secure accreditation without the development money and technical assistance promised in the Act.

Accreditation and Indian Colleges

The statutory definition of "institutions of higher education" incorporates elements of post–high school admission, state authorization, degree credit, public or nonprofit status, and accreditation—all important elements for governmental and institutional quality control mechanisms. The fifth requirement, that institutions be "accredited by a nationally recognized accrediting agency or association," has become a hornets' nest as national political forces tug over accreditation authority and policy.[95] However, it is the exceptions to the accreditation requirements that have proven to be the rub for Indian colleges. The two exceptions to the accreditation requirement allow an unaccredited college to be an "institution of higher education" if it:

> (A) is an institution with respect to which the Commissioner has determined that there is satisfactory assurance, considering the resources available to the institution, the period of time, if any, during which it has operated, the effort it is making to meet accreditation standards, and the purpose for which this determination is being made, that the institution will meet the accreditation standards of such an agency or association within a reasonable time, or (B) is an institution whose credits are accepted, on transfer, by not less than three institutions which are so accredited, for credit on the same basis as if transferred from an institution so accredited.... For purposes of this subsection, the Commissioner shall publish a list of nationally recognized accrediting agencies or associations which he determines to be reliable authority as to the quality of training offered.[96]

Anticipating that the unaccredited status of most Indian colleges would cause eligibility problems, the drafters of the original Tribally Controlled Community College Act bill (which had been proposed as an amendment to the Indian Self-Determination Act)[97] had incorporated the two exceptions into the bill. The legislation that emerged, however, simply incorporated the definition language, eliminating the redundant exemption references.[98]

This final language should not have been problematic, for the two waiver provisions still enabled the Commissioner (now, since the creation of the Department of Education, the Secretary) to interpret the "satisfactory assurance" generously; no regulations have been promulgated by the new Department to guide the Secretary in this regard, but in the face of larger political battles over accreditation, the Department has not chosen to interpret the colleges' status generously. Nor, inexplicably, have the colleges employed the easily available "3-letter" rule to trigger the other exemption provision. All that would be required is to enlist three accredited institutions in order to have credits accepted for transfer, but this waiver has not been widely adopted by the tribal colleges.[99]

As these issues became evident after the passage of the Tribal Act, another twist on the accreditation provisions came into play: feasibility studies. Under the terms of the Act, feasibility studies were required to "determine whether there is justification to start and maintain a tribally controlled community college."[100] These studies, to be conducted by the Secretary of the Interior, were strictly interpreted by the Office of Management and Budget (OMB) and the Bureau of Indian Affairs to require accreditation or candidacy as a measure of feasibility; the Bureau has added to the circularity of this requirement by noting that this criterion could be waived by the 3-letter rule—the accreditation waiver.[101] Thus, the accreditation requirement has an added requirement of feasibility, although accreditation standards are employed in determining feasibility. Indian educators have argued unsuccessfully that these dual requirements are redundant and that a recognized accreditation status should be prima facie evidence of any college's feasibility.[102]

Despite these difficulties, some of the tribal colleges have begun to receive money from the Act.[103] However, a coherent policy for administering Indian programs could have enabled these struggling institutions to receive the money earlier. The OMB has been inflexible in its review of feasibility criteria and has been unwilling to consider these colleges' characteristics as deserving special attention. Many Indian educators have blamed the BIA for its lukewarm support of the Tribal Act;[104] others blame the new Department of Education for its foot dragging.[105]

Both criticisms are accurate, for the BIA was not required to use accreditation as a feasibility criterion, and the Department of Education could have been more flexible in interpreting the colleges' progress toward accreditation. Indeed, the Department, in the absence of regulations governing eligibility, could have employed the discretion accorded it in Title III, where accreditation requirements for Developing Institutions eligibility can be waived in special circumstances where Indian and Spanish-speaking students will be served.[106] In either case, the bureaucratic delays have frustrated legislative attempts to create and enhance these Indian colleges.

The confusion over the Act has continued to mar its delivery of money to Indian colleges. An amendment to the Act was passed by the Senate on January 25, 1980, and was referred to the House Committee on Education and Labor on January 29; it was referred to the Subcommittee on Postsecondary Education, where it has remained since February 1.[107] The amendment clarifies the Indian eligibility requirement and increases the technical assistance authorization provisions.[108] Curiously, however, it further complicates the accreditation issue, for it restores portions of the redundant accreditation waiver provisions incorporated in the statutory definition of "institution of higher education," but gives the Secretary of the Interior (not the Secretary of Education) the authority to determine the reasonableness of the colleges' efforts toward accreditation.[109] This provision, if it were to be adopted, would further complicate the accreditation provisions, for a memorandum of agreement would have to be drafted between Interior and Education Departments to utilize the eligibility staff of the Department of Education, adding yet another layer of administration. A more reasonable approach would employ the Act's present language. Adopting accreditation or its waivers as evidence of feasibility for existing colleges would not require an amendment and would not require any renegotiation of the February 19, 1980, Memorandum of Agreement.[110] Clarifying the difference between accreditation and feasibility would give administrative guidance.

The Department of Interior has opposed passage of the increases in technical assistance authorizations contained in the amendments, predicting it would be too much money: "If all 21 [colleges] were to participate in $10 million worth of technical assistance funds, each college would average approximately $476,000 in [such] funds per year, an amount far in excess of that which can be utilized effectively."[111] That the Act could provide too much money for technical assistance to these institutions seems a curious claim and a false economy, for the money for technical assistance is prerequisite to any developmental activities necessary for accreditation or feasibility. It is not clear whether the fledgling colleges will be able to survive the legislation enacted and administered on their behalf.

Other Financial Issues

As is evident, these small institutions are plagued by rural isolation, lack of property tax bases, lack of experienced Indian personnel, lack of accreditation, and are subject to multiple jurisdictions not always helpful to the unique needs of Indian colleges. Even with special legislation, Navajo Community College, the first and largest tribal college, is in severe financial difficulty.[112]

Further, the "band analysis" means of financing tribal institutions under the Indian Self-Determination Act, whereby tribes set aside their BIA funds for postsecondary programs, is being used by the BIA as a "debit" for money allocated to the tribal colleges under the Tribally Controlled Community College Assistance Act, in apparent disregard for the Tribal Act's prohibition against such substitutions: "Eligibility assistance under this title shall not, by itself, preclude the eligibility of any tribally controlled college to receive Federal financial assistance. . . ."[113] This shell game penalizes the colleges for negotiating the Tribal College Act process and punishes tribes who have assessed themselves for education programs. Analyses of these and other Indian education issues are beyond the scope of this article, but the issues clearly warrant study.

Summary and Conclusions

The enormous problems facing Indian, Chicano, and Puerto Rican colleges have not been addressed by legislative efforts aimed at redressing historic exclusion, nor by educational assistance designed for colleges in general. In the unique case of Indian colleges, specific legislation and program initiatives have not been effective, in part because of the fragile nature of the colleges themselves and in part because of the organizational difficulties Indian people face daily in their relationship with government agencies.

While the great majority of minority students will continue to receive their college education in majority institutions, increasing attention is necessary to ensure minority self-determination, particularly through historically minority colleges. The federal government has only recently recognized and acknowledged its considerable responsibility for assisting black colleges and has moved aggressively to rectify its own exclusionary practices in this regard. The Black College Initiative has given long-overdue notice to these institutions' role in educating Blacks. However, similar "Hispanic Initiatives" and "Indian Initiatives," proposing employment and program emphases for federal agencies, have languished.[114] American higher education, justifiably proud of its diversity, will be denied its most unique institutions if historically minority colleges are allowed to languish.

LULAC NATIONAL EDUCATIONAL
SERVICE CENTERS

Notes

1. 430 F. Supp. 118 (D.D.C. 1977).

2. Haynes, *A Conceptual Examination of Desegregation in Higher Education* (Washington, DC: Institute for Services to Education, 1978); Fleming, *The Lengthening Shadow of Slavery* (Washington, DC: Howard University Press, 1976).

3. Morris, *Elusive Equality* (Washington, DC: Howard University Press, 1979). p. 180.

4. *Education Directory, Colleges and Universities, 1979–80* (Washington, DC: National Center for Educational Statistics [NCES], 1980), p. 468.

5. Haynes, supra at note 2.

6. Title III, Sec. 307 (2) prohibits payments "for an activity that is inconsistent with a State plan for desegregation of higher education applicable to such institutions."

7. Turner and Michaels, *Traditionally Black Institutions of Higher Education: Their Identification and Selected Characteristics* (Washington, DC: NCES, 1978).

8. *Minority Higher Education Reports*, 1, no. 7 (15 August 1980), pp. 1–3.

9. Title III, Sec. 347 (e). See also *House Conference Report to Accompany H.R. 5192*, p. 165. Under the Education Department's reorganization (PL 96-88), the college Housing Program has been transferred from Housing and Urban Development (HUD) to ED. Under the appropriations process (PL 96-103), 10% of the $85 million is to be reserved for black colleges. *Federal Register*, 1 August 1980, p. 51510.

10. *Minority Higher Education Reports*, 1, no. 8 (12 September 1980), p. 5.

11. Turner and Michaels, note 7, at p. 2.

12. Turner and Michaels, note 7, at p. 1.

13. Deloria, *Legislative Analysis of the Federal Role in Indian Education* (Washington, DC: Office of Indian Education. 1975); Thompson, ed., *The Schooling of Native America* (Washington, DC: American Association of Colleges for Teacher Education, 1978); Samora, ed., *La Raza: Forgotten Americans* (Notre Dame: University of Notre Dame Press, 1966); Carter and Segura, *Mexican Americans in School: A Decade of Change* (NY: College Board, 1979); *Puerto Ricans in the Continental United States: An Uncertain Future* (Washington, DC: U.S. Commission on Civil Rights, 1976).

14. Van Amringe et al., *A History of Columbia University, 1754–1904* (NY: Columbia University Press, 1904). p. 32; Rudolph, *The American College and University, A History* (NY: Vintage, 1962).

15. Rudolph, note 14, at p. 104.

16. American Indian Policy Review Commission, *Report on Indian Education* (Washington, DC: GPO, 1976), pp. 61-73.

17. Deloria, *A Brief History of the Federal Responsibility to the American Indian* (Washington, DC: GPO, 1979), p. 13.

18. *Report on Indian Education*, note 16, at p. 66.

19. 7 Stat. 210; *Report on Indian Education*, note 16, at p. 268.

20. *Report on Indian Education*, note 16, at pp. 268–69.

21. *Education Directory*, note 4, at p. 9.

22. Chavers, *The Feasibility of an Indian University at Bacone College* (Muskogee, OK: Bacone College, 1979).

23. *Pembroke State University Catalog*, 1980–1981, pp. 15–16, 26–27.

24. *Report on Indian Education*, note 16, at pp. 51–60. Chavers, "Indian Education: Failure for the Future," *American Indian Law Review*, 2 (1974), 61–84.

25. Cited in *Report on Indian Education*, note 16, at p. 57.

26. See, generally, *Report*, note 16, at pp. 273–75; *Southwestern Indian Polytechnic Institute Bulletin, 1975–1977*.

27. Navajo Community College Assistance Act of 1978, 25 U.S.C. 640a.

28. *Education Directory*, note 4 at p. 383; *Report*, note 16, p. 351.

29. *Report*, note 16, at p. 352.

30. Table 1 could have included several more institutions, but adequate information was not available for Tanana Land Claims College, Ojibwa College, United Tribes Educational Technical Center, Gila River Community College.

31. Cited in Carter and Segura, note 13, at p. 16.

32. Fleming, note 2, at pp. 59–101.

33. Pitt, *The Decline of the Californios: A Social History of the Spanish-Speaking Californians. 1846–1890* (Los Angeles: UCLA Press, 1966); Sánchez, *Forgotten People* (Albuquerque: University of New Mexico Press, 1940); Berger, "Education in Texas during the Spanish and Mexican Periods," *Southwestern Historical Quarterly*, 51, No. 1 (July 1947), pp. 41–53; Independent School District v. Salvatierra, 33 S.W. 2d. 790 (1930).

34. Carter and Segura, note 13, at p. 16.

35. Hendrick, "Early Schooling for Children of Migrant Farmworkers in California: The 1920's," *Aztlan*, 8 (1977), p. 14.

36. Hendrick, note 35, at pp. 11–26.

37. Berger, supra at note 33; Barrera, *Race and Class in the Southwest: A Theory of Inequality* (Notre Dame: University of Notre Dame Press, 1979).

38. *Chicano Alternative Education* (Hayward, California: Southwest Network, 1974); Macias et al., *Educación Alternativa: On the Development of Chicano Bilingual Schools* (Hayward, CA: Southwest Network, 1975).

39. *Education Directory*, note 4, at pp. 33, 341. Other Chicano schools do remain, but have chosen not to seek accreditation or to offer collegiate courses. Schools such as Colegio de la Tierra in California and La Academia de la Nueva Raza in New Mexico have chosen to focus on community development or folklore projects.

40. *Accredited Postsecondary Institutions and Programs* (Washington, DC: GPO, 1979), pp. 5, 42.

41. Discussions with officials of D-Q University and Colegio César Chávez, Summer 1980.

42. Olivas, *The Dilemma of Access* (Washington, DC: Howard University Press, 1979). With reference to the recent denial of accreditation to Colegio César Chávez, see "Coast Hispanic College Fights to Survive," *New York Times*, 15 Nov. 1981, p. 75.

43. Olivas and Hill, "Hispanic Participation in Postsecondary Education," in *The Condition of Education for Hispanic Americans* (Washington, DC: NCES, 1980), pp. 117–215.

44. Arce, in Smith, ed., *Advancing Equality of Opportunity: A Matter of Justice* (Washington, DC: Howard University Press, 1978), pp. 165–75.

45. Olivas, "Hispanics in Higher Education: Federal Barriers," *Educational Evaluation and Policy Analysis* (forthcoming).

46. *Condition of Education for Hispanic Americans*, note 43, at p. 100.

47. Ibid.

48. *Social Factors in Educational Attainment Among Puerto Ricans in U.S. Metropolitan Areas, 1970* (NY: Aspira, 1976), p. 2.

49. *Puerto Ricans in the Continental United States* (Washington, DC: U.S. Commission on Civil Rights, 1976).

50. 39 Stat. 951 (1917): 64 Stat. 319 (1950); 48 U.S.C. § 73.1 et seq.; De Lima v. Bidwell, 182 U.S. 1 (1901).

51. *Puerto Ricans in the Continental United States*, note 49, at Table 7, pp. 19–35; *Condition of Education*, note 43, at Table 1.01; Hernández, "La migración puertorriqueña como factor demográfico; solución y problema," *Revista Interamericana*, 4 (1975), pp. 526–34.

52. *Condition of Education*, note 43, at Table 1.04; *Puerto Ricans in California* (Washington, DC: U.S. Commission on Civil Rights, 1980).

53. *Puerto Ricans in the Continental United States*, note 49, at p. 119.

54. Lavin et al., "Open Admissions and Equal Access: A Study of Ethnic Groups in the City University of New York," *Harvard Educational Review*, 49, no. 1 (February 1979), pp. 53–92; Rossman et al., *Open Admissions at the City University of New York: An Analysis of the First Year* (Englewood Cliffs, NJ: Prentice Hall, 1975).

55. *Puerto Ricans in the Continental United States*, note 49, at Tables 35, 36.

56. Castro, "Hostos: Report from a Ghetto College," *Harvard Educational Review*, 44, No. 2 (May 1974), pp. 270–94.

57. *Fall Enrollment in Higher Education, 1978* (Washington, DC: NCES, 1979), p. 132.

58. *Accredited Postsecondary Institutions*, note 40, at p. 22.

59. When CUNY closed early in 1976, the state appropriated a special fund to the system, including $3 million for Hostos. *Puerto Ricans in the Continental United States*, note 49, at p. 119.

60. *Boricua College Catalog*, pp. 1–2.

61. *Catalog*, note 60, at p. 19.

62. Ibid.

63. *Condition of Education*, note 43, at Table 2.32.

64. *Puerto Ricans in the Continental United States*, note 49, at Table 3.

65. Olivas and Hill, note 43, at Tables 3.10 and 3.21.

66. Olivas and Hill, note 43, at Tables 3.19 and 3.20.

67. Jones, *The Changing Mood in America* (Washington, DC: Howard University Press, 1977).

68. *Black College Primer* (Washington, DC: Institute for the Study of Educational Policy, Howard University, 1980); Turner and Michaels, note 7, at p. 1.

69. Olivas and Hill, note 43, at pp. 118–19; Olivas, "Hispanics in Higher Education," supra at note 45; Nichols, "Testimony in Hearings on Title III of the Higher Education Act," 29 March 1979; Middleton, "Indian Tribal Colleges Accuse U.S. Bureraucrats of Delaying $85 Million Congress Authorized," *Chronicle of Higher Education,* 11 February 1980, pp. 1, 12; Chavers, supra at note 22.

70. Deloria, "Legislation and Litigation Concerning American Indians," *Annals of the American Academy of Political and Social Science,* vol. 436 (March 1978), pp. 86–96.

71. Turner and Michaels, note 7, at p. 2. Another classification problem occurs when institutions mislabel their students. Alice Lloyd College reported its racial data for 1976 as if its enrollment were 90.1% American Indian, although its population is predominantly Appalachian whites (Olivas, note 42, at p. 196). Conversations with school officials, however, revealed that they considered their students "minorities," apparently "Native" Americans.

72. See Appendix D.

73. Nichols, note 69; Bad Wound, Testimony before Select Committee on Indian Affairs, U.S. Senate, 10 June 1980.

74. *American Indians, 1970 Census of Population* (Washington, DC: GPO, 1973), p. ix. For a discussion of minority census issues, including undercounts, see *Conference on Census Undercounts* (Washington, DC: GPO, 1980).

75. 85 Stat. 688.

76. The recently revised Indian Education Act regulations, for instance, drew several comments and incorporated several changes to clarify Indian eligibility. See, for example, *Federal Register,* 21 May 1980, pp. 34180–34181, 34184–34185.

77. Indian Education Act, Sec. 453(a); 20 U.S.C. 1221 (h)(a). See, generally, Yinger and Simpson. "The Integration of Americans of Indian Descent," *Annals of the American Academy of Political and Social Science,* Vol. 436 (March 1978), pp. 137–51.

78. United States *ex rel.* Rollingson v. Blackfeet Tribal Court, 244 F. Supp. 474 (D. Mont. 1965).

79. United States v. Consolidated Wounded Knee Case, 389 F. Supp. 235 (D. Neb. and W.D.S.D. 1975).

80. Mashpee Tribe v. New Seabury Corp., 427 F. Supp. 899, *aff'd,* 592 F. 2d 575 (1st Cir. 1979). For a sample of legislative attempts to extinguish Indian claims, see S.J. Res. 86, 95th Cong. 1st Session, 123 *Congressional Record* (1977), p. 16232, concerning Mashpee claims in Massachusetts. See Newton, "At the Whim of the Sovereign: Aboriginal Title Reconsidered," *Hastings Law Journal* 31, No. 6 (1980), pp. 1215–85. See, generally, Brodeur, "The Mashpees." *New Yorker,* 6 November 1978, pp. 62–150; Deloria, "Indian Law and the Reach of History." *Journal of Contemporary Law* 4 (1977). pp. 1–13.

81. Although it is beyond the scope of this study, there is a small network of minority institution programs scattered throughout the federal government; many of these are being mobilized by the Executive Order on Black Colleges. They include, for example, the Minority Access into Research Careers (National Institutes of Health), Minority Institution Science Improvement Program (Department of Education, relocated from the National Science Foundation), and the Minority Institutions Research Support Program (Environmental Protection Agency).

82. 86 Stat. 334 (as amended); the regulations will be recodified under 34 C.F.R., replacing the 45 C.F.R. regulations. See *Federal Register,* 21 May 1980, p. 34153.

83. 20 U.S.C. 241 (a) (a).

84. 20 U.S.C. 1801.

85. Navajo Community College Assistance Act of 1978, 25 U.S.C. 640(a); Amendments to the Navajo Community College Act [sic], Education Amendments of 1980, Title XIV, Part F, Sec. 1451.

86. Although the institutions are community colleges, they need not be sub-baccalaureate. Higher Education Act of 1965, Title XII, Sec. 1201 (a)(3).

87. 25 U.S.C. 1801.

88. 25 U.S.C. 1804.

89. Locke, *A Survey of College and University Programs for American Indians* (Boulder, CO: WICHE, 1978), p.24.

90. See Table 1.

91. Supra, at note 38. See also Table 1.

92. See Appendix D for the distribution of Title III awards in 1979–1980 to Indian programs; Appendix E is the awards to Hispanic programs.

93. Grafe, *The Trustee Profile of 1976* (Washington, DC: Association of Community College Trustees, 1976), pp. 4–5. See Olivas, note 42, at pp. 86–90.

94. 25 U.S.C. 1801; 20 U.S.C. 1141.

95. Higher Education Act of 1965, Title XII, Sec. 1201 (a)(5); 20 U.S.C. 1141. See, generally, Orlans et al., *Private Accreditation and Public Eligibility* (Washington, DC: National Academy of Public Administration, 1974); *Approaches to State Licensing of Private Degree-Granting Institutions* (Washington, DC: Institute for Educational Leadership, 1975); Kaplin, *The Law of Higher Education* (San Francisco: Jossey-Bass, 1978), pp. 439–59: Finkin, "Federal Reliance and Voluntary Accreditation: The Power to Recognize as The Power to Regulate," *Journal of Law and Education* 2, No. 3 (July 1973), pp. 339–76.

96. Higher Education Act of 1965, Title XII, Sec. 1201 (a)(5); 20 U.S.C. 1141.

97. S. 1215, 95th Congress, 1st Session (1 April 1977). See Senate Report 95–582, *Hearing Before the United States Senate Select Committee on Indian Affairs* (28 July 1977).

98. 25 U.S.C. 1801. In the Act, the requirement that "institutions" be "legally authorized within such State" (Higher Education Act of 1965. Title XII, Sec. 1201 (a) (2); 20 U.S.C. 1141) was deleted, recognizing that tribes were independent governmental bodies.

99. Discussions with BIA and Indian college officials suggested that the 3-letter rule had a stigma and that senior institutions were reluctant to recognize the rule for fear it would jeopardize their own status. This subject deserves further scrutiny.

100. 25 U.S.C. 1806. Section 105 of the Act requires an agreement between the Departments of Interior and Education (then the Office of Education, HEW); this memorandum of agreement was signed on 19 February 1980. The feasibility study form is 73 pages long, not including its required appendices.

101. 25 C.F.R. 32b. See *Federal Register,* 21 November 1979, pp. 67040–67048. In testimony on implementation of the Act, Earl Barlow, BIA Director of Indian Education Programs, said: "One of the criteria for feasibility is that it be an accredited institution or a candidate for accreditation, or its credits must be accepted by three accredited institutions. Each of the 10 schools that have been deemed feasible has either been accredited or has been approved as a candidate for accreditation. . . . Our idea was that [technical assistance] funds would be used to assist colleges that were having some problems with either accreditation or candidacy, but the ruling was made that in order to be eligible for technical assistance grants the institution has to be feasible. It put us in a predicament. The schools that really need technical assistance are not feasible and therefore cannot get technical assistance. That is a major problem." *Hearing Before the Select Committee on Indian Affairs* (10 June 1980), Committee draft, p. 9. See also *Guidelines for the Tribally Controlled Community Colleges.*

102. Testimony of Leroy Clifford, American Indian Higher Education Consortium, note 101, at Committee draft, p. 17.

103. Blackfeet Community College had received its 1979–80 check the week before the June 10, 1980, Senate hearing.

104. Middleton, note 69, at pp. 1, 12.

105. *Hearing,* note 101, at Committee draft, pp. 11–34; *Higher Education Daily,* 12 June 1980, pp. 5–6.

106. Higher Education Act, Title III, Sec. 302 (a) (2). The newly reauthorized Education Amendments of 1980 have widened the waivers to include rural people, low-income individuals, and black students. Title III, Part D, Sec. 342 (b) (1–5); *Conference Report* No. 96–1251, p. 164.

107. Senate Calendar, 24 September 1980, p. 199 [S. 1855].

108. S. 1855, 96th Congress, 1st Session, *Senate Report*, No. 96–538, p. 6.

109. *Senate Report*, note 108, at pp. 2–3. Congressional staffers have suggested that this reassignment was in anticipation of Higher Education Act reauthorization changes in Sec. 1201. These changes were not made in the final version of 1201.

110. 25 U.S.C. 1808; supra, note 100.

111. Letter from Forrest Gerard, Assistant Secretary, Department of the Interior, to Senator John Melcher, 21 November 1979. *Senate Report*, note 108, at pp. 4–5.

112. *Hearing*, note 101, at Committee draft, p. 25. The Education Amendments of 1980 include special provisions for Navajo Community College, Title XIV, Part F, Sec. 1451; *Conference Report*, note 106, at p.209.

113. 25 U.S.C. 189; 20 U.S.C. 1001 *et seq.*

114. Olivas, supra, note 45. Whereas the Black College Initiative was a Presidential Executive Order, the Hispanic and Indian Initiatives were Secretarial. Additionally, the tribal college reporting requirements of PL 95-471 have not been met by either the Department of the Interior or by NCES, despite their responsibility for an annual report to Congress [Sec. 107 (c) (2); 25 U.S.C. 1808].

Appendix A

Executive Order

Historically Black Colleges and Universities

By the authority vested in me as President by the Constitution of the United States of America, and in order to overcome the effects of discriminatory treatment and to strengthen and expand the capacity of historically Black colleges and universities to provide quality education, it is hereby ordered as follows:

1-101. The Secretary of Education shall implement a Federal initiative designed to achieve a significant increase in the participation by historically Black colleges and universities in Federally sponsored programs. This initiative shall seek to identify, reduce, and eliminate barriers which may have unfairly resulted in reduced participation in, and reduced benefits from, Federally sponsored programs.

1-102. The Secretary of Education shall, in consultation with the Director of the Office of Management and Budget and the heads of the other Executive agencies, establish annual goals for each agency. The purpose of these goals shall be to increase the ability of historically Black colleges and universities to participate in Federally sponsored programs.

1-103. Executive agencies shall review their programs to determine the extent to which historically Black colleges and universities are unfairly precluded from participation in Federally sponsored programs.

1-104. Executive agencies shall identify the statutory authorities under which they can provide relief from specific inequities and disadvantages identified and documented in the agency programs.

1-105. Each Executive agency shall review its current programs and practices and initiate new efforts to increase the participation of historically Black colleges and universities in the programs of the agency. Particular attention should be given to identifying and eliminating unintended regulatory barriers. Procedural barriers, including those which result in such colleges and universities not receiving notice of the availability of Federally sponsored programs, should also be eliminated.

1-106. The head of each Executive agency shall designate an immediate subordinate who will be responsible for implementing the agency responsibilities set forth in this Order. In each Executive agency there shall be an agency liaison to the Secretary of Education for implementing this Order.

1-107. (a) The Secretary of Education shall ensure that an immediate subordinate is responsible for implementing the provisions of this Order.

(b) The Secretary shall ensure that each President of a historically Black college or university is given the opportunity to comment on the implementation of the initiative established by this Order.

1-108. The Secretary of Education shall submit an annual report to the President. The report shall include the levels of participation by historically Black colleges and universities in the programs of each Executive agency. The report will also include any appropriate recommendations for improving the Federal response directed by this Order.

Source: Minority Higher Education Reports (15 August 1980), p. 9.

Appendix B

Treaties Dealing With Indian Education

Treaty of August 18, 1804, with Delaware Tribe, 7 Stat. 81; treaty of August 29, 1821, with Ottawa, Chippewa, and Pottawatamie, 7 Stat. 218; treaty of February 12, 1825, with Creek Nation, 7 Stat. 237; treaty of February 8, 1831, with the Menominee Indians, 7 Stat. 342; treaty of September 21, 1833, with the Otoes and Missourias, 7 Stat. 429; treaty of March 2, 1836, with the Ottawa and Chippewa, 7 Stat. 491; treaty of September 17, 1836, with the Sacs and Foxes, etc., 7 Stat. 511; treaty of October 15, 1836, with the Otoes, etc., 7 Stat. 524; treaty of January 4, 1845, with the Creeks and Seminoles, 9 Stat. 821, 822; treaty of October 13, 1846, with the Winnebago Indians, 9 Stat. 878; treaty of August 2, 1847, with the Chippewas, 9 Stat. 904; treaty of October 18, 1848, with the Menominee Tribe, 9 Stat. 952; treaty of July 23, 1851, with the Sioux, 10 Stat. 949; treaty of August 5, 1851, with the Sioux Indians, 10 Stat. 954; treaty of May 12, 1854, with the Menominee, 10 Stat. 1064; treaty of December 26, 1854, with the Nisqually, etc., Indians, 10 Stat. 1132; treaty of October 17, 1855, with the Blackfoot Indians, 11 Stat. 657; treaty of September 24, 1857, with the Pawnees, 11 Stat. 729; treaty of January 22, 1855, with The Dwamish, etc., 12 Stat. 927; treaty of January 26, 1855, with the S'Klallams, 12 Stat. 933; treaty of January 31, 1855, with Makah Tribe, 12 Stat. 939; treaty of July 1, 1855, with the Qui-nai-elt, etc., Indians, 12 Stat. 971; treaty of July 16, 1855, with the Flathead, etc., Indians, 12 Stat. 975; treaty of December 21, 1855, with the Molels, 12 Stat. 981; treaty of October 18, 1864, with the Chippewa Indians, 14 Stat. 657; treaty of June 14, 1866, with the Creek Nation, 14 Stat. 785; treaty of February 18, 1867, with the Sac and Fix Indians, 15 Stat. 495; treaty of February 19, 1867, with the Sissiton, etc., Sioux, 15 Stat. 505.

Treaty of May 6, 1828, with the Cherokee Nation, 7 Stat; treaty of New Echota, December 29, 1835, with the Cherokee, 7 Stat. 748 (provides for common schools and "a literacy institution of a higher order"); treaty of June 5 and 17, 1846, with the Pottowautomie Nation, 9 Stat. 853; treaty of September 30, 1854, with the Chippewa Indians, 10 Stat. 1109; treaty of November 18, 1854, with the Chastas, etc., Indians, 10 Stat. 1122; treaty of April 19, 1858, with the Yancton Sioux, 11 Stat. 743; treaty of June 9, 1855, with the Walla-Wallas, etc., tribes, 12 Stat. 945; treaty of June 11, 1855, with the Nez Perce, 12 Stat. 957; treaty of March 12, 1858, with the Poncas, 12 Stat. 997; treaty of October 14, 1865, with the Lower Brule Sioux, 14 Stat. 699; treaty of February 23, 1867, with the Senecas, etc., 15 Stat. 513; treaty of October 21, 1867, with the Kiowa and Comanche Indians, 15 Stat. 581; treaty of October 21, 1867, with the Kiowa, Comanche, and Apache Indians, 15 Stat. 589; treaty of October 28, 1867, with the Cheyenne and Arapahoe Indians, 15 Stat. 593; treaty of March 2, 1868, with the Ute Indians, 15 Stat. 619; treaty of April 29 et seq., 1868, with the Sioux Nation, 15 Stat. 635; treaty of May 7, 1868, with the Crow Indians, 15 Stat. 649; treaty of May 10, 1868, with the Northern Cheyenne and Northern Arapahoe Indians, 15 Stat. 655; treaty of June 1, 1868, with the Navajo Tribe, 15 Stat. 667; treaty of July 3, 1868, with the Eastern Band Shoshones and Bannock Tribe of Indians, 15 Stat. 673.

Treaty of November 15, 1827, with the Creek Nation, 7 Stat. 307; treaty of September 15, 1832, with the Winnebago Nation, 7 Stat. 370; treaty of May 24, 1834, with the Chickasaw Indians, 7 Stat. 450; treaty of June 9, 1863, with the Nex Perce Tribe, 14 Stat. 647; treaty of March 19, 1867, with the Chippewa of Mississippi, 16 Stat. 719.

Treaty of October 18, 1820, with the Choctaw Nation, 7 Stat. 210; treaty of June 3, 1825, with the Kansas Nation, 7 Stat. 244; treaty of August 5, 1926, with the Chippewa Tribe, 7 Stat. 290; treaty of October 21, 1837, with the Sac and Fox Indians, 7 Stat. 543; treaty of March 17, 1842, with the Wyandott Nation, 11 Stat. 581; treaty of May 15, 1846, with the Comanche, etc., Indians, 9 Stat. 844; treaty of June 5, 1854, with the Miami Indians, 10 Stat. 1093; treaty of November 15, 1854, with the Rogue Rivers, 10 Stat. 1119; treaty of November 29, 1854, with the Umpqua, etc., Indians, 10 Stat. 1125; treaty of July 31, 1855, with the Ottowas and Chippewas, 11 Stat. 621; treaty of February 5, 1856, with the Stockbridge and Munsee Tribes, 11 Stat. 663; treaty of June 9, 1855, with the Yakima Indians, 12 Stat. 951; treaty of June 25, 1855, with the Oregon Indians, 12 Stat. 963; treaty of June 19, 1858, with the Sioux bands, 12 Stat. 1031; treaty of July 16, 1859, with the Chippewa bands, 12 Stat. 1105; treaty of February 18, 1861, with the Arapahoes and Cheyenne Indians, 12 Stat. 1163; treaty of March 6, 1861, with the Sacs, Foxes and Iowas, 12 Stat. 1171; treaty of June 24, 1862, with the Ottawa Indians, 12 Stat. 1237; treaty of May 7, 1864, with the Chippewas, 13 Stat. 693; treaty of August 12, 1865, with the Snake Indians, 14 Stat. 683; treaty of March 21, 1866, with the Seminole Indians, 14 Stat. 755; treaty of April 28, 1866, with the Choctaw and Chickasaw Nation, 14 Stat. 769; treaty of August 13, 1868, with the Nez Perce Tribe, 15 Stat. 693.

Treaty of October 16, 1826, with the Potawatomie Tribe, 7 Stat. 295; treaty of September 20, 1828, Potawatamie Indians, 7 Stat. 317; treaty of July 15, 1830, with the Sacs and Foxes, etc., 7 Stat. 328; treaty of September 27, 1830, with the Choctaw Nation, 7 Stat. 333; treaty of March 24, 1832, with the Creek Tribe, 7 Stat. 366; treaty of February 14, 1833, with the Creek Nation, 7 Stat. 417; treaty of January 14, 1846, with the Kansas Indians, 9 Stat. 842; treaty of April 1, 1850, with the Wyandot Tribe, 9 Stat. 987; treaty of March 15, 1854, with the Delaware Tribe, 10 Stat. 1048; treaty of May 10, 1854, with the Shawnees, 10 Stat. 1053; treaty of May 17, 1854, with the Ioway Tribe, 10 Stat. 1165; treaty of June 22, 1855, with the Choctaw and Chickasaw Indians, 11 Stat. 611; treaty of August 2, 1855, with Williamette Bands, 10 Stat. 1143; treaty of February 22, 1855, with the Chippewa Indians of Mississippi, 10 Stat. 1165; treaty of June 22, 1855, with the Choctaw and Chicasaw Indians, 11 Stat. 611; treaty of August 2, 1855, with the Chippewa Indians of Saginaw, 11 Stat. 633; treaty of August 7, 1856, with the Creeks and Seminoles, 11 Stat. 699; treaty of June 28, 1862, with the Kickapoo Tribe, 13 Stat. 623; treaty of October 2, 1863, with the Chippewa Indians (Red Lake and Pembina Bands), 13 Stat. 667; treaty of September 29, 1865, with the Osage Indians, 14 Stat. 687.

Source: Thompson, ed., *The Schooling of Native America* (Washington, DC: American Association of Colleges for Teacher Education, 1978), pp. 183–85.

Appendix C

Selected Characteristics of Institutions of
Higher Education in Puerto Rico: Fall 1978

| Institution | Control | | Level | | Hispanic[1] |
	Public	Private	2-year	4-year	enrollment
Total	10	24	16	18	123,329
American College of Puerto Rico		X	X		1,141
Antillian College		X		X	749
Bayamón Central University		X		X	2,911
Caguas City College		X	X		651
Caribbean Center for Adv. Studies		X		X	0
Caribbean University College		X		X	1,204
Catholic University of P.R.		X		X	11,380
Conservatory of Music of P.R.	X			X	249
Electronic Data Processing College	X		X		1,226
Fundación Educativa Ana E. Méndez/					
Colegio Universitario del Turabo		X		X	5,401
Puerto Rico Junior College		X	X		7,686
Instituto Comercial de P.R. Jr. College		X	X		1,800
Instituto Técnico Comercial Jr. College		X	X		1,256
InterAmerican University of P.R./					
Hato Rey Campus		X		X	8,067
San Germán Campus		X		X	6,337
7 branches[2]		X	X		13,038
Ramírez College of Business & Tech.		X	X		609
San Juan Tech. Community College	X		X		919
Universidad Politécnica de P.R.		X		X	143
Universidad de Ponce	X			X	347
University of Puerto Rico/					
Río Piedras Campus	X			X	23,535
Mayaguez Campus	X			X	8,871
Medical Sciences Campus	X			X	2,583
Cayey University College	X			X	2,601
Humacao University College	X			X	3,282
Regional Colleges Administration	X		X		7,016
University of the Sacred Heart		X		X	5,929
World University		X		X	4,398

[1]Hispanics comprised between 95 and 100 percent of total enrollment in virtually all institutions in Puerto Rico.

[2]All branches could not be listed due to space limitations.

Source: Olivas and Hill, "Hispanic Participation in Postsecondary Eduction," *The Condition of Education for Hispanic Americans* (Washington, DC: NCES, 1980), Table 3.17.

Appendix D

Indian Programs Funded in FY-1979

Strengthening Developing Institutions
Title III, HEA of 1965

Institution & State	Control	Amount	Project Duration	Total Multi-year Award
Alaska Pacific University, AK	4 Pvt	$ 150,000	1	
Bacone College, OK	2 Pvt	190,000	2	$ 379,000
Baker University, KS	4 Pvt	187,000	1	
Black Hills State College, SD	4 Pub	515,000	1	
Bismarck Junior College, ND	2 Pub	312,000	1	
College of Ganado, AZ	2 Pvt	315,000	2	630,000
Connors State College, OK	2 Pub	192,630	4	770,520
Flaming Rainbow University, OK	4 Pvt	75,000	1	
Flathead Valley Community College, MT	2 Pub	352,000	1	
Fort Lewis College, CO	4 Pub	144,000	1	
Huron College, SD	4 Pvt	595,000	3	595,000
Lake Region Junior College, ND	2 Pub	140,000	1	
Mary College, ND	4 Pvt	600,000	1	
Mount Senario College, WI	4 Pvt	200,000	1	
Murray State College, OK	2 Pub	100,000	1	
Navajo Community College, AZ—Consortium	2 Pub	547,000	1	
Navajo Community College, AZ—Adv. Funding	2 Pub	50,000		
Navajo Community College, AZ—Bilateral	2 Pub	147,000	1	
Northern State College, SD—Consortium	4 Pub	380,000	1	
Northland College, WI	4 Pvt	689,000	3	689,000
Pembroke State University, NC	4 Pub	800,000	4	800,000
San Juan College, NM	2 Pub	193,000	2	386,000
Seminole Junior College, OK	2 Pub	92,000	1	
Sheldon Jackson College, AK	2 Pvt	185,000	1	
Southwestern Technical Institute, NC	2 Pub	170,000	1	
Turtle Mountain Community College, ND	2 Pvt	200,000	1	
Yavapai College, AZ	2 Pub	435,000	3	1,306,000
FY-1979 Total Awards to Indian Programs		$7,955,630		
25 Institutions Funded				

Source: Department of Education, Office for Postsecondary Education.

Appendix E

Hispanic Programs Funded in FY-1979
Strengthening Developing Institutions
Title III, HEA of 1965

Institution & State	Control	Amount	Project Duration	Total Multi-year Award
Arizona Western, AZ	2 Pub	$ 320,000	2	$ 640,000
Bayamón Central University, PR	4 Pvt	351,000	1	
Bee County College, TX	2 Pub	100,000	1	
Biscayne College, FL	4 Pvt	200,000	1	
Boricua College, NY	2 Pvt	310,000	1	
Bronx Community College, NY	2 Pub	175,000	1	
Catholic University of Puerto Rico, PR	4 Pvt	220,000	1	
Cayey University College, PR	4 Pub	200,000	1	
Central Arizona College, AZ	2 Pub	209,000	2	417,000
Colegio César Chávez, OR	4 Pvt	216,000	2	216,000
Colegio Univ. del Turabo, PR	4 Pvt	595,547	3	595,547
College of Santa Fe, NM	4 Pvt	450,000	3	450,000
Eastern Arizona College, AZ	2 Pub	125,000	1	
Eastern New Mexico University—Portales	4 Pub	1,067,000	3	1,067,000
El Paso Community College, TX—Consortium	2 Pub	276,000	1	
Fresno City College, CA	2 Pub	95,000	1	
Humacao University College, PR	4 Pub	200,000	1	
Imperial Valley College, CA	2 Pub	227,000	2	454,000
Incarnate Word College, TX	4 Pvt	900,000	3	900,000
Inter American Univ., San Juan, PR	4 Pvt	465,500	2	465,500
LaGuardia Community College, NY	2 Pub	175,000	2	350,000
Laredo Junior College, TX	2 Pub	289,000	3	866,000
Miami-Dade Community College, FL	2 Pub	300,000	3	900,000
New Mexico Highlands University, NM	4 Pub	755,000	3	755,000
Oxnard College, CA	2 Pub	69,766	1	
Puerto Rico Junior College, PR	2 Pvt	130,000	2	260,000
Saint Philips College, TX	2 Pub	97,983	2	195,966
San Juan Tech. Community College, PR	2 Pub	175,000	1	
Southwestern College, CA	2 Pub	100,000	1	
Texas Southmost College, TX	2 Pub	200,000	2	400,000
Trinidad State Junior College, CO	2 Pub	140,000	2	280,000
University of Albuquerque, NM	4 Pvt	275,000	1	
University of the Sacred Heart, PR	4 Pvt	222,000	1	
Western New Mexico University, NM	4 Pub	390,000	2	390,000
World University, PR	4 Pvt	232,000	1	
FY-1979 Total Awards to Hispanic Programs 35 Institutions Funded		$10,252,796		

Source: Department of Education, Office for Postsecondary Education.

The Ignominious Origins of Ethnic Pluralism in America

STEPHEN STEINBERG

"If there are sordid, servile, and laborious offices to be performed, is it not better that there should be sordid, servile, and laborious beings to fill them?"

Chancellor William Harper,
A Memoir on Slavery, 1837

Ethnic pluralism in America has its origins in conquest, slavery, and exploitation of foreign labor. Conquest, first, in the case of native Americans who were systematically uprooted, decimated and finally banished to reservation wastelands; and second, in the case of Mexicans in the Southwest who were conquered and annexed by an expansionist nation. Slavery, in the case of the millions of Africans who were abducted from their homelands and forced into perpetual servitude on another continent. Exploitation of foreign labor, in the case of the tens of millions of immigrants who were initially imported to populate the nation's land mass, and later to provide cheap labor for industrial development.

To say that ethnic pluralism in America had its origins in conquest, slavery, and exploitation is not to deny that in the course of American history ethnic diversity has come to assume positive value. Nor is it to deny that minorities have often reaped the benefits of an affluent society, notwithstanding the circumstances of their origins. Nevertheless, it is imperative to come to terms with the essentially negative basis on which pluralism developed. Only in this way is it possible to begin to understand why virtually all the nation's racial and ethnic minorities have confronted intense and virulent bigotry, why all have had to struggle to preserve their ethnic identities and institutions, and why the history of race and ethnicity has been fraught with tension, rivalry, and conflict.

It might be said of the United States that it is a nation without a people. With the notable exception of the American Indian, the American people are not ethnically rooted on American soil. When the first colonial settlements were established in the seventeenth century, the Indian population amounted to roughly 800,000 people. Here was a vast expanse of virginal land—nearly three million square miles—that was virtually unpopulated, a remarkable circumstance that would profoundly influence the course of ethnic history in America.

In contrast to the European colonization of Asia and Africa, there was no large indigenous population that could be exploited by the colonial power. This dearth of population had different implications for the nation at different points in its economic development, and concomitantly, different expediencies were employed to secure the necessary population and labor. It was in this process of aggregating population that the nation came to acquire the racial and ethnic diversity that is characteristic of American society today.

For the purpose of this analysis, it is useful to distinguish four stages of national development: (1) settlement, (2) expansion, (3) agricultural development, and (4) industrial development. Each stage brought about major changes in the ethnic profile of the American people; each introduced new racial and ethnic stocks into the national population; and each defined new sets of relationships between the society at large and its constituent minorities.

Settlement

Franklin Roosevelt once began a speech to the Daughters of the American Revolution by addressing them as "fellow immigrants." Though one might applaud the equalitarian sentiment behind this gesture, it is not really correct to refer to the colonial settlers as "immigrants." They came not as migrants entering an alien society, forced to acquire a new national identity, but as a colonial vanguard that would create a new England in the image of the one they had left behind. Colonists even referred to themselves as "emigrants" rather than "immigrants," and it was not until the late 1780s that newcomers began to be identified with the country they entered rather than the one they had left behind.[1]

In their quest for legitimacy, various minority groups have made much of the fact that one or another of their forebears was present in the colonies or crossed the Potomac with Washington's army. Whatever validity these claims may have, the truth of the matter is that the colonial population was predominantly British. As one historian writes of the seventeenth century:

> For despite the Dutch on the Hudson, and small groups of Swiss, Swedes, Finns, and French Huguenots pocketed along the coast, the small vessels which set out on the American voyage were chiefly English built and English manned. their cargoes, moreover, consisted of Englishmen and, later and in smaller numbers, Englishwomen. Even the Scots and Irish, who in the next century would crowd the harbors of the New World, were a minority in the first century.[2]

. . .

The most obvious sign of the cultural preeminence of the English was the establishment of the English language as the lingua franca. In 1814 De Witt Clinton, soon to become the governor of New York, commented with undisguised pleasure: "The triumph and adoption of the English language have been the principal means of melting us down into one people, and of extinguishing those stubborn prejudices and violent animosities which formed a wall of partition between the inhabitants of the same land."[7] The early history of the United States seems to bear out Clinton's contention that the establishment of the English language was a critical first step in the gradual assimilation of the various ethnic stocks of the colonial period. Even before the Revolution, French and Swedish were in decline, and gradually Dutch and German gave way to English also.

After the Revolution the pace of assimilation gained momentum. Aside from the rising nationalism engendered by the War for Independence, the lull in immigration, according to Marcus Hansen, "not only allowed the melting pot to simmer gently, but also hastened the Americanization of those non-British groups which had not yet lost their distinctive identity."[8]

Given the ethnocentrism and xenophobia that reigned during the colonial period, one might ask why the British admitted non-British settlers in the first place. Obviously, had they been guided by their prejudices alone, they would have restricted entry to their own countrymen. The simple truth is that English were not coming in sufficient numbers to populate the colonies. Aside from the high costs of travel and the hardships of colonial life, the economy was not sufficiently developed to sustain large-scale immigration. Except for a small class of artisans, traders, and skilled workers, most settlers eked out their livelihoods as subsistence farmers. Of course, pariah religious groups had non-economic reasons for subjecting themselves to the perils of the New World, and this is why they figured prominently among the earliest settlers.

. . .

Thus it was out of economic necessity rather than a principled commitment to the idea of America as an asylum that the United States imposed no nationality restrictions on immigration, either before or after Independence. Indeed, foreigners were generally regarded with suspicion, if not outright hostility. As one historian writes of the colonial period: "At one time or another, immigrants of practically every non-English stock incurred the open hostility of earlier comers."[13]

Furthermore, xenophobia pervaded all levels of colonial society. When Madison Grant sought to legitimize nativist opposition to immigration in the early part of the twentieth century, he published a compendium entitled *The Founders of the Republic on Immigration, Naturalization, and Aliens,* in which the founding fathers eloquently warned of the dangers that foreigners posed for the new republic.[14] For example:

> Why should the Palatine boors be suffered to swarm into our settlements, and, by herding together, establish their language and manners, to the exclusion of ours? Why should Pennsylvania, founded by the English, become a colony of aliens, who will shortly be so numerous as to Germanize us, instead of us Anglifying them. . . . ?
>
> Benjamin Franklin, 1751

> But are there no inconveniences to be thrown into the scale against the advantage expected from a multiplication of numbers by the importation of foreigners? . . . They will bring with them the principles of the governments they leave, imbided in their early youth; or, if able to throw them off, it will be in exchange for an unbounded licentiousness, passing, as is usual, from one extreme to another. . . . In proportion to their numbers, they will share with us the legislation. They will infuse into it their spirit, warp and bias its directions, and render it a heterogeneous, incoherent, distracted mass.
>
> Thomas Jefferson, 1782

> My opinion, with respect to immigration, is that except of useful mechanics and some particular descriptions of men or professions, there is no need of encouragement, while the policy or advantage of its taking place in a body (I mean the settling of them in a body) may be much questioned; for, by so doing, they retain the language, habits, and principles (good or bad) which they bring with them.
>
> George Washington, 1794

> To admit foreigners indiscriminately to the rights of citizens, the moment they put foot in our country, as recommended in the message, would be nothing less than to admit the Grecian horse into the citadel of our liberty and sovereignty.
>
> Alexander Hamilton, 1802

It is especially noteworthy that these sentiments flourished at a time when the population was relatively homogeneous and the level of immigration rather low. Predictably, as immigration grew in volume and complexity, xenophobia developed into a full-fledged ideology and political movement.

. . .

Expansion

The fact that the United States originated as a British colony affected no group more profoundly than the American Indian. Even the claim that "Columbus discovered America" is symptomatic of an enduring colonialist mentality that denies the very existence of Native Americans, whose ancestors had migrated from Asia and "discovered" America some 15,000 years earlier.

An inveterate disregard for the Indian's humanity was in evidence from the earliest contact with white men. Columbus himself had abducted six Indians in full regalia and decorated them with war paint to display to Queen Isabella. Four centuries later, when the Indian had been vanquished and reduced to utter dependency, Buffalo Bill carried his Wild West Show to Europe, replete with stone-faced Indians in headdress. These two events bracket an epoch of almost unrelenting violence and inhumanity to Native Americans, the dimensions of which have yet to penetrate the American conscience.

Many factors contributed to the endless series of Indian wars, but the overriding issue was land. By issuing generous land grants to colonial settlers, European monarchs unleashed forces that resulted in several centuries of internecine warfare with the indigenous populations of the New World. Each step in the extension of American dominion precipitated renewed conflict, which invariably ended with the forced cession of Indian land. The advancing frontier, so celebrated in American folklore, inevitably meant the dispossession of Indian land and the elimination of the Indians themselves.

The dispossession of Indian land and the displacement of the Indian population occurred gradually over several centuries, though it is possible to discern several stages. During the early colonial period, the settlers were obligated to recognize Indian nations as independent powers because of their relative strength. As Indian historian Wilcomb Washburn writes:

> The period of Indian-white equality . . . was based first of all upon the power of the Indian to maintain that equality. . . . The Iroquois Confederacy possessed the requisite power and political organization to command respect from all interested European governments.[15]

In addition, early settlers were dependent upon Indians for protection and trade, not to mention tutelage in agricultural techniques suitable to the New World. Consequently, settlers were temporarily compelled to negotiate with Indians for the purchase of land. Even where this theoretical "equality" prevailed, however, it was qualified by images of the Indian as savage and beastlike—images that served to justify land grabs by whites. The utter contempt for Indians and their land rights is manifested in one early-seventeenth-century document which held that "savages have no particular propertie in any part or parcel of that country, but only a general residencie there, as wild beasts have in the forests."[16]

As the balance of power shifted in their favor—thanks to their superior technology and weapons—settlers were even less inclined to recognize Indian land rights. From the seventeenth century on, Europeans claimed for themselves the right of "dominion," acknowledging only "possessory rights" of Indians to the lands actually occupied by them.[17] Furthermore, occupancy came to be defined in terms of agricultural settlement, thus denying Indian ownership of land used for hunting or fishing. A series of Indian wars during the colonial period effectively secured English rule over the entire eastern seaboard, thereby establishing a beachhead for further penetration of the mainland.

. . .

The Cherokee contradicted the prevailing stereotypes of Indians as nomadic hunters and uncivilized savages. They had assimilated a great deal of white culture, and lived in cultivated settlements replete with mills, schools, and churches. The Cherokee were also unique in that they had their own written language, and in 1827 drafted a constitution modeled after that of the surrounding white society. Despite the fact that the Cherokee had fought courageously on the American side of the War of 1812, their land was coveted for white settlement, especially after gold was discovered in the heart of the Cherokee nation in 1829.

It is noteworthy that the ultimate removal of the Cherokee from their ancestral homeland did not occur by dint of force alone, but was legitimized through the nation's highest political and judicial institutions. The legal groundwork was laid in an 1823 Supreme Court decision in which Chief Justice John Marshall effectively nullified all previous treaties by declaring that Indians did not have unqualified sovereignty over their territories. Marshall reasoned that discovery gave exclusive title to those who made it, and in effect, placed a stamp of legitimacy on the conquest of the Indian by the colonists. On the basis of this decision, the State of Georgia proceeded to invalidate all statutes adopted by the Indians, including those that restricted the sale of land. When the Cherokee appealed to the federal government for protection of their treaty rights, Jackson replied that "the President of the United States has no power to protect them against the laws of Georgia."[20] The coup de grâce was delivered by Chief Justice Marshall in *The Cherokee Nation* v. *The State of Georgia*. Marshall ruled that the Cherokee Nation, though a "state," was not a "foreign state" but a "domestic dependent nation," and disavowed any jurisdiction in the case. In 1830 Congress passed a Removal Act that empowered the President to deport Indians east of the Mississippi to Indian Territory. Finally, in 1838 some 12,000 Cherokee were rounded up at bayonet point, interned in stockades, and finally forced on a grueling midwinter march to Kansas. An estimated 2,500 died on what the Cherokee called the Trail of Tears.

. . .

By 1880 the last of the Indian wars had been fought, and the surviving Indian population was isolated on reservations.

. . .

Finally, increasing numbers of Indians—at least a third today—live not on reservations, but in the red ghettos of cities like Minneapolis, Chicago and Los Angeles. Here the cycle of Indian-white conflict has gone full circle, and it is the Indians who find themselves, like immigrants, on strange terrain, forced to adapt to the imperatives of an alien society.

Indians were not the only group to be engulfed by a land-hungry nation. In 1803 the United States doubled its national domain by prevailing upon Napoleon to sell Louisiana. Mexico was less accommodating, and its territories were conquered and annexed in 1848 under a treaty ending the Mexican-American War.

The conquest of Mexican territory and the treatment of Mexican nationals were foreshadowed by the Indian experience. The seeds of territorial conquest had been planted long before the nation arrogantly pronounced that it was its "manifest destiny" to extend its dominion from coast to coast.

. . .

In 1846 the United States deliberately provoked a war with Mexico, and after seizing Mexico City itself, forced Mexico to cede one-half her national territory, an area corresponding to Germany and France combined, and today encompassing Arizona, California, Nevada, New Mexico, Utah, half of Colorado, and the part of Texas that had not been annexed a decade earlier.[31]

Nearly 80,000 Mexican citizens lived in the ceded territory, most of whom elected to become citizens of the United States under the terms of the peace treaty. The treaty also guaranteed that their property rights would be protected, but as in the case of the Indians, the Mexicans were gradually dispossessed of their land through a combination of legal chicanery and outright violence. When gold was discovered in California in 1848, Spanish-speaking miners were driven from the mines by vigilante groups.

Unlike Indians who were isolated on reservations, Mexicans of the Southwest—augmented by a steady migration of Mexican nationals—became an integral part of the regional economy, providing the cheap labor that was necessary for the growth of agriculture, ranching, mining, and industry. Since the 1880s special interest groups have actively recruited Mexican nationals whenever labor has been in short supply, as it was during the two world wars. Immigration policy has also been manipulated according to need, and under the bracero program, which operated between 1942 and 1964, over four million Mexican workers were admitted for limited periods, usually coinciding with the seasonal harvest of crops.

. . .

As in the case of the Indian, conquest was only a devastating first step in a long history of expropriation. Paradoxically, the fact that Indians and Mexicans have ancestral claims to the land and its resources has not mitigated their oppression, but on the contrary, has given rise to a more extreme form of exploitation and control.

Agricultural Development

Unlike European nations, the United States in the seventeenth and eighteenth centuries had no surplus population, and in particular, no class of serfs to provide cheap agricultural labor. Attempts were made in colonial times to enslave the Indian, but these generally proved unsuccessful, in part because the supply of Indian slaves was never adequate, in part because the presence of Indian slaves posed danger to the colonies, and in part because Indians did not adapt well to agricultural labor and escape was relatively easy.[34] Long before chattel slavery was introduced, southern planters had experimented with a system of white servitude by importing indentured servants from Europe. However, indentured servants were both scarce and expensive. Furthermore, as contract laborers they could bargain for acceptable terms, and once their contracts expired, they entered the ranks of free labor. In the end, a system of chattel slavery, which reduced blacks to perpetual servitude, was more expedient and more profitable. In his book on *Capitalism and Slavery*, Eric Williams put it well:

The servant expected land at the end of his contract; the Negro, in a strange environment, conspicuous by his color and features, and ignorant of the white man's language and ways, could be kept permanently divorced from the land. Racial differences made it easier to justify and rationalize Negro slavery, to exact the mechanical obedience of a plough-ox or a cart horse, to demand that resignation and that complete moral and intellectual subjection which alone make slave labor possible. Finally, and this was the decisive factor, the Negro slave was cheaper. The money which procured a white man's service for ten years could buy a Negro for life.[35]

Yet slavery also had its disadvantages, which planters weighed as they experimented with different labor systems. In the first place, the purchase of a slave involved a large capital outlay, thereby limiting slave ownership to the wealthy planters. In addition, slaves had to be fed, clothed, and maintained even during periods of their life cycle when their productivity was low. An elaborate and costly system of controls was also necessary in order to deal with recalcitrant and runaway slaves, and to protect the larger community from the constant danger of slave revolts. Self-interest alone might have led planters to avoid the reprehensible trade in human flesh, if other sources of cheap labor had been available.

. . .

Initially slaves were employed in tobacco and indigo production, but it was cotton that would eventually create the greatest demand for slaves. Cotton production was uniquely adapted to slavery. Unlike seasonal crops, cotton's 200-day growing season required continuous employment of labor for most of the year. After cotton was harvested, the ginning, hauling to shipping points, and other farm operations continued so that one year's growing cycle actually overlapped that of the next. Planters gradually discovered that economies could be achieved by employing a large number of laborers who could work in teams and shift from one field to another. The result was a plantation system. Though a few slaves acquired skills as craftsmen and others worked as domestic servants, the overwhelming majority were employed in agriculture, and by 1850 about two-thirds of these were employed in cotton production.[37]

. . .

Yet slavery was more than an expedient for southern agriculture. Though the vast majority of slaved did work in the cotton fields of the South, the benefits of slavery redounded to the entire nation. It is not possible to comprehend the significance of slavery either as an economic institution or as an abomination of American ideals without understanding the role that cotton played in the economic development of the North as well as the South.

. . .

It was cotton that eventually provided the United States with an export staple that could sustain an expansive export market. The invention of spinning machinery and the power loom in the late nineteenth century revolutionized the manufacture of cloth, leading to the first textile factories and generating an almost unlimited demand for raw cotton. At first the technological capacity to use raw cotton exceeded the capacity to produce it, but this was remedied with the invention of the cotton gin in 1793. By automatically separating the cotton fibers from the husk and seed—a laborious operation so long as it was done by hand—Whitney's cotton gin accomplished in one hour what had previously required ten, thereby allowing for the mass production of raw cotton. The result was a cotton boom in the southern states, where the climate and soil were ideally suited to the cotton culture.

. . .

Virtually all of America's vast cotton export went to Britain, which in turn relied on the United States for 80 percent of its raw cotton. This cotton went into production of a wide range of textiles both for domestic use and for export, and in 1860 British-produced textiles constituted about a third of American imports. Clearly, cotton was at the center of Anglo-American trade in the nineteenth century. As one economic historian notes: "The key to American growth before the Civil War must be sought in European and largely British markets, European and again largely British, capital resources; in other words, in the dynamics of an Atlantic economy. . . . Cotton was the most important stimulus to growth in both countries."[41]

Not only was the United States the major supplier of cotton for Britain's expanding textile industry, but it rapidly developed its own thriving domestic industry.

. . .

The enslavement of the African, like the earlier conquest of the Indian, required a rationalizing ideology. It is facile to think that blacks were enslaved because they were seen as inferior; it would be closer to the truth to say that they were defined as inferior so that they might be enslaved. . . . Consider the following characterization of "the Negro," which appeared in the 1910 *Encylopaedia Britannica*:

> . . . . the negro would appear to stand on a lower evolutionary plane than the white man. . . . Mentally the negro is inferior to the white. . . . [T]he remark of F. Manetta, made after a long study of the negro in America, may be taken as generally true of the whole race: "the negro children were sharp, intelligent and full of vivacity, but on approaching the adult period a gradual change set in. The intellect seemed to become clouded, animation giving place to a sort of lethargy, briskness yielding to indolence. . . . " On the other hand negroes far surpass white men in acuteness of vision, hearing, sense of direction and topography. . . . For the rest, the mental condition is very similar to that of a child, normally good-natured and cheerful, but subject to sudden fits of emotion and passion during which he is capable of performing acts of singular atrocity. . . . [45]

. . .

Such was the inauspicious beginning of the nation's first minority whose roots were outside the Western Hemisphere. If the benefits of slavery had been limited to a small class of slaveholders, or even to the regional economy of the South, it is hardly conceivable that the "peculiar institution" would have persisted for so long. But the benefits redounded to the nation as a whole, which helps to explain why blacks were kept in quasi-servitude even after slavery itself was abolished. . . .

Industrial Development

The relationship between southern cotton and northern industry was only one element in a complex pattern of regional specialization and interdependence that facilitated the nation's economic development. As Louis Schmidt described it in 1920:

> The rise of internal commerce after 1815 made possible a territorial division of labor between the three great sections of the Union—the West, the South, and the East. . . . The South was thereby enabled to devote itself in particular to the production of a few plantation staples contributing a large and growing surplus for the foreign markets and depending on the West for a large part of its food supply and on the East for the bulk of its manufactured goods and very largely for the conduct of its commerce and banking. The East was devoted chiefly to manufacturing and commerce, supplying the products of its industries as well as the imports and much of the capital for the West and the South while it became to an increasing extent dependent on the food and the fibers of these two sections. The West became a surplus grain- and livestock-producing kingdom, supplying the growing deficits of the South and East. [46]

Corresponding to this pattern of regional specialization was a distinctive pattern of ethnic concentration. All three regions were confronted with an acute deficit of population and labor, and all three were compelled to import settlers and workers. Just as the South came to depend primarily on slave labor, at least in the critical area of cotton production, the North, and to a lesser extent the West, came to depend heavily on foreign labor imported primarily from Europe.

Immigration began as a trickle, gradually gained momentum during the nineteenth century, and finally assumed the dimensions of a flood by the beginning of the twentieth century. A few figures will help to convey the immensity of this movement.[47] As late as 1820, when the first official immigration statistics became available, only about 8,000 immigrants entered the country annually. In the six decades between Independence and 1840, total immigration was only three quarters of a million people. After 1840, however, there were two great waves of immigration that provided the necessary manpower for sustained economic growth. Between 1840 and 1880 over eight million Europeans entered the country. Between 1880 and 1930 the figure rose to over 23 million. This extraordinary population movement—the largest in recorded history—was fundamentally the result of an extraordinary economic expansion—also the largest and most concentrated in history.

Demographers and historians have identified a host of push and pull factors that operated on different groups, and much effort has gone into assessing the relative importance of each. However, the push and pull factor that was of overriding significance was on and the same: the process of industrialization which, paradoxically, had contrary effects on opposite sides of the Atlantic.

. . .

In short, the economic dislocations associated with the industrialization of European societies provided the major stimulus for mass immigration.[49] Eastern European Jews are a notable exception to this pattern, in that religious persecution and political oppression provided the chief motivation for emigrating. Although some immigrants, especially among the Jews, British, and Germans, were industrial workers or skilled craftsmen, the overwhelming number of European immigrants were peasants or farm laborers.

Virtually all of the eight million immigrants who came to America between 1840 and 1880 had their origins in northwestern Europe. Most came from Germany, Britain, Ireland, and Scandinavia, in that order. In contrast, the 24 million immigrants who constituted the second wave between 1880 and 1930 largely had their origins in eastern and southern Europe. Italians, Poles, and Russian Jews were by far the largest groups, but numerous other nationalities had significant representation: Slavs, Slovaks, Croatians, Serbs, Czechs, Bulgarians, Hungarians, Lithuanians, Romanians, Spanish, Portuguese, and others. Even though eastern and southern Europeans constituted the bulk of the "new immigration," especially after 1890, this second wave included substantial numbers of "old" immigrants from northwestern Europe. For example, Germany, Ireland, and England each contributed more than one million immigrants between 1891 and 1930.

At the same time that industrialization uprooted millions of Europeans it generated an almost unsatiable demand for labor in the Untied States.

. . .

It would be difficult to overestimate the critical role that immigrant labor played in the industrialization of American. The volume of immigration itself closely followed the vagaries of the economy, as Harry Jerome has shown in his book on *Migration and the Business Cycle*.[51] With every peak and trough in the business cycle, immigration tended to rise and fall accordingly.

. . .

What overall judgment is to be made with respect to the mass immigration of the late nineteenth and early twentieth centuries? Did immigration represent opportunity to the "huddled masses" of Europe, as has been proclaimed in American folklore? or would it be more accurate to say that immigration involved the exploitation of foreign labor on a colossal scale? This question cannot be answered simply. Unlike the millions of Africans who were imported against their will, and unlike Indians and Mexicans who were conquered by force, European immigrants came as a matter of choice. Clearly, no matter how dire their circumstances were in America, conditions were still worse in their countries of origin, which is why they wrenched themselves away from their homes and families, and why they so frequently sent for relatives and friends after they arrived. Contrary to legend, few immigrants came with illusions of streets paved with gold; most were lured primarily by industrial wages and had fairly realistic expectations of a better life. If the moral calculus depends on such a comparison between the lives of immigrants before and after their arrival in America, then the question of whether immigration was exploitation or opportunity must be decided in favor of the latter.

But can the question be so easily dismissed? Can the injustices visited upon immigrants be dismissed because most of them would have been still worse off in Europe? Apologists for slavery had also contended that blacks had been rescued from "barbarism and paganism," but not only is such an argument based on a false assumption—Africans lived in stable and highly developed agricultural settlements—the circumstances of blacks in Africa can hardly mitigate the inhumane aspects of slavery. Whatever benefits eventually came to immigrants, it must be remembered that immigration was anything but a work relief program for Europe's masses. If America did not desperately need immigrant labor, then tens of millions of immigrants would never have been permitted to come in the first place. To put it simply, America needed the immigrant at least as much as the immigrant needed America.

. . .

Mass immigration had adverse effects on organized labor in at least two respects. The abundance of cheap labor provided incentive to industrialists to introduce new technology which substituted unskilled machine operators for skilled workers, triggering a nativist reaction among craft workers. Secondly, so long as there was a surfeit of labor, industrial unions were practically doomed to failure, which in turn helped to keep wages low. Thus, immigrants were not only exploited themselves, but they were also used as an instrument for more effective exploitation of others, whether native or immigrant. For this reason, immigrant workers were sometimes compelled to put aside their ethnic loyalties and to join the chorus agitating for immigration restriction. . . .

In his 1912 study of *Immigration and Labor*, Isaac Hourwich argued that by spurring economic growth, immigration actually created opportunities for native workers, a view that is widely held among contemporary historians as well.[54] Nevertheless, the immediate effects were not always favorable, especially for workers who were in direct competition with immigrants. For example, between 1880 and 1914 there was little or no improvement in the real wages of workers, despite a rising level of affluence generally.[55] Thus, there was more than xenophobia and irrationality behind the nativist backlash among rank-and-file workers.[56]

Despite over half a century of nativist agitation and repeated efforts to restrict immigration by introducing a literacy test or some other device, the floodgates of immigration remained open so long as cheap foreign labor was in demand. By the 1920s, however, the rate of capital growth declined from its previous heights, and the application of new labor-saving technology further reduced the demand for labor. Besides, nearly a century of mass immigration, consisting largely of adults in their childbearing ages, had swelled the population to a point where the nation was assured of an adequate labor supply in the future without depending on massive infusions of foreign labor. With the passage of the Immigration Acts of 1921 and 1924, the door was rudely shut on the "huddled masses of Europe."

. . . Roughly 32 million Europeans immigrated between 1820 and 1930. . . . Germans had the largest representation, with nearly six million immigrant arrivals. next are the Italians and Irish, with about four and a half million each, followed the Poles, Canadians, Jews, and English. Together these seven groups account for about 80 percent of all immigration from Europe between 1820 and 1930, though numerous other nationalities are represented in smaller but substantial numbers. For a nation that once prided itself on its ethnic homogeneity, the United States had become the most polyglot nation in history.

. . .

Notes

1. John Higham, *Send These to Me* (New York: Athenaeum, 1975), pp. 5–6; Marcus Lee Hansen, *The Immigrant in American History* (New York: Harper, 1948), p. 11.

2. Mildred Campbell, "Social Origins of Some Early Americans," in James Smith, ed., *Seventeenth-Century America* (Chapel Hill: University of North Carolina Press, 1959), p. 63.

7. Maldwyn Allen Jones, *American Immigration* (Chicago: University of Chicago Press, 1969), p. 76.

8. Marcus Lee Hansen, *The Atlantic Migration* (New York: Harper & Row, 1961), p. 70.

13. Jones, op. cit., p. 44.

14. Madison Grant, *The Founders of the Republic on Immigration, Naturalization, and Aliens* (New York: Scribner, 1928). Excerpts come from pp. 26, 59–60, 90, and 51, respectively.

15. Wilcomb E. Washburn, *The Indian in America* (New York: Harper & Row, 1975), p. 85.

16. Quoted in John Miller, *This New Man* (New York: McGraw-Hill, 1974), p. 171.

17. Washburn, op. cit., p. 82; also, Wilcomb Washburn, *Red Man's Land/White Man's Law* (New York: Scribner, 1971), pp. 27–46.

20. Washburn, *Red Man's Land/White Man's Law*, op. cit., p. 66.

31. Matt S. Meier and Feliciano Rivera, *The Chicanos* (New York: Hill & Wang, 1972), p. 70.

34. Almon Wheeler Lauber, *Indian Slavery in Colonial Times within the Present Limits of the United States* (New York: Columbia University, 1913), pp. 296–98; Winthrop Jordan, *White over Black* (Baltimore: Penguin Books, 1969), pp. 89–90.

35. Eric Williams, *Capitalism and Slavery* (New York: Capricorn Books, 1966), p. 19. In 1844 one writer's calculations led him to conclude: "Where the free man or laborer would require one hundred dollars a year for food and clothing alone, the slave can be supported for twenty dollars a year, and often is. This makes the wages of one forty cents a day, of the other six cents only." Nathaniel A. Ware, *Notes on Political Economy* (New York: Augustus M. Kelley, 1967; orig. 1844), p. 201.

    For other secondary sources on the relative costs of slave labor, see Jordan, op. cit., pp. 76–77; Lewis Gray, *History of Agriculture*, vol. 1 (Gloucester, Mass.: Peter Smith, 1958), pp. 361–71; M. B. Hammond, *The Cotton Industry*, Publications of the American Economic Association, new series, no. 1 (December 1897), pp. 36–37.

37. It is estimated that only 5 percent of the total slave population worked in industry. See Robert Starobin, *Industrial Slavery in the Old South* (New York: Oxford University Press, 1970), p. 11. Richard Wade estimates that of 3,200,000 slaves in 1850, about 2,800,000 worked on farms and plantations. Cited in *The American Negro Reference Book* (Englewood Cliffs, N.J.: Prentice-Hall, 1966), p. 29.

45. *Encyclopaedia Britannica* (1911), vol. 19, pp. 344–45.

46. Quoted in Douglass C. North, *The Economic Growth of the United States, 1790–1860* (New York: W. W. Norton, 1966), p. 103. It should be noted that North's sectional trade hypothesis has been criticized by economic historians who argue that, notwithstanding the tendency toward sectional specialization, each region had a diversified economy that resulted in a significant degree of regional independence and self-sufficiency. For example, see Diane Lindstrom, *Economic Development in the Philadelphia Region, 1810–1850* (New York: Columbia University Press, 1978), chap. 1. This is a valid qualification, and the complexity of regional economies should not be minimized, but it is still true that there was an overall pattern of regional specialization that spurred economic development. Of paramount importance here is the fact that the unique economic character of each region required different solutions to the labor deficit that hampered growth in all regions.

47. *Historical Statistics of the United States,* (Washington, D.C.: Government Printing Office, 1975), pp. 105–6.

51. Harry Jerome, *Migration and the Business Cycle* (New York: National Bureau of Economic Research, 1926).

52. United States Immigration Commission, *Immigrants in Industries* (Washington, 1911), vol. VIII. Gerald Rosenblum, *Immigrant Workers* (New York: Basic Books, 1973), pp. 70–81.

54. Isaac Hourwich, *Immigration and Labor* (New York: Putnam, 1912).

55. Economic historians disagree on whether there was an absolute increase in the real wages of manufacturing workers during the quarter century prior to the First World War. However, as Gabriel Kolko has written in *Main Currents in Modern American History* (New York: Harper & Row, 1976), p. 169: "Whatever the exact truth, America's growth was below known European rates, and all agree that 1900–1914 saw the lowest expansion of real income during the past century, and this was largely due to immigration."

56. See John Higham, "Another Look at Nativism," in *Send These to Me*, op. cit., pp. 102–15.

The Minority Student in College:
A Historical Analysis

MICHAEL WASHINGTON

Minority students in college are those students who have been legitimately categorized by university officials as being members of a minority group. While in most universities throughout the United States the term "minority" is an explicit reference to Afro-American students, there are regions such as the American West and Southwest where other oppressed minority groups such as Native Americans, Asian Americans and Chicanos are also considered minorities. Moreover, although university officials do not generally regard female students as minorities, the sexism which they often experience in their pursuit of a college education qualifies them to be included in this work. In addition, because handicapped students have historically experienced great difficulty in their pursuit of higher education, they too will benefit from the principles addressed herein. Hence the minority student in college, according to the analysis and the strategies described in this book, includes members of oppressed ethnic groups or more specifically Native Americans, Asian Americans, Puerto Ricans, Chicanos or Latinos, and Afro-Americans, as well as handicapped students and women.

In short, minority students in college are those students who have enrolled in the university whose race, sex-oppressed ethic status and/or physical condition have rendered their historical presence in institutions of higher education a minor one based on their status in American society. What is more, it is assumed that because they are labeled as minorities they are expected to be victims of unjust discrimination. The very sociological meaning of a minority group, for example, is that it must be a subordinate group who suffers from discrimination regardless of whether it is large or small in proportion to the dominant community. This sociological definition is thus useful in explaining why oppressed minorities are discriminated against despite their monumental contributions to the development of the American economy; why handicapped people are continuously discriminated against despite their capacities to be developed into healthy-minded, productive citizens; and why women are considered a minority group despite their invaluable contributions to society not to mention the fact that they outnumber the men who are responsible for treating them as minorities.

At this point it is useful to describe some of the historical conditions of each of the aforementioned groups so that the relationship between the discrimination they face in the American society and their status as minority college students may be made more apparent.

Women as Minority Students in College

As mentioned earlier, because the classification of "minority" is associated for the most part with the Afro-American student in college, women are generally not considered by university officials as a minority group. Yet the discrimination faced by women in society at large as well as within the context of the university setting more than qualifies them to be considered a minority. Ever since the founding of America, women have been treated as second-class citizens. Although patriotic women served the American Revolution as camp followers, fund-raisers and in rare instances, soldiers in battle, from a legal and political point of view, the Revolution was a conservative one from the perspective of the American woman. Neither interest in politics nor avid patriotism transformed women into citizens. Property ownership remained the basis for suffrage, and since married women lost control over whatever property they owned upon getting married, they had no free political will. Moreover, unmarried women were also excluded from participation in politics. Most of all, women suffered from limited professional and social opportunities. They were refused admission to most secondary schools and universities. Practically all careers but marriage were considered "unfeminine." With the advent of the Industrial Revolution during the second half of the 19th century, thousands of women entered the workforce as factory workers and in white-collar occupations—both for extremely low pay. In fact certain white-collar jobs such as clerks, stenographers, and secretaries as well as professions like nursing and teaching came to be regarded as occupations for women and each became characteristic of low status and low pay. Nursing, for instance, was still classified as "domestic service" in most areas and as women moved into teaching the status of the occupation fell. When the salaries dropped, very few middle-class men were willing to take teaching jobs.

Furthermore, with the growth of urbanization there was a corresponding increase in underemployment, unemployment and poverty. And as men increasingly viewed women as objects of sexual pleasure, prostitution grew as a profession and tens of thousands of women earned a living in this trade.

By 1920 the long, hard struggle for political suffrage for women finally paid off and for the first time in the history of the United States women had the right to vote. Their political victory, however, did not alter their function to the economy as being low paid workers, neither did it transform the stereotypes of them as sex objects. Clothing designers and cosmetic enterprises amassed huge fortunes making women appear more sexy, and by mid-twentieth century it became popular for editors and publishers of magazines to promote pornography featuring women as mindless, immoral creatures of explicit sexuality whose only desire was to satisfy the prurient and lascivious fantasies of sex-craved men or even other women.

By the second half of the 20th century women began to pursue higher education in greater numbers than ever before. This meant that their educational destinies rested almost completely in the hands of a traditionally conservative elitist and sexist institution. The quest to earn a college degree placed most women in a powerless situation whereby middle-class men held almost total control over their future careers. The presence of women as college students, moreover, brought with it a corresponding increase in instances of sexual harassment and by the decade of 1980's many institutions had created guidelines, definitions and policies for this offense in an effort to curtail its pervasive existence. For example, in November 1983, the University of California's Assembly of the Academic Senate adopted a proposal to ban sex between teachers and their students stating that even "consenting" relationships can inflict "irreparable" damage to the educational environment.

In addition to the proposal adopted by the University of California's Assembly of the Academic Senate, several other institutions adopted definitions and guidelines including the Equal Employment Opportunity Commission (EEOC), the National Advisory Council on Women's Educational Programs, Yale University and Harvard Faculty Councils, just to name a few. In fact, instances of sexual harassment have become so widespread in universities and colleges throughout the United States that specific organizations and associations have come into existence for the sole purpose of advocating women in education. For example, "The Project on the Status and Education of Women of the Association of American Colleges" provides information concerning women in education and works with institutions, government agencies and other associations and programs affecting women in higher education.

Hence because of the probability of being faced with discrimination and/or sexual harassment in their pursuit of higher education, women, according to the analysis and suggestions provided in this book, must also be considered as minority students in college.

The Handicapped Student as a Minority in College

Because of the past and present discrimination experienced by handicapped persons in pursuit of a quality education, as well as in society at large, they too must be considered a minority, particularly in the context of the university. The conditions of handicapped people throughout American history have been appalling and atrocious. Persons whose conditions did not conform to the physical or mental standards of what was considered "normal" were often unmercifully incarcerated in insane asylums. There they were often "confined in cages, closets, cellars, stalls, and pens, where they were chained, naked, beaten with rods" and "lashed into obedience," testified Dorothea Dix, a Boston school teacher who spent many years during the antebellum decades studying the conditions of the handicapped who had been placed into the country's insane asylums. Dix's detailed reports to state legislatures on the hideous conditions, and her long campaign for public recognition of the problem led to many improvements in the nation's state-supported mental hospitals. Yet, despite the efforts of Dix and other reformers for the handicapped, disabled persons continue to suffer from stereotypes and discrimination in their efforts to be mainstreamed into society.

Until the decade of the 1970s most cities, towns and public institutions were built with no consideration for handicapped persons. Moreover, city officials have often been reluctant to grant such persons the right of equal access to public facilities even when they pursued their rights through the courts. For instance, in 1870 in a small New Hampshire town called Sandown, a blind man named David T. Sleeper brought suit against the town for being negligent in keeping a bridge railing maintained. After falling into the water because of the absence of a protective railing, the blind farmhand sued the town for the injuries he suffered, alleging that the town had been negligent in failing to keep the bridge railing maintained. When a jury awarded a verdict in his favor, the town appealed the case to the Supreme Court of New Hampshire arguing that Mr. Sleeper himself had been negligent in traveling, as a blind person, unaided on the highways in his customary way of traveling. With the intent of barring Mr. Sleeper from recovering damages for his injuries, the city of Sandown pursued the case. Fortunately though for Mr. Sleeper and indeed for all blind persons residing in the town, the Supreme Court of New Hampshire upheld the lower court's judgment in favor of David Sleeper. In its opinion, the court rejected the notion that Mr. Sleeper had been negligent in traveling alone. The fact remains, however, that the city officials in Sandown, New Hampshire, like other public officials all over the nation, were willing to deny a disabled person the enjoyment of his equal rights on the basis of his handicap.

As a result of the legacy of discrimination, being looked down upon, and being regarded as incompetent, handicapped people tend to suffer with a low self-image and share the low expectations of themselves that prevail in the larger society. In other words, no one expects them to achieve, so they don't expect themselves to. This is especially true of handicapped persons who enroll in college, particularly when there are no support services for them. As a result, many of them never complete their college education.

Despite the fact that a significant number of the population is considered handicapped with one or more disabling conditions, colleges and universities continue to be unable or unwilling to create the type of educational environment which does not intimidate these students. Recent estimates suggest that more than 15 percent of the population or one in every six Americans have a physical or mental impairment of a chronic or continuing nature. What this means in terms of higher education is that over 35 million United States citizens who may be victimized by deafness and hearing impairments; blindness and visual impairments; mobility impairments; epilepsy; speech impairments; paralysis; cerebral palsy; etc., may expect to experience various forms of discrimination in their quest to earn a college degree.

Oppressed Minorities as Minority Students in College

An oppressed minority is any member of a non-European ethnic group who is an American citizen yet whose cultural experience is one of exploitation and oppression because of the policies of the United States government and U.S. corporate interest. While the term "minority" as used by university officials is usually an explicit reference to Afro-Americans, other groups including Native Americans, Asian Americans, Puerto Ricans, and Chicanos or (Latinos or La Raza) are also considered minorities because of their generally oppressed condition. Because each of these groups has been denied full participation in society, their social presence in the United States is considered a minor one. Furthermore, although each group has played a significant role in the emergence of America as one of the wealthiest nations in the world, they, for the most part, have been relegated to the lowest economic sectors and are to function as sources of cheap labor to the American economy. Hence, the discrimination they face when they enter American colleges and universities is merely part of the total process of keeping them subordinated within the context of the American society.

Native Americans

The Native Americans, for example, who once occupied the vast land we now call the United States as well as Latin America, Central America, South America and Canada have been excluded from sharing in the American dream because they have been forced by the U.S. government to live on reservations. It was the policy of the Europeans from the very beginning to subdue and conquer these people and subjugate them for the purpose of exploiting their land. In his own words, Christopher Columbus describes the motives of the Europeans upon his very first interaction with the natives of the New World. According to Columbus:

> They . . . brought us parrots and balls of cotton and spears and many other things, which they exchanged for the glass beads and hawk's bells. They willingly traded everything they owned. . . . They were well-built, with good bodies and handsome features. . . . They do not bear arms, and do not know them, for I showed them a sword, they took it by the edge and cut themselves out of ignorance. They have no iron. Their spears are made of cane. . . . They would make fine servants. . . . With fifty men we could subjugate them all and make them do whatever we want.

Columbus continued:

> As soon as I arrived in the Indies, on the first Island which I found, I took some of the natives by force in order that they might learn and might give me information of whatever there is in these parts.

The information Columbus wanted most was: where is the gold?

The Spaniards' treatment of the natives in 1492 established a precedent for the English who landed in Jamestown, Virginia in 1607 and who, like the Spanish, initiated a policy of genocide against the Indian populations. From 1607 until the American Revolution of 1776 the English settlers adhered to the policy that "the only good Indian is a dead Indian" and ruthlessly robbed them of their land and murdered them in cold blood. Moreover, the founding fathers saw fit to legally deny them citizenship by writing into the Constitution of the United States of America a section which excluded them from being counted for the apportionment of congressional representatives and direct taxes.

According to Article I, section 2 of the Constitution of the United States of America:

> Representatives and direct taxes shall be apportioned among several States which may be included within this Union, according to their respective numbers, which shall be determined by adding to the whole number of free persons, including those bound to Service for a term of years, and excluding Indians not taxed, three-fifths of all other Persons. (Three-fifths of all other persons means Afro-American slaves who were viewed as 3/5ths of a human being.)

The ratification of the Constitution meant to the Indians that they had become legal captives on their very own land to be deprived of all human rights. Moreover, a full-scale attack, now sanctioned by the law of the land, was unmercifully unleashed against the native Americans to destroy their social organizations, their cultures and indeed their very existence. The racist policies of President Andrew Jackson who had 16,000 Indians in Georgia forcibly removed to dry wastelands of Oklahoma so that Southern planters could expand the institution of slavery was but one of the many injustices spearheaded by the U.S. government against these people. In 1890 at the massacre of Wounded Knee the Western Indians were finally subdued and the American West had officially been won. For the American Indian, however, this meant the loss of their homes, sacred lands, and their traditional ways of life. This meant too that their presence would no longer be of major importance to the preservation of the ecological system of the Western Frontier; but instead their existence would be relegated to a minor one in the eyes of a racist system whose goal it was to rape the land of its resources in the name of truth, justice and the American way. Hence, they have officially become minorities, that is, a subordinated ethnic group within the context of the United States and since colleges and universities were created for those with social privileges, Native American students in college can expect to face discrimination in their quest for higher education.

Asian Americans

Asian Americans are another oppressed minority group who has historically faced oppression as citizens of the United States and are therefore viewed as minorities within the context of universities and college settings. While the presence of Asians in the United States did not occur until after the 1849 California gold discovery, they have nevertheless made tremendous contributions to the United States by providing a constant source of labor. It was the Asian people, for example who helped build the sugar, pineapple, longshore and shipping industries in Hawaii as well as the mine, railroad, agriculture, fishing, fish cannery and sawmill industries on the mainland, especially in the Western states. Yet, despite such monumental contributions to building the economy of the United States, Asian people have suffered brutal exploitation, racial discrimination and special repressive measures. In Hawaii, for instance, the first sugar plantation was opened in 1835 on Kauai, using native Hawaiians as the labor force. Unhappy with the strict rules and low pay, the workers struck in 1848, demanding 25 cents per day instead of 15 cents. The strike was lost after eight days, as was a similar action two years later.

The first 180 Chinese contracted laborers came to Hawaii in 1852 to work sugar plantations under a five-year agreement at $3.00 per month pay. They also struck many times against the overseers' constant beatings for not working fast enough.

The year 1868 saw the first group of 148 Japanese arrive in Hawaii under a three-year contract at $4.00 per month pay. The conditions were so unbearable that three of the workers committed suicide rather than face the inhumanity of the overseers and planters.

During the decade of the 1890s the government of the Hawaiian Islands was overthrown by white American planters and the entire population of people from Polynesian, Chinese and Japanese ancestry were effectively subdued and reduced to the subordinate status of a minority group. This is how Hawaii became the 49th state.

Meanwhile on the mainland, Asian Americans faced constant and sometimes violent discrimination. From the 1850s to the 1880s, the Chinese played an instrumental role in building the foundation of the west coast's economy. Forbidden to prospect for gold and excluded from entering the skilled trades, many Chinese were hired by emerging capitalists to build roads, reclaim swampland, construct wineries and wrap cigars. By 1880, Chinese immigrants, brought in by the railroads to do the backbreaking labor at pitiful wages, numbered 75,000 in California, almost one-tenth of the population. One of the few areas of work the Chinese could enter with little training, capital or protest was the service trades, traditionally considered "women's work"—washing clothes, cooking and being servants to the rich. Outside of these occupations, virtually every area of work they entered, the Chinese encountered violent racial hatred. They became objects of continuous violence. Labor unions were a prime source of massive anti-Chinese campaigns. In 1870 over 10,000 representing unions, "anti-coolie" clubs and others, met in San Francisco to organize the Anti-Chinese Convention of the State of California. The following year a white mob invaded the Los Angeles Chinatown lynching 19 Chinese. In 1877, white hoodlums and unemployed workers attacked the San Francisco Chinatown for three days and nights, demolishing buildings, including 25 laundries. The storm of anti-Chinese sentiment gathered such force during the 1870s and 1880s, that in 1882 the United States Congress with the aid of Samuel Gompers, secretary of the Federation of Organized Trade Unions of the U.S.A. and Canada, passed the Chinese Exclusion Act. The Act specifically forbade the immigration of Chinese Laborers. Subsequent legislation outlawed the wives of laborers joining their husbands. Additional local, state, and national laws prohibited the Chinese from becoming naturalized citizens, marrying whites and testifying against whites in court. Such laws helped to intensify the persecution of Chinese. Many were expelled from California mining towns and attempts were made to remove them from all Pacific coast states. In 1885 the Union Pacific Railway Company recruited 200 Chinese to work their Rock Springs, Wyoming mine. This aroused strong opposition from union members and during the summer of 1885 irate white miners raided and attacked a camp of five hundred Chinese miners burning it down and massacring twenty-eight of them in cold blood.

The persecution and discrimination was not restricted to Chinese-Americans but affected all Americans of Asian decent, especially those of Japanese ancestry. From 1888 on, large numbers of Japanese began migrating to Hawaii and the mainland to work in industries where Chinese had formerly toiled. As their numbers increased, the racist cry of "yellow peril" grew louder. By 1924 such forces as the Hearst and McClatchy press, Native Sons and Daughters, the American Legion and others sparked the passage of the 1924 Japanese Exclusion Act. With the December 7, 1941 attack by Japan on Pearl Harbor, the "yellow peril" forces again crawled out of the woodwork and whipped up such racist hatred against the Americans of Japanese ancestry that posters such as "Jap Hunting License Sold Here—Open Season Now No Limit" appeared as commonplace wherever large concentrations of Asian-Americans lived. Racist hysteria and vigilantism prevailed over decency and common sense and many Asians began wearing buttons proclaiming "I am Chinese" or "Korean American" to protect themselves from racist attacks. Anti-Japanese hysteria spread in the government and one congressman said: "I'm for catching every Japanese in America, Alaska, and Hawaii now and putting them in concentration camps. . . . Damn them! Let's get rid of them!"

Franklin D. Roosevelt did not share this frenzy, but he calmly signed Executive Order #9066 on February 19, 1942, giving the Army power, without warrants or indictments or hearings, to arrest every Japanese-American on the west coast—120,000 men, women, and children, 77,000 of whom were U.S. citizens by birth—to take them from their homes, transport them to 10 concentration camps far into the interior, and keep them there under prison conditions. In 1944 the Supreme Court upheld the forced evacuation on the grounds of military necessity and the Japanese remained in the camps for over three years.

By the second half of the twentieth century the people of Southeast Asia had become the centerfold of world events. Indeed, it was the war in Vietnam which began in full-scale for the U.S. in 1964, that led to the discrimination of Vietnamese-Americans on American soil in the latter 1970s. The contempt held by American citizens toward Vietnamese-Americans after the war had ended was but a mere reflection of the genocidal attitude of the United States government toward the Vietnamese people during the war itself. In an attempt to gain control of the immense supply of rice, rubber, coal, iron ore, teak, corn, tin, spices, oil and other natural resources in Southeast Asia, the United States made a maximum military effort from 1964 to 1972 with everything short of atomic bombs to defeat the nationalist revolutionary movement in Vietnam and reduce the people to a "minority" status within their very own country. By the end of the war, for example, 7 million tons of bombs had been dropped on Vietnam, an area the size of the state of Massachusetts, which was more than twice the total bombs dropped on Europe and Asia in World War II. This was equivalent to almost one 500-pound bomb for every human being in Vietnam. It was estimated that there were 20 million bomb craters in the country. Moreover, poisonous sprays were dropped by airplanes to destroy trees and all other forms of natural growth. As a result of contaminating the vegetation with such poison, Vietnamese mothers reported birth defects in their children.

The bombings and poisonous sprays were not the only concerns of Vietnamese mothers—they had also to contend with the cold-blooded murderers in U.S. military uniforms who massacred their families, burned their homes and destroyed their personal possessions, food and livestock. On March 16, 1968, for example, a company of American soldiers went into the hamlet of My Lai 4, in Quang Ngai Province. They rounded up the inhabitants, including old people and women with infants in their arms. These people were ordered into a ditch, where they were methodically shot to death by American soldiers. The testimony of rifleman James Dursi at the later trial of Lieutenant William Calley was reported in the *New York Times*. According to Dursi, Lieutenant Calley and a weeping rifleman named Paul D. Meadlo—the same soldier who had fed candy to the children before shooting them—pushed the prisoners into the ditch:

> There was an order to shoot by Lieutenant Calley, I can't remember the exact words—it was something like "Start Firing!"
>
> Meadlo turned to me and said: "Shoot, why don't you shoot?"
>
> He was crying.
>
> I said, "I can't. I won't."
>
> Then Lieutenant and Meadlo pointed their rifles into the ditch and fired.
>
> People were diving on top of each other; mothers were trying to protect their children . . .

The My Lai massacre was not an isolated event and except for specific details neither was it unique. Journalist Seymour Hersh reported a letter sent by a G.I. to his family and published in a local newspaper. The letter reads in part:

> Dear Mom and Dad:
>
> Today we went on mission and I am not very proud of myself, my friends, or my country. We burned every hut in sight!
>
> It was a small rural network of villages and the people were incredibly poor. My unit burned and plundered their meager possessions. Let me try to explain the situation to you . . .
>
> Everyone is crying, begging and praying that we don't separate them and take their husbands and fathers, sons and grandfathers. The women wail and moan.
>
> Then they watch in terror as we burn their homes, personal possessions and food. Yes, we burn all rice and shoot all livestock.

Despite the awesome atrocities committed against the Vietnamese people they neither gave up nor lost hope and in March of 1972 the Vietcong and North Vietnam launched a massive offensive capturing the provincial capital of Quang Tri and scoring other successes. Three years later in March of 1975 the North Vietnamese troops launched a major offensive and the South Vietnamese retreat quickly turned into a rout. By mid-April the armies of North Vietnam had captured the capital of Cambodia and by the end of the month Saigon, the capital of South Vietnam which was created by the United States to prevent the unification of the Vietnamese people, had finally fallen. The war was over and a unified regime was established by the North Vietnamese.

If, however, the Vietnamese nationalists were successful in preventing the U.S. government from reducing their people to a "minority" status in their own country, those who had cooperated with the American forces were often not as successful. Thousands of Vietnamese who had aligned themselves with the American forces tried desperately to get aboard departing American helicopters and ships. Many had been promised passage out of the country. Yet, American Marines fought off thousands of terrified Vietnamese swarming over the walls of the American embassy begging to be taken along. Rather than stick to their promises, many American soldiers used the same tactic as did one clever American who devised a simple rule of thumb to make easier the discrimination which was to be spearheaded against these people: "Don't look in their eyes."

Being motivated by an intense desire to find their way to America, the land of golden opportunity, thousands of Vietnamese boarded boats and set as their destination the shores of the

United States. Once they arrived, however, they were greeted by the welcoming committee of hardship and discrimination. Indeed the racist and genocidal attitude of the American service-man toward the Vietnamese during the war had become characteristic of the American populace after the war had ended and instead of meeting with golden opportunity, they were confronted with racial hostility and discrimination. In many instances they were discriminated against because of their willingness to work longer and harder than American workers who were engaged in the same occupations. Despite their willingness to labor, the discrimination experi-enced by the Vietnamese-Americans has caused them to suffer economically. For instance accord-ing to the July 8, 1985, issue of *Time* magazine, while all other Asian groups as of 1980 had median household incomes which exceeded that of American families in general ($19,900) the Vietnamese was the only group that fell below that figure with a median family income of only $12,840.

Hence, because of their history of discrimination in the United States, Vietnamese-Americans, like all Asian-Americans may expect to be treated as minorities when they attend American colleges and universities. It is significant to note, though, that any sign of discrimination in institutions of higher learning would be particularly alarming to Asian immigrants because they almost universally see their children's future in terms of higher education. Yet, according to *Time* magazine:

> Many Asians complain that they are frequently the victims of racial prejudice. Lucie Cheng, head of the Asian Studies Center at the University of California, Los Angeles, charges that administrators, intent on curbing the decline in white enrollment, are actually causing an unfair reduction in admissions of Asian students.

Therefore Asian-American students who plan to attend American universities must recog-nize that because of their history as minorities in the United States they should expect to face discrimination in their pursuit of higher education.

Spanish-Speaking Minorities (Latinos and Puerto Ricans)

Still another group that should expect to face discrimination in pursuing higher education in American colleges and universities is the Spanish-speaking Americans, that is Latinos or Chicanos and Puerto Ricans. While the term "Hispanic" is the commonly used reference to these groups, it is more or less a catchall term embracing new immigrants and some families that have been living in what is now the southwestern United States for more than 300 years. It applies to people of white, black, Indian, and frequently thoroughly mixed ancestry who hail from countries that sometimes seem to have little in common except historical traditions and the Spanish language itself.

As recently as 1950, the census counted fewer than 4 million residents on the U.S. mainland who would today fall under the catchall category of Hispanic, the majority of them were of Mexican descent. Yet, according to *Time* magazine in 1984 there were an estimated 17.6 million, with roughly 60 percent tracing their ancestry to Mexico and the rest to Puerto Rico, Cuba, El Salvador, the Dominican Republic, Columbia, Venezuela and about two dozen other countries of Central and South America. Some analysts think that by the year 2000 they will total 30 million to 35 million, or 11 percent to 12 percent of all U.S. residents, vs. 6.4 percent in 1980. If so, they would constitute the largest American minority, outnumbering blacks as well as people of English, Irish, German, Italian or any other single ethnic background.

Despite their increasing numbers, the Latino population in the United States continue to face discrimination. For instance, in 1978 the median annual income for Latino families was $12,566 as compared to $17,912 for non-Latino families. A major factor contributing to both the growth of the Latino population in the United States and their disparity in income is the existence of U.S. military operations and U.S. based multinational corporations in Latin, South and Central American countries. For instance, according to the National Committee for Peace in Central America, by the summer of 1985 the United States government had a 10,000-person army trained and equipped by the Central Intelligence Agency (CIA) to fight and defend the United States' interest in Central America and particularly to do battle in Nicaragua. The Committee also reported that the U.S. have also provided arms to the right-wing "Death Squads" of El Salvador. The report, moreover, states that these "Death Squads" roam the countryside, killing anyone suspected of dissent, and that troops using American weapons have killed a dozen priests and hundreds of church workers. The casualty total in the Civil War in this small country exceeds 40,000. In addition, the report reveals that children, first and foremost, are the war's victims. They must flee as refugees—food supplies and family life destroyed by the ravages of conflict. And do they have any hope of education, or a better tomorrow? No, the only future most will know is poverty, despair, oppression—and more violence.

Another reason for the growth in the Latino population in the United States is the existence of U.S. corporations in Central American countries. Just as the North American Indians lost their lands to the U.S. corporate interest during the 19th century, the native populations of Central America are being pushed off their lands in the 20th century by multinational corporations which are based in the United States. According to the *Workers Viewpoint* (May 16–May 22, 1964) there are fifteen companies which are considered the most important U.S. corporations in Central America because of the size of their operations and their presence in a number of countries. Such corporations include: Bankamerica, Borden, Dole, Chase Manhattan, Citicorp, Coca-Cola, Colgate-Palmolive, Exxon, Goodyear, Nabisco Brands, Pepsico, R.J. Reynolds, Standard Oil Company of California, Texaco and United Brands (Chiquita Bananas, A&W restaurant and root beer). Because of the policy of such corporations (which have directly invested $10 billion in Central American countries) of using the natives for cheap labor, there exists wide-scale poverty in the majority of these countries. Moreover, the corporate policy of confiscating the best possible lands for themselves causes many natives to be pushed off their own land and tremendous numbers of them flee to neighboring countries including the United States.

Puerto Ricans are also victimized by the policies of corporations based in the United States. Ever since 1898 Puerto Ricans in Puerto Rico have been uprooted a number of times as a result of U.S. corporate control of the island's economy. This pattern began after the invasion of Puerto Rico by the U.S. government during the era referred to by historians as the "Age of Imperialism." Using the rationale that it was the burden of the white race to bring civilization to darker people around the globe, the U.S. government launched a military invasion of Puerto Rico. After this military takeover, U.S.-based agribusiness corporations began paying paltry sums for large plots of fertile land, and in the process, forced large numbers of agricultural workers from the countryside to the cities of Puerto Rico.

Although the Puerto Ricans were granted U.S. citizenship in 1917, the exploitation of Puerto Rican workers by U.S. corporations continued to push them off their lands. By the mid-1940s there occurred a second major shift in the population when an influx of U.S. industrial corporations moved onto the island, set up light manufacturing industries and forced many families off the land. This resulted in the emigration of Puerto Rican workers during the mid-1940s to the United States. The majority of these workers came to New York.

In the years between these two major population shifts, other additional factors played a role in forcing Puerto Ricans to leave their homeland. The two most important were the growing need for labor by U.S. agribusiness and the strategy of population control as a means of dealing with the people's response to colonial injustices.

The jobs of Puerto Rican workers as a whole became even more insecure with the infusion of heavy industrial capital into Puerto Rico during the 1950s. The character of these industries became highly technological, hence the need for large numbers of workers was greatly reduced.

Over two million Puerto Rican workers live in the U.S. today. The majority hold some of the lowest paying service-oriented jobs in the nation, and many more are forced to travel from state to state in search of more steady employment. The 1980 census revealed that among persons living in the United States of 16 years and older, Puerto Ricans had the highest rate of unemployment, with the possible exception of American Indians. One reason for this is the low rate of labor participation (those working or actually looking for work) among Puerto Rican males and females, which was nationally 76 percent and 32 percent respectively. Moreover, it was revealed in a report commissioned by an English-based group in 1982 that "One of every three Puerto Rican workers in the United States is jobless."

The conditions of Latino people from Puerto Rico who are U.S. citizens are worsened by the exploitation by U.S. employers of Latino immigrants from Latin, South and Central America who came to the United States in pursuit of employment opportunities. The willingness of such employers to exploit Spanish-speaking people for cheap labor has caused many Latino immigrants to seek job opportunities in the U.S. to better the condition of their lives. Once they arrive, however, they discover that they have been labeled by the U.S. government as "illegal aliens" and the entire Latino community, citizens and immigrants alike, are heavily and sometimes unmercifully scrutinized by the U.S. Immigration and Naturalization Service regarding their legal status as American citizens.

The question thus becomes "why are Latino people, including Puerto Ricans, discriminated against and are therefore considered minorities in the United States?" The answer to this question requires an historic overview of the relationship between the United States government and the Latino people or those people who are generally referred to as Hispanics.

To begin with, the concept "Hispanic" arrived in the Western Hemisphere in 1492 with Christopher Columbus when he named the island which we now know as Haiti and the Dominican Republic, "the Spanish Island," or "Hispaniola." The brutal mistreatment of the native populations by the Spanish was but one dimension of the conquest of these people. The other dimension took the form of interracial sexual relations and the imposition of Spanish culture on the offspring of the interracial unions as well as on the natives who survived the onslaught. Hence, within a few years after Columbus' arrival in the Caribbean Islands the original cultures of the natives had been transformed into a Spanish hybrid culture and the pattern was established for other Spanish conquistadors who were to conquer the natives in Central and South America. Between 1518 and 1522, for instance, Hernando Cortez defeated the most majestic civilization in the Western Hemisphere, the Aztecs, who lived in what is now Mexico. The pattern was repeated by Francisco Pizarro in his conquest of the Incas, a vast civilization along the western coast of South America. In each case the indigenous cultures were destroyed and replaced by what we now term Hispanic culture. Just as this new culture had come into existence as a result of being conquered by Europeans, it was destined to face similar atrocities in its relationship with the descendants of England who would come to control the government of the United States.

Since the Spanish were the first Europeans to cross the Atlantic Ocean in the 15th century and to control the gold (Aztecs) and silver (Incas) of the Western Hemisphere, they were the first Europeans to heavily populate the New World. But in 1607 the English established their first successful settlement in Jamestown, Virginia, and by the mid-eighteenth century there were 13 English colonies. In 1776 the leaders of the Colonies declared war on the mother country so that they would be able to rule themselves. Hence, the American Revolution was fought and in 1781 the Colonists defeated their mother country. By 1792 the Colonists agreed to be governed by one central government and thus the United States of America emerged as a result of the ratification of the Constitution by all 13 states. Because of the new nation's need to grow and expand, the U.S. government was destined to seize all of the land from "sea to shining sea." It was precisely this expansionist role that brought the government into contact with the Mexican people and thus established the pattern of cultural relations which would survive the twentieth century.

The Mexican people owned almost all of the territory now considered the Southwestern United States. Because the Spanish had conquered the Aztecs during the early 16th century, the people of Mexico were of Spanish and Indian descent and were therefore not of an Anglo-Saxon ancestry. During the early 1820s the Mexican government permitted Americans of English descent to settle in Texas providing they would not bring slavery into the territory. The white planters, though, were eager to expand their cotton kingdom into Texas and therefore they completely disrespected the will of the Mexican government when they brought in thousands of black slaves to work the huge plantations. On March 2, 1836, the white Texans declared their independence from Mexico, adopted a constitution legalizing slavery and established a provisional government. In short, they took Texas from the Mexicans. This happened, moreover, with a considerable amount of bloodshed on both sides.

Texas was not the only territory taken from the Mexicans. When Texas became a state in 1845, Mexico broke off diplomatic relations with the United States and there immediately ensued a boundary dispute as to how far the Texas boundary extended into Mexico. Moreover, President James Polk wanted to take California from the Mexicans and instigated a revolt among the American settlers living there. Consequently, the United States waged a war against Mexico in 1846 for the sole purpose of taking Mexican land. Once the United States gained military control of the Southwest and defeated Mexico, the Treaty of Guadalupe Hidalgo was signed in 1848 which ceded California, Arizona, New Mexico and Colorado to the United States. The treaty also approved the prior annexation of Texas.

When the treaty of Guadalupe Hidalgo was signed, some 75,000 Spanish-speaking people were living in the Southwest, approximately 7,500 in California, a thousand or so in Arizona, 60,000 in New Mexico and perhaps 5,000 in Texas. The moment the war was over a struggle began to dispossess the Mexican people from their land. All kinds of devious schemes were devised to carry out this objective. Sam Houston, ex-president of the Texas republic, and who to this day is portrayed as a hero in the "Winning of the West," brazenly declared: ". . . since Mexicans are no better than Indians, I see no reason why we should not go on the same course now and take their land."

Hence, the pattern was established for the treatment of Mexican Americans and indeed all Hispanics for the remainder of the 19th and 20th centuries. Between 1910 and 1930, for instance, there was a massive flow of immigration by Mexicans into the United States. Thousands and thousands of immigrants came pouring to the southwest with promises of jobs in agriculture. The white power structure was afraid that the revolutionary-inspired Mexicans (because of the 1910 Revolution in Mexico which smashed feudalism) would take over the region. Segregation was prevalent. Mexicans were not allowed to eat in white restaurants, live in the white sections of town, or go to the same schools. In fact, the period from 1903 to 1925 has been called "open killing season on Mexicans." On November 13, 1922, the *New York Times* stated, "the killing of Mexicans without provocation is so common as to pass as almost unnoticed." While it is difficult to pinpoint an exact number for the immigrants who came to the U.S. between 1910 and 1920, it is generally agreed that it was well over one million people. Labor shortages and the quest for cheap labor, especially during World War I, accelerated the immigration of the Mexican workers.

Despite the severe exploitation of Latino workers in the U.S., by the fourth quarter of the twentieth century the growth of the Latino population was one of the most startling phenomena in American social history threatening to be the largest single minority group in the United States by the turn of the twenty-first century. Yet, because of their history of being victimized by racist discrimination, Latino students who pursue degrees in institutions of higher education may expect to face continued discrimination as they attempt to better the conditions of their lives.

Afro-Americans

As mentioned earlier, the very definition of a minority group is that it must be a subordinate group who suffers from discrimination regardless of whether it is large or small in proportion to the dominant community. In the United States Afro-Americans comprise about 12 percent of the total population and represent the largest oppressed ethnic group in the country. Moreover, the very existence of the Afro-American is the result of forced subordination. While European immigrants came to this country in pursuit of liberty and freedom, Africans were kidnapped from Africa and forced to give up their language, their religions, and their identities as human beings so that they could provide the labor power to build the economic foundation of the Western Hemisphere. Implicit then, in the name Afro-American is the history of forced subordination of African peoples by Euro-Americans.

Despite the history of this ethnic group, the name Afro-American is not a negative one. On the contrary, the name represents the attempt of the old American "Negro" to redefine his new identity in the United States in the 1960s. The term "Negro" came into existence by Europeans sometime during the late 15th or early 16th centuries as the scientific classification of the people who would be human cargo and enslaved in the new world. The word itself comes from the Latin word "niger" which means black and the affix "necro" means dead or corpse. Literally translated the word "Negro" means "black corpse" or a people dead from their cultural heritage to be treated inhumanely and discriminated against because of their race.

It is precisely the legacy of racist discrimination that Afro-American college students are represented in very small numbers and thus considered minority students in American institutions of higher education. In order to make huge profits, the founding fathers of America discriminated against African people so that they would be a permanently enslaved workforce. The discrimination became institutionalized when the racist policy of enslavement and subordination was written into law. Once legalized it became a punishable offense for a white to associate with an Afro-American in any way other than as a superordinate, or a superior. In other words, it became illegal for whites to consider Afro-Americans as equal. The legalization of racist practices was buttressed by a belief system which held that whites were a superior race and that African peoples were genetically inferior. Once these ideals were internalized by the American populist it became normal and natural to discriminate against African descendants because of the belief that they were inferior beings. Thus the ideology of racism became the justification for white Americans to enjoy liberty and freedom at the expense and the sacrifice of the Afro-American. As an ideology, this belief became an unconscious dimension of the structure of the American consciousness. In short, racism became the id of the American personality; that is, it emerged as the subconscious rationalization for the racist organization of society. Because higher education is viewed by whites as institutions designed to serve the privileged and not the "inferior" masses, such institutions were not designed to insure the success of the Afro-American student.

This should not be interpreted to mean, though, that the Afro-American was not to receive an education. On the contrary, from the very beginning of slavery, Africans were to be educated to play the role of "Negro slave." In other words, the African slave was to internalize the belief that he was nothing more than a culturally dead commodity of production to exist in a state of subjugation as an inferior to the white dominant race. The education, or as Carter G. Woodson, the father of Afro-American history put it, the "miseducation" of the Afro-American was based on a curriculum of brutality with little distinction between prenatal and adult training. In discussing the prenatal education received by unborn African children in the Caribbean or West Indian Islands, Malcolm X described how pregnant African slave women were made to watch the torturing of their husbands so that the grief and fear experienced by the mother would be transmitted into the soul of the unborn baby (*Malcolm X on Afro-American History*, pp. 33–34). The newborn baby would thus be born out of and into an environment of fear and would, theoretically at least, be easier to discipline. The educational program for African children and other adults was no less brutal. While the numerous beatings and dismembering of Afro-Americans were considered their basic education, the lynchings, burnings and decapitations of rebellious slaves constituted a program of advanced educational indoctrination for those who were forced to watch, and after a slave had experienced several of these learning experiences he/she was considered well "seasoned" for his/her role in the occupational hierarchy on the plantation. Whether the slave became a skilled laborer such as a blacksmith or an unskilled cottonpicking fieldhand, the educational motivation for learning and mastering the job was based on instilling fear in the mind and soul of the Afro-American using various means of brutality.

While it is true that a few Afro-American slaves benefited from literacy training such as that provided by the Society for the Propagation of the Gospel in Foreign Parts (SPG) and the Quakers, the overwhelming majority of slaves were conditioned to believe that they would be severely punished if they were caught trying to read a book. To the master, the ideal condition for the slave was to exist in a state of perpetual ignorance. Since the ideology of the master had to become the dominant belief throughout the South, the Southern Aristocracy used the colleges and universities to unfurl scientific racism so that the intellectuals of Southern society could sanction and spread the gospel of the genetic inferiority of the Afro-American. In a book entitled *Racism and Psychiatry*, Alexander Thomas and Samuel Sillen provide a wealth of documentation as to how medical physicians, psychologists and other intellectuals, flooded the professional journals with scientific evidence, all fabricated of course, to demonstrate that the Afro-American was suited for bondage because of his supposedly "genetically inferior condition." By using science to defend their racist ideology, scientific knowledge became synonymous with the defense of white supremacy and the university curriculum became the training grounds for racist ideologues who indoctrinated their students with the belief that the universe was designed for the Afro-American to be the servant of whites. Although the Civil War ended slavery in 1865, the racist attitudes among professors have survived the twentieth century and it is not uncommon for a psychology professor to explain that the reason blacks score 15 points on the national average lower than whites on I.Q. tests is because they are either genetically or culturally inferior.

The main reason why racism and racial prejudice continue to dominate university policies and classroom practices is because Afro-Americans continue to occupy the lowest sector of the American economy and are still viewed by white society as being socially inferior. To the racially prejudiced college professor, a student from a "racially inferior" ethnic group should not have the same privileges as students from the "superior race." As a consequence, these professors set very low expectations for the Afro-American student and because of a phenomenon known as the self-fulfilling prophecy such students almost always receive very low grades. As if being victims of low expectations by racially prejudiced professors is not detrimental enough to the intellectual development of the Afro-American college student, these students often become victims of their instructors, stereotypic thinking. When such students enter college classrooms they are often viewed as illiterate, lazy, inarticulate and unqualified.

This perception of Afro-American students is worsened by the fact that most college professors are not aware of the cultural differences in the learning behavior of Euro-American and Afro-American students. According to behavioral scientists who have studied the field of Black Psychology, the Afro-Americans' learning mode is based on the African world-view and assumes that learning is primarily an affective process or a process which involves the emotions. Moreover, according to the African way of learning, the most important function of knowledge is to develop the total "self." Hence, self-knowledge is the ultimate source of all knowledge, that is, knowledge of one's self is the ultimate source of one's enlightenment. This relates to the Afro-American college student in that if learning is primarily an affective process then encouragement toward self or intellectual development is a critical component to the method of teaching. Moreover, since the African way of learning is based on self-knowledge, test scores are less meaningful as a means of evaluating what an Afro-American student knows than permitting the student to apply his/her knowledge in some meaningful situation. Consequently, because most white professors do very little to encourage Afro-American students to learn, but more often than not actually discourage them with stereotypic thinking and racial prejudices, the intellectual needs of many Afro-American students go almost completely unmet. Also, because Afro-American students are forced into relying on test scores as a means of evaluating their intelligence, as opposed to an actual demonstration of their abilities, they are often penalized with low test scores and no effort is made to liberate the hidden genius which lurks in the subconsciousness of their minds.

In short, when an Afro-American youth makes the decision to go to college, the decision itself is an act which defies the tradition of the racist myths of America. In the United States, Afro-Americans are expected to be the lowest paid workers in the economy. Their role in the labor force is to be the surplus workers. They are to be the most unemployed and underemployed workers so that they will be on hand to provide cheap labor when white workers either go on strike or enter the armed forces in a wartime era. Because of this, the university system was not designed to insure the success of the Afro-American student. The few students of African descent who are audacious enough to go to college are in such small numbers that they are considered a "minority group" in comparison to the total population of students. Moreover, because the U.S. society is structured to prevent the majority of Afro-Americans from entering the mainstream of society, they are considered an "oppressed minority." Hence, as with all other oppressed minorities in the United States, Afro-American students in college should expect to be confronted with various forms of racial discrimination in their quest for higher education.

Conclusion

In conclusion, minority students in college are those students who face discrimination because of their sex, physical handicap, race and/or oppressed ethnic status. Moreover, because of the history of discrimination they have experienced in the American society, they should expect to be confronted with discriminatory practices by university officials and/or faculty members. While women and handicapped students are not technically classified as minorities by most university guidelines, the sexism experienced by female students and the exclusion of handicapped students from the mainstream of college life, qualifies them as minorities because of the structural difficulties they face in their pursuit of higher education. Hence, women and handicapped students, like the American Indians, Asian-Americans, Latinos and Afro-Americans must recognize that because of the discrimination they face in American society, university personnel may regard their presence on college campuses as a minor one.

It should be recognized too that not all members of minority groups will face the same degree of discrimination. For instance, those persons who are members of a particular minority group who live in an area where there is a very small population of people from the same group, are likely not to face the same degree of noticeable discrimination as would the minority student attending a university with a large constituency of minorities in the area. Whatever the case though, all students who are likely to be considered a minority by either the society at large or by specific institutions of higher learning should be familiar with the necessary strategies which will allow them to experience success in college.

References

Berlowitz, Marvin and Edari, Ronald. *Racism and the Denial of Human Rights: Beyond Ethnicity*, MEP Publications, Minneapolis, Minnesota, 1984.

Duran, Richard P. *Hispanics Education and Background,* College Entrance Examination Board, New York, 1983.

Franklin, John Hope. *From Slavery To Freedom*, Fifth Edition, Alfred A. Knopf, New York, 1980.

Ichioka-Richardson, Yowko. "Exiled in the Promised Land: The Internment of Japanese Americans During World War II," *Third World Caucus Bulletin,* Third World Caucus/CALC, New York, New York, Issue no. 4, December 1983.

Lightfoot, Claude M. *Human Rights U.S. Style*, International Publishers Co., Inc., New York, New York, 1977.

Markey, Edward J. A newsletter by the "National Committee for Peace in Central America," P.O. Box 37123, Washington, D.C. 20013-7123.

Malcolm X. *Malcolm X on Afro-American History,* Pathfinder, New York, 1970.

Mirocha, Kay. "U.S. Corporations in Central America," *Workers Viewpoint*, vol. 9, no. 13, May 16–May 22, 1984.

Murphy, Michael; Starks, Nancy; Cheatham, Betty. *Beyond Paternalism,* International City Management Association, Washington, D.C., 1981.

New York China Town History Project. "Washing and Ironing: Chinese Laundry Workers in the U.S." *TWC* (Third World Caucus), issue no. 4, December 1983.

Project on the Status and Education of the Association of America Colleges—A Packet on Race and Sex Harassment, 1818 R. Street, N.W., Washington, D.C. 20009.

Smith, William D.; Burlew, Kathleen H.; Mosley Myrtis, H.; W. Monty. *Reflections on Black Psychology*, University Press of America, Washington, D.C., December 1979.

Spencer, Metta. *Foundation of Modern Sociology*, Second Edition, Prentice-Hall, Inc., Englewood Cliffs, N.J., 1979.

Time, July 8, 1985.

Thomas, Alexander, and Sillen, Samuel. *Racism and Psychiatry*, Citadel Press, Secaucus, N.J., 1972.

Torres, Zoilo. "Puerto Ricans in the U.S.", *CALC Report/TWC Bulletin*, October/November 1984, vol. X, nos. 6 and 7, pp. 20–22.

Washington, Michael. "Comprehensive Approach to Assessing and Remediating Learning Disabilities in Learning Disabled College Students," The Eric Clearinghouse on Handicapped and Gifted Children, ED 218 839, December 1982 (RIE).

Weinstein, Allen, and Wilson, R. Jackson. *Freedom and Crisis*, vol. 1, Random House, 1978.

Wilson, Arthur. *The Emotional Life of the Ill and Injured*, Social Science Publishers, New York, 1950.

Woloch, Nancy. *Women and the American Experience*, Alfred A. Knopf, New York, 1984.

Yoneda, Karl. *A Brief History of U.S. Asian Labor*, A Political Affairs Report, New York, 1976.

Zinn, Howard. *A People's History of the United States*, Harper and Row, New York, 1980.

The 'Untameable Savage Spirit': American Indians in Colonial Colleges

Bobby Wright

I have long thought the Savages of America very inferior in respect of intellectual endowments to the inhabitants of the civilized world. Indeed it does not appear to me that the Savage and the Christian life can meet together & that men must cease to be Savage before they can be truly converted to the truth of the Gospel.

—Dr. John Kemp, Secretary of the Society in Scotland
for Propagating Christian Knowledge, 1803

English schools we do not approve of here, as seviceable to our spiritual interest, and almost all those who have been instructed in English are a reproach to us. . . . We don't say to what our minds are most strongly attached, but of this we are confident, that they [the Indians] are not disposed to embrace the Gospel.

—Iroquois Spokesman, 1772 (McCallum 1939, 127)

The Roots of Resistance

American Indian participation and success in higher education rank among the lowest of any ethnic group in the nation. The comparative absence of Indians from academe stems in part from their avoidance of and attrition from colleges and universities (Astin 1982, 36, 40, 51; McNamara 1984, 72–78, 104). For the most part, native Americans have not eagerly embraced the education enterprise, despite nearly four centuries of exposure to institutions of higher learning. To more fully understand how such a culturally distinct minority reacts to mainstream intitutions today, educators must not only explore the nature of the current minority experience but also examine their responses to education over time. That is, to appreciate the difficulties minorities currently face in academe, educators must illuminate the historical contexts in which culturally different and oppressed peoples have encountered formal education.

When we contemplate the historic mission of higher education, particularly in relation to American Indians, and, more importantly, when we view that mission from a native perspective, we discover the historic roots of cultural persistence that continue today to result in their rejection of the higher education enterprise. American Indians have adamantly refused to surrender to an institution which for centuries has sought to assimilate them, to remake them in the image of their European subjugators. A historical analysis of American Indian responses to missions in the colonial colleges reveals that the issue of failed participation is far from new. As the introductory quotations illustrate, American Indian resistance has its roots in the centuries-old ethnocentrism that has shaped both European missions and Indian responses.

The Colonial Mission Schools

Throughout the British colonial era in America, the English maintained that their primary purpose in settling the new world was to propagate Christianity among native "infidels," who—although possessing rich and viable religious traditions of their own—were believed lost in the grip of the devil. Invariably the royal charters which sanctioned settlement of the colonies declared Indian conversion and the enlargement of God's kingdom as the ultimate aims of colonization. In granting the 1606 charter to the Virginia Company of London, for example, King James I made clear his interest "in [the] propagating of *Christian* Religion to such People, as yet live in Darkness and miserable Ignorance of the true Knowledge and Worship of God" (McDonald 1906, 2–3). Establishing a like mission for the New England colonists, the 1629 Charter of the Massachusetts Bay Company proclaimed its commitment to "wynn and incite the natives . . . to the knowledge and obedience of the onlie true God and Saviour of mankinde" (Shurtleff 1:17, 384).

In executing their divine mission, the English viewed education as a powerful tool with which to Christianize and "civilize" the "heathens." As early as the 1580s, the Roanoke settlers hoped "that they [the Indians] may in short time be brought to civilitie, and the imbracing of true religion" through the diligent application of "education, friendship, obedience, civilization, [and] Christianity" (Quinn 1:372). In 1609 Robert Gray advocated using the same means to civilize the Indians, since "it is not the nature of men, but the education of men, which makes them barbarous and uncivill, and therefore chaunge the education of men, and you shall see that their nature will be greatly rectified and corrected" (Collier 2:18).[1]

This belief in a divine mission and the efficacy of education prompted several educational schemes that went beyond teaching the rudiments of reading, writing, and catechism. Indeed, enterprising colonists and their English benefactors advanced a loftier design to bring higher learning—the "benefits" of the classical liberal arts education—to illiterate "savages." The "pious" plan was to educate selected Indians as schoolmasters and preachers, who would then assist the work of conversion among their people. In fact, within a decade of Jamestown's 1607 founding, the English had already unfolded plans for an Indian college.

King James I of England launched this initial design in 1617 when he enjoined the Anglican clergymen to collect contributions for "the erecting of some Churches and Schools for ye education of ye children of those [Virginia] Barbarians" (Walne 1922, 141; see also Kingsbury 3:102; Land 1938). The following year, the Virginia Company of London, sponsors of the colonial enterprise, apportioned 10,000 acres at Henrico to endow a "College for Children of the Infidels." Despite the availability of substantial land and capital for the college, however, the Virginia Company diverted most of the money from the prospective Henrico College toward its own economic programs. Finally, a 1622 rebellion led by the Powhatan Indians abruptly ended plans for an Indian college in Virginia.

In New England, the 1650 charter of Harvard College heralded the next educational scheme, providing for the "education of the English & Indian youth of this country in knowledge and godlines" (Forbes 1935). Funds donated in England financed the construction of the Indian College building at Harvard, completed in 1656. Although constructed for twenty students, the structure never housed more than six during its four decades of existence. The building was demolished in 1693, along with all pretexts of educating native converts (Morison 1936, 359).

More than seven decades after the first effort, Virginia revived its plans for an Indian college. In 1693, a royal charter established the College of William and Mary in part so "that the Christian faith may be propagated amongst the Western Indians" (Young 1932, 267). Accordingly, although no other evidence indicates that the college originally intended to educate native scholars, its charter professed a renewed commitment to spread the gospel among the Indians. Robert Boyle, English scientist and philathropist, inspired this "godly" mission with a generous bequest to William and Mary for unspecified "Charitable and other pious and good uses" (Boyle 1691). Motivated by the promise of a share of the charity, the president of William and Mary College used the proceeds from the gift to build the Brafferton School for native scholars in 1723. William and Mary did not actually enroll Indian students as baccalaureate candidates. At best, the

Brafferton School served as a preparatory school with the ultimate aim of matriculation for its Indian students. Furthermore, no Indian students were in residence for two decades following its completion, and only five or six at a time attended during the remainder of the school's existence. Even this record of feeble efforts and insignificant results ended when the American Revolution stopped the flow of missionary funds from England, and the school abruptly closed its doors to Indians (Stuart 1984).

The final colonial college mission arose in the mid-eighteenth century, when Eleazar Wheelock, a Congregational minister at Lebanon, Connecticut, assumed the task of providing academic training for Indian youth. In 1754 he founded Moor's Charity School which operated until the nineteenth century and enrolled as many as 150 Indian students during the reverend's lifetime. Wheelock's passion for education led to his founding of Dartmouth College, chartered in 1769 for "the education & instruction of Youth of the Indian Tribes in this Land in reading wrighting and all parts of Learning which shall appear necessary and expedient for civilizing and christianizing Children of Pagans as well as in all liberal Arts and Sciences; and also of English Youth & any others" (Wheelock 769663.2). He built the college with charitable funds collected by Samson Occom, a converted native scholar, who successfully solicited 12,000 pounds in Great Britain—the largest endowment available to any college of that time. These funds were presumably for Indian education; nonetheless, by the time Wheelock established Dartmouth, his waning interest in Indian education rendered the college increasingly inaccessible to potential native converts (Wright 1988, 10–12). Consequently few Indian scholars benefited from the charity which had accumulated on their behalf.

The College of New Jersey (later Princeton University), although not specifically professing an Indian mission, admitted at least three Indian students during the colonial era. The first, a Delaware youth, attended the college in 1751 under the sponsorship of the Society in Scotland for Propagating Christian Knowledge, also benefactors of Dartmouth College. Although reportedly proficient in his learning and "much beloved by his classmates and the other scholars," the unfortunate Delaware died of "consumption" (tuberculosis) a year later (Szasz 1988, 216–17). Jacob Woolley, one of Wheelock's first students at Moor's Charity School, entered Princeton in 1759, though he was expelled before graduating. As Woolley confessed later, he had been "scandalously guilty of several gross Breaches of the Law of God," including the sin of "drinking strong Drink to Excess" (Wheelock 763425.2). Finally, Shawuskukhkung—also known by his English name, Bartholomew Scott Calvin—attended the college in 1774. During his second year of residence, however, the Revolutionary War interrupted the flow of charitable funds from Great Britain that supported his attendance, forcing Calvin to abandon his studies (Harrison 1981, 16–21).

Thus, American Indian missions in the colonial colleges were lamentable failures. Henrico College, despite a substantial endowment of land and capital, never materialized. The Indian College at Harvard, during its four decades of existence, enrolled only six natives and graduated one, who contributed nothing toward the hoped-for conversion of his people since he died within a year of receiving his bachelor's degree. Although the Boyle bequest generously endowed the Brafferton School at the College of William and Mary, the college neglected Indian education for more than eight decades, making advances in this direction only when political and economic ends could be served. And Dartmouth College produced only three Indian graduates during the last three decades of the eighteenth century.

Reasons for Failure

The Reverend Thomas Bradbury Chandler, discussing Indian missions in his *Appeal to the Public* in 1767, "confessed, that the Success has not been proportionable to the Pains that have been taken" (Goodwin 1973, 104). Indeed, these missions had possessed all the necessary ingredients for success—money, land, innumerable "lost souls," and certainly an abundance of pious rhetoric. Why then did they consistently fail? What accounted for the poor return on such an enormous investment of time, energy, and capital?

A major reason is that the promoters of Indian colleges lacked the integrity and singleness of purpose to make their ventures fruitful (see Wright 1988; Szasz 1988; Axtell 1985). But further compounding the effects of duplicity and specious use of charity among colonial leaders, the intended Indian beneficiaries also reacted in ways that doomed the success of these educational missions.

In 1773, reflecting on 150 years of unsuccessful missionary work, Jonathan Shipley, then bishop of St. Asaph concluded that Indians possessed "an untameable savage spirit, which has refused to hear the voice of instruction; which has obstinately rejected the arts and improvements of the Europeans" (Goodwin 1973, 105–6). From a native perspective, perhaps, it was the Indian people—not the missionaries—who enjoyed victory in this battle of ideologies. American Indians were far from being passive recipients of the extended hand of Christian Knowledge portrayed in the condescending portrait colonial leaders sketched for English contributors. Rather, they responded to missions from a deeply entrenched cultural base which frustrated the English efforts to convert them. If the colonial assault can be read as chauvinism and cultural arrogance, then the Indian resistance can be seen as heroic. A more balanced view of both, of course, is to acknowledge the goodwill, misguided though it was, that existed on both sides of the enormous cultural chasm. Realistically, there was probably no way to bridge this chasm during the colonial period, when the power of religious paradigms left no options for either culture to understand or accept the other except in largely negative terms and where the balance of power disproportionately favored the colonists.

However, this image of assault and resistance oversimplifies the picture. American Indians in the colonies—both individually and collectively—exhibited a full range of responses to missions and education. At the one extreme, some Indian tribes and individuals eagerly embraced opportunities to receive schooling in the liberal arts and Christianity. At the other, many native people violently rejected Christian influence. Between these two extremes, depending on time and place, the broad spectrum of Indian responses to missionary endeavors included genuine conversion, accommodation, intense theological debate and criticism, and finally violent opposition.

Cultural persistence and the rejection of English civilization proved formidable barriers to the Indian college movement from the first proposal at Henrico, Virginia, to the founding of Dartmouth College. Because the Henrico Indian College was never built, little evidence remains to gauge the Virginia Indians' potential response to education and Christianity. However, early observers expressed both dismay and surprise that one of the strongest and most persistent aspects of native life was religion. "Among these Infidells," wrote William Strachey in 1612, "both the knowledge of our Saviour be questioned and the ymmortality of the sowle not rightly understood: howbeit to divert them from this blyndnesse many of our people have used their best endeavours . . . though as yet we have not prevayled [upon the Indian] to forsake his falce godes" (1612, 101).

Even at the end of the seventeenth century, after most Virginia Indians had migrated under duress of war or had simply died off, John Clayton, a contemporary minister, appeared surprised that native religion remained one the most striking cultural patterns among the survivors (Lurie 1959, 56, 58). Of course, their most dramatic displays of resistance to the cultural onslaught were the uprisings of 1622 and 1644, during which they made valiant attempts to rid their lands of the English influence forever. Considering such resistance—at least while the Powhatans remained politically and culturally viable—the English colonists, had they established the Henrico Indian College, would likely have encountered difficulty in locating college recruits among the Virginia natives.

A century later, when recruiting Indian scholars for the College of William and Mary, Virginia leaders found their native counterparts equally reluctant. Hugh Jones reported in 1724 that, while the southern Indians left several of their children under the Governor's care, "they themselves would not relinquish their barbarity; for they in reasoning with us by interpreters, asked leave to be excused from becoming as we are; for they thought it hard, that we should desire them to change their manners and customs, since they did not desire us to turn Indians" (Jones 1956, 59).

The same antipathy to Christian missions may be witnessed among other Indian tribes through the time of the American Revolution. New England missionaries proselytizing among the Narragansetts, the Mohegans, and the Iroquois found that as long as tribes maintained political independence the primary response to European religion was, with few exceptions, one of staunch resistance. Believing that the New England Indians would eagerly embrace the gospel, the English colonists were surprised when the native people "manifested indifference if not aversion" (J. Hammond Trumball in Weis 1959, 141). Roger Williams reported in 1654 that the Narragansett chiefs had asked him "to present their petition to the high Sachems of England, that they might not be forced from their religion, and for not changing their religion, be invaded by war" (Washburn 1975, 112). King Philip of the Wampanoag, who led a rebellion against the English in 1675, likewise expressed his people's hostility to Christianity. When the famous "Apostle to the Indians" John Eliot made an offer "of the everlasting salvation to that king; . . . the monster entertained it with contempt and anger, and, after the Indian mode of joining *signs* with *words*, he took a *button* upon the *coat* of the reverend man, adding, 'That he cared for his gospel, just as much as he cared for that button'" (Mather 1:566). Similarly, the Reverend Experience Mayhew of Martha's Vineyard in 1713 offered to "open the mysteries of Religion" to a Nintic tribe, "as being that which was greatly for their good," but the chief "did not seem at all inclinable to what I proposed" (Ford 1897, 110).

Only when disease, warfare, starvation, and other calamities engendered by European contact had weakened the fabric of traditional culture did New England tribes embrace Christianity. Essentially Indians converted where colonial populations were strong and traditional native communities weak. The Indian groups which inhabited northeastern Massachusetts and the shores of Massachusetts Bay, the peripheral coastal regions of southeastern Massachusetts, and Martha's Vineyard converted to Puritan Christianity. All of these groups were fully colonized by English settlers and were politically weak compared to other Indian groups as well as the colonial English. Among these dependent native groups, such famous missionaries as John Eliot and the Mayhews enjoyed their much-acclaimed success.[2] Among these converts were the few Indian scholars who attended the Harvard Indian College during the last half of the seventeenth century.

By the time the College of William and Mary in Virginia made its pledge to educate native youth, most Powhatan Indians had long vanished from the Tidewater region. When colonial leaders attempted to enlist Indian scholars, therefore, they began to recruit students from considerable distances outside Virginia. Those who eventually came to Williamsburg were Indian slaves, who had no choice in the matter, or political hostages, children of the tributary tribes whose friendship with the preeminent English could be guaranteed only "by yielding up several of their chief rulers' children to be educated at our College." Virginia leaders realized, after previous unsuccessful efforts, that "this fair step towards their conversion, is the more valuable by how much all attempts of this kind have hitherto proved ineffectual" (Perry 1870, 129). In the face of parental reluctance, then, coercion appeared to be the only effective means to stock the Indian school, and this method was not very successful.

Later in the eighteenth century, when Eleazar Wheelock recruited students for Moor's Charity School and Dartmouth College, he found the New England Indians—once resistant to cultural pressures—in a state of decline and consequently more susceptible to missionary work. In 1745 Thomas Prince reported optimistically:

> The surprizing Effusion of his [God's] SPIRIT on diverse Tribes of Indians in these Ends of the Earth, who wou'd never before so much as outwardly receive the Gospel, notwithstanding the Attempts which have been made this hundred Years to persuade them to it. Their extream love of Hunting, Fishing, Fowling, Merry-Meeting, Singing, Dancing, Drinking, and utter aversion to Industry, have render'd them extremely averse to the Christian Religion.

He added that, while the tribes in Plymouth and Massachusetts Bay colonies and on Martha's Vineyard had received the gospel for a hundred years, "very small Impressions of Religion have been ever made 'till now, on the Mohegan Indians in Connecticut, and scarce any at all on the Montauk Indians in Long Island, or the Narragansetts in Rhode Island Colony" (Simmons 1979, 28).

Thus, in 1743, when the young Mohegan Samson Occom went to Wheelock to learn to read and write, he was the first among many prime candidates for Moor's Charity School and Dartmouth College. By this time, Wheelock found ready recruits among the southern New England tribes, but he was consistently exasperated by the reluctance of the Iroquois Six Nations who maintained considerable political autonomy. Even at the turn of the nineteenth century, the Six Nations continued to resist missionary efforts. In his reply to a missionary named Cram in 1805, the Seneca chief Red Jacket later expressed the continuing sentiments of his people. "The Great Spirit has made us all," he said,

> but he has made a great difference between his white and red children. He has given us different complexions and different customs. To you he has given the arts. To these he has not opened our eyes. We know these things to be true. Since he has made so great a difference between us in other things, why may we not conclude that he has given us a different religion according to our understanding? . . . We do not wish to destroy your religion, or take it from you. We only want to enjoy our own. (Stone 1841, 192).

Native Resistance to Missionary Education

Throughout the colonial period, then, early missionaries and educators met considerable resistance to their zealous efforts among the native peoples. Still, despite the prevailing tribal attitudes from Virginia to New England, small numbers of Indian youth from many tribes left their homes to attend the colonial schools and colleges. What were their responses to these new experiences, and how did their attitudes and behaviors affect the outcomes of the colonial college missions?

The young natives, both boys and girls, who attended the colonial schools were generally very young, most not having reached adolescence. Nonetheless, by the time they left their own communities they already had been well socialized into their native cultures. Children grew up in a home environment where care and attention came from an extended family. Their parents and other kin displayed great affection for their young. From the earliest attempts to obtain Indian candidates, the English recognized the parents' intense love for their children as an obstacle in obtaining them for schooling. Virginia Governor George Yeardly reported in 1619 that the Powhatans were "very loath upon any tearmes to part with theire children." Three years later, he repeated "howe difficult a thinge it was at that time to obtain any of their Children wth the consent and good likinge of their Parents by reason of their tenderness of them." Recognizing this difficulty, the Virginia leaders proposed to people the Henrico Indian College with captives and slaves (Kingsbury 1:588; 3:128–29, 228).

A century later, when Virginia leaders resumed an interest in Indian education, they found native parents no less attached to their offspring. Governor Alexander Spotswood affirmed that Indian parents "could never be persuaded to let their Children stay any time among the [English] Inhabitants to attain a tolerable knowledge of our language without which they are incapable of receiving Instruction in the principles of Christianity" (Brock 1:126). Robert Beverly explained in 1705 that "Children are not reckon'd a Charge among them, but rather Riches" (Szasz 1988, 8). As late as 1744, when Virginia leaders were recruiting Iroquois scholars for William and Mary College, they encountered the same obstacle. "We must let you know," the Iroquois leaders told them, "we love our Children too well to send them so great a Way, and the Indians are not inclined to give their Children Learning. We allow it to be good, and we thank you for your Invitation; but our customs differing from yours, you will be so good as to excuse us" (Van Doren 1938, 36).

In New England, colonial educators encountered the same rebuff. In 1708 the Company for the Propagation of the Gospel in New England, a major missionary society, advised Massachusetts Bay leaders that the company heartily approved of schools for Indian children. They cautioned that even "as the fondness of ye Indians for their Children is likely to be a great obstruction to it, yet we would have you continue [the efforts]." Over a decade later, "notwithstanding the obstruction you mention you meet with in the Education of Indian Youth from the fondness of their Parents and perticularly their aversion to part with them," the missionary society was still encouraging "endeavours to train up as many of those youths as you can, in order for the Ministry" (Gordon 1969, 85–86, 171).

Those native parents who perhaps sought a better life for their children or who were coerced to surrender their young for education probably could not fathom the hardships and tragedy to which they submitted their offspring. They had no way of understanding the cultural shock which their children must endure. The Indian children's customs—indeed their entire way of life—were different from those they found in the towns of Virginia and New England. When they traveled the hundreds of miles from their home communities, they were ill prepared for the physical and psychological assaults they encountered upon their arrival. The schools certainly did not prepare the children for the dramatic environmental change. If anything, they compounded the stress by enforcing a sudden and direct change in life-style—in their dress, language, behaviors, values, and diet.

In 1761 Wheelock, with customary ethnocentrism, lamented over the cultural differences. "None know, nor can any, without experience, well conceive of," he complained, "the difficulty of educating an Indian. They would soon kill themselves with Eating and Sloth, if constant care were not exercised for them at least the first year. . . . They are as unpolished & uncultivated within as without" (Wheelock Papers 761404). Thus, colonial educators like Wheelock saw their educational missions as stripping potential converts of their Indian life-style and remolding them in the English image. Reverend Wheelock, like all English missionaries, took "much Pains to purge all *the Indian* out" of his students (Wheelock 764560.1).

The unhappiness of the Indian students can be deduced from their varied reactions. Many of them tried to run away, and some succeeded. A large number of them died. Many who survived the educational system returned to their tribal communities where they rapidly shed the thin veneer of English civilization they had acquired. Other educated converts returned to their native communities where they administered successful schools and churches. Still others became marginal men, hopelessly caught between two separate worlds.

Even after the colleges obtained small numbers of recruits, runaways consistently drained them of their Indian scholars. In the mid-eighteenth century, Mark Catesby noted that, among Indian students of William and Mary, it was "common for them to elope several hundred miles to their native country, and there to resume their skins and savage way of life, making no further use of their learning." He illustrated his observation with the heroic story of a young Indian boy, sent to school in Williamsburg at the age of nine or ten. He "ran from school," Catesby recounted, "found means (nobody knew how) to pass over [the] *James* river, and then travelled through the woods to his native home, though the nearest distance was three hundred miles, carrying no provision with him, nor having any thing to subsist on in his journey but berries, acorns, and such like as the wood afforded" (Catesby 1754, xii). Wheelock's school was also plagued by students who left without completing their course of study. In 1772 alone, four of ten recruits returned home within a year. "They soon began to discover the Indian Temper," Wheelock explained, "grew impatient of Order and Government in the School, shew'd a great Inclination to be hunting and rambling in the Woods" (1773, 7–8).

The students' "Indian Temper" rebelled against the European sense of "Order and Government." Their upbringing already had accustomed them to a great deal of personal freedom, since, compared to their white counterparts, Indian parents were extremely permissive. George A. Pettitt, in his landmark study of native education, commented that "probably no trait of primitive society, particularly in North America, has been more generally commented upon by observers than that of parental indulgence of children" (1946, 6). Youth in their native surroundings were rarely subjected to the harsh discipline and corporal punishment which they routinely encountered in the English schools. Indian parents and their children alike found such treatment intolerable. "There is nothing for which these people have a greater horror than restraint," wrote a Jesuit in 1657. "The very children cannot endure it, and live as they please in the houses of their parents, without fear of reprimand or chastisement" (Szasz 1988, 18). A Cherokee leader complained to a missionary that "he had seen children at school among the English [in Virginia] & ye

Master loved ym yt [them that] read well but corrected ym yt [them that] did not with a rod" (Conard 1979, 467).

In these foreign colonial schools, no less than in their native homes, the Indians would accept no restraint. Even the Indian teachers, schooled in such "educational" methods, rebelled against corporal punishment. Joseph Woolley, Wheelock's student and the first Indian schoolmaster to teach among the Iroquois, reported that his colleague David Fowler "begins to beat his Schollers very much; makes their hands to Swell very much which the Indians don' like very well; They say, he ought to have suppressed it longer" (Wheelock Papers 765406.2). Similarly, in rejecting Wheelock's proposal to educate their children, an Iroquois leader asked, "Do you think we are altogether ignorant of your methods of instruction? . . . You were too hasty, & strong in your manner of speaking, before the children & boys have any knowledge of your language." In a biting addendum, the speaker referred to the example of the Jesuit missionaries, bitter rivals of the English clergy, who "know how to treat Indians. They don't speak roughly; nor do they for every little mistake take up a club & flog them" (McCallum 1932, 287–88).

Floggings were not the only indignities thrust on the young students. The strict discipline of the school routine was equally offensive to the "Indian Temper," for native life was much less rigidly structured and routinized than that in colonial English schools. In Wheelock's school, for example, students were expected to be dressed and ready to attend worship before sunrise. Their school day began with prayers at nine o'clock, with studies continuing until noon. The schedule proceeded again from two until five o'clock, followed by evening prayer. Afterwards, they again attended to their studies (Wheelock 1763, 36). Such a schedule allowed little time for the carefree activities which Indian children enjoyed in their own communities. No wonder, then, these budding scholars yearned to return to their homes. A 1784 observer explained:

> Experience has indeed demostrated that the Indian youth, on whose instruction and moral up-bringing time and pains have been spent, and apparently not without good promise of shaping them into civilized subjects, grasp nevertheless every opportunity of escaping from restraint and oversight, and joyfully return again to their inborn way of life, wild, rude, and careless, finding in it vastly more attractions than in all the pleasures and conveniences which cities can offer. (Schoepf 1788, 79).

If the reluctant students did not leave on their own accord, they risked sickness and death, for the mortality rate among Indian scholars was alarmingly high. Yet it should have been no surprise. Removed several hundred miles from their homelands, as several contemporaries observed, Indian youth were subjected to sudden changes of climate, diet, clothing, and other environmental conditions. Living in close quarters in an urban environment, they were vulnerable to foreign diseases. Writing of the failure of the Harvard Indian College in 1674, Daniel Gookin concluded:

> The design . . . proved ineffectual to the end proposed. For several of the said youth died, after they had sundry years at learning. . . . Sundry of those Indian youths died [of tuberculosis] that were bred up to school among the English. . . . Some have apprehended other causes of the mortality of these Indian scholars. Some have attributed it unto the great changes upon their bodies, in respect of their diet, lodging, apparel, studies; so much different from what they were inured to among their countrymen. (1792, 172–73).

Surviving records amply support Gookin's observation. The only Indian to graduate from Harvard in the colonial period, Caleb Cheeshahteaumuck, class of 1665, died of tuberculosis within months of his graduation. His classmate Joel Iacoomes had died only months before. Similarly, a third Indian scholar identified only as Eleazar, of the class of 1679, died shortly before his commencement; and the final Indian student to attend Harvard, Benjamin Larnell, a promising junior, succumbed to disease in 1713. These unfortunate deaths accounted for a 50 percent mortality rate among colonial Harvard's eight Indian residents. The College of William and Mary experienced the same tragedy. Hugh Jones, writing in 1724, lamented that "hitherto but little good has been done therein, . . . where abundance of them used to die, either through sickness, change of provision, and way of life" (1956, 114). Similarly, at Moor's Charity School and Dartmouth

College, Wheelock lamented the untimely death of his Indian scholars. Of nearly forty youth whom he had educated by 1771, he wrote despairingly, six of the most accomplished were already dead (Wheelock 1771, 19–20).

The students did not want for medical attention, as the school accounts amply demonstrate; but the treatments may have proven worse than the ailments. The frequent administration of "vomit[s]," "purge[s]," and "bleeding" may well have sapped the strength of many ailing Indian students, contributing to the premature deaths of promising young scholars (Brafferton Account, 1765).

To make matters worse, loneliness, alienation, hopelessness, and low self-esteem added psychological stresses which compounded the physical pressures. Perhaps most damaging were the alien Christian concepts so immediately thrust upon them: guilt, sin, fear of death, individual perseverance, distrust of other people, and rigid discipline—concepts foreign to their consciousness. It is no wonder that Indian Christians found conversion an agonizing experience—as John Eliot interpreted it in 1671, "a bitter pill, too hard for me to get down and swallow" (Ronda 1982, 23–25). And the missionaries, seeing the Christian salvation of their defenseless, vulnerable charges as an overriding priority, made no effort to reduce the burden or cushion the intense psychological attacks. The truth is, I believe, that they were simply blind to the psychological stresses, believing that the Christian way of life was superior in all respects.

Of the native scholars who survived and acquired the rudiments of English civilization, most returned to their native communities. Few educated Indians, however, left school with more than a thin veneer of "civilization"; and most, upon returning to their tribal communities, reverted quickly to their traditional life ways. A contemporary historian observed in 1725 that the Indian students at the College of William and Mary who survived and "have been taught to read and write, have for the most part returned to their home, some with and some without baptism, where they follow their own savage customs and heathenish rites. . . . Some indeed," he explained, "after seeming conversion have apostatized and returned to their own ways, chiefly because they can live with less labour, and more pleasure and plenty, as Indians, than they can with us" (Jones 1956, 61–62).

Expressing similar disillusionment, William Byrd complained: "Many of the children of our neighboring Indians have been brought up in the College of William and Mary. They have been carefully instructed in the Principles of the Christian Religion until they came to be men. Yet after they return'd home, instead of civilizing and converting the rest, they have immediately Relapst into Infidelity and Barbarism themselves" (1841, 118). In his travels through Virginia in 1732, William Hugh Grove encountered an Indian who "was Educated at the College, could read and write, and had been christened [with] Alexander Spotswood, then Governor, Standing [as his] Godfather. But [he] was returned to his old Way" (Stiverson and Butler 1977, 30). As late as 1784, seven years after the demise of the Brafferton School, Elkanah Watson encountered "savage warriors, and among them one who had been educated at William and Mary College, a sensible and well-informed [man]; but a perfect Indian in his appearance and habits" (Watson 1856, 257).

The persistent lapse of educated Indians plagued Wheelock's "great design" as well. In 1771 he reported to his English benefactors that what "has occasioned me the greatest weight of sorrow, has been the bad conduct, and behaviour of such as have been educated here, after they left the school, and been put into business abroad." Some, he lamented, "are sunk down into as low, savage, and brutish a manner of living as they were in before any endeavours were used with them to raise them up" (Wheelock 1773, 18–19). Even as late as 1901, after more than a century of financial support, Wheelock's sponsors complained that "only one of those who have in recent years returned to their own people after having been educated at Dartmouth College, at the expense of the [Scottish] Fund, had done any good work; the others having either soon lapsed into the ways of the tribes with whom they lived, or obtained employment among the whites" (Nisbet 1901, 8–9).

Those who were able to shed the ornamental veneer of civilization and reclaim their true sense of identity were the fortunate ones—perhaps, in Indian terms, the successful ones. Less fortunate were those who found themselves caught hopelessly between two worlds, marginal men, accepted by neither the white man nor the Indian. "For the Indian convert," Wilcomb E.

Washburn, a scholar of Indian history, explained sympathetically, "the state was one of personal isolation from both the white world and the Indian world in which he had been born. It was a private world whose sorrow—induced by alienation from both the real white world and the traditional Indian world—could be overcome only by the self-justification of a pure life" (1975, 115–16).

No one understood this marginality more clearly than the Indians who were victimized by it. "Instead of producing that happy effect which you so long promised us," Seneca Chief Red Jacket rebuked the two missionaries—Cram and Alexander:

> . . . [education] so far has rendered us uncomfortable and miserable. You have taken a number of our young men to your schools. You have educated them and taught them your religion. They have returned to their kindred and color, neither white men nor Indians. The arts they have learned are incompatible with the chase, and ill adapted to our customs. They have been taught that which is useless to us. They have been made to feel artificial wants, which never entered the minds of their brothers. They have imbibed, in your great towns, the seeds of vices which were unknown in the forest. They become discouraged and dissipated,—despised by the Indians, neglected by the whites, and without value to either,—less honest than the former, and *perhaps* more knavish than the latter. (Stone 1841, 206).

Even those who supported Indian education acknowledged this tragically wasteful and alienating outcome. The Society in Scotland for Propagating Christian Knowledge, trustees of Samson Occom's collections, graphically illustrated the tragedy in its 1769 report. "Some experiments of what is called civilization and a polite education," the report concluded," . . . have served rather to disgust the Indians, and retard the progress of improvement." A native youth who has been "put to school," the report continued with telling candor,

> is neither a white man nor an Indian; as he had no character with us, he has none with them. If he has strength of mind sufficient to renounce all his acquirements, and resume the savage life and manners, he may possibly be again received by his countrymen; but the greater probability is, that he will take refuge from their contempt in the inebriating draught; and when this becomes habitual, he will be guarded from no vice, and secure from no crime. His downward progress will be rapid, and his death premature. . . . Such persons must either entirely renounce their acquired habits, and resume the savage life; or, if they live among their countrymen, they must be despised, and their death will be unlamented. (Belknap and Morse 1798, 29–30)

As the report suggests, many educated Indians—faced with intense cultural conflict—escaped through alcohol and other destructive behavior. Jacob Woolley, one of Wheelock's first students, confessed that he had been "scandalously guilty of drinking Strong Drink to Excess; and of being in a very sinful passion of Anger, which I shewed by a very boisterous Behaviour." After being expelled from the College of New Jersey (Princeton) in 1763, he was reportedly unemployed and "Melancholly" (Wheelock 763425.2;764120.2). Hezekiah Calvin, approved as a school teacher in 1765 and commissioned to teach among the Iroquois, by 1769 was characterized as a drunk and apostate. He was finally sentenced to prison "for forging a pass for a Negro," while Joseph Johnson, a Mohegan school teacher, reportedly "danc'd—drank & whor'd it" (McCallum 1932, 47, 141).

The Scottish Society's report also affirmed the racism to which the native student in English communities was subjected. White students, the society concluded, "make him sensible of his inferiority to themselves. To treat him as an equal would mortify their own pride, and degrade themselves in the view of their neighbours. He is put to school; but his fellow students look on him as a being of an inferior species" (Belknap and Morse 1798, 29–30).

The society's report may well have alluded to Samson Occom himself. Even this most successful Indian scholar was a victim of intense racial bigotry. Although he was more learned and genteel than most colonists and though highly regarded among Englishmen abroad, Occom never found a place as an equal among the colonists, a realization which probably contributed to his occasional bouts with alcohol. (Wheelock Papers 767604.1). A group of colonial Englishmen exemplified the prevailing racist attitude which frustrated Occom's transition to "civilized" society. In a conversation reported to Wheelock, they spoke openly of the hopelessness of converting Indians by anything but "Powder & Ball." One of them denounced Wheelock's experiment as "absurd & fruitlis" because of the "ireconsilable avertion, that white people must ever have to black. . . . So long as the Indians are dispised by the English we may never expect success in Christianizing of them," they said. The colonists further related that "they could never respect an Indian, Christian or no Christian so as to put him on a level with white people on any account especially to eat at the same Table, no—not with Mr. Ocham himself be he ever so much a Christian or ever so Learned" (Wheelock Papers 767604.1).

Intense cultural conflict, then, was perhaps the most important force that condemned the colonial college efforts to failure. Certainly just as the English considered their Indian neighbors inferior, the natives appraised the white culture and found their own values and life ways equal—if not superior—in integrity. Perhaps it was this cultural chauvinism, more than any other factor, that doomed the Indian colleges from the beginning.

Modern Echoes

Nearly four hundred years later, the methods used to "civilize" (or, in more contemporary terms, to "assimilate" and "acculturate") Indian youth, as well as the tragic outcomes which result, remain much the same. A contemporary researcher, in a recent study of American Indian college students, found that

> Indians do poorly in school because the educational system has been one of the major battlegrounds in the confrontation between Indian and white worlds. . . . As the substance, networks, and activities of education in white schools typically champion white values and practices to the exclusion of Indian ones, fitting in and succeeding in school create special problems for Indian students committed to Indian culture.

"Indian students have been counseled to become 'less Indian,'" he added, "as a conscious strategy for doing better in school. If this is what is meant by success, many Indians would not consider dropping out of school a mark of failure. For many, success in education means mastering white ways on one's own terms by maintaining some commitment to Indian values and tradition. And for those unable to resolve the "cultural conflict," the same isolation, alienation, low self-esteem, melancholy, and deviant behavior which oppressed Jacob Woolley and Samson Occom in the eighteenth century often become the by-products of the present educational process. No wonder, then, that Indians continue to regard higher education with aversion as an institution which for centuries has sought to remold them in the image of the white man. Their cultural persistence remains a centuries-old tribute to peoples who continue to prevail on the battleground of ideologies and cultures, even if they do not always triumph in the academic arenas.

Endnotes

1. For the purpose of this paper, colonial college missions are defined as those educational programs which were designed as instruments of the missionary enterprise and were promoted among some of the early American colleges. Although colonial colleges professed an interest in converting Indians, the efforts and outcomes did not match this pious rhetoric. For a discussion of ethnohistorical treatments of Indian education in the colonial period see Szasz (1988) and Axtell (1985).

2. Indian tribes did not necessarily accept Christianity wholesale. The Massachusetts and Martha's Vineyard groups incorporated Christian concepts into their own traditional religion without significant disruption. (See Sheehan 1980, 165–66; Ronda 1982, 12).

3. Unfortunately, before Wheelock's students began to write during the 1750s, no Indian scholars' writings have survived. Thus, it is difficult, if not impossible, to understand their personal reflections and sentiments; and this paper reports native responses as seen through the filter of contemporary English observers with some reconstructions from ethnographic and anthropological sources.

References

Astin, Alexander W. *Minorities in American Higher Education.* San Francisco: Jossey-Bass, 1982.

Axtell, James. "The Little Red School." Chap. 8 In *The Invasion Within: The Contest of Cultures in Colonial North America.* New York: Oxford University Press, 1985.

Belknap, Jeremy, and Jeremiah Morse. "The Report of a Committee of the Board of Correspondents of the Scots Society for the Propagating Christian Knowledge, Who Visited the Oneida and Mohekunuh Indians in 1796." *Collections of the Massachusetts Historical Society for the Year 1798,* 1st. ser. 5 (1798): 29–30.

Boyle, Robert. "A Contemporary Copy of the Will of Robert Boyle, 18 July 1691." William and Mary College Papers, Folder 7. College of William and Mary, Williamsburg.

Brafferton School. Account Book, 1765. William and Mary College Papers, Folder 288.

Brock, R. A., ed. *The Official Letters of Alexander Spotswood, Lieutenant-Governor of the Colony of Virginia, 1710–1722.* 2 vols. Richmond: Virginia Historical Society, 1882.

Byrd, William. *Histories of the Dividing Line Betwixt Virginia and North Carolina.* 1841. Reprint. Raleigh: North Carolina Historical Commission, 1929.

Catesby, Mark. *The Natural History of Carolina, Florida, and The Bahama Islands.* 2 vols. London: C. Marsh, T. Wilcox, and B. Stitchall, 1754.

Collier 2:18. Due to the author's death, this reference is unidentifiable.

Conard, Arlyn Mark. "Christianization of Indians in Colonial Virginia." Th.D.diss., Union Theological Seminary in Virginia, 1979.

Forbes, Allyn Bailey, ed. *Harvard College Records.* Volume 31, Publications of the Colonial Society of Massachusetts. Boston, Mass.: Colonial Society of Massachusetts, 1935.

Ford, John W. *Some Correspondence between the Governors and Treasurers of the New England Company in London and the Commisioners of the United Colonies in America, the Missionaries of the Company and Others, Between the Years 1657 and 1712.* London: Elliot Stock, 1897.

Goodwin, Gerald J. "Christianity, Civilization and the Savage: The Anglican Mission to the American Indian." *Historical Magazine of the Protestant Episcopal Church* 42 (1973): 93–110.

Gookin, Daniel. "Historical Collections of the Indians in New England." *Collections of the Massachusetts Historical Society.* 1st. ser. 1 (1792): 172–73.

Gordon, Vesta Lee, ed. *Letter Book, 1688–1761, of the Company for the Propagation of the Gospel in New England.* Charlottesville: University of Virginia, 1969. Microfilm in my possession.

[Gray, Robert.] *A Good Speed to Virginia.* 1609. Reprinted in *Illustrations of Early English Popular Literature,* 2 vols., edited by J. Payne Collier. London: n.p., 1864.

Harrison, Richard, ed. *Princetonians, 1776–1783: A Biographical Dictionary.* Princeton, N.J.: Princeton University Press, 1981.

Jones, Hugh. *The Present State of Virginia From Whence is Inferred a Short View of Maryland and North Carolina.* 1724. Reprint. Edited by Richard L. Morton. Chapel Hill: University of North Carolina Press, 1956.

Kemp, John. Letter to Dr. Jedediah Morse, 22 July 1803. Records of the Society in Scotland for the Propagation of Christian Knowledge, GD95/12/1. Scottish Record Office, Edinburgh.

Kingsbury, Susan Myra, ed. *The Records of the Virginia Company of London.* 4 vols. Washington, D.C.: GPO, 1906–35.

Land, Henry H. "Henrico and Its College," *William and Mary Quarterly* 2nd. ser. 18 (1938): 453–98.

Lurie, Nancy Oestreich. "Indian Cultural Adjustment to European Civilization." In *Seventeenth-Century America: Essays in Colonial History*, edited by Richard Morton Smith, 33–60. Chapel Hill: University of North Carolina Press, 1959.

MacDonald, William, ed. *Select Charters and Other Documents Illustrative of American History, 1606–1775*. New York: Macmillan Co., 1906.

Mather, Cotton. *Magnalia Christi Americana, or The Ecclesiastical History of New England*. 2 vols. 1702. Reprint., New York: Russell & Russell, 1967.

McCallum, James Dow. *The Letters of Eleazar Wheelock's Indians*. Dartmouth College Manuscripts Series, No. 1. Hanover: Dartmouth College Publications, 1932.

_____. *Eleazar Wheelock: Founder of Dartmouth College*. Hanover, N.H.: Dartmouth College Publications, 1939.

McNamara, P. P. *American Indians in U.S. Higher Education*. Los Angeles: Higher Education Research Institute, 1984.

Morison, Samuel Eliot. *Harvard College in the Seventeenth Century*. Cambridge: Harvard University Press, 1936.

Nisbet, C. C. *Report to the Society in Scotland for the Propagation of the Gospel of a Visit to America*. Records of the Society in Scotland for the Propagation of the Gospel. GD 95/12/20/1. Edinburgh: By the Society, 1901.

Perry, William Steven, ed. *Papers Relating to the History of the Church in Virginia, 1650–1776*. N.p.: Privately printed, 1870.

Pettitt, George A. *Primitive Education in North America*. Berkeley: University of California Press, 1946.

Quinn, David Beers, ed. *The Roanoke Voyages, 1584–1590*. 2 vols. Cambridge: University Press, 1955.

Ronda, James P. "The Bible and Early American Indian Missions." In *The Bible and Social Reform*, edited by Ernest R. Sandeen. Philadelphia: Fortress Press, 1982.

Schoepf, Johann David. *Travel in the Confederation [1783–1784]*, translated by Alfred J. Morrison. 1788. Reprint. New York: Bergman Publishers, 1968.

Scott, Wilbur J. "Attachment to Indian Culture and the 'Difficult Situation': A Study of American Indian College Students." *Youth and Society* 17 (1986): 381–95.

Sheehan, Bernard W. *Savagism and Civility: Indians and Englishmen in Colonial Virginia*. New York: Cambridge University Press, 1980.

Shurtleff, Nathaniel B., ed. *Records of the Governor and Company of the Massachusetts Bay in New England*. 5 vols. Boston: William White Press, 1853–54.

Simmons, William S. "The Great Awakening and Indian Conversion in Southern New England." *Papers of the Tenth Algonquian Conference*, edited by William Cowan, 25–36. Ottawa: Carleton University, 1979.

Stiverson, Gregory A., and Patrick H. Butler III. "Virginia in 1732: The Travel Journal of William Hugh Grove." *Virginia Magazine of History and Biography* 85 (1977):18–44.

Stone, William L. *The Life and Times of Red-Jacket, Sa-Go-Ye-Wat-Ha; Being the Sequel to the History of the Six Nations*. New York: Wiley and Putnam, 1841.

Strachey, William. *The Historie of Travell into Virginia Britania, 1612*. Edited by Louis B. Wright and Virginia Freund. London: The Hakluyt Society, 1953.

Stuart, Karen. "'So Good a Work': The Brafferton School, 1691–1771." M.A. thesis, College of William and Mary, 1984.

Szasz, Margaret Connell. *Indian Education in the American Colonies, 1607–1783*. Albuquerque: University of New Mexico Press, 1988.

Van Doren, Carl. *Indian Treaties Printed by Benjamin Franklin, 1736–1762*. Philadelphia: Historical Society of Pennsylvania, 1938.

Walne, Peter. "The Collections for Henrico, 1616–1618." *Virginia Magazine of History and Biography* 30 (1922): 259–66.

Washburn, Wilcomb E. *The Indian in America*. New York: Harper & Row, 1975.

Watson, Winslow C., ed. *Men and Times of the Revolution, or, Memoirs of Elkanah Watson*. New York: Dana and Co., 1856.

Weis, Frederick L. "The New England Company of 1649 and Its Missionary Enterprises." *Publications of the Colonial Society of Massachusetts* 38 (1959): 134–218.

Wheelock, Eleazar. Papers, 1772–79. Microfilm. Archives, Library, Dartmouth College, Hanover, New Hampshire.

_____. *A Plain and Faithful Narrative of the Original Design, Rise, Progress and Present State of the Indian Charity-School at Lebanon, in Connecticut*. Boston: Richard and Samuel Drake, 1763.

_____. *A Continuation of the Narrative of the Indian Charity-School in Lebanon, in Connecticut: from the Year 1768, to the Incorporation of it with Dartmouth-College, and Removal and Settlement of it in Hanover, in the Province of New Hampshire, 1771*. N.p., 1771.

_____. *A Continuation of the Narrative of the Indian Charity-School, Begun in Lebanon, in Connecticut; Now Incorporated with Dartmouth-College, in Hanover, in the Province of New-Hampshire*. Hartford: N.p.: 1773.

Wright, Bobby. "'For the Children of the Infidels'?: American Indian Education in the Colonial Colleges." *American Indian Culture and Research Journal* 12 (1988): 1–14.

Young, Robert Fitzgibbon. *Comenius in England: The Visit of Jan Amos Komensky (Comenius) The Czech Philosopher and Educationist to London in 1641–1642; Its Bearing on the Origins of the Royal Society, on the Development of the Encyclopaedia, and on Plans for the Higher Education of the Indians of New England and Virginia*. London: Oxford University Press, 1932.

PART II
CURRICULUM, TEACHING, AND LEARNING

Multicultural Literacy and Curriculum Reform

James A. Banks

Changes in our demographic makeup and in the nature of the work force are among several factors contributing to a growing recognition of the need for curriculum reform. James Banks suggests a curriculum designed to foster multicultural literacy—one that helps students and teachers to know, to care, and to act in ways that develop and cultivate a just society.

Most reports urging educational reform in the 1980s paid scant attention to helping citizens develop the knowledge, attitudes, and skills necessary to function effectively in a nation and world increasingly diverse ethnically, racially, and culturally.[1] Two of the most influential works published late in the decade not only failed to describe the need for multicultural literacy and understanding, but also ran counter to the U.S. multicultural movement.[2]

E. D. Hirsch's and Allan Bloom's widely reviewed and discussed books, both published in 1987, were regarded by many as having cogently made the case for emphasizing the traditional western-centric canon dominating school and university curricula, a canon threatened, according to Bloom and other western traditionalists, by movements to incorporate more ethnic and women's content into curricula.[3] Hirsch's works appear more sympathetic to ethnic and women's concerns than Bloom's. However, Hirsch's formulation of a list of memorizable facts is inconsistent with multicultural teaching, since it ignores the notion of knowledge as a social construction with normative and political assumptions.[4] Regarding knowledge as a social construction and viewing it from diverse cultural perspectives are key components of multicultural literacy.

There is growing recognition among educators and the general public that tomorrow's citizens should acquire the knowledge, skills, and attitudes critical to functioning in a diverse, complex world. Several factors contribute to this growing recognition, including the *demographic imperative*,[5] significant population growth among people of color, and increasing enrollments of students of color in the nation's schools. Because of higher birthrates among people of color compared to whites and the large influx each year of immigrants from Asia and Latin America, one in three Americans is forecast to be a person of color by the turn of the century.[6] Between 1981 and 1986, about 89 percent of legal immigrants to the United States came from non-European nations. Most came from Asia (47 percent) and Latin America (38 percent).[7] This significant population growth will have tremendous impact on the nation's social institutions, including the work force, the courts, the economic system, and the schools. The ethnic texture of the nation's schools will become increasingly diverse as well as low income as we enter the twenty-first century. About 46 percent of school-age youths will be of color by the year 2000.[8] This will contrast sharply with the ethnic and racial makeup of teacher populations; teachers of color are expected to decline from about 12.5 percent of the nation's teaching force in 1980 to about 5 percent by the year 2000.[9]

Growing recognition of the changing nature of the nation's work force and the predicted gap between needs and skills are other factors motivating educators and the general public to focus on multicultural concerns. When the twenty-first century arrives, there will be a large number of retirees and too few new workers. People of color will constitute a disproportionate share of the work force in the next century. Between 1980 and 2000, about 83 percent of new entrants to the labor force will be women, people of color, or immigrants; native white males will make up only 15 percent.[10] However, if the current educational levels of students of color are not increased significantly, most students will not have the knowledge and skills to meet the requirements of a global, primarily service-oriented job market. Consequently, corporations will export work to foreign nations that have more skilled workers—a trend that already has begun. While work opportunities are exported, low-income inner-city residents become increasingly disempowered in the process.

The rash of recent racial incidents on the nation's campuses is yet another factor stimulating discussion and concrete action regarding multicultural education and curriculum reform. More than two hundred such incidents were reported in the press between 1986 and 1988[11]; an unknown number has not been publicized. Racial incidents have occurred on all types of campuses, including liberal ones like the University of California, Berkeley; Stanford University; and the University of Wisconsin, Madison. African Americans and Jews have been frequent victims in such incidents, which have stunned and perplexed administrators and motivated many students of color and their white allies to demand ethnic studies requirements and reform of required general studies courses to include ethnic content.

Despite rough beginnings and a tenuous status, ethnic studies courses are becoming institutionalized at most major universities, including Berkeley, the University of Minnesota, and Bowling Green State University. The ethnic studies program at Berkeley, for example, grants a doctoral degree; the University of Washington has established an interdisciplinary Department of American Ethnic Studies. Amid a bitter campus controversy and national debate, Stanford replaced a required freshman western culture course with one called "Culture, Ideas, and Values," which includes the study of at least one non-western culture and works by women, minorities, and people of color.

Ethnic studies courses in high schools have not fared as well as those at universities. Most school districts have tried to incorporate such content into the existing curriculum rather than establishing separate courses. The rationale for this approach is intellectually defensible and laudable, but the approach has had mixed results. In most schools, the *textbook* is the curriculum. In the early 1970s, when the civil rights movement was at its apex and publishers were being pressured to integrate textbooks, large bits and pieces of ethnic content were introduced.

But when the civil rights movement lost much of its momentum and influence during the Reagan years, the impetus for textbook publishers to include this content waned, and publishers consequently slowed their pace. However, the momentum has now resumed as a result of changing demographics and pressure exerted by people of color, especially those in large urban school districts and in populous states with state textbook adoption policies, such as California and Texas.

The Curriculum Canon Battle

Parents and students of color are now pushing for reforms that go beyond separate ethnic studies courses and programs. They are urging public school educators and university faculties to integrate ethnic content into mainstream curricula and to transform the canons and paradigms on which school and university curricula are based. Acrid and divisive controversies have arisen on several campuses over attempts to incorporate ethnic content into the mainstream curriculum or to require all students to take ethnic studies courses. A heated and bitter debate also has arisen over attempts to incorporate ethnic content into public school curricula.[12] Much of this controversy focuses on attempts to infuse curricula with content about African Americans and African contributions to western civilization—efforts often called *Afrocentric*.[13] Today's curriculum controversies are in some ways more wrenching than those of the 1960s and 1970s, when attempts were made to establish separate ethnic studies courses and programs.

At universities throughout the United States, a vigorous debate is raging between those who defend the established Eurocentric, male-dominated curriculum and those who argue that the curriculum and its canon must be transformed to more accurately reflect race, ethnic, and cultural diversity.

A canon is a "norm, criterion, model or standard used for evaluating or criticizing."[14] It is also "a basic general principle or rule commonly accepted as true, valid and fundamental."[15] A specific and identifiable canon is used to define, select, and evaluate knowledge in school and university curricula in the United States and other western nations. Rarely is this canon explicitly defined or discussed, and it is often taken for granted, unquestioned, and internalized by writers, researchers, teachers, professors, and students. Consequently, it often marginalizes the experiences of people of color, Third World nations and cultures, and the perspectives and histories of women.

African-American scholars such as George Washington Williams, Carter G. Woodson, and W.E.B. DuBois challenged the established canon in social science and history in the nineteenth and twentieth centuries.[16] Their scholarship was influential in the African-American academic community but largely ignored by the white world. The ethnic studies movement, growing out of the civil rights movement of the 1960s and 1970s, seriously challenged the Eurocentric canon. Later, this canon also was challenged by the women's studies movement. These movements are forcing an examination of the canon used to select and judge knowledge imparted in school and university curricula.

Feeling that their voices often have been silenced and their experiences minimized, women and people of color are struggling to be recognized in the curriculum and to have their important historical and cultural works canonized. This struggle can best be understood as a battle over who will participate in or control the formulation of the canon or standard used to determine what constitutes a liberal education. The guardians and defenders of the traditional, established canon apparently believe it best serves their interests and, consequently, the interests of society and the nation.[17]

A struggle for voice has emerged because of a powerful resistance movement to multicultural studies. Two organizations were founded to resist multicultural curriculum reform: the Madison Center, organized by William Bennet when he was secretary of education, and the National Association of Scholars. Resistance also has been articulated in a series of popular and education articles and editorials severely critical of the multicultural education movement.[18]

Special Interests and the Public Interest

Ethnic and women's studies often are called *special interests* by individuals and groups now determining and formulating curricula. *Special interest* is defined as a "person or group seeking to influence policy often narrowly defined."[19] The term implies an interest that is particularistic and inconsistent with the paramount goals and needs of the nation. To be in the public good, interests must extent beyond the needs of a unique or particular group.

An important question is, Who formulates the criteria for determining what is a *special interest*? Powerful, traditional groups already have shaped curricula, institutions, and structures in their image and interests. The dominant culture tends to view a special interest as any one that challenges its power, ideologies, and paradigms, particularly if interest groups demand that institutional canons, assumptions, and values be transformed. History is replete with examples of dominant groups defining their own interests as being in the public interest.

One way those in power marginalize and disempower those who are structurally excluded from the mainstream is by labeling such individuals' visions, histories, goals, and struggles as "special interests." This serves to deny excluded groups the legitimacy and validity of full participation in society and its institutions.

Only a curriculum that reflects the collective experiences and interests of a wide range of groups is truly in the national interest and consistent with the public good. Any other curriculum reflects only special interests and, thus, does not meet the needs of a nation that must survive in a pluralistic, highly interdependent global world. Special interest curricula, such as history and literature emphasizing the primacy of the West and the history of European-American males, are detrimental to the public good, since they do not help students acquire life skills and perspectives essential for surviving in the twenty-first century.

The ethnic and women's studies movements do not constitute efforts to promote special interests. Their major aims are to transform the curriculum so that it is more truthful and inclusive and reflects the histories and experiences of the diverse groups making up American society. Such movements serve to democratize school and university curricula, rather than strengthen special interests.

For a variety of complex reasons, including the need to enhance our nation's survival in a period of serious economic and social problems, it behooves educators to rethink such concepts as special interests, the national interest, and the public good. Groups using such terms should be identified, along with their purposes for using them, and the use of these terms in the context of a rapidly changing world should be evaluated.

Our concept of cultural literacy should be broader than Hirsch's, which is neutral and static. Knowledge is dynamic, changing, and constructed within a social context. Rather than transmitting knowledge in a largely uncritical way, as Hirsch suggests, educators should help students recognize that knowledge reflects the social context in which it is created and that it has normative and value assumptions.

A Multicultural Curriculum

It is imperative that curricula be transformed to help students view concepts, issues, and problems from diverse cultural perspectives. Merely inserting ethnic and gender content into existing curricular structures, paradigms, and assumptions is not enough. Totally transformed, multicultural curricula motivate students to view and interpret facts, events, concepts, and theories from varying perspectives.

Students and teachers also bring their own biases and points of view to the knowledge they encounter. What students learn reflects not only what they encounter in the curriculum, but also the perceptions of the medium (the teacher). The multicultural classroom is a place where multiple voices are both heard and legitimized, including the vanquished and victims, students and teachers, the textbook writer, and those whose culture is transmitted by oral traditions.

Hirsch's contention that all U.S. citizens should master a common core of knowledge is logical and defensible.[20] But who will participate in formulating this knowledge? And whose interests will it serve? There must be broad participation in identifying, constructing, and formulating the knowledge we expect all our citizens to master. Such knowledge should reflect cultural democracy and serve the needs of all citizens.

Knowledge that satisfies these criteria can best be described as multicultural, and when mastered by students, multicultural literacy is acquired. Multicultural literacy is far preferable to cultural literacy, which connotes knowledge and understanding selected, defined, and constructed by elite groups within society. Multicultural literacy, on the other hand, connotes knowledge and understanding that reflect the broad spectrum of interests, experiences, hopes, struggles, and voices of society.

Knowledge as Social Construction

The knowledge construction process is an important dimension of multicultural education.[21] It describes ways teachers help students understand, investigate, and determine how implicit cultural assumptions, frames of references, perspectives, and biases within a discipline influence how knowledge is created. This process teaches students that knowledge reflects the social, political, and economic context in which it is created. Knowledge created by elite and powerless groups within the same society also tends to differ in significant ways.[22]

Students can analyze the knowledge construction process in science, for example, by studying how racism has been perpetuated by genetic theories of intelligence, Darwinism, and eugenics. In his important book *The Mismeasurement of Man*, Stephen Jay Gould describes how scientific racism developed and was influential in the nineteenth and twentieth centuries.[23] Scientific racism also has influenced significantly the interpretations of mental ability tests in the United States.[24] When students are examining how science has supported racist practices and ideologies, they also should examine how science has contributed to human justice and equality. Biological theories about the traits and characteristics that human groups share, as well as anthropological theories that challenged racist beliefs during the post–World War II period, especially the writings of Franz Boas and Ruth Benedict, are good examples of how science and scientists have helped eradicate racist beliefs, ideologies, and practices.[25] Students should learn how science, like other disciplines, has been both a supporter and eradicator of racist beliefs and practices.

Students can examine the knowledge construction process in the social sciences and humanities when they study such units and topics as the European discovery of America and America's westward movement. Students can discuss the latent political messages contained in these concepts and how they are used to justify the domination and destruction of Native American cultures.

Students can be asked why the Americas are called the *New World* and why people from England are often called *settlers* and *pioneers* in textbooks, while people from other lands are usually called *immigrants*. Students can be asked to think of words that might have been used by the Lakota Sioux to describe the same people that a textbook might label *settlers* and *pioneers*. Such terms as *invaders, conquerors,* and *foreigners* may come to their minds. The goal of this exercise is not to teach students that Anglo immigrants who went West were invaders, but to help them view settlers from the perspective of both Anglos and Lakota Sioux.

Other important goals are to help students develop empathy for both groups and to give voice to all the participants in U.S. history and culture. Students will gain a thorough understanding of the settlement of the West as well as other events only when they are able to view these from diverse ethnic and cultural perspectives and construct their own versions of the past and present.

When studying the westward movement, a teacher might ask, Whose point of view does the westward movement reflect, European Americans' or the Lakota Sioux's? Who was moving West? How might a Lakota Sioux historian describe this period in U.S. history? What are other ways of thinking about and describing the westward movement?

The West, thus, was not the West for the Sioux; it was the center of the universe. For people living in Japan, it was the East. Teachers also can help students look at the westward movement from the viewpoint of those living in Mexico and Alaska: The West was the North for Mexicans and the South for Alaskans. By helping students view the westward movement from varying perspectives, teachers can help them understand why knowledge is a social construction that reflects people's cultural, economic, and power positions within a society.

Teaching Students to Know, to Care, and to Act

The major goals of a curriculum that fosters multicultural literacy should be to help students to know, to care, and to act in ways that will develop and foster a democratic and just society where all groups experience cultural democracy and empowerment. Knowledge is an essential part of multicultural literacy, but it is not the only component. Knowledge alone will not help students develop empathy, caring, and a commitment to humane and democratic change. To help our nation and world become more culturally democratic, students also must develop commitment to personal, social, and civic action as well as knowledge and skills to participate in effective civic action.

Although knowledge, caring, and action are conceptually distinct, in the classroom they are highly interrelated. In my multicultural classes for teacher education students, I use historical and sociological knowledge about the experiences of different ethnic and racial groups to inform as well as enable students to examine and clarify their personal attitudes about ethnic diversity.

These knowledge experiences are also vehicles that enable students to think of actions they can take to actualize their feelings and moral commitments.

Knowledge experiences that I use to help students examine their value commitments and think of ways to act include reading *Balm in Gilead: Journey of a Healer*, Sara Lawrence Lightfoot's powerful biography of her mother, one of the nation's first African-American child psychiatrists; the historical overviews of various U.S. ethnic groups in my book, *Teaching Strategies for Ethnic Studies*; and several video and film presentations, including selections from "Eyes on the Prize II," the award-winning history of the civil rights movement produced by Henry Hampton.[26] To enable students to focus their values regarding these experiences, I ask them such questions as, How did the book or film make you feel? and Why do you think you feel that way? To enable them to think about ways to act on their feelings, I ask such questions as, How interracial are your own personal experiences? Would you like to live a more interracial life? What are some books you can read or popular films you can see that will enable you to act on your commitment to live a more racially and ethnically integrated life? The power of these kinds of experiences is often revealed in student papers, as illustrated by this excerpt from a paper by a student after he had viewed several segments of "Eyes on the Prize II":

> I feel that my teaching will now necessarily be a little bit different forever simply because I myself have changed . . . I am no longer quite the same person I was before I viewed the presentations—my horizons are a little wider, perspectives a little broader, insights a little deeper. That is what I gained from "Eyes on the Prize II."[27]

The most meaningful and effective way to prepare teachers to involve students in multicultural experiences that will enable them to know, care, and participate in democratic action is to involve teachers themselves in multicultural experiences that focus on these goals. When teachers have gained knowledge about cultural and ethnic diversity, looked at that knowledge from different ethnic and cultural perspectives, and taken action to make their own lives and communities more culturally sensitive and diverse, they will have the knowledge and skills needed to help transform the curricular canon as well as the hearts and minds of their students.[28] Only then will students in our schools and colleges be able to attain the knowledge, skills, and perspectives needed to participate effectively in next century's global society.

Notes

1. National Commission on Excellence in Education, *A Nation at Risk: The Imperative for Educational Reform* (Washington, DC: U.S. Department of Education, 1983); Task Force on Federal Elementary and Secondary Education Policy, *Making the Grade* (New York: Twentieth Century Fund, 1983).

2. Allan Bloom, *The Closing of the American Mind* (New York: Simon and Schuster, 1987); E. D. Hirsch, Jr., *Cultural Literacy: What Every American Needs to Know* (New York: Vintage Books, 1987).

3. Bloom, *The Closing of the American Mind*.

4. Peter L. Berger and Thomas Luckman, *The Social Construction of Reality: A Treatise in the Sociology of Knowledge* (New York: Doubleday, 1966).

5. James A. Banks, *Teaching Strategies for Ethnic Studies*, 5th ed. (Boston: Allyn and Bacon, 1991), 4–5.

6. American Council on Education and the Education Commission of the States, *One-Third of a Nation: A Report of the Commission on Minority Participation in Education and American Life* (Washington, DC: American Council on Education, 1988).

7. Bureau of the Census, *Statistical Abstract of the United States: 1989*, 109th ed. (Washington, DC: GPO, 1989).

8. Aaron M. Pallas, Gary Natriello, and Edward L. McDill, "The Changing Nature of the Disadvantaged Population: Current Dimensions and Future Trends," *Educational Researcher* 18 (June–July 1989): 16–22.

9. American Council on Education and the Education Commission of the States, *One-Third of a Nation*.

10. William B. Johnson and Arnold H. Packer, *Work Force 2000: Work and Workers for the 21st Century* (Indianapolis: Hudson Institute, 1987).

11. Philip G. Altbach, "The Racial Dilemma in American Higher Education" in *The Racial Crisis in American Higher Education*, ed. Philip G. Altbach and Kofi Lomotey (Albany, NY: State University of New York Press, 1991), 8.

12. Arthur Schlesinger, Jr., "When Ethnic Studies Are Un-American," *Social Studies Review 5* (Summer 1990): 11–13; Andrew Sullivan, "Racism 101," *The New Republic*, 28 November 1990, 18–21; "Common Culture and Multiculture," *Social Studies Review 7* (Winter 1991): 1–10.

13. Molefi Kete Asante, *Afrocentricity* (Trenton, NJ: African World Press, Inc, 1988); Asa G. Hillard III, Lucretia Payton-Stewart, and Larry Obadele Williams, eds., *Infusion of African and African American Content in the School Curriculum* (Morristown, NJ: Aaron Press, 1990).

14. *Webster's New International Dictionary*, 3rd ed., s.v. "canon."

15. Ibid.

16. John Hope Franklin, *George Washington Williams: A Biography* (Chicago: University of Chicago Press, 1985); Carter G. Woodson, *The History of the Negro Church* (Washington, DC: Associated Publishers, 1921); W.E.B. DuBois, *Black Reconstruction in America 1860–1880* (New York: Harcourt, Brace; Russel & Russel; Philadelphia: A. Saifer, all 1935; Atheneum, 1962).

17. Irving Howe, "The Value of the Canon," *The New Republic*, 18 February 1991, 40–44.

18. John Leo, "Teaching History the Way it Happened," *U.S. News and World Report*, 27 November 1989, 73; Gerald Sirkin, "The Multiculturalists Strike Again," *Wall Street Journal*, 18 January 1990; Diane Ravitch, "Multiculturalism Yes, Particularism, No," *The Chronicle of Higher Education*, 24 October 1990, A44.

19. *Webster's Ninth Collegiate Dictionary*, s.v. "special interest."

20. Hirsch, *Cultural Literacy*.

21. James A. Banks, "The Dimensions of Multicultural Education," *Multicultural Leader*, in press.

22. Karl Mannheim, *Ideology and Utopia: An Introduction to the Sociology of Knowledge* (New York: Harcourt Brace, 1936).

23. Stephen Jay Gould, *The Mismeasurement of Man* (New York: W.W. Norton and Company, 1981).

24. Jane R. Mercer, "Alternative Paradigms for Assessment in a Pluralistic Society," in *Multicultural Education: Issues and Perspectives*, ed. James A. Banks and Cherry A. McGee Banks (Boston: Allyn and Bacon, 1989), 289–304.

25. See Franz Boas, *Race, Language and Culture* (New York: Macmillan, 1948) and Ruth Benedict, *Patterns of Culture* (Boston: Houghton Mifflin, 1934).

26. Sara Lawrence Lightfoot, *Balm in Gilead: Journey of a Healer* (Reading, MA: Addison-Wesley, 1988); Banks, *Teaching Strategies; Eyes on the Prize II*, a television series produced by Blackside, Inc., for public television station WGBH, Boston, 1990.

27. Kevin Muir, "Eyes on the Prize: A Review" (Paper submitted to James A. Banks as partial requirement for EDUC 423, "Educating Diverse Groups," University of Washington, Seattle, 1990).

28. James A. Banks and Cherry A. McGee Banks, eds., *Multicultural Education: Issues and Perspectives* (Boston: Allyn and Bacon, 1989).

Complicating the Question:
Black Studies and Women's Studies

Johnnella E. Butler

Many of us who grew up in the sixties, inspired as we discovered Charlotte Perkins Gilman and Charlotte Forten Grimke, Emma Goldman and Shirley Chisholm, W.E.B. DuBois and Simone de Beauvoir, seek to know more about our pasts and present as women, as members of racial, cultural and ethnic groups. We need also to find a means to reinterpret cultural history in order to effect social change and achieve a plural, equitable society. As teachers and scholars we seek conceptual frameworks to reshape the curriculum so that it will reflect the multicultural reality of the world and the experience of men and women. New frameworks are necessary, for much that has been immortalized in the liberal arts curriculum as "truth" is, in reality, vicious, self-serving fiction.

Scholars and teachers in black studies and women's studies have been working to develop frameworks that not only account for the additional data gathered about Black culture and women's experience, but that reinterpret all cultural history through a truly multicultural perspective. Black studies and women's studies professors have led the way in identifying the changes in content, method, and pedagogy that must take place for the liberal arts curriculum to reflect fully the truth about humanity. Yet no formal, full-scale, faculty development project bringing those two groups together was made until 1981. That was the first year the Fund for the Improvement of Postsecondary Education (FIPSE) sponsored "Black Studies/Women's Studies: An Overdue Partnership," which I codirected with Margo Culley in the Five College consortium. An analysis of why we undertook this project, our goals and expectations at its outset, what we learned with the twenty participants during our two years together, and how the teaching of a course growing from the project expanded my understanding of the curriculum transformation process clearly reveals the difficulty and necessity of pursuing this work.

Why Black Studies and Women's Studies?

In black studies, we have set many tasks for ourselves: to correct distortions, to revise the history and other studies of people of African ancestry, and to critique the educational process itself by identifying how the colonization of minds is characteristic of American education. Black studies gives us the underside of what has been touted as American reality, past and present. It reveals the lies of the so-called mainstream in society and in the curriculum. Part of the burden for other black studies professors like myself, as the first generation of blacks to teach in significant numbers on predominantly white campuses, has been to act as "cultural translators" even as we advocate a transformation of the curriculum.

Black studies professors are good translators because we understand the interaction of community and culture. Our recognition of the need to examine curricular content contextually emerges from a study of African traditional thought and its expression in the diaspora and from the experience of teaching black studies. Culture is seen as a dynamic process composed of interdependent systems: belief, economics, politics, the arts, language. Cultural pluralism, from this perspective, is a generative process, promoting change and valuing difference.

In women's studies, the need to recover and reconstruct the past, to correct distortions that have come about through the omission of women's experience has also led to a reconsideration of the liberal arts curriculum. Many white women scholars document in their work and realize in their lives the extent to which women are considered "other" in the dominant culture. They understand how the experience of women is systematically devalued in white American culture. They have thus been able to hear and accept the assertions of Afro-American women's studies scholars who warn that women's studies must not be exclusively white and middle class, but must strive for diversity. Reading their own lives contextually, reconsidering claims of "universality," and identifying systematic gender discrimination have led to the desire for conceptual frameworks that are inclusive of difference, in order to understand as fully as possible human acts and creations.

Black studies and women's studies have clear affinities. Both enterprises have strong roots in movements for social change, both cement the connections between theory and practice, between the academy and the world. Black studies and women's studies offer definitions and critiques of culture, analyses of oppression and, as interdisciplinary undertakings, challenge the traditional compartmentalization of knowledge. For these reasons, as well as for reasons having to do with the persistence of racism and sexism within the academy, black studies and women's studies programs and faculty have too often remained on the periphery of educational institutions and have even been forced to compete for the limited resources available to "peripheral" programs.

Black studies and women's studies, despite many affinities and common agendas, also have their own biases and blind spots. Just as black studies as a discipline has too often focused largely on the contributions of black men, women's studies is marked by its early focus on white, middle-class women. Although educators working in these two fields need each other's expertise, they often work in isolation from each other, and have sometimes regarded each other's enterprise with a suspicion that blocks mutual learning.

We undertook the FIPSE project because we felt that neither black studies nor women's studies alone could produce a transformed curriculum and pedagogy. We asked, how can black studies and women's studies transform each other to bring about social, cultural and curricular change so we can know and tell the full truth of human experience? How can the experience of black studies and women's studies teachers working together lay the groundwork for more interdisciplinary work involving other ethnic studies?

An Overdue Partnership: Goals, Expectations, Lessons

Jointly sponsored by the Afro-American Studies Department at Smith College and the Women's Studies Program at the University of Massachusetts in Amherst, the project brought together twenty faculty members from five area colleges in a two-year effort to build the intellectual, methodological, curricular, and pedagogical connections between the interdisciplinary fields of black studies and women's studies.

Goals and Guidelines

After reviewing other projects that had brought women's studies and/or black studies to the attention of a wide audience of students and teachers, and after assessing the strengths and weaknesses of previous faculty development efforts in our area, we determined that the FIPSE project needed to:

1. Provide a *sustained context* beyond the successful but isolated and occasional events that had focused on the issues of race and gender in our area.

2. Be oriented toward *products*: annotated bibliographies, new courses designed and taught in the home institution during the second year of the project.

3. Demand active participation of all members of the seminar, creating a *learner-centered* experience in which faculty members become resources for each other.

4. Make available to a wider group of faculty members both the thinking and the products of the seminar through a *regional dissemination conference*.

5. Incorporate regular *evaluation* components throughout the two years: entry and exit statements by participants, review of new courses while in progress, on-site visits by outside evaluators.

6. Demonstrate the importance of interdepartmental, interinstitutional, as well as interpersonal cooperation through a *codirectorship*.

The Five College area was ready for this type of faculty development, we felt, because conferences, colloquia, and lectures had already focused on issues of race and gender. Also, the many faculty members in the Five Colleges who had done research and/or teaching on race and gender provided a solid base of local expertise that we could draw on and develop further.

Participants

We publicized the project to all area faculty working in black studies and/or women's studies whether or not they were formally connected to programs or departments. We asked applicants to submit a statement of interest that would include a proposal for a curriculum development project. Selection was based on the strength of the statement of interest and the proposed project as well as on the applicant's demonstrated achievements in black studies and/or women's studies. We also wanted to achieve a balance of black and white participants, a variety of disciplines within these two fields, a mixture of male and female participants, and representation from each of the five area institutions.

Forty area faculty members submitted applications. We chose twenty participants, including four black women, four black men, and twelve white women, all of varying ethnic backgrounds. Two white males were among the forty applicants; neither was accepted. In retrospect, we think we should have accepted at least one of them for the sake of balance.

Components and Products of the Project

Each semester of the two years, and the intervening summer, had specific goals and were oriented toward different products. The first year of the faculty seminar produced syllabi for new courses designed to be taught at the participants' home institutions the following year (see appendix). Discussions focused on theoretical readings and debates, such as the racism/sexism debate that has been pursued in both black and feminist scholarly publications. We felt it was also desirable to go beyond the questions of racism within women's studies and sexism within black studies and to explore the theoretical and methodological affinities between the fields. The second semester was designed to focus more specifically on the topic of black women in an effort to assist participants in their efforts to create new courses.

The product at the end of the summer between the two years was an annotated bibliography by each participant focusing on race and gender in the area of a newly developed course. This facilitated in-depth preparation of the new courses and further encouraged participants to become resources for each other. Summer stipends helped to free participants from summer teaching responsibilities and provided a modest incentive for participation over the two-year period. We chose stipends rather than released time during the year because released time would have been too costly financially. Even more important, we could not afford to lose for two years the black studies and women's studies courses taught by the participants.

During the second year of the seminar, participants tried out their courses and prepared the regional conference that took place in April 1983. The focus of the second year was pedagogy, addressing issues such as:

1. *Ideology and Learning*: How does ideology (overtly or covertly) shape, motivate, hinder learning?

2. *Authority in the Classroom*: How are the claims of intellectual traditions and the claims of life experience balanced in the classroom?

3. *The Affective Dimensions of Learning*: How does one recognize and direct anger? How and why are feelings expressed and disguised in black studies and women's studies classrooms?

4. *The Insider/Outsider or Oppressor/Oppressed Dialogue*: What challenges does the white student in the black studies classroom pose, or the male student in the women's studies classroom? What are the challenges to a white instructor teaching black studies, to a male instructor in women's studies?

An explicit goal of the final semester of the grant (and the regional conference that followed) was to codesign strategies for survival within our institutional contexts, to address the long-term goal of moving the concerns of black studies/women's studies toward the center of higher education, and by realizing these goals, to transform the liberal arts.

Surprises and Lessons

The twenty participants who started in the project were tough-minded, eager to tackle difficult issues. Because we were committed to compatible goals, some expected trust at the start; but we discovered that trust is built only after shared experience. What was needed, rather, was real tolerance so that we could begin to listen to each other. We ultimately developed tolerance as participants became open and vulnerable to each other. One of the surprises of the project, however, was that even this highly select group of colleagues from neighboring institutions, all of whom had demonstrated a commitment, through scholarship and teaching, to issues of race and gender, had initial, sometimes volatile, problems listening to each other and learning from each other's experience.

At first we did not recognize the problem. After a number of confrontations and considerable reflection, we discovered that cultural differences, particularly in the area of styles of conflict and communication, were an initial obstacle even in a group that shared so much. Although committed to cultural diversity in principle, we failed at first to recognize the operation of difference in our own interactions. Styles of expressing conflict that were rooted in culture and manifested through body gestures, different tolerance of voice level, and interruption in debate became, in themselves, sources of conflict. Whereas black participants (male and female) were comfortable with interruptions and direct assertions, many of the white women preferred more controlled patterns of debate (such as hand-raising) and interpreted some gestures as negative when they were not intended that way. Only after we sorted out the origins and meanings of differing styles of conflict could we move on to fruitful examination of issues. Our recognition of the role of cultural diversity in the seminar was to prove useful later in discussions of pedagogy and the implementation of the new courses.

Similarly, as we moved to substantive discussion, we learned the importance of reading contextually, interpreting seemingly similar language according to cultural context. One example involved efforts of white women to equate their own experience of alienation, being relegated to the status of "other" in white American culture, to what black participants called "double consciousness." The black experience of "double consciousness," as originally defined by DuBois, entails a constant awareness of oppression, of outsider status in a racist culture. Black participants resisted equating the white feminist experience with their own. They urged the white women to refine the meaning of their own terms rather than falsely to conflate black and white experiences. "Otherness" is not constant in the same way for white women as "double consciousness" is for black men or women, because white women are nevertheless served by white American culture; they benefit from racial privilege. Only by understanding the differences in perception and experience that marked participants could we then move on to a useful discussion of commonalities.

In bringing together black studies and women's studies, we find that we must reconstruct the past, redefine ourselves, extricate our norms from the illusions and deceptions of history as it has been taught, destroy cultural hegemony and cultural submission, classism, and gender discrimination, and recreate identities based on truly pluralistic norms. What did we learn about transforming the liberal arts curriculum? We must incorporate race, gender, class, and culture as categories of analysis throughout the curriculum.

All this means simply that we are not alike. To include Afro-American literature or sociology in established courses, for example, requires a through reading of scholarship on the Afro-American literacy tradition and the black family structure. It is not enough to add on a unit to a course in literature or sociology; to teach the material responsibly requires attention not only to the black cultural context that shaped the literature of the family, but to the interaction of that context with the dominant white culture. That requires, in turn, an explicit analysis of the cultural norms that define white literature and social structures. Efforts to transform the curriculum through incorporation of black studies and women's studies reveal the need to reformulate and redefine the disciplines.

Testing the Product: Teaching Women and Philosophy

The course I developed in the seminar with Vicky Spelman of the Smith College Philosophy Department, and that we've now team-taught, is an interdisciplinary course called "Women and Philosophy." We wanted to pay explicit attention to ethnicity and how it operates, to challenge conventional definitions of philosophy and of feminism, to engage the students in a generative process moving from the familiar to the unfamiliar. The class was mixed by race, ethnicity, and class, and it struggled in microcosm to achieve the dialogue we seek between women's studies and black studies, much as the faculty seminar had.

Students were hampered, as we all have been, by an inadequate definition of culture and ethnicity due to the tendency to see people in an either/or (rather than a richer, both/and) fashion. We confuse ethnicity with geographical distinctions and further distort perception by our simplistic reduction of everything to the racial. African traditional thought has produced in the New World, West Indian culture, Haitian culture, Brazilian culture, and Afro-Brazilian culture, among others. Asian traditional thought (which we reduce to a monolith called Eastern thought) has produced in this country Japanese-Americans, Chinese-Americans Korean-Americans, Filipino-Americans, Vietnamese-Americans. Native-American worldviews are, in a sense, the least accessible in what we call American culture because of the history of American Indian persecution.

This brief listing of cultures that are American illustrates that the insights of black studies (and other ethnic studies) complicate the question of what is American. Even in a classroom where there is ethnic diversity, habits of reduction keep students from understanding the complexities of American culture. We have Euro-Americans of various European-based ethnic backgrounds, an Anglo-American ethnic-value dominance, and people of color, of varying types and degrees of color, who share some combination of the Euro-American, Afro-American, Native-American, Asian-American, and Hispanic-American ethnicities. The complexities of culture are particularly acute for those whose ethnic sensibility is based on a European continuum as well as an African or Asian continuum. The negation of the both/and possibility is central to the oppression of black Americans; it means, for example, that I cannot be perceived as racially and culturally of African and Euro-American descent. In our class, we learned to allow for the tension that emerges when WASP students discover the lie they've been told—that they are just American, the norm, and not that their is an ethnicity that holds power.

In the "Women and Philosophy" course we also wanted to complicate the question of what is feminism. For example, we put Toni Cade Bambara (*The Salt Eaters*) on the syllabus, as the first work to be read, to insist that the students begin the course dealing with feminism in a way that demands recognition of women other than simply white women. Virginia Woolf (*A Room of One's Own*) immediately followed. We felt that Bambara's work challenged Woolf's definition in serious ways, particularly in regard to racism and classism, and would facilitate a more inclusive, complex definition of feminism. Real transformation, we learned, requires a willingness to revise even while teaching, a willingness to be surprised.

We had not anticipated the loyalty that many of the students (white and black) felt toward Woolf. Because we challenged that loyalty, they resisted the effort to articulate a new definition of feminism. We learned through the experience that we should first validate the students' feelings and understand their basis and origins, and *then* engage them in imagining an expanded definition of feminism. The incident brought into sharp focus a problem central to the transformation process: establishing credibility with a class. Briefly, a black professor teaching black literature and favoring a specific text risks being dismissed as chauvinistic. A white professor challenging conventional expectations may be dismissed as idiosyncratic. Identifying and engaging the students' feelings is not only a means of validating them, but also of establishing the teacher's credibility.

Ultimately, the students identified insights they had gained through our dialogue with one another on issues of feminism:

1. We cannot assume that friendship alone, or the desire for friendship, will bring about either knowledge or transformation.

2. Good intentions are important, but are not sufficient to help move beyond the guilt felt when one confronts the fact s/he may belong by birth and color to an oppressive group. Guilt encourages inertia rather than responsible action.

3. Recognizing and understanding cultural differences does not hinder growth. Cultural differences prevent growth only when they are made into deficits or benefits that create structural inequalities.

4. Insisting that we are all "just" human and implying that we are color-blind and not culture-bound or class-bound does not lead to cooperation and understanding, because societal restrictions and our history do not allow us to act in human ways toward each other without a concerted effort.

5. Each of us must recognize (and resist) the ease of falling back into the system. Beliefs are not easily changed; to do so involves a conscious process that encourages people to think critically.

6. We cannot assume that people are well-meaning or that mutual trust is a given. Our society does not encourage mutual trust; it must be worked for.

Underlying these observations is the realization that most human beings desire to see information as finite and define progress in terms of material comfort. Frequently, when we speak of "gaining knowledge for progress in human affairs," we are not talking about progress at all, but about how to use knowledge for a more elegant order. For women's studies and black studies, the desire for such an artificial order is a trap we must not fall into. We are not engaged in the pursuit of order; we must, rather, be genuinely interested in progress, even if it produces the *appearance* of turmoil and chaos. We do not yet have the knowledge or conceptual frameworks necessary to define a truly inclusive, pluralistic order. What we are engaged in is a long journey toward understanding the diversity within and the complexities of women's studies and black studies, both as separate entities and together. We are working toward the end of understanding the diversity of the human universe in order to create a more humane world and a more truthful curriculum.

Notes

1. The Five College consortium is comprised of five institutions in the Connecticut Valley: the University of Massachusetts, Amherst, a large, public university; Amherst, a small, formerly men's college;

Hampshire, a ten-year-old experimental college; Mount Holyoke, the oldest women's college in the country; and Smith, the largest private women's college in the United States.

Much of this essay grows out of my collaborative work with Margo Culley. We are currently editing a volume of materials produced by the FIPSE project that further analyzes the experience: *Black Studies/ Women's Studies: An Overdue Partnership*.

2. See, for example, Johnnella E. Butler, *Black Studies Pedagogy and Revolution* (Lanham, Md.: University Press of America, 1981); Philip T. K. Daniel, "Theory Building in Black Studies," *The Black Scholar* 12, no. 3 (May–June 1981): 29–36; Charles A. Frye, *Towards a Philosophy of Black Studies* (Saratoga, Calif.: R. and E. Research Associates, 1978); Merrill Harvey Goldwyn, "Teaching Literature and Human Rights Curricular Possibilities," *Improving College and University Teaching* 31, no. 4 (Fall 1983): 149–54; and Thaddeus H. Spratten, "The Educational Relevance of Black Studies: An Interdisciplinary and Intercultural Interpretation." *Western Journal of Black Studies* 1, no. 1 (March 1977): 38–45.

3. See, for example, Robert Staples, "The Myth of Black Macho: A Response to Angry Feminists," *The Black Scholar* 10, no. 2 (March–April 1979); and Elly Bulkin, "Racism and Writing: Some Implications for White Lesbian Critics," *Sinister Wisdom* 13 (Spring 1980): 3–22.

The Social Construction of Black Feminist Thought

PATRICIA HILL COLLINS

Sojourner Truth, Anna Julia Cooper, Ida Wells Barnett, and Fannie Lou Hamer are but a few names from a growing list of distinguished African-American women activists. Although their sustained resistance to Black women's victimization within interlocking systems of race, gender, and class oppression is well known, these women did not act alone.[1] Their actions were nurtured by the support of countless, ordinary African-American women who, through strategies of everyday resistance, created a powerful foundation for this more visible Black feminist activist tradition.[2] Such support has been essential to the shape and goals of Black feminist thought.

The long-term and widely shared resistance among African-American women can only have been sustained by an enduring and shared standpoint among Black women about the meaning of oppression and the actions that Black women can and should take to resist it. Efforts to identify the central concepts of this Black women's standpoint figure prominently in the works of contemporary Black feminist intellectuals.[3] Moreover, political and epistemological issues influence the social construction of Black feminist thought. Like other subordinate groups, African-American women not only have developed distinctive interpretations of Black women's oppression but have done so by using alternative ways of producing and validating knowledge itself.

A Black Women's Standpoint

The Foundation of Black Feminist Thought

Black women's everyday acts of resistance challenge two prevailing approaches to studying the consciousness of oppressed groups.[4] One approach claims that subordinate groups identify with the powerful and have no valid independent interpretation of their own oppression.[5] The second approach assumes that the oppressed are less human than their rulers and, therefore, are less capable of articulating their own standpoint.[6] Both approaches see any independent consciousness expressed by an oppressed group as being not of the group's own making and/or inferior to the perspective of the dominant group.[7] More important, both interpretations suggest that oppressed groups lack the motivation for political activism because of their flawed consciousness of their own subordination.

Yet African-American women have been neither passive victims of nor willing accomplices to their own domination. As a result, emerging work in Black women's studies contends that Black women have a self-defined standpoint on their own oppression.[8] Two interlocking components characterize this standpoint. First, Black women's political and economic status provides them with a distinctive set of experiences that offers a different view of material reality than that available to other groups. The unpaid and paid work that Black women perform, the types of communities in which they live, and the kinds of relationships they have with others suggest that African-American women, as a group, experience a different world than those who are not Black and female.[9] Second, these experiences stimulate a distinctive Black feminist consciousness concerning that material reality.[10] In brief, a subordinate group not only experiences a different reality than a group that rules, but a subordinate group may interpret that reality differently than a dominant group.

Many ordinary African-American women have grasped this connection between what one does and how one thinks. Hannah Nelson, an elderly Black domestic worker, discusses how work shapes the standpoints of African-American and white women: "Since I have to work, I don't really have to worry about most of the things that most of the white women I have worked for are worrying about. And if these women did their own work, they would think just like I do—about this, anyway."[11] Ruth Shays, a Black inner city resident, points out how variations in men's and women's experiences lead to differences in perspective: "The mind of the man and the mind of the woman is the same. But this business of living makes women use their minds in ways that men don't even have to think about."[12] Finally, elderly domestic worker Rosa Wakefield assesses how the standpoints of the powerful and those who serve them diverge: "If you eats these dinners and don't cook'em, if you wears these clothes and don't buy or iron them, then you might start thinking that the good fairy or some spirit did all that. . . . Blackfolks don't have no time to be thinking like that. . . . But when you don't have anything else to do, you can think like that. It's bad for your mind, though."[13]

While African-American women may occupy material positions that stimulate a unique standpoint, expressing an independent Black feminist consciousness is problematic precisely because more powerful groups have a vested interest in suppressing such thought. As Hannah Nelson notes, "I have grown to womanhood in a world where the saner you are, the madder you are made to appear."[14] Nelson realizes that those who control the schools, the media, and other cultural institutions are generally skilled in establishing their view of reality as superior to alternative interpretations. While an oppressed group's experiences may put them in a position to see things differently. Their lack of control over the apparatuses of society that sustain ideological hegemony makes the articulation of their self-defined standpoint difficult. Groups unequal in power are correspondingly unequal in their access to the resources necessary to implement their perspectives outside their particular group.

One key reason that standpoints of oppressed groups are discredited and suppressed by the more powerful is that self-defined standpoints can stimulate oppressed groups to resist their domination. For instance, Annie Adams, a southern Black woman, describes how she became involved in civil rights activities.

> When I first went into the mill we had segregated water fountains. . . . Same thing about the toilets. I had to clean the toilets for the inspection room and then, when I got ready to go to the bathroom, I had to go all the way to the bottom of the stairs to the cellar. So I asked my boss man, "What's the difference? If I can go in there and clean them toilets, why can't I use them?" Finally, I started to use that toilet. I decided I wasn't going to walk a mile to go to the bathroom.[15]

In this case, Adams found the standpoint of the "boss man" inadequate, developed one of her own, and acted upon it. In doing so, her actions exemplify the connections between experiencing oppression, developing a self-defined standpoint on that experience, and resistance.

The Significance of Black Feminist Thought

The existence of a distinctive Black women's standpoint does not mean that it has been adequately articulated in Black feminist thought. Peter Berger and Thomas Luckmann provide a useful approach to clarifying the relationship between a Black women's standpoint and Black feminist thought with the contention that knowledge exists on two levels.[16] The first level includes the everyday, taken-for-granted knowledge shared by members of a given group, such as the ideas expressed by Ruth Shays and Annie Adams. Black feminist thought, by extension, represents a second level of knowledge, the more specialized knowledge furnished by experts who are part of a group and who express the group's standpoint. The two levels of knowledge are interdependent; while Black feminist thought articulates the taken-for-granted knowledge of African-American women, it also encourages all Black women to create new self-definitions that validate a Black women's standpoint.

Black feminist thought's potential significance goes far beyond demonstrating that Black women can produce independent, specialized knowledge. Such thought can encourage collective identity by offering Black women a different view of themselves and their world than that offered by the established social order. This different view encourages African-American women to value their own subjective knowledge base.[17] By taking elements and themes of Black women's culture and traditions and infusing them with new meaning, Black feminist thought rearticulates a consciousness that already exists.[18] More important, this rearticulated consciousness gives African-American women another tool of resistance to all forms of their subordination.[19]

Black feminist thought, then, specializes in formulating and rearticulating the distinctive, self-defined standpoint of African-American women. One approach to learning more about a Black women's standpoint is to consult standard scholarly sources for the ideas of specialists on Black women's experiences.[20] But investigating a Black women's standpoint and Black feminist thought requires more ingenuity than that required in examining the standpoints and thought of white males. Rearticulating the standpoint of African-American women through Black feminist thought is much more difficult since one cannot use the same techniques to study the knowledge of the dominated as one uses to study the knowledge of the powerful. This is precisely because subordinate groups have long had to use alternative ways to create an independent consciousness and to rearticulate it through specialists validated by the oppressed themselves.

The Eurocentric Masculinist Knowledge-Validation Process[21]

All social thought, including white masculinist and Black feminist, reflects the interests and standpoint of its creators. As Karl Mannheim notes, "If one were to trace in detail . . . the origin and . . . diffusion of a certain thought-model, one would discover the . . . affinity it has to the social position of given groups and their manner of interpreting the world.[22] Scholars, publishers, and other experts represent specific interests and credentialing processes, and their knowledge claims must satisfy the epistemological and political criteria of the contexts in which they reside.[23]

Two political criteria influence the knowledge-validation process. First, knowledge claims must be evaluated by a community of experts whose members represent the standpoints of the groups from which they originate. Second, each community of experts must maintain its credibility as defined by the larger group in which it is situated and from which it draws its basic, taken-for-granted knowledge.

When white males control the knowledge-validation process, both political criteria can work to suppress Black feminist thought. Since the general culture shaping the taken-for-granted knowledge of the community of experts is one permeated by widespread notions of Black and female inferiority,[24] new knowledge claims that seem to violate these fundamental assumptions are likely to be viewed as anomalies.[25] Moreover, specialized thought challenging notions of Black and female inferiority is unlikely to be generated from within a white-male-controlled academic community because both the kinds of questions that could be asked and the explanations that would be found satisfying would necessarily reflect a basic lack of familiarity with Black women's reality.[26]

The experiences of African-American women scholars illustrate how individuals who wish to rearticulate a Black women's standpoint through Black feminist thought can be suppressed by a white-male-controlled knowledge-validation process. Exclusion from basic literacy, quality educational experiences, and faculty and administrative positions has limited Black women's access to influential academic positions.[27] Thus, while Black women can produce knowledge claims that contest those advanced by the white male community, this community does not grant that Black women scholars have competing knowledge claims based in another knowledge-validation process. As a consequence, any credentials controlled by white male academicians can be denied to Black women producing Black feminist thought on the grounds that it is not credible research.

Those Black women with academic credentials who seek to exert the authority that their status grants them to propose new knowledge claims about African-American women face pressures to use their authority to help legitimate a system that devalues and excludes the majority of Black women.[28] One way of excluding the majority of Black women from the knowledge-validation process is to permit a few Black women to acquire positions of authority in institutions that legitimate knowledge and to encourage them to work within the taken-for-granted assumptions of Black female inferiority shared by the scholarly community and the culture at large. Those Black women who accept these assumptions are likely to be rewarded by their institutions, often at significant personal cost. Those challenging the assumptions run the risk of being ostracized.

African-American women academicians who persist in trying to rearticulate a Black women's standpoint also face potential rejection of their knowledge claims on epistemological grounds. Just as the material realities of the powerful and the dominated produce separate standpoints, each group may also have distinctive epistemologies or theories of knowledge. It is my contention that Black female scholars may know that something is true but be unwilling or unable to legitimate their claims using Eurocentric masculinist criteria for consistency with substantiated knowledge and Eurocentric masculinist criteria for methodological adequacy.

For any particular interpretive context, new knowledge claims must be consistent with an existing body of knowledge that the group controlling the interpretive context accepts as true. The methods used to validate knowledge claims must also be acceptable to the group controlling the knowledge-validation process.

The criteria for the methodological adequacy of positivism illustrate the epistemological standards that Black women scholars would have to satisfy in legitimating alternative knowledge claims.[29] Positivist approaches aim to create scientific descriptions of reality by producing objective generalizations. Since researchers have widely differing values, experiences, and emotions, genuine science is thought to be unattainable unless all human characteristics except rationality are eliminated from the research process. By following strict methodological rules, scientists aim to distance themselves from the values, vested interests, and emotions generated by their class, race, sex, or unique situation and in so doing become detached observers and manipulators of nature.[30]

Several requirements typify positivist methodological approaches. First, research methods generally require a distancing of the researcher from her/his "object" of study by defining the researcher as a "subject" with full human subjectivity and objectifying the "object" of study.[31] A second requirement is the absence of emotions from the research process.[32] Third, ethics and values are deemed inappropriate in the research process, either as the reason for scientific inquiry or as part of the research process itself.[33] Finally, adversarial debates, whether written or oral, become the preferred method of ascertaining truth—the arguments that can withstand the greatest assault and survive intact become the strongest truths.[34]

Such criteria ask African-American women to objectify themselves, devalue their emotional life, displace their motivations for furthering knowledge about Black women, and confront, in an adversarial relationship, those who have more social, economic, and professional power than they. It seems unlikely, therefore, that Black women would use a positivist epistemological stance in rearticulating a Black women's standpoint. Black women are more likely to choose an alternative epistemology for assessing knowledge claims, one using standards that are consistent with Black women's criteria for substantiated knowledge and with Black women's criteria for methodological adequacy. If such an epistemology exists, what are its contours? Moreover, what is its role in the production of Black feminist thought?

The Contours of an Afrocentric Feminist Epistemology

Africanist analyses of the Black experience generally agree on the fundamental elements of an Afrocentric standpoint. In spite of varying histories, Black societies reflect elements of a core African value system that existed prior to and independently of racial oppression.[35] Moreover, as a result of colonialism, imperialism, slavery, apartheid, and other systems of racial domination, Blacks share a common experience of oppression. These similarities in material conditions have fostered shared Afrocentric values that permeate the family structure, religious institutions, culture, and community life of Blacks in varying parts of Africa, the Caribbean, South America, and North America.[36] This Afrocentric consciousness permeates the shared history of people of African descent through the framework of a distinctive Afrocentric epistemology.[37]

Feminist scholars advance a similar argument. They assert that women share a history of patriarchal oppression through the political economy of the material conditions of sexuality and reproduction.[38] These shared material conditions are thought to transcend divisions among women created by race, social class, religion, sexual orientation, and ethnicity and to form the basis of a women's standpoint with its corresponding feminist consciousness and epistemology.[39]

Since Black women have access to both the Afrocentric and the feminist standpoints, an alternative epistemology used to rearticulate a Black women's standpoint reflects elements of both traditions.[40] The search for the distinguishing features of an alternative epistemology used by African-American women reveals that values and ideas that Africanist scholars identify as being characteristically "Black" often bear remarkable resemblance to similar ideas claimed by feminist scholars as being characteristically "female."[41] This similarity suggests that the material conditions of oppression can vary dramatically and yet generate some uniformity in the epistemologies of subordinate groups. Thus, the significance of an Afrocentric feminist epistemology may lie in its enrichment of our understanding of how subordinate groups create knowledge that enables them to resist oppression.

The parallels between the two conceptual schemes raise a question: Is the worldview of women of African descent more intensely infused with the overlapping feminine/Afrocentric standpoints than is the case for either African-American men or white women?[42] While an Afrocentric feminist epistemology reflects elements of epistemologies used by Blacks as a group and women as a group, it also paradoxically demonstrates features that may be unique to Black women. On certain dimensions, Black women may more closely resemble Black men, on others, white women, and on still others, Black women may stand apart from both groups. Black feminist sociologist Deborah K. King describes this phenomenon as a "both/or" orientation, the act of being simultaneously a member of a group and yet standing apart from it. She suggests that multiple realities among Black women yield a "multiple consciousness in Black women's politics" and that this state of belonging yet not belonging forms an integral part of Black women's oppositional consciousness.[43] Bonnie Thornton Dill's analysis of how Black women live with contradictions, a situation she labels the "dialectics of Black womanhood," parallels King's assertions that this "both/or" orientation is central to an Afrocentric feminist consciousness.[44] Rather than emphasizing how a Black women's standpoint and its accompanying epistemology are different than those in Afrocentric and feminist analyses, I use Black women's experiences as a point of contact between the two.

Viewing an Afrocentric feminist epistemology in this way challenges analyses claiming that Black women have a more accurate view of oppression than do other groups. Such approaches suggest that oppression can be quantified and compared and that adding layers of oppression produces a potentially clearer standpoint. While it is tempting to claim that Black women are more oppressed than everyone else and therefore have the best standpoint from which to understand the mechanisms, processes, and effects of oppression, this simply may not be the case.[45]

African-American women do not uniformly share an Afrocentric feminist epistemology since social class introduces variations among Black women in seeing, valuing, and using Afrocentric feminist perspectives. While a Black women's standpoint and its accompanying epistemology stem from Black women's consciousness of race and gender oppression, they are not simply the result of combining Afrocentric and female values—standpoints are rooted in real material conditions structured by social class.[46]

Concrete Experience as a Criterion of Meaning

Carolyn Chase, a thirty-one-year-old inner city Black woman, notes, "My aunt used to say, 'A heap see, but a few know.'"[47] This saying depicts two types of knowing, knowledge and wisdom, and taps the first dimension of an Afrocentric feminist epistemology. Living life as Black women requires wisdom since knowledge about the dynamics of race, gender, and class subordination has been essential to Black women's survival. African-American women give such wisdom high credence in assessing knowledge.

Allusions of these two types of knowing pervade the words of a range of African-American women. In explaining the tenacity of racism, Zilpha Elaw, a preacher of the mid-1800s, noted: "The pride of a white skin is a bauble of great value with many in some parts of the United States, who readily sacrifice their intelligence to their prejudices, and possess more knowledge than wisdom."[48] In describing differences separating African-American and white women, Nancy White invokes a similar rule: "When you come right down to it, white women just *think* they are free. Black women *know* they ain't free."[49] Geneva Smitherman, a college professor specializing in African-American linguistics, suggests that "from a black perspective, written documents are limited in what they can teach about life and survival in the world. Blacks are quick to ridicule 'educated fools,' . . . they have 'book learning' but no 'mother wit,' knowledge, but not wisdom."[50] Mabel Lincoln eloquently summarizes the distinction between knowledge and wisdom: "To black people like me, a fool is funny—you know, people who love to break bad, people you can't tell anything to, folks that would take a shotgun to a roach."[51]

Black women need wisdom to know how to deal with the "educated fools" who would "take a shotgun to a roach." As members of a subordinate group, Black women cannot afford to be fools of any type, for their devalued status denies them the protections that white skin, maleness, and wealth confer. This distinction between knowledge and wisdom, and the use of experience as the cutting edge dividing them, has been key to Black women's survival. In the context of race, gender, and class oppression, the distinction is essential since knowledge without wisdom is adequate for the powerful, but wisdom is essential to the survival of the subordinate.

For ordinary African-American women, those individuals who have lived through the experiences about which they claim to be experts are more believable and credible than those who have merely read or thought about such experiences. Thus, concrete experience as a criterion for credibility frequently is invoked by Black women when making knowledge claims. For instance, Hannah Nelson describes the importance that personal experience has for her: "Our speech is most directly personal, and every black person assumes that every other black person has a right to a personal opinion. In speaking of grave matters, your personal experience is considered very good evidence. With us, distant statistics are certainly not as important as the actual experience of a sober person."[52] Similarly, Ruth Shays uses her concrete experiences to challenge the idea that formal education is the only route to knowledge: "I am the kind of person who doesn't have a lot of education, but both my mother and my father had good common sense. Now, I think that's all you need. I might not know how to use thirty-four words where three would do, but that does not means that I don't know what I'm talking about. . . . I know what I'm talking about because I'm talking about myself. I'm talking about what I have lived."[53] Implicit in Shay's self-assessment is a critique of the type of knowledge that obscures the truth, the "thirty-four words" that cover up a truth that can be expressed in three.

Even after substantial mastery of white masculinist epistemologies, many Black women scholars invoke their own concrete experiences and those of other Black women in selecting topics for investigation and methodologies used. For example, Elsa Barkley Brown subtitles her essay on Black women's history, "how my mother taught me to be an historian in spite of my academic training."[54] Similarly, Joyce Ladner maintains that growing up as a Black woman is the South gave her special insights in conducting her study of Black adolescent women.[55]

Henry Mitchell and Nicholas Lewter claim that experience as a criterion of meaning with practical images as its symbolic vehicles is a fundamental epistemological tenet in African-American thought-systems.[56] Stories, narratives, and Bible principles are selected for their applicability to the lived experiences of African-Americans and become symbolic representations of a whole wealth of experience. For example, Bible tales are told for their value to common life, so their interpretation involves no need for scientific historical verification. The narrative method requires that the story be "told, not torn apart in analysis, and trusted as core belief, not admired as science."[57] Any biblical story contains more than characters and a plot—it presents key ethical issues salient in African-American life.

June Jordan's essay about her mother's suicide exemplifies the multiple levels of meaning that can occur when concrete experiences are used as a criterion of meaning. Jordan describes her mother, a woman who literally died trying to stand up, and the effect that her mother's death had on her own work:

> I think all of this is really about women and work. Certainly this is all about me as a woman and my life work. I mean I am not sure my mother's suicide was something extraordinary. Perhaps most women must deal with a similar inheritance, the legacy of a woman whose death you cannot possibly pinpoint because she died so many, many times and because even before she became your mother, the life of that woman was taken. . . . I came too late to help my mother to her feet. By way of everlasting thanks to all of the women who have helped me to stay alive I am working never to be late again.[58]

While Jordan has knowledge about the concrete act of her mother's death, she also strives for wisdom concerning the meaning of that death.

Some feminist scholars offer a similar claim that women, as a group, are more likely than men to use concrete knowledge in assessing knowledge claims. For example, a substantial number of the 135 women in a study of women's cognitive development were "connected knowers" and were drawn to the sort of knowledge that emerges from first-hand observation. Such women felt that since knowledge comes from experience, the best way of understanding another person's ideas was to try to share the experiences that led the person to form those ideas. At the heart of the procedures used by connected knowers is the capacity for empathy.[59]

In valuing the concrete, African-American women, may be invoking not only an Afrocentric tradition, but a women's tradition as well. Some feminist theorists suggest that women are socialized in complex relational nexuses where contextual rules take priority over abstract principles in governing behavior. This socialization process is thought to stimulate characteristic ways of knowing.[60] For example, Canadian sociologist Dorothy Smith maintains that two modes of knowing exist, one located in the body and the space it occupies and the other passing beyond it. She asserts that women, through their child-rearing and nurturing activities, mediate these two modes and use the concrete experiences of their daily lives to assess more abstract knowledge claims.[61]

Amanda King, a young Black mother, describes how she used the concrete to assess the abstract and points out how difficult mediating these two modes of knowing can be:

> The leaders of the ROC [a labor union] lost their jobs too, but it just seemed like they were used to losing their jobs. . . . This was like a lifelong thing for them, to get out there and protest. They were like, what do you call them—intellectuals. . . . You got the ones that go to the university that are supposed to make all the speeches, they're the ones that are supposed to lead, you know, put this little revolution together, and then you got the little ones . . . that go to the factory everyday, they be the ones that have to fight. I had a child and I thought I don't have the time to be running around with these people. . . . I mean I understand some of that stuff they were talking about, like the bourgeoisie, the rich and the poor and all that, but I had surviving on my mind for me and my kid.[62]

For King, abstract ideals of class solidarity were mediated by the concrete experience of motherhood and the connectedness it involved.

In traditional African-American communities, Black women find considerable institutional support for valuing concrete experience. Black extended families and Black churches are two key institutions where Black women experts with concrete knowledge of what it takes to be self-defined Black women share their knowledge with their younger, less experienced sisters. This relationship of sisterhood among Black women can be seen as a model for a whole series of relationships that African-American women have with each other, whether it is networks among women in extended families, among women in the Black church, or among women in the African-American community at large.[63]

Since the Black church and the Black family are both woman-centered and Afrocentric institutions, African-American women traditionally have found considerable institutional support for this dimension of an Afrocentric feminist epistemology in ways that are unique to them. While white women may value the concrete, it is questionable whether white families, particularly middle-class nuclear ones, and white community institutions provide comparable types of support. Similarly, while Black men are supported by Afrocentric institutions, they cannot participate in Black women's sisterhood. In terms of Black women's relationships with one another then, African-American women may indeed find it easier than others to recognize connectedness as a primary way of knowing, simply because they are encouraged to do so by Black women's tradition of sisterhood.

The Use of Dialogue in Assessing Knowledge Claims

For Black women, new knowledge claims are rarely worked out in isolation from other individuals and are usually developed through dialogues with other members of a community. A primary epistemological assumption underlying the use of dialogue in assessing knowledge claims is that connectedness rather than separation is an essential component of the knowledge-validation process.[64]

The use of dialogue has deep roots in an African-based oral tradition and in African-American culture.[65] Ruth Shays describes the importance of dialogue in the knowledge-validation process of enslaved African-Americans: "They would find a lie if it took them a year . . . the foreparents found the truth because they listened and they made people tell their part many times. Most often you can hear a lie. . . . Those old people was everywhere and knew the truth of many disputes. They believed that a liar should suffer the pain of his lies, and they had all kinds of ways of bringing liars to judgment."[66]

The widespread use of the call and response discourse mode among African-Americans exemplifies the importance placed on dialogue. Composed of spontaneous verbal and nonverbal interaction between speaker and listener in which all of the speaker's statements or "calls" are punctuated by expressions or "responses" from the listener, this Black discourse mode pervades African-American culture. The fundamental requirement of this interactive network is active participation of all individuals.[67] For ideas to be tested and validated, everyone in the group must participate. To refuse to join in, especially if one really disagrees with what has been said is seen as "cheating."[68]

June Jordan's analysis of Black English points to the significance of this dimension of an alternative epistemology.

> Our language is a system constructed by people constantly needing to insist that we exist. . . . Our language devolves from a culture that abhors all abstraction, or anything tending to obscure or delete the fact of the human being who is here and now/the truth of the person who is speaking or listening. Consequently, *there is no passive voice construction possible in Black English*. For example, you cannot say, "Black English is being eliminated." You must say, instead, "White people eliminating Black English." The assumption of the presence of life governs all of Black English . . . every sentence assumes the living and active participation of at least two human beings, the speaker and the listener.[69]

Many Black women intellectuals invoke the relationships and connectedness provided by use of dialogue. When asked why she chose the themes she did, novelist Gayle Jones replied: "I was . . . interested . . . in oral traditions of storytelling—Afro-American and others, in which there is always the consciousness and importance of the hearer."[70] In describing the difference in the way male and female writers select significant events and relationships, Jones points out that "with many women writers, relationships within family, community, between men and women, and among women—from slave narratives by black women writers on—are treated as complex and significant relationships, whereas with many men the significant relationships are those that involve confrontations—relationships outside the family and community."[71] Alice Walker's reaction to Zora Neale Hurston's book, *Mules and Men*, is another example of the use of dialogue in assessing knowledge claims. In *Mules and Men*, Hurston chose not to become a detached observer of the stories and folktales she collected but instead, through extensive dialogues with the people in the communities she studied, placed herself at the center of her analysis. Using a similar process, Walker tests the truth of Hurston's knowledge claims: "When I read *Mules and Men* I was delighted. Here was this perfect book! The 'perfection' of which I immediately tested on my relatives, who are such typical Black Americans they are useful for every sort of political, cultural, or economic survey. Very regular people from the South, rapidly forgetting their Southern cultural inheritance in the suburbs and ghettos of Boston and New York, they sat around reading the book themselves, listening to me read the book, listening to each other read the book, and a kind of paradise was regained."[72]

Their centrality in Black churches and Black extended families provides Black women with a high degree of support from Black institutions for invoking dialogue as a dimension of an Afrocentric feminist epistemology. However, when African-American women use dialogues in assessing knowledge claims, they might be invoking a particularly female way of knowing as well. Feminist scholars contend that males and females are socialized within their families to seek different types of autonomy, the former based on separation, the latter seeking connectedness, and that this variation in types of autonomy parallels the characteristic differences between male and female ways of knowing.[73] For instance, in contrast to the visual metaphors (such as equating knowledge with illumination, knowing with seeing, and truth with light) that scientist and philosophers typically use, women tend to ground their epistemological premises in metaphors suggesting speaking and listening.[74]

While there are significant differences between the roles Black women play in their families and those played by middle-class white women, Black women clearly are affected by general cultural norms prescribing certain familial roles for women. Thus, in terms of the role of dialogue in an Afrocentric feminist epistemology, Black women may again experience a convergence of the values of the African-American community and woman-centered values.

The Ethic of Caring

"Ole white preachers used to talk wid dey tongues widdout sayin' nothin', but Jesus told us slaves to talk wid our hearts."[75] These words of an ex-slave suggest that ideas cannot be divorced from the individuals who create and share them. This theme of "talking with the heart" taps another dimension of an alternative epistemology used by African-American women, the ethic of caring. Just as the ex-slave used the wisdom in his heart to reject the ideas of the preachers who talked "wid dey tongues widdout sayin' nothin'," the ethic of caring suggests that personal expressiveness, emotions, and empathy are central to the knowledge-validation process.

One of three interrelated components making up the ethic of caring is the emphasis placed on individual uniqueness. Rooted in a tradition of African humanism, each individual is thought to be a unique expression of a common spirit, power, or energy expressed by all life.[76] This belief in individual uniqueness is illustrated by the value placed on personal expressiveness in African-American communities.[77] Johnetta Ray, an inner city resident, describes this Afrocentric emphasis on individual uniqueness: "No matter how hard we try, I don't think black people will ever develop much of a herd instinct. We are profound individualists with a passion for self-expression."[78]

A second component of the ethic of caring concerns the appropriateness of emotions in dialogues. Emotion indicates that a speaker believes in the validity of an argument.[79] Consider Ntozake Shange's description of one of the goals of her work: "Our [Western] society allows people to be absolutely neurotic and totally out of touch with their feelings and everyone else's feelings, and yet be very respectable. This, to me, is a travesty. . . . I'm trying to change the idea of seeing emotions and intellect as distinct faculties."[80] Shange's words echo those of the ex-slave. Both see the denigration of emotion as problematic, and both suggest that expressiveness should be reclaimed and valued.

A third component of the ethic of caring involves developing the capacity for empathy. Harriet Jones, a sixteen-year-old Black woman, explains why she chose to open up to her interviewer: "Some things in my life are so hard for me to bear, and it makes me feel better to know that you feel sorry about those things and would change them if you could."[81]

These three components of the ethic of caring—the value placed on individual expressiveness, the appropriateness of emotions, and the capacity for empathy—pervade African-American culture. One of the best examples of the interactive nature of the importance of dialogue and the ethic of caring in assessing knowledge claims occurs in the use of the call and response discourse mode in traditional Black church services. In such services, both the minister and the congregation routinely use voice rhythm and vocal inflection to convey meaning. The sound of what is being said is just as important as the words themselves in what is, in a sense, a dialogue between reason and emotions. As a result, it is nearly impossible to filter out the strictly linguistic-cognitive abstract meaning from the sociocultural psycho-emotive meaning.[82] While the ideas presented by a speaker must have validity, that is, agree with the general body of knowledge shared by the Black congregation, the group also appraises the way knowledge claims are presented.

There is growing evidence that the ethic of caring may be part of women's experience as well. Certain dimensions of women's ways of knowing bear striking resemblance to Afrocentric expressions of the ethic of caring. Belenky, Clinchy, Goldberger, and Tarule point out that two contrasting epistemological orientations characterize knowing—one, an epistemology of separation based on impersonal procedures for establishing truth, and the other, an epistemology of connection in which truth emerges through care. While these ways of knowing are not gender specific, disproportionate numbers of women rely on connected knowing.[83]

The parallels between Afrocentric expressions of the ethic of caring and those advanced by feminist scholars are noteworthy. The emphasis placed on expressiveness and emotion in African-American communities bears marked resemblance to feminist perspectives on the importance of personality in connected knowing. Separate knowers try to subtract the personality of an individual from his or her ideas because they see personality as biasing those ideas. In contrast, connected knowers see personality as adding to an individual's ideas, and they feel that the personality of each group member enriches a group's understanding.[84] Similarly, the significance of individual uniqueness, personal expressiveness, and empathy in African-American communities resembles the importance that some feminist analyses place on women's "inner voice."[85]

The convergence of Afrocentric and feminist values in the ethic-of-care dimension of an alternative epistemology seems particularly acute. While white women may have access to a women's tradition valuing emotion and expressiveness, few white social institutions except the family validate this way of knowing. In contrast, Black women have long had the support of the Black church, an institution with deep roots in the African past and a philosophy that accepts and encourages expressiveness and an ethic of caring. While Black men share in this Afrocentric tradition, they must resolve the contradictions that distinguish abstract, unemotional Western masculinity from an Afrocentric ethic of caring. The differences among race/gender groups thus hinge on differences in their access to institutional supports valuing one type of knowing over another. Although Black women may be denigrated within white-male-controlled academic institutions, other institutions, such as Black families and churches, which encourage the expression of Black female power, seem to do so by way of their support for an Afrocentric feminist epistemology.

The Ethic of Personal Accountability

An ethic of personal accountability is the final dimension of an alternative epistemology. Not only must individuals develop their knowledge claims through dialogue and present those knowledge claims in a style proving their concern for their ideas, people are expected to be accountable for their knowledge claims. Zilpha Elaw's description of slavery reflects this notion that every idea has an owner and that the owner's identity matters: "Oh, the abominations of slavery! . . . every case of slavery, however lenient its inflictions and mitigated its atrocities, indicates an oppressor, the oppressed, and oppression."[86] For Elaw, abstract definitions of slavery mesh with the concrete identities of its perpetrators and its victims. Blacks "consider it essential for individuals to have personal positions on issues and assume full responsibility for arguing their validity."[87]

Assessments of an individual's knowledge claims simultaneously evaluate an individual's character, values, and ethics. African-Americans reject Eurocentric masculinist beliefs that probing into an individual's personal viewpoint is outside the boundaries of discussion. Rather, all views expressed and actions taken are thought to derive from a central set of core beliefs that cannot be other than personal.[88] From this perspective, knowledge claims made by individuals respected for their moral and ethical values will carry more weight than those offered by less respected figures.[89]

An example drawn from an undergraduate course composed entirely of Black women, which I taught, might help clarify the uniqueness of this portion of the knowledge-validation process. During one class discussion, I assigned the students the task of critiquing an analysis of Black feminism advanced by a prominent Black male scholar. Instead of dissecting the rationality of the author's thesis, my students demanded facts about the author's personal biography. They were especially interested in concrete details of his life such as his relationships with Black women, his marital status, and his social class background. By requesting data on dimensions of his personal life routinely excluded in positivist approaches to knowledge validation, they were invoking concrete experience as a criterion of meaning. They used this information to assess whether he really cared about his topic and invoked this ethic of caring in advancing their knowledge claims about his work. Furthermore, they refused to evaluate the rationality of his written ideas without some indication of his personal credibility as an ethical human being. The entire exchange could only have occurred as a dialogue among members of a class that had established a solid enough community to invoke an alternative epistemology in assessing knowledge claims.[90]

The ethic of personal accountability is clearly an Afrocentric value, but is it feminist as well? While limited by its attention to middle-class white women, Carol Gilligan's work suggests that there is a female model for moral development where women are more inclined to link morality to responsibility, relationships, and the ability to maintain social ties.[91] If this is the case, then African-American women again experience a convergence of values from Afrocentric and female institutions.

The use of an Afrocentric feminist epistemology in traditional Black church services illustrates the interactive nature of all four dimensions and also serves as a metaphor for the distinguishing features of an Afrocentric feminist way of knowing. The services represent more than dialogues between the rationality used in examining biblical texts/stories and the emotion inherent in the use of reason for this purpose. The rationale for such dialogues addresses the task of examining concrete experiences for the presence of an ethic of caring. Neither emotion nor ethics is subordinated to reason. Instead, emotion, ethics, and reason are used as interconnected, essential components in assessing knowledge claims. In an Afrocentric feminist epistemology, values lie at the heart of the knowledge-validation process such that inquiry always has an ethical aim.

Epistemology and Black Feminist Thought

Living life as an African-American woman is a necessary prerequisite for producing Black feminist thought because within Black women's communities thought is validated and produced with reference to a particular set of historical, material, and epistemological conditions.[92] African-American women who adhere to the idea that claims about Black women must be substantiated by Black women's sense of their own experiences and who anchor their knowledge claims in an Afrocentric feminist epistemology have produced a rich tradition of Black feminist thought.

Traditionally, such women were blues singers, poets, autobiographers, storytellers, and orators validated by the larger community of Black women as experts on a Black women's standpoint. Only a few unusual African-American feminist scholars have been able to defy Eurocentric masculinist epistemologies and explicitly embrace an Afrocentric feminist epistemology. Consider Alice Walker's description of Zora Neale Hurston: "In my mind, Zora Neale Hurston, Billie Holiday, and Bessie Smith form a sort of unholy trinity. Zora *belongs* in the tradition of Black women singers, rather than among 'the literati.' . . . Like Billie and Bessie she followed her own road, believed in her own gods, pursued her own dreams, and refused to separate herself from 'common' people."[93]

Zora Neale Hurston is an exception for, prior to 1950, few Black women earned advanced degrees, and most of those who did complied with Eurocentric masculinist epistemologies. While these women worked on behalf of Black women, they did so within the confines of pervasive race and gender oppression. Black women scholars were in a position to see the exclusion of Black women from scholarly discourse, and the thematic content of their work often reflected their interest in examining a Black women's standpoint. However, their tenuous status in academic institutions led them to adhere to Eurocentric masculinist epistemologies so that their work would be accepted as scholarly. As a result, while they produced Black feminist thought, those Black women most likely to gain academic credentials were often least likely to produce Black feminist thought that used an Afrocentric feminist epistemology.

As more Black women earn advanced degrees, the range of Black feminist scholarship is expanding. Increasing numbers of African-American women scholars are explicitly choosing to ground their work in Black women's experiences, and, by doing so, many implicitly adhere to an Afrocentric feminist epistemology. Rather than being restrained by their "both/and" status of marginality, these women make creative use of their outsider-within status and produce innovative Black feminist thought. The difficulties these women face lie less in demonstrating the technical components of white male epistemologies than in resisting the hegemonic nature of these patterns of thought in order to see, value, and use existing alternative Afrocentric feminist ways of knowing.

In establishing the legitimacy of their knowledge claims, Black women scholars who want to develop Black feminist thought may encounter the often conflicting standards of three key groups. First, Black feminist thought must be validated by ordinary African-American women who grow to womanhood "in a world where the saner you are, the madder you are made to appear."[94] To be credible in the eyes of this group, scholars must be personal advocates for their material, be accountable for the consequences of their work, have lived or experienced their material in some fashion, and be willing to engage in dialogues about their findings with ordinary, everyday people. Second, if it is to establish its legitimacy, Black feminist thought also must be accepted by the community of Black women scholars. These scholars place varying amounts of importance on rearticulating a Black women's standpoint using an Afrocentric feminist epistemology. Third, Black feminist thought within academia must be prepared to confront Eurocentric masculinist political and epistemological requirements.

The dilemma facing Black women scholars engaged in creating Black feminist thought is that a knowledge claim that meets the criteria of adequacy for one group and thus is judged to be an acceptable knowledge claim may not be translatable into the terms of a different group. Using the example of Black English, June Jordan illustrates the difficulty of moving among epistemologies: "You cannot 'translate' instances of Standard English preoccupied with abstraction or with nothing/nobody evidently alive into Black English. That would warp the language into uses antithetical to the guiding perspective of its community of users. Rather you must first change those Standard English sentences, themselves, into ideas consistent with the person-centered assumptions of Black English."[95] While both worldviews share a common vocabulary, the ideas themselves defy direct translation.

Once Black feminist scholars face the notion that, on certain dimensions of a Black women's standpoint, it may be fruitless to try to translate ideas from an Afrocentric feminist epistemology into a Eurocentric masculinist epistemology, then the choices become clearer. Rather than trying to uncover universal knowledge claims that can withstand the translation from one epistemology to another, time might be better spent rearticulating a Black women's standpoint in order to give African-American women the tools to resist their own subordination. The goal here is not one of integrating Black female "folk culture" into the substantiated body of academic knowledge, for that substantiated knowledge is, in many ways, antithetical to the best interests of Black women. Rather, the process is one of rearticulating a preexisting Black women's standpoint and recentering the language of existing academic discourse to accommodate these knowledge claims. For those Black women scholars engaged in this rearticulation process, the social construction of

Black feminist thought requires the skill and sophistication to decide which knowledge claims can be validated using the epistemological assumptions of one but not both frameworks, which claims can be generated in one framework and only partially accommodated by the other, and which claims can be made in both frameworks without violating the basic political and epistemological assumptions of either.

Black feminist scholars offering knowledge claims that cannot be accommodated by both frameworks face the choice between accepting the taken-for-granted assumptions that permeate white-male-controlled academic institutions or leaving academia. Those Black women who choose to remain in academia must accept the possibility that their knowledge claims will be limited to those claims about Black women that are consistent with a white male worldview. And yet those African-American women who leave academia may find their work is inaccessible to scholarly communities.

Black feminist scholars offering knowledge claims that can be partially accommodated by both epistemologies can create a body of thought that stands outside of either. Rather than trying to synthesize competing worldviews that, at this point in time, may defy reconciliation, their task is to point out common themes and concerns. By making creative use of their status as mediators, their thought becomes an entity unto itself that is rooted in two distinct political and epistemological contexts.[96]

Those Black feminists who develop knowledge claims that both epistemologies can accommodate may have found a route to the elusive goal of generating so-called objective generalizations that can stand as universal truths. Those ideas that are validated as true by African-American women, African-American men, white men, white women, and other groups with distinctive standpoints, with each group using the epistemological approaches growing from its unique standpoint, thus become the most objective truths.[97]

Alternative knowledge claims, in and of themselves, are rarely threatening to conventional knowledge. Such claims are routinely ignored, discredited, or simply absorbed and marginalized in existing paradigms. Much more threatening is the challenge that alternative epistemologies offer to the basic process used by the powerful to legitimate their knowledge claims. If the epistemology used to validate knowledge comes into question, then all prior knowledge claims validated under the dominant model become suspect. An alternative epistemology challenges all certified knowledge and opens up the question of whether what has been taken to be true can stand the test of alternative ways of validating truth. The existence of an independent Black women's standpoint using an Afrocentric feminist epistemology calls into question the content of what currently passes as truth and simultaneously challenges the process of arriving at that truth.

Department of Afro-American Studies
University of Cincinnati

Notes

Special thanks go out to the following people for reading various drafts of this manuscript: Evelyn Nakano Glenn, Lynn Weber Cannon, and participants in the 1986 Research Institute, Center for Research on Women, Memphis State University; Elsa Barkley Brown, Deborah K. King, Elizabeth V. Spelman, and Angelene Jamison-Hall; and four anonymous reviewers at *Signs*.

1. For analyses of how interlocking systems of oppression affect Black women, see Frances Beale, "Double Jeopardy: To Be Black and Female," in *The Black Woman*, ed. Toni Cade (New York: Signet, 1970); Angela Y. Davis, *Women, Race and Class* (New York: Random House, 1981); Bonnie Thornton Dill, "Race, Class, and Gender: Prospects for an All-Inclusive Sisterhood," *Feminist Studies* 9, no. 1 (1983): 131–50; bell hooks, *Ain't I a Woman? Black Women and Feminism* (Boston: South End Press, 1981); Diane Lewis, "A Response to Inequality: Black Women, Racism, and Sexism," *Signs: Journal of Women in Culture and Society* 3, no. 2 (Winter 1977): 339–61; Pauli Murray, "The Liberation of Black Women," in *Voices of the New Feminism*, ed. Mary Lou Thompson (Boston: Beacon, 1970), 87–102; and the introduction in Filomina Chioma Steady, *The Black Woman Cross-Culturally* (Cambridge, Mass.: Schenkman, 1981), 7–41.

2. See the introduction in Steady for an overview of Black women's strengths. This strength–resiliency perspective has greatly influenced empirical work on African-American women. See, e.g., Joyce Ladner's study of low-income Black adolescent girls, *Tomorrow's Tomorrow* (New York: Doubleday, 1971); and Lena Wright Myers's work on Black women's self-concept, *Black Women: Do They Cope Better?* (Englewood Cliffs, N.J.: Prentice-Hall, 1980). For discussions of Black women's resistance, see Elizabeth Fox-Genovese, "Strategies and Forms of Resistance: Focus on Slave Women in the United States," in *In Resistance: Studies in African-Caribbean and Afro-American History*, ed. Gary Y. Okihiro (Amherst, Mass.: University of Massachusetts Press, 1986), 143–65; and Rosalyn Terborg-Penn, "Black Women in Resistance: A Cross-Cultural Perspective," in Okihiro, ed., 188–209. For a comprehensive discussion of everyday resistance, see James C. Scott, *Weapons of the Weak: Everyday Forms of Peasant Resistance* (New Haven, Conn.: Yale University Press, 1985).

3. See Patricia Hill Collins's analysis of the substantive content of Black feminist thought in "Learning from the Outsider Within: The Sociological Significance of Black Feminist Thought," *Social Problems* 33, no. 6 (1986): 14–32.

4. Scott describes consciousness as the meaning that people give to their acts through the symbols, norms, and ideological forms they create.

5. This thesis is found in scholarship of varying theoretical perspectives. For example, Marxist analyses of working-class consciousness claim that "false consciousness" makes the working class unable to penetrate the hegemony of ruling-class ideologies. See Scott's critique of this literature.

6. For example, in Western societies, African-Americans have been judged as being less capable of intellectual excellence, more suited to manual labor, and therefore as less human than whites. Similarly, white women have been assigned roles as emotional, irrational creatures ruled by passions and biological urges. They too have been stigmatized as being less than fully human, as being objects. For a discussion of the importance that objectification and dehumanization play in maintaining systems of domination, see Arthur Brittan and Mary Maynard, *Sexism, Racism and Oppression* (New York: Basil Blackwell, 1984).

7. The tendency for Western scholarship to assess Black culture as pathological and deviant illustrates this process. See Rhett S. Jones, "Proving Blacks Inferior: The Sociology of Knowledge," in *The Death of White Sociology*, ed. Joyce Ladner (New York: Vintage, 1973), 114–35.

8. The presence of an independent standpoint does not mean that it is uniformly shared by all Black women or even that Black women fully recognize its contours. By using the concept of standpoint, I do not mean to minimize the rich diversity existing among African-American women. I use the phrase "Black women's standpoint" to emphasize the plurality of experiences within the overarching term "standpoint." For discussions of the concept of standpoint, see Nancy M. Hartsock, "The Feminist Standpoint: Developing the Ground for a Specifically Feminist Historical Materialism," in *Discovering Reality*, ed. Sandra Harding and Merrill Hintikka (Boston: D. Reidel, 1983), 283–310, and *Money, Sex, and Power* (Boston: Northeastern University Press, 1983); and Alison M. Jaggar, *Feminist Politics and Human Nature* (Totowa, N.J.: Rowman & Allanheld, 1983), 377–89. My use of the standpoint epistemologies as an organizing concept in this essay does not mean that the concept is problem-free. For a helpful critique of standpoint epistemologies, see Sandra Harding, *The Science Question in Feminism* (Ithaca, N.Y.: Cornell University Press, 1986).

9. One contribution of contemporary Black women's studies is its documentation of how race, class, and gender have structured these differences. For representative works surveying African-American women's experiences, see Paula Giddings, *When and Where I Enter: The Impact of Black Women on Race and Sex in America* (New York: William Morrow, 1984); and Jacqueline Jones, *Labor of Love, Labor of Sorrow: Black Women, Work and the Family from Slavery to the Present* (New York: Basic, 1985).

10. For example, Judith Rollins, *Between Women: Domestics and Their Employers* (Philadelphia: Temple University Press, 1985); and Bonnie Thornton Dill, "'The Means to Put My Children Through': Child-Rearing Goals and Strategies among Black Female Domestic Servants," in *The Black Woman*, ed. LaFrances Rodgers-Rose (Beverly Hills, Calif.: Sage Publications, 1980), 107–23, report that Black domestic workers do not see themselves as being the devalued workers that their employers perceive and construct their own interpretations of the meaning of their work. For additional discussions of how Black women's consciousness is shaped by the material conditions they encounter, see Ladner (n. 2 above); Myers (n. 2 above); and Cheryl Townsend Gilkes, "'Together and in Harness': Women's

Traditions in the Sanctified Church," *Signs* 10, no. 4 (Summer 1985): 678–99. See also Marcia Westkott's discussion of consciousness as a sphere of freedom for women in "Feminist Criticism of the Social Sciences," *Harvard Educational Review* 49, no. 4 (1979): 422–30.

11. John Langston Gwaltney, *Drylongso: A Self-Portrait of Black America* (New York: Vintage, 1980), 4.

12. Ibid., 33.

13. Ibid., 88.

14. Ibid., 7.

15. Victoria Byerly, *Hard Times Cotton Mill Girls: Personal Histories of Womanhood and Poverty in the South* (New York: ILR Press, 1986), 134.

16. See Peter L. Berger and Thomas Luckmann, *The Social Construction of Reality* (New York: Doubleday, 1966), for a discussion of everyday thought and the role of experts in articulating specialized thought.

17. See Michael Omi and Howard Winant, *Racial Formation in the United States* (New York: Routledge & Kegan Paul, 1986), esp. 93.

18. In discussing standpoint epistemologies, Hartsock, in *Money, Sex, and Power*, notes that a standpoint is "achieved rather than obvious, a mediated rather than immediate understanding" (132).

19. See Scott (n. 2 above); and Hartsock, *Money, Sex, and Power* (n. 8 above).

20. Some readers may question how one determines whether the ideas of any given African-American woman are "feminist" and "Afrocentric." I offer the following working definitions. I agree with the general definition of feminist consciousness provided by Black feminist sociologist Deborah K. King: "Any purposes, goals, and activities which seek to enhance the potential of women, to ensure their liberty, afford them equal opportunity, and to permit and encourage their self-determination represent a feminist consciousness, even if they occur within a racial community" (in "Race, Class and Gender Salience in Black Women's Womanist Consciousness" [Dartmouth College, Department of Sociology, Hanover, N.H., 1987, typescript], 22). To be Black or Afrocentric, such thought must not only reflect a similar concern for the self-determination of African-American people, but must in some way draw upon key elements of an Afrocentric tradition as well.

21. The Eurocentric masculinist process is defined here as the institutions, paradigms, and any elements of the knowledge-validation procedure controlled by white males and whose purpose is to represent a white male standpoint. While this process represents the interest of powerful white males, various dimensions of the process are not necessarily managed by white males themselves.

22. Karl Mannheim, *Ideology and Utopia: An Introduction to the Sociology of Knowledge* (New York: Harcourt, Brace, 1936, 1954), 276.

23. The knowledge-validation model used in this essay is taken from Michael Mulkay, *Science and the Sociology of Knowledge* (Boston: Allen & Unwin, 1979). For a general discussion of the structure of knowledge, see Thomas Kuhn, *The Structure of Scientific Revolutions* (Chicago: University of Chicago Press, 1962).

24. For analyses of the content and functions of images of Black female inferiority, see Mac King. "The Politics of Sexual Stereotypes," *Black Scholar* 4, nos. 6–7 (1973): 12–23; Cheryl Townsend Gilkes, "From Slavery to Social Welfare: Racism and the Control of Black Women," in *Class, Race, and Sex: The Dynamics of Control*, ed. Amy Smerdlow and Helen Lessinger (Boston: G. K. Hall, 1981), 288–300; and Elizabeth Higginbotham, "Two Representative Issues in Contemporary Sociological Work on Black Women," in *But Some of Us Are Brave*, ed. Gloria T. Hull, Patricia Bell Scott, and Barbara Smith (Old Westbury, N.Y.: Feminist Press, 1982).

25. Kuhn.

26. Evelyn Fox Keller, *Reflections on Gender and Science* (New Haven, Conn.: Yale University Press, 1985), 167.

27. Maxine Baca Zinn, Lynn Weber Cannon, Elizabeth Higginbotham, and Bonnie Thornton Dill, "The Cost of Exclusionary Practices in Women's Studies," *Signs* 11, no. 2 (Winter 1986): 290–303.

28. Berger and Luckmann (n. 16 above) note that if an outsider group, in this case African-American women, recognizes that the insider group, namely, white men, requires special privileges from the larger society,

a special problem arises of keeping the outsiders out and at the same time having them acknowledge the legitimacy of this procedure. Accepting a few "safe" outsiders is one way of addressing this legitimation problem. Collins's discussion (n. 3 above) of Black women as "outsiders within" addresses this issue. Other relevant works include Franz Fanon's analysis of the role of the national middle class in maintaining colonial systems, *The Wretched of the Earth* (New York: Grove, 1963); and William Tabb's discussion of the use of "bright natives" in controlling African-American communities, *The Political Economy of the Black Ghetto* (New York: Norton, 1970).

29. While I have been describing Eurocentric masculinist approaches as a single process, there are many schools of thought or paradigms subsumed under this one process. Positivism represents one such paradigm. See Harding (n. 8 above) for an overview and critique of this literature. The following discussion depends heavily on Jaggar (n. 8 above), 355–58.

30. Jaggar, 356.

31. See Keller, especially her analysis of static autonomy and its relation to objectivity (67–126).

32. Ironically, researchers must "objectify" themselves to achieve this lack of bias. See Arlie Russell Hochschild, "The Sociology of Feeling and Emotion: Selected Possibilities," in *Another Voice: Feminist Perspectives on Social Life and Social Science*, ed. Marcia Millman and Rosabeth Kanter (Garden City, N.Y.: Anchor, 1975), 280–307. Also, see Jaggar.

33. See Norma Haan, Robert Bellah, Paul Rabinow, and William Sullivan, eds., *Social Science as Moral Inquiry* (New York: Columbia University Press, 1983), esp. Michelle Z. Rosaldo's "Moral/Analytic Dilemmas Posed by the Intersection of Feminism and Social Science." 76–96; and Robert Bellah's "The Ethical Aims of Social Inquiry," 360–81.

34. Janice Moulton. "A Paradigm of Philosophy: The Adversary Method," in Harding and Hintikka, eds. (n. 8 above)., 149–64.

35. For detailed discussions of the Afrocentric worldview, see John S. Mbiti, *African Religions and Philosophy* (London: Heinemann, 1969); Dominique Zahan, *The Religion, Spirituality, and Thought of Traditional Africa* (Chicago: University of Chicago Press, 1979); and Mechal Sobel, *Trabelin' On: The Slave Journey to an Afro-Baptist Faith* (Westport, Conn.: Greenwood Press, 1979), 1–76.

36. For representative works applying these concepts to African-American culture, see Niara Sudarkasa, "Interpreting the African Heritage in Afro-American Family Organization," in *Black Families*, ed. Harriette Pipes McAdoo (Beverly Hills, Calif.: Sage, 1981); Henry H. Mitchell and Nicholas Cooper Lewter, *Soul Theology: The Heart of American Black Culture* (San Francisco: Harper & Row, 1986); Robert Farris Thompson, *Flash of the Spirit: African and Afro-American Art and Philosophy* (New York: Vintage, 1983); and Ortiz M. Walton, "Comparative Analysis of the African and the Western Aesthetics," in *The Black Aesthetic*, ed. Addison Gayle (Garden City, N.Y.: Doubleday, 1971). 154–64.

37. One of the best discussions of an Afrocentric epistemology is offered by James E. Turner, "Foreword: Africana Studies and Epistemology; a Discourse in the Sociology of Knowledge," in *The Next Decade: Theoretical and Research Issues in Africana Studies*, ed. James E. Turner (Ithaca, N.Y.: Cornell University Africana Studies and Research Center, 1984), v–xxv. See also Vernon Dixon, "World Views and Research Methodology," summarized in Harding (n. 8 above), 170.

38. See Hester Eisenstein, *Contemporary Feminist Thought* (Boston: G.K. Hall, 1983). Nancy Hartsock's *Money, Sex, and Power* (n. 8 above), 145–209, offers a particularly insightful analysis of women's oppression.

39. For discussions of feminist consciousness, see Dorothy Smith, "A Sociology for Women," in *The Prism of Sex: Essays in the Sociology of Knowledge*, ed. Julia A. Sherman and Evelyn T. Beck (Madison: University of Wisconsin Press, 1979); and Michelle Z. Rosaldo, "Women, Culture, and Society: A Theoretical Overview," in *Woman, Culture, and Society*, ed. Michelle Z. Rosaldo and Louise Lamphere (Stanford, Calif.: Stanford University Press, 1974), 17–42. Feminist epistemologies are surveyed by Jaggar (n. 8 above).

40. One significant difference between Afrocentric and feminist standpoints is that much of what is termed women's culture is, unlike African-American culture, created in the context of and produced by oppression. Those who argue for a women's culture are electing to value, rather than denigrate, those traits associated with females in white patriarchal societies. While this choice is important, it is not the same as identifying an independent, historic culture associated with a society. I am indebted to Deborah K. King for this point.

41. Critiques of the Eurocentric masculinist knowledge-validation process by both Africanist and feminist scholars illustrate this point. What one group labels "white" and "Eurocentric," the other describes as "male-dominated" and "masculinist." Although he does not emphasize its patriarchal and racist features, Morris Berman's *The Reenchantment of the World* (New York: Bantam, 1981) provides a historical discussion of Western thought. Afrocentric analyses of this same process can be found in Molefi Kete Asante, "International/Intercultural Relations," in *Contemporary Black Thought*, ed. Molefi Kete Asante and Abdulai S. Vandi (Beverly Hills, Calif.: Sage, 1980), 43–58; and Dona Richards, "European Mythology: The Ideology of 'Progress,'" in Asante and Vandi, eds., 59–79. For feminist analyses, see Hartsock, *Money, Sex, and Power*. Harding also discusses this similarity (see chap. 7, "Other 'Others' and Fractured Identities: Issues for Epistemologists," 163–96).

42. Harding, 166.

43. D. King (n. 20 above).

44. Bonnie Thornton Dill, "The Dialectics of Black Womanhood," *Signs* 4, no. 3 (Spring 1979): 543–55.

45. One implication of standpoint approaches is that the more subordinate the group, the purer the vision of the oppressed group. This is an outcome of the origins of standpoint approaches in Marxist social theory, itself a dualistic analysis of social structure. Because such approaches rely on quantifying and ranking human oppressions—familiar tenets of positivist approaches—they are rejected by Blacks and feminists alike. See Harding (n. 8 above) for a discussion of this point. See also Elizabeth V. Spelman's discussion of the fallacy of additive oppression in "Theories of Race and Gender: The Erasure of Black Women," *Quest* 5, no. 4 (1982): 36–62.

46. Class differences among Black women may be marked. For example, see Paula Giddings's analysis (n. 9 above) of the role of social class in shaping Black women's political activism; or Elizabeth Higginbotham's study of the effects of social class in Black women's college attendance in "Race and Class Barriers to Black Women's College Attendance," *Journal of Ethnic Studies* 13, no. 1 (1985): 89–107. Those African-American women who have experienced the greatest degree of convergence of race, class, and gender oppression may be in a better position to recognize and use an alternative epistemology.

47. Gwaltney (n. 11 above), 83.

48. William L. Andrews, *Sisters of the Spirit: Three Black Women's Autobiographies of the Nineteenth Century* (Bloomington: Indiana University Press, 1986), 85.

49. Gwaltney, 147.

50. Geneva Smitherman, *Talkin and Testifyin: The Language of Black America* (Detroit: Wayne State University Press, 1986), 76.

51. Gwaltney, 68.

52. Ibid., 7.

53. Ibid., 27, 33.

54. Elsa Barkley Brown, "Hearing Our Mothers' Lives" (paper presented at the Fifteenth Anniversary Faculty Lecture Series, African-American and African Studies, Emory University, Atlanta, 1986).

55. Ladner (n. 2 above).

56. Mitchell and Lewter (n. 36 above). The use of the narrative approach in African-American theology exemplifies an inductive system of logic alternately called "folk wisdom" or a survival-based, need-oriented method of assessing knowledge claims.

57. (Missing text).

58. June Jordan, *On Call: Political Essays* (Boston: South End Press, 1985), 26.

59. Mary Belenky, Blythe Clinchy, Nancy Goldberger, and Jill Tarule, *Women's Ways of Knowing* (New York: Basic, 1986), 113.

60. Hartsock, *Money, Sex and Power* (n. 8 above), 237; and Nancy Chodorow, *The Reproduction of Mothering* (Berkeley and Los Angeles: University of California Press, 1978).

61. Dorothy Smith, *The Everyday World as Problematic* (Boston: Northeastern University Press, 1987).

62. Byerly (n. 15 above), 198.

63. For Black women's centrality in the family, see Steady (n. 1 above); Ladner (n. 2 above); Brown (n. 54 above); and McAdoo, ed. (n. 36 above). See Gilkes, "'Together and in Harness'" (n. 10 above), for Black women in the church; and chap. 4 of Deborah Gray White, *Ar'n't I a Woman? Female Slaves in the Plantation South* (New York: Norton, 1985). See also Gloria Joseph, "Black Mothers and Daughters: Their Roles and Functions in American Society," in *Common Differences: Conflicts in Black and White Feminist Perspectives*, ed. Gloria Joseph and Jill Lewis (Garden City, N.Y.: Anchor, 1981), 75–126. Even though Black women play essential roles in Black families and Black churches, these institutions are not free from sexism.

64. As Belenky et al. note, "Unlike the eye, the ear requires closeness between subject and object. Unlike seeing, speaking and listening suggest dialogue and interaction" (18).

65. Thomas Kochman, *Black and White: Styles in Conflict* (Chicago: University of Chicago Press, 1981); and Smitherman (n. 50 above).

66. Gwaltney (n. 11 above), 32.

67. Smitherman, 108.

68. Kochman, 28.

69. Jordan (n. 58 above), 129.

70. Claudia Tate, *Black Women Writers at Work* (New York: Continuum, 1983), 91.

71. Ibid., 92.

72. Alice Walker, *In Search of Our Mothers' Gardens* (New York: Harcourt Brace Jovanovich, 1974), 84.

73. Keller (n. 26 above); Chodorow (n. 60 above).

74. Belenky et al. (n. 59 above), 16.

75. Thomas Webber, *Deep Like the Rivers* (New York: Norton, 1978), 127.

76. In her discussion of the West African Sacred Cosmos, Mechal Sobel (n. 35 above) notes that Nyam, a root word in many West African languages, connotes an enduring spirit, power, or energy possessed by all life. In spite of the pervasiveness of this key concept in African humanism, its definition remains elusive. She points out, "Every individual analyzing the various Sacred Cosmos of West Africa has recognized the reality of this force, but no one has yet adequately translated this concept into Western terms" (13).

77. For discussions of personal expressiveness in African-American culture, see Smitherman (n. 50 above); Kochman (n. 65 above), esp. chap. 9; and Mitchell and Lewter (n. 36 above).

78. Gwaltney (n. 11 above), 228.

79. For feminist analyses of the subordination of emotion in Western culture, see Hochschild (n. 32 above); and Chodorow.

80. Tate (n. 70 above), 156.

81. Gwaltney, 11.

82. Smitherman, 135 and 137.

83. Belenky et al. (n. 59 above), 100–130.

84. Ibid., 119.

85. See Ibid., 52–75, for a discussion of inner voice and its role in women's cognitive styles. Regarding empathy, Belenky et al. note: "Connected knowers begin with an interest in the facts of other people's lives, but they gradually shift the focus to other people's ways of thinking. . . . It is the form rather than the content of knowing that is central. . . . Connected learners learn through empathy" (115).

86. Andrews (n. 48 above), 98.

87. Kochman (n. 65 above), 20 and 25.

88. Ibid, 23.

89. The sizable proportion of ministers among Black political leaders illustrates the importance of ethics in African-American communities.

90. Belenky et al. discuss a similar situation. They note, "People could critique each other's work in this class and accept each other's criticisms because members of the group shared a similar experience. . . . Authority in connected knowing rests not on power or status or certification but on commonality of experience" (118).

91. Carol Gilligan, *In a Different Voice* (Cambridge, Mass.: Harvard University Press, 1982). Carol Stack critiques Gilligan's model by arguing that African-Americans invoke a similar model of moral development to that used by women (see "The Culture of Gender: Women and Men of Color," *Signs* 11, no. 2 [Winter 1986]: 321–24). Another difficulty with Gilligan's work concerns the homogeneity of the subjects whom she studied.

92. Black men, white women, and members of other race, class, and gender groups should be encouraged to interpret, teach, and critique the Black feminist thought produced by African-American women.

93. Walker (n. 72 above), 91.

94. Gwaltney (n. 11 above), 7.

95. Jordan (n. 58 above), 130.

96. Collins (n. 3 above).

97. This point addresses the question of relativity in the sociology of knowledge and offers a way of regulating competing knowledge claims.

Creating the Conditions for Cultural Democracy in the Classroom

Antonia Darder

But democracy, by definition, cannot mean merely that an unskilled worker can become skilled. It must mean that every "citizen" can "govern" and that society places him [or her] in a general condition to achieve this.

Antonio Gramsci
Selections from Prison Notebooks

Cultural democracy in the classroom cannot be discussed, within the context of a critical bicultural pedagogy, outside of the theoretical dimensions that function to position teachers with respect to their educational practice. Gramsci's words support a theory of cultural democracy that not only locates bicultural students within a historical and cultural context, but also addresses questions related to moral and political agency within the process of their schooling and the course of their everyday lives. In short, this critical view suggests that, prior to any engagement with instrumental questions of practice, educators must delve rigorously into those specific theoretical issues that are fundamental to the establishment of a culturally democratic foundation for a critical bicultural pedagogy in the classroom.

This view is also consistent with that of Freire (1970) and other critical educational theorists who emphatically express that any liberatory pedagogy cannot represent a recipe for classroom practice. Rather, it is meant to provide a set of critical educational principles that can guide and support teachers' critical engagement with the forces determining the reality of classroom life. Informed by this tradition, a critical foundation for bicultural education must not be presented in the form of models for duplication or how-to instruction manuals. One of the most important reasons for this thinking is expressed by Simon (1988), who speaks eloquently to the notion that all educational practice must emerge from the contextual relationships defined by the very conditions existing at any given moment within the classroom. Such a practice "is at root contextual and conditional. A critical pedagogy can only be concretely discussed from within a particular 'point of practice,' from within a specific time and place, and within a particular theme" (p. 1).

Hence, efforts to instrumentalize or operationalize a critical perspective outside the context in which it is to function fails to engage with the historical, cultural, and dialogical principles that are essential to a critical learning environment. In addition, this approach also ignores that, prior to the development of practice, there are cultural and ideological assumptions at work determining how educators define the purpose of education, their role, and the role of their students in the process of schooling. The belief that teachers must be provided with "canned" curriculum to ensure their success fails to acknowledge the creative potential of educators to grapple effectively with the multiplicity of contexts that they find in their classrooms and to shape environments according to the lived experiences and actual educational needs of their students.

Teacher education programs are notorious for reducing the role of teachers to that of technicians. Instead of empowering teachers by assisting them to develop a critical understanding of their purpose as educators, most programs foster a dependency on predefined curriculum, outdated classroom strategies and techniques, and traditionally rigid classroom environments that position not only students but teachers as well into physically and intellectually oppressive situations. This occurs to such a degree that few public school teachers are able to envision their practice outside the scope of barren classroom settings, lifeless instructional packages, bland textbooks, standardized tests, and the use of meritocratic systems for student performance evaluation.

Educators of bicultural students must recognize the manner in which these conditions work to disempower both teachers and students in American public schools. Teachers can then begin to refuse the role of technicians in their practice as educators as they struggle together to abandon their dependency on traditional classroom artifacts. This represents an essential step if teachers are to educate students of color to discover themselves and their potential within an environment that permits them to interact with what they know to be their world. This is particularly important, given the fact that values supporting cultural diversity, social struggle, and human rights are so often absent from the curricular materials teachers are forced to use in most public schools.

A critical bicultural pedagogy that is built on a foundation of cultural democracy represents a missing educational discourse in the preparation and practice of most public school teachers. As discussed in Chapter 3, the many different forms in which the bicultural experience manifests itself in American life seldom find their way into traditional classroom settings. Instead, bicultural experiences remain, for the most part, hidden within the reinforced silence of students of color. If the voices of difference are to find a place in the everyday interactions of public schools, educators of bicultural students must create the conditions for all students to experience an ongoing process of culturally democratic life. With this in mind, this chapter will address the major questions and issues that educators face in their efforts to pave the way for a critical bicultural pedagogy.

The Question of Language

It is impossible to consider any form of education—or even human existence—without first considering the impact of language on our lives. Language must be recognized as one of the most significant human resources; it functions in a multitude of ways to affirm, contradict, negotiate, challenge, transform, and empower particular cultural and ideological beliefs and practices. Language constitutes one of the most powerful media for transmitting our personal histories and social realities, as well as for thinking and shaping the world (Cole & Scribner, 1974). Language is essential to the process of dialogue, to the development of meaning, and to the production of knowledge. From the context of its emancipatory potential, language must be understood as a dialectical phenomenon that links its very existence and meaning to the lived experiences of the language community and constitutes a major cornerstone for the development of voice.

The question of language must also be addressed within the context of a terrain of struggle that is central to our efforts to transform traditional educational structures that historically have failed bicultural students. In doing so, it is essential that we do not fall into totalizing theoretical traps—ignoring that human beings are in fact able to appropriate a multitude of linguistic forms and utilize them in critical and emancipatory ways. It is simplistic and to our detriment as educators of bicultural students to accept the notion that any one particular form of language (i.e., "standard" English), in and of itself, constitutes a totalizing dominant or subordinate force, as it is unrealistic to believe that simply utilizing a student's primary language (e.g., Spanish, Ebonics, etc.) guarantees that a student's emancipatory interests are being addressed. Consequently, the question of language in the classroom constitutes one of the most complex and multifaceted issues that educators of bicultural students must be prepared to address in the course of their practice.

The complexity of language and its relationship not only to how students produce knowledge but also to how language shapes their world represent a major pedagogical concern for all educational settings. In public schools, teachers can begin to address this complexity by incorporating activities based on the languages their students bring into the classroom. In this way, the familiar language can function as a significant starting point from which bicultural students can engage with the foreign and unknown elements that comprise significant portions of the required curriculum. An example of how teachers might do this with younger students is to develop language instruction and activities with their student that give them the opportunity to bring the home language into the context of the classroom. This can be done by having students and parents introduce their languages through songs, stories, games, and other such activities. Giving attention to the home language raises it to a place of dignity and respect, rather than permitting it to become a source of humiliation and shame for bicultural students. It should be noted that the introduction of different languages must also be accompanied by critical dialogues that help students examine prevailing social attitudes and biases about language differences. These discussions can assist students to consider typical discriminatory responses to such situations as when people speak with foreign accents, or when people do not understand the language being spoken. In addition, students from similar cultural and language communities can be encouraged and made to feel comfortable when they converse together in their primary language as part of the classroom experience. Such opportunities support the development of voice, as well as affirm the bicultural experience of students of color. Bell Hooks addresses this point:

> Learning to listen to different voices, hearing different speech challenges the notion that we must all assimilate—share a single similar talk—in educational institutions. Language reflects the culture from which we emerge. To deny ourselves daily use of speech patterns that are common and familiar, that embody the unique and distinctive aspect of our self is one of the ways we become estranged and alienated from our past. It is important for us to have as many languages on hand as we can know or learn. It is important for those of us who are Black, who speak in particular patois as well as standard English, to express ourselves in both ways. (Hooks, 1989, pp. 79–80)

With older students, the issue of language can be addressed in more complex terms. As mentioned previously, bicultural students must find opportunities to engage in classroom dialogues and activities that permit them to explore the meaning of their lived experiences through the familiarity of their own language. But also important to their development of social consciousness and their process of conscientization is the awareness of how language and power intersect in ways that include or exclude students of color from particular social relationships. Although it is paramount that bicultural students fully develop and strengthen their bicultural voices (as Puerto Ricans, Chicanos, African-Americans, etc.) through their interactions with others in their own communities, it is also imperative that, in order to understand more fully the impact of language on social structures and practices, students of color enter into critical dialogues with those outside their cultural communities. Through the process of these cross-cultural dialogues, students come to better recognize for themselves the manner in which language works to define who they are, and how language as a tool can assist them to explore critically those possibilities that have remained hidden and out of their reach.

It is significant for teachers to recognize that it is more common for bicultural students to reflect on these issues and to express themselves predominantly through a *language of practice*—a highly pragmatic language that is primarily rooted in notions of common sense and concrete experiences. Although this process represents a necessary step in the empowerment of bicultural students, their transformative potential can only be extended when they are able to unite practice with theory, or when they are able to recognize themselves as critical beings who are constantly moving between concrete and abstract representations of experiences that influence how they make decisions about their actions in the world.

In order to create the conditions for students to determine their own lives genuinely within a multiplicity of discourses, teachers must introduce their students to the *language of theory*. The language of theory constitutes a critical language of social analysis that is produced through human efforts to understand how individuals reflect and interpret their experiences and, as a result, how they shape and are shaped by their world. Although it is a language generally connected to the realm of abstract thinking, its fundamental function of praxis cannot be fulfilled unless it is linked to the concrete experiences and practices of everyday life. Such language also encourages the use of more precise and specific linguistic representations of experience than is generally expected—or even necessary—in the course of everyday practice. Challenging bicultural students to engage openly with the language of theory and to understand better its impact on their lives can awaken them to the tremendous potential available to them as social agents.

At this point it is significant to note that what has been traditionally considered theoretical language has also been—almost exclusively—controlled and governed by those who have held power in academic circles: namely, elite, White males. As a result, the greatest number of formal theoretical texts considered as legitimate knowledge, reflect conservative, Eurocentric, patriarchal notions of the world. Generally speaking, these texts uniformly support assumptions that reinforce racism, classism and sexism, while written in such a way as to justify claims of neutrality and objectivity.

In their efforts to resist conservative forms of language domination, many educators disengage from all forms of theoretical language, thereby relegating the language of theory exclusively to a sphere of domination. Not surprisingly, this uncritical view comes dangerously close to being little more than a less recognized form of anti-intellectualism. The greatest danger is that it abandons the struggle for a liberatory language of theory by its refusal to challenge academic work that perpetuates all forms of domination and to assert the need for multiple forms of theoretical language rooted in culturally diverse perspectives and a variety of styles (Hooks, 1989).

From another standpoint, efforts to resist the inequality and alienation reinforced by traditional uses of theoretical language can result in protective mechanisms of resistance among students of color, and this too can give rise to unintentional forms of anti-intellectualism. Given the nature of such responses, it is not unusual for bicultural students, who have suffered the negative impact of domination in their lives, to reject indiscriminately those cultural forms and social institutions that they come to associate with hostility and alienation. As a consequence, it is no simple task to challenge attitudes of anti-intellectualism in the classroom. To do so requires that teachers recognize that attitudes of resistance manifested by students of color are very often rooted in legitimate fears and subsequent responses to support community survival. In addition, these fears and responses are strongly fostered by a *legacy of resistance*, which is reinforced daily through their personal and institutional relationships. These relationships include interactions with their parents, who often harbor unspoken fears that they may lose their children forever if they should become educated. Hooks describes this parental fear:

> They feared what college education might do to their children's minds even as they unenthusiastically acknowledged its importance. . . . No wonder our working class parents from poor backgrounds feared our entry into such a world, intuiting perhaps that we might learn to be ashamed of where we had come from, that we might never return home, or come back only to lord it over them. (Hooks, 1989, pp. 74–75)

Also included among these interactions are relationships with many of their teachers, who themselves have never successfully moved beyond the language of practice. Consequently, it is not unusual for many teachers, when asked to engage with the language of theory, to respond by feeling almost as fearful, intimidated, and disempowered as their students. Simon (forthcoming) addresses this *fear of theory* among teachers who are graduate students in his classes: "A fear of theory [is] more often expressed by students who have had to struggle for acceptance and recognition within the dominant institutions which define the terrain of everyday life. These are students whose lives have been lived within the prescriptive and marginalizing effects of power inscribed in relations of class, gender, ethnicity, race and sexual preference" (p. 7).

These responses by teachers are often used by teacher preparation programs around the country to justify astute arguments against the widespread use of theoretical language. More often than not, these arguments are shaped by a lack of critical engagement with the emancipatory potential of language and by a reproductive ideology that reduces students to simple objects who are somehow mystically stripped of all dignity and voice by expecting them to engage in disciplined critical thought and to address abstract concepts related to practice in more precise ways. These complaints are generally accompanied by a call for more visual language, more anecdotal accounts, or more how-to discussions. In essence, such requests for the predominant use of a language of practice inadvertently perpetuate a nondialectical and dichotomized view of theory and erode the teacher's potential for creative social action. If one listens carefully between the lines of this pragmatic educational discourse, it echoes a "false generosity of paternalism" (Freire, 1970) built on assumptions that arise from a lack of faith in the ability of oppressed groups to appropriate, transform, and utilize the language of theory in a liberatory fashion.

Educators in bicultural communities must grapple with their own language biases and prejudices beyond simply the issue of language differences, and work to encounter the deep frustrations and anxieties related to their fear of theory. This significant area of concern also needs to be adequately addressed by teacher preparation programs. This is particularly true for those programs that have traditionally neglected or ignored altogether this fundamental issue, as evidenced by curricula that place a greater imphasis on numerous predefined ways to teach the standard subjects rather than on exploring the complexity inherent in the human dynamics of creating meaning and producing knowledge in the classroom.

Language represents one of the most significant educational tools in our struggle for cultural democracy in the public schools. It is intimately linked to the struggle for voice, and so is essential to our struggle for liberation. Through language we not only define our position in society, but we also use that language to define ourselves as subjects in our world. Herein lies one of the most important goals for a critical bicultural pedagogy: creating the conditions for the voices of difference to find their way to the center of the dialogical process, rather than to remain forever silent or at the fringes of American classroom life.

The Question of Authority

The question of authority represents one of the most heated areas of contention among major educational theorists in this country. This should not be surprising, for the manner in which we conceptualize authority truly represents a necessary precondition for the manner in which we define ourselves, our work, and our very lives—so much so that it is impossible to discuss cultural democracy in the classroom without addressing the issues that directly stem from this question.

In order to engage critically with the notion of authority, it is vital that teachers come to understand that authority does not automatically equal authoritarianism. Authority, within the context of a critical bicultural pedagogy, is intimately linked to the manner in which teachers exercise control, direct, influence, and make decisions about what is actually to take place in their classrooms. To engage with the question of authority in a liberatory fashion clearly requires an understanding of power and how power is used to construct relationships, define truth, and create social conditions that can potentially either subordinate or empower bicultural students. Hence, authority must be understood as a dialectical "terrain of legitimation and struggle," rather than simply as an absolute, hierarchical, and totalizing force (Giroux, 1988b).

Efforts to examine the question of authority in the classroom also require teachers to address their personal contradictions related to how they formulate ideas of control, power, and authority in their own lives. This is particularly necessary given the manner in which teachers in public schools are consistently subject to administrative dictates and school conditions that undermine their power and authority. As teachers struggle together to challenge their conflicts and contradictions in this area, they are more able to build environments that support an emancipatory view of authority, stimulating their students to rethink critically their values, ideas, and actions in relation to the consequences these might have on themselves and others.

Although the question of authority is seldom discussed in liberatory terms by either conservative or liberal educators, it is essential that it be critically addressed in teacher preparation programs. As mentioned above, it is difficult for teachers to address the issue of authority if they themselves hold uncritical, conflicting, and contradictory attitudes about power and its relationship to human organization. Such attitudes are apparent in prevailing commonsense beliefs about the nature of power. While conservative educators are more likely to see power as a positive force that works to maintain order, earn respect, and "get the job done," liberals—and even many radical educators—are more prone to believe that "power corrupts" and that, despite human efforts, power ultimately leads to destruction. As a consequence, power is commonly perceived either as an absolute force for good, or else as an evil or negative force that dehumanizes and divests the individual's capacity for justice and solidarity with others. Understanding how these views of power are enmeshed in the contradictory thinking of teachers can help to shed light on the inadequacy and helplessness that so many educators express. This is of particular concern, given the fact that so many liberal and radical educators who hold negative assumptions related to power also speak to the necessity of *empowering* students, communities, and teachers alike.

The contradictory assumptions that underscore the question of authority also function to perpetuate the status quo, through the manner in which they sabotage, limit, and distort teachers' perceptions of classroom authority and their ability to alter the conditions they find in public schools. Such teachers, who do not possess a dialectical view of authority, generally lack the critical criteria to challenge attitudes, beliefs, and actions that perpetuate social injustice. In light of this, authority can be more readily understood in terms of its potential to uphold those emancipatory categories essential to the foundation of critical democratic life.

In our efforts to address this dimension, it must be explained that contradictory assumptions of authority cannot be deconstructed by simply utilizing a language of practice. The task of challenging society's contradictions requires educators to delve fearlessly into both the abstract and concrete experiences that unite to inform the theoretical realm. Through uniting their critical reflections of practice with theory, teachers come to discover the manner in which distorted views of power inform those classroom practices that reinforce undercurrents of oppression, perpetuating conditions that marginalize and alienate students of color.

The authoritarian nature of a conservative view of teacher authority is often hidden beneath the guise of traditional notions of respect, which can incorporate objective, instrumental, and hierarchical relationships that support various forms of oppressive educational practices at the expense of student voice. On the other hand, the oppressive impact of the liberal view of teacher authority, which all but disengages with questions of authority, often functions in an equally perverse manner. Hidden under the values of subjectivity, individualism, and intentionality, this view easily deteriorates into a crass relativism, asserting that all expressed values and ideas are deserving of equal time (Giroux, 1981). This is put into practice to the extent that some teachers proudly proclaim that they always consider all ideas generated by their students as equal, irrespective of personal histories, ideologies, or cultural differences—thus professing a specious notion of shared power. Although this perspective may ring true when entertained exclusively in the language of practice, theoretically it reflects an uncritical disengagement with issues related to social forms of domination and the manner in which ideas are generated and informed by particular interest that silence and oppress students from subordinate groups. Therefore it is fraudulent to pretend that a teacher does not possess the authority and power over students to determine how the classroom will be governed; and it is an act of irresponsibility for teachers to abdicate their duty to challenge critically the oppressive nature of student ideas when these ideas constitute acts of racism, sexism, classism, or other forms of psychological violence that attack the dignity and self-worth of students of color.

Unlike traditional views on teacher authority, an emancipatory view of authority suggests that, although teachers hold knowledge that is considered to render them prepared to enter the classroom, they must come to recognize that knowledge as a historical and cultural product is forever in a creative state of partiality. And, as a consequence, all forms of discourse represent only one small piece of the larger puzzle that constitutes all possible knowledge at any given moment in time. Hence, all forms of knowledge must be open for question, examination, and critique by and with students in the process of learning. In this way, teachers actively use their authority to create the conditions for a critical transformation of consciousness that takes place in the process of the interaction of teacher, students, and the knowledge they produce together. Grounded in criteria informed by a liberatory vision of life, teachers embrace the notion of authority in the interest of cultural democracy, rather than against it.

Redefining Fairness and Equality

If American public schools are to establish classroom environments that are culturally democratic, teachers will have to undertake a critical analysis of what has been traditionally defined as *fair and equal*. Just as the principles of democracy have so often been reduced to numerical head-counts and majority rule, concepts of fairness and equality have also been reduced to such quantifiable forms. Therefore, it is not unusual to hear teachers across the country express the belief that fair-and-equal is equivalent to providing the same quantity and quality of goods to all students across the board, irrespective of differences in social privilege and economic entitlement.

Clearly inherent in this perspective of fair-and-equal is the elimination of any transformative impact that these principles might have on the lives of disenfranchised students. The consequence in public schools is that students from the dominant culture who enter with major social and economic advantages receive as much—and at times even more—than students from subordinate cultures who arrive with far fewer social advantages. In an analysis of resource distribution among students in public schools, it is unquestionably apparent that poor children, who receive the least at home, receive the least from public education (Kozol, 1990). This painfully reminds us that the American educational system has little to do with cultivating equality. For if equality was, in fact, a part of the philosophical vision of education, the educational system would prioritize its resources in such a manner as to ensure that the majority of students were placed in settings where they could achieve successfully. Under such conditions, students from disenfranchised communities who require more educational opportunities by way of teacher contact, educational materials, nutritional support, and health care would receive more, while those students who arrive with greater privileges and with many more resources already in place would receive less.

Instead, what we find in most schools is the opposite. Students from the dominant culture who excel because they have been raised in homes that can provide them with the social, economic, and cultural capital necessary to meet the elitist and ethnocentric standards of American schools enjoy greater advantages and more positive regard than those from disenfranchised communities who must consistently struggle to succeed under social conditions working to their detriment. For decades it has been well documented that students from the dominant culture, who are raised in environments of privilege, score higher on standardized examinations. Hence, these students are perceived as superior when compared to most bicultural students. In addition, many of these superior students are also considered by public schools to be exhibiting mentally gifted abilities, while the majority of students of color are stigmatized and shamed by assignments into basic and remedial classes. This mentally gifted status has then been used as a justifiable rationale for appropriating additional resources to the already privileged—a group that just happens to include very few working-class students of color.

The consequence here is that the majority of bicultural students who are in need of greater school resources and educational opportunities find themselves in less challenging and less stimulating environments—environments that operate under the assumption that the students themselves, their parents, and their culture are to blame for their deficiency, while ignoring the deficiencies of a larger social caste system that replicates itself in public schools. Efforts by the White House in the past decade have merely functioned to make the situation worse. Plans that had been made to equalize school funding among districts have been replaced by a major reduction of funding to educational programs and an emphasis on building student motivation and self-control. Jonathan Kozol suggests that the consequences of tougher conservative rhetoric and more severe demands have led to further discrimination toward disenfranchised students:

> Higher standards, in the absence of authentic educative opportunities in early years, function as a punitive attack on those who have been cheated since their infancy. Effectively, we now ask more of those to whom we now give less. Earlier testing for schoolchildren is prescribed. Those who fail are penalized by being held back from promotion and by being slotted into lower tracks where they cannot impede the progress of more privileged children. Those who disrupt classroom discipline are not placed in smaller classes with more patient teachers; instead, at a certain point, they are expelled—even if this means expulsion of a quarter of all pupils in school. (Kozol, 1990, p. 52).

Buried deep within traditional institutional views of fairness and equality is a stubborn refusal to engage with the reality of social conditions that marginalize students of color in this country. As a consequence, not only are bicultural students perceived as somehow less intelligent and therefore less deserving than middle-class students from the dominant culture, but also they are taught through their interactions with the system to perceive themselves in this way. If conditions in public schools are to change, teachers must openly challenge traditional views of fairness and equality and expose how these have functioned to reinforce notions of entitlement and privilege based on a doctrine of Social Darwinism that has proven to be incompatible with any emancipatory vision of social justice and equality.

The Use of Multicultural Curriculum

When educators first begin to think about how they can meet the needs of students of color, one of the most common places to begin is by bringing traditional cultural objects and symbols into the classroom. In fact, most multicultural curricula place a major emphasis on such cultural artifacts because they can be easily seen, manipulated, and quantified, although they ignore the more complex subjectivities of cultural values, belief systems, and traditions that inform the production of such cultural forms. Also problematic are depictions of cultural images and symbols that promote Eurocentric interpretations of cultural groups—depictions that function to dissolve cultural differences and reinforce mainstream expectations of assimilation. As a consequence, these traditional multicultural approaches operate to the detriment of students of color because they fail to respect and affirm their cultural differences and to help them understand the social and political implications of growing up bicultural in American society.

This is not to imply that bicultural students should not be exposed to curriculum that seeks to present cultural artifacts affirming their cultural traditions and experiences, but rather to emphasize that such multicultural materials and activities do not, in and of themselves, ensure that a culturally democratic process is at work. As mentioned above, this is in fact the case with most traditional efforts to promote cultural diversity. And many situations exist in which students are presented with games, food, stories, language, music, and other cultural forms in such a way as to strip these expressions of intent by reducing them to mere objects disembodied from their cultural meaning.

In order to prevent such an outcome, educators must become more critical not only of the actual curriculum they bring into the classroom, but also of the philosophical beliefs that inform their practice. First, they can begin to assess carefully their personal assumptions, prejudices, and biases related to issues of culture. Since it is far more common for teachers to think of themselves as neutral and unbiased toward all students, many racist, classist, and sexist attitudes and behaviors are most often disguised by faulty common-sense assumptions utilized extensively to assess student academic performance or classroom behavior. For example, most teachers still retain notions of culture that reflect color-blind or melting-pot assumptions and a bootstrap mentality. Simply put, these teachers believe that all people are the same in spite of race or culture, that the United States is a place where all cultures have (or should have) melted together to form one culture, and that anyone who wants to succeed *can* succeed, irrespective of social or economic circumstances.

Unfortunately these assumptions work to undermine the emancipatory potential of multicultural curricula. This is primarily because, when educators engage with issues related to cultural diversity based on these beliefs, they are unable accurately to address cultural issues related to power and dominance, as well as the impact that these forces have on the lives of bicultural students. For instance, in situations where students of color act out their resistance to cultural domination by passively refusing to participate in classroom activities or by actively disrupting the process, these student behaviors are interpreted by the majority of teachers as simply a classroom management problem—or, at most, as cause for concern about the emotional stability or well-being of the student. Seldom does it occur to most teachers who are faced with such behaviors to consider the manner in which cultural subordination and prevailing social hostility toward differences might represent the genesis of classroom resistance. Consequently, despite well-meaning efforts by teachers to intervene, their faulty assumptions generally hinder their effectiveness with bicultural students through unintentional acts of cultural invasion and further cultural subordination of students of color.

Second, in order to approach effectively the need for culturally relevant curriculum in the classroom, educators must be willing to acknowledge their limitations with respect to the cultural systems from which bicultural students make sense of their world. This requires teachers to recognize that students and their families bring to the classroom knowledge about their cultures, their communities, and their educational needs. This can best be accomplished by creating conditions for students to voice more clearly what constitutes the cultural differences they experience and to unfurl the conflicts as they struggle together to understand their own histories and their relationships with others. In addition, teachers must take the time to learn about the communities in which their students live. As teachers gain a greater understanding of students' lives outside of school, they are more able to create opportunities for classroom dialogue, which assists bicultural students to affirm, challenge, and transform the many conflicts and contradictions that they face as members of an oppressed group.

Third, educators also need to become more critical in their assessment of multicultural curricula and activities with respect to the consequences of their use in the classroom. For example, many teachers believe that making feathered headbands and teaching students about the Indians' contributions to the first Thanksgiving are effective activities for the study of Native Americans. In reality, these types of activities constitute forms of cultural invasion that reinforce stereotypical images of American Indians and grossly distort the history of a people. Although this is a deeply problematic representation of culture for all students, it has a particularly perverse effect on students who have had little or no exposure to Native Americans other than what they have seen on television and in films, and a destructive impact on the self-esteem and identity of Native American students who are victimized by such distorted depictions of their cultural histories.

And fourth, teachers must come to realize that no multicultural curriculum, in and of itself, can replace the dialogical participation of bicultural students in the process of schooling. This is to say that even the most ideologically correct curriculum is in danger of objectifying students if it is utilized in such a way as to detach them from their everyday lives. Gramsci (1971) observes, "Thus, we come back to the truly active participation of the pupil in the school, which can only exist if the school is related to life. The more the new curricula nominally affirm and theorize the pupil's activity and working collaboration with the teacher, the more they are actually designed as if the pupil were purely passive" (p. 37). Gramsci's words support the notion that a genuine affirmation of cultural diversity in the classroom requires the restructuring of power relations and classroom structures in such a manner as to promote the *active* voice and participation of bicultural students. Through the creation of culturally democratic classroom conditions that also place bicultural voices at the center of the discourse, all students can come together to speak out about their lives and engage in dialogues that permit them to examine their cultural values and social realities. In this way, students can learn to make problematic their views of life, search for different ways to think about themselves, challenge their self-imposed as well as institutionally defined limitations, affirm their cultural and individual strengths, and embrace the possibilities for a better world through a growing sense of solidarity built on love, respect, and compassion for one another and a commitment to the liberation of all people.

Challenging Racism in the Classroom

No matter how much a teacher might feel committed to the notion of cultural diversity, it is impossible to create a culturally democratic environment that can effectively meet the educational needs of bicultural students if that teacher is ill equipped to challenge incidences of racism when they surface in the curriculum or in student relationships. As described earlier, racism results from institutionalized prejudices and biases that perpetuate discrimination based on racial and cultural differences. When educators fail to criticize discriminatory attitudes and behaviors, they permit bicultural students to suffer needless humiliation and psychological violence that nega-tively reinforce feelings of disentitlement and marginalization in society.

Despite attitudes to the contrary, cultural differences do not constitute the problem in public schools; rather, the problem is directly related to the responses of the dominant culture to these differences—responses that function to perpetuate social, political, and economic inequality. Instead of adopting the neutral position of most multicultural approaches, Carol Phillips suggests that educators teach students

> how to recognize when cultural and racially different groups are being victimized by the racist and biased attitudes of the larger society; how these behaviors are institutionalized in the policies and procedures of [school] and programs; how these practices of excluding people are so mystified that well-meaning advocates for change fail to see them operating; [and] how to act against prevailing forces that perpetuate racism. (Phillips, 1988, p. 45)

The inability to address racism, as suggested by Phillips, is commonly observed in the failure of educators to address even racial slurs when they occur. A common scenario may find two or more students in a disagreement, and one or more may yell out at the other, "You nigger!" or "You greaser!" More times than not, educators who overhear such comments—unable to deal with their own discomfort—let them go by altogether, or they may tell the students to stop fighting, or that it is against the rules to call each other names. Unfortunately, despite good intentions, these approaches ignore the social circumstances that inform such behavior and the consequences for all students involved. In addition, it does nothing to assist these students and their peers to understand their actions critically, nor will it transform their relationships in any way.

Educators who strive for culturally democratic environments will need to call on their courage and inner strength to challenge the tension and discomfort they experience when confronting issues of discrimination in the classroom. Instead of looking for quick-fix methods to restore a false sense of harmony at such moments of confrontation, educators must seek to unveil the tensions, conflicts, and contradictions that perpetuate discriminatory attitudes and behaviors among their students. In a situation such as the one described above, the teacher can bring students together into a critical dialogue about racial epithets and their role in perpetuating injustice. This may begin with questions about the feelings that precipitate these words: Where did they learn the words? What is the intent behind their use? What are the effects of these epithets on the victim? On the victimizer? How does this behavior relate to other forms of racism in the community? How could students engage in resolving their differences in other ways?

Dialogues such as this should be consistently introduced and encouraged among students within the context of the classroom, so that they may come to understand how their attitudes and behaviors affect others and, more importantly, so that they may come to act in behalf of all who are oppressed. Through their participation in this process, students have the opportunity to speak their feelings about race and how it relates to their lived experiences, and to become conscious of their own investment in racist attitudes and behaviors. In addition, they also learn to analyze how racism affects the conditions that exist in their communities, and to develop strategies for countering racism when they encounter it in their own lives (Giroux, 1990). For bicultural students, the dialogue must extend further. It must also assist them to identify the different ways in which their relationships with the dominant culture have conditioned them to take on contra-dictory attitudes and beliefs about themselves that cause them to participate unintentionally in the perpetuation of their own oppression.

The Culture of the Teacher

Whenever educators begin seriously to confront the complexity of teaching in bicultural commu-nities, they also begin to question what impact the teacher's cultural background has on her or his ability to educate successfully students of color. It is an important question to consider within the context of a critical bicultural pedagogical discourse—particularly because of the profound nature of cultural belief systems and their relationship to issues of identity and social power. In addition, it brings into the arena of discussion notions of cultural differences with respect to the roles that teachers play if they are from the dominant culture, versus those who come from subordinate cultures.

As suggested earlier, in their efforts to learn about different cultural communities, teachers generally pursue materials that address the more visible or tangible aspects of cultural experience, while neglecting the deep structural values that inform the cultural worldviews of subordinate groups. In conjunction with this, teachers have been socialized to believe that by simply gathering or obtaining information on any particular subject they can come to know. From a critical bicultural perspective, learning about a culture from a book or a few seminars does not constitute knowing that culture. This is particularly true with respect to understanding the daily lived experiences of the group and the historicity of social forces that work to shape and shift how its members interact in the world. For example, someone who is not Hopi might read many books or articles about the Hopi people and yet still not know what it means to grow up as a Hopi in American society.

To even begin to comprehend the bicultural experience requires that teachers from the dominant culture invest time and energy into establishing critical dialogues with people of color if they wish to understand their communities better. Even then, these teachers must recognize and respect that their process of learning and knowing is inherently situated *outside* that cultural context, and is therefore different from the knowledge obtained from living *within* a particular cultural community. This is an essential understanding for teachers who have been raised in the dominant culture and whose cultural reference point is based on White Euroamerican values— which are the predominant values informing most American institutions. This is not to say that all Anglo-Americans conform to these values, but rather to suggest that, even in states of nonconformity, Euroamerican values represent the central reference point that individuals of the dominant culture move toward or move away from in the course of their personal and institutional relationships. This reference point also dictates the multitude of subject positions that individuals from the dominant culture assume in their lives with respect to class, gender, sexual orientation, spirituality, politics, and other ideological categories related to worldview.

The biculturation process . . . represents an attempt to describe the dynamics by which people of color interact with the conflicts and contradictions arising when growing up in a primary culture that dictates a reference point and subject positions in conflict with those of the dominant culture. As a consequence, members from subordinate groups must find ways to cope and function within institutional environments that on the one hand generally undermine and curtail their rights to equality, and on the other hand push them to assimilate the values of the dominant culture. The different ways in which bicultural people attempt to resolve the tension created by such forces are reflected in the predominant response patterns they utilize to survive. What complicates this process further is the manner in which Euroamerican values are perpetuated through hegemonic forces of social control, while the primary values of African-Americans, Latinos, Native Americans, Asians, and other subordinate groups are relegated to subordinate positions in American society.

The consequence is that very often people of color whose bicultural voices and experiences have been systematically silenced and negated are not necessarily conscious of the manner in which racism and classism have influenced their individual development, nor how they have functioned to distort perceptions of their cultural group within an Anglocentric world. Therefore, the fact that a person is bicultural does not guarantee that she or he occupies a position of resistance to such domination. In fact, under current social conditions, it is not unusual to find people of color in positions of power who ignore issues of social power and perpetuate ideas and beliefs that function to the detriment of their own people. Such prominent figures include the likes of Senator Samuel Hayakawa, who was an outspoken advocate for a national English-only initiative; Linda Chavez, a former member of the National Human Relations Commission; and Shelby Steele, the author of *The Content of Our Character*. This is also the case with the many teachers of color who have naively made attempts to assimilate into the dominant culture without critically engaging with the impact of their beliefs on their lives and work.

This perspective is offered here because it represents a reality that must be understood if educators are honestly to consider questions related to the cultural background of the teachers who educate bicultural students. It is a reality that must be acknowledge if we are to prevent falling into the trap of essentialist arguments, such as those proclaiming that only teachers of color can effectively educate students of color. Instead, what is needed is the courage, willingness, and desire to speak honestly to those issues that relate directly to how individuals define their cultural identity and how this influences their work with bicultural students. How teachers perceive the notion of cultural identity is especially important, given that the majority of educators in the United States are members of the dominant culture, and that most educators—of all cultures—have been schooled in traditional pedagogical models. Hence, the teacher's cultural background, espoused ideology, and academic preparation embody equally important areas of concern in our efforts to create conditions that are conducive to a culturally democratic life in the classroom.

If public schools are to provide successfully for the educational needs of bicultural students, they must work in collaboration with bicultural educators, students, parents, and their communities. Anything short of this effort suggests an educational process that is in danger of oppressing and disempowering students of color. This is not to imply that all teachers in bicultural communities must necessarily be teachers of color, but rather to emphasize that it is an arrogant and patronizing gesture for educators from the dominant culture to think that they can meet the needs of a culturally different community when they fail to work in solidarity with educators and other members of that community.

Efforts to establish solidarity among culturally diverse groups require relationships based on mutual respect and equality. White teachers need to abandon, willingly, unfair notions of entitlement and privilege so they may enter into relationships with people of color that support the struggle for freedom and a better world. This requires that White educators acknowledge the manner in which people of color have been historically discriminated against and subordinated to inferior positions in the society at large and the manner in which public education has perpetuated this process. They must come to see how these injustices actually exist in their own profession by the very nature of the assumptions that inform their practice. For example, it is not unusual to find bicultural/bilingual instructional aides with ten or more years of experience in the classroom working under inexperienced White middle-class teachers who know very little about the actual needs of bicultural students. Yet, when such conditions are challenged as part of a wider struggle for more bilingual/bicultural teachers, it is interesting to note the manner in which questions of social control ultimately inform the responses of many public school districts. Rather than create the conditions for well-experienced instructional aides to complete their education and receive certification, many large urban school districts have decided to import teachers from Spain. These are teachers who, in fact, are less knowledgeable of the American bicultural experience than Euroamerican educators. This illustrates only one of the ways in which a process of hegemony operates in public schools to sabotage the transformative struggles of oppressed communities and to ensure the perpetuation of the status quo. Such forms of hegemony can be understood by teachers and challenged in the course of their work.

Further, in order for bicultural students to develop both an individual and social sense of empowerment in their lives, they need to establish relationships with both White and bicultural teachers who are genuinely committed to a democratic vision of community life. When students actually experience the process of White teachers and bicultural teachers working together to address issues related to cultural differences and conflicts, they also come to better understand cultural democracy and learn to participate in cross-cultural dialogues in ways that truly respect and honor the emancipatory rights of all people.

Critical educators from the dominant culture demonstrate a spirit of solidarity and possibility when they willingly challenge both cultural values and institutional conditions of inequity despite the fact that these potentially function to their material benefit. Their refusal to accept social conditions of entitlement and privilege for themselves at the expense of oppressed groups helps to lay the groundwork for relations with people of color based on a solidarity and commitment to social justice and equality. Such educators truly recognize the need to create conditions in the classroom that empower students of color and to open opportunities that historically have remained closed to these students. Operating from this perspective, programs developed under such mandates as affirmative action and equal educational opportunity are given support as beginning efforts toward social equality, rather than seen as somehow taking away from members of the dominant culture. The way in which teachers themselves address these issues in the larger world is significant, because it usually also reflects how they relate with students of color in the course of their daily interactions with them in the classroom.

It is also essential that students of color experience a variety of teachers of color during the course of their schooling. Bicultural educators who are socially conscious bring a wealth of knowledge and experience that often resonates with the realities that students of color experience in their own lives. Many of these teachers are bilingual, understand the complexity of their students' cultural worldviews, are knowledgeable about their history and literature, are cognizant of the different styles in which students learn and communicate, are conscious of the rules of appropriate relationships and interactions among people, and know the communities from which their students come. As a consequence, bicultural teachers are generally more able to use their own learning experiences and knowledge of their cultural values to develop effective curricula that engage with issues related to cultural diversity. In addition, through their knowledge of community, they are able to find ways in which to integrate the students' lived culture into classroom relationships. They are also more genuinely able to affirm and support the development of the bicultural voice, given their ability to engage with the lived conditions of cultural domination and resistance. Hence, it must be recognized that bicultural teachers serve vital roles as models for students of color—many of whom have seldom witnessed people of color in positions of power and influence. Most importantly, through their experiences with critical bicultural educators, bicultural students are more concretely challenged and supported as they come to redefine their possiblities within the context of American society.

Restructuring Public Schools

Critical educators of bicultural students must consider creative ways in which they can work to restructure public school environments that support experiences of culturally democratic life. The manner in which this is done must take into account not only the specific needs that bicultural students bring into the classroom, but also the needs that teachers have in order to be more effective educators. Through gaining a better understanding of the lived histories and daily lives of both students of color and their teachers, classroom structures can be transformed to reflect meaningful social relationships and critical pedagogical approaches that are built on the principles of cultural democracy. Just as students are critically challenged to redefine the possibilities for transforming the world, their teachers should be actively involved in such a process within the context of their own profession.

First of all, efforts by teachers to promote the development of voice, participation, social responsibility, and solidarity are strongly reflected in the way they physically structure and situate the learning environment in their classrooms. A few classroom changes that would address this concern include these examples:

- The furniture, and in particular the seating in the room, is arranged so as to permit free physical movement of students about the classroom.

- Classroom spaces promote working in groups and on collaborative projects.

- Classroom bulletin boards are generated in conjunction with the participation of students, who are encouraged to utilize materials that are meaningful to them. These forms of cultural expression are then used to stimulate dialogues about their relationship to the context of students' lives and communities.

- Curricular activities are created for students to have opportunities to converse in their home languages with each other and to introduce various aspects of their language experience to other students.

- Students are actively involved in the development of classroom rules and in making decisions about classroom activities whenever possible. In addition, they are involved in dialogues designed to help them consider the consequences of rules and decisions made with respect to themselves as individuals and the class as a whole.

It is important to note that none of these suggestions, in and of itself, constitutes *the* way to incorporate a critical bicultural pedagogy, for the manner in which a critical pedagogy evolves in any particular classroom environment must be based on the contextual conditions present. No lesson plan or curriculum should ever supersede the actual learning needs expressed by students or identified by the teacher. Learning is a contextual experience by which knowledge and meaning are produced within the complexity of a multitude of potential responses generated by students and teacher alike.

The few suggestions mentioned above focus on what teachers can do to transform the structures and relationships within their own classrooms. But outside the classroom, there is also much to be done related to the general restructuring of the working conditions that teachers find in public schools. Critical educators must explore some possible ways in which to transform these conditions so that schools may function to support their own empowerment as well as an emancipatory vision for education. Some suggestions to consider with respect to this concern are as follows:

- The development of cross-cultural teaching teams in schools with large bicultural student populations.

- The initiation of professional development opportunities for all teachers to become knowledgeable in the principles of a critical bicultural pedagogy. This would provide teachers the opportunity to better understand the bicultural experience of students and to examine together their own prejudices and biases related to issues of cultural diversity.

- A greater involvement of teachers in the development, evaluation, and selection of texts, films, and other instructional materials.

- An ongoing collaborative effort with parents and community members to transform the educational environments of public schools.

- Establishment of regular public forums within schools to discuss issues related to bicultural students, such as bilingualism, the bicultural process, the academic needs of students, parent involvement in the classroom, and so forth.

In addition, teachers must also struggle to transform the structural conditions related to both out-of-class work and class size. Much of the demoralization teachers experience is not, for the most part, a consequence of low pay; rather, it is more closely linked to the powerlessness generated by working in an environment that is fundamentally incompatible with engaging in the complexities of teaching a culturally diverse student population. In order to address this issue, public school teachers might begin by demanding that the number of students in their classrooms be limited to approximately twenty. It is not unusual to find public schools in large urban settings where teachers are assigned up to forty students, with limited assistance from an instructional aide. One of the most revolutionary actions that public school teachers can take, at this point in time, is to assume an uncompromising posture with respect to the issue of class size. It is well documented that students are more successful when they receive more individualized attention from the teacher. So completely conscious of this fact are private schools that they use as a major selling point their policy of small class size. Teacher unions and other teacher organizations need to become advocates for themselves as well as for disenfranchised students by asserting the entitlement of the latter to the rights enjoyed by students from privileged classes. Most importantly, teachers who are less burdened by the tremendous demands placed on them by large class size are more able to engage consistently and critically with the actual needs of bicultural students and issues related to cultural diversity.

Also of major importance is the struggle for the redefinition of the teacher's workday. Seldom are teachers afforded opportunities to come together on an ongoing basis to reflect and dialogue critically about the concerns they experience in their efforts to meet the needs to their students. And even more seldom do they have the time to maintain some consistent form of personal contact with parents, despite the fact that studies clearly indicate this to be a significant factor in the achievement of bicultural students (Rashid, 1981; Goldenberg, 1987; Cummins, 1986). Teachers require institutional support in their efforts to develop working relationships with their colleagues, students, parents, and the communities in which they work. This can only take place when the teacher's work is redefined more realistically to include both what teachers are required to implement daily in their classrooms and those important functions they must perform outside the classroom setting to be effective educators. But this redefinition can only take place when teachers struggle to transform the conditions of their labor within the context of a critical process that is generated by working together for a better life—not only as educators, but as workers and free democratic citizens.

Beyond Despair

Much frustration is evident in the attitudes and responses of many educators to the conditions they find in public schools. Many teachers blame the problems they experience on the increasing number of students of color. Others are acutely aware that they were insufficiently prepared by teacher education programs to meet the needs of a culturally diverse student population. Still others experience a deep feeling of personal frustration, which they attribute to their own individual failure as teachers. Whatever the manner in which teachers define the cause of their frustration, it is clear that their perceptions echo a great sense of despair and powerlessness.

It is important to note that those teachers who find themselves within public school conditions—where their voices are silenced and their opportunities to decide on curricula, texts, and other classroom requirements are limited—are most in danger of experiencing a sense of despair. Public school teachers in these environments must work together to challenge themselves and each other to move beyond the limitations that they find in these schools. In addition, they must also move beyond their own dependency on traditional classroom structures and the artifacts that support the perpetuation of their disempowerment.

For example, under such conditions as described above, teachers must initially cultivate their creative abilities to utilize commonplace materials and natural environments that can serve as ideal conditions for students to investigate the ordinary, and through acting on it discover their potential power to create and change their world. Given this approach, any classroom situation can potentially be converted into a critical environment as educators discover the multitude of pedagogical possibilities at their disposal. But this can only take place when educators courageously abandon old and disempowering notions of what is necessary and certain, and move beyond the boundaries of prescribed educational practice and into the realm of creativity and discovery.

As emphasized earlier, fundamental to creating the conditions for cultural democracy is a political commitment to a liberatory vision. A critical bicultural pedagogy can only emerge within a social context where teachers are grounded in a commitment to both individual and social empowerment. Hence, the smaller political endeavor of the classroom is not seen as simply an encapsulated moment in time, but rather it is consistently connected to a greater democratic political project. From this vantage point, teachers function as empowered social agents of history, who are firmly committed to collaborative struggles for transformation as they seek to change and redefine the conditions that threaten the opportunities for voice, participation, and solidarity in their schools. As teachers work in solidarity with their colleagues, parents, students, and the community, they discover their tremendous collective power, and through this process of affirmation move beyond despair. It is, in part, this critical commitment to act in behalf of freedom and social justice that also serves as a model for their students to discover their own personal power, social transformative potential, and spirit of hope.

Embodied in this emancipatory spirit of hope is also a faith in the capacity of human beings to transform the oppressive and dehumanizing conditions that disconnect, fragment, and alienate us from one another. Grounded in this struggle by a collective vision of liberation, critical educators search out creative ways to expand the opportunities for students of color to become authentic beings for themselves, in spite of the limitations of traditional curricula and prevailing social conditions. Students are encouraged to question the conflicts, contradictions, disjunctions, and partiality of standardized knowledge forms—in their own lives as well. Consistently, liberatory educators support and challenge bicultural students to struggle together so that they may come to know all the possibilities that might be available to them as free citizens. For it is through this critical process of discovery and empowerment that teachers and students move in solidarity across the terrain of cultural differences to arrive at the knowledge that hidden in the complexity of these differences are many ways to be human, and many ways to struggle for a world in which we can all be free.

Talking about Race, Learning about Racism:
The Application of Racial Identity Development Theory in the Classroom

BEVERLY DANIEL TATUM

The inclusion of race-related content in college courses often generates emotional responses in students that range from guilt and shame to anger and despair. The discomfort associated with these emotions can lead students to resist the learning process. Based on her experience teaching a course on the psychology of racism and application of racial identity development theory, Beverly Daniel Tatum identifies three major sources of student resistance to talking about race and learning about racism, as well as some strategies for overcoming this resistance.

As many educational institutions struggle to become more multicultural in terms of their students, faculty, and other staff, they also begin to examine issues of cultural representation within their curriculum. This examination has evoked a growing number of courses that give specific consideration to the effect of variables such as race, class, and gender on human experience—an important trend that is reflected and supported by the increasing availability of resource manuals for the modification of course content (Bronstein & Quina, 1988; Hull, Scott, & Smith, 1982; Schuster & Van Dyne, 1985).

Unfortunately, less attention has been given to the issues of process that inevitably emerge in the classroom when attention is focused on race, class, and/or gender. It is very difficult to talk about these concepts in a meaningful way without also talking and learning about racism, classism, and sexism.[1] The introduction of these issues of oppression often generates powerful emotional responses in students that range from guilt and shame to anger and despair. If not addressed, these emotional responses can result in student resistance to oppression-related content areas. Such resistance can ultimately interfere with the cognitive understanding and mastery of the material. This resistance and potential interference is particularly common when specifically addressing issues of race and racism. Yet, when students are given the opportunity to explore race-related material in a classroom where both their affective and intellectual responses are acknowledged and addressed, their level of understanding is greatly enhanced.

This article seeks to provide a framework for understanding student's psychological responses to race-related content and the student resistance that can result, as well as some strategies for overcoming this resistance. It is informed by more than a decade of experience as an African-American woman engaged in teaching an undergraduate course on the psychology of racism, by thematic analyses of student journals and essays written for the racism class, and by an understanding and application of racial identity development theory (Helms, 1990).

Setting the Contest

As a clinical psychologist with a research interest in racial identity development among African-American youth raised in predominantly White communities, I began teaching about racism quite fortuitously. In 1980, while I was a part-time lecturer in the Black Studies department of a large public university, I was invited to teach a course called Group Exploration of Racism (Black Studies 2). A requirement for Black Studies majors, the course had to be offered, yet the instructor who regularly taught the course was no longer affiliated with the institution. Armed with a folder full of handouts, old syllabi that the previous instructor left behind, a copy of *White Awareness: Handbook for Anti-racism Training* (Katz, 1978), and my own clinical skills as a group facilitator, I constructed a course that seemed to meet the goals already outlined in the course catalogue. Designed "to provide students with an understanding of the psychological causes and emotional reality of racism as it appears in everyday life," the course incorporated the use of lectures, readings, simulation exercises, group research projects, and extensive class discussion to help students explore the psychological impact of racism on both the oppressor and the oppressed.

Though my first efforts were tentative, the results were powerful. The students in my class, most of whom were White, repeatedly described the course in their evaluations as one of the most valuable educational experiences of their college careers. I was convinced that helping students understand the ways in which racism operates in their own lives, and what they could do about it, was a social responsibility that I should accept. The freedom to institute the course in the curriculum of the psychology departments in which I would eventually teach became a personal condition of employment. I have successfully introduced the course in each new educational setting I have been in since leaving that university.

Since 1980, I have taught the course (now called the Psychology of Racism) eighteen times, at three different institutions. Although each of these schools is very different—a large public university, a small state college, and a private, elite women's college—the challenges of teaching about racism in each setting have been more similar than different.

In all of the settings, class size has been limited to thirty students (averaging twenty-four). Though typically predominantly White and female (even in coeducational settings), the class makeup has always been mixed in terms of both race and gender. The students of color who have taken the course include Asians and Latinos/as, but most frequently the students of color have been Black. Though most students have described themselves as middle class, all socioeconomic backgrounds (ranging from very poor to very wealthy) have been represented over the years.

The course has necessarily evolved in response to my own deepening awareness of the psychological legacy of racism and my expanding awareness of other forms of oppression, although the basic format has remained the same. Our weekly three-hour class meeting is held in a room with movable chairs, arranged in a circle. The physical structure communicates an important premise of the course—that I expect the students to speak with each other as well as with me.

My other expectations (timely completion of assignments, regular class attendance) are clearly communicated in our first class meeting, along with the assumptions and guidelines for discussion that I rely upon to guide our work together. Because the assumptions and guidelines are so central to the process of talking and learning about racism, it may be useful to outline them here.

Working Assumptions

1. Racism, defined as a "system of advantage based on race" (see Wellman, 1977), is a pervasive aspect of U.S. socialization. It is virtually impossible to live in U.S. contemporary society and not be exposed to some aspect of the personal, cultural, and/or institutional manifestations of racism in our society. It is also assumed that,

as a result, all of us have received some misinformation about those groups disadvantaged by racism.

2. Prejudice, defined as a "preconceived judgment or opinion, often based on limited information," is clearly distinguished from racism (see Katz, 1978). I assume that all of us may have prejudices as a result of the various cultural stereotypes to which we have been exposed. Even when these preconceived ideas has positive associations (such as "Asian students are good in math"), they have negative effects because they deny a person's individuality. These attitudes may influence the individual behaviors of people of color as well as of Whites, and may affect intergroup as well as intragroup interaction. However, a distinction must be made between the negative racial attitudes held by individuals of color and White individuals, because it is only the attitudes of Whites that routinely carry with them the social power inherent in the systematic cultural reinforcement and institutionalization of those racial prejudices. To distinguish the prejudices of students of color from the racism of White students is *not* to say that the former is acceptable and the latter is not; both are clearly problematic. The distinction is important, however, to identify the power differential between members of dominant and subordinate groups.

3. In the context of U.S. society, the system of advantage clearly operates to benefit Whites as a group. However, it is assumed that racism, like other forms of oppression, hurts members of the privileged group as well as those targeted by racism. While the impact of racism on Whites is clearly different from its impact on people of color, racism has negative ramifications for everyone. For example, some White students might remember the pain of having lost important relationships because Black friends were not allowed to visit their homes. Others may express sadness at having been denied access to a broad range of experiences because of social segregation. These individuals often attribute the discomfort or fear they now experience in racially mixed settings to the cultural limitations of their youth.

4. Because of the prejudice and racism inherent in our environments when we were children, I assume that we cannot be blamed for learning what we were taught (intentionally or unintentionally). Yet as adults, we have a responsibility to try to identify and interrupt the cycle of oppression. When we recognize that we have been misinformed, we have a responsibility to seek out more accurate information and to adjust our behavior accordingly.

5. It is assumed that change, both individual and institutional, is possible. Understanding and unlearning prejudice and racism is a lifelong process that may have begun prior to enrolling in this class, and which will surely continue after the course is over. Each of us may be at a different point in that process, and I assume that we will have mutual respect for each other, regardless of where we perceive one another to be.

To facilitate further our work together, I ask students to honor the following guidelines for our discussion. Specifically, I ask students to demonstrate their respect for one another by honoring the confidentiality of the group. So that students may feel free to ask potentially awkward or embarrassing questions, or share race-related experiences, I ask that students refrain from making personal attributions when discussing the course content with their friends. I also discourage the use of "zaps," overt or covert put-downs often used as comic relief when someone is feeling anxious about the content of the discussion. Finally, students are asked to speak from their own experience, to say, for example, "I think . . . " or "In my experience, I have found . . . " rather than generalizing their experience to others, as in "People say . . . ."

Many students are reassured by the climate of safety that is created by these guidelines and find comfort in the nonblaming assumptions I outline for the class. Nevertheless, my experience has been that most students, regardless of their class and ethnic background, still find racism a difficult topic to discuss, as is revealed by these journal comments written after the first class meeting (all names are pseudonyms).

The class is called Psychology of Racism, the atmosphere is friendly and open, yet I feel very closed in. I feel guilt and doubt well up inside of me. (Tiffany, a White woman)

Class has started on a good note thus far. The class seems rather large and disturbs me. In a class of this nature, I expect there will be many painful and emotional moments. (Linda, an Asian woman)

I am a little nervous that as one of the few students of color in the class people are going to be looking to me for answers, or whatever other reasons. The thought of this inhibits me a great deal. (Louise, an African-American woman)

I had never thought about my social position as being totally dominant. There wasn't one area in which I wasn't in the dominant group. . . . I first felt embarrassed. . . . Through association alone I felt in many ways responsible for the unequal condition existing in the world. This made me feel like shrinking in a hole in a class where I was surrounded by 27 women and 2 men, one of whom was Black and the other was Jewish. I felt that all these people would be justified in venting their anger upon me. After a short period, I realized that no one in the room was attacking or even blaming me for the conditions that exist. (Carl, a White man)

Even though most of my students voluntarily enroll in the course as an elective, their anxiety and subsequent resistance to learning about racism quickly emerge.

Sources of Resistance

In predominantly White college classrooms, I have experienced at least three major sources of student resistance to talking and learning about race and racism. They can be readily identified as the following:

1. Race is considered a taboo topic for discussion, especially in racially mixed settings.

2. Many students, regardless of racial-group membership, have been socialized to think of the United States as a just society.

3. Many students, particularly White students, initially deny any personal prejudice, recognizing the impact of racism on other people's lives, but failing to acknowledge its impact on their own.

Race as Taboo Topic

The first source of resistance, race as a taboo topic, is an essential obstacle to overcome if class discussion is to begin at all. Although many students are interested in the topic, they are often most interested in hearing other people talk about it, afraid to break the taboo themselves.

One source of this self-consciousness can be seen in the early childhood experiences of many students. It is known that children as young as three notice racial differences (see Phinney & Rotheram, 1987). Certainly preschoolers talk about what they see. Unfortunately, they often do so in ways that make adults uncomfortable. Imagine the following scenario: A White child in a public place points to a dark-skinned African-American child and says loudly, "Why is that boy Black?" The embarrassed parent quickly responds, "Sh! Don't say that." The child is only attempting to make sense of a new observation (Derman-Sparks, Higa & Sparks, 1980), yet the parent's attempt to silence the perplexed child sends a message that this observation is not okay to talk about. White children quickly became aware that their questions about race raise adult anxiety, and as a result, they learn not to ask questions.

When asked to reflect on their earliest race-related memories and the feelings associated with them, both White students and students of color often report feelings of confusion, anxiety, and/ or fear. Students of color often have early memories of name-calling or other negative interactions with other children, and sometimes with adults. They also report having had questions that went both unasked and unanswered. In addition, many students have had uncomfortable interchanges around race-related topics as adults. When asked at the beginning of the semester, "How many of you have had difficult, perhaps heated conversations with someone on a race-related topic?", routinely almost everyone in the class raises his or her hand. It should come as no surprise then that students often approach the topic of race and/or racism with both curiosity and trepidation.

The Myth of the Meritocracy

The second source of student resistance to be discussed here is rooted in students' belief that the United States is a just society, a meritocracy where individual efforts are fairly rewarded. While some students (particularly students of color) may already have become disillusioned with that notion of the United States, the majority of my students who have experienced at least the personal success of college acceptance still have faith in this notion. To the extent that these students acknowledge that racism exists, they tend to view it as an individual phenomenon, rooted in the attitudes of the "Archie Bunkers" of the world or located only in particular parts of the country.

After several class meetings, Karen, a White woman, acknowledged this attitude in her journal:

> At one point in my life—the beginning of this class—I actually perceived America to be a relatively racist free society. I thought that the people who were racist or subjected to racist stereotypes were found only in small pockets of the U.S., such as the South. As I've come to realize, racism (or at least racially oriented stereotypes) is rampant.

An understanding of racism as a system of advantage presents a serious challenge to the notion of the United States as a just society where rewards are based solely on one's merit. Such a challenge often creates discomfort in students. The old adage "ignorance is bliss" seems to hold true in this case; students are not necessarily eager to recognize the painful reality of racism.

One common response to the discomfort is to engage in denial of what they are learning. White students in particular may question the accuracy or currency of statistical information regarding the prevalence of discrimination (housing, employment, access to health care, and so on). More qualitative data, such as autobiographical accounts of experiences with racism, may be challenged on the basis of their subjectivity.

It should be pointed out that the basic assumption that the United States is a just society for all is only one of many basic assumptions that might be challenged in the learning process. Another example can be seen in an interchange between two White students following a discussion about cultural racism, in which the omission or distortion of historical information about people of color was offered as an example of the cultural transmission of racism.

"Yeah, I just found out that Cleopatra was actually a Black woman."

"What?"

The first student went on to explain her newly learned information. Finally, the second student exclaimed in disbelief, "That can't be true. Cleopatra was beautiful!" This new information and her own deeply ingrained assumptions about who is beautiful and who is not were too incongruous to allow her to assimilate the information at that moment.

If outright denial of information is not possible, then withdrawal may be. Physical withdrawal in the form of absenteeism is one possible result; it is for precisely this reason that class attendance is mandatory. The reduction in the completion of reading and/or written assignments is another form of withdrawal. I have found this response to be so common that I now alert students to this possibility at the beginning of the semester. Knowing that this response is a common one seems to help students stay engaged, even when they experience the desire to withdraw.

Following an absence in the fifth week of the semester, one White student wrote, "I think I've hit the point you talked about, the point where you don't want to hear any more about racism. I sometimes begin to get the feeling we are all hypersensitive." (Two weeks later she wrote, "Class is getting better. I think I am beginning to get over my hump.")

Perhaps not surprisingly, this response can be found in both White students and students of color. Students of color often enter a discussion of racism with some awareness of the issue, based on personal experiences. However, even these students find that they did not have a full understanding of the widespread impact of racism in our society. For students who are targeted by racism, an increased awareness of the impact in and on their lives is painful, and often generates anger.

Four weeks into the semester, Louise, an African-American woman, wrote in her journal about her own heightened sensitivity:

> Many times in class I feel uncomfortable when White students use the term Black because even if they aren't aware of it they say it with all or at least a lot of the negative connotations they've been taught goes along with Black. Sometimes it just causes a stinging feeling inside of me. Sometimes I get real tired of hearing White people talk about the conditions of Black people. I think it's an important thing for them to talk about, but still I don't always like being around when they do it. I also get tired of hearing them talk about how hard it is for them, though I understand it, and most times I am very willing to listen and be open, but sometimes I can't. Right now I can't.

For White students, advantaged by racism, a heightened awareness of it often generates painful feelings of guilt. The following responses are typical:

> After reading the article about privilege, I feel very guilty. (Rachel, a White woman)

> Questions of racism are so full of anger and pain. When I think of all the pain White people have caused people of color, I get a feeling of guilt. How could someone like myself care so much about the color of someone's skin that they would do them harm? (Terri, a White woman)

White students also sometimes express a sense of betrayal when they realize the gaps in their own education about racism. After seeing the first episode of the documentary series *Eyes on the Prize*, Chris, a White man, wrote:

> I never knew it was really that bad just 35 years ago. Why didn't I learn this in elementary or high school? Could it be that the White people of America want to forget this injustice? . . . I will never forget that movie for as long as I live. It was like a big slap in the face.

Barbara, a White woman, also felt anger and embarrassment in response to her own previous lack of information about the internment of Japanese Americans during World War II. She wrote:

> I feel so stupid because I never even knew that these existed. I never knew that the Japanese were treated so poorly. I am becoming angry and upset about all the things that I do not know. I have been so sheltered. My parents never wanted to let me know about the bad things that have happened in the world. After I saw the move (*Mitsuye and Nellie*), I even called them up to ask them why they never told me this. . . . I am angry at them too for not teaching me and exposing me to the complete picture of my country.

Avoiding the subject matter is one way to avoid these uncomfortable feelings.

"I'm Not Racist, But . . . "

A third source of student resistance (particularly among White students) is the initial denial of any personal connection to racism. When asked why they have decided to enroll in a course on racism, White students typically explain their interest in the topic with such disclaimers as, "I'm not racist myself, but I know people who are, and I want to understand them better."

Because of their position as the targets of racism, students of color do not typically focus on their own prejudices or lack of them. Instead they usually express a desire to understand why racism exists, and how they have been affected by it.

However, as all students gain a better grasp of what racism is and its many manifestations in U.S. society, they inevitably started to recognize its legacy within themselves. Beliefs, attitudes, and actions based on racial stereotypes begin to be remembered and are newly observed by White students. Students of color as well often recognize negative attitudes they may have internalized about their own racial group or that they have believed about others. Those who previously thought themselves immune to the effects of growing up in a racist society often find themselves reliving uncomfortable feelings of guilt or anger.

After taping her own responses to a questionnaire on racial attitudes, Barbara, a White woman previously quoted, wrote:

> I always want to think of myself as open to all races. Yet when I did the interview to myself, I found that I did respond differently to the same questions about different races. No one could ever have told me that I would have. I would have denied it. But I found that I did respond differently even though I didn't want to. This really upset me. I was angry with myself because I thought I was not prejudiced and yet the stereotypes that I had created had an impact on the answers that I gave even though I didn't want it to happen.

The new self-awareness, represented here by Barbara's journal entry, changes the classroom dynamic. One common result is that some White students, once perhaps active participants in class discussion, now hesitate to continue their participation for fear that their newly recognized racism will be revealed to others.

> Today I did feel guilty, and like I had to watch what I was saying (make it good enough), I guess to prove I'm really *not* prejudiced. From the conversations the first day, I guess this is a normal enough reaction, but I certainly never expected it in me. (Joanne, a White woman)

This withdrawal on the part of White students is often paralleled by an increase in participation by students of color who are seeking an outlet for what are often feelings of anger. The withdrawal of some previously vocal White students from the classroom exchange, however, is sometimes interpreted by students of color as indifference. This perceived indifference often serves to fuel the anger and frustration that many students of color experience, as awareness of their own oppression is heightened. For example, Robert, an African-American man, wrote:

> I really wish the White students would talk more. When I read these articles, it makes me so mad and I really want to know what the White kids think. Don't they care?

Sonia, a Latina, described the classroom tension from another perspective:

> I would like to comment that at many points in the discussions I have felt uncomfortable and sometimes even angry with people. I guess I am at the stage where I am tired of listening to Whites feel guilty and watch their eyes fill up with tears. I do understand that everyone is at their own stage of development and I even tell myself every Tuesday that these people have come to this class by choice. Some days I am just more tolerant than others. . . . It takes courage to say things in a room with so many women of color present. It also takes courage for the women of color to say things about Whites.

What seems to be happening in the classroom at such moments in a collision of development processes that can be inherently useful for the racial identity development of the individuals involved. Nevertheless, the interaction may be perceived as problematic to instructors and students who are unfamiliar with the process. Although space does not allow for an exhaustive discussion of racial identity development theory, a brief explication of it here will provide additional clarity regarding the classroom dynamics when issues of race are discussed. It will also provide a theoretical framework for the strategies for dealing with student resistance that will be discussed at the conclusion of this article.

Stages of Racial Identity Development

Racial identity and racial identity development theory are defined by Janet Helms (1990) as

> a sense of group or collective identity based on one's *perception* that he or she shares a common racial heritage with a particular racial group...racial identity development theory concerns the psychological implications of racial-group membership, that is belief systems that evolve in reaction to perceived differential racial-group membership. (p. 3)

It is assumed that in a society where racial-group membership is emphasized, the development of a racial identity will occur in some form in everyone. Given in the dominant/subordinate relationship of Whites and people of color in this society, however, it is not surprising that this developmental process will unfold in different ways. For purposes of this discussion, William Cross's (1971, 1978) model of Black identity development will be described along with Helms's (1990) model of White racial identity development theory. While the identity development of other students (Asian, Latino/a, Native American) is not included in this particular theoretical formulation, there is evidence to suggest that the process for these oppressed groups is similar to that described for African Americans (Highlen, et al., 1988; Phinney, 1990).[2] In each case, it is assumed that a positive sense of one's self as a member of one's group (which is not based on any assumed superiority) is important for psychological health.

Black Racial Identity Development

According to Cross's (1971, 1978, 1991) model of Black racial development, there are five stages in the process, identified as Preencounter, Encounter, Immersion/Emersion, Internalization, and Internalization-Commitment. In the first stage of Preencounter, the African American has absorbed many of the beliefs and values of the dominant White culture, including the notion that "White is right" and "Black is wrong." Though the internalization of negative Black stereotypes may be outside of his or her conscious awareness, the individual seeks to assimilate and be accepted by Whites, and actively or passively distances him/herself from other Blacks.[3]

Louise, an African-American woman previously quoted, captured the essence of this stage in the following description of herself at an earlier time:

> For a long time it seemed as if I didn't remember my background, and I guess in some ways I didn't. I was never taught to be proud of my African heritage. Like we talked about in class, I went through a very long stage of identifying with my oppressors. Wanting to be like, live like, and be accepted by them. Even to the point of hating my own race and myself for being a part of it. Now I am ashamed that I ever was ashamed. I lost so much of myself in my denial of and refusal to accept my people.

In order to maintain psychological comfort at this stage of development, Helms writes:

> The person must maintain the fiction that race and racial indoctrination have nothing to do with how he or she lives life. It is probably the case that the Preencounter person is bombarded on a regular basis with information that he or she cannot really be a member of the "in" racial group, but relies on denial to selectively screen such information from awareness. (1990, p. 23)

This de-emphasis on one's racial-group membership may allow the individual to think that race has not been or will not be a relevant factor in one's own achievement, and may contribute to the belief in a U.S. meritocracy that is often a part of a Preencounter worldview.

Movement into the Encounter phase is typically precipitated by an event or series of events that forces the individual to acknowledge the impact of racism in one's life. For example, instances of social rejection by White friends or colleagues (or reading new personally relevant information about racism) may lead the individual to the conclusion that many Whites will not view him or her as an equal. Faced with the reality that he or she cannot truly be White, the individual is forced to focus on his or her identity as a member of a group targeted by racism.

Brenda, a Korean-American student, described her own experience of this process as a result of her participation in the racism course:

> I feel that because of this class, I have become much more aware of racism that exists around. Because of my awareness of racism, I am now bothered by acts and behaviors that might not have bothered me in the past. Before when racial comments were said around me I would somehow ignore it and pretend that nothing was said. By ignoring comments such as these, I was protecting myself. It became sort of a defense mechanism. I never realized I did this, until I was confronted with stories that were found in our reading, by other people

of color, who also ignored comments that bothered them. In realizing that there is racism out in the world and that there are comments concerning race that are directed towards me, I feel as if I have reached the first step. I also think I have reached the second step, because I am now bothered and irritated by such comments. I no longer ignore them, but now confront them.

The Immersion/Emersion stage is characterized by the simultaneous desire to surround oneself with visible symbols of one's racial identity and an active avoidance of symbols of Whiteness. As Thomas Parham describes, "At this stage, everything of value in life must be Black or relevant to Blackness. This stage is also characterized by a tendency to denigrate White people, simultaneously glorifying Black people. . . . " (1989, p. 190). The previously described anger that emerges in class among African-American students and other students of color in the process of learning about racism may be seen as part of the transition through these stages.

As individuals enter the Immersion stage, they actively seek out opportunities to explore aspects of their own history and culture and the support of peers from their own racial background. Typically, White-focused anger dissipates during this phase because so much of the person's energy is directed toward his or her own group- and self-exploration. The result of this exploration is an emerging security in a newly defined and affirmed sense of self.

Sharon, another African-American woman, described herself at the beginning of the semester as angry, seemingly in the Encounter stage of development. She wrote after our class meeting:

> Another point that I must put down is that before I entered class today I was angry about the way Black people have been treated in this country. I don't think I will easily overcome that and I basically feel justified in my feelings.

At the end of the semester, Sharon had joined with two other Black students in the class to work on their final class project. She observed that the three of them had planned their project to focus on Black people specifically, suggesting movement into the Immersion stage of racial identity development. She wrote:

> We are concerned about the well-being of our people. They cannot be well if they have this pinned-up hatred for their own people. This internalized racism is something that we all felt, at various times, needed to be talked about. This semester it has really been important to me, and I believe Gordon [a Black classmate], too.

The emergence from this stage marks the beginning of Internalization. Secure in one's own sense of racial identity, there is less need to assert the "Blacker than thou" attitude often characteristic of the Immersion stage (Parham, 1989). In general, "pro-Black attitudes become more expansive, open, and less defensive" (Cross, 1971, p. 24). While still maintaining his or her connections with Black peers, the internalized individual is willing to establish meaningful relationships with Whites who acknowledge and are respectful of his or her self-definition. The individual is also ready to build coalitions with members of other oppressed groups. At the end of the semester, Brenda, a Korean American, concluded that she had in fact internalized a positive sense of racial identity. The process she described parallels the stages described by Cross:

> I have been aware for a long time that I am Korean. But through this class I am beginning to really become aware of my race. I am beginning to find out that White people can be accepting of me and at the same time accept me as a Korean.

> I grew up wanting to be accepted and ended up almost denying my race and culture. I don't think I did this consciously, but the denial did occur. As I grew older, I realized that I was different. I became for the first time, friends with other Koreans. I realized I had much in common with them. This was when I went through my "Korean friend" stage. I began to enjoy being friends with Koreans more than I did with Caucasians.

> Well, ultimately, through many years of growing up, I am pretty much in focus about who I am and who my friends are. I know before I took this class that there were people not of color that were understanding of my differences. In our class, I feel that everyone is trying to sincerely find the answer of abolishing racism. I knew people like this existed, but it's nice to meet with them weekly.

Cross suggests that there are few psychological differences between the fourth stage, Internalization, and the fifth stage, Internalization-Commitment. However, those at the fifth stage have found ways to translate their "personal sense of Blackness into a plan of action or a general sense of commitment" to the concerns of Blacks as a group, which is sustained over time (Cross, 1991, p. 220). Whether at the fourth or fifth stage, the process of Internalization allows the individual, anchored in a positive sense of racial identity, both to proactively perceive and transcend race. Blackness becomes "the point of departure for discovering the universe of ideas, cultures and experiences beyond blackness in place of mistaking blackness as the universe itself" (Cross, Parham, & Helms, 1991, p. 330).

Though the process of racial identity development has been presented here in linear form, in fact it is probably more accurate to think of it in a spiral form. Often a person may move from one stage to the next, only to revisit an earlier stage as the result of new encounter experiences (Parham, 1989), though the latter experience of the stage may be different from the original experience. The image that students often find helpful in understanding this concept of recycling through the stages is that of a spiral staircase. As a person ascends a spiral staircase, she may stop and look down at the spot below. When she reaches the next level, she may look down and see the same spot, but the vantage point has changed.[4]

White Racial Identity Development

The transformations experienced by those targeted by racism are often paralleled by those of White students. Helms (1990) describes the evolution of a positive White racial identity as involving both the abandonment of racism and the developments of a nonracist White identity. In order to do the latter,

> he or she must accept his or her own Whiteness, the cultural implications of being White, and define a view of Self as a racial being that does not depend on the perceived superiority of one racial group over another. (p. 49)

She identifies six stages in her model of White racial identity development: Contact, Disintegration, Reintegration, Pseudo-Independent, Immersion/Emersion, and Autonomy.

The Contact stage is characterized by a lack of awareness of cultural and institutional racism, and of one's own White privilege. Peggy McIntosh (1989) writes eloquently about her own experience of this state of being:

> As a white person, I realized I had been taught about racism as something which puts others at a disadvantage, but had been taught not to see one of its corollary aspects, white privilege, which puts me at an advantage. . . . I was taught to see racism only in individual acts of meanness, not in invisible systems conferring dominance on my group. (p. 10)

In addition, the Contact stage often includes curiosity about or fear of people of color, based on stereotypes learned from friends, family, or the media. These stereotypes represent the framework in use when a person at this stage of development makes a comment such as, "You don't act like a Black person" (Helms, 1990, p. 57).

Those Whites whose lives are structured so as to limit their interaction with people of color, as well as their awareness of racial issues, may remain at this stage indefinitely. However, certain kinds of experiences (increased interaction with people of color or exposure to new information about racism) may lead to a new understanding that cultural and institutional racism exist. This new understanding marks the beginning of the Disintegration stage.

At this stage, the bliss of ignorance or lack of awareness is replaced by the discomfort of guilt, shame, and sometimes anger at the recognition of one's own advantage because of being White and the acknowledgment of the role of Whites in the maintenance of a racist system. Attempts to reduce discomfort may include denial (convincing oneself that racism doesn't really exist, or if it does, it is in the fault of its victims).

For example, Tom, a White male student, responded with some frustration in his journal to a classmate's observation that the fact that she had never read any books of Black authors in any of her high school or college English classes was an example of cultural racism. He wrote, "It's not my fault that Blacks don't write books."

After viewing a film in which a psychologist used examples of Black children's drawings to illustrate the potentially damaging effect of negative cultural messages on a Black child's developing self-esteem, David, another White male student, wrote:

> I found it interesting the way Black children drew themselves without arms. The psychologist said this is saying that the child feels unable to control his environment. It can't be because the child has notions and beliefs already about being Black. It must be built in or hereditary due to the past history of the Blacks. I don't believe it's cognitive but more biological due to a long past history of repression and being put down.

Though Tom's and David's explanations seem quite problematic, they can be understood in the context of racial identity development theory as a way of reducing their cognitive dissonance upon learning this new race-related information. As was discussed earlier, withdrawal (accomplished by avoiding contact with people of color and the topic of racism) is another strategy for dealing with the discomfort experienced at this stage. Many of the previously described responses of White students to race-related content are characteristic of the transition from the Contact to the Disintegration stage of development.

Helms (1990) describes another response to the discomfort of Disintegration, which involves attempts to change significant others' attitudes toward African Americans and other people of color. However, as she points out,

> due to the racial naiveté with which this approach may be undertaken and the person's ambivalent racial identification, this dissonance-reducing strategy is likely to be met with rejection by Whites as well as Blacks. (p. 59)

In fact, this response is also frequently observed among White students who have an opportunity to talk with friends and family during holiday visits. Suddenly they are noticing the racist content of jokes or comments of their friends and relatives and will try to confront them, often only to find that their efforts are, at best, ignored or dismissed as a "phase," or, at worst, greeted with open hostility.

Carl, a White male previously quoted, wrote at length about this dilemma:

> I realized that it was possible to simply go through life totally oblivious to the entire situation or, even if one realizes it, one can totally repress it. It is easy to fade into the woodwork, run with the rest of society, and never have to deal with these problems. So many people I know from home are like this. They have simply accepted what society has taught them with little, if any, question. My father is a prime example of this. . . . It has caused much friction in our relationship, and he tells me as a father he has failed in raising me correctly. Most of my high school friends will never deal with these issues and propagate them on to their own children. It's easy to see how the cycle continues. I don't think I could ever justify within myself simply turning my back on the problem. I finally realized that my position in all of these dominant groups gives me power to make change occur. . . . It is an unfortunate result often though that I feel alienated from friends and family. It's often played off as a mere stage that I'm going through. I obviously can't tell if it's merely a stage, but I know that they say this to take the attention off the truth of what I'm saying. By belittling me, they take the power out of my argument. It's very depressing that being compassionate and considerate are seen as only phases that people go through. I don't want it to be a phase for me, but as obvious as this may sound, I look at my environment and often wonder how it will not be.

The societal pressure to accept the status quo may lead the individual from Disintegration to Reintegration. At this point the desire to be accepted by one's own racial group, in which the overt or covert belief in White superiority is so prevalent, may lead to a reshaping of the person's belief system to be more congruent with an acceptance of racism. The guilt and anxiety associated with Disintegration may be redirected in the form of fear and anger directed toward people of color (particularly Blacks), who are now blamed as the source of discomfort.

Connie, a White woman of Italian ancestry, in many ways exemplified the progression from the Contact stage to Reintegration, a process she herself described seven weeks into the semester. After reading about the stages of White identity development, she wrote:

> I think mostly I can find myself in the disintegration stage of development. . . . There was a time when I never considered myself a color. I never described myself as a "White, Italian female" until I got to college and noticed that people of color always described themselves by their color/race. While taking this class, I have begun to understand that being White makes a difference. I never thought about it before but there are many privileges to being White. In my personal life, I cannot say that I have ever felt that I have had the advantage over a Black person, but I am aware that my race has the advantage.

> I am feeling really guilty lately about that. I find myself thinking: "I didn't mean to be White, I really didn't mean it." I am starting to feel angry towards my race for ever using this advantage towards personal gains. But at the same time I resent the minority groups. I mean, it's not our fault that society has deemed us "superior." I don't feel any better than a Black person. But it really doesn't matter because I am a member of the dominant race. . . . I can't help it. . . . and I sometimes get angry and feel like I'm being attacked.

> I guess my anger towards a minority group would enter me into the next stage of Reintegration, where I am once again starting to blame the victim. This is all very trying for me and it has been on my mind a lot. I really would like to be able to reach the last stage, autonomy, where I can accept being White without hostility and anger. That is really hard to do.

Helms (1990) suggests that it is relatively easy for Whites to become stuck at the Reintegration stage of development, particularly if avoidance of people of color is possible. However, if there is a catalyst for continued self-examination, the person "begins to question her or his previous definition of Whiteness and the justifiability of racism in any of its forms. . . . " (p. 61). In my experience, continued participation in a course on racism provides the catalyst for this deeper self-examination.

This process was again exemplified by Connie. At the end of the semester, she listened to her own taped interview of her racial attitudes that she had recorded at the beginning of the semester. She wrote:

> Oh wow! I could not believe some of the things that I said. I was obviously in different stages of the White identity development. As I listened and got more and more disgusted with myself when I was at the Reintegration stage, I tried to remind myself that these are stages that all (most) White people go through when dealing with notions of racism. I can remember clearly the resentment I had for people of color. I feel the one thing I enjoyed from listening to my interview was noticing how much I have changed. I think I am finally out of the Reintegration stage. I am beginning to make conscious efforts to seek out information about people of color and accept their criticism. . . . I still feel guilty about the feeling I had about people of color and I always feel bad about being privileged as a result of racism. But I am glad that I have reached what I feel is the Pseudo-Independent stage of White identity development.

The information-seeking that Connie describes often marks the onset of the Pseudo-Independent stage. At this stage, the individual is abandoning beliefs in White superiority, but may still behave in ways that unintentionally perpetuate the system. Looking to those targeted by racism to help him or her understand racism, the White person often tries to disavow his or her own Whiteness through active affiliation with Blacks, for example. The individual experiences a sense of alienation from other Whites who have not yet begun to examine their own racism, yet may also experience rejection from Blacks or other people of color who are suspicious of his or her motives. Students of color moving from the Encounter to the Immersion phase of their own racial identity development may be particularly unreceptive to the White person's attempts to connect with them.

Uncomfortable with his or her own Whiteness, yet unable to be truly anything else, the individual may begin searching for a new, more comfortable way to be White. This search is characteristic of the Immersion/Emersion stage of development. Just as the Black student seeks to redefine positively what it means to be of African ancestry in the United States through immersion in accurate information about one's culture and history, the White individual seeks to replace racially related myths and stereotypes with accurate information about what it means and has meant to be White in U.S. society (Helms, 1990). Learning about Whites who have been antiracist allies to people of color is a very important part of this process.

After reading articles written by antiracist activists describing their own process of unlearning racism, White students often comment on how helpful it is to know that others have experienced similar feelings and have found ways to resist the racism in their environments.[5] For example, Joanne, a White woman who initially experienced a lot of guilt, wrote:

> This article helped me out in many ways. I've been feeling helpless and frustrated. I know there are all these terrible things going on and I want to be able to do something. . . . Anyway this article helped me realize, again, that others feel this way, and gave me some positive ideas to resolve my dominant class guilt and shame.

Finally, reading the biographies and autobiographies of White individuals who have embarked on a similar process of identity development (such as Barnard, 1987) provides White students with important models for change.

Learning about White antiracists can also provide students of color with a sense of hope that they can have White allies. After hearing a White antiracist activist address the class, Sonia, a Latina who had written about her impatience with expressions of White guilt, wrote:

> I don't know when I have been more impressed by anyone. She filled me with hope for the future. She made me believe that there are good people in the world and that Whites suffer too and want to change things.

For White students, the internalization of a newly defined sense of oneself as White is the primary task of the Autonomy stage. The positive feelings associated with this redefinition energize the person's efforts to confront racism and oppression in his or her daily life. Alliances with people of color can be more easily forged at this stage of development than previously because the person's antiracist behaviors and attitudes will be more consistently expressed. While Autonomy might be described as "racial self-actualization, ... it is best to think of it as an ongoing process . . . . wherein the person is continually open to new information and new ways of thinking about racial and cultural variables" (Helms, 1990, p. 66).

Annette, a White woman, described herself in the Autonomy stage, but talked at length about the circular process she felt she had been engaged in during the semester:

> If people as racist as C. P. Ellis (a former Klansman) can change, I think anyone can change. If that makes me idealistic, fine. I do not think my expecting society to change is naive anymore because I now *know* exactly what I want. To be naive means a lack of knowledge that allows me to accept myself both as a White person and as an idealist. This class showed me that these two are not mutually exclusive but are an integral part of me that I cannot deny. I realize now that through most of this class I was trying to deny both of them.
>
> While I was not accepting society's racism, I was accepting society's telling me as a White person, there was nothing I could do to change racism. So, I told myself I was being naive and tried to suppress my desire to change society. This is what made me so frustrated—while I saw society's racism through examples in the readings and the media, I kept telling myself there was nothing I could do. Listening to my tape, I think I was already in the Autonomy stage when I started this class. I then seemed to decide that being White, I also had to be racist which is when I became frustrated and went back to the Disintegration stage. I was frustrated because I was not only telling myself there was nothing I could do but I also was assuming society's racism was my own which made me feel like I did not want to be White. Actually, it was not being White that I was disavowing but being racist. I think I have now returned to the Autonomy stage and am much more secure in my position

there. I accept my Whiteness now as just a part of me as is my idealism. I will no longer disavow these characteristics as I have realized I can be proud of both of them. In turn, I can now truly accept other people for their unique characteristics and not by the labels society has given them as I can accept myself that way.

While I thought the main ideas that I learned in this class were that White people need to be educated to end racism and everyone should be treated as human beings, I really had already incorporated these ideas into my thoughts. What I learned from this class is being White does not mean being racist and being idealistic does not mean being naive. I really did not have to form new ideas about people of color; I had to form them about myself—and I did.

Implications for Classroom Teaching

Although movement through all the stages of racial identity development will not necessarily occur for each student within the course of a semester (or even four years of college), it is certainly common to witness beginning transformations in classes with race-related content. An awareness of the existence of this process has helped me to implement strategies to facilitate positive student development, as well as to improve interracial dialogue within the classroom.

Four strategies for reducing students resistance and promoting student development that I have found useful are the following:

1. the creation of a safe classroom atmosphere by establishing clear guidelines for discussion;

2. the creation of opportunities for self-generated knowledge;

3. the provision of an appropriate developmental model that students can use as a framework for understanding their own process;

4. the exploration of strategies to empower students as change agents.

Creating a Safe Climate

As was discussed earlier, making the classroom a safe space for discussion is essential for overcoming students' fears about breaking the race taboo, and will also reduce later anxieties about exposing one's own internalized racism. Establishing the guidelines of confidentiality, mutual respect, "no zaps," and speaking from one's own experience on the first day of class is a necessary step in the process.

Students respond very positively to these ground rules, and do try to honor them. While the rules do not totally eliminate anxiety, they clearly communicate to students that there is a safety net for the discussion. Students are also encouraged to direct their comments and questions to each other rather than always focusing their attention on me as the instructor, and to learn each other's names rather than referring to each other as "he," "she," or "the other person in the red sweater" when responding to each other.[6]

The Power of Self-Generated Knowledge

The creation of opportunities for self-generated knowledge on the part of students is a powerful tool for reducing the initial stage of denial that many students experience. While it may seem easy for some students to challenge the validity of what they read or what the instructor says, it is harder to deny what they have seen with their own eyes. Students can be given hands-on assignments outside of class to facilitate this process.

For example, after reading *Portraits of White Racism* (Wellman, 1977), some students expressed the belief that the attitudes expressed by the White interviewees in the book were no longer commonly held attitudes. Students were then asked to use the same interview protocol used in the book (with some revision) to interview a White adult of their choice. When students reported on these interviews in class, their own observation of the similarity between those they had interviewed and those they had read about was more convincing than anything I might have said.

After doing her interview, Patty, a usually quiet White student, wrote:

> I think I learned a lot from it and that I'm finally getting a better grip on the idea of racism. I think that was why I participated so much in class. I really felt like I knew what I was talking about.

Other examples of creating opportunities for self-generated knowledge include assigning students the task of visiting grocery stores in neighborhoods of differing racial composition to compare the cost and quality of goods and services available at the two locations, and to observe the interactions between the shoppers and the store personnel. For White students, one of the most powerful assignments of this type has been to go apartment hunting with an African-American student and to experience housing discrimination firsthand. While one concern with such an assignment is the effect it will have on the student(s) of color involved, I have found that those Black students who choose this assignment rather than another are typically eager to have their White classmates experience the reality of racism, and thus participate quite willingly in the process.

Naming the Problem

The emotional responses that students have to talking and learning about racism are quite predictable and related to their own racial identity development. Unfortunately, students typically do not know this; thus they consider their own guilt, shame, embarrassment, or anger an uncomfortable experience that they alone are having. Informing students at the beginning of the semester that these feelings may be part of the learning process is ethically necessary (in the sense of informed consent), and helps to normalize the students' experience. Knowing in advance that a desire to withdraw from classroom discussion or not to complete assignments is a common response helps students to remain engaged when they reach that point. As Alice, a White woman, wrote at the end of the semester:

> You were so right in saying in the beginning how we would grow tired of racism (I did in October) but then it would get so good! I have *loved* this class once I passed that point.

In addition, sharing the model of racial identity development with students gives them a useful framework for understanding each other's processes as well as their own. This cognitive framework does not necessarily prevent the collision of developmental processes previously described, but it does allow students to be less frightened by it when it occurs. If, for example, White students understand the stages of racial identity development for students of color, they are less likely to personalize or feel threatened by an African-American student's anger.

Connie, a White student who initially expressed a lot of resentment at the way students of color tended to congregate in the college cafeteria, was much more understanding of this behavior after she learned about racial identity development theory. She wrote:

> I learned a lot from reading the article about the stages of development in the model of oppressed people. As a White person going through my stages of identity development, I do not take time to think about the struggle people of color go through to reach a stage of complete understanding. I am glad that I know about the stages because now I can understand people of color's behavior in certain situations. For example, when people of color stay to themselves and appear to be in a clique, it is not because they are being rude as I originally thought. Rather they are engaged perhaps in the Immersion stage.

Mary, another White student, wrote:

> I found the entire Cross model of racial identity development very enlightening. I knew that there were stages of racial identity development before I entered this class. I did not know what they were, or what they really entailed. After reading through this article I found myself saying, "Oh. That explains why she reacted this way to this incident instead

of how she would have a year ago." Clearly this person has entered a different stage and is working through different problems from a new viewpoint. Thankfully, the model provides a degree of hope that people will not always be angry, and will not always be separatists, etc. Although I'm not really sure about that.

Conversely, when students of color understand the stages of White racial identity development, they can be more tolerant or appreciative of a White student's struggle with guilt, for example. After reading about the stages of White identity development, Sonia, a Latina previously quoted, wrote:

> This article was the one that made me feel that my own prejudices were showing. I never knew that Whites went through an identity development of their own.

She later told me outside of class that she found it much easier to listen to some of the things White students said because she could understand their potentially offensive comments as part of a developmental stage.

Sharon, an African-American woman, also found that an understanding of the respective stages of racial identity development helped her to understand some of the interactions she had had with White students since coming to college. She wrote:

> There is a lot of clash that occurs between Black and White people at college which is best explained by their respective stages of development. Unfortunately schools have not helped to alleviate these problems earlier in life.

In a course on the psychology of racism, it is easy to build in the provision of this information as part of the course content. For instructors teaching courses with race-related content in other fields, it may seem less natural to do so. However, the inclusion of articles on racial identity development and/or class discussion of these issues in conjunction with the other strategies that have been suggested can improve student receptivity to the course content in important ways, making it a very useful investment of class time. Because the stages describe kinds of behavior that many people have commonly observed in themselves, as well as in their own intraracial and interracial interactions, my experience has been that most students grasp the basic conceptual framework fairly easily, even if they do not have a background in psychology.

Empowering Students as Change Agents

Heightening students' awareness of racism without also developing an awareness of the possibility of change is a prescription for despair. I consider it unethical to do one without the other. Exploring strategies to empower students as change agents is thus a necessary part of the process of talking about race and learning about racism. As was previously mentioned, students find it very helpful to read about and hear from individuals who have been effective change agents. Newspaper and magazine articles, as well as biographical or autobiographical essays or book excerpts, are often important sources for this information.

I also ask students to work in small groups to develop an action plan of their own for interrupting racism. While I do not consider it appropriate to require students to engage in antiracist activity (since I believe this should be a personal choice the student makes for him/herself), students are required to think about the possibility. Guidelines are provided (see Katz, 1978), and the plans that they develop over several weeks are presented at the end of the semester. Students are generally impressed with each other's good ideas, and, in fact, they often do go on to implement their projects.

Joanne, a White student who initially struggled with feelings of guilt, wrote:

> I thought that hearing others' ideas for action plans was interesting and informative. It really helps me realize (reminds me) the many choices and avenues there are once I decided to be an ally. Not only did I develop my own concrete way to be an ally, I have found many other ways that I, as a college student, can be an active anti-racist. It was really empowering.

Another way all students can be empowered is by offering them the opportunity to consciously observe their own development. The taped exercise to which some of the previously quoted students have referred is an example of one way to provide this opportunity. At the beginning of the semester, students are given an interview guide with many open-ended questions concerning racial attitudes and opinions. They are asked to interview themselves on tape as a way of recording their own ideas for future reference. Though the tapes are collected, students are assured that no one (including me) will listen to them. The tapes are returned near the end of the semester, and students are asked to listen to their own tapes and use their understanding of racial identity development to discuss it in essay form.

The resulting essays are often remarkable and underscore the psychological importance of giving students the chance to examine racial issues in the classroom. The following was written by Elaine, a White woman:

> Another common theme that was apparent in the tape was that, for the most part, I was aware of my own ignorance and was embarrassed because of it. I wanted to know more about the oppression of people in the country so that I could do something about it. Since I have been here, I have begun to be actively resistant to racism. I have been able to confront my grandparents and some old friends from high school when they make racist comments. Taking this psychology of racism class is another step toward active resistance to racism. I am trying to educate myself so that I have a knowledge base to work from.
>
> When the tape was made, I was just beginning to be active and just beginning to be educated. I think I am now starting to move into the redefinition stage. I am starting to feel OK about being White. Some of my guilt is dissipating, and I do not feel as ignorant as I used to be. I think I have an understanding of racism; how it effects [*sic*] myself, and how it effects this country. Because of this I think I can be more active in doing something about it.

In the words of Louise, a Black female student:

> One of the greatest things I have learned from this semester in general is that the world is not only Black and White, nor is the United States. I learned a lot about my own erasure of many American ethnic groups. . . . I am in the (immersion) stage of my identity development. I think I am also dangling a little in the (encounter) stage. I say this because a lot of my energies are still directed to White people. I began writing a poem two days ago and it was directed to White racism. However, I have also become more Black-identified. I am reaching to the strength in Afro-American heritage. I am learning more about the heritage and history of Afro-American culture. Knowledge = strength and strength = power.

While some students are clearly more self-reflective and articulate about their own process than others, most students experience the opportunity to talk and learn about these issues as a transforming process. In my experience, even those students who are frustrated by aspects of the course find themselves changed by it. One such student wrote in her final journal entry:

> What I felt to be a major hindrance to me was the amount of people. Despite the philosophy, I really never felt at ease enough to speak openly about the feelings I have and kind of watched the class pull farther and farther apart as the semester went on. . . . I think that it was your attitude that kept me intrigued by the topics we were studying despite my frustrations with the class time. I really feel as though I made some significant moves in my understanding of other people's positions in our world as well as my feelings of racism, and I feel very good about them. I feel like this class has moved me in the right direction. I'm on a roll I think, because I've been introduced to so much.

Facilitating student development in this way is a challenging and complex task, but the results are clearly worth the effort.

Implications for the Institution

What are the institutional implications for an understanding of racial identity development theory beyond the classroom? How can this framework be used to address the pressing issues of increasing diversity and decreasing racial tensions on college campuses? How can providing opportunities in the curriculum to talk abut race and learn about racism affect the recruitment and retention of students of color specifically, especially when the majority of the students enrolled are White?

The fact is, educating White students about race and racism changes attitudes in ways that go beyond the classroom boundaries. As White students move through their own stages of identity development, they take their friends with them by engaging them in dialogue. They share the articles they have read with roommates, and involve them in their projects. An example of this involvement can be seen in the following journal entry, written by Larry, a White man:

> Here is our fifth week of class and more and more I am becoming aware of the racism around me. Our second project made things clearer, because while watching T.V. I picked up many kinds of discrimination and stereotyping. Since the project was over, I still find myself watching these shows and picking up bits and pieces every show I watch. Even my friends will be watching a show and they will say, "Hey, Larry, put that in your paper." Since they know I am taking this class, they are looking out for these things. They are also watching what they say around me for fear that I will use them as an example. For example, one of my friends has this fascination with making fun of Jewish people. Before I would listen to his comments and take them in stride, but now I confront him about his comments.

The heightened awareness of the White students enrolled in the class has a ripple effect in their peer group, which helps to create a climate in which students of color and other targeted groups (Jewish students, for example) might feel more comfortable. It is likely that White students who have had the opportunity to learn about racism in a supportive atmosphere will be better able to be allies to students of color in extracurricular settings, like student government meetings and other organizational settings, where students of color often feel isolated and unheard.

At the same time, students of color who have had the opportunity to examine the ways in which racism may have affected their own lives are able to give voice to their own experience, and to validate it rather than be demoralized by it. An understanding of internalized oppression can help students of color recognize the ways in which they may have unknowingly participated in their own victimization, or the victimization of others. They may be able to move beyond victimization to empowerment, and share their learning with others, as Sharon, a previously quoted Black woman, planned to do.

Campus communities with an understanding of racial identity development could become more supportive of special-interest groups, such as the Black Student Union or the Asian Student Alliance, because they would recognize them not as "separatist" but as important outlets for students of color who may be at the Encounter or Immersion stage of racial identity development. Not only could speakers of color be sought out to add diversity to campus programming, but Whites who had made a commitment to unlearning their own racism could be offered as models to those White students looking for new ways to understand their own Whiteness, and to students of color looking for allies.

It has become painfully clear on many college campuses across the United States that we cannot have successfully multiracial campuses without talking about race and learning about racism. Providing a forum where this discussion can take place safely over a semester, a time period that allows personal and group development to unfold in ways that day-long or weekend programs do not, may be among the most proactive learning opportunities an institution can provide.

Notes

1. A similar point could be made about other issues of oppression, such as anti-Semitism, homophobia and heterosexism, ageism, and so on.

2. While similar models of racial identity development exist, Cross and Helms are referenced here because they are among the most frequently cited writers on Black racial identity development and on White racial identity development, respectively. For a discussion of the commonalities between these and other identity development models, see Phinney (1989, 1990) and Helms (1990).

3. Both Parham (1989) and Phinney (1989) suggest that a preference for the dominant group is not always a characteristic of this stage. For example, children raised in households and communities with explicitly positive Afrocentric attitudes may absorb a pro-Black perspective, which then serves as the starting point for their own exploration of racial identity.

4. After being introduced to this model and Helms's model of White identity development, students are encouraged to think about how the models might apply to their own experience or the experiences of people they know. As is reflected in the cited journal entries, some students resonate to the theories quite readily, easily seeing their own process of growth reflected in them. Other students are sometimes puzzled because they feel as though their own process varies from these models, and may ask if it is possible to "skip" a particular stage, for example. Such questions provide a useful departure point for discussing the limitations of stage theories in general, and the potential variations in experience that make questions of racial identity development so complex.

5. Examples of useful articles include essays by McIntosh (1988), Lester (1987), and Braden (1987). Each of these combines autobiographical material, as well as a conceptual framework for understanding some aspect of racism that students find very helpful. Bowser and Hunt's (1981) edited book, *Impacts of Racism on Whites*, though less autobiographical in nature, is also a valuable resource.

6. Class size has a direct bearing on my ability to create safety in the classroom. Dividing the class into pairs or smaller groups of five or six students to discuss initial reactions to a particular article or film helps to increase participation, both in the small groups and later in the large group discussion.

References

Barnard, H. F. (Ed.). (1987). *Outside the Magic Circle: The Autobiography of Virginia Foster Durr*. New York: Simon & Schuster. (Originally published in 1985 by University of Alabama Press)

Bowser, B. P., & Hunt, R. G. (1981). *Impacts of Racism on Whites*. Beverly Hills: Sage

Braden, A. (1987, April–May). "Undoing racism: Lessons for the peace movement." *The Nonviolent Activist*, pp. 3–6.

Bronstein, P. A., & Quina, K. (Eds.). (1988). *Teaching a psychology of people: Resources for gender and sociocultural awareness*. Washington, DC: American Psychological Association.

Cross, W. E., Jr. (1971). The Negro to black conversion experience: Toward a psychology of black liberation. *Black World, 20* (9), 13–27.

Cross, W. E., Jr. (1978). The Cross and Thomas models of psychological nigrescence. *Journal of Black Psychology, 5*(1), 13–19.

Cross, W. E., Jr., (1991). *Shades of black: Diversity in African-American identity*. Philadelphia: Temple University Press.

Cross, W. E., Jr., Parham, T. A., & Helms, J. E. (1991). The stages of black identity development; Nigrescence models. In R. Jones (Ed.), *Black psychology* (3rd ed., pp. 319–338). San Francisco: Cobb and Henry.

Derman-Sparks, L., Higa, C. T., & Sparks, B. (1980). Children, race and racism: How race awareness develops. *Interracial Books for Children Bulletin, 11* (3/4), 3–15.

Helms, J. E.. (Ed.). (1990). *Black and white racial identity: Theory, research and practice.* Westport, CT: Greenwood Press.

Highlen, P. S., Reynolds, A. L., Adams, E. M., Hanley, T. C., Myers, L. J., Cox, C., & Speight, S. (1988, August 13). *Self-identity development model of oppressed people: Inclusive model for all?* Paper presented at the American Psychological Association Convention, Atlanta, GA.

Hull, G. T., Scott, P. B., & Smith, B. (Eds.). (1982). *All the women are white, all the blacks are men, but some of us are brave: Black women's studies.* Old Westbury, NY: Feminist Press.

Katz, J. H. (1978). *White awareness: Handbook for anti-racism training.* Norman: University of Oklahoma Press.

Lester, J. (1987). *What happens to the mythmakers when the myths are found to be untrue?* Unpublished paper, Equity Institute, Emeryville, CA.

McIntosh, P. (1988). *White privilege and male privilege: A personal account of coming to see correspondence through work in women's studies.* Working paper, Wellesley College Center for Research on Women, Wellesley, MA.

McIntosh, P. (1989, July/August). White privilege: Unpacking the invisible knapsack. *Peace and Freedom*, pp. 10–12.

Parham, T. A. (1989) Cycles of psychological nigrescence. *The Counseling Psychologist, 17* (2), 187–226.

Phinney, J. (1989). Stages of ethnic identity in minority group adolescents. *Journal of Early Adolescence, 9*, 34–39.

Phinney, J. (1990) Ethnic identity in adolescents and adults: Review of research. *Psychological Bulletin, 108* (3), 499–514.

Phinney, J. S., & Rotheram, M. J. (Eds.). (1987). *Children's ethnic socialization: Pluralism and development.* Newbury Park, CA: Sage

Schuster, M. R., & Van Dyne, S. R. (Eds.). (1985). *Women's place in the academy: Transforming the liberal arts curriculum.* Totowa, NJ: Rowman & Allanheld.

Wellman, D. (1977). *Portraits of white racism.* New York: Cambridge University Press.

American Indian Studies Programs:
Surviving the '80s, Thriving in the '90s

BOBBY WRIGHT

Introduction

American Indian Studies[1] emerged as an academic field from the turbulent student protests of the late 1960s and early '70s, when minority students demanded more relevant college curricula. Angry and often militant students charged that the traditional curriculum was ethnocentric, and it ignored, distorted and denigrated their ethnic experiences.

Since that time, academe has given birth to a growing number of programs which have as their foundation the study of American Indian culture, history and contemporary affairs. Heth and Guyette (1984) identified 107 two- and four-year institutions with American Indian studies programs, most in colleges and universities serving significant Indian student populations.[2] These researchers also found several institutions which were planning additional programs. The movement continues today as diverse institutions such as Lake Superior State University in Michigan and Stanford University explore new academic programs in American Indian studies—indicative of the growing acceptance and importance of this emerging field of study.

The academic structure of the programs which house this developing field varies, ranging from autonomous departments with their own roster of interdisciplinary courses and their own faculty to decentralized interdepartmental, interdisciplinary programs. Often, too, American Indian studies is part of a more encompassing ethnic studies department which may include African-American, Hispanic and Asian studies. In 1984, almost half of the Native American studies programs enjoyed full departmental status or were programs administered by another academic unit (Heth & Guyette, 1984).

The roles these programs play in their respective institutions also range in scope. Nonetheless, to varying degrees, they perform the same traditional functions as other academic departments; that is, teaching, research and service. Unlike most academic units, however, American Indian Studies programs assume other unique roles, including American Indian student support services, student recruitment, and affirmative action responsibilities. This article discusses each of the major functions in light of issues and prospects which will affect their status in the 1990s.[3]

Teaching

American Indian studies programs typically offer instruction in interdisciplinary courses of study focusing on Native American culture, history and contemporary affairs. Their offerings range from a few courses to a comprehensive curriculum leading to a graduate degree. Of the 107 programs identified by Heth and Guyette (1984), 18 (16.8 percent) offer a major in American Indian studies, while 40 (37.4 percent) deliver a minor. Six institutions including the University of

California at Los Angeles and the University of Arizona offer graduate degrees in American Indian studies.

Since the emergence of this new field of study, faculty from more established disciplines have critically questioned the academic integrity of the Native American studies curriculum. Ethnic studies, they've argued, has no academic substance, no theoretical foundation, no scholarly tradition—all of which characterize the traditional disciplines. However, like other interdisciplinary area studies—Women's studies and American studies, for example—American Indian studies programs have stemmed the tide of conservatism and elitism that characterize the academy. They have demonstrated their academic quality and importance and over the past two decades have gained at least grudging acceptance by the academic community. Indeed, Native American studies has earned a significant place in the academy, and its role will become even more important in the 1990s, as institutions respond to emerging issues in higher education.

One of the main issues concerns diversity. During the past few years, student unrest has revisited the college campus—at such diverse institutions as the university of Massachusetts at Amherst, Citadel, Fairleigh Dickinson University, Manhattanville College, New Jersey Institute of Technology, the University of Wisconsin at Madison, Rutgers University and the University of California at Berkeley (Wilson & Justiz, 1987–1988). The list goes on. Meanwhile, civil rights organizations have documented episodes of racial harassment at more than 250 colleges over the past three years (*Black Issues* Wire Services, 1990). These tensions call attention not only to the needs of culturally diverse student populations, but of all students who must learn to function in an increasingly multicultural, interdependent global society. In response to these needs, many colleges and universities have mandated, as part of their general education requirements, coursework in multicultural and/or global perspectives. Among those which have adopted diversity requirements in the last year or two are the State University of New York College at Cortland, Penn State University, Williams College and the Universities of Cincinnati, California at Berkeley, Wisconsin at Madison, Wisconsin at Milwaukee, and Vermont (Magner, 1990). These and other institutions rely on ethnic studies programs to respond to this general education need. Consequently, the American Indian studies role is expanding beyond providing a scholastic specialization for a limited audience. Today their academic importance penetrates the very core of college curriculum, addressing a critical need for diversity in the academy.

Research

American Indian studies faculty, like those in any established academic unit, conduct research. Although the interdisciplinary field of American Indian Studies claims no theory or methodology independent of the established disciplines, scholars of American Indian studies scrutinize theories and facts stemming from the traditional academic fields and consequently contribute fresh perspectives to existing bodies of knowledge.

Equally important, the research activities of American Indian studies programs have effectively addressed socioeconomic and educational problems facing Indian communities. Applied research conducted through these programs has included business feasibility studies, tribal historical research for federal recognition petitions, recreation market research, and student outcomes assessment for tribally controlled community colleges. Academic researchers in the traditional departments have largely ignored such lines of inquiry. In response, several larger institutions have established American Indian studies research centers,[4] some supported by a professional refereed journal which offers a forum for scholarship by and about American Indians. The American Indian Studies Center at the University of California, Los Angeles, for example, publishes the *American Indian Culture and Research Journal,* and the *American Indian Quarterly* is a scholarly publication of the University of California, Berkeley.

A decade ago, Thornton (1980) identified research as the most pressing American Indian studies need for the 1980s. He argued that

> since the initial "creation," American Indian studies had not sufficiently developed intellec-
> tually for it to flourish or even perhaps survive in the academic system, and if it was to do

so, it must "come to grips' with the scholarly activities characteristic of other disciplines (p. 5).

American Indian studies, he concluded from this premise, "needed to develop greater scholarly and research activities" (p. 5). He also stressed the need for more American Indian scholars, who can bring new sensitivities and fresh approaches to existing lines of inquiry.

A decade later, these needs remain as critical as ever, particularly in four-year institutions where scholarship production is a primary measure of departmental quality.[5] In the 1990s, the academic acceptance and integrity of American Indian studies will continue to depend on its quality of research and its contributions to the knowledge base.

Service

Institutional and public service activities are important and time-consuming expectations of academic units and their faculty. Service to the institution encompasses such endeavors as campus committee work, guest lecturing, and student recruitment. Public service entails activities which support community and professional organizations—consulting and technical assistance to local communities, program planning and evaluation, participation on governing boards, and leadership in professional associations, for example.

Institutional service has become particularly problematic for Native American studies faculty, especially among the severely underrepresented few who are women and American Indian. College committees, many of which mandate minority representation, overutilize available Indian faculty. As a consequence, their research programs, as well as their tenure and promotion opportunities, often suffer. However, because the Indian voice is important to institutional decision-making, Native American studies faculty are reluctant to decline participation and thereby risk the advancement of American Indian student and community concerns. This is a dilemma that must be addressed through expanded and concerted affirmative action measures.

In their public service, American Indian studies programs have made special commitments to Indian communities and organizations. They serve as liaisons between the institution and its Indian constituents and seek to extend institutional resources for the benefit of native communities. The Center for native American Studies at Montana State University, for example, recently established an Office of Tribal Service. Staffed by a tenure-track Indian faculty member, this office is charged to coordinate University-Indian community interactions and to extend the institution's resources to meet needs identified by the tribes of Montana. The Center's faculty development activities on behalf of Montana's tribally controlled colleges have been lauded as a national model of inter-institutional cooperation. (Carnegie Foundation for the Advancement of Teaching, 1989, pp. 33–34, 82–83). Such service and outreach commitments to Indian people are costly and place additional demand on program resources, especially in times of retrenchment. Nevertheless, the commitment to service is essential to the unique identity of American Indian studies and must persist with equal vigor in the 1990s.

American Indian Student Support Services

Unlike typical academic departments, American Indian programs assume the additional responsibility for academic, social and cultural support to increase American Indian student enrollment and retention. Heth and Guyette (1984) found that 62 of the 107 programs (57.9 percent) administered minority student support programs and that 74 (or 69.2 percent) had special counselors for American Indian students. Other support includes scholarship and fellowship programs, tutoring, cultural/social/educational centers for Indian students, American Indian student organizations, developmental coursework and the like.

In assuming this special role, American Indian studies programs offer social-cultural enclaves for students, especially those from rural reservations, who can often experience alienation and isolation from the mainstream. Wright (1985) demonstrated that American Indian studies programs and the special support services they embrace "are meeting the serious needs of American Indian college students" and contribute significantly to their success (pp. 1–7).

Like the service and outreach functions, this unique student services role imposes unusual demands on American Indian studies faculty and program resources. However, American Indian students remain severely underrepresented in higher education institutions and their retention is disproportionately low. As long as these conditions persist, Native American studies programs will remain a vital resource for Indian students in the coming decade.

Summary and Recommendations

Institutions which house and fund American Indian Studies fully expect that these programs and their faculty will perform the traditional teaching, research, and service functions of all academic units. Meanwhile, American Indian Studies programs have assumed several roles which extend beyond those of typical academic departments. First, they assist institutions in meeting their diversity goals through the multicultural dimension of their faculty, students, and curriculum. Second, they assume an active role in minority student recruitment and retention. Third, they serve as a vital link between the academic and Indian communities. And finally, these programs represent and advance Indian concerns within the academic community. These special and important responsibilities which American Indian Studies programs shoulder remain relatively unnoticed and unrewarded by the institutions they serve.

> In 1980 Lujan and Hill concluded that with questionable integrity and continuous accommodation to external pressures, the [American Indian studies] programs become all things to all people. This results in reduced academic respect and the image of ethnic studies as an administrative sop to pacify minorities (1980, p. 196).

The present article has stressed that the image and importance of American Indian Studies programs have changed positively in the decade since Lujan and Hill advanced their cynical but grounded remarks. Still, the multiple demands placed on these programs remains troublesome.

Looking to the 1990s—after a decade of stabilization, growth, proliferation, and academic acceptance of these programs—American Indian studies will need less to legitimize itself, as institutions increasingly view their presence on campus and their roles as central to their mission. They will, in short, become institutional assets, instead of fleeting liabilities. Still, in spite of this optimism, this paper highlights several issues which institutions and their Native American programs must address to ensure the continued development of these emerging academic units. Considering these concerns and with sensitivity to the already great expectations of these programs, the following recommendations for the 1990s are offered:

1. American Indian studies programs should reexamine their role in the college curriculum. Once viewed by institutions and by some programs themselves as a smattering of "relevant" courses primarily for Indian students (Lujan & Hill, 1980, pp. 195–197), the Native American studies curriculum can now assume a more prominent role, especially as higher education continues to confront the issue of diversity in the 1990s. Emerging from the academic isolation that once characterized Native American studies programs, they can infuse the curriculum in a variety of ways—by offering coursework to satisfy core curriculum or general education requirements, by encouraging interdepartmental agreements which permit appropriate American Indian studies courses to satisfy major requirements of other departments, by providing opportunities for Indian studies faculty to team-teach in other departments, and by proposing courses for such special programs as women's studies and university honors programs.

2. In light of the limited availability of qualified Indian doctorates, many of whom have found an academic home in American Indian studies, and in recognition of the unusually heavy demands on minority faculty, institutions should develop special faculty development programs designed to recruit, nurture and tenure American

Indian faculty. Such programs might encompass research support funds, release time provisions, early sabbatical leaves, mentorships with senior faculty, and financial support for Indian faculty pursuing their doctorates. Moreover, institutions must recognize that, in recruiting American Indian faculty, they are entering a fiercely competitive marketplace where minority doctorates are a rare commodity (Mooney, 1990b: Nitzschke et al., 1990). Accordingly, they must be prepared to offer competitive, often higher salaries which reflect this market consideration—much in the same vein as the salaries that engineering and science faculty command.

3. American Indian studies programs must place quality scholarship at the top of their priorities. Faculty should no longer accept the burden of institutional service and other unrewarded activities at the expense of their academic advancement and tenure. Likewise, programs should encourage research which serves the American Indian people while it contributes new perspectives to existing lines of inquiry. And to address the critical future need for American Indian scholars, Native American studies programs should develop fellowships, cross-campus mentorship programs and other efforts to recruit and nurture Indians for the professoriate.

4. American Indian Studies programs should be recognized and adequately funded for their distinctive community outreach and student services activities. These programs remain in a unique position to meet institutional commitments to American Indian communities and their students. Their efforts must be duly rewarded. In a recent report, the Carnegie Foundation for the Advancement of Teaching recommended "a fresh concept of scholarship," which rewards faculty activities other than academic publications—teaching, service and other professional activities (Mooney, 1990b, p. 1). American Indian studies programs should embrace this movement to broaden the definition of scholarship, so that the unusual faculty demands of institutional and public service, student support, and teaching are appropriately rewarded in the faculty review process.

American Indian studies has emerged from the 1980s, realizing the importance of its visibility in the curriculum, the power of providing an institutional home for American Indian faculty and students, and the significance of creating safe, analytic spaces to discover and express its own scholarly voice. The coming decade, then, promises to be one during which American Indian Studies crosses the ledger from the credit to the debit side, as institutions increasingly recognize that these programs are vital assets rather than liabilities.

Notes

1. American Indian Studies is variously called Native American Studies, Alaska Native Studies, or for an individual tribe—for example, Navajo and Crow Studies. Heth and Guyette (1984) found an approximate 50/50 ratio between programs using the term "American Indian" and those employing "Native American" (p. 8). While I prefer the use of "American Indian Studies," I have alternated terminology in the interest in writing style and readability.

2. All identified programs do not have an academic program. Some rather focus their activities on American Indian student support. Heth and Guyette (1984) failed to include in their count most of the current 24 tribally controlled colleges, where Native American Studies constitute a major focus of their missions and consequently of their curricula. Accordingly, although no national surveys of Native American studies programs have been conducted since 1984, clearly their number is now significantly greater.

3. The degrees to which the individual programs assume the various roles vary, of course, dependent on institutional type and character. For example, community colleges, primarily teaching institutions, do not emphasize research and service. However, at tribally controlled community colleges, where American Indian studies is central to their mission of cultural renewal, preservation, and transmission, many of these institutions have assumed important research and service functions. I have not highlighted Native American Studies at tribal colleges, leaving that important topic to a later discussion.

Instead, I have discussed the program roles which would be typical of four-year, particularly land-grant institutions, though I expect that the issues will apply to all institutional types.

4. Heth and Guyette (1984) identified 15 institutions which had research units.

5. Native American Studies programs at community colleges do not emphasize research. Neither is research typically a faculty expectation. However, because of their awareness of and responsiveness to community needs, many tribal college programs have engaged in important research activities such as tribal histories, community needs assessments, and native language studies. I would add, too, that, while research should be a priority, it must not be advanced at the expense of undergraduate teaching excellence.

References

Black Issues Wire Services (1990). Officials set up efforts to eradicate racist incidents on campus. *Black Issues in Higher Education*, 6 (21), 32.

Carnegie Foundation for the Advancement of Teaching (1989). *Tribal Colleges: Shaping the Future of Native America.* Princeton, NJ: Carnegie Foundation for the Advancement of Teaching.

Heth, C., & Guyette, S. (1984). *Issues for the Future of American Indian Studies: A Needs Assessment and Program Guide.* Los Angeles: American Indian Studies Center.

Lujan, P., & Hill, L. B. (1980). Intercultural communication as an academic haven for American Indian Studies. In *American Indian Issues in Higher Education.* Los Angeles: American Indian Studies Center.

Magner, D. (1990). Difficult questions face colleges that require students to take courses that explore issues related to race. *The Chronicle of Higher Education*, 36 (28), A19–A20.

Mooney, C. J. (1990a). Higher-education conferees applaud Carnegie plan to broaden definition of faculty scholarship. *The Chronicle of Higher Education*, 36 (30), A1, A16.

Mooney, C. J. (1990b). Universities awarded record number of doctorates last year; foreign students thought to account for much of the increase. *The Chronicle of Higher Education*, 36 (30), A1, A11.

Nitzschke, D. F., Cleckley, B. J., & Satcher, D. (1990) Ethnically and racially diverse faculty: A response to change. In R. W. Hively (Ed.). *The Lurking Evil: Racial and Ethnic Conflict on the College Campus* (pp. 104–110). Washington, DC: American Association of State Colleges and Universities.

Thornton, R. (1980). American Indian studies as an academic discipline: A revisit. *In American Indian Issues in Higher Education.* Los Angeles: American Indian Studies Center.

Wilson, R., & Justiz, M. J. (1987, Fall; 1988, Winter). Minorities in higher education: Confronting a time bomb. *Educational Record*, 68 (4), 69 (1), 8–14.

Wright, B. (1985). Programming success: Special student services and the American Indian college student. *Journal of American Indian Education*, 24 (1), 1–7.

Bobby Wright is currently a Research Associate and Assistant Professor in the Center for the Study of Higher Education, The Pennsylvania state University. He is a former Director of Montana State University's Center for Native American Studies and is an enrolled member of the Chippewa-Cree Tribe, Rocky Boy's Reservation.

PART III
STUDENTS

Improving Black Student Access and Achievement in Higher Education

Walter R. Allen

Over the past thirty years, profound changes have occurred in black student patterns of college attendance in the United States, and black college students now face a crisis (Ballard 1973; Billingsley 1981). Until 1950, more than seventy-five percent of black college students enrolled in historically black institutions; by 1973, that percentage had dropped to roughly one-quarter (Anderson, 1984). An estimated 57 percent of all black baccalaureates for the 1978–79 school year came from white colleges and universities (Deskins, 1983). As of 1982, three-fourths of all black college students were still in predominantly white institutions (National Center, 1982).

But these blacks on white campuses are severely disadvantaged compared to white students in terms of persistence rates (Astin, 1982; Di Cesare, Sellacek, & Brooks, 1982; Thomas, 1981), academic achievement levels (Nettles *et al.*, 1985; Smith and Allen, 1984); enrollment in advanced degree programs (Hall, Mayes and Allen, 1984; Astin, 1982); and overall psychosocial adjustments (Allen, 1985, 1986; Fleming, 1984). Black students on historically black campuses are disadvantaged compared to black *and* white students on white campuses in terms of family socioeconomic status (Morris, 1979; Thomas, 1984), high school academic records (Astin and Cross, 1981), caliber of university instructional faculty and facilities (Fleming, 1984; Williams, 1981), academic specializations selected (Haynes, 1981; Thomas, 1984), and enrollment in advanced study (Blackwell, 1982; Miller, 1981; Pearson and Pearson, 1985).

What happens to black students at such critical steps as college entry, selecting a major, and graduation or dropping out? This paper looks at three student outcomes: academic performance, racial attitudes, and college satisfaction. It compares conclusions in the literature with those of a national study of black students—both those who attended predominantly white and those who attended historically black state-supported universities. The paper explores relationships between student outcomes, student background characteristics, the nature of student experiences on the campus, and the student's particular personality orientation.

Race and Gender Differences

Past research suggests that the fit between black students and white colleges is not very good. Black students differ in fundamental ways from the white students these schools commonly serve. They, therefore, experience more difficulties in adjusting, more limited academic success, and higher attrition rates with definite consequences for their aspirations.

Black Students on White Campuses

Studies of black students attending predominantly white postsecondary institutions commonly report (1) their social and economic characteristics (Allen, 1986; Blackwell, 1982); (2) their levels of adjustment (Fleming, 1984; Webster, Sedlacek, and Miyares, 1979); and (3) their academic success/attrition rates (Nettles, *et al.*, 1985).

The parents of black students are typically urban, have fewer years of education, earn less, and work at lower-status jobs than do the parents of white students (Bayer, 1972; Blackwell, 1982; Boyd, 1974).

Yet despite these social and economic disadvantages, black college students have the same or higher aspirations than their white counterparts (Allen, 1985, 1986; Bayer, 1972; Gurin and Epps, 1975), even though they attain these aspirations less often than white students. Lower educational attainment is pronounced for black students in general, and for black women in particular (Allen, 1986; Hall, Mays, and Allen, 1984; Smith and Allen, 1984; Gurin and Epps, 1975). All students must adjust to college (Webster, Sedlacek, and Miyares, 1979), but black students face additional problems. Many must create their own social and cultural networks, given their exclusion (self- and/or other-imposed) from the wider university community. Of all problems faced by black students on white campuses, those arising from isolation, alienation, and lack of support seem to be most serious (Allen, 1985, 1986; Smith and Allen, 1984; Rosser, 1972).

Black students' academic performance is lower than that of their white peers. Their academic difficulties are often compounded by the absence of remedial/tutorial programs and information exchange with whites (i.e., faculty and students) (Hall, Mays, and Allen, 1984).

Despite the initial difficulties *most* black students experience, *many* make the required adjustments and are academically successful in predominantly white institutions (Allen, 1986; Ballard, 1973; Peterson et. al., 1978).

Black Students on Black Campuses

Research on black students attending historically black colleges can be usefully organized into student background and academic skills, student academic development, and student psychosocial development.

Studies of black students on white campuses do not necessarily assume a fit between students and institution, and yet nonetheless assume that white campuses provide superior environments for black student education. Typically, the parents of black students on black campuses earn less money, have lower educational achievement, hold lower-status jobs, and are more often separated or divorced than the parents of black students at white schools (Gurin and Epps, 1975; Morris, 1970; Thomas, 1984). Black students on black campuses typically have lower standardized test scores and weaker high-school backgrounds than do typical black students on white campuses (Astin and Cross, 1981).

This condition grows naturally from the special mission of black colleges. To a large extent, they enroll students who might not otherwise be able to attend college because of financial or academic barriers (Miller, 1981; Morris, 1979; Thomas, McPartland, and Gottfredson, 1981). They pride themselves on their ability to take poor and less well-prepared black students as they are, correct their academic deficiencies, and graduate them equipped to compete successfully for jobs or graduate/professional school placements in the wider society (Miller, 1981; Morris, 1980).

Furthermore, when black students on black and white campuses are compared for psychosocial development, those on black campuses seem to fare much better. In an early study, Gurin and Epps (1975) found that black students who attend black colleges had positive self images, strong racial pride, and high aspirations. More recently,. Fleming (1984) demonstrated much higher levels of psychosocial adjustment for blacks on black campuses than for those on white campuses.

In sum, the evidence suggests that black students on black campuses are more disadvantaged socioeconomically *and* academically than are black (or white) students on white campuses but that students on black campuses display more positive psychosocial adjustments, significant academic gains, and greater cultural awareness/commitment.

Gender Differences

Researchers have identified persistent differences in the college experiences of men and women—differences that cross the color line. In their early, comprehensive comparison of black men and women attending ten black colleges between 1964 and 1974, Gurin and Epps (1975) found that black women experienced a clear disadvantage compared to black men:

- Women's educational and occupational goals were lower on all measures.

- Males were three times more likely to plan for Ph.D.'s.

- Women were more likely to aspire to "female sector" jobs requiring less ability/effort and providing lower prestige.

- Males were more likely to be influenced in their goals and aspirations by the college attended.

A decade later, Fleming (1984) studied a comparable sample of 3,000 black college students, including students attending predominantly white colleges. Fleming found that white men on white campuses, and black men on black campuses, derived far more benefits from college than black women. On white campuses, black men were withdrawn and unhappy, felt unfairly treated, and experienced considerable lack of academic motivation while black men on black campuses, like white males on white campuses, felt potent and "in charge."

Findings from a study of over 700 black undergraduates on white campuses revealed that black men were more likely than black women to have both high aspirations and good grades. This was surprising, since black women in this sample had higher grade point averages than black men (Smith and Allen, 1984; Allen, 1986). When black males and black females with comparable achievement levels were compared, the males consistently reported higher post-graduate aspirations. Thomas (1984) found that black women's occupational aspirations are highest and least traditional in private schools.

National Study of Black College Students

A National Study of Black College Students (NSBCS), housed at the University of Michigan, Ann Arbor, has collected several waves of data on the achievements, experiences, attitudes, and backgrounds of black undergraduates attending selected state-supported universities. The 1981 phase of study collected data from black undergraduates at six predominately white, public universities (University of Michigan, Ann Arbor; University of North Carolina, Chapel Hill; University of California, Los Angeles; Arizona State University, Tempe; Memphis State University; and the State University of New York, Stony Brook). The 1983 phase collected data from black undergraduates at eight predominantly black, public universities (North Carolina Central University, Durham; Southern University, Baton Rouge, Louisiana; Texas Southern University, Houston, Texas; Jackson State University, Mississippi; North Carolina A&T State University, Greensboro; Central State University, Wilberforce, Ohio; Morgan State University, Baltimore, Maryland; and Florida A&M University, Tallahassee).

Both data sets were merged to compare and contrast students at predominantly white universities and those at traditionally black universities. The final response rate for the 1981 undergraduate study was 27 percent, while the 1983 undergraduate response rate was 35 percent; together the data sets include 1,583 students.

This study used three measures of student outcomes: academic performance, satisfaction with college, and racial attitudes. Academic performance was measured by the respondent's reported grade point average. Racial attitudes were measured by asking respondents to indicate whether they strongly agreed, agreed, disagreed or strongly disagreed with each of the following statements:

There is a need for a national black political party. . . .

Interracial dating and marriage are equally as acceptable as within-race dating and marriage. . . .

Schools with majority black student populations should have a majority of black teachers and administrators. . . .

There is a great deal of unity and sharing among black students at this university. . . .

"Conservatives" rejected the national black party, opposed interracial dating or marriage, opposed majorities of teachers/administrators in black majority schools, and judged black unity and sharing as low.

Student satisfaction with college was measured by four items:

1. How much do you, as a black student, feel part of general campus life, insofar as student activities and government are concerned? not at all . . . (1) to considerable . . . (4).

2. Have you considered leaving school?

3. How would you characterize *your* relations with whites at this university? Faculty?: excellent . . . (1) to very poor . . . (4)

4. Staff people? excellent . . . (1) to very poor . . . (4)

Three other groups of variables were collected for the study: (1) Background factors, including campus race, student sex, mother's education, and high school grade point average; (2) Campus experience factors, including feelings of involvement in campus life, and level of academic competition at the university; (3) Social/psychological factors, including respondent's self-concept, racial attitudes, and occupational aspirations.

The NSBCS has been described elsewhere in greater detail (Allen 1985; 1986). An expanded treatment of the study is also available from the National Center for Postsecondary Governance and Finance in the proceedings of the conference from which this paper has been excerpted (Allen, 1988).

Academic Performance

Black students on black campuses reported higher grade point averages than did their peers on white campuses. Three-quarters of the students in the white campus group, versus two-thirds of the students in the black campus group, reported grade point averages of less than 3.0 on a four-point scale. Men reported significantly higher grade point averages than women. These differences were less pronounced, however, than the differences between black and white campuses. Women were only slightly more likely than men to report grade point averages below 3.0 (72 percent versus 68 percent). Grades were higher for students who had not seriously contemplated leaving school and for students who found their interests reflected in campus activities. Grades were also higher for students who reported favorable relationships with faculty and staff, and who had high educational aspirations.

Student Racial Attitudes

Racial attitudes varied by student background, campus experiences, and personality orientation. A sizable 62 percent of the women (54 percent of the men) considered interracial dating unacceptable. Women were also less likely to see a high degree of unity on their campuses; 52 percent of women versus 57 percent of the men reported a great deal of unity among black students.

Black students on white campuses were more likely to describe unity among black students on the campus negatively; 44 versus 62 percent judged black student unity "very low." Black students on both race campuses seemed equally likely to consider interracial dating acceptable; 41 percent approved. Students from higher-income families were more accepting of interracial dating. Student assessment of the degree of unity among black students on campus was strongly related to positive feelings about and greater involvement with campus life.

Student Satisfaction with College

On black campuses, two-thirds of the students reported campus activities as "somewhat" or "considerably" representative of their interests. The comparable figure for white campuses was 38 percent. While 26 percent of the students on black campuses felt that campus activities were "considerably" representative of their interests, only 8 percent those on white campuses were similarly positive. At the other extreme, twice as many students on white campuses reported campus activities as "not at all" representative of their interests (19 percent) as their counterparts on black campuses (10 percent).

Student Gender and Campus Race Effects

Overall, men were more likely than women to claim "excellent" relations with white faculty and staff—24 versus 19 percent. Twenty percent of the men (15 percent of women) reported "excellent" relations with white staff.

Black students were more likely to report favorable relationships with white faculty and staff on predominantly black campuses. Differences were striking. The proportion of black students on black campuses claiming excellent relations with white faculty (26 percent) and with white staff (22 percent) exceeded by nearly twice the proportions on white campuses claiming similar relationships (15 percent and 12 percent respectively).

The mothers of students attending white campuses tended to be better educated than their black campus counterparts. Nearly a third of the students on white campuses reported that their mothers had graduated from college; 11 percent reported that their mothers held advanced degrees. By comparison, only 22 percent of the mothers of students attending black schools had graduated from college and 9 percent held advanced degrees. At the lower end of the educational ladder, a third of the mothers of children attending black colleges had not graduated from high school compared with a quarter of the mothers of students on white campuses.

The high school academic superiority of black students on white campuses was uncontestable; nearly half the students on white campuses, versus 18 percent of students on black campuses, reported high-school averages of 3.5 or better. When high-school grades were compared with college grade-point averages, the observed declines in academic performance were nothing short of spectacular. Women's grade point averages declined more drastically than men's.

Black men and women followed traditional differences in college majors. Women were overrepresented in the social sciences (21 versus 18 percent), the humanities (7 versus 4 percent), and the human service professions—e.g., social work, nursing (14 versus 10 percent) and the entrepreneurial professions like business, engineering (48 versus 56 percent).*

Seventy-three percent of the students on black campuses, versus half of those on white campuses, chose to major in some profession. The entrepreneurial professions attracted 57 percent of the professional majors on black campuses and 43 percent of those on white campuses. Fifteen percent of the professional majors on black campuses, versus 8 percent of those on white campuses, were in the human service professions. The percentage of black students majoring in the natural and life sciences were about the same on both black and white campuses. Black students on white campuses were, however, considerably more likely to major in the social sciences (24 versus 16 percent) and the humanities (9 versus 3 percent).

The differences by predominant race of campus in the sensed level of academic competition was nothing short of profound. Sixty-one percent of the students on white campuses reported that the level of academic competition was "considerable"; an additional 28 percent said there was "some" competition. The comparable figures for black students on black campuses were 13 and 64

---

*This is how the sentence appears in the original publication.

percent. Women were more likely than men to use the highest category ("considerable amount") in describing the level of academic competition.

The two categories of students who felt the most academic pressure—women and those on white campuses—also reported the least favorable relationships with faculty. Women less often claimed "excellent" relations with faculty (19 versus 24 percent); the same is true for students on white campuses (15 versus 26 percent).

Black students on white campuses were considerably more likely than those on black campuses to anticipate future occupations in the highest prestige category (e.g., judge, corporate executive, physician), by a margin of 26 to 13 percent. This fact, coupled with the greater intensity of academic competition, may explain why black students on white campuses reported aspirations for lower status occupations. Black students on white campuses may well adjust their "prestige" aspirations downward because they understand more clearly the competitive odds they are likely to encounter. Women were significantly less likely to report occupational goals in the highest prestige category (16 versus 22 points). Women's career strivings and career goals were also consistently depressed, suggesting gender discrimination and psychological impact on possible factors restricting the goal-focused behaviors of women.

Black students on black campuses were more likely to set their sights on master's degrees (44 versus 32 percent), probably because of the disproportionate enrollment on black campuses in professional training programs where the terminal degree was in social work (MSW), business (MBA), or regional planning (MRP). Black students on black campuses were more likely than black students on white campuses to report the Ph.D. as their ultimate goal (17 versus 8 percent). On the other hand, black students attending white universities were more likely than black students on black campuses to aspire to prestigious terminal degrees in medicine or law (29 versus 8 percent).

Implications and Recommendations

Interpersonal relationships are crucial in determining how individual and institutional characteristics influence black student experiences in higher education. Interpersonal relationships form the bridge between individual dispositions and institutional tendencies; together these factors determine student outcomes. How a student perceives and responds to events in the college setting influences the value derived from the college experience.

Black student college outcomes can be reasonably viewed as resulting from two factors. Whether a student successfully completes college and graduates with honors is unquestionably influenced by such individual characteristics as how bright the student is, his or her level of background preparation, the intensity of personal ambition, and the seriousness and discipline of his or her striving. Beyond these personal traits, however, lies a set of more situational and interpersonal factors and characteristics: the quality of life at the institution, the level of academic competition, university rules/procedures/resources, relationships with faculty, and friend-support networks.

In discussing the aspiration-attainment process twenty years ago, Rehberg and Westby (1967) introduced the vital notion of facilitation. The concept is useful here to point up that the attainment process is influenced by a combination of institutional, individual, and interactional factors. Black students act out their educational goals in special social environments which affect how likely they are to realize those goals. Other actors in the setting—indeed the setting itself—can either facilitate or frustrate the efforts of black students to perform well academically (Allen, 1985).

The challenge confronting researchers, educators, and policymakers is to identify key factors and to formulate strategies to improve the educational experiences and outcomes of black students in U.S. higher education. In seeking answers to a wide range of complex questions, it is helpful to compare student experiences on black and white campuses. Black students on black campuses purchase richly endowed physical circumstances and bureaucratic efficiency at the cost of less favorable interpersonal relations and peace of mind. Black women are forced to choose between self-assertion and male companionship or between the pursuit of nontraditional careers and personal happiness.

These are unfair, unnecessary choices, bred from our society's historic institutionalization of the inequities of race, gender, and class. Until these inequities are corrected at their source, black students in higher education—indeed the entire educational process at this level—will continue to suffer. The ideal goal of educational change for black students in higher education over the coming years should be to combine the better qualities of black and white campuses.

A significant study by Ogbu (1978) comparing, minority education in Japan, Israel, the United States, Britain, New Zealand, and India revealed similarities in the negative myths about the inferior educational opportunities provided to disadvantaged groups. The universal effect of this pattern was to "institutionalize" the low status of discriminated groups and, by so doing, to perpetuate their low educational attainment. Education is a valued social resource; thus, its allocation is subject to the dynamics of power in any society. In the United States prevailing views of blacks, other minorities, women, and the poor have encouraged cultural definitions of them as uneducable, poorly motivated, and low achievers. These views have reinforced (and been reinforced by) their concentration in society's deviant categories, low-prestige occupations, low-income neighborhoods, and low-educational achievement categories.

Improving the effectiveness of black postsecondary education remains a pivotal issue in the future of our society. For "education remains the primary lever by which the racial situation in this country can be controlled and changed—not simply at the college level, but also in high schools, elementary schools, and day-care centers, where today hundreds of thousands of black youth are being separated from the elemental knowledge necessary for them to compete equally with whites when they become adults" (Ballard 1973, 143). It is, therefore, incumbent upon universities and the education system in general to improve the quality of schooling for black Americans.

Over the past thirty years, black Americans have made unparalleled gains in the literacy, in the proportion enrolled in school, and the mean years of schooling completed (Reid 1982). In fact, by 1980, black Americans were indistinguishable from whites by these measurements. However, what does distinguish blacks from whites is the return on their educations and the consequent, persistent economic inequities. Thus, the average white male high school graduate earns more than the average black male college graduate (Abramowitz 1976, 204). The 1977 unemployment rate for white male high school dropouts was the same as that of black male college graduates (Hill 1979).

A common response to such glaring inequities is to retreat into questions about the "quality" of education received by black Americans. Hidden in this ploy is the implicit and unacceptable assumption that all white Americans—by virtue of their color—receive the same quality of education. Previously, black Americans were told that they did not have enough education; now the message is that they have enough education *but*, unfortunately it is the wrong kind. The suspicion of black Americans about such a message is well founded. Hare and Levine (1983) remind us:

> The school plays a unique role in allocating people to different positions in the division of labor through routing and grading practices. Relative success in school is, in fact, the major avenue through which discrimination in the job market is justified. Given racism as well as sexism and classism in a stratified America, it can be argued that the disproportional allocation of blacks, other people of color, women, and people of lower class origin to the lowest labor slots is functional and their relative academic failure is essential to getting the job done (p. 19).

Bibliography

Abramowitz, E. A. *Equal Educational Opportunity for Blacks in U.S. Higher Education: An Assessment.* Washington, D.C.: Howard University Press, 1976.

———. Allen, W. R. "Race Consciousness and Collective Commitments among Black Students on White Campuses." *Western Journal of Black Studies* 8 no. 3 (1984): 156–66.

_____. "Black Student, White Campus: Structural, Interpersonal and Psychological Correlates of Success." *Journal of Negro Education* 54, no. 2 (1985): 134–47.

_____. *Gender and Campus Race Differences in Black Student Academic Performance, Racial Attitudes, and College Satisfaction.* Atlanta: Southern Education Foundation, 1986.

Allen, W. R. "Improving Black Student Access and Achievement in U.S. Higher Education" in *From Access to Achievement: Strategies for Urban Institutions.* Edited by R. C. Richardson, Jr. and A. G. de los Santos, Jr. College Park, Maryland: National Center for Postsecondary Governance and Finance, 1988.

Anderson, J. D. "The Schooling and Achievement of Black Children: Before and After Brown. Topeka, 1900–1980." *Advances in Motivation and Achievement* 1 (1984): 103–22.

Astin, A. *Minorities in Higher Education.* San Francisco: Jossey-Bass, 1982.

Astin, H., and P. H. Cross. "Black Students in White Institutions." In (ed.) *Black Students in Higher Education in the 1970's,* edited by Gail E. Thomas, Westport, Conn.: Greenwood Press, 1981.

Ballard, A. B. *The Education of Black Folk: The Afro-American Struggle for Knowledge in White America.* New York: Harper & Row, 1973.

Bayer, A. E. *The Black College Freshmen: Characteristics and Recent Trends.* Washington, D.C.: American Council on Education Research Reports, (3), 1972.

Billingsley, A. "The Case for Black Colleges." *Essence.* (Aug. 1981): 124.

Blackwell, J. E. "Demographics of Desegregation." In *Race and Equity in Higher Education,* edited by Reginald, Washington, D.C.: American Council on Education, 1982.

Boyd, W. M. *Desegregating America's Colleges: A Nationwide Survey of Black Students, 1972–1973.* New York: Praeger, 1974.

Braddock, J., and M. P. Dawkins. "Predicting Black Academic Achievement in Higher Education." *Journal of Negro Education* 49 (Summer 1984): 310–25.

Deskins, D. R., Jr. *Minority Recruitment Data: An Analysis of Baccalaureate Degree Production in the U.S.* Totowa, N. J.: Rowman and Allanheld, 1983.

DiCesare, P. C., W. E. Sedlacek, and G. C. Brooks. "Nonintellective Correlates of Black Student Attrition." *Journal of College Student Personnel,* 13 (1972): 319–24.

Fleming, J. *Blacks in College.* San Francisco: Jossey-Bass, 1984.

Gurin, P., and E. G. Epps, *Black Consciousness, Identity and Achievement: A Study of Students in Historically Black Colleges.* New York: Wiley Press, 1975.

Hall, M., A. Mayes, and W. Allen. "Dreams Deferred: Black Student Career Goals and Fields of Study in Graduate/Professional Schools." *Phylon* 45 no. 4 (1984): 271–283.

Hare, B. R., and D. U. Levine. "Toward Effective Desegregated Schools." Unpublished paper. Department of Sociology, State University of New York at Stony Brook, 1983.

Haynes, Leonard, III. "The Adams Mandate: A Format for Achieving Equal Educational Opportunity and Attainment." In Thomas 1981, 329–95.

Hill, R. B. *The Widening Economic Gap.* Washington, D.C.: National Urban League Research Department, 1979.

House. "Social Structure and Personality." In *Social Psychology: Sociological Perspectives,* edited by M. Rosenberg and Ralph Turner. New York: Basic Brooks, 1981.

Miller, C. "Higher Education for Black Americans: Problems and Issues." *Journal of Negro Education* 49 (Summer 1981): 208–24.

Morris, L. *Elusive Equality: The Status of Black Americans in Higher Education.* Washington, D.C.: Howard University Press, 1979.

_____. *Still a Lifeline: The Status of Historically Black Colleges and Universities,* 1975–1978. National Advisory Committee on Black Higher Education and Black Colleges and Universities. Washington, D.C.: U.S. Department of Education, 1980.

National Center for Education Statistics. *The Traditionally Black Institutions of Higher Education,* 1860–1982. Washington, D.C.: U.S. Department of Education, 1984.

National Center for Education Statistics. *Fall Enrollment in Colleges and Universities,* 1980, Washington, D.C.: U.S. Department of Education, (June 1982).

Nettles, M., C. Gosman, A. Thoeny, and B. Dandrige. *The Causes and Consequences of College Students' Attrition Rates, Progression Rates and Grade Point Averages.* Nashville, Tenn.: Higher Education Commission, 1985.

Newman, D. K. *Protest, Politics and Prosperity: Black Americans and White Institutions,* 1940–75. New York: Pantheon Books, 1978.

Ogbu, J. U. *Minority Education and Caste: The American System in Cross-Cultural Perspective.* New York: Academic Press, 1978.

Pearson, W., and L. C. Pearson. "Baccalaureate Origins of Black American Scientists. Cohort Analysis." *Journal of Negro Education* 54 (1985): 24–34.

Pentages, T. J., and C. F. Creedon. "Studies of College Attrition: 1950–1975." *Review of Educational Research* 48 (?1978): 49–101.

Peterson, M., R. T. Blackburn, Z. F. Gamson, C. H. Arce, R. W. Davenport, and J. R. Mingle. *Black Students on White Campuses: The Impacts of Increased Black Enrollments.* Ann Arbor: Institute for Social Research, University of Michigan, 1978.

Ramist, L., and S. Arbeiter. *Profiles, College-Bound Seniors,* 1983. New York: College Entrance Examination Board, 1984.

Reed, R. J. "Increasing the Opportunities for Black Students in Higher Education." *Journal of Negro Education* 47, no. 2 (1979): 189–203.

Rehberg, R., and D. Westby. "Parental Encouragement, Occupation, Education and Family Size: Artifactual or Independent Determinants of Adolescent Educational Expectations." *Social Forces* 45 (?1967): 362–73.

Reid, J. "Black America in the 1980's." *Population Bulletin* 37, no. 4 (?1982): 1–38.

Rosser, J. M. "Higher Education and Black Americans: An Overview." *Journal of Afro-American Issues* 1, no. 2 (1972): 189–203.

Smith, A. W., and W. R. Allen. "Modeling Black Student Academic Performance in Higher Education." *Research in Higher Education* 21, no. 2 (1984): 210–24.

Smith, J. *The Impact of Desegregation on Higher Education.* Durham: Institution on Desegregation, North Carolina University, 1981.

Thomas, G. E. *Equality of Representation of Race and Sex Groups in Higher Education: Institutional and Program Enrollment Statuses.* Center for Social Organization of Schools, Johns Hopkins University, Report No. 263, October 1978.

_____. *Black Students in Higher Education: Conditions and Experiences in the 1970's.* Westport, Conn. Greenwood Press 1981.

_____. *Black College Students and Factors Influencing Their Major Field Choice.* Atlanta: Southern Education Foundation, 1984.

Thomas, G. E., J. M. McPartland, and D. C. Gottfredson. *The Status of Desegregation and Black-White Participation in Higher Education*. Baltimore, M. D.: Center of Social Organization of Schools, Johns Hopkins University, Report No. 598, 1981.

Webster, D. W., W. E. Sedlacek, and J. Miyares. "A Comparison of Problems Perceived by Minority and White University Students." *Journal of College Student Personnel* 20, no. 2 (1979): 165–70.

Wells, A. ed., *Contemporary Sociological Theories*. Santa Monica Calif.: Goodyear Publishing Co., Inc., 1978.

Williams, C. A. *The Black/White College: Dismantling the Dual System of Higher Education*. Washington, D.C.: U.S. Commission on Civil Rights, Clearinghouse Publication 66, 1981.

Getting In
Mexican Americans' Perceptions of University Attendance and the Implications for Freshman Year Persistence

LOUIS C. ATTINASI, JR.

In view of its importance for social advancement [11] and its contribution to the improvement of personal well-being [2, 51], it is not surprising that higher education in the United States has become a cynosure for efforts to improve the condition of economically and socially disadvantaged subpopulations. Ironically, the present condition of these subpopulations exists because, in the past, higher education's service as an instrument for social mobility was seldom indiscriminate. America's racial and ethnic minorities have been and continue to be "grossly underrepresented in higher education and in almost all occupational fields that require a college education" [2], and do not, as a consequence, enjoy equitable participation in the larger society's social, economic, and political life.

One racial minority that has been particularly underserved by American higher education, in general, and by the four-year institution, in particular, is the Mexican American. In 1979, according to an estimate by the Bureau of the Census [47], the rate of baccalaureate degree attainment in the general population was more than four times the rate in the Mexican American subpopulation alone. Data presented by Brown [10] tend to confirm the link between social and economic advancement and college graduation. Relative to the total population, Mexican Americans are overrepresented in lower-level, poorer-paying positions, such as those occupied by service workers, artisans, operatives, farm and nonfarm laborers; they are underrepresented in more prestigious, better-paying positions, including those held by professional and technical workers, managers and administrators, and farmers and farm managers.

The low percentage of the Mexican American subpopulation graduating from college is attributable, in part, to high attrition rates at the elementary and secondary school levels, which effectively decrease the number of individuals eligible for college attendance, and to the failure of a substantial number of high school graduates from the subpopulation to enroll in college. Data based on the Bureau of the Census' Current Population Surveys from 1974 through 1978 [2] indicate nationwide a rate of college entry of 23 percent. The corresponding rates for whites are 83 percent and 38 percent, respectively.

The Persistence of Mexican Americans in College

The low percentage of college graduates among Mexican Americans is also due to the failure of many Chicanos, once enrolled in an institution of higher education to persist to degree completion. Numerous studies involving national [4], regional [11], state [13], and institutional [23, 36, 37] data have shown that Mexican American students graduate from college within a normal time frame—four to five years —at a rate that is from one and a half to two times smaller than the rate for Anglo students. Even if a longer time frame—nine or ten years—is considered, the discrepancy persists. Tracking students who entered college in 1971 until 1980, Astin [2] found that 55 percent of the Anglos but only 40 percent of the Mexican Americans in his national sample had achieved baccalaureate degrees during the nine-year period.

It is clear that addressing the low percentage of college graduates in the Chicano subpopulation necessitates examinations of Mexican American school-going behavior before, at the point of, and after college entry. The study of Chicano persistence in the elementary and secondary schools [28] has a history of several decades, beginning most notably with the U.S. Commission on Civil Rights' Mexican American Education Study in 1971 [48]. Similarly, there has been extensive investigation of the issue of Mexican American access to college [28, 38]. Much less attention, however, has been focused on the persistence of Chicanos at the baccalaureate level.

Of the few attempts to date to isolate factors that influence the persistence of Mexican Americans in college, the most significant is a study by Astin and Burciaga [3] for the Commission on Minorities in Higher Education. Astin and Burciaga analyzed data based on two different longitudinal samples—one covering the first two years of undergraduate work (1975 freshmen followed up in 1977) and the other a nine-year span covering undergraduate and graduate work (1971 freshmen followed up in 1980). For the first sample, persistence was examined as continuous enrollment over the first two years of college; for the second, as attainment of the baccalaureate degree by the ninth year following matriculation. In each case, analysis was by means of a two-stage stepwise linear multiple regression "so that the students' entering characteristics were first controlled before any attempt was made to assess the influence of environmental characteristics" [2, p. 90].

Astin and Burciaga [3] found that the persistence of Chicanos is related statistically to a number of factors, including performance and preparation in high school, the education and occupational status of parents, various expectations about the college experience, the nature of financial support, and the institution of initial matriculation. As their analysis was not theory-driven, however, Astin and Burciaga could provide no overarching conceptualization to tie these statistical associations together. Establishing the associations did not lead to a coherent explanation of Chicano persistence in college.

Methods of Studying Persistence in College

Astin and Burciaga's study is not atypical of research on the persistence/attrition of college students. Studies of this subject have either lacked the guidance of a conceptual framework or have uncritically accepted frameworks developed for other sociopsychological phenomena. Investigators not using conceptual frameworks have been content with establishing the correlates of persistence, rather than understanding the phenomenon as a dynamic process.

Since 1967 a number of "models" of persistence/attrition behavior have been developed and tested. These models have been based on selective findings of the correlational research, together with certain sociological and/or psychological constructs adapted from theoretical frameworks for explaining other social phenomena. For example, both Spady [41] and Tinto [45, 46] have proposed conceptualizations of attrition behavior heavily influenced by Durkheim's [15] sociological explanation of suicide. Other prominent models [7, 42] derive their basic theoretical orientations from one another of the recent conceptualizations of disengagement from work (for example, Price's [34] model of work turnover or Dawis, Lofquist, and Weiss' [12] theory of work adjustment).

Undoubtedly, with the emergence of these conceptual models, the study of student persistence in college has moved in a potentially more fruitful direction. As the preoccupation with the identification of correlates has been replaced by an interest in explaining the processes that lead to persistence and withdrawal behaviors, the models have held out the possibility of reaching an understanding of the underlying dynamics of persistence/attrition phenomena. Still, none of the available models has proved more than very modestly successful in explicating those dynamics [31]. This is the result, in my judgment, of certain conceptual and methodological shortcomings shared by the existing models.

First, as mentioned above, each of the present persistence/attrition theorists has chosen to ground his model in a framework used to explain some other social or sociopsychological phenomenon. But an assumption *at the outset* that dropping out of college is like committing suicide or leaving a job has turned out to be too severe a constraint upon the conceptualizing process [31]. In addition, the models have been developed on the basis of, and tested with, data collected from institutional records and/or by means of fixed-choice questionnaires. These are methods of data collection that effectively strip away the context surrounding the student's decision to persist or not to persist in college and exclude from consideration the student's own perceptions of the process.

Yet, given the present level of our understanding of that decision, it is precisely those characteristics—the context of the decision and the student's perspective on the context—that investigations of student persistence in college must include. What are needed then are naturalistic, descriptive studies guided by research perspectives that emphasize the insider's point of view. [46].[1]

An Exploratory Study

In this article, I report an exploratory study undertaken to collect and analyze qualitative data describing, from the Mexican American student's point of view, the context surrounding his or her decision to persist or not to persist in the university and, on the basis of that description, to develop concepts of the university-going process. The concepts so developed were used to propose hypotheses about the context within which Mexican American students make decisions to persist or not to persist in the university.

In lieu of one of the existing conceptual frameworks of persistence/attrition, the study was guided only by a broad research perspective—the sociology of everyday life [14]. The latter is actually a collection of research perspectives in sociology, all of which focus on everyday social interaction in natural situations and have as their starting points (1) the experience and observation of people interacting in concrete, face-to-face situations, and (2) an analysis of the actors' meanings.

In particular, two of the sociologies of everyday life—symbolic interactionism and ethnomethodology—were used in conducting the inquiry. Symbolic interactionism emphasizes social interaction as a process that forms human conduct: It is from the interaction of the individual with others that the meanings of things arise, and it is on the basis of their meaning that the individual acts toward things. The concern of symbolic interactionists then is shared emergent meanings. Ethnomethodology seeks to understand how actors go about the task of seeing, describing, and explaining the world in which they live, that is, the process of creating shared emergent meanings and using them to account for things in one's everyday world. Two assumptions, following from the research perspective, underlay the study: (1) Persistence behavior is the consequence of a process in which the student is an active participant: He or she takes account of various things in his or her everyday world and acts on the basis of how he or she interprets them. (2) Persistence behavior is related to the manner in which the university becomes and remains, through everyday social interaction, a reality for the student.

Data Collection and Analysis

The conceptualization of Chicano university-going reported here is based on Mexican American university students' perceptions of their own and others' college-going experiences and attitudes, as reported to the author in open-ended interviews. Eighteen students and former students from a single entering class of a large, public southwestern university were interviewed by the author eight to eleven months following the end of their freshman year to obtain their perceptions of their college-going behavior during, and prior to, their freshman year.

Informants for the study were selected from a list provided to the author by the Office of Academic Computing Services at the study university. The list contained the names, addresses, and telephone numbers of individuals who: (1) were new freshman at the university in the fall of 1981, (2) were registered as full-time students (more than eleven credit hours) for that semester, (3) at the time of admission reported their ethnicity to be Hispanic,[2] and (4) at the time of admission were citizens or permanent residents. The list also indicated whether or not and, if so, when each student had withdrawn from the university prior to the twenty-first day of the fall semester of 1982.

The selection of informants from the sampling frame was guided by a single consideration: the sample had to include both persisting and nonpersisting students. In all other respects, the selection process was arbitrary, producing, in essence, a sample of convenience. Individuals who agreed to be interviewed and did, in fact, participate in interviews constituted the sample. Representativeness was not an important consideration in the selection process because the purpose of the study was to discover, rather than to validate, the patterns in a process as it naturally occurs and is understood.

Thirteen of the informants were persisters, that is, they exhibited continuous enrollment through the beginning of their sophomore year; the other five were nonpersisters, having withdrawn at some point between the beginning of the freshman year and the beginning of the sophomore year. A demographic and academic profile of the informant is provided in table 1, together with comparable profiles of all new full-time Hispanic freshmen and of all new full-time freshmen matriculating at the study university in fall 1981. Table 2 identifies (pseudonymously) the eighteen informants and provides additional background information on them.

Open-ended interviewing, that is, without an interview schedule, was used in the study so that the author would be free to pursue any area of inquiry suggested by an informant's responses, and the informant would be free to draw upon his or her own experience, rather than prestated alternatives, in responding to the author's questions. The interviews were in-depth modified "life history" interviews; the informants were encouraged to think back over their lives and recount experiences related to their own and others' college-going behavior. For each experience, informants were asked to describe the ways in which other persons were involved in the experience and to recall their own perceptions of it. The interviews were conducted in person at sites of the informants' choosing.

Analysis of the data was accomplished by qualitative induction [17]. That is, concepts and hypotheses emerged from an examination of concrete data collected in the field. The induction process was constrained only by the research perspective: any concept or hypothesis that emerged would, perforce, be consistent with the assumptions of the sociology of everyday life.

To initiate the analysis, the interviews were open-coded, that is, the contents were coded in as many different ways as possible [9]. A total of one hundred nineteen codes were used in this study. These related to context and setting, informants' definitions of situations, informants' ways of thinking about people and objects, process, activities, events, strategies, and relationships. Some coding categories—those most related to the study's research perspective—were more likely to be used than others. Examples of the former are everyday social interaction and perceptions of the university. Often the coding categories were labeled with the very words (for example, "getting in" and "preparing") used by the informants themselves.

Coding was followed by a data reduction step in which the number of coding categories was reduced and the analysis became more conceptually oriented. Decisions about the retention, merging, and discarding of codes initially were made on the basis of the saliency of the categories, that is, the number of cases they contained and the extent of their relationships to other categories. Further data reduction was accomplished by "clustering" [44] the remaining coding categories. Connections or linkages between categories were established by identifying higher-order categories under which a number of coding categories fit. Conceptually, the coding categories became subcategories or properties of the higher-order category. For example, the categories "scaling down" and "getting to know" were seen to be linked, because they were both processes that helped students negotiate, or penetrate, the campus geographies. Thus, it was possible to "reduce" these two categories to form the broader category "getting in." "Scaling down" and "getting to know" then became subcategories of "getting in."

Table 1
Demographic and Academic Profiles of Various Groups of Fall 1981
Matriculants at the Study University

	All Full-Time, First-Time Freshmen	All Full-Time, First-Time Hispanic Freshmen	The Informants
Number:	3126	147	18
Gender:			
% Male	48.9	50.3	44.4
% Female	51.1	49.7	55.6
Residency status:			
% Resident of state	77.2	81.0	88.9
% Non-resident of state	22.8	19.0	11.1
Average age:	18.4	18.5	18.6
Average rank in high-school graduating class (% from the top):	N/A	24.3	23.1
Average ACT composite score:	N/A	18.5	18.7
Area of major:			
% Agriculture	0.6	0.7	
% Business Administration	23.2	24.5	27.9
% Communication	6.1	2.1	
% Computer Science	6.0	6.8	5.6
% Education	3.3	6.9	
% Engineering	15.2	15.0	16.7
% English	0.5	0.7	
% Fine Arts	5.0	5.5	
% Home Economics	0.7	1.4	11.1
% Mathematics & Natural Science	2.8	2.1	
% Medical Technology	0.6		
% Pre-Professional	13.2	14.4	22.4
% Pre-Architectural	5.2	4.8	5.6
% Pre-Criminal Justice	0.5	0.7	5.6
% Pre-Law	2.5	2.7	5.6
% Pre-Medicine	2.8	3.4	5.6
% Pre-Nursing	1.8	1.4	
% Pre-Social Work	0.4	1.4	
% Psychology	2.0		
% Social Science	2.2	1.4	5.6
% Spanish	0.1	0.7	
% Other foreign language	0.3		
% No Major	18.1	18.4	11.1
Freshman-Year Persistence Status:			
% Persisting	83.5	68.7	72.2
% Non-Persisting	16.5	31.3	27.8

This process of "moving out of the data" was facilitated by the writing of research memos [16]. Research memos were notes of varying length that the author wrote to himself in order to capture, on the spot, insights into the data and its analysis. As the analysis proceeded, there was increasing interplay between data reduction and memo writing. Progress is reducing the data and generating conceptual categories expanded the contents of memos and suggested connections between the ideas in separate memos. The latter resulted in "rememoing," that is, writing memos based on other memos. At the same time, memoing and rememoing facilitated data reduction by

Table 2
Comparative Background Data for Informants

Name	Sex	Age*	Marital Status	Location of High School(s) Attended	Location of Residence While Attending University	Academic Major*	Persistence Status
Anita†	F	18	Single	In-state	On-campus	Bus./Pre-Law	Persister
Barbara	F	18	Single	In-state	Off-campus	Undecided	Persister
Carlos	M	18	Single	In-state	Off-campus	Computer Sci	Persister
David	M	18	Single	Out-of-state/ In-state	Off-campus	Pre-Medicine	Persister
Emmanuel	M	18	Single	In-state	On-campus	Electr. Eng.	Persister
Frances	F	18	Single	In-state	On-campus	Electr. Eng.	Persister
Gregory	M	18	Single	In-state	Off-campus	Bus. Adm.	Persister
Helen	F	17	Single	In-state	Off-campus	Home Ec.	Non-Persister
Isabelle	F	19	Single	In-state	Off-campus	Pre-Architect.	Persister
Jose	M	19	Single	Out-of-state/ In-state	Off-campus	Management	Persister
Karen	F	18	Single	In-state	On-campus	Crim. Justice	Persister
Linda	F	17	Single	In-state	On-campus	Sociology	Persister
Michael	M	17	Single	In-state	Off-campus	Aerospace Eng.	Non-Persister
Natalie	F	19	Single	Out-of-state	Off-campus/ On-campus	Marketing	Persister
Thomas	M	19	Single	Out-of-state	On-campus	Pre-Law	Persister
Peter	M	23	Married	In-state	Off-campus	Gen. Construction	Non-Persister
Theresa	F	18	Single	In-state	Off-campus	Home Ec.	Non-Persister
Rose	F	18	Single	In-state	Off-campus	Bus. Adm.	Non-Persister

*At time of matriculation
†All names are fictitious.

suggesting how categories might be collapsed into other categories, and, thus, categories of a higher conceptual level generated.

Getting Ready

Two conceptual schemes for interpreting the college-going behavior of Chicano university students emerged from the study. One of these schemes has reference to behaviors and attitudes of these students prior to college matriculation, the other to behaviors and attitudes after matriculation. Each scheme centers around a major organizing concept. For prematriculation experiences, the concept is "getting ready"; for postmatriculation experiences, it is "getting in."

Among experiences before college attendance reported by the informants were activities that variously engendered a college-going frame of mind; modeled college-going behavior; or simulated, in some way, the experience of going to college. These experiences were seen to constitute five categories, or patterns, of getting-ready behavior: (1) Initial expectation engendering, (2) Fraternal modeling. (3) Mentor modeling, (4) Indirect simulation, and (5) Direct simulation (table 3).

"Initial expectation engendering" refers to experiences very early in the life of an informant that led to a belief or perception, held long before actual college attendance, that the informant would be going to college. Although such an expectation could be encouraged by elementary school teachers and classmates, it was most frequently perceived to be the result of parental

Table 3
Dimensions of the "Getting Ready" Categories

Category	Type of Activity	Other Participants	Message Conveyed	Outcome
Initial expectation engendering	Oral communication	Parents Friends Classmates	*You* are a *future* college-goer.	Expectation of being a college student.
Fraternal modeling	Observation Oral communication (a description)	Siblings Other relatives	*You* are a *future* college-goer. This is what college is like for me, your brother.	Expectation of being a college student. Expectation of what being a college student is like.
Mentor modeling	Oral communication (a description)	High-school teachers (especially mentors)	This is what college *was* like for me, your teacher.	Expectation of what being a college student is like.
Indirect simulation	Oral communication (a prescription or prediction)	High-School teachers (especially mentors)	This is what you *should do* in college. This is what college *will be* like for you.	Expectation of what being a college student is like.
Direct simulation	Participant observation	Campus people	Oh, so this is what college will be like for me, the informant	Expectation/ experience of what being a college student is like.

exhortation. For example, Julius (all names are pseudonyms) recalled: "That's all [my father] ever preached—college." Rose, after quoting her father's advice: "Go to college. Go to college,'" added, "You know, going to college and getting an education was just everything to my father."

Despite the obvious importance of parents and others in engendering this early college-going expectation, the informants often described the expectation as though it were a conclusion they had reached independently. Some recalled coming to think about college as part of a natural progression. In the words of Anita: "So I thought: 'After high school comes college, after college comes work'." Other informants linked college-going to future benefits. For example, David recalled this sentiment: "I knew I wanted to go to college anyway because I wanted to be better off." Frances specifically connected the self-realization aspect with the influence-of-others aspect of initial expectation engendering: "Deep down [my sister] doesn't really want to go to school but it's been expected and she knows if she wants to make anything of herself and if she really wants to do something she's going to have to go."

Whatever the particular characteristics of the initial expectation engendering process, the outcome was always perceived to be an expectation that the informant would be a college-goer. Experiences belonging to the remaining categories of getting ready provided substance, in the form of descriptions, prescriptions, and predictions *about* college-going, for the generalized expectation *of* college-going that resulted from initial expectation engendering.

"Fraternal modeling" refers to the informant's having observed, and/or having received information about, the college-going behavior of a relative, usually a sibling. There appear to have been at least two aspects, or features, of this category of getting ready. First, the informant's knowing *that* his or her relative has gone to college often led to a kind of "turn-taking" mind set.

Linda provides a description of this feature: "When my brother first went to college, . . . I just assumed at that point, that when I was that age, I would go to college."

The second aspect of fraternal modeling involved the informant's coming to know something *about* the college-going behavior of the relative. Cues given by the relative provided the informant with information about how one went about being a college student, about negotiating the college campus. Oral cues were forthcoming during face-to-face interactions when the relative returned home from college, or, occasionally, over the telephone. Barbara recounted what she learned from her sister: "Well, my sister was in engineering. And she was one of the few girls, which made things worse. She talked about some of her classes and stuff which I knew from then I didn't want to get into anything that I was going to have to be that involved and that so precise and everything." A few informants actually observed if only in limited contexts, the college-going behavior of a sibling during visits to the campus. Anita reported: "I came and visited my sister a couple of times and . . . I remember going through all the hassles of getting her registered and everything and it was just like uh, it was a big hassle."

Knowing something about the experiences and/or attitudes of the modeler sometimes led to early apprehension about college-going. As a result of experiences like the one described above and of her sister's expressed anxieties, Anita recalled being "scared" about the idea of going to college. This kind of knowledge also resulted in "negative exampling," that is, the modeler's behavior causing the informant to decide to approach college-going differently than the modeler. Barbara's remarks about how her sister's experiences with the engineering major influenced her own choice of major are quoted above. Barbara also made this observation: "I saw the mistake my sister made of thinking she was going to get A's and then she didn't and so I taught myself to be the opposite way around, to know that I wasn't going to."

Modeling behavior which provided the informants with knowledge about college-going behaviors and attitudes also was exhibited by particular high-school instructors. Because the informants reported close relationships with these instructors, they are referred to here as mentors. Invariably, "mentoring modeling" took the form of the mentor relating his or her own experiences in, and attitudes about, college. Anita recalled a high school physics teacher who talked a lot about the subject: "He went [to college] all over but [mentions a university by name] was mostly all he talked about. . . . He is really intelligent and anything he said, we knew it was true." Barbara provided a very specific example of her mentor's influence on her attitude development toward college-going: "One of my high school teachers, probably the best teacher I ever had, flunked out of college two times. He didn't tell his parents when he flunked out. . . . He was real good because all my life everybody's always expecting me to get A's. . . . So that was the first time I really had a different perspective."

In the case of fraternal or mentor modeling, informants came to have knowledge about college-going as the result of interactions that produced *descriptions* of college-going behaviors and attitudes. Such knowledge could also be the consequence of interactions that led to *prescriptive* or *predictive* statements about college-going. Experiences of the latter kind are examples of "indirect simulation."

Two subcategories of indirect simulation can be differentiated on the basis of the formality of the simulative experience. First, there were the formal, well-planned simulative experiences. These included preparation for college classes. David provided this description of a "college class" that he had taken in high school: "They told us about ACT's and college. It was mainly . . . to prepare us. . . . That's the only class where they really pushed us to go [to college]." Career-day seminars were also simulative experiences of this kind.

Although planned simulations seem to be common to all informants, simulations that were less formal and more spontaneous apparently made a stronger impression. Anita recalled vividly a prediction her high-school chemistry teacher had made about what college-going was going to be like for her and her classmates: "He would expect everybody to go to college, right? And he'd say, 'You think I'm easy now but wait until you get to the university. Those profs are just going to eat you alive if you're like this in class.' He goes, 'I'm very easy compared to some of those profs that you're going to meet'."

While indirect simulations, like modeling experiences, involved the informants in the vicarious acquisition of knowledge about college-going behavior and attitudes, the final category of getting ready—"direct simulation"—includes a whole range of what might be called "quasi-college-going" experiences involving the informants' actual participation. Sorting of these experiences into subcategories of direct simulation (table 4) was accomplished by evaluating them in the light of six criteria: (1) the intention of the informant, that is, whether his or her purpose was essentially or incidentally related to college-going; (2) the nature of the informant's activity, particularly the kinds of interactions he or she had with campus people; (3) the extent of such interactions; (4) the nature and extent of the informant's use of campus resources; (5) the duration of the experience; and (6) the role the informant occupied during the experience.

"Incidental visiting" refers to experiences that were essentially unrelated to college-going activity, that were typically short in duration and not recurrent, and that involved limited interaction with campus people and limited use of resources. An example is Peter's infrequent visits to the campus to use the gym. Experiences that belong to the subcategory called "related visiting" were related to college-going but indirectly, that is, to the college-going of a person other than the informant. Like incidental visiting, related visiting tended to be characterized by limited interaction with campus people, limited use of campus resources, and a time frame that was short. Informants who participated in visiting experiences often reported that they came away feeling that they had "just barely walked on campus" (Isabel) and had not been "exposed to the real aspect of the university being a university" (Linda).

Experiences that involved extensive use of campus resources, extensive interaction with campus people, and extended or repeated presence on the college campus belong to a subcategory of direct simulation called "attending." One kind of attending (Attending I) refers to activities that extensively imitated college-going per se. Nevertheless, each experience of this type involved the informant in considerable interaction with campus people, extensive usage of campus resources, and a relatively lengthy or recurrent campus stay. Emmanuel recounted his participation in a summer institute sponsored by the study university: "In the summer of my junior year, between my junior and my senior year, the university, the engineering department,

Table 4
Subcategories of "Direct Simulation" and their Dimensions

Subcategory	Intention	Example(s) of Activities	Amount of Interaction	Duration	Use of Resources	Role of Informant
Incidental visiting	Not related to college-going	Taking test Going to gym	None or limited	Short	Very limited	User
Related visiting (1)	Related to college-going (prospectively)	Touring campus	Limited	Short	Very limited	Tourist
Related visiting (II)	Related to college-going (indirectly)	Accompanying sibling	Variable but usually limited	Variable but generally short	Limited	Visitor
Attending (I)	Variable	Participating in summer workshop	Extensive	Relatively long	Relatively extensive	Pseudo-student
Attending (II)	Related to college-going (directly)	Going to college class	Extensive	Long	Extensive	Quasi-student

sent me to a summer institute, a seminar for a week. And they try to familiarize you with the campus."

A second level of attending (Attending II) included experiences that, to some degree, constituted college-going, for example, attending college classes as an official enrollee or as the companion of an official enrollee. As an example of the latter, Natalie reported: "My mother was also going to college when I was in high school. So I used to go to classes with her. Sometimes I would just accompany her . . . or if she said that she had a interesting class, I'd listen to it. . . . [I'd go] to classes and the cafeteria." Participation in Attending II experiences blurred the boundary between simulation and the experience, and it is difficult, on the basis of the available data, to estimate the extent to which such experiences only simulated postmatriculation college-going experiences visa-vis actually embodying them. Still, the findings to be presented in the next section indicate that having had Attending II experiences did not exempt informants, after official matriculation at the university, from obstacles to their effective negotiation of the university campus.

It should be clear to the reader that each getting-ready experience resulted in either (1) an expectation that the informant would eventually go to college, or (2) an expectation of what it would be like to be college-going. Expectations resulting from experiences belonging to all categories, save direct simulation, were externally prompted, that is, the impetus for the expectation was something said or done by an individual other than the informant. Expectations from direct simulation experiences tended to derive from self-reflexive activity and, hence, were internally prompted.

Each expectation may be understood to be the outcome of an evaluative experience. That is, associated with the prompting of the expectation was a valuation—either positive or negative—of college-going. All of the experiences identified as instances of initial expectation engendering involved only positive valuations. It is hypothesized that experiences of this kind involving negative evaluations do occur, probably to individuals who decide not to attend college. Experiences assigned to the other four categories involved both positive and negative valuations. An interesting case of the latter (an example is described above) is the high-school teacher's use of future college-going as a disciplinary mechanism. However, most experiences in these categories reported by the informants resulted in positive valuations of college-going.

Although experiences belonging to any single category of getting ready were not temporally discrete from those belonging to all others, there was an overall chronological pattern to the occurrence of the experiences relative to their categorical assignments. For example, initial expectation engendering, as is implied by its name, generally took place very early in an informant's life. Fraternal modeling, mentor modeling, and indirect simulation were experienced, more or less simultaneously, some variable length of time after initial expectation engendering. Direct simulation was characteristic of late precollegiate life.

One consequence of this patterning was that experiences belonging to later occurring categories tended to build upon those belonging to earlier ones. As noted above, experiences of the fraternal modeling, mentor modeling, and indirect simulation types provided substance, in the form of descriptions, prescriptions, and predictions about college-going, for the kind of generalized expectation of college-going that resulted from initial expectation engendering. The self-expectation that characterized experiences in the direct simulation category was the result of a valuation of college-going that took into account not only the immediate events but also valuations and expectations resulting from (earlier) experiences belonging to the other categories.

Getting In

Postmatriculation behaviors and attitudes can be understood in terms of a second organizing concept—"getting in." In describing their early impressions of the university, the informants were virtually unanimous in emphasizing a perception of "bigness." The descriptor "big" turned out to be a gloss for articulating the perceived dimensions; namely, mass, distance, and complexity, of three campus geographies: (1) the physical geography, (2) the social geography, and (3) the academic/cognitive geography (table 5).

For example, mass, distance, and complexity of the physical geography referred to the fact that for some informants the campus was larger in size than their entire hometowns (mass), that from one end of the campus to the other was much longer than the single block their high schools occupied (distance), and that it was not easy to resolve the physical campus into what would be for the informants logical and easily recognizable spaces (complexity). As an aspect of the social geography, mass was often described in terms of the literally hundreds of students with whom the informants attended class, distance as the gap between student and instructor that prevented a close working relationship, and complexity as the total ignorance of one another's lives exhibited by members (including the informants) of the campus population. Mass as an aspect of the academic/cognitive geography exhibited itself in what was perceived to be a seemingly unlimited number of potential fields of study, distance as the giant cognitive step the informants had to make in moving from "easy" high-school curricula to "hard" university ones, and complexity as the perceived obtuseness of professor talk. The inability to deal with these dimensions led to feelings of "being lost" in one or more of the geographies.[3]

Many of the postmatriculation behaviors reported by the informants may be understood as strategies to fix themselves in the physical, social, and/or academic/cognitive geographies. The behaviors employed in this way, which constitute the categories of getting in, took account, quite naturally, of the perceived dimensions of the geographies. Each represents a potential component of the process by which the informant initiated his or her negotiation of the geographies. Two categories of getting in emerged from an analysis of the date: (1) "getting to know" and (2) "scaling down."

A seemingly obvious way for an individual to deal with a milieu that overwhelmed him or her with its size, placed him or her at a distance from important people and things, and posed complexity was to increase his or her familiarity with that milieu. The informants reported two different sets of behaviors that led to increased knowledge of the campus geographies. The first set, called "mentoring," involved interactive experiences with students, already at the university for some time when the informant matriculated, who functioned as guides or interpreters of the geographies. Frances reported such a person, who had had a profound influence on her early behavior at the university: "She influenced my decision to stay here [in the dorm]. . . . She told me basically what goes on around here and how to get along around here. . . . Some of the things she said, you know, about the Engineering College and about how band was. I wanted to be in a good band so. And engineering—she told me a lot of things that go on in engineering. She told me what classes to take my first semester because [from] the trouble she had . . . she knew, you know, what you should do first. . . . She just kind of paved the way and guided me through making decisions, you know, as to where to go."

Table 5
The Perceived Geographies and Their Features

	Geography		
Feature	Physical	Social	Academic/Cognitive
Mass	"Is this place large!"	"So many people!"	"So many fields, so many classes one could take."
Distance	"You can't see from one side of the campus to the other."	"I was like in an audience and he had a micro-phone."	"High school to college is a bigger step."
Complexity	"There were all these little signs telling you to go over here, go over there. I got lost."	"You're constantly running into people you don't know."	"They made instruction more complicated than it had to be."

The second set of getting-to-know experiences—"peer knowledge sharing"—includes experiences with fellow newcomers in which there was a kind of cooperative exploring of the geographies. Barbara provides a good description of such activity: "It kind of helps if you have somebody to relate to and somebody who's having the same problem. And they find out something you're supposed to do that you didn't know about. So just kind of giving information back and forth." In Barbara's case, it was with high-school friends, co-matriculants at the university, that she engaged in peer knowledge sharing. In other cases, peer knowledge sharing occurred with individuals who were not known to the informants prior to their arrival on campus. Anita reported her strategy of sitting by someone in each class and introducing herself to that person: "That way it makes the class a lot easier. . . . Because, you know, they learn it different, they can explain it in their terms and you can catch on easily and that way you're not so insecure when you go in [-to class]."

Scaling down refers to behaviors and attitudes which resulted in the informant's perception of a more narrowly defined geography, effectively reducing the amount of the geography with which the informant had to be familiar in order to locate himself or herself. In effect, the mass, distance, and complexity dimensions of the geographies were "scaled down." Barbara, for example, explained how she had learned to avoid the "biggest places" on campus. Rather, she ran her "own little circle": "It's not like I'm at [the university]. It's kind of like I'm here in this part of it."

One focus of both the getting-to-know and the scaling-down kinds of experiences was the process of "majoring in." In addition to its manifest function—initiating a focused study of that area of the curriculum that is most closely related to one's life and career goals, selecting an academic major had another, more latent function: it provided a vehicle for locating oneself in the physical, social, and academic geographies; it provided a way of getting in. For the informants, the assumption of an academic major meant that the physical environment was circumscribed, the curriculum was bracketed, an important element of one's self-identity vis-a-vis the campus community was created, and a cynosure for social activities was realized. Hence, the expression, "I am majoring in——-" [a particular academic major is named] or, more simply, "I am in——-" [a particular academic major is named], was not merely an idiom but an oral affirmation of the locating function of the academic major. With respect to the role of the major in negotiating the social geography, it is interesting to note that the campus organization most frequently mentioned by the informants—an organization for Hispanic business students—had as its *raison d'être* the sharing of an academic major (figure 1).

Figure 1
The Categories and Subcategories of "Getting In" and their Relationships to "Majoring In."

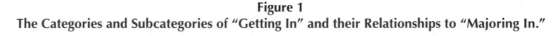
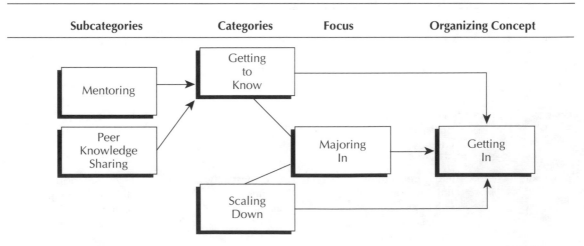

Theoretical Interpretations and Hypotheses

Following Stern [44], who argues that the process of concept development in qualitative research is facilitated by selective sampling of the literature for concepts that can be compared as data, the author looked for available social and/or sociopsychological constructs that could be used to draw out the theoretical significance of the getting ready and getting in concepts.

The construct "significant other," particularly as worked out by Haller and Woelfel [18], is useful for considering the significance of getting ready. In their study of the occupational and educational goals of high-school students, Haller and Woelfel [18, pp. 594–95] came to define a "significant other" as:

> A person, known to the focal individual, who either through direct interaction (a definer) or by example (a model) provides information which influences the focal individual's conception of himself in relation to educational or occupational roles or influences his conception of such roles (a conception of an object).

In the present study, parents, high-school teachers and, less frequently, siblings were definers with respect to college-going: These individuals communicated to the informant the fact that he or she belonged to the category of future college-goers and defined for him or her what is meant to be a college-goer. In addition, high-school teachers and siblings created expectations with respect to college-going by modeling college-going behavior. The mere departure of an older sibling for college might have signaled to the informant his or her membership in the category of (future) college-goers. Subsequently, the informant's observations of college-going behavior by siblings and teachers provided insight into the nature of the college-going role.

A second construct that was useful for drawing out the theoretical significance of getting ready was anticipatory socialization.[4] Anticipatory socialization refers to a premature taking on or identification with the behavior and attitudes of an *aspired to* group which "may serve the twin functions of aiding [an individual's] rise into [the aspired to] group and of easing his adjustment after he has become part of it" [24, p. 87]. The concept has been primarily worked out in relation to occupational preparation [33] and the formation of political views [39], but there has been some consideration of it with respect to the role of college student.

Parsons [30], for example, has argued that because, as early as elementary school, high achievers are culled from their classmates so they can be directed toward a college preparatory curriculum, the decision of a high achiever to attend college may be the result of a long period of anticipatory socialization. Silber and his colleagues [40] have reported that some high-school students prepare themselves for college by rehearsing forms of behavior they associate with college students. This role rehearsing may include taking special courses that are viewed as trial college experiences and carrying out assignments the teacher identifies as what one does in college.

Role-rehearsing was clearly an element of the getting ready experiences recorded here. It may have been very indirect as, for example, the simulation of certain aspects of college-going in the college preparatory classes. A more direct kind of rehearsing occurred when the individual participated in on-campus activities: living in dormitories, going to parties, attending classroom lectures. Another component of anticipatory socialization, the forecasting of future situations, was a feature of getting ready; as, for example, when the informant, upon observing an older sibling depart for college, predicted his or her own matriculation, or when a high-school teacher predicted that college professors would treat the informant and his or her co-students much differently than he or she (the high-school teacher) did.

In drawing out the theoretical significance of the concept "getting in," the author again referred to two existing constructs. The author's consideration of "social integration" as a theoretical datum for comparison with the concept of getting in was initially prompted by his reading of other conceptually oriented investigations of the behavior of undergraduate students. As mentioned above, Spady [41] and later Tinto [45] borrowed the concept from the French sociologist Emile Durkheim as he had elaborated it in his treatise on the causes of suicide [15], in order to conceptualize student withdrawal from college. Durkheim argued that suicide was likely in populations where rates of interaction (collective affiliation) were too low, because this leads to a lack of common sentiments and values (moral consensus) and the precedence of individual interests over social ones. As the individual increasingly frees himself or herself from the social control of the group, he or she removes himself or herself from its prophylactic influence and finds little meaning in life, which comes to appear as an intolerable burden.

Spady (and Tinto after him), in adapting these concepts to an explanation of student withdrawal from college, specified a lack of collective affiliation (friendship) and a lack of moral consensus (cognitive congruence) as having separate effects on dropping-out behavior, that is, independently influencing the level of one's social integration. Neither Durkheim nor Spady provides a clear definition of the construct "social integration."

The results of the study reported here suggest that moral consensus is neither the (principal) outcome of collective affiliation (as postulated by Durkheim) nor an independent cause of one's persisting in life or college (as indicated by Spady and Tinto). A student's interaction with others is important for his or her persistence in college not simply or primarily because it leads to the sharing of general values and orientations, but because it assists the student in developing specific strategies for negotiating the physical, social, and cognitive/academic geographies. The getting-to-know category of getting in defines "collective affiliations" with specific individuals—mentors and peers—that "integrate" the student into the physical and academic/cognitive geographies as well as the social geography by providing him or her with knowledge of these geographies and the skills to negotiate them. According to this interpretation, then, students become integrated for distinctly more cognitive, and less moral, reasons.

In theorizing about how exactly students, with the assistance of mentors and peers, come to locate themselves in the perceived geographies, the concept of the "cognitive map" may be important. It is hypothesized [43] that when significant environments (for example, a large university campus) are too large to be apprehended at once, people will form "conceptions" of them. These conceptions, or cognitive maps, are a complex of things learned about the environment, including expectations, stereotypes, and value judgments. In developing cognitive maps of large and complex spaces, individuals make certain simplifications and adjustments in accordance with their own needs and experience. This means, of course, that cognitive maps and mapmaking exhibit considerable interpersonal variation.

The basis of cognitive map formation is the identification of significant objects in the environment, the establishment of the connectedness of the objects to one another and to the observer, and the assignment of meaning, whether emotional or practical, to the objects and their relationships. As the word "map" implies, the origin and major implication of the cognitive map lie in the spatial domain. But people are thought to organize other phenomena, for example, social interrelations, affective bonds, and temporal relationships, in the same way [22]. Cognitive mapping is similar to the "sense-making activity" of organizational members as described by Weick [49, pp. 148–149]:

> People in organizations try to sort . . . chaos [which is flowing and equivocal] into items, events, and parts which are then connected, threaded into sequences, serially ordered, and related. . . . [Because it is] the individual [who] breaks up chaos so that other forms of order can be created, . . . it stands to reason that what is eventually available for inspection is something very much of the individual's own making.

The student's initial perceptions of the campus geographies may be understood to reflect the absence of cognitive maps. Thus the geographies were perceived to be large-scale environments (mass) in which objects stood separated from one another (distance) and seemed incapable of being resolved into meaningful components (complexity). The student's strategies for getting in are conceptualized to be mechanisms for facilitating the acquisition of these maps. For example, getting-to-know behaviors—knowledge sharing with other neophytes and mentoring relationships with veteran students—are shortcuts to acquiring representations of specific objects within the various geographies and the associations between these representations. Scaling-down behaviors result in more detailed maps of smaller proportions of the geographies—areas of particular concern to the individual.[5,6]

On the basis of the findings and theoretical interpretations of the research reported here, the following hypotheses regarding the context of the Mexican American's decision to persist in the university are proposed.

(1) For Mexican American freshmen, the effects of so-called "background" variables (for example, high school curriculum, parents' education, parents' occupations) on persistence in college are mediated by significant-other influences. Most of the existing models of college student persistence/withdrawal posit, and are successfully used to test for, the influence of prematriculation factors on persistence. The findings of the present study suggest that where these factors influence the persistence of Mexican Americans in the university it is because they increase these students' exposure to modeling and defining experiences relative to college-going.

(2) For Mexican American freshmen, the extent and nature of anticipatory socialization for college-going has an influence not only on the decision to go to college but, once there, on the decision to stay. Haller and Woelfel [18] have shown that the level of anticipatory socialization for college, in the form of defining and modeling experiences, has a positive impact on an individual's educational goals, that is, the decision to go to college. The results of the present study suggest that these experiences also have an impact on the decision to remain in college. That is, a student's willingness to "stick it out" may reflect early and thorough socializing by family, teachers, and friends for college-going.

(3) For Mexican American freshmen, the extent to which social integration influences persistence is not the extent to which it promotes the individual's moral conformity to the institution but rather the extent to which it endows the individual with the capacity to cognitively manage the university environment, that is, helps him or her to perceive the physical, social, and academic/cognitive geographies as negotiable.

(4) For Mexican American freshmen, persisting at the university is positively related to the development and use of cognitive maps of the physical, social, and academic/cognitive geographies. The persister is more likely to employ strategies (the result of other cognitive maps?) that facilitate the development of such maps.

Implications for Practice

The results of the research reported here suggest a number of strategies that the university might adopt to improve the college-going experience of Mexican Americans and promote their persistence during the freshman year. Consider, for example, early anticipatory socialization for college-going. Parents, teachers, and siblings are generally the key agents for such socialization, and it is not easy to conceive of how the university community could have much direct impact upon it. There are ways, however. An example is an experimental program currently underway at the study university in which members of the staff of the Student Affairs Office are bringing Chicano junior high-school girls and their mothers to the campus in order to introduce them, gradually, to the university and to the college-going process. Each of the girls in the project was selected from a family without any previous college experience. By including mothers, the project directors have acknowledged the important role of parents in socialization for college attendance.

The opportunities for constructive intervention by the university in later anticipatory socialization are many and varied. Indeed, most institutions, including the study university, already play a role in this kind of socialization. For example, universities regularly provide tours of their campuses for high-school students and conduct college day programs. But it is common for host institutions to look upon such events as nothing more than marketing strategies. This is unfortunate, because the results of the present study suggest their potential for significant socialization to college-going; they represent opportunities for orienting the prematriculant to the university experience.

For example, the traditional campus tour might be conducted in such a way that it assists the student to begin to develop a cognitive map of the physical geography. This would involve, for example, the tour director highlighting the importance of places (not just their histories) and indicating their connections with one another. Visual aids might include, in addition to commercial products, sketch maps of the university drawn by veteran students.

Of course, in those situations where the high-school student is on the university campus for an extended period of time, the opportunity for influencing his or her socialization to college-going is maximal. Each case of an extended stay mentioned by the informants in the present study (for example, a yearbook editors' conference and a statewide summer enrichment program) was the result of an effort underwritten by the high school. The university itself should sponsor extended stays, so that students (particularly those being little socialized to college-going at home) can "practice" going to the university.

Still another way for the university to influence later anticipatory socialization would be involvement in the design of curricula for college preparatory classes (for example, writing for college) which are offered by many high schools. Again, the object would be to assist the prematriculant to initiate the processes of developing cognitive maps of the campus geographies.

With respect to getting-in phenomena, the results of the present study have several implications for university intervention to positively influence the process of college-going after matriculation. For example, most institutions, including the study university, introduce new freshmen to their campus by conducting a special program, traditionally called "freshman orientation."[7] The duration of the program varies from institution to institution, being as short as a day and as long as several weeks. Its purpose is to "orient" individuals to a new environment.

The present study should prove useful to the university student affairs office in the conduct of the freshman orientation for Chicano freshmen inasmuch as it provides a conceptualization of how these students "orient" themselves. They build up internal mental representations, or cognitive maps, of the physical, social and academic/cognitive geographies; these maps are mechanisms for finding one's way in a large-scale environment. The map-making process is gradual and apparently exhibits interpersonal variation. For example, students who persist through their freshman year may form maps more quickly than those who do not. This, in turn, may be related to the possession by the persisters of still other cognitive maps—cognitive maps that are, essentially, instructions on how to negotiate new environments. It would behoove university personnel designing orientation sessions to understand the components (for example, knowledge-sharing and mentoring strategies) of such "how to" cognitive maps so that such information can be passed on early to new students. The results of this study also argue for an orientation that continues through the freshman year rather than being limited to one or two weeks at the beginning of the fall semester. This would reflect the gradualness of the process of building cognitive maps and, hence, the importance of monitoring it on a continuous basis.

Future Research

In-depth, nonscheduled interviews of Mexican American university students and former university students conducted from the perspective of the sociology of everyday life proved useful for generating concepts of Chicano university-going. But these concepts need to be refined and verified in subsequent research. This can be accomplished, in the first place, by expanding the qualitative data base on Mexican American university-going initiated by the present study. Although further in-depth interviewing of university sophomores and nonpersisting members of their freshman classes would be useful, interviews of individuals at other points in the life cycle should be conducted as well. The research reported here suggests that the nature of college-going in the freshman year is influenced profoundly by experiences that occur much earlier in life.

Undoubtedly, it would be illuminating to interview individuals on a continuous basis from, say, the time they entered first grade in order to ascertain their immediate perceptions of people and events ultimately influencing their college-going and persistence at the university. To do so would be logistically and financially impractical. More feasible is a research design in which informants are interviewed periodically from the time they enter high school until the time they complete, or fail to complete, their freshman year of college. At minimum, the research design of the present study should be extended so that individuals are interviewed *while* they are in their freshman year.

The findings of the present study suggest specific areas of inquiry for future interviewing. Thus, questioning ought to be focused, for example, on experiences in which college-going is modeled or defined for future college-goers, or on social interactions that contribute to the development and use of cognitive maps of the university. Information on these topics would be collected by means of an interviewing technique that was more structured than that used here so that data obtained from different individuals would be more comparable. In addition to the question-and-answer format, other procedures for eliciting information would be employed. For example, the notion that there is variation among students in the acquisition and use of cognitive maps might be "tested" by having individuals draw maps of the campus geographies or list categories of objects to be found within them [20].

Qualitative data collection by methods other than interviewing also should be considered in future research. Two of these methods would seem to be particularly useful. Because experiences related to college-going and persistence at the university are extensive in time and occur ubiquitously, the possibility of a researcher's observing and recording even a fraction of these experiences is nil. This problem cannot be circumvented, but comparable kinds of data can be collected by having informants be the observers and recorders of their own experiences. Cooperative and articulate individuals would be trained to record in diaries or logs their experiences and their immediate reactions to their experiences. Periodically, these individuals would be debriefed by the researcher.

The extensiveness of the temporal and spatial contexts of behavior related to college-going and persistence does not mean that direct observation of such behavior is lost to the researcher as a strategy for data collection. The results of the present study (and presumably of interviews in follow-up studies) suggest (or will suggest) places where and time when observation of behavior related to college-going can be conducted most propitiously. For example, on the basis of the present investigation, a researcher wishing to observe various getting-ready experiences might focus on the college preparatory class, the university tour, and/or the high-school career day. Foci for observation of getting-in experiences would include freshman-level classes of varying sizes and extracurricular organizations (such as the Hispanic Business Students' association) that form around the academic major.

In addition to initiating a qualitative database on Mexican American college-going, the present study has hypothesized factors that influence the persistence of Chicanos at the university during the freshman year. Future research should seek to test the relationships specified in these hypotheses. Most likely, this would involve the design of a survey instrument and its administration to a large, random sample of Chicano students stratified on the basis of whether or not they persisted into the sophomore year. Alternatively, first-time university freshmen could be surveyed and their persistence status subsequently ascertained.

Still another way in which the research described here might be followed up would involve examining, with comparable research methods, the college-going and persistence of students from other ethnic backgrounds, of other academic levels, and in other kinds of institutions. One wonders, for example, to what extent the patterns of college-going and persistence described in this study are tied to unique aspects of Mexican American culture. Ramirez and Castaneda [35] have identified four major value clusters within the Mexican American value system, including identification with family, community and ethnic group; personalization of interpersonal relationships; status and role definition in family and community; and Mexican Catholic ideology. Given the centrality of the family to the total socialization of the Chicano child, the importance of parents, siblings, and other relatives for getting-ready behavior is not surprising. Should we expect that for Anglos significant others for socialization to college-going might be drawn more heavily from among elementary and secondary school teachers and counselors? Similarly, in what ways do cultural differences between minority and Anglo students affect how and how effectively cognitive maps of the university environment are "drawn" and utilized?

The present dearth of meaningful studies of Hispanic college students[8] parallels the primitive state of research on Latino education in general [27]. The investigation reported here was undertaken in the spirit of Olivas' [27] call for improvement in both the quality of Hispanic data and theoretical constructs for explaining them. The author hopes it will encourage others to begin to fill the "fertile void in the literature of Hispanic students" [27, p. 136].

Notes

1. This approach was adopted by Neumann [25] in a study of the persistence of community college students.

2. Virtually all of the Hispanics who attend the university are Mexican American. For purposes of university reporting, ethnic/racial background is based on the student's response to an item on the university's admission form. Because an unknown number of Hispanics either (along with Anglos) selects the alternative "Other" or declines to respond at all to this item, it is unlikely that the list included *all* new full-time Hispanic freshmen entering in fall 1981. For the purpose of the research reported here, it was not necessary that it do so (see below).

3. Mass, distance and complexity all seem to be related to the sociopsychological concept of alienation, which has been defined as [19, p. 9]: "Different kinds of dissociation, break or rupture between human beings and their objects, whether the latter be other persons or the natural world, or their own creations in art, science and society; and subjectively, the corresponding states of disequilibrium, disturbance, strangeness and anxiety."

4. Other researchers [8, 21, 31] have noted the potential usefulness of this concept for understanding persistence in college.

5. Scaling down behavior may be an example of what Weick [50] calls the "small win" strategy. According to Weick [50, p. 44]: "People with limited rationality have sufficient variety to visualize, manage, and monitor the smaller amount of variety present in scaled-down problem environments. When people initiate small-scale projects there is less play between cause and effect; local regularities can be created, observed, and trusted; and feedback is immediate and can be used to revise theories. Events cohere and can be observed in their entirety when their scale is reduced."

6. The nature of scaling down attitudes and behavior presumably would be of interest to campus ecologists [5] who wish to understand how specific groups and even individual students visualize and use the campus, in order to design environments that better meet these students' needs [6].

7. Pascarella and his colleagues [31] have found participation in freshman orientation to have a significant indirect effect (through social integration) upon the persistence of college students.

8. The recently published *Latino College Students* [28], an edited volume of research studies, is an attempt to address this omission.

References

1. Anderson, K. L. "Student Retention Focused Dialogue: Opening Presentation." paper presented at the annual meeting of the Association for the Study of Higher Education, Chicago, 1985.

2. Astin, A. W. *Minorities in Higher Education: Recent Trends, Current Prospects, and Recommendations.* San Francisco: Jossey-Bass, 1982.

3. Astin, H. S., and C. P. Burciaga. *Chicanos in Higher Education: Progress and Attainment.* ERIC 226–690. Los Angeles: Higher Education Research Institute, 1981.

4. Astin, H. S., and P. H. Cross. *Student Financial Aid and Persistence in College.* ERIC 221–078. Los Angeles: Higher Education Research Institute, 1979.

5. Banning, J. H. "The Campus Ecology Manager Role." In *Student Services: A Handbook for the Profession,* edited by U. Delworth, G. R. Hanson and Associates, pp. 209–27. San Francisco: Jossey-Basey, 1980.

6. Banning, J. H., and L. Kaiser. "An Ecological Perspective and Model for Campus Design." *Personnel and Guidance Journal,* 52 (February 1974), 370–75.

7. Bean, J. P. "The Application of a Model of Turnover in Work Organizations to the Student Attrition Process." *Review of Higher Education,* 6 (Winter 1983), 129–48.

8. _____. "Interaction Effects Based on Class Level in an Explanatory Model of College Student Dropout Syndrome." *American Educational Research Journal*, 22 (Spring 1985), 35–64.

9. Bogdan, R. C., and S. K. Biklen. *Qualitative Research for Education: An Introduction to Theory and Methods*. Boston: Allyn & Bacon, 1982.

10. Brown, G. H. "The Outcomes of Education." In *The Condition of Education for Hispanic Americans*, edited by G. H. Brown et al., pp. 117–215. Washington, D.C.: U.S. Government Printing Office, 1980.

11. Carter, T. P., and R. D. Segura. *Mexican Americans in School: A Decade of Change*. New York: College Entrance Examination Board, 1979.

12. Dawis, R. V., L. H. Lofquist, and D. J. Weiss. *A Theory of Work Adjustment A Revision*. Minnesota Studies in Vocational Rehabilitation, No. 23. Minneapolis: Center for Industrial Relations, University of Minnesota, 1968.

13. De Los Santos, A. G., Jr., J. Montemayor, and E. Solis. *Chicano Students in Institutions of Higher Education: Access, Attrition, and Achievement*. Research Report Series, Vol. 1, No. 1. ERIC 205–360. Austin: Office for Advanced Research in Hispanic Education, College of Education, University of Texas at Austin, 1980.

14. Douglas, J. D. "Introduction to the Sociologies of Everyday Life." In *Introduction to the Sociologies of Everyday Life*, edited by J. D. Douglas, pp. 1–19. Boston: Allyn & Bacon, 1980.

15. Durkheim, E. *Suicide: A Study in Sociology*. Edited by G. Simpson. Translated by J. A. Spaulding and G. Simpson. Glencoe, Ill.: Free Press, 1951. (Originally published 1897.)

16. Glaser, B. G., and A. L. Strauss. *The Discovery of Grounded Theory: Strategies for Qualitative Research*. New York: Aldine, 1967.

17. Goetz, J. P., and M. D. LeCompte. *Ethnography and Qualitative Design in Educational Research*. Orlando, Fla.: Academic Press, 1984.

18. Haller, A. D., and J. Woelfel. "Significant Others and Their Expectations: Concepts and Instruments to Measure Interpersonal Influence on Status Aspirations." *Rural Sociology*, 37 (December 1972), 591–622.

19. Heinemann, F. H. *Existentialism and the Modern Predicament*. New York: Harper Torchbooks, 1958.

20. Herman, J. F., R. V. Kail, and A. W. Siegel. "Cognitive Maps of a College Campus: A New Look at Freshman Orientation." *Bulletin of the Psychonomic Society*. 13 (March 1979), 183–86.

21. Iverson, B. K., E. T. Pascarella, and P. T. Terenzini. "Informal Faculty-Student Contact and Commuter College Freshmen." *Research in Higher Education*, 21 (1984), 123–36.

22. Kaplan, S., and R. Kaplan. "Introduction to Chapter 3." In *Humanscape: Environments for People*, edited by S. Kaplan and R. Kaplan, pp. 42–43. North Scituate, Mass.: Duxbury Press, 1978.

23. Kissler, G. R. *Retention and Transfer: University of California Undergraduate Enrollment Study*. ERIC 215–597. Berkeley, Calif.: Office of the Academic Vice President, University of California, 1980.

24. Merton, R. K. and A. S. Kitt. "Contributions to the Theory of Reference Group Behavior." In *Continuities in Social Research: Studies in the Scope and Method of the American Soldier*, edited by R. K. Merton and P. F. Lazarsfeld, pp. 40–105. Glencoe, Ill.: Free Press, 1950.

25. Neumann, W. F. "Persistence in the Community College: The Student Perspective." Ph.D. Dissertation, Syracuse University, 1985.

26. Olivas, M. A. *The Dilemma of Access: Minorities in Two-Year Colleges*. Washington, D.C.: Howard University Press, 1979.

27. _____. "Research and Theory on Hispanic Education: Students, Finance, and Governance." *Aztlan*, 14 (Spring 1983), 111–46.

28. _____ (ed.) *Latino College Students*. New York: Teachers College Press, 1986.

29. Ortiz, V. "Generational Status, Family Background, and Educational Attainment Among Hispanic Youth and Non-Hispanic White Youth." In *Latino College Students*, edited by M. A. Olivas, pp. 29–46. New York: Teachers College Press, 1986.

30. Parsons, T. "The School Class as a Social System: Some of Its Functions in American Society." *Harvard Educational Review*, 29 (Fall 1959), 297–318.

31. Pascarella, E. T., and D. W. Chapman. "A Multi-Institutional, Path Analytic Validation of Tinto's Model of College Withdrawal." *American Education Research Journal*, 20 (Spring 1983), 87–102.

32. Pascarella, E. T., P. T. Terenzini, and L. M. Wolfle. "Orientation to College and Freshman Year Persistence/Withdrawal Decisions." *Journal of Higher Education*, 57 (March/April 1986). 155–75.

33. Pavalko, R. M. *Sociology of Occupations and Professions*. Itasca, Ill.: Peacock, 1971.

34. Price, J. L. *The Study of Turnover*. Ames, Iowa: Iowa State University Press, 1977.

35. Ramirez, M., III, and A. Castaneda. *Cultural Democracy, Bicognitive Development, and Education*. New York: Academic Press, 1974.

36. Richardson, R. C., Jr., and L. C. Attinasi, Jr. *Persistence of Undergraduate Students at Arizona State University: A Research Report on the Class Entering the Fall, 1976*. ERIC 223–138. Tempe, Ariz.: College of Education, Arizona State University, 1982.

37. Rosenthal, W. *Summer 1980 Report of Persistence-Attrition of Members of Ethnic Groups*. ERIC 191–412. East Lansing, Mich.: Office of Institutional Research, Michigan State University, 1980.

38. Santos, R. "Hispanic High School Graduates: Making Choices." In *Latino College Students*, edited by M. A. Olivas, pp. 104–27. New York: Teachers College Press, 1986.

39. Sheinkopf, K. G. "Family Communication Patterns and Anticipatory Socialization." *Journalism Quarterly*, 50 (Spring 1973), 24–30, 133.

40. Silber, E., et al. "Adaptive Behavior in Competent Adolescents: Coping with the Anticipation of College." *Archives of General Psychiatry*, 5 (October 1961), 354–65.

41. Spady, W. G. "Dropouts from Higher Education: A Interdisciplinary Review and Synthesis." *Interchange*, 1 (April 1970), 109–21.

42. Starr, A., E. L. Betz, and J. Menne. "Differences in College Student Satisfaction: Academic Dropouts, Nonacademic Dropouts, and Nondropouts." *Journal of Counseling Psychology*, 19 (July 1972), 318–22.

43. Stea, D. "The Measurement of Mental Maps: An Experimental Model for Studying Conceptual Spaces." In *Behavioral Problems in Geography: A Symposium* (Northwestern University Studies in Geography, No. 17), edited by K. R. Cox and R. G. Golledge, pp. 228–53. Evanston, Ill.: Department of Geography, Northwestern University, 1969.

44. Stern, P. N. "Grounded Theory Methodology: Its Uses and Processes." *Image*, 12 (February 1980), 20–23.

45. Tinto, V. "Dropout From Higher Education: A Theoretical Synthesis of Recent Research." *Review of Educational Research*, 45 (Winter 1975), 89–125.

46. _____. *Student Leaving: Rethinking the Causes and Cures of Student Attrition*. Chicago: University of Chicago Press, 1987.

47. U. S. Bureau of the Census. *Persons of Spanish Origin in the United States: March 1979*. Current Population Reports, Series P–20, No. 354. Washington, D.C.: U.S. Government Printing Office, 1980.

48. U.S. Commission on Civil Rights. *The Unfinished Education: Outcomes for Minorities in the Five Southwestern States*. Mexican American Educational Series, Report 2. Washington, D.C.: U.S. Government Printing Office, 1971.

49. Weick, K. E. *The Social Psychology of Organizing*. 2nd ed. Reading, Mass.: Addision-Wesley, 1979.

50. _____. "Small Wins: Redefining the Scale of Social Problems." *American Psychologist*, 39 (January 1984), 40–49.

51. Withey, S. B. "Summary and Conclusions." In *A Degree and What Else: Correlates and Consequences of a College Education*, edited by S. B. Withey, pp. 127–32. New York: McGraw-Hill, 1971.

The author wishes to thank Elizabeth Fisk Skinner for research advice; John Weidman and others who commented on the version of this article presented at the Annual Meeting of the Associations for the Study of Higher Education, San Antonio, Texas, February 1986; and the anonymous referees. The research for this article was supported in part by a Dissertation Research grant from the Arizona State University Graduate Research Council.

Experiences of Multiple Marginality:
A Case Study of Chicana "Scholarship Women"

GLORIA HOLGUIN CUADRAZ

In *Hunger of Memory*, Richard Rodriguez (1982) writes poignantly of his educational experiences as a Mexican American scholarship boy. The scholarship boy is portrayed as an "uprooted and anxious" individual, who, through the scholarship system, transcends class lines, only to remain an outcast in the new more privileged class (Hoggart, 1957). For Rodriguez, his path as a scholarship boy resulted in the loss of his Spanish language, culture, and intimacy between himself and family members.

The case study reported here explores the educational and life experiences of ten Chicana scholarship students. To illustrate their lives as scholarship students, childhood accounts were contrasted to their experience as graduate students at a major elite university. The first objective was to consider the unique role of working class achievers in the conjunction of education and the social structure. The second objective was to locate the social and political context for their experiences in graduate education. As Rodriguez (1982) laments, "I was a scholarship boy who belonged to an earlier time. I had come to the campus singly; they had come in a group" (p. 160). The point is that the scholarship path was no longer simply a matter of individual achievement, but was structural opportunity which became accessible to those who achieved but had historically been excluded. The third objective was to explore their life experiences as scholarship students, which were experiences of multiple marginality. In this context, "the simultaneity of experience" (Moraga, 1983; Zavella, 1989) may be best expressed as "simultaneous marginality": that is, their journeys out of the working class and into the predominantly middle-class environment of a major university (Karabel, 1975), combined with their membership in a racial group historically underrepresented in higher education (Astin, 1982; Clewell, 1987; National Board on Graduate Education, 1976; Olivas, 1986), and their socialization into the professional world of academia, an occupation historically reserved for middle-class white men (Adams, 1983; Hochschild, 1975; Ladd and Lipset, 1975; Ryan and Sackrey, 1984) resulted in a specific form of class, race, and gender-based experiences of "marginality."

Conceptual Framework

Marginality

The concept of marginality has been widely used in social science literature to describe the malaise of the individual caught between two cultures (Park, 1928; Stonequist, 1937). The concept has been criticized for its statistical and analytic limitations, its basis upon a stereotype, and its largely descriptive nature, at the expense of social structural analysis (Antonovsky, 1956; Garz, 1984; Golovensky, 1952; Green, 1947). For this study, however, Stonequist's (1937) argument that the marginal man plays a key role in social change is relevant, for it is their relationship to dominant groups that enables marginal individuals to affect the course of future social relationships between members of both groups. Discussing its applicability to Chicano intellectuals, Garza (1984, p. 27) argues that the concept of marginality is useful because it conveys the information "that something is *peripheral* to or *removed* from something else." Stonequist's attribution of the marginal individual's role in social change its usefulness as a device to capture the experience of "not belonging," is important for the combined race, class, and gender tensions of women who moved from one status to another. I argue that as scholarship students, the women experienced the constraints of a social structure that set them up to experience their daily lives as "others." Yet, as Freire (1982, p. 61) argues, "the oppressed are not 'marginals,' . . . They have always been 'inside'—inside the structure which *made them beings for others* (emphasis added). As insiders to a social structure which reproduces inequality, the irony is that because these women gained greater access to the 'centers' of elite institutions via the scholarship path, their simultaneous marginality became one of a privileged nature relative to their communities of original. Thus, as individuals from working-class backgrounds, as members of a racial group, and as women, who had in common the trajectory of the scholarship path, they were in a unique position to experience the contradictions of being 'inside' in an 'outside' way.[1]

Cultural Capital

In Bourdieu's (1977) view, educational institutions play a central role in the reproduction of class relations. While education in modern democratic societies is believed to play a role in reducing social inequalities, Bourdieu claims that educational systems reinforce, perpetuate, and legitimate the present "cultural and status cleavages" by converting social class inequalities into academic inequalities. Rather than reduce inequalities, the schools exacerbate the differences. The transmission of social inequality occurs because children from dominant-group families possess "cultural capital" similar to that of the educational system and minority group families do not. Working-class and non-dominant group children possess cultural capital too, but it is incongruent with the symbolic and social expectations of the school system. When children enter the schools, Bourdieu maintains that a child's attitudes and perceptions toward education are part of a "class ethos"—a system of implicit and deeply internalized values which helps to define attitudes toward cultural capital and educational institutions" (Bourdieu & de Saint-Martin, 1974, p. 32).

The schools play as important a role as the family in determining an individual's educational expectations. The schools rely on the student's possession of the appropriate cultural capital, acquired prior to entering school, to determine who will succeed. The schools require of its students that "they should have what it does not give" (Bourdieu, 1977, p. 494). The socialization that takes place in schools is thus merely a continuation of the socialization middle- and upper-class students receive in the home.

Working-class high achievers enter the educational system without the requisite cultural capital but they have acquired "scholastic cultural capital" because of "exceptional intellectual ability, individual effort, and unusual home or social circumstances" (Swartz, 1977, p. 550). Because these students do not possess broad cultural knowledge, their social mobility is limited. The controlled social mobility of working-class high achievers contributes to the social stability of the class structure. Moreover, the meritocratic ideology of democratic societies is reinforced by the educational attainment of a few individuals, which masks the social reality of inequality. The educational system reproduces the existing class hierarchies and supports meritocratic ideology by allowing a few working class individuals to acquire status and economic rewards through education; by implication, through their own efforts working-class children who fail to acquire scholastic cultural capital can then be held responsible for their failure to achieve.

From this perspective, Chicanas from the working-class enter the schools without dominant cultural capital. The Chicana scholarship students, however, acquired scholastic cultural capital, which enabled them to proceed through institutions of higher education. Bourdieu's image of incorporation for those from the working class who achieve scholastic cultural capital overemphasizes adaptation to and legitimation by the dominant culture. He underestimates contradictions, resistance and nonconformity and overestimates the extent to which these individuals rely solely on their own efforts to succeed (for critical review, see Lamont & Lareau, 1988). As they proceeded on the scholarship path, their experiences as scholarship students went far beyond individual achievement.

Social and Political Context

The presence of Chicanas in institutions of higher education, particularly graduate education programs, is a relatively recent phenomena. In order to understand the experiences of the Chicanas I interviewed, it is important to include both "troubles and issues, both biography and history" (Mills, 1959), for they form a particular generation (Mannheim, 1952). The women in my sample entered graduate school during the second decade of what has been called the "golden age of higher education," 1960–1980 (Hodgson, 1978). During the 1960s, the United States economy experienced tremendous economic growth (Ryan and Sackrey, 1984) and institutions of higher education underwent "democratization" (Finkelstein, 1984; Ryan & Sackrey, 1984). The role of the federal government became increasingly significant by providing financial assistance to working-class students historically disenfranchised from institutions of higher education (Garza, 1984; Karabel, 1983; Ryan & Sackrey, 1984). In response to civil rights protests by Blacks, Chicanos, women, and others, the federal government also played a role in implementing the Civil Rights Act of 1964, which laid the legal basis for affirmative action in higher education.

This generation of Chicanas in doctoral programs was part of the "wave" of Chicanas who entered the stratum of the academy "in a group" and became part of an intelligentsia that originated out of a highly politicized era. Even though the 70s signified a retrenchment of some civil rights gains, the early seventies were marked by the drive to increase the number of students of color in graduate school. By the middle of the decade, the National Board on Graduate Education (1976) was reporting a decline for Blacks and a stasis for Chicanos.

The University of California participated in the national impetus to increase the presence of students of color and women in its graduate programs. As a flagship campus, the University of California, Berkeley holds a national reputation for its graduate programs; as a result of increased federal support, private scholarship monies, and the establishment of its own campus funding source and programs, it joined in the national effort to expand the provision of opportunity at the graduate level.

The University of California, Berkeley is also well-known as a site of numerous social protests that erupted during the sixties. The Free Speech Movement in 1964, anti-war rallies, the New Left, the Grape Boycott launched on behalf of the labor struggles by the United Farm Workers, the Third World Strike, People's Park, the Women's Movement, and countless other political mobilizations were centered on the campus (Rorabaugh, 1989). Because Berkeley is renowned for its liberal political perspectives, it may partially account for the experiences and perspectives the women conveyed in the interviews.

National Research Council data (1985) on doctorate recipients, 1975–1985, found that Hispanic women increased their proportion of total doctorates earned by United States citizens and increased their proportion within their own ethnic group during this ten-year period. Hispanics as a group (men and women) increased their national percentage of all United States citizens earning the Ph.D. from 303 (1.2 percent) in 1975 to 559 (2.5 percent) in 1985. Hispanic women earned 61 (20.1 percent) of the doctorates within their own ethnic group in 1975, and by 1985, had narrowed this gap, earning 261 (46.7 percent) of the doctorates earned by Hispanics, representing an increase of 328 percent. The proportion of all U.S. Ph.D.'s. earned by Hispanic women increased from 0.2 percent in 1975 to 1.1 percent in 1985.[2]

The systematic collection of enrollment and graduation data, by ethnicity and gender, does not begin until the 1975–76 academic year. This is the case for both state and national data. Studies with a focus on Hispanics consistently note the problem of unreliable and incompatible data sets (Olivas 1982a). Thus, accurate data on the number of Chicanas enrolled in doctoral programs on the Berkeley campus during the decade in question is not available. Data was obtained, however, for UCB doctorates conferred for the thirteen-year period between 1975-76 and 1977-88. These figures do not inform us of how many Chicanas entered doctoral programs during the 70s and did not complete their degrees; they do provide us with a clue about the low number of doctorates awarded to Chicanas. Across all disciplines for this time period on the Berkeley campus, out of the 10,294 doctoral degrees awarded, Chicanas earned a total of 29 (0.3 percent) Out of 1621 doctoral degrees conferred in the social sciences, the academic field in which Chicanas are most highly represented a total of 11 (0.6 percent) were earned by Chicanas.[3]

Research Design

Sample Selection

The sample consisted of ten Chicana scholarship students who enrolled in a social science doctoral program between the years 1970 and 1980 at the University of California, Berkeley. At the time of the interviews, five of the women were in the midst of their programs and five had completed their programs. The women were identified and selected based on knowledge about their existence and information obtained from key informants.

Class background was based on respondents' description and identification; those parents' whose occupations fell under traditionally defined blue-collar or service sector and operative work were classified as working-class. Eight Chicanas identified their backgrounds as working-class. Two women described their original family backgrounds as working-class but indicated their families had experienced mobility into the lower middle class.

Data Collection

I conducted open-ended interviews that ranged from two to four hours, guided by a list of topic areas. The first area covered the respondents' families, their parents' education and occupations, childhood experiences, and the communities in which they were raised. In the second topic area, the women were asked questions about the kinds of schools they attended, their attitudes toward school, major successes or failures in school, aspirations, relationships with teachers, awards, and achievements. Similar questions were asked about their experiences in higher education. In the interview, I also inquired about the significance of education upon their political and personal development. The third topic area asked the respondents' reasons for attending graduate school, and for choosing their field of study, their relationships with faculty, and the development of their educational and research interests.

Findings

As the daughters of farm workers, meatpackers, maids, homemakers, and the unemployed, the Chicanas conveyed a "matter-of-factness" about what their parents did for a living, keenly aware that their parents' occupations were low-paying, no status, many times back-breaking labor. That their parents had limited opportunities in life was a reality to which they had grown accustomed. It was a reality made all the more stark by the fact that the majority of students they eventually encountered within their doctoral program had parents whose occupational statuses placed them squarely among the successful, middle and upper-middle classes.

Whether their parents were first generation immigrants from Mexico or whether they could trace familial roots in the United States several generations back, the majority of the parents' educational attainment was low. Eight of the mothers had not attended school beyond the sixth grade, while two of the mothers had graduated from high school. The one college graduate was the father of the one woman whose family became middle-class. With the exception of Vera's father, who obtained a GED later in life, none of the other women's fathers had but a few years of schooling at the elementary level. In some cases, no formal schooling had taken place.

Six of the women in my sample reported being labeled early in their schooling years as "bright students." On the one hand, as scholarship students, they were assured of their worth; on the other hand, as women of Mexican descent, they experienced blatant and subtle occurrences of racism, which devalued and demeaned them. They felt they were perceived as something special in one context, yet something less in another. Norma conveyed the mixed messages of her early educational experiences:

> One real vivid impression is always being the new kid in class, so always going through a process where the teacher checked me out and immediately assumed that as a Mexican girl I was dumb. Of course, I was pretty quiet. It was always the spelling test; that was usually the first indication of what I was most capable of. It was almost predictable. After the first spelling test, then the teachers would say something to the effect, "Gee, you're so different from the other Mexicans," or "It's going to be so nice working with you."

Helen on the other hand, who was tracked into remedial groups until the fourth grade, spoke of her efforts to be included among the bright students. After becoming aware that she was not being placed in the top group, as a "redbird" she asked to be allowed into the "white group," as she referred to it (the orange birds). After completing the red bird series, she recalls saying to the teacher:

> I want to go to the orange book. Well, the teacher said, "You can't." See, the orange book was where all the white kids were. . . . And my group was where all the Mexicans and Asians were. There were some Asians in the orange book, but there were no Mexicans *at all*. I remember that, because I was the smartest Mexican in the class. I know that. . . . So I said, "What do I have to do to get in the orange book, because I'm *done* with the red book."

Her story continued to explain how she took a succession of tests until she got into the orange group. Stories such as these, of their attempts to persevere, and at some level to basically overcome others' assumptions about their limitations as Mexican women, became a common theme as they proceeded on their scholarship paths.

When asked what they remembered the most about growing up and their early educational experiences, the women talked about feelings of "being different" or feelings of "separation" from their peers. Nellie shared such feelings about her peers.

> I can remember feeling separated from the other kids in a classroom as far back as second grade. I still remember sitting in the back of the room helping the kids who didn't know English with their schoolwork. Because I knew both Spanish and English, I was serving as an interpreter and teacher for my own peers at a very early age.

Feelings of being different derived from mixed messages about their racial identity. The pervasiveness of such powerful messages quickly developed into an acute sensitivity to their "differences." As scholarship students, their achievements and the experience of being perceived as unlike "the other Mexicans" most often placed them amongst white students in the high-tracked groups. Their racial marginality within this context then intersected with their gender in an interesting manner. The issue which arose centered around being "smart and pretty." The women shared vivid memories of who received the attention from teachers and classmates in this regard. At very early ages, the women were forced to assimilate how they were special because they were "smart," but because of the negative attributions about their racial identity, expressed feelings that they were still not quite as "good" as the other girls. Elba, for example, in spite of being fair-skinned, described racism as the overriding experience of her childhood. In this context, she described how at the age of seven she was determined to change her name so she could be more like her friends, who were predominantly white. She thoughtfully reminisced:

> It's a strong sense of wanting to be different than I was. And I could even be specific. I knew I wanted to have blonde hair and blue eyes. And I wasn't too upset about the color of my skin; if I could just add the blonde hair and blue eyes.

Feeling "different" also resulted in feelings of being "left out." The following excerpt hints at the effects these feelings had for the development on self-esteem. When asked what she remembered the most about growing up, Vera responded:

I remember a lot of times people would have parties and a lot of other girls in my class would be invited but it wouldn't be me. And the ones that would be invited, would of course, be the Italian girls and the white girls. But, I sort of never understood why I wasn't being invited. I always thought it was because I was ugly. In my own understanding, I just thought I was plain ugly.

Along with the developed sensitivity to their racial identity came an understanding that being Mexican meant learning there were certain socially prescribed limitations. Vera shares her early memories of developing racial awareness.

You know, every girl's dream is to be a cheerleader, so I always wanted to be a cheerleader. I remember Mrs. Sandoval telling me, "Are you crazy, you can't be a cheerleader; they don't let the Spanish girls be cheerleaders." So that was the first time I said, "Oh, hmm." That was the first time anyone articulated that to me.

Vera, as other respondents, came to understand that being Mexican meant a climate of presumptuous limitations on what could or could not be accomplished.

Class marginality is the most difficult dimension of their marginality to capture. Unlike the ascriptive nature of racial and gender marginality, class marginality became more pronounced as they advanced into the culture of the academy. On the one hand, the scholarship trajectory rendered them marginal to their class of origin; on the other hand, they were marginal to the middle-class environment in which they came to achieve. For example, Norma, one of twelve children, spoke of how books became a refuge for her as a child and how it became one means through which she escaped the crowded conditions of the converted garage which she and her three sisters shared. After weekly trips to the library, where she was allowed to check out five books per week, she would "read and read and read." Such stories about finding "refuge" in the scholarship path were common.

Graduate School: "What Am I Doing Sitting Here?"

These Chicanas were among a select few within their own racial and cultural group engaged in the attainment of doctoral degrees at a major institution where their daily reality included interactions with an elite white culture. One dimension of their marginality, therefore, involved the cultural conflict they experienced as members of an ethnic minority that has historically been assigned second-class status in the United States.

Perceptions about how they came to be in a doctoral program were often portrayed by the women as one of "chance" and "luck." Yet, when probed to elaborate on this viewpoint, it became evident there was a basis for this "luck," resulting from the opening of structural opportunities in higher education and the increased availability of monies and institutional resources especially targeted for racial minorities during this specific historical period. The "bottom line," as Sandra put it, "was the financial aid. No matter how smart or motivated I was, I couldn't have done it without the money that I've gotten." All the women had been recipients of one form or another of financial aid, grants, and scholarships, in addition to working their way through school.

Time and time again, the women spoke about the significant influence that one or two key individuals had in guiding their persistence through the scholarship path. For example, when Sandra had been denied admission to the undergraduate institution of her choice, a Chicana counselor on the university staff stepped in and agreed to take full responsibility for her progress. The exception was granted and Sandra graduated with a 3.4 grade point average. Stories of such intervention were common throughout the interviews, strongly suggesting the critical role that "institutional insiders" played in these women's lives as scholarship students. Nellie explained how she "didn't even know what graduate school was, had never heard of it" until a Chicano counselor identified her as a good student and encouraged her to pursue a doctorate.

Then there was Alicia's story, whose path into a doctoral program began when she took a course as an undergraduate with a group of Chicano graduate students. She declared:

They encouraged me, practically forced me to apply to graduate school. Without them I would've never done it. They practically sat me down and forced me to do this thing.

Unlike middle-class students, whose attainment of postsecondary education is perceived as a continuation of their parents' achievements and lifestyle, for these Chicanas, acquiring an education instead represented the opportunity to take advantage of opportunities their parents had not had. It meant doing "good" by the sacrifices their parents had made in order for them to have better opportunities.

In response to a question about her early experiences in graduate school, it came of no surprise that Alicia was indeed sensitive to her "differences." She clamored,

> I remember one time sitting in the class and I started writing and asking myself—what am I doing sitting here? What am I doing with my life sitting in this room, listening to all this garbage that has absolutely no relevance to anything—at least I couldn't see any relevance to anything.

Vera relates the following analysis, which reflects a sensitivity to their differences, present in the accounts by the Chicanas.

> When I stop to consider what I was saying and thinking my first year here, I had nowhere near the articulation powers I have now. There was a great deal of logical inconsistency, impreciseness to my language. By my first year my confidence was thrashed because I couldn't write, couldn't speak; I mean, I was a minority kid who hadn't had the training all those people had and was basically being given a chance.

Norma recalled one incident in graduate school which involved Elba, another Chicana member of her cohort. Interestingly, both women separately raised this particular incident as an example of how their concerns and perspectives were often treated with disdain by faculty members unaccustomed to their world views. Elba recounted:

> Probably the worst experience I've ever had was in a theory course where I wrote a paper about _____, for writing as if he was in a vacuum, not recognizing the realities of racism from all over the world. And the professor wanted me to read the paper before the class. Without telling me he invited the widow of _____ to sit in on the class. He didn't introduce her until I had delivered the paper. He did it deliberately. He proceeded to destroy my paper and to talk about how it was ideology and not (discipline x).

For Norma, the incident had the following significance:

> He lectured her (Elba) and told her, if you want to change the world, then get out of (department X). This is not about social change. This is about learning (discipline x). Of course, those stories circulated and we got the message to shut up. We were not allowed to ask certain questions. It was devastating. I remember after the quarter I was so unhappy. I was so depressed.

For both Elba and Norma, the source of tension came both from the outright suppression of certain political views and the extent to which such action restimulated painful memories of the past.

Profoundly, in spite of their advancement within their respective graduate programs, their "acceptance" was rarely without problematic qualifications. Vera vividly recalled the parting words of her department chairperson, a year before she actually completed her doctorate.

> I don't care about your process; you may very well have come the furthest of anybody who has ever come into this department—the person who has started the lowest and come the furthest. That doesn't mean anything to me. I don't care about the process. All I care about is where you end up.

Why Don't You Just Come Out of the Closet and Call Yourself a Feminist?

Gender marginality for these women goes beyond the tension over traditional and modern roles, although this is certainly one level of strain. At the heart of it is the universal issue of patriarchal domination and women's subordination. But the experience of subordination takes on different forms of meanings, depending on their structural and cultural relationship to the particular social group in question (Zinn, 1982).

As scholarship women, their gender socialization provides another dimension to their class dislocation. Recent works by Chicana scholars argue it is necessary to explore family ideology, particularly Chicano family ideology, in order to understand the conflict experienced with the domain of the family unit (Pesquera, 1985; Segura, 1986; Zavella, 1987). By family ideology, Zavella (1987) is referring to the assumptions about proper men's and women's roles, where, "traditionally, men are breadwinners, whereas women are supposed to sacrifice their careers and minister to family needs, especially those of children" (p. 5). Literature on traditional Chicano families places overriding importance on the extended family, the sex-role segregation between men and women, age-based authority, while little value is placed on independence, achievement and deferred gratification. The process of acquiring degrees in higher education, however, places high value on the latter characteristics. To the extent that traditional family ideology has affected these women, it is important to understand this source of strain, primarily because it provides insight into one of the barriers they traversed in order to proceed on their scholarship paths. By pursuing advanced degrees and the scholarship path into academia, these women have defied traditional family ideology.

A major finding which surfaced in the interviews was the gradual transition from the cultural nationalism of the Chicano Movement to the feminism of the Women's Movement. As their lives unfolded, it became evident that an ideological shift occurred, based on their daily experiences as scholarship women and their involvement in political activities of the time. The shift, however, did not entail a complete abandonment of either ideology, but instead, involved a reconceptualization which would more accurately reflect their own daily realities as Chicanas.

The woman had varying degrees of involvement at different points in their lives with the Chicano Movement. Most of the women became involved with the activities of the Movement through their roles as students. At one end of the spectrum was Alicia, who was involved in activities ranging from the organizing of farm workers for the United Farm Workers to efforts to establish Chicano Studies programs on college campuses:

> At some point I decided education was useful as a tool to help you understand your own reality and then figure out how to transform your reality. So that was what motivated me, what interested me, that particular process—not so much a career orientation. At that point all I wanted to do was be a full-time political activist. I didn't care about anything else. I didn't care how I survived; that was kind of immaterial.

The impact of the Movement on the development of their academic interests was tremendous. In fact, several of the women attributed their presence in academia now to the beliefs which the Chicano Movement instilled. Elba clearly articulated her viewpoint:

> The reason I got my education was more to do with my political leaning than anything else. If I were to credit one thing for being where I am, it is the politics of the time and my anger at the injustices, and my anger at the racism. Anger can be a very motivating emotion.

Their participation in Chicano organizations provided a concrete basis for the women to identify with the issues being raised by the Women's Movement. It was their experiences within these organizations that led them to question the sexism within the Chicano Movement. As massive protests declined in the early 70s, Elba recounts what happened, "At some point, the few women that were around were recognizing that these meetings were being dominated by men. In the Chicano Movement as a whole, women were saying—we went through this major struggle with you in the campus and the community as a whole, but now that the main struggle has subsided, and we're going along into building, it's time to take a more assertive role."

An example of becoming aware of their role as women was shared by Norma in this account of her early days of involvement in United Mexican American Students (UMAS):

> I remember at the first meeting I was elected secretary and came away from the meeting feeling real excited. I came across this Chicano who had not been at the meeting and told him. He responded, "Well, what do you expect, of course you were elected secretary!"

There was a resentment there. I didn't quite understand it so I shined it on. The thing that's interesting is that I was one of the original organizers, yet, I ended up being the secretary. And it never occurred to me that there was any problem with that. The people who had been elected president and vice-president were men I had recruited and were men who had initially resisted.

It was incidents such as the above, however, which led them to establish networks with other graduate students and respond to the alienation and frustrations graduate school. The Chicana Colectiva, comprised of Chicana graduate students from various disciplines, formed in 1976 and was instrumental in providing a forum for discussion of feminist issues. The women utilized the group as both an academic and personal support group. Norma explained, "Part of participating in Chicano academia was having a women's group that would help deal with the sexism by the men, their lack of legitimation of women's issues and their lack of concern with what we were interested in." Norma recalled:

> In the Colectiva we used to talk about feminism—whether we were feminists or not. I used to lean towards feminism because it seemed appropriate. We came to the conclusion that we acted like feminists even though we didn't call ourselves feminists. I remember a friend of mine (outside of the group) just got impatient one time and said, "Why don't you just come out of the closet and call yourself a feminist?" I thought, she's right. If I act like a feminist, why don't I identify with them, with their support and the feminist movement? So I started doing it.

Evident in this quote, however, is the tenuousness with which feminism was initially embraced (others have also cited this tendency: see Garcia, 1989; Zavella, 19891). Just as sexism in the Chicano Movement presented problems, the women also spoke about the ways in which the Women's Movement was limited in its ability to address non–middle class concerns and issues of racism.

Support versus Sabotage: The Private Sphere

In the private sphere, two kinds of stories were conveyed. At least three of the women said they could not have achieved their accomplishments without the support of their husbands. While not without its difficulties, the support rendered to them by their spouses was vital to their development and progress. Conversely, several of the women attributed a partial development of their feminism to power struggles with the men in their lives. For example, Alicia spoke of her ex-husband's support, or rather, lack of it, as "subtle sabotages" and "not-so-subtle sabotages." As a first-year graduate student she had written a research proposal that would have involved field-work in Mexico. She asked him to read it and recalled his response. "He read it and he looked at it, threw it down and said, 'What the hell do you expect me to do with this place for a couple of years while you do this?'" She said, "I never even thought of doing it after that."

Nellie spoke of an argument where her partner threw two shelves of an entire wall's worth of her books to the floor, in the midst of telling her he was "sick of her university." Similarly, Elba recalled the unhappiness of her first marriage. Having left school to get married, she later recognized that she really wanted school:

> I subscribed to book clubs and had all these books coming. I read everything I could get my hands on. In fact, some of my arguments with my husband were around the books. He didn't like me reading books. He'd tear them up on occasion. Finally, after four years I decided I didn't want anymore of this, took my son, pinned a note to the door and said, "I'm leaving" and left everything. I couldn't drive at the time so a girlfriend came and got me and drove me straight to College X. And I enrolled . . . that same day. I never looked back.

When their constraints in the home are placed in the context of their struggles in graduate school and the larger social environment, the marginality of their experiences as scholarship women become ever more apparent. Like the mixed messages they received as children about their special worth, on the one hand, and their demeaned value, on the other, the duality of the messages continued through their adult lives. Alicia's version of one such contradiction illustrates the complexity: "One of the things my ex-husband said that really attracted him to me was the fact that I was strong, that I had a mind, that I had things to say. So he was apparently attracted to a strong woman. But when it came down to the daily reality of it all, it just wasn't quite attractive to him."

I Can't Be a Quitter

There was not a single strategy utilized by all the Chicanas to cope with the strains and demands of their programs. Instead, they used an assortment of strategies and coping mechanisms. While one "avoided the department like the plague" another spoke of "hanging around with the white Harvard males." For others, their involvement in political activities allowed them the ability to place their graduate school experiences in perspective. For several, family obligations and childrearing served as a deterrent to agonizing over the graduate school process. Family thus became one safe "haven" which allowed them to maintain a distance from departmental politics. For those women without immediate family, contact with extended family members and friendships became another way in which they reconstructed a semblance of family life.

The major finding was the critical importance played by the formation of Chicano academic support groups to these women's negotiations through graduate school. When asked about their positive experiences in graduate school, the women often referred to the critical difference involvements in such organizations made in continuing their programs. Vera, whose most positive experience in graduate school was organizing women of color, described her academic role as a clear extension of her political commitments. "The way I see my political role as it relates to my academic work is that I see myself as basically a soldier of ideas, a soldier of meaning, fighting the battle over meaning, fighting the battle over how ideas are constructed."

Several of the women initially belonged to one group of Chicano/a faculty and graduate students, the Chicano Political and Economic Collective (CHPEC), who reviewed and critiqued each other's work. As the women within this group developed a critique of patriarchy as a system of domination, a splintering occurred, with the women charging that sexism within that group was preventing a feminist analysis from moving forward. In its place, *Mujeres en Marcha* was formed in 1981. Since then, another organization was formed in 1982, *Mujeres Activas en Letras y Cambio Social*, which involved Chicana graduate students and faculty from other Northern California campuses.

Regardless of how the women chose to construct their respective academic and political roles, the grounds were inevitably politically based. For the very essence of what they represent, as working class Chicanas surviving at an elite university, is constantly brought to bear on their experiences. Alicia's struggle to complete her doctoral program became one of sheer determination. She confessed, "I can't be a quitter. I can't quit, because then I'm just reinforcing the stereotypes they have of us anyway. So I just kept going."

Thus, the women's graduate schooling years provided one context for the development of their research interests in Chicano and Chicana Studies and feminist scholarship. Yet, pursuing the academic career for the sake of the profession itself was virtually absent from their discussions. Instead, their concerns were directly tied to issues of a political nature. As Alicia commented, "If I come to the position where all I can do is be an academic, I'm going to be extremely upset, disappointed and traumatized." Such a sentiment was common among the women, as their attention to issues of the "oppressed," particularly those of women within their own ethnic group, formed the basis for the future direction of their research and academic interests.

I'll Always Be a Misfit. That's My Life

The women's narrative about their early schooling years revealed a pervasive marginality based on their race, gender and class. Their early childhood accounts, as they relate both to their educational experiences and family lives, contrasted sharply with issues prominent in their lives as graduate students. Their initial domestic worlds of the working class were displaced and replaced. Education was the medium through which they entered other worlds.

In accordance with Hoggart's (1957) claim about the scholarship boy, the Chicana scholarship women became equipped for hurdle-jumping. They acquired the scholastic cultural capital necessary to achieve in school and to transcend class lines; yet, they have "neither the comforts of simply accepting the big world's values, nor the "recompense of feeling firmly critical towards them" (Stonequist, 1937). In the process of hurdle-jumping, they acquired many of the traits characteristic of Stonequist's marginal man. The simultaneity of their marginality is exemplified by their initial self-consciousness and sensitivity about their identity. In their childhood experiences, this is amply demonstrated in their accounts about coming to racial awareness.

Bourdieu's thesis about the unequal distribution of cultural capital and the perpetuation of social inequality provided a theoretical framework from which to understand the relationship of education and the social structure. In his quest to explain how the systems of domination are kept intact, however, Bourdieu excludes, as Swartz (1977) notes, "the consideration of contradiction as a generator of human action and social transformations. Symbolic violence and domination persist; only their disguises are altered." As the study conveyed, the scholarship trajectories of these Chicana scholarship women abounded with tensions. The acknowledgment of these tensions is important because their presence in institutions of higher education during the politically turbulent years of the "golden age of higher education" demystified and unmasked the very systems of domination which created the structural opportunities and conditions for their scholarship paths.

The social networks, formed in response to the political movements, to the conflicts within these movements, and their efforts to succeed academically, played an important part in their development. The ideologies prevalent during this period were instrumental in shaping these women's lives and directions they took. The women met resistance and contradictions throughout their scholarship paths. Their portrayal as high achievers is not so much a testimony of their exceptional talent, although they succeeded in spite of the barriers, as it is to collective action. The process of achievement during this historical period necessitated continuing the legacy of prior collective action in order to survive. They climbed the educational ladder and became scholarship women. They continue to negotiate the simultaneous marginality in their lives.

Notes

1. An excellent essay that describes the phenomena of marginality for Black women in the academy as a status of "outsider within" is put forth by Patricia Collins (1986).

2. We do not know from this national data, however, what proportion of those within the Hispanic category are Chicanos. Astin (1982) estimates the Chicano population represents 60 percent of the Hispanic category. We do not know to what extent this estimate would hold for men versus women, particularly given the existence of gender discrepancies, as those noted here.

3. Office for Institutional Research. Doctoral Degrees: 1975–76 to 1987–88. Data Files. UC Berkeley.

References

Adams, H. F. (1983). Work in the interstices: Women in academe. *Women's Studies International Forum*, 6, 135–141.

Antonovsky, A. (1956). Toward a refinement of the 'marginal man' concept. *Social Forces* 35, 57–62.

Astin, A. W. (1982). *Minorities in American higher education*. San Francisco, California: Jossey-Bass Publishers.

Bourdieu, P. (1977). Cultural reproduction and social reproduction. In J. Karabel & A. Halsey (Eds.), *Power and Ideology in Education*. New York: Oxford University Press.

Bourdieu, P. & M. de Saint-Martin, (1974). The school as a conservative force: Scholastic and cultural inequalities. In J. Eggleston (Ed.), *Contemporary Research in the Sociology of Education*. New York: Harper & Row.

Clewell, B. C. (1987). Retention of Black and Hispanic doctoral students. Graduate Record Examination, Princeton, NJ: Educational Testing Service.

Collins, P. A. (1986). Learning from the outsider within: The sociological significance of Black feminist thought. *Social Problems*, 33, S14–31.

Finkelstein, M. J. (1984). *The American academic profession: A synthesis of social scientific inquiry since World War II*. Columbus, OH: Ohio State University Press.

Freire, P. (1982). *Pedagogy of the oppressed*. New York: Continuum.

Garza, H. A. (1984). Nationalism, consciousness, and social change: Chicano intellectuals in the United States. Ph.D. diss., University of California, Berkeley.

Golovensky, D. I. (1952). The marginal man concept: An analysis and critique. *Social Forces* 30, 333–339.

Green, A. W. (1947). A re-examination of the marginal man concept. *Social Forces* 26, 167–171.

Hochschild, A. (1975). Inside the clockwork of male careers. In F. Howe (Ed.), *Women and the power to change*. New York:McGraw-Hill.

Hodgson, G. (1978). *America in our time: From World War II to Nixon, what happened and why*. New York: Random House.

Hoggart, R. (1957). *The uses of literacy*. London: Chatto and Windus.

Karabel, J. (1975). Social class, academic ability, and college "quality." *Social Forces*, 53, 381–398.

Karabel, J. (1983). The politics of structural change in American higher education: The case of open admissions at the City University of New York. In H. Hermanna, U. Teichler, & H. Wasser (Eds.), *The compleat university*. Cambridge, MA: Schenkman Publishing Company.

Ladd, E. C., & Lipset, S. M. 1975. *The divided academy*. The Carnegie Commission on Higher Education. New York: McGraw Hill Book Company.

Lamont, M. & Lareau, A. (1988). Cultural capital: Allusions, gaps and glissandos in recent theoretical developments. *Sociological Theory* 6, 153–168.

Mannheim, K. (1952). *Essays on the sociology of knowledge*. London: Routledge & Kegan Paul.

Mills, C. W. (1959). *The sociological imagination*. New York: Oxford University Press.

Moraga, C. (1983). *Loving in the war years: lo que nunca paso por sus labios*. Boston, MA: South End Press.

National Board on Graduate Education. (1976). *Minority group participation in graduate education*. Washington, DC: National Academy of Science.

Olivas, M. A. 1982a. Federal higher education policy: The case of Hispanics. *Educational Evaluation and Policy Analysis* 4, 301–310.

Olivas, M. A. (Ed.) (1986). Latino college students. New York: Teachers College Press.

Park, R. E. (1928). Human migration and the marginal man. *American Journal of Sociology* 33, 881–893.

Pesquera, B. (1985). Work and family: A comparative analysis of professional, clerical and blue-collar Chicana workers. Ph.D. diss., University of California, Berkeley.

Rodriguez, R. (1982). *An autobiography: Hunger of memory*. Boston, Massachusetts: Godine Publisher.

Rorabaugh, W. J. (1989). *Berkeley at war*. New York: Oxford University Press.

Ryan, J. & C. Sackrey. (1984). *Strangers in paradise: academics from the working class*. Boston, Massachusetts: South End Press.

Segura, D. A. (1986). Chicanas and Mexican immigrant women in the labor market: A study of occupational mobility and stratification. Ph.D. diss., University of California, Berkeley.

Stonequist, E. (1937). *The marginal man*. New York: Charles Scribner.

Swartz, D. (1977). Pierre Bourdieu: The cultural transmission of social inequality. *Harvard Educational Review* 47, 544–555.

Zavella, P. (1989). The problematic relationship of feminism and Chicana studies. *Women's Studies*.

Zavella, P. (1987). *Women's work and Chicano families: Cannery workers of Santa Clara Valley*. Ithaca, New York: Cornell University Press.

Zinn, M. Baca. (1982). Mexican American women in the social sciences. *Signs: Journal of Women in Culture and Society* 8, 259–72.

Black Women in Black and White College Environments:
The Making of a Matriarch

JACQUELINE FLEMING

The social science literature portrays conflicting images of black women: as dominant and assertive, and as the victims of the "double jeopardy" of being both black and female. This paper discusses how predominantly black or predominantly white college environments differentially encourage characteristics associated with each image. Samples of over 500 black females who were freshman or seniors, in one of two all black or four predominantly white colleges, were given a large battery of questionnaires to assess the impact of college. The results show that the adverse conditions of predominantly white colleges were more likely to encourage self-reliance and assertiveness, characteristics reminiscent of the "matriarchal" image in social science literature. In contrast, the supportive conditions of predominantly black schools were more likely to encourage a social passivity that may undercut the simultaneous greater academic gains at black colleges. This suggests a dilemma that is characteristic for white women, and perhaps also suggests the image of black women as the victims of double discrimination.

There are two conflicting images of black women in social science literature. On the one hand, black women are often portrayed as strong, competent, self-reliant, even dominant—the "matriarch" image introduced by Frazier (1939). On the other hand, black women are often viewed by social scientists as "victims," suffering under the double jeopardy of being both black and female in a society that is both racist and sexist. How can we reconcile both images of black women? Is one right and the other wrong? Or are both true, at least under certain conditions? If both images do capture some truth, then the important research question is to identify the conditions and contexts that promote and reinforce each image. The existing research on black women provides very few clues as to the situational and contextual factors that produce women who appear to be either strong and self-reliant or helpless victims.

This paper explores the impact of two similar yet very different situations—predominantly black and predominantly white college environments—on the behavioral and psychological orientations of black college women. The major purpose is to determine whether each kind of college environment facilitates the development of characteristics associated with one or both of the two images described above.

The college years are an appropriate critical period of human development for this kind of investigation. They coincide with the formation of personal and social identity (Erikson, 1968). Yet there has been little research on the impact of college upon black women, even though the impact of college on that group is especially interesting because they have the choice of going to either a predominantly black or a predominantly white college.

In this paper, therefore, we ask two questions. First, do black women develop differently in black and white college settings? Second, does the differential development of black women in these two college settings tend toward or resemble the different images of black women in the social science literature? (Of course some of the same questions could be asked abut black men, and in the larger research project of which this paper is a part, those questions are also being explored. This paper is written for this issue of the *Journal of Social Issues,* and in it we focus on black women only.)

Images

The favored view of black women in the social science literature is that of strength, self-reliance, and a strong achievement orientation (see Staples, 1970). No doubt this view goes back to Frazier's (1939) idea of a black matriarchy; that is, maternal households and husbands absent, which Frazier believed to be a common family form that emerged just after slavery. In support of this description, Frazier noted the self-reliance and self-sufficiency that black women learned during slavery, and their familiarity with playing the dominant role in marital and family relations. It was further alleged that the social ascendancy black women gained during slavery led to favoritism toward the black female child. Girls are said to be openly preferred, with greater sacrifices made and greater educational opportunities provided for their futures (Ausubel, 1956; Grossack, 1963; Rohrer & Edmonsen, 1960). While Frazier's original notion referred to father-absent families, it has more recently been widely asserted and accepted that, even when the father is present, the mother is the dominant partner. A further implication is that mother dominance (with or without the father present) is beneficial for daughters but maladaptive for sons, in terms of emotional and intellectual adjustment (Clark, 1965; Gans, 1970; Hyman & Reed, 1969; Kardiner & Ovesey, 1951; Schwartz, 1965). Indeed, black women are often judged to be better educated than black males (Bernard, 1966; Bressler & McKinney, Note 1); to demonstrate superior scholastic performance (Bernard, 1966; Jackson, 1973); and to be more represented in high-status occupations and generally more successful than black males (Bock, 1969; Scanzoni, 1971). This, then, is the image of assertive strength that has dominated much of the thinking in social science about black women.

Yet much of the evidence supporting the "black matriarchy" theory, often coming from impressions and observational research methods, has now been shown to be inaccurate or misleading (see Fleming, in press). Several authors have demonstrated with census figures that the alleged educational advantage of black women over men is actually very slight; even this slight advantage obscures the fact that black males predominate in terms of advanced degrees, elite professional attainment and income (Epstein, 1973; Jackson, 1973; Almquist, Note 2). In studies of occupational aspirations, some investigators do find higher aspirations among women, but the bulk of evidence is that black women express *lower* occupational goals that men, often aspiring to goals that are stereotypically feminine and surprisingly inconsistent with the image of the "dominant" black woman (Cater, Little & Barabus, 1972; Fleming, 1983; Gurin & Gaylord, 1976; Mednick & Puryear, 1975; Picou, 1973; Smith, 1975; Turner, note 3). Studies of family relations also find little support for the matriarchal theory (Blood & Wolfe, 1963; Geismar & Gerhart, 1968; Hyman & Reed, 1969; Mack, 1971). Especially vis-a-vis black males, black women seem to show no superiority in dominance or social power.

How can we account for the persistent stereotype of black women as assertive, strong, and dominant? In studies directly comparing black women and white women, most researchers find that black women show stronger work orientation, longer history of participation in the work force, and stronger commitment to professional goals (Epstein, 1973; Fichter, 1967; Kuvelsky & Obordo, 1972; Smuts, 1971; Gump, note 4). Perhaps the truth is not that black women are stronger or more dominant than black men, but rather that they are less passive and dependent—less "feminine," in terms of white stereotypes—than white women. Their long history of instrumentality in the service of family functioning may well have built in black women an air of self-reliance that arouses further stereotyping among those (largely white) social scientists more accustomed to white traditional norms for women.

A more recent but less widely held social science view of black women portrays them as the helpless victims of double discrimination or "double jeopardy" (Epstein, 1973; Almquist, note 2). In this view, the negative statuses of blackness and femaleness combine to make black women the most disadvantaged of the four sex-race groups. According to Almquist, the scientific community ignores working women and prefers, for some reason, to concentrate on the small minority who have attained professional status. But professionals constitute only a small part of the labor force, and in the remaining occupational categories black women are seriously disadvantaged compared to black males (although the gap between black and white women is narrowing). Almquist's analyses also suggest that black women are more disadvantaged because of sexism (non-equal pay with men for equal work) than because of racism (inequalities in occupational distribution). All in all, black women are concentrated at the bottom of the occupational pyramid, with low status and low earnings. In terms of personal characteristics and traits, this second image may imply that black women are uncomplaining and docile (instead of assertive and strong), content to endure at the bottom of both the racial and sexual hierarchies.

Impact of Black and White Colleges on Black Women

Although there is not much research on the subject, the situations of black women in black and white college settings are very different, in at least two important dimensions: social environment and institutional climate. Jencks and Riesman (1968) argued that predominantly black colleges help to perpetuate a black matriarchy because more women than men are enrolled in these schools. However, there are surely a substantial number of both men and women in black colleges, and a national survey of the impact of colleges on black students show that the sex ratio is in fact more nearly equal in black than in white colleges (Fleming, in press). This means that with a substantial presence of black males, black women have a more normal social life in black colleges. On the other hand, if black and white women are at all similar, then other previous research suggests that the presence of men may interfere with the development of achievement drives in black women. Tidball (1976), for example, has shown that among white females, the presence of male peers in the college environment is negatively related to the level of outstanding post-college accomplishments. Thus, according to this hypothesis, in predominantly black colleges, black women may have more social opportunities, but the presence of men may aid or impede their achievement potential.

A second important situational factor is the institutional climate. While there is much variation among black colleges, they often do have features and conditions fostering high aspirations that are not generally present in predominantly white colleges. Gurin and Epps (1975) report that for black students in black colleges, achievement potential is enhanced by the following: informal contact with faculty, strong academic values, administration and faculty beliefs that every individual can and will succeed, diverse curricular and extracurricular options, and attention to remedying poor high school preparation. Thus although not all black colleges are the same, they seem more likely to provide a supportive institutional climate for black students than do white colleges. (Of course given Tidball's point, in a coeducational environment these supportive effects may only be true for black male students.)

Previous research suggests that a sharply contrasting social environment prevails for black students in predominantly white colleges. Here several studies report that black students have a poor social life, few dating opportunities, and a constricted range of personalities with whom to interact. As a result, they suffer from isolation (Hedegard & Brown, 1969). Fleming's (in press) study of college environments documents that the absolute numbers of black males on these campuses are small, especially among seniors, so that they problem of social isolation falls hardest on black women. Given Tidball's (1973) findings, however, the relative absence of black male peers may help to release the achievement potential of black women, even though they are more likely to be faced with an impoverished social life on white college campuses.

Evidence suggests that the institutional climate for black students on white campuses is also less than favorable. Kilson (1973) claims that because of racial prejudice, black students on white campuses lead restricted lives, failing to participate in the life on the campus where so many opportunities for informal learning exist. Isolation and restricted access to campus life also adversely affect the academic lives of students, so that they perform below par. Furthermore, black students feel that their difficulties are the result of not only alienating social conditions, but also feelings of institutional nonsupport and abandonment.

We might well expect the psychological and social development of black women to be different in colleges that offer such contrasting environments. While predominantly black institutions are more likely to offer a good social life and a supportive institutional climate, predominantly white colleges are far more likely to offer the harsh conditions of an impoverished social life and a nonsupportive institution.

College Type and the Image of Black Women

Clearly, black colleges and white colleges should have very different effects on black women. What are these differences, and can they be formulated in terms of the two "images" of black women in the social science literature discussed earlier? There is very little research to help us form a cogent hypothesis. Although black colleges have been accused of perpetuating a matriarchy, the evidence seems inconsistent. For women, the supportive institutional climate of black colleges might help to develop self-reliance and achievement concerns, but the presence of substantial numbers of black male peers could be a cross-pressure toward passivity, at the very least directing achievement into relatively traditional unassertive channels. On the other hand, at white colleges the demands of achievement might be strong, but the poor social life (relatively few black males) and nonsupportive institutional climate might erode the development of achievement concerns.

One purpose of the study to be reported in this paper was to explore whether the situation pressures and contextual factors that black women face in black versus white colleges differentially contribute to the development of qualities such as self-assertion and an achievement orientation, personal characteristics that are intimately bound up with either of the two stereotypes of black women in the existing social science literature.

Design of the Study

The research reported in this paper was a series of comparative, cross-sectional studies in which samples of freshmen and seniors were compared in order to infer the impact of college. Over 500 black female students were recruited from six colleges (two predominantly black and four predominantly white) in greater Atlanta, a cosmopolitan area that attracts many black students to its great variety of educational environments.

Both predominantly black institutions were located in Atlanta: (1) Spelman College, a private, female, liberal-arts school (adjacent to a male "brother" college) with an enrollment of about 1,200; and (2) Clark College, a private coed, liberal-arts school with an enrollment of about 1,500. The predominantly white institutions were: (1) Emory University, a private liberal-arts school located in Atlanta, with a total enrollment of about 7,000, including about 50 black students; (2) Georgia Institute of Technology, a state school in Atlanta with a primarily engineering curriculum, enrolling about 6,300 undergraduates, of whom about 400 were black; (3) the University of Georgia, a state liberal-arts school in Athens, enrolling about 15,000 white and 360 black undergraduates; and (4) Georgia College, a state liberal-arts school located in Milledgeville, with a student body including about 2,500 white and 350 black students.

Both of the predominantly black schools were private institutions, as opposed to only one of the white colleges. One of the predominantly black schools was a single-sex institution, whereas all of the predominantly white schools were coeducational. All of the white institutions were considerably wealthier than either of the black schools. It seemed important for this exploratory effort to match students' characteristics (that is, anticipated background and aptitude variables), rather than matching institutional characteristics; the latter will be a major focus for succeeding years of the study.

Subjects

Data were collected during the five-month period from January through May 1977. From lists made available by the colleges, students were recruited by letter, by follow-up phone calls, and by class announcements. The final sample of 532 students included 333 (204 freshmen, 129 seniors) from black colleges and 199 (134 freshmen, 65 seniors) from white colleges. Response rates ranged from 36 to 84 percent of those students actually contacted by letter. Despite the effort to match background characteristics, students in black schools had substantially lower scores on socioeconomic status and in aptitude tests than counterparts in predominantly white schools. These considerations should be kept in mind in evaluating the results.

All subjects were tested in mixed-sex groups (except at Spelman, of course). Testing groups varied from twenty to one hundred students. Each session was conducted by one male and one female member of the project staff. Subjects filled out a lengthy questionnaire and participated in several other procedures, and were paid $5 for the 3—4 hour session. About three-quarters of the subjects gave permission to release transcripts and aptitude test scores.

Instruments

While a wealth of information was obtained from the students, only those instruments and items of special interest and relevance to the present paper will be described in detail here. The long questionnaire asked for the usual background and demographic information, and then asked students to describe their academic and other campus activities in some detail. Open-ended questions asked about students' perceptions of college climate. For example, one question asked what were the most enjoyable and most disappointing things in college? Another asked how much, and in what ways, had college influenced or changed them? Several coding categories were developed to score answers to these questions. The influence of college, for example, could be categorized as cognitive growth ("I learned a lot"), identity formation ("I found myself"), or coping and survival ("I learned to look out for myself"). Other open-ended questions investigated students' plans after college and vocational ambitions. Students were asked to rate the favorableness of several aspects of their college experience (for example, administration, faculty, quality of instruction, and other students), as well as the appropriateness of thirty-six self-descriptive adjective phrases, all on typical six-point rating scales. Finally, three personality measures used in previous studies of college students and presumed to be especially relevant to the problems facing black students in college situations, were incorporated in the questionnaire: (1) an overall measure of *social assertiveness* (Rathus, 1973) containing separate factor scales for fear of confrontation, shyness, submissiveness, and emotional suppression; (2) a measure of *black ideology* (Ramseur, Note 5) which also has overtones of social assertion; and (3) a measure of test anxiety conceived as reflecting fear of failure (Atkinson & Litwin, 1960; Mandler & Sarason, 1952).

Analysis

For purposes of this paper, the effects of predominantly black and predominantly white colleges were estimated by comparing, within each college type, the scores of freshmen and seniors, through a series of one-way analyses of variance. (As noted above, there were substantial differences in social class and aptitude test scores between students attending black and white colleges. Because these differences could create spurious college-type effects, and because of widely different numbers of cases per cell, a two-way analysis of variance design was not employed at this stage of the research.) In effect, the analyses treat two parallel cross-sectional designs, one for each type of college.

In educational research, such cross-sectional studies often yield results in agreement with those from longitudinal designs (see the review by Feldman & Newcomb, 1969). Yet the use of cross-sectional designs, so often dictated by practical problems of field research, poses certain problems for the interpretation of development change. For example, freshman-senior cross-sectional differences could be interpreted as not reflections of college effects, but rather as the result of generational (cohort) differences among students, or as changes in the colleges' recruit-ment and/or selection patterns, or as the result of attrition among students over three years of college (see Baltes, Reese, & Nesselroade, 1977; Baltes, Reese, & Lipsitt, 1980; Campbell & Stanley, 1963). The first two of these three alternative interpretations seems unlikely on the basis of our knowledge of the particular student bodies and institutional practices during the years of study. The effects of attrition cannot be dismissed. In our analyses, we made covariance adjustments for aptitude test scores and for social class, which are two of the most critical influences on attrition (Astin, 1975), in an effort to minimize the spurious effects of attrition. Still, we cannot rule out effects from these or other uncontrolled factors within the study.

The interpretive approach taken in this study, therefore, is to assume that identified fresh-man-senior differences suggest hypotheses about the presumed impact of different kinds of college on black women that must be tested in further research. Indeed, a larger longitudinal study to test these cross-sectional findings is already underway.

Academic Performance, Confidence, and Motivation

In general, black colleges seem to foster improved academic performance among black women students as shown by freshman-senior differences on a variety of measures. For example, seniors score significantly higher than freshmen on cumulative grade-point-average, and "honors" sta-tus, even when freshman-senior differences in aptitude tests scores and social class are taken into account. (Similar effects are found on a variety of other grade-based measures.) Over time, of course, college students should learn to study, to write papers, and to take exams, so that improvements such as these might have been expected. It is interesting, therefore, that black female students attending white schools do not, in general, experience significant academic gains during the college years.

The performance results are paralleled by changes in students' confidence and motivation. At black schools, seniors were more likely than freshmen to describe themselves as "intelligent" and less likely to describe themselves as "lazy" or to think of themselves as intellectually incompetent. They also showed lower fear of failure levels. In contrast, seniors at white schools were *less* likely to describe themselves as "energetic," and there were no significant differences on the other measures. In terms of confidence and motivation, as well as actual academic performance, then, the black schools seem to be more encouraging of their women than are the white schools.

Development of Social Assertiveness

The most compelling set of findings in this study concerned the differential encouragement of social assertiveness. In black colleges, there appears to be a significant *loss* in assertive abilities, while in white colleges consistent gains in assertiveness are strongly suggested by the observed differences. If an air of self-reliant and confident assertion constitutes the essential ingredient in the strong, dominant, "matriarch" image of black women, then that image may be fostered by predominantly white college settings.

The overall social assertiveness measure, taken from Rathus (1973), is composed of four negatively defined factors. In the predominantly black colleges, senior women actually scored higher than freshmen on three of these factors: fear of confrontation, shyness, and submissiveness. These findings clearly suggest that seniors in these schools are less able than their freshman counterparts to deal effectively in many social situations. But if seniors are in fact less assertive socially, they may be unaware of this fact, because they report feeling more independent than do freshmen. In more ideological terms, seniors at the black college also show higher scores on a measure of acceptance of white authority.

In predominantly white schools, several different findings indicate enhanced assertiveness among seniors. Senior women scored high on the total social assertiveness scale, and lower on the emotional suppression factor. They describe themselves more often as "outspoken" and less often as "inarticulate" than do their freshman counterparts. Also, seniors scored higher than did freshmen on the black ideology scale, a measure which incorporates many social assertion indicators. Thus, the evidence points to a consistent pattern of enhanced social assertiveness over time, for black women at predominantly white colleges.

Perceptions of College Impact

Students at black and white colleges come to perceive the nature and effects of their respective institutions in quite different ways. Correspondingly, their own reactions and feelings about college also differ. These differences are quite consistent with the two patterns of findings already discussed.

At black colleges, seniors tend more than freshmen to describe the major influence of college on themselves in ways that can be classified as "cognitive growth." As might be expected, they also show higher levels of satisfaction with the institution as a whole, and with the quality of instruction and contact with faculty in particular. Overall, seniors at black colleges are more satisfied than are freshmen with their decision to come to college.

At the white colleges, black female seniors apparently grow increasingly critical of their institutions. As compared to freshmen, they have more negative feelings about the college administration, faculty, and other students. They are *less* satisfied than are freshmen with their decision to come to college. While they do not see college as particularly influential in cognitive ways, they do tend more often than freshmen to describe the influences of college on them as involving coping and survival, the ability to deal with other people, and a general cultural broadening. Interestingly enough, black women at white colleges increasingly come to believe that marriage interferes with a career, while this belief diminishes at black colleges.

In sum, students at the black colleges believe that it has affected their cognitive development, which is consistent with the other data about academic performance discussed above. These effects are clearly satisfying and positive for them. Students at the white colleges believe that college has most affected their social skills, again consistent with the observed increases in assertiveness. These changes, however, are neither satisfying nor positive; for over time, attendance at a white college appears to entail increased negative feelings and even doubt about the basic choices associated with going to college. We see, in other words, two quite different patterns of college impact, each with its own characteristic emotional tone. Black colleges facilitate academic achievement in the narrow sense, though perhaps (at least for women) at the cost of confidential social assertion. Subjectively, this appears to be a comfortable change. White colleges increase dissatisfaction and negative feelings, but they facilitate assertion, articulateness, ideological consciousness, and similar broadly defined social skills.

Discussion

The results of this first stage of a long-term research project show that two groups of colleges, one predominantly black and the other predominantly white, have substantially different effects on black women students. White colleges appear to develop what can be termed a "confident, assertive" response pattern in black women that is accompanied by dissatisfaction, while black colleges appear to foster an "academic achievement" pattern that has further overtones of social passivity.

These two patterns reflect some aspects of the two contrasting social science images of black women discussed at the beginning of this paper. The "matriarchal" or strong and dominant stereotype best fits the kind of development found at predominantly white colleges, which encourages social assertiveness and an articulate outspokenness. Although these qualities are potentially positive ones, the circumstances that produce them are not. For black women in white schools, confident assertiveness seems to arise under unhappy conditions—an unpleasant college experience may even create doubts about the wisdom of college itself. Thus harsh conditions seem to elicit assertive responses from black college women. The actual conditions facing black women on these white college campuses (social isolation, lack of opportunity for heterosexual relationships, a nonsupportive institution) may provide clues as to what societal conditions have contributed to whatever "germ of truth" underlies the popular matriarchal stereotype. Indeed, many of the conditions on white college campuses are highly reminiscent of the social realities with which black women have always had to cope. The social history of black women in America has been characterized by adverse economic conditions and men unable to lend sufficient support, so that black women have been forced to call upon their own resources and become instrumental and assertive. Historically, this was not a choice but a necessity. In many respects, the necessity continues even today. Researchers still report a low male:female sex ratio at colleges (Jackson, 1971) that makes black males relatively unavailable. And on the average, black men are less able to provide the same level of economic support as do other men (Almquist, Note 2). To some extent, then, the conditions that originally forced black women into a self-reliant and assertive stance persist today.

On the other hand, predominantly black colleges present black women with an entirely different set of circumstances and encourage quite different characteristics. From the results represented, black women do well academically and feel comfortable and supported in black colleges. In objective terms, there are large numbers of black men on these campuses (or on "brother" campuses) so that dating opportunities are more plentiful. Probably because of a more supportive faculty and administration, academic achievement seems greater. Yet the presence of academic and social supports does not encourage self reliance in these women, but the opposite. On a number of different measures, black women on black campuses seem far more likely to become more passive during the college year. Thus, although black college environments seem to promote good academic and cognitive development in the college years, they do not appear to encourage black women to become active and assertive. In the long view, this "atrophy" of assertive skills, and the development of a more passive dependent orientation that this implies, may act to undermine the ambition associated with academic achievement.

To some extent, then, the image of the black woman as "victim" of the double jeopardy of being both female and black—striving for achievement, perhaps, but in unassertive ways—seems to fit the kind of development found at predominantly black colleges. Such a conclusion is in direct contradiction to the argument of Jencks and Riesman cited above. It suggests, ironically, that black colleges, presumably intended to facilitate the academic development of black men and black women, may at the same time limit the social development and assertiveness of black women.

Why should this be so? One explanation would be that confident social assertion is in fact best fostered by a difficult, even "abandoning" environment (see Winter, McClelland, & Stewart, 1981; pp. 138–140, 142–143, 150). Another interpretation would be that it is the relative absence of significant competition from male peers (albeit perceived as a poor social life with inadequate dating opportunities) that fosters a confident assertive style among black women. The dilemma of the black woman at a black college—urged to achieve yet also pressured to be unassertive while doing so—looks much like the dilemma usually facing white women. In this regard Tidball's (1976) findings, that the presence of male peers acts to discourage white female achievement, would seem to apply also for black college women. This second interpretation may be supported by the findings about views on marriage and career. It could be explored better with data on the effects of different types of colleges on black men, and on white students of both sexes.

To some extent, then, each of the social science images, or stereotypes, of black women is a characteristic response to an identifiable set of social conditions, whether in the history of black American women or on American college campuses today. As we look toward the future, however, it is important to go beyond these stereotypes and styles. Each pattern of response has strong and weak points. Confident and strong assertion is undoubtedly a positive response for black women, just as it is for anybody else; but without the tools of academic accomplishment and confidence, it can be a dead end. And even the brightest academic accomplishments can be eroded by social passivity. Perhaps the most important question for black women, then, is to find the conditions under which the best of both styles can be developed.

Notes

1. Bressler, T., & McKenney, N. *Negro women in the United States.* Paper presented at the annual meeting of the Population Association of America, Boston, MA, 1968.

2. Almquist, E. M. *Black women in the labor force: The experience of a decade.* Unpublished manuscript, North Texas State University, 1975.

3. Turner, B. F. *Perception of the occupational opportunity structure and socialization to achievement as related to sex and race.* Paper presented at the meeting of the Eastern Psychological Association, New York, 1971.

4. Gump, N. N. *Reality and myth: Employment and sex role ideology in black women.* Prepared for conference on New Directors for Research on Women, Howard University, 1975.

5. Ramseur, H. *Continuity and change in black identity: A study of black students at an interracial college.* Unpublished doctoral dissertation, Harvard University, 1975.

References

Astin, A. W. *Preventing students from dropping out.* San Francisco, CA: Jossey-Bass, 1975.

Atkinson, J. W., & Litwin, G. H. Achievement motive and test anxiety conceived as motive to approach success and motive to avoid failure. *Journal of Abnormal and Social Psychology,* 1960, *60,* 52–63.

Ausubel, D. P. Ego development among segregated children. *Mental Hygiene,* 1956, 42, 362–369.

Baltes, P. B., Reese, H. W. & Lipsitt, L. P. Life-span developmental psychology. *Annual Review of Psychology 1980.* Palo Alto, CA: Annual Reviews, 1980.

Baltes, P. B., Reese, H. W., & Nesselroade, J. R. *Life-span Developmental psychology: Introduction to research methods.* Monterey, CA: Brooks/Cole, 1977.

Bernard, J. *Marriage and family among negroes.* Englewood Cliffs, NJ:Prentice-Hall, 1966.

Blood, R. O., & Wolfe, D. M. *Husbands and wives: The dynamics of married living.* New York: Free Press, 1963.

Bock, E. W. Farmer's daughter effect: The case of the negro female professionals. *Phylon,* 1969, 30. 17–26. Also in A. Theodore (Ed.), *The professional woman.* Cambridge, MA: Schenkman, 1971.

Campbell, D. T., & Stanley, J. C. *Experimental and quasi-experimental designs for research.* Chicago, IL: Rand McNally, 1963.

Carter, D. E., Little, C. A., & Barabas, Z. S. Comparative study of Negro and white attitudes associated with educational-occupational aspirations. *Journal of Negro Education,* 1942, 41, 361–364.

Clark, K. B. *Dark ghetto: Dilemmas of social power.* New York: Harper & Row, 1965.

Epstein, C. F. Positive effects of the double negative: Explaining the success of black professional women. In J. Huber (Ed.) *Changing women in a changing society.* Chicago, IL: University of Chicago Press, 1973.

Erikson, E. H. *Identity, youth and crisis.* New York: Norton, 1968.

Feldman, K., & Newcomb, T. *The impact of college on students.* San Francisco, CA: Jossey-Bass, 1969.

Fichter, J. H. Career expectations of Negro women graduates. *Monthly Labor Review,* 1967, 90, 36–42. Also in A. Theodore (Ed.) *The professional woman.* Cambridge, MA: Schenkman, 1971.

Fleming, J. Sex differences in the educational and occupational goals of black college students: Continued inquiry into the black matriarch theory. In M. S. Horner, M. Notman, & C. Nadelson (Eds.). *The challenge of change.* New York: Plenium, 1983.

Fleming, J. *The impact of college environments on black students.* San Francisco, CA: Jossey-Bass, in press.

Frazier, E. F. *The Negro family in the United States.* Chicago, IL: University of Chicago Press, 1939.

Gans, H. J. The subcultures of the working class, lower class, and middle class. In E. O. Lauman et al. (Eds.) *The logic of social hierarchies.* Chicago, IL: Markham, 1970.

Geisman, L. L., & Gerhart, U. C. Social class, ethnicity, and family functioning: Explaining some issues raised by the Moynihan report. *Journal of Marriage and the Family,* 1968, 30, 480–487.

Grossack, M. M. (Ed.) *Mental health and segregation.* New York: Springer, 1963.

Gurin, P., & Epps, E. *Black consciousness, identity and achievement.* New York: J. C. Wiley Co., 1975.

Gurin, P., & Gaylord, C. Educational and occupational goals of men and women at black colleges. *Monthly Labor Review,* 1976, 99, 10–16.

Hedgegard, J., & Brown, D. Encounters of some negro and white freshmen with a public multi-university. *Journal of Social Issues,* 1969, 25, 131–144.

Hyman, H. H., & Reed, J. S. Black matriarchy reconsidered: Evidence from secondary analysis of sample surveys. *Public Opinion Quarterly,* 1969, 33, 346–354.

Jackson, J. J. Black women in a racist society. In C. V. Willie, B. M. Kramer & B. S. Brown (Eds.) *Racism and mental health.* Pittsburgh, PA: University of Pittsburgh Press, 1973.

Jencks, C., & Riesman, D. *The academic revolution.* New York: Doubleday, 1968.

Kardiner, A., & Ovesey, L. *The mark of oppression.* New York: World Publishing Company, 1951.

Kilson, M. The black experience at Harvard. *New York Times Sunday Magazine,* Sept. 2, 1973.

Kuvelsky, W., & Obordo, A. S. A racial comparison of teenage girls' projections for marriage and procreation. *Journal of Marriage and the Family,* 1972–34, 75–83.

Mack, D. Where the black matriarchy theorists went wrong. *Psychology Today,* 1971, 4; 24.

Mandler, G., & Sarason, S. A study of anxiety and learning. *Journal of Abnormal and Social Psychology,* 1952, 47, 166–173.

Mednick, M. T. S., & Puryear, G. R. Motivational and personality factors related to career goals of black college women. *Journal of Social and Behavioral Sciences,* 1975, 21, 1–30.

Picou, J. S. Black-white variations in a model of the occupational aspiration process. *Journal of Negro Education,* 1973, 42, 117–122.

Rathus, S. A. A 30-item schedule for assessing assertive behavior, *Behavior Therapy,* 1973 4; 398–406.

Rohrer, J. H. & Edmonson, M. S. (Eds.) *The eighth generation: Cultures and personalities of New Orleans negroes.* New York: Harper, 1960.

Scanzoni, J. H. *The black family in modern society.* Boston, MA: Allyn & Bacon, 1971.

Schwartz, M. Northern United States Negro matriarchy: Status versus authority. *Phylon,* 1965, 26, 18–24.

Smith, E. J. Profile of the black individual in vocational literature. *Journal of Vocational Behavior,* 1975, 6, 41–59.

Smuts, R. W. *Women and work in America.* New York: Schocken Books, 1971.

Staples, R. The myth of the black matriarchy. *Black Scholar,* 1970, 1, 9–16.

Thorpe, C. B. Status, race and aspiration: A study of the desire of high school students to enter a professional or a technical occupation. *Dissertation Abstracts,* 1969, 29, (10-A), 3672.

Tidball, E. M. Of men and research: The 1973 dominant themes in American higher education include neither teaching nor women. *Journal of Higher Education,* 1976, 47, 373–389.

Winter, D. G., McClelland, D. C., and Stewart, A. J. *A new case for the liberal arts: Assessing institutional goals and student development.* San Francisco, CA: Jossey-Bass, 1981.

Historically Black Colleges
Models for Increasing Minority Representation

WILLIAM B. HARVEY AND LEA E. WILLIAMS

The enrollment patterns of Black college students have shifted dramatically in the past generation. In 1950, for example, over 90% of Black students were educated in traditionally Black institutions of higher education. That situation has changed substantially since the 1960s, when higher education, like the larger society, began to move toward desegregation, and it is now estimated that approximately 18% of Black college-going students attend historically Black colleges and universities (American Council on Education, 1987: 8). This shift in college choices is significant because it reflects a drastic change in earlier social norms that restricted the range of educational opportunities available to Black people.

However, recent studies, (Fleming, 1984; Allen, 1987) and a litany of racist occurrences at several predominantly White institutions (Glover, 1988; Wells, 1988), reaffirm the important function that historically Black colleges and universities continue to serve by providing supportive environments in which Black students receive positive psychosocial reinforcement as well as academic growth and development.

The realization that the historically Black institutions still grant a disproportionate share of the baccalaureate degrees that are earned by Black students is perhaps as significant as the change in enrollment patterns. Approximately 37% of the undergraduate degrees received by Black students were conferred by these initiations in 1985 (see Table 1). The higher attrition and noncompletion rates of Black students at predominantly White colleges and universities underscore the reality that, particularly for this population, merely gaining access to these institutions is hardly synonymous with realizing success with them.

Despite the problems that Black students continue to face at predominantly White institutions of higher education, there are people who oppose the continuation of Black colleges and universities. Some individuals who take such a position do not believe that it is counter to the best interests of Black people, and frequently these individuals base their objections on philosophical and/or fiscal grounds. Philosophically, they contend that the society should strive to achieve a greater degree of racial integration than presently exists. Through Black colleges' continued existence, such colleges allow, if not encourage, Black students to be segregated from the larger society at a key time in their intellectual and emotional development. From a fiscal perspective, concern is sometimes expressed that duplicated facilities and programs are an inevitable result of the presence of Black colleges and that higher education dollars are spent less efficiently than they would be if these institutions were no longer in existence.

These arguments cannot be ignored. Indeed, they must be responded to in order for Black institutions of higher education to receive continued political and financial support from the public at large and its elected representatives. In the best of all possible worlds, where racism and discrimination do not exist and where equal opportunity is a statement of fact rather than one of

Table 1
Degrees Conferred by Historically Black Colleges and Universities
Compared to Total Degrees Conferred to Blacks in the U.S., 1984–85

	Bachelor's	Master's	Doctorate	First Professional	Total
Blacks in the U.S.	57,473	13,939	1,154	3,029	75,595
Historically Black Colleges & Universities	21,467	4,213	174	942	29,943
% of Degrees Conferred by Historically Black Colleges & Universities	37.3	30.2	15.0	31.0	39.6

Source: American Council on Education, Office of Minority Concerns, sixth annual status report, 1987.

intent, Black colleges and universities might not be needed. But the terribly slow pace at which American society moves toward the ideal state of human relations means, for both practical and symbolic reasons, that Black institutions of higher education remain critical to the continued progress of Black Americans.

Hodgkinson (1985) points out that the well-being of Black Americans, including their educational development, is becoming increasingly significant to the condition of the entire nation. The historical pattern suggests, as well as do current conditions, that Black colleges will continue to play a critical role if society is to achieve the important goal of bringing larger numbers of Black people into the nation's economic mainstream.

From Humble Origins

The important functions played by Black colleges and universities can best be understood within a historical context. Black participation in higher education began at the conclusion of the Civil War, for prior to that time slavery was the operating reality in the South, few free blacks were prepared to attend college, and, given the prevalence of racial segregation, few institutions were willing to admit them. There were three distinct phases that occurred in the development of higher-education institutions for Blacks. The first phase took place from 1865 to 1875, when various White church denominations founded schools for newly freed slaves. Phase two occurred from about 1875 to about 1890, when various Black church denominations started colleges. The third phase lasted from about 1890 to about 1950, when the land-grant and state colleges for Black students were established in the South (Wright, 1978).

In the first phase, despite their designations as colleges and universities, most of these institutions actually enrolled large numbers of students who studied secondary- or even elementary-level work. The preparatory education departments at the Black institutions provided the elementary/secondary education that their students had not previously received because of those students' lack of formal schooling. Several of the institutions began with the most meager of resources. One school was reportedly founded in a railroad car, another in an abandoned hospital barrack, and yet another in an abandoned jail. Though the early Black colleges and universities were mostly offering secondary education, they increasingly devoted themselves to work at the college level as the years passed.

The second phase of development exemplifies the concept of self-help that was particularly typical of Southern Blacks during the latter half of the nineteenth century. The strongest social institution in the Black community was the church, so it is not surprising that the different religious denominations were active in the establishment of institutions of higher education. From tithes, the congregations provided financial support to the schools, and the ministers and members of the church hierarchy frequently served as teachers and administrators. For many of these former slaves, their belief in education was second only to their belief in God, and the church and the college were seen as partners in preparing Black people for what they hoped would be a brighter future.

In phase three, public funding was provided to begin state colleges for Black students, but this was a process that the legislatures usually did not approach with a great deal of urgency. When Congress provided financial support for state land-grant institutions of higher education through the passage of the Morrill Act in 1862, it seemed possible that Black colleges might receive funding. However, it was not until 1890, when the Morrill Act was amended to require equal distributions between Blacks and Whites, that the Black institutions received regular appropriations. Despite the amendment, the distributions were hardly equal, though, for after a decade of the amended Morrill Act, White colleges were still receiving appropriations at a rate 26 times greater than Black colleges (Sekora, 1968).

Apart from funding, the biggest issue facing Black colleges, whether they were public or private, was the kind of curriculum they should offer. One Black leader, Booker T. Washington, promoted the idea that the institutions should be most concerned with teaching job-related skills, while another important figure, W. E. B. Du Bois, argued that the colleges should concentrate on the intellectual development of Black students. "Thus the ground was laid for the great controversy over the relative merits of industrial as opposed to higher education" (Frazier, 1949). Both men thought that the format they advocated might result in a better life for the Black masses. Ultimately, both industrial and classical education became part of the curricular design for Black colleges.

The funding problem was a more difficult one to resolve. Compared to most White colleges, the Black institutions of higher education were drastically underfinanced, as many continued to be. The private colleges relied on gifts, donations, and payments by students, while the allocated funding that was earmarked for the Black land-grant institutions was often diverted to the White land-grant colleges and universities (Clark and Kirwin, 1967).

Not only were the inadequacies of the Black colleges obvious, but it has also been argued that these colleges were also intentionally maintained in an inferior condition by those who wielded power and authority in the society. The shortcomings of Black colleges "must be located in the total social order that insisted that the institutions of higher learning for Blacks be nothing more than second- and third-class imitations of White institutions" (Bullock, 1970). Still, given the obstacles that the Black colleges and universities faced, these institutions served their clientele with a considerable degree of effectiveness. The institutions have been able to upgrade the quality of their offerings over the years, while maintaining a commitment to individual student development, and thus these institutions have been able to attain the stature of viable academic centers of higher learning.

A Pattern of Success

Following the desegregation of higher education, proponents of the historically Black institutions have pointed out that these schools are, on the whole, considerably more successful than their predominantly White counterparts at educating Black students. This realization is, for these proponents, a sufficient justification for their continuation and support. While the historically Black colleges and universities are often thought to be quite similar, "the colleges differ considerably in their academic quality, financial health, physical facilities, student body attributes and faculty strength" (Williams, 1988). A range of quality and effectiveness differentiates these institutions, just as it does at their White counterparts. However, Black institutions, unlike other colleges, are united around their central mission of meeting the educational and developmental needs of Black students. Allen (1987) argues that "traditionally Black institutions are necessary since they educate a sizeable group of Black students who might otherwise not be able to obtain college degrees."

The success that Black colleges have realized, frequently with meager resources, is indisputable. Yet most Black institutions of higher education suffer from "serious shortages of funds and employ underpaid faculties that devote disproportionate amounts of their time to teaching" (Fleming, 1984). In spite of these shortcomings, Jordan (1975) estimates that 75% of all Black Americans who hold Ph.D.s, 75% of all Black army officers, 80% of all Black federal judges, and 85% of all Black doctors received their undergraduate education at historically Black institutions. It is precisely this record of success, and the inability of predominantly White institutions to achieve similar results, that suggests that some insights might be gained by an examination of Black colleges and universities, particularly their organizational structures, instructional styles, and operational approaches. Several general characteristics can be seen as being common to the modus operandi of the historically Black institutions, such as

> A set of interwoven circumstances on Black college campuses that causes them to be much more successful in graduating Black students than are White institutions.

> The nature of the relationship between students and faculty on Black college campuses that apparently differs from the relationship on White college campuses.

> The atmosphere of the Black college campus, which seems to give the students a greater sense of confidence and builds higher self-esteem.

Thus the Black college experience prepares students to enter and succeed in the wider world beyond the campus. This counters the argument that students attending Black colleges are artificially protected from the "real" world and therefore are less able to cope with the realities of that world once they leave the campus. In many ways, Black college graduates can make a smoother transition from college to the larger society because, during the critically important years of adolescence, they have been nurtured in a supportive environment and encouraged to develop to their fullest intellectual potential.

Certain structural and intangible characteristics seem to have developed at Black institutions of higher education that result in successful educational experience for their students. These characteristics can be identified as a participatory ethos, an inclusive environment, an expectation of success, nonpunitive remediation, positive role models, and a sense of historical affirmation. Without the oppressive weight of institutional bigotry, limited faculty expectations, and the daily struggle against overt and subtle forms of racism, students at Black colleges are freer to concentrate on academic pursuits. Removing the burden of these crippling distractions, which can be more psychologically damaging to students than the inadequacies of physical facilities and instruction by less widely recognized faculty, is perhaps one explanation for why students, especially those who enter with lower levels of preparation, succeed in catching up academically and graduate in higher proportions from Black colleges.

Further, the assumptions that Black colleges are anachronistic, monocultural environments are simply untrue. Since the inception of Black colleges, they have been racially mixed, except when prohibited by law. When initially founded in the late nineteenth century, the Black institutions had administrators and faculty who were mainly White missionaries from the northern states. While the leadership began shifting to Blacks by the mid-twentieth century, today the faculties remain fully integrated.

Though accurate data are not available on the racial composition of faculty members at state-supported colleges, at the private Black colleges, which comprise the membership of the United Negro College Fund, more than one-third of the faculty (38%) were non-Black in 1987–88 (United Negro College Fund, 1988). This is an enviable ethnic balance, when compared to the severe underrepresentation of Black faculty on White campuses. In addition, Black colleges have always served as welcoming forums for visiting scholars, political statesmen, and business leaders, irrespective of their race, creed, or religion. Thus Black colleges' students receive wide exposure to a variety of racial and ethnic groups, and they benefit from the exchange of diverse opinions and views, which is excellent preparation for dealing with the wider world beyond the campus.

The Comfort Level

For the most part, there appears to be a general level of satisfaction and comfortability among Black students on Black college campuses. The physical condition of these institutions is likely to be less luxurious than that of predominantly White colleges and universities, but the ambience is apparently much more comforting. Allen (1987) points out that the historically Black institutions offer their students "psychological well-being, cultural affinity, nurturing academic relations, and happiness at the cost of limited physical facilities, fewer resources, and more restricted academic programs." Similarly, Fleming (1984) observes that "the black college environments are more effective, because they are 'supportive.'"

The sense of affirmation that Black students receive in Black institutions of higher education is highlighted when one compares their positive experiences on these campuses with the negative interactions that they frequently experience at predominantly White institutions. In considering the factors that impact upon student growth and development, without question an "important feature is the campus milieu, the 'inner life of the institution'" (Barthelemy, 1984).

Allen's research indicates that Black students feel welcome(d) at Black colleges and universities, and consequently they are better able to focus their energies on matters related to the pursuit of their degrees without experiencing counterproductive distractions. Conversely, they are faced with alienation, stress, and sometimes outright hostility at predominantly White institutions. Rather than feeling affirmed in such settings, Black students are more likely to feel attacked. It is obvious that "where these students are able to feel less 'under siege,' the quality of their educational experiences and educational outcomes will be vastly improved" (Allen, 1987).

At Black colleges and universities, Black students are expected and encouraged to be involved, both in academic and extracurricular activities. Obviously the thrust of their learning experiences occurs in classroom settings, but the benefit and value of participation in various clubs and organizations should not be minimized. The opportunity to be actively involved in activities of this kind adds an experiential dimension to the more theoretical base that the student receives in the classroom. The benefits of serving in leadership positions in student governments, fraternities, sororities, or other extracurricular organizations are both immediate and long-term. "Through these involvements, student-support networks are developed and students build a sense of confidence in their ability to lead and a strong measure of pride" (Barthelemy, 1984). Thus the climate of the predominantly Black institutions invites participation on the part of the students and provides them with opportunities to be meaningfully involved. This situation contrasts graphically with the predominantly White institutions where Black students most often find themselves on the periphery of campus activity.

Bringing Out the Best

In trying to decipher the contributions of Black colleges to the success of Black students in higher education, the literature on minority student retention offers some understanding of the reasons for these colleges' success. Research by Astin (1982) on minority persistence identifies several key factors that contribute to students' remaining in college.

Astin groups these factors into entry characteristics of college-going students and environmental factors existing at the institutions. To expand on the former category, it seems that the minority students who persist in college generally have pursued a rigorous academic course of study in high school and are confident in their academic ability, especially in math, science, and foreign languages. These students have a higher chance of success if they come from the middle class and are relatively young. Once a minority student arrives on campus, the environmental factors that nurture achievement include being a residential student at a four-year selective college or university, majoring in education, and not having an outside job.

It is interesting to note that the entry profile of many of the students who enter Black colleges is the opposite of Astin's profile of success. Because most Black colleges are open-admissions institutions, many students have not taken a rigorous academic course of study, nor are they particularly strong in math, science, or foreign languages. In addition, they are not necessarily from the middle class. Yet Black colleges seem to overcome students' weaker entry characteristics. The significant question regarding this situation is: How do Black colleges succeed in educating Black students when other colleges are failing in this endeavor?

One key is obviously the positive environmental climate that exists at Black colleges. Most of Astin's environmental factors—factors that also contribute to student success—can be found in the Black colleges. Most of these institutions are residential, and they provide a racially comfortable environment for the students. Researchers (Allen, 1986, Fleming, 1984) have confirmed that Black students find Black colleges more hospitable ethnically and socially. In addition, the relatively small enrollments of Black colleges assure a low faculty/student ratio. This facilitates student/faculty interaction and is conducive to the development of late bloomers, those students with academic potential not previously recognized or awakened. Moreover, because strengthening basic skills is inherently a part of the Black college mission, remedial courses have traditionally been available, and thus are less likely to be viewed as a recent and perhaps unwelcome(d) accommodation.

Ultimately, the fact that the majority of faculty and students at Black colleges share a common racial kinship and identity cannot be minimized. Whatever weaknesses students bring to Black colleges, the general attitude of the institution, as epitomized by the faculty, administrators, and staff, has to be more understanding, more accepting and less prejudicial than at predominantly White institutions. The high percentage of White faculty at the historically Black colleges suggests that the effective transmission of information is not bound by color, and that in these institutions the expectation of student success, rather than failure, engenders a set of behaviors and interactions that facilitates successful academic experiences. When students can identify positively with faculty in the classroom, students tend to feel more at ease and their confidence is raised, which are likely to have a positive influence on their overall performance.

Remediation as Reinforcement

Black colleges have often been viewed as academically weak because they invest time and resources in developmental education. However, since the 1960s, more developmental educations programs have been offered by all colleges because of the need for such courses. In addition, the society has demanded wider access to higher-education opportunity, which has brought many first-generation students to the classrooms. In 1983–84, the National Center for Educational Statistics reported that 82% of all higher-education institutions offered at least one remedial course. This included 87% of the public colleges and 44% of the private institutions. In the same year, 16–25% of all college freshmen took at least one remedial course in reading, writing and mathematics (U.S. Department of Education, 1985).

Developmental education at the collegiate level recognizes the importance of giving students with inadequate secondary educational preparation a chance to bridge the learning gap between their existing knowledge and the requirements of the college classroom.

At its best, developmental education provides a chance for students to improve their skills and acquire the basic knowledge needed to succeed in college without having to suffer prejudice for past inequities and omissions. Because of the circumstances of their founding and the continuing educational needs of the students they serve, Black colleges have traditionally embraced this approach to learning. In a sense, Black colleges have always favored an egalitarian view of education that is inclusive rather than exclusive. Students are the ultimate beneficiaries of this climate of acceptance.

Present and Future Considerations

Traditionally, within the higher education sector, Black colleges have been viewed as special focus institutions that serve—almost exclusively—a racially defined constituency. As long as Black colleges educated a population of students that was of marginal interest to other segments of higher education, the relative health of these institutions and the quality of education provided by them were issues seldom raised. Perhaps the most notable exceptions to this rule were the higher education philanthropic agencies and accrediting associations. Their long-standing involvement with Black colleges derived from a vested interest; these colleges either received financial support from these sources or sought to be accredited by them. Thus, it was self-interest that motivated educational philanthropists and regional accrediting bodies to raise questions about the health and quality of Black colleges.

Today, the situation is quite different. Black colleges now exist in an educational milieu that is acutely aware of the changing racial demographics of the American population, with its steadily declining majority being gradually replaced by ever-increasing ethnic minorities. Educators are keenly attuned to the reality of a "minority majority" in America as we move closer to the 21st Century. Coming to this realization, colleges across the nation have begun eagerly seeking ethnic students. Black colleges, once the only institutions providing a higher education for substantial numbers of Black students, no longer hold this distinction. Furthermore, they must now compete for Black students in the same marketplace as the other institutions of higher education, many of which are better financed and endowed than the Black colleges.

How do such changes affect Black colleges as they endeavor to remain viable institutions, committed especially to increasing minority participation in higher education?

For the foreseeable future, Black colleges will undoubtedly have to work harder to attract students. To succeed, they must expand beyond their traditional recruitment base to include other populations of students, such as Hispanics, Whites and international students. In this regard, Black public colleges began increasing their White enrollment in the mid 1970s because of the Supreme Court decision in the *Adams* case, which mandated that institutions supported by state funding maintain a racial balance.

The Black colleges most likely to be successful in the future will be those that boldly confront the task of rethinking their educational objectives. The focus should be at least twofold: (1) to better prepare students for living and working in a highly technological world that will demand very sophisticated knowledge; and (2) to equip them with the tools to grapple with extremely complex personal, professional and ethical issues.

The ability of Black colleges to meet these challenges will, of course, require both financial and human resources. But beyond more money and additional staff, visionary leadership and a high level of faculty expertise are needed. Of absolute necessity, the president must have a vision for the institution, one who sees beyond the moment and who captures the imagination of the college's many constituencies. That vision, based on college-wide, mutually agreed-upon goals, should determine a course of action for the future. Next to the president, the faculty carries the heaviest responsibility. They are the linchpin in determining whether the institutional objectives are met, and they are absolutely key to enhancing the college's reputation within the higher education sphere. This requires faculty who are steeped in their disciplines, are constantly renewing themselves, and who have the know-how to convey their subject matter through skillful teaching.

Visionary leadership and expertise in teaching are indispensable for any college wishing to expand and grow. This combination would place Black colleges in a better position to recruit and retain their present students. Moreover, it would allow them to broaden their base to include various other ethnic groups, many segments of which could benefit from the teaching/learning modes which have made Black institutions particularly successful with first-generation college students. Casting a wider recruitment net will not necessarily diminish the historical role Black colleges have played in educating Blacks, and to which most want to remain committed. Quite the contrary, it should strengthen the colleges, enhancing their reputations as institutions truly committed to increasing student access and assuring equal higher education opportunity for all.

References

Adams v. Bennett, 675 F. supp. 668 (D.D.C. 1987).

Allen, W. (1986) *Gender and Campus Race Differences in Black Student Academic Performance: Racial Attitudes and College Satisfaction*. Atlanta, GA: Southern Education Foundation.

Allen, W. (1987) "Black colleges vs. white colleges." *Change* 19, 3:28–39.

American Council on Education (1987) *Minorities in Higher Education: Sixth Annual Status Report.* Washington, DC: American Council on Education.

Astin, A. (1982) *Minorities in American Higher Education.* San Francisco: Jossey-Bass.

Barthelemy, S. (1984) "The role of black colleges in nurturing leadership," In A. Garibaldi (ed.) *Black Colleges and Universities.* New York: Praeger.

Bullock, H. (1970) *A History of Negro Education in the South, from 1619 to the Present.* New York: Praeger.

Clark, T. and A. Kirwin (1967) *The South since Appomattox.* New York: Oxford.

Fleming, J. (1984) *Blacks in College.* San Francisco: Jossey-Bass.

Frazier, E. (1949) *The Negro in the United States.* New York: Macmillan.

Glover, C. (1988) "The other side of racism." *Journal of the National Society of Black Engineers* 4, 1:42–46.

Hill, S. (1985) *The Traditionally Black Institutions of Higher Education: 1860 to 1982.* Washington, DC: National Center for Educational Statistics.

Hodgkinson, H. (1985) *All One System.* Washington, DC: Institution for Educational Leadership.

Jordan, V. (1975) "Blacks in higher education: some reflections." *Daedalus* 104: 160–165.

Sekora, J. (1968) "Murder relentless and impassive: the American academic community and the Negro college." *Soundings* 51:259.

U.S. Department of Education (1985) Many College Freshman Take Remedial Courses. National Center for Education Statistics Bulletin (September).

United Negro College Fund (1988) Statistical Report. New York.

Wells (1988) "Facing the current of campus racism." *Journal of the National Society of Black Engineers* 4, 1:36–40.

Williams, L. (1988) "Public policies and financial exigencies: Black colleges twenty years later." *Journal of Black Studies* 19, 2: 135–149.

Wright (1978) "The Black college in historical perspective" in P.E. Jones (ed.) *Historical Perspectives on the Development of Equal Opportunity.* Iowa City, IA: American College Testing Program.

The Demographics of Diversity
Asian Americans and Higher Education

Jayjia Hsia and Marsha Hirano-Nakanishi

Today's media attention on Asian American talent and college-going—the stories about Westinghouse talent search winners, allegation of bias in Ivy League administrations—is best understood in a shifting demographic context. Asian Americans this decade have been the nation's fastest-growing group of college-goers. In 1976, there were 150,000 Asian American undergraduates in U.S. higher education. A decade later, in the fall of 1986, there were almost three times as many—448,000. If this phenomenal growth had *not* drawn attention, one might be surprised.

Beyond the headlines, though, there has been too thin an information base for higher education policymakers as they plan services for a set of students for its commitment to education—and striking diversity.

The Numbers

The numbers of Asian American college-goers tripled in no small measure because of growth in the larger Asian American population. The 1980 census reported a total of 3.5 million Asian Americans; they constituted a mere 1.5 percent of the total U.S. population. The 1980 count, however, represented more than a doubling of the previous Asian American count in 1970. The rate of growth of Asian Americans (141 percent) over that decade exceeded increases recorded among Hispanic (39 percent) and black (17 percent) persons—and for the population as a whole (11 percent).

Population estimates for Asian Americans *after* 1980, unlike those for larger minority groups, are at best informed approximations. None of the inter-decennial national surveys of population collect enough sampled Asian Americans to provide statistically reliable estimates. Population projections of Asian American growth by researchers from the East-West Population Institute in Honolulu put the total figure for Asian Americans at 5 million in 1985, making Asian Americans about 2 percent of the total U.S. population. Some estimate that the 1990 Asian American population will number about 6.5 million, or just under 3 percent of the total U.S. population. Some demographers postulate that ethnic Asians could become as much as 10 percent of the U.S. population by the year 2080.

Projections aside, we address the more modest question: How did the number of Asian Americans escalate so dramatically between 1970 and 1980? It did not come about through what demographers would call "natural increase," wherein recorded live births exceed recorded deaths. Asian American women of child-bearing age recorded lower fertility rates than white, black, and Hispanic women. U.S.-born Asian American women, aged 25 to 34, recorded only 951 children per 1,000 women, while the foreign-born averaged 1,268 children. The equivalent figure among white women was 1,404. By ethnic group, fertility was highest among Vietnamese women, predominantly newcomers whose rate of 1,785 approached those reported for Hispanic and black women. Native-born Japanese and Chinese American women, who tend to be well-educated professionals living in urban centers, recorded the lowest fertility rates of all groups, with 768 and 669 children per 1,000 respectively. (For a group to "naturally increase," fertility rates need to approach 2,000 births per 1,000 women of child-bearing age.) In short, Asian Americans have not given birth to enough children to maintain their numbers, let alone explain the explosive growth among Asians.

That growth has been due principally to a steady stream of Asian immigrants and refugees. It must be noted that the last 20 years of Asian immigration have been unlike any other in the history of Asians in America. Beginning with the Chinese Exclusion Act of 1882, a series of racially motivated, restrictive immigration laws, such as the 1924 National Origins Act, virtually halted immigration from Asia. The year 1968 is a landmark in changing that situation: it was the year the Immigration Act of 1965 took effect. The 1965 law abolished the national-origin quota system and classified immigrants according to whether they originated from the Eastern or Western hemispheres. The annual quota for the Eastern Hemisphere, which included Asia, was set at 170,000, with no more than 20,000 permitted to emigrate from any single country.

A preference system for ranking potential immigrants also was established, which emphasized reunification of families of U.S. citizens. Since 1980, the family-reunification preference has been the driving force for admission among all Asian immigrant groups. In earlier years, the third preference, which favored specified professionals, scientists, and artists of exceptional ability, and the sixth preference, which focused on skilled and unskilled workers in occupations that suffered from labor shortages in the U.S., were important vehicles for Asian immigration. As examples, one out of five immigrants from the Philippines was admitted under the third or sixth preference in 1970; 19 percent of Asian Indian immigrants in 1975 entered under an occupational preference.

For perspective, it is worth noting that, from 1971 to 1980, Asian immigration totaled about 1.6 million; this was the first time Asian immigration ever exceeded 500,000 in any 10-year period. For immigrants from the Americas the figures were higher. Asian and other immigration remained much lower than the historic inflow from Europe. In the decades between 1841 and 1971, the median decade-long immigration figure for Europeans to the U.S. was a little over 2 million.

Current U.S. immigration policy, then, may be viewed as one that seeks to remediate past imbalances and that recognizes that Asian peoples constitute over half of the world population. The figures continued to rise from fiscal 1981 through 1988. According to the Immigration and Naturalization Service, 1.75 million East, Southeast and South Asian immigrants were admitted legally to the U.S., with Asians now constituting the largest group of legal immigrants annually. (The numbers of illegal Asian immigrants in this country are quite small.) Perhaps the most remarkable point that can be made here is that the number of Asian immigrants coming to the U.S. during the '80s exceeded all Asian Americans counted in the 1970 census.

Parallel with immigrants, Southeast Asian *refugees* have also been admitted under a series of parole authorizations granted by the U.S. Attorney General since 1975, with the flow enhanced by events abroad and a broadened definition for "refugees" in the 1980 Refugee Act. Refugees can take new steps to become permanent residents after a year's residence in this country; most eventually acquire U.S. citizenship through naturalization. In the 1980 census, just over 300,000 Vietnamese, Laotians, and Cambodians were counted in the U.S. From 1980 to May 30, 1989, a total of 657,000 refugees identified as Vietnamese, Khmer, Cambodian, Laotian, or Highlanders were admitted, with the trendline decreasing in successive years from a high of 168,000 in FY 1981 to 26,000 during the first half of FY 1989. Thus, even before we get to the 1990 census count, we know there are more than a million Southeast Asians in the United States today—a substantial new addition to the mix called Asian Americans.

In the 1990 census, which begins in April, we can expect that the Asian American population will have lost some individuals through death, emigration, or repatriation and gained others through birth, immigration, refugees, and asylees. Asylees? Refugees come from abroad; asylees are already in the U.S., or a port of entry, when they seek shelter. Recent events in Tiananmen Square and the response of U.S. leaders suggest that some fraction of the 26,000 students and additional numbers of political students and additional numbers of political dissidents from the People's Republic of China may be granted asylum. The uncertain political climate in Hong Kong as of 1997 also may increase emigration; some U.S. legislators have urged that the current quota of 5,000 from Hong Kong be increased several-fold. Indeed, political or economic instability in any of the Asian nations can act as a push to increase future migration.

Finally, it should be noted that definitional changes in the 1980 census also increased the count of Asian Americans. Asian Indians have been treated historically as Asians—indeed, they were barred for decades from migration to the U.S., and were denied U.S. citizenship through naturalization until 1965. Somewhat startlingly, through 1970 the Census Bureau generally classified Asian Indians as Caucasians. The contradictory categorizations occurred despite, or because of, the fact that India is the second most populous nation in the world and has enormous racial, ethnic, and linguistic diversity. Some of the discrepancy here, of course, stems from the use of forced choices about race, which until recently were limited to Caucasoid, Mongoloid, and Negroid. Given the social, economic, and political uses of the census, Asian Indian organizations lobbied effectively to be counted as Asian Americans for the 1980 census, a step that increased the count of Asian Americans by over 200,000.

Change and Diversity

Until the recent influx of immigrants and refugees, the structure of the Asian American population had remained relatively stable for decades. Chinese, Japanese, and Filipino Americans comprised the three largest ethnic groups. In the decades up to 1970, the Asian American population became increasingly U.S.-born.

The new influx changed the picture. By 1980, the proportion of foreign-born Asian Americans had jumped to 62 percent. That census, for the first time, counted six specific Asian ethnic groups. In descending numerical order, these were Chinese (812,178), Filipino (781,894), Japanese (716,331), Asian Indian (387,223), Korean (357,393), and Vietnamese (245,025). According to demographers, Filipinos will have surpassed Chinese as the largest group by 1990, and the number of Japanese probably will have fallen below those of Vietnamese and Korean Americans.

The proportion of foreign-born among Asian American groups varies widely, from 28 percent among Japanese Americans to 91 percent among the Vietnamese.

With the exception of scholars, bureaucrats, and political activists, Americans of Asian ancestry rarely think of themselves first and foremost as "Asian American." Most ethnic Asians, particularly newcomers, are more likely to identify with their specific national or regional identities: Vietnamese, Korean, Hmong, Punjabi, Sikh, Cantonese or Taiwanese, Visayan or Ilocano. A third-generation Japanese American would be fluent in English and well assimilated in the mainstream society but have only passing knowledge of Japanese language or culture. A first-generation Asian Indian—admitted under the third preference—with a good job, possessing advanced degrees and proficient in several languages including English, typically would fit with ease into a professional milieu and live in a middle-class neighborhood. By contrast, a Laotian refugee who disembarked from a jumbo jet after years in refugee camps might have considerable trouble communicating in English and find life in the U.S. almost as alien as Alice found Wonderland. Yet, all are classified "Asian American" and are too often treated as members of a homogeneous population.

Beyond the six groups reported by the 1980 census, 166,000 persons were counted in a catch-all "other Asian" category. The designation included 22 specified ethnic groups. Laotian, Thai, Kampuchean (Cambodian), Pakistani, Indonesian, and Hmong people were each counted in the thousands. The remainder consisted of more than 26,000 East, Southeast, and South Asians who identified themselves as everything from Bangladeshi and Bhutanese to Singaporean to Sri Lankan.

Asian newcomers speak hundreds of mutually unintelligible languages and dialects. They transmit their diverse cultures by means as ancient as the oral traditions of pre-literate societies and as modern as the weekend classes for Korean students in Hangul, an orthography developed by a royal commission in the fifteenth century but officially adopted by the Korean government only at the end of World War II. In short, when most Asian American ethnic groups communicate across sub-group lines, the only real language of common communication is—as one should expect in America—English.

Along other dimensions that define ethnicity and cultural identity, there are Asian Americans affiliated with virtually all the world's faiths, from Buddhist to Zoroastrian. And while country of origin often is the manner by which people identify themselves, country of *ancestry* is the choice of many, such as people from Vietnam of Chinese ancestry.

Finally, striking variations abound *within* each Asian American ethnic group. These are associated with a panoply of factors—time or generation in the U.S., origin from regions at peace or strife, socioeconomic status in the country of origin and in the U.S., and the transferability of skills and foreign credentials to the U.S. As an example, the early Vietnamese refugees were predominantly of the educated, urban, middle-to-upper class, with a working knowledge of English, having lived in the United States for many years now. The more recent wave of Vietnamese "boat people" consisted of people much less advantaged in almost every way upon entry into the United States. Their trek to our shores was harrowing and tragic. Unfortunately, bringing so little with them, their days here have also been fraught with stress and pain. In 1980, 9.6 percent of U.S. families lived below the poverty line; the proportions of Vietnamese (33.5 percent), Cambodian (48.7 percent), Hmong (62.8 percent), and Laotian (65.9 percent) families living at poverty level were many times greater.

Participation in Higher Education

Differences notwithstanding, there are characteristics shared by most of the groups that magnify impact upon higher education.

The most important of these characteristics is that education has long been associated with status and respect in most Asian societies. For early waves of Asian immigrants, heavy investments in education provided one of the only avenues of mobility in an otherwise restrictive environment. That value is strong too, among Asian newcomers. Between 1976 and 1986, while the Asian population doubled, its post-secondary participation rose threefold—accounting, in the process, for a big chunk in higher education's total growth over those years.

This valuing of education is demonstrated also in the superior levels of educational attainment held by almost every older-adult Asian subgroup in 1980. With the exception of Vietnamese, Asians (25 and older) held high school degrees in higher proportions than the U.S. average. Significantly greater proportions of Asians over 25 (with the exception of Vietnamese) hold the equivalent of at least a four-year college degree. Over 50 percent of older-adult Asian Indians have college degrees—more than the national average.

Japanese Americans apparently *under*attain in higher education in comparison to Asian peers. Among Japanese American older adults, over 70 percent of whom are native-born, the lower rate reflects the fact that many were prevented from attending college by various restrictive policies, not the least by their wholesale incarceration in concentration camps during World War II.

Depressed as degree-earning is among the Nisei, it is high when compared with the proportion of college graduates among the older-adult Hmongs (2.9 percent), Cambodians (7.7 percent), and Laotians (5.6 percent), most of whom found no opportunity for advanced study in their homelands—and precious little here.

Asians' educational commitment translates into the phenomenon that the children—newcomers and native Asian Americans alike—enter *and* stay in school. In every age range, from kindergarten to young adult, higher proportions of Asian Americans enroll in school than their white, black, and Hispanic peers. Asian American high school sophomores and seniors, followed for six years beyond the 1980 High School and Beyond (HS&B) survey, recorded the lowest high school dropout rates and the highest cumulative grade point averages among all groups. A higher proportion of Asian high school graduates went right on to college than graduating peers. Among Asian American seniors who enrolled in four year colleges, 86 percent persisted, and 12 percent transferred to a different institution, only 2 percent reporting they had completed a short-term program or withdrawn. Among all students, 75 percent persisted, 15 percent transferred, and 10 percent completed a short course or withdrew. The persistence and transfer figure for Asian

Americans attending two-year colleges was 91 percent compared with 75 percent among all community college students.

In the jargon of higher educational research, there is little "leakage" of Asian Americans from the U.S. educational pipeline.

Note, however, that the sample of Asian American students in HS&B was inadequate for analysis by subgroups. But there is growing evidence that all is not uniformly rosy for Asian ethnics, especially for the growing segment of Southeast Asian refugees and immigrants. There have been reports of higher dropout rates among students from some Southeast Asian refugee groups in urban areas. Public schools in Boston and a number of Midwestern cities report high school dropout rates of Khmer, Hmong, and Laotian students that approach the rates of other disadvantaged minority students. To the extent that these phenomena are validated, Asian-ethnic students may be polarized over time into two segments, one in grave need of all forms of special assistance, the other a group appearing at first blush to exceed all expectations. Worse, the former may be lumped with the latter and lose sorely needed help.

Besides Asian cultural traditions of support for education, practical reasons for investing in higher education have always been a driving force for Asians. The socioeconomic position of ethnic Asian families in American society has improved markedly in recent decades, accomplished in no small measure by the Asian family's overinvestment in higher educational credentials, that is, getting the highest degrees possible even while earning less than white counterparts with equivalent qualifications. Asians also tend to pool resources by living in larger households and having more family members work. Overinvestment in education, with family members sharing the earnings load, has been a principal strategy of Asian Americans to gain entry to good jobs and a more comfortable life.

A common strategy, too, has been to optimize academic strengths in choosing a college major. First-generation and children of first-generation Asian Americans generally have shown above-average quantitative skills and compiled enviable high school records, but many have yet to achieve ease in speaking or writing English. For them, majors of choice have been those that take advantage of their mathematical reasoning abilities and minimize the need for eloquence. Thus, as first-generation students, Asians have focused on engineering, computer science, the physical sciences, and mathematics. Often coupled with this optimization strategy is the pragmatic view that study in technical fields will provide marketable skills and entry to secure, high-status, well-paying jobs.

Given these strategies, and the fact that future increases in Asian American college enrollment will come from immigrant families, it doesn't take a crystal ball to make reasonable guesses about the major fields that enrollment will head for. An important key to steering these talented students into broader fields will be to find ways of addressing their limited English proficiency.

We know also that Asian Americans choose public over private institutions. In 1986, 83 percent enrolled in public colleges and universities, compared with 77 percent of all college students. Financially limited, predominantly urban newcomers take advantage of community colleges. While 63 percent of all postsecondary students are enrolled in four-year colleges, only 58 percent of Asian Americans did so.

Demographic factors help explain the generally heightened participation of Asian Americans in higher education, but that participation is not spread evenly across institutions. According to Dr. Sam Peng of NCES, this 2 percent of the U.S. population accounted for 37 percent of the 23,000 students at the City College of San Francisco (fall of 1986), 25 percent of all students at UC-Irvine, 20 percent of Cooper Union, and 12 percent of the women at Wellesley. How could there be 758 Asian Americans out of 9,757 students at MIT, but only 427 Asian Americans out of 100,000 students in the entire state of Mississippi?

The short answer is that Asian Americans are concentrated geographically. In 1980, 56 percent lived in the West and only 12 percent in the Midwest. There are, of course, differences among ethnic groups. In 1980, the Japanese (80.3 percent), Filipinos (68.8 percent), and, to a lesser extent, the Chinese (52.7 percent) lived in the West. Proportionately more Asian Indians (34 percent) and Chinese (27 percent) lived in the Northeast than Asian Americans in general (17 percent). Southeast Asians are more widely distributed as a result of a dispersal policy in the refugee resettlement program. But there has been a migration over time, with resulting clusters of

Southeast Asians in Texas, Louisiana, Northern Virginia, and California. Six out of 10 Asian Americans live in California, Hawaii, or New York. Nine out of 10 live in urban areas. Seven states had 100,000 or more Asian Americans, and 20 standard metropolitan statistical areas had 25,000 or more.

An examination of recent higher education enrollment shows parallel concentrations of students in specific regions, states, and institutions. In the fall of 1986, there were a total of 12.5 million students enrolled in higher education institutions. About 448,000, or 3.6 percent, were Asian or Pacific Islander Americans. Asian enrollments were highest in the three states with large Asian American populations: California (192,837 students), Hawaii (36,478 students), and New York (32,532 students). In California, for example, with its pyramidal system of 106 community colleges, 19 campuses of California State University (CSU), and nine campuses of the University of California (UC), Asian students in 1987 constituted about 9 percent of all high school graduates (20,640 Asians), 7.3 percent of all community college first-time freshmen (5,439 Asians), 16 percent of all CSU freshmen (3,574 Asians), and 20 percent of all UC first-time freshmen (3,578 Asians).

When some observers see these figures, they are quick to point out that Asian Americans are *not* primarily attending the "flagship" UC campuses—that over 40 percent attend the basic level of postsecondary education, the community colleges. In the hands of others, the same figures were used to raise questions of Asian "overrepresentation" in the more selective CSU and UC sectors. Others still, who know that 26 percent of Asian high school graduates are academically eligible for the UC (double the eligibility of the total high school graduate pool) and that 49 percent are academically eligible for CSU (about 1.7 times the eligibility rate of the total high school graduate pool), wonder if Asian Americans are underrepresented, given their qualifications. Suffice it to say here that the increase in the Asian American college-age population in California, coupled with its strong educational record and propensity to participate in higher education, have created tension and placed Asian admissions in the political spotlight.

In 1985, a sample survey of students was undertaken by the CSU system across its campuses. Overall and on individual campuses, Asian American students were uniformly more critical of academic programs and practices than students of any other ethnic group. They wanted a greater variety of course offerings, enhanced instruction, improved career guidance, and personal counseling. Cognizant that the "model minority" image of Asian Pacific students conceals real problems that students face, CSU has a system-wide committee at work to assess needs and recommend ways of more effectively meeting them.

This review of demographic trends highlights the striking diversity of the nation's Asian American population. In years to come, that diversity will increase—somewhat unpredictably, given pending changes in immigration policies and political instabilities around the Pacific Rim. One certainty is that the nation and its colleges must increase assistance for the current and coming waves of refugees and immigrants from Southeast Asia—people who sink under the poverty line and leak along our educational pipeline.

At the other end of the distribution, it will be increasingly important for educational decisionmakers to be mindful that Asian Americans have believed in the meritocracy that is part of the American promise. Asian Americans have not only invested in education, they have invested in that promise. All evidence points to the observation that Asian American students work hard on studies and on the job, do well on tests, and, despite allegations to the contrary, participate in extracurricular activities. They seek stronger academic programs, courses, guidance, and counseling. The tensions over Asian American participation in higher education must and eventually will be settled, for more is at stake than a seat in a class.

Jayjia Hsai is chair of the American Educational Research Association's Special Interest Group Regarding Research on the Education of Asian and Pacific Americans (AERA SIG/REAPA). She is a senior research scientist emeritus of Educational Testing Service. Marsha Hirano-Nakanishi, director of institutional research and assistant professor of education at California State University—Northridge, is immediate past chair of the AERA SIG/REAPA.

Comparative and Predictive Analyses of Black and White Students' College Achievement and Experiences

MICHAEL T. NETTLES, A. ROBERT THOENY, AND ERICA J. GOSMAN

Introduction

Ever since the 1954 landmark Supreme Court case of *Brown v. The Board of Education of Topeka, Kansas,* efforts have been made to achieve greater desegregation at all levels of formal education. As a result of the gradual elimination of racially discriminatory barriers to higher education, more blacks began attending college in the 1960s and 1970s. In fact, even though those two decades were the greatest overall enrollment growth years in the history of American higher education, black enrollment increased more than twice as much as total enrollment. In 1965, for example, black undergraduates represented 4.8 percent of all undergraduates in the United States, compared to 10.2 percent in 1980 [42]. This remarkable increase in black enrollment appears on the surface to herald a great movement toward the achievement of equality in higher education. However, an examination of students' college performance reveals that some formidable challenges remain to be faced by American colleges and universities in the quest for equality.

Because of the enormous increase in the interest of minority students in attending college, many barriers to access have been challenged. Perhaps none has been challenged as strongly as traditional admissions standards of colleges and universities. Throughout the 1960s and 1970s, there were many debates regarding traditional college admissions policies, which were viewed by many as being racially and socioeconomically discriminatory. On one side were the advocates of more liberal admissions policies that would offer greater options for increasing minority access to higher education. These advocates argued in favor of nontraditional predictors of college performance, suggesting that students' potential college achievement should not be predicted solely on the basis of their performance on college entrance tests, but rather on the basis of a variety of student characteristics. This view was supported by several researchers who suggested that the significant predictors of black students' performance were different from the predictors for white students. Clark and Plotkin [13] discovered that for black students entering predominantly white universities, success in college was dependent upon their motivation and goals regardless of their precollegiate performance or entrance examination indices. Beasley and Sease [9] discovered that students' biographical characteristics and their extracurricular participation in student government, music, speech, science, mathematics, art, or writing organizations, as well as their reasons for attending college, were all valid in predicting black students' college grade point averages and persistence. The findings of Beasley and Sease were supportive of similar findings in earlier studies conducted by Anastasi [2] and Aiken [3]. Other researchers, such as Sedlacek and Brooks [36], Gibbs [21], and Pruitt [31] recommended that for black students such measures as educational aspirations, motivation, precollegiate preparation and experiences, and social and academic support be used as alternative college admissions criteria to traditional standardized tests, high school rank, and high school grade point averages.

During the same time period, counterarguments were advanced by several researchers who gave little or no attention to the validity of the nontraditional admissions criteria suggested above. Rather, these researchers focused upon showing the validity of standardized entrance tests for predicting both black and white students' college performance. Thomas and Stanley [39] reported the results of correlational analyses which showed that aptitude tests are better predictors of the college performance of black students than high-school grades. Studies conducted by Stanley and Porter [37] and Cleary [14] found no significant racial differences in the value of standardized entrance tests and other precollegiate academic characteristics (i.e., high-school grades and rank) as predictors of college performance. Thus, these researchers supported the view of maintaining traditional admissions criteria as valid indicators for both minority and majority population groups.

During the latter half of the 1960s and throughout the 1970s, many colleges and universities adopted open admissions policies in order to provide opportunities for everyone to pursue a college education. By 1970 it was estimated by McDaniel and McKee [25] on the basis of extensive surveys of colleges and universities that over 80 percent of American colleges and universities had adopted open admissions or some form of special admissions policies for black students. There are many reasons educators supported the open-door movement—funding formulas based upon student credit hours and the Great Society programs of the 1960s, to name just two. Efforts to desegregate higher education also played a role in admissions policy decisions in the 1960s and 1970s. In the 1980s, however, greater pressure has been applied to college administrators to reduce cost and increase quality. Higher admissions standards are believed by many to be the best means to achieve both cost reduction and higher quality; however, higher standards may also result in fewer minority students being educated at the college level. This movement necessitates a reexamination of the admissions criteria that predict success in college. This is especially important if the performance of different population groups is predicted on the basis of different sets of criteria.

In a comprehensive review of population validity studies involving college entrance examinations and various population groups, Breland [12] concluded that when identical regression equations (using traditional admissions criteria, particularly SAT and ACT scores) are applied to black and white students, the tendency is to overpredict the college performance of black students. This conclusion suggests that although the same predictors may be adequate for students of both races, some events may occur during the college experiences of black students that cause surprisingly lower performance levels than would be predicted by regression equations utilized for white students. It further implies that noncognitive variables that describe the college experience may have some impact upon students' college performance, particularly for black students.

Population validity studies like the ones cited above generally have several limitations that cause attenuation in correlation coefficients [15, 12]. First is the problem of locating and stabilizing criterion variables. In the case of studies of college admissions, the criterion variable is usually college grade point average in the freshman year or cumulative grade point average including grades earned beyond the freshman year. These serve as the best available proxies of college students' academic and cognitive achievement, yet instability is caused by their representation of different types of students taking different types of courses from different instructors who utilize different instructional and grading techniques. This problem is compounded when pooled samples are utilized, representing a variety of institutions with different standards and programs. Another common problem of population validity studies in which GPA is the criterion variable is the restriction of range due to limited admissions and high attrition, which also results in attenuation of correlation coefficients. In other words, if a larger number of students were admitted with lower academic skills and if no or less attrition occurred, the relationship between predictor variables and criterion variables would be stronger. A third problem is the time interval between the criterion measurement and the occurrence of the predictor variable. The longer the time between these two measures, the greater the likelihood of extraneous factors occurring that confound validation. This is one reason why freshman grade point average is the most commonly used criterion variable—the time lapse between measurements is small. The final confounding effect is likely to occur in population validity studies in which the criterion variable is subject to systematic bias. Systematic bias is difficult or impossible to identify but is most suspected when the rater is of different gender or race than the person(s) being rated.

These limitations in population validity studies are typical of limitations in all correlation studies in educational and social science research, and even though they cause imperfection in the measure of criterion variables, they do not interfere with the usefulness of these analyses in understanding students' college performance. In the study presented in this article, we have attempted to reduce the effect of time lapse between predictor and criterion measures by including a variety of student in-college experiences, faculty attitudes and behaviors, and institutional characteristics that are usually excluded. We have also tried to reduce the effect of systematic bias, typically caused by race and gender, by including these two variables in the regression equations. Thus, any significance of these two predictor variables may indicate the existence of bias. The restriction of range due to limited admissions and high attrition rates, as well as the imperfection of the criterion variables, cannot possibly be controlled. However, the criterion variable of the college grade point average represents the best currently available proxy of cognitive development and academic achievement in college, which can only be changed if standard outcomes assessments are developed to measure students' academic achievement.

Because many earlier researchers of higher education desegregation focused on increasing enrollment and access, it was perhaps appropriate for earlier studies to concentrate upon entering students' intellectual qualities. It is important in the context of predicting students' college performance and achievement, however, to broaden the scope to include noncognitive and campus environmental variables that affect students' learning and performance outcomes. These include students' in-college attitudes and behaviors, faculty attitudes and behaviors, and other institutional characteristics. Studies of student retention have shown that the college environment and other institutional factors are important considerations in predicting students' college performance [6, 41]. The implication in these studies on retention is that it is important to understand a great deal more than precollegiate biographical and intellectual factors in order to explain students' overall college performance.

In addition to achieving racial equality in student performance, a major goal in higher education desegregation is the equality of the college experiences. These experiences have changed for both black and white students over the past two decades. Peterson and his associates [30] depict a high degree of student activism among black students on white campuses, most of which resulted from students' dissatisfaction with their university's response (or lack thereof) to their special needs as a new student population group. Peterson describes black students as feeling a great deal of racial discrimination, which many college administrators simply chose to ignore. As a result, black students demanded changes through any means necessary to receive a favorable response. Today, however, there is little evidence of black student activism on college campuses.

The data presented and analyzed in this article address the two issues of racial equality in students' performance and equality in their college experience. The article addresses three specific questions: (1) Is there a difference in the college performance of black and white students? (2) What are the significant predictors of black and white students' college performance? (3) How do differences in the quality of the college experiences of black and white students affect their college performance? The criterion variable of performance is students' cumulative college grade point averages (CCGPAs). The predictor variables include a variety of student, faculty, and institutional characteristics.

Procedures

This study is based upon analyses of the survey responses of 4,094 students and 706 faculty from 30 colleges and universities located in the southern and eastern regions of the United States. Both samples are stratified by race such that 50 percent of the students are black and 50 percent are white; 30 percent of the faculty sample is black and 70 percent is white.

The original student sample was designed to randomly select 300 students from each campus—50 white and 50 black students from each of the sophomore, junior, and senior classes for a total of 9,000. However, on several campuses there were not enough students in the minority racial group to select the 50 desired from each class. In these cases, all minority students from those classes were selected, and the result was an original sample size of 7,428. The 4,094 responses represent a 55.1 percent return rate.

The faculty sample was also randomly selected. Thirty faculty members were selected from the total faculty at each of the 30 institutions, with one-third of the sample from each campus representing the minority racial group (black or white) at that institution. The 706 faculty responses represent a 78 percent return rate from the original sample.

Because the sampling procedure involved selecting equal numbers of black and white students at each institution and disproportionate numbers of black and white faculty, a weighting scheme was applied to the data analyses to control oversampling of minority (whites at black institutions and blacks at white institutions) students and faculty at each campus. Students and faculty at small institutions were also oversampled. The formula used to weight each student and faculty response is as follows:

$$\text{Weight} = \frac{\begin{array}{c}\text{Percent of students}\\\text{at the institution}\\\text{who are of}\\\text{respondent's race}\end{array}}{\begin{array}{c}\text{Percent of}\\\text{institutional sample}\\\text{who are of}\\\text{respondent's race}\end{array}} \times \frac{\begin{array}{c}\text{Percent of total}\\\text{student population}\\\text{who attend}\\\text{respondent's}\\\text{institution}\end{array}}{\begin{array}{c}\text{Percent of total}\\\text{sample who attend}\\\text{respondent's}\\\text{institution}\end{array}} \times \frac{N}{En}$$

The 30 universities were equally divided by type and predominant race into the following five categories: (1) large white state universities (flagship); (2) regional white state universities; (3) black state universities; (4) white large private universities; and (5) black private universities. The universities are located in 10 southern and eastern states.

Each student in the sample received a survey instrument entitled "The Student Opinion Survey" (SOS), which was designed to collect various personal, academic, demographic, and attitudinal data. The SOS was developed specifically for this study, but other instruments were used as references in its development. Of particular value were the Student Descriptive Questionnaire administered by the College Board to SAT examinees, the Educational Testing Services' College and University Environmental Scale (CUES II), and the Higher Education Evaluation KIT of the Center for the Study of Evaluation at the University of California, Los Angeles [26]. Each faculty member in the sample received a survey instrument entitled "The Faculty Opinion Survey," which was designed specifically for this study.

Methodology

The analyses utilized in this article serve two purposes: (1) to compare black and white students' college performance and their academic, personal, attitudinal, and behavioral characteristics; and (2) to illustrate the predictive validity of a variety of students' academic, personal, and attitudinal characteristics, as well as of faculty attitudes and behaviors. Chi-square analyses were used to compare black and white students on several categorical variables, F-tests were used to compare students on interval variables, and multivariate analyses of variance (MANOVA) were used to make racial comparisons of groups of similar or related variables. The Pearson Product Moment Correlation procedure was applied to illustrate the relationship of numerous student and faculty variables to student performance without controlling for the effects of other variables. Finally, two types of multiple regression analyses were used to illustrate the significant predictors of students' performance. The first regression is a full model with all variables entered into the equation concurrently to obtain the independent effects of each predictor variable with all others in the model statistically controlled. The resulting partial t-values from this regression were used to eliminate predictors that did not contribute significantly at the 0.05 level. In the second regression, setwise and stepwise inclusion techniques were combined to isolate interaction terms that added significantly (0.05 level) to the reduced model obtained through the first regression procedure. All significant main effects from the first regression were entered concurrently on step one of the second regression. Cross-product interaction terms between race and each of the main effects were then allowed to enter the model in stepwise fashion on subsequent steps if they added to the explanatory power of the equation at at least the 0.05 level of significance. The result was partial regression coefficients and t-values representing the independent contribution of each significant main effect and each significant interaction effect.

Dependent Variable

The dependent variable in these analyses, the students' CCGPAs, represents a measure of students' overall college performance. This information was self-reported by students on the SOS, on which they were asked to indicate their letter grade equivalent GPA by choosing one grade from a list of nine. The nine-point scale is 1 = A, 2 = A-, 3 = B+, 4=B, 5 = B-, 6 = C+, 7 = C, 8 = C-, 9 = D or less. These letter grades were statistically analyzed by using the 9-point ordinal scale.

Independent Variables

Our study includes a total of 31 student, faculty, and institutional variables in the regression equation used to predict students' college grade point averages. Twenty-three of the variables are students' personal, academic, attitudinal, and behavioral characteristics obtained from the SOS. The student variables include demographics, precollege academic and racial experiences, and in-college attitudinal and behavioral characteristics. The in-college attitudinal and behavioral variables are factor scales developed from a computerized factor analysis of 72 items from the SOS. Items were included if they correlated at least 0.35 with the factors. Seven promax rotated factors were selected for inclusion in these analyses. The seven factor scales are (1) academic integration, (2) feelings that the university is nondiscriminatory, (3) student satisfaction, (4) peer group relations, (5) interfering problems, (6) study habits, and (7) socioeconomic status. Cronbach's alpha coefficients [16], measuring internal consistency reliability, ranged from 0.66 to 0.82 for the seven student factor scales. The factor items and correlations for the seven student factors, as well as the reliability coefficients, are illustrated in Appendix A.

The remaining 15 student independent variables are the following: (1) composite SAT score, (2) race, (3) sex, (4) age, (5) high-school grade point average, (6) marital status, (7) type of high school attended, (8) number of hours spent working on a job while attending college, (9) where student lives while attending college, (10) racial majority minority status, (11) transfer status, (12) number of miles between permanent home and college, (13) racial similarity of high school and college, (14) degree aspirations, (15) whether student worked while attending college.

The faculty variables include 5 attitudinal/behavioral characteristics of faculty at the 30 universities. These 5 variables were selected using 53 items and the same type of factor analyses used for the student factors. Each student file contains the average factor score for faculty on his/her campus; thus, the relationship of faculty attitudinal/behavioral characteristics and student performance is based upon the average faculty attitudes/behaviors on each student's campus. Cronbach's alpha reliability coefficients for the five factors range from 0.58 to 0.83. The factor names, the item correlations with the factors, and the factor reliability scores are listed in Appendix A. Two institutional characteristics are included as independent variables. These two variables are: (1) predominant race of university and (2) total enrollment. Data for both of these variables were reported directly by the 30 universities.

Findings

To illustrate the bivariate relationships between the dependent and independent variables, Table 1 shows the weighted Pearson Product Moment correlation coefficients (r) for the interval level independent variables in the equation. Since the sample size (4,094 students and 706 faculty) is large, significance at the bivariate level is relatively easy to obtain. This results in statistical significance for relationships that are not very strong. Therefore, the significance levels for the bivariate relationships are excluded from Table 1, because the important point in these bivariate analyses is the size of the correlations.

The weighted Pearson correlations reveal some interesting relationships between student and faculty characteristics and attitudes and students' cumulative college grade point averages. The strongest predictors of CCGPAs at the bivariate level are high-school grade point average . ($r= 0.410$), interfering problems ($r=0.387$), SAT score ($r=0.313$), age ($r= -0.313$), study habits ($r=0.303$), academic integration ($r=0.192$), total enrollment ($r=-0.158$), and socioeconomic status ($r=0.121$). According to these correlation coefficients, students with high cumulative college grade point averages have high high-school grade point averages, have a low number of interfering problems while attending college (financial, social, and psychological), have high SAT scores, are younger students, have relatively good study habits, have high academic integration, attend smaller universities, and have relatively high socioeconomic status backgrounds. The remaining nine variables in the Pearson analyses yield very low relationships to students' cumulative college grade point averages. This is especially important regarding such student factors as feelings of racial discrimination ($r = 0.038$), students' peer group relations ($r=0.000$), and students' satisfaction with their institution ($r= 0.043$). It is also interesting that at the bivariate level, none of the five faculty scales have a strong relationship with CCGPA—ranging from only $r=0.064$ to $r=0.015$.

The multivariate regression results also shown in Table 1 provide stronger inferences than the correlations, because they show the independent effect of each variable in the equation while all others are simultaneously controlled. Multivariate regression analyses are considered more discriminant than individual correlations and therefore are more useful in determining significant predictors of CCGPA. The multivariate regression also allows for the inclusion of dichotomous categorical variables that could not be analyzed through the Pearson correlation procedure.

Table 1 illustrates seventeen significant predictors of students' CCGPAs in the full model of main effects. The results of the multivariate analyses differ in some important ways from the results of the bivariate analyses. Many of the variables that have very low direct relationships at the bivariate level are significant at the multivariate level, and others with high direct correlations at the bivariate level are nonsignificant when the effects of other variables in the regression equation are controlled. The multivariate regression analysis in Table 1 reveals that, in order of importance, students with high CCGPAs (1) have low feelings of racial discrimination, (2) have a low number of interfering problems, (3) have high high-school grade point averages, (4) have high SAT scores, (5) have high satisfaction with their university, (6) have relatively good study habits, (7) have relatively high academic integration, (8) attend institutions where faculty have a low level of influence upon student development, (9) have degree aspirations beyond the Bachelor's degree, (10) are members of the racial majority on their campus, (11) are married, (12) have relatively strong peer relationships, (13) are female, (14) attended a private high school, (15) live in on-campus housing, (16) are older students, and (17) are non-transfer students. The only two variables that have a relatively high correlation with the CCGPAs but are nonsignificant in the regression analysis are socioeconomic status and total enrollment. In other words, when controlling for all other factors in the equation, students' socioeconomic status (SES) and the size of their institutions are not significant predictors of their CCGPAs. This suggests that parents' education, occupation, and income, which are the components of the SES factor, are not contributors to students' college performance if all other matters (i.e., high school preparation, feelings of discrimination, interfering problems, etc.) are equal. Likewise, all things considered, students' grades are not dependent upon whether they attend a large university or a small college.

Table 1
Pearson Product-Moment Correlations and Regression of Students' College Grade Point Averages on Student, Faculty, and Institutional Characteristics: Full Model of Main Effects

Independent Variable	B^1	Beta[2]	t	r	N
SAT score	0.003	0.233	12.37**	0.313	4039
Socioeconomic status	0.000	−0.001	−0.08	0.121	4040
Race (0 = white; 1 = black)	0.273	0.049	1.84		
Sex (0 = female; 1 = male)	−0.160	−0.042	−2.86**		
Age	0.040	0.037	2.02*	0.313	4017
High-school GPA	0.360	0.299	18.70**	0.410	4020
Marital status (0 = single; 1 = married)	0.357	0.053	−3.48**		
Type high school attended (0 = public; 1 = private)	0.230	0.040	2.87**		
Number of hours spent working on a job	0.019	0.014	0.66	0.030	4008
Housing (0 = private home or apt.; 1 = on-campus housing)	0.150	0.039	2.44**		
Racial minority status (0 = majority; 1 = minority)	−0.634	−0.074	−4.21**		
Transfer (0 = yes; 1 = no)	0.138	0.035	2.40*		
Miles from permanent home	−0.028	−0.020	−1.28	−0.010	4017
Fit between racial composition of high school and college (0 = different; 1 = alike)	0.056	0.014	0.98		
Fit between racial composition of home neighborhood and college (0 = different; 1 = alike)	0.039	0.009	0.61		
Highest expected degree (0 = Bachelor's or less; 1 = Master's or more)	0.334	0.082	5.70**		
Whether worked while in college (0 = yes; 1 = no)	0.110	0.029	1.43		
Academic integration	0.376	0.171	9.77**	0.192	4040
Feelings of racial discrimination	−0.269	−0.553	−5.19**	0.038	4040
Student satisfaction	0.408	0.177	9.29**	0.043	4040
Peer group relations	0.116	0.050	3.14**	0.000	4040
Interfering problems	−0.816	−0.344	−20.75**	−0.387	4040
Study habits	0.395	0.175	10.62**	0.303	4040
Faculty satisfaction with institution	0.012	0.015	0.660	0.064	4040
Faculty conservative teaching style	0.029	0.011	0.51	−0.029	4043
Faculty influence on student development	−0.202	−0.120	−5.03**	−0.049	4043
Faculty feelings of racial discrimination	0.009	0.006	0.24	0.015	4040
Faculty contact with students	0.005	0.048	1.37	0.034	4040
Predominant race	0.104	0.027	0.64		
Total enrollment	0.000	−0.033	−1.02	−0.158	4043
Constant	5.92				
F (equation)		83.02**			
R^2		0.447			

*Significant at the 0.05 level (two-tailed).   [1]Unstandardized regression coefficient.
**Significant at the 0.01 level (two-tailed).   [2]Standardized regression coefficient.

On the other hand, four variables that have very low correlations with CCGPA at the bivariate level are significant at the multivariate level. These include three student factor scales—student satisfaction, feelings that the university is racially nondiscriminatory, and peer group relations—and one faculty factor scale—faculty influence upon student development. In other words, with all of the other variables held constant, students who feel that their university is not racially discriminatory, who are satisfied with their university, and who have strong peer group relations have higher CCGPAs. Also, students at universities where faculty have relatively little influence upon student development have higher CCGPAs when all else is constant. Some possible explanations for these findings are provided in the discussion section of this article.

Table 2 illustrates the reduced model regression equation which includes all of the significant variables (0.05) from the full model. This regression equation also includes the significant interaction terms wherein race is multiplied by each variable in the equation to illustrate any racial differences in the predictors of CCGPAs. While the full model regression equation accounts for 44.7 percent of the variance in students' CCGPAs, the reduced model is a slightly better model, accounting for 45 percent of the variance.

Table 2 illustrates that, with the exception of age, all variables that were significant in the full model are also significant in the reduced model. The introduction of interaction terms revealed four significant interactions with race: SAT scores, student satisfaction, peer group relations, and interfering problems. The interaction terms demonstrate that these four variables have differen-

Table 2
Regression of Students' College Grade Point Averages on Student, Faculty, and Institutional Characteristics: Reduced Model of Significant Main Effects and Interaction Terms

Independent Variable	B^1	Beta[2]	t
SAT score	0.002	0.236	12.67**
Race (0 = white; 1 = black)	−0.258	−0.049	−0.447
Sex (0 = female; 1 = male)	0.211	0.055	3.78**
Age	0.029	0.027	1.50
High-school GPA	0.357	0.297	18.14**
Marital status (0 = single; 1 = married)	0.351	0.052	3.42**
Type high school attended (0 = public; 1 = private)	0.297	0.051	3.88*
Housing (0 = private home or apt.; 1 = on-campus housing)	0.195	0.050	3.33*
Racial minority status (0 = majority; 1 = minority)	0.533	0.065	2.39**
Transfer (0 = yes; 1 = no)	0.177	0.045	3.12**
Highest expected degree (0 = Bachelor's or less; 1 = Master's or more)	0.358	0.088	6.25**
Academic integration	0.390	0.182	11.13**
Feelings of racial discrimination	−0.224	−0.079	−4.26**
Student satisfaction	0.506	0.224	11.94**
Peer group relations	0.127	0.055	3.60**
Interfering problems	−0.870	−0.365	−22.81**
Study habits	0.402	0.178	11.31**
Faculty influence on student development	0.069	0.042	2.80**
Interaction terms:			
SAT x race	−0.001	−0.175	−2.07*
Student satisfaction x race	0.224	0.044	2.36*
Peer group relations x race	0.178	0.033	2.19*
Interfering problems x race	−0.283	−0.049	−3.06**
Constant	6.17		
F (equation)		87.96**	
R^2		0.450	

*Significant at the 0.05 level (two-tailed).   [1]Unstandardized regression coefficient.
**Significant at the 0.01 level (two-tailed).   [2]Standardized regression coefficient.

tial impacts on the CCGPAs of black and white students. While all four variables are significant predictors of CCGPAs for both black and white students, the interaction terms show that SAT scores tend to overpredict black students' CCGPAs. Student satisfaction, peer group relations, and interfering problems all have greater significance as predictors for black students' than for white students' CCGPAs. These are all important matters explored in the discussion section of this article.

The interaction terms in Table 2 are important in showing how some variables operate differently as predictors of black and white students' CCGPAs. Additional insight can be gained by comparing black and white students on some of the significant variables included in the regression model. Significant racial differences on significant predictor variables help to explain some of the racial difference in students' CCGPAs. In Table 3 weighted Chi-square analyses are used to show racial differences on seven categorical variables that are significant predictors of CCGPAs. Table 3 shows that black and white students are significantly different in terms of the type of high school attended, their transfer status, gender representation, majority/minority status, housing patterns, and degree aspirations. Black students are less likely to have attended private high schools, a background characteristic which is related to a high CCGPA. They are also less likely to be in the racial majority on their college campus and less likely to live in on-campus housing, both of which contribute to high CCGPAs. On the other hand, black students are more likely not to be transfer students and more likely to have degree aspirations beyond a baccalaureate degree, both of which contribute to high CCGPAs. They are also significantly more likely to be female, and being female is a contributor to a high CCGPA. It would appear from Table 3 that racial differences on three of the categorical variables are likely to have a negative impact upon black students' college performance—their greater tendency to attend public high schools; their

Table 3
Weighted Chi-Square Tests Comparing Black and White Students

Independent Variable	White Students		Black Students		Chi-Square	df
	%	n	%	n		
Type of High School						
Public	86.3	2945	91.07	599	11.07**	1
Private	13.7	467	8.93	59		
Transfer Status						
Taken courses elsewhere	41.70	1426	34.60	227	11.49**	1
Never taken courses elsewhere	58.30	1994	65.40	430		
Gender						
Female	49.13	1667	61.74	404	34.93**	2
Male	50.87	1726	38.26	250		
Majority/Minority						
Majority status	98.33	3373	71.73	476	699.46**	1
Minority status	1.67	57	28.27	188		
Marital Status						
Single	90.82	3036	89.93	588	0.505	1
Married or living together	9.18	307	10.07	66		
Housing						
Private home or apt. off-campus	43.65	1492	50.29	3331	9.84*	1
On-campus housing	56.35	1926	49.71	327		
Degree Aspirations						
Bachelor's or less	36.24	1233	20.51	134	60.80**	1
More than a Bachelor's	63.76	2169	79.49	521		

**Significant at the 0.001 level.

greater tendency to live off-campus; and their greater frequency of attending a university where they are in the racial minority.

Table 4 provides a comparison of black and white students' CCGPAs, high-school GPAs, SAT scores, and socioeconomic status. The F-tests in Table 4 show that black students have significantly lower CCGPAs (C+ compared to B-), significantly lower high-school GPAs (B- compared to B+), lower composite SAT scores (819 compared to 1074), and lower socioeconomic status than white students. It is interesting to observe through these analyses that the gap between black and white students' high-school grades persists throughout college. Since SES is not a significant predictor of students' college grades, the two most important racial differences in Table 4 are high-school grades and SAT scores, both of which are discussed in relation to CCGPAs later in this article.

Table 5 illustrates comparisons of black and white students on the six student factor scales representing attitudes and behaviors that are significant predictors of CCGPAs. Both univariate analysis of variance and multivariate analysis of variance are used to indicate single variable racial differences and vector significance, respectively. Table 5 shows that black students and white students differ significantly in the quality of their college experience. The only attitudinal/ behavioral variable showing no significant difference is peer relations. Otherwise, black students have significantly lower academic integration, are less likely to feel that their university is nondiscriminatory, are less satisfied with their university, have more interfering problems, and have poorer study habits. Each of these racial differences, as well as the overall model, are significant at the 0.001 level. We suggested earlier that the lower quality college experience of black students (as measured by the attitudinal/behavioral factors) may explain why such variables as SAT scores overpredict their college performances. However, this is probably an unsatisfactory explanation, because SAT scores were found to be a significant predictor in the regression analyses controlling for the effects of these other factors. It is especially important to note that

Table 4
Racial Comparisons of Students' CCGPAs, HSGPAs, Composite SATs and SES's

Variable	White Mean	SD	Black Mean	SD	F
Cumulative college GPA	4.41 (B–)	1.92	5.34 (C+)	1.79	120.20**
High-school GPA	2.81 (B+)	1.56	3.74 (B–)	1.63	191.64**
SAT score (composite)	1,073.81	54.85	819.29	133.08	1,551.52**
SES	1.80	2.64	–1.23	3.09	556.83**

Table 5
Multivariate Analyses of Variance of Students' Attitudes and Behaviors

Variable	White Mean	SD	Black Mean	SD	F
Academic integration	0.263	0.872	–0.161	0.972	126.85**
Feelings that the university is nondiscriminatory	0.302	0.606	0.118	0.957	41.21**
Student satisfaction	0.337	0.814	0.226	0.907	255.81**
Peer relations	–0.025	0.831	–0.007	0.872	0.257
Interfering problems	–0.287	0.787	0.173	0.816	187.44**
Study habits	0.217	0.856	–0.229	0.819	152.37**

Note: Hotelling Lawley Multivariate Test of Significance $F = 123.43**$, $df = 4086.00$.
  *Significant at the 0.05 level.
**Significant at the 0.01 level.

although these two factors in particular are strong predictors of black students' CCGPAs, black students have lower satisfaction with their universities and more interfering problems than white students. Colleges and universities attempting to address black students' college performance difficulties should give special attention to these two attitudinal variables.

The data presented above support the following four major conclusions:

1. A variety of students' academic, personal, and attitudinal/behavioral characteristics, both precollege and in-college, are significant predictors of their CCGPAs.

2. For the most part, the significant predictors of CCGPAs are equally effective predictors for black and white students. However, four variables—SAT scores, student satisfaction, peer relationships, and interfering problems—have differential predictive validity for black and white students.

3. Significant racial differences on several significant predictors help to explain racial differences in college performance. The most important are type of high school attended, high school preparation, majority/minority status in college, where students live while attending college, academic integration, feelings that the university is racially discriminatory, satisfaction with the university, interfering problems, and study habits.

4. With the exception of faculty influence upon student development, none of the faculty attitudinal/behavioral characteristics included in the analyses exerts significant effects upon students' CCGPAs.

These four major conclusions are discussed below.

Discussion

The first conclusion, that a variety of students' academic, personal, and attitudinal characteristics predict their college performances, is supportive of the arguments advanced by advocates of broader admissions policies for colleges and universities. Researchers have been equivocal in concluding that standardized test scores have racially equal effects upon the college performance. Wilson [42], for example, found in a study of two college settings that SAT scores in one university had a significantly lower correlation with performance for black students than for whites in the freshman year, and the differences were even greater for the latter years. The results were the reverse on a second campus measured at the same time. Wilson found similar differential effects for blacks and whites when combining standardized test scores with high school grades to predictor college freshman GPAs and CCGPAs. Although the traditional admissions criteria of high-school grade point averages and SAT scores are found in the present study to be among the very strongest predictors of both black and white students' college performances, there are many other factors that explain why students perform the way they do in college.

Nevertheless, improvements by black students in both high-school GPAs and SAT scores will likely lead to improved college performance. The improvement in high-school preparation of black students is an important public policy concern in need of greater attention. Lee [24] recently discovered, using the *High School and Beyond* data base, that only 25 percent of black students in America's public high schools are enrolled in academic curricula, compared to 47 percent of white students. In order to expect improvements in college performance as well as higher SAT scores, the racial gap in high-school preparation will have to be eliminated. National reports such as *A Nation at Risk* and *Involvement in Learning* provide a sound basis for improving the quality of American education, but much more attention should be directed toward the elimination of the racial gap in the quality of elementary- and high-school preparation.

Based upon the analyses presented earlier in this article, efforts by colleges and universities to provide greater access are likely to benefit greatly from incorporating many variables in addition to high-school GPAs and SAT scores into the admissions and advising processes. For applicants with marginal credentials on traditional criteria, the data reported in Tables 1 and 2 suggest that with a combination of other intellectual and nonintellectual characteristics, many marginal students are likely to be successful in college. On the nonintellectual side, for example, students' decisions to live on campus as opposed to off campus is found in this study to contribute to high CCGPAs. Studies conducted by Blai [10], Ainsworth and Maynard [1], Duncan and Stoner [19], and Pascarella and Terenzini [29] have provided consistent evidence that residential peer influence as well as on-campus academic environments have a significant effect on students' college achievements for both high- and low-aptitude college students. These studies are particularly convincing in showing the positive effect of residential hall placement upon the performance of low-aptitude students when matched as roommates with high-aptitude students of similar personality type [1]. Blimling and Hample [11] have also found that students living in campus residence halls with structured emphases upon studying improve their academic performances in college.

The on-campus versus off-campus finding is only one example of the additional considerations needed in admissions and advising processes aimed at promoting greater access and higher achievement. Such additional variables as students' goals and aspirations were also shown in Tables 1 and 2 to be significant predictors of students' performances and are supportive of the findings reported by Clark and Plotkin [13] and Sedlacek and Brooks [36]. Good study habits are another important characteristic; as might be expected, students with good study habits have higher CCGPAs. Astin [7] discovered that students entering college with well-developed study habits earn higher grades and have higher rates of persistence in college. This finding suggests that efforts by universities to assure that their students possess or learn good study habits will contribute to higher college performance. Poor study habits may also be a major reason for lower precollegiate performance. Remedial and developmental efforts to improve the study habits of college students are likely to have a favorable impact upon their college performances regardless of their race.

Among the most important findings reported in this paper are those regarding the student-environment fit as measured by students' feelings that the university is nondiscriminatory, academic integration, students' satisfaction, peer group relations, and interfering problems. These factors measure the quality of the college experience, sometimes referred to as person X environment fit, which is found to exert significant positive effects upon students' college performance. Most research on this subject concludes that the better the fit between the student and his or her institution the better the chances for his or her academic success. Graham and his colleagues [22], for example, conclude that black students with interracial educational experience prior to college adjust more easily in white colleges. What Graham observes is a reduction in students' feelings of discrimination as a result of their past experiences in desegregated environments. What is observed in the present study is that lower feelings of discrimination contribute to higher college performance for both black and white students alike. However, the analyses presented in this article indicate that neither the racial fit between students' high school and college nor the racial fit between their home neighborhood and college are related to their CCGPAs. This suggests that integrated experiences prior to college may contribute to the college experiences of both black and white students, but perhaps only indirectly to their academic performance—mediated by their positive college experiences.

Academic integration is a scale which measures students' perceptions about the availability and attitudes of faculty with regard to providing informal and formal contact to discuss school work or career plans and the like. High academic integration has been found to contribute to high CCGPAs. Pascarella and Terenzini [27, 28], for example, found that the actual frequency and quality of student contact with faculty contributed to higher freshman-year grade point averages as well as to students' personal and intellectual development. Similar results were obtained by Bean and Kuh [8]. It is interesting that in the present study, however, the faculty factor labeled "faculty contact with students" exerts no significant effect upon students' college performance. There is an important distinction between academic integration and faculty contact. Academic integration represents students' perceptions about the attitudes and behaviors of faculty. Perceptions of favorable attitudes (academic integration) is significantly associated with high CCGPA.

On the other hand, the faculty contact scale measures the actual frequency of interaction. The findings in this study suggest that students' perceptions of a high degree of faculty concern for students' academic and career plans are far more important than the actual frequency of interaction between faculty and students. One would believe that faculty contribute greatly to students' feelings of academic integration, but frequency of contact may not be the key ingredient to creating that perception among students. Endo and Harpel [20], for example, found that informal faculty contact with students had a far greater effect upon attitudes about and satisfaction with their college experience than formal contacts.

The significance of the interfering problems scale as a predictor of a lower CCGPA is not surprising, because that scale reflects problems that students may encounter—personal, financial, and family— that directly compete with their academic efforts. While no comparable measure is found in the literature related to students' college grades, such measures are consistently associated with student attrition [6, 7]. As indicated by the interaction terms, this measure is particularly important for black students and is further compounded by the fact that black students have significantly lower SES's than white students. Thus, improvements in financial aid programs should not only have a positive effect upon black students' persistence, but should also have a positive effect upon their academic performance.

Student satisfaction is also a significant predictor of students' CCGPAs, an observation not found in the literature. One difficulty with this satisfaction measure is that one cannot know whether high satisfaction is the result of a high CCGPA or vice versa. Like interfering problems, however, high satisfaction has shown a consistent relationship to persistence [41, 17].

The second major conclusion from this study is that four variables—SAT scores, student satisfaction, peer group relations, and interfering problems—have differential predictive value for black and white students. Specifically, black students' college grades are lower than would be predicted by their SAT scores; and satisfaction, peer relations, and interfering problems have a much greater impact upon their CCGPAs than do these same factors for white students.

Since the effects of such factors as feelings of discrimination and racial minority status are controlled, as well as the effects of other college experience measures, it is not reasonable to explain that the overprediction of black students' college grades through SAT scores is due to their differential college experience (as hypothesized earlier in this article). This overprediction of black students' performance, as well as the lower CCGPAs of black students, is very important and will need more focused analyses in order to be clearly understood. As a start, it may be useful to study black students' aspirations for grades in comparison with students of other racial/ethnic groups, or to discover if some form of systematic bias exists in the grading process that is not measured by the variables in this study. However, contrary to findings of a recent study by Roueche and his associates [32], high school performance serves as a strong and stable predictor of both black and white students' college performance, and is a more stable predictor for black students' CCGPAs. Again, a major concern of great consequence for the desegregation process is that black students have significantly different precollegiate educational experiences than white students, and these experiences may be partially reflected in their SAT scores.

The observed interactions between race and student satisfaction, peer relations, and interfering problems and the relationships of these variables to CCGPA demonstrate the need for greater sensitivity on the part of colleges and universities to the particular needs of black college students. The data in Table 5 illustrate that black students experience significantly less satisfaction with their universities than white students, and they have significantly greater interfering problems. On the other hand, there is no significant difference in their peer group relations. Despite the absence of visible and widespread student protests in the 1980s (as described by Peterson [30] in the early 1970s), there are differences in the quality of black and white students' college experiences that appear to have a negative impact upon black students' performance. These differential experiences represent major challenges for colleges and universities in the desegregation process.

There are additional racial differences on other variables that are equally significant predictors of CCGPAs for students of both races. This brings us to the third major conclusion of this study—that the racial differences on several significant variables may account for racial differences in students' CCGPAs. Black students have significantly lower levels of precollege preparation than white students, they are less academically integrated, have less satisfaction with their universities, experience more interfering problems, and have less well developed study habits. These are matters that must be addressed by educators and policy makers in order to achieve equality in college performance and in the quality of the college experience.

The final general conclusion is that, surprisingly, faculty factors contribute very little to the prediction of students' CCGPAs. In fact, only one factor—faculty influence upon student development—is a significant predictor of students' CCGPAs and its relationship is counterintuitive— low faculty influence on student development is associated with high student performance. This factor represents faculty members' perceptions about the amount of influence they have upon students' career plans, major fields of study, and personal and social values.

The remaining faculty factors exert no significant effect upon students' CCGPAs. This is especially interesting in the case of the faculty contact factor, which measures frequency of faculty contact with students. The result, as reported earlier, is contrary to findings by Pascarella and Terenzini [27, 28], in which frequency of contact is found to be a contributor to students' GPAs in the freshman year. On the other hand, this finding is consistent with those of Endo and Harpel [20], who found that neither the frequency of informal nor formal student-faculty interaction has a significant influence upon academic achievement. In light of the fact that academic integration, which measures students' perceptions of faculty accessibility and interest, is a significant predictor of CCGPAs, it is surprising that faculty contact is not. This suggests a clear difference between actual contact as reported by faculty and *perceived* contact and concern as reported by students. In any case the latter effect is found in this study to be the contributor to students' CCGPAs.

Finally, it is surprising that neither teaching style nor faculty satisfaction with their universities is a significant contributor to students' CCGPAs. It has been rather broadly suggested in the literature that nontraditional teaching styles are causes for grade inflation and that students' performance is a major cause of faculty satisfaction. Neither claim is supported by the analyses in this paper. The remaining faculty factor measures feelings that the university is discriminatory, which also does not significantly impact upon students' college performance.

Conclusion

During the 1970s, the vast majority of colleges and universities made extensive efforts to provide greater access to students. Surveys of three thousand colleges and universities conducted by Roueche et al. [32] reveal that even the most prestigious institutions have not only admitted greater numbers of students but have also developed special programs and services to assure that admitted students succeed. In fact, in a recent survey by Roueche and Snow [33], only one hundred and sixty of the three thousand institutions surveyed reported not having special remedial or developmental programs to help students' academic achievement. It appears, however, that with increasing demands for scarce resources, efforts by universities to provide greater access will be continually challenged.

The data reported in this study are supportive of the validity of traditional admissions criteria—high-school grades and SAT scores—for both black and white students. However, SAT scores, while valid, appear not to be as strong a predictor for black students' as they are for white students' CCGPAs. Additionally, several student personal and attitudinal/behavioral characteristics contribute far too much to the prediction of CCGPAs to be ignored in the admissions process. Therefore, colleges and universities should include consideration of both nonintellectual and intellectual factors in the college admissions process.

Appendix A
Student Factors

Item	Correlation with Factor	Item	Correlation with Factor	Cronbach's Alpha Reliability
Student Factor 1: Academic Integration				
1. There is very little contact between professors & students outside the classroom. (1 = strongly agree, 5 = strongly disagree)	0.61	6. It is easy to develop close relationships with faculty members on this campus. (1 = strongly agree, 5 = strongly disagree)	−0.77	
2. Most faculty members here are sensitive to the interests, needs & aspirations of students. (1 = strongly agree, 5 = strongly disagree)	−0.61	7. How often have you socialized informally with a faculty member? (1 = very often, 5 = almost never)	−0.46	
3. At least one faculty member here has had a strong impact on my intellectual development. (1 = strongly agree, 5 = strongly disagree)	−0.45	8. How often have you discussed career plans and ambitions with a faculty member? (1 = very often, 5 = almost never)	−0.48	
4. Faculty members here are good teachers. (1 = strongly agree, 5 = strongly disagree)	−0.48	9. How often have you discussed personal problems and concerns with a faculty member? (1 = very often, 5 = almost never)	−0.46	
5. If a student seems to be doing poorly, this university goes out of its way to help the student stay in school. (1 = strongly agree, 5 = strongly disagree)	−0.52	10. Are you satisfied with the faculty-student relations? (1 = very satisfied, 5 = very dissatisfied)	−0.71	0.83
Student Factor 2: Feelings of Discrimination				
1. This institution makes an effort to attract students of diverse ethnic backgrounds. (1 = strongly agree, 5 = strongly disagree)	0.35	5. Faculty members on this campus are sensitive to issues that are important to students of my race. (1 = strongly agree, 5 = strongly disagree)	0.57	
2. I often feel discriminated against because of my race by faculty members on this campus. (1 = strongly agree, 5 = strongly disagree)	−0.75	6. I often feel discriminated against by students on this campus whose race is different from my own. (1 = strongly agree, 5 = strongly disagree)	0.65	
3. There is administrative support of minority group organizations and programs on this campus. (1 = strongly agree, 5 = strongly disagree)	0.51	7. There is open discussion of racial issues on this campus. (1 = strongly agree, 5 = strongly disagree)	0.36	
4. There is little or no racial discrimination on this campus. (1 = strongly agree, 5 = strongly disagree)	0.74	8. The administration on this campus discriminates against students of my race. (1 = strongly agree, 5 = strongly disagree)	−0.75	0.70

Appendix A (continued)
Student Factors

Item	Correlation with Factor	Item	Correlation with Factor	Cronbach's Alpha Reliability
		Student Factor 3: Student Satisfaction		
1. Are you satisfied with the student housing at your university? (1 = very satisfied, 5 = very dissatisfied)	−0.43	5. Are you satisfied with the student employment services at your university? (1 = very satisfied, 5 = very dissatisfied)	−0.40	0.74
2. Are you satisfied with your university's academic reputation? (1 = very satisfied, 5 = very dissatisfied)	−0.58	6. Are you satisfied with the student organization at your university? (1 = very satisfied, 5 = very dissatisfied)	−0.42	
3. Are you satisfied with the quality of classroom instruction at your university? (1 = very satisfied, 5 = very dissatisfied)	−0.42	7. Are you satisfied with the administration at your university? (1 = very satisfied, 5 = very dissatisfied)	−0.49	
4. Are you satisfied with the variety of courses offered at your university? (1 = very satisfied, 5 = very dissatisfied)	−0.58	8. Are you satisfied with the libraries, learning centers, etc., at your university? (1 = very satisfied, 5 = very dissatisfied)	−0.58	
		Student Factor 4: Peer Group Relations		
1. It has been difficult for me to meet and make friends with other students. (1 = strongly agree, 5 = strongly disagree)	0.40	4. How often have you studied with other students since enrolling in college? (1= very often, 5 = almost never)	−0.41	0.65
2. How often have you participated in activities with other students since enrolling in college? (1= very often, 5 = almost never)	−0.71	5. How often have you participated in some art, drama, or music activity on campus since enrolling in college? (1= very often, 5 = almost never)	0.38	
3. How often have you attended a meeting of a club, organization, or student government group since enrolling in college? (1= very often, 5 = almost never)	−0.63	6. How often have you sat around in the student center talking with other students since enrolling in college? (1= very often, 5 = almost never)	−0.36	

Student Factor 5: Interfering Problems

1. I have done as well academically at this university as I thought I would. (1 = strongly agree, 5 = strongly disagree)		
4. Have you experienced financial difficulties since enrolling in college? (yes or no)	0.56	0.61
2. Have you experienced emotional problems since enrolling in college? (yes or no)	−0.41	
5. Problems outside of school cause me to neglect my schoolwork. (yes or no)	0.43	
3. Have you experienced academic difficulty since enrolling in college? (yes or no)	0.42	
6. How difficult is it for you to finance your college education? (1 = not difficult, 5 = very difficult)	0.47	
	0.55	

Student Factor 6: Study Habits

1. I see to it that my schoolwork is carefully planned and organized. (1 = almost always, 5 = rarely)	−0.62
3. I keep my assignments up to date. (1 = almost always, 5 = rarely)	0.66
2. Unless I really like a course I don't work as I should. (1 = almost always, 5 = rarely)	−0.57

Student Factor 7: Socioeconomic Status (SES)

1. Parents' education	0.71
2. Parents' income	0.73
3. Parents' occupation	0.86

Appendix B
Faculty Factors

Item	Correlation with Factor	Item	Correlation with Factor	Cronbach's Alpha Reliability
Faculty Factor 1: Satisfaction with the University				
1. How satisfied are you with opportunities for career advancement at your institution? (1 = very satisfied, 5 = very dissatisfied)	−0.54	5. How satisfied are you with the quality of research by faculty on your campus? (1 = very satisfied, 5 = very dissatisfied)	−0.70	
2. How satisfied are you with opportunities for personal growth at your institution? (1 = very satisfied, 5 = very dissatisfied)	−0.56	6. How satisfied are you with resources for instructional programs and courses? (1 = very satisfied, 5 = very dissatisfied)	−0.65	
3. How satisfied are you with the quality of students on your campus? (1 = very satisfied, 5 = very dissatisfied)	−0.56	7. How satisfied are you with resources for faculty research? (1 = very satisfied, 5 = very dissatisfied)	0.65	
4. How satisfied are you with the overall instructional competency of faculty on your campus? (1 = very satisfied, 5 = very dissatisfied)	−0.60	8. How would you rate the overall academic reputation of your institution? (1 = very satisfied, 5 = very dissatisfied)	−0.65	0.83
Faculty Factor 2: Teaching Style				
1. I strongly encourage students to meet with me outside of class. (1 = strongly agree, 5 = strongly disagree)	0.52	4. Black and other minority perspectives should always be included in courses related to American life or institutions. (1 = strongly agree, 5 = strongly disagree)	0.45	
2. I frequently digress from prepared materials during class to pursue questions or comments from students. (1 = strongly agree, 5 = strongly disagree)	0.46	5. Do you invite student criticism of your ideas in class? (1 = almost always, 5 = almost never)	0.47	0.58
3. Informal out-of-class contacts with faculty members are crucial to a student's development. (1 = strongly agree, 5 = strongly disagree)	0.63			

Faculty Factor 3: Faculty Influences upon Student Development

1. How much influence do you believe you have upon students' decisions about their major field of study? (1 = a great deal, 5 = almost none)   −0.80

2. How much influence do you believe you have upon formulating students' career plans? (1 = a great deal, 5 = almost none)   −0.82

3. How much influence do you believe you have upon students' emotional and social development? (1 = a great deal, 5 = almost none)   −0.49

4. How much influence do you believe you have upon students' acceptance of people of different racial and ethnic backgrounds? (1 = a great deal, 5 = almost none)   −0.38   0.80

5. How much influence do you believe you have upon students' personal philosophy and outlook on life? (1 = a great deal, 5 = almost none)   −0.43

Faculty Factor 4: Feelings of Discrimination

1. Students of different racial/ethnic origins generally get along well with one another on this campus. (1 = strongly agree, 5 = strongly disagree)   −0.54

2. This institution makes a determined effort to attract students of diverse ethnic and social backgrounds. (1 = strongly agree, 5 = strongly disagree)   −0.54

3. Some faculty members discriminate against students who are the racial minority on this campus. (1 = strongly agree, 5 = strongly disagree)   0.49   0.69

4. Many of the policies and practices of this institution are racially biased or discriminatory. (1 = strongly agree, 5 = strongly disagree)   0.62

Faculty Factor 5: Faculty Contact with Students

1. I have met with _____ (no.) students during the past week to provide basic information about their academic programs.

2. I have met with _____ (no.) students during the past week to discuss intellectual or course-related matters.

3. I have met with _____ (no.) students during the past week to assist them in considering matters related to their future careers.

4. I have met with _____ (no.) students during the past week to assist them in resolving personal problems.

5. I have met with _____ (no.) students during the past week to socialize informally.

References

1. Ainsworth, C., and D. Maynard. "The Impact of Roommate Personality on Achievement: An Exploratory Study and Model of Analysis." *Research in Higher Education*, 4 (1976), 291–301.

2. Anastasi, A., J. J. Meade, and A. A. Schneiders. "The Validation of a Biographical Inventory as a Predictor of College Success." Princeton, N.J.: College Entrance Examination Board, 1960.

3. Aiken, L. R. "The Prediction of Academic Success and Early Attrition by Means of a Multiple-Choice Biographical Inventory." *American Educational Research Journal*, 1 (1964), 127–35.

4. Astin, A. W. "Personal and Environmental Factors Associated with College Drop-Outs Among High Aptitude Students." *Journal of Educational Psychology*, 55 (1964), 219–27.

5. _____. *Predicting Academic Performance in College*. New York: Free Press, 1971.

6. _____. *Preventing Students from Dropping Out*. San Francisco: Jossey-Bass, 1975.

7. _____. *Minorities in American Higher Education: Recent Trends, Current Prospects, and Recommendations*. San Francisco: Jossey-Bass, 1982.

8. Bean, J., and G. Kuh. "The Reciprocity Between Student-Faculty Informal Contact and the Undergraduate Grade Point Average of University Students." Paper presented at the annual meeting of the Association for the Study of Higher Education, Chicago, 1984.

9. Beasley, S. R., and W. A. Sease. "Using Biographical Data as a Predictor of Academic Success for Black University Students." *Journal of College Student Personnel*, 15 (May 1974), 201–6.

10. Blai, B. "Roommate-Impact upon Academic Performance." Bryn Mawr, Pa.: Harcum Junior College, 1971.

11. Blimling, G., and D. Hample. "Structuring the Peer Environment Residence Halls to Increase Performance in Average-Ability Students." *Journal of College Student Personnel*, 20 (1979), 31–316.

12. Breland, H. M. "Population Validity and College Entrance Measures." Princeton, N.J.: Educational Testing Service, 1978.

13. Clark, K. B., and L. Plotkin. "The Negro Student at Integrated Colleges." New York: National Scholarship Service and Fund for Negro Students, 1964.

14. Cleary, A. T. "Test Bias: Prediction of Grades of Negro and White Students in Integrated Colleges." *Journal of Educational Measurement*, 5 (1968), 115–24.

15. Cohen, J., and P. Cohen. *Applied Multiple Regression/Correlation Analysis for the Behavioral Sciences*. Hillsdale, N.J.: Lawrence Erlbaum, 1975.

16. Cronbach, L. J. "Coefficient Alpha and the Internal Structure of Tests." *Psychometricka*, 16 (1951), 297–334.

17. Cross, P. H., and H. Astin. "Factors Affecting Black Students' Persistence in College." In *Black Students in Higher Education*, edited by G. Thomas. Westport, Conn.: Greenwood Press, 1981.

18. Decoster, D. "Effects of Homogeneous Housing Assignments for High Ability Students." *Journal of College Student Personnel*, 8 (1968), 75–78.

19. Duncan, C., and K. Stoner. "The Academic Achievement of Residents Living in a Scholar Residence Hall." *Journal of College and University Student Housing*, 6 (1977), 7–9.

20. Endo, J. J., and R. L. Harpel. "The Effect of Student-Faculty Interaction of Students' Educational Outcomes." *Research in Higher Education*, 16 (1982), 115–38.

21. Gibbs, J. L. "Black Students/White University: Different Expectations." *Personnel and Guidance Journal*, 51 (1973), 463–69.

22. Graham, C., R. W. Baker, and S. Wapner. "Prior Interracial Experience and Black Student Transition into Predominantly White Colleges." *Journal of Personality and Social Psychology,* 47 (1985), 1146–54.

23. Lavin, D. *The Prediction of Academic Performance.* New York: Russell Sage Foundation, 1965.

24. Lee, V. "Explaining the Relationship between Social Class and Academic Achievement in Public and Catholic Schools." Ph.D. dissertation, Harvard Graduate School, 1985.

25. McDaniel, R., and J. McKee. "An Evaluation of Higher Education's Response to Black Students." Bloomington: Indiana University, 1971.

26. Pace, C. R. "Higher Education Measurement and Evaluation Kit." Los Angeles: University of California, Graduate School of Education, Center for Study and Evaluation.

27. Pascarella, E., and P. Terenzini. "Student-Faculty Informal Relationships and Freshman Year Educational Outcomes." *Journal of Educational Research,* 71 (1978), 183–89.

28. _____. "Student-Faculty Informal Contact and College Outcomes." *Review of Educational Research,* 50 (1980), 545–95.

29. _____. "Contextual Analysis as a Method for Assessing Residence Group Effects." *Journal of College Student Personnel,* 23 (1982), 108–14.

30. Peterson, M. W., et al. "Black Students on White Campuses: The Impact of Increased Black Enrollments." Ann Arbor, Mich.: The University of Michigan, 1978.

31. Pruitt, A. S. "Minority Admissions to Large Universities: A Response." *Journal of College Student Personnel,* 14 (1973), 22–24.

32. Rouche, J. E., et al. "College Responses to Low Achieving Students: A National Study." *American Education* (June 1984), 31–34.

33. Roueche, J. E., and J. J. Snow. *Overcoming Learning Problems.* San Francisco: Jossey-Bass, 1977.

34. Sample, D. D., and W. R. Seymour. "The Academic Success of Black Students: A Dilemma." *Journal of College Student Personnel,* 12 (1971), 243–47.

35. Scott, C. M. "Background and Personal Data as Factors in the Prediction of Scholastic Success in College." *Journal of Applied Psychology,* 22 (February 1938), 42–49.

36. Sedlacek, W. E., G. C. Brooks, and L. A. Mindus. "Black and Other Minority Admissions to Large Universities: Three-Year National Trends." *Journal of College Student Personnel,* 9 (1968), 177–79.

37. Stanley, J. C., and A. C. Porter. "Correlation of SAT Scores with College Grades for Negroes versus Whites." *Journal of Educational Measurement,* 4 (1967), 199–218.

38. Terenzini, P., and E. Pascarella. "Voluntary Freshman Attrition and Patterns of Social and Academic Integration in a University: A Test of a Conceptual Model." *Research in Higher Education,* 6 (1977), 25–43.

39. Thomas, C. L., and J. C. Stanley. "Effectiveness of High School Grades for Predicting College Grades of Black Students: A Review and Discussion." *Journal of Educational Measurement,* 6 (1969), 203–16.

40. Thomas, G. E. "The Effects of Standardized Achievement Test Performance and Family Status on Black-White College Access." In *Black Students in Higher Education: Conditions and Experiences in the 1970s,* edited by G. E. Thomas. Westport, Conn.: Greenwood Press, 1981.

41. Tinto, V. "Dropout from Higher Education: A Theoretical Synthesis of Recent Research." *Review of Educational Research,* 45 (1975), 89–125.

42. Wilson, K. M. "Predicting the Long-Term Performance in Colleges of Minority and Nonminority Students: A Comparative Analysis in Two Collegiate Settings." Princeton, N.J.: Educational Testing Service, 1978.

Michael T. Nettles is research scientist at the Educational Testing Service, Princeton, New Jersey. A. Robert Thoeny is associate director of academic affairs, Tennessee Higher Education Commission, Nashville, Tennessee. Erica J. Gosman is research associate at the Western Interstate Commission on Higher Education, Boulder, Colorado.

Hispanic Student Retention in Community Colleges:
Reconciling Access with Outcomes

AMAURY NORA AND LAURA RENDÓN

The extraordinary diversity of the American higher education system assures that those who graduate from high school or earn a GED, regardless of academic preparations, race, class, age, or sex, will be accepted for admission at some institution. However, there is evidence that a student's educational choice tends to be delimited not only by academic preparation, but by race and social class.[1] Community colleges, the capstone of American equal opportunity, have evolved as the primary access to higher education for ethnic minorities and students from low social class origins. A controversy presently exists that community colleges may have a negative effect on ethnic minorities, who represent their primary source of students (particularly Hispanic students), and that the colleges may actually serve to perpetuate race and class inequities in the American society. The controversy stems from the fact that Hispanic students are differentially concentrated in the nation's community colleges, but that their educational achievement, retention, and transfer rates to senior institutions have been less than satisfactory.[2]

Hispanics in Community Colleges

Hispanic students are largely dependent on community colleges to initiate college-based programs of study. In the fall of 1984, 54.3 percent of all Hispanics enrolled in public and private postsecondary institutions were found in two-year colleges, compared to 42.7 percent for blacks and 35.9 percent for whites.[3] The disproportionate presence of Hispanics, ethnic minorities, and students of low to modest social origins in two-year colleges raises concern about the type and extent of the educational opportunities afforded to selective students in the stratified hierarchy of postsecondary institutions. Economically and academically disadvantaged students appear to be primarily attending colleges which rank at the bottom of a stratified institutional hierarchy, have the most modest resources, and have had the lowest levels of student achievement and persistence. The limitations inherent in the structure and nature of community colleges only serve to exacerbate the problems associated with these institutions' high Hispanic and ethnic minority student attrition and low transfer rates to senior institutions.

Hispanic Student Retention

The academic achievement of Hispanic students in community colleges has been less than satisfactory, and is marked by low retention and transfer rates to senior institutions. Data are available to suggest that the uneven flow of Hispanic students through the postsecondary educational pipeline may be due to the cohort's disproportionate enrollment in community colleges. In a survey taken two years after 1980 seniors enrolled in postsecondary institutions, 50 percent of the Hispanics were not enrolled in college.[4] In a study of minority student participation in higher education, the Commission on the Higher Education of Minorities[5] indicated that one of the most important reasons that Chicanos, Puerto Ricans, and American Indians are underrepresented in graduate programs is their greater-than-average attrition from undergraduate colleges, particularly community colleges.

Data from the National Longitudinal Study indicated that of the students who entered college in the fall of 1973, 47 percent of the Hispanic two-year college students, compared to 28 percent of four-year college Hispanics, had withdrawn by 1977.[6] Further, a National Longitudinal Study of the class of 1972[7] established race/ethnicity differences in educational attainment. Seven-and-one-half years after high school, Hispanics had the greatest proportion (38%) of persons with only a high school diploma and the lowest proportion (8%) with a baccalaureate degree. In a separate study, Haro[8] found that in seven states with the largest enrollment of Hispanics there is "an average college attrition rate for the Spanish-surnamed student population of 80.4 percent, compared to 62.3 percent for the majority population." The state of California, which accounts for nearly one-third of all Hispanic enrollments in higher education,[9] had a five-year college graduation rate of 15.4 percent for Mexican-Americans, 34.2 percent for white, non-Hispanics, and three year graduation rate for 27.9 percent for Mexican-Americans and a 38 percent for white, non-Hispanics.[10]

Transfer Rates to Senior Institutions

Slippage in the educational pipeline also occurs during student transition from a two- to four-year institution. Estimates on baccalaureate degree intentions of community college students range from a low of 52 percent to a high of 74 percent.[11] However, it is estimated that only 5 to 25 percent actually achieve this initial goal.[12] A case in point is illustrated by the state of California, which has the largest number of Hispanics in the largest system of community colleges in the country. In California, community colleges experiencing the largest transfer losses tended to be those with a very high proportion of Chicano or black freshman students.[13] Affirming that initial intentions of community college minority students rarely translate to reality are figures which substantiate their gross underrepresentation in the share of college degrees earned. In 1980 Hispanics comprised approximately six percent of the U.S. population. Yet, they earned only 2.3 percent of the bachelors, 2.2 percent of the masters, 1.4 percent of the doctorates, and 2.2 percent of the first professional degrees.[14]

The factors associated with poor Hispanic student retention are varied. The problem of minority and low-SES student underrepresentation really begins at the precollege level. Hispanics have lower high school graduations rates than whites. In 1982, only 40.3 percent of Hispanics graduated from high school. Exacerbating this problem is the fact that Hispanic high school graduates are less likely to attend college than whites. About 32 percent of white students attend college, compared to 29.9 percent for Hispanics. Factors which may be attributed to high dropout rates and low levels of college participation among Hispanics include poverty, unemployment, poor quality of education at inner-city schools, infrequent student/faculty interaction, the absence of role models, lack of commitment to educational goals, institutional right-to-fail policies, declining literacy demands, and lack of academic preparation in reading, writing, and math.[15]

Student financial aid has recently received attention as a determinant of student retention. Astin,[16] Voorhees,[17] Brooks,[18] and Herndon[19] have found that student financial aid has a positive effect on student persistence. However, a study of Olivas[20] on Hispanic financial aid recipients found that not only were students uninformed about their parents' income, but that half of all Hispanic students in the study overestimated their actual income. In a separate study on financial aid packaging policies and Hispanics in higher education, Olivas[21] found that over 60 percent in a representative sample of over 16,000 Hispanic students received only a single-source aid and that this one source of aid was "almost exclusively Basic Educational Opportunity Grants (or BEOGs, known as Pell Grants since 1981)." Even when multiple-source aid is awarded to Hispanic students, 95 percent of all multiple sources in the study included a Pell Grant award, a non-campus-based grant. If Hispanic community college students, who may qualify for financial assistance, are overestimating actual income on financial aid forms and being denied financial aid, not only are the students having to bear the entire cost of a college education, but their chances of succeeding and attaining some form of credential may be reduced.

In summary, Hispanic students may be enrolling in institutions which limit their ability to attain their educational goals and reduce their chances to move up the social and economic ladder. Despite open access, Hispanic retention, academic achievement, and transfer rates remain inadequate. Equal opportunity, the democratic ideology which fueled the community college movement, appears to be contradicted by the social reality that gross education achievement inequities persist between majority and minority student cohorts. The net effect is that individuals from selective ethnic backgrounds and social classes are granted a prolonged social niche, at the bottom of a diversified class structure.

Factors Affecting Hispanic Student Retention: Two Research Studies

To what extent do community colleges have a negative effect on Hispanic students? Critics of community colleges contend that the colleges ill serve minorities, serve as tracking mechanisms that divert students from more prestigious institutions, restrict opportunities to earn baccalaureate degrees, and perpetuate the existing hierarchical class structure. In short, community colleges are viewed as academic graveyards for ethnic minorities. These are serious indictments against community colleges which more often than not are based on perceptions and observations unsupported by empirical evidence. The research literature has been deficient in explaining how multiple student- and institution-related factors limit Hispanic student achievement and persistence in community colleges. Given that community colleges are not research-based institutions and have been poorly studied, they remain most vulnerable in terms of being targets for adverse criticism and for responding to disparaging accusations. Nevertheless, enough evidence exists to question whether or not community colleges, the vehicles of egalitarianism, perpetuate inequities in access and educational achievement for Hispanic students who are disproportionately concentrated in these institutions. This critical issue serves as the major basis for analyzing the complex factors which may account for the differential progress of Hispanic students in community colleges.

Two retention studies[22] employing a structural equation model[23] provide the most recent empirical information about Hispanic student retention in community colleges. The first study[24] examines student and institution-related determinants of Hispanic student retention. The second study[25] addresses the relative effects of student financial aid on Hispanic student retention. Both studies modified Tinto's[26] student attrition model to explain the effects of student background characteristics and academic and social integration on retention.

Determinations of Retention among Chicano Community College Students

Nora tested the hypothesis that high levels of congruency between students and their environments lead to high levels of credential attainment, hours earned, and goal satisfaction. Through the modification of Tinto's[28] attrition model, the study examined how six constructs affected student integration. The model examined the direct and indirect effects of background characteristics and initial commitments on academic integration and social integration; and direct and indirect effects of background characteristics and initial commitments on retention; and the direct effects of academic integration and social integration on retention. Structural equation modeling[29] was used to examine the structural coefficients and measurement model of the hypothesized causal model.

Population and Sample

The study was drawn from 3,544 first-time Chicano students who were enrolled full- or part-time in 1977 or 1978 in each of three South Texas community colleges. The colleges were Laredo Junior College (Laredo), Texas Southwest College (Brownsville), and Del Mar College (Corpus Christi).

A systematic random sample of every other Chicano student was taken to arrive at a total N of 1,786. To gain longitudinal data between 1977 and 1982, a South Texas Student Survey (Rendon, 1982) was mailed to the sample population. After three mailing efforts, the final number of respondents was 227. Proportions from the mailings were tabulated to yield a conservative, estimated response rate of 23.71 percent.

Results

The mean age of the sample population was 23.57 with 59 percent of the sample being females. Although the mean was twenty-three, 77 percent of the student population was under twenty-three years of age. The sample population was relatively young and was unmarried (72.85%). Over half (56.44%) of the students were in the third quartile of their graduating class, but eighty-six percent of the total student population graduated in the third quartile or above. The two largest categories for grades were Mostly A's and B's (28%) and Mostly C's (36.44%). Most of the students (89%) reported having made Mostly B's and C's and above. The mean number of years for mother's education was 8.30 and 8.62 for father's education. Moreover, 54.95 percent of the student population initially wanted to attend a two-year college. Among the reasons given for selecting a community college over a four-year institution were: (1) close to home (11.41%), (2) cheaper (13.69%), (3) work while studying (10.51%), (4) "try out" college work (10.50%), and (5) take courses for self-improvement (13.24%). Those students who graduated (or received some form of credential) represented 29.91 percent of the population. In the four-year period from 1977–1978 to 1981–1982, the mean total number of hours enrolled by students was 65.17. It is important to note that with sixty-five hours or less, students could have received some form of two year credential.

Although measures used in testing the fit of the model reflected the overall strength of the causal model (see Table 1), the findings were not entirely supportive of Tinto's model. Both academic and social integration did not have the significant direct effects on retention which have been reported in other studies[30] testing Tinto's model. Tinto's model specifies effects which are mediated through academic and social integration.

Students entering an institution with higher levels of institutional/goal commitments will have higher levels of academic and social integration at their respective institutions and consequently higher levels of retention. For Hispanic community college students, however, institutional/goal commitments not only have a significant direct effect on retention, but are considerably more important in determining retention (see Table 2). The total effect for academic integration was only .218, while the total effect of social integration (.092) on retention signified that there was no causal path between these two integration variables. There were no significant direct

Table 1
Measures of Goodness of Fit for the Whole Model

Measures	Test of Significance
Goodness of Fit Index	.920
Adjusted Goodness of Fit Index	.840
Root Mean Square Residual	.093
Total Coefficient of Determination for Structural Equations	.341

effects of grades, parents' education, and encouragement on retention rates, but two of the three variables, grades and encouragement, directly affected initial institutional/goal commitments.

Institutional/goal commitments. Although the effect of parents' education on institutional/goal commitments[31] was hypothesized to be positively related, the strength of the structural coefficient (gamma=.019) was not what had been expected. Students' initial commitments to the institution and to their educational goals were not affected significantly by their parents' education. It was believed that for most Mexican-Americans education was highly valued, whether it was because parents who had not themselves earned a college degree provided strong incentives for their children to "succeed" where they did not[32] or because it was expected by parents who had "succeeded" in earning a college degree.

Social integration. None of the hypothesized direct effects of the background characteristics on social integration were supported in the findings. More importantly, though, was the positive direct effect (.683) which initial institutional/goal commitments had on social integration. Students who entered college with higher levels of commitment to the institution and to their educational goals had more informal interactions with faculty members, met more often with counselors, and attended and participated more in peer-related activities.

Academic integration. The direct effects of students' initial institutional/goal commitments on students' academic perceptions about the faculty, counselors, and administrators and about their academic experiences (including career preparation) was supported by the findings and substantiates research conducted by Fox[33] and by Pascarella, Terenzini, and Wolfle.[34]

Retention. The last structural equation examined the direct and indirect effects of grades, parents' education, encouragement, and institutional/goal commitments, academic integration, and social integration on the dependent variable, retention. Students whose parents had higher levels of education were more likely to enroll in more semester hours, to be more satisfied with their present goal attainment, and to have earned some form of credential. Although this direct effect was hypothesized, and the findings supportive (gamma = .134), it was expected to have had a smaller impact on retention. The direct effect of academic integration on retention was the second largest structural coefficient in the equation (beta = .218).

One precollege variable, high school grades, and one endogenous variable, social integration, had direct effects on retention as hypothesized; however, even with total effects taken into

Table 2
Effect Coefficients of Exogenous and Endogenous Variables

Variable	Direct Effect	Total Effect
Retention		
Grades	.059	.170
Parents' education	.134	.138
Encouragement	−.052	.092
Institutional/goal commitments	.651	.904
Academic integration	.218	.218
Social integration	.092	.092
Institutional/Goal Commmitments		
Grades	.138	.138
Parents' education	.019	.019
Encouragement	.157	.157
Social Integration		
Grades	−.154	−.059
Parents' education	−.146	−.133
Encouragement	.029	.137
Institutional/goal commitments	.683	.683
Academic Integration		
Institutional/goal commitments	.871	.871

account, the strength of the relationship was minimal. Although it was hypothesized in the causal mode, the degree (strength) of the direct effect of institutional/goal commitments on retention was unexpected, the direct effect on the latent variable was .651, the effect coefficient .904. Students with higher levels of commitments to the institution and to educational goals enrolled in more semester hours, were more satisfied with their present educational goal attainment, and graduated with some form of credential.

Fox[35] has consistently found that high levels of academic integration have more of an impact on persistence than any other variable in Tinto's model. The findings in the present research, however, revealed that for a community college Chicano student population, neither academic integration nor social integration affected retention rates significantly more than academic and social integration measures.

Student Finances and Retention Rates

A causal model examining the effect of campus- and noncampus-based financial aid on Hispanic community college student retention was employed by Nora.[36] Campus-based financial program included Supplemental Education Opportunity Grants (SEOG), College Work Study (CWS), and National Defense Student Loans (NDSL). Non–campus-based resources were Pell Grants. The paradigm represented a multi-equation model with five endogenous variables. The five endogenous variables included academic performance, three campus-based resources (National Direct Student Loans, College Work Study, and Supplemental Educational Opportunity Grants), and the dependent variable, retention. Exogenous variables included non–campus-based resources, high school grades, and student financial need. Background characteristics were examined to determine the direct effects and indirect effects (through intervening variables) these factors had on minority retention rates and the direct and indirect effect of campus-based resources and academic performance on minority retention rates. Based on Tinto's[37] model of student retention, the LISREL[38] model in the study incorporated a modification of the measurement model made earlier by Nora[39] and included measures of student finances examined by Voorhees.[40]

Population and Sample

The study population (N=170) was drawn from a total population of 883 first-time Chicano students who were enrolled full- or part-time in 1982 in a community college (Laredo Junior College) in South Texas.

Results

The mean financial need for the sample population was $3,560, ranging from a need of $180 to a high of $12,227. The mean high school grade for financial aid recipients was 83.38. The mean for non–campus-based awards (Pell Grants) was $1,617 with only twelve (6.31%) students not receiving this particular form of financial assistance. Once enrolled in the community college, students were enrolled for a mean of 6.17 semesters (including summer sessions), earned a mean of 55.26 semester hours, and received a mean GPA of 2.524. Although the mean number of semester hours earned would indicate that many students could have received a community college certificate or associate degree, only 17.64 percent of the sample population received some form of credential from the two-year institution in which they were enrolled; a total of 140 (82.38%) students did not. The means for campus-based resources (Supplemental Educational Opportunity Loans, College Work Study, National Direct Student Loans) were $811, $674, and $51, respectively. However 29.47 percent, 70.52 percent, and 96.84 percent of the students in the sample population did not receive Supplemental Educational Opportunity Loans, College Work Study, and National Direct Student Loans, respectively. These findings are supported by Olivas[41] in that, among Hispanic college students, financial aid is restricted to Pell Grants almost exclusively.

The effect coefficients for the structural model are included in Table 3. The Goodness of Fit Index for the causal model was .970, the Adjusted Goodness of Fit Index .949, and the Root Mean Square Residual .07. The total Coefficient of Determination for the overall model was .805; the squared multiple correlations (R^2) for the latent constructs (campus-based resources, academic performance, and retention) were .524, .216, and .764. All the measures of the overall strength of the structural model indicated that the modified model in the study represented a plausible model of retention.

The results indicated that two factors had a significant impact on Hispanic community college retention rates: non–campus-based resources (Pell Grants) and campus-based resources (Supplemental Educational Opportunity Loans, College Work Study, National Direct Students), total effects being .774 and .402, respectively. The impact of campus-based resources on retention, however, was enhanced when it was mediated through academic performance; the direct effect of campus-based resources was only .197, the effect coefficient (direct and indirect effects) was .402. Moreover, the findings indicated that these factors had a significantly larger effect on retention than GPA as reported by Fox[42] and Voorhees.[43]

Other variables in the model which were significant included the direct effect of high school grades on the student's academic performance in the two-year institution (gamma=.381) and the direct effect of campus-based resources on academic performance (B=.271). More importantly, the direct effect of high school grades on retention, although significant, was only .110. Even when the total effects were examined, the effect coefficient was .189. Another direct effect which was significant was that of need on retention (gamma = –.132). Again, however, this effect was negated by the intervening variables (total effects = –.084). There were no significant direct effects of need (gamma = .017) and non–campus-based resources (gamma = –.076) on academic performance.

In sum, Hispanic community college students who received higher levels of non-campus and campus-based financial aid award were enrolled in more semesters, earned more semester hours, and received some form of credential. Moreover, Hispanic students who received higher levels of campus-based resources earned higher grade point averages. Although the direct effect of campus-based resources on retention was not as large as that of non-campus resources or academic performance, students who received Supplemental Educational Opportunity Loans, College Work Study, and National Direct Student Loans did considerably better in their academic performance and, consequently, had higher levels of retention.

Table 3
Effect Coefficient of Exogenous and Endogenous Variables

Variable	Direct Effect	Total Effect
Retention		
Non–campus-based resources	.613	.774
Grades	.110	.189
Need	–.132	–.084
Campus-based resources	.197	.402
GPA	.208	.208
Campus-based resources		
Non–campus-based resources	.700	.441
Need	.179	.113
GPA		
Non–campus-based resources	–.076	.114
Grades	.381	.381
Needs	.017	.065
Campus-based resources	.271	.430

Discussion, Implications, and Recommendations

The key findings of Nora's[44] study of Hispanic community college student retention indicated that the largest impact on retention was of high levels of student institutional and goal commitments. Hispanic students who were committed to attending a two-year institution and who had strong commitments about their educational goals tended to enroll in more semester hours, were more satisfied with their educational goal attainments, and earned some form of college credential. Unlike other studies[45] social integration was not found to be a determinant of retention. Academic integration had only a slight effect on retention.

The results of Nora's[46] regarding the relationship between campus and non-campus financial aid resources and student retention indicated that the largest effect on retention was Pell Grants. The second largest effect was produced by Supplemental Education Opportunity Loans, College Work Study, and National Direct Student Loans; the third largest effect came from student GPAs. Nora's study contradicts those of Voorhees[47] which have indicated that campus-based resources (Supplemental Educational Opportunity Loans, College Work Study, National Direct Student Loans) have the most effect on retention.

The implications of these findings must be viewed in the context that the results come from studies which, although confirmatory in nature, have only begun to explore how diverse variables operate in complex ways to influence Hispanic dropout decisions in community college settings. Nonetheless, Nora's studies do shed additional light on the debate about whether or not community colleges are having a negative effect on Hispanic students.

A pronounced contradiction appears in both of Nora's studies that awakens doubts about the true opportunities afforded to Hispanic students in community colleges. In both studies, a substantial number of students earned enough credit hours to earn a college credential. In the first study, the mean credit hour earned was 65.17; in the second, 52.25. However, only 29.91 percent of the students in the first study had earned some form of credential, and only 17.64 percent received a degree or certificate in the second study. In short, while Hispanic students do enroll and earn enough credit hours to make them eligible for some form of college credential, relatively few graduate or earn degrees or certificates.

This contradiction may be explained through an analysis of the finding that students with strong institutional and goal commitments tended to earn more college credit hours and to earn college credentials. Many students may be enrolling in community colleges without a clear conception of what their educational goals are. Some may attend to get a Pell Grant because they don't have a job; those who have a job or family problems may have external preoccupations that preclude institutional affiliation and commitment to studies; others may attend for personal satisfaction as opposed to earning a college degree. Still others may have spent most of the time taking remedial courses, paying more attention to "catching up" than to developing other educational goals. In any case, having unclear, diffuse goals appears to work against Hispanic student retention and ultimate graduation. Students with uncertain goals may never develop strong goal commitments and may consequently never finish their program of study.

This generalized finding has important implications for Hispanic students who indicate they wish to transfer to earn baccalaureate degrees. Nationwide, as many as 74 percent of community college students indicate they wish to earn a four-year degree, yet only a small fraction actually transfer to achieve this goal.[48] Explanations for the poor student transfer rates may be attributed to lack of commitment to the goal of transferring, or to the setting of educational goals based on a lack of information about what it takes to complete a four-year degree, and a misconception about the structure of higher education.[49] The implication is that community colleges need to do more in the way of providing assistance and information to help students develop clear, realistic educational goals at an early enrollment point.

"Front-loading"[50] is a proposal that would give top priority for the allocation of faculty and institutional resources to first- and second-year undergraduate students. In community colleges, students need early counseling and advisement about setting realistic educational and career goals, getting serious and committed to studying, selecting proper course sequences, and acquiring materials and information about transferring to senior institutions. Assigning students to a faculty mentor who can provide consistent advisement and follow-through can provide students with a contact person who can help them to shape their goals as well as to become actively involved in the studying and learning process. These centers can help early-identified, potential transfer students with proper course selection and sequence, the selection of an appropriate curricular program at a senior institution, and the completion of admissions, financial aid, and housing forms.

On the issues of financial aid, one must consider the nature of the Hispanic community college student. Most students come from low-socioeconomic-status backgrounds and from families where the precedent of attending college is not established. Because both campus- and non–campus-based resources have been found to have a significant impact on retention rates among Hispanic community college students, two-year institutions need to do more than simply meet a student's financial need. The colleges need to develop a comprehensive financial aid advisement program that reaches out to students and their parents before they graduate high school. Hispanic parents need to understand and appreciate the higher education system, as well as its costs and the financial assistance available for their children. Parents and students also need information about the cost of going to college and about diverse financial resources available to them. Parents and students can also be educated about the importance of completing IRS and student financial aid applications in a correct and timely fashion, making correct estimates about their income and selecting a comprehensive financial aid package.

Although campus- and non–campus-based resources are deciding factors in whether or not Hispanic students stay in college, the fact remains that the majority of Hispanic students receiving Pell Grants do not necessarily earn degrees. This fact creates some fundamental questions. Does simply staying in college (for whatever reason) define retention, even if students don't earn some form of credential? Why aren't Hispanic students earning community college credentials? Are they merely escaping a poor job market, wasting time, or uninterested in earning a credential? Are other factors such as poor advisement and lack of involvement with the college community operating to negate student achievement? Too many unanswered issues force one to conclude that more research needs to be conducted on the diverse and complex factors which may be operating to impact Hispanic student achievement in community colleges.

Do community colleges short-change Hispanic students? In some ways they do, in others they don't. Clearly community colleges have done more than any other postsecondary sector to increase access for Hispanics. And, to their credit, many two-year colleges are doing more with regard to affirmative action policies and strategies to not only attract Hispanics to their campuses, but to retain them, assist them to complete their program of study, and facilitate transfer to senior institutions. However, the weight of the evidence does more to challenge the dubious nature of equal opportunity than it does to confirm true equity. For example, the present flow of Hispanic students through the educational pipeline suggests that Hispanics have made few appreciable gains in either their participation or achievement in community colleges. The fact remains that few Hispanics earn college credentials, graduate, or transfer to senior institutions.

Community colleges need to do more to provide demonstrable evidence that they are more than the "end-of-the-line" for Hispanic students. A crucial lesson learned from the expansion of higher education and the provision of equal opportunity for all students through a differentiated system of higher education is that increased access does not automatically lead to reduced social and economic inequalities between majority and minority groups. In the end, the critical issue is not how many gain access to higher education, but rather what happens to students once they get there. This is true for community colleges as it is for other postsecondary sectors. That community colleges can make systemic reform and devise interventions to turn the present condition of Hispanic education around remains to be seen.

Notes

1. Commission on the Higher Education of Minorities. *Final Report on the Higher Education of Minorities*. (Los Angeles: Higher Education Research Institute, Inc., 1982); J. Karabel and A. W. Astin, "Social Class, Academic Ability and College Quality," *Social Forces 53* (1975), pp. 381–397; J. Karabel, "Community

Colleges and Social Stratification," *Harvard Educational Review 42(4)* (1972), pp. 521–558; and J. Karabel, "Open Admissions: Toward Meritocracy or Democracy?; *Change* 4 (1972), pp. 30–44.

2. Amaury Nora, "Determinants of Retention Among Chicano College Students: A Structural Model," *Research in Higher Education 26(1)*, (1987), pp. 31–59; Laura Rendon, *Chicanos in South Texas Community Colleges: A Study of Student and Institutional-Related Determinants of Educational Outcomes.* (Unpublished doctoral dissertation, University of Michigan, 1982); Commission on the Higher Education of Minorities, *Final Report*; A. W. Astin, *Minorities in American Higher Education* (San Francisco: Jossey-Bass, 1982); and Michael Olivas, *The Dilemma of Access* (Washington, D. C.: Howard University Press, 1979).

3. S. Jaschik, "States Called Key to College Gains for Minorities," *The Chronicle of Higher Education* July 23, 1986.

4. V. Lee, *Access to Higher Education: The Experience of Blacks, Hispanics and Low Socio-Economic Status Whites.* (Washington, D. C.: American Council on Education, 1985).

5. Commission on the Higher Education of Minorities, *Final Report.*

6. R. Wilson and S. Melendez, *Minorities in Higher Education.* (Washington, D. C.: American Council on Education, 1982).

7. H. J. Burkheimer and T. P. Novak, *A Capsule Description of Young Adults Seven and One-Half Years after High School.* (Research Triangle Park, Center for Educational Research and Evaluation, 1981).

8. C. M. Haro, "Chicanos and Higher Education: A Review of Selected Literature," *Aztlan* 14:1 (1983), pp. 35–76.

9. Michael Olivas, "Financial Aid and Self-Reports by Disadvantaged Students: The Importance of Being Earnest," *Research in Higher Education* 25(3), (1986), pp. 245–262.

10. The California State University and Colleges, *Those Who Stay—Phase II: Student Continuance in the California State University and Colleges.* Technical memorandum No. 8 from the Office of the Chancellor, California State University and Colleges, 1979.

11. R. C. Richardson and L. W. Bender, *Students in Urban Settings: Achieving the Baccalaureate Degree* (Washington, D.C.: Association for the Study of Higher Education, 1986).

12. Ibid; E. M. Bensimon and M. J. Riley, *Student Predisposition to Transfer: A Report of Preliminary Findings* (Los Angeles: Center for the Study Community Colleges, 1984); and Astin, *Minorities in American Higher Education.*

13. California State Postsecondary Education Commission, *Update of Community College Transfer Student Statistics, Fall 1984.* Commission Report 85–21 (Sacramento: CSPEC ERIC Document No. ED 256399, 1979); and G. Hayward, *Preparation and Participation of Hispanic and Black Students: A Special Report* (Sacramento: California Community Colleges, Office of the Chancellor ERIC Document No. ED 254285, 1985).

14. Wilson and Melendez, *Minorities in Higher Education.*

15. Rendon, *Chicanos in South Texas.* Nora, "Determinants of Retention"; and Wilson and Melendez, *Minorities in Higher Education.*

16. Astin, *Minorities in American Higher Education.*

17. Richard A. Voorhees, "Student Finances and Campus-Based Financial Aid: A Structural Model Analysis of the Persistence of High Need Freshmen," *Research in Higher Education* 22:1 (1985), pp. 65–91.

18. J. W. Brooks, "Academic Performance and Retention Rates of Participants in the College Work Study Program and Recipients of National Direct Student Loans" (Doctoral dissertation, Indiana University, 1980). *Dissertation Abstracts International* 40, 3440-A. (University Microfilms No. 8103407).

19. M. S. Herndon, "A Longitudinal Study of Financial Aid Persister, Dropouts, and Stopouts: A Discriminant Analysis" (Doctoral dissertation, University of California, Los Angeles, 1981). *Dissertation Abstracts International* 42, 4736A–4737A. (University Microfilms No. DA8206026).

20. Olivas, *Financial Aid.*

21. Olivas, "Financial Aid and Self-Reports."

22. Nora, "Determinants of Retention"; and Amaury Nora, *Campus-Based Aid Programs as Determinants of Retention Among Hispanic Community College Students* (Paper presentation at the American Educational Research Association, Washington, D. C., 1987).

23. Structural equation modeling combine a measurement model and structural (causal) model into a complete model and are analogous to a combination of factor analysis and path analysis. The measurement model is similar to factory analysis; however, it is confirmatory in nature, unlike traditional factor analysis. Confirmatory factor analysis does not have the rotation problems found in exploratory factor analysis and unique variables (residuals) can be correlated (see note 47). The structural model is similar to path analysis (simultaneous regression equations) except that these regression equations are based on latent (unobserved) variables and there is the possibility of correlated residuals.

24. Nora, "Determinants of Retention."

25. Nora, "Campus-Based Aid Programs."

26. Vincent Tinto, "Dropout from Higher Education: A Theoretical Synthesis of Recent Research," *Review of Educational Research* 45:1 (1975), pp. 89–125.

27. Nora, "Determinants of Retention."

28. Tinto, "Dropout from Higher Education."

29. P. M. Bentler, "Multivariate Analysis with Latent Variables: Causal Modeling," *Annual Review of Psychology* (1980), pp. 419–456; P. M. Bentler and G. Speckart, "Attitudes 'Cause' Behaviors: A Structural Equation Analysis," *Journal of Personality and Social Psychology* 40:2 (1981), pp. 226–238; P. M. Bentler and J. A. Woodward, "A Head Start Reevaluation: Positive Effects Are Not Yet Demonstrable," *Evaluation Quarterly* 2 (1978), pp. 493–510; Karl G. Joreskog and Dag Sorbom, LISREL: *Analysis of Linear Structural Relationships by the Method of Maximum Likelihood* (Version IV) (Chicago: National Ed. Resources, 1981); D. Kenny, *Correlation and Causality* (New York: Wiley, 1979); J. Scott Long, "Estimation and Hypothesis Testing in Linear Models Containing Measurement Error," *Sociological Methods and Research* 5:20 (1976), pp. 157–203; and Elazar Pedhazur, *Multiple Regression in Behavioral Research: Explanation and Prediction* (2nd ed.) New York: Holt, Rinehart & Winston, (1982).

30. J. Fox, *Application of a Conceptual Model of College Withdrawal to Disadvantaged Students* (Paper presented at the annual meeting of the American Educational Research Association, Chicago, Ill., March 1985).

31. This variable measured the initial institutional commitment that students had upon entering a community college for that particular institution. Secondly, it was a measure of the students' initial goal commitments when they first entered their community college.

32. W. Sewell and V. Shah, "Parents' Education and Children's Educational Aspirations and Achievements," *American Sociological Review* 33:2 (1968). pp. 191–209.

33. Fox, *Application of a Conceptual Model.*

34. Pascarella, Terenzini, and Wolfle, *Orientation to College.*

35. J. Fox, "Effect Analysis in Structural Equation Models," *Sociological Methods and Research* 9:1 (1980), pp. 3–28; and Fox, *Application of a Conceptual Model.*

36. Nora, "Campus-Based Aid Programs."

37. Tinto, "Dropout from Higher Education."

38. Joreskog and Sorbom, LISREL.

39. Nora, "Determinants of Retention."

40. Voorhees, "Student Finances."

41. Olivas, "Financial Aid and Self-Reports."

42. Fox, *Application of a Conceptual Method.*

43. Voorhees, "Student Finances."

44. Nora, "Determinants of Retention."

45. Ernest Pascarella and Patrick Terenzini, "Interaction Effects in Spady's and Tinto's Conceptual Models of College Dropout," *Sociology of Education* 52 (1979), pp. 197–210; and Pascarella, Terenzini, and Wolfle, *Orientation to College.*

46. Nora, "Campus-Based Aid Programs."

47. Voorhees, "Student Finances"; and Richard Voorhees, "Financial Aid and Persistence: Do the Federal Campus-Based Aid Programs Make a Difference?" *The Journal of Student Financial Aid* 15:1 (1985), pp. 21–30.

48. Richardson and Bender, *Students in Urban Settings.*

49. Bensimon and Riley, *Student Predisposition to Transfer.*

50. Study Group on the Conditions of Excellence in Higher Education, *Involvement in Learning* (Washington, D.C.: National Institute of Education, 1984).

From the Barrio to the Academy:
Revelations of a Mexican American "Scholarship Girl"

LAURA RENDÓN

People of color are often changed by higher education, but now institutions themselves must change in order to accommodate culturally diverse student populations.

It was during my first year of graduate school at the University of Michigan, far away from the Laredo, Texas, barrio where I spent my youth, that I read Richard Rodriguez's (1975) poignant essay "Going Home Again: The New American Scholarship Boy." Reading this story of how the academy changes foreigners who enter its culture (more than it is changed by them) inspired a powerful emotional response in me. My own odyssey through higher education had taken me along an unusual path—from a community college to one of the nation's most prestigious universities. Engaged in Rodriguez's revealing thoughts and feelings in a dark library reading room, which I presumed too much like the British Museum, where Rodriguez had worked on his dissertation, I, too, began to experience, although not quite fully understand, the pain that comes from cultural separation. I began to think about how the rewards of academic success were in stark conflict with most of my past. And I began to empathize with the portrait that Rodriguez had read about in Richard Hoggart's (1970) *Uses of Literacy*—the image of a scholarship boy who can attain academic success only if he replaces allegiance to his native culture with loyalty to a new academic culture. "In the end . . . he must choose between the two worlds; if he intends to succeed as a student, he must, literally and figuratively, separate himself from his family, with its gregarious life, and find a quiet place to be alone with his thoughts. . . . For the loss he might otherwise feel, the scholarship boy substitutes an enormous enthusiasm for nearly everything having to do with school" (Rodriguez, 1975, p. 17).

To become an academic success, Rodriguez, too, had learned that he must sever his ties with the past. For example, he discovered that he had to forget the Spanish language in favor of English. He began to believe that assimilation into the mainstream culture was the key to total success. He described the regrets his parents had about how education had changed him and had "put big ideas into his head." He recounted the anguish of feeling uncomfortable with his parents when he went home with his newfound identity. What had been intimate conversations now became polite interviews.

The parallels between Rodriguez and me were obvious. Both of us had Mexican American parents who wanted their children to have a better life than they did. Our parents had never acquired a firm command of the English language but understood that learning English was essential for social advancement. Nonetheless, my parents did not understand what higher education could offer (or even take away), as they had only received a second- and third-grade education. Both Rodriguez and I were unique within our families. Rodriguez had conducted research to obtain a Ph.D. in English Renaissance literature, and I was working on a doctorate in higher education administration. As the first in my family to take this long journey into the mystifying world of higher education, I asked myself, if Rodriguez was the new American "scholarship boy," was I the new American "scholarship girl"? Did I really need to reject my past in order to attain success in the present? Was there some way in which to reconcile days gone by with my contemporary experiences?

For the young scholar who first experiences academic shock—a feeling of alienation that moves the student from concrete to abstract experience and that takes the student from an old culture that is vastly different in tradition, style, and values to a new world of unfamiliar intellectual conventions, practices, and assumptions—these questions are not easily answered. I did not know at the time that the barometer the academy uses to differentiate the academic elite from the mediocre is precisely the measure of how well young scholars negotiate academic shock. If the student, like Rodriguez, silences the past and humbly waits to be confirmed into the community of scholars, the academy swiftly offers its greatest rewards. If the student persists in using past experience to affirm himself or herself, not only do rewards become more difficult to attain, but the student is also riddled with the guilt, pain, and confusion that arise from daring to live simultaneously in two vastly different worlds while being fully accepted in neither.

My Own Journey

My early beginnings are in stark contrast with my present. Recently, as I was being recruited for a faculty position at a southwestern university, I was told that I was one of the most marketable Hispanic females in the field of higher education. I sometimes wonder how I merit such praise. My trip from the barrio to the academy has hardly been silky smooth. I still remember the first time I actually made a decision to attend college. I was thirteen and in the eighth grade when a counselor came to my English class and announced that on that day we had to make a decision about whether we were going to be on the academic or the vocational track. When I asked the counselor to explain the difference, she forthrightly explained that the academic track was for those who were going to college and that the vocational track was for those who planned to get a job after high school graduation. I had always dreamed of being a teacher, so the choice was an easy one for me. I remember going home that afternoon and proudly telling my mother of my decision. Her response triggered the first painful feelings of academic shock. Dismayed and frustrated, she said, *"Estas loca. Como piensas ir al colegio si nadie de nuestra familia ha ido? Eso es para los ricos."* (You're crazy. How can you think of going to college if no one in the family has? That is for the rich.) For my mother, the choice would have been clear. In our family going to college was not an option; it had never been and it never would be. Higher education belonged to the elite, the wealthy, and we clearly were not in that group.

My pain and disappointment did not, however, interrupt my plans. I persisted in following my dream, and on graduating from high school I promptly enrolled in my local community college. Little did I know then that despite its self-proclaimed magnanimous goal of being a "people's college," the community college has also served to ghettoize people of color. In general, Hispanics, Native Americans, and African Americans tend to enroll in community colleges as opposed to four-year institutions. People like me, whom Madrid (1990) describes as *flor de tierra* (plants whose roots do not go deep), are not likely to enter higher education through the front door. We do not apply to wealthy liberal arts colleges or to institutions whose prestige is unquestioned. With Madrid, I believe that most students like me enter higher education through its windows, only to find that all around us are walls that keep us secluded and marginalized. Nonetheless, Laredo Junior College became for me the first access point to the world of higher education.

At Laredo Junior College I found both the comforts and discomforts of attending college with my friends; we were not only uncertain about our future but perplexed about what it would take to succeed in this new world of higher education. It was here, in this illusory intellectual oasis of the Laredo community, that I experienced some of the sensations of academic shock as I faced new academic demands and tried to reconcile my new world with my culture. I knew that my mother was feeling angry and frustrated with my tenacious desire to go to college, although we never really talked about it. It was a subject that was broached in different ways. She would explain that she was tired of being a waitress. She would be irritable that she had to work night shifts in order to sustain the family (my two sisters and me). I knew that for her the ideal daughter would promptly, after graduating from high school, get a job so that her mother would not have to work anymore. Even today I often find myself trying to make up for the fact that I did not fit this ideal vision.

My friends at Laredo Junior College not only shared my family's experience of economic hardship but they also seemed lost in this new world of abstraction. Suddenly, our professors expected us, with no guidance, to have clarity about our vague dreams and goals, to express ourselves in rational, analytic forms, and to put aside our personal anxieties and frustrations so that we could be successful college students.

The few of us who tried to transfer to an institution away from home experienced the pain and conflict of academic shock even more acutely. My parents told me that if I must transfer, I should go to a nearby institution. I felt, however, that I needed to get further away, to experience something dramatically different. The pull of the academy was overwhelming. During my sophomore year, due to poor counseling, I found both that it was too late to apply to a four-year institution and that my local community college was not offering any more courses in my program of study (English and journalism education). Feeling the need to stay on track and continue my studies, I transferred to San Antonio College. It was here, 150 miles away from home, that I experienced the loneliness that often overcomes scholarship boys and girls. In this community college, I felt isolated and disconnected. None of my professors was minority, and the other Mexican American students also seemed lost and alienated. I felt that my white professors did not recognize my academic potential. None made any special effort to encourage me to perform at my best. In San Antonio, I not only felt alienated from my family but I found myself being perceived differently by them. Living away from home was, indeed, changing me. To cope, I found comfort in reading, and I was especially intrigued by what I read for my philosophy class. Yet I never talked about Sartre or Plato with any of my family members. These new ideas seemed to belong only within the confines of the collegiate environment. Subconsciously, I must have felt that the language of college did not belong in my family life. The two were separate and incompatible. Reflecting on new learning while at the same time coping with the feeling of not belonging made me more introverted.

When I transferred again to the University of Houston, the pain of separation became even greater. My mother, wanting to be certain that I was living in a safe place, took the long bus trip with me to Houston. She wept when I told her that I had gotten a grant, that I had a dormitory room, and that everything would be all right. It was in Houston that I came face to face with being a minority. Academic shock was compounded by ethnic and racial shock. In Laredo, a community of over 90 percent Mexican Americans, we were all the same, but here I was keenly aware of being different. At the University of Houston in 1968, during the thick of racial and social unrest, there were few Mexican American or black students. I met no Mexican American professors, and there was only one black faculty member, who taught journalism on a part-time basis. My dorm roommates were white, but despite our differences, we learned from each other and became good friends. Coping with academic life was difficult and exacerbated by my separation from my family and culture. When I would call my mother and explain how busy I was, she would encourage me to come home and give up everything. *"Vente, hija"* (Come back daughter), she would say, *"ya deja todo eso"* (and leave everything behind). It was her motherly duty to protect her child from the unknown.

When I graduated from college, I wanted to stay and teach in Houston, but my parents insisted that I return to Laredo. "You have much education," my father explained, "but you lack experience," emphasizing that experience was necessary for coping with real life. Once I asked my mother why she resisted my leaving home to be by myself. *"Tengo miedo, hija"* (I am afraid, daughter), she would say. When I asked her what she was afraid of, she simply responded, *"No se"* (I don't know). I sensed that deep in my mother's soul she felt resentful about how this alien culture of higher education was polluting my values and customs. I, in turn, was afraid that I was becoming a stranger to her, a stranger she did not quite understand, a stranger she might not even like.

Connections with the Past

Today, I am asked to speak to educators about people like me, people of color who come to the academy as strangers in a strange land. And often what intrigues them the most is not what I have to say about how education can best serve these students but how my own journey progressed. "How did you succeed?" they ask. "If you succeeded, why can't others?" While these questions are often asked out of genuine curiosity and concern, I sometimes become irritated because they seem to me to be tied to the belief that if only students like me were not lazy, if only they would shed their past, if only they would be truly loyal and dedicated to schooling, they, too, could succeed. "Pure" academics who subscribe to Euro-centered rationalism and objectivity do not wish to read personal, emotional, or intuitive essays like mine that focus on the past. To them, these recollections are, at best, primitive and self-serving and, at worst, romanticized nonsense. True scholarship "boys and girls" would focus on objective modes of expression, on the present and future, and if the past must be recalled, it must be only as something that should be left behind or neatly put away. To succeed we must assimilate, become one of "them," and learn what Rodriguez (1975) calls "the great lessons of school"—that in order to have a public identity, we must use only English, for if Spanish or other foreign languages are employed, feelings of public separateness will be reinforced. The academy is set up so that students most likely to succeed are those that can successfully disconnect from the past and turn over their loyalty to the conventions and practices of the academy. Yet, academic success can be attained without total disconnection, and many educators either do not want to accept this or fail to recognize this.

Certainly there are many times now when I feel alienated from the world from which I came. What keeps me separate are my education, where I live, who my new friends are, my career, my values, and my command of the English language. For seven years I lived away from the Southwest. When I lived in Virginia, South Carolina, and North Carolina, I was invariably asked what a person like me was doing, living in the South away from my culture. But I have never been totally separate, and I never really will be or want to be. Leaving Texas led to a deeper appreciation of the world from which I came, to an enhanced understanding of other cultural values and ideologies, and to a stronger commitment to conducting research that could help two- and four-year colleges enhance the educational experience of students of color. I have learned that the past is always with me. What connects me to my past is what gives me my identity—my command of the Spanish language, the focus of my research, my old friends, and my heritage. What makes Laura Rendon an individual is not only who she is now but what happened to her along the way. What gives me strength is my newfound ability to trust and follow my own natural style and to encourage others to do the same.

Lessons to Be Learned

What is to be learned from a Mexican American scholarship girl/woman who felt intense pressure to assimilate into the academy and who is now a university professor who publishes in juried journals, attends meetings comprised predominantly of white males, and addresses predominantly white audiences? I contend that the most important lesson to be learned is *not* that higher education must increase access for new scholarship "boys and girls" or must offer them better financial aid packages, more role models, and better counseling and mentoring. These standard solutions, while important, do not focus on the larger and more important issue, which is that higher education must begin to think in new ways about what constitutes intellectual development and about whether the traditional manner with which education prepares new students is appropriate for people of color as well as for white women and men. The model that higher education now follows is based on what the authors of *Women's Ways of Knowing* (Belenky, Clinchy, Goldberger, and Tarule, 1986) describe as the "masculine myth." In this model, the scholarship boy/man is admitted into the fraternity of powerful knowers only when he has learned to think in complex, abstract ways, when he has learned to recognize that past experience is a source not of strength but of error. Once certified as a thinker who thinks like "them," students have learned that doubt precedes belief. The great lesson learned is that separation leads to academic power.

This paradigm validates the portrait of the "scholarship boy" with which Richard Rodriguez identified. If this model most appropriately describes the course of male intellectual development, where confirmation to a community of scholars is calculated to occur only at the end of a program of study, then so be it. But I believe this model is not appropriate for women or for people of color. For us, it is important that from the beginning of our college career, our professors express their sincere belief that we are capable of learning and can be taught to learn. Often we enter higher education consumed with self-doubt. We doubt our intellectual capacity; we question whether we really belong in the academy; we doubt whether our research interests are really valid. This doubt is reinforced by the subtle yet powerful messages that higher education institutions communicate. For example, we hear loud and clear that only white men can do science and math, that only the best and the brightest deserve to be educated, that white students are inherently smarter than nonwhites, and that allowing people of color to enter a college diminishes its academic quality.

When I entered the University of Michigan, I remember being overwhelmed by its intellectual ethos. I recall listening to my white graduate student counterparts talk about their undergraduate experiences in liberal arts colleges and prestigious universities that appeared to be of higher quality than the institutions I had attended. I wondered whether I could compete with these students whose expediences were so different from my own. One white woman graduate student actually found the courage to reveal her stereotyped views of Hispanics and said, "You know, Laura, you're pretty smart. I'll have to admit that when I first met you, I thought you were kind of dumb." Higher education often requires not only that students be humble but that they tolerate humiliation. I remember wanting to study Chicanos in community colleges and wondering if the focus of my research would typecast me as a unidimensional (and therefore less worthy) scholar, capable of studying, writing, and thinking only about minority issues. I also wondered why, even when I had penetrated the walls of an esteemed university, I continued to focus my research on community colleges. I remember one of my friends telling me, "Why are you studying community colleges? I mean, community colleges—who cares?" He did not understand that I cared because community colleges were where people like me were gaining access to higher education, and because, unlike me, many of these people entered college, got nowhere, and left. Nonetheless, I asked myself why I wasn't breaking away from this niche and studying other kinds of institutions.

My story's lesson is that it is not only students who must adapt to a new culture but institutions that must allow themselves to be changed by foreign cultures. A few years ago, I read Galarza's (1970) perspective on institutional deviancy. Institutions become deviant, he explained, when they inflict pain on individuals, when they begin to depart from their moral and statutory commitment. There is no doubt in my mind that higher education has inflicted great pain on students of color.

To become academic success stories we must endure humiliation, reject old values and traditions, mistrust our experience, and disconnect with our past. Ironically, the academy preaches freedom of thought and expression but demands submission and loyalty. Scholarship "boys and girls" are left only with what Rodriguez (1982) calls "hunger of memory," a nostalgic longing for the past—the laughter of relatives, the beautiful intimacy of the Spanish language, the feeling of closeness with one's own parents.

How can institutions change? It is my belief that institutions must consider past experience, language, and culture as strengths to be respected and woven into the fabric of knowledge production and dissemination, not as deficits that must be devalued, silenced, and overcome. We need to validate students' capacities for intellectual development at the beginning, not at the end, of their academic careers. This means that early on we must communicate that students of color are capable of academic thought and expression and that we believe and trust that their experience will guide them as they develop their intellectual capacities. An ideal classroom is one in which the teacher allows students to write about their culture and experiences, where the learning climate encourages creativity and freedom of expression, where teachers help students see the connection between what is taught and what is experienced in real life. We must find ways to change the linear model of teaching, where knowledge flows only from the teacher to student. Instead, we must focus on collaborative learning and dialogue that promotes critical thinking, interpretation, and diversity of opinion.

We must set high standards, while helping students to reach them. Most faculty fail to give students the support they need in order to break free from belief systems that stifle their creativity. For example, many nontraditional students who come to college believe they cannot compete with other students, that their perspectives are not valued in college, and/or that they will be "just a number" in college.

When I talk with college faculty, I often hear how they are tired of spoon-feeding students, how they have had to lower their standards, how students aren't motivated, how students don't care. Yet when I tell them that they must help and nurture these students, they balk. Most faculty believe that college students should be held accountable for their own actions, no matter what their past experience has been. While there is some truth to this, I agree with the authors of *Women's Ways of Knowing* (Belenky, Clinchy, Goldberger, and Tarule, 1986) that we need to find ways of caring that make the ones we care for stronger rather than weaker. Taking care need not necessarily equate to taking over. We need to create ways to look after our students so that they may develop the strength needed to assume responsibility for their own learning.

Most important, we must stop inflicting pain on students by demeaning and devaluing their past. If I had allowed myself to be molded into a student who rejected her past in order to attain success, I never would have been able to give something back that would strengthen my community. Recently, I decided to return to the Southwest, in large part to be closer to the people and issues to which I am most committed. My academic success has made my parents proud of me, even when they don't fully understand what I do or what I write. And I am most proud of them for enduring an often agonizing experience with me.

Today we are witnessing the power of diversity. If higher education has up until now been able to validate scholarship "boys and girls" only when they have paid the high price of disconnection with their culture, it will become increasingly difficult to continue to do so. There are more and more of us (including white men and women) who are not buying into this flawed model of academic success. In the 1990s, as our numbers multiply, our power grows. If the academy refuses to change, we will change it. We will claim the curriculum, for we have always been a part of history, science, math, music, art, and literature. We will change teaching and learning to accommodate diversity. We will find our voice and use it to assert our rights and control our destiny.

I do not hunger for the past; it is always with me. Instead, I yearn for the future and believe that the time will come when higher education will be served by caring faculty, counselors, and administrators who know that they must do, not what is "politically correct," but what is morally and ethically the right thing. Many more like me will come to partake of the academy, classic scholarship men and women who leave home to find success in an alien land. We will change the academy, even as the academy changes us. And more and more of us will experience academic success—with few, if any, regrets.

References

Belenky, M. F., Clinchy, B. M., Goldberger, N. R., and Tarule, J. M. *Women's Ways of Knowing: The Development of Self, Voice, and Mind.* New York: Basic Books, 1986.

Galarza, E. "Institutional Deviancy: The Mexican American Experience." In *Mexican American Mental Health Issues: Present Realities and Future Strategies.* Boulder, Colo.: Western Interstate Commission for Higher Education, 1970.

Hoggart, R. *The Uses of Literacy: Aspects of Working-Class Life, with Special Reference to Publications and Entertainments.* New York: Oxford University Press, 1970.

Madrid, A. "Diversity and Its Discontents." *Academe,* 1990, 76 (6), 15–19.

Rodriguez, R. "Going Home Again: The New American Scholarship Boy." *American Scholar*, 1975, 44 (1), 15–28.

Rodriguez, R. *Hunger of Memory: The Education of Richard Rodriguez—An Autobiography* Boston: Godine, 1982.

The Effects of Student Financial Aid on Access to Higher Education:
An Analysis of Progress with Special Consideration of Minority Enrollment

EDWARD P. ST. JOHN AND JAY NOELL

An objective of the federal student financial aid programs is to promote access to higher education, especially for students from disadvantaged backgrounds. During the past few years, concern has been expressed by diverse segments of the higher education community that this objective is not being met for black and Hispanic students. This article analyzes the effects of aid offers on enrollment decisions by college applicants from the classes of 1972, 1980, and 1982, and analyzes the effects of the type of aid offered had on enrollment by minority students in the classes of 1980 and 1982. The principal findings from this analysis are that (1) all types of aid packages had a positive impact on enrollment decisions by college applicants in all three classes, and (2) all types of aid had a positive influence on enrollment by minority students.

One of the objectives of the U.S. Department of Education's (ED's) student financial aid programs is to promote access to higher education for the disadvantaged. In the 1980s, concern has been expressed by diverse segments of the higher education community that recent changes in federal student aid could be impeding progress of this goal. The fact that the rate of college enrollment by blacks has declined since 1976 seems well established (Mingle, 1987). Concern has fueled speculation that the increasing emphasis placed on loans in the 1980s has contributed to this downturn (Newman, 1985; Wilson, 1986). However, it is not easy to determine whether a shift in emphasis from grants to loans actually influenced college attendance decisions by low-income students, because (1) federal grant aid (especially Pell) has been targeted to low-income students; and (2) institutional and state aid policies, as well as federal policy, influence the types of aid packages offered to college applicants. Therefore, to analyze the effects that loans have on access, it is necessary to evaluate the effects of different types of aid offers on student enrollment decisions.

It is important periodically to assess the impact that the type of financial aid packages offered to college applicants has had on their enrollment decisions and to consider how these patterns have changed over time. In this article we analyze (1) trends in college enrollment between the early 1970s and early 1980s, and (2) the impact that the type of student aid offered had on enrollment decisions of high school seniors in the high school classes of 1980 and 1982. College enrollment behavior is influenced by a wide range of factors in addition to the type of financial aid that students are offered. To estimate the effects of financial aid on student college enrollment, it is first necessary to control for a student's social background, academic achievement, prior school experience, and postsecondary plans. Based on a review of the literature on educational attainment, student demand, and student choice, we developed and tested a model to measure the additional effects that the receipt of an offer has on a student's college enrollment behavior. First, we describe the study approach, including the model we used to analyze enrollment decisions. Second, we present the study findings. Finally, conclusions and implications are considered.

Study Approach

There are at least two approaches to the cross-sectional analysis of the effects of aid on student decisions to enroll in college that merit further exploration. One involves estimating the amount of aid they would be likely to receive if they applied to college, then estimating whether the availability of aid made a difference in student decisions, or would have made a difference if the amounts of aid available were different, the approach used by Manski and Wise (1983) in their well-regarded study. More recently Schwartz (1985, 1986) estimated the effects of eligibility for Federal grants and loan subsidies on college attendance and wealth equalization. These recent studies refine the methodologies used in more traditional student demand studies used in the late 1960s and early 1970s. For a review of these early demand studies, see Jackson and Weathersby (1975), McPherson (1978), and Leslie and Brinkman (1988).

The second approach involves estimating the marginal effects of an aid offer on the college enrollment decisions by college applicants. This approach was used by Jackson (1977, 1978) and was favorably reviewed by Jensen (1983) as being the most sound methodologically of the prior studies of the effects of student aid on access. It should be noted that when this approach was used, the relative impact of financial aid was smaller than in more traditional student-demand studies (Brinkman and Leslie, 1988). However, this approach is appropriate for this assessment because it is the best way to evaluate the impact that the type of aid offered has had on student enrollment decisions. Therefore, our model for analyzing the effects of aid offers on the decisions of college applicants to enroll was derived from studies by Jackson (1977, 1978). Jackson (1988) has recently published a study that compares the effects of aid offered on enrollment decisions by students in the high school classes of 1972 and 1980.

This study extends beyond past research by (1) comparing the effects of aid offers on the enrollment decisions by students in three high school classes (1972, 1980, and 1982); (2) examining the effects of different types of aid packages on enrollment decisions; and (3) analyzing the influence of aid offers on enrollment decisions of minority students. In a recent review of research on the effects of student aid on access, McPherson and Shapiro (1989) observe that analysis of response of students from different racial and ethnic backgrounds to aid offers is important in assessing the effectiveness of federal student aid spending as a device for expanding minority participation. The databases, model specifications, analysis methods, and study limitations are described below.

Databases

The primary focus of this assessment is on the impact that the type of financial aid offered had on the enrollment decisions of college applicants. We analyzed the effects of aid offers on college enrollment behavior of members of the high school classes of 1972, 1980, and 1982. However, because the enrollment rates have historically been lower for blacks and Hispanics, special consideration is given to the impact that student aid has had on the enrollment decisions by these subpopulations. Enrollment by Native Americans has also been lower, historically, than for whites or Asian Americans, but there is not a sufficient subsample of this population in HSB or NLS for separate analysis on this population. With the databases used for this study—the National Longitudinal Survey (NLS) of the High School Class of 1972 and the High School and Beyond (HSB) study—it is only possible to conduct separate analyses of blacks and Hispanics in the 1980s. NLS did not contain the additional sampling of these subpopulations that is necessary to analyze these groups separately.

The two national longitudinal studies—NLS and HSB—developed by ED's Center for Education Statistics (CES) are used for the analysis because they represent the best available databases for assessing the effects of aid on access on student enrollment decisions. These databases provide national samples of high school seniors with follow-up surveys during their freshman or sophomore year. They allow us to assess the effects of background on college enrollment during the first year after high school. NLS contains data on high school seniors in the class of 1972. HSB contains data on seniors in 1980 (in the senior cohort) and in 1982 (in the sophomore cohort). Weights for the first year after high school were used for all analyses and were rescored to the number of cases in the sample.

The base year for NLS-72 was 1972–72 academic year, when a stratified two-stage probability sample of twelfth graders was conducted (Tourangeau et al., 1987). It provides data on student social background, high school experience, and achievement test scores. The first follow-up was conducted from October 1973 to October 1974 and was used for information on college enrollment and aid offers.

For HSB-80 the base survey and first follow-up survey were used (Sebring et al., 1987a). The base-year survey was conducted in the spring of 1980, using a highly stratified national probability sample. The base-year surveys collected information on student background, high school experience, and ability/achievement tests. The first follow-up was conducted in the winter and spring of academic year 1981–82, and contains information on college enrollment and aid offers.

For HSB-82, the first follow-up—conducted during the senior year for the high school class of 1982—was used for data on social background, high school experience, and ability/achievement (Sebring et al., 1987b). The second follow-up provided information on college enrollment and aid offers.

In our analyses a high school senior is considered a college applicant if he/she applied as a senior or attended college the first year after high school. For all three classes, there was a larger number of students who attended college the first year after high school than indicated they applied as seniors. We assume it is because many colleges, including most community colleges, do not require advance applications. Therefore, we adjusted the applicant group to include those who attended but did not apply during their senior year of high school. The information on student aid offers was taken from the first follow-up survey conducted after high school. CES's longitudinal databases are the best available data sources for this type of analysis because they contain information for all high school seniors who apply to college.

Model Specifications

Our model assumes that student financial aid is only one of several variables that can influence a student's enrollment decision. The following factors are controlled for in our analyses:

Region (South, Northeast, and North Central were coded as 1)
Social Background, as measured by
    Ethnicity (Black and Hispanic are coded as 1),
    Gender (Males are coded as 1),
    Mother's Education (a five-category measure was used for all three years), and
    Family Income (a ten-category measure for the class of 1972 and a seven-category
       measure for the classes of 1980 and 1982)
Ability/Achievement (a three-category measure derived from a composite score on
    standardized tests)
High School Experience, as measured by
    High school track (vocational and academic tracks are coded as 1), and
    High school grades (an eight-point scale coded so that high grades have the highest
       value)
Presecondary Aspirations, as measured by the highest level of educational attainment
    expected by high school seniors (a six-level scale was used for the class of 1972 and a
    five-level scale for the classes of 1980 and 1982)

Our outcome variable for college attendance was constructed from a set of questions about student applications to their first-, second-, and third-choice schools. We decided this variable was the most appropriate for analyzing the effects of student aid on access, because these questions were also used to construct the composite attendance variable and to construct our variables on aid offers. Also, since we plan to analyze the effects of tuition and the amount of aid offered on attendance in a subsequent analysis, it was necessary to use the composite attendance variable because it is possible to determine tuition for the school students applied to, at least for the class of 1982, if this variable is used.

Analysis Methods

To analyze the effects that financial aid has on enrollment, we undertook three analytical steps. First, we analyzed the effects of student background on whether or not students enroll in college. This step is similar to educational attainment research (e.g., Alexander and Eckland, 1975; Wolfle, 1985) and was undertaken because it demonstrates the importance of these background factors on college enrollment.

Second, we analyzed the effects that these same background variables have on student decisions to apply to college. We feel this step is important because it identifies the social and environmental factors that influence the decision to apply to college. Because blacks and Hispanics have historically had lower attendance rates, we consider this analytical step necessary.

Third, we analyzed the effects that student aid offers have on the enrollment decisions of college applicants. To develop these treatment variables we first examined whether students reported being offered aid by their top-choice schools. Students in the classes of 1972 and 1980 were asked about their top three choices, whereas students in the class of 1982 were only asked about their top two choices. To construct the aid offer we first examined the aid package offered to the students by the school they attended. If they did not attend college, then we used the aid package offered by the highest-choice school. Since most schools make the admissions decision before aid is awarded to new applicants, we assumed that students with aid offers also had the opportunity to attend. Four types of packages were used: grant/scholarship only, loan only, work-study only, and a package containing more than one type of aid. In our initial analyses we used all types of aid packages, but the percentages of students with most types of aid packages were too small to include separately, so they were combined.

Because all three of these steps involve use of dichotomous outcome variables, logistical regressions are used in each step of the analysis. We convert the coefficients for each variable in our three models to a measure of change in probability (a Delta-p statistic) using a methodology proposed by Peterson (1984, p. 130–131):

$$\text{Delta-}p = \exp(L_1)/[1 + \exp(L_1)] - \exp(L_0)/[1 + \exp(L_0)]$$

where

$$L_0 = \text{Ln } p/(1 - p) \qquad (p = \text{``baseline } p\text{'' in table})$$

and

$$L_1 = L_0 + \text{Beta}$$

Study Limitations

There are three limitations that influence our ability to analyze the effects of aid offers on college attendance decisions. One limitation is that high school classes are studied infrequently. There were major changes in student aid policy between the fall of 1972, when high school seniors in the high school class of 1972 first entered college, and the fall of 1980, when the seniors from the class of 1980 entered. For example, the Pell program (formerly Basic Education Opportunity Grants) went into effect in fall 1973, and the Middle Income Student Assistance Act (MISAA) went into effect in fall 1978. Both of these programs expanded the number of students who received aid offers and could have increased the effect of student aid on access. The gap has an impact on this study because the peak Black enrollment rate among 18- to 24-year-olds was in 1976.

A second limitation is that the CES data contained self-reported data on aid offers. Presumably students might not recall their exact amount or type of aid offered, especially aid offered by schools they did not attend. Unfortunately, most databases that can be used to assess progress on access have this limitation. It would be necessary to survey the financial aid offices of every college to which a student applied to overcome this deficiency.

Findings

Our analysis of the effects of aid is presented in five parts. First, we briefly examine trends in minority enrollment to establish the fact that the percentage of minority students enrolling in college has declined and, therefore, merits special consideration. Second, we analyze the effects of student background on college enrollment by all seniors in three high school classes (1972, 1980, and 1982). Sophomores in the class of 1982 who did not enroll in high school during their senior year were excluded, so the three cohorts would be similar. Third, we analyze the effects of these same background characteristics on whether students apply to college. This analysis considers changes in who applies for college. Fourth, we analyze the effects of these same background characteristics on whether students apply to college. This analysis considers the type of aid packages offered to entering freshmen and how these offers have influenced the enrollment decisions by college applicants in the three high school classes. Fifth, we analyze the effects of aid offers on the enrollment decisions of applicants from the high school classes of 1980 and 1982. This final step analyzes the effects that the type of aid offered had on whites, blacks, and Hispanics. Separate analyses were conducted of the three ethnic groups to see if the type of aid offered had different effects among these groups. Since there was not a sufficient sample of blacks and Hispanics in NLS for separate analysis of each group, we excluded the class of 1972 from the final step in our analysis.

Enrollment Trends

Trends in participation rates can easily be illustrated by a review of statistics from Current Population Reports. The percentage of the traditional college-age group currently or previously enrolled in college remained relatively constant between the early 1970s and the early 1980s (Table 1). In contrast, the enrollment rate for blacks and Hispanics increased between the early 1970s and the early 1980s. However, it should also be noted that enrollment rates by blacks and Hispanics peaked in 1976. These trends are consistent with other research on minority participation (e.g., Mingle, 1987). Given these trends, there is indeed reason for public concern about minority enrollment.

Effects of Background on College Enrollment

The analysis of the effects of background on enrollment (Table 2) shows that a basic set of social background variables—including mother's education, being on an academic track in high school, having high grades and test scores, and having high postsecondary aspirations—have a strong impact on enrollment decisions by seniors in all three classes. In addition, being from Northeastern, North Central, and Southern states had a positive impact on attendance compared to being from the West. It should also be noted that when other variables in the model are controlled for, ethnicity was neutral for seniors in the 1980s, but positive for blacks in the 1970s.

The effects of several variables changed during the ten-year period. First, when other variables in the model are controlled for, being from a low-income family has a slight negative influence on college attendance by seniors in the high school class of 1972, but not on seniors in the high school class of 1980 and 1982. This finding suggests that the negative effects of being from a low-income family were reduced in the early 1980s, at least when background, achievement, and aspiration are controlled for. Second, there were also changes in the effects of gender (being male) on college attendance. Being male did not have a significant impact on college attendance by high

Table 1

Percentage of 18- to 24-Year-Olds Enrolled or Previously Enrolled in Two- or Four-Year College, by Sex, Race, and Hispanic Origin
(In thousands)

	1970	1971	1972	1973	1974	1975	1976	1977	1978	1979	1980	1981	1982	1983	1984
All Groups															
Enrolled	8,163	8,871	8,950	8,878	8,788	9,288	9,620	9,285	9,180	9,049	9,339	9,879	9,978	9,908	9,899
Total	20,832	21,813	22,160	22,522	2,530	22,959	23,380	23,338	23,313	23,358	23,541	24,388	24,388	24,291	23,203
%	39.8	40.1	40.4	39.4	39.0	40.4	41.1	39.8	39.4	38.7	39.7	40.5	40.9	40.8	41.7
Male															
Enrolled	4,278	4,578	4,713	4,819	4,406	4,703	4,691	4,558	4,443	4,302	4,379	4,667	4,751	4,807	4,703
Total	9,498	10,071	10,447	10,890	10,873	10,915	11,108	11,166	11,107	11,159	11,300	11,748	11,830	11,757	11,310
%	45.0	45.4	45.1	43.2	42.0	43.1	42.2	40.8	40.0	38.8	38.8	39.7	40.2	39.2	41.8
Female															
Enrolled	3,885	4,095	4,245	4,259	4,302	4,565	4,929	4,729	4,737	4,747	4,960	5,212	5,227	5,299	4,998
Total	11,134	11,542	11,713	11,832	11,857	12,044	12,272	12,170	12,208	12,197	12,241	12,640	12,558	12,534	11,973
%	34.9	35.5	36.2	38.0	36.3	37.9	40.2	38.9	38.8	38.9	40.5	41.2	41.8	42.3	41.7
White															
Enrolled	7,481	7,805	8,073	7,976	7,807	8,191	8,454	8,149	7,970	7,842	8,089	8,524	8,527	8,573	8,282
Total	17,900	18,737	19,155	19,322	19,358	19,668	20,003	19,912	19,774	19,726	19,863	20,406	20,260	20,198	19,182
%	41.8	42.1	42.1	41.3	40.3	41.7	42.3	40.9	40.3	39.8	40.7	41.8	42.1	42.4	43.2
Black															
Enrolled	587	800	753	748	803	883	981	927	971	987	993	1,040	1,111	1,034	1,121
Total	2,502	2,837	2,755	2,892	2,828	2,890	2,987	3,038	3,099	3,152	3,186	3,300	3,509	3,433	3,428
%	22.7	25.3	27.3	25.9	28.4	30.6	32.8	30.5	31.3	31.3	31.2	30.8	31.7	30.1	32.7
Hispanic Origin															
Enrolled	N.A.	N.A.	214	278	358	368	383	327	332	349	400	459	468	462	472
Total	N.A.	N.A.	1,217	1,183	1,300	1,312	1,405	1,429	1,448	1,507	1,677	1,813	1,809	1,830	1,755
%	N.A.	N.A.	17.8	23.5	25.9	28.0	27.3	22.9	22.9	23.2	24.2	25.3	25.9	25.2	26.9

Source: Calculated from the U.S. Bureau of the Census. Current Population Reports, Series P-20: No. 222, Table 14; No. 241, Table 13; No. 280, Table 12; Nos. 272, 286, 303, 319, 333, 346, 360, Table 13; No. 400, Table 13 and Table 39. N.A. indicates that the data are not available. Data for 1982, 1983, and 1984 are unpublished data calculated from the U.S. Bureau of the Census, Current Population Survey.

school seniors in 1972, but it did in 1980 and 1982, when males were less likely to attend. This finding is consistent with the trend toward a larger percentage of female enrollments in the late 1970s and early 1980s.

In combination, these findings suggest that there were gains in access to higher education between the early 1970s and early 1980s. Unfortunately, since we do not have data on the mid-1970s, we can reach no conclusions about the period when the rate of participation by minorities was at its peak.

Effects of Background on College Applications

The background of college applicants has frequently overlooked implications for policy. The effects of background on application decisions merit consideration as an intermediate step in the assessment of the effects of student aid on access. With only a few exceptions, most background variables in the model have an impact on the decision to apply similar to what they have on attendance (Table 3).

One notable difference between this analysis and the prior one is that blacks were more likely than other ethnic groups to apply for college in the early 1970s as well as the early 1980s. Although being black is positive and significant for all three classes, the size of the effects decreases during the period when other variables in the model are held constant. When other background variables are controlled for, blacks in the senior class of 1972 were 11.8 percentage points more likely than other ethnic groups to apply, whereas blacks in the classes of 1980 and 1982 were only 8.3 percentage points more likely to apply.

Table 2
Effect of Background on College Attendance During the Fall
After School for Seniors in the High School Classes of 1972, 1980, and 1982

	Logistic Regression Delta-p Statistical Probabilities High School Classes of		
	1972	1980	1982
Northeast	0.129**	0.098**	0.184**
North Central	0.102**	0.153**	0.183**
South	0.048**	0.103**	0.129**
Black	0.050*	0.009	0.026
Hispanic	0.060	0.040	−0.010
Male	−0.023	−0.035*	−0.041**
Family Income	0.005*	0.006	0.004
Mother's Education	0.046**	0.037**	0.042**
Academic Program	0.073**	0.140**	0.081**
Vocational Program	−0.063**	−0.054**	−0.041*
High School Grades	0.043**	0.061**	0.089**
Test Score	0.071**	0.044**	0.037**
Postsecondary Plans	0.154**	0.174**	0.186**
Sample Size	8237	7877	7578
Model Chi-Square	3326.70**	2686.91**	2883.62**
*Baseline p	0.464	0.577	0.546

Source: National Longitudinal Study of the High School Class of 1972, Base Survey and First Follow-Up; and the High School and Beyond Study Base Survey and Follow-Ups.
  *significant at .05 level.
**significant at .01 level.

Effects of Aid Offers on Attendance by College Applicants

Between the early 1970s and the early 1980s, there were substantial changes in the types of aid packages offered to college applicants (Table 4). First, the percentage of applicants receiving aid offers increased from 26.8% of the applicants in 1972 to 30.7% of the applicants in 1980, and to 35.2% for senior applicants in 1982. The percentage of applicants receiving offers that included scholarships or grants as part of their packages increased from 16.1% in 1972 to 17.9% in 1980, and to 21.4% in 1982. The percentage of applicants receiving offers that included loans as part of their packages dropped from 16.5% in 1972 to 15.9% in 1980 but increased to 21.1% in 1982. Thus, the percentage of students with grants/scholarships and loans in their packages increased between 1980 and 1982. The increasing use of institutional resources for grants and scholarships helps explain this increase in grants and scholarships in the early 1980s, and the expansion in federal loan programs explains the increase in the percentage of students with loans between 1980 and 1982.

When the effects of aid on access were analyzed (Table 5), all types of aid offers had a strong positive impact on the decision of applicants to enroll in college. The Delta-p statistics for the four types of aid packages compare the effect of that particular aid offer to no aid offer. Thus, it is possible to compare the relative effects of different types of packages. In 1972 and 1982, aid offers with loans as the only form of aid increased the probability of attending slightly more than offers with grants or scholarships; however, the reverse was the case in 1980. Therefore, it is not possible to conclude that one type of aid was more or less effective than another. In all three years, financial aid offers with work only and packages with two or more types of aid had a slightly stronger impact than offers with scholarships or loans as the only source of aid. However, these differences are slight. Therefore, we conclude that all forms of aid were effective in promoting access in all

Table 3
**The Effect of Background on College Application by Seniors
in the High School Classes of 1972, 1980, and 1982**

	Logistic Regression Delta-p Statistics High School Classes of		
	1972	1980	1982
Northeast	0.121**	0.096**	0.174**
North Central	0.080**	0.150**	0.166**
South	0.031	0.096**	0.129**
Black	0.118**	0.083**	0.083**
Hispanic	0.076*	0.064*	0.005
Male	−0.050*	−0.047**	−0.067**
Family Income	0.004	−0.005	0.002
Mother's Education	0.038**	0.032**	0.047**
Academic Program	0.096**	0.143**	0.108**
Vocational Program	−0.084**	−0.053**	−0.035
High School Grades	0.028**	0.049**	0.082**
Test Score	0.075**	0.056**	0.046**
Postsecondary Plans	0.145**	0.169**	0.191**
Sample Size	8235	7451	7553
Model Chi-Square	3609.66**	2775.12**	3178.56**
*Baseline p	0.576	0.660	0.620

Source: National Longitudinal Study of the High School Class of 1972, Base Survey and First Follow-Up; and the High School and Beyond Study, Base Survey and Follow-Ups.
  *significant at .05 level.
**significant at .01 level.

three time periods. Since the percentage of students receiving aid offers was larger in the early 1980s than in 1972, it would appear that the total effect of financial aid on access was greater in the early 1980s than it was in 1972, the last year before Pell. Presumably expansion in federal aid did contribute to the increased attendance rate during the decade.

Family background continues to have a strong influence on college enrollment by college applicants. However, family income has a strong positive influence on attendance all three years and being black has a strong negative impact on attendance by applicants. Because of these conditions, we decided separate analyses of the effects of aid on attendance by minority groups merited special consideration.

Effects of Aid Offers on Minority Enrollment

There is widespread concern in the higher-education community about the decline in the college enrollment rates of blacks. There has been speculation that an increased emphasis on loans could have influenced this decline (Newman, 1985; Wilson, 1986). Below we analyze the effects of aid on white, black, and Hispanic applicants and compare these results to those for all students already reported. Unfortunately, only two of the three high school classes (1980 and 1982) had sufficient sample sizes for analyzing the effects of aid offers on minority college applicants. The HSB survey included an oversampling of minority populations, which was not done in NLS. However, the absence of the 1972 cohort does not dampen the value of examining the classes of 1980 and 1982, since NLS predated Pell and the peak of minority enrollments in the late 1970s, and a comparison of the classes of 1980 and 1982 is sufficient to see if an increased emphasis of loans influenced applicants' enrollment decisions.

The comparison of the types of aid packages offered to black and Hispanic college applicants from the classes of 1980 and 1982 shows that the types of packages offered to minority students did change between 1980 and 1982 (Table 6). The percentage of black applicants receiving aid offers changed very little between 1980 (47.8%) and 1982 (47.7%), but the percentage of Hispanic applicants receiving aid offers dropped slightly, from 36.2% to 35.4%. However, the percentage of whites receiving aid offers increased, from 28% in 1980 to 33.2% in 1982. There was a slight decrease between 1980 and 1982 in the percentage of students in all three groups who received aid packages with scholarships or grants as the only form of aid. However, the total percentage with scholarships or grants in their packages increased slightly for whites and blacks but decreased slightly for Hispanics. The percentage of blacks receiving loans as the only form of aid offered increased, from 14.4% to 15.2%, whereas the percentage of Hispanics receiving loans as the only

Table 4
Financial Aid Packages Offered to College Applicants
from the High School Classes of 1972, 1980, and 1982

	Percent Receiving Aid		
	1972	**1980**	**1982**
No Aid	73.2%	69.3%	64.8%
Scholarship/Grant only	7.5	12.8	11.6
Loan only	7.3	10.0	9.7
Work-Study only	1.5	1.3	0.9
Scholarship/Grant and Loan	4.4	1.5	5.6
Loan and Work-Study	2.0	0.9	2.2
Scholarship/Grant and Work-Study	1.4	0.6	1.6
All Three Types	2.8	3.5	3.6

Source: National Longitudinal Study of the High School Class of 1972, Base Survey and First Follow Up; and the High School and Beyond Study, Base Survey and Follow-Ups.

Table 5
Effect of Background and Aid Packages on Enrollment by College Applicants
by Seniors in the High School Classes of 1972, 1980, and 1982

	Logistic Regression Delta-*p* Statistics High School Classes of		
	1972	**1980**	**1982**
Northeast	0.034*	−0.008	0.033*
North Central	0.044**	0.019	0.036**
South	0.032*	0.015	0.029*
Black	−0.104**	−0.084**	−0.059**
Hispanic	0.009	−0.013	−0.022
Male	0.015	0.015	0.009
Family Income	0.010**	0.020**	0.013**
Mother's Education	0.025**	0.016**	0.008
Academic Program	−0.001	0.029*	−0.020
Vocational Program	0.008	−0.004	−0.012
High School Grades	0.021**	0.015**	0.022**
Test Score	0.017	0.008	−0.012
Postsecondary Plans	0.044**	0.032**	0.025**
Scholarship only	0.062**	0.101**	0.062**
Loan only	0.108**	0.095**	0.078**
Work only	0.149**	0.110**	0.097*
Package	0.147**	0.082**	0.095**
Sample Size	4488	4338	4887
Model Chi-Square	565.81 **	400.40 **	311.75 **
*Baseline *p*	0.805	0.876	0.889

Source: National Longitudinal Study of the High School Class of 1972, Base Survey and First Follow-Up; and High School and Beyond Study, Base Survey and Follow-Ups.
 *significant at .05 level.
**signiflcant at .01 level.

form of aid offered dropped from 9.7% to 6.3%. The percentage of all three ethnic groups receiving offers with grants/scholarships and loans increased.

When the decision of college applicants to attend college is analyzed separately for the three groups, some important differences emerge (Table 7). Being from the Northeast had a slight negative impact on college attendance by blacks in 1980 but not in 1982. In contrast, for Hispanics, being from the South was negative in 1980 but not in 1982. Being from the Northeast was also positive for Hispanics in 1982. For whites, being from the Northeast and North Central regions was positive in 1982 but not in 1980. Family income was neutral for blacks in 1980 and positive in 1982. It was positive for Hispanics and whites in both years.

When the effects of aid on access were analyzed (Table 7), all types of aid offers (except work only) had a strong positive impact on the decision of white applicants to enroll in college; scholarships only and loans only had a positive influence on enrollment by black applicants in 1980 and 1982, and all types of packages had a positive influence on black applicants in 1982; scholarships had a positive influence on enrollment by Hispanic applicants from the classes of 1980 and 1982, and aid combinations had a positive impact for the class of 1982. The Delta-*p* statistics for the four types of aid packages compare the effect of that particular aid offer to no aid offer. Thus, it is possible to compare the relative effects of different types of packages.

The analysis of the effects of aid offers on the college enrollment decisions of black applicants shows that most forms of aid offered have a significant and positive impact on their enrollment decisions. However, the size of the effect of loans is less than grants/scholarships or aid packages

Table 6
Student Financial Packages Offered to Black and Hispanic Applicants in Fall 1980 and 1982

	Percent Receiving Aid Fall 1980		
	White	Black	Hispanic
No Aid	72.0%	52.2%	63.8%
Scholarship/Grant only	10.8	22.6	19.0
Loan only	9.7	14.4	9.7
Work-Study only	1.1	3.1	1.4
Scholarship/Grant & Loan	1.4	1.9	1.8
Loan and Work	0.9	1.4	0.6
Scholarship/Grant & Work	0.6	1.0	0.6
All Three Types	3.7	3.4	3.2
	Fall 1982		
No Aid	66.8%	52.3%	64.6%
Scholarship/Grant only	10.3	19.3	14.2
Loan only	9.1	15.3	6.3
Work-Study only	0.8	1.5	1.2
Scholarship/Grant & Loan	5.7	4.2	7.0
Loan and Work	2.3	2.5	2.0
Scholarship/Grant & Work	1.4	2.0	2.9
All Three Types	3.8	2.9	1.8

Source: High School and Beyond Study, Base Survey and Follow-Ups.

for both years. Also the size of the effects of loans deceased in 1982 compared to 1980. In fall 1980, a black applicant was 14.5 percentage points more likely to attend if a loan was the only source of aid offer received. However, in fall 1982, the black applicant who received a loan as the only type of aid offered was only 11.2 percentage points more likely to attend. Also, a lower percentage of black applicants received loans as the only type of aid offered in the fall of 1982 compared to the fall of 1980.

The effect of packages with two or more types of aid, most of which include loans as part of the package, was larger for blacks in 1982 than in 1980. Further, these combined packages had a larger impact than other types of aid offers in 1982 for blacks, Hispanics, and whites. Blacks receiving a package with two or more types of aid in 1982 were 18.6 percentage points more likely to attend when all other variables were held constant, and Hispanics who received aid packages with two or more types of aid were 15.0 percentage points more likely to attend. Scholarships and grants as the only source of aid had a positive impact on enrollment in both years for all three groups.

The models had less predictive power for blacks and Hispanics than for whites, although all model chi-squares are significant at the .01 level. It should also be noted that financial aid was the only variable in the model that was significant (at a .05 level or higher) for blacks in 1982 and for Hispanics in 1980.

Student aid appears to have a stronger impact on college attendance by blacks and Hispanics than whites. When other factors in the model are controlled for, all forms of aid had a stronger impact on access for minority students than for whites. Work as the only source of aid for Hispanics in the fall of 1980 and for whites in the fall of 1982 was the only type of aid that was not significant. Otherwise, all types of aid offers had a positive impact on the enrollment decisions by all three groups.

Table 7
Effects of Background and Aid Packages on College Enrollment by
Black and Hispanics in the High School Classes of 1980 and 1982

	Logistic Regression Delta-p Statistics Class of 1980		
	White	Black	Hispanic
Northeast	0.000	−0.362	−0.060
North Central	0.017	−0.190	0.006
South	0.016	0.172	−0.103
Male	0.023*	0.039	−0.007
Family Income	0.020**	0.014	0.030
Mother's Education	0.014*	0.031	0.054
Academic Program	0.029*	0.078	0.066
Vocational Program	0.003	−0.003	−0.035
High School Grades	0.016**	0.014	−0.002
Test Score	−0.015	0.029	0.005
Postsecondary Plans	0.031**	0.043**	0.023
Scholarship only	0.089**	0.177**	0.141*
Loan only	0.088**	0.145**	0.123
Work only	***	0.153	**
Package	0.071**	0.119	0.169
No. of Cases	2432	886	721
Model Chi-Square	279.56**	59.41**	29.66**
Baseline p	0.888	0.792	0.826
	Class of 1982		
Northeast	0.027	−0.052	0.154**
North Central	0.033**	−0.100	0.071
South	0.017	0.018	0.007
Male	0.019*	−0.045	−0.008
Family Income	0.013**	0.020	0.016
Mother's Education	0.010*	0.006	0.023
Academic Program	−0.010	−0.054	−0.260
Vocational Program	−0.005	0.007	−0.256
High School Grades	0.024**	0.023	0.027
Test Score	−0.021	−0.010	0.074
Postsecondary Plans	0.024**	0.036	0.025
Scholarship only	0.042**	0.150**	0.038**
Loan only	0.072**	0.112**	0.131*
Work only	0.084	***	0.121
Package	0.081**	0.186**	0.150
Sample Size	3420	613	591
Model Chi-Square	216.11*	51.11**	32.22**
Baseline p	0.901	0.811	0.837

Source: High School and Beyond Study Base Survey and Follow-Ups.
   *significant at the .05 level.
  **significant at the .01 level.
***too few cases to analyze separately and therefore were excluded from the analysis.

Conclusions

In conclusion, this analysis shows progress has been made in promoting access to higher education, and student financial aid has played an important role in this progress. When background variables are controlled for, blacks had the same probability as other students of attending college in the 1980s. Blacks were also more likely than other ethnic groups to apply to college.

First, when we analyzed the effects that the type of financial aid offered had on enrollment by college applicants, we found that all forms of student aid had a positive association with attendance. This conclusion was true for applicants in the classes of 1972, 1980, and 1982.

Second, all types of aid were effective in promoting access for minority students. Since black applicants were less likely than other applicants to attend college, and since there has been speculation that the increased use of loans could have contributed to the downturn in black enrollment, special consideration was given to the impact that the type of aid offered had on minority applicants in the high school classes of 1980 and 1982. When loans were the only form of aid offered, they had a positive effect on enrollment decisions for whites and blacks in both years, but not on Hispanics. The percentage of students receiving loans as part of their aid offers expanded between 1980 and 1982, but the percentage of students receiving loans as the only type of aid offered actually declined for whites and Hispanics.

However, our findings also suggest that caution should be used when packaging aid for minority applicants. The impact of loans as the only source of aid decreased between fall 1980 and fall 1982 for blacks and whites. In 1982, all other types of aid had a stronger impact on attendance than loans as the only type of aid offered for blacks and whites. For blacks, grants had a stronger impact than loans in 1980 and 1982. And for Hispanics, grants were the only type of package that was significant in 1980.

These conclusions do have a few important implications. First, to the extent possible, it would appear that if loans are offered to minorities and other disadvantaged college applicants, they should be combined with other types of aid in aid packages. Packaging loans with grants and work appears to be more effective in promoting access than giving minority applicants loans as the only student aid. Whenever possible, grants should be the first form of aid offered to low-income and other disadvantaged students.

Second, the types of aid packages that are offered to minorities who apply to college should be closely monitored in future studies. Most large surveys, including the forthcoming National Postsecondary Student Aid Survey, collect data on the types of aid offered to applicants who attend but not on the types of aid that were offered to applicants who do not attend. It is certainly important to monitor the types of packages that different types of students receive. However, it is also important, periodically, to sample students who did not attend to determine the types of aid that are being offered to them. In the past, longitudinal studies have not been initiated frequently enough to monitor the impact of changes in student aid programs.

Acknowledgments. The research reported in this article was originally conducted under contract with the Office of Planning, Budget, and Evaluation, U.S. Department of Education. The views express in this article do not necessarily reflect any positions or policies of the U.S. Department of Education. An earlier version of this article was presented at the American Educational Research Association Annual Meeting, April 1988, New Orleans, Louisiana. The authors would like to thank Rita J. Kirshstein, Charles L. Masten, and John W. Curtis for their assistance.

References

Alexander, K., and Eckland, B. (1975). Basic attainment processes: a replication and extension. *Sociology of Education* 48 (fall): 457–495.

Jackson, G. A. (1977). Financial Aid to Students and the Demand for Higher Education. Unpublished Doctoral Dissertation, Harvard University.

Jackson, G. A. (1978) Financial aid and student enrollment. *Journal of Higher Education* 49(6): 548–574.

Jackson, G. A. (1988). Did college choice change during the 1970s? *Economics of Education Review* 7(1): 15–27.

Jackson, G. A., and Weathersby, G. B. (1975). Individual demand for higher education. *Journal of Higher Education* 46(6): 623–652.

Jensen, E. L. (1983). Financial aid and student outcomes. *College and University*, Spring: 287–301.

Leslie, J. L., and Brinkman, P. T. (1988). *The Economic Value of Higher Education*. San Francisco: Jossey-Bass.

Manski, C. F., and Wise, D. A. (1983). *College Choice in America*, Cambridge, MA: Harvard University Press.

McPherson, M. S. (1978). The demand for higher education, in *Public Policy and Private Higher Education*, D. W. Brenneman and C. E. Finn, Jr. (eds). Washington, DC: Brookings Institution, pp. 143–196.

McPherson, M. S., and Schapiro, M. O. (1989). Measuring the effects of federal student aid: An assessment of some methodological and empirical problems. (Unpublished).

Mingle, J. R. (1987). *Focus on Minorities: Trends in Higher Education Participation and Success*. A joint publication of the Education Commission of the States and the State Higher Education Executive Offices, Denver, CO, July.

Newman, F. (1985). *Higher Education and the American Resurgence*. Princeton, NJ: Carnegie Foundation for the Advancement of Teaching.

Peterson, T. (1984). A comment of presenting results from logit and probit models. *American Sociological Review* 50 (1): 130–131.

Schwartz, J. B. (1985). Student financial aid and the college enrollment decision: The effects of grants and interest subsidies. *Economics of Education Review* 4(7): 129–144.

Schwartz, J. B. (1986). Wealth neutrality vs. higher education: The effects of student grants. *Economics of Education Review* 5(2): 107–117.

Sebring, P., Campbell, B., Glusberg, M., Spencer, B., and Melody, S. (1987a) *High School and Beyond 1980 Senior Follow up (1986) Data File User's Manual*. Washington, DC: Center for Education Statistics, U.S. Department of Education.

Sebring, P., Campbell, B., Glusberg, M., Spencer, B., Singleton, M., and Turner M., (1987b). *High School and Beyond 1980 Sophomore Cohort and Third Follow-Up (1986) Data File User's Manual*. Washington, DC: Center for Education Statistics, U.S. Department of Education.

Tourangeau, R., Sebring, P., Campbell, B., Glusberg, M., Spencer, B., Singleton, M. (1987). *The National Longitudinal Study of the High School Class of 1972 (NLS-72) Fifth Follow-Up (1986) Data File User's Manual*. Washington, DC: Center for Education Statistics, U.S. Department of Education.

Wilson, R. (1986). Overview of the issue: Minority/poverty student enrollment problems. *Third Annual NASSGAP/NCHELP Conference on Student Financial Aid, May 28–30, 1986, Loyola University of Chicago, The Proceedings*, Vol. 1. Springfield: Illinois State Scholarship Commission, pp. 125–130.

Wolfle, L. M. (1985). Postsecondary educational attainment among blacks, *American Education Research Journal* 22(4): 501–525.

The College Experience
of Native Americans:
A Critical Analysis

WILLIAM G. TIERNEY

The literature on the Native American experience in postsecondary institutions is generally relegated to footnotes in books about other minorities in the United States. Further, what little information exists pertains to statistical summaries about where Indian students go to college, their rates of participation, leave-taking, and the like. In many respects, Native Americans are invisible in academe; researchers neither study them nor do institutions devise specific strategies to encourage Indian students to attend, to participate, and to graduate.

Yet "invisibility" is a social construct. Simply stated, those students who are Native American are not invisible to themselves, to their parents, to their tribes. Although national surveys may provide faulty data that reduces an Indian student to an asterisk, the Indian student does not perceive his or her experience in that manner.

How do Indian students perceive academe? What are the challenges that await Indian students when they enter college? How we interpret those experiences depends upon the theoretical frameworks from which we operate. Accordingly, in this chapter I undertake two tasks. First, I make the invisible visible. Through the case history of one Indian student we hear of some of the struggles he has encountered as a student at a mainstream community college. Second, I offer two contrasting frameworks—a model of social integration and a critical perspective—for interpreting the student's experience. I argue that Indian students are invisible because of assimilationist attitudes based on the widely utilized social integration model. I conclude with the implications for this interpretation, and I raise issues for further research.

A Voice

On a cold, clear February morning Delbert Thunderwolf (a pseudonym) and I sat down with one another for the third time in eighteen months. He is a thirty-one-year-old community college student who is an American Indian from the upper Midwest. He is majoring in business. Delbert is a tall man, over six feet, and has the frame of a runner. He grew up "in my mother's house and in some other relatives' families," throughout his adolescence. Although he was born on the reservation, he moved to a city near the reservation until he left the area for college. He attended a boarding school for high school; when he finished school he worked for about six months and then chose to go to college.

Delbert is one of the individuals I interviewed for a two-year research project concerning the recruitment and retention of Native American students to two- and four-year colleges and universities. By the end of the project I had interviewed over two hundred individuals—other Indian students such as Delbert, as well as faculty, staff, and administrators at eleven institutions.

The first time I spoke with Delbert he had recently arrived at the public community college, and he discussed his reasons for going to college. He said:

> I attended Southwestern Indian Polytechnic Institute for two semesters, but I drank myself out of there. I was drunk for a long time. I sobered up four years ago, and in that time I had a chance to reevaluate my educational needs. I worked as assistant manager in a clothing and feed store here in town. I started seeing a bunch of people around me with college educations and they were going for what they wanted. And me, I couldn't do that on $5.50 an hour. I hurt myself physically on the job twice, and I said, "This is dumb." At first I was afraid to come back to college. I was afraid I wouldn't make it. It took a lot to do it, and I'm glad I did. I'm still afraid, though.

When I met with Delbert the second time, he spoke about the other Indian students at the public community college.

> Some students come here, and it's hard for them to get adjusted. A lot of them, they have fifth-, sixth-, sometimes third-grade reading levels, because the reservation schools aren't any good. Some of these reservations here are so big that it's hard to change that philosophy that you've got to be by your mom and dad in order to survive. They come off the res. and they don't have the survival instinct for the big city.

> I think white people think education is good, but Indian people often have a different view. I know what you're going to say—that education provides jobs and skills. It's true. That's why I'm here. But a lot of these kids, their parents, they see education as something that draws students away from who they are.

> And then there's the obstacles. There's no money. You go from one financial aid office and get told to go somewhere and then somewhere else. You give up. You can't figure out the papers, and you wind up thinking you're dumb. So you leave. I've seen a lot of them leave. . . . They go home. I try to explain to them, "What are you going to do? What are you gaining for yourself inside?" There's never no answers. They just go home.

Delbert expects to graduate soon. During our final interview he reflected on college and expanded on his thoughts about education.

> Drugs and alcohol are a terrible problem. I've seen students behave like I did. They sort of drink themselves out of the place. But sometimes I think that's not the problem. I think somewhere you have to give Indian people a different view of why they are here, what education is, so they can help keep the focus on why they want to stay in school.

> A lot of teachers might know a lot about business or accounting, but they don't know anything about Indians or what it's like to be away from home. One problem for students is that they don't find people to help. . . . No one tells Indian students to go after their dream.

> I would like to take all of my instructors and lead them through my life. Show them what it's like to come off the reservation. They would see how Indian people hold onto each other real fast in order to hold the old ways together. They'd see how much trouble it is to make the decision to leave home and come to school, how Indian people love staying around and being on the reservation, at home. How it's really a struggle to come here. I would love to have my instructors see that. Just to have them see the bonding that takes place. They'd see us right.

> I would like to tell them that education shouldn't try and make me into something I'm not. That's what I learned when I wasn't here. Who I am. And when I learned that, then I could come back here. I sort of walked away for a while and then came back. It's one of the best gifts I've ever had. But a lot of us just walk away.

Contextualizing Indian Voices

How are we to interpret the comments of Delbert Thunderwolf? The purpose in listening to him is surely not to call upon one student's voice to highlight how all American Indian students perceive higher education, as if Delbert were a symbolic "Everyman." Although their population is undeniably smaller than other cadres of postsecondary students, such as Anglos and African Americans, in some respects the Native American student population is more diverse than any other student group.

In addition to traditionally conceived variables pertaining to college students, such as male/female, urban/rural, parents who attended college and those who did not, and the like, we also need to think of Indian students according to additional variables, such as where they grew up—on a reservation or off—what role tribal language played in their lives, and how traditional or nontraditional they are according to Indian mores.

According to more common notions of college going, for example, Delbert Thunderwolf might be described as an adult male whose parents did not attend college and who grew up in a city. Yet because he is a Native American, some would say it is also pertinent to find out how much time he spent on a reservation (very little), whether he speaks a tribal language (he does not), and if he is "traditional" in the sense that he partakes of American Indian ceremonies and rituals (he does to a certain extent).

Consequently, Delbert's voice should be interpreted as nothing more than what it is—one voice among many. Indeed, he has several voices of his own, such as the autobiographical voice and that of someone caught between two worlds. Yet his comments also are echoed by other students involved in this study who spoke of similar dilemmas when they attended college. Delbert's voice, then, is both unique and representative; his perceptions and reactions to the world are unique to himself, yet they also are situated within a tribal culture that is shared with other American Indians.

My objective here is to utilize Delbert's comments to highlight the differences between two theoretical perspectives on minority college-going and participation, which in turn influence the actions and policies we take in academe pertaining to minority students. Prior to discussing these

Table 1
Racial and Ethnic Enrollment Data from Institutions of Higher Education, 1968–1984

Year	Total (in thousands)	Percentage						
		White	Minority	Black	Hispanic	Asian	American Indian	Alien
1968	4,820	90.7	9.3	6.0	Other	3.5		—
1970	4,966	89.4	10.6	6.9	Other	3.7		—
1972	5,531	87.7	12.3	8.3	Other	4.0		—
1974	5,639	86.5	13.5	9.0	Other	4.5		—
1976	10,986	82.6	15.4	9.4	3.5	1.8	.7	2.0
1978	11,231	81.9	15.9	9.4	3.7	2.1	.7	2.2
1980	12,087	81.4	16.1	9.2	3.9	2.4	.7	2.5
1982	12,388	80.7	16.6	8.9	4.2	2.8	.7	2.7
1984	12,162	80.3	17.0	8.8	4.3	3.1	.7	2.7

Source: 1968–1974 U.S. Department of Education, "Racial and Ethnic Enrollment Data from Institutions of Higher Education," biennial, as reported in *Statistical Abstract of the United States 1986,* 106th edition, U.S. Department of Commerce, Bureau of Census, table 259, page 153.

1976–1984: U.S. Department of Education, National Center for Education Statistics, "Fall Enrollment in Colleges and Universities" surveys, as reported in *Digest of Education Statistics 1986–87* and *Digest of Education Statistics 1980.*

perspectives, however, it will be helpful to contextualize his voice. What do we know about Native American participation in academe? Where do Indian students go to college, and what happens to them when they enter?

College-Going Patterns

As noted at the outset of this chapter, there is a notable lack of research and information about Native American participation in higher education. We do know that the history of American Indian participation in general, and in higher education in particular, has revolved around notions of assimilation and cultural genocide. Since 1617, when King James sought to establish a "college for the Children of the Infidels," Euro-Americans have persistently sought to remake Native Americans in the image of the white man—to "civilize" and assimilate the "savages." Dartmouth College, William and Mary, and Princeton University, among others, began as institutions with explicit mission statements to educate Indian people and "civilize" them. Yet native peoples have steadfastly struggled to preserve their cultural integrity. The college campus, then, has historically been a stage for this cross-cultural drama. And again, because American Indians are a small percentage in the overall framework of college participation, few studies or books have documented the educational struggles native peoples have faced or the manner in which they have met these challenges.

Even surveys that include Native Americans as part of their studies note the concerns the researchers have in utilizing data on Native Americans. Astin, for example, commented in *Minorities in American Higher Education* that the size of the sample of Native Americans "was often so small as to raise serious questions about the reliability of the results." Judith Fries recently completed a report specifically about Native Americans in higher education for the Center for Education Statistics. She, too, noted, "Most sample surveys are either too small to produce reliable estimates for American Indians, or Indians are grouped into an 'other' category."

What we do know is that the composite population of Native Americans is economically poorer, experiences more unemployment, and is less formally well-educated than the national average. A greater percentage of the population lives in rural areas than the rest of the country, where access to postsecondary institutions is more difficult. By all accounts the Native American population of the United States is becoming increasingly youthful. Current estimates place the total population of Native Americans as slightly less than two million. Between 1970 and 1980, the number of Indians between the ages of eighteen and twenty-four increased from 96,000 to 234,000. The average age of the population is sixteen.

Several different surveys suggest that less than 60 percent of those students who are ninth-graders will eventually graduate from high school. Eighty-five percent of those students who enter a postsecondary institution will not receive a four-year degree. Only one-third of those who graduate from high school will go on to college. Well over half of the college-going population will attend a two-year institution, compared to a third of the Anglo college-going cohort.

Table 2
Percentage Enrollment of Racial/Ethnic Groups by Type of Institution, 1986–1987

Institution	Black	American Indian	Asian American	Hispanic	White	Nonresident Alien
2-Year Public	40.6	54.3	44.7	56.3	36.9	23.4
2-Year Private	3.7	3.9	0.8	2.3	2.4	1.8
4-Year Public	39.2	34.3	41.4	31.2	42.3	42.9
4-Year Private	16.5	7.5	13.1	10.2	18.4	31.9
TOTAL	100.0	100.0	100.0	100.0	100.0	100.0

Source: Unpublished data: National Center for Education Statistics, Integrated Postsecondary Education Data Systems (1986–87).

Native Americans are among the smallest of student populations on four-year campuses; as of 1986 only seven four-year institutions had over five hundred American Indians in attendance. Those institutions that enroll a predominantly Native American population are essentially tribally controlled colleges—most of which are located on Indian reservations. In sum, if one hundred students enter the ninth grade, sixty of them will graduate from high school and about twenty will enter academe. Of those twenty students, about three will receive a four-year degree.

The challenge now turns to how we might interpret this data. How might we locate Delbert Thunderwolf's comments and perceptions of academe, given the generalized context of Native Americans in postsecondary education? To answer these questions I turn to two theoretical formulations that afford competing interpretations of Delbert's comments.

Two Perspectives of College Going and Leaving

Social Integration

The manner in which researchers have conceptualized minority participation in education is in keeping with much of the current research on student development and attrition. An abundance of Durkheimian "social facts" have been discovered that have led to different hypotheses. Researchers, for example, believe that parental education, individual motivation, age of student, and socioeconomic status (SES) are important factors in determining college participation and retention. The implications of such research, obviously, are that if a student's parents went to college, or if a student is "motivated," or if a student is of a traditional age, then it is more likely the student will attend and persist in postsecondary education.

Vincent Tinto has synthesized previous research efforts pertaining to student attrition and posited his own theory of student leave-taking. Tinto's work is important for a discussion of Native American students for at least three reasons. First, his work has gained wide respect amongst researchers in academe. Tinto's formula is the most popular model to describe college participation and departure. Second, he has struggled to take into account the cultural contexts in which students reside, and in doing so, he had laid to rest the more harmful psychological assumptions that have tended to "blame the victim" for school departure. Third, based on extensive quantitative analyses, Tinto persuasively argues in his recent book, *Leaving College,* that most students do not leave college because they have "failed." He states, "Leaving has little to do with the inability to meet the formal academic requirements of college persistence. The majority of student institutional departures are voluntary in character." As we shall see, such a finding is of key importance when we consider Delbert Thunderwolf's comments: first, however I elaborate on Tinto's model.

The scaffolding for Tinto's model rests on two ideas: (a) Van Gennep's rituals of passage and (b) Durkheim's theory about suicide, anomie, and the need for social integration. To summarize these two concepts, Van Gennep assumed that the members of a society underwent a variety of rituals throughout their lives that moved them from one stage to another—from childhood to adolescence, from adolescence to adulthood—and so on. Durkheim postulated that the cause of suicide in society was due to the lack of an individual's integration with larger societal structures such as the church, the state and the family.

Basically, Tinto argues that college life implies a passage from one stage to another and that college-going depends upon how well the college can integrate the student into the social and academic life of the institution. He comments that the model "argues that some degree of social and intellectual integration must exist as a condition for continued persistence."

Although Tinto does not directly discuss Native Americans in his book, the implications are far-reaching, given the strength of Native American culture, their "roots," and the different cultural values they presumably have from the culture of the mainstream institutions they attend. Indeed, the implicit assumption is that Native Americans will need to undergo a cultural suicide of sorts in order to avoid an intellectual suicide. As Tinto notes, "to become fully incorporated into the life of the college, they have to socially as well as physically disassociate themselves from the communities of the past. Their persistence in college depends upon their becoming departers from their former communities." The implication is that Indian students must depart from their culture if they are to succeed at the "ritual" of college.

To summarize the pertinent points of Tinto's theory of social integration for Native Americans, I offer five axioms:

1. Postsecondary institutions are ritualized situations that symbolize movement from one stage of life to another.

2. The movement from one stage of life to another necessitates leaving a previous state and moving into another.

3. Success in postsecondary education demands that the individual become successfully integrated into the new society's mores.

4. A postsecondary institution serves to synthesize, reproduce, and integrate its members toward similar goals.

5. A postsecondary institution must develop effective and efficient policies to insure that the initiates will become academically and socially integrated.

In the next section I will take issue with the axioms that have been outlined, and I will suggest an alternative way we might think of Native American participation in postsecondary education.

A Critical Perspective

Tinto's work is a significant contribution to understanding the problems of retention. He has demonstrated how colleges and universities often differ dramatically from the communities that students leave. Certainly, the problems a Native American student encounters upon entering the culture of a mainstream organization demonstrates on a grand scale what Tinto seeks to explain.

In advancing a critical agenda, however, I argue that our theoretical propositions need to do more than causally explain why particular groups of students encounter difficulty when they enter a postsecondary institution. Theory needs to explain not only what is (the understood reality of a situation) but also what *could* be. With regard to student participation in postsecondary education, we need to develop theoretical horizons that do not call upon a unitary synthesis of what we want students to become, but rather allow for the multiple voices that exist among students to be heard. Peter McLaren is worth quoting at length with regard to where the inquiry needs to go:

> We need to further develop a language of representation and a language of hope which together will allow the subaltern to speak outside the terms and frames of reference provided by the colonizer, whether or not the colonizer in this case happens to be the teacher, the researcher, or the administrator. We need a language of analysis and hope that . . . does not prevent minorities and the excluded to speak their narratives of liberation and desire. . . . The project of critical pedagogy is positioned against a pedantic cult of singularity in which moral authority and theoretical assurance are arrived at unproblematically without regard to the repressed narratives and suffering of the historically disenfranchised.

Most would agree that Native Americans have been "historically disenfranchised" in American society. From various histories of Native Americans or from investigations of the current economic conditions of Native Americans, consistent policies of discrimination against tribal peoples become readily apparent. What should be done to end discriminatory practices and to promote strategies that will allow for the conditions wherein American Indians "speak their [own] narratives of liberation and desire?"

From the perspective advanced here, each of the underlying assumptions of Tinto's framework must be brought into question. Tinto's model is one of integration, yet he never questions what such a focus will do to those whose values and culture are different from the norm. Or rather, Tinto highlights what will happen—those who do not integrate will depart—and he creates a framework based on integration. What are the consequences of such a view? I am suggesting that Tinto's overreliance on an integrative model of persistence offers potentially harmful consequences for minority students in general, and Indian students in particular. The anthropologist Ray McDermott is helpful here. He says:

> There is a preoccupation among us: Because we claim to offer good education to all and because many minority people seem to reject it, we are plagued with the question—"What is it with them, anyway?" Or, "What is their situation that school seems to go so badly?"

What McDermott and I are arguing is that we need to step back and ask more primary questions about the nature of college-going. We need to ask how failure is arranged and institutionalized in colleges and universities. From this perspective, the inherent assumptions of Tinto's model must be brought into question. What follows is an analysis of the five axioms of Tinto's formulation; I utilize the scaffolding of critical theory and the commentary of Delbert Thunderwolf to offer an alternative framework for thinking of minority student participation in academe.

College as Ritual/Choice. Postsecondary institutions may be ritualized situations, as Tinto suggests, but they do not fit the framework of anthropological rituals, for the simple reason that, with regard to American Indian students, one culture is trying to integrate another culture into its system. Van Gennep's "rituals of passage" were never conceived as acts perpetrated on one culture by another. Van Gennep's rituals also were not choice options; everyone underwent the ritual. Yet with regard to Delbert, he did need to make a choice. His first decision was to undergo the "ritual" of college, but he then chose to leave, and then he chose to return. The ritual system in which he was involved—the public community college—was not of his own culture, but of the mainstream culture.

Further, as the Spindlers have effectively argued, when we think of traditional cultures and rituals of passage we do not find the concept of "dropout," and we do not discover adolescents choosing whether to undergo the ritual. The Spindlers offer examples from the Hutterites in North America and the Arunta of Australia to point out how mainstream American society differs from traditional societies. To be sure, education is a form of initiation, and all societies struggle to educate their young. But with the Arunta and others, the Spindlers argue, "all of the initiates succeed, none fail, in this intensive, compressive school. To fail would mean at least that one could not be an Arunta, and usually this must mean death . . . social death." Van Gennep's rituals in a traditional society are managed to produce success. To fail to initiate the young into society is unthinkable; the continuity of culture would be destroyed, and society would disintegrate. There are no dropouts. Yet in American society, education does produce dropouts, and success is not assured, especially for American Indian students.

With regard to Delbert, we hear that he believed college was a mixed opportunity, a good and bad choice. He went to an institution, dropped out, worked, and realized that he needed to go back to college when he saw people who had college degrees. "They were going for what they wanted," said Delbert, "and I couldn't do that on $5.50 an hour." In Delbert's eyes, then, college offered the ability to make choices about his life that he otherwise could not have. Delbert viewed college as an avenue that would enhance his economic potential.

Yet he also saw colleges as a harmful and difficult choice. He commented that Indian parents "see education as something that draws students away from who they are." He wanted his teachers to "see how much trouble it is to make the decision to leave home and come to school . . . how it's really a struggle to come here." From a critical perspective, then, the ritual of college is a decision for Indian students that forces them to choose between the world of their tribe and that of academe.

College as Leave-Taking. This assumption follows naturally from the previous argument. If one accepts that individuals exist in developmental patterns, then initiation rituals can be seen as moving initiates from one stage to the next. The problem with such a view when we apply it to college again is highlighted when we think of the Native American experience.

Initiation rituals are not predicated on the belief that the initiates must leave their previous culture and accept a new one. Indeed, initiation rituals exist to provide individuals with more knowledge about the culture in which they reside. Mainstream institutions, however, are based on the assumption that all students, including minority students, not only must leave a developmental stage, but implicitly also must depart from their own cultures as they assume the mantle of adulthood. "There is an assured and assumed continuity," the Spindlers' comment about the rituals of the Hutterites. "The system is self-sustaining." Yet the system we have in place in colleges and universities is not culturally self-sustaining for minority students; instead, it is based on the belief that for success to occur, cultural disruption must take place.

Delbert pointed out how difficult the cultural disruption was for his friends. "It's hard for them to get adjusted," he said. Delbert argued that "education shouldn't try and make me into something I'm not." Delbert resisted cultural disruption, and he implied that the only way he was able to succeed in college was first to understand who he was as an Indian. "I sort of walked away for a while and then came back," he commented. "It's one of the best gifts I've ever had." Although Delbert was able to avoid assimilation, he stated what the national figures confirm: "A lot of us just walk away."

Postsecondary Success. From an integrationist model, when one succeeds in academe, one has adopted the new culture's mores and become integrated. I am not suggesting that integration is bad or harmful. However, to adopt a model predicted on integration and not to attempt to define what one means by the term underscores the problems that will arise for those not in the mainstream. By not delineating what he means by *integration*, Tinto leaves the term open for self-definition. And those in power in academe will define integration the way it has traditionally been done. As we know, in the case of American Indians, integration has been a code word for assimilation. Assimilation has meant the loss of their culture.

One difference between an integrationist and a critical analysis comes with Delbert's comment about education. He acknowledged that "education provides jobs and skills." But he also went on to state that Indian people did not necessarily see education only in that manner; he argued that "somewhere you have to give Indian people a different view of why they are here, what education is." His point was that education in mainstream institutions was alienating and foreign for Indian students and that alternative venues needed to be created.

According to the model of social integration described above, one would agree with Delbert's comment that education caused cultural disruption. College is a ritualized situation that makes students into new people. To the extent that students do not engage in the process, the social integrationist would argue, they are at risk of dropping out. Success or failure in college turns on how an individual and the family interpret the educational process. Because education "draws students away from who they are," it has the potential of being interpreted as a positive, negative, or neutral influence. A social integrationist might see the influence as positive, or at least neutral; nonetheless, the influence exists.

Within the context of Delbert's comments, however, we see that drawing "students away from who they are" was perceived as negative, harmful. Presumably, Delbert viewed education in terms of integration, and integration was seen as a form of assimilation. A critical perspective acknowledges how the two "worlds"—that of the institution and that from which Delbert comes—are different. The educational process is seen as trying to remake people into something different from who they are, and such attempts are viewed in a negative light.

Postsecondary Goals. We are led to believe that the goals of education will be similar for all. In one light, one cannot argue with such an assumption. All students need to be equipped with the intellectual and vocational skills necessary to function in the twenty-first century. Yet Pottinger succinctly elaborates the dilemma for Native Americans: "Few individuals wish to be handicapped by inadequate preparation for the 'real world,' a real world which demands skills relevant to the latest advances in technology. But how does one achieve this competence without losing touch with one's heritage?

The integrative framework that Tinto proposes implicitly demands that students choose: either maintain your culture and risk economic and social problems, or eschew your culture and gain a college degree and all the benefits that will be forthcoming. Framed in this manner, if we return to the data of Native American participation in academe, we see that they have overwhelmingly chosen their culture rather than to undergo the initiation rituals of an oppositional culture in a mainstream institution.

Yet, one is hard-pressed to look upon nonparticipation or attrition from postsecondary education as a "success" if the consequences are a student's inability to earn an income or take control of her or his life. I am suggesting that we ought to investigate how organizational participants might develop strategies framed by a concern for redefining the parameters of the organization. Rather than assimilate minorities into the organization, we need to shift our emphases so that alternative discourses can be heard. Henry Giroux defines such an educational strategy as "border pedagogy":

> Students must engage knowledge as a border-crosser, as a person moving in and out of borders constructed around coordinates of difference and power. These are not only physical borders, they are cultural borders historically constructed and socially organized within maps of rules and regulations that limit and enable particular identities, individual capacities, and social forms. In this case, students cross over into borders of meaning, maps of knowledge, social relations, and values that are increasingly being negotiated and rewritten as the codes and regulations which organize them become destabilized and reshaped.

Giroux means more than simply that students should be able to understand their own cultures and also exist in others. He does not mean to imply that students' cognitive capacities are like different television channels with which they can flip back and forth depending upon their desire. Nor does he intend to suggest that educators should be concerned merely with creating the conditions whereupon Native Americans or any other minority may appropriate the dominant discourse. Rather, the implications of a critical approach for postsecondary organizations necessitate redefining how we think, and hence act, in the organizational world.

The Role of Colleges. Delbert spoke about the "obstacles" Indian students face, with an example about financial aid. He said, "You go from one financial aid office and get told to go somewhere else. . . . You give up." A social integrationist will see Delbert's comments as identifying organizational barriers to be overcome. The assumption is that the organization is ineffective and policies need to be developed so that the organization will become more efficient. On the one hand the organization must provide more assistance, so that students are not lost and do not "give up." On the other hand, Indian students must be taught to learn the process, so that they can successfully navigate the bureaucratic waters.

In some respects the critical response is problematic. Student departure from college may be viewed as a point of resistance. In effect, Indian students reject the cultural requisites that the organization places upon them. Rather than seeing them as victims, a critical theorist might view such an action as a form of cultural integrity and strength. Indian students reject being assimilated into mainstream society, and the only avenue for their rejection is to depart.

The problem turns, for the critical theorist, on the consequences of departure. Delbert commented that he asked students when they leave, "What are you going to do," and he found, "There's never no answers." The point is not that cultural resistance is wrong or futile, but surely there are organizational responses other than the assumption that students must become integrated into the mainstream culture. Critical theorists, however, have yet to operationalize such a response, but clues about how one might act arise with a comment by Delbert.

He commented that most whites "don't understand," and that he wanted "to lead them through [his] life." His hope was that in doing so, his instructors would "see right." Again, the integrationist model assumes that the purpose of "seeing right" is to create a more effective system so that students will successfully undergo the rituals of transition.

Delbert, however, was not speaking about "seeing right" in order for Indian students to become assimilated to the ways of the mainstream. Indeed, he referred again to the need to resist the mainstream. "Education shouldn't try to make me into something I'm not," said Delbert. "That's what I learned when I wasn't here. . . . Who I am." Yet Delbert's time away from school involved alcohol abuse and a job that he did not find particularly challenging; it was the spiritual and ceremonial learning activities with his people that forced him to think about "who he was," which in turn enabled him to return to school. One wonders what kinds of activities minority students must undergo to maintain their identity and grasp the tools that a college education offers.

I am suggesting that organizations need to be constructed where minority students' lives are celebrated and affirmed throughout the culture of the institution. The point is not simply to have a Native American studies center or a course or two devoted to native peoples. Minority students need institutions that create the conditions where the students not only celebrate their own histories but also are helped to examine critically how their lives are shaped and molded by society's forces. Such a theoretical suggestion has implications for virtually all areas of the organization—from how we organize student affairs to the manner in which we construct knowledge, from the role of assessment to the role of the college president.

The emphasis of a critical analysis shifts away from what strategies those in power can develop to help those not in power to analyzing how power exists in the organization and, given how power operates, to developing strategies that seek to transform those relations. All organizational participants will be encouraged to come to terms with how they may reconstruct and transform the organization's culture. As opposed to a rhetoric of what mainstream organizations will *do* for Native Americans—a top-down managerial approach—the struggle is to develop strategies and policies that emerge from a vision of working *with* Native Americans toward a participatory goal of emancipation and empowerment.

Conclusion

I have offered two different theoretical constructs that have direct implications for Native American participation in academe. Tinto's model of social integration offers a wealth of explanatory evidence about why individuals do not persist and what strategies institutional participants might develop to help them persist.

Critical theory offers an alternative lens with which to analyze Native American college-going patterns. I provided a critique of social integration and argued that a Durkheimian model of college as a ritual of passage has two conceptual flaws. First, anthropologists who subscribe to the notion of rituals of transition have never defined rituals as individual choices that move people from one culture to another but, rather, have defined them as stages of human development. Second, a model based on an implicit understanding of integration will inevitably subscribe to cultural assumptions that pertain to mainstream culture and deny or overwhelm alternative interpretations of other cultures.

Delbert Thunderwolf's perceptions of his experiences afforded an opportunity to think about Native American involvement in academe and to contrast the two perspectives. Participants in an academic world that subscribe to a model of cultural integration will not hear Delbert's words in a manner similar to how the critical theorist hears them. In effect, Delbert's voice is not heard. Yet for critical theorists, "seeing right" or "hearing right" is not enough; the question before us must be: If our theoretical notions enable us to hear Delbert's voice, then what must we do? What are the implications for action? These are the questions that now await us.

PART IV
FACULTY

Faculty Issues:
The Impact on Minorities

James E. Blackwell

One-third of a century has passed since the U.S. Supreme Court decreed in *Brown v. Board of Education,* a Topeka, Kansas, case, that racial segregation is unconstitutional. Fifteen years have disappeared since affirmative action in higher education became national policy. Fifteen years have also passed since the decision in the *Adams v. Richardson* case ordered the dismantling of dual systems of publicly supported colleges and universities. Collectively, these decisions have been sources of immense inspiration, heightened expectations, and strengthened beliefs that laws, if fully implemented, could be powerful instruments for creating the type of change necessary to expand educational opportunities for all Americans.

Yet a compelling argument can be made in 1988 for the proposition that even the most fundamental promises emanating from such momentous court actions have not been fulfilled—have not approximated the original expectations. Instead, there are significant signs of retrogression. Those modest but important achievements toward equality of educational opportunity are under assault. These retreats coincide with widespread pronouncements that America must become more competitive and that the nation needs to shape all of its human resources toward improving national economic achievement.

Perhaps it is precisely that recognition of unfulfilled promises and the apprehensions expressed by many educators and policymakers that frames the current context for urgent actions. For without immediate purposeful intervention, even those gains already attained may be diluted. Hence, understanding the problems associated with generating a more equitable share of baccalaureate degrees among members of minority groups achieves a special salience as we approach the end of the current decade.

A central purpose of this paper is to delineate and analyze pertinent faculty issues that affect minorities' receiving baccalaureate degrees in the United States. However, it is also appropriate to underscore the importance of parallel issues about the status of minorities in faculty positions in American colleges and universities. This discussion will illuminate the complex nature of the problem. Among these faculty issues are slippages in efforts to move increasing numbers of underrepresented minority persons into the educational mainstream, fluctuations and declines in the numbers of faculty members from minority groups, downturns in the college-going rates of students identified as members of racial or ethnic minority groups, impediments to retaining minority students, reasons that they fail to earn baccalaureate degrees, and the quality of life experienced by members of minority groups at American colleges and universities.

The Educational Pipeline for Faculty

Systematic analyses of the educational pipeline reveal a number of slippage points in the postsecondary education of students from minority groups (Astin 1982; Blackwell 1987; Reed 1983). This slippage is critical to other vital faculty issues. One major concern is that minority group members are not available for teaching and/or administrative positions in institutions that require each faculty member to have a doctoral degree.

Almost 40,000 fewer blacks were enrolled in college in 1984 than in 1976 (Christoffel 1986). Astin's (1982) research identifies slippage points for blacks, native Americans, Chicanos, Puerto Ricans, and whites at such transition points as college, graduate, and professional-school levels. Each of these points can be described as filters that screen out the proportions of subjects who move on to the next point within the educational system.

Not unexpectedly, there is a white monopoly on enrollment in graduate schools. This monopoly has far-reaching implications for access, training, and production of minorities with the educational requisites for faculty positions in colleges and universities. Simply put, if minorities cannot gain access to graduate education and if significant numbers do not attain the doctoral degree, then obviously the pool of minority group members is limited while a sustained volume of white candidates continues.

What factors contribute to the continuing underrepresentation of minority group students in graduate schools? The discussion must focus on enrollment trends.

Total enrollment in graduate schools in the United States declined by 1.4 percent between 1976 and 1984, the last year for which reliable data are available. White students comprised 83.9 percent of graduate enrollment in 1976, a figure which declined 5.4 percent by 1984. Still, white students held about eight of every ten (80.5 percent) slots in our nation's graduate schools in 1984. Minority decline was less—3.0 percent; but the most alarming attrition was among black graduate students, whose representation fell by 22.4 percent in less than ten years. The loss for native Americans was almost 10 percent. In contrast, Asian Americans saw a gigantic increase of 48.1 percent and Hispanic enrollment in graduate schools climbed by 14.4 percent. In absolute numbers, Asians gained almost 9,000 graduate students, and Hispanics gained approximately 3,000 graduate students. White Americans lost almost 50,000 graduate students and, blacks about 15,000, and native Americans about 300 students.

Many explanations have been offered to account for these patterns. For whites, the most consistent theme appears to be that upturns in the economy have accelerated economic opportunities in business and industry, making graduate school less appealing and profitable. These opportunities, even in an economic growth situation, are not as readily available to racial and some ethnic minorities in the United States.

Explanations offered to account for the declining presence of blacks in graduate schools include inadequate financial aid and lack of institutional commitment to recruiting black students. Unlike the decade of the 1960s and pre-*Bakke* 1970 years, recruiting black students for graduate education does not now have a high priority. Other reasons include the paucity of black faculty, an unfavorable institutional climate, inadequate college preparation, and faculty indifference to the need for diversity among the graduate student body (Blackwell 1987).

Many black students are unwilling to incur enormous debts to finance graduate education. The average annual cost of post-secondary education ranges from $5,900 to $17,900. Federal support for graduate education is less stable and, in many cases, less available. Many potential graduate students have family and personal financial obligations or responsibilities. However although finance is a major factor in the declining enrollment of some minority group members, it is clearly not the sole factor.

Irrespective of the explanations offered for the declining enrollment of blacks and native Americans in graduate schools or for the increase in the numbers of Hispanics matriculated, the most important fact is that the nation has not fully opened its graduate school doors to these three groups. As a result, there is a critical shortage of blacks, Hispanics, and native Americans for faculty positions. That shortage is a direct consequence of the underproduction of minorities with doctoral degrees.

Doctoral Degree Levels

A dramatic downturn occurred between 1980 and 1986 in the total number of doctorates earned by American citizens. Although all doctorates dropped from 26,394 in 1980 to 22,984 six years later, white Americans still claimed 89.3 percent. Black Americans suffered the most conspicuous loss: from 4.1 percent in 1980 to 3.5 percent in 1986, or 275 black doctorates.

American Indians had a net loss of six doctorates. The percentage of American Indians with doctorates remains at a dismal 0.4 percent. Puerto Rican Americans experienced an increase from 69 in 1980 to 137 in 1986 or 0.6 percent of the total number of doctorates conferred. The absolute number of doctorates earned by Mexican Americans also rose from 109 in 1960 to 182 in 1986 or 0.8 percent. It is apparent from these data that those minorities in the United States who comprise more than a fifth of the nation's total population experience less than 50 percent parity in the total number of doctorates awarded American citizens each year. Their underrepresentation in the number of doctorates produced is a serious indictment of both the American educational system and society as a whole for its failure to increase and maintain the access of, retention in, and achievement within graduate education.

Underproduction of doctorates among minority groups generates especially troublesome problems. For instance, uneven distribution of academic majors exacerbates an already disturbing pattern. While blacks, Mexican Americans, Puerto Ricans, and native Americans are not overrepresented in any field of specialization, certain concentrations of degree attainment are particularly striking. As recently as 1986, approximately half of all blacks with doctorates earned them in education. By comparison, 43.2 percent of Mexican Americans, 32 percent of Puerto Ricans, slightly more than 24 percent of American Indians, less than 20 percent of the white population, and about 10 percent of Asian Americans were awarded degrees in education.

Among the minority groups, Asian Americans were more likely to concentrate their doctoral training in the physical sciences, life sciences, and engineering, while blacks, Mexican Americans, and Puerto Ricans were more likely to pursue degrees in education, the social sciences, and psychology and strikingly less likely to undertake doctoral programs in such fields as mathematics, computer science, physics, chemistry, earth and environmental science, engineering, agricultural sciences, health and medical sciences, and languages and literature. That type of maldistribution inevitably leads to the "ghettoization" of minorities in higher education whenever they are hired beyond token numbers.

This abysmal situation observed in the underrepresentation of blacks, Mexican Americans, native Americans, and Puerto Ricans need not continue. Indeed, some institutions have implemented strategies designed to expand the pool of minorities for graduate education and, ultimately, for faculty positions in colleges and universities. The interventions they have found effective are reported in detail in the paper on which this article is based (Blackwell 1988).

Minority Faculty: Recruiting, Employing, Retaining

The underrepresentation of minorities in faculty positions in our nation's colleges and universities is extremely serious. Alarming trends indicating declines in the hiring and retention of minorities have been observed recently (Arce and Manning 1985; Blackwell 1984; Harvey 1986; Matthews 1987). As early as 1973, Bayer stated that blacks comprised 2.9 percent of the total number of faculty positions in colleges and universities. Asians accounted for 2.1 percent and other minorities constituted 2.8 percent of total faculty positions.

Blackwell (1984) and Harvey (1986) claim that blacks comprised about 4 percent of total faculty a decade later, but this percentage represented a decrease from an estimated high level of approximately 6 percent in the late 1970s—before the severity of the effects of the "revolving door" of junior faculty had been realized. A major problem with the 4 percent figure is that it includes all black faculty employed at historically black colleges and universities. When that number is disaggregated from the total number of blacks holding faculty positions in postsecondary education, blacks account for approximately 1 percent of the faculty in predominantly white colleges and universities.

While Asians were the only minority group to register significant gains in faculty positions between 1975 and 1983, blacks were the only minority to experience both a decline in absolute numbers and a percentage loss of the total number of faculty positions in the United States. During that period, an additional 257 American Indians received faculty positions. The number of Hispanics in college teaching positions rose by 1,133 while the number of Asians rose from 9,763 to 16,899, a gain of 7,126. The number of whites rose from 409,947 in 1975 to 440,505 in 1983, a net gain of 9,442. Nevertheless, whites continue to claim nine of every ten faculty positions in American colleges and universities, while minorities had slightly less than 10 percent of the total.

Minorities are substantially more likely to hold nonfaculty positions in institutions of higher learning. As a group, they constitute 22.2 percent of all nonfaculty positions. Nonfaculty personnel range from service positions (such as janitorial, custodial and maintenance services, and dining room assistants), to clerical positions and higher-graded administrative positions. According to 1983 data on minorities in administrative positions in colleges and universities, blacks held 7.2 percent of the administrative positions, Hispanics 1.6 percent, Asians 1.1 percent, and whites 89.7 percent. These data are not disaggregated by institutional affiliation. If they were, they would reveal that more than half of the black administrators are employed at historically black colleges and universities and that specific institutions, such as New Mexico Highlands, account for a disproportionate number of administrators from the Hispanic population. Again, there is a major problem of maldistribution.

Affirmative Action

During the 1960s and early 1970s, several postsecondary institutions made apparently genuine efforts to recruit and employ minorities for faculty and nonfaculty positions. Those efforts were stimulated by the tumultuous events of the 1960s, demands from students, the commitment of some white faculty to institutionalize diversity in their departments, and the intervention of affirmative action in higher education in 1972.

Inasmuch as affirmative action is a sociopolitical construct it is not particularly surprising that several researchers focused on general descriptions of affirmative action in higher education (Banks 1984; Exxum 1983; Exxum et al. 1984; L. S. Lewis 1975; Matthews 1987; Menges and Exxum 1983; Reed 1983, 1986), others on the benefits of affirmative action (Leinwood-Jones 1983; Penn et al. 1986), others the needs and policies about recruiting minorities for faculty positions (Reed 1986; Sandler 1974). The attitudes of whites toward affirmative action have been the subject of a number of empirical investigations (Burstein 1979; Klugel and Smith 1983; Lipset and Schneider 1978; Ponterotto et al. 1986; Taylor, Sheatsley, and Greeley 1979), as have the criteria for affirmative action programs (Exxum et al. 1984; Hitt and Keats 1984).

The most fundamental objective of affirmative action is to end discrimination in recruitment, hiring, and retraining and to "remedy the effects of past discrimination through the implementation of a variety of positive steps." One of those steps is expanding the pool of eligible individuals to include representatives of all groups, especially those who have been victimized by past discrimination. Affirmative action programs are most effective when there is a clear and unequivocal institutional commitment to its basic principles (Exxum et al. 1983; Menges and Exxum 1983; Hitt and Keats 1984; Reed 1983). That commitment begins with higher administration and pervades the entire institutional structure.

Hitt and Keats (1984) demonstrated that attitudinal and procedural factors were crucial to effective affirmative action programs. These factors encompassed "commitment from higher administration, receptive attitudes from key personnel, and formal and informal grievance procedures" (p. 203). Other factors important to effectiveness include "credibility of the affirmative action officers, development and implementation of creative approaches to affirmative action, social and academic support systems, current and accurate information regarding available occupational minority candidates by discipline, and regular review of affirmative action programs and goals" (Hitt and Keats 1984, 203).

Whites hold 90.7 percent of all faculty positions and 89.7 percent of all administrative positions in American colleges and universities. Therefore, white attitudes and perspectives on whether affirmative action effectively helps minorities move into the mainstream have enormous salience. These attitudes and perspectives are highly complex and varied. Researchers who expound endogenous and exogenous explanations of discrimination in the marketplace (Blackwell 1982; Becker 1971; Reich 1971; Swinton 1977) argue that people are primarily motivated by economic self-interests. Hence, their responses to programs like affirmative action will arise from their perceptions, real or imagined, of what impact such programs will have on individual economic entitlements. However, the sense of economic entitlements is not unrelated to one's position in a racially stratified system.

For example, actions of those who believe that their mere membership in a racially dominant group thereby entitles them to the best rewards, irrespective of their own qualifications or even if minority members are equally or better qualified, are greatly influenced by that belief system. Symbolic racism (McConahay and Hough 1976) often associated with political conservatism and traditional racial prejudice posits that minorities, by demanding transformations in the racial status quo, are not only making illegitimate demands but are "violating cherished values" (Klugel and Smith 1983, 800).

Attitudes of whites toward affirmative action often seem so contradictory that many minorities claim that the obfuscation is a purposeful effort to mask their real opposition. Poll data continue to show that a significant majority of white Americans registered support for programs aimed at helping minorities get jobs or access to higher education. However, a significant white majority opposed programs defined as "preferential treatment for members of minority groups" (Klugel and Smith 1983; Ponterotto et al. 1986). If one accepts the symbolic racism thesis that minorities are attempting to violate "cherished values" of meritocracy and white privilege in a racially stratified society, and if minorities pose a threat to the economic rewards generally received by whites, then it is understandable how these attitudes influence affirmative action policies in higher education at levels controlled by whites.

Furthermore, many who oppose affirmative action are not racially biased but firmly believe that the opportunity structure, which served them well in the past, will also serve racial and ethnic minorities if they meet the traditional criteria for getting jobs and moving upward. In short, opposition to affirmative action in higher education is a complex phenomenon; so are white attitudes about it. It is also important to note Klugel and Smith's admonition that verbal support for affirmative action does not necessarily transform itself into behavioral support in promoting affirmative action policies (1983, 778).

Hence, circumvention techniques or strategies for subverting affirmative action in faculty hiring have developed. They include:

1. The absence of clearly defined job descriptions in advertisements (Exxum et al. 1984).

2. Advertising in specialties that are not traditional for minorities. Ambiguities in job descriptions often permit shifts in specializations whenever minorities appear in the pool of candidates.

3. Advertising for temporary, nontenure-track positions to which minorities seeking tenure-track lines are far less likely to apply.

4. Transmitting negative signals during the interview process.

5. Having no minorities on search committees to review the curriculum vitae of all applicants.

6. Having no tenured minority faculty on search committees who would not be afraid to argue without fear of reprisals.

7. Inadequate searches resulting in claims that "we can't find any."

8. Continuing to use white male networks.

Despite such subversion, persistent insensitivity to the need for affirmative action, ignorance about effective recruiting strategies, some colleges have been successful in recruiting faculty minorities. For example, the University of Massachusetts/Boston ranks first among all New England colleges and universities in the percentage of minorities on its faculty—approximately 13.4 percent. That success is attributed to the unqualified priority assigned to affirmative action by Chancellor Robert Corrigan, the authority of the affirmative action officer, and the monitoring roles performed over the past seventeen years by the Association of Black Faculty and Staff of the University of Massachusetts/Boston.

Effective strategies include institutional commitment to affirmative action as an instrument for increasing diversity needed by the institution as a whole. From this commitment must emerge clearly defined policies accompanied by rewards for compliance and sanctions for noncompliance. It also means hiring affirmative action officers who have clout and who are willing to use that clout as they monitor the recruitment and hiring process. In addition, the following suggestions are offered:

1. Aggressive recruitment, including obtaining lists of potential candidates from institutions that produce significant numbers of doctoral minorities.

2. Using "grow-our-own" programs.

3. Using postdoctoral fellowships to make permanent faculty positions more appealing to minorities.

4. Instituting all-but-the-dissertation slots to attract minorities with a follow-up program of faculty development that permits completing the degree. Williams College has instituted this program. (It has also been a standard practice at several black colleges for many years).

5. Advertising in media outlets likely to be used, seen, or read by minorities.

6. Being willing to overcome departmental jealousies that impede market prices for minority faculty, a scarce commodity.

7. Housing subsidies in areas of high housing-market prices.

8. Supporting travel to professional meetings.

9. Research opportunities.

10. Course loads that enable the person to meet tenure expectations.

11. Senior faculty members to mentor junior faculty members.

12. Stating tenure/retention requirements clearly during the interview so that the individual will have an unambiguous understanding of expectations.

13. Joint appointments with other departments and/or with nearby institutions.

14. Using visiting professorships and endowed chairs to recruit senior faculty from minority groups.

15. Communicating genuineness of commitment to collegiality unencumbered by racial or ethnic considerations.

Retaining Minorities

Many junior minority faculty experience a "revolving door" syndrome. Individuals are hired, kept on the faculty for five or six years, evaluated negatively for tenure, and are required to move on to another institution. Sometimes the process is repeated until the individual leaves college and university teaching.

This situation may be explained by ambiguous tenure policies and practices in many institutions as well as the extraordinary time demands made upon minority faculty members. Most institutions, except the historically black institutions and the few institutions that have become predominantly native American and predominantly Hispanic, hire minorities in token numbers. As a result, they are often drawn into "Activities unrelated to their competencies or interests" (Banks 1984), competing with research and publication demands. Yet, as Pruitt (1987) stated, minority faculty often feel that they must respond to the needs of minority students who often feel alienated in predominantly white institutions.

A dilemma is, on the one hand, to work hard and meet the traditional requirements for tenure and, on the other, respond directly to student demands and departmental and institutional expectations to not only work with minority students but be the "minority representative" on every committee. Many who choose the latter course received the impression that such responsiveness was appropriate and would compensate for lower scholarly output at the time of tenure consideration. They are disillusioned when the same persons in their departments who encouraged them to "assume responsibility for all things minority" penalize them for "inadequate scholarly productivity" during tenure considerations.

Even those who opt to avoid responses to such demands often find the tenure process painfully disheartening and unrewarding. Many minorities have reported that white faculty pay little attention to the actual quality of their research and writing but focus on "where they published." If they have not published in those journals or with publishing houses that white professors have defined as "prestigious organs," neither the quality nor the quantity of their publications counts; demerits are assigned on quantifiable scales employed in evaluations of publications. In addition, some white faculty members claim that research by minority faculty is not "relevant" for the field or that it does not represent a significant "breakthrough" in the discipline and, hence, is not meritorious. Those demerits can block tenure and reduce the number of minorities available to teach college students or to encourage them to obtain their baccalaureate degrees.

A third alternative, more demanding and taxing, requires exceptional discipline and planning. That alternative combines meeting the traditional requirements for tenure through outstanding performance as a scholar and teacher as well as being available to assist students as needed. Many scholars who are employed in major research universities have risen to that challenge. For those who opt for this choice, there should be a clear understanding that exceptionally hard work and a strong commitment to scholarly pursuits and to assisting minority students will demand unparalleled self-discipline. Inescapably, whenever a minority person is hired in a faculty position, he or she is a role model, expected to be an advisor, a counselor, an advocate, and a sympathetic listener for minority students. Even so, the dilemmas posed by competing demands and that sense of responsibility to minority students place a heavy burden on some minority faculty.

As evidenced in Banks' research (1984), some minority scholars do not display compassion for minority students. Nor did they agree that special attention to minority students was a central responsibility for them. Some took the position that their only duty was to be the best scholar they could be and that they should do no more for minority students than they would for any other student. In that category, it appeared that such persons were among that group of professors who, at best, could be characterized as indifferent to student concerns. Most persons in his study, however, did not fall into that category.

It is time for universities and colleges to reevaluate existing tenure policies. While research is essential and must be done, the primary function of colleges and universities is to impart knowledge to students. The most effective method of accomplishing that task is through quality teaching. Therefore, tenure policies should assign at least the same weight to teaching as to research competence. In addition, if institutions are committed to participatory democracy and to the value of faculty involvement in governance, they must find ways of rewarding service. Finally, as long as minority faculty members are expected to respond to the needs of minority students over and above regular duties, that work should be factored into the scale of values used to determine merit for tenure.

Faculty Roles in Minority Baccalaureates

Once minorities have been employed in faculty positions, what roles can they perform that will help minority students earn baccalaureate degrees? What strategies can they develop or execute that will spark a greater interest among minority students in graduate education—ultimately, in college or university teaching as a profession? I believe faculty members can and do play major roles in students' academic outcomes and career aspirations.

First and foremost, professors can demonstrate competence in their subject matter. Excellent teaching is characterized by extraordinary competence, knowledge of the subject matter, the ability to convey ideas in an interesting manner, the ability to stimulate interest in the subject matter, preparation for every classroom activity, and the ability to engage students in civilized discussions about ideas. Excellent teaching requires professors to communicate a profound interest to students as individuals and the capacity to listen to students. Students quickly identify with faculty members, irrespective of race, who communicate that sense of caring to them.

Excellent teaching will articulate expectations of high student performance and, simultaneously, a commitment to help students measure up to those standards. It is not patronizing students. It is not "talking down to them." It does mean recognizing the demonstrated achievement levels of students and making the adjustments necessary to facilitate comprehension and utilization of the subject matter. It is that commitment to excellence, sense of caring, and fairness in evaluations of students that will promote self-confidence, a determination to succeed, and a healthy use of role modeling and mentoring. In these processes, minority students, who may not have understood the real value of a baccalaureate degree, may develop an even more profound appreciation for higher levels of professional training (Garibaldi 1984, 1986).

To be more specific, professors must understand not only the norms of language but cultural variations in the meanings attached to language styles and usage. Mainstreaming minorities who may be either outside or marginal to the mainstream may take special attention, particularly in avoiding stigmas, stereotypes, and personally injurious labels. It also means using a classroom management style that facilitates involvement in learning, that appreciates diverse cultural styles, multiculturalism, and diversity, and that uses these features to stimulate interest in learning.

Many minority students matriculated at predominantly white institutions report the negative impact of encounters with indifferent, insensitive, or racist professors and "elitists" of any race. Examples are racist remarks ("Why don't you go to some college where you belong?") the use of pejorative and racially insensitive examples in classroom situations (e.g., when speaking about "welfare queens," look to minority students for an explanation), and failing to keep appointments with minority students. Such encounters often influence students to drop out before earning a baccalaureate degree.

Mentoring

One of the most important interventions that minority faculty can use is mentoring. Since Daniel Levinson's 1978 description of the mentoring process in *Seasons of a Man's Life*, considerable attention has been given to definitions of the mentoring process (Blackwell 1983; Busch 1985; Levinson 1978; Stein 1981) and mentoring functions (Kaufman 1986; Prehm and Issacson 1985; Schein 1978; Shapiro et al. 1978).

Mentoring means using one's own experiences and expertise to help guide the development of others. It is a close, interpersonal relationship that benefits both mentor and protégé. The process demands that the mentor be available to the protégé, takes time and in helping the protégé achieve aspirations and goals, offers encouragement and constructive criticism, and develops a relationship sufficiently strong with the protégé that criticism will not damage it.

Effective mentoring requires the mentor to spend time with students outside the classroom situation. It can be achieved through involving the student in the mentor's research and scholarly endeavors. This involvement exceeds mere apprenticeship, since the student is not only learning more about methodology and procedures but also how to think critically, how to use knowledge, and how to appreciate the value of scholarly endeavors. This process creates a stronger sense of involvement within the university and stimulates understanding of the range of exciting dimensions of faculty life.

The teaching component of effective mentoring helps the student sharpen writing skills, appreciate strong self-discipline, and see value in high personal standards and expectations. Spending the time to read, critically assess or evaluate, and offer praise while simultaneously encouraging even better performance also are essential activities.

Intrusive Advising

A valuable strategy for helping students earn baccalaureate degrees is aggressive or intrusive advising. Advising has been the subject of extensive research recently (Asher 1984; Avakian et al. 1982; Bennett and Okinaka 1984; Bynum and Thompson 1983; Glennen et al. 1985; Guloyan 1986; J. J. Lewis 1987; Mallinckrodt and Sedlacek 1987; McKenna and Lewis 1986; Perry 1981; Richardson and Gerlach 1980; Rugg 1982; Suen 1983; Varheley and Applewhite-Lorzano 1985; White and Brown 1980). Glennen and associates' concept of intrusive advising seems particularly appropriate for minority students:

> To be intrusive in advising means to be duly concerned about the academic affairs of one's students. The intrusive advisement system takes an aggressive approach in requiring the students to come in for advising at frequent intervals. It does not wait for students to get into academic difficulty, but continually checks on their progress and provides academic support in the form of developmental course work and/or tutoring assistance in areas identified by the advisor as needing course work according to the students needs, abilities and degree plan (1985, 335).

Faculty members are selected for participation, intensively trained, and given released time that permits their involvement. Students are required to visit a centralized counseling center a specified number of times and encouraged to visit beyond the requirement as needed. Students learn about the support services available so that they can use them before major problems arise. Special foci include interpretations of learning styles, the importance of regular class attendance, problems of low grades and the advantages of enrollment in advanced courses. Through a network of faculty, advisors, administrators, and support staff, information about students and an alert system, identifying students in potential trouble, develop. As Casas and Ponterotto (1984) and Maldonado and Cross (1979) point out, this advising system raises the level of campus consciousness about minority problems wherever they exist, emphasizes the need for minorities to maintain pride in their own culture, and creates greater cultural awareness among nonminorities on the campus

Intrusive advising has been used at HBCUs for several years. In fact, this system of faculty involvement in student life, the nurturing of and caring for students and their lives may help to explain why HBCUs enroll about one-fifth of America's black college students but annually graduate about half of all black baccalaureate degree recipients.

Faculty representatives at predominantly white institutions could visit HBCUs and observe programs with particularly high graduation rates. Examples are the Business and Management Program offered at Florida A & M University and the premedical education and pharmacy programs at Xavier University of New Orleans.

Finally, faculty members can participate at all levels of the governance structure bearing upon the institutional life of minority students. It is that governance structure which establishes parameters of performance, rules, expectations, normative patterns, and procedures. Wise faculty members understand these activities and learn how academic systems work either to the advantage or disadvantage of students.

Ultimately, responsibility for facilitating baccalaureate degree attainment among minority students does not rest on the shoulders of minority faculty. It is a total institutional responsibility. However, it is foolish to assume that the greater share of that task will not be borne by minority faculty members if and wherever they are employed in colleges and universities. A prior responsibility is to identify, train, graduate, and hire minorities in far greater numbers than colleges and universities are doing today if they are serious about meeting present and future needs.

References

Arce, C., and W. H. Manning. *Minorities in Academic Careers: Experiences of Ford Foundation Fellows.* New York: Ford Foundation, 1985.

Asher, C. "Helping Minority Students with Nontraditional Skills to Enter and Complete College." *Urban Review* 16, no. 1 (1984): 57–61.

Astin, A. *Minorities in Higher Education.* San Francisco: Jossey-Bass, 1982.

Avakian, A. N., et al. "Race and Sex Differences in Student Retention at an Urban University." *College and University* 57 (Winter 1982): 160–65.

Banks, W. M. "Afro-American Scholars in the University." *American Behavioral Scientist* 23, no. 3 (Jan./Feb.): 325–38.

Bayer, A. E. *Teaching Faculty in Academe.* Washington, D.C.: American Council on Education, 1973.

Becker, G. *The Economics of Discrimination.* Chicago: University of Chicago Press, 1971.

Bennett, C., and A. Okinaka. "Explanations of Black Universities." *Integrated Education* 22 (Jan./June 1984): 73–80.

Blackwell, J. E. "Persistence and Change in Inter-group Relations: The Crisis upon Us." *Social Problems* 29, no. 4 (April 1982): 325–46.

———. *Networking and Mentoring: A Study of Crossgenerational Experiences of Blacks in Graduate and Professional Schools.* Atlanta: Southern Education Foundation, 1983.

———. *Desegregation of State Systems of Higher Education: An Assessment.* Atlanta: Southern Education Foundation, 1984.

———. *Mainstreaming Outsiders: The Production of Black Professionals.* 2nd ed. Dix Hills, N.Y. General Hall Pub. Co., 1987

———. "Faculty Issues: Affecting Minorities in Higher Education." *From Access to Achievement: Strategies for Urban Institutions.* Edited by R. C. Richardson, Jr. and A. G. de los Santos, Jr. College Park, Maryland: National Center for Postsecondary Governance and Finance, 1988.

Burstein, P. "Public Opinion, Demonstrations and the Passage of Anti-discrimination Legislation." *Public Opinion Quarterly* 79 (1979): 157–72.

Busch, J. W. "Mentoring in Graduate Schools of Education." *American Educational Research Journal* 22, no. 2 (Summer 1985): 257–65.

Bynum, J. E., and W. E. Thompson. "Drop-outs, Stopouts and Persisters: The Effects of Race and Sex Composition of College Classes." *College and University* 59, no. 1 (Fall 1983): 39–48.

Casas J. M. and J. G. Ponterotto. "Profiling an Invisible Minority in Higher Education: The Chicano." *Personnel and Guidance Journal* 62, no. 6 (1984): 349–53.

Christofel, P. "How Can My College Recruit and Retain Minority Students?" New York: College Board's Research and Development Update, October 1986.

Exxum, W. H. "Climbing the Crystal Stairs: Values, Affirmative Action, and Minority Faculty." *Social Problems* 30 (April 1983): 383–99

Exxum, W. H., et al. "Making It to the Top: Women and Minority Faculty in the Academic Labor Market." *American Behavioral Scientists* 27, no. 3 (Jan./Feb. 1984): 301–4.

Garibaldi, A. *Black Colleges and Universities: Challenges for the Future.* New York: Praeger, 1984.

———. *The Decline of Teacher Production in Louisiana, 1976–1983 and Attitudes Toward Their Profession.* Atlanta: Southern Education Foundation, 1986.

Glennen, R. E., et al. "Impact of Intrusive Advising on Minority Student Retention." *College Student Journal* 19 (Winter 1985): 335–38.

Grant, R. E., and L. J. Eiden. *Digest of Education Statistics 1983–1984.* Washington, D.C.: National Center for Educational Statistics, 1985.

Guloyan, E. V. "An Examination of White and Non-white Attitudes of University Freshmen as They Relate to Attrition." *College Student Journal* 20 (Winter 1986): 396–402.

Harvey, W. B. "Where Are the Black Faculty Members? *Chronicle of Higher Education* Vol? (Jan. 22, 1986): 96.

Hitt, M. A., and B. W. Keats. "Empirical Identification of the Criteria for Effective Affirmative Action Programs." *Journal of Applied Behavioral Science* 20, no. 3 (1984): 203–22.

Kaufmann, F. A., et al. "The Nature, Role and Influence of Mentors in the Lives of Gifted Adults." *Journal of Counseling and Development* 64 (May 1986): 576–78.

Klugel, J. R., and E. R. Smith. "Affirmative Action Attitudes: Effects of Self-interest, Racial Affect, and Stratification Beliefs on Whites' Views." *Social Forces* 61, no. 3 (March 1983): 797–820.

Leinwood-Jones, A. "Reconciling Search Policies with Affirmative Action Regulations." *Educational Record* 64, no. 2 (Spring 1985): 34–37.

Lewis, J. J. "Do Black Students on a White Campus Value the University's Efforts to Retain Them? *Journal of College Student Personnel* 28, no. 2 (March 1987): 176–77.

Lewis, L. S. *Scaling the Ivory Tower.* Baltimore: Johns Hopkins University Press, 1975.

Levinson, D. *The Seasons of a Man's Life.* New York: Knopf, 1978.

Lipset, S. M., and W. Schneider. "The Bakke Case: How Would It Be Decided at the Back of Public Opinion? *Public Opinion* 1: 38–44.

Maldonado, B., and W. Cross. "Today's Chicano Refutes the Stereotype." In *Understanding and Counseling Ethnic Minorities,* edited by G. Henderson, pp. 138–149. Springfield: Charles C. Thomas, 1979.

Mallincrodt, B., and W. E. Sedlacek, "Student Retention and the Use of Campus Facilities by Race." *NASPA Journal* 24 (Winter 1987): 28–32.

Matthews, F. L. "Affirmative Action Officers: Higher Education's Catalyst for Change Persevere." *Black Issues in Higher Education.* 3, no. 2 (March 1, 1987): 1–5.

McConahay, J. B., and J. C. Hough, Jr. "Symbolic Racism." *Journal of Social Issues* 32 (1976): 23–45.

McKenna, P. G., and V. Lewis. "Tapping Potential: Ten Steps for Retaining Underrepresented Students." *Journal of College Student Personnel* 27 (Summer 1986) 452–53.

Menges, R. J., and W. H. Exxum. "Barriers to the Progress of Women and Minority Faculty Members." *Journal of Higher Education* 4, no. 2 (1983): 123–44.

Ponterotto, J. G., et al. "Student Affirmative Action Programs: A Help or Hindrance to Development of Minority Graduate Students." *Journal of College Student Personnel* 27, no. 4 (July 1986): 318–25.

Penn, N. E. et al. "Affirmative Action at Work: A Survey of Graduates of the University of California, San Diego, Medical School." *American Journal of Public Health* 76, no. 9 (Sept. 1986): 1144–46.

Perry, F., Jr. "Factors Affecting Academic Performance and Persistence among Mexican-American, Black and Anglo Students." *College Student Journal* 15 (Spring 1981): 53–62.

Prehm, H. J., and S. L. Issacson. "Mentorship: Student and Faculty Perspectives." *TESE* 8, no. 1 (1985): 12–16.

Pruitt, A. S., and P. D. Isaac. "Discrimination in Recruitment, Admission and Retention of Minority Graduate Students." *Journal of Negro Education* 54, no. 4 (Fall 1985): 5267–536.

Reed, R. J. "Affirmative Action in Higher Education: Is It Necessary?" *Journal of Negro Education* 52, no. 3 (1983): 332–49.

———. "Faculty Diversity: An Educational Moral Imperative in Search of Institutional Commitment." *Journal of Educational Equity and Leadership* 6, no. 4 (Winter 1986): 274–94.

Reich, M. "The Economics of Racism." In *Problems in Political Economy*, edited by D. M. Gordon, 107–113. Lexington, Mass.: D. C. Heath, 1971.

Richardson, R. L., and S. C. Gerlach. "Black Dropouts: A Study of Significant Factors Contributing to a Black Student's Decision." *Urban Education* 14 (Jan. 1980): 489–94.

Rugg, E. A. "Longitudinal Composition of Minority and Non-minority College Dropouts: Implications for Retention Improvement Programs." *Personnel and Guidance Journal* 61 (Dec. 1982): 230–35.

Sandler, B. "The Hand that Rocked the Cradle Has Learned to Rock the Boat." *New Directions for Institutional Research* 3 (Autumn 1974): 1–21.

Schein, E. *Career Dynamics: Matching Individuals and Organizational Needs*. Reading, Mass.: Addison-Wesley, 1978.

Shapiro, E. C., et al. "Moving Up: Role Models, Mentors, and the Patron System." *Sloan Management Review* 19, no. 3 (1978): 51–56.

Stein, S. L. "Sex Differences in Expectations of Mentors." Paper presented at the American Educational Research Association meeting, Los Angeles, California, April 1981, (Cited in Busch, 1985).

Suen, H. K. "Alienation and Attrition of Black College Students on a Predominantly White Campus." *Journal of College Student Personnel* 24 (March 1983): 117–21.

Swinton, D. H. "Racial Discrimination: A Labor Force Competitive Theory of Discrimination in the Labor Market." *American Economic Association* (Feb. 1977): 400–405.

Taylor, D. G., P. B. Sheatsley, and A. M. Greeley, "Attitudes toward Racial Integration." *Scientific American* 238 (1979): 42–49.

Varhely, S. C., and S. R. Applewhite-Lozano. "A Recruitment and Retention Plan for Students from Minority Groups." *Journal of College Student Personnel* 26, no. 1 (Jan. 1985): 77–78.

White, A. J., and S. E. Brown. "Relationship Between the Attrition Rates of Black and White College Students at the University of Georgia." *Negro Education Review* 31 (July/Oct. 1980): 137–39.

Pathway to the Professoriate;
The American Indian Faculty Pipeline

WILLIAM T. CROSS

One of the least known segments of American higher education is the American Indian/Alaskan Native (hereafter referred to as American Indian or Indian) professoriate. The literature has been silent on the number, location, rank, discipline and tenure status of American Indian faculty. Faculty in the 1990s will play an increasingly important role in the education and economic advancement of our tribal communities. In terms of the number of Indian faculty participating in this development, the jury is still out. This article explores the current nature of the literature regarding the American Indian professoriate including an examination of the Indian educational pipeline.

On February 9, 1990 a significant agreement (New Momentum) was initiated between Northern Arizona University and the Navajo Nation. This compact is designed to assist with tribal economic development and to improve Navajo education achievement from elementary through postsecondary levels. Two of the main ingredients of this agreement are: (1) the effort to enhance the faculty of the Navajo Community College, and (2) utilize the faculty at Northern Arizona University to advance the educational and economic development of this tribal community.

This agreement between the university and the Navajo Nation is an indication of an ever increasing role that colleges and universities are playing in the future development of Indian communities. As college and university faculty take part in this important role, one important question emerges: if college and university professors are to perform a greater function in the development of Indian communities, how many of these faculty will be Indian? In order to fully address this question we must ask an even more basic question. What do we actually know about the Indians who serve as faculty in our nation's colleges and universities? Presently there is insufficient literature on the participation of Indian faculty within the American professoriate. Even recent studies completed on the condition of the American professoriate make no reference to Indians who serve as part of this assembly. Illustrating this point is a 1987 special report, *The Academic Life: Small Worlds, Different Worlds* by the noted scholar on the subject of higher education, Burton Clark. The report summarizes the condition of the American professoriate and provides a unique and detailed insight into the world of the American professoriate. However, this important work did not enlighten its readers on the condition of Indian faculty. In reference to professors of color, Clark (1987) stated, "We largely ignored the play of social background in the lives of American academics, subordinating stratification issues posed by students of class and race . . ." (p. 280).

Additional recent works have taken the same approach on the subject of minority professors. In their recent work, *Prospects for Faculty In The Arts and Sciences.* William G. Bowen and Julie Ann Sosa (1989) stated ". . . to have included cross-tabulations by gender and race would have produced an overwhelming mass of statistics concerning subjects that deserve separate and intensive analysis. . ." (p.9). The landmark study published by Bowen and Schuster (1986), *The American Professors: A National Resource Imperiled*, devoted two and one-half pages to the issue of Black faculty. Regarding other racial groups the authors stated, "We did not address issues related specifically to other under-represented ethnic minorities. . ." (pp. 152–153). In other words these major research efforts, for one reason or another, also chose not to embrace Indian faculty issues.

The *Almanac of Higher Education*, produced by the Chronicle of Higher Education for 1989–90, also made no mention of Indian faculty but does provide a summary of the total American professoriate for 1987 as follows: There were some 824,700 full-time, part-time and temporary faculty members in 3,587 public and private institutions of higher education. The proportion of these faculty with tenure was 68.9 percent in public and 54.7 percent at private institutions. The average income was $37,903 at public four-year institutions and $35,747 at private four-year institutions. There were 991,339 bachelors, 289,557 masters, and 34,120 doctoral degrees conferred. The lack of descriptive statistics for Indian faculty indicates a significant limitation of the data and confirms that Indians remain an unknown quantity in the American professoriate.

This article presents, from the data available, a descriptive analysis of the pathway to the professoriate for American Indians. The statistics for this description of the Indian educational pipeline were generated from the National Center for Education Statistics. Digest of Educational Statistics (1990), and a report by Thurgood and Coyle, entitled "Summary Report 1987: Doctorate Recipients from United States Universities."

Education Pipeline

The educational pipeline for Indians, as with all children, begins with 100 percent entering first grade; however, it is estimated that only 51 percent of Indian students complete high school, 17 percent enter college, 4 percent enter graduate school and only 2 percent complete graduate school (Astin, 1982). The number of Indian students currently in school forms the pool of possible Indian professors for the future. It stands to reason that the number of Indian faculty in the professoriate is directly related to the success Indians have throughout the educational pipeline.

While it is not within the purview of this article to present a comprehensive analysis of the current educational pipeline, presentation of recent statistics will provide some enlightenment on the subject of the American Indian professoriate. The number of Indian students who are participating at the upper division levels in colleges and universities, along with the current number of Indian faculty, can provide some approximation of the number of possible Indian professors that may exist in the future.

Undergraduate Enrollment and Degree Attainment

The number of Indians who enter college has been steadily increasing. In 1976 there were 76,110 students compared to 92,500 students in 1988. This represents a difference of some 16,400 students in a twelve year period as indicated in Table 1.

However, in 1984, college enrollment for Indian students decreased from 87,700 students in 1982 to 83,600 students in 1984; a loss of 4,100 students.

The most recent data, however, indicate that Indian student enrollment increased in 1986 to 90,100 students and again in 1988 to 92,500 students.

Table 1
Total Enrollment in Higher Education (number in thousands)

American Indian	1976	1978	1980	1982	1984	1986	1988
Enrollment	76.1	77.9	83.9	87.7	83.6	90.1	92.5

The basis for this decline remains unknown since research on this phenomena is apparently non-existent. An analysis of federal support for programs and individuals during years of decline may reveal a cause and effect situation.

Two-Year Enrollment

The number of Indian students enrolled at two-year colleges increased by 9,200 from 1976 to 1988. However, the same decrease that was reported previously for the general enrollment of Indian students also existed for those at the two-year level as demonstrated by the decrease of 3,600 Indian students from 1982 to 1984 as illustrated in Table 2.

Table 2
Two-Year College Enrollment (number in thousands)

American Indian	1976	1978	1980	1982	1984	1986	1988
Enrollment	41.2	43.1	47.0	49.1	45.5	50.5	50.4

The most recent statistics demonstrate that approximately one-half (50,400) of all Indian students enrolled at the undergraduate level in 1988 were enrolled in two-year or community colleges.

The Two-Year Degrees

The two-year degree is the most prevalent degree awarded to Indian students. In 1986 there were a total of 3,196 associate degrees awarded to Indian students of which 1,263 went to men and 1,933 went to women (see Table 3 for total degrees).

The six most favored fields of study selected by Indian students at the two-year college level included liberal/general studies, business and management, health, engineering, art and education. The fields of study are presented in Table 3.

Since 1987 Indian women have outnumbered men in receiving the associate degree. The field of study selected most frequently was business and management. Indian men selected liberal/general studies most often as their number one choice of major field of study.

Table 3
Associate Degrees Conferred by Sex, Top Five Major Fields of Study and Total Number of American Indian Students, All Fields

Major Field of Study	Total	Men	Women
All Fields	3,196	1,263	1,933
Liberal/General Studies	813	351	462
Business/Management	811	203	608
Health Professions	403	51	352
Engineering Technologies	332	298	34
Visual/Performing Arts	175	55	120
Education	134	33	101

Four-Year Enrollment

The number of Indian students enrolled in four-year colleges (both public and private) has fluctuated slightly over the years from 1976 to 1988. However, this 12 year period has recorded an enrollment increase of Indian students in both public and private schools.

The increase in the number of Indian students enrolled in four-year colleges is comparable to the sluggish growth in the number of college students in general, except for Black enrollment which actually dropped during the period 1978 to 1988.

There was a slight drop in the number of Indian students in public institutions in 1978 and 1984. Private schools experienced a slight drop in Indian student enrollment in 1982 and 1986 as shown in Table 4.

Table 4
American Indian Four-Year College Enrollments by Type of Institution

Enrollment/Type of Institution	1976	1978	1980	1982	1984	1986	1988
Public	28.2	27.2	29.0	30.9	30.1	31.7	33.3
Private	6.8	7.6	7.9	7.6	7.9	7.8	8.8
Total	35.0	43.8	36.9	38.5	38.0	39.5	42.1

Bachelors Degrees

Overall, the number of bachelors degrees granted to Indian students increased from 1976 to 1984; however, 1978 and 1986 showed a decrease. The difference of 645 degrees awarded between 1976 and 1986 represents a small increase for an eight year span. The number of Indian woman receiving a bachelors degree outnumbered Indian men between 1980 and 1986 as revealed in Table 5.

Table 5
American Indian Bachelor's (number of degrees)

Number of Degrees	1976	1978	1980	1984	1986
American IndianWomen	1,522	1,674	1,893	2,248	2,152
American Indian Men	1,804	1,736	1,700	1,998	1,819
Total	3,326	3,410	3,593	4,246	3,971

Of special note is the decline of bachelors degrees exhibited in the data for the year 1986. This decline comes at a time when both Indian student high school and college enrollments were increasing.

A sample of the fields of study most frequently selected by Indian students is shown in Table 6.

Table 6
Bachelor's Degrees Conferred by Sex, Top Six Fields of Study and Total Number of American Indian Students, All Fields

Major Field of Study	Total	Women	Men
All Fields	3,971	2,152	1,819
Business/Management	783	383	400
Social Science	464	249	215
Education	452	328	124
Health Professions	274	228	46
Engineering	214	30	184
Psychology	186	212	65

There is no known long-term study on the selection of majors by Indian students; consequently, it is impossible to compare changes or trends in selection of academic majors. Nevertheless we can observe from the data presented for the year 1986 that the selection of major fields of study are identical to students in the general population who had selected business and management, social science, and health professions, in that sequence.

Graduate Enrollment and Degree Attainment

The number of Indian students who chose to pursue a graduate degree since 1971 has only slightly increased. An examination of the graduate enrollment data between 1976 and 1988 indicates a total increase of 500 Indian students as depicted in Table 7. Graduate enrollment decreased in the years 1978 and 1984. These two decreases amounted to a total of 800 Indian graduate students; a loss which is irreplaceable to Indian communities. The comparison of women to men in terms of graduate enrollment demonstrates that women have outnumbered men in enrollment since 1980 and that the number of men has either decreased or remained at the same level since 1978.

Table 7
Graduate Enrollment by Sex (number in thousands)

Graduate Enrollment	1976	1978	1980	1982	1984	1986	1988
Women	2.4	2.4	2.7	2.9	2.6	3.2	3.3
Men	2.7	2.5	2.5	2.5	2.2	2.3	2.3
Total	5.1	4.9	5.2	5.4	4.8	5.5	5.6

Masters Degrees

The number of Indian students receiving masters degrees during the period 1976 to 1986 demonstrated a steady growth until 1986 when the number decreased by 152.

In 1976 Indian students received a total of 967 degrees compared to 1,104 in 1986, a total increase of 137 degrees. Indian women have outpaced Indian men in achieving a masters degree since 1978, with a total of 191 more degrees received during the period 1978 to 1988. The decrease of 152 masters degrees in 1988 mentioned previously had an impact of representing 66 fewer degrees for Indian men and 86 fewer degrees for women than were reported previously in 1984. This decrease assuredly reduces the potential number of Indian doctoral prospects for the future. Because of the small number of Indian students in the masters degree pool, any decrease can have a dramatic consequence on the number of Indians who may later enter the professoriate.

Table 8
Master's Degrees Conferred by Sex

Number of Degrees and Sex	1976	1978	1980	1984	1986
American Indian Women	446	504	533	673	587
American Indian Men	521	495	501	583	517
Total	967	999	1,034	1,256	1,104

An analysis of data on major fields of study for 1986 indicates the most prevalent field chosen by Indian students for their masters degree was that of education. Education was the first choice as the field of study with Indian women receiving 256 masters degrees compared to only 120 for Indian men; or a ratio greater than two-to-one as shown in Table 9.

The top two choices for major fields of study selected by Indian students, Education and Business Management, are the same choices selected by the general population of students at the masters degree level. Table 9 includes the major fields of study.

Table 9
Master's Degrees Conferred by Sex, Top Six Fields of Study and Total Number of American Indian Students in All Fields

Major Field of Study	Total	Women	Men
All Fields	1,104	587	517
Education	376	256	120
Business and Management	170	58	112
Public Affairs	135	83	52
Health Professions	62	50	12
Visual/Performing Arts	47	23	24
Engineering	39	6	33

Doctoral Degrees

The doctorate as a degree has received the most attention in regard to predicting future minority faculty members and is sometimes referred to as the union card for academia (Page, 1990).

The number of Indians awarded the doctorate increased during the period 1976 to 1980 but then declined in both 1984 and 1986 as indicated in Table 10.

Table 10
Doctorate Degrees Conferred by Sex

Year and Sex	1976	1978	1980	1984	1986
American Indian Women	28	35	35	55	46
American Indian Men	67	69	95	64	58
Total	95	104	130	119	104

In the years 1976 and 1978, Indian men outnumbered Indian women two-to-one in receiving the doctorate, and in 1980, almost three-to-one. In 1984 the number of Indian men receiving the doctorate degree decreased by 31 from 1980 and decreased again in 1986 by six from 1984. This represents a loss of 37 doctorates from the number achieved in 1980. The number of Indian women receiving the doctorate degree increased slightly from 1976 to 1984 then decreased along with the Indian men in 1984.

The gap between Indian men and women is closing as the number of men receiving the doctorate diminishes and the number of women receiving the degree increases. The difference in 1980 was 60 doctoral degrees compared to only 12 in 1986.

Education was the field of study most often selected by Indian students for the doctorate. In 1986 almost 50 percent of all doctorates were awarded in the field of education. The top six fields of study selected by Indian students are listed in Table 11 with engineering, health professions and physical sciences equally selected in the sixth position.

Table 11
Doctorate Degrees Conferred by Sex, Top Six Fields of Study,
and Total Degrees Awarded for 1986–87

Major Field and Sex	Total	Women	Men
All Fields	104	46	58
Education	49	24	25
Psychology	16	10	6
Letters	6	3	3
Life Sciences	5	1	4
Social Sciences	4	2	2
Engineering	3	3	0
Health Professions	3	2	1
Physical Sciences	3	3	0

Professional Degrees

The educational pipeline of possible Indian professors also includes individuals who were awarded the professional degree. It is interesting to note that the number of professional degrees earned by Indians outnumbered the doctorates earned almost three-to-one as presented in Table 12.

Table 12
Professional Degrees Conferred by Field of Study and Sex

Major Fields of Study and Sex	Total	Women	Men
All Fields	304	121	183
Dentistry (D.D.S. or D.M.D.)	13	2	11
Medicine (M.D.)	66	30	36
Optometry (O.D.)	4	1	3
Osteopathic Medicine (D.O.)	13	3	10
Pharmacy (D.Phar.)	6	0	6
Podiatry (Pod.D., D.P., D.P.M.)	2	2	0
Veterinary Medicine (D.V.M.)	31	15	16
Chiropractic Medicine (D.C., D.C.M.)	4	1	3
Law, General (LL.B. or J.D.)	152	68	84
Theological (B.D., M.Div., Rabbi)	13	1	12

In 1986 Indian students received a total of 304 professional degrees; 183 men and 121 women. In attempting to explain this difference, it should be noted that the financial rewards from a professional degree far exceed that of the professoriate. The need and incentive in the Indian community has also given greater emphasis to professional careers rather than the professoriate.

Faculty

The following description of the American Indian professoriate is the result of assembling fragments of data from a report by Judy Fries entitled "The American Indian in Higher Education 1975–76 to 1984–85," and the U.S. Equal Employment Opportunity Commission (EEOC) reports for the years 1983 and 1985. Data on Indian faculty for other years remain unpublished.

In 1983 there was a total of 1,307 faculty identified as Indian; 962 men and 355 women. Faculty for this year were evenly distributed across the ranks, and 52 percent of the men had achieved tenure while only 35 percent of the women had achieved tenure.

In 1985 there were 1,735 faculty identified as Indian; 1,394 men and 341 women. The breakdown of tenure status for men and women was not reported in the data.

These statistics are too small in number to establish any trends, but we do observe a decrease in the number of Indian women in the faculty between 1983 and 1985, while the number of Indian men has increased as presented in Table 13.

Table 13
Faculty by Sex and Total for 1983 and 1985

American Indian Faculty by Year and Sex	Total	Women	Men
1983	1,307	355	962
1985	1,735	341	1,394

Tenure

The acquisition of tenure by Indian faculty is the last step in the educational process toward becoming a full-fledged member of the professoriate. Except for the few Indian men and women professors identified earlier as having achieved tenure, no other information was found in the literature regarding the number of Indian faculty who have been granted tenure. Tenure in higher education is intended to insure freedom in teaching and research as well as providing economic security. Tenure is one of the most important concerns pertaining to the production of Indian professors, for without achieving tenure Indian faculty either leave the profession or remain at its lower ranks. Non-tenure for many minority professors has created a "revolving door" in which minority faculty are forced to leave an institution only to seek tenure at another (Blackwell, 1988, p. 426). The most important function of any junior faculty member in the attempt to gain tenure is to conduct research and publish the findings (Swinn & Witt, 1982, p. 1242). However, the research produced by many Indian scholars on such subjects as tribal management, economic development, American Indian rights or American Indian history, may not be viewed as relevant or scholarly by some non-Indian faculty members and can prevent the promotion to tenured positions.

In addition to regular teaching, research and publication responsibilities necessary to gain tenure, Indian professors are also expected by their institutions to be counselors, financial aid representatives, and advocates for Indian students. They must also sit on various institutional committees and attend meetings to provide Indian input for the institution. Such duties take valuable time away from research and publication, the charge most important to earning tenure (Blackwell, 1988, p. 428). Indian professors are constantly confronted with the expectations of public service that includes conducting research for tribal communities or governments, assisting with proposal writing, representing the community at meetings, or serving as tribal council members or non-profit board members. These tasks also take time away from research and publication efforts.

American Indian Values

Many Indian faculty who attempt to join the professoriate are confronted by economic and social hardships. Indians continue to be one of the most impoverished minority groups in this country and given this situation, the likelihood of ever reaching the professional status of a college or university professor is almost insurmountable.

Further, the value conflict between American Indians and the mainstream culture only serves to make the aspiration of Indians who wish to join the professoriate that much more difficult. Indian values are often in direct conflict with the established process of becoming a full-fledged member of the professoriate. For example, the social value and preeminent goal in life for many American Indians is the survival of the Indian people (Forbes, 1973, p. 205). This value conflicts with the educational values of mainstream society, in that this Indian value requires a total life commitment to one's community. On the other hand, the educational value of mainstream society is enhanced when one excels as an individual, who, for example, has become the top academic achiever in the class. The mainstream educational system is established on this individualistic and competitive premise, and therefore, structurally may not be suited for Indian academic success.

In order to reduce many of these conflicts between individualistic versus collective values, tribal governments are taking control of their educational systems operating within tribal communities. Numerous tribal governments now operate their own K-12 schools and some have established tribally controlled colleges. There are currently 24 such tribal colleges, the majority of which are located on reservations (Carnegie Foundation for The Advancement of Teaching, 1989).

Conclusion

The educational research literature, except for a few fragmented efforts, has been silent on the number, location, rank, tenure status and other information relating to Indians in the professoriate. To pursue this issue more closely, an investigation of the limited data regarding the American Indian professoriate was examined along with other data that distinguishes the American Indian pipeline.

This inquiry was made because of the growing importance higher education and its faculty are performing in the educational and economic development of Indian communities. A further attempt was made to shed some light on how little is really known about the individuals who make up the American Indian professoriate and to hopefully provide a glimpse of what it takes to travel the pathway to the professoriate.

In reference to the pipeline, the number of Indian students graduating from high school and choosing to attend college at both the undergraduate and graduate level has been increasing since 1976, but recently (1988) the number of Indian students who graduate from institutions of higher education is, for some reason, decreasing.

Indian women have been making consistent gains in all categories in the pipeline of higher education, including outnumbering Indian men in enrollments (both graduate and undergraduate) and degrees earned at the associate, bachelor, masters levels. Additionally, if current trends continue, Indian women will lead men in the number of doctorates awarded. In reference to the professoriate, however, the feelings of triumph from these achievements made by Indian women in the pipeline are discounted by the lack of progress women are achieving within the professoriate. In fact, the minimal data released on this point indicate that Indian women are actually losing the few faculty positions they hold.

The literature provides no clues as to why Indian men are not achieving as well as women in academia. This point must be pursued in subsequent research.

On the subject of major fields of study in the pipeline, Indian students are selecting the same majors as the general population of students. In terms of more immediate importance to the American Indian professoriate, the fact that one-third of all masters degrees and almost one-half of all doctorates awarded to Indians are in the field of education tends to limit the pool of possible Indian professors to mainly one discipline. Otherwise these individuals must find employment, teach, and earn tenure out of their discipline, which is not an easy task.

In closing, it is actually possible for the 92,100 Indian undergraduate and 3,971 graduate students to complete their college careers without ever having the benefit of being taught by an Indian professor. It is also possible that as higher education plays an ever increasing role in the development of Indian communities, this undertaking will be realized without the involvement of any Indian faculty.

Further research is required in order to more fully understand the means necessary to cultivate additional Indian faculty and to better understand the contributions and potential contributions of Indians who are not serving in that capacity.

References

Astin, A. (1982). *Minorities in Higher Education*, San Franciso: Jossey Bass.

Blackwell. J. E. (1988). "Faculty Issues: The Impact on Minorities." *The Review of Higher Education*, 11(4), 428.

Bowen, H. & Schuster, J. (1986). *American Professors: A National Resource Imperiled* (pp.152–153). New York: Oxford University Press.

Bowen, W. & Sosa. J. (1989). *Prospects for Faculty in the Arts and Sciences* (p. 9). Princeton, NJ: Princeton University Press.

Carnegie Foundation for the Advancement of Teaching (1989). *Tribal Colleges: Shaping the Future of Native America*. Princeton, NJ.

Carnegie Foundation for the Advancement of Teaching (1987). *A Classification of Institutions of Higher Education*. Princeton, NJ.

Chronicle of Higher Education (1989). *The Almanac of Higher Education 1989–90* (pp. 3.5). Chicago and London: University of Chicago Press.

Clark, B. (1978). *The Academic Life: Small Worlds, Different Worlds* (p. 280). Princeton, NJ: The Carnegie Foundation for the Advancement of Teaching.

Forbes, J. (1973). "Teaching Native American Values and Cultures." In J. Banks, (Ed), *Teaching Ethnic Studies: Concepts and Strategies* (pp. 201–225). Washington, DC: National Council for the Social Studies.

Fries, J. E. (1987). "The American Indian in Higher Education, 1975–76 to 1984–85." Washington, DC: National Center for Educational Statistics, Office of Educational Research and Improvement. U.S. Department of Education.

National Center for Educational Statistics (1990). *Digest of Education Statistics*, Washington, DC.

Smith, P. (1990). *Killing the Spirit* (p. 108). New York: Viking Penguin.

Swinn, R. M. & Witt, J. C. (1982). "Survey on Ethnic Minority Faculty Recruitment and Retention." *American Psychologist, 30* (11), 1242.

Thurgood, D. & Coyle, S. (1989). "Summary Report 1987 Doctorate Recipients from United States Universities." Washington, DC: National Academy Press.

Wilson, R. & Melendez, S. (1987). Annual Status Report: Minorities in Higher Education. Washington, DC: American Council on Education.

William T. Cross, *Ph.D., is assistant professor of Communications Arts and Sciences at Michigan State University, East Lansing, Michigan. The research for this article was completed at the Graduate School of Education, Harvard University, while completing a fellowship in administration.*

Racism in Academia:
The Old Wolf Revisited

María de la Luz Reyes and John J. Halcón

In this article, the authors modify and use the metaphor of "a wolf in sheep's clothing" as the theme in uncovering racism aimed at Chicanos in higher education. The authors, who are new to the academic profession, as are many Chicanos in the field, discover that the old wolf, racism, is as active in academia as in their previous educational settings. In elementary and secondary schools the wolf's disguises include educational tracking, low expectations, and negative stereotypes. Chicanos who have overcome these obstacles and who are attempting to break into the faculties and administrations of U.S. higher education institutions are finding the wolf in a new wardrobe. The authors identify the various disguises used to hide racism by higher education faculties and administrations.

A Chicano candidate was being interviewed for a tenure-track faculty position. The small conference room, with a seating capacity of twelve, was filled beyond its limits. Extra chairs were brought in as faculty from various departments sat elbow to elbow. Just a week before, it had been impossible to round up four warm bodies to interview a White male candidate applying for another faculty position in the School of Education.

At the head of the table, in a dark pin-striped suit, sat the invited candidate. He smiled as he waited for another question. At the center of the table, an older Anglo professor leaned forward, brushed back his thinning white hair, adjusted his glasses and peered at the waiting candidate.

"Dr. Fuentes,[1] I see here in your vita that you have a bachelor's degree in Chicano Studies, a specialization in bilingual education, your publications deal mostly with minority issues, and you have been keynote speaker at two Chicano commencements."

"Yes, that's correct," replied Dr. Fuentes.

"Well, Dr. Fuentes, I have a problem with these things."

"What's the problem?" queried Dr. Fuentes.

"Frankly, I am concerned that if we hire you, you will be teaching separatism to our impressionable young administrators. . . . "

The blood rushed to the candidate's face, and the anger in his eyes was difficult to conceal. The audience grew silent.

* * *

As minorities, we know from personal experience that racism in education is vigorous and pointed. We realize that, in spite of bona fide college degrees, our credentials are challenged by pervasive racist attitudes, and our efforts toward full incorporation into academic positions in institutions of higher education (IHEs) are hampered by layers of academic stratification. We find that, even with earned Ph.D.s, the academic road is the beginning of another Sisyphean climb. If current patterns of minority hiring persist, the best we can expect is to occupy positions outside the mainstream ranks, those most peripheral to the hub of governance and power.

Not long ago, as graduate students, we believed that successful completion of our graduate programs would be our license to "play in the big leagues." In our naiveté, we assumed that attainment of our advanced degrees would mark the end to our "language problems," our experiences with educational tracking, low expectations, negative stereotyping, use of tests to denote our ranking and placement in the system, and a myriad of other institutional obstacles. In a sense, we assumed—or maybe hoped— that the frequent encounters with racism which we experienced in schools were confined to the lower echelons of the educational ladder. We believed that our Ph.D.s paved the way to an egalitarian status with mutual respect among professional colleagues, where the new rules of competition would be truly based on merit. We were wrong. Instead, we find that even in academia, we face the same racism under different conditions—the old wolf in new clothing.

The racism experienced by Chicanos in academia is not new. Chicano scholars have characterized it as "academic colonialism" (Arce, 1978; Ornelas, Ramirez & Padilla, 1975). Many Chicano writers blamed this form of racism for their inability to penetrate the elitist, White, male-dominated system which excluded them from full and significant participation (Arvizu, 1978; Candelaria, 1978; Casso & Roman, 1975; Valverde, 1975). But to those of us new to academe, the manifestations of racism at the professorial level appear new. This sense of newness may be attributed to the fact that the majority of racial incidents are generally associated with the experiences of minorities at elementary, secondary, and baccalaureate levels. The very idea that racism could exist among the *educated* elite is disconcerting to new academicians of color, and might come as a surprise to aspiring novices looking in from the outside.

In the early 1970s, some believed that there were only about one hundred Chicano PhD.s in the United States (C. de Baca, 1975). The most recent data indicate that full-time Hispanic faculty (including Cubans, Chicanos, Puerto Ricans, and South Americans) in higher education institutions as of fall 1983 numbered 7,356 (*Digest of Education Statistics 1985–86* and *1987*) There is no specific breakdown for Chicanos provided in these data, but the fact is clear that today we have more Hispanic academics than ever before.

From personal observations and from what we have learned through our interactions with other Hispanics in academe, we believe that for the first time there exists a noticeable number of over-qualified, under-employed Hispanic Ph.D.s, unable to gain access to faculty positions in IHEs. Ten to fifteen years ago we might not have been able to name ten Chicano Ph.D.s; today many of us can easily name six to ten Hispanic Ph.D.s unable to obtain academic positions. This observation is at once ironic and paradoxical: we are considered the elite and best-educated members of a minority community that is still struggling desperately to graduate its members from high school, and yet, rather than finding a payoff at the end of the educational tunnel, we find a dark path draped in full academic regalia—for aspiring Chicano academics, this is indeed a sobering and humbling reality.

As Chicano academics, we have personally met or have come to know about a large number of Chicano Ph.D.s, through a loose, informal network across the country. This network provides information about the experiences of other Chicano academicians from which we have collected examples of racism in IHEs. This essay is an attempt on the part of two Chicanos to describe incidents of racism in IHEs that we, and other Chicano colleagues, have experienced.

Definition of Racism

Dube's (1985) definition of racism provides a useful framework for our discussion of racism in academia. He describes three types of racism: overt, covert, and reactive. This paper will focus on the overt and covert forms found in academia. According to Dube, overt racism is based on the notion that some races are inherently superior to others. It is the most easily identified form, "open and up-front" (p. 88), and publicly displayed like that of the Ku Klux Klan, for example. In contrast, covert racism stems from a more subtle philosophy, "at times taking the form of superior virtue . . . believed to be common only to virtuous 'races'" (p. 88). Although not easy to identify, it has negative consequences for minorities.

In our experiences within educational systems, we find that examples of these two types of racism occur regularly. In some cases, long and well-established patterns of behavior are so entrenched that they function as standard operating procedures. In the following pages we will discuss manifestations of these types of racism primarily as they affect Chicano academics.

Overt Racism

Overt racism at IHEs usually occurs in isolated events such as the interview described at the beginning of this article. Although "open and up-front," overt racism is usually not exhibited publicly beyond the campus. It is most common in situations where minorities are being considered for positions occupied primarily by Whites, as in the case of minorities vying for tenure-track faculty positions at predominantly White colleges and universities.

A recent series of incidents comes to mind. Five Chicano Ph.D.s applied for various faculty positions at a southwestern college located in a community with a 40 percent Chicano constituency. Over the course of a year and a half, they each surfaced as finalists and were interviewed for tenure-track positions. The strong pool of Chicano candidates resulted from active recruitment efforts by Chicano faculty who wanted to improve academic opportunities for other Chicanos.

Some faculty and school deans were surprised to learn that five Chicano applicants had been invited to interview, especially since the dean of arts and sciences had reported that previous faculty recruitment efforts had yielded "no qualified minorities." Although the number of candidates seemed significant compared to previous searches, it was small when compared to the twenty-five to thirty-five White candidates interviewed during the same period. Chicano candidates drew a large number of faculty spectators to their interviews, while non-minority applicants went virtually unnoticed—even in the departments to which they had applied. On at least two occasions, one department chair in education reported at a faculty meeting that only two faculty members had attended the interviews for the math and science education candidates (two White males). Given the predominance of White faculty across the campus, the seemingly frequent and obvious presence of Chicanos within a relatively short span of time prompted one school dean to remark, "What do they think this is, Taco University?" That racial slur resurfaced each time another Chicano was to be interviewed.

Optimistically, one might believe that the faculty came to meet and listen to the candidate, but that was not the case. Instead, many appeared to attend the interviews chiefly to find fault with the candidate or to offer their reasons for not hiring the candidate. In one case some faculty members came with copies of previously circulated petitions, attempting to halt the search on the grounds that they did not agree with the job description used in the national search. No formal objection to the job description had been made before the search committee let it be known that a Chicano had emerged as the top candidate.

The tragedy was that those overt racist tactics were successful—none of the five Chicanos was hired. According to personal accounts from the candidates in subsequent communications, they were told they were rejected on the basis of "inexperience," "lack of sufficient qualifications," or "incompatibility" with the faculty in the departments in which they had applied. Four of the five positions were left vacant, and in the fifth, a White male who had served as an adjunct instructor was hired on a temporary basis. A year later, one of the Chicano applicants was hired, but only after a series of confrontations between minority faculty and the administration as well as pressure from Chicano and Black students and from members of the Hispanic community.

Covert Racism

Covert racism is the most pervasive form of racism in higher education. Because of its elusive nature, however, covert racism is ignored by those who have never experienced it, and denied by those who contribute to it. As discussed previously, our interactions with other Chicanos in academe have allowed us to compile typical examples of covert racism in higher education. We have organized those examples under the following categories: tokenism, the type-casting syndrome, the one-minority-per pot-syndrome, the brown-on-brown research taboo, and the hairsplitting concept. Below we discuss each category, examining closely the implications for Chicano academics.

Tokenism. The civil rights movement of the 1960s ushered the way for Executive Order 11246, the federal blueprint for affirmative action (Holmes, 1975). This Department of Labor regulation required that all federal contractors and subcontractors take affirmative action in all employment activity, assuring equal opportunity to job applicants and barring discrimination on the basis of "race, color, religion, sex, or national origin." For Hispanics, this order opened up new opportunities. They found themselves appointed to important positions in both private and public agencies. During the same period, fellowships to pursue graduate degrees at universities across the country, especially in education, became available primarily through the Ford Foundation and Title VII of the Elementary and Secondary Education Act. Those funding sources and others like them allowed a larger number of Hispanics, who might not otherwise have afforded it, to pursue higher education.

In the mid-1970s, when minority quota systems were being implemented in many nonacademic agencies, the general public was left with the impression that Chicano or minority presence in professional or academic positions was due to affirmative action, rather than to individual qualifications or merit. But that impression was inaccurate. Generally, IHEs responded to the affirmative action guidelines with token positions for only a handful of minority scholars in nonacademic and/or "soft" money programs. For example, many Blacks and Hispanics were hired as directors for programs such as Upward Bound, Talent Search, and Equal Opportunity Programs (EOP) (Valverde, 1975). Other minority faculty were hired for bilingual programs and ethnic studies programs, but affirmative action hires did not commonly extend to tenure-track faculty positions. The new presence of minorities on college campuses, however, which occurred during the period when attention to affirmative action regulations was at its peak, left all minority professionals and academics with a legacy of tokenism—a stigma that has been difficult to dispel.

Actual gains in academic faculty positions due to affirmative action regulations could not have been anything but minuscule. As early as 1975, Peter Holmes, then Director of the Civil Rights Commission, reported at the National Institute on Access to Higher Education for the Mexican American that the spirit of the affirmative action regulations was based on the notion of an "availability pool." This concept was interpreted such that the regulations applied *only* in situations where it could be proven that there were significant numbers of available minorities in the respective employment areas. Since the number of Hispanics with Ph.D.s constituted less than one percent of available persons in many academic fields at that time (*Minorities in Higher Education*, 1984), Holmes believed it was impossible for higher education institutions to comply with the regulations (see also "Discrimination in Higher Education," 1975). The University of California at Berkeley, for example, negotiated an affirmative action plan with the former Department of Health, Education and Welfare, and mutually identified *only three* departments where projected goals for minority hiring were required under affirmative action regulations (Holmes, 1975).

Despite the minimal gains for minorities in tenure-track positions, we continue to be plagued with the assumption that we are mere tokens and have been hired without the appropriate credentials, experience, or qualifications. The legacy of tokenism and its negative implications has led to a current situation, in which unspoken pressure is put on minority academics to continually prove that they are as good as White academics. Tokenism has also had the effect of reducing minority-occupied positions to a subordinate status, providing an easy excuse to ignore or minimize our presence and our efforts.

The Typecasting Syndrome. A by-product of tokenism is the typecasting syndrome. This is an underlying attitude or belief that Hispanics can only, or should only, occupy minority-related positions, such as those in Bilingual Education, Chicano Studies, foreign languages (Spanish), or student support services such as EOP.

An actual case of this typecasting syndrome occurred recently to a Chicana colleague during the negotiation of her contract with a state university on the West Cost. Two tenure-track positions were announced at the university where she applied for a faculty position. One position was in the teacher education program with a rank of associate professor, and the other position was in the bilingual education program at the assistant professor level. Although her qualifications and experience were equally strong in both areas, she applied for the teacher education position, because she had recently been promoted to associate level and because she recognized the need for integrating minority scholars into the mainstream programs. Much to her surprise, she received an invitation to interview for the teacher education and the bilingual position, without having applied for the latter.

When the interviews were completed, she was informed that she was the top candidate for both positions and that the university would make her an offer. A couple of weeks later, the dean called to offer her the bilingual position because "they believed that it was her main area of expertise" and that it was "where she would be most happy." She was quite aware that the position in teacher education meant breaking through an all-White faculty, while the position in bilingual education would have confined all Hispanics to the same unit. As a result, she refused the offer for the bilingual position, reminding the dean that she had not applied for it, and that since she was the top candidate in both positions, she should be allowed to select the position she preferred.

The negotiations slowed as she was informed of a "new policy" requiring candidates to "update" all college transcripts, provide proof of earned doctorate degree, and proof of good teaching evaluations from previously taught classes. She learned from the other Chicanos at the university that the "new" requirements were familiar tactics intended to discourage her from accepting the position. It took the threat of legal action to convince the Dean to offer her the associate level position in teacher education.

Arce (1978) and Olivas (1986) argue that this practice of specialized minority hiring for minority slots "is a more formal co-optation of Hispanic concerns . . . which relieves the institution of the need to integrate throughout their ranks" (Olivas, 1986, p. 14). The worst part for the few Chicanos in academia is that the typecasting syndrome segregates them in ethnically related professions. Arciniega and Morey (1985), for example, reported that in 1983 only 3.5 percent of the California State University faculty were Hispanic, and that the majority of those were in ethnic studies departments.

Another negative consequence of the typecasting syndrome is that often the only avenues for Hispanic promotion are in ethnically related fields. A recent report entitled, "The Status of Chicanos/Latinos at the University of California" (Gordon, 1988) bears this out. A coalition of Hispanic faculty members from the U.C. system complained in the report that there were only three Chicanos/Latinos in high-level academic administrative positions, and they reported that "there are no, repeat no, Chicano or Latino academic deans or department heads outside of the ethnic or Chicano Studies" (Fields, 1988, p. A17). If this is the case at the University of California system, in a state with 6.6 million Hispanics (Fields, 1988), it is not likely that Hispanic academics are faring much better in other states where their numbers are smaller.

Typecasting is indeed pervasive, and is simply another form of stereotyping that prevents Chicanos from becoming fully integrated into all areas of academia. The larger social consequences of confining minorities to the outer fringes of academia includes severely limiting White students' access to ethnically diverse points of view—resulting in a shallow education from a monocular perspective (Fishman, 1975). In an increasingly pluralistic society, this practice has the added effect of depriving White students of social skills necessary for mutual respect and co-existence with other cultural groups. The alarming increase in racial incidence involving White college students against minorities (Farrell, 1988a, b, c, d; McCurdy, 1988; Williams, 1987) is ample evidence of this deprivation.

The "One-minority-per-pot" Syndrome. Many colleges and universities operate under an unwritten quota system that manifests itself as reluctance to hire more than one minority faculty member per department. We refer to this practice as the "one-minority-per-pot" syndrome. Two or three minority faculty may be hired for ethnic studies, bilingual education, or foreign languages, but too often, departments of education, sociology, history, English, or psychology, for example, seldom hire more than one minority per department.

We believe that implicit in this practice is a deep-seated belief that minorities are not as qualified as non-minorities. This conviction stems from an unspoken fear that the presence of more than one minority faculty member in a mainstream, traditional department might reduce the department's academic reputation. We have participated in faculty meetings in which the subject of additional faculty has been discussed. In these meetings, the suggestion that minority candidates be considered has generally evoked pat responses along these lines: "We don't want to hire anyone because of their ethnicity, we want *fully qualified* candidates" (see Blum 1988a; Heller 1988), or "this isn't a position for bilingual education," or "We hired a minority last year." Typically, consideration of minority candidates occurs only when there is pressure applied to diversify the faculty.

Scott Heller (1988) offers evidence of the deeply ingrained belief among faculty that hiring minorities reduces the caliber of the faculty already on board. In one college president's attempt to discover the reasons for the institution's inability to hire Black faculty, several faculty members revealed their reservations in private interviews when they "questioned whether affirmative action hiring wasn't tantamount to lowering academic standards" (p. A16). In a seeming contradiction, these same faculty members welcomed a pool of candidates that included minorities. Apparently, an applicant pool that includes minorities is considered by White faculty as evidence of a "good faith effort" in hiring and integrating minorities—even if minorities are not ultimately hired.

The "one-minority-per-pot" concept applies to administrators as well as faculty. Recently, a Chicano colleague of ours applied for an associate deanship at his institution. Prior to completing his application, he was forewarned by the academic vice president that he was not likely to be considered for this position. According to our colleague, the vice president told him that "there were already three other Chicano administrators at the college." Recognizing the futility of his effort, the candidate withdrew his name from consideration.

Another familiar theme closely associated with the "one-minority-per-pot" syndrome is the practice of requiring additional documentation from minorities above and beyond the standard curriculum vitae, transcripts, and letters of recommendation. For example, it is not uncommon for minorities to be required to submit copies of their dissertations, evaluations of their teaching, bibliographies from their published papers, and copies of funded proposals. Since it is usually minorities who are singled out to provide additional documentation and the requests are usually made *after* they have become top candidates, there is adequate ground for suspecting that covert racism is at work. The intent of this tactic is to discourage minority candidates from accepting faculty positions. Both points were illustrated previously in the case of our Chicana colleague who was offered a position for which she had not applied. For minority academics, this particular practice has the simultaneous effect of publicly demeaning their professional reputations while chipping away at their self-esteem.

Additionally, the limitation on minority hiring that is part of the "one-minority-per-pot" syndrome has the effect of restricting the career goals and aspirations of Hispanics and other minority faculty. We believe that the lack of minority faculty in academic departments today (Blum, 1988a, b; Fields, 1988; *Higher Education Research Institute,* 1982; Harvey, 1987; *Minorities and Strategic Planning at the University of Colorado,* 1987) is more likely the result of this unwritten quota system than it is of the lack of available candidates in some hypothetical pool.

The "Brown-on-Brown" Research Taboo. As Hispanic academics, our research interests often stem from a recognition that we have endured racial discrimination and from a compelling need to lend a dimension of authenticity to the prevailing theories about our communities. Said another way, we want to provide our own perspectives regarding prevailing negative assumptions about our values, culture, and language. This explains our interest in such topics as dropouts, bilingual education, second-language literacy, Chicano literature, and the education of minority students. Our interest in these research areas is also motivated by a concern for assisting our community in improving its second-rate status in the educational, economic, and political arenas. Tired of reading about ourselves in the social science literature written by non-minorities, we want to speak for ourselves, to define, label, describe, and interpret our own condition from the "inside out." We feel strongly about providing a balance to the existing literature and research on Chicanos.

Our efforts, like those of other minority scholars, often meet with covert disapproval by our White colleagues, who judge the quality and validity of our scholarly work, our research, and our publications (Blum, 1988a, b). Quite often, our research interests are dismissed as minor or self-serving. The general perception is that minority-related topics do not constitute academic scholarship—as was the case in the incident described in the introduction—and that they are inappropriate and narrow in scope. The assumption is that minority researchers cannot be objective in their analyses of those problems which are so close to their life experiences. In this regard we have to agree with Kushner and Norris (1980–1981) who suggest that the devaluing of minority research interests deprives minorities of the "dignity of contributing to theorizing about their worlds" (quoted in Lather, 1986, p. 264).

The perception that "brown-on-brown" research is somehow not valuable pervades academic circles. This paternal attitude from a White, male-dominated profession is a double standard that lends full credibility to Whites' conducting research on White populations, but discredits minority academics' research on minority issues. White-on-White research is accorded legitimacy, but "brown-on-brown" research is questioned and challenged at the same time that many White social scientists are establishing their professional careers as experts on minority issues.

Many minorities believe that another objection to "brown-on-brown" research is that the traditional Euro-centric perspective used to evaluate their scholarship puts nontraditional research at a disadvantage because predominantly White male academics lack the appropriate cultural perspectives from which to judge its real merit (O'Neale in Blum, 1988a; Wilson in Blum 1988b). The problem of judging minority scholarship may also be exacerbated by the high concentration of minority academics in education, the arts, and the humanities, "where the evaluation of research is more subjective than in such fields as engineering or the natural sciences" (Wilson in Blum, 1988b, p. A17).

Referring to women in academia who share experiences similar to those of ethnic minorities, especially regarding the devaluing of their research, Simeone (1987) states:

> While the system employs the rhetoric of merit, its determination is far from objective. Even if there were agreement on the most important criteria, for example, agreement on means of assessment and actual performance would be difficult to reach. The process which is constructed to sort out the mediocre and the merely good at each level may be sorting factors other than merit, as well. Some of these may include political or social affiliations, intellectual perspective, or perceived congeniality. (p. 28).

The devaluing of minority research in promotion and tenure decisions is difficult to prove. Yet many Hispanics, Blacks and Native Americans cite cases from their own experiences, or that of their colleagues, as examples of unfair evaluation of their research during promotion and tenure reviews (see Blum, 1988b, and Fields, 1988). A recent example is that of a Black woman in the English Department at Emory University, who lost a three-year battle to overturn her denial of tenure (Blum, 1988a). She was the only Black woman in the department, and her expertise was in Black literature. The scholar in question and her supporters claim that the decision to deny her tenure was based on institutional racism that devalues scholarship by minorities on ethnically related subjects. On the other hand, both the committee on tenure who reviewed her case and university administrators claim that the decision was based on "her weakness as a scholar" (p. A15). Several students and faculty who were interviewed did not discount racism as a factor. A member of the committee stated, "it's a kind of covert or unconscious racism deflected into the belief that a certain specialty or a certain journal that is outside of established fields is not good enough" (Baker in Blum, 1988a, p. A17).

The devaluing of "brown-on-brown" research stems from the values undergirding institutions of higher education, which reflect culturally monolithic systems. These systems judge the quality of scholarship from the normative perspective of their own cultural group. As a result, the work of those individuals who depart from those standards is deemed inferior (Ramirez, 1988). The obvious consequence, then, of the tenure and promotion processes based on White males' definition of research and scholarship is that few minorities make the grade.

The Hairsplitting Concept. This last type of covert racism is rather elusive, but it is no less real. We describe the hairsplitting concept as a potpourri of trivial technicalities, or subjective judgment calls, which prevent minorities from being hired or promoted. When minorities have met all the academic criteria, jumped the hurdles, and skipped through all the specified hoops, the final decision is based on highly subjective and arbitrary points. At times, these decisions border on paternalism, with White males defining and deciding what is best for us, as in the case cited earlier of the Chicano professor being told in which department she would be most happy. At times minority candidates are second-guessed and eliminated, not on the basis of their qualifications, but on the personal opinions of the decision makers (Heller, 1988). A minority candidate, for example, might not get a position because the committee might assume that she or he would not be happy in a predominantly White community (Wilson in Blum, 1988; Fields, 1988; Heller, 1988). Decisions that are publicly acclaimed as objective are, in fact, highly subjective. Politics, personality, and even intellectual orientation almost always color decisions and serve to exclude those who are different (Candelaria, 1978; Ramirez, 1988; Simeone, 1987).

Hairsplitting practices are dangerous because the exclusion of Chicanos is justified by minor, arbitrary, and inconsequential factors that prevent them from reaping the benefits of their education. What appears to be consistent in the application of hairsplitting practices is that often when White-dominated selection committees feel threatened by a minority candidate, they base their selection decision on an arbitrary, hairline difference favoring the White candidate. When IHEs use arbitrary hairsplitting practices as grounds for their final decision, the unspoken rule seem to be that it is better to support the candidate who best reflects the status quo.

Each of the above forms of covert racism has contributed to the current status of Chicanos in academia and in part, explains the dearth of minority academicians. We have discovered a painful truth: It is difficult to escape the tentacles of racism, which touched our earlier educational experiences. The sad reality is that the "old wolf" is still around, now dressed in token assumptions, the typecasting syndrome, the one-minority-per-pot syndrome, the brown-on-brown research taboo, and the hairsplitting tactics.

Some Responses to Racism

Chicanos, like other minority academics, find ways to cope with racism. In talking with other Chicanos, we have identified four prevalent responses to racism: give in, give up, move on, or fight back.

Chicanos in the "give in" group play the academic game at all costs. They yield easily to the demands to assimilate. In some cases, they attempt to divert themselves of all obvious cultural traits. At the same time, they work diligently at mainstreaming their research interests, and steer clear of minority-related issues. Individuals in this group might even deny racism, explaining the dearth of minority academics simply from a "pick-yourself-up-by-your-bootstraps" philosophy. They behave as if they were convinced that the key to success in academia is simply a matter of hard work and that politics, personal preferences, and subjectivity have little to do with merit. A few in this group succeed in infiltrating the system and blending well in their academic settings. Others give in completely, but despite their full conversion, they encounter rejection by those in the system who continue to perceive them as outsiders, or "tokens." Chicanos who deal with racism in this manner may feel alienated and out of touch with the Hispanic community at large. Indeed, their own Chicano community may have little respect for them and may perceive them as sell-outs.

Chicanos in the "give up" group are usually found in institutions and departments where displays of racism are overt. These Chicanos tend to struggle against academic racism at all costs. Most of their energies are used to combat injustices instead of pursuing scholarship. These individuals tend to become so demoralized that racism destroys both their spirit and their self-esteem. The lack of a support network to assist them to survive and succeed in such an academic environment makes it almost impossible to tolerate any direct or subtle attack.

These individuals soon experience "burnout" as they see the futility of their efforts to change the system. At times, the direct or underlying hostility and alienation that these individuals experience have a disabling effect that gradually leads to a self-fulfilling prophecy regarding their academic potential. Repeated invalidation of their work serves to convince them that their efforts are substandard and their work inferior. Instead of hanging on, they give up—becoming disillusioned or convinced that they "don't have what it takes" to be an academic; that academia is not suited to their ultimate priorities, or that they "don't need the hassles." These Chicanos may leave academia altogether, and they may not return.

Chicano academics who cope with institutionalized racism by moving on to greener pastures compose the "move on" group. Individuals in this group maintain a strong affiliation with their community and feel a strong sense of responsibility to improve the status of other Chicanos in the larger community. They neither assimilate easily, nor readily ascribe to mainstream perspectives. As a result of their strong cultural awareness and assertiveness, they may often be perceived by their White peers as "arrogant." These individuals recognize manifestations of racism in the academy and fully understand that as minority academics they are in "tenuous-track" positions. They are realists. And, although they clearly fight against racism, they learn how to "pick their fights," realizing that taking on every minority issue can render them totally ineffective. They carefully evaluate their situations, looking at such factors as the key players, their support networks, and the odds of succeeding in their institutions. When they recognize that the price of the struggle isn't worth their efforts *in that particular environment*, they move on. They do so instead of seriously jeopardizing their careers, damaging their self-esteem, and exhausting all their energies in futile struggles. Although few find the ideal university, many of these Chicanos eventually find the "best fit" for them.

Finally, Chicano academics in the "fight back" group respond in two ways, one of which is similar to the response of the "move on" group. That is, they fight back but recognize their limitations and the importance of succeeding in the system. They do so—not because institutions of higher education are perfect systems—but because they recognize that if institutional racism is to be eradicated, they must participate in the decision making arenas controlled by tenured faculty, and where the key decisions for admission and full incorporation are made. They understand that this must be done from the inside out. So they persevere. They learn to play the game, without compromising either their integrity or their ethnicity. They comply with the rules only insofar as issues related to scholarship will earn them tenure. They may temporarily limit their involvement with the Chicano community in order to attain tenure. Once they are tenured, however, many redirect their attention to minority concerns and minority-related research that will help improve the condition of their community. A characteristic of Chicanos in this group is an unwavering tenacity and resilience that enables them to continue their efforts even when they encounter stiff opposition. Chicanos in this group often join together to plan effective strategies for combating racism and demanding equity. Their fight against racism motivates them to surpass the limited expectations the dominant community has for them as minorities.

Another response of Chicanos in the "fight back" group is to exert every effort to prove the oppressor wrong, regardless of the consequences. These Chicanos often sacrifice their academic careers to effect a significant change that will pave the way for other Chicano academics. They are generally politically astute and know how to mobilize the minority community behind certain issues. They are often perceived as the martyrs and prophets of the community, who appear to be filled with a kind of reckless zeal to right injustices. As a result, they may pay the price of being excluded from academia altogether.

The different responses to racism that we have observed are often variations of the above four themes. For example, an individual may respond to racism in any of these four ways, depending on the specific circumstances. The most critical dividing line in these responses lies between the coping strategies that ultimately separate Chicano academics from their community and those that allow Chicanos to maintain close ties with their community.

Conclusions

Discriminatory policies and the manifestations of racism in educational institutions have changed very little over the years. In spite of the changing demographics that indicate a dramatic rise in the Hispanic populations, and in spite of the new focus on recruitment and retention of minorities by educational institutions, Chicano academics today are generally experiencing many of the same kinds of racial prejudices experienced by those who preceded them into the academy a generation ago. Forms of tokenism, typecasting, limitations on minority hiring, devaluing of Chicano research, and hairsplitting practices are prevalent manifestations of racism in academia. Each of these factors contributes to maintaining the small number of Chicano academics currently in IHEs, and to the inability of a growing number of Chicano Ph.D.s to break into the system. The latter are experiencing the disillusionment of being over-qualified, under-employed, or unemployed. They are in a Catch-22 situation: unable to get an academic job because they lack university teaching and publishing experience, and unable to acquire that experience because they cannot get an academic position. To our knowledge, no surveys have been conducted to determine the actual count, but we know that a good number of unemployed potential Chicano academics exist because the network is small, and we know many of them. This is a disturbing reality for members of a minority community who work hard to convince their youth that education is the great social equalizer that generally brings with it a guaranteed economic return.

How can we eliminate or reduce racism in academia? Eradicating institutional racism in academia will not be an easy task. Hispanic Ph.D.s (which includes Cubans, Chicanos, Puerto Ricans, and Central and South Americans) compose a mere 2.1 percent of all doctorate degrees (*Minorities in Higher Education*, 1987). Of those, Chicano academics in universities across the country represent an even smaller number. Further, we know from experience that unless the dominant majority recognizes the value of a culturally diverse professoriate, we cannot expect them to take the lead in eliminating precisely the kind of racism they tacitly condone.

On the other hand, we cannot change the system alone. Chicano academics will have to form coalitions and join forces with other Hispanic, Black, Native American, and Asian academics who share similar experiences. Together we must work at dispelling the myth of tokenism that surrounds minority hiring. We must press for an end to the typecasting syndrome, to the limit on minority hiring by certain departments, and to hairsplitting practices. We must promote instead the idea that departments should be rewarded when they can demonstrate diversity among their faculty, and at the same time, we must lobby and press for a reexamination of the criteria for review, promotion, and tenure, for a redefinition of scholarship, and for inclusion of so-called "minority journals" among those classified as premier journals.

Minority academics will have to work at convincing their institutions that minority faculty are the *key* to recruitment, retention, and promotion of other minorities, both students and faculty. They will have to press for *full incorporation* and *integration* into the various branches of the institution, not just in minority slots. Anything less than that will render them powerless to assist other minorities to move successfully through the academic hurdles. Without minority role models at all levels of the educational structure, but especially in the centers of power—the ranks of tenured professors—it will be difficult to convince young Hispanic, Black, and Native American students that they can benefit from higher levels of education.

As minority academics, we realize that we need an exceptional amount of ability, drive, dedication, and discipline to meet the requirements for academic advancement and the added demands of serving as role models for minority students. One way to compensate and to make allowances for this extra work is to exert pressure to have universities assign some weighted value to minority contributions of this type. We believe Valverde (1975) had a good idea in arguing that universities should give Chicanos (and other minorities) their "full measure by ascribing proportional value to such characteristics as language, ethnic perspective, cultural knowledge, diversity of ethnic mix in the network of people, and the power to attract other minority students into higher education" (p. 110).

To accomplish these goals, we will have to be each other's biggest fans; that is, we must seize and even create opportunities for publicly recognizing the qualifications and the contributions made by members of our own ethnic group and other minorities. We must go out of our way to promote minority scholars, to highlight their expertise, to disseminate minority publications among our non-minority colleagues, to suggest ways in which they can integrate minority perspectives into their classes and use books written by, or which include articles written by minority scholars. We must push for diversification of the curriculum.

We recognize that it will take courageous leadership among minority academics to effect changes in the current situation and that the burden of initiating those changes lies squarely on our shoulders. No one else has the vested interest that we have. No one else can do it for us. We must tackle it ourselves because it is obvious that non-minority academic leaders are ambivalent about the role of minorities in higher education. On one hand, they pay lip service to the diversification of faculty on their campuses, but on the other hand, they do nothing to bring that about. Once we fully understand this and once we understand how institutions have excluded us from full participation, we can join forces with other people of color, set priorities, and harness our energies to combat racism in academia. If we fail to do this, we will find ourselves a generation from now still facing the same "old wolf" . . . in yet another fleecy robe.

Note

1. In the tradition of ethnographic field work and because of politically sensitive settings for other minorities, pseudonyms for actual persons and institutions are used throughout the essay to protect their identities and to maintain confidentiality. Accounts are based on actual interviews (May, 1986). The incidents reported in this article were either experienced by us personally or were reported to us by others.

References

Arce, C. (1978). Chicano participation in academe: A case of academic colonialism. *Grito del Sol: A Chicano Quarterly, 3,* 75–104.

Arciniega, T., & Morey, A. I. (1985). *Hispanics and higher education: A CSU imperative.* Long Beach, CA: Office of the Chancellor.

Arvizu, S. F. (1978). Critical reflections and consciousness. *Grito del Sol: A Chicano Quarterly, 3,* 119–123.

Bayer, A. E. (1973). *Teaching faculty in academe: 1972–73.* American Council on Education Research Report 8(2). Washington, DC: American Council on Education.

Blum, D. E. (1988a, June 22). Black woman scholar at Emory U. loses 3-year battle to overturn tenure denial, but vows to fight on. *The Chronicle of Higher Education,* pp. A15–A17.

Blum, D. E. (1988b, June 22). To get ahead in research, some minority scholars choose to "play the game." *The Chronicle of Higher Education,* p. A17.

C. de Baca, F. (1975). White house perspective. In H. J. Casso & G. D. Roman (Eds.), *Chicanos in higher education.* Albuquerque: University of New Mexico Press.

Candelaria, C. (1978). Women in the academy. *Rendezvous: Journal of Arts and Letters, 13*(1), 9–18.

Casso, H. J., & Roman, G. D. (Eds.). (1975). *Chicanos in higher education.* Albuquerque: University of New Mexico Press.

Digest of education statistics, 1985–86 and *1987.* Washington, DC: U.S. Department of Education, Office of Educational Research and Improvement.

Discrimination in higher education. (1975, Spring). *Civil Rights Digest, 7*(3), 3–21.

Dube, E. (1985). The relationship between racism and education in South Africa. *Harvard Educational Review, 55,* 86–100.

Farrell, C. S. (1988a, January 27). Black students seen facing "New Racism" on many campuses. *The Chronicle of Higher Education,* pp. A1, A37–A38.

Farrell, C. S. (1988b, January 27). Stung by racial incidents and charges of indifference, Berkeley to become integrated university. *The Chronicle of Higher Education,* pp. A37–A38.

Farrell, C. S. (1988c, February 17). Rising concerns over campus racial bias marked at Northern Illinois University. *The Chronicle of Higher Education*, pp. A37–A38.

Farrell, C. S. (1988d, February 24). Students protesting racial bias at U. of Massachusetts end occupation of campus building after 5 days. *The Chronicle of higher Education*, p. A41.

Fields, C. M. (1988, May 11). Hispanics, state's fastest-growing minority, shut out of top positions at U. of California, leaders say. *The Chronicle of Higher Education*, pp. A9–A10.

Fishman, J. (1975). *An international sociological perspective of bilingual education.* Keynote Address. National Association for Bilingual Education Conference, San Antonio, Texas.

Gordon, L. (1988, June 14). Second report criticizes UC on its policy towards hiring Latinos. *Los Angeles Times*, p. 3.

Harvey, W. B. (1987, May/June). An ebony view of the ivory tower. *Change, 19*(3), 46–49.

Heller, S. (1988, February 10). Some colleges find aggressive affirmative action efforts are starting to pay off, despite scarcity of candidates. *The Chronicle of Higher Education*, p. A12.

Higher Education Research Institute, Inc. (1982). *Final report of the commission on the higher education of minorities.* Los Angeles: Jossey-Bass, Inc.

Holmes, P. (1975. The ineffective mechanism of affirmative action plans in an academic setting. In H. J. Casso & G. Roman (Eds), *Chicanos in higher Education* (pp. 76–83). Albuquerque: University of New Mexico Press.

Kushner, S., & Norris, N. (1980–81). Interpretation, negotiation and validity in naturalistic research. *Interchange, 11*(4), 26–36.

Lather, P. (1986). Research as praxis. *Harvard Educational Review, 56*, 257–277.

McCurdy, J. (1988, June 8). Nullification of Latino students' election sparks melee at UCLA. *The Chronicle of Higher Education*, p. A23.

Minorities and strategic planning at the University of Colorado. (1987). Boulder: Office of the Associate Vice President for Human Resources.

Minorities in higher education. Third Annual Status Report. (1984). Washington, DC: American Council on Education.

Minorities in higher education. Sixth Annual Status Report. (1987). Washington, DC: American Council on Education.

Olivas, M. A. (1986). Research on Latino college students: A theoretical framework and inquiry. In M. A. Olivas (Ed.), *Latino college students* (pp. 1–25). New York: Teachers College Press.

Ornelas, C., Ramirez, C. B., & Padilla, F. V. (1975). *Decolonizing the interpretation of the Chicano political experience.* Los Angeles: UCLA Chicano Studies Center Publications.

Professional women and minorities: A Manpower data resource service. (1984). Washington, DC: Scientific Manpower Commission.

Ramirez, A. (1988). Racism toward Hispanics: The culturally monolithic society. In P. A. Katz & D. A. Taylor (Eds.), *Eliminating racism profiles in controversy* (pp. 137–157). New York: Plenum Press.

Simeone, A. (1987). *Academic women working towards equality.* South Hadley, MA: Bergin & Garvey.

Valverde, L. (1975). Prohibitive trends in Chicano faculty employment. In H. J. Casso & G. D. Roman (Eds.), *Chicanos in higher education* (pp. 106–114). Albuquerque: University of New Mexico Press.

Williams, A. A. (1987, Oct. 12). Advice/Dissent. *Colorado Daily*.

Faculty Responsibility and Tolerance

WILLIAM B. HARVEY

"Always do the right thing. That's it? That's it! I got it . . . I'm gone."
—Spike Lee

The "ivory tower" image of academia, so carefully cultivated by institutions of higher education, conveys the impression that these organizations are conveniently removed from the problematic day-to-day concerns most other individuals and institutions have to contend with. The image also carries with it a sense that colleges and universities operate with implicit ethical and moral sensibilities that would brook no tolerance for petty prejudices and personal intolerance. Some disagree: "Although a pleasant fiction, this is far from true" (Robinson and Moulton, 1985).

The world of academe does not operate in a vacuum. The values of the larger society—including the pernicious malady of racism—are found on college and university campuses, and are practiced by the individuals who study and work there.

Examples of racism can be found in the recent wave of antagonistic actions directed against African American students. These incidents have occurred at numerous predominantly white colleges and universities throughout the country (Glover, 1988; Wells, 1988).

Acts of intolerance range from psychological intimidation to outright physical attacks that, from an idealistic standpoint, would seem to be more out of place in higher education settings than in others. In actuality, these unsavory collegiate activities mirror the practices and perspectives that are manifested in the "real world." And, just as in the larger society, individuals on college and university campuses having status and power tend to be reactive, rather than proactive, on racial issues.

Barber (1989 takes to task those "administrators and their critics (who) wring hands and rue the social crises of higher education but, hesitate when faced with hard decisions, and prefer to follow rather than challenge the national mood" (p. 62). While his criticism is certainly appropriate, it should have been more pointedly directed at the professoriate. For—even to a greater degree than college and university administrators—it is the faculty whose silence is deafening on the subject of racism. Faculty maintain their silence on racism when it is manifested in American society generally and within institutions of higher education specifically.

This paper examines how faculty at predominantly white colleges and universities set the mission, objectives, practices, and policies of these institutions. The paper also looks at the responses of these academicians to various social and academic phenomena that affect the institutional ethos and style of operation. Specifically, faculty values, perspectives, and outlooks are analyzed as they relate to the presence of students, faculty, and staff of color, most specifically African Americans.

The focus here on African Americans is not intended to diminish the significance of patterns of discrimination that have been practiced against other underrepresented groups, such as American Indians and Hispanics. Any corrective actions taken to reduce the level of racial exclusion and isolation of African Americans should benefit members of these other groups as well.

Moral and Ethical Considerations

Some would argue it is unfair to single out faculty as the primary group responsible for failing to respond to racism in higher education. Faculty provide knowledge, insight, guidance, direction, and inspiration. Faculty influence students beyond the bounds of their subject matter; faculty wisdom and experience make them role models in matters of behavior, decorum, and values as well.

Bowen and Schuster (1986) have observed that:

> [F]aculties, individually and collectively, usually occupy a prominent role in the policies, decisions, and ongoing activities falling within the wide-ranging realm of institutional governance and operation . . . faculty members are intelligent and highly educated people who feel qualified to have opinions not only on matters affecting them personally and their departments, but also on matters pertaining to the institution as a whole (pp. 21–22).

It seems reasonable to presume that faculty also have opinions on important national issues, such as the presence of racism in society.

Embodied in its faculties is the sense that institutions of higher education are places where ethical and moral considerations are viewed with extreme gravity. It is disturbing, then, that at many predominantly white colleges and universities the degree of sensitivity and concern faculty show to matters of racial discrimination is minuscule.

For institutions of higher education and individual faculty members who work within them, the failure to deplore racist and discriminatory behavior in society—or even to point out that such actions are indirect contradictions to the national ideals of liberty and justice for all—amounts to an implicit endorsement of racial bias. To pursue a course of silent observation, rather than one of vocal condemnation, allows members of the professoriate to shield themselves, their colleges, and their universities from the prospect of criticism or retaliation from other political or economic agencies, powerful individuals, and the general public.

Even in private institutions, which are unlikely to be as dependent on public appropriations as state-supported institutions, stances taken by most faculty on social issues seem to reflect the prevailing views of the larger population. Occasional public dissent by a crusading eccentric academician is tolerated, but, in general, faculty members seem to tacitly acknowledge that institutional prosperity depends on public acceptance. Consequently, faculty do not "rock the boat" by pointing out the shortcomings of society. To cite a past example, the professoriate did not become substantially involved in the anti-Vietnam War movement or the environmental movement until such causes received widespread support in the non-academic community.

In the case of racism, its covert acceptance by academicians would seem to be directly contrary to concepts of moral and ethical behavior that higher education has come to stand for. But, as Robinson and Moulton (1985) posit, "academic values sometimes appear to take precedence over moral values." In other words, despite the lofty tone of academic rhetoric, pragmatism rather than idealism appears to be the operative philosophy. Thus, actions may be academically justified even when they are *not* morally justified.

An historical reference point is the lunch counter sit-ins in the South that fueled the civil rights movement and helped end racial segregation. The sit-ins were led by African American college students. Why were the predominantly white colleges and universities on the "wrong" side of this issue? One wonders what white professors were teaching their students about the nature of American society, human rights, and moral justice. Why had faculty not seen fit to challenge the obvious contradiction between word and deed? Indeed, why do their contemporaries not voice this challenge even now in regard to the continued prevalence of racist attitudes and behaviors across the nation?

Some academicians would argue that in dealing with controversial social issues like racism, neutrality is the only appropriate position in a classroom setting. Further, they would argue, neither they nor their institutions should take a side. Robinson and Moulton (1985) counter: "it is sometimes impossible for an institution with power and influence to be neutral since doing nothing in a political crisis constitutes a kind of action" (p. 18).

Thus, when segregation determined the lifestyle of the South, it appears that sanctity of the established order was more important to academicians than society's fair treatment of all citizens. The attitude of complacence and "benign neglect" seems to be prevalent in current times as well, though it may be argued that the neglect is more malign than benign.

The Faculty Role in Promoting Change

If predominantly white colleges and universities are to move toward the ideal of equal treatment, mutual respect, and dignity for all members of the academic community, key players must be faculty members. In most cases, faculty establish criteria for admission to the institution, determine curricula of the institution, and decide who should be hired or fired. Faculty have the power to modify fundamental operational aspects of the college or university, including those areas most problematic to success for African Americans and members of other minority groups.

Unfortunately, an implicit contradiction exists within faculty ranks. Ladd and Lipset (1975) consider faculty members to be liberal in thinking, but not prone to making fundamental changes or modifications in the operation of institutions from which they derive income, status, and power. Many white faculty members may indicate tacit support for a larger African American presence in predominantly white colleges and universities, but these faculty also embrace the concept of meritocracy, as used in its current restrictive sense. For example, in one of the most sensitive and critical areas within academe—the determination of appropriate standards for hiring faculty—Carnegie Foundation data indicate that only 8 percent of faculty members believe that normal academic requirements should be relaxed in appointing members of minority groups to the faculty at their institutions. (*The Chronicle of Higher Education Almanac*, 1990, p. 24).

In fact, the relaxation or reduction of normal requirements is a misnomer. Faculty have always reserved the right to employ flexible standards and criteria when making appointments. African American candidates ask that such flexibility be employed when they are considered, as it has been so often for whites. This concept is a simple one—it is sometimes referred to as affirmative action—and many institutions endorse, but do not implement it.

One hears, then, rhetorical support for increasing opportunities for African American and other minority persons within predominantly white colleges and universities. But this support stipulates that opportunities be initiated within the existing framework of meritocracy.

Unfortunately, such propositions merely extend the current dilemma. They do not change or challenge the inherent value system—or mechanisms used to maintain it—that placed African Americans and other people of color at a decided disadvantage from the very beginning. Faculty may recognize that pluralism and diversity are qualities that enrich institutions of higher education. But, at the same time, faculty holds fast to procedures and approaches that have in effect limited access for non-whites.

A recent analysis of the professoriate indicates that college faculty members are demoralized and disenchanted (Clark, 1987). Despite this apparent dissatisfaction with working situations, faculty have not advocated major alterations in the structure or operation of institutions of higher education. In American higher education, whites hold approximately 90 percent of the faculty positions, and they clearly seem more oriented towards maintaining the status quo than in promoting significant change. Recent findings indicate that "nearly half of full-time faculty members at four-year institutions and 55 per cent [sic] of those at two-year institutions said they were satisfied with their institutions' affirmative action results" (Mooney, 1989, pp. A1, A18).

These results, according to 1987 data, indicate an African American faculty presence in predominantly white institutions at "somewhere between a high of 2.9 percent to a low of 1.3 percent" (Saunders, 1990, p. 32). This information hardly suggests a ground swell of support for hiring new African American faculty by white persons who already hold such positions. Nor are other efforts to make the academic world more amenable to African Americans—by setting criteria other than those traditionally used in the admissions review process or revising curricula to include an Afrocentric perspective—usually heartily embraced by white faculty members.

Admission Considerations

Faculty have significant responsibility as far as admission practices are concerned. Demographic projections show that educated African Americans and Hispanics will be critical to the economic well-being of the country in the century ahead. These demographic data alone should prompt faculty to insist that new and more appropriate methods be developed for assessing student potential for college.

These new methods would limit institutional reliance on instruments or tests that are culturally biased and directly correlate to socio-economic standing. Since the income levels of African Americans remain substantially below those of whites, these instruments place African Americans at a clear disadvantage. Astin makes the point that "if one accepts the idea that colleges exist to educate, the model of selective admissions based on test scores and prior grades makes little sense" (1982, p. 148).

Standardized examinations and test scores currently serve as a sorting mechanism that excludes African Americans and other minorities from access to white universities. Navarro writes:

> minority student performance on tests reflects not simply past educational inequity but also a greater degree of anxiety in text situations, greater difficulty on speeded tests, and fewer opportunities to develop good test-taking skills either in school, at home, or through test preparation courses. In addition, because [minority] students tend to score so close to minimum levels of performance, failure on the part of test users to take into consideration the standard error measurement may result in denial of admission . . . to students whose real ability may be above the cut (1985, pp. 20–21).

The National Alliance of Black School Educators (1984) takes the position that virtually all standardized tests fail to meet the rigorous standards of psychometric science, arguing that standardized tests have more often been instruments of politics than science.

Astin (1982) argues that the heavy reliance institutions place on standardized test scores in the admissions process is not only to the special disadvantage of minorities. This reliance tends to subvert the overall post-secondary educational mission. That mission is to provide educational opportunity for those who have talent, rather than to serve as a mechanism to restrict access—to increased economic and social advantages—to students from certain backgrounds. Colleges and universities clearly do serve a screening function in society. Restrictive measures in the admissions process impact prospective students from minority groups to a greater degree than they impact whites.

Bailey (1978) contends that standardized tests are often used as a screening device to control higher education and preserve its hierarchical structure. Morris (1981) claims that "it is clear that testing has a negative effect on Black admissions at most colleges and universities" (p. 72). It is also clear that only intervention by white faculty members can modify the admissions process so that the inordinate significance given to standardized tests can be reduced. This will provide African American and other minority group students an opportunity to gain admission to predominantly white colleges and universities in greater numbers.

Astin (1982) calls for a new educational model that reduces or eliminates the significance placed on standardized exams so that all students who desire access to higher education may attain it. He concedes, however, that "until such a utopian system is achieved, the standardized test and the predictive model of admissions will continue to represent serious barriers to the educational development of minority students" (p. 169).

Rather than using standardized test scores to restrict admission of African American and other minority students, faculty could call for flexible approaches in the admission process. Performance levels and graduation requirements would still reflect high standards of quality. The flexible admission process could result in substantially greater numbers of African American student admissions, without risking decreases in the quality and value of institutional degree offerings—if more supportive environments and more effective means of instruction were created for the 82 percent of African American students who now attend predominantly white institutions of higher education.

Graduation rates for African American students have been substantially lower at predominantly white institutions than at historically Black colleges and universities. In part, the differential rates reflect a fundamental dichotomy between the two kinds of institutions. Unlike their predominantly white counterparts, historically Black colleges and universities expect "student success, rather than failure" and engender "a set of behaviors and interactions that facilitates successful academic experiences" (Harvey and Williams, 1989).

Curricular Modifications

Faculty must clearly and precisely stipulate that it is no longer intellectually, morally, or ethically acceptable to exclude curricular representation of any significant population groups. Omission diminishes the perceived worth of excluded group members as human beings. Academicians must acknowledge and forcefully articulate the limitations of the Eurocentric curriculum. Faculty, after all, are responsible for determining the body of knowledge appropriate for an educated person. College faculty must also remove ethnocentric blinders and recognize that students need and deserve a complete record of information, not a selective one that exalts certain groups and devalues others.

Though the connection is frequently overlooked, the hostility and insensitivity that emanate from campus culture is tied to the limitations of curricula. Whether or not the institution provides multicultural education to its students will influence how these impressionable young people respond to persons from different racial and ethnic groups. Feagin (1989) writes: "the attitudes of white students are insensitive because of the way they are being taught, or not taught, about American race relations and race history" (p. 13).

With rare exception, students graduate from high school and enter colleges and universities with a profound miseducation about the development of American society and the world. Elementary and secondary schools offer only scanty bits of information about the economic, legal, and sociocultural contributions of African Americans, American Indians, Hispanics, and Asian Americans to the development and maintenance of this country. Despite some improvement over the past two decades, schools still tend to convey the notion that white men from Western Europe and their descendants have been responsible for nearly all of the ideas and artifacts that have ever been generated in North America.

Rather than correcting widespread misconceptions, predominately white colleges and universities tend to support and extend them. Students receive no accurate historical or global context—they are not told that ancestors of minority Americans created sophisticated civilizations and cultures that contribute to our reservoir of human knowledge and understanding. Experiences, sacrifices, and contributions of Americans from minority groups to the development of this country are not represented in the college curricula.

White students come to campus after overt and subtle messages of racial prejudice have been communicated to them for years. Many are likely to have come from communities that are racially segregated. Misinformation and biased assumptions about people who are not white must be countered—by the university or college—with facts.

As long as the critical academic responsibility of providing the truth, *in its totality, to all students*, is ignored, it is unrealistic to expect any fundamental change in racial intolerance. Clearly, faculty members have abdicated their responsibility to present an accurate rendering of events and situations to students. More inclusive curricula are believed to contribute to greater racial tolerance on college campuses, although this link has yet to be validated.

At Stanford University, the University Committee on Minority Issues points out that "the potential of the undergraduate curriculum to promote greater interracial understanding is a persistent issue—indeed, an issue we are painfully reminded of every time a racial incident occurs on campus involving ignorance and insensitivity" (*Stanford Observer*, 1989). The absence of information in the curriculum on people of color helps drive the fiction of the meritocratic scenario that envelopes higher education. This fiction implies that people who are not white have no merit—otherwise their experiences would be studied with the same measure of dedication and zeal as that of the experiences of Western Europeans.

Diversity in Faculty Ranks

Increasing the numbers of African American faculty on campuses of predominantly white colleges and universities has proved to be extremely difficult. Though many institutions of higher education identify themselves as affirmative action employers, they have minimally increased from year to year their hiring of African Americans. On some campuses, the number of African American hires has actually decreased. In this situation, more than any other, the behavior of white institutions belies the rhetorical positions they profess.

Since the 1960s, African Americans have dramatically increased their presence in higher education. But they remain underrepresented relative to their proportion of the national population, and, in some categories, African American representation is declining (Carter and Wilson, 1989). In most higher education institutions, the hiring of new faculty is generally controlled by incumbent faculty members. Most frequently, the mechanism used in the hiring process is the search and screening committee.

Based on criteria established by the committee, members define and describe the vacant position and its responsibilities, identify minimal qualifications, advertise the position in various outlets, and screen the vita and letters of candidates to determine which of the applicants are most highly regarded. Ultimately, a small number of the most impressive applicants interview with the search committee. A selection list is then forwarded to the appropriate institutional official, who identifies the preferred candidate for the position, usually in concurrence with the views of the search committee. The problem with this procedure is that it tends to perpetuate the exclusion of African Americans from faculty positions.

"Old boy" connections, latent racism, common interests and backgrounds, or other factors may cause search committees to be less than fair and objective in fulfilling their responsibilities. Some of them "are sufficiently sophisticated that a minority will always be among the finalists but somehow never get selected for the position" (Wilson, 1987, p. 13).

There are several significant reasons why the faculties of predominantly white colleges and universities ought to be racially and culturally diverse. An increase in African American faculty will not necessarily guarantee a transformation of attitudes toward African American and other minority students. But this increase will:

- broaden and enrich the perspectives and outlooks that are presented to all students.
- provide opportunities for white students to interact with African Americans in a capacity that may be unique for many of them.
- provide role models for African American students.
- counter myths and stereotypes that may exist even among white faculty colleagues.

Given that hiring decisions remain in the hands of incumbent faculty members, the ranks of African Americans who hold faculty positions at predominantly white colleges and universities can only increase if traditional barriers to their employment are removed. Wilson (1987) asserts that only the appearance of change has taken place in the academy, and, as a result, the African American presence is still at risk in predominantly white colleges and universities.

Without question, the substantial underrepresentation of African Americans in the professoriate indicates that more needs to be done. While the availability of African Americans in certain fields and specialties is limited, the lack of progress for African American faculty in predominantly white colleges and universities cannot be fully explained by arguments about the availability pool (Washington and Harvey, 1989). Even in the high demand fields of science and engineering, where they are significantly underrepresented and presumably in high demand, African American professors have attained tenure and have been promoted at a lower rate than their white counterparts (Brown, 1988).

Wilson (1987) debunks the myth that African Americans receive favored treatment once they accept a professorial appointment. Sudarkasa (1987) contends that subtle measures are still being used by white faculty to restrict opportunities available to African Americans. Whether at the faculty or student level, Thresher's observation (1966) rings true: access to higher education is primarily a social process that is deeply imbedded in societal cultural patterns and value systems. The value system must be expanded to celebrate pluralism and diversity. Academia must mount the campaign. Professors must lead the charge.

Campus Climate

The degree of receptivity or hostility faced by African Americans at predominantly white colleges and universities can be gauged by what had been called the "campus climate" (American Council on Education, 1989). This term is used to describe the culture, habits, decisions, practices, and policies that make up campus life—the sum total of the daily environment. The degree to which the climate is hospitable determines the "comfort factor" for African Americans and other nonwhite persons on campus. A general reluctance to modify traditional practices and policies of academe (Lyons, 1990), accentuated by demonstrative actions against the presence of African Americans and other minority groups at predominantly white colleges and universities, keeps the campus climate chilly for nonwhites. Keller (1988–89) maintains that "the campus climate is still hostile to Blacks at many institutions, and the faculty and deans are often insensitive to the particular needs of Black students" (p. 50).

Currently, there are no studies published that indicate that white universities with a greater percentage of Black faculty have fewer racial incidents than other campuses. This is an issue that deserves future study. Researchers who have examined experiences of African American students on predominantly white college campuses, however, repeatedly stress the need for institutional sensitivity toward the structural and attitudinal roadblocks to their progress. Nettles (1988) contends that "universities must retool their programs, expectations, and operations to bring these in line with the new demographic reality" (p. 38).

According to Fleming (1984), "the enrollment of Black students in white colleges constituted the beginnings of fundamental adjustment problems that have yet to be worked through to the mutual satisfaction of both Black students and predominantly white educational institutions" (p. 13). Allen's (1987) research on Black students indicates that "their intellectual growth is undermined by inhospitable conditions where every action is scrutinized for evidence to support the foregone conclusion that 'Blacks are not qualified and really don't belong at this university' (p. 31). Richardson and Bender (1987) argue that to solve problems of racial bias in higher education institutions, "all that is needed are leadership and commitment" (p. 7).

At present, the race relations situation on the nation's campuses can best be described as problematic. In a front-page story, *The Chronicle of Higher Education* recently reported that "a resurgence of racist incidents in the past two years has led some educators, students, and others associated with higher education to warn of 'a new racism' on college and university campuses" (Farrell, 1988, p. A1.). On a similar note, another *Chronicle* issue revealed that:

> almost 30 years after the civil-rights movement made improved race relations a top priority for higher education, ugly and embarrassing incidents continue to plague colleges and universities across the country. Hundreds of institutions of all sizes have been affected. . . . Many administrators and scholars who have studied the incidents have concluded that they are not simply isolated and extremist acts, but that they reflect a disturbing pattern (Magner, 1989, p. A1).

Still, even with these new data in hand, scholars remain silent about the abhorrent nature of these attacks and the climate that spawns them. They refrain from issuing a public rebuke to the participants.

Wilson (1987) opines that "these incidents are only symptoms of a more pervasive problem in academia," (p.13) the problem presumably the institutional racism that is overlooked or unnoticed by the professoriate.

Reed (1989) poses two provocative questions related to these deplorable incidents when he asks what the role is of the university in the development of racial incidents and whether the university is culpable. Reed posits that "universities have cultural goals, often so deeply implicit as to be transparent. One of these deeply implicit goals is the preservation of the belief system and the value orientations of the society" (p. 19).

This comment suggests that the superiority of whites over African Americans remains the operative belief system in America and that racist actions are simply a manifestation of these beliefs. The statement also implies that universities have failed to acknowledge the degree to which they also transmit these beliefs—and that, indeed, this transmission occurs in such a subtle fashion as to be scarcely noticeable to the casual observer, or even to the unsuspecting participant. In response to Reed's questions then, the answer would seem to be yes, universities are culpable in regard to racist incidents on campus. The role played by universities in the development of these hideous incidents is related to their failure to denounce racism as an acceptable base for thought and action among individual citizens and in societal organizations and policies.

Ending a Bitter Legacy

Though few academicians would admit to such feelings, Katz (1983) identifies racism among faculty members as a major cause of the continuation of discrimination on campuses of predominantly white colleges and universities. He comments that:

> I found no one who proudly voiced naive or vicious prejudices. Indeed, the faculty members whom I encountered were afraid and embarrassed to discover prejudicial thinking in themselves. But many faculty tended to look away from the problems of race and thereby deprived themselves and their white students of the opportunity of becoming aware of their attitudes toward race and they deprived Black students of the essential opportunity of being treated unequivocally as equals.

Recent research by Bem and Allen (1990) further dispels the prevalent contention that African American students are not victimized in the classroom by their white professors. If faculty members refuse to face the realization that in the academic world—among the intellectual elite—racism continues to flourish both at the personal and institutional level, then predominantly white colleges and universities will not be modified, in any substantive fashion, to make them fairer and more equitable to African Americans or other minority group members.

Conclusions

Considerable evidence supports the realization that barriers to African American participation in higher education have existed for centuries, and that these impediments continue to exist and to frustrate the advancement of members of this group. The implicit values and operational approaches of colleges and universities have essentially mirrored the dominant attitudes of the larger social system. As far as making higher education more amenable to the views and concerns of African Americans and other minority groups, Wilson, Justiz, and Bjork (1988) assert that "the key to reversing poor minority participation in higher education is not a mystery . . . what has been lacking in the past decade is commitment from higher education leadership and faculties to sustain the gains of the early 1970s" (p. 21).

There are, of course, both similarities and differences in respect to the situations that African Americans on white campuses face and the experiences of other minority groups. According to Feagan (1989), "the actions of many (perhaps most) white administrators and faculty members suggest the conscious or unconscious commitment to keeping the campus subculture white-dominated" (p. 10).

If one accepts the contention that college subcultures are typically white-normed and white-dominated, then the presumption could be made that members of various minority groups have qualitatively different kinds of experiences—depending on how closely their values and actions appear to correspond to those of the dominant group. In that respect, Asian Americans have come to be regarded as the "model minority."

On the other hand, the historical patterns of widespread discrimination practiced against American Indians and Hispanics would suggest that their experiences on predominantly white campuses would be similar to those of African Americans. In addition, like African Americans, American Indians and Hispanics tend to have a lower socioeconomic standing than both whites and Asian Americans, and this factor has been consistently correlated with academic success.

The grassroots of academe—the members of the professoriate—have expounded precious little energy to make the college environment more racially inclusive. From the standpoint of faculty involvement, the situation has been discouraging. Among faculty, efforts to overcome racial intolerance in higher education institutions are likely to be borne exclusively by African American and other minority group members. This should not be the case, as all faculty members should be accountable for bringing about a more diverse and tolerant campus. But most faculty seem to miss the wisdom of Wilkerson's (1982) observation that "meritocracy and egalitarianism are not contradictory and do not require compromise" (p. 11).

The sad reality of the current social condition is that "America is moving backward—not forward—in its efforts to achieve the full participation of minority citizens in American life" (Melendez, 1988, p. vii). Obviously, "one of the most pressing issues facing higher education today is the role of colleges and universities in enabling minorities to share fully in the best experience that American society can offer" (Ostar, 1988, p. iv). College administrators and students can help overcome faculty inertia by actively speaking out in support of tolerance and open-mindedness throughout the academic year. By clearly articulating and reiterating that bigotry has no place in the scholarly community, students and administrators facilitate respect for diversity as a key ingredient in the process of social and academic development. Having such leadership in other segments of the academic community may embolden faculty to endorse statements and efforts that would create a tolerant atmosphere.

Two arenas where faculty members look for acknowledgment and reinforcement of their professional standing are the major disciplinary and professional associations, and foundations and other funding agencies. The involvement of these groups—through recognition and creative funding possibilities—could do much to overcome faculty inertia in this critical area. As new faculty are hired, institutions should assure that candidates are sensitive to and supportive of diversity, pluralism, and the realization of democratic ideals. The college or university should also make clear, before finalizing a prospective faculty appointment, that the institution stands committed to these concepts.

Only when the rhetoric of equal opportunity is translated into action and only when faculty members recognize that their responsibilities transcend their professions will this urgent national problem of racial prejudice and discrimination begin to be resolved.

Without the meaningful inclusion and involvement of African Americans and other minority groups in predominantly white colleges and universities, America will continue as a disconnected set of subcultures. On the other hand, with the positive leadership of college faculty members—leadership that has been conspicuous by its absence—the values of the nation can be shaped so that fair and equal treatment becomes a basic tenet of daily life. Behavior is cued by values which are articulated by leaders. Accordingly, institutions and individuals will respond to a value orientation that emphasizes inclusion. This will make America more truly the accepting and participatory society that it has always claimed to be—and that many of its citizens still wait for it to become.

References

American Council on Education. (1989). *Minorities on campus: A handbook for enhancing diversity.* Washington, D.C.: Author.

Allen, B. & Niss, J. (1990, April). A chill in the college classroom. *Phi Delta Kappan, 71,* 607–609.

Allen, W. R. (1987, May/June). Black colleges vs. white colleges: The fork in the road for Black students. *Change, 19,* 28–34.

Astin, A. (1982). *Minorities in American higher education.* San Francisco: Jossey-Bass.

Barber, B. (1989 Fall). The civic mission of the university. *Kettering Review,* 62–72.

Bailey, R. L. (1978). *Minority admissions.* Lexington: D.C. Heath and Company.

Bonner, T. (1986 Sept-Oct). The unintended revolution in America's colleges since 1940. *Change*, 18(5), 44–51.

Brown, S. V. (1988). *Increasing minority faculty: An elusive goal.* Princeton, NJ: Educational Testing Service.

Bowen, H. R. & Schuster, J. H. (1986). *American professors: A national resource imperiled.* New York: Oxford University Press.

Bundy, M. (1977 November). The issue before the court: Who gets ahead in America. *The Atlantic*, 48.

Carter, D. & Wilson, R. (1989). *Minorities in higher education.* Washington, D.C.: American Council on Education.

Clark, B. (1987). *The academic life; Small worlds, different worlds.* Princeton: Carnegie Foundation for the Advancement of Teaching and Princeton University Press.

Committee sets goal of doubling ethnic studies course offerings. (1982, April). *Stanford Observer*, 23(5), 12.

Faculty attitudes and activities, 1988–89. (1990, September 5). *The Almanac of Higher Education*, p. 24.

Farrell, C. S. (1988, January 27). Black students seen facing 'new racism' on many campuses. *Chronicle of Higher Education*, p. 1.

Feagin, J. R. (1989). *Minority group issues in higher education.* Paper presented at the Center for Research on Minority Education, University of Oklahoma, Norman.

Fleming, J. (1984). *Blacks in college.* San Francisco: Jossey-Bass.

Glover, C. (1988). The other side of racism. *Journal of the National Society of Black Engineers, 4*(1), 42–46.

Harvey, W. B. & Williams, L. (1989). Historically Black colleges: Models for increasing minority representation. *Journal of Black Studies, 21*(3), 328.

Katz, J. (1983). White faculty struggling with the effects of racism. In J. H. Cones, III, J. F. Noonan, & D. Janha (Eds.), *Teaching minority students:* New directions for teaching and learning (No. 16). San Francisco: Jossey-Bass.

Keller, G. (1988–89). Black students in higher education: Why so few? [Review Essay]. *Planning in Higher Education, 17*(3), 43–59.

Knowles, L. L. & Prewitt, K. (Eds.). (1969). *Institutional racism in America.* Englewood Cliffs: Prentice-Hall.

Ladd, E. C. & Lipset, S. M. (1975). *The divided academy: Professors and politics.* New York: McGraw Hill.

Lyons, N. L. (1990, February 1). Once you're in, you gotta hold your own. *Black Issues in Higher Education*, p. 1.

Magner, D. K. (1989, April 26). Blacks and whites on the campuses: Behind ugly racist incidents, student isolation and insensitivity. *Chronicle of Higher Education*, p. 1.

Melendez, S. (1988). *Educating One-Third of a Nation: The Conference Report.* Washington, D.C.: American Council on Education.

Mooney, C. J. (1989, November 8). Professors are upbeat about profession but uneasy about students, standards. *Chronicle of Higher Education, 36*(10), pp. A1, A18.

Morris, L. (1981). The role of testing in institutional selectivity and Black access to higher education. In G. Thomas (Ed.), *Black students in higher education* (pp. 64–75). Westport: Greenwood Press.

National Alliance of Black School Educators. (1984). *Saving the African American child*. Washington, D.C.: Author.

Navarro, M. S. (1985). The quality education movement: New state standards and minority access to college. In E. Freeman (Ed.), *Educational standards, testing and access.* (pp. 15–22). Princeton: Educational Testing Service.

Nettles, M. T. (Ed.). (1988). *Toward Black undergraduate student equality in American higher education.* Westport: Greenwood Press.

Newman, F. (1985). Standards, testing and access in the year 2001. In E. Freeman (Ed.). *Educational standards, testing and access.* (pp. 97–107). Princeton: Educational Testing Service.

Ostar, A. (1988). *Educating One-Third of a Nation: A Conference Report*. Washington, D.C.: American Council on Education.

Reed, W. (1989). The role of universities in racial violence on campuses. *Trotter Institute Review*, 3(2), 1–4.

Richardson, R. Jr. & Bender, L. (1987). *Fostering minority access and achievement in higher education*. San Francisco: Jossey-Bass.

Robinson G. M. & Moulton, J. (1985). *Ethical problems in higher education*. Englewood Cliffs: Prentice Hall.

Saunders, D. (1990, April 12). Tenure for Black Faculty an illusion in the white academy. *Black Issues in Higher Education*, (p. 32).

Sudharkasa, N. (1987, February). Affirmative action or affirmation of the status quo. *AAHE Bulletin*, *39*, 3–6.

Thresher, B.A. (1966). *College Admissions and the Public Interest*. New York: College Entrance Examination Board.

Washington, V. & Harvey, W. (1989). *Affirmative rhetoric, negative action: African American and Hispanic faculty at predominately white institutions.* (1989 ASHE-ERIC Higher Education Report 2). Washington, D.C.: The George Washington University.

Wells, R. (1988). Facing the current of campus racism. *Journal of the Society of Black Engineers*, 4(1), 36–40.

Wiley, E. III. (1989, September 28). Nation's racial climate made Virginia Beach inevitable, scholars say. *Black Issues in Higher Education*, 6(14), 10.

Wilkerson, M. B. (1982, Winter). The masks of meritocracy and egalitarianism. *Educational Record*, 63(1), 4–11.

Wilson, R. (1987, February). Recruitment and retention of minority faculty and staff. *AAHE Bulletin*, 39(6), 11–14.

Wilson, R., Justiz, M. & Bjork, L. (1988). Minority faculty opportunities in higher education. In M. Justiz & L. Bjork (Eds.), *Higher education research and public policy*. Washington, D.C.: American Council on Education/Macmillan.

Young, M. (1985). *The rise of meritocracy: 1870–2033*. Harmondsworth, England: Penguin Books.

Black Women Intellectuals

BELL HOOKS

Often I was in some lonesome wilderness, suffering strange things and agonies . . . cosmic loneliness was my shadow. Nothing and nobody around me really touched me. It is one of the blessings of this world that few people see visions and dream dreams.

Zora Neale Hurston
Dust Tracks on the Road

We have an obligation as Black women to project ourselves into the revolution . . .

Kay Lindsey
The Black Woman as a Woman

The enormous space that work occupies in Black women's lives today follows a pattern established during the very earliest days of slavery. As slaves, compulsory labor overshadowed every other aspect of women's existence. It would seem, therefore, that the starting point for an exploration of Black women's lives under slavery would be an appraisal of their roles as workers.

Angela Davis
Women, Race, and Class

Living in a society that is fundamentally anti-intellectual, it is difficult for committed intellectuals concerned with radical social change to affirm in an ongoing way that the work we do has meaningful impact. Within progressive political circles, the work of intellectuals is rarely acknowledged as a form of activism, indeed more visible expressions of concrete activism (like picketing in the streets or traveling to a Third World country and other acts of challenge and resistance) are considered more important to revolutionary struggle than the work of the mind. It is this devaluation of intellectual work that often makes it difficult for individuals from marginalized groups to feel that intellectual work is important, that it is a useful vocation. Throughout our history as African Americans in the United States, Black intellectuals have emerged from all classes and conditions of life. However, the decision to consciously pursue an intellectual path has always been an exceptional and difficult choice. For many of us it has seemed more like a "calling" than a vocational choice. We have been moved, pushed, even, in the direction of intellectual work by forces stronger than that of individual will.

Offering an account of the factors that may motivate Black folks to become intellectuals, Cornel West asserts in his essay "The Dilemma of the Black Intellectual," "The choice of becoming a Black intellectual is an act of self-imposed marginality; it assures a peripheral status in and to the Black community. The quest for literacy indeed is a fundamental theme in Afro-American history and a basic impulse in the Black community. But for Blacks, as with most Americans, the uses for literacy are usually perceived to be for more substantive pecuniary benefits than those of the writer, artist, teacher, or professor. The reasons some Black people choose to become serious intellectuals are diverse. But in most cases these reasons can be traced back to a common root: a conversion-like experience with a highly influential teacher or peer that convinced one to dedicate one's life to the activities of reading, writing, and conversing for the purposes of individual pleasure, personal worth, and political enhancement of Black (and often other oppressed) people." Though these may be common reasons Black people choose intellectual work, they may co-exist with motivations that are more difficult to name, especially in public space. In my case, I turned towards intellectual work in a desperate search for an oppositional standpoint that would help me survive a painful childhood. Growing up in a segregated, southern, poor and working-class community where education was valued primarily as a means of class mobility, "intellectual life" was always linked to the career of teaching. It was the outward service as a "teacher" helping to uplift the race, where teachers could gain an individual acceptance within Black community, rather than a privatized, intellectual "inner" life. Growing up in such a world, it was more than evident that there was a socially understood difference between excelling academically and becoming an intellectual. Anyone could teach but not everyone would be an intellectual. And while the role of teacher earned one status and respect being "too learned," being too intellectual, meant that one risked being seen as weird, strange, and possibly even mad.

Learning early on that good grades were rewarded while independent thinking was regarded with suspicion, I knew that it was important to be "smart" but not "too smart." Being too smart was synonymous with intellectuality and that was cause for concern, especially if one was female. For a smart child in underclass and poor Black communities, to ask too many questions, to talk about ideas that differed from the prevailing community world view, to say things grown Black folks relegated to the realm of the unspeakable was to invite punishment and even abuse. There have yet to be extensive psychoanalytic studies discussing the fate of gifted Black children raised in homes where their brilliance of mind was not valued but made them "freaks" who were persecuted and punished.

During adolescence, I underwent a conversion process that pushed me towards intellectual life. Constantly persecuted and punished in our family, my attempts to understand my lot pushed me in the direction of critical analytical thought. Standing at a distance from my childhood experience, looking at it with a detached disengagement, was for me a survival strategy. To use psychoanalyst Alice Miller's term, I became my own "enlightened witness," able to analyze the forces that were acting upon me, and through that understanding able to sustain a separate sense of my self. Wounded, at times persecuted and abused, I found the life of the mind a refuge, a sanctuary where I could experience a sense of agency and thereby construct my own subject identity. This lived recognition of how the mind engaged in critical thought could be used in the service of survival, how it could be a healing force in my struggle to fight childhood despair enabled me to become an autonomous self in the dysfunctional household and led me to value intellectual work. I valued it not because it brought status or recognition but because it offered resources to enhance survival and my pleasure in living.

Never thinking of intellectual work as being in any way divorced from the politics of everyday life, I consciously chose to be come an intellectual because it was that work which allowed me to make sense of my reality and the world around me, to confront and comprehend the concrete. This experience provided the groundwork for my understanding that intellectual life need not lead one to be estranged from community but rather might enable one to participate more fully in the life of family and community. It early confirmed what Black leaders in the 19th century well knew—that intellectual work is a necessary part of liberation struggle, central to the efforts of all oppressed and/or exploited people who would move from object to subject, who would decolonize and liberate their minds.

When Black scholars write about Black intellectual life, they usually focus solely on the lives and works of Black men. Unlike Harold Cruse's massive work *The Crisis of the Negro Intellectual*, which focuses no attention on the work of Black women intellectuals, Cornel West's essay "The Dilemma of the Black Intellectual" was written at a historical moment when there was a feminist focus on gender that should have led any scholar to consider the impact of sex roles and sexism. Yet West does not specifically look at Black female intellectual life. He does not acknowledge the impact of gender or discuss the way sexist notions of male/female roles are factors that inform and shape both our sense of who the Black intellectual is or can be, as well as their relation to a world of ideas beyond individual productions. Despite the historical evidence that Black women have always played a major role as teachers, critical thinkers, and cultural theorists in Black life, particularly in segregated Black communities, there is very little written about Black female intellectuals. When most Black folks think about "great minds" they most often conjure up male images.

Whenever I ask students to name Black intellectuals, without requesting that they be gender-specific, they invariably name Black men: Du Bois, Delaney, Garvey, Malcolm X, and even contemporary folks like Cornel West and Henry Louis Gates are mentioned. If I request that they be gender specific they readily name these Black men and hesitate as they mentally search for the names of Black women. After much pause, they begin to call out the names of famous contemporary Black women writers, usually Alice Walker or Toni Morrison. Now and then Angela Davis's name appears on the list. They do not know the work of 19th century Black women intellectuals. Black women critical thinkers who would be perfect counterparts to Du Bois and Delaney are not known. The names of Anna Julia Cooper, Mary Church Terrell and even the more widely circulated name of Ida B. Wells are not on the tip of everybody's tongue. In her introduction to the Schomburg edition of Anna Julia Cooper's 1892 text A Voice From The South, Mary Helen Washington emphasizes both the importance of Black female intellectual work and the reality that it has yet to receive deserved acknowledgment and recognition. Washington asserts: "Without women like Fannie Barrier Williams, Ida B. Wells, Fannie Jackson Coppin, Victoria Earle Matthews, Frances Harper, Mary Church Terrell, and Anna Julia Cooper, we would know very little about the conditions of nineteenth-century Black women's lives, and yet the Black intellectual tradition, until very recently, has virtually ignored them and devalued their scholarship as clearly subordinate to that produced by Black men."

While it is not too surprising that students are unable to name 19th century Black women intellectuals, it is shocking that they do not know the work of contemporary Black women thinkers like Hortense Spillers, Hazel Carby, Patricia Williams, and Beverly Guy-Sheftall, to name a few. Sexist subordination in Black intellectual life continues to obscure and devalue the work of Black female intellectuals. This is why it is so difficult for students to name us. And those students who invoke the names of Walker and Morrison have rarely read their non-fiction work, and often have no clue as to the scope and range of their thought. Black women intellectuals who are not "famous writers" (and not all writers are intellectuals) remain virtually invisible in this society. That invisibility is both a function of institutionalized racism, sexism, and class exploitation, and a reflection of the reality that large numbers of Black women do not choose intellectual work as their vocation.

Working with Black female students within the academy who express extreme reticence about the value and importance of intellectual work has motivated me to critically examine the relationship of Black women to intellectual work, to ask questions: how many Black women would see themselves as being intellectuals? How do we make a living? Are we all in the academy? Where are our essays on intellectual production, etc.? Many of the Black female students I encounter are uncertain about intellectual work. I am awed by the depths of anti-intellectualism they are assaulted by and internalize. Many of them express contempt for intellectual pressed on everyone's consciousness the notion that Black women were all body and no mind. Their cultural currency continues to inform how Black females are perceived. Seen as "sexual sign," Black female bodies are placed in a category that, culturally speaking, is deemed far removed from the life of the mind. Within the sex/race/class hierarchies of the United States, Black women have always resided at the bottom. Lowly status is reserved in this culture for those deemed incapable of social mobility because they are perceived in sexist, racist, and classist terms as deficient, inadequate, inferior.

Overall representations of Black females in contemporary mass media continue to identify us as more sexual, as earthy freakish, out of control. And the popular success of a polemical work like Shahrazad Ali's The Black Man's Guide to Understanding The Black Woman, which insists that Black women are the intellectual inferiors of Black men, have smaller brains, etc., indicates the extent to which many Black people internalize sexist/racist thinking about Black female identity. Like those misogynist Renaissance treatises, Ali's book associates Black women with nature, with sexuality, asserting the primary thesis that we must be "controlled."

Running counter to representations of Black females as sexual savages, sluts, and/or prostitutes is the "mammy" stereotype. Again, this image inscribes Black female presence as signified by the body, in this case the construction of woman as mother, as "breast," nurturing and sustaining the life of others. Significantly, the proverbial "mammy" cares for all the needs of others, particularly those most powerful. Her work is characterized by selfless service. Despite the fact that most households in the United States do not have Black maids or nannies working in them, racist and sexist assumptions that Black women are somehow "innately" more capable of caring for others continues to permeate cultural thinking about Black female roles. As a consequence, Black women in all walks of life, from corporate professionals and university professors to service workers, complain that colleagues, co-workers, supervisors, etc. ask them to assume multi-purpose caretaker roles, be their guidance counselors, nannies, therapists, priests; i.e., to be that all nurturing "breast"—to be the mammy. While these Black women are no longer forced by racist exploitative labor practices to "serve" solely in jobs deemed menial, they are still expected to clean up everyone's mess. And it is not simply the White world that brings these expectations to bear on Black women; they are also imposed by Black men and children who also believe that Black women should serve them. Sexist assumptions about women's roles inform the Black communities' expectations of Black women. Many Black folks share the assumptions held by diverse groups in this society that women are "inherently" destined to selflessly serve others. This thinking is often reinforced in Black communities by religious teaching emphasizing the necessity of selfless service as the highest expression of Christian charity. Collectively, many Black women internalize the idea that they should serve, that they should always be available to meet the need of someone else whether they want to or not.

Cultural insistence that Black women be regarded as "service workers" no matter our job or career status as well as Black female passive acceptance of such roles may be the major factor preventing more Black women from choosing to become intellectuals. Intellectual work, even when it is deemed socially relevant, is not seen as "selfless work." Indeed, a prevailing cultural stereotype of an intellectual is someone who is usually self-centeredly preoccupied with their ideas. Even in those cultural arenas where intellectual work is most respected, it is most often seen as work that emerges from self-engagement and self-involvement. Even though Black intellectual men like Du Bois have linked the life of the mind to various forms of political activism, they were self-focused in their pursuit of ideas. Talking with Black women, both academic and non-academic, about our relation to the world of ideas, to seeking knowledge and knowledge production, one of the consistent themes that emerged was the fear of appearing selfish, of not doing work that was seen as directly recognizable as extending beyond the self and "serving" others. Many Black females, myself included, described childhood experiences where the longing to read, contemplate, and talk about a broad range of ideas was discouraged, seen as frivolous activity, or as activity that indulged in too intensely would lead us to be selfish, cold, cut off from feelings and estranged from community. In childhood, if I did not place household chores above the pleasures of reading and thinking, grown-ups threatened to punish me by burning my books, by forbidding me to read. Although this never happened, it impressed on my consciousness the sense that it was somehow not only "wrong" to prefer being alone reading, thinking, writing, but was somehow dangerous to my well-being and a gesture insensitive to the welfare of others. In adulthood, I spent years believing (and therefore making it so) that it was important for me to complete every other task no matter how inconsequential before doing intellectual work. Of course, I would often arrive at the space intended for such work tired, weary, lacking in energy. Early sexist socialization that teaches Black women, and indeed most women, that mind work must always be secondary to housework, childcare, or a host of other caretaking activities has made it difficult for women to make intellectual work a central priority even when our social circumstances would indeed offer rewards for this activity.

Among Black women thinkers who work as academics, many individuals that I spoke with, felt that their longing to devote time and energy to intellectual work could not be fulfilled because they found themselves perpetually juggling multiple demands. Rightfully complaining that they lack time to pursue intellectual work freely and fully, they also expressed fear that too passionate pursuit of intellectual goals would cut them off from meaningful relational activity. Still, they did not seem eager to interrogate the reasons why they are reluctant, or in some cases downright unable, to claim intellectual work as worthy of primary attention. Focusing particularly on Black females who had completed graduate courses but had stopped at the dissertation writing level, I found they were the most mired in contradictory feelings about the value of academic and/or intellectual work, and that these feelings psychologically blocked their ability to complete this final requirement. It occurred to me that dissertation writing is that moment in one's graduate work where we confront most directly what it means to engage in solitary thinking and writing. For most students, it is that graduate experience which best exemplifies the individualistic character of scholarly thought and work.

One writes alone, usually spending much time in isolation. Often it is difficult to maintain a sense of engagement in community. Black women who have been socialized to devalue or feel guilty about time spent away from others may not be able to claim or create space for isolated writing. This is especially so for Black women who are parents. Single parents must often grapple with concrete material hindrances that do not enable them to focus intensely on thinking and writing even if they so desired. Still, there are individuals without relational or material constraints who are as reluctant as their less advantaged counterparts to claim intellectual work as their primary vocation. Again and again the fear of "isolation" from community or the sense that life was not well lived if not experienced in community was identified as a barrier preventing Black women from wholeheartedly choosing intellectual work. For these barriers to be overcome, individual Black women who are able to remain devoted to an intellectual vocation even as we experience ourselves as connected in community must chart this journey, naming the process.

In "The Dilemma of the Black Intellectual," Cornel West addresses the conflicts that arise when Black intellectuals are faced with a "bourgeois model of intellectual activity" that puts us on the defensive: "There is always the need to assert and defend the humanity of Black people, including their ability and capacity to reason logically, think coherently, and write lucidly. The weight of this inescapable burden for Black students in the White academy has often determined the content and character of Black intellectual activity." These conflicts seem particularly acute for Black women who must also fight against those racist/sexist stereotypes that continually lead others (and even ourselves) to question whether or not we are competent, whether we are capable of intellectual excellence. For Black women scholars and/or intellectuals, writing style may evoke questions of political allegiance. Using a style that may gain one academic acceptance and recognition may further estrange one from a wider Black reading audience. Again, one confronts in a different way questions of isolation and community involvement. Choosing to write in a traditional academic style may lead to isolation. And even if one writes along the lines of accepted academic style there is no guarantee that one's work will be respected.

Often Black thinkers fear our work will not be taken seriously by a larger audience, that it will be seen as lacking in some manner. Such fears inhibit intellectual production. Writing essays that include confessional reflections, I initially felt uncertain about whether they would speak to an audience beyond myself and my friends. When I published my first collection of essays, *Talking Back*, I was surprised by the many letters I received from Black women discussing the essay which focused on the difficulties I faced as a graduate student. Stories of persecution by professors, peers, and professional colleagues poured in. Accounts of Black females being interrogated by those seeking to ferret out whether the individual was capable of completing work, of thinking logically, of writing coherently were a norm. These forms of harassment often undermine Black women's capacity to convey skill and intellectual ability. Then there were the stories—told through letters—of depression and life-threatening despair. Overall, these letters confirm that the choice to pursue an academic and/or intellectual career in the socially legitimate manner continues to be an arduous task for Black females. Even though there are certainly many more Black women academics than ever before, they are often anti-intellectual (a stance which is often a consequence of the pain they have endured as students or as professors who are regarded with suspicion and contempt by peers). In their daily life they may insist that work which speaks directly to concrete experience is more valuable than those forms of intellectual work that are not produced to be marketed to a mass audience. Given the lack of sustained public admiration and support for Black females choosing intellectual vocations, when confronting such work in isolation, in private spaces, it is not surprising that individual Black women may find themselves overwhelmed by doubts, that such spaces may intensify fears of lack, fears that one's ideas could not possibly be worthy of a hearing. Black women must re-vision notions of intellectual work that enable us to embrace a concern with a life of the mind and the welfare of community.

In "The Dilemma of the Black Intellectual," West is extremely critical of those bourgeois models of intellectual life that conceive of it solely in individualistic or elitist terms, offering the "insurgency" model as an alternative. He asserts: "Instead of the solitary hero, embattled exile, and isolated genius—the intellectual as star, celebrity, commodity—this model privileges collective individual work that contributes to communal resistance and struggle." While the idea of insurgency provides a useful counterpoint to the bourgeois model in theory, West does not address the concrete reality of what circumstances, what material conditions enable and promote intellectual work. Indeed, without privileging the notion of "isolated" genius one must honestly name the reality that much intellectual work takes place in isolation, is informed by time spent in contemplation, revery, and active writing. How can Black women grapple with choosing needed isolation without buying into the bourgeois model? Any discussion of intellectual work that does not emphasize the conditions that make such work possible misrepresents the concrete circumstances that allow for intellectual production. Indeed, Black women struggling to strengthen and deepen our commitment to intellectual work know that we must confront the issue of "isolation," our fear of it, our fear that it estranges us from community inhibits full pursuit of intellectual work. Within patriarchy, men have always had the freedom to isolate themselves from family and community, to do autonomous work and re-enter a relational world when they chose, irrespective of their class status. It is the image of a male figure seeking aloneness to do the work of the mind that is common in mass media, and not that of the female. That patriarchal world which supports and affirms male re-entry into family and community after time apart often punishes females for choosing to do autonomous work. Recent studies (like Arlie Hochschild's The Second Shift) which examine the gendered nature of household chores indicate that working women continue to do most housework. So, before that isolated Black woman intellectual can re-enter a relational community, it is likely that she must first assume responsibility for a variety of household chores.

Clearly, Black women academics and intellectuals often are unable to claim necessary alone time to do their work. Discussing the question of isolation with Black women peers and students, I was not surprised to discover that the majority of us had little experience of being alone or working alone. This may be especially true for Black females from poor and working-class backgrounds where limited space and sheer numbers of bodies in a given household made time alone an impossibility. Raised in a large household, it was only when I went to college that I realized I had never been alone a day in my life. Black females raised in sexist households were not placed in situations where we could spend time alone. In fact, it was usually the opposite. We were constantly placed in settings with chaperones or company (in the old days, of course, this was to protect female virtue). Concurrently, it was deemed "unnatural" for a girl who needed to learn how to parent and be a homemaker to spend time alone.

Feminist research on parenting indicates that females are socialized to develop relational skills that enhance our ability to care for others. Such socialization was and is usually made explicit in traditional Black households. Since many Black females have been raised in homes with working mothers, they assumed responsibility for household chores and the care of others early on. Time alone for thinking has not been traditionally valued for Black girls. And even though poor and working-class Black males may not have been raised in settings that overtly valued time alone, males were able to inhabit spaces by themselves, to stand on corners alone and contemplate the universe, sit on rooftops etc. In discussion with other Black females, I found that our time to think usually happened only when domestic chores were done. It was often stolen time. And at times one had to choose between having that space or relational pleasures, hanging out with friends or family. Black women intellectuals know the value of time spent alone. Many Black female thinkers that I interviewed talked about finding it difficult to sit down and write for long stretches of time. Some of this difficulty emerges because individuals may not know how to be comfortable in alone space with alone activity. Certainly not all intellectual work occurs in isolation (some of our best ideas emerge in the context of exchange) but this reality co-exists with the reality that solitary contemplation of ideas is a crucial component of the intellectual process. To feel we have a right to solitary time, Black women must break with conventional sexist/racist notions of woman s role.

Within a White supremacist, capitalist, patriarchal social context like this culture, no Black woman can become an intellectual without decolonizing her mind. Individual Black women may become successful academics without undergoing this process and, indeed, maintaining a colonized mind may enable them to excel in the academy but it does not enhance the intellectual process. The insurgency model that Cornel West advocates, appropriately identifies both the process Black females must engage to become intellectuals and the critical standpoints we must assume to sustain and nurture that choice. To counter the internalized low self-esteem that is constantly actively imposed on Black females in a racist/sexist, anti-intellectual culture, those of us who would become intellectuals must be ever vigilant. We must develop strategies to gain critical assessment of our worth and value that do not compel us to look for critical evaluation and affirmation from the very structures, institutions, and individuals who do not believe in our capacity to learn. Often, we must be able to affirm that the work we do is valuable even if it has not been deemed worthy within socially legitimized structures. Affirming in isolation that work we do can have a meaningful impact in a collective framework, we must often take the initiative in calling attention to our work in ways that reinforce and strengthen a sense of audience.

As a Black woman intellectual writing feminist theory from a standpoint that has as its central scholarly agenda understanding the specific nature of Black gender politics, and as its political task challenging racist and sexist thinking, I began this work in an academic context even though few people in the academy affirmed my efforts. Talking with working-class Black people at various jobs, with folks in the communities I was raised and/or lived in, I found individuals to affirm and encourage my work. This encouragement was crucial to my success. I could not have continued to work in isolation—my spirits would have been depressed. And even though my work is now widely affirmed in academic settings, I remain most grateful for those non-academic individuals who encouraged me when that support was not there in the socially legitimate place. It is impossible for Black female intellectuals to blossom if we do not have a core belief in ourselves, in the value of our work, and a corresponding affirmation from the world around us that can sustain and nurture. Often we cannot look to traditional places for recognition of our value; we bear the responsibility for seeking out and even creating different locations.

The politics of patriarchy makes the situation of Black male intellectuals distinct from that of Black women. Though they confront racism, they do not confront gender biases. And as has already been stated, since they are seen as legitimate members of an established intellectual tradition, their work is less suspect and often more rewarded than that of Black women. Importantly, Black female intellectuals need the support and encouragement of Black male peers. Often sexism stands in the way of Black males offering this support. Concurrently, academic competitiveness militates against the formation of Black intellectual communities that cross institutions and disciplines. Such communities emerge from the resistance efforts of Black women and men who recognize that we strengthen our positions by supporting one another.

West insists that "the major priority of Black intellectuals should be the creation or reactivation of institutional networks that promote high-quality critical habits primarily for the purpose of Black insurgency." Taking this proposition a step further, it is crucial that such efforts encompass Black intellectuals who may not have any formal institutional affiliation. This is especially crucial for Black women since many exceptional female critical thinkers do not work in academic settings. Asserting that "the central task of postmodern Black intellectuals is to stimulate, hasten, and enable alternative perceptions and practice by dislodging prevailing discourses and powers," West offers a paradigm that allows for an emphasis on ending sexism and sexist oppression as a necessary pre-condition for Black intellectual insurgency. For it is only as Black females and Black males work against the sexist conditioning that promotes the assumption that intellectual work is exclusively the domain of males, or that their work is more important, that we can create communities and environments, that fully promote and sustain our intellectual work. And it is only our vigilant interrogation of sexist biases and practices that will enable Black men to encourage and value the work of Black female peers. This would mean that Black male intellectuals would take our work seriously, that they would cease to pay lip-service to the idea of ending sexism while continually ignoring or appropriating ideas. When Black male intellectuals refer to the work of Black female peers and use it constructively in diverse settings (classrooms, lectures etc.), they help bring greater visibility to Black women, strengthening bonds of solidarity. We see this in the work of Black male intellectuals, Manning Marable, Derrick Bell, and Kobena Mercer, to name a few. Concurrently, non-Black allies could best express solidarity by not condoning and supporting Black male appropriation of Black female scholarly labor.

As diverse Black communities grapple with issues of gender, and as the work of feminist scholars is read and/or talked about more widely in such settings, Black female intellectuals will not only have greater recognition and visibility; there will be greater encouragement for young scholars to choose intellectual paths. Despite the many difficulties that surface when Black women choose intellectual work, the possibilities of meaningful reward serve as a counterforce motivating and sustaining us. These rewards may not always be conventional expressions of regard. They may be given by communities who have no contact with academic institutions. Letters from Black men who are in prison and using that time to educate themselves for critical consciousness have been a source of inspiration for my work. When an imprisoned Black male comrade writes me to say, "Your work has touched me in ways that made me strive to be whole," it affirms that intellectual work can connect us with a world outside the academy, can deepen and enrich our sense of community. This is the message I most want to share with young Black females who fear that intellectual work estranges us from the "real" world. In fact, when we do insurgent intellectual work that speaks to a diverse audience, to masses of people with different class, race, or educational backgrounds, we become part of communities of resistance, coalitions that are not conventional. Intellectual work only estranges us from Black communities when we do not relate or share in myriad ways our concerns. That sharing has to go beyond the written word since many Black folks are barely literate or are illiterate. Talking in churches and homes, in both formal and informal ways, we can share the work we do. By acknowledging that reward, understanding, and recognition is, can be, and will be given to us from unconventional places and by valuing these sources of affirmation Black intellectuals call attention to a counter hegemonic system of legitimation and valuation that either in conjunction with the work we do in institutions or as an alternative to it can legitimize and sustain our work.

The affirmation that has come to me from individuals and locations that are on the margins strengthens and inspires me. I call attention to it not to be self-serving but to provide a countertestimony, one that opposes the usual insistence that there can be no meaningful exchange, contact, influence, of intellectuals with everyday folks who may have no educational background. West ends his essay "The Dilemma of the Black Intellectual," with the uplifting comments: "The predicament of the Black intellectual need not be grim and dismal. Despite the pervasive racism of American society and anti-intellectualism of the Black Community, critical space and insurgent activity can be expanded. This expansion will occur more readily when Black intellectuals take a more candid look at themselves, the historical and social forces that shape them, and the limited though significant resources of the community from whence they come." Ongoing critiques of sexism expand that space and make it possible for the contributions of Black women to be valued. Until then, racism and sexism will continue to inform how the work of African American women is regarded.

My awareness of the particular dilemmas Black women intellectuals face was deepened when I began my first full-time teaching job at Yale University. At that time, I was one of two African American women in Yale college. During my stay there the senior Black woman, art historian Sylvia Boone, was tenured. Whenever I called attention to the relative absence of Black women scholars at this institution, naming the impact of sexism and racism, I was told again and again by White male colleagues, "If Black women are not here, it is not because Yale is racist, it is that Black women are simply not good enough." These comments compelled me to critically focus on the ways sexist and racist representations of Black women intellectuals inform the way we are perceived, put in place structures that legitimate the devaluation of our work.

Until my time at Yale, I had not really thought it important or necessary to openly declare myself an "intellectual" and to encourage other Black women to do the same, to make their presence known, to convey our thoughts about the intellectual process. Yearly, I see many brilliant young scholars turn their backs on intellectual work because they feel so diminished in institutions, because they feel their voices are not valued in the larger society. Concern for the future of Black female students, whose intellectual ideas, scholarship and writing are sorely needed has motivated me to do the "critical self-inventory" West advocates and to publicly discuss personal experience, giving personal testimony that may encourage and uplift. In the process of critical self-evaluation I realized how I had been socialized not to speak about commitment to intellectual life, but rather to see that as a private, almost "secret" choice. By not speaking about this choice, I was also not conveying to Black female students the joys and pleasures of intellectual work. If I and other Black women, particularly those of us who work in academic settings, only talk about the difficulties, we paint a gloomy picture that may lead students to see intellectual work as diminishing and disenabling. Often in conversations with students, particularly young Black females, I am asked by students to discuss aspects of my personal journeying. This passionate inquiry and interrogation often challenges my sense of privacy (such as it is), yet it is rooted in a profound desire on their part to understand the process by which Black women choose intellectual life, where and how we find personal fulfillment. Their longing for Black women intellectuals to chart the journey often places a demand for openness, for candid, honest revelation that may not be placed on male colleagues, or non-Black women. Yet, Black women intellectuals committed to insurgent practices must recognize the call to speak openly about the intellectual life as we know it, about our work as a form of activism.

Oftentimes intellectual work compels confrontation with harsh realities. It may remind us that domination and oppression continue to shape the lives of everyone, especially Black people and people of color. Such work not only draws us closer to the suffering, it makes us suffer. Moving through this pain to work with ideas that may serve as a catalyst for the transformation of our consciousness, our lives, and that of others is an ecstatic and joyous process. When intellectual work emerges from a concern with radical social and political change, when that work is directed to the needs of the people, it brings us into greater solidarity and community. It is fundamentally life-enhancing.

References

Baker, Houston A., *Afro-American Poetics: A Revision of Harlem and the Black Aesthetic*, Madison, Wisconsin: University of Wisconsin Press, 1988.

—— *Blues, Ideology and Afro-American Literature: A Vernacular Theory*, Chicago: University of Chicago Press, 1984.

—— *The Journey Back: Issues in Black Literature and Criticism*, Chicago: University of Chicago Press, 1980.

—— *Modernism and the Harlem Renaissance*, Chicago: University of Chicago Press, 1987.

Bambara, Toni Cade, *Gorilla, My Love*, New York: Random House, 1972.

—— *The Salt Eaters*, New York: Vintage Books, 1981, c1980.

—— *The Seabirds Are Still Alive*, New York: Random House, 1977.

—— *Tales and Stories for Black Folks*, Garden City, New York: Zenith Books, 1971.

Baraka, Amina and Amiri Baraka, *Confirmations: An Anthology of African American Women*, New York: Morrow, 1983.

Baraka, Imamu Amiri, Blues People; Negro Music in White America, New York: W. Morrow, 1963.

—— *Daggers and Javelins: Essays, 1974–1979*, New York: Morrow, 1984.

—— *Dutchman and The Slave: Two Plays*, New York: W. Morrow, 1964.

Baudrillard, Jean, *Revenge of the Crystal: Selected Writing on the Modern Object and Its Destiny, 1968–1983*, London and Concord, MA: Pluto Press in association with the Power Institute of Fine Arts, University of Sydney, 1990,

Bell, Derrick A., *Race, Racism, and American Law*, Cambridge, Massachusetts: Harvard Law School, 1970.

Asian Pacific Americans in Higher Education:
Faculty and Administrative Representation and Tenure

DON T. NAKANISHI

The widely prevalent image of Asian Pacific Americans as a successful, model minority group serves to disguise their lack of representation and influence in major American social institutions, including higher education. Although there has been a dramatic increase in their enrollments at the undergraduate level in colleges and universities during the past decade (Hsia and Hirano-Nakanishi, 1989), the representation of Asian Pacific Americans at other levels of the academic hierarchy has been far less substantial. My own tenure case, which attracted considerable media attention during its three-year duration, demonstrates the unresponsiveness of the university hierarchy to racism so blatant even "so-called 'conservative' students" in campus fraternities and sororities at UCLA became involved (Omatsu, 1990a, p. 65). My attorney, Dale Minami, noting the wider implications of the case, stated that I "was a symbol of a New California where due to changing demographics, the majority of inhabitants would soon be people of color . . .

[M]any in the Ivory Tower, subconsciously or consciously, feared this" (Minami, 1990, p. 94). Because these demographic shifts are taking place so rapidly and with such widespread implications, greater policy and programmatic attention should be devoted to fair representation of and full participation by Asian Pacific Americans at all levels of higher education. My own protracted tenure battle has convinced me that Asian Pacific Americans must take a more active stand in our own behalf if we are to achieve fair representation in the academy.

In this discussion I will not review the details of my case, which are fully documented elsewhere (Omatsu, 1990b). Instead, I will focus on three widely prevalent myths or misconceptions regarding Asian American faculty and administrative representation and tenure. To do so, I will draw on several recent institutional studies and commission reports, as well as the experiences of over fifty professors from across the nation—over half of whom were Asian Pacific Americans and practically all of whom were women or scholars of color—who have contacted me since I received tenure in June 1989, and have sought my advice about what they should do in dealing with situations that resemble mine. Finally, I will summarize some of the political actions taken in my own tenure case, actions that unfortunately proved necessary although they challenged the myth of Asian Americans as the "model minority."

Misconceptions about Asian Pacific American Faculty and Administrators

The first misconception is that Asian Pacific Americans are well represented in college faculties and key administrative positions. This view is a simple and yet mistaken extension of the notion that Asian Pacific Americans are a successful minority, and that they are especially successful and talented in academics. Indeed, one might assume that since Asian Pacific Americans appear to be well represented in the freshman classes of many of America's leading colleges and universities (some have even charged that they are overrepresented, particularly in the fall of 1991 when three University of California campuses—Berkeley, with 34 percent Asian American; UCLA, with 40 percent; and Irvine, with 51 percent—had freshman classes in which Asian Pacific Americans outnumbered whites), then by extension they must be equally well represented at other levels of these institutions.

The reality, however, is quite different. Like other minority groups and women in general, there is a substantial decline in the representation of Asian Pacific Americans as one moves up the academic pyramid from high school graduation to freshman admissions to graduate admissions and then to the ranks of faculty and administrators. At UCLA, for example, in 1987, the representation of Asian Pacific Americans followed a common downward pattern of declining representation (found at practically all major colleges and universities): 20 percent of the entering freshman class were Asian Pacific Americans, but they constituted only 10 percent of all entering graduate students, 6 percent of the nontenured faculty, and 4 percent of the tenured faculty (Minami, 1990). As I mentioned above, this pattern of diminishing presence in the academic hierarchy holds true not only for Asian Pacific Americans, but also for all other racial minority groups as well as women. On the other hand, at practically every major university in America, Whites reflect the opposite, upward pattern of increasing representation in the academic pyramid. For example, in 1987 at UCLA, Whites constituted 48 percent of the entering freshman class, 67 percent of all entering graduate students, 81 percent of all nontenured faculty, and 90 percent of all tenured faculty (Minami, 1990). Furthermore, Asian Pacific Americans in top administrative posts at UCLA and most major universities are practically nonexistent (Chan, 1989). Currently, only two of the top seventy-five administrators at UCLA are Asian Pacific American (Minami, 1990). Nationally, Asian Pacific Americans in administration constitute less than 1 percent of all administrators (Escueta and O'Brien, 1991).

To be sure, at most major universities it does not appear that Asian Pacific Americans are as grossly underrepresented in the faculty ranks as African Americans, Chicanos and other Latinos, and American Indians. In contrast to the situation of other minority faculty, there are usually some Asian professors on most college faculties (and usually more than the numbers of other minorities), where they usually are concentrated in specific fields like the sciences, engineering, medicine, or the teaching of Asian languages. However, this presence may be misleading, because often the professors in these fields are Asian foreign nationals who received a substantial portion of their higher educational training in Asian countries, rather than Asian Pacific Americans. For example, in one of the few empirical studies to address this issue, Stanford University (1989) found that in 1987 thirty-nine of the fifty-two tenure and nontenure line Asian faculty at its institution (75 percent) were born outside the United States, and thirty-one of these fifty-two Asian faculty members (60 percent) received their bachelor's degrees abroad. This situation, as the Stanford report pointed out, has several potentially unwarranted consequences for others in the campus community:

> While the committee feels that all faculty are an asset to the University and the Stanford community, including all minority faculty by any definition, we also note that foreign-born and foreign-educated faculty members may not be as effective as role models for minority undergraduates, who are for the most part American-born. Students have described gaps in communication, especially in advising and counseling, arising from what they feel are the very different life experiences of minority faculty born and raised abroad. In such instances, mentoring—so important for the successful academic experience of minority students—can be strained (Stanford University, 1989, p. 19).

The second misconception is that Asian Pacific Americans do not face discriminatory or unfair employment practices in higher educational institutions. This view combines two widely accepted but false notions. First, it is an extension of the claim that Asian Pacific Americans have been fully accepted in American life, and that they no longer encounter either overt or covert racial discrimination that might limit their opportunities for social and professional advancement. The second underlying assumption is that colleges and universities are unique places of employment, that they are somehow more tolerant, more enlightened, more objective, and more open to new ideas and perspectives than institutions in the so-called real world, be they corporations, factories, or law firms, and that they are free of bias and subjectivity.

I do not believe that every Asian Pacific American faculty member faces racial discrimination. However, there is ample evidence from several studies, as well as the personal experiences of many individual professors who have publicly aired their situations, that Asian Pacific Americans from a variety of academic fields at different types of institutions across the nation have faced unusual and unfair treatment in their evaluations for tenure and promotions (Attorney General's Asian Pacific Islander Advisory Committee, 1988; Escueta and O'Brien, 1991; Minami, 1990). In the past few years the list of Asian Pacific Americans who have filed internal campus grievances or outside lawsuits in order to gain fair, unbiased, and equitable treatment for tenure and promotion has grown quite extensive and provides a brief glimpse of a potentially broader phenomenon. The disciplines represented in recent cases include business, medicine, architecture, biology and genetics, psychology, law, English literature, and my own field of education, to name just a few. These cases have involved major universities throughout the United States.

In higher educational institutions Asian Pacific Americans have encountered at least two major forms of unfair and potentially discriminatory treatment. First, like other minority and women scholars who pursue research in ethnic and gender studies, Asian Pacific American professors whose scholarship focuses on topics and issues concerning the historical and contemporary experiences of the Asian Pacific American population encounter the same misinformed, culturally disparaging, and often hostile reactions to and evaluations of their work by faculty colleagues. Ethnic and gender research that frequently confronts and challenges prevailing analytical perspectives and explores sensitive issues of racism and intergroup relations has yet to be fully accepted and embraced as important, relevant, or exciting subjects of study by many faculty members.

At the same time, Asian Pacific American professors have also encountered both covert and overt forms of racial discrimination. The significance of Professor Rosalie Tung's landmark Supreme Court lawsuit (*E.E.O.C.* v. *University of Pennsylvania*) is that the Court agreed with her attorneys and the Equal Employment Opportunity Commission that colleges and universities have no special privileges that should shield or protect them from fully disclosing relevant personnel review documents in a formal investigation of discrimination in employment. My own case also illustrates the absolute necessity of being able to have access to all original, unedited versions of tenure review documents rather than so-called redacted summaries that many universities like the University of California provide while pursuing internal campus grievances, as well as formal lawsuits. Although university officials claim that these edited summaries merely remove signatures, letterheads, and other identifiers to ensure confidentiality, they usually eliminate far more than that.

My case has some parallels with Professor Tung's because it involved high-ranking administrators of my professional school who worked in an unprecedented manner to influence and intimidate professors in my department and those who served on various independent reviewing committees to vote against my bid for tenure. The "redacted" summaries that I received completely eliminated all relevant information about the discriminatory actions of these individuals that was contained in my review documents. It was only because a dozen faculty members who sat on various reviewing committees in the multitiered tenure evaluation process had the courage to take the extraordinary action of breaking with the honored tradition of academic confidentiality, and to testify on my behalf in grievance hearings, as well as to provide me with the copies of unedited versions of my review documents, that we were able to lift the veil of discrimination in my case. And even in the seemingly enlightened and tolerant confines of a contemporary university community, there was ample evidence from several faculty witnesses that the top administrators in my professional school had referred to me privately on several different occasions as a "dumb Jap" or a "fat Jap." For three years, even after an independent academic senate grievance committee at my campus had ruled, on two separate occasions, that I had received unfair and biased treatment and that the top departmental official had engaged in "a deliberate attempt to deny tenure," the very highest ranking administrators of the university protected and supported this individual.

The third misconception is that Asian Pacific American professors who encounter problems in their employment or promotion are more inclined than other minority-group faculty to walk away and not contest an unfair denial of tenure or promotion. The decision to fight is a very difficult one, but as I indicated earlier, a growing number of Asian American professors across the nation and in different disciplines are asserting their rights and standing up for what they believe is right and proper—for their own sake, to be sure, in protecting their jobs or careers, or in gaining a fair and equal evaluation of their scholarly accomplishments, but also for the sake of other Asian Americans, other people of color, and women in all fields of employment, especially for those who are making their way up the academic pyramid and those who will be attempting to have meaningful and productive academic careers in the future. Asian Pacific Americans in general and Asian Pacific American professors in particular have been viewed stereotypically as passive and docile, and are expected (even more than the average assistant professor) to quietly fade away when a decision is made to deny them tenure. However, I know from my own case and those of many older assistant professors with whom I have spoken that this kind of passivity is no longer appropriate. Many of us have come to the belief that it is our obligation to assert our rights and to stand up for what we believe—just as laborers did in an earlier period in Asian Pacific American history, and just as other Asian Americans have done and are doing in confronting glass ceilings in careers and fields that have been traditionally closed to Asian Pacific Americans. Without being overly rhetorical, there simply does come a time when one has to be the one that takes a stand. It is only by doing so that we can ever hope to advance in this society (Nakanishi, 1989).

Until recently the issue of Asian Pacific American faculty representation and tenure was not as forcefully or explicitly pursued by Asian Pacific American students, community leaders, or even other Asian American professors. I believe Asian Pacific Americans have paid a very heavy price for not fully advancing this issue. Both nationally and in the University of California system, Asian Pacific Americans have the lowest rate of tenure of all groups (Escueta and O'Brien, 1991). At the same time, as a special Asian Pacific American task force to California's state attorney general recommended in a recent report on Asian Pacific American civil rights issues, "Asian Pacific Islander Americans cannot continue to be represented predominantly as students within California's educational institutions. The poor representation of Asian Pacific Americans among the faculty and staff in those institutions can only perpetuate institutional biases that result in unfair admissions policies, financial aid decisions, academic curriculum planning and employment policies that are oblivious to the needs of Asian Pacific Islanders" (Attorney General's Asian and Pacific Islander Advisory Committee, 1988, p. 99).

The interest focused on my tenure case at UCLA during a three-year period and the support activities that surrounded it serve to highlight the extraordinary mobilization that the Asian Pacific American community of the 1990s is capable of mounting and willing to undertake to enhance the presence of Asian Pacific Americans in higher educational institutions, particularly in relation to their hiring and promotion as faculty and administrators. These actions share a number of features with the highly visible and effective lobbying and protest activities that were launched in relation to allegations concerning the possible use of admissions quotas for Asian Pacific American applicants to undergraduate colleges, reflecting this group's willingness to marshall support and resources to protect what they believe is their most important vehicle for social mobility (Nakanishi, 1989). I preface this list by noting that during the three years of this battle, my own department faculty voted five times to recommend tenure; and I won two internal campus grievances of discrimination. Prior to resolution of this case, the following actions occurred:

The *Los Angeles Times, New York Times,* and other media—especially the Asian American press—carried personal stories on my case.

Over 150 Asian American studies scholars from across the nation wrote letters of support.

Many members of the University of California Board of Regents called the highest ranking officials at the university about the case.

The entire Asian American congressional delegations from Hawaii and California wrote letters demanding that I receive tenure.

The Republican governor of California, at the urging of the Southeast Asian community in Orange County, called for tenure.

Tens of thousands of dollars were raised for a legal defense fund for my case.

An extraordinary array of major civil rights organizations, bar associations, chambers of commerce, and labor unions in the State of California wrote and endorsed resolutions demanding tenure.

UCLA students held three large rallies in support of my tenure on campus; the third rally received endorsements for the rally from over half of the California state legislature, the mayor of Los Angeles, every top Asian American elected official, a number of civil rights groups, and the undergraduate and graduate student body governments. It also attracted every television station in Los Angeles, along with reporters from all the city's newspapers.

Every major UCLA Asian American alumni donor demanded a meeting with top administrators to discuss my case.

Finally, the California legislature held up a $60 million appropriations bill to build a new business school building at UCLA, and requested a closed-door meeting with the chancellor, a meeting that ultimately resulted in an end to the struggle.

The extraordinary array of expressions of support that emerged on behalf of my own case reads like a handbook for political action. As my attorney noted, "Victory brought Asian Americans to a new understanding of our political power" (Minami, 1990, p. 81). The struggle also communicates the powerful resistance that Asian Pacific Islanders may encounter in their quest for equitable treatment. During my tenure case numerous doctoral students indicated to me that the outcome of my case would influence their decision to pursue doctoral research and careers in Asian American studies.

Recommendations

The representation and professional experiences of Asian Pacific Americans in the faculty and administrative ranks of American colleges and universities has not received sufficient policy or programmatic attention. As institutions grapple with an array of issues concerning the ethnic and intellectual diversity, they should fully and positively consider the concerns of Asian Pacific American students, professors, staff, and administrators. I here offer several recommendations to assist institutions in their deliberations and planning activities:

1. Contact and work with a variety of national and regional professional organizations, representing a wide range of academic disciplines, to assist in the hiring and retention of Asian Pacific American faculty and administrators, and to gain a fuller understanding of the issues facing Asian Pacific Americans in higher education. These include, among others, the Association of Asian American Studies, California's Asian Pacific Americans in Higher Education organization, and Asian Pacific caucuses to professional associations like the American Psychological Association and the American Educational Research Association. Relevant organizations are listed in the November-December 1989 issue of *Change* magazine, which focused on Asian Pacific Americans.

2. Include Asian Pacific Americans as participants and as a focus of attention in all institutional planning activities and studies dealing with faculty diversity issues, and in efforts to augment the presence of scholars of color at your institution.

3. Be sensitive to the fact that Asian Pacific American faculty members from a wide range of disciplines have encountered both overt and covert forms of discrimination and prejudice in their professional careers, particularly in the consideration of tenure and promotion. In many cases, they represent the first scholars of color in a department, and may encounter difficulties that other pioneers have faced in entering new fields.

4. Take positive steps to recruit and train Asian Pacific Americans for academic and nonacademic administrative positions at your institution. Do not make unwarranted assumptions about their interest, or lack of interest, in becoming administrators, or their potential leadership talents.

5. Be cognizant of demographic projections, all of which suggest that the population of Asian Pacific Americans will continue to grow in all regions of the country. Issues about the fair representation of Asian Pacific Americans at faculty and administrative levels will continue to be compelling.

6. Recognize the diversity of Asian Pacific Americans, and the differences among them with respect to their participation at different levels of American higher education. Academic pipeline issues are still very important for the representation of all Asian Pacifics in certain fields, particularly the humanities, and for certain groups like Southeast Asians, Pacific Islanders, and Filipino Americans in practically all academic fields. Special attention should be paid to increasing the numbers of doctoral students from the latter three groups, and in increasing their opportunities for future professorial and administrative positions.

References

Attorney General's Asian Pacific Islander Advisory Committee, *Final Report*. Sacramento, Calif.: Office of the Attorney General, 1988.

Chan, S. "Beyond Affirmative Action: Empowering Asian American Faculty." *Change*, Nov.–Dec. 1989, pp. 48–51.

Escueta, E., and O'Brien, E. "Asian Americans in Higher Education: Trends and Issues." (American Council on Education) *Research Briefs*, 1991, 2(4), 1–11.

Hsia, J., and Hirano-Nakanishi, M. "The Demographics of Diversity: Asian Americans and Higher Education." *Change*, Nov.–Dec. 1989, pp. 20–27.

Minami, D. "Guerrilla War at UCLA: Political and Legal Dimensions of the Tenure Battle." *Amerasia Journal*, 1990, 16(10), pp. 81–107.

Nakanishi, D. "A Quota on Excellence? The Asian American Admissions Debate." *Change*, Nov.–Dec. 1989, pp. 38–47.

Nakanishi, D. "Why I fought." *Amerasia Journal*, 1990, 16 (1), 139–158.

Omatsu, G. "Movement and Process: Building Campaigns for Mass Empowerment." *Amerasia Journal*, 1990a 16 (1), 63–80.

Omatsu, G. (ed.). "'Power to the People!' The Don Nakanishi Tenure Case at UCLA." *Amerasia Journal*, 1990b, 16 (1), 61–169.

Stanford University. *Building a Multiracial, Multicultural University Community: Final Report of the University Committee on Minority Issues*. Stanford, Calif.: Stanford University, 1989.

Latino Faculty at the Border
Increasing Numbers Key to More Hispanic Access

MICHAEL A. OLIVAS

This is not your usual *Change* essay but, then again, this is not your usual problem.

I am regularly asked why Latinos do not fare better in school and society, usually by well-meaning colleagues who are genuinely troubled by the problem. Having spent eight years in the Catholic seminary studying for the priesthood, I tend to be an optimist and put the best gloss on any problem. So, for all the years I've been writing about the education of Latinos, I have always taken the high road: I have variously "relied upon the reservoir of goodwill in the majority," counted upon colleagues to "follow their own institutional self-interest in seeking and graduating Hispanic students," and encouraged need-based aid programs because "in any need-based aid program, Latinos, who constitute one of the most impoverished communities, will more likely participate." I have delivered dozens of lectures (usually during Hispanic Awareness Weeks or Cinco de Mayo celebrations) exhorting my people to do well and encouraging institutional leaders to help my people.

But, like the Reverend Leon Sullivan's finally giving up on White South Africans, I have come to believe, reluctantly, that the majority of persons in higher education do not think a problem exists, do not act as if a problem exists, or do not care about minority achievement. I say this, knowing how sharply critical and pessimistic this will seem to readers. However, I believe Anglo racism is at the heart of the problem. Even the self-help I have urged and the patronage of a small number of majority colleagues cannot resolve the clear and long-standing legacy of historical racism toward Latino populations in the United States.

For this proposition I could cite historical evidence, from the annexation of the southwestern United States to the colonization of Puerto Rico, to the Bracero Program and "Operation Wetback," to the English-only movement and long-standing immigration practices; I could cite more subtle practices, such as the heightened reliance on standardized testing and the indifference of philanthropy to Hispanic communities. This laundry list could continue but advances no purpose. Instead, I choose one issue on which to focus my point: the need for more Latino professors. I believe that this need is the single most important key to any hope for increasing Latino access.

While the need may be self-evident to *Change* readers and intuited by many educators, the extraordinary extent of the problem is not widely known, or is misunderstood. According to the most recent Office for Civil Rights figures (lamentably inadequate as they are), Hispanics constitute 1.5 percent of all faculty and just 1.1 percent of all tenured faculty.

As paltry as these figures are, they mask an even more startling under-representation, for the numbers include *all* fields of the professoriate and report *all* Hispanics, even some who would be surprised to find themselves carried on their colleges' books as minority faculty. I have found institutions that pad their figures shamelessly and that list retired, resigned, and temporary faculty as if they were active participants in institutional life. After teaching one special course as an adjunct on an extension campus for a university, I found myself listed seven years later in the institution's catalogue (one law school lists a 70-year old emeritus a decade later). Such examples are legion and probably double the true number of Hispanic faculty. Professors from Spain, Brazil, Portugal, and South America are routinely identified and misleadingly tallied as "minority" faculty. In several universities, Anglo women married to Latinos have been counted.

While I do not have the space here to dissect racial enumeration practices, suffice it to say that institutions employ far too few Latino faculty, employ far too many statistical tricks in their reporting, and that both practices evidence bad faith.

Although all fields are under-represented, I am going to use law faculty as an example, both because I know the practices in it better than in other fields, and because law professors have an influence in higher education beyond their small numbers. However, the problems Latinos face in entering the teaching of law mirror the problems of minorities in the academy at large: exceedingly small numbers, arbitrarily employed hiring criteria, and sheer prejudice. With adjustments for different trade usages and academic customs, the case I now recite resembles that in most disciplines.

First, one starts with exceedingly small numbers: fewer than three dozen of the 5,700 law teachers two-thirds of 1 percent) in the approximately 180 accredited law schools in the fifty states and the District of Columbia are Latinos; of these 35, there are 20 Mexican-Americans, 5 Puerto Ricans, and the remainder are Cuban or of other Hispanic origin.

Although law faculty positions are not as plentiful now as when law enrollments were soaring, a substantial number of vacancies are filled each year. In 1986-87, the most recent year for which data are available, 570 law professors (10 percent of the total) entered teaching. In that year, only one new Latino entered law teaching in the nation, and two left . . . if it's possible to lose ground, under the circumstances, we lost ground last year. Because several schools have more than one Latino teaching law, the 35 are concentrated in 24 schools (the University of New Mexico has 5 Latinos on its law faculty, earning it a designation as a nuclear-free zone or historical landmark). A recent study by the Society of American Law Teachers (SALT) found that 30 percent of respondent law schools had *no* minority faculty, either Latino or black, while another 34 percent had only one minority teacher. (Even if one includes black and Puerto Rican law schools, only 7 percent of the law professoriate is minority.)

These extraordinary data show the extent to which minorities, especially Mexican-Americans and Puerto Ricans, have entered the legal academy. Of course, these data are similar to other fields, from the least to the most prestigious. Data gathered by National Chicano Council on Higher Education officials report there are only three Chicano professors of higher education, seven physicists, a dozen in chemistry, with slightly higher numbers in sociology, psychology and bilingual education. By any measure, these numbers are appalling.

These figures constitute the demand What about the supply side? In 1987, all minority law students constitute 10.6 percent of law enrollments. Of these, 1,512 were Chicanos (1.3 percent), the same percentage of law enrollments as in 1975-76, when 1,443 Mexican-Americans were enrolled. To be sure, there are relatively few Latinos in the law school "pipeline," but the metaphor is misleading. First, the consumers (law schools) are also the producers; why don't they see their responsibility to recruit and graduate more Latino lawyers? Second, even 1,400 graduates a year produce a very large pool of eligible Latinos over time, certainly sufficient to produce more than the *one* Mexican-American lawyer hired to teach in 1986-87.

What went wrong? What can be done? Is law teaching the pantheon, with law review membership and Supreme Court clerkships the essential requirements for entry, and we're simply not qualified?

Hardly. Considerable data have been gathered on last year's new teachers, and their quality is indeed high. Nonetheless, of the 577 new law teachers hired, only 38 percent had law review experience (versus 48 percent of the total professoriate); 16 percent had been elected to Coif membership (the national honorary reserved for the top 10 percent of graduates); 10 percent held the L.L.M., an advanced graduate degree in law (versus 23 percent of the total); and only 14 percent had ever published an article or legal writing. Most interestingly, one-third had no legal experience before they entered teaching; 30 percent had not even passed a bar exam. It was not minority teachers who pulled down these data; the minorities who were hired statistically resemble their majority counterparts.

What is operating here? A powerful mythology permeates law hiring, as it does hiring in nearly all academic fields—that there are too few minority candidates for too few positions, and they possess unexceptional credentials for the highly credential demand. I believe these data paint the opposite picture—that, for most schools, white candidates with good (but not sterling) credentials are routinely considered and hired, while the high-demand/low-supply mythology about minorities persists.

As I have alleged, not only does this myth not square with available data, but the practices ignore the supply-side responsibility of law schools and the lack of marketplace alternatives for Latinos in other legal employment. After all, major firms and governments are not much more accessible to Latinos than are law faculties. The answer is an unpopular one because it entails racism, which permeates the academy as it does all of society.

That this is so should not surprise us, as higher education reflects our society, draws from it, and collaborates with it. After all, the legal road to *Brown v. Board of Education* was a series of higher education cases, suits in our lifetime that assaulted a segregated citadel. The poisonous residue of those practices remains. Many of today's senior faculty directly benefited from having it all to themselves, from not having to compete—in school or the academic marketplace—with women or minorities. To a large extent, they still don't compete, particularly not with Latinos.

After all my cynicism, what can be done? My suggestions are aimed at law teaching, but they apply to many professions and fields of study.

As in many professions, there is a formal hiring fair, or "meat market," for law hiring, one that inadequately reaches or serves Latino applicants—the conference of the American Association of Law Schools (AALS). Law schools could make that meeting a far more effective device for recruiting minorities. Recent minority alumni could be encouraged to register for the conference, and the forms could be sent to recent graduates who express an interest. I regularly carry AALS forms to conferences, scouting out minority talent; I send out dozens of forms each year, encouraging minority attorneys to consider teaching. Others could do this, thereby widening the formal stream of applicants.

Similarly, faculty could keep in touch with recent graduates who are undertaking advanced legal studies, making legal presentations, clerking, and engaging in private or government practice. Law deans should identify minority practitioners who may not wish to leave their firm but who might be persuaded to teach as an adjunct, judge a moot court, or lecture on their field of expertise in a lunch forum, continuing legal education seminar, or other teaching situation. This would expose students to minority professionals and encourage minority attorneys to consider teaching as a possible alternative career opportunity.

Many full-time teachers began teaching as adjunct or part-time faculty. Every legal writing program staffed by local attorneys or senior law students should be required to include minorities on its teaching staff. Faculty in all disciplines should encourage promising minority students by hiring them as research assistants or teaching assistants, to mentor them, inculcate scholarly values, and ensure a fuller stream of persons who will aspire to eventual careers in teaching. Schools should always "be on the prowl" for promising prospects, especially minority prospects.

Schools could structure interviews so that minorities can succeed, and can increase the likelihood of minorities succeeding by interviewing several minority candidates and by hiring more than one. One of the first law schools to hire Chicano faculty hired two at once in the early 1970s. That school (New Mexico) now has five Latino and a total of seven minority faculty members. It is clear that much more effort needs to be made to increase the critical mass of minority teachers in individual schools (remember: only a third of all law schools have two or more minorities). Minority faculty should be appointed to chair search committees, not merely serve as the lone member charged with affirmative action responsibilities.

A combination of formal and informal methods must be used to identify faculty. As with recruiting graceful seven footers, strong-armed quarterbacks, or musical prodigies, recruitment requires diligent looking. Historically black law schools and Puerto Rican institutions have always been able to recruit lawyers, yet few majority schools recruit faculty or graduates from them. Minority legal organizations have contributed many extraordinarily talented attorneys to the teaching ranks and regularly attract excellent minority law graduates. Government service has recruited a disproportionate array of minority attorneys because of less elite hiring criteria, more perceived openness to minorities, and few opportunities at elite law firms—which tend to have very few minority partners or associates. Indeed, faculty enter legal teaching from a variety of backgrounds; in this regard, law schools have a larger stream of candidates than do other academic fields, which recruit new faculty directly from doctoral programs. However, almost no field is without minority candidates. I believe it is self-serving mythology that minority candidates are "flooded with offers" when every year, qualified and interested minorities are looking for academic work but do not find it.

One way for a university to encourage the recruitment of minority faculty is to provide an additional "slot," or position, reserved for the minority teacher. Most universities have funding mechanisms that reserve resources for the occasional superstar, faculty spouse, senior administrator, or other out-of-the-ordinary hiring; let resources be reserved that same way for minority hiring. To turn up the heat, insist that schools or departments with one or no minority faculty members cannot hire any majorities until they achieve success in attracting minorities. Only courageous provosts, deans, and presidents can effect this practice, but courage is what we need.

One more idea: placement and search firms are regularly used by major law firms and by universities in administrative searches; they could be used by law schools and other departments to find the minority faculty talent we so desperately need.

The several ideas suggested here are not revolutionary or even that unusual. Most law schools employ them, or versions of them, when looking for hard-to-find specialists; every law faculty has had to search for a specialized tax or bankruptcy or decedents-estates teacher, all of whom have been less readily available than, say, a contracts or torts teacher. The same diligence should be used in looking for minority law teachers.

I am convinced that there is a good supply of Latinos in most fields who are interested in and qualified for teaching. This is more a demand-side issue, and institutions should take more seriously their obligation to demand more minority faculty.

It is little wonder that Latinos have not fared well in the academy. The condition of Hispanic education is appalling, as noted throughout this issue of *Change*. Even spending more money has not drastically improved matters, since majority decision makers and educators simply do not appear to be concerned. The best concern that could be shown is to hire more Latino teachers, in all disciplines, and to make it a priority to produce more teachers. Teachers and scholars make a difference in their instruction, their writing, their service, and their characterization of social issues. They serve as useful irritants, interpreters of society, and as role models for their students.

I have chosen to critique law professor hiring practices, but any field could be similarly analyzed. The lamest excuses exist in the social and behavioral sciences, to which many Latino scholars have been drawn. Many minority faculty work in minority institutions or low-prestige colleges, which then removes them from consideration in more prestigious schools. One of the most distinguished Chicano historians labors at a state teachers college, with a teaching load of four courses per semester. This pattern is extremely common. Given the proper support and opportunities, many more minority faculty members could successfully perform at research institutions. In an earlier book (*The Dilemma of Access*), I found startling evidence that minority faculty were not even reasonably represented in the least prestigious sector—community colleges—where few faculty hold the doctorate or engage in research.

In an eloquent law review essay, law professor Rachel Moran described the phenomenon of being "a society of one":

> The psychological and social consequences of membership in a Society of One are pervasive and severe. The lone minority or woman professor is likely to encounter two extreme

reactions. Some students and faculty will expect the minority or woman professor to serve as a representative of all minorities and women. These expectations will manifest themselves in demands for compliance with an impossible standard of performance. Another group will stigmatize the isolated minority or woman professor by assuming that he or she is inherently less capable than white male colleagues and was only appointed because of affirmative action. These dehumanizing views ignore the unique individual characteristics of minority and women law professors by either elevating them to superhuman symbol or reducing them to substandard political appointment. Both reactions have devastating consequences. An impossible standard of performance is a sure-fire formula for disappointment and failure. A negative expectation about academic promise may become a self-fulfilling prophecy. . . . A lone minority or woman law professor cannot discount the salience of race, ethnicity, and gender in the legal academy. Yet, in standing apart as a Society of One, these professors cannot assume the limited diversity on law faculties implies equality or even a grudging respect.

To be sure, many faculty of all stripes will find their work alienating, solitary, or unsatisfactory. I believe, however, that minority faculty are made to feel more isolated than are their majority colleagues and that isolation leads to disaffection and attrition. My discussions with disaffected Latino academics, both former law faculty and those in other disciplines, lead me to conclude that many of these instances could have been avoided with better support and reduced tension. Most encountered the "Society of One" syndrome and felt that they had regularly encountered hostile colleagues or racist students. While some feel relieved to be away from their situation, many feel bitterly betrayed that their original choice of careers was curtailed by prejudice. This attrition, like Latino attrition generally, seems an extraordinary waste in light of dire needs.

As a Chicano law professor, I fully appreciate the extent to which I and Latino colleagues have greater responsibilities; our service contributions and informal duties at times seem overwhelming. However, unless higher education takes more seriously *its* responsibilities to seek out others like us, and to behave differently toward Latinos, the extraordinary cycle of exclusion from faculty ranks will continue. Higher education is poorer for its loss.

Michael A. Olivas is professor of law, University of Houston, and a consulting editor of Change magazine.

A Comparative Study of Occupational Stress Among African American and White University Faculty: A Research Note

EARL SMITH AND STEPHANIE L. WITT

Today, it is finally becoming more common to openly discus the fact that African Americans, in all areas of academe, are losing ground (American Council on Education, 1989; Loury, 1987; Murray, 1984; Thomas, 1987). The *silence* that previously accompanied the precipitous decline of both African American students (Fiske, 1985) and African American faculty in American universities is no longer acceptable, if we are at all serious about reversing this trend. Many faculty, administrators, and even students are now engaged in a thorough debate about how to rectify the situation and move closer toward solutions that ensure African American faculty will have equal access to the opportunity structure that exists within the university system in the United States. These issues are timely for the healthy survival of our society.

The specific problem this paper addresses is the occupational environment of African American faculty members teaching at predominantly white colleges and universities in the U.S. We approach our subject through research on occupational stress. For more than a decade there has been an increase in interest among both researchers and practitioners toward the understanding as well as improving of employees' quality of life at work. The main outcome of this dual concern is the proliferation of research on better understanding employees' job stress (Gmelch, 1988). We take this route for we feel that the adverse trends in overall faculty decline (many through retirements) on the one hand, and decline in the numbers of African American faculty on the other, suggests that by the year 2,000 there will be fewer African American faculty employed in the academy than at the present time.[1]

The number of African American faculty holding full-time tenure-track positions at predominantly white institutions of higher learning, although never large, has been on the decline since the mid-1970s (College Board, 1985; Exum, 1983; Thomas, 1986).[2] This dwindling presence of the African American professorate has not received a great deal of scholarly attention. Two scholars who have examined this problem are Howard Bowen and Jack Schuster. In their book, *American Professors: A National Resource Imperiled* (1986, p. 152), they note the following:

> No aspect of our campus visits was more alarming than the situation we found with respect to minority faculty members. Over the past two decades, higher education has made considerable progress in opening the faculty to ethnic minorities, but that movement seems to have ground to a halt and may even be in reverse gear. Almost everywhere we went, we

were struck by the scarcity of minority faculty. More unsettling still, a decline in their numbers is anticipated for the near future.

This alarm about the number of African American faculty presently employed, and the fewer numbers that will be employed as professors on university campuses in the future, compelled us to ask questions about the experiences of African American faculty members that transcend the usual exercise reporting basic demographic characteristics of these faculty, especially their numerical count.

The issues we address and hope others will become more concerned about are related to the occupational environment that African American faculty inhabit. Specifically, we ask *what* do we really know about the work environment of African American professors? We feel the most obvious answer to this question is "not very much."

Literature Review

National-level research on African American academicians is rare. Banks (1984) seems to feel that one of the primary reasons for this lack of research focus is that prior to 1965 few African American faculty members were employed at traditionally white American colleges and universities. Because of low numbers of African American faculty, and because of both discrimination is hiring and widespread social segregation, we can surmise that nationwide studies of African American faculty teaching at historically black colleges and universities would not have been viewed as an important problem choice for research.

More recently, though, some scattered research has appeared on African American faculty that suggests sources of job-related stress. Exum (1983) found that competition between institutional values, such as merit, and affirmative action policies have created several difficult contradictions in academe that are not easily settled. Palmer (1983), in another analysis of the careers of African American faculty who teach at predominantly white colleges and universities, reports that the *fear of failure* is one of the most significant stresses that African American faculty face: "Most stressful of all, some blacks say, is a gnawing fear that a professional failure will not only cause them personal humiliation, but prompt white colleagues to doubt the abilities of all blacks to survive in academe" (p. 18).

In his essay entitled "Afro-American Scholars in the University," Banks (1984) finds that questions about incorporation, overall happiness, and specific duties that are asked of African American scholars leave little doubt that environmental factors impact heavily on African American faculty in that they report more stress and anxiety than their white counterparts.

Banks tells us that white administrators are interested in hiring African American faculty for a variety of reasons; among them are motives linked to *specific role expectations* they will play once they are actually hired and on campus. Although these expectations vary from campus to campus, they tend to fall outside of the norm of what faculty are typically hired to do. He says (1984, pp. 326–327):

> The administrators of universities expected black scholars to function quite differently from their White counterparts. The often troublesome realities of black students on White campuses seemed to call for a new set of insights and efforts, and the newly hired black faculty members were expected to provide both the insights and efforts. . . . Sometimes the recruitment was subtle, at other times quite explicit. Rarely did administrators spell out the special kinds of expectations they had for black professors prior to employing them. Consequently, many individuals who had been trained for serious intellectual work and took jobs expecting to do such work found that their orientation was not compatible with what the institutions expected of them. Scholarly work had to be accomplished in combination with the extra-academic responsibilities hoisted on to their shoulders and consciences.

In order to test these assertions, we undertook a nationwide study of university faculty and placed at the center of this work questions related to occupational stress. The following discussion is geared toward explaining what we did and what we ultimately found in our analysis.

From the outset, it is useful to offer a definition for the term *stress*. An examination of the relevant literature shows no firm, generalizable definition of stress. In a 1973 paper, Selye noted that "stress, like relativity, is a scientific concept which has suffered from the mixed blessings of being too well known and too little understood" (p. 127). Furthermore, the literature on stress does not specify the social determinations of stress except in a vague and confusing manner (Dodge and Martin, 1970, p. 58; Murphy, 1985).

Originally, a good portion of work on stress was based on Selye's (1956) definition of stress as "the nonspecific response of the body to any demand." Building on the original thrust of Selye, recent work in the occupational stress arena refers more to the stresses that arise from psychological and social processes that result from the personal interactions with other persons within the occupational environment (Baker, 1985).

Much of the current work on stress has often been based on conditions set forth in a study by McGrath (1976, p. 1352). Building on earlier work about the conception of a necessary perception by the individual of a stressful situation, McGrath observes: "So there is a potential for stress when an environmental situation is perceived as presenting a demand which threatens to exceed the person's capabilities and resources for meeting it, under conditions where he expects a substantial differential in the rewards and costs from meeting the demand versus not meeting it." Along with the differential between rewards and costs, the uncertainty of the results is also central to McGrath's conception of stress. In line with this body of literature on occupational stress, our study utilizes questions that tap the psychological as well as the psychosocial levels of stress that are perceived by individual faculty members within their respective university work environments.

Caplan and Associates (1980) reported that university faculty represent, overall, one of the *least stressed professions*. They made this assessment based on the fact that unlike laborers in industry—where, heretofore, most of the stress research has been conducted—university faculty have the capacity to manage their workday and work week and therefore are able to make critical choices about teaching schedules, how much time to devote to research projects, and how much time they can spend away from teaching and research (Gmelch, 1982, pp. 88–89). Other studies, however, report that nationwide, university faculty are under extreme pressure and are reporting high levels of workplace stress. A very perceptive passage from the *Chronicle of Higher Education* (February 4, 1987) says: "What turns a professor into a bundle of nerves? 'Too many tasks in too little time' is a chief complaint. Faculty members have classes to teach, papers to grade, grant applications to write, committee work to complete, students to advise, and books and articles to write and publish."

In sum, our review of the literature indicates that African American scholars may be subject to higher levels of job-related stress than their white counterparts. Reasons for this suggested in the literature include the pressures and visibility ("fish-bowl effect") associated with being a "token," and, second, the pressure that results from the "extra-academic" demands frequently placed on African American faculty. In our analysis we will determine whether significantly different levels of work-related stress are reported by African American and white faculty and whether the previously reported low level of stress among university faculty still holds. Further, we will examine whether different aspects of the working environment are important sources of stressors for African Americans as opposed to white faculty.

Methodology

The data used in this research paper are derived from a sample of male, female, African American, and white college and university faculty. The data for the study were collected by the Fellows of the Interdisciplinary Research Center for Faculty Stress and Productivity at Washington State University utilizing the *National Faculty Stress Survey*. The questionnaire asked respondents about their perception of stress primarily within the university work environment.

Since securing an adequate sample of nonwhite faculty has been a problem in previous research, our sample was constructed in such a way as to ensure an adequate representation of African American faculty. Major professional organizations from all academic disciplines (e.g., the American Sociological Association) were asked to share their lists of minority members. University-based affirmative action officers and ethnic studies program directors from a cross-section of American colleges and universities were also contacted for lists of minority faculty. All professional associations as well as the institutions contacted responded positively to our requests.[3] Personal letters were sent to eminent African American scholars asking for the other African American scholars employed at their institutions and within the nationwide university system. Again, the cooperation of all individuals was quite high. Several selection criteria were adhered to for this study. To be included in the sample, scholars had to have an earned doctorate (Ph.D. or Ed.D.) and to have been employed, full time, as a member of the instructional faculty of their respective college or university. Scholars who had changed their career paths to work outside of instruction were not included in the sample.

For the development of the original sample, each African American female was matched to a white female and each African American male was matched with two white males and one white female whose names were gathered by using individual college catalogs for those universities in the study. Matching was done by tenure status, discipline (Biglan, 1973), and type of institution following the Carnegie classification of institutions of higher education (see Witt, 1990 for a list and discussion of the Carnegie classification of institutions).

A total sample of 2,095 faculty were drawn from 233 colleges and universities. Responses were obtained from 193 colleges and universities. When accounting for those questionnaires that were nondeliverable (e.g., deceased faculty, moved—no forwarding address, etc.), the response rate was 51.2 percent. Given the length of the survey as well as time constraints of university faculty, the response rate is satisfactory.

From our total sample, a "matched-pairs" sample was created for analysis in this paper (Hays, 1973). The matching was done to control for any differences due to the effects of status. By controlling for status factors and differences among the respondents, the precision of the analysis was increased, so that a true difference between the matched groups would be much more discernible (Kolstoe, 1973, p. 223). The African American and white respondents were matched along the following dimensions: tenure status, type of institution, race, age, gender, marital status, rank and academic discipline. The matched pair sample consists of 246 matched pairs of male and female full-time faculty, yielding a total matched pairs sample of 492 individuals (the total sample for the unmatched study in 893 faculty). Comparisons of stresses of African American faculty with those of the matched white faculty in the sample will suggest the extent to which African American faculty are like their match and the ways that they may differ.

The Faculty Stress Index used in this analysis is based on previous work done by Gmelch (1982), which led to the development of the Administrative Stress Index. This index forms the core (30 items) of the Faculty Stress Index. The Faculty Stress Index was created by reviewing relevant literature and having faculty keep "stress logs" of the situations and demands that pressured them. Gmelch and co-workers report that the test/retest results indicate that the Faculty Stress Index has a mean item reliability coefficient of .83, "indicating a high degree of consistency of measurement in the items finally included in the national faculty survey" (Gmelch, Wilke, and Lovrich, 1986). For each of the 49 items in the Faculty Stress Index, faculty indicated their stress levels on a Likert-type scale of ranging from (1) "no pressure" to (5) "high or excessive pressure." Using the responses obtained on these stress items, additive scales were computed for the three major areas of faculty activity: teaching, research, and service.[6]

The items used to create the teaching stress scale are the following: evaluating the performance of students; having students evaluate my teaching performance; teaching or advising inadequately prepared students; inadequate time for teaching preparation; having repetitious teaching assignments; resolving differences with students; receiving inadequate recognition for teaching performance; making classroom presentation; teaching subject matter that I'm not prepared for.

The items used to create the research stress scale are the following: having unclear criteria for the evaluation of research activities; receiving insufficient recognition for research; preparing a manuscript for publication; securing financial support for research; insufficient time to keep up with developments in my field; making presentations at meetings.

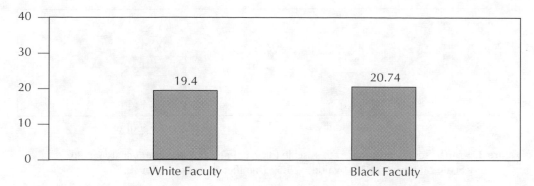

Figure 1. Mean scores on teaching stress scale for matched samples of university faculty. Scale range = 8 to 40; t-value = –1.79 (not significant).

The items used to create the service stress scale are the following: Participating on committees; Inadequate recognition for community service; Frequent requests for community service; Insufficient reward for institutional and departmental service; No clear criteria for the evaluation of service activities; Insufficient time for service activities.

Results

In order to conduct an analysis to see whether African American and white university faculty report different levels of occupational stress, a matched-pair difference of means test was computed on each of the three scales addressing stress from teaching, research, and service. Figure 1 displays the mean scores on the scale addressing stress from teaching for African American and white respondents. As expressed in the chart, African American respondents report slightly higher mean levels of stress from teaching than do whites (20.74 versus 19.40, out of a possible 40 points), but the difference is not statistically significant.

Figure 2 is a display of the mean score on the scale addressing stress from research for matched pairs of African American and white faculty. In this case, African American faculty report higher stress levels from research than white faculty (17.59 versus 16.50, out of a possible 30 points). A difference of mean test indicates that this difference in reported stress is statistically significant at the .05 level.

Figure 3 is a display of the mean score on the scale addressing stress from service activities (including campus governance) for the matched pairs of African American and white faculty. African American respondents reported higher mean levels of stress from service activities (16.36) than white faculty members (12.82 out of a possible 30 points). A difference of means test for the matched pairs of faculty indicates that the difference in the mean reported stress levels from service activities for the two groups is statistically significant ($p \leq .01$).

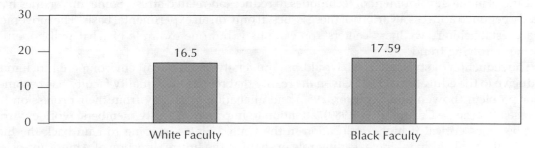

Figure 2. Mean scores on research stress scale for matched samples of university faculty. Scale range = 6 to 30; t-value = –2.01 (significant at the .05 level).

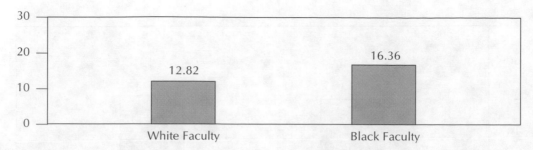

Figure 3.   Mean scores on service stress scale for matched samples of university faculty. Scale range = 6 to 30; t-value = –5.57 (significant at the .01 level).

Conclusion and Recommendations

This analysis comparing the reported stress levels of African American and white university faculty for teaching, research, and service activities indicates that in some areas important differences in their stress levels exist. Specifically, African American and white faculty have different levels of stress in regard to research and service activities. In many ways, this reflects the findings of previous studies detailing the additional demands and time constraints imposed on African American faculty (Witt, 1990). Our understanding of why these different stress levels exist is based on what we learned from respondents about their tasks, responsibilities and, overall, their position within the university organizational structure. Banks (1984, p. 327) addressed a similar issue and found:

> Rather than being allowed—and indeed encouraged—to concentrate on their academic work, many black professors were sucked into a plethora of activities often unrelated to their competence and interests. Institutions that have traditionally discouraged younger faculty members from participating in administrative committees and in community affairs drafted young black scholars for these activities.

To be sure, the two areas of faculty activities that require uninterrupted free blocks of time (e.g., research and service) are most likely to be negatively impacted by additional time commitments in meetings, student advising, and other non-teaching/research-related duties. As we found in our analysis, these are the areas in which African American and white faculty levels of stress differ the most.

Furthermore, this insight also provides a starting point for both university faculty and university administrators to initiate systematic discussions on ways to reduce, cope with, and then eliminate stress-producing anxieties. Medical practitioners, based on longitudinal epidemiological studies, have long known that occupational stress can result in serious heart disease, which ultimately leads to early death (Eliot, 1988; Syme, 1988 and forthcoming). It is only recently, though, that stress has begun to receive the kind of medical attention that it deserves (Karasek and Theorell, 1990). It is our hope that the identification of the major areas of difference in the sources of stress among African American and white college and university faculty will be of value to institutions in the development of techniques to reduce job-related stress. Some universities have already begun to address a variety of these issues, if only on an experimental basis. The movement toward establishing "wellness centers" on campus is but one example of what will hopefully become a growing trend.

The reduction of stress, we feel, would put university faculty in an environment much more conducive to the educational task. Given the reality that retention of quality faculty has become a major problem (Bowen and Schuster, 1986) and alienation of faculty from their profession has increased (Carnegie Corporation, 1989), attention to improving faculty members' work environment becomes critical if higher education in the United States is going to gain back the high rankings it once held in taking a leading role in shaping the future direction of American society (Pearson, 1985).

We believe that although our work points to problems of workplace pressure among two groups of university faculty, the study has several limitations, mainly the use of self-report data. Regardless, this paper does offer some important indicators for further research. We strongly feel that further research is needed to help clarify both conditions and relationships in regard to faculty environmental milieu and how this affects the levels of stress found among the underrepresented ranks of African American faculty. Finally, the data presented here point to the critical need to address these concerns longitudinally, which could significantly enhance our predictive powers that address issues of the overall faculty effectiveness (e.g., learning outcomes, productivity) within institutions of higher learning. In so doing, we increase the opportunity to become much more competitive in the world marketplace with other nations (e.g., Japan) that have in the past and continue to place higher education at the top of their priority lists for the twenty-first century.

Acknowledgments. We would like to acknowledge the assistance of two of our colleagues at Washington State University. Professors Nicholas Lovrich (Political Science) and Walter Gmelch (Education Administration) gave generously of their time and critical insight in the preparation of this study. We also thank the two anonymous reviewers for their helpful comments. Send reprint requests to Professor Earl Smith, Department of Sociology, Pacific Lutheran University, Tacoma, WA 98447.

Notes

1. We should point out that this assessment is in opposition to the relatively optimistic viewpoint shared by liberal blacks writing in the 1970s who based their entire assumption on the goodness of affirmative action policies (cf. Fleming, 1978).

2. African American faculty representation at all types of institutions—large and small, public and private, two-year and four-year—is less than 5 percent of all college and university faculty. African American faculty make up only 4.4 percent of all full-time university faculty (Zimbler, 1990).

3. We followed the "snowball" method outlined in Babbie (1986, p. 263). For a good explanation of this procedure, especially the critical nature of trying to generate a nationwide sample of African American scholars (see Pearson, 1985. *Black Scientists, White Society and Colorless Science*).

4. For African Americans, this almost always means a change from faculty status to that of administration.

5. Respondents assessed the level of pressure that they felt on the stress questions on the following scale:

No or Slight Pressure		Noticeable or Moderate Pressure		High or Excessive Pressure
1	2	3	4	5

6. Scale reliability's were computed for each scale. Teaching—white faculty Cronbach's alpha = .81; Teaching—African American faculty Cronbach's alpha = .80; Research—White faculty Cronbach's alpha = .65; Research—African American faculty Cronbach's alpha = .56; Service—White faculty Cronbach's alpha = .64, Service—African American faculty Cronbach's alpha = .63.

References

American Council on Education (1989). *Minorities in Higher Education*. Washington, DC: Office of Minority Concerns, 8th Annual Report.

Baker, Dean (1985). The study of stress at work. *Annual Review of Public Health* 6: 367–381.

Banks, William (1984). Afro-American scholars in the university. *American Behavioral Scientist* 27: 325–338.

Biglan, Arthur (1973). The characteristics of subject matter in academic areas. *Journal of Applied Psychology* 57: 195–203.

Bowen, Howard, and Schuster, Jack (1986). *American Professors: A National Resource Imperiled*, New York: Oxford University Press.

Brown, Shirley Vining (1988). *Increasing Minority Faculty: An Elusive Goal*. Princeton, NJ: Educational Testing Service.

Caplan, Robert, et al. (1980). *Job Demands and Worker Health*. Survey Research Center, Institute for Social Research. Ann Arbor: The University of Michigan.

Caplow, Theodore, and McGee, R. (1958). *The Academic Marketplace*. New York: Basic.

Carnegie Corporation (1989). The condition of the professoriate: Attitudes and trends. *Chronicle of Higher Education*, November 8.

Carnegie Foundation (1985). Carnegie Foundation survey of faculty members. *The Chronicle of Higher Education*, December 18.

College Board (1985). *Equality and Excellence: The Educational Status of Black Americans*. New York: College Board Publications.

Dillman, Donald (1978). *Mail and Telephone Surveys*. New York: John Wiley and Sons.

Dodge, D., and Martin, W. (1970). *Social Stress and Chronic Illness*. Notre Dame: University of Notre Dame Press.

Eliot, Robert S. (ed.) (1988). *Stress and the Heart*. New York: Futura Publishing Company.

Exum, William (1983). Climbing the crystal stair: Values, affirmative action, and minority faculty. *Social Problems* 30: 383–399.

Fiske, Edward (1985). Minority enrollment in colleges is declining. *New York Times*, October 27.

Franklin, John Hope (1976). *Racial Equality in America*. College: University of Chicago Press.

Gmelch, Walter (1982). *Beyond Stress to Effective Management*. New York: John Wiley and Sons.

Gmelch, Walter (1988). Educators' response to stress. *The Journal of Educational Administration* 26: 222–231.

Gmelch, Walter, Lovrich, Nicholas, and Wilke, Phyllis (1984). Stress in academe: A national perspective. *Research in Higher Education* 20: 477–490.

Gmelch, Walter, Wilke, Phyllis K., and Lovrich, Nicholas P. (1986). Dimensions of stress among university faculty. *Research in Higher Education* 24: 255–286.

Harvey, William (1986). Where are the black faculty members. *Chronicle of Higher Education*. January 22.

Hays, William (1973). *Statistics for the Social Sciences*. New York: Holt Rinehart Publishers.

Karasek, Robert, and Theorell, Tores (1990). *Healthy Work: Stress, Productivity, and the Reconstruction of Working Life*. New York: Basic Books.

Kolstoe, Ralph (1973). *Introduction to Statistics for the Behavioral Sciences*. Glencoe, Illinois: Dorsey Press.

Loury, Glenn (1987). Why preferential treatment is not enough for blacks. *The Chronicle of Higher Education*, March.

Mason, John (1975a). A historical view of the stress field—Part I. *Journal of Human Stress* 1(1): 6–12.

Mason, John (1975b). A historical view of the stress field—Part II. *Journal of Human Stress* 1(2): 22–36.

Massey, Walter (1987). If we want racially tolerant students, we must have more minority professors. *The Chronicle of Higher Education*, July 17.

McGrath, J. E. (1976). Stress and behavioral organizations. In M. Dunnette (ed.), *Handbook of Industrial and Organizational Psychology*, pp. 1351–1395. Chicago: Rand McNally.

McMillen, Liz (1987). Job-related tension and anxiety taking a toll among employees in academe's stress factories. *The Chronicle of Higher Education*, February 4.

Mingle, James (1981). The opening of white colleges and universities to black students. In Gail Thomas (ed.), *Black Students in Higher Education*, pp. 18–29. Westport, CT: Greenwood Press.

Moore, William, and Wagstaff, L. (1985). *Black Educators in White Colleges.* San Francisco: Jossey-Bass.

Murphy, Lawrence (1985). Occupational stress management: A review and appraisal. *Journal of Occupational Psychology* 57: 1–15.

Murray, Charles (1984). *Losing Ground: American Social Policy, 1950–1980.* New York: Basic Books.

Palmer, Stacy (1983). In the fishbowl: When blacks work at predominantly white colleges. *Chronicle of Higher Education*, September 14.

Pearson, Willie, Jr. (1985). *Black Scientists, White Society, and Colorless Science.* New York: Associated Faculty Press.

Selye, Hans (1956). *The Stress of Life.* New York: McGraw Hill.

Selye, Hans (1973). The evolution of the stress concept. *American Scientist* 61: 692–699.

Smith, Earl, and Pearson, Willie, Jr. (1991) Scientific productivity among a sample of black and white female Ph. D.'s. *Journal of Social and Behavioral Sciences* 35: 163–174.

Syme, S. Leonard (1988). Social epidemiology and the work environment. *International Journal of Health Services* 18: 635–645.

Syme, S. Leonard (forthcoming). Social determinants of disease. Department of Biomedical and Environmental Health Sciences, School of Public Health, University of California at Berkeley.

Thomas, Gail, ed. (1981). *Black Students in Higher Education.* Westport, CT: Greenwood Press.

Thomas, Gail (1986). *The Access and Success of Blacks and Hispanics in U.S. Graduate and Professional Education.* Washington, DC: National Academy Press.

Thomas, Gail (1987). Black students in U.S. graduate and professional schools in the 1980s: A national and institutional assessment. *Harvard Educational Review* 57: 261–282.

Witt, Stephanie (1990). *The Pursuit of Race and Gender Equity in American Academe*, New York: Praeger.

Witt, Stephanie, and Lovrich, Nicholas (1988). Sources of stress among faculty: Gender differences. *The Review of Higher Education* 2: 269–284.

Zimbler, Linda (1990). *Faculty in Higher Education Institutions, 1988.* 1988 National Survey of Postsecondary Faculty (NSOPF-88). National Center for Education Statistics. Washington, DC: U.S. Department of Education.

The Survival of American Indian Faculty

Wayne J. Stein

More American Indian faculty teach in four-year institutions in the United States today than at any time in the past. Yet a recent survey of these faculty indicates that many are so frustrated by their experiences in higher education that they intend to move on to other careers.

This recent survey—the unpublished *American Indian Faculty Survey*—was sent to 30 Indian faculty members at four-year institutions during the spring of 1992. Twenty-two of those faculty responded. The survey was aimed at extracting information relative to how—and whether—American Indian academics survive in four-year institutions. Specifically, the survey asked:

- What differences do American Indians bring to the world of higher education in the United States?

- What process must American Indians go through to gain entry into the world of higher education and what roles must they play once entry has been gained?

- What perceptions do American Indian faculty hold about the roles they play in higher education?

- What are Indian faculty doing to overcome barriers, to achieve success as faculty members in academic departments—especially to get their work published in meaningful journals?

- What can authorities in higher education do to help make a career accessible and rewarding to American Indian faculty?

This paper discusses some answers to these questions and offers recommendations designed to help colleges and universities ensure the survival of American Indian faculty. That survival is at risk. It is certainly true that the percentages of Indian candidates in doctoral programs have increased, as have the percentages of all minorities in doctoral programs: American Indians and Alaska Natives from .2 percent to .4 percent; Asian Americans from 3.8 percent to 4.4 percent; African Americans from 3.8 percent to 4.3 percent; and Hispanics from 1.2 percent to 2.6 percent.[1]

The problem is that fewer non-white candidates indicate they will pursue a faculty position once they graduate with their doctorate. The higher education pipeline is drying up.[2] Institutions of higher education usually give five reasons to explain why they are not hiring more faculty:

- Minorities aren't qualified enough.
- Minority faculty just aren't out there.
- Minority faculty want astronomical salaries.
- Minority faculty wouldn't want to live here.
- We're already doing everything we can.[3]

Part Myth, Part Luck

Professor Janet Thomas[4] is one American Indian who *was* hired for a faculty position. A member of a Southwest tribe and a junior faculty at a large Midwestern research university, she was queried by the *American Indian Faculty Survey* about why and how she entered academe.

Thomas came to higher education after a successful career in the federal government. She made the choice to change careers based on personal considerations upon completing her terminal degree.

Professor Thomas is that rare individual known in affirmative action circles as a "two for one." She is a woman *and* a member of a minority group. Such individuals are counted twice by institutions when reporting their affirmative action programs for the year.

Thomas has heard all the conventional wisdom about higher education and minority faculty. She considers the widespread idea that a non-white and especially a non-white female can pick and choose her desired position in higher education to be a myth. She feels that she herself gained some advantage in securing her position because she was female—not necessarily because she was Indian— because the institution only interviewed women for the position.

Other American Indian faculty who answered the survey described their search for faculty positions as both intensely frustrating and a learning experience. Institutional affirmative action offices often require that departments interview any qualified minority candidate, a mandate that places Indian candidates repeatedly into interview pools where they have little chance of being hired.

Prospective Indian faculty have learned that the most crucial ingredient for a successful search is who they knew or how well they could cultivate important members of the search committees.[5]

Jason Red Wing, a member of an East Coast tribe and a junior faculty member of a large research university in the Southwest, is currently not tenured. He expects to gain tenure after undergoing the promotion and tenure process at his university.

Professor Red Wing is somewhat representative of the most recent generation of American Indian scholars. He chose higher education as a medium for his scholarly work while in his 30s. He came to that decision after a career that took him through a host of positions in tribal and community service and eventually to a community college. Why did Red Wing chose higher education as a career?

"I needed a job and a friend worked in a community college and invited me to apply," he explained. "From there, my interest grew."

Like many of today's American Indian faculty, Red Wing took a circuitous route to higher education. He didn't see collegiate teaching as a career choice early on, but, instead, serendipitously began his career due to circumstances rather than plan.[6]

The *American Indian Faculty Survey* found that this may be the case for many American Indian faculty. Not many American Indians in higher education actually envisioned a higher education career. They arrived in academe after first beginning careers in another phase of education, tribal government, federal government, or, rarely, business.

Mentoring Works

Red Wing was fortunate to find a caring and interested mentor in the higher education system who just happened to be American Indian. His mentor guided his graduate work and helped him secure his present position.

American Indian faculty generally find mentors while pursuing their advanced degrees, but rarely are these persons of American Indian descent. But once the Indian person has secured a position with a four-year institution, gaining the friendship and guidance of a mentor has proven much more difficult.

Only 50 percent of today's American Indian faculty, the *American Indian Faculty Survey* finds, have found mentors in their departments or universities. Those faculty who have are quick to share stories about mentor guidance that helped them overcome obstacles that could have proven career-ending.

Those American Indian faculty without mentors express frustration and worry that they may not be making the right career choices.

Today, in most four-year institutions, mentors—minority and nonminority—are self-identifying. Most of the time, the mentor is a senior faculty member in a department who makes a personal commitment to mentor a junior faculty member. Sometimes the junior faculty member is American Indian. Senior faculty and department heads are the true gatekeepers of their particular disciplines and of higher education in general. Without their support and approval, most junior faculty, minority or nonminority, will not succeed.[7]

Perceptions and Misperceptions

American Indian faculty fulfill the expected faculty roles of researcher, teacher, and servant to the community in four-year institutions. But a number of other factor—real or perceived—do come into play as American Indian faculty members work their way through the tenure and promotion maze.

One of the most damaging perceptions that must be overcome by American Indian and other minority faculty is that they were hired only because they were a member of a minority group and, therefore, possess inferior qualifications or credentials. Non-white women have a double problem because women often face this same perception regardless of color. Many American Indian faculty who responded to the survey often feel that they must work twice as hard as their non-Indian counterparts to prove themselves.

What is interesting about this attitude is that American Indian faculty, who recall past discriminatory treatment, often give it more credence than their non-Indian colleagues, Unfortunately, misperceptions can be as powerful as facts to those who hold them.

It is true that nonminority faculty see being a minority as a benefit in the promotion and tenure hunt and 67 percent see minorities as facing no barriers to promotion and tenure. This finding, a sharp contrast to the 78 percent of minority faculty who feel they face widespread barriers, illustrates the tremendous gap between the two groups and the perceptions of reality they hold.[8]

Most universities and four-year colleges publicly state that research, teaching, and service are valued equally on their campuses. Faculties of most universities and four-year colleges answer the question about equality among research, teaching, and service by stating that research is number one, teaching number two, and that service to university and community is a distant third.

Minority faculty, including American Indians, agree with their nonminority colleagues when asked the same question. There is no doubt in their minds that research is king on their campuses. Teaching is rewarded but not nearly as well as research and publication. Community service, again, is a distant third.[9]

Quality Journals

Professor Allen T. Whitt, a member of a south central tribe and a faculty member of a large four-year institution in the Southwest, has tenure in his department. He tells a story of vacillating departmental pressure and benign neglect at his university.

Whitt's department demands research of high quality and publication in journals it deems worthy. Whitt has problems with both requirements and has fought a running battle for years over these two standards held by his department. His quarrel isn't with requiring quality research or publishing that research, but with what non-Indian faculty view as worthy of research and where it should be published.

Whitt understands that his personal area of research is not highly valued by his colleagues because it is outside the mainstream and is on American Indian issues. Further, many journals in his field suspect his work because it is about Indians and he is an American Indian. Dr. Whitt has been told that it would be impossible for him to do objective scientific research on his own people.

Non-Indian authors publishing on American Indians are routinely published ahead of Whitt, who must seek out lesser-known journals to publish his work. Often, these are journals published by Indian academic departments for the express purpose of publishing research about American Indian issues. It seems ironic that nonminority academicians or publishers would hold such rigid beliefs when one notes that most research and published articles about the nonminority population of this country are done by those very same nonminorities.

Dr. Whitt's experience is not an isolated incident. A number of other American Indian scholars reported the same problems in a recent survey. A report done by Stanford University in 1989 on building diversity on their campus found that their minority faculty also had problems with their research being undervalued by their departmental colleagues.[10]

The problem of undervaluing research done by American Indian and other minority faculty is of real concern. Research and publication have become the key criteria considered when a junior faculty member is up for tenure and when tenured faculty are up for promotion. American Indian faculty must have the support of their departmental colleagues if they are to gain tenure or promotion. If their research and the journals in which it is published are not valued, their chances for tenure or promotion are greatly reduced.

American Indian faculty generally find teaching to be the area where they receive the most reward, personal and professional, and receive the best professional criticism. With the call to diversify the curriculum for all disciplines on university campuses through the use of core requirement for graduation, Indian studies has become an attractive source of core courses.

Indian faculty in departments other than Indian studies, minority studies, or ethnic studies also have much to offer when teaching course work with an American Indian perspective. Often, they are able to greatly assist their departments to meet core course requirements by such offerings.

This fairly recent phenomenon in higher education does have a down side for American Indian faculty. They are often asked to carry heavier than normal teaching loads, to take larger than normal student enrollment in their classes, and are asked to develop new courses on a frequent basis. Couple this with the mistaken belief of nonminorities that American Indian faculty members must be expert on *all* things Indian regardless of their field of study or tribal affiliation, and stress can quickly build for these American Indian academics.[11]

Community Service

Service is an area that has long plagued the American Indian higher education faculty community. It is the multi-faceted nature of university service that gives most American Indian faculty their greatest joy and greatest headaches. Though service other than through teaching and research is the least rewarded activity in the tenure and promotion hierarchy of departments, colleges, and universities, it puts the most demand on the American Indian faculty member.

Minority faculty are such a rarity on most campuses that university committees compete vigorously for their time and services. American Indian faculty can find themselves serving on numerous committees if they or their departmental chairs don't put limits on such service. Most American Indian faculty feel compelled to serve when asked, and junior faculty members can soon find themselves with little time to do research or class preparation.[12]

Universities also often expect American Indian faculty to participate in fund-raising efforts through grant writing. These efforts, most often directed at the federal government, seek to raise the income and prestige of the university and assist American Indian people.

After helping to secure the funds, whether public or private, the American Indian faculty member is often asked to administer the resulting program. These additional responsibilities can be devastating to the tenure efforts of an American Indian junior faculty member. Neither grantsmanship nor administration of resulting programs are given much weight in the tenure process for neither is a true scholarly activity.

American Indian faculty members can gain real importance on campus through such activities, but it is a reality that if they are junior and haven't kept up with their research and publications, they are in serious trouble. On the majority of four-year institution campuses, it is still "publish or perish."

Neighboring or in-state tribal and urban Indian groups also often expect American Indian faculty to serve in nonuniversity organizations cations or to write grants. American Indian faculty often see themselves as part of the much larger extended American Indian community. They gain much satisfaction from service to that larger community, but get little or no reward from their university or four-year college for having performed it.[13]

American Indian faculty, junior or senior, find they are expected by students, colleagues, and administrators to serve as mentors, advisers, and role models to all American Indian students, and even all other minority students on campus. This can be a truly heavy burden not often shared by their non-Indian colleagues. At the very least it isn't *expected* of their non-Indian colleagues as it is of them, by others and themselves.

American Indian faculty find themselves spending inordinate amounts of time and effort in mentoring and advising Indian students who may or may not be in any of the classes they teach or on their student advising rolls. American Indian faculty see this as an important role and most often do it willingly and joyfully.[14] They know the importance of being there for American Indian students seeking help, advice, or just assurance that everything will work out with hard work and perseverance.

The dangers for American Indian Faculty assuming these roles, as they most often do, are threefold:

- They take on another stressful, unrewarded, time-consuming activity.
- The administration begins to hold them responsible for the success or failure of Indian students.
- Other non-Indian professionals and faculty are relieved of their responsibilities toward Indian students.[16]

American Indian faculty must weigh carefully the joy they get from working with all Indian students on campus against the real problems that overcommitment can cause. If they are junior faculty, they must take even greater care than their senior colleagues.

The Survival of American Indian Faculty

Given that retention of American Indian faculty has been fair to poor on many American campuses, universities and colleges must try harder to find American Indian faculty and must be more creative in keeping them on campus and away from burn-out.[16]

Universities and four-year colleges can take a series of steps to enhance the chances that American Indian faculty members will be successful members of their campus communities.

Institutional Commitment

Institutions can begin by making a serious and creative effort to hire more American Indian faculty. This commitment should start at the top of the institution and be accompanied by workshops, seminars, and other communication programs sponsored by the university.

These efforts should be directed toward changing how faculty, administrators, and students view American Indian faculty. Affirmative action needs to be presented as an opportunity to add new and enriching elements to the environment of the university, not as a system of enforced equality imposed on everyone. These communication efforts must be well-planned and ongoing, if the cultural environment is truly going to change on any campus.[17]

Such a commitment also means not accepting the many excuses used to avoid the effort to seek qualified American Indian candidates, or used not to hire American Indians who might apply for faculty positions.

By increasing the number of American Indian faculty, several good things happen for an institution and for other Indian faculty. The institution has met its responsibility to diversify, and there are more American Indian faculty members to share the many expectations placed on minority faculty.

Universities and four-year colleges can also create career paths for promising American Indian students that lead to faculty positions. This can be done by searching out talented and intelligent American Indian students and encouraging them to consider a life in higher education.

Once identified, institutions need to support such students in graduate school with teaching and research assistantships. This philosophy of "growing your own" or joining a consortium of institutions "growing their own" has great merit. Institutions can truly select the best and the brightest to enter the disciplines of higher education.

Mentoring and American Indian Faculty

Once an American Indian faculty member is hired, appropriate administrators need to take time to ensure that this person becomes acclimatized to the institution. It is here that the chairperson of a department can make a major difference. By ensuring that the new faculty member is comfortable in the institutional environment, the chances are greatly enhanced that the faculty member will stay with the university.

The best way to accomplish this acclimatization is through a mentoring relationship.[18] The department chair can seek out senior faculty members within the department who would be willing to take on this important duty and assign such faculty as mentors to incoming American Indian faculty. This simple courtesy would help the new faculty member learn the departmental ropes and expectations quickly and accurately and help the new person understand what is needed for tenure. A mentor could also guide the new American Indian faculty member through the wide range of roles expected of faculty and warn against overcommitment.

Equality in Research

Institutions, departments, and senior faculty must rethink how they view research done by American Indian faculty. For too long, they have undervalued such research for what may be ethno-centric and possibly racist reasons. A fundamental change here would greatly help American Indian faculty gain recognition for the research they do that pertains to American Indians.

Rethinking the value of American Indian faculty research would have a positive ripple effect and change how journals view such work, for it is the senior faculty in any discipline who referee the articles that go into the most important journals in a given discipline.

This rethinking would also change—for the better—how smaller, more specialized journals dealing mainly with American Indian issues are viewed. This may be the toughest change and improvement recommended because it asks for a change in old, oftentimes strongly-held, beliefs and values of the majority faculty members.

Departments need to take care when assigning courses to junior American Indian faculty to develop and teach. They must give junior American Indian faculty the appropriate support when course assignments are made. This can be done by being realistic when evaluating the time commitments each course will take.[19]

The Reality: There are Few Indian Faculty

Department chairs and non-Indian—nonminority—faculty need a better understanding of what service expectations they and others have of American Indian faculty. If American Indian faculty are expected to serve on numerous committees, participate in grantwriting, serve the extended noninstitutional Indian community, and be role models for Indian and minority students, they must be rewarded for these services when it comes time for tenure or promotion.

If an institution or department don't see these as important to the tenure or promotion process, then the dean of the college and the department chair must make this crystal clear to the

American Indian faculty. By doing so at each stage of the relationship between institutions and American Indian faculty, from the interview for a position to promotion to a higher rank, much confusion and heartache could be avoided.

Yes, there are more American Indian faculty than ever serving in institutions of higher education in the United States. Yes, conditions are better than ever for American Indian students and faculty in higher education. Nevertheless, many of the conditions that make it hard for American Indian faculty to survive as professionals in the institutions of higher education continue to exist.

Higher education must continue to evolve in such a way as to encourage more American Indians and other minorities to become active and successful faculty in the institutions of higher education of the United States. The country is changing in many ways at a rapid pace, none more rapidly than the roles and numbers of its many minority citizens.

Notes

1. Stanford University, 1989, p. 21.
2. Pepion, 1992, p. 5.
3. Spann, 1988, pp. 5–8.
4. The names used in this paper are fictitious, but their responses are accurate and based on the 1992 American Indian Faculty Survey.
5. Pepion, 1992.
6. Stein, 1992.
7. Pepion, 1992, p. 3.
8. Pepion, 1992, p. 100.
9. Pepion, 1992, pp. 92–93; Stanford University, 1989, pp. 22–23.
10. Stanford University, 1989, pp. 23.
11. American Indian Faculty Survey, 1992; Kidwell, 1990.
12. American Indian Faculty Survey, 1992; Pepion, 1992; Stanford, 1989.
13. Kidwell, 1990.
14. American Indian Faculty Survey, 1992.
15. Kidwell, 1990.
16. Kidwell, 1990; Stanford, 1989.
17. Sanchez, 1992–93.
18. The National Education Association's Office of Higher Education recently published *Mentoring Minorities: Passing the Torch*, which offers a thorough look at how the mentoring relationship among faculty can evolve into a workable—and successful—experience for all concerned.
19. Kidwell, 1990.

References

Stein, W. J. "American Indian Faculty Survey." (Unpublished survey), 1992.

Kidwell, C. S. "Indian Professionals in Academe: Demands and Burn-out. In *Opening the Montana Pipeline*. Sacramento: Tribal College Press, 1990.

LaCounte, D., Stein, W. J., and Weasel, Head, P. *Opening the Montana Pipeline*. Sacramento: Tribal College Press, 1990.

Pepion, K. "American Indian and Other Minority Faculty." (Ph.D., diss. research), University of Arizona, 1992.

Sanchez, A. A. "Diversity in Leadership, Diversity in the Classroom." *Community College Journal* 63, no. 3 (December/January 1992–93).

Spann, J. *Achieving Faculty Diversity.* Madison: The University of Wisconsin System, 1988.

Stanford University. *Building a Multi-Racial, Multi-Cultural University Community.* Palo Alto: Author, 1989.

Wayne J. Stein (Turtle Mountain Chippewa) is an assistant professor of higher education and director of the Center for Native American Studies at Montana State University in Bozeman, Montana. He works closely with tribal communities, governments, and the seven tribal colleges of Montana on a wide variety of topics and programs. He recently published his first book, Tribally Controlled Colleges: Making Good Medicine.

Socializing Women Doctoral Students: Minority and Majority Experiences

Caroline Sotello Viernes Turner
and Judith Rann Thompson

The doctorate is a ticket to employment in faculty positions, particularly at major research universities. Yet few minority men complete doctorates, and even fewer minority women complete doctorates. The 32,943 doctorates awarded nationwide in 1984–85 went differentially to majority men (45.6 percent), majority women (27.1 percent), minority men (5.6 percent) and minority women (3.6 percent) (Anderson et al. 1989, 219). In their discussion of the American professoriate, Howard Bowen and Jack Schuster (1986) conclude that minorities continue to be severely underrepresented in higher education.

Some reasons for this phenomenon are crumbling inner-city schools, a lack of role models, and a growing number of financially rewarding alternatives such as law, medicine, and business. In addition, many scholars suggest that current academic policies and practices may present barriers for both women and minorities while facilitating the progress of majority males (Finkelstein 1984; Baird, in press; Mitchell 1982; Menges and Exum 1983; Nettles 1990). Patrick Hill (1991) describes higher education institutions as organized to perpetuate "self-containment" and "marginalization." Several researchers assert that race and gender are interlocking sources of marginalization in higher education (Aisenberg and Harrington 1988; Collins 1989; hooks 1989; Carter, Pearson and Shavlik 1988; Aronson and Swanson 1991).

The literature thus suggests that a subtle but critical source of this marginalization is a professional social environment that fails to support or encourage women (Clark and Corcoran 1986). Both majority and minority women apparently lack access to socialization experiences. Yet proportionately fewer minority women have doctorates than majority women. As a consequence, we asked: What is the difference between minority and majority women's socialization experiences in graduate education programs? Do minority women receive fewer? Does racial discrimination add significantly to the gender barrier they are already experiencing?

To address these questions, we asked minority women doctoral students about their professional social experiences in graduate school.[1] We then compared their perceptions with those of majority women. Finally, from narrative data and related literature we drew implications for recruiting and retaining minority women as faculty. A conscious and well-planned effort to make the academic environment as attractive and supportive as possible for minority women could increase the number of minority women faculty in the future.

Theoretical Perspectives: Doctoral Student Socialization

Socialization is the process by which a person learns the ways of a group or society in order to become a functioning participant (Kozier and Erb 1988, 47). John Van Maanen defines socialization as a "life-long process that helps to determine a person's ability to fulfill the requirements for membership in a variety of life groups . . . work, school, clubs, family" (1984, 213).

Doctoral programs typically involve a lengthy period of adult socialization in cognitive skills, appropriate attitudes toward research and scholarships, and field-specific values. Shirley Clark and Mary Corcoran define three stages in this process: (1) anticipatory socialization, recruitment, and choice of field, (2) occupational entry and induction focusing on extensive formal training in graduate school including attendance in classes, advising, preparation for exams and dissertation, internships, mentoring, publishing, presenting, and getting a job, and (3) faculty role continuance or retention.

Naturally, as Beverly Lindsay (1988) points out, both institutional and individual forces influence this process. First, the departmental context in which students are socialized is created by institutional influences—federal and state laws and policies, institutional policies and practices, and the traditions and values of the institution, the department, and the discipline. Second, how individual students experience socialization opportunities is influenced by their cultural values, prior experiences with socialization, personalities, individual support system, level of commitment, and gender-related issues and values.

A successful socialization process is critical for a successful graduate career. Historically, the socialization of graduate students has been controlled by the prevailing culture which, until rather recently, has been overwhelmingly white and almost exclusively male. Acculturation has been generally most successful for those who could fit the status quo most comfortably (Boulding 1983; Hughes 1988; Martin and Siehl 1983). Women and minorities of both genders frequently come to academe with traditions very different from the majority culture. In fact, their values may actually conflict with those of the white male academic culture (Hall, Mays, and Allen 1984; hooks 1989; Sandler 1986; Collins 1989). In addition, racism and sexism have been cited as primary reasons for the marginalization of minorities and women in higher education (Baird, forthcoming; McClelland and Auster 1990; Menges and Exum 1983).

Nevertheless, Clark and Corcoran's work shows that socialization opportunities are extremely important to successful professional academic careers for women. This study examines whether minority women who are currently in graduate programs do, in fact, receive the socialization opportunities they need and whether they receive as many opportunities as majority women. We examined student experience using the stages of doctoral program socialization identified by Clark and Corcoran and found four indices of social opportunity in the experiences of the women in our study: (1) recruitment of student by department, (2) participation in apprenticeship and mentoring experiences, (3) perception of the departmental environment as competitive or cooperative and whether they found support networks in the department, and (4) experience of discrimination.

Methodology

We call our study site Midwestern University. It is a 123-year-old land grant institution with several campuses and research stations around the state. The main campus boasts one of the highest single campus enrollments in the United States and attracts students from every state and from 900 countries. Approximately 8,000 students are enrolled in the university's 180 graduate programs, making it one of the nation's top doctoral-granting institutions. This research university is located in a large metropolitan area in the upper Midwest.

The data on doctoral students that Midwestern University has collected for the last nine years follow national trends with remarkable fidelity. To provide a historical context for the study, we collected institutional data on self-identified minority and majority doctoral students attending Midwestern University from the winter of 1981 to spring 1990: statistics on enrollment, years to degree, and degrees completed.

Minority women doctoral students made up 1.5 percent (199) of the total doctoral student enrollment (12,847) during this period; majority women students comprised 28.7 percent (3,687); minority males comprised 2.2. percent; and majority males comprised 36.8 percent. Forty-six percent of the minority females and 30 percent of the majority females were in education. The only other major with an enrollment of more than ten minority female doctoral students was psychology.

Data on completed degrees indicated that minority women earned 1.5 percent (67) of the total doctoral degrees granted (4,593); majority women earned 26.9 percent (1,234); minority males earned 2.5 percent, and majority males earned 42.8 percent. Mean years to degree was 7.8 for minority women; 7.6 for majority females; 7.8 for minority males; and 6.5 for majority males. Few minority women enrolled in research doctoral programs; consequently, they receive few doctorates. Minority enrollment is largely confined to education and the liberal arts disciplines. Compared to majority males, minorities and women take longer to complete their degrees.

After examining these data, we took a closer look at the experiences of minority and majority women currently enrolled in doctoral programs. The graduate school gave us the names, addresses, and phone numbers of women registered during the fall of 1987 to the spring of 1990. A hundred and one were minority women. We then generated a random list of 101 majority women doctoral students registered during the same period. The graduate school sent all potential respondents a letter inviting them to take part in the study. Thirteen minority students and twenty majority students declined to participate. From those willing to participate, we interviewed a random sample of thirty-seven minority women doctoral students (ten blacks, seven Native Americans, fourteen Asian Americans, and six Hispanics) and twenty-five majority women doctoral students. Time, funding, and logistical constraints did not allow us to interview as many majority women as we wished, but all interviews were conducted in person and face-to-face.

To elicit information about backgrounds and future career plans, we asked interviewees to complete a two-page questionnaire of demographic data, including ethnic/racial background, marital status, number of dependents, full-time/part-time student status, department affiliation, and intent to pursue an academic career. Most respondents, both minority and majority, intended to pursue a faculty career, were in their mid-thirties, attended school full-time, commuted to campus, had no dependents, and reported high undergraduate (3.3 or better) and graduate (3.8 or better) grade point averages. Approximately half were married. Twenty-seven (73 percent) of the minority respondents and twenty (80 percent) of majority respondents were enrolled in the humanities and social sciences, including education. Ten (27 percent) of the minority respondents and five (20 percent) of the majority respondents were enrolled in the physical and life sciences, including engineering.

We also conducted an interview in which we used a semi-structured questionnaire as a guide to examine the process of personal and professional development of respondents. We asked each student to describe the kinds of relationships she had with other students and faculty members, and the range and type of opportunities that she has had for acquiring professional values and skills inside and outside the classroom. Interviews lasted from forty-five minutes to an hour and a half, depending on the length of responses given by the interviewee. All interviews were audio-recorded, transcribed, and separately coded by two researchers.

We identified student perceptions on four points from the interview data: the university recruitment process, departmental opportunities for apprenticeship and mentoring experiences, a cooperative or competitive departmental environment, and racial and gender discrimination in the department.

Findings

Our study found that minority women generally had fewer opportunities for professional socialization experiences than majority women. Although a few more minority women reported being actively recruited by graduate departments, the social environment for majority women was generally much richer. More majority women had apprenticeship and mentoring experiences. More frequently they reported the presence of support networks inside their departments.

Interestingly, minority women students reported little racial discrimination except for a lack of curricula on race issues. (This was also true of gender and class.) However, both minority and majority women overwhelmingly reported gender discrimination. Still, the comparative lack of socialization for minority women suggests that racism provides a double barrier for them, one they may not even be aware of, since they feel gender bias so conspicuously.

Recruitment

Despite strong verbal concerns expressed by Midwestern University administrators about the need to recruit solid minority candidates into graduate programs, only six of the thirty-four minority students (three Asian, one Native American, one African American, and one Hispanic) said they had been actively recruited by their department. Ironically, even fewer majority women—only two—had been departmentally recruited. In most cases, minority women reported that they had investigated the top institutions in their field and had chosen Midwestern University. As one minority women stated, "No one recruited me or talked me into it. I investigated some of the programs on my own. I talked to some of the people in the department, and I felt good about [it]."

One majority woman had worked with a professor whose doctoral degree was from Midwestern University and who had encouraged her to apply. The second student had received a call from a professor in the department offering her a three-year appointment if she became a doctoral student.

Apprenticeship Experiences

In general, majority women participating in this study had more opportunities than women of color for such apprenticeship opportunities as research and teaching assistantships, coauthoring papers with a faculty member, making presentations at professional conferences, and being introduced by faculty to a network of influential academics who could provide support for students seeking entry-level jobs.

Forty-nine percent of minority students held research or teaching assistantships, while 60 percent of the majority women did. Coauthoring articles ran 52 percent for the majority, 27 percent for the minority. Forty-eight percent of majority women students had opportunities to copresent papers with faculty members at professional conferences, while 38 percent of minority women did. When asked about help with entry-level job searches, 64 percent of the majority respondents and 51 percent of the minority respondents reported receiving such assistance.

Most minority women doctoral students who did not work full-time received financial support such as fellowships. However, only a few (those in the physical and life sciences) had research or teaching assistant positions leading to close working relationships with faculty. Some minority students believed that they were left out of funding and apprenticeship opportunities.

Although minority students reported getting along reasonably well with faculty, with few exceptions they did not have mentors—someone who takes a personal interest in providing apprenticeship opportunities for a given student. These minority women described their lack of sponsorship in graduate school this way:

> I guess I don't feel mentored. He [graduate advisor] doesn't seem as actively a mentor as my undergraduate advisor. So far I haven't seen the possibility of coauthoring articles with professors. I've only seen it with male students. I'm not participating in research projects. . . . So far for me, none of that has happened.

> Sometimes I feel very marginal. I attribute this to being off campus, although sometimes I wonder if it has to do with my age too. It's clear that there is a cohesiveness among the TAs that I don't participate in.

> I've noticed that several graduate students have had the fortunate opportunity to work collaboratively with professors. I don't know of any students of color who have enjoyed that same opportunity.

> I had no opportunities. I was left to figure things out for myself, and I didn't always know what I was doing. I don't feel I got the kind of advice I really needed.

Minority students who have mentors initiated the process. One minority graduate student described her advisor:

> He is accessible and has given me opportunities that have been really good. . . . But you see, I had to initiate them. . . . I think that is part of the process of being a graduate student. At first I was kind of expecting to be helped a little bit more and it didn't come, but he's one of the people who also says, "Well, we don't coddle you in grad school," but if you ask for something he will give it. . . . He's great. I just wish I had hooked up with him earlier, especially considering he's the reason I came here, but I was so intimidated by him that it took a while.

This student pointed out that the mentor-student relationship is utility-based:

> They care about the ones [graduate students] that work with them. Faculty in general don't care about graduate students. There are exceptions. And if you work for someone, then they are more helpful to you.

In contrast, majority women were more likely to mention both apprenticeship and mentorship opportunities provided within Midwestern University. One majority student provided this description:

> I feel very well mentored by my advisor, who is really well known in the field and the reason I came here. Also, I work with another professor on a research project and I feel like he is really taking time to not only have me work for him but teach me the ins and outs of research. I have participated in research projects and have been invited to co-author an article which is just at the beginning process. A professor invited me to apply to present at a conference (I haven't heard yet) and I know they'll help me get a job.

> This past year I really felt that my advisor was watching out for me. He provided me with an assistantship and then a fellowship. Both my program director and my advisor have really gone out of their way to make sure that I'm okay [financially] . . .

> I think [publications are] one thing our faculty is really supportive of. In fact, they really push you on it, which is good because, you know, sometimes you might not do anything if you're not pushed a little bit. Then most of the faculty I think really help you write and revise and get [the paper] ready for publication.

Most minority and majority students were first generation academics, and both minority and majority women reported being mentored by someone, usually a relative or a coworker, outside Midwestern University. However, relatives as mentors, in or out of the university, benefited majority women more often. Approximately one-third of the minority women doctoral students reported that at least one other family member held a doctoral degree, whereas almost half of the majority students interviewed did.

Departmental Environment and Support Networks

Majority respondents perceived their departments as cooperative, while minority respondents saw the department as competitive. Majority women doctoral students perceived themselves as part of the academic community at Midwestern University, and minority women doctoral students typically reported feeling detached from that community, even though they had positive relationships on campus.

During their interviews, most minority women made assertions of their autonomy—and isolation. A typical statement is: "I would say student relationships are supportive. . . . but I don't study with other students. . . . There is a formal student organization, but I haven't been a part of it because my job takes a lot of time." More minority students than majority students report that they work outside the university at least part time.

Minority students characterized the departmental environment as individualistic and competitive, particularly at the faculty level. Although they reported friendly relationships with other doctoral students in their programs, they did not generally have close friends on campus, and few lived on or very near the campus. When asked further about support, many reported that they achieved a sense of balance in their lives by being part of a broader ethnic/racial community. One student praised her community: "They'll support me! I've got a relationship in my community that's pretty wonderful. I go into my community a lot. . . . I retain a lot of connections."

Minority respondents wanted more opportunities to meet and hear about others like themselves. Said one: "Every once in a while I'll meet a black woman graduate student, and I'll wish I had more time to talk to her and I don't, and that's hard for me. . . . I don't think there are any resources really for minority graduate students, and it seems to me that most of things on campus are remedial, but where are the things that applaud us when we do well? We don't hear as much about them."

Majority students, on the other hand, reported a cooperative environment and described participating in collaborative study groups:

> Students are primarily supportive, some cooperative work done. Students do study together. . . . Probably my strongest supporters at the university are the people that I work with [on-campus].

> Students are very supportive and cooperative. Students study together.

> I would say it's a real cooperative environment as far as the students. . . . I go to students before I go to my professor to talk about what classes to take and what are useful classes. We have a real close-knit group of students working together.

Discrimination

Minority women seemed to perceive gender discrimination as a stronger barrier than racial discrimination to success in graduate school. They reported little racism, but, like majority women, reported extensive gender discrimination.

Most minority respondents said they had not experienced racial discrimination in either their programs or at Midwestern University in general. However three minority students provided the following perceptions:

> The students were not friendly toward me at all. Part of it, I know, is racism.

> Experience racial discrimination? Well, of course, but of course. I live in America. Yes, I've experienced racism and sexism in my program, on this campus and in the community. . . . I feel that some females, my white counterparts probably are aware of fellowship money and other types of moneys and are encouraged to apply.

> There is a difference in how students of color are treated, but it is subtle. I am not even sure that the faculty is aware of what is going on. "They" have a way of making you feel that what you have said is not as important as what the other students say.

In contrast to these three examples, both majority and minority respondents were vociferous and almost unanimous in reporting passive gender discrimination in their programs—a sense of being passed over in favor of less able male students—in every major. Only one or two students reported more active sexual discrimination ("put downs" in class), and in both cases it involved the same department. Typical reports of passive discrimination were:

> I took a seminar with him. There were five students. He spoke to the men. . . . When I would start to say something and be interrupted, it really bothered me. . . . I attribute it to sexism. He did not interrupt the men that way. (Minority)

> I think the students that get treated best are young white males because they do what they are supposed to do. They play the appropriate role. (Minority)

> The perfect graduate student is a young white male. (Majority)

> They're not trying to actively do you in, but there is not that extra effort to help someone get along and get a job and to keep yourself supported during it. I think that people have certain people that they decide are special people, mostly the white men, and they're the ones that start getting everything right from the beginning. (Majority)

I have a coadvisor situation. My advisor in the field is a man who's very good, but it's not the same kind of relationship. I get more advice from [my coadvisor in a different field]. Both of them are helpful [but] she understands what my struggles are much more than he does. (Majority)

It's a recurring theme that the grad students want more women to come and speak. Something like 50 percent of the active researchers in the biological sciences are women and maybe 40 percent in our particular field and last year three men were on the committee (organizing department seminars) and there wasn't a single woman speaker. It just doesn't occur to them. (Majority)

Some (graduate students) are treated better, typically the males. Male grad students tend to be the stars and females aren't, and that may change. In the second year class, there is one woman who is doing really well, but she just had a kid—she's doing well in research, but she is in a different track now, because she took time off. (Minority)

Most minority and majority respondents reported inattention to race and gender issues in curricula, a form of racial and gender discrimination by omission rather than commission. They said that their departments do not address issues of diversity or the role of class, gender, and race in research and teaching.

We have one faculty member, that's kind of her role is to look at cross-cultural issues and gender, but you know there's not specific coursework in that . . . no readings, no mention of works by minorities. (Majority)

They don't address it at all. . . . I don't really think the department . . . plans to address issues of student diversity and the role of gender and race in research and teaching. . . . I'd like to see the departments modify their curriculums in such a way that we do see other perspectives. (Minority)

Only one minority student provided an example of diversity consciousness in her department:

My advisor was one of the few people to really address the issue of race in terms of research and teaching and that was in our—class. He assigned a chapter on testing minorities and some of the issues.

Policy Implications

The literature makes it abundantly clear that socialization experiences are critical to success in graduate school and in a subsequent academic career. In our study, minority women report less access to such experiences than majority women, a finding verified by information from current tenured faculty. Thus, we can conclude that minority women have less opportunity for successful academic careers.

The relation of graduate school socialization and doctoral degree completion, as well as in subsequent career success in academe, are discussed extensively in the literature. Robert Bargar and Jane Mayo-Chamberlain (1983) found that the advisor-advisee relationship is crucial to the successful completion of a doctoral degree. Karen Winkler (1988) indicates that apprenticeship experiences help to pave the way to acceptance as faculty members. Clark and Corcoran (1986) provide narrative evidence that successful, tenured women faculty had the opportunity for socialization experiences with advisors and colleagues. Elizabeth Whitt found that "administrators expected [new faculty] to bring with them much of what they needed to know about being faculty members. They were expected to have prior socialization in research and teaching; appropriate values, expectations, and work habits; a research orientation; and a program of research already in progress" (1991, 191). Carole Bland and Constance Schmitz (1986) conclude that research knowledge and skills by themselves are insufficient to make a successful researcher; a supportive environment and role models are also required.

Yet despite the well-documented need for socialization experiences, minority graduate women in our study reported relative isolation, a lack of faculty mentoring experiences, and a lack of collegiality with other doctoral students. Few attend conferences, coauthor papers with faculty, or collaborate on faculty research projects. On the other hand, majority women doctoral students report more mentoring relationships and experiences, both student-initiated and faculty-initiated.

All respondents are doing well in the coursework, preliminary exams, and other formal requirements for the degree; however, minority women do not have the richness of mentoring experiences and apprenticeship experiences that majority women reported.

One of us received, in February 1992, a letter from a colleague that corroborated the accuracy of the minority women's perceptions. This colleague wrote:

> As a professor, when I look for a graduate student to fulfill these roles, I look for the brightest, the most advanced, the easiest to work with, the ones who have a beginning of their own network, and who have a schedule compatible with mine. . . . [Minorities and women in your study] are progressing through their program at a slower rate, are not around the university as much because they are working off campus, and may be more involved in their community outside the University than in the University and in the discipline. . . . Few faculty, out of the goodness of their hearts are going to choose a woman, minority, or disabled graduate student to work with them on their grants and articles if there is a white male who is perceived as slightly better on these features, because faculty see their own productivity and future at stake. . . . Our minority programs do not address the complex professional/social interaction within the system that facilitates or inhibits, in small but significant ways, the future success of graduate students and young faculty.

James Blackwell also underscores the accuracy of minority women's perceptions:

> Those who teach are often guilty of subconscious (though sometimes conscious and deliberate) efforts to reproduce themselves through students they come to respect, admire, and hope to mentor. As a result, mentors tend to select as protégés persons who are of the same gender and who share with themselves a number of social and cultural attributes or background characteristics such as race, ethnicity, religion, and social class. Because minorities are presently underrepresented in faculty positions, such practices inevitably result in the underselection of minorities as protégés. (1989, 11)

Doctoral degree granting institutions, like the one examined in this study, must make a more conscious effort to foster the development of minority women scholars. However, providing successful socialization experiences for all doctoral students may require not only behavioral changes but dramatic changes in institutional structures or the creation of new structures. According to Hill (1991), marginalization is perpetuated if new voices are added while the priorities and core of the organization remain unchanged. He states: "Were a college or university truly committed to democratic pluralism, it would proceed to create conditions under which the representatives of different cultures need to have conversations of respect with each other in order to do their everyday teaching and research," then continues, "Marginalization ends and conversations of respect begin when the curriculum is reconceived to be unimplementable without the central participation of the currently excluded and marginalized" (1991, 44, 45).

Specifically, first a way must be found to implement current official policies to actively recruit minority students. We found little evidence that minority (or majority) women were being sought for doctoral studies. Second, some of the funding for programs to serve minority students should be directed toward the social needs of minority women, who are often the only minority women in their departments. Third, an effort must be made to modify the curriculum to include contributions of men and women of color. Fourth, efforts must be increased to recruit and retain minority women faculty. Not only would such efforts provide role models, but a diverse faculty also means a diverse research and teaching agenda, increasing possible avenues for students to connect with faculty of similar backgrounds and interests. Finally, and perhaps most importantly, ways must be found to encourage current faculty to provide mentoring and apprenticeship opportunities for minority women. As Blackwell points out, mentoring minority students should not be the sole responsibility of minority faculty members. All faculty must share in the mentoring process. He also states that while mentoring is very time consuming, it is neither appreciated nor adequately rewarded in academe.

The letter cited earlier from one of our faculty colleagues sums the situation succinctly: "What needs to happen is [that] our influential, primarily older, white male faculty members need to want to work with, and find it to their advantage to work with research assistants, teaching assistants, and co-authors who are minority women."

While this study is persuasive, further research is needed to support the kinds of institutional changes necessary to provide minority women with the socialization experiences critical to successful academic careers. National studies are needed so that responses can be compared across ethnic and racial groups and across disciplines and fields. If academia is to be truly inclusive—and it must become so to maintain a position in the world that is relevant—then discrimination at the more subtle level of socialization opportunities must be addressed. Moreover, it must be addressed in an institutional context with consequences or incentives that are effective.

Note

1. We invited women who self-identified as black, Native American, Asian American, and Hispanic to participate in this study. Few minority women are enrolled in doctoral programs at Midwestern University and, in most instances, our respondent was the only minority woman in her department. Thus, for purposes of confidentiality, we do not designate ethnic and department affiliation.

Bibliography

Aisenberg, Nadya and Mona Harrington. *Women of Academe: Outsiders in the Sacred Grove*. Amherst: University of Massachusetts Press, 1988.

Anderson, Charles J., Deborah J. Carter, Andrew G. Malizio, with Boichi San. *1989–90 Fact Book on Higher Education*. New York: American Council on Education and Macmillan Publishing Company, 1989.

Aronson, Anne L., and Diana L. Swanson. "Graduate Women on the Brink: Writing as 'Outsiders Within.'" *Women's Studies Quarterly* 19, nos. 3–4 (December 1991): 156–74.

Baird, Leonard L. "The Melancholy of Anatomy: The Personal and Professional Development of Graduate and Professional School Students." In *Higher Education: Handbook of Theory and Research, Vol. 4*, edited by John C. Smart. New York: Agathon Press, forthcoming.

Bargar, Robert R., and Jane Mayo-Chamberlain. "Advisor and Advisee Issues in Doctoral Education." *Journal of Higher Education* 54, no. 4. (July/August 1983): 407–31.

Blackwell, James E. "Mentoring: An Action Strategy for Increasing Minority Faculty." *Academe* 75, no. 5 (September/October 1989): 8–14.

Bland, Carole J., and Constance J. Schmitz. "Characteristics of the Successful Researcher and Implications for Faculty Development." *Journal of Medical Education* 61 (January 1986): 22–31.

Boulding, Elise. "Minorities and Women: Even Harder Times." *Academe* 69 (January/February 1983): 27–28.

Bowen, Howard R., and Jack H. Schuster. *American Professors: A National Resource Imperiled*. New York: Oxford University Press. 1986.

Carter, Deborah, Carol Pearson, and Donna Shavlik. "Double Jeopardy: Women of Color in Higher Education." *Educational Record* 68, no. 4 and 69, no. 1 (Fall 1987–Winter 1988): 98–103.

Collins, Patricia Hill. "The Social Construction of Black Feminist Thought." *Signs: Journal of Women in Culture and Society* 14, no. 41 (1989): 745–73.

Clark, Shirley M., and Mary Corcoran. "Perspectives on the Professional Socialization of Women Faculty." *Journal of Higher Education* 57 (January/February 1986): 21–43.

Finkelstein, Martin J. *The American Academic Profession: A Synthesis of Social Scientific Inquiry Since World War II.* Columbus: Ohio State University Press, 1984.

Hall, Marcia L., Arlene F. Mays, and Walter R. Allen. "Dreams Deferred: Black Student Career Goals and Fields of Study in Graduate/Professional Schools." *Phylon* 45, no. 4 (1984): 271–83.

Hill, Patrick J. "Multi-Culturalism: The Crucial Philosophical and Organizational Issues." *Change* 23, no. 4 (July/August 1991): 38–47.

hooks, bell. *Talking Back.* Boston, Mass.: South End Press, 1989.

Hughes, Marvalene S. "Developing Leadership Potential for Minority Women." *Empowering Women: Leadership Strategies on Campus,* edited by Mary Ann Sagaria. New Directions for Student Services No. 44. San Francisco: Jossey-Bass, 1988.

Kozier, Barbara, and Glenora Erb. *Concepts and Issues in Nursing Practice.* Menlo Park, Calif.: Addison-Wesley Publishing Company, 1988.

Lindsay, Beverly, "Public and Higher Education Policies Influencing African American Women." *Higher Education* 17 (1988): 563–80.

McClelland, Katherine E., and Carol J. Auster. "Public Platitudes and Hidden Tensions." *Journal of Higher Education* 61, no. 6 (1990): 607–42.

Martin, Joanne, and Carol Siehl. "Organizational Culture and Counterculture: An Uneasy Symbiosis." *Organizational Dynamics* 12, no. 2 (1983): 52–64.

Menges, Robert J., and William H. Exum. "Barriers to the Progress of Women and Minority Faculty." *Journal of Higher Education* 54, no. 2 (1983): 123–44.

Mitchell, Jacqueline. "Reflections of a Black Social Scientist: Some Struggles, Some Doubts, Some Hopes." *Harvard Educational Review* 53 (February 1982): 27–44.

Nettles, Michael T. "Success in Doctoral Programs: Experiences of Minority and White Students." *American Journal of Education* 98, no. 4 (August 1990): 494–522.

Sandler, Bernice R. "The Campus Climate Revisited: Chilly for Women Faculty, Administrators and Graduate Students." Pamphlet. Washington, D.C.: The Project on the Status and Education of Women/Association for American Colleges, 1986.

Van Maanen, John. "Doing New Things in Old Ways: The Chains of Socialization." In *College and University Organization: Insights from the Behavioral Sciences,* edited by James L. Bess. New York: University Press, 1984.

Whitt, Elizabeth J. "'Hit the Ground Running': Experiences of New Faculty in a School of Education." *The Review of Higher Education* 14, no. 2 (Winter 1991): 177–97.

Winkler, Karen J. "Minority Students, Professors Tell of Isolation, Anger in Graduate School." *Chronicle of Higher Education* 35, no. 11 (9 November 1988): A15–A17.

Caroline Sotello Viernes Turner is Assistant Professor of Educational Policy and Administration at the University of Minnesota, Minneapolis. Judith Rann Thompson is Associate Professor in the Division of Education at Bennett College, Greensboro, North Carolina. We are grateful to Linda Heyne, Kathy James, LaVon Lee, and Jill Beaulieu-Wilkie, who conducted several interviews for this project. We also thank Estela M. Bensimon, Elizabeth Higginbotham, Shirley M. Clark, Karen Seashore Louis, Carole J. Bland, and members of The Review staff for their helpful comments and criticisms. This research was supported by funds from the University of Minnesota Commission on Women and the College of Education. An earlier vision of this paper was presented at the Annual Meeting of the American Educational Research Association, San Francisco, April 1992.

Minority Faculty Recruitment Programs at Two-Year Colleges

RONALD D. OPP AND ALBERT B. SMITH

Increasing the representation of minorities among full-time faculty is a particularly important issue at the two-year college level. In a current study from the U.S. Department of Education, two-year colleges were reported to enroll a disproportionate share of all minority students enrolled in higher education (*Chronicle of Higher Education Almanac*, 1991). Fifty-six percent of all Hispanics, 54 percent of all American Indians, and 42 percent of all African-Americans enrolled in higher education are attending two-year colleges.

Given the disproportionate number of minority students enrolled in two-year colleges, the need for adequate minority representation among full-time faculty in this sector is particularly critical. In a recent study, it was reported that minority students account for 19.2% of the nation's 13.7 million college students in 1990, up from 18.7% in 1980 (*Chronicle of Higher Education*, March 18, 1992). As minority students become a larger proportion of all higher education enrollments, finding ways to increase the recruitment and retention of minority college students is becoming an increasingly important concern in higher education. The significant presence of minority full-time faculty can help two-year colleges become more successful in recruiting and retaining minority students.

Minority faculty on two-year college campuses can also help increase the educational aspirations of minority students by providing positive role models of individuals with high levels of educational achievement. They can also help white students overcome prejudicial thoughts about the intellectual capabilities of people of color, and help white faculty gain a deeper understanding and appreciation for different cultural heritages (Linthicum, 1989). For all of these reasons, adequate representation of minority faculty is essential to excellence and equity in two-year colleges.

Federal data on the representation of minorities among full-time faculty in higher education are readily available. In a 1989–90 Equal Employment Opportunity Commission survey, it was reported that African-Americans represent 4.5%, Hispanics 1.9%, and American Indians .3% of all full-time faculty (*Chronicle of Higher Education Almanac*, 1991). The representation of these minority groups among full-time faculty is significantly less than their proportional representation in the overall U.S. population: African-Americans make up 12.1%, Hispanics make up 9.0% and American Indians make up .8% (*Chronicle of Higher Education Almanac*, 1991). Clearly, African-Americans, Hispanics and American Indians are significantly underrepresented in higher education compared to their representation in the general population.

Although Equal Employment Opportunity Commission (EEOC) data regarding the distribution of faculty by race/ethnicity are readily available, these data are typically not reported by *institutional type*. Thus, researchers interested in the distribution of faculty by race/ethnicity within two-year colleges have to rely on sources other than the EEOC for data. Most of the data about the racial/ethnic distribution of two-year college faculty comes from the work of individual researchers. In the most recent national study, based on a weighted sample of faculty in 89 community colleges, Astin found that about 9.8% of full-time faculty were minority (1991).

Purposes of the Study

One of the purposes of this study was to provide current *institutional* data on the number and percentage of underrepresented minorities among full-time faculty in two-year colleges. Unlike previous studies reporting data on minority two-year college faculty (Russell, 1991; Astin, 1991), this study was based on information gathered directly from two-year institutions rather than from faculty surveys. Thus, the number of minorities reported by institutions can be compared with the weighted estimates of the number of minority faculty derived from national faculty surveys.

Another purpose of the study was to examine empirically what academic administrators felt about a number of barriers to minority faculty recruitment. A number of researchers have posited attitudinal and structural factors which hinder the recruitment of minorities in four-year institutions (Smelser & Content, 1980; Reed, 1983; Menges & Exum, 1983; Exum, 1983; Exum et al. 1984; Reed, 1986; Banks, 1988; Bunzel, 1990; Mickelson & Oliver, 1991). This study was designed to test empirically whether these same factors are perceived as barriers to recruiting minority faculty at the two-year college level as well.

This study was also designed to examine empirically what institutions were *actually* doing to recruit minority faculty. Much of the existing literature on minority faculty recruitment consists of suggestions about what *should* be done to improve recruitment programs (Harris, 1989; Lessow-Hurley, 1989; Boyd, 1989). In only one recent national study was there an examination of what two-year colleges were *actually* doing to recruit minority faculty. That study contained a report on what *states* were doing to recruit minority faculty, but provided little information about what individual *institutions* were doing (Linthicum, 1989). This study complements that research on *state* programs by providing information on what is being done at the *individual campus* level to recruit minority faculty.

A final purpose of this study was to determine empirically what characterizes successful programs of minority faculty recruitment. Much of the existing literature has focused primarily on describing strategies for improving minority faculty recruitment, without testing empirically how successful these strategies actually are. In this study an analysis is provided about what strategies are related to having a high number of underrepresented minority full-time faculty. Hopefully, information about strategies which facilitate minority faculty recruitment can be utilized by two-year college administrators in designing more successful programs and practices.

Research Design

Definitions, sampling methodology, questionnaire design, data gathering procedures and response rates will be discussed in the sections that follow.

Definitions

In this study *underrepresented minorities* are defined as those minority groups whose presence among full-time faculty in higher education is not proportionate with their overall representation in the U.S. population. Using this definition of underrepresentation, the investigators focused on four different minority groups: African-Americans, Mexican-Americans, Puerto Rican-Americans, and American Indians. In this study *full-time faculty* were further defined as those individuals for whom teaching was their principal activity and who were considered full-time employees at their institution for at least nine months of the 1991–92 academic year.

Sampling Methodology

The researchers utilized individual two-year institutions as the unit of analysis, rather than college districts or state systems. Within each two-year institution, the vice president of academic affairs or a person in an equivalent position was surveyed to obtain information about the college's minority faculty recruitment program. Given the major responsibility that this administrator typically has for faculty recruitment, it was assumed that this individual would be knowledgeable both about the number of full-time minority faculty employed at the college, and about the college's minority faculty recruitment program.

The vice president of academic affairs at each two-year college was identified by using *Who's Who in Community, Technical and Junior Colleges* (AACJC, 1991). This particular reference guide was chosen because it is an authoritative source of recent information about administrative leaders at virtually every two-year institution in the country. A total of 1,293 vice presidents of academic affairs at individual two-year college campuses was identified through the use of this reference guide. In short, virtually every two-year college vice-president of academic affairs in the country was included in the sample for this study, with the exception of those vice-presidents at two-year campuses not listed in this AACJC reference guide.

Questionnaire Design

The questionnaire instrument was designed to test many of the assumptions found through a review of the literature on minority faculty recruitment. The questionnaire was field tested utilizing 34 community college faculty and administrators representing a number of community colleges in West Texas. As a result of this validation process, the questionnaire was revised to eliminate any questions which were found to be ambiguous or misleading. The final instrument which emerged was a four-page instrument divided into five sections.

Appendix A

A National Survey of Recruitment Practices for Minority Full-Time Faculty at Two-Year Colleges

Directions: Please answer each question by circling the appropriate number.
Example: This is a survey on minority faculty recruitment practices.

1	Yes	2	No

Part I: Demographic Background

1. Your sex:

1	Male	2	Female

2. Racial/ethnic group (Circle *all* that apply):

1	White/Caucasian	5	Mexican-American
2	Black/African-American	6	Puerto Rican-American
3	American Indian	7	Other
4	Asian-American		

3. How old will you be on December 31 of this year? _____

4. What is the highest degree that you have earned?

1	Bachelor's	4	Ed.D.
2	Master's	5	Ph.D.
3	Ed. Specialist	6	Other Degree

5. What is the highest level of education reached by your mother?

1	Grammar school or less	5	Some college
2	Some high school	6	College degree
3	High school graduate	7	Some graduate school
4	Postsecondary school other than college	8	Graduate degree

6. What is the highest level of education reached by your father?

1	Grammar school or less	5	Some college
2	Some high school	6	College degree
3	High school graduate	7	Some graduate school
4	Postsecondary school other than college	8	Graduate degree

7. Number of years of two-year college administration experience: _____

How much contact do you have with each of the following groups:

1 = Extensive
2 = Some
3 = None at all

8. Minority students 1   2   3

9. Minority faculty 1   2   3

10. Minority administrators 1   2   3

Part II: Campus Demographics

11. How many *full-time* African-American faculty do you have?_____

12. How many *full-time* Mexican-American faculty do you have? _____

13. How many *full-time* Puerto Rican-American faculty do you have? _____

14. How many *full-time* American Indian faculty do you have? _____

15. How many *full-time* faculty do you have? _____

16. In recruiting minority *full-time* faculty in the 1980s, this college:

1	made progress	3	lost ground
2	stayed about the same		

17. How much gain (if any) do you expect to make in recruiting minority *full-time* faculty during the 1990s?

1	substantial	3	little
2	moderate	4	none

Part III: Barriers to Recruiting Minority Faculty

Below are some statements about your current college. Indicate the extent to which you agree or disagree with each of the following: (Circle one response for each item)

> 1 = Agree Strongly
> 2 = Agree Somewhat
> 3 = Disagree Somewhat
> 4 = Disagree Strongly

18. Current economic constraints make it difficult to hire additional minority faculty here 1   2   3   4

19. Affirmative action requirements significantly raise the costs of faculty searches here 1   2   3   4

20. Minority faculty are hired at this college primarily to staff ethnic studies programs..1   2   3   4

21. Attempts to influence departments here to hire minority faculty evoke the red flag of interference with faculty prerogatives 1   2   3   4

22. Departments/divisions here avoid the issue of hiring minority faculty by arguing that there are few minorities in their field 1   2   3   4

23. Minority faculty would have difficulty fitting in socially with the community here 1   2   3   4

24. Minority faculty are not available for positions here in arts and science fields 1   2   3   4

25. Minority faculty are not available for positions here in technical and occupational fields 1   2   3   4

26. Women and minorities are competing with each other at this college for the same faculty positions................................1   2   3   4

27. Prospective minority faculty prefer employment in business and industry to employment here....................................1   2   3   4

Part IV: Minority Faculty Recruitment Strategies

Which of the following strategies for recruiting minority faculty has your institution used? (Circle one response for each item).

> 1 = Yes
> 2 = No
> 3 = Not Applicable

28. Advertising in media outlets used by minorities 1   2   3

29. Inviting minority professionals for guest lectures...............................1   2   3

30. Inviting minority professionals for part-time adjunct assignments 1   2   3

31. Recruiting minorities in private enterprise jobs with the
    support of their employers to teach part-time 1   2   3

32. Encouraging faculty to make contact with minority scholars
    in their fields to publicize available positions 1   2   3

33. Including faculty from diverse cultural backgrounds
    on search committees 1   2   3

34. Including minority community members on search committees 1   2   3

35. Having minorities serve on college advisory boards
    to remind institutions of their commitments to minorities 1   2   3

36. Having minorities serve on the board of trustees
    to remind institutions of their commitments to minorities 1   2   3

37. Having college representatives meet with minority
    representatives of civic organizations 1   2   3

38. Having college representatives meet with minority
    representatives of churches 1   2   3

39. Having college representatives meet with minority
    representatives of businesses 1   2   3

40. Having college representatives attend conferences held by
    professional organizations concerned with minority issues 1   2   3

41. Funding teaching internships for minority graduate
    students at two-year colleges 1   2   3

42. Creating faculty exchange programs between two-year
    colleges and predominantly minority four-year colleges 1   2   3

43. Conducting staff development sessions and workshops
    about affirmative action 1   2   3

44. Utilizing an applicant tracking system of resumes
    and applications of minorities 1   2   3

45. Asking deans or department chairs to justify
    nonminority hires 1   2   3

46. Rewarding departments with an extra position
    for each minority hire 1   2   3

47. Filling on a temporary basis positions where minority
    candidateshave not been recruited into the applicant pool 1   2   3

48. Cancelling positions where minority candidates have not
    been recruited into the applicant pool 1   2   3

49. Hiring a high level campus affirmative action officer
    to enforce campus affirmative action policies 1   2   3

50. Making affirmative action part of collective bargaining 1   2   3

Part V: Description of Minority Faculty Recruitment Program

Please briefly describe below your minority faculty recruitment program (or send under separate cover material that describes your college's policies and practices and success in this area).

The first section contained a number of questions related to the respondents' personal backgrounds, including their age, sex, race, and educational level. Also included in this first section was a question on the number of years of respondents' two-year college administrative experience, and the amount of contact the respondents had with minority students, faculty, and administrators. In the second section, respondents provided information on the number of minority faculty and total full-time faculty at their institutions, and whether their institutions expected to make progress in hiring minority faculty in the 1990s. In the third section, respondents were asked to indicate the degree to which they agreed or disagreed with a number of statements about attitudinal and structural barriers to recruiting minority faculty. The fourth section consisted of questions designed to determine which strategies institutions had actually utilized in recruiting minority faculty. The final section contained questions that asked respondents to briefly describe their minority faculty recruitment program, or to send material that described their college's policies, practices, and success in this area.

Data-Gathering Procedures

The first wave of the questionnaire was mailed out in mid-February 1992 to 1,293 vice-presidents of academic affairs listed in *Who's Who in Community, Technical and Junior Colleges* (AACJC, 1991). The first-wave packet contained a cover letter explaining the purpose of the study, a sheet defining underrepresented minorities and full-time faculty, the questionnaire, and a self-addressed business-reply envelope. After a three-week interval, a second-wave packet was mailed out in early March to all non-respondents to the first wave. This paper is based on a preliminary analysis of data received up to this point.

Responses

Out of the 1,293 questionnaires mailed out with the first wave, a total of 391 surveys were received, for a response rate of 30.4%. Out of the additional 902 questionnaires mailed out in the second wave, 222 additional questionnaires have been received to date, for a response rate of 24.6%. Thus, at present, the overall response rate for the survey after two waves is 47.4%. The final response rate is expected to exceed 50% when all second wave questionnaires are received.

Discussion of Results

Results will be discussed in the following sections: characteristics of the sample, percentages of underrepresented minority faculty, barriers to minority faculty recruitment, recruitment strategies, and the prediction of minority faculty recruitment success.

Characteristics of the Sample

The vice-presidents of academic affairs who responded to this survey tended to be white males, 51 years of age, with either an Ed.D. or Ph.D., and 13 years of community college experience. Slightly more than one-quarter of the respondents were female, and slightly more than one-tenth were members of a minority group. This profile of respondents is quite similar to findings by Hankin (1985) that 29.8% of two-year college administrators were female and 13.4% were minority. In short, the respondents to this study have demographic backgrounds similar to community college administrators nationally.

Table 1
Characteristics of Sample

Demographic Characteristics	Percentage or Mean	Number of Respondents
Sex		
Female	27.4%	167
Male	72.6%	442
Race		
White	88.3%	542
Black	6.8%	42
American Indian	2.1%	13
Asian-American	.7%	4
Mexican-American	2.9%	18
Puerto Rican-American	.2%	1
Other	.5%	3
Educational Background		
Bachelors	1.8%	11
Masters	26.4%	160
Ed.D.	31.9%	193
Ph.D.	37.9%	229
Other	2.0%	12
Average Age	51 years	607
Average Number of Years of Community College Experience	13 years	

Percentages of Minority Faculty

Percentages of minority faculty were calculated by dividing the number of a particular minority group by the number of full-time faculty to be found within the total sample of institutions. Separate percentages were calculated for African-American, American Indian, Mexican-American, and Puerto Rican-American faculty, as well as for the percentage of all of these minority groups combined. There were a total of 53,628 full-time faculty across the 616 institutions included in this study, which represents 60.7% of the 88,252 full-time faculty found in the two-year college sector (Astin, 1991).

Table 2
Percentage of Underrepresented Minority
Faculty at Two-Year Colleges (in percentages)

Institutional Minority Group	Astin[1] Self-Report	NCES[2] Study	Study
African-Americans	5.1	4.0	3
American Indians	1.4	1.2	1
Mexican-Americans	1.7	1.7	—
Puerto Rican-Americans	.3	.2	—
Total	8.5	7.1	—

[1]Percentages obtained from *National Norms for the 1989–90 HERI Faculty Survey*, A. W. Astin et. al, 1991.
[2]Percentages obtained from *Profiles of Faculty in Higher Education Institutions, 1988*, NCES. Data are for public two-year colleges only.

There was a total of 3,103 full-time African-American faculty reported, or 5.1% of all full-time faculty. This figure is one percentage point higher than the percentage reported in either of the two recent national faculty studies. There was a total of 1,075 Mexican-American faculty reported, or 1.7% of all full-time faculty. This figure exactly coincides with the percentage of Mexican-American faculty reported in the national study by Astin. Similar data were not available from NCES, since they reported aggregated data for Hispanics, rather than disaggregated data for Mexican-Americans and Puerto Rican-Americans. There was a total of 125 Puerto Rican-American faculty reported, or 0.3% of all full-time faculty. This figure is again slightly above the percentage reported in the study by Astin. Finally, the percentage of American Indians is slightly above the percentages reported in the two national faculty studies.

Comparing the minority data gathered from this study with the data from the two recent national faculty studies indicates that there is considerable agreement in the percentages of minority full-time two-year college faculty across all three studies. With the exception of the percentage of Mexican-American faculty, there is a trend for the institutional self-reported data to be slightly higher than the weighted data gathered from faculty samples. There might be several reasons for these differences in the percentages of minority full-time faculty across studies. One possible reason is that minority faculty may be less likely to respond to faculty surveys than their non-minority counterparts. This underrepresentation of minority faculty respondents may have had an effect on the weighting schemes used by Astin and NCES to estimate the total full-time faculty population from their faculty samples. For example, Astin's weighting scheme took into account *gender* and *rank* nonresponse bias within institutions, but did not address nonresponse bias by *minority status*. Another possible reason is that the institutions who reported to this study may not have been representative of the total population of two-year institutions with regards to their percentage of minority faculty. Vice presidents of academic affairs at institutions with a higher percentage of underrepresented minorities may have been more likely to respond to this survey than those at institutions with a lower percentage. In short, *between-institution* nonresponse bias may account for the differences between these studies.

Barriers to Minority Faculty Recruitment

Respondents were asked to indicate the extent to which they agreed or disagreed with a list of statements regarding barriers to minority faculty recruitment at their college. In order to shorten the presentation, only the top nine barriers are displayed in Table 3.

Table 3
Percent Agreeing or Strongly Agreeing
with Barriers to Minority Faculty Recruitment

Recruitment Barrier	Number of Institutions (n=616)	Percentage of Institutions
Economic constraints make it difficult to hire additional minority faculty	422	68.5
Minority faculty are not available in technical and occupational fields	339	55.0
Minorities prefer jobs in business and industry	308	50.0
Minority faculty are not available in arts and science fields	285	46.3
Women and minorities are competing with each other	246	39.9
Affirmative action significantly raises the cost of recruitment	196	31.8
Departments argue that there are few minorities in their fields	185	30.0
Minorities would have difficulty fitting in socially with community	151	24.5
Minority recruitment interferes with faculty prerogatives	133	21.6

Over two-thirds of the 616 respondents indicated that current economic constraints make it difficult to hire additional minority faculty at their institution. In a period of tight state budgets across the country, it is perhaps not surprising that two-year colleges administrators mentioned finances as their biggest barrier in hiring more minority faculty. The large percentage who agreed with this barrier underscores the difficulty many two-year institutions are having in achieving their minority faculty recruitment goals given the condition of their state and local economies. There may be little improvement in the number of underrepresented minority full-time faculty at two-year colleges until this economic situation improves.

Another set of structural barriers mentioned by a large number of respondents is the unavailability of minority faculty in both technical and occupational as well as arts and science fields. A number of researchers have noted the uneven distribution of academic majors among minority students (Astin, 1982; Garza, 1988; Blackwell, 1988). African-Americans, Mexican-Americans, Puerto Rican-Americans and American Indians are much more likely to pursue advanced degrees in education and the social sciences than degrees in such fields as mathematics, sciences, and languages and literature. Given the severity of this maldistribution, it is very difficult to recruit minority full-time faculty for a number of arts and science as well as occupational and technical fields. One of the reasons for this maldistribution of academic majors is minority students' lack of adequate preparation in mathematics and science at the secondary level. Clearly, two-year college faculty and administrators interested in increasing the representation of minority groups among full-time faculty need to collaborate with elementary and secondary schools in increasing minority student interest in and preparation for science and math-related areas.

The other structural barrier to minority faculty recruitment mentioned by a majority of the respondents is that prospective minority faculty prefer employment in business and industry to employment in two-year colleges. A number of researchers have noted that academic salaries rank far below salaries in business and industry (Bowen and Schuster, 1986; Bunzel, 1990). There are several approaches that two-year college administrators might use to compete with business and industry for prospective minority candidates. One possible recruitment approach is to stress the intrinsic satisfactions involved in a two-year college academic career. These intrinsic motivators include the considerable personal and professional autonomy of an academic career and the critical role that two-year college faculty play in educating minority students in higher education. A second possible approach is to try to recruit minorities in private enterprise jobs to teach part-time with the support of their employers. This study provides evidence that having minorities from private enterprise teach part-time is a particularly successful strategy for increasing the number of minority full-time faculty. One possible reason for the success of this strategy is that teaching part-time at a two-year college may provide minorities with a better sense of the intrinsic satisfactions of a full-time academic career.

Recruitment Strategies

A comparison of recruitment strategies between institutions with high versus low percentages of underrepresented minority faculty is presented in Table 4. In order to shorten the presentation, only those recruitment strategies where there was a difference of 12 or more percent between high and low percentage institutions are displayed.

A high percentage of underrepresented minority faculty was defined as 5 or more percent, while a low percentage was defined as less than 5 percent. Institutions with higher percentages of minority faculty are much more likely than those with lower percentages to include minority faculty and community members on search committees, and to have minorities serve on college advisory boards and on boards of trustees. These findings provide evidence that minorities on search committees and governance bodies of two-year college facilitate the recruitment of minority faculty. One possible explanation for this finding is that an institution's commitment to diversity is demonstrated to prospective minority candidates through this recruitment strategy. Another possible explanation is that minorities on search committees and governing bodies may serve as institutional or departmental advocates for the need for greater faculty diversity. Such advocacy would be expected to lead to higher numbers of minority faculty.

Institutions with a high percentage of underrepresented minority faculty are more likely than other institutions to have faculty make contact with minority faculty to recruit minorities in private enterprise to teach part-time, to cancel positions that have not attracted minorities in the applicant pool, and to have college representatives attend conferences held by professional organizations concerned with minority issues. These strategies hold in common a proactive stance to the recruitment of minority faculty. These findings provide evidence that proactive recruitment strategies facilitate the recruitment of minority faculty. One possible explanation for the success of these recruitment strategies is that they all tend to enlarge the pool of potential minority applicants for faculty positions. Such an enlarging of the pool would be expected to increase the number of minority faculty ultimately hired. Another possible explanation is that these proactive strategies also serve as concrete demonstrations of the institution's commitment to diversity. As a consequence, more minority candidates may be encouraged to apply for faculty positions at these institutions.

Table 4
A Comparison of Recruitment Strategies between Institutions
with High versus Low Percentages of Underrepresented Minority Faculty

Recruitment Strategy	Low Percentage (Less than 5%)	High Percentage (5% or more)	Difference
Have minorities serve on board of trustees	59.7	86.6	26.9
Include minority community members on search committees	23.4	50.2	26.8
Include minority faculty on search committees	66.7	92.9	26.2
Have faculty make contact with minority faculty	46.6	66.1	19.5
Recruiting minorities to teach part-time	48.1	29.6	18.5
Have minorities serve on college advisory boards	72.0	90.2	18.2
Canceling positions without minority applicants	7.1	24.1	17.0
Attend conferences concerned with minority issues	70.0	87.0	17.0
Meet with minority business representatives	64.3	80.9	16.6
Hire minorities as part-time adjunct faculty	75.1	91.6	16.5
Filling positions on a temporary basis	13.9	30.2	16.3
Meet with minority civic organizations	71.2	83.8	12.6
Funding teaching internships for minority graduate students	8.0	20.9	12.0

Predicting Minority Faculty Recruitment Success

The results of a regression analysis predicting the percentage of underrepresented minority faculty are displayed in Table 5.

Table 5
Prediction of the Percentage of Underrepresented Minority Faculty

				Final Step	
Step	Variable	Zero r	Step Beta	Beta	F Ratio*
1	African-American	.36	.36	.33	57.9
2	Amount of contact with minority students	.29	.24	.11	44.6
3	Mexican-American	.18	.18	.15	36.4
4	Fitting in socially within the community	−.33	−.26	−.17	33.3
5	Amount of progress recruiting in the 1980s	.22	.15	.12	30.4
6	Minority faculty not available in arts/sciences	−.25	−.13	−.12	28.0
7	Interfering with faculty prerogatives	−.05	−.12	−.14	25.8
8	Minorities on board of trustees	.24	.14	.11	24.7
9	Recruiting minorities in private industry	.24	.10	.10	23.0
10	Cancelling positions without minority applicants	.19	.10	.10	21.7

*F Ratio greater than 1.81 significant at the .05 level.
Multiple R = 62 Adjusted R^2 = .36
Mean = 8.1, S.D. = 12.2
Number of cases = 402

In this analysis, it was found that being an African-American or Mexican-American vice president of academic affairs are positive predictors of the percentage of underrepresented minority faculty. There are several possible explanations for this positive influence for racial background. One possible explanation is that minority chief academic administrators may serve as strong advocates for the need for greater minority representation at their institutions. Such advocacy would be expected to lead to an increase in the number of minority faculty hired. Another possible explanation is that having a minority in such a highly visible position sends a positive message to prospective minority faculty about the institution's commitment to diversity. Because of this commitment, more minority candidates may be encouraged to apply for faculty positions.

The amount of contact with minority students is also a positive predictor of the percentage of minority faculty. The more contact the chief academic administrator has with minority students, the greater the percentage of underrepresented minority faculty at the institution. The positive influence of contact with minority students has several possible explanations. One possible explanation is that contact with minority students simply serves as a proxy measure for institutions with a high percentage of minority students. Such institutions might be expected to have a vigorous minority faculty recruitment program. Another possible explanation is that extensive contact with minority students serves to make the chief academic administrator more aware of the needs of minority students. As a consequence of this greater awareness of minority student needs, the chief academic administrator might be more motivated to recruit more minorities for faculty openings.

Three of the barriers to minority faculty recruitment were negative predictors of the percentage of minority faculty. The greatest barrier was the difficulty in having minorities fit in socially with the community. The more strongly respondents agreed with this statement, the lower was the percentage of minority faculty at the institution. There are several possible explanations for the negative influence of this finding. One possible explanation is that two-year institutions may not actively recruit minority faculty because of the difficulties they anticipate with minorities fitting in socially with the community. Without an active recruitment program, institutions would be expected to have a low percentage of minority faculty. Another possible explanation is that minority faculty may simply not apply to institutions in communities where they expect to have difficulty fitting in socially. In short, minority candidates may self-select themselves from applying to these two-year institutions.

Another barrier to minority faculty recruitment which was a negative predictor was the unavailability of minority faculty for arts and science positions. The more strongly the respondents agreed with this statement, the lower the percentage of minority faculty at the institution. One possible explanation for this finding is that there are simply not enough prospective minority faculty in a number of arts and science fields. This shortage may be the result of the maldistribution of academic majors among minority students. Such a maldistribution would be expected to lower the number of minority faculty available to be hired. Another possible explanation is that chief academic officers who strongly agree with this statement may not actively recruit minority faculty because of their perception that few, if any, prospective minority faculty are available. In short, this lack of minority faculty recruitment may result in a self-fulfilling prophecy.

Attempts to influence departments to hire minority faculty evoke the red flag of interference with faculty prerogatives was another negative predictor. The more strongly respondents agreed with this statement, the lower was the percentage of minority faculty at the institution. One possible explanation for this finding is that academic administrators may not attempt to actively recruit minority faculty in order to "maintain normative consensus and collegial relationships. . . ." (Exum, 1983, p. 390). The absence of active minority recruiting would be expected to lead to low numbers of minority faculty. Another possible explanation is that academic administrators may actively recruit minority faculty applicants, but these applicants may be rejected by faculty as threats to their prerogatives. The rejection by faculty of all minority candidates recruited by administrators would be expected to lead to lower numbers of minority faculty.

Finally, three recruitment strategies served as positive predictors of the percentage of minority faculty. Of these three recruitment strategies, having minorities serve on boards of trustees was the most influential predictor. Institutions that used this recruitment strategy were more likely to have a higher percentage of underrepresented minority faculty. One possible explanation for this finding is that such a minority presence serves as a concrete demonstration of an institutional commitment to diversity for prospective minority faculty. More minority candidates may be encouraged to apply for faculty positions at these institutions. Another possible explanation is that minorities on the board serve as advocates for improving the diversity on campus. Such advocacy would be expected to lead to more minority faculty being hired.

Another recruitment strategy which served as a positive predictor was recruiting minorities in private enterprise jobs to teach part-time with the support of their employers. Institutions which used this strategy were more likely to have a high percentage of underrepresented minority faculty. One possible explanation for this finding is that institutions using this strategy are more aware of qualified minority applicants when positions became available. Such an awareness would be expected to lead to more minority faculty being hired. Another possible explanation is that minority faculty teaching part-time may be more likely to apply for full-time faculty positions when they become available. Any increase in the number of minority candidates applying for faculty jobs would be expected to lead to an increased number of minorities eventually being hired.

The final recruitment strategy which served as a positive predictor was cancelling positions where minority candidates had not been recruited into the applicant pool. Institutions that utilized this recruitment strategy were more likely to have a higher percentage of underrepresented minority faculty. One possible explanation for this finding is that institutions that utilize this recruitment strategy motivate departments to widely disseminate information about faculty job openings to prospective minority candidates. Such an active recruitment process would be expected to increase the number of minority faculty eventually hired. Another possible explanation is that canceling positions without minority candidates serves as a concrete demonstration to prospective minority faculty of the institution's commitment to diversity. Such a demonstration of commitment would be expected to motivate more prospective minority candidates to apply for faculty positions at these institutions.

Policy Implications and Conclusions

In this study evidence is provided that African-American, American Indian, Mexican-American, and Puerto Rican-American full-time faculty at two-year colleges are significantly underrepresented compared to the proportional representation of these minority groups in the U.S. population. Clearly, two-year colleges administrators need to address this issue of equity in their full-time faculty hiring.

The underrepresentation of minority faculty is also an issue of excellence as well as equity. Astin has argued that institutions of higher education cannot have excellence without promoting the cause of equity (Astin, 1985). Minority full-time faculty on two-year campuses serve to more fully develop the talents and cultural sensitivity of both minority and white students. Minority faculty not only play a vital role as positive role models for minority students, but also help white students overcome prejudicial thoughts about the intellectual capabilities of people of color. Minority faculty also help white faculty gain a deeper understanding and appreciation for different cultural heritages (Linthicum, 1989). In short, minority full-time faculty promote both the cause of excellence as well as equity within two-year institutions.

In this study it was shown that many of the attitudinal and structural barriers which hinder the recruitment of minority full-time faculty at four-year institutions also serve as barriers at two-year institutions as well. Structural barriers were found to be much greater hindrances to minority faculty recruitment than attitudinal barriers within institutions. The most influential structural barrier for a majority of two-year institutions is the economic constraints which prevent hiring additional minority full-time faculty. Given the current economic situation facing many two-year colleges, individual institutions may have few resources to hire *any* full-time faculty. This is a problem which probably needs to be addressed at the state, rather than at the local level. A state incentive program targeting additional funds for each minority full-time faculty hired at two-year colleges would provide the resources two-year college administrators need to enhance their minority recruitment programs.

The other set of structural barriers mentioned by a majority of respondents is the unavailability of prospective minority faculty for many arts and science as well as technical and occupational fields. A large part of this problem is due to a maldistribution of majors, with minority students tending to avoid majors in math and science-related fields because of their lack of preparation in these subjects at the secondary level. Clearly, two-year college faculty and administrators need to collaborate with elementary and secondary schools in increasing minority student interest in and preparation for these math and science-related areas. One possible collaboration is for two-year colleges to sponsor science fairs for elementary and secondary students in their catchment area. Another possible approach is for two-year institutions to offer summer programs for elementary and secondary students focusing on science, math, and technology-related areas. It is clearly in the best interest of two-year colleges to develop early outreach programs to try to interest and prepare minority students for faculty positions in math, science, and technology-related areas at their institutions.

Two of the most important variables in the prediction of the percentage of underrepresented minority faculty were being an African-American or Mexican-American vice president of academic affairs. These findings provide evidence that having minorities in highly visible positions of leadership facilitates the recruitment of minority faculty. Many two-year institutions might argue that they already have an administrator, often a minority, responsible for affirmative action. Slightly under one-half of the respondents reported that they had just such an affirmative action officer. However, having such an officer responsible for affirmative action was found not to be significantly related to the number of minority faculty at an institution. This finding underscores the importance of hiring minorities for highly visible administrative positions. In summary, the single most important step that an institution can take to increase the number of underrepresented minority full-time faculty is to hire a minority as the chief academic administrator.

Three recruitment strategies were also found to be positively related with the percentage of underrepresented minority full-time faculty. The most influential of these recruitment strategies is having minorities on the board of trustees. Minorities on the board of trustees serve as advocates promoting the cause of equity in full-time faculty hiring. They also remind the institution of its commitment to equity and to the community that it represents. Perhaps most importantly, the institution's commitment to diversity is clearly demonstrated by having minorities on the board of trustees. Additional minority candidates for faculty positions may be attracted to the institution because of this commitment. In short, appointing minorities to the board of trustees is a successful means of increasing the number of underrepresented minority full-time faculty at an institution.

Another recruitment strategy which is positively related to an institution's percentage of underrepresented minorities is recruiting minorities in private enterprise jobs to teach part-time with the support of their employers. One of the important structural barriers mentioned by a majority of two-year respondents is the fact that careers in business and industry tend to pay far more than careers in academe. One way to effectively compete with business and industry for minority candidates is to hire minorities for part-time teaching assignments. This strategy serves to make institutions more aware of minority candidates when full-time positions become available. It also serves to make minorities more aware of the intrinsic satisfactions of a career as a two-year college faculty member. Although two-year college administrators may not be able to outbid business and industry for prospective minority candidates, they may be able to woo them away from business and industry with intrinsic rather than extrinsic motivators. In summary, hiring minorities as part-time teachers is another successful recruitment strategy for increasing the number of underrepresented minorities.

A final recruitment strategy which is positively related to the number of underrepresented minorities is cancelling positions where minority candidates have not been recruited into the candidate pool. Institutions that utilize this strategy tend to have a high number of minority faculty. Interestingly, less than 15% of respondents reported using this particular recruitment strategy. One might expect that chief academic administrators would have some reluctance in using this strategy, given that it often evokes among faculty the red flag of interference with their prerogatives. Despite potential opposition from faculty, this recruitment strategy is a particularly effective means of increasing the number of underrepresented minority full-time faculty. Many more two-year college administrators should consider utilizing this strategy in addressing the issue of equity in faculty hiring.

References

American Association of Community and Junior Colleges (1991). *Who's Who in Community, Technical, and Junior Colleges 1991*. Washington: Author.

Astin, A. W. (1982). *Minorities in American Higher Education*. San Francisco: Jossey-Bass.

Astin, A. W. (1985). *Achieving Educational Excellence*. San Francisco: Jossey-Bass.

Astin, A. W., Korn, W. S., & Dey, E. L. (1991). *The American College Teacher*. Los Angeles: Higher Education Research Institute.

Banks, W. M. (1984). Afro-American scholars in the university. *American Behavioral Scientist*. Vol. 27, No. 3, 325–338.

Blackwell, J. E. (1988). Faculty issues: the impact on minorities. *The Review of Higher Education*, Vol. 11, No. 4, 417–434.

Boyd, W. M. (1989). Affirmative action: a way to win. *AGB Reports*, Vol. 31, No. 4, 22–25.

Bunzel, J. H. (1990). Faculty hiring: problems and practices. *American Scholar*, Vol. 59, No. 1, 39–52.

Exum, W. H. (1983). Climbing the crystal stair: values, affirmative action, and minority faculty. *Social Problems*, Vol. 30, No. 4, 383–399.

Exum, W. H., Menges, R. J., Watkins, B., & Berglund, P. (1984). Making it at the top. *American Behavioral Scientist*, Vol. 27, No. 3, 301–324.

Garza, H. (1988). The "barriorization" of Hispanic faculty. *Educational Record*, Vol. 68, No. 4, 122–124.

Hankin, J. N. (1984). Where the (affirmative) action is: the status of minorities and women among the faculty and administrators of public two-year colleges. *Journal of College and University Personnel Association*, Vol. 35, No. 4, 36–39.

Harris, P. G. (1989). Almost 50 ways. . . . *AGB Reports*, Vol. 31, No. 4, 32–33.

Lessow-Hurley, J. (1989). Recruitment and retention of minority faculty. *CUPA Journal*, Vol. 40, No. 3, 22–26.

Linthicum, D. S. (1989). *The Dry Pipeline: Increasing the Flow of Minority Faculty*. Washington: National Council of State Directors of Community and Junior Colleges.

Menges, R. J., & Exum, W. H. (1983). Barriers to the progress of women and minority faculty. *Journal of Higher Education*, Vol. 54, No. 2, 123–144.

Mickelson, R. A., & Oliver, M. L. (1991). The demographic fallacy of the Black academic: Does quality rise to the top? in W. R. Allen, E. G. Epps, & N. Z. Haniff, ed. *College in Black and White*. Albany: State University of New York Press.

Moore, W. (1988). Black faculty in white colleges: a dream deferred. *Educational Record*, Vol. 68, No. 4, 116–121.

Reed, R. J. (1983). Affirmative action in higher education: is it necessary? *Journal of Negro Education*. Vol. 52, No. 3, 332–349.

Reed, R. J. (1986). Faculty diversity: an educational and moral imperative in search of institutional commitment. *Journal of Educational Equity and Leadership*, Vol. 6, No. 4, 274–294.

Russell, S. H., Fairweather, J. S., Hendrickson, R. M., & Zimbler, L. J. (1991). *Profiles of Faculty in Higher Education Institutions, 1988*. Washington: National Center for Education Statistics.

Smelser, N. J., & Content, R. (1980). *The Changing Academic Market*. Berkeley: University of California Press.

The Chronicle of Higher Education (1991). *The Chronicle of Higher Education Almanac*, Washington, D.C.: Author.

The Chronicle of Higher Education. (1992, March 18), 1.

Community College Faculty: A Profile

DEBORAH J. CARTER AND CECILIA A. OTTINGER

Over the last several years, there has been much discussion about the profile of faculty in higher education and likely trends in the future. Higher education institutions and researchers have begun to look at the faculty pool to determine its characteristics in terms of tenure, fields of expertise, and working conditions. However, very little of this discussion has been addressed to trends in community colleges or to the racial ethnic makeup of faculty members in these institutions. Community colleges have experienced considerable growth in enrollments and have greatly expanded their role in the higher education community. Yet very little is known about the faculty at these institutions.

This research brief offers a profile of this vital segment of college faculty. Particular attention is paid to the differences between the conditions of full-time and part-time faculty, as well as racial, ethnic, and gender distribution. Data are taken from two sources: The 1989–90 survey of faculty conducted by the Higher Education Research Institute (HERI) at UCLA and the 1988 National Survey of Postsecondary Faculty (NSOPF-88) conducted by the National Center for Education Statistics.

Highlights and Implications

- Part-time faculty are a major component at two-year institutions. In 1987, more than half of faculty at two-year colleges were employed part-time (58 percent). In the future, this part-time faculty pool could represent a potential source of new faculty if shortages in the full-time market occur.

- Faculty of color held only 8 percent of full-time faculty positions at public two-year colleges and 3 percent at independent two-year colleges.

- In 1987, men clearly outnumbered women in full-time faculty positions at public two-year institutions.

- Contrary to popular belief, part-time faculty are not short-timers, moving from institution to institution during each term. On average, part-time faculty at two-year institutions stay at the same institution for about 6 years.

- At all two-year colleges, more than 2 out of 5 full-time faculty are employed at the lecturer/instructor level.

- This is even more true among full-time minority faculty. More than half of African American community college faculty are lecturers/instructors (52 percent). Colleges need to examine their hiring and promotion policies.

I. Characteristics of Full-time Faculty

- In fall 1987, there were an estimated 514,000 full-time faculty in all two-year and four-year institutions (NSOPF-88).

  - In that year, 93,000 full-time faculty were employed in public two-year colleges, and 421,000 were at four-year colleges and universities.

Representation of Faculty of Color

Faculty of color continue to hold extremely small percentages of full-time appointments in two-year institutions, according to data from the HERI 1989–90 Faculty Survey and NSOPF-88.

- Eight percent of full-time faculty at public two-year institutions were members of minority groups; only 3 percent of faculty at private two-year institutions were minorities (table 1).

- In 1989–90, 9 percent of faculty at all colleges and universities were racial and ethnic minorities.

- In 1989–90, African Americans held 4 percent of all full-time faculty appointments in two-year public colleges, followed by Asian Americans and Hispanics[1] (each with 2 percent) and American Indians with only 1 percent.

- NSOPF data revealed similar differences. According to this study, 9 percent (8,370 out of 93,000) of full-time faculty in two-year public colleges are of color and 11 percent (46,310 out of 421,000) of full-time faculty in four-year institutions are faculty of color.

- It is estimated that between 20 and 25 percent of American Indian faculty in two-year colleges are employed in the two-year tribal colleges.[2]

- Additionally, 47 percent of all full-time African American faculty are employed in Historically Black Colleges and Universities (HBCUs), with about 30 percent employed at public four-year HBCUs.[3]

Gender Representation

- In 1987, male faculty clearly outnumbered female faculty at public two-year institutions (62 percent vs. 38 percent). However, a larger proportion of two-year full-time faculty are women than at all four-year institutions (25 percent).

- By comparison, almost three-quarters (73 percent) of all full-time faculty positions at all colleges and universities were held by men in 1987, while women held a little more than one-quarter (27 percent) (NSOPF-88).

Rank and Tenure

The granting of tenure in two-year colleges differs from the system used in four-year institutions. According to Cohen and Brawer, tenure in two-year colleges is "often awarded after a single year, or in many cases, after probation of two or three years; the practice rarely approximates the seven-year standard common in universities" (1982, 73). Also, many two-year colleges do not have ranking systems at all.

The data cited below allow one to review the characteristics of full-time faculty at two-year institutions who are employed in systems with tenure and rank components.

- According to the NSOPF study in 1987, 25 percent of full-time faculty at public two-year colleges did not have a tenure system at their institutions.

- According to HERI, full-time faculty at public two-year colleges were more likely to hold tenure than their counterparts at two-year independent institutions (71 percent vs. 55 percent).

- Women are less likely to be tenured than men. According to the HERI faculty survey, more than three-quarters of all male faculty at two-year colleges were tenured (76 percent), compared with 63 percent of female faculty at those same institutions (table 2).

- Generally, African American and Asian American male faculty at two-year institutions were almost as likely to hold tenured positions, compared with the average tenure rate for all male faculty at two-year colleges.[4]

- Tenure rates for American Indian women and white women approximate the national average for female faculty in two-year colleges.

In 1987, 70 percent of two-year colleges designated faculty by academic rank (NSOPF-88).

- The 1989 HERI faculty survey shows that of full-time faculty at two-year colleges, 25 percent were full professors, 16 percent were associate professors, 12 percent were assistant professors, and 41 percent were lecturers or instructors and 5 percent in the other category.[5]

Like faculty of color at all colleges and universities, Hispanic, African American, and Asian American faculty in two-year colleges are concentrated in the ranks of lecturers and instructors more than is the case for white faculty. Few faculty from minority groups occupy senior faculty positions.

- Of all full-time African American faculty at community colleges, 52 percent were lecturers or instructors. Only 15 percent of African American faculty at two-year colleges were full professors; 15 percent are associate professors, 14 percent held

Table 1
Characteristics of Full-Time Faculty at Two-Year and Four-Year Colleges, 1989

Characteristics	All Institutions	2-year		4-year	
		Public	Independent	Public	Independent
Highest Degree Held					
Bachelor's	3%	10%	4%	1%	2%
Master's	28%	60%	70%	22%	29%
Doctorate	61%	16%	18%	69%	62%
Tenure	67%	71%	55%	68%	57%
Race					
White	90%	91%	97%	87%	92%
African American	4%	4%	3%	7%	4%
Asian-American	3%	2%	0%	4%	2%
Hispanic	1%	2%	0%	1%	1%
American Indian	1%	1%	0%	1%	1%
Other	2%	5%	0%	2%	2%
Academic Rank					
Professor	34%	25%	19%	35%	30%
Associate/Assistant Prof.	49%	28%	33%	57%	59%
Lecturer/Instructor	15%	42%	34%	7%	10%
Other	2%	5%	14%	1%	1%
Principal Activity					
Administration	3%	3%	5%	4%	3%
Teaching	90%	95%	94%	93%	95%
Research	6%	1%	0%	2%	1%
Other	1%	1%	1%	1%	1%

Source: Astin, Korn and Dey. *The American College Teacher: National Norms for the 1989–90 HERI Survey.* Los Angeles: Higher Education Research Institute, UCLA, March 1991.

assistant professor positions, and 5 percent held positions in the other category (figure 1).

- Twenty percent of Mexican American two-year faculty were full professors, compared with 56 percent who were instructors. Of the approximately 200 Puerto Rican faculty employed in two-year colleges, 51 percent are assistant professors and 49 percent are instructors.

- Among white faculty at community colleges, 26 percent were full professors; 16 percent associate professors; 12 percent, assistant professors; and 40 percent, instructors or lecturers.

- Almost half of full-time women faculty at two-year institutions were lecturers/instructors (49 percent); in comparison, 36 percent of male faculty were employed in these ranks (figure 2).

Educational Background

- In 1989, most full-time faculty (61 percent) at two-year colleges held a master's as their highest degree.

- Full-time faculty at independent two-year colleges were somewhat more likely to have a master's as their highest degree than those at public institutions in 1989 (70 percent vs. 60 percent).

- There were some differences by gender. In 1989, 66 percent of full-time women faculty at two-year colleges indicated that the master's was their highest degree, compared with 58% of men (table 2).

- This trend also varied by race and ethnicity. In 1989, 61 percent of white full-time faculty at two-year colleges cited the master's as the highest degrees earned, as did 57 percent of both African Americans and Asian Americans, and 52 percent of American Indians (HERI, 1991).

Figure 1
Distribution of Full-Time Two-Year Faculty by Rank and Race/Ethnicity, 1989

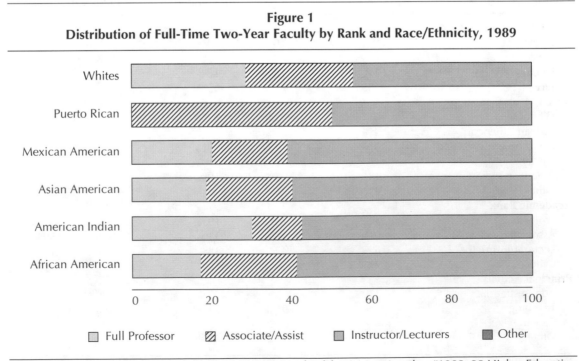

Source: Higher Education Research Institute, University of California, Los Angeles. "1989–90 Higher Education Research Institute Faculty Survey," unpublished data tabulations. March 1991.

Figure 2
Distribution of Full-Time Two-Year Faculty by Rank and Sex, 1989–90

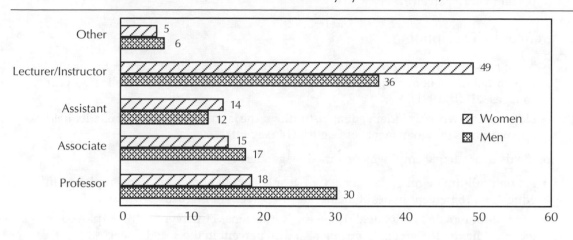

Note: Numbers may not add to 100 due to rounding.
Source: Astin, Korn and Dey, *The American College Teacher: National Norms for the 1989–90 HERI March 1991 Faculty Survey.* Los Angeles: UCLA, Higher Education Research Institute, March 1991.

- In 1989, only 16 percent of full-time faculty at all two-year institutions held a Ph.D. or Ed.D. as their highest degree.

  – At independent two-year colleges, 18 percent of full-time faculty indicated that a Ph.D. or Ed.D. was the highest degree attained, as did 16 percent of full-time faculty at public two-year colleges.

Table 2
Characteristics of Full-time Two-Year Faculty by Sex, 1989

Characteristic	% Distribution	
	Men	Women
Highest Degree Earned		
Bachelor's	9%	11%
Master's	58%	66%
Ph.D/Ed.D.	20%	11%
Tenured	76%	63%
Academic Rank		
Professor	30%	18%
Associate/Assistant Professor	29%	28%
Lecturer/Instructor	36%	49%
Other	6%	5%
Race/Ethnicity		
White	93%	89%
African American	3%	6%
American Indian	2%	1%
Asian-American	2%	3%
Hispanic	2%	2%
Other	2%	1%

Source: Astin, Korn and Dey. *The American College Teacher: National Norms for the 1989–90 HERI March 1991 Faculty Survey.* Los Angeles UCLA, Higher Education Research Institute, March 1991.

- Full-time male faculty at all two-year colleges were almost twice as likely to have attained a Ph.D. or Ed.D. as their highest degree than their female counterparts (20 percent vs. 11 percent).

Differences by Discipline

- At all two-year institutions, the largest share of full-time faculty were in the health-related fields (11 percent); as were 11 percent of full-time faculty at public two-year colleges (HERI, 1991).
- However, at two-year independent institutions, the largest proportion of faculty held appointments in departments of English (14 percent).

The top fields of academic employment varied by gender.

- Among full-time women faculty at two-year colleges, 30 percent were employed in education, 18 percent in health fields, and 10 percent in English.
- For full-time male faculty at all two-year institutions, 11 percent were employed in technical fields, 10 percent in business, and 10 percent in the social sciences.

The top fields of academic employment for minority faculty in two-year colleges generally follow the same patterns as those for all higher education institutions combined.[6]

- African American faculty at two-year colleges are employed predominantly in the social sciences (19 percent), health-related departments (16 percent), and education departments (13 percent). Business departments rank fourth, employing 10 percent of African American faculty in two-year colleges.
- English departments employ approximately 23 percent of all Hispanic two-year college faculty. Health-related departments are second, employing 18 percent of Hispanic faculty, followed by social science departments with 10 percent and mathematics and statistics departments with 10 percent.
- For Asian American faculty, the five top fields of employment at two-year colleges are the social sciences (16 percent), mathematics and statistics (15 percent), other technical departments (11 percent), business (10 percent), and education (9 percent).
- The HERI faculty survey reports that the two largest shares of American Indian faculty are employed in departments that are grouped as "other" or as "other technical" fields (22 percent and 15 percent). Following these two clusters of departments, the two identifiably largest shares of American Indian faculty are in English (11 percent) and the social sciences (8 percent).

Principal Activities and Job Satisfaction

- In 1989–90, full-time faculty at two-year colleges were slightly more likely to identify teaching as their principal activity than full-time faculty at all institutions (95 percent vs. 90 percent) (table 1).
- In 1987, full-time faculty at two-year colleges indicated that 71 percent of their time was spent on teaching, compared with 56 percent for full-time faculty nationally (NSOPF-88).
- In the 1992 Campus Trends Survey, it was found that most two-year public institutions (78 percent) have regular, full-time faculty teach 10 or more courses per year (typically, five courses in each of two terms). In contrast, only 6 percent of their public four-year counterparts did so (El-Khawas, 1992).

Full-time faculty at two-year colleges spent considerably more time teaching than did their four-year counterparts.

- In 1989–90, 78 percent of full-time faculty at public two-year institutions and 70 percent at independent two-year colleges spent more than 12 hours per week teaching (HERI, 1991).
- In contrast, only about one-third of full-time faculty at public and independent four-year colleges spent 12 or more hours teaching (30 percent and 33 percent, respectively).

Much of this difference may be due to institutional demands for research at four-year colleges and universities.

- Thirty-two percent of full-time faculty at public four-year institutions noted that the demand for doing research interfered with their effectiveness as a teacher. Not surprisingly, only 6 percent of faculty at two-year public colleges cited this reason.
- Considering that most full-time faculty hold tenure, it is not surprising that in 1989 three-quarters of full time faculty (61 percent) indicated that they were "very satisfied" with their job security.
- This satisfaction was evident at all types of institutions, although full-time faculty at public two-year institutions were "very satisfied" with their job security to a greater extent than their independent two-year counterparts (79 percent vs. 71 percent).

Recent Trends in Hiring Full-Time Faculty at Two-Year Colleges

- During the periods 1990–91 to 1991–92, 44 percent of two-year institutions reported net gains in hiring full-time faculty (table 3).
- Overall, between academic years 1990 and 1991, less than half of all colleges and universities reported net gains in hiring full-time faculty (48 percent). A slightly larger percentage noted net gains during the period AY 1987 to AY 1988 (50 percent).
- Between 1990–91 and 1991–92, 29 percent of two-year colleges noted a net gain in the number of faculty of color, compared with 45 percent of public four-year colleges.
- During this period, almost half of two-year institutions (49 percent) increased the number of women faculty hired; as did half of all institutions (50 percent).
- Between 1990–91 and 1991–92 public four-year institutions were more likely to increase their female faculty than any other types of institutions.

Table 3
Patterns of Faculty Hiring: Selected Years (Percentage of Institutions with Net Gains)

	Total	2-Year Colleges	Public 2-Year	Public 4-Year
Change in Full-Time Faculty				
1987–88 to 1988–89	50%	49%	48%	48%
1990–91 to 1991–92	48%	44%	44%	49%
Change in Part-time Faculty				
1987–88 to 1988–89	42%	41%	42%	41%
1990–91 to 1991–92	54%	60%	60%	57%
Change in Minority Faculty				
1987–88 to 1988–89	25%	22%	24%	38%
1990–91 to 1991–92	34%	29%	29%	45%
Change in Women Faculty				
1987–88 to 1988–89	42%	40%	50%	43%
1990–91 to 1991–92	50%	49%	49%	59%

Source: Elaine El-Khawas, *Campus Trends,* 1989 and 1992.

II. Characteristics of Part-time Faculty

National data on part-time faculty is more scarce than for their full-time counterparts. One of the few sources is the National Survey of Postsecondary Faculty (NSOPF-88).

There has been much discussion in higher education concerning the growth of part-time faculty. Research has found that during the mid-1970s and 1980s, the number of part-time faculty increased considerably, particularly at two-year institutions (American Association of University Professors, 1992).

- In 1987, there were an estimated 311,000 part-time faculty employed at all colleges and universities in the U.S.
- In 1987, 125,000 part-time faculty were employed at public two-year institutions.
- Part-time faculty comprised more than half (58 percent) of all faculty at public two-year colleges in 1987.

Representation of Faculty of Color

- Faculty of color represented 8 percent of all part-time faculty at public two-year colleges in 1987; nationally, faculty of color comprised 10 percent of all part-time faculty (table 4).
- The racial distributions of part-time faculty at public two-year institutions was: whites 91 percent, African Americans 3 percent; Hispanics and Asian Americans 2 percent; and American Indians 1 percent.
- However, at four-year institutions minorities held a larger share of part-time positions (13 percent).

Gender Representation

- In 1987, men at public two-year colleges held a larger proportion of part-time faculty positions than women (58 percent vs. 42 percent).
- Women held a slightly larger share of part-time faculty positions at four-year colleges (46 percent) than at two-year institutions.

Rank and Tenure

Almost all part-time faculty at two-year colleges (96 percent) were employed in non-tenure positions.

- This was true as well of part-time faculty at four-year colleges and universities (95 percent).
- The vast majority of part-time faculty were hired at the instructor or lecturer level; only 21 percent of part-time faculty were in the ranks of full, associate, or assistant professor.
- This trend was strongest in the public two-year sector, in which only 9 percent of part-time faculty were full, associate or assistant professors.
- Slightly more than half of all part-time faculty held other full-time jobs (52 percent). This held true at all institutional types.
- Very few part-time faculty aspired to full-time employment in academe. In 1987, only 16 percent of all part-time faculty, as well as part-timers at public two-year colleges, aspired to full-time employment.

Table 4
Characteristics of Part-time Faculty, Fall 1987, Percent Distribution

	All Institutions	2-Year Public	4-Year Institutions
Gender			
Male	56%	58%	54%
Female	44%	42%	46%
Highest Degree Held			
Bachelor's and other	27%	40%	17%
Master's	44%	47%	53%
Doctorate	29%	13%	29%
Satisfaction with Job Overall	87%	86%	90%
Race/Ethnicity			
White	90%	91%	87%
African American	4%	3%	4%
Asian	3%	2%	5%
Hispanic	2%	2%	2%
American Indian	1%	1%	2%

Note: Percents may not add to 100 due to rounding.
Source: National Center for Education Statistics. (NSOPF-88).

Educational Background

- Part-time faculty at public two-year institutions were almost equally likely to indicate that a bachelor's or master's was their highest degree earned. In 1987, 47 percent indicated that a master's was their highest degree, and 40 percent noted that a bachelor's was the highest degree held.

Longevity

Contrary to the belief that part-time faculty are short-termers (i.e., move from institution to institution during each term and hold multiple appointments), this does not appear to be the reality.

- In 1987, the mean number of years at an institution for all part-time faculty was 6.5 years; for those at public two-year colleges, the mean was 6.1 years.

Principal Activities and Job Satisfaction

- Part-time faculty at public two-year colleges devoted a larger share of their time to teaching than their counterparts at four-year colleges (65 percent vs. 58 percent).

- Nationally, the majority of part-time faculty experienced overall job satisfaction (87 percent). However, part-time faculty at public two-year institutions were slightly more satisfied with their jobs than their part-time counterparts at four-year colleges or nationally (90 percent and 86 percent).

Recent Trends in Hiring Part-Time Faculty at Two-Year Colleges

There is an increasing trend at two-year institutions to hire part-time faculty.

- Between 1987–88 and 1988–89, 41 percent of two-year institutions increased their hiring of part-time faculty (table 3).

- During the period 1990–91 to 1991–92, 60 percent of two-year institutions increased their hiring of part-time faculty.

This trend may be partly explained by the fact that enrollments have increased at two-year institutions and part-time faculty are needed to address the needs of a growing student population.

- In 1985, 4.7 million students were enrolled in two-year colleges; by 1990, 5.2 million students were enrolled in these institutions—an 11 percent increase (NCES, 1991).

Summary and Implications

The analysis of the data on community college faculty gives only a snapshot of what is going on with the faculty within these institutions. However, it is still very difficult to determine any trends over time on this increasingly important sector of higher education institutions. Ongoing data collection efforts concerning faculty are needed, particularly in a time when colleges and universities may be faced with critical faculty shortages. In addition, more data are needed to monitor the experiences of minority faculty, particularly as institutions address diversity issues on campuses.

Part-time faculty are a burgeoning component of the two-year sector. This is probably in response to the increases in enrollments in two-year colleges. More research and information on these faculty members is needed. What are the implications of institutions having large numbers of part-time faculty? Does it affect the quality of teaching? Is hiring part-time faculty a viable way of addressing budgetary problems? What are the advantages and disadvantages of being a part-time faculty member? What is the long-term economic impact of increasing the number of part-time faculty?

Beyond addressing these general questions, data is needed to help us gauge the role minorities and women play in two-year colleges. Community colleges are just as likely to hire faculty of color as are other institutions. Yet, while people of color are an increasing component of the U.S. population generally and of the student population within community colleges, they remain greatly underrepresented among faculty. Certain minority groups, such as Hispanics and American Indians, already attend community colleges in disproportionate numbers. For example, in 1990, 55 percent of American Indian students were enrolled in two-year colleges (Carter, 1992). The question arises, in what manner can two-year colleges better address the needs of minority students? What role should the composition of the faculty play? How can colleges increase the number of minority faculty into career-track positions?

Many full-time women faculty and faculty of color at two-year and other institutions are at the lower ranks and have little opportunity for tenured positions where those opportunities exist. Colleges need to re-examine hiring and promotion policies and determine how to get more women and minority faculty into the career tenure track or into extended term appointments.

At a time when institutions are facing uncertainty in their environments, current and trend data are key to addressing any issues. Without the ability to have a much fuller picture of what is happening, institutions cannot begin to address the needs of full-time faculty in any type of institution. Community college enrollments are growing, and we need to know how staffing needs are met.

Notes

1. Data for Hispanic faculty in the HERI survey include only faculty who are identified as Mexican American/Chicano or Puerto Rican.

2. The percentage of American Indian faculty employed in two-year tribal colleges is an estimate computed from data from the NSOPF-88 and the American Indian Higher Education Consortium.

3. The percentage of African American faculty employed in four-year public HBCUs is an estimate using data from the HERI faculty survey, the United Negro College Fund, and the Equal Employment Opportunity Commission (EEOC).

4. Only general trends are given on tenure by sex and race/ethnicity. Due to the small number of cases, the data may not be reliable for the various demographic categories.

5. The HERI faculty survey data on academic rank includes institutions that do not identify faculty by rank.

6. For comparisons, information on general academic employment patterns of minority faculty may be found in Carter and Wilson's Tenth Annual Status Report on Minorities in Higher Education.

Resources

1989 Survey of Faculty, conducted by the Higher Education Research Institute (HERI) at the University of California, Los Angeles.

This is a national survey of full-time faculty at 392 colleges and universities across the country, conducted in the fall and winter of 1989–90. It covers full-time faculty who spend at least part of their time teaching undergraduates. Because of the sample size for each racial and ethnic group and the availability of disaggregated data, the survey offers an excellent opportunity for analyzing employment patterns of minority faculty in community colleges. Much of the information for this report is taken from special analyses of the HERI 1989–90 Faculty Survey.

The study's normative report, *The American College Teacher*, is based on responses from 35,478 faculty, statistically weighted to be representative of all full-time faculty in the U.S. This report is the source for references in this research brief to all faculty, when followed by the notation, HERI. For more information, see Alexander W. Astin, William S. Korn, and Eric L. Dey, *The American College Teacher: National Norms for the 1989–90 HERI Faculty Survey* (Los Angeles: UCLA, Higher Education Research Institute, 1991).

1988 National Survey of Postsecondary Faculty (NSOPF-88), conducted by the National Center for Education Statistics, Washington, D.C.

This is a national survey of both full-time and part-time instructional faculty at 449 colleges and universities, which specifically provides data on the percentage of minority faculty employed in the public two-year colleges. Basic findings for 7,408 respondents are available in a report titled *Faculty in Higher Education Institutions, 1988*. (This report includes independent two-year colleges only in the "all institutions" category, because there were too few cases to provide reliable estimates). For more information, see *Faculty in Higher Education Institutions, 1988: Contractor Report* (Washington, D.C.: U.S. Department of Education, National Center for Education Statistics, August 1991).

Equal Employment Opportunity Faculty Survey, conducted by the Equal Employment Opportunity Commission.

Since 1973, the United States Equal Employment Opportunity Commission (EEOC) has required all public and independent institutions of higher education with at least 15 full-time employees to file the Higher Education Staff Information (EEO-6) report biennially. The survey includes information by gender, race/ethnicity, and employment status (part-time or full-time) for the following categories: executive, administrative, and managerial; faculty (by rank and tenure status); professional non-faculty; clerical and secretarial; technical and paraprofessional; skilled craft; and service/maintenance. The survey does not disaggregate data for two-year and four-year institutions. In addition to employment, the EEO-6 report provides annual salary data by job category.

Data are not inputed for institutions that do not report employment figures. Because of nonreporting by institutions and states, the number of institutions included in the EEO-6 survey is different for each survey period. The different number of reporting institutions affects percentage change figures, which measure increases or decreases in employment counts over time. For these reasons, the reader should be extremely cautious when interpreting changes in the actual employment counts over time. For more information, contact Esther

Littlejohn, Equal Opportunity Commission, Office of Research and Surveys, 1801 L Street, N.W. 9th floor, Washington, D.C. 20507, (202) 663-4958.

Campus Trends, by Elaine El-Khawas at the American Council on Education.

Campus Trends is an annual survey of college and university administrators conducted by the American Council on Education. It is designed to provide timely information on changes taking place in the academic and administrative practices of American colleges and universities. The survey collects data such as the financial conditions facing American higher education; the changes in enrollment, curriculum, faculty hiring, and assessment activities. All results are reported by type and control of institution. *Campus Trends*, 1992 is available for $10 for ACE members and $13 for nonmembers from ACE, Division of Policy Analysis and Research, One Dupont Circle, Washington, D.C. 20036-1193. For further information call (202) 939-9450.

The Dry Pipeline: Increasing the Flow of Minority Faculty, prepared by Dorothy S. Linthicum for the National Council of State Directors of Community and Junior Colleges.

The National Council commissioned this study in October 1988 in response to the need to increase the flow of minority faculty and administrators. The report summarizes innovative ideas and programs used by colleges and states across the nation to increase the number of minorities entering the pipeline for future positions and presently serving on faculties. Where possible, names and telephone numbers of appropriate contacts are included. Literature sources are referenced for additional information. The report describes exemplary efforts by colleges and by states in terms of both short-range and long-range strategies. For more information on this report, contact Dorothy S. Linthicum, Education Consultant, 3895 White Rose Way, Ellicott City, MD 21403. For further information call (401) 461-5229.

The American Association of University Professors.

AAUP is the national organization which represents college faculty. AAUP is concerned with issues such as the economic status of women and minorities, and encouraging improvements in teaching and learning. AAUP recently released the report, *The Status of Non–Tenure-Track Faculty*. This report analyzes NSOPF-88 data on faculty who do not hold tenured positions and discusses the implications of these trends for higher education. For more information, contact AAUP, 1012 14th Street, N.W., Suite 500 Washington, D.C. 20005; (202) 737-5900.

References

American Association of University Professors. *The Status of Non–Tenure-Track Faculty*. Washington, D.C.: American Association of University Professors, 1992.

Astin, Alexander W., William S. Korn, and Eric L. Dey. *The American College Teacher: National Norms for the 1989–90 HERI Faculty Survey*. Los Angeles: Higher Education Research Institute, University of California, Los Angeles, 1991.

Brawer, Florence, and Arthur Cohen. *The American Community College*. San Francisco: Jossey-Bass, 1982.

Carter, Deborah J., and Reginal Wilson. *1991 Tenth Annual Status Report on Minorities in Higher Education*. Washington, D.C.: American Council on Education, 1992.

El-Khawas, Elaine. *Campus Trends, 1989*: Washington, D.C.: American Council on Education, 1989, 1991.

El-Khawas, Elaine. *Campus Trends, 1992*: Washington, D.C.: American Council on Education, 1989, 1991.

Higher Education Research Institute, University of California, Los Angeles. "1989–90 Higher Education Research Institute Faculty Survey," unpublished tabulations, November 1991 and March 1992.

U.S. Department of Education, National Center for Educational Statistics. *Faculty in Higher Education Institutions, 1988: National Survey of Postsecondary Faculty* (NSOPF-88). Washington, D.C.: U.S. Department of Education, Office of Educational Research and Improvement, 1990.

U.S. Equal Employment Opportunity Commission, *EEO-6 Higher Education Staff Information Surveys, 1975–1989*.

PART V
ADMINISTRATION, LEADERSHIP, AND GOVERNANCE

Leadership and American Indian Values: The Tribal College Dilemma

ELGIN BADWOUND AND WILLIAM G. TIERNEY

The purpose of this paper is to demonstrate the need for research in organizational governance and decision-making that takes into account the values that are inherent to American Indian culture, and hence, to tribal community colleges.

We begin with a discussion of the rational model of organizational governance and decision-making in higher education; we have chosen the rational model because it is the most prevalent organizational theory to analyze post-secondary organizations (Pfeffer, 1981; Chaffee, 1983). We summarize the model in terms of five elements which serve as a framework for diagnosing organizations (Scott, 1981), and then analyze the model's assumptions from the standpoint of our experiences with tribal colleges. Deficiencies of the model manifest themselves as conflicts between the model's assumptions and the values that underlie the tribal college mission. As a result, we propose an alternative way to view an organization and suggest further avenues for investigation.

As elaborated by Scott, the elements of an organization are: goals, participants, technology, environment, and social structure. According to Scott, these five elements characterize all organizations, regardless of purpose or nature. While the elements serve as standards for diagnosing organizations, the way one interprets elements—such as organizational goals or the environment—depends heavily on the way participants view their organization. How we understand our world in large part determines how we interpret elements such as the social structure. The struggle for tribal community colleges is to understand their organization from their own perspective, as well as that of the dominant society.

The Rational Model

Goals. The rational model assumes that consistent sets of goals exist in organizations (Pfeffer, 1981). Organizations, through decision-making processes of reasoned problem solving, strive to achieve maximal outcomes related to their goals. According to the rational model, when an issue arises that demands action the process of making decisions consists of three basic steps. First, organizational participants develop a set of alternatives. Second, they assess the likely outcomes or consequences of each of the alternatives. Third, decision makers select the alternatives or courses of action which in their view will maximize possibilities for achieving organizational goals. Efficiency is the underlying rationale for the model.

Goals are prerequisites for the decision-making process and act as strategic organizing principles. Organizational participants commit themselves to the goals of the organization and while the recommendations of the participants may vary, they agree on the goals which give meaning to their involvement in the decision-making process (Chaffee, 1985).

Participants. The necessity for a hierarchical organization is predominant to ensure an effective and efficient channel of communication. The unity-of-command principle determines that organizational participants achieve a degree of specialization for their tasks and that all employees receive orders from only one superior. The organization delineates its hierarchy through rules and regulations that spell out chains of command and work expectations of participants. A rigid hierarchy allows the organization to make it clear who is in charge and who is expected to do what.

Technology. Rational and logical problem solving skills are critical to technology in the rational model. Technical competence is particularly critical insofar as decision situations typically consist of complex sets of problems. Participants rely upon extensive and systematic uses of information for decision making and thus information-use skills are important.

Social Structure. The social structure is formal. Given the importance of specialization, the division of labor and differentiation of work tasks is essential. The organization prescribes values, roles, and social positions which are necessary in achieving organizational goals. Participants are united and bound together by common values which are consonant with the goals of the organization. Rather than having the flexibility to pursue divergent interests and to create organizational niches for themselves, participants are constrained by a normative social structure.

Environment. Managers must seal with the environment, but the organization exists divorced from environmental constraints and influences. Leaders derive goals not through interaction with the environment, but through internal discussions about what goals the organization should pursue (Chaffee, 1985). The environment exists "out there" and is a malleable object which managers fit to the organization's goals.

Leadership. Leadership is vested in a central authority who makes the final decisions. The right to give orders and exact obedience is a central tenet of the model. Individuals in the organization participate in decision-making and provide recommendations. However, decisions ultimately rest with the leader. This image of leadership assumes that the central figure is authoritarian; the leader has the confidence of organizational participants to make decisions and to lead the organization.

Tribal College Perspective. The rational model adheres to the Western belief in order, reason, and logic. In some respects, such a view is helpful to all administrators as they confront daily problems. Obviously, some degree of order is warranted in any organization. Otherwise, chaos, intuition, and anarchy may come to dominate organizational life. When such conditions dominate, it is difficult to imagine how any organization can be effective. Since the model emphasizes hierarchy and rigidity, however, it is inappropriate for tribal colleges insofar as they seem to emphasize informality and flexibility in decision-making.

In presenting the tribal college perspective, it is important first of all to discuss the ideals which underlie the rational model and compare them with the fundamental ideals of a tribal college. The rational model emphasizes the Western goals of efficiency and effectiveness with regard to both individual and organizational performance. The ultimate concern of organizations, according to the rational model, is to achieve goals through systematic and orderly processes with minimal waste of resources. The assumption is that all organizations are predicated on similar beliefs.

Our intent is not to call into question Western values such as those that the rational model promotes; rather we intend to demonstrate how American Indian values, and thus, tribally-controlled organizations, have widely divergent concepts about values and goals than those of mainstream organizations. For example, it is worth quoting Astin at length about the meritocratic nature of American higher education:

> In a meritocracy . . . rewards are allocated on the basis of performance. The greatest rewards go to those who perform best. In a meritocratic society, competition plays a central role . . . Meritocratic thinking reflects a peculiarly American preoccupation with measuring, ordering, and ranking (1981, p. 155).

From this perspective, a primary goal of American postsecondary education is to enable individuals to achieve status and success in society. Society measures success by the material rewards which one accrues. The emphasis is on individual competition. Meritocratic values are inherent in practices such as promotion, tenure, and classification/personnel systems.

American Indian culture, however, has goals that are neither competitive nor meritocratic. Instead, generosity, reverence for the earth, and wisdom are basic values (McNickle, 1973). Members of Indian societies demonstrate generosity through informal and formal means of giving or sharing. Indian societies measure status in terms of how individuals openly display generous deeds. The extent to which individuals acquire prestige depends upon the extent to which they share accumulated wealth with less fortunate individuals. Within Indian societies, a prevailing concern exists for the welfare of the group. Indians revere "mother earth" as the provider of life and as a symbolic representation of deeply-held religious beliefs. The earth provides food, shelter, and water, but also is part of the universe which is embedded with legends and supernatural powers that give meaning for Indian existence. Indians view the universe and the environment in a holistic fashion, rather than as a separate entity comprised of distinct parts.

Wisdom is the virtue that is held in highest esteem. Indian societies attribute wisdom to members who have consistently demonstrated adherence to Indian values and who possess visionary qualities to lead. Leadership qualities inherent in individuals endowed with wisdom transcend traditional concepts associated with leadership, such as personality traits or charisma. Central to the qualities possessed by the leader is the notion of spirituality, a condition that is neither learned nor certified, but is attained through the workings of a higher power or being. Indeed, it is wise individuals who sustain Indian culture and whose vision enables Indian societies to endure.

In its purest form, an organization that promotes American Indian values departs fundamentally from the rational organization. The departure stems from the assumptions which underlie the rational organization. For example, tribal colleges do not appear to have preexisting sets of goals which dictate decision-making. Participant welfare is of utmost concern and goals reflect group interests; goals emerge only as a result of extensive group interaction. Participants neither hold allegiance to preexisting goals, nor do they feel compelled by hierarchical chains of command and rigid rules and regulations. Participants tolerate institutional constraints on individual behavior insofar as these constraints do not stifle participatory decision-making.

Specialization, division of labor, and differentiation of work tasks are not predominant technologies as they are in the rational organization. Rather, knowledge of and skills in group dynamics, processes, and interactions are critically important. To be sure, individual labor and program tasks are differentiated, but boundaries between and among positions and programs remain blurred as responsibilities are shared to a high degree.

Unlike the rational organization, where social structure is mainly static and confined to organizational prescriptions for behavior, tribal colleges exhibit social structures that are dynamic and fluid. Participants have a pervasive concern for the group which is demonstrated by constant interactions to share ideas, information, and problems. Organizational values, roles, and social positions develop, but they persist only as long as they contribute to and reflect group interests. These elements of social structure undergo constant change and modification to coincide with emerging ideas and issues.

Instead of remaining distant from the environment, tribal colleges are integral to their environment from both a practical and a spiritual standpoint. Demonstrated concern for group welfare is virtuous, and tribal colleges appear to maintain an active relationship with other entities in the environment. Colleges interact regularly with clientele, tribal government, and other programs. Further, the environment conveys spiritual significance and meaning. Respect for the earth and maintaining harmony with nature are cherished Indian values. In this sense, colleges share a responsibility to protect the environment.

The leader in the tribal college is a facilitator and promoter of group values and interests. Instead of maintaining autocratic power by virtue of position, the tribal college leader develops authority by demonstrating competence and allegiance to the values which underlie the organization. Participants follow the leader not because of rules and regulations, but because the leader has demonstrated appropriate leadership qualities.

Table 1 compares the rational model with the tribal college model we have conceptualized. The table compares the two models across Scott's (1981) five organizational elements and across leadership and philosophical concepts which underlie each model. While the table is an oversimplification of organizational dynamics inherent to each model, it provides a useful means of comparison.

In summary, the rational model of governance and decision-making fails to be an adequate predictor of organizational behavior in tribal colleges. Tribal college interpretations of the various aspects of an organization, such as goals, participants, and social structure digress fundamentally from the perspectives provided by the rational model. Tribal college managers cannot rely upon the rational model to synthesize effective leadership strategies that account for the basic values of American Indian culture. Yet, the development of such strategies is critical if tribal colleges are to effectively fulfill their dual responsibilities, which, in many respects, present a cultural dilemma.

A Cultural Dilemma

Tribal colleges, as entities of tribal governments, promote the self-determination aspirations of Indian People. While the maintenance of Indian culture provides the foundation for tribal college organization, the colleges also strive to integrate traditional disciplinary knowledge of mainstream society into their academic programs. The dual mission of maintaining tribal identity and acquiring knowledge and skills for mainstream society is evident in the mission statement of one tribal college which reads in part, "College students need preparation which will enable them to understand the ways of the larger society, as well as the customs and beliefs of the . . . people." Another college states as part of its mission, ". . . to incorporate the wisdom and beauty of (our) heritage with the knowledge and skills of our modern technological society."

In one sense the mission statements are paradoxical and pose a cultural dilemma. One wonders how an organization can successfully integrate diverging and conflicting concepts of knowledge. Indeed, criticism of tribal colleges from the Indian community often relates to this very question. For example, one tribal community member remarked, "The college is nothing more than a poor replica of existing (mainstream) higher education institutions" (personal corre-

TABLE 1
Two Forms of Governance and Decision Making

Elements	Rational	Tribal College
Goals	Prerequisite; Consistent across the organization; Organizing principles and focuses of decision-making	Consistent across the organization; Reflect group consensus; Emerge from participatory decision-making process
Participants	United by common values which relate to and are consonant with organizational goals	Concern for the welfare of the group; Not bound by organizational prescription
Technology	Rational; Logical problem solving; Extensive and systematic uses of information.	Group interactions and processes; Sharing of information and knowledge
Environment	Closed system; No active interaction with environment; Develop goals through internal discussions	Open system; Active interaction with the environment; Holistic; Practical and spiritual meaning
Social Structure	Normative, participants bound by prescribed values; Formal, social positions defined for participants	Dynamic and fluid; Unity; Values change and modify to meet emerging ideas and issues
Leadership	Centralized; Authoritarian; Ultimate decision making authority	Authority by virtue of demonstrated competence; Ideas and values compatible with those of the group
Philosophy	Efficiency and Effectiveness	Unity; Generosity/sharing; Flexibility

spondence). Another member explained, "The college needs to go beyond offering stock material. It needs to develop curriculum which will account for the total Indian experience" (personal correspondence). To adequately serve the needs of the people a tribal college must have effective strategies that draw upon the history and culture of tribal people.

A growing body of literature has pointed out how an organization reflects the people who exist in the organization (Morgan, 1987; Chaffee & Tierney, 1988). Such a view holds that even though rational and political factors influence organizational life, organizations are also influenced by strong forces that emanate from within. Proponents of a new model termed "organizational culture" assume that organizational life is reflected in what is done, how it is done, and who is involved in doing it—without reference to rational or political goals. Organizational life concerns decisions, actions, and communication both on an instrumental and symbolic level.

The organization is viewed as existing within a dynamic framework where participants help create and define the on-going nature of the organization. "This internal dynamic," notes Tierney, "has its roots in the history of the organization and derives its force from the values, processes and goals held by those most intimately involved in the organization's workings" (1988, page 3). A cultural model of the organization holds much promise for understanding tribal colleges. Rather than rely on rational goals or politically-inspired social structures, proponents of a cultural model seek to understand the reality of the organization from the participant's point of view, and then construct effective decision-making strategies.

Because the model is new, no research has been undertaken that investigates tribal colleges. We have attempted in this article to point out the shortcomings of previous models as they relate to tribal administrators. What remains to be done are studies that incorporate the unique nature of tribally-controlled colleges with a cultural model of the organization. Such a model will allow tribal administrators to develop strategies for their own organizations as they see fit, rather than have the tribal organization adapt to predefined concepts of what constitutes effective goals and decision-making.

References

Astin, A. W. (1982). *Minorities in American higher education.* San Francisco, CA: Jossey-Bass, Inc.

Chaffee, E. E. & Tierney, W. G. (1988). *Collegiate culture and leadership strategy.* New York, NY: MacMillan.

Chaffee, E. E. (1985). Three models of strategy. *Academy of Management Review. 10*(1), 89–98.

Chaffee, E. E. (1983). *Rational decision-making in higher education.* Boulder, CO: National Center for Higher Education Management Systems, Inc.

McNickle, D. (1973). *Native American tribalism: Indian survivals and renewals.* New York, NY: Oxford University Press.

Morgan, G. (1987). *Images of organization.* Beverly Hills, CA: Sage.

Pfeffer, J. (1981). *Power in organizations.* Boston, MA: Pitman Publishing, Inc.

Scott, W. R. (1981). *Organizations: Rational, natural, and open systems.* Englewood Cliffs, NJ: Prentice-Hall, Inc.

Tierney, W. G. (1988). Organizational culture in higher education: Defining the essentials. *Journal of Higher Education, 59* (1), 2–21.

Elgin Badwound was president of Oglala Lakota College on the Pine Ridge Indian Reservation from 1979 to 1986. He is currently a doctoral candidate in higher education at Pennsylvania State University.

William G. Tierney was academic dean at Fort Berthold Community College from 1978 to 1980. He is currently an assistant professor and research associate in the Center for the Study of Higher Education at Pennsylvania State University (133 Willard Building, University Park, PA 16802).

Administrative Commitments and Minority Enrollments:
College Presidents' Goals for Quality and Access

Robert Birnbaum

The decade of the 1970s was remarkable for educational access. Enrollments of minority students in colleges and universities doubled (Blake 1987). Although dropout rates were still unacceptably high, the nation made visible progress towards eliminating disparities in the collegiate representation of minority and ethnic groups. Questions of access, equity, and educational justice were high on the educational policy agenda.

By the middle of the decade of the '80s, however, higher education had a new public policy agenda. Interest in Educational Opportunity Programs was superseded by initiatives identified with names such as Outcomes Assessment, Centers of Excellence, and Honors Programs. The higher education community was put "on notice of pressures to raise admissions standards, to cut support services, and to require higher performance levels for degrees" (Bornholdt 1987, 7).

This renewed concern for "quality" coincided with dropping minority enrollments and waning public interest in the question of access. This paper will assess how a sample of college and university presidents balance the two goals of quality and access and will discuss the implications of this balance for American higher education.

The paper is in four parts. The first part examines the tensions between quality and access as they are reflected in public policy and fiscal arenas. The second part reports on the goals of college and university presidents found in an ongoing study of leaders at thirty-two institutions. Contained in it are analyses of what presidents say about their goals for access and quality and comparisons of their stated goals to changes in minority enrollment patterns at their institutions. The third part is a review of the findings and a discussion of the difficulties in interpreting the data. The fourth and final section proposes acknowledging the cycles of interaction between quality and access at both system and campus levels. Although administrators may play a facilitative role, the major forces that influence access are likely to come from outside rather than inside the campus.

The Tensions Between Quality and Access

The concepts of quality and access do not have standard definitions. As a result, they have often come to be used as "code" words by advocates with different educational and public policy agendas, making dialogue strained or impossible, Protagonists may talk past each other about whether it is or is not possible to have both quality and access without understanding the different meanings they impute to these words.

It is possible to define quality in terms that emphasize the functions of institutions to develop human talent and to provide some "value added" to their students (Astin 1982; Astin 1985). Alternatively, quality can be thought of as the degree to which an institution has appropriate objectives, and uses its resources effectively to achieve them (Council on Postsecondary Accreditation 1986). Both of these definitions are educationally sound and responsive to the diversity of purposes and forms in American higher education, and they are not inconsistent with principles of access. But they are not the definitions generally understood or accepted either by the academic community, or by the publics that support higher education.

Both lay and professional audiences tend to define quality in terms of institutional reputations, the quantity and level of institutional resources, or measurable student achievement (Astin 1985). Quality is thought of as levels of input (raising SAT scores or the percentage of faculty with doctoral degrees), or levels of output (the number of students admitted to Phi Beta Kappa or performance on "rising junior" examinations). Yet accepting these traditional definitions places access and quality in conflict. That does not mean that programs to increase access cannot have sound teaching and learning or that graduates of such programs cannot enter and successfully complete advanced professional and academic study (Rouche and Baker 1987). But access involves admitting students whose academic performance may have been compromised by inadequate preparation, resources, or support. Because the performance of previously disadvantaged students on traditional measures of academic achievement is unlikely, on average, to equal that of students who were initially better prepared, increasing access will, by traditional definitions, decrease "quality."

Astin (1985, 100) summed up the dilemma caused by these traditional definitions of quality when he said that "there is something inherently contradictory about a higher education system where quality and opportunity are in conflict rather than in harmony. If only a few institutions can be regarded as excellent (the reputational view), then most students will be forced to attend 'mediocre' institutions. And if excellence depends mainly upon resources, then the expansion of opportunities requires that finite resources be distributed more thinly, thereby diluting the overall quality of the system."

Access, too, has many potential meanings. It can refer to the college-going rate of the age cohort, to the availability of opportunities for nontraditional students (for example, adults), to the enrollment of students from ethnic and racial minorities, or to equity in distributing faculty and professional staff positions to members of presently underrepresented groups. One common view of access uses the percentage of minority students enrolled as an index with which to measure progress.

For the purposes of this paper, quality will be referred to in the terms that would probably be accepted by most academics—that is, greater rigor in applying traditional academic standards. Access will be defined in several ways when analyzing administrative goals and will be equated to the percentage of minority students when considering enrollment data.

The Politics of Quality and Access

While the conflict between access and quality may to some be an arbitrary one of definition, the practical consequences are real. Resources of all kinds are always limited; and time, attention, political support, and money devoted to one item on an agenda—whether the agenda of public policy or that of an academic institution—are not available for another. Practitioners whose experiences span the period between the early 1970s and the mid-1980s can attest to the change that has taken place during that time. A preoccupation with access during the earlier period has been replaced today by a consuming interest in quality, and it has not appeared possible to attend to both. In considering the conflict between access and quality, Rivlin has asked why it seems that "grown-ups with human brains can't indeed start trying to keep more than one goal in mind at the same time" (College Entrance Examination Board 1987, 8). But what appears reasonable in theory has proven to be exceptionally difficult in practice. During both time periods equal opportunity and enhanced quality have been concerns. But in both cases, concern for one meant comparative neglect of the other.

College Administration, Quality, and Access

If quality and access (as traditionally defined) are in conflict, competing for attention and fiscal resources on the public policy agenda, then college presidents, like other participants in institutional governance and management, will logically be faced with small versions of these same dilemmas. Data reported by a national sample of campus academic leaders indicated that 18 percent of all institutions increased black enrollment in 1987, while 13 percent decreased (comparable figures for Hispanic students were 14 and 9 percent). In contrast, 54 percent of institutions reported increases in enrollment of high-ability students, and only 1 percent reported decreases (El-Khawas 1987). A comparison of the net change of + 5 percent in institutions increasing black student enrollment with the +53 percent in institutions increasing high-ability enrollment provides clear evidence of how the conflict is being resolved.

The quality and access trade-offs appear not only in enrollment but in administrative interests as well. There are many things happening on a campus, and a president cannot attend to all of them. A recent survey of college presidents (College Presidents 1985) reported that 53 percent believed maintaining academic quality was a critical issue at their institution, while only 2 percent believed it was not urgent. In contrast, only 28 percent of the presidents described recruiting minority students (one aspect of access) as extremely important, while almost as many (24 percent) found it not urgent.

Whether one looks at national reports, professional and scholarly publications, institutional emphasis on student ability, or presidential perceptions of important issues, the outcomes are comparable. Recently, more attention has keen given to quality than to access at all levels in the system.

The Goals of Institutional Leaders

Part of an ongoing study of institutional leadership assessed the goals of college and university presidents that are related to quality and access. Although it is common to talk about "organizational goals," the concept is exceptionally problematic (see, for example Simon 1964). The goals of leaders may be influential because they set constraints within which lower participants function. Nevertheless, the interests of people at upper organizational levels often are not fully shared at lower levels, and this may be particularly true in normative, professional organizations such as colleges and universities.

Previous studies of the goals of academic leaders (Gross and Grambsch 1974; Doucette, Richardson, and Fenske 1985) have tended to rely upon questionnaire responses to fixed lists of possible goals. While this approach has many strengths, it has weaknesses as well. The range of responses may be limited by the categories included on the list. Responses may reflect officially approved mission statements or socially accepted values more accurately than the respondent's personally preferred outcomes. Also, respondents can indicate support for large numbers of goals, ignoring the potential conflicts between them. In contrast, the research reported in this paper relied upon responses to an open-ended interview question that attempted to elicit individual "goals" without providing external cues. The question asked was: In what ways do you hope the institution will be different five years from now than it is today?

This question was asked with two intuitively appealing (although not empirically grounded) assumptions in mind: (1) that what a president said would be a valid indication of future outcomes to which he or she was committed; and (2) that to the extent presidents have flexibility in making choices, they are likely to allocate resources of time, energy, political support, and finances to programs consistent with their goals. For the purpose of this study, any desired future condition mentioned by a respondent was considered to be a goal.

There has been little research on the relationship between administrative goals and minority enrollment, and findings tend to be equivocal. One study of minority degree achievement (Richardson, Simmons, and de los Santos 1987) pointed out that "virtually all discussions of minority degree achievement stress the importance of administrative commitment." However, the study itself found that administrators at some institutions that were successful in graduating minority students could not specify particular strategies that they followed. The administrators said that minority students were treated just like everyone else.

Another study that analyzed fourteen externally supported programs designed to help minority students achieve their goals reported four characteristics linked to a successful outcome. One of them was "institutional commitment—the degree to which the institution's top administrators demonstrate interest and support for the project. Strong commitment produces a positive environment for all participants and communicates the project's value to other faculty and staff. A lack of commitment may signal to the wider campus community that the activity is not worthy of their support or involvement" (Helping Minority 1985, 9). However, the data upon which that judgment was based were not described. Although a positive relationship between administrative support and minority enrollments is plausible, there is not yet enough evidence available to justify treating the claim as more than a hypothesis.

The Sample

Data for this study were collected as part of the Institutional Leadership Project, a major research activity of the National Center for Postsecondary Governance and Finance. Intensive, semistructured interviews of trustees, administrators, faculty, and students in leadership roles on thirty-two college and university campuses across the country focused on how these leaders interacted and influenced each other and their institutions. The participating institutions, selected to achieve a wide range of structures, demographic characteristics, and geographical locations, included eight universities, eight state colleges, eight independent colleges, and eight community colleges. Three of the institutions were historically black and one was predominantly Hispanic.

This paper is based primarily upon the responses of institutional presidents. To a lesser extent, it also considers the responses of three other officers; board chair, vice president for academic affairs, and faculty leader (either chair of the faculty senate or analogous body, or president of the faculty union).

I used content analysis to classify interview responses and develop seven categories of goals. Two of these categories, used in this paper, were maintaining and/or enhancing quality, and maintaining and/or enhancing access and equity. Other categories, which are not discussed in this paper, included maintaining and/or enhancing the quantity of resources, concern for educational programs, supporting special administrative or academic interests, improving specific organizational processes, and improving relations with external audiences (Birnbaum 1987). Of the seven categories, qualitative goals were the second most frequently cited, quantitative goals were the most common, and access/equity goals were the least frequently cited.

Responses coded as related to quality fell into four subgroups: quality of students, quality of faculty, quality of programs, and general or undefined quality. Responses coded as related to equity/access fell in three subgroups that emphasized the enrollment of minority or "diverse" students, the participation of adult or other nontraditional students, or the support of minority or other underrepresented faculty. There was no limit to the number of individual goals that could be expressed by any respondent.

Findings

The distribution of the responses of college presidents is shown in Table 1.

Of the thirty-two presidents, seventeen (53.1 percent) indicated one or more qualitative goals, either along or combined with access goals. In contrast, only five (15.6 percent) volunteered one or more access goals, alone or in combination with quality goals; and of these, only three were specifically focused upon access for minority students. Two presidents indicated goals that included both access and quality. The responses of the presidents in this sample about desired outcomes in the next five years appeared to be consistent with general public policy trends placing greater emphasis upon a desire to improve quality rather than upon increasing access.

Table 1
Responses of College Presidents Indicating Concern for Quality and/or Access/Equity Goals

Goal	Number of Presidents	Percent of Presidents
Quality only	15	46.9%
Access/equity only	3	9.4
Both quality and access/equity	2	6.2
Neither	12	37.5
Total	32	100.0%

A complete analysis of these responses by institutional type cannot be reported; all respondents were promised confidentiality, and the small numbers involved would make it impossible to provide complete breakdowns without permitting the identification of institutions. However, it can be stated that community college presidents were more likely than presidents of other institutional types to indicate access as a goal and that they were less likely than other presidents to identify quality as a goal.

Administrative Goals, Institutional Types, and Minority Enrollments

If the assumption that presidential goals would affect institutional performance was accurate, differences in minority enrollments might be expected between institutions in which presidents indicated access as a goal and those in which they did not. This concept does not suggest that future plans affect past enrollments but rather assumes that, if presidential commitments to access remain stable over time, current access goals can be used as a proxy for previous attitudes as well. An alternative explanation for minority enrollment changes might be the mission of the institution, with differences in minority enrollments seen between institutional types generally understood as concerned with access and those usually thought of as emphasizing quality.

To consider the relationship of presidential goals to minority enrollments, I determined undergraduate enrollments of American Indian, black, and Hispanic students for the sample institutions for 1976 and 1984, using data collected by the Office of Civil Rights, U.S. Department of Education. Enrollments of Asian students, usually included in analyses of minority enrollments, were excluded here because they represent a unique enrollment category that can confound summative analyses. I calculated the proportion of minority enrollments and the changes between those two periods separately for three categories of institutions: those whose presidents indicated access as a goal; those whose presidents indicated quality as a goal (and did not also indicate access); and those who indicated neither. The four predominantly minority institutions, and two predominantly white institutions for which ethnic data were not available, were not included in this analysis. See Table 2.

Table 2
Changes in Percentage of Minority Enrollments Between 1976 and 1984, by Presidential Goals

Goals	N	1976 Enrollment	1981 Enrollment	Diff
Access	5	12.6%	11.4%	−1.2%
Quality but not Access	11	5.7	7.7	+2.0
Neither Quality Nor Access	10	9.4	9.4	0.0
Total	26	8.5%	9.1%	+0.6%

The data in Table 2 indicate that the average minority enrollment at the study institutions remained essentially stable during the eight-year period. As expected, institutions in this study whose presidents indicated access as a goal had the highest proportion of minority enrollments during the period, and those expressing a quality but not an access goal had the lowest. However, contrary to expectations, those institutions whose presidents expressed access goals suffered a slight loss in the proportion of minority enrollments during the period, while minority enrollment in those institutions whose presidents indicated quality but not access goals increased somewhat. Minority enrollments decreased on four of the five campuses whose presidents expressed access goals, on four of the ten campuses in which neither quality nor access goals were expressed, and on three of the eleven campuses with quality but not access goals.

I next considered changes in minority enrollments on the basis of institutional program and purpose, using institutional type as a proxy for mission. I expected that minority enrollments would increase most at public community colleges and state colleges and increase least at universities. I made no assumptions about changes in independent colleges, the most diverse group in the sample. See Table 3.

Table 3
Changes in Proportion of Minority Enrollments By Institutional Type

Type	N	1976 Enrollment	1984 Enrollment	Diff
University	8	5.8%	5.7%	−0.1%
State college	5	8.6	12.4	+3.7
Independent college	6	11.4	11.1	−0.3
Community college	7	8.7	8.8	+0.1
Total	26	8.5%	9.1%	+0.6%

The data in Table 3 indicate that minority enrollments were stable in three of the four institutional types. In state colleges, however, the representation of minority students increased from 8.6 to 12.4 percent. Examining the seven institutions with the greatest minority student increase (ranging from +12.8 to +2.4 percentage points) and the seven with the greatest decreases (ranging from −11.3 to −1.8 percentage points) revealed no clear patterns by institutional type. Two community colleges were among the seven with the largest increases and three were among those with the largest decreases; three state colleges increased and one decreased, two independent institutions increased and two decreased; universities had one in the "most decreased" group, and none in the "most gained" category.

Presidential Goals and Goals of Others

Although it is common to think of the goals of the president as reflecting the "goals" of the institution, this view is not always correct. Others in the organization also have goals, and these may be consistent or inconsistent with those of the formal leaders. To assess the institutional consistency of presidential goals concerning access, I analyzed other campus leaders' responses to the question; "In what ways do you hope the institution will be different five years from now than it is today?"

The respondents included trustee chairs, the heads of faculty senates or the presidents of faculty unions, and the vice president for academic affairs. Eleven of these additional respondents stated that access was one of their preferred goals. Of these eleven respondents, three were on campuses whose presidents had also indicated an access goal, and eight were on campuses at which the president had not indicated such a goal. In total, therefore, there were ten campuses upon which either the president and/or one of these three campus leaders indicated an access goal. They included two universities, two state colleges, two independent colleges, and four community colleges.

To consider the possible effects these individuals' concern for access may have had I compared changes in minority enrollments in these ten institutions with changes in the other sixteen. See Table 4.

Table 4
Change in Minority Enrollment Related to Presence of Access
Goals by at Least One of Four Campus Leaders

Access Goal Cited by at Least One Leader	N	1976 Enrollment	1984 Enrollment	Diff
Yes	10	13.0%	12.1%	–0.9%
No	16	5.6	7.2	+1.6
Total	26	8.5%	9.1%	+0.6%

Institutions at which at least one of the four leaders expressed an access goal had significantly higher minority enrollments in 1976 than those institutions at which no such goal was expressed. But compared to a change of +0.6 percentage points for all institutions, the ten institutions in which one or more persons had an access goal experienced a minority enrollment decrease of - 0.9 percentage points. Institutions in which none of the leaders expressed an access goal increased by 1.6 percentage points. The changes in these data indicating combined responses from all four categories of leader are comparable to those based only on presidential responses .

Campuses with the Greatest Changes

Neither the expressed goals of the president nor the institutional type (with the exception of state colleges) appeared to be strongly related to changes in minority enrollments. To explore potential causal factors more carefully, I divided the sample of twenty-six institutions approximately into quarters and compared the enrollment patterns of seven institutions with the greatest increases to those with the greatest decreases of minority enrollments. The data (see Table 5) indicate that the greatest decreases were seen in institutions that began the 1976 period with high minority enrollments. By 1984, minority enrollment in both groups was approximately the same.

Table 5
Changes in Minority Enrollment
of Campuses with the Greatest Increases and Decreases

Changes in Enrollment of Minority Students	N	1976 Enrollment	1984 Enrollment	Diff
Greatest Increases	7	7.9%	13.6	+5.7%
Greatest Decreases	7	16.1	12.2	–3.9%
Total	14	12.0%	12.9%	+0.9%

The interview data reviewed for this study do not indicate the reasons for the decreases. However, decreases in minority enrollment may be due to decreases in institutional commitments or interests, to changes in demographic characteristics of the potential applicant pools, or even to regression effects, which are to be expected statistically (extreme scores during one time period usually are found to be less extreme in another). In the seven institutions with the largest increases in minority enrollment, three presidents expressed quality goals, and one expressed both quality and access goals. In the seven institutions with the greatest decreases, three presidents expressed access goals, one expressed quality goals, and one expressed both access and quality goals. In other words, increases of minority enrollments were seen on campuses where presidents talked about quality; decreases of minority enrollments were seen on campuses where presidents talked about access.

Additional Analyses

In addition to the studies already discussed here, institutional and enrollment data were analyzed with ANOVA. There were no statistically significant relationships between changes of minority enrollment and factors such as institutional category, control, whether the president was new or experienced, whether the president did or did not express access goals, or the actual 1976 level of minority enrollment. I also examined total enrollment levels to determine any relationship between changes in total enrollment and changes in minority enrollment. No differences were found. Institutions with the greatest increases in minority enrollments had a total enrollment increase of 9.2 percent during this period, identical to the changes seen in seven institutions with the greatest minority enrollment decreases.

Interpreting the Findings

On the face of it, the data in this study suggest that college presidents, today are much more concerned with issues of quality than issues of access or equity. Also, changes in minority enrollment do not appear to be related to stated presidential goals for access. Although these conclusions may be valid, before accepting them, we should consider a number of caveats relating to the data and methodology. For example, changes in minority enrollments on some campuses may, in fact, have been related to the presidential commitments of a predecessor rather than to those of the incumbent. For instance, the adequacy of minority enrollments is at least in part a function of local conditions that were not considered in this study. An institution with a 10 percent minority enrollment may be doing well if the area from which it recruits students has a 5 percent minority population, but doing poorly if its pool has a 20 percent minority population. The period may have been relatively stable. These enrollment data were collected during a period that did not reflect the declines in minority enrollments seen since 1984. Also, some administrators with strong commitments to minority enrollments may not have stated them in response to the broadly phrased question asked; and minority enrollment goals may be been important to some presidents, but overshadowed in the president's response by some immediate event (a recent state budget cut, for example).

Goals and Enrollments

This study indicated no simple relationships between presidential goals expressed as desired future states and the changes in minority enrollments of the institutions. The data do not lend much support to the belief that minority enrollment is dependent upon administrators who have the goal of increasing access, but neither do they refute it. The sample is too small to draw supportable and universal generalizations. Nevertheless, the fact that minority enrollment increased on many campuses where the president did not indicate minority enrollment as a goal suggests that too much emphasis may be given to gaining administrative endorsement and not enough to developing structures and processes that activate the pressures that guide administrative actions. In the final analysis, the issue is not what administrators say, but what campuses do.

It may be possible for administrative support of all kinds (for example, financial, staff, and data systems) to exist for a program on a campus even without any particular interest on the part of senior administrators. Those familiar with the complexities of organizational life can understand reasons why this might be so. Institutional programs are characterized by inertia; and even in the presence of administrative indifference (or outright hostility), past financial allocations can continue. Budgets tend to be historical and incremental, staffs once on board are difficult to reduce or remove, and political forces may make withdrawal of support from even an undesired program an unpleasant prospect. On most campuses, the stabilizing and self-correcting properties of organizations make once-started programs difficult to stop (Birnbaum, forthcoming).

By and large, presidents do not initiate either social or educational movements. They respond to them. Presidents have many programs, problems, and constituencies with which to be concerned, and their time is limited. Most (but not all) of what presidents do and how they spend their time is dictated not by their personal interests but by their perceptions of the demands of the environment. This does not mean that presidents do only what is expedient. Rather, it suggests that when presidents, like the rest of us, must make choices among a number of legitimate but competing claims, the most prominent alternatives tend to receive the most attention. For example, when presidents confront an environment that places pressure on them to look like rational managers, they are likely to adopt management systems and processes. When important political and social agencies in their environment emphasize issues of quality, then concerns presumably related to quality will be high on their agenda. In the same way, when society places presidents under pressure to provide programs for access and student support, they will be likely to do so.

There is nothing wrong in attempting to increase a president's personal commitments to programs of minority recruitment or degree completion, but the results may be disappointing in the absence of other pressures that support those efforts. The final section of this paper discusses reasons why generating such support is difficult and offers some simple suggestions about what those concerned with access can do to facilitate change.

Helping Change Happen

The rhetoric of the 1960s asserted, "If you are not part of the solution, you're part of the problem." There is some truth to that claim, but it tends to oversimplify the exceptionally complex web of valid and competing interests within which social issues such as access and equity are considered in democratic societies. It is probably better to have an administrator interested in programs related to access than not, but it is a mistake to overemphasize the presidential role. Presidents find it relatively easy to stop things from happening but difficult to start them. An understanding of what is happening on a campus is probably more likely to come from understanding forces external to it as from analyzing presidential goals or values.

Cycles of Political Concern

In his recent book, *The Cycles of American History,* Arthur Schlesinger, Jr., (1986) proposed that political emphases in America have alternated in regular cycles between concern for public and for private interests. He commented that others also have noted the "patterns of alternation, of ebb and flow, in human history" (p. 22). They have suggested cycles ranging from twelve to thirty years, with each new cycle apparently serving the stabilizing political function of correcting the excesses of the previous cycle.

Because higher education is embedded within the larger social, political, and economic systems of the country, it should not be surprising if these same cycles appeared in a consideration of the relationship between access and quality. Hansen and Stampen (1987) have identified such a "pendulum effect" related to higher education policy, in which attention to larger social goals since the end of World War II "for the most part reflected efforts to resolve problems outside of higher education. However, for higher education these goals were translated into essentially two alternating mandates: to improve quality and to improve equity" (p. 18). These researchers identified five periods or phases since World War II: a period of adjustment between 1946 and 1957; an emphasis upon quality between 1958 and 1967; a concern for equity between 1968 and 1972 with a consolidation of equity gains between 1973 and 1980; and the current emphasis upon quality that began in 1981. During each of these phases, emphasis on one goal came at the expense of the other.

Cycles of Organizational Concern

The cycles of interest seen at the levels of public policy may exist at the campus level as well. Colleges, like all other organizations, have many goals that may be in conflict with one another.

Organizations respond to these conflicts "by attending to different goals at different times. Just as the political organization is likely to resolve conflicting pressures to 'go left' and 'go right' by first doing one and then the other, the business firm is likely to resolve conflicting pressures to 'smooth production' and 'satisfy customers' by first doing one thing and then doing the other. The resulting time buffer between goals permits the organization to solve one problem at a time, attending to one goal at a time" (Cyert and March 1963, 118).

Rivlin has characterized public policy debates in higher education as an "alternation of interest in distributive justice (access or equity) and the quality of the product that is being distributed" (College Entrance Examination Board 1987, 8). Such alternation may be the way in which colleges and universities deal with problems such as "access" and "quality." Relatively little attention is given to either goal as a matter of continuous planning; instead one or the other is likely to receive attention as a consequence of some specific series of events. When access is threatened, or falls below a level deemed acceptable by the institution or the social system, changes are instituted to address it. Little attention is given during that process to the goal of "quality" or to the impact of access programs on achieving quality. When the goal of access is largely accomplished (that is, when discrepancies between desired and actual access levels have become acceptable), administrators may transfer their attention to problems of academic achievement. At such times, the goal of access is largely forgotten. The establishment of specialized units to respond to either of these goals (for example, Equal Opportunity Programs and Honors Programs) increases the probability that the organization itself will deal with them, if for no other reason than the unit will create products (reports, complaints, budget requests, etc.) that will serve as attention cues for others. But the sequential attention to goals means that it is unlikely that they will be considered simultaneously, and so contradictions between them can be ignored.

These process are therefore "cybernetic" in nature; that is they are self-correcting and based upon negative feedback (Birnbaum, forthcoming). Such processes are consistent with findings in this study indicating that presidents with minority enrollment goals are from institutions with minority enrollment decreases; it may be that the enrollment decline leads to the development of a goal, rather than the reverse. In the same way, presidents whose minority enrollments are increasing may no longer need to have that as a goal (that is, a desired future state of affairs) and can turn their attention to other matters.

Administrators and the Access/Quality Dilemma

There are probably two ways presidents may have an effect in increasing minority enrollments. The first way is having presidents who have (or can be convinced to develop) a strong moral commitment to educational equity. Such presidents will place the issue high on their personal agendas, and will make it one of the benchmarks of their administration. Although a great deal of attention has been given to advocating the appointment of such persons, it will probably continue to be the less common means through which the problem of minority enrollments is addressed. This is not because presidents are opposed to principles of access, but rather because most presidents most of the time are likely to have other commitments they consider to be more pressing.

The second way is to make the issue of minority enrollments a crisis. Fortunately, minority enrollment increases need not depend upon the moral commitments of presidents as long as presidents are responsive to pressures by external bodies that exercise some political power. T. Edward Hollander, Chancellor for Higher Education in New Jersey has commented about minority enrollment and retention: "We've found that when presidents make this a concern, there have been dramatic changes" (Jaschik 1987, 22). Presidents need not have a moral commitment to any specific organizational program for that program to become a matter of concern to them. Political pressure, to some extent from inside the campus but to an even greater degree from outside, may be even more effective than moral commitment in getting presidents to spend time and give attention to access, to secure resources, and to hold people accountable for performance.

Getting the Attention of Public Policy

Rivlin has commented that "the first characteristic of policy making is the need for a crisis. In higher education, as in other areas of public policy, the American political system seems unable to engage in a serious debate about policy change—let alone to undertake action—unless some form of doom is widely felt to be impending" (College Entrance Examination Board 1987, 7). To increase public concern for minority enrollments will require that the problem of declining participation rates be defined as a major social crisis.

There are hopeful signs that our educational system, if not our political system, has retained a sensitivity to minority enrollments that may reverse present trends. One of the first such indications was a statement made by President Healy of Georgetown University. He called attention to the decrease in minority enrollments as early as 1984 and reminded his colleagues that "all of us acknowledge the ideal of integration, but our zeal for keeping access open and for working at the integration of our faculties has slipped" (Heller 1984, 1). The American Council on Education meeting at which Healy spoke passed a resolution urging campus attention to integration, and some participants "expressed fear that the problem was being overlooked in the 'band-wagon' of interest in improving the quality of higher education institutions" (Heller 1984, 15). Comparable statements were made at meetings of the College Board and ETS that same year.

Recent developments are encouraging. The State Higher Education Executive Officers (SHEEO) have issued a report recommending that minority student recruitment and achievement be treated as a "preeminent concern for the higher education community" (1987, 33). The Board of Directors of the American Council on Education held a special session in May 1987 focused on campus resources and initiatives for increasing minority enrollments: a blue-ribbon task force is being assembled on the topic, a handbook that campuses can use to improve minority participation in all aspects of campus life is being prepared, and minority participation was identified as ACE's "number one issue" (Green 1987). The number of black students taking the SATs reportedly rose 26 percent between 1985 and 1987, reversing the decline of the early 1980s (Fiske 1987). And the May/June 1987 edition of *Change* was devoted to examining minority enrollments and degree completion. This conference itself furthers the cause by continuing the process of bringing the issue back to public attention .

Schlesinger (1986) quotes Emerson speaking of conflicting elements in American democracy: "It may be safely affirmed of these two metaphysical antagonists, that each is a good half, but an impossible whole. Each exposes the abuses of the other, but in a true society, in a true man, both must combine" (p. 48). The genius of American higher education is that it attempts, to a degree not found elsewhere in the world, to support both quality and access. And indeed, in our educational system, neither quality nor access can survive alone; it is only in combination that they define our educational system. When the system overemphasizes one to the detriment of the other, both are threatened. As the State Higher Education Executive Officers have said, "The priority given equality can be no less than that accorded the issue of quality. A higher education system that fails to equip large numbers of its students to meet requisite standards can never be deemed high in quality, no matter what peaks of performance it inspires in a few" (1987, 33).

Getting the Attention of Campus Presidents

Administrators act when things go wrong. By and large, they respond to deviations from accepted practice or expected performance, rather than initiating new programs. Some administrators may have personal or professional agendas that lead them to respond to problems of access without external pressures, but most probably do not. It is not because they oppose concepts of access, but because they find other things more pressing and therefore more important. Those who are concerned with access should think less about how to get administrators to share their commitments and more about how to get administrative attention.

In public institutions in general, and in institutions that are part of multicampus systems in particular, much administrative attention is given to the concerns expressed by the state chancellor, system head, or state coordinating board. When those concerns are highly publicized, or when they are related to resource allocation decisions, they tend to become critical matters deserving of executive attention. The Institutional Leadership Project pinpointed a number of examples of administrative attention directed by agendas set at higher system levels. Those who wish to influence campus administrators should probably direct some of their energy to influencing the external political and bureaucratic bodies to which campus administrations are responsive. This responsiveness may in part explain why the major increases in minority enrollments were seen in the state college sector.

One of the ways administrators sense that things are going wrong is through data analysis. It is unclear whether on many campuses today administrators regularly see accurate data on minority enrollments and/or degree completion rates. For example, although national data indicate that minority enrollment is declining, academic vice presidents in 1985 (El-Khawas 1986a) were much more likely to report increases rather than decreases in black and Hispanic enrollments during the previous four years and to overwhelming state that their ability to attract minority students had recently improved. One year later they reported that 1986 minority enrollment increased even further (El-Khawas 1986b). Those concerned with questions of access on their campus might find their time to be initially well spent in the mundane and drab activity of collecting, analyzing, and reporting data, even though it is much less glamorous than program development. A campus that publishes and disseminates annual reports on enrollment and attrition by ethnic group is more likely to activate the interest of concerned campus groups than a campus that does not collect or publish such data. Such information might be even more potent if published together with such bench-mark data as national enrollment distributions, enrollments in comparable institutions, and the ethnic distribution in the geographic areas from which the institution draws its students. The availability of such data not only provides attention cues for those sharing similar concerns but also provides people who wish to support the development of programs with powerful arguments for their positions.

In addition to emphasizing data, campus groups concerned with access should give attention to accountability. Most people are not concerned with most issues on most campuses most of the time. Administrators spend much of their time dealing with transitory problems as they come up and moving on to new issues as old ones fade. If concern for minority enrollments and degree achievement is uncoordinated and sporadic, administrative interest will likely follow suit. On the other hand, continuous interest that is demonstrated by responsible advocacy, willingness to participate in program development, requests for regular reports, and the use of public campus forums to confront the issue, will convince administrators that they will be held accountable for responding to this problem. Such a pattern makes it more likely that structures to support such programs will be developed.

Processes for accountability can be developed at all levels of the educational system. The State Higher Education Executive Officers (SHEEOs) who coordinate public systems of higher education at the state level have proposed that the individual campuses should be dealt with, not just by moral suasion, but also through structures and guidelines that focus their efforts. Moreover, they said, "This is an issue of such high priority that institutions need to be put on formal notice that both actions and outcomes will be subject to outside review" (1987, 38).

In the same way, college presidents can be asked to conduct a formal review of minority access progress each year for dissemination to the campus community, thus making presidents accountable to campus constituencies. In turn, when admissions offices are asked for regular reports on minority recruitment activities, academic support programs will be required to produce and distribute analyses of minority student support services and outcomes. Finally, when affirmative action officers are asked to formally describe the ethnic distribution of annual promotion, recruitment, and tenure activity, they more likely will give attention to issues of access and equity than officers who are not required to make such reports .

Influencing the Cycles

Colleges and universities are embedded in webs of interaction with social, political, economic, and cultural forces that have a significant effect upon what they are expected to do. It is implausible that public attention on such issues is a response to the activities and desires of college presidents and much more likely that presidential activities and desires are a response to public attention. Presidential support of a program on most institutions can probably have a marginal effect on campus performance and is therefore desirable, but it is unlikely to overcome other barriers to attendance and degree completion. While educators can engage in activities on every campus that make minority enrollment and completion a matter of concern to the administration of their institution, it is probably true that the greatest impact will come not from administrative behavior on the campus but from public policy decisions at the state and federal level and, in particular, from decisions concerning student financial aid.

If the cyclic theory of a natural succession of alternating concerns for access and quality is correct, we can expect that concern for quality will continue to increase until its excesses (at least in part related to a reduction in minority enrollments) are seen as a crisis. This will then activate groups whose political power will force a realignment of interests in access. To some extent, this process may already be in motion. But the full cycle itself may be a long one, and many potential students may be lost as it plays out. Individual acts responding to the crisis of access as it is reflected in decreased minority enrollments may seem inconsequential in the face of the present public concern for quality, but they nonetheless serve an important function. The cumulative effects of such acts may help to again place access as a major issue on the public policy agenda and bring the current imbalance between these two objectives into a more reasonable equilibrium.

Bibliography

Association of American Colleges. *Helping Minority Students Succeed. Washington*, D.C.: Association of American Colleges, 1985.

Astin, A. W. *Minorities in American Higher Education.* San Francisco: Jossey-Bass, 1982.

——. *Achieving Academic Excellence.* San Francisco: Jossey-Bass, 1985.

Birnbaum, R. "Individual Preferences and Organizational Goals: Consistency and Diversity in the Futures Desired by Campus Leaders." Paper presented at the 1987-88 meeting of the Association for the Study of Higher Education, Baltimore, Maryland, November 1987.

——. *How Colleges Work: The Cybernetics of Academic Organization and Leadership.* San Francisco: Jossey-Bass, forthcoming.

Blake, E., Jr. "Equality for Blacks: Another Lost Decade or New Surge Forward?" *Change* (May / June 1987): 10–13.

Bornholdt, L. "Time for a Second Generation Effort." *Change* (May / June 1987): 6–7.

College Entrance Examination Board. *Educational Access and Achievement in America.* New York: College Entrance Examination Board, 1987.

"College Presidents' Views on Trends and Issues. *Chronicle of Higher Education* 2 (4 Dec. 1985): 42.

Council on Postsecondary Accreditation. *Educational Quality and Accreditation: A Call for Diversity, Continuity, and Innovation.* Washington, D.C.: Council on Postsecondary Accreditation, 1986.

Cyert, R. M., and J. G. March. *A Behavioral Theory of the Firm.* Englewood Cliffs, N.J.: Prentice-Hall, 1963.

Doucette, D. S., R. C. Richardson, Jr., and R. H. Fenske. "Defining institutional mission." *Journal of Higher Education* 56 (1985): 189–205.

El-Khawas, E. *Campus Trends, 1985.* Washington, D.C.: American Council on Education, 1986a.

——. *Campus Trends, 1986.* Washington, D.C.: American Council on Education, 1986b.

——. *Campus Trends, 1987.* Washington, D.C.: American Council on Education, 1987.

Fiske, E. B. Steady gains achieved by blacks on college admission test scores. *New York Times*, 23 Sept. 1987 A1, D30.

Green, M. F. 1987. *Newsletter*, 10, no. 1. [whole issue is Green's No headline] Council of Fellows, American Council on Education.

Gross, E., and P. V. Grambsch. *Changes in University Organization, 1964–1971*. New York: McGraw-Hill, 1974.

Hansen, W. L., and J. O. Stampen. *Economics and the Financing of Higher Education: The Tension Between Quality and Access*. National Center for Postsecondary Governance and Finance, University of Wisconsin-Madison, 1987.

Heller, S. "Reaffirm Drive for Integration, Colleges Urged." *Chronicle of Higher Education* 29 (21 Nov. 1984): 1, 15.

Jaschik, S. "State Leaders Urged to Intensify Colleges' Efforts to Enroll and Graduate More Minority Students. *Chronicle of Higher Education* 32 (15 July 1987): 1, 22.

"Minority Access: A Question of Equity. Change (May/June 1987): 35–39.

Richardson, R. C., Jr., H. Simmons, and A. G. de los Santos, Jr. "Graduating Minority Students." *Change* (May/June 1987): 20–27.

Rouche, J. E., and G. A. Baker, III. *Access and Excellence: The Open Door College*. Washington, D.C.: Community College Press (AACJC), 1987.

Schlesinger, A. M., Jr. *The Cycles of American History*. Boston: Houghton Mifflin, 1986.

Simon, H. A. "On the Concept of Organizational Goal." Administrative Science Quarterly 9 (1964): 1–22.

State Higher Education Executive Officers Task Force on Minority Student Achievement. *A Difference of Degrees: State Initiatives to Improve Minority Student Achievement*. Report and Recommendations of the State Higher Education Executive Officers Task Force on Minority Student Achievement, (Draft). (24 June 1987).

Double Jeopardy: Women of Color in Higher Education

DEBORAH CARTER, CAROL PEARSON, AND DONNA SHAVLIK

At the intersection of race and gender stand women of color, torn by the lines of bias that currently divide white from nonwhite in our society, and male from female. The worlds these women negotiate demand different and often wrenching allegiances. As a result, women of color face significant obstacles to their full participation in and contribution to higher education.

In their professional roles, women of color are expected to meet performance standards set for the most part by white males. Yet their personal lives extract a loyalty to their culture that is central to acceptance by family and friends. At the same time, they must struggle with their own identity as women in a society where "thinking like a woman" is still considered a questionable activity. At times, they can even experience pressure to choose between their racial identity and their womanhood.

For women of color, the combined effect of these pressures can be destructive if they are not recognized and if the faulty premises that underlie them are not addressed. The premises, reduced to their essence, are: first, that there is a single standard by which all people should be judged or defined, and second, that women of color must identify either with their ethnic group or with their sex. In fact, our society, which is experiencing rapid demographic and social transformation, is trying to move toward a more diverse definition of humanity. To that end, this article explores the educational needs and insights of women of color in higher education.

The "New" Majority

Today, women constitute 52 percent of all people enrolled in college in the U. S. and nearly 55 percent of the minority enrollment. In the last decade, women of nearly all racial/ethnic groups have enrolled in college in greater numbers than their male counterparts. In higher education, women currently comprise over 59 percent of the black enrollment, 52 percent of the Hispanic enrollment, and 55 percent of the American Indian enrollment. Asian/Pacific Island women constitute 46 percent of the enrollment of their ethnic group—a tremendous numerical gain in the last 10 years.

Today's college students include, in addition to traditional-age women, a high proportion of "returning women," those who are going back to school to finish an education interrupted for work, family, financial, or other reasons. Collectively, today's women students are diverse in terms of age, social class, race, ethnicity, and religion. Their needs and learning styles often challenge the prevailing culture.

Black Women[1]

Historically, black women have been one of the most isolated, underused, and consequently demoralized segments of the academic community. This third-class academic citizenship has developed despite the fact that more black women enroll in college and receive degrees than black men, although enrollments for both black men and women have declined during the last decade. Black women currently represent 5.2 percent of the college enrollment compared to 3.6 percent for black men. They also maintain a higher proportional representation within their race than their white female counterparts. However, even with these higher participation rates, black women are seriously underrepresented in tenured faculty positions. They comprise only 0.6 percent of the full professorships, compared to 1.6 percent for black men, 9.9 percent for white women, and 83.2 percent for white men.

When black women question this disparity, they often are told that "qualified black women can't be found" or that they should "step back and give black men the opportunity because racism and discrimination have had more serious repercussions for black men than for black women." Both rationales generate a sense of frustration within collegiate black women. The latter argument also creates a deep schism for black women who are reluctant to be seen as stifling the progress of black men.

Although the feminist movement on campuses has tried to represent the cross-cultural and cross-racial orientation of all women, the movement at its best has attempted to transcend, rather than confront, the racial tensions and the complexities resulting from the black woman's involvement in the movement. Black women find themselves in yet another white-dominated group in which their interests as black people are not well represented. Many black women feel that both the women's movement and women's studies programs are basically white and middle class in orientation.

During the last two decades, blacks have been attending predominantly white institutions in greater numbers. Because black women enrolled in these institutions in larger numbers, they, as other women of color face classroom environments that often are unreceptive and unsupportive. They are less likely to receive the same encouragement from their instructors as their white counterparts. There are few black female professors to serve as role models and provide support for their success. The recent resurgence of overt racial hostility and violence on many predominantly white college campuses has added to the stress black females experience.

Most women and women of color will tell you of a belief that underlies all they do: they must be smarter, study longer, work harder, and be more articulate than everyone else in order to overcome both the sexism and racism they face in higher education—and later in the workplace.

Hispanic Women[2]

Hispanic women face many of the same problems that confront black women. They also endure the added pressure of lack of recognition for the richness and diversity of their cultures.

Hispanic women differ from each other, as well as from the majority, in color and physiognomy, degree of adaptation to the dominant culture and ties to their native culture, proficiency in English, social class background, and financial need. Although Hispanic women have achieved greater gains in academe than have Hispanic men, they still remain one of the poorest, least-educated populations in the country.

Sara Melendez and Janice Petrovich write in *Educating the Majority* that some culturally determined behaviors, such as ways of dealing with authority figures, expressing disagreement, communicating (verbally and nonverbally), and finding motivation, often conflict with the counterpart behaviors in the dominant culture. Students are often unaware of these culturally-determined behaviors and beliefs, which can create difficulties for Hispanic women students in the classroom and in individual exchanges with peers and faculty and staff.

Hispanic females are not encouraged to take risks, to move out and away from the family, or to make decisions that run contrary to their parents' wishes. Consequently, for the Hispanic female student, making decisions independently in a collegiate setting may be a new and unsettling experience.

Within the Hispanic culture, a sense of belonging and cooperation are more important values than competition and individual achievement. This tends to be in direct conflict with the nature of the college classroom. Hispanic women also tend to demonstrate communication patterns similar to those of Asian and American Indian women—they are soft-spoken and nonconfrontational. These styles, highly valued in Hispanic culture, are not valued in the academic world.

American Indian Women[3]

Ignorance of the issues facing the American Indian population as a whole shows how little tribal cultures have permeated our national values. American Indian women often are hesitant to discuss what it means to "be Indian," because there are tremendous variations in practices and traditions among the more than 20 distinct tribal groups within the borders of the United States. This is a similar conflict to that experienced by Hispanic women, when Chicanas, Puertoriquenas, and Cubanas are lumped together as an ethnic unit.

Within this diversity, Indian women face common problems and issues when they enter or work in higher education, according to Robbi Ferron, affirmative action recruiting manager for the City of Seattle. These include misperceptions and misunderstandings about the availability of financial aid to this group. "Myths run the gamut, from a belief that every Indian has a free ride through college (treaties, it is imagined, guarantee a free education to every Indian) to the notion that Indian students are unlikely candidates for academic scholarships. These myths are often linked."[4]

American Indian women have considerable responsibilities within the extended family system of tribal culture. These responsibilities may add to the pressures they experience in finding housing, managing finances, and attending classes. Off-campus housing may be difficult for an American Indian woman to find, because of racial discrimination; black and Hispanic students also face such problems. Cultural obligations also are a factor. Robbi Ferron writes: "She [the American Indian student] may have to absent herself from school in order to go home to cook for a ceremony. A professor, administrator, or co-worker may think it foolish, but her acceptance as a tribal member may rest on her participation."

American Indian, Hispanic, and Asian American women often must assume behaviors in the classroom that are foreign to their experiences in their own cultures as women. These women may come to the university with strong cultural prohibitions against questioning authority and speaking up in public. If the value of a classroom discussion is the ability to criticize the work of authorities, they are forced into choosing between their cultural values and success in academic terms. Cultural differences in rules of eye-contact, turn-taking in speech, and other basic approaches to conversation may be an additional source of cultural conflict for these students.

Asian American Women

Asian Americans also tend to be lumped together when more than 60 sub-groups comprise their population, with the largest representations being Chinese, Japanese, Korean, and Filipino. The academic success of Asian Americans has received much attention. A substantial majority of these citizens descend from an ethnic group whose culture places high value on educational achievement and the hard work necessary for success. In response to the large number of high-achieving Asians, some universities have apparently adopted unofficial Asian admissions quotas for certain programs, to reduce their high representation. Such practices can only be viewed as a type of academic anti-Asian discrimination, affecting both sexes.

In addition to facing such institutional discrimination, women students from Asian backgrounds experience the value orientations of their particular ethnic group—which more overtly assigns secondary status to females—and societal stereotyping. The high value placed on academic success within their families and community is both a real strength and a potential source of stress. The constant emphasis on achievement may result in a tremendous amount of psychological and emotional stress on these students. There is also a strong sense of collective responsibility for actions of the individual. Therefore, many Asian students are reluctant to call attention to themselves in any social situation, for fear of ridicule or criticism of not only *their* status but that of their family, community, and ethnic group.

According to research cited by Joanne S. Yamauchi and Tin-Mala, more traditional Chinese, Japanese, and Korean females tend to exhibit more subservience to males in contrast to their white female counterparts. However, Filipinos do not tend to have a secondary role relationship to men since they come from a context in which males and females share similar or equal loads in family planning and work responsibilities.

The communication style of most Asian women—which is subtle, indirect, and emphasizes harmony and cooperation—may be perceived to be less expressive, conflict-minimizing, and unassertive in comparison to their white counterparts, and hence, devalued and misunderstood.

The Power of Language

The difficulties of women of all ethnic groups in academe and the workplace is nowhere better reflected than in the symbolic power of language in affecting perception. Women, and especially women of color, are held back by a form of invisibility in language. Studies have shown that when people hear or use the generic "he," they envision a male or see no image, rather than envision a female. Similarly, the word "people" creates an image of a white person or white group of people unless it is preceded by identifying language describing a specific ethnic group.[6]

Using phrases such as "women and minorities" also tends to render women of color invisible, which then leads to their needs and perspectives being omitted from the larger discussion.

Even the use of "majority" and "minority" can affect the presence of women—and women of color—in cultural awareness. This use of language tends to confer psychological majority status on one privileged group—white males—and minority status on all others.

At present, the generic terms we use confer majority status and visibility on white males as the norm to match and follow. There is no generic term that includes everyone. Although it may seem awkward to say women and men of color and white women, or even to name all of the relevant racial groups, doing so is more clear and inclusive.

The work of gender and ethnic culture scholars is a relatively recent contribution to our body of knowledge. These scholars are countering the unfortunate provincialism that has prevailed for too long under the guise of intellectual elitism. Until a few years ago, higher education in the United States did not recognize diversity, implicitly presenting the majority male perspective as either synonymous with reality, or—if differences were acknowledged—superior to all other realities. Now, recent scholarship is providing terms and categories to help us all benefit from the perspective of majority women and people of many ethnic and cultural heritages.

We know that all over the world women's roles and experiences differ greatly from men's, and that generally such differences affect the ways men and women view the world. Therefore, we cannot simply assume that generalizations about African, Asian, or European cultures reflect as accurately the female view as they do the male point of view, just as we cannot assume that generalizations about majority female systems apply to all minority women. Yet it is not easy to find descriptions of the philosophical points of view of American women of African, Hispanic, or Asian extraction. While they may exist, these points of view are not widely available or recognized.

This situation is a disadvantage not only to women of color, but to everyone. If the unique perspectives of women of different ethnic heritages never enter the realm of academic discourse, it makes these perspectives invisible. The dominant culture has no knowledge of what it is missing, and minority women, to the degree that they internalize values of the dominant culture, will devalue or undervalue their own perceptions. Everyone is the loser in this equation.

Institutional Response

Despite the vast diversity among the various ethnic groups in this country and between the sexes, women of color do share some common concerns and needs in higher education. At the same time that institutions seek to recognize and appreciate their differences, it is important that their commonalities also are recognized.

Women of all colors will have true opportunity in higher education when institutions address the following issues effectively:

1. the impact of ethnic and women's studies upon the design of curricula and extracurricular activities for women of color on historically black and predominantly white college campuses;

2. the importance of role models and campus climate in developing positive self-concepts among women of color;

3. the impact of affirmative action/equal opportunity policy on all women's access to and performance in institutions of higher learning;

4. the impact of current trends in education (such as the shift away from liberal arts to more professionally oriented education) on women's career choices;

5. the importance of critical life events to women's achievement in college; and,

6. the unique cultural heritages Hispanics, Asian Americans, and American Indians embrace as members of smaller ethnic groups or tribes.

To reach this state, institutions must make long-term commitments to self-examination and then design programs to help participants become more knowledgeable about the various racial/ethnic cultures, women's culture, and interaction with dominant white male culture.

This means reviewing all policies and programs to see if they reflect and give appropriate consideration to each person regardless of unalterable group characteristics. It means designing an individual institutional plan for ongoing review and changing the curriculum to incorporate courses that reflect scholarship on women and ethnic/racial minorities. It means having faculty, staff, and administrators who represent the new majorities as well as the old, to teach and establish the appropriate learning environment for the diverse student bodies of the future. Nothing less will enable women of color to reach their full potential in our higher education system or enable our society to have the educated, trained, productive, and fulfilled populace that is within our reach.

The good news is that women are pursuing educational resources in continually growing numbers and, for the first time in statistical history, are approaching financial equity with male counterparts in the work world. If educational institutions make and carry out a commitment to accommodating the presence, learning styles, and contributions that women of all ages and cultures offer, the results will be an exciting diversity and new reality in our society.

Notes

1. Beverly Guy-Sheftall and Patricia Bell-Scott. "Finding a Way: Black Women Students and the Academy." In *Educating the Majority: Women Challenge Tradition in Higher Education,* Carol Pearson, Donna Shavlik, and Judith Touchton (eds.). ACE/Macmillan Series in Higher Education. New York: Macmillan Publishing Company, in press.

2. Sara E. Melendez and Janice Petrovich, "Hispanic Women Students in Higher Education: Meeting the Challenge of Diversity." In *Educating the Majority*, op. cit.

3. Robbi Ferron, "American Indian Women in Higher Education: Common Threads and Diverse Experiences." In *Educating the Majority*, op. cit.

4. Robbi Ferron, ibid.

5. Joanne S. Yamauchi and Tin-Mala, "Undercurrents, Maelstroms, or the Mainstream? A Profile of Asian Pacific American Female Students in Higher Education." In *Educating the Majority*, op. cit.

6. Barrie Thorne, "Rethinking the Ways We Teach." In *Educating the Majority*, op. cit.

Multiculturalism:
The Crucial Philosophical and Organizational Issues

Patrick J. Hill

In higher education today and in American society at large, we are wrestling with an incredible explosion of diversity. There are those who deem higher education complicitous with society's leadership in depreciating or ignoring the diversity of human experience; their attempt is to provide institutional and curricular status of a non-marginal sort for enterprises like women's studies, ethnic studies, and Latin American studies. Then there are those who judge the early responses to diversity to have been more or less appropriate under the circumstances, who worry about incoherence, fragmentation, and "particularism" in the curriculum, and who want to clarify what students should be led to regard as central and what as marginal. In one way or another, all these parties are concerned with the comparative value of the diverse visions and with how we are to conceive their relationship.

This article attempts to clarify the crucial philosophical and organizational issues that underlie the current struggles in higher education about multiculturalism. The article is in two parts. The first examines the explosion of diversity and evaluates four major frameworks that have been employed in the West to comprehend or order diversity. The second part reflects on the ramifications of these frameworks for current and possible approaches to the conduct of higher education.

I. Four Frameworks

"The hallmark of modern consciousness," Clifford Geertz observes insightfully, "is its enormous multiplicity." Diversity of opinion, of course, is hardly new; it was, for example, radical diversity of opinion more than 300 years ago that shaped the philosophical projects of Montaigne and Descartes. The novelty in the contemporary engagement with diversity is a function of four other novelties:

1. Awareness on the part of most Western philosophers of the collapse of the Enlightenment goal of objective reason, in the light of which it was hoped to sort and hierarchize the great diversity of opinion. Gadamer's rehabilitation of the concept of prejudice as an inevitable feature of all human thinking may by itself symbolize how far we have moved from the ideal of a disembodied, objective mind.

2. The related awareness, partly philosophical and partly political, of the socioeconomic and political dimensions to the development and sustaining of knowledge-claims. While the claims of scientists were falsely cloaked in the mantle of pure objectivity, the knowledge-claims of other groups (e.g., women, minorities,

persons of color, and third-world persons) were and are suppressed, invalidated, and marginalized.

3. The growing incapacity of groups hitherto exercising monopolizing control over judgments of truth and worth to sustain such power. The wealth of Japan and the Arab peoples, for example, and the voting power of women and the elderly in the United States, have forced accommodations by the established order to a newly emerging one.

4. The realization on the part of many of the intrinsic beauty and worth of the diverse voices—a realization that came to many people in the United States through the black revolution of the '60s. This shift in consciousness was crisply expressed by Octavio Paz:

> The ideal of a single civilization for everyone, implicit in the cult of progress and technique, impoverishes and mutilates us. Every view of the world that becomes extinct, every culture that disappears, diminishes a possibility of life.

Diversity, again, is not new, and intellectuals have not needed the stimulations of today to construct its analysis. In Western thought, four major frameworks have been employed in the analysis of diversity:

1. *Relativism*, which in one way or another regards all knowledge-claims as self-contained within particular cultures or language communities, and which recognizes no higher or commensurable ground upon which objective adjudication might take place.

2. *Perennialism or universalism*, which see commonalities or constancies in the great variety of human thought, and which frequently (as in the influential work of Frithjof Schuon) regard those constancies as the essential and more important aspect of diverse historical phenomena.

3. *Hierarchism*, which attempts to sort or rank the multiplicity by a variety of means, among them establishing criteria or methods of inquiry that divide knowledge from opinion, or interpreting world history and human development in such a way that certain opinions and behavior are progressive, developed, and/or mature, while others more or less approximate those ideals.

4. *Pluralism*, which in its democratic version is central to the analysis of this article and which I will therefore spend a longer moment here to expand upon.

In the philosophical and political traditions of American pluralism, diversity has played a prominent role. Nowhere was diversity more prominent than in the epistemology and social philosophy of John Dewey. Though aware of the idealized dimension of his thinking, Dewey grounded both science (as a way of knowing) and democracy (as a way of life) in a respect for diverse opinion.

> It is of the nature of science not so much to *tolerate* as to *welcome* diversity of opinion, while it insists that inquiry brings the evidence of observed facts to bear to effect a consensus of conclusions—and even then to hold the conclusions subject to what is ascertained and made public in further new inquiries. I would not claim that any existing democracy has ever made complete and adequate use of scientific method in deciding upon its policies. But freedom of inquiry, toleration of diverse views, freedom of communication, the distribution of what is found out to every individual as the ultimate intellectual consumers, are involved in the democratic as in the scientific method.

In linking science and democracy, Dewey welcomed not just the diversity of opinion of highly trained scientists; he welcomed as an intellectual and political resource the diversity of every human being:

Every autocratic and authoritarian scheme of social action rests upon a belief that the needed intelligence is confined to a superior few, who because of inherent natural gifts are endowed with the ability and the right to control the conduct of others. . . . While what we call intelligence may be distributed in unequal amounts, it is the democratic faith that it is sufficiently general so that each individual has something to contribute.

For Dewey, the inclusion of diverse perspectives becomes an ethical imperative:

> The keynote of democracy as a way of life may be expressed, it seems to me, as the necessity for the participation of every mature being in the formation of the values that regulate the living of men [*sic*] together. . . . All those who are affected by social institutions must have a share in producing and managing them.

Finally, appreciation of diversity is linked by Dewey to visions of human nature and community. The resources of diversity will flourish in those social and political forms that allow the pooling of the experience and insights of diversely constituted individuals. Not that the pooled insight is inherently preferable to the workings of intelligence in an individual or within a single-language community—Dewey is forever appreciative of the value of small communities—but that the pooling is an escalation of the power of human intelligence:

> The foundation of democracy is faith in the capacities of human nature; faith in human intelligence and in the power of pooled and co-operative experience. . . . What is the faith of democracy in the role of consultation, of conference, of persuasion, of discussion, in formation of public opinion, which in the long run is self-corrective, except faith in the capacity of the intelligence of the common man [*sic*] to respond with common sense to the free play of acts and ideas which are secured by effective guarantees of free inquiry, free assembly, and free communication.

In pooled, cooperative experience, Dewey is saying, the powers of human intelligence are increased, and human nature or capacity is completed.

This view, or at least the narrowly epistemological dimension of it, is affirmed in other traditions. In Gadamer, the essential and unavoidable partiality of the human knower must be corrected or supplemented in dialogue. In *The Genealogy of Morals*, Nietzsche states the epistemological value of cooperative inquiry quite succinctly:

> The more affects we allow to speak about one thing, the more eyes, different eyes we can use to observe one thing, the more complete will our concept of this thing, our objectivity, be.

Interpreting Diversity

What is at issue among these four competing philosophic frameworks? How might we go about choosing among them?

The philosophical issue in most general terms is the appropriate interpretation of diversity: how to give it its proper due. In an older style of doing philosophy—what Rorty terms the metaphysical as opposed to the "ironist" view—we would now seek to determine which one of these frameworks is true to the nature of things, in this case to the phenomenon of diversity. In a post-metaphysical mode of doing philosophy, we recognize that each of these frameworks is an interpretation, a value-laden interpretation of the variety of human experience. No neutral ground exists upon which we might stand to evaluate either the values or the frameworks objectively.

The choice among the frameworks is to be made (assuming, as I judge to be the case here, that each has dealt honestly and intelligently with the full range of available data) not in terms of conformity to the nature of things, but in terms of each framework's appropriateness for sustaining the values of the culture or language community. The question of the adequacy of each of the interpretations of diversity, then, will be answered differently in different cultures. All answers will be value-laden answers that cannot be justified without reference to these values.

In the United States and much of the Western world, we are at least nominally committed to a democratic social order. The evaluation that follows of the four frameworks is thus done within the context of that cultural commitment. The judgments reached are not abstract ones about the correspondence of particular frameworks to the nature of things, but judgments about their appropriateness to sustaining the vision of "pooled and cooperative experience" articulated above. Crucial to each of those judgments will be the extent to which diversity is "welcomed" and incorporated democratically into pooled experience as well as the extent to which each framework an suggest a relationship of self and diverse other that might motivate the kind of conversation capable of sustaining a public sphere.

With these considerations and a frank commitment to democratic values in mind, I make the following observations about the frameworks for explaining diversity.

1. *Relativism.* This is the framework that accords enduring centrality to diversity, both to the fact of diversity and to its defense, if not its nurturance. The endless attempts of philosophers to discredit the logical foundations of relativism are convincing to themselves but ineffective in undermining the attractiveness and strength of its straightforward recognition of diverse, frequently non-intersecting (or impermeable) modes of thinking. While those who describe themselves as relativists will endlessly be dogged with logical objections, the opposite position—what Geertz calls "anti-relativism"—can mask a great lack of appreciation for the profound, intractable diversity of our time.

From the standpoint of democratic values, the problem with relativism is less its logical incoherence than its comparative incapacity to motivate interest or conversation—an incapacity which may stem more from the individualism of our culture than from the framework itself. If we all live in separate and/or incommensurate reality-worlds, the motivation to inquire into the world of the diverse other can be readily relegated to the anthropologist or world traveler. For democracy to work, its citizens must sense, if not a commitment to a shared future, then at least an occasional need for each other.

2. *Perennialism or universalism.* These philosophies do not ignore diversity, as is frequently charged. They could not uncover perennial themes in diverse cultures or epochs without first immersing themselves in the diversity. Perennialists would claim that they do accord diversity its proper due; indeed, their system is not incapable of explaining anything.

The problem with perennialism from the standpoint of democratic values is less its capacity to explain diversity than it is the comparative non-centrality it accords it. If the dialogical other is inevitably going to be viewed as an instantiation of a previously known pattern—or, more generously, if the dialogue is at best going to force a modification of a previously known pattern in the light of which I and the other will then be seen as instantiations—it is understandable that the other may feel his/her uniqueness depreciated and forced to fit a mold. Genuine appreciation of diversity must be found to some extent upon an expectation of novelty.

3. *Hierarchism.* Philosophies or theologies or social systems that hierarchize or sort differences according to some historical or developmental scheme are obviously taking diversity—especially inequality—seriously. It is not ignored. It is ranked and explained (or explained away, critics would say).

While inequality is a fact of life and some sort of ranking may for the near term be unavoidable, what is disturbing to a theorist of democracy is the way in which whole epochs and entire peoples—e.g., Native Americans, women, the physically challenged, and the so-called underdeveloped nations—have been and continue to be marginalized and their experience depreciated in such rankings. Democratic social theory cannot in the end be satisfied with an egalitarian epistemology—because some insights and truths are more appropriate than others to particular situations and because we wish to encourage the development of continually diverse perspectives. Still more opprobrious to democratic social theory as an interpretation of human diversity and inequality is a system of ranking joined to a hierarchical structure of association; in any such system, the epistemologically marginalized remain politically vulnerable and effectively voiceless. Whatever inequality currently exists is worsened and perpetuated by structures that de facto operate (in Dewey's words) "as if the needed intelligence" to participate meaningfully "were confined to a superior few."

   4. *Democratic pluralism.* Within the context of a commitment to democratic values, the diversity of the world's peoples is to be welcomed, respected, celebrated, and fostered. Within that context, diversity is not a problem or a defect, it is a resource. The major problem within all pluralistic contexts (including relativism) is less that of taking diversity seriously than that of grounding any sort of commonality. It is the problem of encouraging citizens to sustain conversations of respect with diverse others for the sake of their making public policy together, of forging over and over again a sense of a shared future.

   Conversations of respect and the making of public policy in a democracy cannot be based on mere tolerance—on the "live and let live" or "to each his own" attitudes of individualistic relativism—at least, not in the Jeffersonian and Deweyan, as opposed to the Federalist, vision of democracy. Democracy needs something at once more binding or relating of diverse viewpoints and something that grounds the respect in a public sphere, in a world or situation that is at least temporarily shared. It is impossible to respect the diverse other if one does not believe that the views of the diverse other are grounded in a reality—the democratic version of reality—that binds or implicates everyone as much as do our own views.

   Conversations of respect between diverse communities are characterized by intellectual reciprocity. They are ones in which the participants expect to learn from each other, expect to learn nonincidental things, expect to change at least intellectually as a result of the encounter. Such conversations are not animated by, nor do they result in, mere tolerance of the preexisting diversity, for political or ethical reasons. In such conversations, one participant does not treat the other as an illustration of, or variation of, or a dollop upon, a truth or insight already fully possessed. There is no will to incorporate the other in any sense into one's belief system. In such conversations, one participant does not presume that the relationship is one of teacher to student (in any traditional sense of that relationship), of parent to child, of developed to underdeveloped. The participants are co-learners.

My paradigms of such conversations of respect are drawn from my experience in interdisciplinary academic communities. Not all interdisciplinary conversations, to be sure, are respectful: Social scientists often view English professors as providing a service, the service of illustrative examples of their truths, or as high-class entertainment. Humanists often assume that scientists are value-blind dupes of the military-industrial complex. Other interdisciplinary conversations, somewhat less disrespectful, are so complementary as to involve little or no diversity of substance.

   In genuinely respectful conversations, each disciplinary participant is aware at the outset of the incapacity of his/her own discipline (and, ideally, of him/herself) to answer the question that is being asked. Each participant is aware of his/her partiality and of the need for the other. One criterion of the genuineness of the subsequent conversations is the transformation of each participant's understanding or definition of the question—perhaps even a transformation of self-understanding.

   This definition of a conversation of respect may strike many as too demanding, uncritical, or relativistic. It seems to suggest that the respect easily acknowledged as appropriate to conversations between Christians and Buddhists or between Palestinians and Jews is also appropriate to conversations between biologists and philosophers, between those in higher education and those currently excluded. Or, worse yet, between systems of beliefs on the one hand modernized to accommodate contemporary science and philosophy and, on the other, fundamentalists, traditionalist, pantheists, and all sorts of local and tribal and idiosyncratic cognitive systems.

   I have three responses to these concerns. First, we foreclose the ethnographic task that Geertz and others have urged upon us as appropriate to the contemporary explosion of diversity if we presume that we will not discover something about the life of the mind and something valuable for all of us in a dialogue with the radically diverse other. Second, I do not regard these boundary-crossing conversations as the only conversations worth having or the only activity worth engaging in; they just deserve far more of our energy at this time than we have been allotting to them. Third, in view of the collapse of Enlightenment values, of the crisis of the planetary environment, and in view of the many critiques of universalism, the reluctance of modern thought to engage in conversations with communities that retain pre-industrial values ought to be considerably less than it was a quarter of a century ago. The deep distrust of modernity for everything that originated prior to the 16th century has less and less to recommend it.

One last observation about the four frameworks of interpretation: Although particular versions of the four have done so, none of them (as presented in general terms here) attends adequately to the politics of knowledge, to the postmodern awareness of the interplay between power and truth. Democracy's celebration of the diversity of knowers is a healthy corrective to the alternatives of hierarchism; but democracy's framework attends no more sufficiently than the others to the de facto inequality among these alternatives and to the impact of that inequality upon the pursuit of truth. A fuller analysis of the nature of thinking in democratic contexts, which I have attempted elsewhere, would attend to a) the habits of mind appropriate to participation in a democracy, and b) the creation of conditions under which the power of pooled intelligence might be fully realized.

II.

Having looked at the fact of diversity—at the principal interpretations of it—and attempted to evaluate those interpretations in the context of a democratic pluralism, I turn now to three more topics: 1) the philosophical underpinnings of the current organization of higher education, including the implications of that organization for liberal education; 2) how higher education would be differently organized with the philosophical underpinnings of democratic pluralism; and 3) possible objections to my analysis.

Let me begin with this introductory observation. Higher education, judged by the standards of democratic pluralism, does not take seriously even the diversity within its walls, much less the diversity outside its walls. The diversity of disciplinary or ideological perspectives is muted by what the recent national study of the major conducted by the Association of American Colleges called "the ethos of self-containment." Even in institutions that take interdisciplinarity seriously, the diversity most frequently worked with is not the challenging diversity of unshared assumptions or excluded peoples but the congenial diversity of presumed complementarity. Wedded as most of higher education is to the notion that the point of teaching is to transmit what we already know, few agree with Gerald Graff in seeing a positive pedagogical function for exposing our students to unresolved conflict.

Organizational Philosophy

At first blush, and from the point of view of the student, the organization of the university appears relativistic. It appears that each major, surely each division, constitutes a separate reality-world or, to borrow a recent phrase of Isaiah Berlin's, a "windowless box." The organization of the university seems intended to facilitate each student's discovering a reality-world in which (s)he will feel comfortable. The departments, especially across divisional lines, are at best tolerant of each other, displaying in practice and in their requirements for their majors no great need of each other. Given these assumptions, they pay appropriately little attention to other departments or to general education, both because the major is believed to be self-contained and because there is little to no agreement on what might be significantly common across fields of inquiry. Indeed, the disciplines are often viewed, consistent with their historical origins, as correctives to each other.

From the point of view of the self-contained major, the liberally educated person is defined by the habits of mind appropriate to the particular department. From the point of view of the undeclared student, liberal education is de facto defined in a myriad of ways, and the message of the university as a whole seems to be: Define it whichever way you like.

The university, of course, is only speciously relativistic. Hierarchy pervades the institution. Although messages of what is or is not important frequently escape a student's perusal of the catalogue or passage through the pork-barreled distribution requirements, the truth is that the university oozes with uncoded messages about centrality and marginality. While these messages vary from institution to institution, we are all familiar with the value judgments inherent in distinctions like the hard and soft sciences, graduate and undergraduate, required and optional. Discerning observers see the value judgments in the size of departments and buildings, in grading patterns, in the willingness or unwillingness to waive prerequisites, in the frequency of tenure-track appointments, and in the denial of departmental status and budgets to areas like women's studies.

Liberal education in the hierarchical university is spoken of in much the same individualistic terms that an outright relativist might employ: "Do what you're good at." But there is no mistaking the fact that, in the hierarchical university, all the disciplines are not equally valuable. By and large, it is believed by students and professors alike that the better and more serious students will be found in the prestigious departments. It is not a value-free observation to report that so-and-so majored in biochemistry at Johns Hopkins.

What about universalist or perennialist assumptions in the current organization of the university? These assumptions, of course, pervade the separate disciplines themselves (otherwise there would be no point to Geertz's critique). But the assumptions are not apparent in the organization of the university. General education, wherein one would expect the commonality of human experience or disciplinary paradigms to be addressed, is a poor stepchild in most colleges and universities. The university is organized to encourage research and teaching within unshared paradigms. If there are constancies in human cultures and disciplines, the traditional university is certainly not set up to encourage the boundary-crossings that might uncover them.

Democratic Pluralism?

What about democratic pluralism and the conversations of respect upon which it thrives? To what extent is the traditional university grounded on those assumptions?

In my judgment, most universities are not grounded at all on these assumptions. I will make this point by sketching a few features of what a college/university so grounded might look like.

A college that looked upon diversity as a vital resource for learning and wished therefore to encourage conversations of respect under conditions in which unshared or disparate power would not inhibit those conversations would devote itself to three tasks. Two of the tasks are now being done in a token fashion; the third is not being done at all.

Such a college would make it the *highest priority to* recruit women, minorities, persons of color, and persons from other cultures to their faculties and student bodies as soon as possible. As a temporary measure, a measure of significant inadequacy, such colleges would undertake a massive retraining of their faculties (mis)educated in one discipline and one culture.

The second step is a prerequisite of significant multicultural education. Having hired some women and persons of color from North America and around the world, it would thus be easy to claim, as many colleges now do, that they are giving diversity its due because they have a study-abroad program, because 10 percent of the faculty are tenured women, because they have a Nigerian in the history department, or because they require one course in non-Western culture. These colleges are still in the grips of the windowless boxes of relativism. In such colleges, it is still quite possible for the vast majority of students and faculty to happily go their independent ways with no experience of a conversation of respect—a transforming conversation of respect—with another culture.

Were a college or university truly committed to democratic pluralism, it would proceed to create conditions under which the representatives of different cultures *need* to have conversations of respect with each other in order to do their everyday teaching and research. As colleges are set up now, there is, except in the highly sequenced departments, virtually no interdependence of the various departments and frequently little of the members of the same department. A democratically pluralistic college would make war upon the ethos of self-containment, upon all boundaries that inhibit or make unnecessary conversations of respect between diverse peoples. General education would be radically reconceived to immerse students in such conversations, in full interaction with their majors. Team-taught programs and interdisciplinary/intercultural majors would become the central (though not the exclusive) mode of study.

The point requires even further elaboration. We would not have changed much if all we achieve is a sprinkling of multicultural courses in the departments: "Multicultural Cities" in the sociology department, five courses on the Far East in a 120-course history department, or a cross-listed elective for biology majors on the "History of Chinese Medicine." We need to reconceive and restructure the curriculum so that the inquiry cannot fairly be conducted without the contributions or even the presence of the currently marginalized. We would no longer find separate courses on health taught mostly by white males in separate departments of biology, sociology, and philosophy, but instead a team-taught program of 32 credits on "The Human Body in Interdisciplinary and Intercultural Perspective," or "Health and Sickness in Interdisciplinary and Intercultural Perspective," or "Self, Nature and World in Interdisciplinary and Intercultural Perspective."

Marginalization will be perpetuated, in other words, if new voices and perspectives are added while the priorities and core of the organization remain unchanged. Marginalization ends and conversations of respect begin when the curriculum is reconceived to be unimplementable without the central participation of the currently excluded and marginalized.

This point was made in a different language by a team that visited Brown last year. It contrasted the idea of diversity—of mere diversity—with what I have been calling conversations of respect in democratic pluralism:

> By contrast to the idea of [mere] diversity, which gives primary regard to the mere presence of multiple ethnic and racial groups within the community, pluralism asks of the members of all groups to explore, understand and try to appreciate one another's cultural experiences and heritage. It asks a leap of imagination as well as a growth of knowledge. It asks for a most difficult outcome: cultural self-transcendence.

Meaningful multiculturalism, in other words, transforms the curriculum. While the presence of persons of other cultures and subcultures is a virtual prerequisite to that transformation, their "mere presence" is primarily a political achievement (which different groups will assess differently), not an intellectual or educational achievement. Real educational progress will be made when multiculturalism becomes interculturalism.

What might such an exploration in intercultural education look and feel like to the student in a democratically pluralistic university? I have framed an answer in terms of the habits of mind I have seen developed by the most responsive students in experiments approximating what I am advocating.

Such persons have immersed themselves in a sustained learning community, a community that is intercultural and interdisciplinary. They have studied something of great human significance and have experienced how their understanding deepens with the additions of each relevant perspective of another discipline, culture, or subculture. They have mastered or at least internalized a feeling for more than one discipline, more than one culture. They know the value and indeed the necessity of seeking many and diverse perspectives, most particularly the inevitable *partiality* of those perspectives. They have mastered the skills of access to those perspectives. They have mastered the skills in understanding and integrating these diverse perspectives. They are comfortable with ambiguity and conflict. Tolerance, empathic understanding, awareness of one's own partiality, openness to growth through dialogue in pluralistic communities—all of these things have become part of their instinctive responses to each novel situation they encounter. (They might even characterize those who proceed otherwise as uncritical thinkers.)

There is one last point I wish to make about the organization of democratically pluralistic colleges. I return to the aforementioned report at Brown to preface the point:

The ideal of pluralism toward which we would have the University strive is one that can only be realized when a spirit of civility and mutual respect abounds, when all groups feel equally well placed and secure within the community because all participate in that spirit.

I am less concerned at the moment with the "spirit of civility and mutual respect" than I am with its consequence: "When all groups feel *equally well-placed and secure within the community*." How would an institution make this happen for currently excluded or marginalized peoples?

In a previous age, we might have been content to say that such security would be provided by allowing all voices to have access to or be represented at the decision-making table. We are now too aware of the interplay of power and knowledge and of the partiality of our own listening to be satisfied with such an answer. Colleges serious about "equal placement and security" would have to be concerned with neutralizing the impact of unshared power in teaching and research as well as in personnel decisions.

I see no holding back from concluding that this suggests an end to the currently inhibiting system of rank, tenure, and promotion. I am not saying flatly that the whole system must be abandoned (though I have heard worse ideas), but if it is not, then ways must be found (as they were found in the Federated Learning Communities and its spin-offs) to conduct the conversations of respect fully within the curriculum but entirely without consequences one way or another for promotion and tenure decisions.

Six Objections

Many reasonable objections might be raised to restructuring the university along the lines I have suggested. Less in the hope of responding definitively to them than in the hope of enhancing the plausibility of a democratically pluralistic vision of the university, I will respond briefly to the objections I have most frequently encountered.

1. Granted, we are living in a radically diverse world, runs the first objection. It is impossible, however, without undermining the coherence of the academic enterprise, to take all of that diversity seriously.

   In reply: I am not suggesting that every institution has to mirror all the diversity in the world. The full diversity should be mirrored by the entire system of higher education or (less so) by institutions in a region or state. What is important for a single institution is that a challenging, relevant diversity pervade the curriculum and that its students are thereby exposed to the liberal-education experiences described above.

2. A second objection, inspired by the developmental view of human diversity: It is all well and good to acknowledge the explosion of diversity in our awareness. But all these diverse viewpoints are not equally worthwhile. It is romantic and unreasonable to believe that Native American society, pre-industrial Latin America, or the Gaelic-speaking people of the west of Ireland have as much to contribute to the understanding and shaping of the modern world as do Americans and Europeans and the Japanese.

   In reply: I do not expect Native Americans to leap-frog in the near future over the Japanese and Americans in the production of smart bombs or compact discs. But by and large I will expect, until proven otherwise in sustained conversations of respect, that the marginalized cultures of the world have much to contribute to medicine, to agricultural science, to our understanding of the relationship of humanity and the environment, to child-rearing, to therapy, and to dozens of other important things. The advanced industrial nations of the world have cornered the market on neither wisdom nor science.

3. A related hierarchical objection: Can any education be serious that does not focus centrally on Western civilization? Even ignoring the fact that it is our heritage (and

ought therefore to be the focus of our education), it is the most powerful and influential force on the planet.

In reply: I am not suggesting that we not study Western civilization, nor that it be marginalized or caricatured as the sole root of the world's many problems. I am suggesting, rather: a) that both in its origins (as Martin Bernal has urged) and in its current form it be studied in interaction with other cultures and with its own subcultures (which are also our heritage); and b) that this study take the form of a dialogue with members of those other (sub)cultures in situations of "equal placement and security." Political science majors, for example, ought regularly to encounter professors from Latin America and Africa in dialogue with North American professors on issues of democracy and sociopolitical organization. Biology majors likewise should participate in curricular-based dialogues with Chinese professors who question the assumptions of Western medicine. While students could scarcely come away from such experiences without some awareness of the partiality of Western approaches, they would also likely leave with as much or more appreciation of the strengths of our approaches than is fostered by the current noncomparative, sprawling, unfocused, and unconnected curriculum.

4. A universalist might object: There is no great need to study Buddhist psychology because the essence of it is available in Jung; and no great need to read Vine Deloria because his tribalism is not significantly different from the decentralist tradition in America or Russia.

    In reply: If these intellectual phenomena are as similar as the objection supposes, that conclusion should emerge in a sustained conversation of respect with Buddhists and Native Americans. We are all too familiar with the distortions and depreciations that occur when a dominant culture or an isolated individual attempts to interpret another by incorporating it into what is already familiar. Additionally, the objection presupposes, contrary to the assumptions of democratic pluralism, that the alleged similarities of these intellectual phenomena are more significant than their diversity.

5. A more general (and politically more difficult) version of the previous objection: One or another invasion of diversity has characterized the whole of at least Western history. Geertz and the multiculturalists are exaggerating the significance of contemporary diversity. Diversity is already receiving its appropriate due.

    In reply: In a democratic society, the issue under discussion is not only the philosophical issue of according diversity its proper due, but the politico-philosophical issue of how that judgment is made. Were the predominantly white and male establishment of higher education to decide what changes need to be made to accord contemporary diversity its due, the response would reflect the partiality of their experience and aspirations. Were that decision to emerge from a democratic process in which the currently marginalized and excluded had participated from positions or "equal placement and security," the judgment would understandably be of a different sort. Ultimately, we come face to face with the depth or shallowness of what Dewey (in a text cited earlier) called "the democratic faith."

6. The last, and most frequently heard, objection: Changes of the sort being discussed would inevitably lead to a watering down, if not a complete collapse, of standards.

    In reply: There is little doubt that standards would change, just as the standards of the individual disciplines evolve in many interdisciplinary inquiries or as the skills one values in tennis change from singles to doubles. Whether the new standards are as challenging as the old depends less on the intrinsic nature of these different intellectual enterprises than it does upon the integrity and respectfulness of the conversations.

Conclusion

It is easy to read contemporary experience in the light of simpler times, of a more familiar order, and to regard the explosion of diversity as productive of fragmentation, incoherence, and conflict. From the standpoint of democratic pluralism, wherein diversity is a resource, the explosion is challenging and unsettling but highly welcome. I thus prefer the metaphor of inchoateness to the backward-looking metaphor of fragmentation. We are not staring wistfully at the fragmented ruins of a temple once whole, but poring over the recently discovered jottings for a novel whose form or plot has yet to emerge.

If higher education were to take as its role the creation of new structures of dialogue and invention and cooperative discovery (i.e., structures appropriate to an inchoate world), there may indeed emerge a new world order. I speak not of an order in which technologically powerful Americans try to bring the diversity of the world to heel, but of a new world order that empowers hitherto excluded peoples of our and other nations to contribute their experience on an equal footing to our collective understanding of ourselves, society, and the world.

Developing Leadership Potential for Minority Women

MARVALENE STYLES HUGHES

The push for affirmative action in the 1970s provided a window of hope for women and minorities. A generation of women saw themselves as empowered individuals who could exercise options to be wives, partners, mothers, and professional women. The brief emphasis on laws to ensure equal opportunity and affirmative action provided only a tenative wedge for women to collectively combat stereotypes and external barriers to success. An overarching problem remains: Women have not succeeded at transcending cultural, ethnic, generational, or economic boundaries among themselves. This reality poses immense challenges for those who strive to enhance the development of leadership in women. Minority and majority women are not unified in embracing the challenges facing women in leadership development. They have not combined their insights and resources to begin to shape new visions of leadership. Rather, they have accepted traditional white male leadership models and risked the loss of those characteristics that make women unique. Only in confronting these issues can we begin to create a new vision of leadership.

Inclusion and Exclusion Dynamics for Women

Boyer (1986) reminds us that "equality involves a philosophy of inclusion rather than exclusion . . . it includes the capacity to embrace all humankind in matters that influence the resources and levels of accessibility to be experienced by Americans regardless of their ethnic, racial, economic, or gender profile" (pp. 139–140). This is the ideal against which we must measure the reality of women's positions in higher education.

Women are viewed as marginal to the political and organizational power systems of the world. Minority women are not viewed at all; they are essentially invisible. Minority women do not have access to white patriarchal power and leadership. Excluded even from the social and personal access accorded white women, minority women have scarce entrée into political and organizational power structures.

At first glance, this distance poses major disadvantages to minority women. This chapter, however, hypothesizes that minority women's exclusion from the white patriarchy shields them from indoctrination into the beliefs and values of those systems and positions them to offer keen insights into differences between men's and women's realities. These fresh insights are needed to inform leadership paradigms. The overarching goal is for women as a whole to preserve those qualities uniquely attributed to women and to develop their unique contributions to the world of leadership and power.

The paucity of research studies is a major deterrent to progress toward this goal. Black, Hispanic, Asian, and Native American women are not only invisible in the higher education profession but are also invisible in the related literature.

Thus, it can be concluded that affirmative action is a program that failed (Washington, 1986). Moreover, it is widely perceived in the late 1980s that the federal government has transmitted a clear message to society that affirmative action standards should be relaxed. Indeed, the numbers speak for themselves: As of 1983, there was an average of 1.1 senior female administrators per campus, compared to 0.06 in 1975 (Mark, 1986). Also, although the number of women administrators did increase, women continue to be underrepresented and are clustered in middle management, with few women achieving senior-level positions. The situation is worse for minorities and worse still for minority women.

Actual progress is a salient indicator. Not only have women not overcome gender role barriers, minority women have also lagged notably in their efforts to attain career positions. Between blacks and whites applying for positions at predominantly white institutions, the black female is the last to be hired when selections are made by white males (Harvey, 1986). Washington (1986) views affirmative action officers, persons hired as advocates for qualified minority applicants, as mere processors of information about minority candidates; they have little impact on final selection. Affirmative action officers are rarely in a position to veto hiring decisions.

The relative newness of black women to higher education leadership also complicates opportunities for career mobility (Williams, 1986). This newness is also a reality for all ethnic minority women, including Hispanic women, the Native American women, and Asian women, for whom an even smaller amount of research exists.

Minority women are underrepresented among college and university faculties and administrations. The pervasive underrepresentation of women in leadership positions in higher education filters down to students. Women students discover early that they have few role models and mentors. Minority women students have the most limited access to ethnic role models and mentors like themselves.

The overwhelming majority of leaders in higher education, both male and female, report having had male mentors (Moore, 1982). Given the dominance of white men in higher education (80 percent male and almost 92 percent white), it is no surprise that mentors are predominantly white males. Cross-gender, cross-cultural mentoring does not preclude the value or success of a mentor-protégé relationship. Nevertheless, cross-race and cross-sex mentor-protégé relationships may not be the most desirable relationships. Further, some unanticipated negative outcomes may result (Goldstein, 1979; Collins, 1983). There is evidence that mentors serve protégés best if they are most like them (Kanter, 1977; Alvarez, 1979). Likewise, one may infer that would-be protégés desire mentors most like themselves. The available pool of mentors supports the continuation of white male leadership.

In a white male–other mentor-protégé relationship, white women experience a gender gap; ethnic minority women experience a gap associated with both gender and ethnic identity. Hence, minority women have the least access to a like-self mentor. Minority women who have mentors must therefore settle for similarity in values, philosophy, and style. Mentor-protégé models must be designed to enable protégés to assertively assess and select an appropriate mentor (Styles, 1983).

When women are matched as mentor and protégé, the pairs seek opportunities to work together, increase their contacts to work together, demonstrate empathic understanding, and collaborate on work-experience collegiality (King, 1986). One feminine leadership model (Loden, 1985) that emphasizes cooperation, a team structure, a combination of intuition and rationality, and high-quality output is best demonstrated when women mentor women. In contrast, women who subscribe to a male-mentor model may find themselves in the career mainstream, but they may do so at the risk of losing their unique qualities. Minority women not only sacrifice their gender uniqueness but must also be willing to shed their unique cultural and ethnic heritage. This loss of identity may be subtle, as detected in speech patterns, or blatant, as in dress and hairstyles. Unless sensitivity exists, acculturation may be antithetical to diversity in leadership development for minority women.

The Voices of Minority Women

The roles and experiences of minority women in higher education have been neglected in research. It is time to begin listening to the voices of minority women, to discern the patterns of differences and commonalities in their experience. Through thoughtful and sensitive attention to individual stories, we can enrich our understanding of the varied experience of women and the unique personal, cultural, and ethnic heritage they bring to leadership roles. Exploratory interviews were conducted with Hispanic, black, Native American, and Asian women in a variety of leadership positions in higher education, and highlights of those conversations are presented here. These sketches are suggestive, not definitive. The intent here is to identify perceptions that may stimulate further study. From their reflections on their status as minorities and women, we find common themes, as well as essential differences—reflections we need to draw on to inform our hopes for change in the development of leadership.

This chapter constitutes my effort to underscore some of the complexities of building leadership development programs for minority women and to prompt discussion, mobilize action, and encourage further research. Women from each ethnic group were consulted for the content in this chapter, and while my own experiences as a black female administrator resonate with the voices of the women represented here, readers are encouraged to view the findings as an exploratory contribution, filtered through the experiences of the author.

Hispanic Women. The term *Hispanic* is a generic label that covers a multitude of geopolitical and cultural differences. Thus, the very labels of one's ethnicity—Hispanic, Chicana, or Mexican American—reflect political and social stances that are rarely understood by non-Hispanics, but must be.

In conversations with Hispanic women, it is quickly pointed out that *machismo* originated in the Spanish culture. Nevertheless, the assumptions that traditional Hispanic males prefer that their wives not work, and that traditional Hispanic females value homemaking over jobs, are belied by the growth in the work forces of Spanish-origin women. By 1980, 49 percent of all Spanish-origin women were employed, as compared to 52 percent of all women (Zavella, 1984). Nevertheless, Hispanic women note the threat that their independence presents to some traditional Hispanic male colleagues, and they express concern about conflicts with their ethnic male colleagues. Hispanic women often express a strong sense of ethnic-community identification, which portrays decades of familial roots. These familial and cultural roots seem to be steeped in the bicultural realities of living in two worlds. "Double membership" encumbers Hispanic women with double the stress and double the obstacles of living and working in one world.

Moreover, Hispanic women who achieve leadership positions may not view themselves as tokens. One woman's comment, "I am promotable, a woman, and a Hispanic," conveys the demeaning acknowledgment that advancement may not reflect assessment of her performance exclusive of her ethnicity and gender. Not only is the Hispanic woman denied the affirmation of knowing that she is viewed as competent, she also perceives heightened expectations of her performance: "It is not enough just to be competent or to be average. You must be exceptional."

Black Women. For black women, roles and expectations regarding the external ethnic community are magnified. Interacting with networks in the political, social, and spiritual black community is an added professional responsibility that is often imposed by white administrators. Thus, the black woman faces expectations beyond those of her white colleagues and regardless of her personal preferences.

In addition to involvement in black community leadership, another expectation common to minority experience is to "represent" the minority perspective. She is to "educate" her colleagues about the ethnic and cultural heritage of blacks. A black woman contrasts this role with the assumption of her white colleagues: that blacks automatically know white ethnocentricities. Moreover, an individual woman is called on to be "the" black voice in the white community. Any perspective advanced by her may be attributed to all black people. This practice denies her an individual voice and perpetuates stereotypes and assumptions about blacks.

Black women have acquired a stereotypic image of being the strongest among all ethnic female groups. This strength, "black matriarchy," denies individuality and may result in expectations that are not uniformly applied to all women. High expectations for performance, coupled with the isolation of being one among a few black women on a campus, compounds the stress black women feel. None of the black women interviewed had set a career goal of leadership for themselves. We "tend to be better at being competent than confident."

Native American Women. It is dangerous to generalize about any ethnic group, and it is grossly inaccurate to lump Native American women into one category (LaCounte, 1987, identified a total of 481 tribes as recognized by state governments). Moreover, this is the ethnic group least represented in leadership positions in higher education (Mark, 1986) and least represented in research.

Several recurring themes emerge in conversations with Native American women in leadership positions. Dominance and control are devalued in many tribal groups; they are seen as integral to leadership in the majority society. One woman describes the value of "yielding behaviors," which are intended to allow full expressions from the other to unfold, but to speak softly and show patience is sometimes misinterpreted as an indication of weakness. This woman notes that despite her white male colleague's temptation to "jump in and take charge," he has acknowledged that her style is potent in its unobtrusiveness.

Native American women also describe their role in providing Native American students a "sense of community" and "belonging"—critical elements in their culture. The value of a global sense of purpose beyond personal goals was expressed: "People lose touch, they lose the heart." Thus, there is a special need for clarity of self and purpose. To become too calculating and manipulative and to "lose sight of the mission" may result in personal achievement, but the loss is a sense of what is important. As with the dualistic existence described by Hispanics and blacks, "Indian people must develop two identities—one that is at home looking up at the sky through the poles of the medicine lodge, and one that is comfortable in a business suit" (LaCounte, 1987, p. 76).

One woman recounted a childhood memory of participating in a "talking circle," a Native American custom in which people are invited to share their concerns and support with each other. She recalled that when the snow was very high, her grandfather would clear a path from the house to the street where the bus would come to pick up her sister for school. At that time she had been too young to go to school, yet now she vividly remembered the image of her grandfather undertaking this difficult task. She exclaimed with some surprise, "This is what I do here at the university . . . this is what I am supposed to do. This is very clearly my role. I am to help clear a path for others to enable them to pursue an education."

Asian Women. Like Hispanics and Native Americans, Asian women must be viewed as extremely diverse in their geoethnic cultural backgrounds. Among diverse Asian groups, there are, however, cultural similarities that are rooted in Eastern values. According to Chew and Ogi (1987), the role of women is secondary, and the supreme value of human existence lies in the capacity for loyalty to the group. These beliefs relegate women to a secondary position and view them as commodities (Homma-True, 1980). The importance of family and interdependence are perpetuated through such values as filial piety, which promotes conformity and compliance by children; humility, which is considered more desirable than assertiveness; restrained emotion and the avoidance of conflict through internal resolution; and obligation, which is demonstrated by seeking the advice of parents or grandparents on life choices (Chew and Ogi, 1987).

These values were evident as one Asian woman drew contrasts between Eastern and Western leadership values. She described Asian women as quiet and invisible, behind the scenes but potent in impact. "To do your very best" without aspiring to recognition is a value instilled by the family and the Asian community. She cautioned that this is not a message to compete with others; rather, it is a self-gauge, to perform at your highest level so that your contributions to the group are the very best that you can offer.

"I cannot, under any circumstances, be an average performer," comments another Asian woman. Although this perception seems to echo the heightened standard of performance required of other minority women, there is a difference. Black, Native American, and Hispanic women are combating negative stereotypes of their abilities; Asian women are compelled to live up to a stereotype of excellence—a stereotype internalized by many women, their families, communities, and cultures. "Many people are there to encourage you—your family, your community, your teachers, your peers." All of them expect excellence: "If you are a first, it is a killer. I am not just me, I am related to a better system, which does not allow mediocrity."

Common Themes and Patterns

These highlights of the perceptions and experiences of minority women demonstrate the importance of understanding interethnic differences and intraethnic diversity. Sensitivity to the historical and cultural heritage of each ethnic group is crucial to the design of effective programs for enhancing the leadership of women.

A minority woman's socialization is best understood if placed in the context of her role in her ethnic culture. Superimposed on this complex cultural layer is the dimension of male-female intraethnic relationship. Men in each ethnic group hold views of women's roles in that group. These sex-role expectations often dictate sex-role practices.

All ethnic minority women share the common reality of patriarchal oppression and white oppression, yet it is unusual for one ethnic minority group to overtly support the goals of another. Given scarce resources and few rewards, interethnic competition is more typical. Thus, interethnic relationships among minority women are often minimized, unless career structures create interactions. Minorities are often no more prepared for interethnic and intraethnic minority relationships on the job than their white colleagues are.

Still another issue for minority women is the confusing role of and relationship with white women. Minority women constantly evaluate the primacy of gender loyalty and support among all women, as compared to ethnic loyalty. An unanswered question is whether the absence of white women's cross-ethnic gender loyalty is a collusion with white patriarchy.

Despite significant cultural and ethnic differences in values and orientations toward themselves and their leadership roles, minority women reflect certain common themes as they speak of their experiences. Issues center on their role as ethnic culture bearers, their isolation as minority women, and their struggles with self-identity.

Roles as culture bearers or spokespersons create unrealistic multiple expectations. The burden placed on minority women to maintain a course between institutional demands and external community demands is unreasonable. Administrators, as well as leaders in the ethnic community, place unrealistic expectations on minority women to bond with the external ethnic community. Minority women are required to live in a dualistic world, which imposes double stressors and double obstacles on their ability to balance their lives, both personally and professionally. They are expected to tolerate ignorance of minority ethnography and to educate colleagues and students on specific ethnic cultures. They are expected to serve as role models and mentors for ethnic students of like identity, as well as for other professionals. Each of these multiple roles is an addition to the requirements made of white colleagues; at the same time, the standards for minority performance are higher.

Isolation is more than a matter of statistics. Isolation is a result of feeling as if one is the only person experiencing a given phenomenon. Feeling isolated increases the odds that one can objectify a mainstream reality, but the possibility remains that one may internalize and personalize the negative experience. Minority women are isolated by both gender and ethnicity. They are without the support system of like-ethnic professionals and without the possibility of mentors or role models who share their ethnic or cultural heritage. The lack of interethnic sensitivity and bonding among women exacerbates the loneliness of each woman.

One's sense of strong, competent self is severely challenged by isolation and unrealistic expectations. Unrealistic, heightened, multiple expectations of performance severely challenge one's self-concept. The suspicion that one has been promoted because of gender or ethnicity, rather than ability, undermines one's sense of competence and autonomy. The expectation of a minority woman to speak on behalf of her ethnic group denies her unique voice. The isolation of minority women on college and university campuses also precludes the benefit of support and nurturance from those of like identity.

Informing Leadership Development

Each of these themes is played out in ways that differ subtly for each minority woman. Nevertheless, these themes do provide a foundation from which to build leadership development for women. The lack of interethnic understanding among women dilutes our ability to forge a leadership that serves and honors all women and men. The assumption of homogeneity within minority groups undermines the design of programs addressed to the needs and values of individual women. To incorporate the experiences of minority women in new thinking about leadership, we must address their role as ethnic culture bearers, their isolation, and their struggles with self-identity. Increased numbers of white and minority women on college and university campuses are crucial to our ability to move beyond our token roles, but we cannot wait until our numbers are less skewed; rather, we must build from our strengths. We must engage as women, interdependently and interethnically.

Profound and lasting change is needed to enhance the participation of minority women on college and university campuses. The recommendations made here call for an increased sensitivity to and honoring of diversity in higher education. Diversity must be personally valued and personally espoused; it cannot be dictated or prescribed. Nevertheless, leaders of colleges and universities have a moral obligation to provide leadership and resources to initiate and sustain the changes that will ensure diverse campus communities. Building a supportive campus climate for minority women begins with the recognition that diversity benefits all faculty, students, and staff.

Commitment to the leadership development of minority women is an essential component of the effort to enhance diversity. Institutional leaders must identify and support the development of minority women leaders for the sake of the women themselves, the role they can play in the lives of students, faculty, and staff, and the contributions they can make to the quality of work and learning on the college campus.

To provide a supportive context for the development of women students of color, we must attend to the experiences of all ethnic minority women on campus. Thus, the recommendations offered here begin with those facets of academic life that must be reconsidered to support the participation of minority women on the faculty and staff. These are followed with specific recommendations to enhance the leadership development of minority women students.

1. Senior administrators must influence their campuses with public support and action on issues of diversity and minority participation, at all levels of the institution. A strong institutional statement, committing every participant to work toward interethnic and intercultural understanding, can establish a tone and commitment for the institution that undergirds all other efforts.

2. Institutions must work toward a critical mass of minority women of varied ethnic and cultural backgrounds. Increased numbers are indispensable for changing majority attitudes and eliminating the effects of isolation and tokenism. Recruitment efforts must be aimed at all levels and types of positions on the campus. Mandates to achieve diversity in all aspects of the institution need to be enforced, and success must be rewarded.

3. Administrators in supervisory positions must be held responsible for ensuring the success of minority women in their departments or divisions. Recruitment of minority women is an essential first step. Deans and administrators must also be concerned with the retention of the minority persons they recruit. Retention efforts require an awareness of the issues and problems unique to the minority women on campuses. Specific actions are required to prevent these issues and problems from becoming barriers to success.

4. Senior administrators must be made aware of the inequities faced by minority women in faculty and staff roles. Overload and heightened expectations, roles as liaisons with ethnic communities and spokespersons for ethnic groups, and struggles with isolation and self-identity must be confronted seriously and creatively. To address these issues, institutional leaders must commit resources to study the reality of the professional and personal lives of minority women on their campuses and identify the problems and inequities unique to individual campuses. They must also remedy overload with increased staffing and support. When staffing cannot redress inequities, expectations of performance must be altered. Finally, they must address isolation and self-identity through effective mentoring and networks for minority professionals.

5. Developing the leadership talent of minority women faculty, staff, and students is essential to their full and equitable participation in higher education. Their leadership development requires institutional commitment. Existing programs, both internal and external to the campus, must be identified. Minority women must be encouraged and financially supported to participate in appropriate programs. Institutions must groom talent to meet the need for diverse and qualified women to fill positions of leadership.

6. Minority and majority women must join to transform visions of leadership. If leadership development in higher education is to transform the dominant white male culture, the voices of women in general and minority women in particular must be heard, understood, and recognized. Moreover, only through working together can minority and majority women demonstrate their capacity to cross ethnic boundaries. Task forces, collaborative research, and support groups all provide contexts for working toward the common goals of transforming current leadership patterns and enhancing interethnic understanding.

7. Minority women are in the best position to address major issues in leadership programs regarding gender, ethnic, and cultural differences. Opportunities must be created to encourage minority women to speak out. At the same time, it is important that minority women not be burdened with sole responsibility for educating their colleagues. Thus, institutional leaders need to make resources available to support internal efforts, as well as external consultants who can aid in the work of bringing gender, ethnic, and cultural differences to bear on dominant models of leadership.

8. Opportunities for developing the leadership potential of students are as diverse as the student body. Minority women students will gain from one-to-one relationships with adults committed to their development, and they will benefit from broad-based programs sensitive to the inclusion of minority women. Whatever the structure of the effort to develop leadership, it must be based on a model that honors gender, ethnic, and cultural differences.

9. As minority women students look for mentors and models, they must be taught to assess the values, leadership styles, and goals of their potential mentors (Styles, 1983). To protect the uniqueness of their gender, ethnic, and cultural backgrounds, they must be clear about their own identity when entering mentor-protégé relationships.

10. Minority women students have much to gain from models of minority and majority women working toward common goals of new patterns of leadership. Working interdependently and interethnically, minority and majority women can learn from one another and about one another. Women students will be provided with a model of collaboration and a commitment to understanding differences that will enrich their college experience and, ultimately, their lives.

As minority and majority women, we must look to one another for the support and sustenance we require, and we must incorporate our increased understanding and sensitivity into all our interactions: with students, colleagues, and supervisors, both female and male. We need to know far more about one another—ourselves, our families, our personal cultural orientations. We need to move personally and professionally toward understanding that is based on knowledge. We need to develop a vision of leadership that recognizes and affirms multiple strengths and values, a leadership that honors unique contributions from women of different backgrounds and heritages.

Laster (1986) concludes, "If career success, political empowerment, parenting, male-female relationships, networking, premenstrual syndrome, and menopause are among the main topics of conversation wherever and whenever women gather, then shouldn't we be able to talk? It is time for us to each lay down our petty differences, address the larger issues that divide us, and come together as sisters, regardless of our skin color. We each have problems and we each have solutions. If we were to share our experiences and our expertise and learn to hold each other in higher regard, perhaps we could make this a better world for the next generation of career women, no matter the color of their skin. None of us are free until all of us are free" (p. 3).

References

Alvarez, R. "Institutional Discrimination in Organizations and Their Environments." In R. Alvarez and K. Lutterman (eds.), *Discrimination in Organizations: Using Social Indicators to Manage Social Change*. San Francisco: Jossey-Bass, 1979.

Boyer, J. "Developing a Mentality of Equity: Expanding Academic and Corporate Leadership Challenges." *Journal of Educational Equity and Leadership*, 1986, 6(2), 139–155

Chew, C. A., and Ogi, A. Y. "Asian American College Student Perspectives." In D. J. Wright (ed.), *Responding to the Needs of Today's Minority Students*. New Directions for Student Services, no. 38. San Francisco: Jossey-Bass, 1987.

Collins, R. "Colonialism on Campus: A Critique of Mentoring to Achieve Equity in Higher Education." *Journal of Educational Equity and Leadership*, 1983, 3 (4), 277–287.

Goldstein, E. "The Effect of Same-Sex and Cross-Sex Role Models on Subsequent Academic Productivity of Scholars." *American Psychologist*, 1979, 34, 307–410.

Harvey, W. B. "Where Are the Black Faculty Members?" *Chronicle of Higher Education*, January 22, 1986, p. 96.

Homma-True, R. "Mental Health Issues Among Asian-American Women." In National Institute of Education (ed.), *Conference on the Educational and Occupational Needs of Asian/Pacific American Women*. Washington, D.C.: U.S. Government Printing Office, 1980.

Kanter, R. M. *Men and Women of the Corporation*. New York: Basic Books, 1977.

King, R. *Women Mentors as Leaders*. San Francisco: American Educational Research Association, 1986. (ED 270 411)

LaCounte, D. "American Indian Students in College." In D. J. Wright (ed.), *Responding to the Needs of Today's Minority Students*. New Directions for Student Services, no. 38. San Francisco: Jossey-Bass, 1987.

Laster, J. "Black Women/White Women: Can We Talk?" *Charisma*, 1986, pp. 1–3.

Loden, M. *Feminine Leadership or How to Succeed in Business Without Being One of the Boys*. New York: Random House, 1985.

Mark, S. F. "Gender Differences Among Mid-Level Administrators." Paper presented at the meeting of the Association for the Study of Higher Education, San Antonio, 1986.

Moore, K. M. "The Role of Mentors in Developing Leaders for Academe." *Educational Record*, 1982, 63 (1), 23–28.

Styles, M. "The Mentor-Protégé Relationship: A Career Development Tool." *Spotlight*, 1983, 6 (1), 10.

Washington, E. "Western Michigan University's Black College Program: Swelling the Black Faculty Cohort." Paper presented at the annual conference of the National Association for Equal Opportunity in Higher Education, Washington, D.C., 1986. (ED 268 938)

Williams, A. *A Profile of Black Female Administrators at a Large Urban Public University.* San Francisco: American Educational Research Association, 1986. (ED 270 407)

Zavella, P. "The Impact of 'Sun Belt Industrialization' on Chicanos." *Frontiers*, 1984, 8 (1), 21–27.

The Campus Racial Climate
Contexts of Conflict

SYLVIA HURTADO

Racial conflict was becoming commonplace on American college campuses throughout the 1980s, with more than one hundred college campuses reporting incidents of racial/ethnic harassment and violence in each of the last two years of the decade [40]. The most highly publicized racial incidents, ranging from verbal harassment to violent beatings, occurred at some of the most elite institutions in the country [25, 56]. In many cases students organized protests as a direct response to these problems or to express solidarity with students facing similar problems at other institutions [60]. Although these events have provided the impetus for examining the quality of race relations on individual college campuses, researchers have not explored at any great length the nature of campus race relations across a variety of institutional contexts.

The research on minorities in higher education is extensive, yet a surprisingly small number of empirical studies have focused specifically on campus racial climates. Only a few studies include measures of campus race relations in their models of student persistence [54, 57, 58], academic achievement [2, 41, 42, 46], and social involvement [1]. Although this is an important step toward developing appropriate models that describe the college experiences of minority students, these studies have revealed a conflicting pattern of relations between hostile racial climates and student outcomes [29]. Part of the problem is that we need a better understanding of what constitutes a racially tense interpersonal environment before considering how these climates are related to student development.

Drawing upon previous work on race relations, inequality, and campus diversity, the goal of this study is to examine comparative institutional data that may help identify contexts for racial conflict. This study offers a unique opportunity to examine racial tension on campus because it focuses on the experiences of a student cohort that attended predominantly white colleges from 1985 to 1989, a period when racial incidents occurred on many campuses. A central premise of the study is that such incidents are part of a wide range of climate issues on college campuses that require our attention. Much of what we observe on campus is undoubtedly influenced by the general social context, yet we can learn a great deal about the nature of our campuses by examining black, Chicano, and white student perceptions in institutional contexts associated with campus racial tension.

The Social Context

The civil rights movement, the elimination of *de jure* segregation in the public sector *(Brown v. the Board of Education* [16]), litigation in areas related to the Civil Rights Law (Title VI), and a surge in minority enrollments up until the mid-1970s raised the level of public consciousness regarding inequalities in the education of minority groups. These events represented tremendous strides in progress toward eliminating overt aspects of discrimination in educational institutions, making such practices illegal and unethical in the public mind. However, scholars concede that institutional compliance with legal injunctions for increased minority participation in higher education continues to be problematic [59, 61, 65], the system of higher education remains racially stratified [62], and vestiges of discrimination exist in everyday administrative practices [50]. Thus, important progress has yet to be made in removing some of the more intractable forms of racial inequality and discrimination at both the institutional and individual levels.

The research literature suggests that instances of overt racial conflict can no longer be viewed as aberrations or isolated incidents, but rather are indicators of a more general problem of unresolved racial issues in college environments and in society at large. Researchers investigating racial climates in the mid-1970s found that though college campuses exerted considerable energy in initiating programs and services in response to the initial entrance of black students, institutions did not attend to minority-majority relations or the psychological climate [49]. Recent studies have shown that even on relatively calm campuses there are differences in students' racial attitudes and considerable social distance among students of different racial or ethnic backgrounds [37, 38]. Alienation from the mainstream of campus life is also reported to be particularly acute among minority students on predominantly white campuses [2, 46, 53]. The 1989 American Council on Education (ACE) survey of academic administrators revealed that only one in four felt their campus provided an "excellent" to "very good" climate for black students, and only 21 percent felt they provided a supportive climate for Hispanics [23]. If these issues have been left unattended since the influx of minorities into higher education in the 1960s, it is no wonder that campuses continue to deal with racial tensions.

External forces and the events of the past decade have helped to make these unresolved issues more salient. The resurgence of overt hostilities on campuses, reported as early as 1979 [54], accompanied events that signaled the questioning of affirmative action practices (for example, *Bakke*), declining federal commitment to issues that affect minorities, renewed Ku Klux Klan activity, and increasing racial discord in urban communities [25,33, 59]. At the same time, college campuses reflected a political shift toward conservatism in the country during the 1980s. Students who identified with the far right and political conservatives became more vocal, while their classmates shied away from the liberal label and increasingly characterized their political views as middle-of-the road [22]. Moreover, significant policy trends that are connected with issues of inequality directly affected institutions of higher education. For example, reductions in federal aid programs during the Reagan years resulted in changes in financial aid packaging policy at the institutional level, which many contend have disproportionately affected blacks and Hispanics in their decisions to attend or remain in college [8, 19, 43, 44, 56]. Diminishing federal support for Pell grants and minority-targeted fellowships promises to complicate institutional efforts to stem the decline of college participation rates for low-income and minority groups [17, 18, 30, 45].

Institutional Contexts

Although the general social context influences all institutions, researchers have found considerable institutional variability in reports of racial conflict and responses to improve the racial climate. Early studies found that institutional selectivity and size were both positively associated with student unrest involving campus racial policies [5]. Researchers offered two alternative interpretations: (a) selective institutions and large campuses are environments that are more likely to attract protest-prone students, and (b) large institutions are characterized by an impersonal atmosphere and lack of concern for the individual student, thereby promoting student discontent. The first interpretation suggests that conflict on campus is largely due to the types of students an institution recruits. Studies support the notion that elite institutions tend to attract students with strong ideological commitments and foster political liberalism [7, 28]. The second interpretation states that institutional size may be a proxy for attention to students, suggesting that the extent to which institutions are supportive of students helps maintain a conflict-free environment. Recent research shows that higher rates of institutional spending (per student) in the areas of student services and student aid (non-repayable grants and fellowships) are correlated with student perceptions of relatively low racial tension on campuses [29]. Although there is research support for both interpretations, one focuses on the individual as the source of conflict, while the other suggests that institutional contexts are largely responsible for setting the stage for conflict. These interpretations were tested in the current study, along with others which suggest that both size and selectivity are proxies for other phenomena that include changes in minority enrollment and institutional priorities that help shape the climate.

One of the most comprehensive studies of the racial climate, initiated on the campuses of thirteen four-year institutions, systematically documented the historical and environmental forces that accompanied substantial increases in black student enrollment from 1968 to 1975 [49]. In addition to campus site visits, extensive surveys of administrators, faculty, and students at four of the large institutions explored three broad areas of institutional responsiveness to the entrance of black students: institutional commitment, program responses, and the attitudinal or perceptual climate. Although the large institutions had invested a fair amount of time and funds in minority programs and services, researchers found that these institutions differed substantially in ratings of relative priorities placed on the recruitment of black students, provision for nonacademic support, and commitment to affirmative action. They also observed that campuses paid little attention to the interpersonal aspects of race relations, which were characterized by "voluntary segregation or by indifference thinly covering interracial conflicts and feelings of mistrust" [49, p. 319]. They concluded that a failure to deal with any of the issues at the institutional, programmatic, or individual levels was "likely to become a source of difficulty at some point in these institutions' relationships with minorities" [49, p. 316]. Although researchers anticipated problems with minority students, they did not foresee the extent to which an institution's relationship with majority students would become equally problematic in matters such as admissions (for example, *Bakke*), student organizations (fraternities), and student publications (for example, *Dartmouth Review*). Still, these early findings hold important implications for the examination of contemporary racial tension with regard to the role of institutional priorities and the impact of changing enrollments.

The 1989 ACE survey of academic administrators at 456 institutions revealed distinct differences by institution type in priorities for cultural diversity, programmatic activity, and the amount of racial tension reported on campus [23]. Administrators at doctoral institutions reported the most programmatic activity to improve minority participation at all levels of the university, including efforts to increase the number of minority faculty and increase the enrollment of minority students at the undergraduate level. Comprehensive universities were the next most active in this regard. At the same time, however, racial tensions were reported more often at comprehensive and doctoral institutions than at other types of institutions. In direct contrast, administrators from private baccalaureate institutions reported the least racial tension among the four-year institutions but also gave their institutions the lowest ratings in their ability to attract black and Hispanic students. These ratings, from one of the top academic administrators at each campus, indicate distinct differences among four-year institutions that include both a public/ private dichotomy and contradictions in campus racial climates.

Conducted some fourteen years apart, both studies suggest that despite visible programmatic activity, institutions continue to vary considerably in their commitment to diversity and in the amount of racial conflict on campus. These findings run counter to the commonly held assumption that the introduction of a few programs would essentially lead to better racial climates. Apparently, a shift in institutional priorities for diversity is more difficult to achieve and may involve resolving a more complex set of institutional priorities or problems. Richardson and Skinner's [51] model of institutional adaptation to diversity proposes that goals for quality and diversity may be seen as sources of conflict within institutions. Scholars have raised questions regarding this issue, stating that the assumptions underlying these concepts may inappropriately place the two goals in conflict [53]. Though there has been substantial attention to the debate regarding the relationship between the two priorities, there has been little concern about whether the quest for institutional quality or a shift in priorities of institutional commitment to diversity may be related to racial tension on campus.

The adaptation model has several underlying premises that are reexamined here in relation to the campus climate. The model equates quality with individual achievement, suggesting that the focus of selective institutions is high on achievement and low on diversity, whereas the reverse is true for open-access institutions. The problem with this logic is that all educational institutions have a concern for individual achievement; the difference between these types of institutions is that student achievement must be proven *prior* to admission with selective institutions, whereas open-access institutions are willing to allow students to prove achievement *during* college. Therefore, selective institutions may have less to do with improving individual achievement than with maintaining institutional status and reputation [6]. This forces us to reexamine the conflict in priorities: the source of conflict is not between diversity and achievement but originates from differences in institutional priorities that work to preserve inequalities. For example, although campus race relations is not an aspect of the adaptation model, researchers acknowledge that "our society has historically treated minority populations as inferior" [51] and report that the social environment of the large, predominantly white universities has been problematic, even for minority students with strong academic preparation [52, p. 487]. Traditional notions of quality are often linked to both selectivity and an institutional preoccupation with resource accumulation and reputation enhancement [6]. It may be that minority students are generally undervalued (regardless of their achievement characteristics), whereas high-achieving white students are viewed as resources. Therefore, priorities that guide an institution and its members may have underlying ideological assumptions that are linked with racial issues.

A theoretical tradition supports the view that our institutions, particularly our schools, have embedded ideologies that work to preserve inequality [14, 27]. Research on racial inequality and attitudes has adopted a similar notion of dominant ideological interests. Arce [4] introduced the concept of "academic colonialism" when referring to Chicano participation in academe. Academic colonialism refers to the imposition of dominant ideologies (for example, intellectual premises, concepts, practices) and/or the uncritical acceptance of these ideologies by subordinate groups. Similarly, others assert that dominant group interests are served in maintaining a status quo that justifies unequal social relations and achieves some level of consensus about such arrangements among subordinate groups [31, 32, 38]. Viewed from this perspective, the conflict between quality and diversity appears contrived, and arguments for "quality" may be used as a way to uniformly exclude minorities (faculty and students) and their perspectives.

When "harmonious inequality" is challenged by subordinates, dominant groups are forced to defend their privilege [32]. This perspective suggests that mean-spirited acts of racial harassment on the part of white students may represent a reassertion of group dominance in an era when prevailing dominant group ideologies are in question. However, the defense of dominant group privilege is less often characterized by such acts of "traditional" racism on campus and more often takes on a sophisticated guise as an expressed concern for the individual that is consistent with prevailing democratic values—so long as one chooses to ignore *both* the historical and continuous disadvantages under which subordinate groups operate. As researchers point out, this concern for individual privilege is at the heart of the meritocratic ethic in higher education [38]. It is also at the center of contention with regard to virtually every institutional response to eliminate inequalities and discriminatory practices for various groups, including affirmative action, the development of disciplinary codes to prohibit harassment, and the practice of providing minority-targeted scholarships.[1] Although this view suggests dominant group opposition to institutional commitment to diversity, we have yet to obtain evidence which shows that diversity priorities are related to racial tension on predominantly white campuses.

Race relations theorists propose that racial conflict arises out of a sense of threat to group position, when the dominant group perceives the risk of losing power, resources, or other advantages [12, 63]. Work in the area of relative numbers of underrepresented groups suggests that the proportions of socially and culturally different people in a group are critical in shaping the dynamics of social interaction [35]. Blalock hypothesized that "as the minority percentage increases, we would expect to find increasing discriminatory behavior" [11, p. 148] because more members of the minority group will be in direct competition with someone from the dominant group. Recent research on racial attitudes shows decreases in white support for integration and increases in perceived threat from blacks as the relative size of the black population increased in communities [26]. Thus, differences in minority enrollment may account for variations in racial tension and contradictions observed in studies of institution type and the racial climate. Faced with impending changes in the ethnic composition of the college-age population [24], such effects may have important implications for college campuses.

Student Perceptions and Ethnic Group Differences

Researchers have found that student perceptions vary by race in college environments, yet only a handful of studies have compared perceptions of the racial climate among black, Chicano, and white college students [64]. A study at one predominantly white university showed that although a higher percentage of blacks than Chicanos reported that they have personally experienced discrimination, these reports were positively correlated with feelings of alienation only among Chicano students [46]. Loo and Rolison [37] also found that the majority of white students (68 percent) thought that the university was generally supportive of minority students, while only 28 percent of the black and Chicano students expressed the same opinion. In the same study, certain behaviors (for example, ethnic group clustering) were interpreted by white students as racial segregation, whereas minority students tended to view them as modes of cultural support within a larger unsupportive environment. In a comparative study of two institutions [48], researchers found black students were most likely to perceive a hostile racial climate on campus, but Hispanics were also more likely than white students to perceive such hostility. Perceptions of the racial climate also differed by institution, although it appears that dimensions of location and ethnic composition of the campus were confounded with group differences. These studies show that ethnic groups differ in their views of the racial climate, highlighting the need to conduct comparative group analyses across institutions to understand environments with considerable racial tension.

Method

Conceptual Framework

The structural properties of the environment are central to shaping social interaction and the individual's attitude and behavior within it [36]. These structural properties are often assessed with measures that social psychologists refer to as "contextual variables" [36] or distal characteristics [34]. In higher education research these measures are often institutional characteristics such as size, type, control, selectivity, and racial composition of the college. In Jessor's [34] view, there are a multiplicity of environments in which human interaction takes place. These multiple environments can be ordered along a continuum according to proximity to the individual. Demographic and structural attributes of environments are considered distal, whereas the perceived environment is considered the most proximal and is of immediate significance to the actor. Studies have begun to validate the notion that proximal measures are more important than distal characteristics in relation to student outcomes [47, 55]. Research in social psychology also suggests that proximal measures mediate the effect of these distal characteristics on other outcomes [34, 39]. In this particular study the distal environmental dimensions include size, selectivity, ethnic enrollments, and campus expenditures. The proximal environment is represented by student perceptions of institutional priorities that reflect institutional commitment to cultural diversity, a resource/reputation orientation, and a student-centered orientation. Within this framework, the proximal measures (student perceptions of the environment) are hypothesized to have a greater influence than the distal measures of the environment on student perceptions of racial tension.

Data Sources

This study draws upon several major data sources. The primary source of student data came from responses to a four-year longitudinal survey, the 1989 Follow-up Survey (FUS) to the 1985 Freshman Survey, a project of the Cooperative Institutional Research Program (CIRP) and the Higher Education Research Institute at UCLA. The 1985 Freshman Survey was administered during freshman orientation and the FUS was sent to the student's home address in the summer and fall of 1989, four years after college entry. The FUS was administered according to two different sampling techniques to address the need for national normative data and to facilitate separate group analyses. The first sample was drawn from the population of first-time, full-time freshmen (192,453) responding to the 1985 Survey. A stratified, random procedure was used to ensure representation of students based on sex within the different types of institutions in higher education. (Stratification involved 23 cells reflecting institutional selectivity, control, race, sex, and the type of institution.) Based on patterns of response observed in earlier FUS studies, a random sample (20,317) was selected to yield a minimal number (175) of respondents in each stratification cell. This yielded data on 4,672 respondents (23 percent response rate), which were statistically adjusted for nonresponse and weighted to approximate the national population of students. (The statistical weighting methodology used in HERI Follow-up surveys can be found in all FUS reports [30]).

Although this sampling procedure is well suited for analyses of national normative data, the numbers of minority students drawn randomly across institutions remains extremely small for the purposes of separate group analyses. A second procedure was necessary to yield a sample more conducive to analyses on ethnic groups. Four-year institutions were selected to maximize variability according to student academic programs and minority enrollment in addition to institutional type, control, and selectivity. Full cohorts of students (34,323) were surveyed, yielding 10,640 respondents (31 percent response rate). A secondary data sampling procedure was employed to select only those students representing three ethnic groups (black, Chicano, and white students) from among respondents at 116 predominantly white institutions. Each institution was considered a separate stratum with stratified, random sampling conducted on a 3:1 white/minority ratio. The purpose of this procedure was to yield a sample of white students that was distributed across institutions in a manner similar to the distribution of minority students. Most institutions had both black and Chicano students but in some institutions, due to distinct patterns of college attendance among minorities, white students were matched with only one of these ethnic groups. This final selection criteria yielded a sample of 1,825 white students, 328 black, and 340 Chicano students. The major part of the study utilized the data from this selected sample for separate group analyses.

Institutional characteristics and undergraduate ethnic enrollments were obtained from the data files of the U.S. Department of Education's Integrated Postsecondary Data System (IPEDS, formerly HEGIS).[2] Black, Hispanic, and total enrollment data for 1982, 1986, and 1988 at each institution were obtained from this national source. These years were used to create enrollment change variables for the ethnic groups in each institution. Financial data on 1985 expenditures (per student) for student services and grants/fellowships were similarly obtained, and all institutional data were merged with student survey data for analyses.

Measures

A total of 21 independent variables were selected for the analyses. Variable definitions are shown on table A-1, along with coding schemes and scales. The dependent variable consisted of a factorially confirmed scale representing student perceptions of racial tension among students, faculty, and campus administrators [29]. Items constructing all scales are shown on table A-2. The rationale for including specific measures in analyses is described below.

Because the distribution of students across different college environments is never random, one of the basic features of any research design is to control for student characteristics at the point of initial exposure to the environment. For example, selective institutions tend to attract students who are more critical of their environments (for example, liberal and protest "prone"), come from families with higher incomes, and have higher academic ability [5, 7]. Parental income and student academic performance (high-school grade-point average) served as control variables, along with a number of student self-rating and value measures on the 1985 Freshman Survey. Measures that controlled for predispositions in student perceptions included student self-ratings of political view, estimated chances of becoming involved in campus protest, and the importance attributed to the goal of helping to promote racial understanding. Aside from the need for statistical control, additional student background characteristics were included in analyses because they are established correlates of racial attitudes and perceptions. For example, females are generally more supportive of affirmative action and racial integration [13]; the well-educated tend to be more supportive of principles of racial integration (but not decidedly more willing to support specific equity policies) [31, 32]; and age is negatively associated with racial integration [26]. Previous research has also suggested that a sense of interpersonal accomplishment or social self-confidence may be an important precursor to social involvement among minorities [2] and perceptions of racial tension on campus among white students [29]. Therefore, additional student background variables included gender, mother's and father's level of education, age, and a social self-confidence scale.

Factor scales constructed from student perceptions of their environment included institutional priorities that reflect a commitment to diversity, a reputation/resource orientation, and a student-centered orientation. Parallel measures, obtained independent of student observation, for an institution's student-centered priorities included campus expenditures (per student) in the areas of student services and student aid (non-repayable grants and fellowships). High expenditures in these areas reflect student-centered priorities, particularly in an era of budget constraint and shrinking governmental resources. Measures reflecting the college composition, the proportion of black and Hispanic undergraduate enrollment in 1986, and ethnic enrollment changes over a six-year period (1982–88) served to test race-relations theories based on relative numbers. They also controlled for institutional differences that were observed in previous studies of the racial climate [23] and as parallel measures of institutional commitment to diversity. The enrollment change measures were designed to capture changes in student diversity at each institution prior to and during the enrollment of the 1985–89 cohort. Two additional college composition variables, institutional size and selectivity, served to test alternative interpretations regarding campus conflict [5].

Five factors derived from previous climate studies [20, 29] were used in the regression analyses of campus racial tension on student and institutional characteristics. Because items were on similar scales (table A-2), new variables were created by summing responses on each item to construct a factor scale. Table 1 shows that all the scales have fairly high reliabilities that are similar across groups. The range on reliabilities across groups for a socioeconomic status factor was too wide to be considered a generalizable construct in analyses across groups; therefore, multiple indicators (parental income and the level of mother's and father's education) were entered in the equation with full recognition that this might underestimate the effects of each indicator. The effects of these variables and other complex relationships among the independent variables were carefully monitored prior to and after entry into the equation using a computer software program, *Betaview*, designed for this purpose [21].

Analyses

Student perceptions of racial climate issues at all types of four-year institutions were examined using bivariate analyses of national normative data. Ethnic group differences on all variables were assessed using two-tailed tests of significance on the selected sample of black, Chicano, and white students. Because ethnic groups differed significantly in their perceptions of the environment, separate group analyses were conducted using multiple regression techniques to assess the relationship between perceptions of campus racial tension and student and institutional characteristics. Variables were entered in three stages to observe changes in regression coefficients. The first stage explored the extent to which perceptions of racial tension were a function of the cultural

Table 1
Factor Scales: Estimates of Internal Consistencies (Alpha) by Student Sample

Factor Scale	Number of Items	Black	Chicano	White
Campus racial tension	3	0.66	0.66	0.64
Social self-confidence	3	0.76	0.75	0.73
Institutional commitment to diversity	4	0.88	0.86	0.80
Student-centered orientation	5	0.75	0.80	0.83
Resource/reputation orientation	5	0.77	0.79	0.76

NOTE: Confirmatory and exploratory procedures used to develop factors are reported in Hurtado [29] and Dey [20]. Items constituting each scale are reported in table A-2.

and psychological baggage that students bring with them to college, including demographic attributes and tendencies that might suggest a precollege bias in their views regarding the climate. Institutional priorities, hypothesized to be the primary explanatory variables that would diminish the impact of college composition variables (size and selectivity), were entered in the next stage. College composition variables were entered in the final stage to determine if these structural aspects of the environment remain central to shaping perceptions of the climate. Interaction terms representing (I) high resource/reputation priorities and institutional commitment to diversity and (2) high resource/reputation and student-centered priorities were forward entered in a second regression model for each group to determine if these combinations could account for a significant addition in the proportion of variance in the dependent variable.

Results

National normative data are presented in table 2 to provide an overview of student perceptions of the racial climate, highlighting differences among four-year colleges and universities. Student views on the existence of racial discrimination show the least variation across all institution types. Only about 12 percent of all students at four-year institutions agreed with the statement that "racial discrimination is no longer a problem in America," indicating that most undergraduates feel that this form of discrimination is still an issue to contend with in our society. At the same time, items measuring student perceptions of campus race relations reflect a much wider range of responses between institution types. This suggests that though most students acknowledge the existence of racial discrimination, their perceptions of race relations on campus vary according to their experiences in different institutional contexts.

Data show that approximately one in four students at all four-year institutions perceives considerable racial conflict; however, this proportion is higher in university settings (approximately one in three students). It is also important to note that most students agree that "students of different ethnic origins communicate well with one another" on their campus, with the lowest proportion of students agreeing with this statement at private (59 percent) and public universities (61 percent). When compared with other institution types, students at both public and private universities were also more likely to report a lack of trust between minority student groups and administrators (36 and 39 percent, respectively). These results support accounts of racial incidents and related protests occurring primarily at public and private universities from 1985 to 1989 [25].

Private four-year colleges fared better than universities and public four-year colleges on most racial climate measures. Students at Catholic institutions are least likely to report racial conflict (12 percent) or mistrust between minority groups and administrators (16 percent) and are most likely to report good communication among ethnic groups (82 percent). While over two-thirds of all students report that most faculty are sensitive to the issues of minorities, a higher proportion of students at Protestant (81 percent) and nonsectarian four-year colleges (76 percent) perceive this to be the case. In addition, a general measure of curriculum integration shows that the highest

Table 2
Student Perceptions of Racial Issues at Four-Year Colleges and Universities, 1989 Follow-up Survey of Fall 1985 Freshmen

	All Institutions	Universities		Four-Year Colleges				Institutional Range (high to low)
		Public	Private	Public	Nonsectarian	Private Catholic	Protestant	
Agreement with the Statement:[1]								
Racial discrimination is no longer a problem in America	12	11	9	15	11	8	12	7
Statements about the Institution:[1]								
There is a lot of campus racial conflict here	25	34	34	21	17	12	16	22
Many courses include minority perspectives	47	46	41	49	50	43	47	9
Students of different ethnic origins communicate well with one another	68	61	59	69	77	82	76	23
There is little trust between minority student groups and administrators	31	36	3	34	21	16	19	23
Most faculty here are sensitive to the issues of minorities	67	61	65	65	76	70	81	20
Institutional Priorities:[2]								
Create a diverse multicultural environment on campus	42	43	40	42	42	45	37	8
Develop among faculty and students an appreciation for a multicultural society	31	36	40	42	46	45	45	10
Increase minority representation in the faculty and administration	29	30	25	32	27	23	22	10
Recruit more minority students	41	40	40	47	36	29	33	18

Source: National normative data, Higher Education Research Institute, UCLA. Responses are statistically adjusted to correct for non-response and weighted to approximate the national population of 1985 first-time, full-time freshmen. (For weighting procedures see Higher Education Research Institute, 1991).

[1]Percent who "agree strongly" or "agree somewhat."

[2]Percent rating priority is "high" or "highest."

proportion of undergraduates (50 percent) report that many courses include minority perspectives at nonsectarian four-year colleges.

Two general observations are made regarding student perceptions of specific institutional priorities for cultural diversity. First, there is a somewhat smaller institutional range of student views on diversity priorities compared with views on campus race relations, indicating diversity priorities may be more consistent across institutions. Institutions differed most on priorities to diversify the student body, faculty, and the administration. Students at public four-year colleges (47 percent) and universities (40 percent) are more likely than students at private four-year colleges to report minority student recruitment was a "high" or the "highest priority" at their institution. Students at public institutions were also more likely than students at private institutions to report that increasing the representation of minorities in the faculty and administration was a high priority (30–32 percent).

Although these differences in priorities for diversity may be cause for concern, perhaps a more general concern is related to the second observation: less than a third of the students perceive specific goals to change the racial composition of the institution, and less than half perceive general goals for fostering cultural or racial diversity to be a high institutional priority. Given public statements regarding the importance of diversity and the general nature of items reflecting priorities to "create a diverse multicultural environment on campus" and "develop an appreciation for a multicultural society among faculty and students," one wonders why more students do not perceive these to be a high priority on campuses. To what extent are students' perception of racial tension on campus related to their view of institutional priorities for cultural diversity? What can explain the institutional contradictions between priorities and race relations observed here and in previous studies [49, 23]? While institutional type and control are helpful in locating the problems within the higher education system, they are of limited practical significance to administrators in addressing problems within institutional settings. Subsequent analyses focused on the relationship between institutional priorities and campus racial tension, with appropriate controls for student and institutional characteristics, to provide insights into contexts for conflict and contradiction.

Table 3 shows means, standard deviations, and tests of significance on all measures used in analyses of the selected sample of black, Chicano, and white students. This table describes the sample and shows that significant group differences were detected on most freshmen characteristics and perceptions of the environment. The Chicano students came from families with significantly lower levels of educational attainment and lower incomes ($\overline{X} \approx \$27,850$) than either their black or white classmates. Upon college entry in 1985, Chicanos were also less likely to characterize themselves as politically liberal. Black students entered college with significantly higher social self-confidence. They were more likely than other students in the sample to become involved in campus protest, characterize their views as politically liberal, and place a high value on helping to promote racial understanding. In contrast, white students had significantly higher GPAs, college-educated parents, higher family incomes ($\overline{X} \approx \$42,100$), and were less likely to place a high value on promoting racial understanding than the minority students. These results suggest that these are important student background characteristics to take into account in assessing institutional contexts that inform perceptions of campus racial tension.

Given these freshmen differences in relative status and social views, we would expect their perceptions of the environment to vary considerably four years after college entry. Black students were more critical of their environments than the other student groups: they perceived relatively higher levels of racial tension and lower levels of institutional commitment to diversity at their institutions. Chicanos were least likely to perceive that their institution had student-centered priorities. However, there appeared to be consensus across all groups on institutional priorities for resource and reputation enhancement, as there were no significant differences among groups. Significant group differences were also detected among college composition variables (size, selectivity, ethnic enrollment). This is due primarily to the distinct distribution of Chicano and black students among institution types: Chicanos were concentrated in larger, less selective institutions with a higher proportion of Hispanic enrollment.

Table 3

Means, Standard Deviations, and Tests of Significance on Variables by Group

Variables	White (n = 1821) Mean	S.D.	Black (n = 325) Mean	S.D.	Chicano (n = 340) Mean	S.D.	Significant Differences		
1985 Student Characteristics									
Sex (female)	1.58	0.49	1.61	0.49	1.64	0.48	A**	B**	C*
Age	3.12	0.47	3.03	0.48	3.19	0.53	A**	B**	C*
High-school GPA	6.36	1.39	5.59	1.60	5.95	1.41	A**	B**	C**
Mother's education	5.36	1.78	5.07	1.95	3.50	2.10	A**	B**	C**
Father's education	6.10	1.90	4.87	2.11	3.89	2.37	A**	B**	C**
Income	9.19	2.97	6.73	3.18	6.54	3.12	A**	B**	C**
Social self-confidence	10.78	1.95	10.99	2.17	10.55	2.03		B**	C**
Expect to protest	2.35	0.83	2.44	0.83	2.24	0.87		B**	C**
Political view (liberal)	3.06	0.78	3.32	0.64	3.02	0.71	A**	B**	
Promote racial understanding	2.27	0.83	3.14	0.79	2.55	0.83	A**	B**	C**
Institutional Characteristics									
Institutional Priorities									
Expenditures:									
Student services	865.32	701.54	899.54	618.67	842.93	764.22			
Non-repayable aid	1345.88	939.09	1576.17	1008.69	1124.31	730.68	A**	B**	C**
Student Perceptions:									
Student-oriented	12.45	2.98	12.39	2.66	11.78	3.11		B**	C**
Resource/reputation-oriented	14.33	3.23	14.35	3.30	14.61	3.47			
Commitment to diversity	9.51	2.73	8.94	3.38	9.57	3.08	A**	B**	
College composition:									
Selectivity (Average SAT)	105.38	14.27	108.16	15.72	98.42	13.64	A**	B**	C**
Enrollment:									
Size (total FTE)	6.28	2.16	5.72	1.95	6.39	2.38	A**	B**	C**
Black percent in 1986	4.68	3.10	5.53	3.35	4.21	2.45	A**	B**	C**
Hispanic percent in 1986	5.60	6.84	3.30	5.33	14.29	16.27	A**	B**	C**
Black increase (1982–88)	1.64	0.48	1.57	0.50	1.70	0.46	A*	B**	C*
Hispanic increase (1982–88)	2.55	0.83	2.48	0.87	2.69	0.73	A**	B**	C**
Dependent Variable									
Campus Racial Tension	6.70	1.90	7.85	2.07	6.73	2.03	A**	B**	

Note: Variable scales are reported in table A-1. Significant group differences, *$p \leq 0.05$, **$p \leq 0.01$ (two-tailed probability): A = white/black difference, B = black/Chicano difference, C = Chicano/white difference.

Table 4
Regression of Campus Racial Tension on Student and Institutional Characteristics by Group

Standardized Regression Coefficients and T Ratios for:

	White (n = 1821)			Black (n = 325)			Chicano (n = 340)		
	β¹	β²	t	β¹	β²	t	β¹	β²	t
1985 Student Characteristics									
Sex (female)	0.02	0.06	2.65	0.02	0.05	0.86	-0.05	0.03	0.64
Age	-0.03	-0.01	-0.56	-0.03	-0.01	0.23	-0.02	0.06	1.11
High-school GPA	0.10**	0.01	0.53	0.01	-0.06	-1.10	0.04	-0.04	-0.86
Mother's education	0.04*	0.04	1.64	-0.03	-0.02	-0.32	-0.02	-0.00	-0.04
Father's education	0.02	-0.01	-0.35	-0.01	-0.00	-0.05	-0.10	-0.13	-1.88
Income	0.05*	0.01	0.48	0.05	-0.03	-0.47	0.08	0.01	0.22
Social self-confidence	0.06*	0.03	1.55	0.01	0.05	1.00	0.03	-0.01	-0.21
Expect to protest in college	0.15**	0.12	5.20	0.06	0.04	0.70	0.18**	0.10	1.89
Political view (liberal)	0.02	0.02	0.85	0.23**	0.18	3.41	0.09	0.04	0.88
Goal: helping to promote racial understanding	0.00	0.02	0.68	0.02	0.04	0.70	0.06	0.09	1.70
Institutional Characteristics									
Institutional Priorities									
Expenditures (per student):									
Student services	-0.09**	0.01	0.48	-0.15**	-0.08	-1.17	-0.07	-0.04	-0.60
Non-repayable student aid	-0.09**	-0.00	-0.05	-0.11	-0.12	-1.32	0.19**	0.01	0.14
Student Perceptions of Priorities:									
Student-centered	-0.28**	-0.20	-7.48	-0.29**	-0.22	-3.58	-0.38**	-0.18	-3.06
Resource/reputation	0.17**	0.06	2.64	0.20**	0.12	2.15	0.22**	0.08	1.57
Commitment to diversity	-0.05*	-0.03	-1.28	-0.28*	-0.18	-3.14	0.23**	-0.20	-4.03
College composition:									
Selectivity (Average SAT)	0.16**	0.19	5.56	0.09	0.17	2.13	0.31**	0.29	3.17
Enrollment:									
Size (total FTE)	0.23**	0.14	3.48	0.14**	-0.12	-1.42	0.36**	0.10	0.97
Black percent in 1986	0.07**	0.11	5.09	-0.05	0.00	-0.01	-0.13*	0.05	0.68
Hispanic percent in 1986	-0.08**	-0.05	-2.15	-0.03	0.02	0.42	-0.31**	-0.07	-0.64
Black increase (1982–88)	0.13**	0.06	2.08	-0.06	0.01	0.14	0.28**	0.13	1.94
Hispanic increase (1982–88)	0.07**	-0.02	-0.66	-0.12*	-0.10	-1.65	0.12*	0.04	0.62
R^2	0.19			0.24			0.36		

Note: β¹ is reported at the step where all student characteristics are controlled. (* $p = \le 0.05$, ** $p = \le 0.01$); β² is reported at final step of the equation. T ratios (reported at the final step) of approximately 1.96 or greater are significant at the 0.05 level, and 2.59 or greater at the 0.01 level.

Table 4 shows the regression results for the three ethnic groups. Beta coefficients are shown at two steps: β^1 is the value of each regression coefficient at the step where all student characteristics are controlled, and β^2 represents the value of the coefficient at the final step of the equation. The β^1 coefficient represents the effect of a variable, net of student characteristics and prior to competing with other environmental variables in the equation. These coefficients are shown to (1) consider alternative interpretations that can be derived from other models that may exclude some of the environmental measures, and (2) evaluate the performance of some of the data obtained independent of student observation (expenditures and enrollments) in comparison to student perceptions. T-ratios represent the magnitude of the coefficient, taking into account its standard error of estimate; these values are presented in lieu of unstandardized coefficients to compare effects across groups at the final step of the equation. Overall, the regression models account for 36 percent of the variance in campus racial tension in the Chicano, 24 percent in the black, and 19 percent in the white student samples.

Student Characteristics

Results show that white students who entered college expecting to become involved in campus protest, white females, and black students who characterized their views as politically liberal are inclined to perceive racial tension on campus. It may be that these types of students are predisposed to view the climate critically and are sensitive to issues of racial and social inequality. In the wake of harassment incidents on campus, these students may have also found themselves in the forefront of protests to pressure institutions into formulating a response. Prior to the entry of institutional characteristics in the equations, the significant betas (β^1) of other student variables show that perceptions of racial tension are also prevalent among Chicanos who expected to become involved in campus protest. Additional characteristics of white students who perceive racial tension include those with a higher level of social self-confidence, parental income, mother's education, and a higher GPA. These latter student characteristics do not maintain significant coefficients in the final steps of the regression equations due to their association with institutional characteristics that have relatively strong effects (for example, selectivity). Thus, perceptions of racial tension are not created solely in the minds of specific individuals but rather are rooted in a shared institutional reality.

Institutional Characteristics

Across all groups, students perceive low racial tension at institutions with high student-centered priorities. This relationship remains significant after controlling for institution size, college composition variables, and other institutional priorities. Betas at the step where all student characteristics are controlled (β^1) also indicate that institutional spending priorities may play an indirect role in relation to campus racial tension. Campus expenditures for student aid (among Chicano and white students) and student services (among black and white students) are negatively associated with perceptions of racial tension. The changes in the coefficients for these expenditure measures were monitored throughout the equations, revealing that perceptions of student-centered priorities account for much of their effect on perceptions of racial tension. These institutional spending priorities are associated with perceptions of an overall environment of student support that, in turn, are associated with perceptions of lower racial tension. Results on these parallel measures of student support extend earlier findings that were derived from a model of campus racial tension that included only expenditure measures (distal measures) [29].

Data support the notion that an institutional commitment to diversity can substantially improve minority and, to some extent, white student perceptions of race relations on campus. Perceptions of institutional commitment to diversity maintained a strong negative association with perceptions of racial tension among black and Chicano students. Similarly, white students' perceptions of institutional commitment to diversity were associated with a small negative effect on racial tension prior to controlling for other environmental characteristics (β^1). However, the effect for white students became nonsignificant when measures of student-centered priorities were controlled (β^2). This difference between white and minority groups will be discussed in the latter part of this article. It is important to note here, however, that perceptions of institutional commitment to diversity do not significantly contribute to white student perceptions of racial tension.

Although college selectivity and priorities for resource/reputation enhancement are often associated with traditional notions of quality, they maintain unique effects on racial tension in the black and white student samples and are more closely linked in the Chicano sample. Black and white students who perceive that their institutions have high resource and reputation priorities perceive high racial tension. In addition, institutional selectivity was a positive indicator of perceptions of racial tension across all ethnic groups. The unique effects of selectivity on perceptions of racial tension are maintained over and above student characteristics and campus priorities for resource and reputation enhancement. This suggests that selectivity is not merely a proxy for the type of student an institution recruits, nor can priorities for resource/reputation enhancement fully explain why we observe racial conflict in selective institutions.

Interaction terms that represent (1) high resource/reputation and institutional commitment to diversity and (2) high resource/reputation and student-centered orientation were introduced in subsequent models (not shown) to test whether these combinations of priorities were significantly related to racial tension. The interaction terms did not contribute significantly to the proportion of variance explained in the dependent measure. Therefore, these dimensions of institutional priorities appear to work independently and are not likely to have an additive effect on perceptions of racial tension.

Differences among the ethnic groups are evident in the relationship between enrollments and perceptions of racial tension. The effect of institutional size on perceptions of racial tension was diminished substantially by other institutional measures in all student groups, yet it maintains a positive association with perceptions of racial tension among white students. Similarly, the various effects of the ethnic enrollment measures on minority student perceptions of racial tension were diminished when other institutional characteristics were taken into account (β^2). In contrast, white students' perceptions of racial tension were significantly influenced by minority enrollments. The proportion of black students and increases in black enrollment are positively associated and Hispanic enrollment is negatively associated with white students' perception of racial tension on campus. There are at least two possible explanations for this difference between white and minority students and the contradictory effect of Hispanic enrollment: (1) as some race relations theories propose, white students may feel threatened by the presence of an increasing number of black students [11], or (2) ethnic enrollment differences in the institutional sample may indicate that the effects of the minority composition of a college on racial tension may be nonlinear.

To investigate nonlinear effects, the quadratic and cubic terms of the proportion of black students were added hierarchically to the regression models for each group. Although the cubic term was significant in the white student sample, when compared with the base model, there was no change in the direction of effects and the additional proportion of variance accounted for was too small to determine a nonlinear trend in the data. Still, the different distribution of black and Hispanic enrollments at the institutions in this sample may be indicative of nonlinear effects. None of the institutions had a black student population higher than 26 percent, and two institutions in the sample were Hispanic serving institutions (HSIs)[3] with Hispanic enrollments approaching 30 and 50 percent, respectively. Moreover, these institutions were located in cities with predominantly Hispanic populations. It may be that white students' perceptions of racial tension are lower in these institutional contexts not so much because of the ethnicity of the changing population, but because of the higher proportion of culturally diverse students and the general multicultural context of community in which they are located.

Summary and Discussion

National data show that approximately one in four students perceived considerable racial conflict at four-year institutions in the late 1980s. Considering the substantial media attention devoted to racial issues on campus in recent years, some may think this proportion is small. However, the proportion of students reporting racial conflict was higher in university settings (approximately one-third). This proportion is significant given that racial tension escalated to the point of creating serious disruptions at several campuses [25, 60]. At the same time that institutions were experiencing racial conflict, students were critical of institutional priorities to improve the racial climate. Less than a third of the students reported priorities to increase the representation of minorities through student and administrator/faculty recruitment, and less than half reported that general goals for fostering a multicultural environment were a high priority at their institution.

Although there are slight differences in reporting categories, results from the 1989 Follow-up of students replicate several general findings of the 1989 ACE survey of academic administrators [23]. Perceptions of campus race relations and various diversity priorities are not uniform across different institutional contexts. A higher proportion of universities and public four-year colleges have initiated efforts to diversify their environments, yet these institutions also have relatively higher racial tension than private four-year colleges. There also appears to be a public/private institutional dichotomy among four-year colleges in the quality of race relations and priorities for diversity: students at private four-year colleges perceive better overall campus race relations than at public four-year institutions. At the same time, a smaller proportion of students perceive that the recruitment of minority students and administrators/faculty is a high priority at private four-year institutions. Ethnic group analyses revealed that these contradictory patterns may be due to differences in college composition and distinct institutional priorities that shape the general campus climate.

Institutions may foster racial tension when they support priorities that work against promoting a better climate. Specifically, traditional notions of quality based on selectivity and resource/reputation priorities are associated with perceptions of high racial tension. Selective institutions are unique environments, they are not simply contexts of individual achievement as proposed in the adaptation model for diversity [51]. They represent an extreme in American wealth and privilege, are staunch promoters of tradition, and are the rungs to powerful positions in society. Although resistance to change may be greatest at these institutions, they are also birthplaces for progressive thought. Racial tension may be highest in these contradictory environments because institutional commitment to diversity is often ambivalent, mitigated by other institutional actions that systematically exclude minorities and their perspectives.

In retrospect, the narrow focus on the enhancement of reputation and resources and moves to increase the selectivity of institutions may have more to do with maintaining inequalities than with actually improving the overall quality of college environments. Our definition of quality and its implementations are laden with assumptions that carry implicit messages to members of the campus community. Narrow conceptions of "quality" often favor elitism rather than egalitarianism, homogeneity rather than diversity, and the unequal distribution of resources. Institutions have opposed diversification of the curriculum, student body, and faculty; concentrated resources in a few individuals (for example, "faculty stars"); and often excluded minorities—all in the name of "quality." This justification is constructed to maintain "harmonious inequality" and may heighten racial tension when groups challenge these actions and their underlying assumptions. The apparent link between racial tension and traditional notions of quality should serve as the impetus for reframing our conceptions of quality to focus on improving the overall condition of life on campus. The quality of life on campus includes both the campus racial climate and the environment of support for students.

Along these lines, black and Chicano student perceptions of institutional commitment to diversity are associated with perceptions of relatively low racial tension. Among white students, this relationship is weaker and appears to be indirect: institutional commitment to diversity is tied to how an institution treats students (student-centered priorities), which, in turn, affects perceptions of racial tension on campus. The difference between groups may be partially explained by results that show white students are less likely to perceive racial tension. Minorities are more aware of racial tension both for historical reasons and because they, unlike white students who are a numerical majority, must depend on constant interracial contact in social, learning, and work spheres on predominantly white campuses.

History reflects that substantial barriers delayed minority progress to attain full participation in American life, and removal of these barriers for racial integration and participation in education required both collective action and institutional change [15]. This progress is still in evolution in our society, as minorities continue to enter college from substantially different social backgrounds (income and parental education) compared to white classmates. Black and Chicano students may feel that institutional initiatives can improve the condition of a racial climate that affects daily interactions, whereas white students may feel the same way about more general climate issues. Thus, institutions that increase their commitment to diversity may significantly improve minority student perceptions of the racial climate. Results also indicate that institutional commitment to diversity does not fuel perceptions of racial tension among the majority of white students. A small proportion (12 percent) of students believe that racial discrimination is no longer a problem in our society, suggesting that only a small (sometimes vocal) group may oppose measures designed to improve the climate for diversity.

A central finding of this study is that racial tension may arise in environments where there is a lack of concern for individual students. Across all groups, perceptions of student-centered priorities were important predictors of perceptions of low racial tension. These results provide empirical support for the importance of "setting a 'tone' that is congenial to all students" [47, p. 645] on college campuses. It may be that racial tensions are higher in environments where students believe that particular groups have special privileges or receive more attention when, in fact, all groups are experiencing a decline in the quality of support for students. Expenditures in the areas of student services and student grant/scholarship aid secure the environment of support for student development, resulting in a more favorable climate. Institutions should stand firm on issues that maintain support for students, particularly in light of declining federal commitment to issues that affect minority and low-income students. Campuses should seek opportunities to reconfigure resources and rewards to create student-centered priorities that will benefit all students. For example, institutions may devote more attention to student-centered approaches that involve faculty in both the personal and academic development of students. This approach may both reduce racial tension and improve social and academic outcomes for students.

Researchers have proposed that the effect of institutional size on campus conflict and racial policies was due to the impersonal environment of large campuses and their ability to attract more liberal or protest-"prone" students [5]. Controls for student characteristics and student-centered priorities in the analyses show that these conclusions are only partially supported. While certain types of students may be more critical of the racial climate and an environment of student support was found to be essential, institutional size remains a significant predictor of perceptions of racial tension among white students. This suggests that there is more to large campus environments and their differential impact on racial/ethnic groups than we understand. Minority student perceptions of racial tension may be mediated by other institutional characteristics (for example, ethnic enrollments) and perhaps their ability to develop their own niche in large institutional settings [10]. Although all students may use this adaptive strategy, white students may view the prevalence of "niches" developed along mutual interests and ethnicity as increasing racial tension on large campuses. This area requires further research to understand how minority and white students make sense of large environments and whether their approaches may be conducive to relations across ethnic groups.

Results from assessing the effect of ethnic composition of a college, or the "compositional hypothesis" [26], are mixed. Increases in black enrollment over the last six years and the proportion of black enrollment are associated with white students' perception of high racial tension; however, the proportion of Hispanic enrollment had the opposite effect. It is difficult to determine whether different effects of relative size of the two ethnic groups may be due to substantially different relations with white students or may be explained by institutional sampling variability. Institutions with a broad range of ethnic enrollments should be added to the sample in the future to settle the question of whether there is a population "threshold" point that determines differences in relations among various ethnic groups on college campuses.

In any case, predominantly white campuses may be relatively unprepared for some of the problems accompanying change in their student bodies—particularly in the wake of impending demographic changes [24]. These findings indicate, and reports of racial incidents confirm [25], that black-white relations are generally in need of improvement on college campuses where enrollment shifts are occurring. Race relations theorists would conclude that, due to competition for resources, white students view black students as a threat to their group position [11]. The fact that student-centered priorities are associated with lower racial tension suggests that some campuses may have minimized feelings of competition among groups. The relative status differences among students of different racial/ethnic groups (social background and relative size of the groups) suggest structural conditions that may inform a sense of group position; however, it is not clear whether white students feel they are in competition with black students for limited institutional resources. The actual motivations for racial tension require further research to conclusively determine how different ethnic groups perceive one another in relation to their environments.

Conclusion

This study has shown that perhaps no single element of the environment may work to produce racial tension on college campuses. It is a configuration of external influences (historical and contemporary), structural characteristics of institutions and group relations, and institutionalized ideologies. Each of these areas requires our attention in efforts to promote civility and foster values in students that will serve them in an increasingly multicultural society. These efforts should be guided by a willingness to question our assumptions, consideration of the experiences of different ethnic groups, and an overriding concern for a quality of life on campus that will be conducive to student development. Further research on the experiences of different ethnic groups may help determine elements of our environments that uniquely contribute to the development of each group.

Notes

The Exxon Education Foundation provided generous support for the administration of surveys at selected institutions, thereby facilitating analyses by ethnic group. This funding was provided as part of a project on the outcomes of general education conducted at the Higher Education Research Institute, UCLA. Research was conducted in UCLA's Department of Sociology and the Graduate School of Education with the support of the University of California President's Postdoctoral Fellowship. The author extends her appreciation for Walter R. Allen's and Michael A. Olivas's helpful comments on an earlier draft of this article.

1. In the case of minority-targeted scholarships, the defense of individual privilege ran counter to group norms. As the Bush Administration questioned the legality of minority-targeted scholarships, the 1990 General Social Survey showed that the majority of the American public (69 percent of the white and 95 percent of the black population) supported special college scholarships for black students who maintain good grades [13]. Shaky legal rationale was used to defend individual privilege [45], even while there was widespread public support for minority-targeted scholarships.

2. The U.S. Department of Education still collects and reports data on Chicanos under the umbrella category of "Hispanic," even though census data and educational data show dramatic differences among Latino groups [24]. Chicanos represent the majority of the Hispanic enrollment in this sample of institutions.

3. According to the Hispanic Association of Colleges and Universities (HACU), a Hispanic-serving institution is one that meets a Hispanic enrollment minimum of 25 percent.

Table A-1
Variable Definition and Coding Scheme

Dependent Variable

Campus Racial Tension — Four-item factor scale (see table A-2 for items).

1985 Student Characteristics

Sex	Dichotomous: 1 = "male"; 2 = "female."
Age	Ten-point scale: 1 = "16 or younger," to 10 = "55 or older."
High-school GPA (self-report)	Eight-point scale: 1 = "D," to 8 = "A or A+."
Mother's education	Eight-point scale: 1 = "grammar school or less," to 8 = "graduate degree."
Father's education	Eight-point scale: 1 = "grammar school or less," to 8 = "graduate degree."
Parental Income	Fourteen-point scale: 1 = "less than $6000," to 14 = "$150,000 or more."
Social self-confidence	Three-item factor scale based on student self-ratings (see table A-2).
Expect to protest in college	Four-point scale: 1 = "very little chance," to 4 = "very good chance."
Political view (self-rating)	Five-point scale: 1 = "far right," to 5 = "far left."
Helping to promote racial understanding	Four-point scale: 1 = "not important," to 4 = "essential."

Institutional Characteristics

Institutional Priorities

Expenditures per student:

Student services	Expenditures for admissions and all activities designed to contribute to the emotional, physical, intellectual, cultural, and social development of students outside the formal educational program
Non-repayable aid	Monies given in the form of grants and scholarships to students enrolled in formal coursework. Excludes college work study and Pell grants.

Student Perceptions of Priorities:

Student-centered	Five-item factor scales (see table A-2 for item scales).
Resource/reputation	Five-item factor scales (see table A-2 for item scales).
Commitment to diversity	Four-item factor scales (see table A-2 for item scales).

College composition:

Selectivity	Average SAT of entering freshmen divided by 10 (ACT converted to SAT equivalents using Astin & Henson, 1977).

Enrollment:

Size (total FTE)[1]	Total graduate and undergraduate FTE.
Black percent in 1986	Black undergraduate FTE divided by total undergraduate FTE.
Hispanic percent in 1986 FTE	Hispanic undergraduate FTE divided by total undergraduate.
Black increase (1982–88)[2]	Dichotomous: 1 = "decrease," 2 = "increase" (absolute numbers of undergraduate FTE).
Hispanic increase (1982–88)	Three-point scale: 1 = "decrease," 2 = "no change," 3 = "increase" (absolute numbers of undergraduate FTE).

[1] Three part-time students are equivalent to one FTE.

All institutions in the sample experienced change in black undergraduate enrollment over six years.

Table A-2
Items Constituting Factor Scales

Social Self-Confidence Factor
(Student self-rating compared to the average person his/her age)

    Leadership ability[1]

    Popularity[1]

    Self-Confidence (social)[1]

Campus Racial Tension Factor
(Statements about the freshman college)

    There is a lot of campus racial conflict here[2]

    Students of different racial ethnic origins communicate well with one another[3]

    There is little trust between minority student groups and campus administrators[2]

Institutional Priority: Commitment to Diversity Factor
(Priorities of the freshman college)

    Increase the representation of minorities in the faculty and administration[4]

    Develop among students and faculty an appreciation for a multicultural society[4]

    Recruit more minority students[4]

    Create a diverse multicultural environment on campus[4]

Institutional Priority: Resource/Reputation Factor
(Priorities of the freshman college)

    Increase or maintain institutional prestige[4]

    Enhance the institution's national image[4]

    Hire faculty "stars"[4]

    Raise money for the institution[4]

    Conduct basic and applied research[4]

Institutional Priority: Student-centered Factor
(Statements about the freshman college)

    It is easy to see faculty outside of office hours[5]

    Most students are treated like "numbers in a book"[6]

    Faculty here are interested in students' personal problems[2]

    Faculty here are strongly interested in the academic problems of undergraduates[2]

Note: Full details of the exploratory and confirmatory procedures used to develop factors are reported in Hurtado (1990) and Dey (1991).
[1]Five-point scale: 1 = "bottom 10%" to 5 = "highest 10%."
[2]Four-point scale: 1 = "Disagree strongly" to 4 = "Agree strongly."
[3]Four-point scale: 1 = "Agree strongly" to 4 = "Disagree strongly." (reversed for analyses).
[4]Four-point scale: 1 = "Low Priority" to 4 = "Highest priority."
[5]Three-point scale: 1 = "Not descriptive" to 3 = "Very descriptive."
[6]Three-point scale: 1 = "Very descriptive" to 3 = "Not descriptive." (reversed for analyses).

References

1. Allen, W. R. "Black Student, White Campus: Structural, Interpersonal, and Psychological Correlates of Success." *Journal of Negro Education*, 54 (1985), 134–37.

2. "Black Students in U.S. Higher Education: Toward Improved Access, Adjustment, and Achievement." *The Urban Review*, 20 (1988), 165–87.

3. American Council on Education. "Bush's Plan Would Reduce Pell Grants." *Higher Education and National Affairs*, 40 (11 March 1991).

4. Arce, C. H. "Chicano Participation in Academe: A Case of Academic Colonialism." *Grito del Sol: Chicano Quarterly*, 3 (1978), 75–104.

5. Astin, A. W. "New Evidence on Campus Unrest, 1969–70." *Educational Record*, (Winter 1971), 41–46.

6. *Achieving Educational Excellence*. San Francisco: Jossey-Bass, 1985.

7. *Four Critical Years*. San Francisco: Jossey-Bass, 1977.

8. *The Black Undergraduate: Current Status and Trends in the Characteristics of Freshmen*. Los Angeles: Higher Education Research Institute. 1990.

9. Astin, A. W., and J. W. Henson. "New Measures of College Selectivity." *Research in Higher Education*, 7 (1977), 1–9.

10. Attinasi, L. C., Jr. "Getting In: Mexican Americans' Perceptions of University Attendance and the Implications for Freshman Year Persistence." *Journal of Higher Education*, (May/June 1989), 247–77.

11. Blalock, J. M., Jr. *Toward a Theory of Minority-Group Relations*. New York: Wiley, 1967.

12. Blumer, H. "Race Prejudice as a Sense of Group Position." *Pacific Sociological Review*, 1 (1958), 3–7.

13. Bobo, L., and J. R. Kluegel. "Opposition to Race-Targeting: Self-Interest, Stratification Ideology, or Prejudice?" A paper delivered at the American Association of Public Opinion Research, Phoenix, Arizona, May 1991.

14. Bowles, S., and H. Gintis. *Schooling in Capitalist America*. London: Routledge and Kegan Paul, 1977.

15. Branch, T. *Parting the Waters: America in the Wing Years, 1954–63*. New York: Simon and Schuster, 1989.

16. Brown v. Board of Education. 347 US 483 (1954).

17. Carter, D. J., and R. Wilson. *Minorities in Higher Education: Eighth Annual Status Report*. Washington, D.C.: American Council on Education, 1990.

18. *Minorities in Higher Education: Ninth Annual Status Report*. Washington, D.C.: American Council on Education, 1991.

19. Carter-Williams, M. "The Eroding Status of Blacks in Higher Education: An Issue of Financial Aid." In *Black Education: A Quest for Equity and Excellence*, edited by W. D. Smith and E. W. Chunn. New Brunswick, N.J.: Transaction Publishers, 1989.

20. Dey, E. L. *Perceptions of the College Environment: An Analysis of Organizational, Interpersonal, and Behavioral Influences*. Ph.D. dissertation, University of California Los Angeles, 1991. Ann Arbor: University Microfilms International, No: 9119161.

21. *Beta View*. [Computer program]. Los Angeles: Higher Education Research Institute, 1990.

22. Dey, E. L., A. W. Astin, and W. S. Korn. *The American Freshman: Twenty-Five Year Trends*. Los Angeles: Higher Education Research Institute, 1991.

23. El-Khawas, E. *Campus Trends, 1989*. Higher education panel reports, no. 78. Washington, D.C.: American Council on Education, 1989.

24. Estrada, L. F. "Anticipating the Demographic Future." *Change,* 20 (1988), 14–19.

25. Farrell, W. C. Jr., and C. K. Jones. "Recent Racial Incidents in Higher Education: A Preliminary Perspective." *The Urban Review,* 20 (1988), 211–33.

26. Fossett, M. A., and K. J. Kiecolt. "The Relative Size of Minority Populations and White Racial Attitudes." *Social Science Quarterly,* 70 (1989), 820–35.

27. Giroux, H. A. "Theories of Reproduction and Resistance in the New Sociology of Education: A Critical Analysis." *Harvard Educational Review,* 53 (1983), 257–93.

28. Gunn. P., and E. Epps. *Black Consciousness, Identity, and Achievement: A Study of Students in Historically Black Colleges.* New York: Wiley, 1975.

29. Hurtado, S. *Campus Racial Climates and Educational Outcomes.* Ph.D. dissertation, University of California, Los Angeles, 1990. Ann Arbor: University Microfilms International, No: 9111328.

30. Higher Education Research Institute. *The American College Student. 1989: National Norms for 1985 and 1987 College Freshmen.* Los Angeles: Higher Education Research Institute, 1991.

31. Jackman, M. R. "Prejudice, Tolerance, and Attitudes Toward Ethnic Groups." *Social Science Research,* 6 (1977), 145–69.

32. Jackman, M. R., and M. J. Muha. "Education and Intergroup Attitudes: Moral Enlightenment, Superficial Democratic Commitment, or Ideological Refinement?" *American Sociological Review,* 49 (1984), 751–69.

33. Jacob, J. E. "Black America 1987: An Overview." In *The State of Black America, 1988,* edited by J. Dewart. New York: National Urban League, 1988.

34. Jessor, R. "The Perceived Environment in Psychological Theory and Research." In *Toward a Psychology of Situations: An Interactional Perspective,* edited by D. Magnusson. Hillsdale, N.J.: Lawrence Erlbaum Associates, 1981, 297–317.

35. Kanter, R. M. "Some Effects of Proportions on Group Life: Skewed Sex Ratios and Responses to Token Women." *American Journal of Sociology,* 82 (1977), 965–89.

36. Kiecolt, K. J. "Recent Developments in Attitudes and Social Structure." *Annual Review of Sociology,* 14 (1988), 381–403.

37. Loo, C. M., and G. Rolison. "Alienation of Ethnic Minority Students at a Predominantly White University." *Journal of Higher Education,* 57 (1986), 58–77.

38. McClelland, K. E., and C. J. Auster. "Public Platitudes and Hidden Tensions: Racial Climates at Predominantly White Liberal Arts Colleges." *Journal of Higher Education,* 61 (November/ December 1990), 607–42.

39. Moos, R. H. *Evaluating Educational Environments.* San Francisco: Jossey-Bass, 1979.

40. National Institute against Prejudice and Violence "Conflict Continues on U.S. Campuses." *Forum,* 5 (November 1990), 1–2.

41. Nettles, M. T. "Black and White Students' Academic Performance in Majority White and Majority Black College Settings." In *Desegregating America's Colleges and Universities,* edited by J. B. Williams 111. New York: Teachers College Press, 1988.

42. Nettles, M. T., A. R. Thoeny, and E. J. Gosman. "Comparative and Predictive Analyses of Black and White Students' College Achievement and Experiences." *Journal of Higher Education,* 57 (1986), 289–318.

43. Olivas, M. A. "Research and Theory on Hispanic Education: Students, Finance, and Governance." *Atzlan. International Journal of Chicano Studies Research,* 14 (1983), 111–46.

44. _____. "Research on Latino College Students: A Theoretical Framework for Inquiry." In *Latino College Students,* edited by M. A. Olivas. New York: Teachers College Press, 1986.

45. _____. "Federal Law and Scholarship Policy: An Essay on the Office for Civil Rights, Title VI, and Racial Restrictions." *Journal of College and University Law*, 18 (1991), 21–28.

46. Oliver, M. L., C. J. Rodriguez, and R. A. Mickelson. "Brown and Black in White: The Social Adjustment and Academic Performance of Chicano and Black Students in a Predominantly White University." *The Urban Review: Issues and Ideas in Public Education*, 17 (1985), 3–24.

47. Pascarella, E. T., and P. T. Terenzini. *How College Affects Students*. San Francisco: Jossey-Bass, 1991.

48. Patterson, A. M., W. E. Sedlacek, and F. W. Perry. "Perceptions of Blacks and Hispanics in Two Campus Environments." *Journal of College Student Personnel*, 25 (1984), 513–18.

49. Peterson, M. W., et al. *Black Students on White Campuses: The Impacts of Increased Black Enrollments*. Ann Arbor: Institute for Social Research, 1978.

50. Reyes, M. D., and J. J. Halcón. "Racism in Academia: The Old Wolf Revisited." *Harvard Educational Review*, 58 (1988), 299–314.

51. Richardson, R. C., Jr., and E. F. Skinner. "Adapting to Diversity: Organizational Influences on Student Achievement." *Journal of Higher Education*, 61 (September/ October 1990), 485–511.

52. Skinner, E. F., and R. C. Richardson, Jr. "Making it in a Majority University." *Change*, 20 (May/ June 1988), 34–42.

53. Smith, D. G. "The Challenge of Diversity: Involvement or Alienation in the Academy?" *ASHE-ERIC Higher Education Report* 5, 1989. Washington: George Washington University.

54. Smith, D. H. "Social and Academic Environments of Black Students on White Campuses." *Journal of Negro Education*, 50 (1981), 299–306.

55. Stoecker, J., E. T. Pascarella, and L. M. Wolfe. "Persistence in Higher Education: A 9-year Test of a Theoretical Model." *Journal of College Student Personnel*, 29 (1988), 196–209.

56. Sudarkasa, N. "Black Enrollment in Higher Education: The Unfulfilled Promise of Equality." In *The State of Black America*, edited by J. Dewart. New York: National Urban League, 1988.

57. Tracey, T. J., and W. E. Sedlacek. "A Comparison of White and Black Student Academic Success Using Noncognitive Variables: A LISREL Analysis. *Research in Higher Education*, 27 (1987), 333–48.

58. Tracey, T. J., and W. E. Sedlacek. "Noncognitive Variables in Predicting Academic Success by Race." *Measurement and Evaluation in Guidance*, 16 (1984), 171–78.

59. Trent, W. T. "Student Affirmative Action in Higher Education: Addressing Underrepresentation." In *The Racial Crisis in American Higher Education*, edited by P. G. Altbach and K. Lomotey. Albany: State University of New York Press, 1991.

60. Vellela, T. *New Voices: Student Activism in the '80s and '90s*. Boston: South End Press, 1988.

61. Vera, R. *Texas' Response to the Office of Civil Rights. Progress Made Under the Texas Equal Educational Opportunity Plan for Higher Education*. Claremont: Tomas Rivera Policy Center, 1989.

62. Verdugo, R. R. "Educational Stratification and Hispanics." In *Latino College Students*, edited by M. A. Olivas. New York: Teachers College Press, 1986.

63. Wellman, D. T. *Portraits of White Racism*. New York: Cambridge University Press, 1977.

64. White, T. I., and W. E. Sedlacek. "White Student Attitudes Toward Blacks and Hispanics: Programming Implications." *Journal of Multicultural Counseling and Development*, 15 (October 1987), 171–83.

65. Williams, J. B., III. "Title VI Regulation of Higher Education." In *Desegregating America's Colleges and Universities*, edited by J. B. Williams III. New York: Teachers College Press, 1988.

Understanding the Hiring of Women and Minorities in Educational Institutions

Alison M. Konrad and Jeffrey Pfeffer

The conditions under which women and minorities were hired for managerial positions in higher education administration were studied using data on 821 institutions from the 1978 and 1983 College and University Personnel Association's annual compensation surveys. The percentage of women in a particular job across institutions, the percentage of women in all the administrative positions in an institution, and the fact that the previous occupant of the position was a woman all had a positive, unique effect on the odds that a new hire was a woman. The effects of minority composition on the hiring of minorities were similar.

For some time there has been substantial research interest in the factors that either inhibit or facilitate the entry of women and ethnic minorities into jobs, organizations, and occupations. This interest derives from the fact that the differential allocation of women, for instance, to positions and organizations helps to account for differences in the earnings of women and men with similar human capital endowments (Halaby 1979), as well as from the fact that "sex segregation in the workplace is one of the most visible signs of social inequality" (Bielby and Baron 1984, p. 27). The present study examines the conditions under which women and minorities are hired as administrators in higher education, focusing also on the factors that encourage the hiring of women and minorities for positions that were previously closed to them and the conditions under which students are most likely to come into contact with female and minority authority figures in nontraditional and nonstereotyped positions.

Research on the gender and ethnic composition of educational institutions is particularly important because of recent evidence that demographic composition may affect the educational outcomes of female and minority students. For example, Petersik and Schneir (1980) found a strong positive relationship $(r = .77)$ between the grades obtained by female students and the percentage of female faculty members in the students' departments. Tidball (1980) noted an even stronger positive relationship $(r = .94)$ between the ratio of female faculty to female students of a college and the likelihood that a female graduate from that college would be listed in registries, such as the *Who's Who* series. More recently, Carpenter and Hayden (1987) found that female high school students in single-sex schools had higher enrollments in science courses and higher achievement in general than did their counterparts in coeducational schools in one Australian state, though there was no relationship between the sex composition of the school and the enrollment of female students in science courses or their overall achievement in another Australian state.

Minority students, too, seem to benefit from an academic environment in which minority authority figures are present. Ramirez and Soriano (1982) found that among Hispanic undergraduates who attended high schools with few Hispanic administrators, 67 percent reported that their high school counselors *discouraged* them from attending college, while among those who attended high schools with many Hispanic administrators, 92 percent reported that their high school counselors *encouraged* them to attend college. Because female and minority students appear to benefit from the presence of demographically similar authority figures, it is important to examine the conditions under which female and minority administrators are hired by institutions of higher education.

Previous Research

Previous research on hiring equity in higher education focused almost exclusively on faculty members. A number of findings suggest that female and minority faculty are most underrepresented at wealthy, prestigious, selective research institutions. In a study of 79 universities, Szafran (1984a) found that gender equity in recruitment was associated with low expenditures per student. Tolbert (1986) reported negative correlations between the percentage of female faculty members at an institution and both the selectivity and the revenues per student of that institution. Bach and Perrucci (1984) showed that the proportion of female faculty members increased with a decline in the prestige and selectivity of colleges, but not of universities. Haberfeld and Shenhav (1988) found that the percentage of black faculty members in colleges was double that in universities from 1982 to 1986, although blacks were underrepresented in both sectors of higher education. These findings suggest that female and minority students in selective, prestigious institutions have the least access to demographically similar authority figures.

One factor that affects the placement of women and minorities in the labor market is the proportion of women and minorities in an occupation (Waite and Berryman 1986), community (Semyonov 1988), or organization (Pfeffer and Davis-Blake 1987). Blalock (1956, 1957) and Kanter (1977) both emphasized the importance of numbers and proportions for understanding group processes. Pfeffer and Davis-Blake (1987) found that the proportion of women in a college or university administration affected administrators' earnings, and Wharton and Baron (1987) examined the effects on men's attitudes of the gender composition of the work setting.

Unit of Analysis

The existing research on the position of women and minorities at work has several deficiencies. Most critically, many studies have used the three-digit occupational level of analysis (see, for example, Beller 1984; Bridges 1982; England 1981). As Bielby and Baron (1986) convincingly demonstrated, the occupational level of analysis is less than appropriate for analyzing the place of women or minorities in organizational career and job structures. Occupations are too aggregate a level of analysis because there is substantial within-occupation and between-organization heterogeneity in pay and promotional opportunities (see, for example, Mennerick 1975; Talbert and Bose 1977).

Recent studies have shown that workers experience greater segregation at the level of the job title within the organization than would be expected from the amount of occupational segregation observed. For example, Bielby and Baron (1984, 1986) found that 96 percent of women and men would have to change *jobs* to achieve gender integration of job titles within a large set of (primarily) manufacturing organizations. In comparison, only 70 percent of men and women in the U.S. labor force would have had to change three-digit *occupations* at the same time (1970) to achieve gender integration. Thus, it is important to consider gender and ethnic segregation at all three levels of analysis—the occupation, the organization, and the job within the organization. Szafran (1984b, p. 56) noted, "since the firm is the structural unit within which hiring and promotion decisions are made, there is reason to consider the analysis of labor force processes from an organizational perspective" (see also Tolbert 1986). In spite of this recognition, the unavailability of such data has led to continued analysis at the occupational or industrial level (see, for example, Tienda, Smith, and Ortiz 1987, p. 197). The present data set includes information on specific positions within over 800 comparable organizations, allowing us to examine how between- and within-organization segregation affect hiring outcomes.

Second, studies that have examined the place of women in job categories within organizations (Bielby and Baron 1984, 1986; Mennerick 1975: Rosenbaum 1985) have examined as a dependent variable the percentage of women in classes or categories of jobs. Using the job categories as defined by the organization as the unit of analysis may cause some analytic problems, since job classification systems themselves may be endogenous with respect to the gender composition of organizations. Baron and Bielby (1986) observed that in times of economic hardship, employers eliminated from their organizations prestigious, high-paying, specialty positions held primarily by men, incorporating these tasks into less prestigious, lower-paying jobs held primarily by women. In times of economic boom, employers did the opposite, increasing the number and specialization of job titles to create an internal labor market through which male workers could advance. Baron, Davis-Blake, and Bielby (1986) showed that the characteristics of job ladders, such as their length and whether a given job is dead-end, are related to the gender composition of the job.

That the process of the proliferation or decline of job titles and the structure of jobs in career ladders are linked to gender composition suggests that by taking organizationally defined job categories as the unit of analysis, researchers may miss some of the segregation process. The present data allow us to avoid this problem to some extent because the positions studied were defined by the survey instrument in terms of duties and responsibilities. Moreover, we look at high-level positions in which there is only one incumbent (for instance, there is only one organizational president) and thus can examine the hiring of specific jobs in specific settings by either women or minorities.

It seems a natural extension of the research begun by Bielby and Baron (1984, 1956) and Baron and Bielby (1985) to consider not only gender composition at the level of job title, but individual hiring decisions and their outcomes in organizations. The overall pattern of gender and ethnic segregation is the result of the individual hiring decisions that occur when positions are vacant. Thus, just as "organizational variation is . . . overlooked by studies at the individual and occupational levels" (Baron and Bielby 1985, p. 235), variation in hiring practices with respect in specific positions may be masked by analyses at the organizational or even the job-title level of analysis. Therefore, it seems useful to extend the analysis to investigate how the gender and ethnic composition of organizations is produced and reproduced at an even more detailed level of analysis—the individual hire.

Simulated and Actual Effect

The literature on hiring has seldom been able to examine actual outcomes with respect to ethnicity and gender. Some research has examined the use of various criteria and selectivity (Cohen and Pfeffer 1984; Collins 1979). Numerous experimental studies have presented subjects with résumés that were identical except for something such as a name that signifies gender or a picture that signifies ethnicity. Nieva and Gutek (1980), for instance, summarized the large body of literature on gender bias in evaluations that was comprised almost exclusively of these "hypothetical-person" studies. A more recent review (Powell 1987) summarized the findings of 6 studies on gender effects in actual recruitment situations and over 40 studies of gender effects in "hypothetical-person" situations. Studies of ethnic effects on actual hiring outcomes in work organizations are virtually nonexistent, as far as we know.

This study capitalizes on the availability of a fairly unique data set to examine the conditions under which women or minorities are hired for a set of high-level college and university administrative positions, including such jobs as president, provost, deans, and directors. Predictions concerning the hiring of women and minorities were tested on 6,211 high-level administrative positions in higher education that turned over between 1978 and 1983. In the next section, the relevant literature is described and hypotheses for the present research are formulated. Then the data are described and factors that affect the gender and ethnicity of new hires are examined.

Finally, an analysis exploring the conditions under which women and minorities are hired for jobs, organizations, and positions that have been traditionally closed to them is presented and discussed.

Background and Hypotheses

This study focuses on four conditions on the demand side of the labor market that may affect discrimination and segregation in hiring. These conditions include the relative economic attractiveness of jobs, perceptual biases that are enhanced under conditions of uncertainty, organizations' susceptibility to enforcement of the federal guidelines for equal employment opportunity (EEO), and demographic group power.

The supply of labor that is available to organizations is another critical influence on hiring practices. Ideally, an examination of hiring would consider the pool of applicants available for each job opening, but these data were not available for the present analysis. We were able to introduce two measures of the probable gender and ethnic composition of these applicant pools, however. First, we calculated the proportion of women and minorities in each position in the national sample of institutions. This figure served as a measure of the proportion of the labor force with job-specific experience that was female or minority. Although specific applicant pools may have differed from the national proportion of experienced women and minorities in the job, no published studies of which we are aware include information on specific applicant pools, and the national percentages provide some control for the probable demographic distribution of applicants. This measure does not provide any information about applicants without job-specific experience. However, since experienced candidates are generally preferred for high-level positions like the ones we are studying, the pool of inexperienced candidates probably had less impact on final hiring outcomes.

The second measure we constructed as a control for the probable applicant pool was the percentage of women and minorities who are currently employed at each institution. To the extent that vacancies are filled by promotion from within, the percentage of women and minorities employed offers an estimate of the potential pool of candidates in the internal labor market. In the following discussion of the effects of the demand side on female and minority hiring, it should be kept in mind that demand-side effects are hypothesized to occur when these two measures of supply are controlled.

The Relative Attractiveness of Jobs

Strober (1984) considered the pay level of the job relative to other options to be the most important factor affecting change in the gender assignment of jobs. She suggested that when education and other job requirements are controlled for, White men move into women's jobs when the salaries of those jobs are higher than other available jobs in the labor market and out of those jobs when the salaries are lower. She argued that the feminization of both public school teaching (Strober 1984) and bank telling (Strober and Arnold 1987) could be explained by the relative attractiveness of the salaries.

Strober (1984) also argued that minorities are in more poorly compensated occupations than are Whites. In an analysis of the changing demographic composition of occupations from the 1960 to the 1980 censuses. Strober and Catanzarite (1988) reported that Black men and Black women moved into occupations that White men and White women left. White women also moved into occupations that White men left. Strober and Catanzarite attributed this movement to the relative attractiveness of occupational earnings.

Other research findings also support the notion that relative earnings are important for the gender and ethnic composition of jobs and occupations. Many studies suggest that women and minorities enter nontraditional occupations only when White men have many attractive options, such as when there is high growth and low unemployment (Abrahamson and Sigelman 1987; Albelda 1986). For example, Szafran (1984b) found that the percentage of bank professionals who were women or minorities was negatively associated with high unemployment in the community. Other research has shown that women and minorities are most likely to be hired by low-paying organizations (Blau 1977). Szafran (1984a), Tolbert (1986), and Bach and Perrucci (1984) all reported associations between an increased percentage of female faculty members and factors that are likely to be associated with low faculty salaries—for example, low expenditures per student, low revenues per student, and low selectivity and prestige.

Therefore, on the basis of this existing literature, we expect to find that women and minorities are hired more often for lower-paying jobs and for jobs in organizations with lower levels of resources. We also expect that a low salary level is one of the conditions that allows women and minorities to enter nontraditional jobs (those with a higher percentage of men and Whites, respectively).

Perceptual Biases and Uncertainty

Jobs and occupations come to be seen as typical and more appropriate for men or for women and for Whites or for minorities. The existence of customary gender labels for occupations was documented by Nieva and Gutek (1981). Shepard and Hess (1975), for instance, found that for 28 of 43 different jobs they studied, the respondents showed 90 percent agreement on the gender label of the task. Krefting, Berger, and Wallace (1978) demonstrated that the gender labeling of an occupation is strongly determined by the percentage of women in that occupation in the nation as a whole. Wharton and Baron (1987) reported that men in industries and occupations with a higher percentage of women on a national level were more likely than were other men to say that women could adequately perform their jobs. The existence of ethnic labels of occupations was documented in Moore and Johnson's (1983) research on elementary school teachers' occupational expectations for their minority students, which closely matched the actual percentages of minorities in the national labor force.

In addition to jobs in general, individual positions in organizations may be typified for a particular sex or ethnic group by their particular history. Bielby and Baron (1986, p. 787) noted that "once established, sex labels of job titles acquire tremendous inertia, even when similar work is done by the opposite sex elsewhere in the same establishment or in other settings." This local history may have important effects on hiring because it is information that is widely available to decision makers. Thus, we expect that the gender or ethnicity of the previous incumbent in a position will determine, in part, the gender or ethnicity of the subsequent hire, even when the percentages of women or minorities in the institution and in the job nationally are held constant.

Evidence suggests that the extent to which these typifications affect hiring is determined by the level of uncertainty. According to Kanter's (1977) theory of homosocial reproduction, the level of uncertainty about job activities and the relationships among jobs is important in determining the hiring of women, and this theory may be extended to the situation of minorities. Uncertainty creates the need for fast and accurate communication among workers for organizational success. Since demographic similarity may enhance the speed and quality of communication, a demographically homogeneous group is hired for uncertain jobs (Nieva and Gutek 1980; Salancik and Pfeffer 1978). This reasoning suggests that women and minorities will be hired for administrative jobs only when uncertainty in the situation is reduced in some way.

The complexity of the tasks being accomplished increases uncertainty and thus the tendency to exclude dissimilar others from high-level managerial positions. In the present case, we argue that universities, which are involved in both teaching and research, perform more varied and complex activities than do four-year colleges or two-year colleges, which are much more concerned strictly with teaching. The greater range of activities and uncertainty associated with research may make universities somewhat less likely to hire women or minorities. The higher level of uncertainty in universities also may diminish the prospects of nontraditional employment for women and minorities.

Another potential source of uncertainty in the hiring process is the extent to which the applicant is well known to the employer. Uncertainty about an applicant's abilities and whether an applicant will fit the organization are likely to be diminished when an administrator is promoted from within, rather than hired from outside, the organization. When determining promotions, decision makers have a greater opportunity both to determine the skills and abilities of female and minority candidates and to develop a history of working with these individuals so that communication is enhanced and uncertainty about their fit is reduced. Studies that have found greater sex and ethnic differences in hiring than in promotion support this notion (Eberts and Stone 1985; Grandjean 1981; Lewis 1986).

We hypothesized that women and minorities would be more likely to be promoted from within than hired from outside the organization. Though the literature has examined the relative likelihood of promotion and hiring differences, we found no studies that examined whether promotion was more likely than was hiring to lead to nontraditional employment for women and minorities. We hypothesized that being inside the organization would increase the likelihood that women and minorities would be hired for nontraditional positions or would be hired at all because decision makers would be more likely to assign women and minorities who were well known to them to nonstereotyped positions, since they would be well acquainted with the individuals' particular strengths.

Susceptibility to EEO Enforcement

Salancik (1979) argued that the level of governmental pressure to fulfill affirmative action requirements is an important force toward integration, and the work of DiPrete (1987), DiPrete and Soule (1986, 1988). and Leonard (1985a, 1985b) supports this point. The idea that the enforcement of affirmative action requirements increases the hiring of women and minorities is based on the idea that in the absence of such enforcement, White men are preferred and this "taste for discrimination" is indulged. Factors that may enhance or inhibit the indulgence of discriminatory tastes include the level of resources and governmental surveillance.

High levels of resources enhance the ability to indulge a taste for White male labor because these workers are more expensive than are women or minorities. As was argued previously, when employers have the necessary resources, they can attract White men by offering high wages.

We argue that public institutions are more susceptible to EEO enforcement than are private ones because of their greater reliance on governmental funding and, as a result, that more women and minorities should be hired in public institutions. Private institutions are less dependent on governmental funding and may be subject to different normative and institutional pressures, as well as less public oversight. Research suggests that minorities fare better in public than in private employment settings. Using data from the 1970 census, Kaufman (1986) reported that Blacks were more likely to be employed in the public than in the private sector. In a study of job changes using data from the 1973 Current Population Survey, Pomer (1986) found that Black workers were more likely to advance from low-paying occupations to lower-level manual and nonmanual jobs in the public sector, while such movement was more likely for Whites in the private sector.

Women's comparative employment opportunities in the public and private sectors have received less attention. Szafran (1984a) found that public universities were no more likely than were private ones to show sex equity in recruiting faculty members. Most studies have investigated wage differences by sex and have consistently found fewer differences in organizations that were public (Asher and Popkin 1984; Johnson 1978; Smith 1976).

The research cited here did not examine either specific job titles within organizations or individual hires. In the case of the hiring of administrators in colleges and universities, we expected that public institutions would be more likely to integrate their work forces than would private institutions. Thus, we hypothesized that women and minorities would be more likely to be hired as administrators in public than in private institutions and that women and minorities would be more likely to enter nontraditional jobs in public institutions.

Demographic Group Power

Demographic group power may also be expected to affect the hiring of women and minorities. When they hold more administrative positions, women or minorities can exert more influence on the hiring decision. Given the preference of individuals for similar over dissimilar others (Antill 1983; Hill, Rubin, and Peplau 1976; Kandel 1978), women should be more likely to prefer women and minorities to prefer minorities for administrative positions. In his study of gender equity in the recruitment of faculty members Szafran (1984a) found that as the proportion of female administrators in the university increased, so did the probability that female faculty members would be hired in proportion to their representation in the labor market, a finding that supports our argument.

Since people are least likely to stereotype demographically similar others (Park and Rothbart 1982), institutions with many female or minority administrators should also be most likely to hire women and minorities, respectively, for nontraditional positions. Therefore, the presence of female and minority decision makers should most likely open, through the hiring process, universities, jobs, and positions that have traditionally been closed to women and minorities.

Numerous female or minority administrators in an institution may also affect the probability of hiring a woman or minority through the process of role modeling and the reduction of uncertainty. Decision makers in organizations with a high proportion of female administrators, for example, are more likely than are others to have observed women performing nontraditional administrative roles competently. Therefore, they may be more likely to hire women for nontraditional positions. A parallel argument would hold for minorities. This argument also leads us to expect that women and minorities will have the highest probability of entering universities and nontraditional positions at institutions with a strong representation of their own demographic groups in the administration.

Data

The data used in the present study were taken from the College and University Personnel Association's Annual Administrative Compensation Survey for 1978-79 and 1983-84. The survey is sent to approximately 3,000 colleges and universities each year, and the response rate is usually about 50 percent. The survey asks some general questions about the size, resources, and source of support of the institutions, as well as specific questions about numerous administrative positions. The responding institutions are anonymous, so we have no way of checking the data against other published sources. The form asks respondents to report the salary for each position and the gender, ethnicity, and tenure (in the position) of the current incumbent. The survey also asks whether the current incumbent was promoted from within or hired from outside the organization. The positions included in the survey are managerial-level administrative positions, such as presidents, vice presidents, financial and legal officers, directors of student services (for example, student health services, student union, and student placement), directors of computer centers and other research facilities, directors of alumni and community relations programs, and deans. All the positions included in the survey specified the person heading some administrative unit or department in the college or university. Although an organization may occasionally have two people jointly heading an administrative unit, such instances should be rare, so we can assert with some confidence that each position had only one incumbent.

In 1978–79, 1,328 institutions responded to the survey and reported on 28,100 positions. In 1983–84, 1,517 institutions reported on 38,723 positions. We restricted our sample to two-year colleges, four-year colleges, and universities, eliminating from the analyses institutions that were only law schools, medical schools, or religious seminaries, as well as schools for which data were not available for both periods (we considered only positions that were reported on at both times). The result is a sample of 821 institutions that reported on the same 11,412 positions in both periods.

To analyze the conditions that were related to the hiring of women and minorities, we directed our attention only to those positions that had experienced turnover during the period and thus had a new hire in the job in 1983. Turnover was determined by examining the tenure of the incumbent in 1983–84, as well as in 1978–79 When there was any ambiguity about the validity of the data on tenure or the assessment of turnover (such as when the reported tenure was 7 years in 1983–84 and 10 years in 1978–79), the case was dropped from the analysis. Those positions for which 1983–84 incumbents had fewer than 5 years of tenure in their current positions and all other logical aspects of the data seemed all right were considered to have experienced turnover during the period. Of the 11,412 positions included in the total sample, 6,211 turned over between 1978–79 and 1983–84. Table 1 presents information about the variables used in the reported analyses, including descriptions, means, and standard deviations, and Table 2 presents the correlations.

Results

First, we examined the extent to which women and minorities were segregated in and excluded from certain jobs and organizations. A significant level of segregation in the data must be documented and closed jobs and organizations must be identified before it becomes reasonable to examine conditions under which women and minorities are brought into these previously closed jobs. Second, we investigated how well the hiring of women and minorities could be predicted from the pattern of positions in which women and minorities were most likely to be found in 1978. An examination of the independent variables that measure the demographic composition of jobs, organizations, and positions enables us to see the effects of potential applicant pools and the typification of jobs by gender and ethnicity. Then we added other independent variables to the model to see if the predictions on hiring could be improved. Finally, we explored the conditions under which women and minorities were most likely to be hired for nontraditional positions.

Table 1
Description of Variables, Means, and Standard Deviations for Jobs
Experiencing Turnover, 1978–83 ($N = 6,211$)

Description of variables	Mean	SD
Female '83: Dummy variable indicating that a woman was hired between 1978 and 1983.	.23	.15
Female '78: Dummy variable indicating that the previous incumbent in the position was a woman.	.15	.36
% F job: Percentage of women in the job for the sample of 821 institutions in 1978.	17.0	13.4
Inside hire dummy: New incumbent for the position hired from within the same institution.	.47	.50
Occupational earnings: Average salary reported for the job in the sample of 821 institutions in 1978.	26,197	7,325
Organizational size: A factor score comprised of the four variables, full-time equivalent (FTE) faculty, FTE students, FTE staff, and total budget in 1978.	.29	1.25
Student resources: A factor score comprised of the three variables, FTE faculty/FTE students, FTE staff/FTE students, and total budget/FTE students in 1978.	.00	.97
Faculty resources: A factor score comprised of the two variables, FTE staff/FTE faculty and total budget/FTE faculty in 1978.	.08	.84
Private institution dummy.	.39	.49
University dummy.	.48	.50
% F Organization: Percentage of women in administrative positions in the institution in 1978.	.16	.10
Non-White '83: Dummy variable indicating that a minority person was hired between 1978 and 1983.	.05	.22
Non-White '78" Dummy variable indicating that the previous incumbent in the position was a minority person.	.04	.19
% NW job: Percentage of minority persons in the job for the sample of 821 institutions in 1978.	5.6	5.8
% NW organization: Percentage of minority persons in administrative positions in the institution in 1978.	.04	.06

We studied hiring patterns at three different levels of analysis. First, we examined the job level by calculating the percentage of women and minorities occupying each of the 69 jobs in the entire sample of organizations. All the 69 job categories in our analysis would be considered a single occupation in the three-digit census classification: "administrators, education and related fields." This variable served as a control for the percentage of women and minorities among those who were potentially available in several narrowly defined external labor markets.

Second, we investigated segregation and composition at the *organizational* level of analysis by calculating the percentage of women and minorities occupying any administrative position included in the survey for the college or university administration as a whole. Using this variable, we could control for the potential pool of applicants for internal promotions and determine whether organizations that already had many women or minorities, respectively, in administrative positions had different hiring patterns than did others.

Third, we explored the level of the specific position within the organization by taking into account the gender and ethnicity of the incumbent in the position in 1978–79. In this way, we could determine whether women and minorities were more likely to be hired for specific positions that were previously held by members of their own groups once potential applicant pools in the internal and external labor markets were controlled.

Most of the jobs we examined were numerically dominated by men and Whites. Women made up 18 percent of the incumbents in 1978 and 22 percent in 1983. Minorities constituted 6 percent of the incumbents in both years. Twenty-three percent of the new hires were women, and 5 percent were minorities. Table 3 shows the positions for which 40 percent or more of the new hires were women or minorities. Women made up 40 percent or more of the new hires in 15 of the 69 jobs, and minorities constituted 40 percent or more of the new hires in two jobs (both of which were on the list of jobs for which at least 40 percent of the new hires were women).

To assess the degree of segregation experienced by the sample of workers, we used a well-known measure, Duncan and Duncan's (1955) segregation indexes. Calculation of the segregation indexes showed that the present set of jobs were segregated by gender to a greater extent than by ethnicity. In 1978, 39 percent of men and women would have had to change jobs to produce gender integration. In 1983, this figure dropped slightly to 37 percent. By comparison, in 19781 24 percent of Whites and minorities would have had to change jobs to produce ethnic integration. In 1983, this figure rose slightly to 25 percent. The fact that jobs and labor pools were

Table 2
Correlation Matrix

	2	3	4	5	6	7	8	9	10	11	12	13	14	15
1. Female '83 dummy	29	33	06	−21	−09	01	00	09	−08	16	05	06	13	03
2. Female '88 dummy		36	00	−19	−10	01	−02	10	−10	27	05	04	14	01
3. % F job			00	−48	−01	00	−01	05	−02	03	12	11	41	−01
4. Inside hire dummy				−01	09	01	05	−10	06	−07	00	00	03	02
5. Occupational earnings					10	00	03	−10	05	−05	−04	−06	−20	03
6. Organizational size						23	35	−32	50	−39	05	02	05	03
7. Student resources							08	22	08	02	−02	−01	00	02
8. Faculty resources								10	19	−10	02	02	01	04
9. Private institution dummy									−24	31	−08	−06	−05	−18
10. University dummy										−43	04	02	02	04
11. % F organization											02	02	−03	04
12. Non-White '83 dummy												23	29	16
13. Non-White '78 dummy													32	29
14. % NW job														02
15. % NW organization														

Table 3
Positions for Which Women and Minorities Constituted 40 Percent or More of the New Hires

Position	Percentage of New Hires: Female	Number of New Hires
Dean of nursing	86	14
Director of affirmative action	59	81
Director, bookstore	51	156
Director, student placement	51	214
Dean, special programs	50	6
Director, public relations	46	138
Director, libraries	45	255
Director, legal services	44	25
Director, information office	44	79
Dean, social work	44	18
Director, community service	43	42
Director, housing and food	42	24
Registrar	41	229
Director, personnel	40	135
Director, financial aid	40	302

Position	Percentage of New Hires: Minorities	Number of New Hires
Director, affirmative action	56	81
Dean, social work	44	18

segregated more by gender than by ethnicity suggests that competition with women for desirable jobs is more important than is competition with minorities. Since women make up a much higher proportion of the work force than do minorities, they pose a greater threat of displacement to the more expensive White men.

In addition to estimating segregation by jobs, we also estimated gender and ethnic segregation at the organizational level, that is, the extent to which men and women, Whites and minorities were found in separate organizations. While the jobs were segregated by gender to a greater extent than by ethnicity, the organizations were segregated by ethnicity to a greater extent than by gender. The Duncan segregation indexes showed that 42 percent of men and women would have had to change organizations to produce gender integration in 1978 and that 37 percent would have had to change in 1983.

The analogous figures are strikingly higher for ethnic minorities. In 1978, 68 percent of Whites and minorities would have had to change organizations to produce ethnic integration, and 64 percent would have had to change in 1983. The extremely high level of between-organization ethnic segregation suggests that the maintenance of social distance between ethnic groups may be more important, perhaps, than may the maintenance of social distance between men and women. Men and women may be in different jobs, but they work together in the same organizations more frequently than do Whites and minorities. With regard to predicting the hiring of women and minorities, univariate analyses showed that both women and minorities were significantly more likely to be hired for jobs, organizations, and positions held by members of their own group in the past. As shown by the univariate analyses depicted in Table 4, women were significantly more likely to be hired for (1) jobs having a higher percentage of women in 1978, (2) organizations having a higher percentage of women in 1978, and (3) positions having a previous female incumbent in 1978. The findings for minority hires, also in Table 4, were similar. These findings document the existence of a hiring process during the late 1970s and early 1980s that tended to maintain existing patterns of segregation.

Table 4
Degree to Which Women and Minorities Were Hired
for Positions Typically Held by Members of Their Own Group

Variable	Percentage of Female Hires	Percentage of Male Hires	t	df	p
Male-dominated job (71% male or greater)	68.9	87.8	17.6	6112	<.001
Male-dominated organization (71% male or greater)	70.1	90.5	20.2	6079	<.001
Position previously held by a woman	41.8	10.5	–29.3	6053	<.001

Variable	Percentage of Minority Hires	Percentage of White Hires	t	df	p
White-dominated job (9l% white or greater)	79.4	94.7	12.7	6098	<.001
White-dominated organization (91% white or greater)	52.7	90.7	24.4	6026	<.001
Position previously held by a minority person	41.4	3.3	–35.1	5974	<.001

Multivariate analyses confirmed that there were separate effects at all three levels of analysis—the job, the organization, and the specific position within the organization—on the hiring of both women and minorities. A logistic regression equation predicting the gender of the new hire from the percentage of women in the job, the percentage of women in the organization, and the gender of the previous occupant of the position was conducted to determine the extent to which the gender of new hires could be correctly predicted by these variables alone. A parallel analysis was conducted to predict the hiring of minorities. The results of these analyses are shown in Table 5. Examining the odds coefficients shows that an increase of 1 percent female in the *job* increased the odds that a woman would be hired by a ratio of 1.06 (that is, since the odds of hiring a woman were at a base rate of 23:77, an increase of 1 percent female in the job increased the odds of hiring a woman to 24:76 and an increase of 10 percent female in the job increased the odds of hiring a woman to 76:24). An increase of 10 percent minority in the job increased the odds of hiring a minority from 5:95 to 34:66. An increase of 10 percent female in the *organization* increased the odds of hiring a woman from 23.77 to 38.62. An increase of 10 percent minority in the organization increased the odds of hiring a minority from 5:95 to 40:60. Having a previous woman or minority in a position doubled to tripled the odds that the new hire would be a woman (the odds increased from 23:77 to 42:58) or minority (the odds increased from 5:95 to 13:87), respectively.

Since over a third of the minority hires were women, the two dependent variables of gender and ethnicity were confounded somewhat. To examine whether this confounding affected the specification of the prediction equations, analyses were run to predict the gender and ethnicity of new hires from both the gender-composition (percentage of females in the job, percentage of females in the organization, and a woman previously in the position) and the ethnic-composition variables (percentage of minorities in the job, percentage of minorities in the organization, and a minority person previously in the position). Including all six variables in the analysis significantly improved the fit of the logistic regression model predicting the hiring of women (chi-square = 8.95, $df = 3$, $p < .05$). However, neither the percentage of minorities in the job, the percentage of minorities in the organization, nor the existence of a previous minority incumbent in the position attained statistical significance at the .05 level as predictors of the hiring of women. For this reason, we decided not to include the minority-composition variables in subsequent analyses of the hiring of women. Including all six variables in the analysis had no effect on the fit of the model predicting the hiring of minorities (chi-square = 5.54, $df = 3$, N.S.), so we decided not to include the gender-composition variables in subsequent analyses of the hiring of minorities.

Table 5
Logistic Regressions Predicting the Hiring of Women and Minorities from Previous Segregation

Female Hire in 1983[a]	Logit Coefficient	S.E.	Odds Coefficient
Independent Variables in 1978			
% F job	.05***	.003	1.06
% F organization	3.02***	.23	20.49
Female '78	.89***	.90	2.44

Minority Hire in 1983[b]	Logit Coefficient	S.E.	Odds Coefficient
Independent Variables in 1978			
% NW job	.07***	.006	1.07
% NW organization	4.86***	.38	129.02
Non-White '78	1.08***	.20	2.94

*** $p < .001$.
[a] $-2 \times$ log likelihood = 1088.62, $df = 3$, $n = 5371$.
[b] $-2 \times$ log likelihood = 733.09, $df = 3$, $n = 5357$.

Of course, the demographic composition of jobs and organizations and the race and gender of previous incumbents in positions is not random. Because demographic composition may be affected by a number of properties of organizations and positions, it is necessary to expand the analysis to control for these variables to ensure that the effects of composition and incumbency remain. Furthermore, we have argued that some of these factors, such as resources, being an inside hire, and the salary for the position, have theoretically expected effects on who gets hired.

Adding these variables to the logistic regressions predicting hiring improved the fit of the models for both women (chi-square = 63.57. $df = 7$, $p < .001$) and minorities (chi-square = 15.13, $df = 7$, $p < .05$). The results arc presented in Table 6. As expected, women were less likely to be hired for highly paid jobs and more likely to be hired from inside than from outside organizations. Unexpectedly, women were more likely to be hired by organizations that were rich in faculty resources. Since the faculty-resources variable included the ratio of staff to faculty, perhaps women were hired more often at these institutions because their salaries were lower and by hiring women, these institutions could provide faculty with greater staff support for a lower cost.

Minorities were more likely to be hired by public than by private organizations, as expected, but public control did not affect the hiring of women. In the case neither of sender nor of ethnicity did being in a university significantly affect hiring. For both women and minorities, the percentage in the job, the percentage in the organization, and the presence of a woman or minority previously in the position continued to be statistically significant predictors of hiring even when the new variables were added. Moreover, a comparison of the coefficients with those in Table 5 indicates that the additional variables have almost no effect on the previous estimates of effect sizes.

To explore the conditions under which women or minorities were more likely to be hired for nontraditional locations in the job structure, we estimated an expanded logistic regression model that included six interaction terms. The interaction terms in equation 1 showed whether, for example, the percentage of women in the job predicted the gender of a new hire more strongly in a private than in a public institution, as we would predict. The interaction terms in equation 2 showed whether, for example, the presence of a female incumbent in a job in 1978 predicted the gender of a new hire more strongly in a private than in a public institution, as we predicted.

The results for the interaction effects in the analyses, displayed in Table 7, showed that the conditions producing gender integration in hiring were different from those producing ethnic integration. Women were most likely to be hired for men's jobs and positions that were low paying, as was predicted by Strober (1984) and Strober and Arnold (1987). Also as expected,

Table 6
Logistic Regressions Predicting the Hiring of Women and Minorities
from Segregation and Other Organizational Characteristics

Female Hire in 1983[a]	Logit Coefficient	S.E.	Odds Coefficient
Independent Variables in 1978			
% F job	.05***	.004	1.05
% F organization	2.79***	.27	16.28
Female '78	.87***	.09	2.38
Occupational earnings	−.00002*	7 x 10−6	1.00
Student resources	.04	.04	—
Faculty resources	.08*	.04	1.09
Inside hire (1 = yes)	.45***	.07	1.57
Organizational size	−.14**	.05	.87
Private institution (1 = yes)	.10	.09	—
University (1 = yes)	.03	.09	—

Minority Hire in 1983	Logit Coefficient	S.E.	Odds Coefficient
Independent Variables in 1978			
% NW job	.07***	.006	1.07
% NW organization	4.86***	.39	119.58
Non-White '78	1.08***	.20	2.94
Occupational earnings	−.00001	.00001	—
Student resources	−.06	.07	—
Faculty resources	.03	.08	—
Inside hire (1 = yes)	−.002	.13	—
Organizational size	.05	.07	—
Private institution (1 = yes)	−.40*	.16	.67
University (1 = yes)	.03	.15	—

*$p < .05$.
**$p < .01$.
***$p < .001$.
[a] $-2 \, X \log$ likelihood = 1152.17, $df = 10$, $n = 5,371$.
[b] $-2 \, X \log$ likelihood = 748.22, $df = 10$, $n = 5,357$.

women were more likely to be hired for men's jobs and positions in public than in private institutions, perhaps because of the greater pressure for EEO. Women were also more likely to be hired for men's jobs in organizations with many women in the administration, perhaps because female decision makers are more likely to open up opportunities that were previously closed to women. Unexpectedly, women were more likely to be hired for nontraditional jobs and positions in universities than in colleges. This finding may be due to the fact that universities are more visible than are colleges and therefore are more likely to be targets of affirmative action enforcers.

For minorities, hiring from inside the institution was most likely to produce integration. Minorities who were hired from the inside were more likely to be placed in nontraditional jobs than were minorities hired from the outside. This finding suggests the importance of reducing uncertainty about applicants for the placement of minorities into nontraditional jobs.

Discussion

The main conclusion about the hiring of women and minorities for higher administrative positions is that the segregation of the past is one of the most pervasive influences on the hiring patterns of the present. Job vacancies in labor markets that are comprised of a high proportion of women and minorities are most likely to be filled by women and minorities. Organizations in which many women or minorities are currently employed are most likely to place women and

Table 7
Logistic Regressions Exploring the Conditions Under Which
Women and Minorities Were Hired for Nontraditional Jobs and Positions[a]

Measure of Traditional	Female Hire in 1983	
	Equation 1 — % F Job	Equation 2 — Female '78
Inside hire x traditional	−.0006	.04
	(.006)	(.18)
% F organization x university	−1.30	−.52
	(.90)	(.93)
% F organization x traditional	−.06#	.55
	(.03)	(.96)
University x traditional	−.03***	.49*
	(.007)	(.21)
Private institution x traditional	.02***	.45*
	(.007)	(.19)
Occupational earnings x traditional	$-9 \times 10{-7}$#	$-6 \times 10{-5}$*
	$(5 \times 10{-7})$	$(2 \times 10{-5})$

Measure of Traditional	Minority Hire in 1983	
	Equation 1 — % NW Job	Equation 2 — Non-White '78
Inside hire x traditional	−.03*	.29
	(.01)	(.39)
% NW organization x university	−2.05	−2.53
	(1.59)	(1.71)
% NW organization x traditional	−.08	−.70
	(.13)	(1.99)
University x traditional	.001	.31
	(.01)	(.42)
Private institution x traditional	.002	−.34
	(.02)	(.47)
Occupational earnings x traditional	$-1 \times 10{-6}$	$2 \times 10{-5}$
	$(4 \times 10{-6})$	$(3 \times 10{-5})$

#$p < .10$.
*$p < .05$.
***$p < .001$.

[a] Only the logit coefficients (and their standard errors) for the interaction terms are shown in the table. All main effects in Table 6 were controlled in these analyses. Equation 1 examines the conditions under which women and minorities are hired for nontraditional *jobs*. Equation 2 examines the conditions under which women and minorities are hired for nontraditional *positions* within organizations. These results did not change when controls for region were entered into the equation.

minorities in vacant positions. This finding is partly due to the fact that some vacancies are filled through promotion from within, but these organizations are more likely to hire women and minorities from the external labor market as well.

Positions that previously had a female incumbent are most likely to be filled subsequently by women, and positions that previously had a minority incumbent are most likely to be filled subsequently by minorities, regardless of the demographic composition of the internal and external labor forces. This finding suggests that positions in specific organizations develop gender and ethnic typifications as a result of their local histories of incumbents in the jobs. The conclusion for EEO policies is that it is difficult to get women or minorities placed in positions from which they have been excluded in the past, but once the first woman or minority person is hired, subsequent women and minority persons, respectively, are much more likely to be hired. Adding other organizational factors to the analysis alters this conclusion little.

Because our findings showed evidence of gender and ethnic typification and segmentation at fine levels of analysis, we conclude that the large body of work on the gender and ethnic segmentation of occupations needs to be augmented by attention to segregation among organizations and among positions in an organization. We find gender and ethnic segregation among a set of jobs that are considered a single occupational category in most published studies of segmentation. We also find between- and within-organization segregation that studies using broadly defined occupations as the unit of analysis cannot examine.

The present study did not examine the labor supply that is available to hiring organizations. Clearly, it would have been preferable to have data on the education and work experience of all the applicants for each job vacancy, so these factors could be controlled while sex and ethnicity effects were examined. Like others who have analyzed related issues (DiPrete and Soule 1988; Lewis 1986; Seeborg, Seeborg, and Zegeye 1986), we have no data, nor do we know of extant data, that permit the analysis of specific applicant pools. The present study adds to this substantial literature a focus on organizational features that contribute to the nontraditional hiring and promotion of women and minorities.

Although the present data set did not include information on the specific candidate pools for each vacancy, it did include measures of the demographic composition of the national labor markets for each vacancy. Thus, we were able to include an assessment of the percentage of experienced workers in the labor market who were women or minorities. The data set also included the percentage of women and minority administrators in the institution as a control for the potential pool of individuals who were available for internal promotions. These data were limited because they did not include comparisons of the qualifications of the female and minority labor pools with those of the White male labor pool. However, they provide information on the demographic composition of the labor pools that were defined much more narrowly than previous studies were able to achieve.

After gender and ethnic composition at the different levels of analysis are considered, there are some, but not many, theoretically expected effects of other organizational and positional attributes that often have different consequences for women and minorities. For instance, as expected, the likelihood of women being hired was lower for higher-paying jobs and higher if the women were already in the organization. However, there was no effect of either salary or being an insider on the hiring of minorities, but there was an observed effect of public versus private control.

It is clear, however, that at least for these positions during the periods under study, such factors as resources, type of institution, form of control, and size are much less important than are compositional and incumbency factors in predicting the hiring of women and minorities. The typification of positions, at the various levels of analysis, and the consequent institutionalization of expectations about appropriate hiring is an effect that is substantively significant and important in thinking about public policies to ameliorate segregation.

The results also suggest the need to consider gender and ethnic effects separately when exploring the conditions under which women and minorities were hired for nontraditional positions. Relative economic attractiveness, governmental pressure, and demographic group power were important in bringing about the gender integration of jobs and positions. More important for ethnic integration, however, was the perception of individuals. Once individual minority workers had been inside the institution and become known to decision makers, nontraditional placement (placement in positions other than director of affirmative action) was more likely to occur.

Finally, we found an important difference in the patterns of gender and ethnic segmentation in administrative positions in higher education. Women and men were found to work in separate jobs to a greater extent, while Whiles and minorities were found to work in separate organizations to a greater extent. One possible explanation suggested by an anonymous reviewer, which additional data analyses refuted, was the demographic composition of regional labor markets. Since some regions in the United States have a higher proportion of minorities in the labor force than do others, the finding that Whites and minorities are less likely than are men and women to work in the same organization may simply reflect the composition of the regional labor market.

Additional data analyses indicated, however, that even within regions, organizations were segregated by ethnicity to a greater extent than by gender and jobs were segregated by gender to a greater extent than by ethnicity.

The finding of differences in these patterns also poses an interesting and unexplored question for labor market theorists. Why do Whites and minorities work in different organizations to a greater extent, while women and men work in different jobs to a greater extent? We suggest some possible explanations for the patterns we observed, but these explanations require additional empirical testing. Greater job segregation by gender may be explained by the lack that women make up a much higher proportion of the U.S. labor force than do minorities and, therefore, that they pose a greater threat or displacement to the more expensive White men. Thus, White men may act to keep women out of their jobs. These actions may range from blatant hiring discrimination to subtle social exclusion on the job that keeps women from learning the informal norms of the organization and profession that are necessary to move up.

Greater organizational segregation by ethnicity may be explained by the motivation to maintain social distance between the ethnic groups. There may be little motivation to create and maintain social distance between the genders, with the result that men and women often work together in the same organization, though not in the same job. There may be greater motivation to create and maintain social distance between the ethnic groups, since social contact between members of the ethnic groups is often inhibited and strained by cultural differences. White workers may simply feel more comfortable with other White workers. As a result, subjective assessments of whether a job applicant will fit into the organization or the work group may bias hiring decisions by ethnicity.

One implication of the finding that the genders worked together in the same organization substantially more often than did the two broadly defined ethnic groups is that female students have a fairly good chance of being exposed to female administrators in most colleges and universities, but minority students may find few minority administrators at many institutions. Considering the beneficial effects of demographically similar authority figures to the educational outcomes of female and minority students, this finding is troublesome.

References

Abrahamson, Mark, and Lee Sigelman. 1987. "Occupational Sex Segregation in Metropolitan Areas." *American Sociological Review* 52:588–97.

Albelda, Randy P. 1986. "Occupational Segregation by Race and Gender. 1958–1981." *Industrial and Labor Relations Review* 39:404–11.

Antill. J. K. 1983. "Sex Role Complementarity versus Similarity in Married Couples." *Journal of Personality and Social Psychology* 45:145–55.

Asher, Martin, and Joel Popkin. 1984. "The Effect of Gender and Race Differentials on Public-Private Wage Comparisons: A Study of Postal Workers." *Industrial and Labor Relations Review* 38:16–25.

Bach, Rebecca L., and Carolyn C. Perrucci. 1984. "Organizational Influences on the Sex Composition of College and University Faculty: A Research Note." *Sociology of Education* 57:193–98.

Baron, James N., and William T. Bielby. 1985. "Organizational Behaviors to Gender Equality: Sex Segregation of Jobs and Opportunities." Pp. 233–51 in *Gender and the Life Course*, edited by Alice S. Rossi. New York: Aldine.

_____. 1986. "The Proliferation of Job Titles in Organizations." *Administrative Science Quarterly* 31:561–86.

Baron, James N., Alison Davis-Blake, and William T. Bielby. 1986. "The Structure of Opportunity: How Promotion Ladders Vary within and among Organizations." *Administrative Science Quarterly* 31:248–73.

Beller, Andrea H. 1984. Trends in Occupational Segregation by Sex and Race, 1960–1981." Pp. 11–26 in *Sex Segregation in the Workplace: Trends, Explanations, Remedies*, edited by Barbara F. Reskin. Washington, DC: National Academy Press.

Bielby, William, and James N. Baron. 1984. "A Woman's Place Is with Other Women: Sex Segregation within Organizations." Pp. 27–55 in *Sex Segregation in the Workplace: Trends, Explanations, Remedies*, edited by Barbara F. Reskin. Washington, DC: National Academy Press.

_____. 1986. "Men and Women at Work: Sex Segregation and Statistical Discrimination." *American Journal of Sociology* 91:759–99.

Blalock, H. M. 1956. "Economic Discrimination and Negro Increase." *American Sociological Review* 21:584–88.

_____. 1957. "Per Cent Non-white and Discrimination in the South." *American Sociological Review* 22:677–82.

Blau, Francine. 1977. *Equal Pay in the Office*. Lexington, MA: Lexington Books.

Bridges, William P. 1982. "The Sexual Segregation of Occupations: Theories of Labor Stratification in Industry." *American Journal of Sociology* 88:270–95.

Carpenter, Peter, and Martin Hayden. 1987. "Girls' Academic Achievements: Single-Sex versus Co-educational Schools in Australia." *Sociology of Education* 60:156–67.

Cohen, Yinon, and Jeffrey Pfeffer. 1984. "Employment Practices in the Dual Economy." *Industrial Relations* 23:58–72.

Collins, Randall. 1979. *The Credential Society*. New York: Academic Press.

DiPrete, Thomas A. 1987. "The Professionalization of Administration and Equal Employment Opportunity in the U.S. Federal Government." *American Journal of Sociology* 93:119–40.

DiPrete, Thomas A., and Whitman T. Soule. 1986. The Organization of Career Lines: Equal Employment Opportunity and Status Advancement in a Federal Bureaucracy." *American Sociological Review* 51:295–309.

_____.1988. "Gender and Promotion in Segmented Job Ladder Systems." *American Sociological Review* 53:26–40.

Duncan, Otis Dudley, and Beverly Duncan. 1955. "A Methodological Analysis of Segregation Indexes." *American Sociological Review* 20:210–17.

Eberts. Randall W., and Joe A. Stone. 1985. "Male-Female Differences in Promotions: EEO in Public Education." *Journal of Human Resources* 20:504–21.

England, Paula. 1981. "Assessing Trends in Occupational Sex Segregation, 1900–1976." Pp. 273–95 in *Sociological Perspectives on Labor Markets*, edited by Ivar Berg. New York: Academic Press.

Grandjean, Burke D. 1981. History and Career in a Bureaucratic Labor Market." *American Journal of Sociology* 86:1057–92.

Haberfeld, Yitchak, and Yehouda Shenhav. 1988. "Are Women and Black Scientists Closing the Gap? A Longitudinal Analysis of Discrimination in American Science during the 70's and the 80's." Unpublished manuscript, Department of Labor Studies, Tel-Aviv University, Tel-Aviv, Israel.

Halaby, Charles N. 1979. "Sexual Inequality in the Workplace: An Employer-Specific Analysis of Pay Differences." *Social Science Research* 8:79–104.

Hill, C. T., Z. Rubin, and L. A. Peplau. 1976. "Breakups Before Marriage: The End of 103 Affairs." *Journal of Social Issues* 32(1):147–168.

Johnson, William R. 1978. "Racial Wage Discrimination and Industrial Structure." *Bell Journal of Economics* 9:70–81.

Kandel, D. B. 1978. "Similarity in Real-life Adolescent Friendship Pairs." *Journal of Personality and Social Psychology* 36:306–312.

Kanter, Rosabeth Moss. 1977. *Men and Women of the Corporation*. New York: Basic Books.

Kaufman, Robert L. 1986. "The Impact of Industrial and Occupational Structure on Black-White Employment Allocation." *American Sociological Review* 51:310–23.

Krefting, L. A., P. K. Berger, and M. J. Wallace, Jr. 1978. "The Contribution of Sex Distribution, Job Content and Occupational Classification to Job Sextyping: Two Studies." *Journal of Vocational Behavior* 13:181–91.

Leonard, Jonathan S. 1985a. "The Effect of Unions on the Employment of Blacks, Hispanics, and Women." *Industrial and Labor Relations Review* 39:115–32.

_____.1985b. "What Promises Are Worth: The Impact of Affirmative Action Goals." *Journal of Human Resources* 20:1–20.

Lewis, Gregory 13. 1986. Gender and Promotions: Promotion Chances of White Men and Women in Federal White-collar Employment." *Journal of Human Resources* 21:406–19.

Mennerick, Lewis A. 1975. "Organizational Structuring of Sex Roles in a Nonstereotyped Industry." *Administrative Science Quarterly* 20:570–86.

Moore, H. A., and D. R. Johnson. 1983. "A Reexamination of Elementary School Teacher Expectations: Evidence of Sex and Ethnic Segmentation." *Social Science Quarterly* 64:460–75.

Nieva, Veronica F., and Barbara A. Gutek. 1980. "Sex Effects on Evaluation." *Academy of Management Review* 5:267–76.

_____. 1981. *Women and Work: A Psychological Perspective*. New York: Praeger.

Park, Bernadette, and Myron Rothbart. 1982. "Perception of Out-group Homogeneity and Levels of Social Categorization: Memory for the Subordinate Attributes of In-group and Out-group Members." *Journal of Personality and Social Psychology* 42:1051–68.

Petersik, J., and S. Schneir. 1980. "Sex Role Dynamics in the Grade Book." *SASP Newsletter* 6(1): 7–8.

Pfeffer, Jeffrey, and Alison Davis-Blake. 1987. "The Effect of the Proportion of Women on Salaries: The Case of College Administrators." *Administrative Science Quarterly* 32:1–24.

Pomer, Marshall I. 1986. "Labor Market Structure, Intragenerational Mobility, and Discrimination: Black Male Advancement Out of Lowpaying Occupations, 1962–1973." *American Sociological Review* 51:650–59.

Powell, Gary N. 1987. "The Effects of Sex and Gender on Recruitment." *Academy of Management Review* 12:731–43.

Ramirez, A., and F. Soriano. 1982. "Social Power in Educational Systems: Its Effect on Chicanos' Attitudes toward the School Experience." *Journal of Social Psychology* 118:113–19.

Rosenbaum, James E. 1985. "Persistence and Change in Pay Inequalities: Implications for Job Evaluation and Comparable Worth." Pp. 115–40 in *Women and Work: An Annual Review* (Vol. 1), edited by Laurie Larwood, Ann H. Stromberg, and Barbara A. Gutek. Beverly Hills, CA: Sage.

Salancik, Gerald R. 1979. Interorganizational Dependence and Responsiveness to Affirmative Action: The Case of Women and Defense Contractors." *Academy of Management Journal* 22: 375–94.

Salancik, Gerald R., and Jeffrey Pfeffer. 1978. "Uncertainty, Secrecy, and the Choice of Similar Others." *Social Psychology* 41:246–55.

Seeborg, Irmtraud Streker, Michael C. Seeborg, and Abera Zegeye. 1986. "Training and Labor Market Outcomes of Disadvantaged Blacks." *Industrial Relations* 25:33–44.

Semyonov, Moshe. 1988. "Bi-ethnic Labor Markets, Monoethnic Labor Markets, and Socioeconomic Inequality." *American Sociological Review* 53:256–66.

Shepard, W. O., and D. T. Hess. 1975. "Attitudes in Four Age Groups toward Sex Role Division in Adult Occupations and Activities." *Journal of Vocational Behavior* 6:27–39.

Smith, Sharon P. 1976. "Pay Differentials between Federal Government and Private Sector Workers." *Industrial and Labor Relations Review* 29:179–97.

Strober, Myra H. 1984. "Toward a General Theory of Occupational Sex Segregation: The Case of Public School Teaching." Pp. 144–56 in *Sex Segregation in the Workplace: Trends, Explanations, Remedies,* edited by Barbara F. Reskin. Washington, DC: National Academy Press.

Strober, Myra H., and Carolyn L. Arnold. 1987. "The Dynamics of Occupational Segregation among Bank Tellers." Pp. 107-58 in *Gender in the Workplace,* edited by Clair Brown and Joseph A. Pechman. Washington, DC: Brookings Institution.

Strober, Myra H., and Lisa M. Catanzarite. 1988. April. "Changes in Black Women's Representation in Occupations and a Measure of the Relative Attractiveness of Occupations." Paper presented at the annual Standford Organizations Conference, Asilomar, CA.

Szafran, Robert F. 1984a. *Universities and Women Faculty: Why Some Organizations Discriminate More than Others.* New York: Praeger.

Szafran, Robert F. 1984b. "Female and Minority Employment Patterns in Banks: A Research Note." *Work and Occupations* 11:55–76.

Talbert, Joan, and Christine E. Bose. 1977. "Wage-Attainment Processes: The Retail Clerk Case." *American Journal of Sociology* 83:403–24.

Tidball, M. E. 1980. "Women's Colleges and Women Achievers Revisited. *Signs: Journal of Women in Culture and Society* 5:504–17.

Tienda, Marta, Shelley A. Smith, and Vilma Ortiz. 1987. "Industrial Restructuring, Gender Segregation, and Sex Differences in Earnings." *American Sociological Review* 52:195–210.

Tolbert, Pamela S. 1986. "Organizations and Inequality: Sources of Earnings Differentials between Male and Female Faculty." *Sociology of Education* 59:227–35.

Waite, Linda J., and Sue E. Berryman. 1986. "Job Stability among Young Women: A Comparison of Traditional and Nontraditional Occupations." *American Journal of Sociology* 92:568–95.

Wharton, Amy S., and James N. Baron. 1987. "So Happy Together? The Impact of Gender Segregation on Men and Work." *American Sociological Review* 52:574–87.

Diversity and Its Discontents

ARTURO MADRID

My name is Arturo Madrid. I am a citizen of the United States, as are my parents and as were my grandparents and my great-grandparents. My ancestors' presence in what is now the United States antedates Plymouth Rock, even without taking into account any American Indian heritage I might have.

I do not, however, fit those mental sets that define America and Americans. My physical appearance, my speech patterns, my name, my profession (a professor of Spanish) create a text that confuses the reader. My normal experience is to be asked, "And where are *you* from?" My response depends on my mood. Passive-aggressive, I answer, "From here." Aggressive-passive, I ask, "Do you mean where I am originally from?" But ultimately my answer to those follow-up questions that will ask about origins will be that we have always been from here.

Overcoming my resentment I try to educate, knowing that nine times out of ten my words fall on inattentive ears. I have spent most of my adult life explaining who I am not. I am exotic, but—as Richard Rodriguez of *Hunger of Memory* fame so painfully found out—not exotic enough . . . not Peruvian, or Pakistani, or whatever. I am, however, very clearly the *other*, if only your everyday, garden-variety, domestic *other*. I will share with you another phenomenon that I have been a part of, that of being a missing person, and how I came late to that awareness. But I've always known that I was the other, even before I knew the vocabulary or understood the significance of otherness.

I grew up in an isolated and historically marginal part of the United States, a small mountain village in the state of New Mexico, the eldest child of parents native to that region, whose ancestors had always lived there. In those vast and empty spaces people who look like me, speak as I do, and have names like mine predominate. But the *americanos* lived among us: the descendants of those nineteenth-century immigrants who dispossessed us of our lands; missionaries who came to convert us and stayed to live among us; artists who became enchanted with our land and humanscape and went native; refugees from unhealthy climes, crowded spaces, unpleasant circumstances; and, of course, the inhabitants of Los Alamos, whose sociocultural distance from us was accentuated by the fact that they occupied a space removed from and proscribed to us. More importantly, however, they—*los americanos*—were omnipresent (and almost exclusively so) in newspapers, newsmagazines, books, on radio, in movies, and, ultimately, on television.

Despite the operating myth of the day, school did not erase my otherness. It did try to deny it, and in doing so only accentuated it. To this day what takes place in schools is more socialization than education, but when I was in elementary school—and given where I was—socialization was everything. School was where one became an American, because there was a pervasive and systematic denial by the society that surrounded us that we were Americans. That denial was both explicit and implicit.

Quite beyond saluting the flag and pledging allegiance to it (a very intense and meaningful action, given that the United States was involved in a war and our brothers, cousins, uncles, and fathers were on the frontlines), becoming American was learning English, and its corollary: not speaking Spanish. Until very recently ours was a proscribed language, either *de jure*—by rule, by policy, by law—or *de facto*—by practice, implicitly if not explicitly, through social and political and economic pressure. I do not argue that learning English was not appropriate. On the contrary. Like it or not, and we had no basis to make any judgments on that matter, we were Americans by virtue of having been born Americans, and English was the common language of Americans. And there was a myth, a pervasive myth, to the effect that if only we learned to speak English well—and particularly without an accent—we would be welcomed into the American fellowship.

Sam Hayakawa and the official English movement folks notwithstanding, the true text was not our speech, but rather our names and our appearance, for we would always have an accent, however perfect our pronunciation, however excellent our enunciation, however divine our diction. That accent would be heard in our pigmentation, our physiognomy, our names. We were, in short, the *other*.

Being the *other* involves contradictory phenomena. On the one hand, being the other frequently means being invisible. Ralph Ellison wrote eloquently about that experience in his magisterial novel *Invisible Man*. On the other hand, being the *other* sometimes involves sticking out like a sore thumb. What is she/he doing here?

For some of us being the *other* is only annoying; for others it is debilitating; for still others it is damning. Many try to flee otherness by taking on protective colorations that provide invisibility, whether of dress or speech or manner or name. Only a fortunate few succeed. For the majority of us otherness is permanently sealed by physical appearance. For the rest, otherness is betrayed by ways of being, speaking, or doing.

The first half of my life I spent downplaying the significance and consequences of otherness. The second half has seen me wrestling to understand its complex and deeply ingrained realities; striving to fathom why otherness denies us a voice or visibility or validity in American society and its institutions; struggling to make otherness familiar, reasonable, even normal to my fellow Americans.

I spoke earlier of another phenomenon that I am a part of: that of being a missing person. Growing up in northern New Mexico I had only a slight sense of us being missing persons. *Hispanos*, as we called (and call) ourselves in New Mexico, were very much a part of the fabric of the society, and there were *hispano* professionals everywhere about me: doctors, lawyers, schoolteachers, and administrators. My people owned businesses, ran organizations, and were both appointed and elected public officials.

My awareness of our absence from the larger institutional life of the society became sharper when I went off to college, but even then it was attenuated by the circumstances of history and geography. The demography of Albuquerque still strongly reflected its historical and cultural origins, despite the influx of Midwesterners and Easterners. Moreover, many of my classmates at the University of New Mexico were *hispanos*, and even some of my professors. I thought that would obtain at UCLA, where I began graduate studies in 1960. Los Angeles had a very large Mexican population and that population was visible even in and around Westwood and on the campus. Many of the groundskeepers and food-service personnel at UCLA were Mexican. But Mexican-American students were few and mostly invisible, and I do not recall seeing or knowing a single Mexican-American (or, for that matter, African-American, Asian, or American Indian) professional on the staff or faculty of that institution during the five years I was there. Needless to say, people like me were not present in any capacity at Dartmouth College, the site of my first teaching appointment, and of course were not even part of the institutional or individual mind-set. I knew then that we—a we that had come to encompass American Indians, Asian-Americans, African-Americans, Puerto Ricans, and women—were truly missing persons in American institutional life.

Over the past three decades the *de jure* and *de facto* types of segregation that have historically characterized American institutions have been under assault. As a consequence, minorities and women have become part of American institutional life. Although there are still many areas where we are not to be found, the missing persons phenomenon is not as pervasive as it once was.

However, the presence of the *other*, particularly minorities, in institutions and in institutional life resembles what we call in Spanish a *flor de tierra* (a surface phenomenon): we are spare plants whose roots do not go deep, vulnerable to inclemencies of an economic, or political, or social, nature.

Our entrance into and our status in institutional life are not unlike a scenario set forth by my grandmother's pastor when she informed him that she and her family were leaving their mountain village to relocate to the Rio Grande Valley. When he asked her to promise that she would remain true to the faith and continue to involve herself in it, she asked why he thought she would do otherwise. "Doña Trinidad," he told her, "in the Valley there is no Spanish church. There is only an American church." "But," she protested, "I read and speak English and would be able to worship there." The pastor responded, "It is possible that they will not admit you, and even if they do, they might not accept you. And that is why I want you to promise me that you are going to go to church. Because if they don't let you in through the front door, I want you to go in through the back door. And if you can't get in through the back door, go in the side door. And if you are unable to enter through the side door I want you to go in through the window. What is important is that you enter and stay."

Some of us entered institutional life through the front door; others through the back door; and still others through side doors. Many, if not most of us, came in through windows, and continue to come in through windows. Of those who entered through the front door, some never made it past the lobby; others were ushered into corners and niches. Those who entered through back and side doors inevitably have remained in back and side rooms. And those who entered through windows found enclosures built around them. For, despite the lip service given to the goal of the integration of minorities into institutional life, what has frequently occurred instead is ghettoization, marginalization, isolation.

Not only have the entry points been limited, but in addition the dynamics have been singularly conflictive. Gaining entry and its corollary, gaining space, have frequently come as a consequence of demands made on institutions and institutional officers. Rather than entering institutions more or less passively, minorities have of necessity entered them actively, even aggressively. Rather than waiting to receive, they have demanded. Institutional relations have thus been adversarial, infused with specific and generalized tensions.

The nature of the entrance and the nature of the space occupied have greatly influenced the view and attitude of the majority population within those institutions. All of us are put into the same box; that is, no matter what the individual reality, the assessment of the individual is inevitably conditioned by a perception that is held of the class. Whatever our history, whatever our record, whatever our validations, whatever our accomplishments, by and large we are perceived unidimensionally and dealt with accordingly. I remember an experience I had in this regard, atypical only in its explicitness. A few years ago I allowed myself to be persuaded to seek the presidency of a well-known state university. I was invited for an interview and presented myself before the selection committee, which included members of the board of trustees. The opening question of that brief but memorable interview was directed at me by a member of that august body. "Dr. Madrid," he asked, "why does a one-dimensional person like you think he can be the president of a multidimensional institution like ours?"

Over the past four decades America's demography has undergone significant changes. Since 1965 the principal demographic growth we have experienced in the United States has been of peoples whose national origins are non-European. This population growth has occurred both through birth and through immigration. A few years ago discussion of the national birthrate had a scare dimension: the high—"inordinately high"—birthrate of the Hispanic population. The popular discourse was informed by words such as "breeding." Several years later, as a consequence of careful tracking by government agencies, we now know that what has happened is that the birthrate of the majority population has decreased. When viewed historically and comparatively, the minority populations (for the most part) have also had a decline in birthrate, but not one as great as that of the majority.

There are additional demographic changes that should give us something to think about. African-Americans are now to be found in significant numbers in every major urban center in the nation. Hispanic-Americans now number over 15 million people, and although they are a regionally concentrated (and highly urbanized) population, there is a Hispanic community in almost every major urban center of the United States. American Indians, heretofore a small and rural population, are increasingly more numerous and urban. The Asian-American population, which has historically consisted of small and concentrated communities of Chinese-, Filipino-, and Japanese-Americans, has doubled over the past decade, its complexion changed by the addition of Cambodians, Koreans, Hmongs, Vietnamese, et al.

Prior to the Immigration Act of 1965, 69 percent of immigration was from Europe. By far the largest number of immigrants to the United States since 1965 have been from the Americas and from Asia: 34 percent are from Asia; another 34 percent are from Central and South America; 16 percent are from Europe; 10 percent are from the Caribbean; the remaining 6 percent are from other continents and Canada. As was the case with previous immigration waves, the current one consists principally of young people: 60 percent are between the ages of 16 and 44. Thus, for the next few decades, we will continue to see a growth in the percentage of non-European-origin Americans as compared to European-Americans.

To sum up, we now live in one of the most demographically diverse nations in the world, and one that is increasingly more so.

During the same period social and economic change seems to have accelerated. Who would have imagined at mid-century that the prototypical middle-class family (working husband, wife as homemaker, two children) would for all intents and purposes disappear? Who could have anticipated the rise in teenage pregnancies, children in poverty, drug use? Who among us understood the implications of an aging population?

We live in an age of continuous and intense change, a world in which what held true yesterday does not today, and certainly will not tomorrow. What change does, moreover, is bring about even more change. The only constant we have at this point in our national development is change. And change is threatening. The older we get the more likely we are to be anxious about change, and the greater our desire to maintain the status quo.

Evident in our public life is a fear of change, whether economic or moral. Some who fear change are responsive to the call of economic protectionism, others to the message of moral protectionism. Parenthetically, I have referred to the movement to require more of students without in turn giving them more as academic protectionism. And the pronouncements of E.D. Hirsch and Allan Bloom are, I believe, informed by intellectual protectionism. Much more serious, however, is the dark side of the populism which underlies this evergoing protectionism—the resentment of the *other*. An excellent and fascinating example of that aspect of populism is the cry for linguistic protectionism—for making English the official language of the United States. And who among us is unaware of the tensions that underlie immigration reform, of the underside of demographic protectionism?

A matter of increasing concern is whether this new protectionism, and the mistrust of the *other* which accompanies it, is not making more significant inroads than we have supposed in higher education. Specifically, I wish to discuss the question of whether a goal (quality) and a reality (demographic diversity) have been erroneously placed in conflict, and, if so, what problems this perception of conflict might present.

As part of my scholarship I turn to dictionaries for both origins and meanings of words. Quality, according to the *Oxford English Dictionary*, has multiple meanings. One set defines quality as being an essential character, a distinctive and inherent feature. A second describes it as a degree of excellence, of conformity to standards, as superiority in kind. A third makes reference to social status, particularly to persons of high social status. A fourth talks about quality as being a special or distinguishing attribute, as being a desirable trait. Quality is highly desirable in both principle and practice. We all aspire to it in our own person, in our experiences, in our acquisitions and products, and of course we all want to be associated with people and operations of quality.

But let us move away from the various dictionary meanings of the word and to our own sense of what it represents and of how we feel about it. First of all we consider quality to be finite; that is, it is limited with respect to quantity; it has very few manifestations; it is not widely distributed. I have it and you have it, but they don't. We associate quality with homogeneity, with uniformity, with standardization, with order, regularity, neatness. All too often we equate it with smoothness, glibness, slickness, elegance. Certainly it is always expensive. We tend to identify it with those who lead, with the rich and famous. And, when you come right down to it, it's inherent. Either you've got it or you ain't.

Diversity, from the Latin *divertere*, meaning to turn aside, to go different ways, to differ, is the condition of being different or having differences, is an instance of being different. Its companion word, diverse, means differing, unlike, distinct; having or capable or having various forms; composed of unlike or distinct elements. Diversity is lack of standardization, of regularity, of orderliness, homogeneity, conformity, uniformity. Diversity introduces complications, is difficult to organize, is troublesome to manage, is problematical. Diversity is irregular, disorderly, uneven, rough. The way we use the word diversity gives us away. Something is too diverse, is extremely diverse. We want a little diversity.

When we talk about diversity, we are talking about the *other*, whatever that other might be: someone of a different gender, race, class, national origin; somebody at a greater or lesser distance from the norm; someone outside the set; someone who possesses a different set of characteristics, features, or attributes; someone who does not fall within the taxonomies we use daily and with which we are comfortable; someone who does not fit into the mental configurations that give our lives order and meaning.

In short, diversity is desirable only in principle, not in practice. Long live diversity . . . as long as it conforms to my standards, my mind set, my view of life, my sense of order. We desire, we like, we admire diversity, not unlike the way the French (and others) appreciate women; that is, *Vive la différence!*—as long as it stays in its place.

What I find paradoxical about and lacking in this debate is that diversity is the natural order of things. Evolution produces diversity. Margaret Visser, writing about food in her latest book, *Much Depends on Dinner,* makes an eloquent statement in this regard:

> Machines like, demand, and produce uniformity. But nature loathes it: her strength lies in multiplicity and in differences. Sameness in biology means fewer possibilities and therefore weakness.

The United States, by its very nature, by its very development, is the essence of diversity. It is diverse in its geography, population, institutions, technology; its social, cultural, and intellectual modes. It is a society that at its best does not consider quality to be monolithic in form or finite in quantity, or to be inherent in class. Quality in our society proceeds in large measure out of the stimulus of diverse modes of thinking and acting; out of the creativity made possible by the different ways in which we approach things; out of diversion from paths or modes hallowed by tradition.

One of the principal strengths of our society is its ability to address, on a continuing and substantive basis, the real economic, political, and social problems that have faced and continue to face us. What makes the United States so attractive to immigrants is the protections and opportunities it offers; what keeps our society together is tolerance for cultural, religious, social, political, and even linguistic difference; what makes us a unique, dynamic, and extraordinary nation is the power and creativity of our diversity.

The true history of the United States is one of struggle against intolerance, against oppression, against xenophobia, against those forces that have prohibited persons from participating in the larger life of the society on the basis of their race, their gender, their religion, their national origin, their linguistic and cultural background. These phenomena are not consigned to the past. They remain with us and frequently take on virulent dimensions.

If you believe, as I do, that the well-being of a society is directly related to the degree and extent to which all of its citizens participate in its institutions, then you will have to agree that we have a challenge before us. In view of the extraordinary changes that are taking place in our society we need to take up the struggle again, irritating, grating, troublesome, unfashionable, unpleasant as it is. As educated and educator members of this society we have a special responsibility for ensuring that all American institutions, not just our elementary and secondary schools, our juvenile halls, or our jails reflect the diversity of our society. Not to do so is to risk greater alienation on the part of a growing segment of our society; is to risk increased social tension in an already conflictive world; and, ultimately, is to risk the survival of a range of institutions that, for all their defects and deficiencies, provide us the opportunity and the freedom to improve our individual and collective lot.

Let me urge you to reflect on these two words—quality and diversity—and on the mental sets and behaviors that flow out of them. And let me urge you further to struggle against the notion that quality is finite in quantity, limited in its manifestations, or is restricted by considerations of class, gender, race, or national origin; or that quality manifests itself only in leaders and not in followers, in managers and not in workers, in breeders and not in drones; or that it has to be associated with verbal agility or elegance of personal style; or that it cannot be seeded, nurtured, or developed.

Because diversity—the *other*—is among us, will define and determine our lives in ways that we still do not fully appreciate, whether that other is women (no longer bound by tradition, house, and family); or Asians, African-Americans, Indians, and Hispanics (no longer invisible, regional, or marginal); or our newest immigrants (no longer distant, exotic, alien). Given the changing profile of America, will we come to terms with diversity in our personal and professional lives? Will we begin to recognize the diverse forms that quality can take? If so, we will thus initiate the process of making quality limitless in its manifestations, infinite in quantity, unrestricted with respect to its origins, and more importantly, virulently contagious.

I hope we will. And that we will further join together to expand—not to close—the circle.

Organizing for Diversity: Fundamental Issues

DARYL G. SMITH

Higher education is faced today with the necessity—and the opportunity—to once again rethink what it does and how it does it. At the core of this effort is the organization's improved capacity to educate in a pluralistic society for a pluralistic world. But to do so requires a shift in our thinking from a focus on the issues surrounding students and "the problems" they create for the institution. In addition to whether students are prepared for learning is a serious question as to whether institutions are prepared for diversity. Such a shift requires a different rationale for thinking about change. If the institution is concerned about the capacity to deal with diversity, then the attention is on the entire community. Diversity among faculty, staff, and students is seen as important not only for the support such individuals provide for specific groups but also for the importance of diverse perspectives to institutional success and quality. The institution recognizes that remediation is an issue for many students and that concern for effective teaching and learning must be a paramount objective throughout the institution. Readiness to deal with diversity requires asking about the attitudes and information of traditional students as well as nontraditional students. Indeed, at a number of institutions, programs have been developed that focus on multicultural awareness for all students through workshops and course credit. Such programs assume that individuals need education about and awareness of pluralism. The message is that educating for diversity is important for everyone to create a suitable environment for diversity, both in the university and in society (Banks 1981; Barbarin 1981).

On many campuses across the country, the challenges of creating an organization that embraces diversity so that it can truly begin to educate all students has begun.

Institutional self-reflection, let alone transformation, is not an easy process. It raises questions about the institution and its assumptions about the academic enterprise. Moreover, the picture of what colleges and universities should look like is not yet clear, though the research on successful institutions suggests some of the issues that institutions must address. Higher education is a highly complex, decentralized system, and within that system is an enormous array of institutions. Thus, the process of change and the specific goals for change will necessarily be specific to the institution. Nevertheless, the existing review of the literature suggests that colleges and universities—large and small, commuter and residential, public and private, urban and rural—will be asked to confront a number of challenges as diversity is addressed.

Diversification of Faculty and Staff

The call for a more diversified faculty and staff in the literature is viewed almost universally as important. The literature is clear about the importance of faculty support in general and the importance of this role in particular for nontraditional students, whether adult learners, disabled students, or minority students. Certainly an important aspect of the success of historically African-American colleges and women's colleges rests on the important role of African-American faculty and staff and women faculty and staff in running the institution. The emphasis on a diverse faculty and staff is indeed critical but for more reasons than are often articulated.

Five reasons emerge. The first three deal with faculty and staff roles relating to students. The most common reason given for the need to diversify faculty and staff is to provide support for the benefit of students from particular groups. Observers generally acknowledge that students in the minority will seek out a faculty member who, they perceive, understands their experience. Often this selection is based on gender, racial or ethnic commonality, or disability. Given the environment on many campuses, such faculty and staff play a very important role. Indeed, evidence suggests that such faculty and staff, because of their relatively small numbers, are often burdened by the advising and counseling that accompany their role as a member of a visible minority.

A second reason for encouraging the diversification of faculty and staff is that diversification is an important symbol to students from these groups about their own futures and about the institution's commitment to them. Third, diversification of the campus community creates a more comfortable environment for students as well as for faculty and staff. The strains suffered by students also exist for faculty and staff members who represent diverse groups. These individuals assume the burden of being spokespersons, mentors, support persons, and symbols, while also trying to perform to rigorous professional standards. At the same time, they may endure the same kind of loneliness and insensitivities also experienced by students (Blackwell 1988; Olivas 1988; Smith 1980).

The last two reasons for the importance of a diversified faculty and staff relate to benefits to the institution. Diversification of the faculty and staff is likely to contribute to what is taught, how it is taught, and what is important to learn, contributions that are vital to the institution. Faculty trained in traditional pedagogy and in traditional methodologies often find it difficult to fundamentally change courses and curricula. Diversification of the faculty and staff make it easier, because the likelihood is greater for the introduction of different perspectives and approaches and for many more opportunities or professional collaboration. People like administrators and faculty in decision-making positions who have had their own experiences with aspects of institutional life that create barriers or even alienate students offer the institution an invaluable service by providing their perspectives on potential problem areas. It should be remembered, however, that no single individual can represent any more than his or her own perspective or be sensitive to all the issues, needs, and concerns of each disparate group that has been described. An African-American faculty member, for example, cannot reflect all the issues of a disabled or a Latino student. Thus, what is needed is true diversity. Fifth, a diverse faculty and staff reflect one measure of institutional success for an educational institution in a pluralistic society. As long as the leadership of our institutions contains only token representation of persons from diverse backgrounds, institutions will not be able to claim that the goals for society or our educational institutions have been achieved.

Thus, the issue of diversity in faculty and staff assumes direct as well as indirect importance for campus efforts. While these efforts are important for students from those groups, they are also important for the institution. Concern is great, however, that being able to achieve this goal in the near future is highly unlikely (Blackwell 1988; Sudarkasa 1987; Valverde 1988; Wilson 1987a). The lack of growth in higher education over this past decade and the increased use of part-time faculty have combined to produce fewer opportunities for faculty and staff advancement. Now, projections for openings in the next decade are more optimistic, but it is almost universally recognized that the lack of retention and the lack of attractiveness in pursuing advanced degrees for today's and yesterday's undergraduates threaten institutional goals for increasing the hiring of more women and minorities (Blackwell 1988). If the presence of a truly diversified faculty and staff is critical, this situation jeopardizes institutional efforts.

It is important to note that the barrier to diversification is not simply an issue of numbers. Availability of individuals to assume these positions is clearly a problem. Evidence suggests, however, that institutions are also having difficulty retaining faculty and staff of different backgrounds for the same reasons they have had problems retaining students. The current revolving-door pattern is an extravagant waste of human resources and a major obstacle to change. Efforts to retain and develop staff and graduate students already within the institution are therefore as important as increasing the pool of applicants to the institution.

Mission and Values

As indicated earlier, some of the values rooted in the academic tradition are now coming into question. Issues of values are not easily identified, discussed, or dealt with. Given the literature on organizational effectiveness, however, it is probably very important to identify those values that are central to the institution's mission and those that are not. It is also critical that this discussion be held in such a way that traditional assumptions may be open to question. Two sets of values are frequently cited as important: competition/cooperation and individualism/concern for community. The increasing evidence on the effectiveness of cooperative learning, for example, suggests that traditional structures that encourage competitiveness may be counterproductive to the institution and to all students (Astin 1987; Palmer 1987). Rather than being viewed as a threat to institutional quality, such changes may well turn out to improve institutional effectiveness. Discussions about individualism and community touch not only on matters of importance to a number of ethnic and racial groups but also on the increasing concern about narcissism and unethical behavior in society (Harris, Silverstein, and Andrews 1989; McIntosh 1989; Minnich 1989). Have we gone too far in encouraging competitive and highly individualistic practices at the expense of concern for the community and at the expense of good learning?

Questions about values emerge at all levels of the institution. Perhaps one of the most challenging has to do with the ways in which students perceive that the values and perspectives they bring with them to the academic community are not appreciated and may even put them into conflict with institutional norms and behaviors. At its worst, students may perceive that they must abandon the values of their own cultures or background to succeed (Ogbu 1978). The resulting phenomenon of alienation is contradictory to the central role being given to the importance of involvement in one's education and with the institution.

The question of values also extends to how the campus functions and to the norms and expectations for performance. As has been suggested in this monograph, grading practices, decision making, approaches to learning, residence hall life styles, dress, and interpersonal manners are very much affected by values and by background. Creating a campus environment in which one is free to discuss these issues and in which one can create alternative practices can be difficult. The overall pattern of teaching practices in higher education, for example, has never adequately reflected what we know about learning. Large lecture classes, lack of immediate feedback, multiple choice tests, and so on do not reflect the necessary variety in pedagogy for adequate learning (Smith 1983). One might conjecture that as long as students could succeed despite this kind of teaching and as long as one did not care about those who did not succeed, we did not need to connect teaching with learning. Now those conditions must change. Fewer and fewer students succeed. To connect teaching with learning requires knowing about students, knowing about the subject matter, and knowing about conducive environments for learning. Perhaps because of their marginal status, more of these issues are being raised today as they relate to nontraditional students. Just one example of alternative forms of pedagogy is described in *Women's Ways of Knowing* (Belenky et al. 1986). Despite methodological issues about the study's ability to generalize about gender, the report does vividly describe a group of women's preference for "connected" learning. The authors describe connected learning as an interactive experience in which involvement facilitates learning. In this form of learning, empathy, care, and understanding are viewed as important parts of the process of making judgments. Class participation, collaborative projects, and students contributing to one another's views would be seen as critical. In contrast, the values implicit in many traditional forms of pedagogy are isolation, cynicism, and competition.

Areas of new inquiry, however, are not always well received, particularly if they are not in the accepted tradition of one's colleagues or institution (Pearson, Shavlik, and Touchton 1989). Many have viewed feminist scholarship and ethnic studies, for example, as peripheral to the curriculum and as subjects of nonserious inquiry. Moreover, some view such scholarship as contributing to the weakening of the curriculum (1987). The issues involved go to the heart of such questions as what constitutes a good education, what we mean by equality and how we evaluate it, and the appropriate methodologies in the search for truth. For faculty members interested in asking new questions in new areas, the risk can be great unless those areas are already seen as legitimate or unless they themselves have the status to alter approaches in their fields. And it can be very difficult for those who represent minorities in the decision-making process.

Institutions face a challenge in differentiating between those values and goals that facilitate learning and serve the institution's mission and those values that leave some groups on the margin. At the same time, it is important to be open to new ways of accomplishing goals. Evidence on the benefits of cooperative learning for all students, for example, suggests that traditional structures that build in competition may be counterproductive. Such environments may be detrimental to most students. Values and the clarification of assumptions about values are at the heart of the issue of diversity.

Dealing with Conflict

Even the most superficial analysis of what is happening on many college campuses suggests that conflict is either openly present or just under the surface. Some degree of conflict would be expected when individuals and groups from diverse backgrounds try to come together in an institutional setting (Jones 1987). While increased numbers may be more comfortable to a member of a minority group, they may be more threatening to a member of the majority. Thus, conflict may be intensified on many campuses as they become more diverse or more explicit in their efforts to diversity. A look at the literature on intergroup relations suggests moreover that the conditions are present for conflict, given the competitive environment, unequal status of individuals and groups, frustration caused by hostile environments, and perceptions of the responsiveness by some and favoritism by others and given that little exists to bring groups together in meaningful contact (Amir 1969; Gamson, Peterson, and Blackburn 1980). Building on the literature of cultural pluralism, we can expect conflict when desirable values are incompatible. Campuses, for example, are struggling with having to choose between setting desirable standards for speech and behavior and supporting rights of free speech given in the First Amendment (*Stanford Observer* 1989). Yet the existence of conflict may be a good sign that the institution is grappling with many of these issues and is in the process of fundamental change. Indeed, a very significant study of the patterns of adaptation that occur in institutions dealing with issues of diversity suggests that conflict may be part of the process that will assist institutions to identify essential changes (Skinner and Richardson 1988). Conflict can therefore be a pathway to learning (Green 1989).

Though higher education is rooted in a tradition of debate and the free exchange of ideas, it is not clear that dealing with conflict, particularly the kind of conflict apt to become emotional, is one that institutions can deal with very effectively. The conflicts that can emerge from trying to create truly pluralistic environments are uncomfortable and may need to be so. The challenge is to create vehicles for dealing with conflict in an environment that is open to differences. Indeed, a characteristic of many successful campuses has been the creation of strong policies, procedures, and even special programs of mediation and arbitration to recognize the existence of conflict and to use it as a vehicle for learning by the institution (Green 1989).

The Quality of Interaction on Campus

The body of research cited that reflects the importance of students' involvement with the institution requires an institutional assessment about involvement, how students can become involved, the level of interaction among students and between students and faculty, and the general climate of the campus for involvement. The literature on intergroup relations that suggests the need for students and faculty to participate together in meaningful and important work also supports the involvement. While residential campuses and smaller institutions have more natural potential to develop involvement, the challenge is present for all institutions. Many campuses use mentor programs, programmatic efforts at the college and departmental levels within the university, residence halls, and athletic programs to build communities of involved students and faculty. For large public institutions, the challenging question is whether meaningful learning communities can be developed that benefit from diversity.

Educating for Diversity

As institutions begin to evaluate the quality of climate for diversity, one inevitable discussion centers around the role of the educational process and in particular the role of the curriculum (Slaughter 1988). Many more institutions are beginning to articulate a commitment to educate students for living in a pluralistic world and to create environments that embrace diversity. The content of the curriculum insofar as it serves these goals, the styles of teaching, and the modes of assessment are all being evaluated. Schools like Stanford and the University of California-Berkeley have now moved to require that all students develop some familiarity with the diversity of American cultures and with issues of race, class, and gender. Curricular transformation involves the same kind of developmental process as institutional transformation in moving from courses that address the voids in the curriculum to efforts to ask new questions that more naturally embrace the pluralism of perspectives in the field (McIntosh 1989).

The role of pedagogy is very important to this aspect of education. Recognizing that groups and individuals may learn in different ways requires rethinking the ways in which teaching occurs. The increasing community of students with learning disabilities has focused attention on this issue, but the discussion touches on the literature concerning the adult learner, racial and ethnic groups, and women as well. In other words, it touches on more than a majority of all students.

The issue of assessment is another component of this educational challenge. Not only are the goals for assessment ambiguous in terms of the kinds of learning being evaluated; significant questions also exist about many of the forms of assessment now in place. For example, for those with learning disabilities, multiple choice, time-limited tests may be invalid indicators of learning. The controversy concerning the role of standardized tests for women and minorities reflects similar concerns about the validity of present testing approaches. Without valid indicators of learning, underestimating the performance of many populations of students is a significant risk. This controversy is being highlighted by court challenges to the *means* of awarding New York State scholarships to women and by criticisms of the national movement to require examinations for teachers (Duran 1986; National Center 1989).

The Perceived Conflict between Access and Quality

The continuing message that a fundamental conflict exists between issues of access to the institution and quality is perhaps the most disturbing indication that present institutional approaches to diversity are inadequate (Adolphus 1984; Birnbaum 1988; Mingle 1987; Rendon and Nora 1987; Skinner and Richardson 1988; Stewart 1988). Given the number of national studies concerned about the effectiveness and quality of higher education and the call for increasing standards, the higher education community needs to carefully and thoughtfully address this apparent conflict.

Much of the discussion about improving institutional quality focuses on perceptions about the quality of the students being admitted and concern about lowering standards, although these perceptions can also be found in discussions about hiring and retaining faculty and staff (Gamson 1978; Mingle 1987; Peterson et al. 1978; Willie and McCord 1979). There is reason to believe that the questions being asked and the assumptions being made result in an inappropriate conflict between these two central values. Several important points must be made:

- The concern about the preparation of students, while affecting many minority students, is not a minority problem. While the impact of poor preparation on those who come from disadvantaged backgrounds is more devastating, declining preparation of students is a national issue affecting virtually all schools and all students. Indeed, most poorly prepared students are white (SHEEO 1987).

- The concern that the admission of many minority groups represents a lowering of test scores ignores the fact that the goals of higher education with regard to admissions have always reflected different levels of preparation among its students. Even the most highly selective institutions have sought diversity in geography, artistic and athletic talent, and leadership among their students rather than populations of perfect GPAs and SATs. With these types of diversity, quality was discussed hardly at all because the educational community and the public understood that quality presumably embraced the contributions of those with different strengths. Moreover, it was widely recognized that grades and test scores could not define all that was needed for success in academics and the community. The value of diversity when it comes to students that differ markedly from the majority seems to be recognized far less, however.

- Much of the evidence concerning the tension between quality and diversity rests on lower standardized scores. As indicated elsewhere, serious questions exist about the predictive validity and the power of these instruments for women, for many minorities, and for those with learning disabilities (Duran 1986; Grubb 1986; Morris 1979: National Center 1989; Sedlacek 1986; Thomas 1981; Wilson 1980). The same could be said for learning assessment programs that rely on these kinds of measures. Changing measures of assessment does not mean lowering standards for learning. Indeed, one characteristic of institutions described earlier as successful is that they set high standards and expectations. We are challenged to develop adequate assessment programs and to avoid relying on inadequate programs that, because of expediency, have the effect of diminishing the evidence of performance for particular groups. Though assessment takes a different form for faculty and staff, concern exists that many institutions do not know how to evaluate the quality of scholarship or performance of those from different faculty groups as well.

- The problem about quality also involves how we define success in school and a student's capacity to *learn*. *If we assume* that only one way to learn is correct and at the same time place individuals in environments that are only marginally dedicated to their success, we are setting up whole groups of students for failure. Early evidence focused attention on academic preparation as the most significant factor in achievement, leading many researchers to conclude that academic success is a function of preparation, not race (Richardson and Bender 1987). As this monograph has suggested, however, to the degree that issues of racism, sexism, homophobia, and the general presence of an alienating environment also affect performance, then lack of performance cannot be focused entirely on the student. All too often we have assured the institution's perfection and students' incompetence. Care must be exercised in how we teach, about the environment in which teaching takes place, and about how we assess learning.

Numerous references in the literature suggest that the fundamental predisposition of higher education has been to maintain homogeneity and to adapt only when necessary (Morris 1979; Verdugo 1986). A critical example of it may be occurring now in the discussions about whether some institutions have set limits on access for Asian-American students because they are "overrepresented" in the student body. The credibility of higher education's commitment to quality and diversity is weakened when access of Asian-Americans is limited in the name of diversity and access of African-American and Latino students is limited in the name of quality. The net result of both is to perpetuate homogeneity.

If these two concepts—diversity and quality—remain in conflict, the challenge of diversity will not be met. The questions once again are whether the conflict is real and whether we are asking the right questions. When quality is measured in one way only, conflict between quality and diversity is created (Madrid 1988). The implications are that we can broaden our understanding about quality without diluting expectations for learning or for the curriculum. The institution will need to carefully evaluate its standards, its performance criteria, and the climate in which learning occurs, however.

The Changing Climate

At the same time that institutions that genuinely wish to change face significant challenges, other forces facilitate a recognition of the need for change. As troubling as some of the incidents of racial harassment and sexual harassment have been, they have served to bring to the forefront the nature and depth of some of the problems within the community of higher education. Some institutions have begun to study themselves, listening to the experiences of their staff, students, and faculty while acknowledging the need for change. Many institutions, including some of the more prestigious ones, are now leading the way in their efforts to address some of these issues. At the same time, awareness is growing at the national level that major public policy and social implications are involved. Some of the recent national commissions on the achievements of minorities have been both urgent and eloquent in their calls for change and action.

Changing student demographics and the increased voice that students and staff can find in influencing institutional policy have facilitated the awareness of a need for change. It has combined with continuing institutional concern for enrollments to put students in a more influential position than they have been in during other times. This is now a time of increasing student activism. Over the next decade as large numbers of faculty retire and larger numbers of students enter the collegiate generation, we can anticipate a shift in institutional priorities from a concern for enrollment to a concern about hiring faculty, and it may well shift the focus away from the quality of students' experience to the quality of the faculty's experience (Bowen and Schuster 1986; Smith 1988). The improved environment for faculty, their salaries, and their hiring may assist in attracting more minorities and women to faculty positions. Some evidence suggests, for example, that it may already be occurring. While the overall numbers of minority Ph.D.s has declined in recent years, the number has actually increased for minority women (Coyle and Bae 1987).

An organizational approach to diversity has significance for virtually all institutions regardless of the diversity within their student bodies, for it acknowledges the importance of diversity for society and for its future. The reality of demographic shifts is such that Hawaii's minority student enrollment is 66.4 percent and Maine's is 3.8 percent. The approach to educating for all forms of diversity—minorities, women, disabled adult learners, and part-time learners—and the importance of educating all students to live in a pluralistic world are as relevant to Maine as they are for Hawaii, however.

By creating an organization that can deal with diversity and by taking a comprehensive approach to diversity, institutions will find themselves less fragmented in dealing with the numbers of groups with special needs. It will then be more likely that the special needs and perspectives of any number of groups will be more easily accommodated. Moreover, an institution that organizes for diversity will derive many benefits from this approach, not the least of which is the increased capacity to respond to change (Weick 1979). Other opportunities are present as well:

- Revitalizing the curriculum;
- Developing new approaches to policy and organization;
- Modeling the development and growth of "global villages";
- Increasing dialogue and thus success concerning the characteristics of the environment that foster good teaching and learning;
- Creating an environment that appreciates the ways in which difference contributes to education;
- Clarifying the values that are essential to the academic mission and to the creation of community;
- Benefiting from the diversity of teaching approaches;
- And for students, particularly but not only in residential institutions, experiencing the excitement and opportunities to learn from diversity.

In other words, opportunity is greater for much enhanced institutional success and quality.

Assessment and Implications

While the challenge of diversity is indeed a national challenge, so clearly marked paths are present to creating educational organizations prepared for this process, given the complexities involved in the concept itself and in human and organizational behavior in general. Nevertheless, consistencies emerge from a wide-ranging set of literatures suggesting some of the steps needed.

Institutional Assessment

Information is an important element in efforts to create change and to assess the need for change. One of the important initial strategies that can be applied in an institution is an assessment in which all aspects of the college or university are evaluated and can serve as a point of reference. A fundamental question frames the assessment: How is the institution doing with respect to diversity?

Because the effectiveness of research is critically related to its design, an institutional audit needs to be sure

- That generalizations across groups are not made until the validity of such groups is confirmed;

- That the perspectives of a diverse set of constituencies and groups are involved in the design and interpretation of the results;

- That the instruments used to collect data, whether surveys, interviews, or tests, are checked for their validity and appropriateness for the campus and its constituencies and that, where possible, multiple methods are used;

- That the aspects of campus life and individual and group characteristics studied are inclusive enough to tap a broad range of issues.

Minorities on Campus (Green 1989) provides additional questions to broaden the focus.

Research

The need for continued research on diversity in higher education is great. Efforts to identify successful programs that may serve as models for other institutions are very important. The use of national data bases, not only to track students but also to identify institutional characteristics that facilitate success, provides important perspectives. Studies addressing institutional characteristics, however, must move beyond measures of selectivity and resources to ensure that a broader range of institutional qualities is addressed. We also need to know more about the varieties of ways in which students can be involved and how, if at all, those ways differ among specific populations. A parallel need exists, however, to track the presence and retention of faculty and staff and to look at the institutional experiences of those individuals, not only at the professional level but also at the graduate level. The Council of Graduate Schools (1986) has called for such efforts because of the centrality of faculty and staff for the efforts being considered.

A profound need also exists for greater dialogue concerning the results of empirical studies and for synthesis of results that address both theoretical and applied questions. Part of this dialogue could entail efforts to clarify apparent contradictions so that accurate conclusions can be drawn or so that further research could be developed to clarify these differences. The array of studies available that address similar questions with different methodologies and analyses and all too often reach different conclusions limits the role of the scholar and the researcher in contributing to what is actually occurring in our institutions. The loss is significant not only for educational research but also for effective institutional change.

Because institutions vary in their missions, size, complexity, and makeup, the need continues for institutional research on a number of topics that will allow individual institutions to assess their own success in educating students from widely diverse backgrounds as well as the climate of the institution for these students, for faculty and staff, and for more traditional students. Institutional research on who comes, who stays, students' satisfaction, factors associated with retention and graduation, and alumni perceptions can be very helpful in identifying issues and in creating a climate for change (Smith 1982). Great care must be exercised in framing questions for research, however, so that "deficit" models are not reintroduced.

Coordination among Sectors

Some of the data on educational preparation continue to reinforce the importance of quality preparation in kindergarten through grade 12 to students, to higher education, and to society as a whole. Traditionally, higher education has not directly addressed these issues except through schools of education. This review reinforces the degree of self-interest that higher education should have in issues of precollegiate education. Clearly, higher education cannot address all these issues on its own, but it is responsible for training the teachers and educators who run schools and has an important role in the nature of school systems and in the importance given to the educational profession. Higher education also produces the scholars for future generations of faculty. Moreover, the standards set for entrance and for assessment have an impact throughout the school years. The presidents of Stanford and Harvard are two leading educators who have acknowledged the importance of the role higher education should take in this effort. The nature of the education all students receive concerning issues of diversity can have a major impact throughout the educational system.

Additionally, in states where community colleges assume a significant role in the education of students—and in particular, minority and adult students—articulation between two-year and four-year institutions must be strengthened. This priority is addressed in California, which is actively attempting to address this issue through the development of a revised master plan for higher education in the state (Joint Committee 1988). Following up on students' progress, early intervention, articulation of courses, and coordinated student services are all important features of this effort (Cohen 1988; Donovan, Schaier-Peleg, and Forer 1987; Richardson and Bender 1987). Gathering data is a critical element, though trying to assess the retention and transfer rates from two-year institutions to four-year institutions is a challenge, given the diverse reasons students have for attending community colleges.

State higher education executive officers have developed an important report outlining the particularly significant role that states can play in setting policies and expectations to facilitate institutional and cooperative responses. In addition to financial support, programmatic support, and policy, states have important roles in the design and implementation of effective programs to gather data (Callan 1988; SHEEO 1987).

National Issues

In addition to the national studies that clarify, study, and bring attention to the challenges of diversity, a need exists for support in encouraging students to enter teaching and those fields where women and minorities have traditionally been underrepresented. Sufficient evidence suggests that previous national, corporate, and foundation efforts to encourage students to enter graduate and professional schools have been successful. That need is emerging once again as higher education prepares for a new wave of challenges and opportunities presented through the attrition of faculty hired during the growth of the sixties (Council of Graduate Schools 1986). Related to these kinds of programs is the need to focus once again on financial assistance so that students can more reasonably choose programs appropriate to their goals. They can involve direct assistance as well as programs that forgive loan obligations for students going into certain fields, such as teaching.

Costs and Commitment

Some students are very much affected by issues of cost. Yet federal and state funding of financial aid has decreased during the last 10 years, and many institutions have seen the percentage of their resources allocated to financial aid growing larger and faster than any other portion of the budget

(Stampen and Fenske 1988). The pressures on institutional budgets and national pressure to limit the increase in growth for the costs of higher education place significant strain on institutions to limit spending. To the degree that some of the changes needed, such as increased financial aid to minority students or part-time students, add to costs, the changes will be slowed.

Perhaps one of the greatest challenges presented is the need for sustained commitment and effort. The need for change is urgent, but institutional change will not be easy or quick. With equal parts of dismay and cynicism, numbers of writers observe that higher education's concerns for such issues run in cycles. Indeed, "unless we recognize the systemic nature of persistent racial inequalities, progress . . . may never be more than marginal and episodic" (Morris 1979, p. 269). Others suggest that it is only in response to a crisis that institutions or those involved in public policy will respond. The implication is that when the crisis ends, the commitment also ends (Adolphus 1984). While many are calling it a crisis, the nature of the change needed will no doubt require sustained commitment. "What is needed is a level of commitment such that the risk of retreat is forever banished" (SHEEO 1987, p. 12).

Leadership

While some authors are inclined to debate the importance of leadership in creating change, studies to date reflect the importance of institutional leadership in creating a climate for change and in achieving change. Leadership is required not only to set explicit goals and provide the resources for change but also to frame relevant questions and set the tone for the resulting discussions. For example, the dichotomy between quality and diversity needs to be eliminated so that the necessary discussions can occur in a climate that does not assume that being different is synonymous with being inferior. Energetic leadership will be required to achieve the diversity in faculty and staff that is essential to success.

Throughout the literature is the implication that some of the prevailing attitudes and values in higher education not only create a chilly climate but also may actually impede learning for many more than a minority of students. Indeed, it impedes learning for the majority. Addressing issues of cooperation versus competition and individualism versus community may result in a far healthier community and a far stronger educational system. These issues, however, require careful analysis and discussion. Sensitive and educated leadership will be required.

Conclusion

Twenty years ago a concerted effort was begun to change the shape of American higher education. In that it resulted in changes in the programs and curricula of the academy and in the makeup of its students, faculties, and staffs, these efforts have been successful. If the perspective of several decades can provide a single prevailing lesson from such changes, however, it is that to simply "add and stir" is not enough. Whether or not the melting pot will be the metaphor for pluralism, embracing diversity in all its obvious and subtle forms will be its necessary ingredient. Nearly 400 years ago, the poet John Donne observed that the loss of one person represents more than the loss of one small piece of humanity; it represents a loss to all humanity. Donne's ancient bell tolls still, for clearly the issues of diversity have significance beyond those of the disenfranchised, beyond communities that exclude rather than include. If higher education is to meet the needs of all its constituents, these issues must be confronted—not just because they are important to a special group, but because they are vital to all institutions and the nation.

PART VI

RESEARCH ISSUES

Diverse Students and Complex Issues:
A Case for Multiple Methods in College Student Research

LOUIS C. ATTINASI, JR. AND AMAURY NORA

In chapter 1 of *Diverse Methods for Research and Assessment of College Students,* Frances K. Stage presents a number of arguments for increased flexibility in our choice of methods for conducting research on and assessing college students. Underlying many of these arguments is the position that because of their extreme diversity today's college students cannot be studied adequately through the use of the structured survey instrument alone. In this chapter the authors expand this argument by examining directly the increasing diversity of the students in our institutions of higher education and its implications for research and assessment. They consider as well the complex student-related issues that researchers of college students strive to understand and the implications of this for the selection of research and assessment methods. Finally, they present some alternative research strategies for examining the experiences of diverse student bodies relative to complex issues, and illustrate their use by describing a recent series of studies that they have, independently and jointly, conducted on the persistence of Hispanic college students.

The Diversity of the American College Student Body

Background Characteristics

During the last two decades there have been dramatic changes in the face, or more accurately, faces, of the American college-going population. Figures on nationwide enrollment during the period 1976–1986 compiled by the U.S. Department of Education (Editors, 1990, pp. 30–31) indicate the growing diversity of our students. According to these figures, the decade saw substantial increases in the numbers of individuals from nonmajority racial and ethnic groups and in the number of women who were enrolled in American colleges and universities. Between 1976 and 1986 the number of Native Americans enrolled in all institutions of higher education increased by 19%, the number of Hispanics by 63%, and the number of Asian Americans by 126%. After a more substantial increase in the preceding decade (1966–1976), the number of Blacks increased by 5%. In addition, the total number of women enrolled increased by 27%. (During the 10-year period the total number of men remained nearly the same, while the number of White men actually decreased by 4%.)

The increasing ethnic and racial pluralism of the American college student body can be attributed to a number of factors, particularly the civil rights activities and legislation of the 1960s and 1970s, the growth in size of the subpopulations native to the North American continent (Mexican Americans and Native Americans) and their demands for full participation in American life, and the recent waves of immigration, particularly from Southeast Asia following the Vietnam

War. The greater representation of women in our student bodies certainly reflects changes in traditional views regarding educational and vocational objectives for women together with the ever-growing need of single mothers and displaced homemakers to be educated for work. The percentage of women has increased to the point that it now equals, indeed in most instances surpasses, the percentage of men in the total enrollment of institutions that enroll both men and women.

Today's college students are more diverse than their predecessors in other ways as well. For example, the numbers of students with special needs, including the physically challenged and those with learning disabilities, have grown as society's increasing sensitivity to problems of physical and educational access has been translated into legislation. In addition, older students constitute an ever-increasing percentage of higher education enrollment, reflecting both the aging of the general population and the growing trend of career changes during adulthood. Finally, the increasing availability of financial aid and targeted recruiting have resulted in the enrollment of more individuals from financially disadvantaged families.

Campus Subcultures

The students on our campuses are diverse not only in terms of the background characteristics they bring with them but also with respect to membership in student subcultures (Kuh & Whitt, 1988). Student subcultures, which are present in every institution of higher education, are based on particular "orientations" toward (Clark & Trow, 1966) or "perspectives" on (Hughes, Becker, & Geer, 1962), a college education. For example, a subculture may be oriented around a view of college as providing intellectual challenge, preparation for work, peer-group socialization, or even a place for "killing time." Campus subcultures are important because they provide their members with the means of coping with the difficulties of college life through social support and guidelines for living. They influence the way the members interpret events and problems, providing them with attitudes and values on the basis of which they "can build consistent patterns of response, enabling them to fit into the activities of the school" (Hughes et al., 1962, p. 529). Through their effects on the orientation of students toward learning and extracurricular activities, student subcultures can have profound consequences for the institutions in which they exist (Kuh & Whitt 1988).

The variety of subcultures present on a campus are the consequence of characteristics of both the institution and its students (Kuh & Whitt 1988). Students' precollege characteristics (e.g., values and attitudes) and prior acquaintance with one another as well as their postmatriculation characteristics (residential, class and organizational propinquity) influence the development of subcultural groups. So, too, does the institutional context, including the institutional ethos, interests of persons within the institution, authority structure, and institutional size and complexity (Clark & Trow, 1966).

Some (e.g., Clark & Trow, 1966; Katchadourian & Boli, 1985) have proposed general typologies of student subcultures. One of the best known of these is a typology developed by Clark and Trow (1966) that has four categories: the collegiate, vocational, academic, and nonconformist subcultures. A more recent typology (Katchadourian & Boli, 1985) based on a longitudinal study of Stanford University students in the early 1980s also includes four categories: the careerists, the intellectuals, the strivers, and the unconnected. Such typologies are largely heuristic or analytic devices intended to illustrate the concept of student subcultures in higher education, not descriptions of specific groups on a particular campus (Clark & Trow, 1966). Furthermore, the included categories often fail to meet generally accepted criteria for subcultures, such as persistent interaction, processes of socialization, mechanisms for social control, and norms that differ from the parent (overall institutional) culture (see Bolton & Kammayer, 1972; Horowitz, 1987; Van Maanen & Barley, 1985; Warren, 1968).

Still, typologies of student subcultures such as those proposed by Clark and Trow and Katchadourian and Boli underscore the fact that there are fundamental differences among students in their postmatriculation orientations toward a college education and begin to suggest the diversity of campus peer groups to which college students can become attached. On any particular campus, the variety of such groups is likely to be large and, at least in some respects, unique vis-a-vis what is to be found in other institutions (Clark & Trow, 1966). If, as case studies of student subcultures at particular institutions have shown (Becker, Geer, & Hughes, 1968; Becker, Geer, Hughes, & Strauss, 1961; Snyder, 1971), the influence of these subcultures is pervasive in the lives of their members, it would behoove the researcher of college students to take them fully into consideration.

Researching a Diverse Student Body

Students who come from different ethnic backgrounds are likely to be culturally different. Furthermore, even students who share the same ethnic culture may differ subculturally because of differences in their sex, age, physical, financial, or educational status, or their campus peer group membership. That is, we can expect that on one level (i.e., that of the general culture) the same "collective, mutually shaping patterns of norms, values, practices, beliefs, and assumptions" will be guiding their behavior and providing them with "a frame of reference within which to interpret the meaning of events and actions on and off campus" (Kuh & Whitt, 1988, pp. 1213). On other levels (i.e., the subcultural ones), however, the shaping factors will be quite different.

Not only must the research of today's college students contend with their cultural and diversity but also with their individual subcultural, even cultural, distinctiveness. Under such circumstances the inadequacy of the structured survey instrument constructed largely from the perspective of the researcher becomes apparent. The user of such an instrument makes the assumption, albeit usually implicitly, that he or she "knows exactly what is important to ask about the college student experience," and as a consequence, the research process remains closed "to the possible emergence of hidden issues, new themes, and unpredicted discoveries". Can we expect such a data collection device alone to lead us to an understanding of the experiences of diverse students in institutions of higher education? And if not, how is the researcher of a culturally, or at least subculturally, diverse student body to proceed?

Fortunately, such a researcher has a rich research tradition upon which to draw. Cultural anthropologists have long studied groups of people culturally different from themselves with ethnography (Pelto & Pelto, 1978), a methodology appropriate for cross-cultural research. The methodology provides an insider's perspective on what is happening in the group's natural setting. (Anthropologists typically study groups in their natural settings.) This has been referred to as the *emic* perspective (Pike, 1967), and it is uncovered by research methods such as participant observation and in-depth interviewing. These methods allow the researcher to understand an experience (e.g., what it is like to be a Black student in a largely White institution) from the point of view of the experiencer himself or herself. This is accomplished without the imposition of prior researcher conceptions. It is only after uncovering the insider's perspective through "thick" qualitative data collection that the researcher then seeks to interpret his or her observations from an outsider's, or *etic*, perspective (Pike, 1967).

Open-ended research techniques such as participant-observation (Spradley, 1980) and in-depth interviewing (Spradley, 1979) allow the researcher to study culturally different people in an open-minded (but not empty-headed) way. Initially, relative to the broad topic under investigation, anthropologists permit their informants (they prefer this term to *subjects*, as it recognizes the active role of the researched in the research project) to define the relevant areas of inquiry. While recognizing that there are likely to be multiple realities—informants carry around in their heads, and act on the basis of, many different views of what is going on in the setting—they look for convergence of information. This is referred to as *triangulation* and is accomplished when different sources and/or methods of data collection inform findings. In addition to participant-observation and in-depth interviewing, document analysis and the examination of unobtrusive informational residues are typically used in efforts to achieve triangulation.

As the study proceeds and the investigator achieves increasing triangulation of sources and methods, he or she is likely to begin focusing on some particular aspect of what is happening in the setting. This research process is often compared to a funnel: it is broad at the top, or beginning, and gradually tapers to a narrow bottom, or end. However, although some singular aspect of the setting eventually becomes the research focus, the rest is not ignored. The researcher continues to pay attention to as much of the context as he or she is able. This is because the anthropologist believes that the culture of any group is an integrated whole and that any part is incomprehensible unless interpreted relative to the whole.

An anthropologist collects and analyzes data simultaneously. Decisions about what to do next are largely based on the sense made of where he or she has already been. This refers not only to the identification of new observations to be made and new questions to be asked (and of where, when, and from whom to make or ask them) but also to the emergence and clarification of concepts and working hypotheses. The research process is largely inductive as the investigator seeks to derive more general concepts and understandings from the welter of concrete details he or she compiles. Tentative concepts and understandings are tested against the evidence resulting from a subsequent wave of data collection. Ethnographic research has often been referred to as *qualitative,* since the data that are collected and analyzed are preponderantly verbal, Geertz (1973) called this "thick description"—not numerical.

It is not unusual for an anthropologist to spend 1 or 2 years in the field collecting and initially analyzing data, and then a comparable period of time in completing the analysis and writing up the results. The termination of an ethnographic study is always arbitrary, reflecting as much the exhaustion of resources—time and money—as any belief that the culture (or the particular aspect that is under investigation) is finally understood (Lincoln & Guba, 1985). The findings are typically written up as a case study (Lincoln & Guba, 1985; chapter 4) so that the ethnographer can weave a rich narrative based on what he or she has seen and heard, a narrative that captures both the emic—as much as possible the ethnographer uses the actual words of the informants themselves—and the etic perspectives on what has happened.

Wolcott (1988) drew the distinction between conducting a full-scale ethnography, on the one hand, and borrowing from the repertoire of (qualitative) methods typically employed by an ethnographer to conduct a field study that is not truly ethnographic, on the other. The distinction lies primarily in the ethnographer's attention to the broad cultural context within which the particular events of interest take place. Thus an ethnography of schooling that fails to deal with the context of schooling beyond the bounds of the school itself is not an ethnography at all.

Wolcott's distinction called attention to the fact that researchers of many stripes make use of the qualitative research techniques typically associated with ethnography. Some of these researchers come from other disciplinary backgrounds, most notably sociology, and others from no identifiable disciplinary background at all. The latter is true of many researchers who use qualitative methods to study aspects of education. The particular scholarly orientation underlying their use notwithstanding, the openness of these methods to frames of reference different from those routinely used by researchers of college students makes them particularly well suited for investigating our culturally and subculturally diverse study bodies.

The Complexity of Student-Related Issues

Today's researcher of college students must contend not only with a diverse population of students but also with a diverse and complex set of issues. Thus, to adequately explain why college students exhibit various levels of retention and achievement, or to adequately assess their academic progress, it is necessary to consider more than one or two potentially influencing factors at a time. Reviewers of the research literature on student retention (Attinasi & Nora, 1987) have shown how the failure to do so for years slowed progress in the study of this phenomenon.

Many of the topics of interest to researchers and assessors of college students have not been examined, or are only just beginning to be examined, in terms of theoretical perspectives or conceptual frameworks. Such frameworks are often (and certainly ought to be) the basis of multifactor, explanatory models of such phenomena as college student retention and achievement. By identifying and clarifying the processes leading to various outcomes of college attendance, naturalistic research, including ethnographic inquiries, can be helpful in generating these frameworks, which then can be verified quantitatively. Moreover, such studies can generate hypotheses concerning relationships among factors in existing frameworks that can be tested through qualitative research. In addition, naturalistic research is capable of producing findings that will enhance our understanding of processes underlying cause-and-effect relationships established through quantitative research. This argues for researching student outcomes and assessing student progress with a variety of methods.

An Example: Investigations of the Retention of Hispanic Students

Student retention is one area that has been investigated by means of both naturalistic and quantitative (survey) inquiries. Duran (1987), Nora (1987), and Attinasi (1989) have all conducted studies in which the issue of the persistence of undergraduate Hispanic students, in particular, has been addressed. The use of various methodologies, (i.e., trend analysis, multivariate analysis, structural modeling, and naturalistic research) in these investigations helped to increase understanding of Hispanic student retention, an issue that is complex not only because of the complicated nature of the retention phenomenon itself but also because of the additional factor of the cultural uniqueness of Hispanics. This section now describes the various methods that have been used to investigate the retention of Hispanic students and discusses the unique contributions of qualitative (in-depth interviewing of persisters and nonpersisters) and quantitative (causal model testing with survey data) research approaches and the potential contribution of their integration.

Trend Analysis

In a study of Hispanics' precollege and undergraduate education, Duran (1987) identified specific trends related to Hispanics' participation in higher education and discussed the implications for the issues of access, retention, academic performance, and degree attainment. In particular, he documented the underrepresentation of Hispanic students relative to non-Hispanic Whites and the substantial differences between these groups in degree attainment rates, retention rates, test score level, and overall academic performance, and with respect to many other indicators of success in college. Duran did not propose potential causes of Hispanics' underrepresentation and underachievement in institutions of higher education, but his profile made clear the need to move beyond statistical description of the condition to an understanding of why the condition existed and what could be done to ameliorate it.

Many questions left unanswered by Duran's study beg to be addressed: Why are Hispanic students underrepresented in undergraduate degree attainment in all areas of higher education? Is it a matter of aspirations, high school features, institutional factors, or all of these things? Are aspirations affected by characteristics specific to 2- and 4-year institutions? What insights about the condition of Hispanic students can we obtain by talking directly and in-depth with those who are affected? Answers to these questions require both quantitative and naturalistic studies of Hispanic experiences in higher education, studies that could lead to the building and testing of theory in this area (Olivas, 1983).

A Quantitative Model

One attempt to address these questions was made by Nora (1987), who developed a quantitative causal model of student retention based on Tinto's (1975, 1987) theoretical framework and tested it with a sample of Hispanic students drawn from a 2-year college population. Nora's model includes the four key sets of variables conceptualized by Tinto to explain retention: (a) the levels of the student's integration into the academic and social lives of the institution, (b) the level of the student's commitment to an educational goal and to the institution, (c) the nature of the student's (precollege) background, and (d) a withdrawal/persistence decision. In sum, Tinto hypothesized that higher levels of social and academic integration result in higher levels of commitment both to the institution and to educational goals. The latter, in turn, increases the likelihood of persistence.

Nora used structural equation modeling to assess the appropriateness of the hypothesized causal model. The analysis provides substantiation for the relationships hypothesized in the study and indicates that the causal model is a plausible representation of influences on student retention specific to Hispanic students in 2-year institutions. Although the model can explain a good deal of the variance in Hispanic student attrition, several factors found to be significant in predicting student persistence for majority students in 4-year residential institutions do not appear to have an impact on the retention of the Hispanic community college students Nora studied.

Thus the findings are only partially supportive of the hypothesized relationship between measures of academic integration and retention found in previous retention studies. A relationship between measures of social integration and retention can not be substantiated for Hispanics in 2-year institutions, although social integration had been found to have the largest influence on withdrawal decisions for majority students. For Hispanic students, measures of initial commitments (to the institution and educational goals) have a significantly large direct effect on retention.

A Naturalistic Study

At about the same time as Nora's study, Attinasi (1989) took a different tack on the problem and conducted a naturalistic study of Hispanic retention. This was an exploratory investigation with the purpose of determining factors related to retention that could be identified through an in-depth interviewing of both persisting and nonpersisting Mexican-American students. Attinasi sought qualitative data to describe, from the student's point of view, the sociopsychological context within which he or she decided to persist or not to persist through the freshman year. In lieu of one of the existing conceptual frameworks of persistence/attrition, the inquiry was guided only by a broad research perspective, the sociology of everyday life (Douglas, 1980). This perspective focuses on everyday social interaction in natural situations and emphasizes initiating research with (a) the experience and observation of people interacting in concrete, face-to-face situations and (b) an analysis of the actors' meanings.

Data were collected through in-depth, open-ended interviewing of persisting and nonpersisting students, and analyzed inductively to generate grounded concepts for interpreting the context within which these students made persistence decisions. The analysis began with open-coding of the interview transcriptions, that is, the coding of their contents in as many ways as possible. The coding categories related to context and setting, informants' definitions of situations, informants' ways of thinking about people and objects, process (sequence of events, changes over time), activities, events, strategies, relationships, and social structure. This was followed by a data reduction step in which the number of coding categories was reduced, and the analysis began to take shape conceptually. Saliency of the categories, as judged by frequency of occurrence, uniqueness, and apparent connectedness to other categories, was the criterion for initial decisions to retain, merge, and/or discard coding categories. That is, it became possible to link categories to one another through higher-order categories. A higher-order category, or concept, was one under which another category could be fitted without sacrificing the latter's integrity. In this way initial coding categories became subcategories or properties of higher-level categories. Eventually, connections between higher-level categories were established.

From this data analysis, two conceptual schemes emerged: "getting ready" and "getting in." The getting-ready concept includes acquiring early in life through parental communication an expectation of going to college, witnessing early in life the college-going of family members, having vicarious experiences of college through communications from high school teachers, and having direct experience of college through prematriculation visits to college campuses. Getting in includes postmatriculation experiences associated with the student's management of the new environment. Here two subconstructs, "getting to knows" and "scaling downs," emerge. Getting to know involves acquiring familiarity with the physical, social, and academic spheres of the campus through contacts with veteran students and through information sharing with fellow neophytes. Scaling down is the tendency of informants to confine their activities to narrow portions of the three campus spheres (physical, social, academic), in effect reducing the amount of new knowledge they have to acquire to successfully negotiate them. As persisters and nonpersisters differ in terms of both getting-ready and getting-in experiences, Attinasi concluded that these concepts are important for understanding Hispanic student retention.

Combining Naturalistic and Quantitative Approaches

As the investigations of Hispanic student retention by Nora and Attinasi illustrate, research on college students (or the assessment of their progress) may involve either the establishment of relationships between variables (through quantitative survey methods, for example) or in-depth examination of behavioral processes (through naturalistic research methods). But it may also be desirable to integrate the two approaches in order to address the issue of unexplained variance in quantitative models and enhance understanding of relationships established between factors in these models. When tested empirically, causal models of phenomena such as college student retention and achievement typically have accounted for only a very modest amount of the variance in the behavior (e.g., persistence) of interest. The large unexplained variance associated with most of these models is probably due to either (a) the failure of the researcher to adequately operationalize the factors specified in the conceptual framework from which the model is constructed or (b) some misspecification of factors in the conceptual framework itself.

Suppose, for example, there is a conceptual framework that posits a direct effect of some factor, say commitment to the institution, on the student's persistence in the institution. Suppose further that a researcher operationalizes the conceptual framework as a quantitative causal model, measuring the commitment to the institution and persistence variables in specific ways, and then tests the causal model. If in repeated tests of the model the researcher consistently finds no direct effect of the measure(s) of commitment on the measure(s) of persistence, he or she might be tempted to conclude that a direct relationship between the factors is misspecified in the conceptual framework. This conclusion is unwarranted, however, as it is equally plausible that the failure to find a direct relationship between the factors is due to inappropriate operationalization of one or both of them in the causal model.

The exclusion of relevant varieties from a causal model leads to exaggerated or underestimated effects and reduction in the variance accounted for by variables in the model (Pedhazur, 1982). Even the exclusion of variables that are not correlated with other variables in the model can have adverse effects because, by increasing error terms (unexplained variance), such exclusion can distort the relationships between the included variables (Pedhazur, 1982).

One way to reduce the size of the error terms associated with existing quantitative models of college student outcomes such as persistence is to begin to incorporate into these models findings from naturalistic research (Fry, Chantavanich, & Chantavanich, 1981). Naturalistic research has the potential for identifying factors that influence outcomes that will otherwise remain unidentified, hence unmeasured, and thus subsumed under error terms. The inclusion of these omitted factors in conceptual models, and of appropriate measures of them in causal models, should not only reduce the risk of specification error but also increase our understanding of the processes underlying relationships established in these models.

The above logic led Nora, Attinasi, and Matonak (1990) to undertake a study seeking to improve the explanatory capacity of a quantitative model. The study combined Tinto's (1975, 1987) framework for explaining retention with some of the qualitative factors Attinasi (1989) identified in his naturalistic investigation. The result was a causal model that includes new measures of Tinto's background component based on Attinasi's getting-ready concept. It was tested through path analysis on a sample of academically underprepared students drawn from a community college population.

Most previous studies found, contrary to Tinto's conceptualization, that the precollege background of students has little or no direct effect on persistence decisions. The previous failure to find such an effect could be due to the failure to operationalize the background factor appropriately. Measures based on the getting-ready concept might specify the precollege component better and allow us to confirm a direct effect of it on retention.

The new causal model has a good overall fit to the data in explaining the variance in both integration and retention factors. The getting-ready measures affect positively and directly the two major intervening variables in the model: social integration and academic integration. However, contrary to what was hypothesized, they have a significant negative direct effect on retention itself, perhaps because the getting-ready measures are based on university students oriented principally to the 4-year institution. We may expect that the greater the number and intensity of these experiences the more quickly the decision will he made to transfer out of the community college.

In any event, this study illustrates the potential of combining naturalistic and quantitative methods to investigate college student outcomes. The findings of Attinasi's interview study suggest a new, perhaps better, operationalization of the background component of Tinto's theoretical framework. It is not difficult to conceive of improved measurement of other factors in Tinto's framework (and factors in other models of retention and other phenomena) through the findings of naturalistic research, which would be subsequently tested with survey data. Naturalistic research also has the potential for providing in-depth understanding of relationships between factors that are well established through the testing of causal models with survey data. For example, although we might have established a statistically significant relationship between particular quantitative measures of, say, social integration and persistence through causal model testing, we might still wish to understand how the relationship plays itself out in the everyday life of individual students; after all, there is only so much of human behavior that can ultimately be captured in numbers. To achieve such understanding is the object of naturalistic research.

Conclusion

We have described both the increasing diversity of American college students and the complexity of the issues typically addressed by those who conduct research on them. Both have implications for research methods. The cultural and subcultural diversity of students calls for the use of methods that allow the researcher to be sensitive to diverse frames of reference, many of which may be quite different from the investigator's own. A standardized questionnaire developed from the researcher's own frame of reference will not adequately capture the experiences and attitudes of students who have diverse racial or ethnic backgrounds or who are subculturally diverse due to differences in age, sex, special needs, financial status, or campus peer-group affiliation. Rather, the researcher also needs to be able to draw upon the rich research methodology developed by anthropologists and others who have traditionally engaged in cross-cultural research. The researcher needs to ground his or her understanding of what happens to students in college in the students' own understanding of these events.

The complexity of potential issues—for example, retention and achievement—also argues for the use of a variety of methods, both naturalistic and quantitative, in the research and assessment of college students. To understand student retention or achievement requires both the development and testing of multifactor quantitative models and detailed understanding of student perceptions of influences on these outcomes. The findings of naturalistic approaches can both assist in the development of the conceptual frameworks from which quantitative models are drawn and illuminate our understanding of the processes that underlie associations identified in these models. The authors have used their own independent and joint investigations of the retention of undergraduate Hispanic students to illustrate the potential of this kind of multiple-method approach for studying a unique cultural group.

Further Reading

For further reading on the experiences of diverse college students, see particularly Fleming's *Blacks in College* (1984) Olivas' *Latino College Students* (1986), or *Evolving Theoretical Perspectives on College Students* (1990) edited by Moore. (For complete publications data, see the reference list.)

References

Attinasi, L. C. Jr. (1989). Getting in: Mexican Americans' perceptions of university attendance and the implications for freshman year persistence. *Journal of Higher Education 60,* 247–277.

Attinasi, L. C., Jr., & Nora, A. (1987, November). *The next step in the study of student persistence in college.* Paper presented at the meeting of the Association for the Study of Higher Education, Baltimore, MD.

Becker, H. S., Geer, B., & Hughes, E. C. (1968) . *Making the grade: The academic side of college life.* New York: Wiley.

Becker, H. S., Geer, B., Hughes, E. C., & Strauss, A. L. (1961). *Boys in white.* Chicago: University of Chicago Press.

Bolton, C. D., & Kammayer, K C. W. (1972). Campus cultures, role orientations, and social types. In K. Feldman (Ed.), *College and student: Selected readings in the social psychology of higher education.* New York: Pergamon.

Clark, B. R., & Trow, M. (1966). The organizational context. In T. M. Newcomb & E. K. Wilson (Eds.), *College peer groups: Problems and prospects for research.* Chicago: Aldine.

Douglas J. D. (1980). Introduction to the sociologies of everyday life. In J. D. Douglas, *Introduction to the sociologies of everyday life.* (pp. 1–19). Boston: Allyn & Bacon.

Duran, R. P. (1987). Hispanics' precollege and undergraduate education: Implications for science and engineering students. In L. S. Dix (Ed.), *Minorities: Their underrepresentation and career differentials in science and engineering* (pp. 73–128). Washington, DC: National Academy.

Editors of *The Chronicle of Higher Education.* (1990). The almanac of higher education (1989–1990). Chicago: University of Chicago Press.

Fleming, J. (1984). *Blacks in college: A comparative study of students' success in Black and White institutions.* San Francisco: Jossey-Bass.

Fry, G., Chantavanich, S., & Chantavanich, A. (1981). Merging quantitative and qualitative research techniques: Toward a new research paradigm. *Anthropology and Education Quarterly 12,* 145–48.

Geertz, C. (1973). *The interpretation of cultures.* New York: Basic Books.

Horowitz, H. I. (1987). *Campus life: Undergraduate cultures from the end of the 18th century to the present.* New York: Knopf.

Hughes, E. C., Becker, H. S., & Geer, B. (1962). Student culture and academic effort. In N. Sanford (Ed.), *The American College.* New York: Wiley.

Katchadourian, H. A., & Boli, J. (1985). *Careerism and intellectualism among college students.* San Francisco: Jossey-Bass.

Kuh, G. D., & Whitt, E. J. (1988). *The invisible tapestry: Culture in American colleges and universities* (ASHE-ERIC Higher Education Report No. 1). Washington, DC: Association for the Study of Higher Education.

Lincoln, Y., & Guba, E. (1985). *Naturalistic inquiry.* Beverly Hills, CA. Sage.

Moore, L. (1990). *Evolving theoretical perspectives on students* (New Directions for Student Services, No. 51). San Francisco: Jossey-Bass.

Nora, A. (1987). Determinants of retention among Chicano college students: A structural model. *Research in Higher Education, 26,* 31–59.

Nora, A., Attinasi, L. C., Jr., & Matonak, A. (1990). Testing qualitative indicators of precollege factors in Tinto's attrition model: A community college population. *Review of Higher Education, 13,* 337–356.

Olivas, M. A. (1983). Research and theory on Hispanic education: Students, finance, and governance. *Atzalan, 14,* 111–146.

Olivas, M. (1986). *Latino college students.* New York: Teacher's College Press.

Pedhazur, E. J. (1982). *Multiple regression in behavioral research* (2nd ed.). New York: Holt, Rinehart and Winston.

Pelto, P. J., & Pelto, C. H. (1978). *Anthropological research: The structure of inquiry* (2nd ed.). New York: Cambridge University Press.

Pike, K. L. (1967). *Language in relation to a unified theory of the structure of human behavior.* Hague: Mouton.

Snyder, B. R. (1971). *The hidden curriculum.* Cambridge: M.I.T. Press.

Spradley, J. P. (1979). *The ethnographic interview.* New York: Holt, Rinehart and Winston.

Spradley, J. P. (1980). *Participant observation.* New York: Holt, Rinehart and Winston.

Tinto, V. (1975). Dropout from higher education: A theoretical synthesis of recent research. *Review of Educational Research, 45,* 89–125

Tinto, V. (1987). *Student leaving: Rethinking the causes and cures of student attrition.* Chicago: University of Chicago Press.

Van Maanen, J., & Barley, S. R. (1985). Occupational communities: Culture and control in organizations. *Research in Organizational Behavior, 6,* 287–365.

Warren, J. R. (1968). Student perceptions of college subcultures. *American Educational Research Journal, 5,* 213–232.

Wolcott, H. F. (1988). Ethnographic research in education. In R. M. Jaeger (Ed.), *Complementary methods for research in education* (pp. 187–206). Washington, DC: American Educational Research Association.

Recognizing Diversity:
A Need for a Paradigm Shift

Li-Rong Lilly Cheng

The number of language-minority students in the United States has increased significantly in the past 2 decades. Consequently, a paradigm shift has been proposed in an attempt to restructure the present curriculum by encompassing cultural and linguistic characteristics of minorities, which, in turn, will greatly enhance the teaching/learning process. A brief survey of past, present, and expected language-minority students illustrates the need to adopt a paradigm shift. In 1970, 20% of the U.S. public school students were minorities, and in 1986, 29.1% were minorities. Many of the recent foreign-born immigrants and refugees came from Asia and Latin America. In 1990, ethnic minority students constituted half of California's and a third of the nation's student population. According to the U.S. Bureau of Census, African-Americans will increase by 12.8% over the next decade, and the Latino population will grow by 26.8%. It is expected that by the year 2000, there will be 10 million Asian-Americans in the U.S. There are students sitting at the doorways of universities who are not unqualified but are unprepared (Grant, 1989).

The aforementioned influx of language-minority students has caused inevitable repercussions at our schools that can no longer be ignored. This article explores the implications for faculty members as well as students. Educators must be reeducated in how to relate to students and how to better adapt their teaching techniques to this new breed of students. The paradigm shift provides a detailed guideline that will generate new insights by the students in our classrooms and new approaches to current teaching methods. An assessment of today's student body profile must be made in order to properly instruct the students.

Diverse Populations

African-Americans

In 1986, college enrollment in the U.S. totaled 12,161,778, including 1,070,000 African-American students. The enrollment of African-American students in 4-year, predominantly White institutions has fallen short of anticipated goals. African-American faculty and administrators have remained a minute proportion of the tenured and senior staff in colleges and universities. The National Study data (Allen, 1987) classified African-American students as socially, culturally, and academically excluded individuals. Students also reported problems with social adjustment, cultural alienation, racial discrimination, and strained interpersonal relations, especially with the largely White faculty.

Other Language-Minority Students

By the year 2000, the number of limited-English-proficient (LEP) school-age children in the U.S. will have increased from the present 2.8 million to an estimated 3.4 million. The percentage of Asians was approximately 1% in 1970 and is expected to reach 4% by the year 2000. This represents a growth of 400% in 30 years. The Hispanic/Latino population has increased to 17 million and is expected to reach 21 million by the year 2000. Three quarters of all LEP students speak Spanish, and most of the others speak an Asian language (4.4% speak Vietnamese, 2.8% speak Cantonese, 2.4% speak Cambodian, 2.1% speak Filipino/Tagalog, and 2.19% speak Hmong).

The majority of Asian LEP students are from the People's Republic of China, Hong Kong, Taiwan, Korea, Cambodia, Laos, Vietnam, and the Philippines. The majority of Middle Eastern LEP students come from Iran, Syria, Jordan, and Lebanon. In summary, 40% of the immigrants come from Asia and 40% from Latin America. The majority of Hispanic/Latino students come from Mexico (61%), Puerto Rico (15%), and Cuba (6%).

International Students

The United States has 25% of the world's higher education institutions. Eight percent of the population in higher education are from foreign countries. The majority of foreign students come from Taiwan, China, India, and Korea. These student populations are heterogeneous in terms of native language, degree of acculturation, country of birth, immigration experience, and socioeconomic status.

The overall limited and unsuccessful past experiences of African-Americans and Latinos in higher education, coupled with vast increase in LEP minority and international students in all levels-of education, has provoked the need to alert faculty to better accommodate each and every student in the usage of diverse dialects. Teaching strategies to enhance communications and bridge cultural gaps need to be infused into the curriculum.

Bridging the Gap

In the United States, teachers allow greater freedom and more informality in the classroom, encouraging creativity, discussion, and debate. Students are expected to volunteer information and to ask questions. Most foreign-born students have to shift from the lecture method of teaching to the freer learning environment, from memorization of facts to problem solving, from dependence on teachers to self-reliance in finding information which may be alien to them (Cheng, 1987).

Not all people from the same culture have the same values and beliefs: there are tremendous individual differences. An awareness of the general cultural and linguistic values of diverse populations is an essential tool for educators that makes possible more effective communication with diverse populations, while recognizing many of their difficulties, avoiding potential conflicts, and establishing an atmosphere that will facilitate learning.

It is critical that university courses address the realities of serving people who are diverse in terms of cultural orientation, economic standing, and academic background. The educational attainment of minorities in this country is not keeping pace with their growth in numbers. If left uncorrected, this situation will create serious problems for our society as a whole (Grant, 989).

Universities must adopt educational approaches that emphasize individual instruction, identify areas of concern, and design programs to enhance learning. This must be done so that all students have the opportunity to achieve to their maximum ability (Allen, 1987). Indeed, it is important for us to infuse multicultural and pluralistic perspectives into our course content, design, instruction, and evaluation processes (Cole, 1989; Erickson & Iglesias, 1986; Hakuta, 1987; Powell & Collier, this issue; Taylor, 1986; Westby, in press).

Paradigm Shift

From Compensatory to Enhancement

If we are serious about teaching in a multicultural university of the 21st century, then we must embrace diversity and endorse shifting of our paradigms. We need to challenge our traditional mode of operation when we discuss issues of language and language use. Custred (this issue) stresses the importance of standard English and urged institutions of higher education to provide *compensatory education* to individuals who use "folk speech." Perhaps we need to rethink the process. Instead of compensating for the *deficiency*, can we not enhance and add to the student's repertoire? Custred indicates that minority students experience alienation in school. Only when they feel that they are accepted can they feel the school is "their" school. Such acceptance comes from faculty as well as fellow students, who are sensitive to diverse styles of writing, speaking learning, socializing, and communicating (Vaughn-Coke, 1983).

From Deficit to Asset

Instead of looking at the diverse patterns of writing and speaking as deficient, perhaps we can be enriched by the different modes and ways with words (Heath, 1983). Society attaches a stigma to those who have "deficits." If our students bring to us differing forms of communication, they need to be considered as assets and be discussed in the context of diversity. Hoover advocates a change from the deficit model to the excellence/vindicationist model, which fits well with this paradigm shift.

Languages are continually undergoing change, and the results of various changes are reflected in the different varieties of the language (Wolfram, 1986). The following elements are often subject to language variation: verbs, verb auxiliaries, negatives, inflectional suffixes in nouns, and various forms of pronouns, articles, and adverbs. Phonological differences across languages and dialects are among the most obtrusive characteristics of language. One source of variation comes from "within the language" itself, as languages naturally adjust and readjust their phonological systems over time. Other sound differences come from "outside the language," as English has adopted sounds from other languages with which it has come into contact.

From Reduction to Addition

This section offers instructional strategies to enhance teaching learning. Code-switching, which means alternation in the use of two languages/dialects, is a natural occurrence and serves important social functions. When code-switching is used to maximize communication and to strengthen not only the content but the essence of the message, it is considered an asset (Cheng & Butler, 1989). Culture is transcended by the use of language only when the dialect and the code-switching are considered legitimate. Instead of reducing one's accent, one can add another style or articulation to one's repertoire and code-switch to meet communicative demands of various social and cultural situations (Grosjean,1982). Linguistically and culturally diverse students need to add to their existing repertoire the various forms of academic, social, and public discourse. Powell and Collier observe a large disparity between the types of public speaking skills that faculty teach and the types of public speaking demands that graduates reported. Therefore, additional materials need to be included in public speaking courses not only to enhance the students' public speaking skills but to add cultural literacy in the course content so that they will improve the form, content, and function of their public discourse (Condon & Yousef, 1975; Hall, 1959; Philips, 1983; Scollon & Scollon, 1981).

Many programs designed to reduce foreign accents (Biederman, 1989; Compton, 1983) are gaining recognition in the field of speech pathology. These programs range from focusing on training in English phonology to enhancing communication skill, including interpersonal communication. Many students have mastered English grammar, have a repertoire of vocabulary sufficient for everyday conversation, and appear to be fluent in conducting their daily business.

However, they have voiced their concerns and are self-conscious about their lack of social, cultural, and conversational competence in English (Shaw, 1985; Wald, 1987). Most say that they want to "sound like an American." Comments such as "You speak very well" or "There is no need for you to receive training in English" are often met with disbelief. One must ask why these students disagree with such evaluations.

Many graduates from such programs continue to feel socially isolated, are frustrated with their inability to communicate effectively (Heller, 1986; Molholt, 1988; Weade & Greene, 1985), and receive negative feedback on their lack of communication skills during evaluations. In the workplace, they are victims of the "glass ceiling" phenomenon: an unseen and unperceived constraint on promotion or advancement.

MacKay (1978), Dreher (1981), and Wiener (1983) maintained that speech pathologists in urban settings need to broaden their knowledge base in order to serve the nonnative speakers. To be successful with nonnative speakers of English, the teacher must understand how the communication styles of other cultures contrast with what Americans consider "effective." Dialectician Stern, as reported by Biederman (1989), indicated that the goal of accent reduction training is to gain greater intelligibility and that nonnative speakers often make false or negative impressions due to their "foreign accent."

From Tolerance to Acceptance

The notion of tolerating differences connotes an underlying disregard and indifference, while accepting differences connotes approval and support. When social dialects are tolerated, they are considered "harmless" but not "useful" and are often not encouraged. Powell and Collier, joined by many researchers (Cole & Deal, in press), further advocate the need for a more pluralistic perspective in course content, instructional processes and evaluation processes. The true essence of pluralism is not to tolerate differences but to embrace diversity. One might tolerate the "folk" speech of another individual because of its differences and yet not understand that the "folk" speech of that individual represents a different world-view and set of experiences. An attempt to modify that speech presents a message that violates the person's right to choose.

Language involves considerably more than the transmission of literal content. The term pragmatics refers to how the forms of language are used to perform the particular functions of language in its social setting. Given the variety of factors that have to be considered by a native speaker of English in choosing a strategy for performing a speech act, it is easy to imagine how problematic the appropriate choice of a strategy can become in a multicultural context.

The distinction between literal and nonliteral context is not always obvious, particularly in a cross-cultural setting, where both the knowledge of the form and the situational knowledge must be shared by the participants for the communication to be completed successfully. For example, "She drives me up the wall." How can you drive up a wall? The failure to distinguish between literal and nonliteral intention is particularly subject to misinterpretation and intolerance across cultural groups.

From Disenfranchisement to Empowerment

Educators must redefine their roles in the classroom, community, and the society so that their role definitions result in interactions that empower students rather than disenfranchise them (Cummins, 1986). To be empowered, students need to feel confident about themselves and not feel embarrassed or inhibited about speaking and communicating. Because dialect styles may not be approved by their instructors, they may feel inadequate and thus perform poorly in the classroom, resulting in disenfranchisement and alienation. Hoover also advocates the power of self-esteem and fearlessness.

From Standard to Diverse

Custred stresses the importance of teaching the standard form of English to our students. On the surface, his concern for our students' lack of command in standard English seems totally legitimate. We should provide every opportunity for our students to practice standard English. However, this should not be done at the expense of losing one's diverse social and regional dialect or one's mother tongue. Hoover (this issue) emphasizes the importance of recognizing the role of ebonics in higher education and identified linguistic and cultural strengths of ebonics. The complexity of the ebonics lexicon as described by Hoover requires careful linguistic studies and research. Hence, proposing the exclusive use of standard English denies scholars the opportunity to conduct legitimate research and prohibits students' active participation using diverse social and regional dialects.

From Assimilation to Acculturation

As Powell and Collier state, "the public speaking 'form' is based on a Western ideology of communication that is grounded in classical Greek and Roman philosophy" (p. 241). Those instructors who advocate assimilation will demand that their students follow the Eurocentric rules. Kaplan (1966) and Westby (in press) believed that there were diverse cultural thought-patterns which framed one's oral and literary presentations. Providing our students the opportunities to acculturate and learn the Eurocentric style will be beneficial. However, instructors must realize the potential harm of enforcing assimilation, which may be extremely difficult for some and impossible for others (Gollnick & Chinn, 1986). On the other hand, the process of acculturation is essential for our students with linguistic and cultural diversities so that they can cope with academic discourse and simultaneously maintain their own cultural identities.

Professors need to go beyond the linguistic and superficial cultural differences toward recognizing cognitive style differences. We are aware that "hypothetical thinking" and "critical thinking" are parts of the American academic cultural system that students must acquire (Bloom, 1981). The foreign-born student needs to have a detailed understanding of the cultural and cognitive assumptions underlying Western reading and writing activities. Because these assumptions are implied rather than taught directly, exercises should be given that review in detail the whys and wherefores of the reasoning process that native English speakers take for granted. Such issues are rarely discussed in training foreign-born students to function within a sociocultural context that has hidden cognitive agendas.

Essay topics can be challenging and present barriers for the training/learning process. Some topics are culturally inappropriate and others may be socially irrelevant. For example, the essay topic "What are the characteristics of fashion that seem most important within American culture today?" sounds acceptable on the surface, but on closer examination, we find that the topic of fashion is taboo for men in some cultures (Cheng & Ima, 1988).

Although many programs claim to be dealing with cultural training, they are often ethnocentric in nature (Powell & Collier) and seldom take into consideration the affective domain of foreign students and their need to maintain their own cultural identity. In sum, instructional approaches need to embrace the following paradigm shift in order to truly serve our diverse student population.

Existing Model	*Paradigm Shift*
Compensatory	Enhancement
Reduction	Addition
Standard	Diverse
Assimilation	Acculturation
Deficit	Asset
Tolerance	Acceptance
Disenfranchise	Empower

Accepting the paradigm shift means that one has to learn about, understand, and respect one's culturally diverse students. One has to talk with them about their experiences and present a curriculum that is relevant, valid, and paints a picture of reality (Hilliard, 1990).

Second-Language Instructions

Many students speak a social dialect other than standard English. There are several basic principles on second-dialect instruction described by Taylor (1986), such as that both teacher and learner must believe it possible to acquire a second dialect, instruction in a second dialect must be proceeded by a nonbiased assessment of the learner's knowledge of the first dialect and knowledge of the targeted second dialect. Students learn to be bidialectal and to code-switch depending on the social contexts.

Many foreign-born students share some of the following characteristics:

1. Display insufficient overall communication skills in English
2. Lack sociocultural knowledge
3. Evidence sufficient technical/professional knowledge
4. Speak English that is influenced by their native language
5. Exhibit moderate difficulty in auditory comprehension (especially nonliterate interpretation)
6. Demonstrate mild to moderate difficulty with English writing skills
7. Lack prior knowledge and experience in American schools
8. Lack opportunities to practice English outside school

The following guidelines for educators might be useful (Cheng, 1987):

- Perfecting language means increasing cultural literacy, providing training beyond phonology, morphology and syntax by nurturing bicultural identity, working on stress and intonation, realizing present social reality, and practicing ritualized patterns.

- Providing opportunities for experiencing a variety of narrative styles and an explanation of the written and unwritten rules that govern these styles

- Being specific and explicit in discussing similarities and differences and comparing, what is and is not appropriate, especially when using jargon or colloquialisms

- Learning to be sensitive to cultural differences and understanding cultural beliefs, perceptions, and values

- Making no assumptions about what students know or do not know, anticipating needs as well as sources of anxiety

- Expecting frustrations and possible misunderstandings; students benefit from practice

- Encouraging students to join social activities, clubs, student government and organizations to increase their exposure to various forms of discourse, as language is a social tool and should be used for fulfilling multiple social needs and requirements

- Facilitating the transition into mainstream culture through such activities as role-playing, preparing scripts for commonly occurring activities, using culturally unique experiences as topics of discussion, and conducting social/pragmatic activities

- Encouraging students to (a) read children's literature, including fairy tales, comic books, newspapers (especially cartoons), magazines (especially jokes); (b) read about famous people, current and historical; (c) know the best-sellers; (d) do crossword puzzles; (e) read poetry; (f) listen to great orators; and (g) learn new words and find the multiple social meanings of words

With such a linguistically and culturally diverse population represented in the present school system, it is imperative that educators be aware of the differences in students' attitudes, cultural backgrounds, communication styles, language and dialect usage, expectations toward school and educators, and exposure to educational systems and knowledge about community resources.

Ignorance of these factors may result in unforeseen academic troubles among minority and international students.

Potential Risk Factors

Students bring to us diverse linguistic, paralinguistic, stylistic, and discourse backgrounds and experiences, some of which may be viewed as at-risk factors for academic and professional success. This section highlights some of these characteristics.

Linguistic Characteristics

The issues surrounding social dialects have been controversial and complex. Opposing views have emerged over the past few decades. Cole (1985) proposed contrasting models: the idealization model that promoted standard English as the "linguistic archetype" and other dialects as inferior, and the social reality model that recognized the many varieties of English, of which standard English is only one. The American Speech-Language-Hearing Association (ASHA) published position papers on social dialects (ASHA, 1983, 1989), proposing that "the role of the speech-language pathologist is to provide the desired competency in standard English without jeopardizing the integrity of the individual's first dialect" (ASHA, 1983, p. 24). Furthermore, ASHA urged that

> competencies are also necessary in the provision of services to nonstandard English speakers including knowledge of the particular dialect; knowledge of phonological and grammatical feature of the dialect; knowledge of effects of attitudes toward dialects; thorough understanding and appreciation for the community and culture of the nonstandard speaker. (p. 24)

Custred believes that both standard language and folk speech have their places in the purview of the university. However, he does not stress an attitudinal shift toward appreciation of dialect diversity.

Communication Characteristics

Like most native speakers, few clinicians can define what constitutes "effective" communication from the American perspective. American style tends to be more informal and yet time- and results-oriented. Americans expect immediate responses, have difficulty tolerating delayed responses, find silent periods uncomfortable, and may view more reflective communicators as slow or unmotivated. The American belief in independence, individualism, assertiveness, and competition corresponds to a direct and assertive communication style; other styles may be judged evasive, inscrutable, inappropriate, or incompetent.

What is considered effective communication by African-American, Latino, and Asian/Pacific-Americans may be very different. Cultural differences in communication styles may affect social, academic, and professional success. All of these tendencies are at times dysfunctional for students in typical U.S. educational settings. Information on cultural patterns of communication is essential for educators dealing with nonnative speakers of English.

Akbar (1975) proposed a description of the African-American style of communication as highly affective; the use of language requiring many coined interjections; expression through considerable body language; reliance on words that depend on context for meaning and have little meaning in themselves; adoption of systematic use of nuance of intonation and body language, such as eye movements and positioning; preference of oral-aural modalities for learning communication; and sensitivity to others' nonverbal cues (Cole & Terrell, in press; Payne, 1986; Taylor, 1986; Wolfram, 1986).

The range of styles used by individual speakers and the conditions for adjusting along a continuum of formality vary considerably. The more attention paid to speech, the more formal the style. For example, it is important for Asian students to be orderly and obedient. They learn by observation, memorization, and pattern practice. In contrast, the American educational system stresses critical thinking and discovery in a less stressful and more open atmosphere. Such incongruencies in educational practices may result in communication breakdown and failures to achieve.

Nonverbal Characteristics

Nonverbal expression is extremely important in the communication process. Leubitz (1973) identified four functions of nonverbal communication: to relay messages, to augment verbal communication, to contradict verbal communication, and to replace verbal communication. Knapp (1972) suggested that 35% of the social meaning is transmitted by words, whereas 65% of the social meaning is conveyed through nonverbal channels. Other features of nonverbal communication, including proximity, social distance, facial expression, and so on, must also be included in our discussion.

Topics on cultural differences must be addressed to empower both the student and the instructor. Awareness of diverse forms of verbal and nonverbal communication is essential to maximize the teaching/learning process. Acknowledgment of and sensitivity to these diverse communicative mannerisms signals acceptance of the students' unique traits. The educator should address these issues before the class to eliminate the feeling of isolation and to empower the student to speak and participate in the class. Furthermore, awareness of nonverbal forms of communication will provide the instructor with greater ability to determine whether or not the student really understands. For example, knowing that an Asian student may say "yes" when meaning "no" is of vital importance to an educator. The educator must not merely take such responses at face value; rather, one must verify or reemphasize the point and ensure that all students really do comprehend. By the same token, the student must share the responsibility and make it known when there is a failure to understand. In addition to the diversity among nonverbal communication, there are a great many noticeable differences among narrative characteristics that are directly related to one's cultural identity.

Narrative Characteristics

Most studies of the language of African-American children view language from a linguistic perspective; that is, the structure of its usage. However, it might also be useful to study the verbal skills of Black children, including such expressions as "rappin'" (an art form originated in African-American communities that conveys messages set to a rhythmic beat). The need for a paradigm shift is evident in light of the ever-increasing number of nonnative speakers of English. A new approach to teaching is needed regarding the methods of discourse. An acceptance and enhancement of unique cultural characteristics, if incorporated into the present curriculum, will result in a more effective and interesting teaching/learning process. Guidelines for the execution of the paradigm shift follow.

Implications

Given the ethnic/cultural/linguistic diversity of our student population, it is difficult for educators to develop in-depth knowledge of the language, cultural, and social backgrounds of each student. However, it is possible to develop cross-cultural communicative competence. The concept of cross-cultural competence is defined as the ability to communicate effectively across cultures. Professionals need to nurture personal knowledge about cultures, language and discourse styles, family and support systems, and skills and attitudes about serving diverse populations. A period of adjustment may be required by international students. What is expected by teachers must be explicitly explained to culturally diverse students. Educators must examine and reexamine their own assumptions about what their students know. Teachers and students must enter into a dialogue about how to bridge the linguistic and cultural gap. Furthermore, the incongruencies between the expectations of American teachers and those of diverse students must be considered in teaching culturally/linguistically diverse students.

Faculty

Excellence in education will require a culturally heterogeneous cadre of professionals who are knowledgeable in and understand related social, linguistic, cultural, educational, and economic factors. If faculty are to be motivated to change their teaching, a system of rewards or appraisal may be necessary to help promote individual, personal, and professional growth (Hart, 1989). Multicultural and social literacy are necessary across the educational continuum. The following are some of the questions which need to be asked to challenge faculty members (Banks, 1990; Banks, Cortes, Gay, Garcia, & Ochoa, 1976):

1. Am I prepared to teach multicultural students?

2. How do my instructional strategies reflect and accommodate the learning/communication styles of diverse students?

3. Have I updated my knowledge and skills with regard to issues of diversity?

4. Do my students receive frequent, timely, performance-based feedback that supports improved performance?

Curriculum

There is a need to transform the curriculum. Questions may include

1. Are topics that have social and cultural relevance being used?

2. How does the course capitalize on the rich diversity of students?

3. How does the course help students develop writing and communication skills?

4. Does the course promote a positive attitude toward linguistically diverse students?

5. Are rules of writing and speaking explained explicitly?

6. Are models of good writing and speaking styles presented?

There is a need for educators to examine their methods of teaching and to endorse the foregoing paradigm shifts, to embrace diversity and to debunk the monolithic myth, and to move toward cultural pluralism (Hollins, this issue). Leadership must be provided to have educators embrace this change when engaged in a "noble initiative of human development" (Farrell, 1989).

Conclusion

There is a need for systematic change in institutions' culture, self-perceptions, and operations. These institutions must redefine themselves as culturally plural, in keeping with the true fabric of the American tapestry, and recognizing the many contributions of African, Asian, European, and native cultures and peoples. In the words of Oliver and Johnson (1988):

> As we approach an increasingly multiracial and multiethnic 21st century, higher education must play an important role in educating and training this and future generations of American students—white and black, yellow and brown, immigrant and non-immigrant— if we are to continue to meet the human capital needs that our technologically advanced society demands. (p. 144)

References

Akbar, N. (1975, October). Address before the Black Child Development Institute annual meeting, San Francisco.

Allen, W. R. (1987, May/June). Black colleges vs. white colleges: The fork in the road for Black students. *Change*, pp. 25–34.

American Speech-Language-Hearing Association. (1983). Position paper on social dialect. *ASHA*, 25(9), 23–24.

American Speech-Language-Hearing Association. (1987). Social dialects position paper. *ASHA*, 29, 1.

Banks, J. A. (1990). *Transforming the curriculum: Conference on diversity*. Oakland, CA: California Teacher Credentialing Commission.

Banks, J. A., Cortes, C. E, Gay, G., Garcia, R., & Ochoa, A. S. (1976). *Curriculum guidelines for multiethnic education*. Washington, DC: National Council for the Social Studies.

Biederman, P. W. (1989, November 23). Dialectician puts accent on the stars. *Los Angeles Times*, p. J10.

Bloom, A. H. (1981). *The linguistic shaping of thought: A study on the impact of language on thinking in China and the West* Hillsdale, NJ: Lawrence Erlbaum.

Cheng, L. (1987). *Assessing Asian language performance: Guidelines for evaluating limited English proficient students*. Rockville, MD: Aspen.

Cheng, L., & Butler, K. (1989). Code-switching: a natural phenomenon vs. language 'deficiency.' *World Englishes, 8*(3), 293–309.

Cheng, L., Ima, K. (1988), The California Basic Educational Skills Test (CBEST) and Indochinese teacher interns: A case of a cultural barrier to foreign-born Asian professionals? In G. Y. Okihiro, S. H. Hune, A. A. Hansen, & J. M. Liu (Eds.), *Reflections on shattered windows* (pp. 68–79). Pullman: Washington State University Press.

Cole, L. (1985). *Nonstandard English: Handbook for assessment and instruction*. Silver Springs, MD: Author.

Cole, L. (1989). E pluribus pluribus: Multicultural imperative for the 1990s and beyond. *ASHA 22*(4), 317–318.

Cole L., & Deal, V. R. (Eds.). (in press). *Communication disorders in multicultural populations*. Rockville, MD: American Speech-Language-Hearing Association.

Cole, L., Terrell, S. (in press). Philosophical and practical approaches to second dialect instruction. In *Communication disorders in multicultural populations*. Rockville, MD: American Speech-Language-Hearing Association.

Compton, A. J. (1983). *Compton phonological assessment of foreign accents*. San Francisco: Carousel.

Condon, J., & Yousef, F. (1975). *An introduction to intercultural communication*. Indianapolis, IN: Bobbs-Merrill.

Cummins, J. (1986). Empowering minority students: A framework for intervention. *Harvard Educational Review, 56*, 18–36.

Dreher, B. B. (1981). Response to Gandour. *Journal of Speech and Securing Disorders, 46*, 216–218.

Erickson, J. G., & Iglesias, A. (1986). Assessment of communication disorders in non-English proficient children. In O. L. Taylor (Ed.), *Nature of communication disorders in culturally and linguistically diverse populations* (pp. 181–218). Austin, TX: Pro-Ed.

Farrell, W. C. (1989). *Our new urban students, Part 1: Implications for school personnel.* Paper presented to the Office of Education Outreach, School of Education, University of Wisconsin—Milwaukee.

Gollnick, D. M., & Chinn, P. C. (1986). *Multicultural education in a pluralistic society.* Columbus, OH: Merrill.

Grant, B. (1989). *Making an educated decision.* Phoenix: Arizona State University Business School.

Grosjean, F. (1982). *Life with two languages: An introduction to bilingualism.* Cambridge, MA: Harvard University Press.

Hakuta, K. (1987). *Mirror of language: The debate on bilingualism.* Rowley, MA: Newbury House.

Hall, E. T. (1959). *The silent language.* New York: Doubleday.

Han, K. (1989). *Faculty performance appraisal: A recommendation for growth and change. Accent on improving college teaching and learning.* Ann Arbor: National Council for Research to Improve Post Secondary Teaching and Learning, Regents of the University of Michigan.

Heath, S. B. (1983). *Ways with words: Language, life and works in communities and classrooms.* New York: Cambridge University Press.

Heller, S. (1976, October 29). Teaching assistants get increased training: Problems arise in foreign student programs. *Chronicle of Higher Education*, pp. 9–11.

Hilliard, A. (1976) *Alternatives to IQ testing: An approach to the identification of gifted minority children.* (Final report). Sacramento: California State Department of Education.

Hilliard, A. (1990). *Validity & equity in curriculum and teaching.* Multicultural lecture series. San Diego State University, San Diego, February 22.

Kaplan, L. (1966). Cultural thought patterns in intercultural education. *Language Learning, 16,* 1–20.

Knapp, L. (1972). *Nonverbal communication in human interaction.* New York: Holt, Rinehart & Winston.

Leubitz, L (1973). *Nonverbal communication: A guide for teachers.* Skokie, IL: National Textbook Press.

MacKay, I. R. (1978). *Introducing practical phonetics.* Boston: Little, Brown.

Molholt, G. (1988). Computer-assisted instruction in pronunciation for Chinese speakers of American English. *TESOL Quarterly, 22*(1), 91–111.

Oliver, M. I., & Johnson, J. H., Jr. (1988). The challenge of diversity in higher education. *Urban Review, 20*(3), 139–145.

Payne, S. (1986). Cultural and linguistic groups in the United States. In O. L. Taylor (Ed.), *Nature of communication disorders in culturally and linguistical diverse populations.* Austin, TX: Pro-Ed.

Philip, S. (1983). *The invisible culture: Communication in classroom and community on the Warm Springs Indian Reservation.* New York: Longman.

Scollon, R., & Scollon, S. B. K. (1981). *Narrative, literacy and face in interethnic communication.* Norwood, NJ: Ablex.

Shaw, A. G. (1985). *Student frustration, expected peer and faculty relationships as correlates of college dropout behavior.* Unpublished doctoral dissertation, Northeastern University, Boston.

Taylor, O. L (Ed.). (1986). *Nature of communication disorders in culturally and linguistically diverse populations.* Austin, TX: Pro-Ed.

Vaughn-Coke, R. (1983). Improving language assessment in minority children. *ASHA, 25,* 29–34.

Wald, M. (1987, January). A thicker foreign accent. *New York Times Educational Supplement*, p. 16.

Weade, R., & Green, J. L (1985). Talking to learn: Social and academic requirements for classroom participation. *Peabody Journal of Education, 62,* 6–19.

Westby, C. E. (in press). Cross-cultural differences in adult-child interaction. In L. Cole & V. Deal (Eds.), *Communication disorders in multicultural populations.* Rockville, MD: American Speech-Language-Hearing Association.

Wiener, F. D. (1983). Native English speakers. *ASHA, 25,* 19–22.

Wolfram, W. (1986). Language variation in the United States. In O. L Taylor (Ed.), *Nature of communication disorders in culturally and linguistically diverse populations* (pp. 73–116). Austin, TX: Pro-Ed.

Prediction of Hispanics' College Achievement

Richard P. Durán

This article examines issues and trends of research findings regarding prediction of Hispanics' undergraduate college achievement in selective colleges, and it also suggests directions for improvement in existing approaches. The first portion of the article focuses on the use of high school grades and college admissions test scores to predict early college grades in selective college institutions. Basic assumptions underlying use of measures are discussed, as are characteristics of Hispanics' performance on measures. The emphasis of the first part of the article is on the question of population validity in the prediction of grades for nonminority college students versus Hispanic college students. The main issue is whether existing research evidence using correlation methods or regression methods shows us that we can predict college grades in a similar manner and to a similar level of accuracy for both nonminority and Hispanic populations. No attempt is made to discuss technical details of procedures, nor is there any attempt to describe alternative statistical frameworks other than the procedures described.

The weight of current research findings suggests that high school grades and admissions test scores do not do as good a job at predicting Hispanics' college grades as they do for nonminority students. This conclusion, however, does not invalidate the use of high school grades and admissions test scores for Hispanics; it does suggest that we need to understand how differences between Hispanic and nonminority students should affect the interpretation of admissions information and also how our conception of different measures of college aptitude and college achievement affects the ability to predict success in college for Hispanics. The implication for admissions policy is that college admissions staff need to be very cautious in interpreting Hispanics' admissions profiles. High school grades and admissions test scores have their place in evaluating Hispanics' preparation for college, but they should be examined critically, with due weight given to other factors that may affect their interpretation.

The second part of this paper is devoted to discussion of a broader conceptual framework for improving prediction of Hispanics' college success, and this will entail development of additional indicators of college ability and college success. This broader framework also includes identification of interventions that might benefit Hispanics' chances for success in college. Ideally, a broader framework would help admissions staff in applying more critical judgment to the value of high school grades and admissions tests in making admissions decisions regarding Hispanics. In addition, a broader framework would permit institutions to investigate empirically what sorts of additional information about Hispanics and about institutions can help predict Hispanics' success in their local college contexts and how interventions might affect Hispanics' college success.

Predictive Validity Studies

Predictors of College Achievement

Not all college institutions are alike. Colleges vary in the importance they place on candidates' previous academic achievement and college aptitude test scores. Almost all selective four-year institutions rely heavily on high school grades or rank in high school class and college aptitude test scores as primary evidence of candidates preparation for the academic demands of college.

Among admissions staff, the importance of high school grade-point average or rank in high school class is weighed judgmentally in terms of students' areas of study in high schools and sometimes by the academic reputation of a high school. High school grade-point average and rank in high school class based on grades have the advantage that they are numerical measures and, as such, embody objective, quantitative characteristics that should be interpreted in the same manner by different persons. High school grade-point average and rank in high school class also have a cumulative and representatively stable character; they reflect a history of academic achievement rather than just a one-shot evaluation of academic skills.

High school grade-point average and rank in high school class as predictors of college aptitude also have some limitations, and these limitations are of special significance to minority populations such as Hispanics. Achievement information alone, based on high school grades or rank in high school class, is incapable of indicating whether students' performance has been moderated by the quality of schooling and students' opportunity to learn in classroom settings. Such information is also incapable of capturing personal and background characteristics of students that influence opportunity to learn, given the characteristics and resources of a school. Thus, if we wish to be sensitive to factors moderating students' achievements in high school, we must go beyond simple numerical measures of high school achievement.

Figure 1
Academic Achievement of High School Seniors

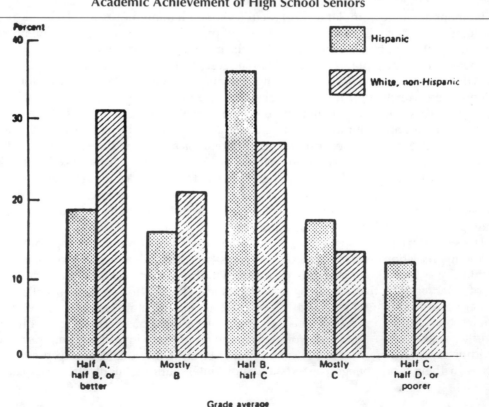

Source: Brown et al. (1980).

Research findings from the National Longitudinal Study of the High School Class of 1972 suggest that Hispanics overall are not achieving at the same level in high school as are non-Hispanics (U.S. Department of Education, 1980). Figure 1, for example, indicates that Hispanics tended to earn lower grades in high school than did non-Hispanic white students. A similar but less dramatic pattern of grade differences also obtains for Hispanic and non-Hispanic white students who aspired to go to college and who took the Scholastic Aptitude Test. Table 1, based on the report *Profiles: College-Bound Seniors, 1983* (Ramist & Arbeiter, 1984), indicates a small difference in the high school grade-point average of whites versus Mexican Americans and Puerto Ricans residing in the fifty states and the District of Columbia. Closer inspection of table 1, however, reveals that a noticeable difference occurs in the proportion of whites versus Hispanics who earn a grade-point average of 3.0 and above; about 60 percent of whites earned a grade-point average of 3.0 or better as compared to about 55 percent of Mexican Americans and about 47 percent of Puerto Ricans. Such differences, when examined more closely for the proportion of persons in the highest grade-point average categories above 3.0, imply that Hispanics are less likely than whites to meet high school grade standards for admission among highly selective college institutions.

As mentioned previously, areas of high school study are an important adjunct to evaluating high school grades. Table 2, taken from the College Board data for 1982–83 (Ramist and Arbeiter, 1984), summarizes difference in high school areas of study for Mexican Americans, Puerto Ricans, and whites. As the table shows, Hispanic SAT test takers in 1982–83 were almost 15 percent less likely than white test takers to have been enrolled in college-preparatory programs during high school. Almost 80 percent of whites had such a background versus about 65 to 67 percent of Hispanics. Particularly important is the length of prior study of English and mathematics; 94 percent of whites have studied English for four or more years, while about 88 percent of Mexican Americans have studied this much English. Ninety percent of Puerto Ricans have studied four or more years of English, but this figure probably also reflects Puerto Ricans' exposure to English-as-a-second-language training among Puerto Rican test takers who have had some schooling in Puerto Rico. Moreover, with regard to length of mathematics study, 65 percent of

Table 1
Self-Reported High School Grade Averages of Hispanic and White SAT Test Takers in 1982–83

Overall High School Grade Average[a]	Percent Mexican Americans	Percent Puerto Ricans[b]	Percent Whites (non-Hispanics)
3.75–4.00	12.1	8.1	16.5
3.50–3.74	11.2	8.9	12.4
3.25–3.49	13.2	10.9	13.4
3.00–3.24	18.1	18.8	17.6
2.75–2.99	13.2	14.1	12.1
2.50–2.74	13.1	15.3	11.9
2.25–2.49	9.0	10.6	7.6
2.00–2.24	6.1	7.7	5.4
Under 2.00	4.1	6.1	3.2
Mean GPA by group	3.01	2.89	3.09
N	15,496	7,959	701,345

Source: Ramist & Arbeiter (1984).

[a]Calculated by weighting the latest self-reported grade in each of the six subject areas (English, Mathematics, Foreign Languages, Biological Sciences, Physical Sciences, and Social Studies) by the number of years of study in the subject and dividing by the total number of years of study in all six subjects. If a grade was not reported in a subject, that subject was not used in the calculation of overall grade average.

[b]Puerto Ricans in the 50 states and District of Columbia only.

whites have studied mathematics for four or more years, as compared to a little over 50 percent of Hispanics. The data suggest that Hispanics show nearly a 15 percent disadvantage in mathematics experience in comparison to whites.

A level of four years or more of English and mathematics study is used for the foregoing comparisons for a good reason. Students who are candidates for the most selective colleges are likely to show a more intensive background in English and mathematics than are other college candidates. English and mathematics study are often assumed to be the most important and most generalizable areas of high school study; they are more likely to be studied sequentially over a longer period of years, and they also emphasize training in academic skills that are required across a wide range of academic study areas in college.

Table 2 also shows data on the average number of years of study spent by students in foreign languages, biological sciences, physical sciences, and social studies. The average length of study in these areas tends to be just a little longer for whites than for Hispanics. The data of table 2 do not convey to us differences in the academic track of students; these data do not reveal whether Hispanics and whites have received the same quality and intensity of instruction in the areas indicated.

The high school data also indicate that Hispanics who take the SAT tend to show lower high school grades and less intensive academic study in core areas related to college work than do whites. From the point of view of college admissions staff evaluating high school credentials, Hispanic college candidates for selective institutions tend to show lower college qualifications than nonminority college candidates.

Longitudinal educational survey research suggests that high school experiences and background of Hispanics can differ from the experiences and background of nonminority students. It may be that such differences are allied not only with evidence of lower high school academic achievement among Hispanics versus white non-Hispanics but also with more inaccuracy in use of such information for prediction of college achievement for Hispanics than for whites. Consider, for example, figure 2, drawn from data from the National Longitudinal Study of the High School class of 1972 (Brown, Rosen, and Olivas, 1980). The figure reports differences between Hispanic students' replies to survey questions concerning various factors that interfere with their high school work. Both Hispanics and whites reported in significant numbers that money worries, family obligations, poor place to study, and parents' disinterest were impediments to high school work. Hispanics, however, were 15 to 20 percent more likely than whites to respond that the factors cited were a detriment to high school work. Whether or not similar data would obtain for Hispanics and nonminority students planning attendance at selective college institutions is an open question meriting further investigation based on the 1972 NLS educational survey data base or perhaps based on the more recent High School and Beyond longitudinal data base. There is the

Table 2
Areas of High School Study, 1982–83 College Board Data on SAT Test Takers

	Mexican Americans	Puerto Ricans[a]	White Non-Hispanics
Percentage enrolled in academic or college preparatory programs	67.3	65.2	79.9
Percentage with four years or more of English	88.3	90.4	94.0
Percentage with four years or more of mathematics	53.5	50.1	65.3
Average number of years of foreign language	1.99	2.36	2.27
Average number of years of biological sciences	1.31	1.38	1.39
Average number of years of physical sciences	1.50	1.64	1.87
Average number of years of social studies	3.06	3.15	3.24

Source: Ramist & Arbeiter (1984).
[a]Puerto Ricans in the 50 states and District of Columbia only.

possibility, then, that Hispanics' high school achievement may show more variation than would be expected because of the effects of home and family obligations and concerns.

College Board data (Ramist and Arbeiter, 1984) from 1982–83 suggest that there are both similarities and differences in the nonacademic characteristics of Hispanic and white non-Hispanic test takers. In considering such similarities and differences, it is essential to note the populations represented are not representative of high school students as a whole. This is particularly so for Hispanics, since Hispanics who take the SAT are a very select and small subsample of all Hispanics because of the operation of factors that inhibit receipt of a quality education among Hispanics. Table 3 compares Hispanic and white non-Hispanic SAT test takers in 1982–83 on answers to several survey questions of background and personal characteristics. White college candidates tend to have parents with more education than Hispanics. On the average, white parents demonstrate access to college, while this is not the case for Hispanics—the latter showing averages influenced by a failure to complete high school. White parents show a considerable advantage in income level, $31,200, in comparison to Hispanics—$19,600 for Mexican Americans and $14,700 for Puerto Ricans. Other data in the table indicate that the family sizes

Figure 2
Factors Interfering with School Work of High School Seniors

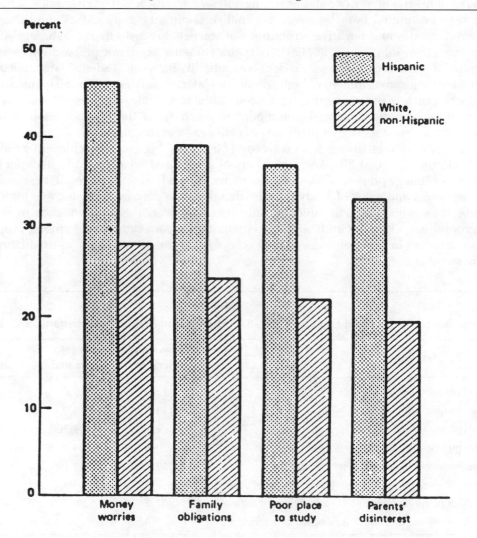

Source: Brown et al. (1980).

of white and Hispanic students were about the same for students taking the SAT in 1982–83. About 10 percent more white than Hispanic SAT test takers indicated that they worked part time out of school, and among those who worked, about an equal number of hours was spent in this endeavor (seven to eight hours per week). About 15 percent more Hispanics than whites indicated that they planned to ask for financial aid to attend college; from 88 to 90 percent of Hispanics had such plans, as opposed to 74 percent of whites. All told, the figures cited indicate clearly that 1982–83 Hispanic test takers were not as economically able as whites to plan pursuit of a college education.

Hispanics in 1982–83 were more likely than whites to answer no to the question "Is English your best language?" Almost 10 per Puerto Ricans and a little over 7 percent of Mexican Americans answered this question no. These figures compare to a no answer for under 2 percent of white examinees. The figures suggest that a small but significant proportion of Hispanic test takers face the prospect of college education in their less familiar language—English. It is possible, however, that many subtle and important features of English-language familiarity are not re-flected in the language question cited. Sociolinguistic research I reviewed (Durán, 1983) indicated that some Hispanics could maintain that they were more familiar with English than Spanish and still manifest limited familiarity with English occurring in academic settings. Limited familiarity with English in academic settings could be manifested not only in lack of familiarity with academic vocabulary, reading skills, and written usage but also in oral comprehension and speaking skills required in academic settings. Research indicates that Hispanics' school achieve-ment may be limited both by students' English familiarity and, just as significantly, by the negative attitudes and negative attributions of teachers toward Hispanic students in academic interactions (Durán, 1983; Buriel, 1983). Hispanic students' academic preparation for college may be limited in a number of ways by lack of compatibility between students' language background and the language environment of high school (and later on, college). Some Hispanic students may be quite resourceful in overcoming such incompatibilities, while others may not be so resourceful. The resulting variation in this accommodation could affect the interpretation of high school grades (and also test scores) as predictors of college achievement.

A hypothesis to be drawn from reviewing Hispanics' high school achievement in relation to their background is that Hispanics' high school grades and areas of study may not be as valid measures of college preparation as are those of white non-Hispanics. Overall, Hispanics' patterns of achievement and areas of study indicate that they less prepared for study in highly selective colleges than white non-Hispanics. In addition, however, there is evidence to suggest that background heterogeneity and heterogeneity in high school experiences among Hispanics may lead to variation in the usefulness of high school achievement measures as predictors of college achievement.

Table 3
College Board Background Data on 1982–83 Hispanic and White Non-Hispanic SAT Test Takers

	Mexican Americans	Puerto Ricans[a]	White Non-Hispanics
Median years of father's education	12.0	12.0	14.3
Median years of mother's education	11.8	11.9	13.5
Median parental income	19,600	14,700	31,200
Median number of parent dependents	4.8	4.3	4.3
Percentage working part time in high school	52.7	52.6	62.6
Mean number of part-time work hours outside of school	7.3	7.4	7.8
Percentage planning to request financial aid for college	87.7	89.7	73.5
Percentage indicating English is not their best language	7.4	9.7	1.8

Source: Ramist & Arbeiter (1984).
[a]Puerto Ricans in the 50 states and District of Columbia only.

College Admissions Test Scores

Two college aptitude tests are used widely in admissions to selective institutions: the American College Testing Program (1980) college admissions test (ACT) and the College Board Scholastic Aptitude Test. While the tests differ in terms of their structure and the scores they report, they both are described as tests of developed academic abilities needed for college. College admissions test scores, like high school grade-point average, have an advantage in being numerical. Presumably, the same numerical value of a test score for a given candidate should signify the same level of college potential for admissions staff at different colleges with similar academic standards. Since the ACT and SAT are administered nationally, scores on each of these tests ought to be comparable across all candidates taking the same test. Numerical comparison is much less tenable with high school grades, since the quality of high schools, the difficulty of study areas, and the grading standards applied may differ from student to student. Just like high school grade-point average, college admissions test scores have inherent limits. They are incapable of indicating how much they are influenced by background and schooling factors that spuriously affect test performance. These limitations will be discussed later.

Table 4 displays mean ACT test scores in 1978–79 for a large sample of self-identified Mexican American/Chicano students, Puerto Rican/Spanish-speaking American students, and Caucasian American/white students. (The ethnic category labels given are the same as those used by the American College Testing Program.) Average standardized scores for each group are shown for each four subtest areas and also for a composite score across areas. Scores on all subtests and the composite score have a range from a low of 1 to a high of 36. The entries in parentheses beneath scores are the standard deviations of the scores. Examination of table 4 reveals that both Hispanic subgroups scored about one standard deviation below Caucasian American/white students in all subscore areas. Puerto Rican/other Spanish-speaking students scored slightly higher than Mexican American/Chicano students in all subtest areas and on the composite score.

Table 5 displays SAT verbal and mathematics test scores in 1982–83 for self-identified Mexican Americans, Puerto Ricans, and whites.[1] Standardized scores on each section vary between 200 and 800. Standard deviations of scores for each group and subscore are indicated in parentheses. The data in table 5 indicate that white non-Hispanics scored about three-quarters of one standard deviation higher than Mexican Americans and Puerto Ricans. Mexican Americans scored slightly higher than Puerto Ricans on both verbal and mathematics subscores. Taken at face value, the ACT and SAT test data cited suggest that Hispanics seeking enrollment in selective colleges show less college aptitude than white non-Hispanic college candidates. Questions of construct and

---

Table 4
Mean ACT Scores and Standard Deviations in 1978–79 for Representative Samples of Hispanic and Caucasian American/White Students

Group	ACT Subtest				
	English	Mathematics	Social Studies	Natural Sciences	Composite
Mexican American/Chicano students —sample: N = 931	14.1 (5.2)	12.6 (6.7)	12.5 (6.5)	16.6 (5.9)	14.1 (5.2)
Puerto Rican/Spanish-speaking American students— sample: N= 190	14.5 (5.6)	13.7 (7.3)	14.0 (7.2)	17.5 (6.2)	15.1 (5.8)
Caucasian American/white students—sample: N= 34,172	19.1 (4.9)	19.0 (7.3)	18.7 (6.9)	22.4 (6.0)	19.9 (5.4)

Source: American College Testing Program (1980, pp. 90–91, 93). Reprinted by permission of the publisher.
Note: Sample sizes given arise from a 10 percent random sampling of the full population of examinees in 1978–1979 who enrolled in college as freshmen 1979. Parentheses enclose standard deviations.

content validity aside, the pattern of differences between Hispanics and whites on test scores is consistent with the interpretation of differences reported earlier concerning high school grades and years of study in important academic study areas.

As with measures of high school achievement, one may raise questions about the usefulness of admissions test scores as predictors of Hispanics' college achievement. Admissions test scores result from isolated encounters with a test. Test scores thus do not have a cumulative history of repeated assessment over high school years, as is the case with high school grade-point average. Since tests are encountered only in isolated situations, they are subject to all the personal and situational factors that limit the reliability of assessment for any variable measured on a single occasion or on just very infrequent occasions.

The instructions for taking a test and the elementary content of test items ought to be equally intelligible to all examinees, regardless of background. A further concern is that the speed or pace of an admissions test is not excessive across populations, so that ability to answer items is not affected by "racing" or inability to reach an item. Limitations in interpreting test scores for a population may result when we are not confident that test items are measuring exactly and only those skills they are supposed to assess for that population (Osterlind, 1983).

A review of the foregoing question suggests that some Hispanics' admissions test behavior may be influenced by familiarity with academic English, personality factors, and speededness (Durán, 1983). The extent and intensity of such influences are not well understood or documented at this point. Results across studies vary. There is a fair-amount of evidence that, by and large, SAT admissions test items measure the same abilities across Hispanic and nonminority populations, although language familiarity and speededness can affect this interpretation. The results thus far seem clearest for the language-familiarity question. Alderman's (1981) research, for example, indicated that SAT scores of Spanish-dominant Puerto Ricans, tested in Puerto Rico, were more related to their Prueba de Aptitud Académica scores (the Spanish version of the SAT) as students' proficiency in English rose. The relationship between SAT and PAA scores was more unstable when students had less English-language proficiency. As one might suspect, low English-language familiarity might also lower scores on English-language college aptitude tests. Table 6, taken from 1982–83 College Board data, shows the median SAT verbal and mathematics test scores of Mexican Americans, Puerto Ricans, and white non-Hispanics broken down according to a yes versus no answer to the question, "Is English your best language?"

As the table 6 data indicate, Hispanics who indicated that English was not their best language earned lower SAT scores than other Hispanics; these Hispanics, as expected, also earned much lower SAT scores than white non-Hispanics who indicated that English was their best language. As mentioned previously, there is the possibility that some Hispanics who answer yes to the question "Is English your best language?" may be persons whose familiarity with academic

Table 5
Mean Scholastic Aptitude Test Scores 1982–83 for Hispanics and Whites (Non-Hispanics)

Group	Verbal	Mathematics
Mexican Americans	375 ($S = 100$)[a] ($N = 15,315$)	417 ($S = 105$) ($N = 15,314$)
Puerto Ricans[b]	365 ($S = 107$) ($N = 7,479$)	397 ($S = 108$) ($N = 7,479$)
Whites	443 ($S = 102$) ($N = 685,219$)	484 ($S = 114$) ($N = 684,957$)

Source: Ramist 8; Arbeiter (1984).
[a]Standard deviations (S) are given in parentheses along with sample sizes (N).
[b]Puerto Ricans in the 50 states and District of Columbia only.

English is not commensurate with the English-language background and English-language familiarity of non-minority-group white students. Thus the data from table 6 confirm the possibility that low levels of English-language familiarity may depress SAT scores, but this does not inform us fully about the underlying issue. The data do not reveal how examinees' SAT performance changes as a function of their degree of English-language proficiency.

Other College Candidate Information

In addition to the high school record and college aptitude test scores, other widely used pieces of information are weighed by admissions staff of selective institutions, including the candidate's letter of application, letters of recommendation, and, in some instances, oral interview performance. Apparently, very little apart from anecdotal knowledge is known about how such information affects the admission of Hispanics to college. Among the important advantages of the additional forms of information is that they can help establish candidates' maturity and motivation for college and its academic demands. In addition, such information can assist a college in ascertaining personal qualities of candidates that may not be directly related to academic endeavors but might contribute to the well-roundedness and representativeness of a college community, should a candidate be admitted. Recent research by Willingham and Breland (1982) indicates that information on the personal qualities of candidates can be useful in deciding the nonacademic characteristics of admittees but that such information has less value than the high school record and admissions test scores in predicting college grades. Willingham and Breland's work was not intended as a study of minority access to institutions per se. Hence, one may legitimately suggest that the issue of how best to use personal qualities in minority admissions to college is an area in need of further research. Given the unequal educational opportunity that Hispanics face prior to college, evidence shows that personal qualities such as motivation to achieve may be very useful as indicators of Hispanics' ability to succeed in college.

The use of letters of intent, letters of recommendation, and interview information in the actual process of admissions decision-making is difficult to research. Moll (1979), in an account of the admissions decision-making process for private colleges, suggests that the process itself has

Table 6
Hispanic and White Non-Hispanic SAT Verbal and Mathematics Median Scores
in Relation to Answers About English as Best Language (1982–83 SDQ Question 38)

Group	SDQ Question 38 Response: English as Best Language	Percentage of a Group	Median SAT Verbal Score[b]	Median SAT Mathematics Score[b]
Mexican Americans	Yes	92.6	374	407
(N = 16.438)[a]	No	7.4	290	360
Difference in medians to yes/no responses			80	47
Puerto Ricans[c]	Yes	90.3	365	385
(N = 8.089)	No	9.2	282	337
Difference in medians to yes/no responses			83	48
White Non-Hispanics	Yes	98.2	439	481
(N = 706,923)	No	1.8	360	443
Difference in medians to yes/no responses			79	38

Source: Ramist & Arbeiter (1984).

[a]*N* is based on those examinees who responded to SDQ question 38 *and* who had an SAT verbal section score.
[b]Median scores rather than mean scores are reported since the tabulations reviewed used only median statistics.
[c]Puerto Ricans in the 50 states and District of Columbia only.

characteristics affected by the nature of institutions, institutional policies, and the social interaction of admissions staff in admissions decision-making. The manner in which admissions staff evaluate the relative importance of the high school record, college admissions test scores, and personal characteristics of candidates is often not a rational decision-making process. How Hispanics fare in this process, given their tendency to present lower high school grades and admissions test scores, is not well documented. There is a persistent belief among many Hispanic students and educators that too much importance is placed by admissions staff on high school grades and admissions test scores relative to other information on Hispanic candidates. Also, admissions staff unfamiliar with Hispanics' social, cultural, and historical background may be unable to provide a sensitive interpretation of Hispanic candidates' personal characteristics indicative of college potential. Further discussion is given to some of these concerns in the last section of the paper.

Predictive Validity Research

This section presents a discussion of findings of research studies using high school grade-point average (or rank in class) and college admissions test scores to predict Hispanics' and white non-Hispanics' early college grades.[2] A fuller discussion of studies and findings is given in Durán (1983) and to some extent in Breland (1979). College grades earned early in a college experience—typically in the first year—are a commonly adopted indicator of propensity to succeed in college. Predictive validity studies most often follow a model using high school grade-point average (or rank in high school class) and college admissions test scores as variables predicting college grade-point average.

Early college grade-point average has the advantage of being a quantitative measure and hence is capable of being interpreted in an identical numerical manner by different observers. The temporal proximity of early college grades to high school experience is an important quality enhancing the use of information based on performance at the high school level in predicting college grades. It is a well-known phenomenon of social science research that relationships among variables that are collected across different points in time grow weaker as the interval separating points of measurement increases. In the case of college grades and information gathered in high school, this decrease in relationship among variables results from changes, growth, and learning in individuals in college that stem from experiences after leaving high school. As will be mentioned in the last part of this paper, more attention ought to be given to such college experience factors—particular those that are allied with Hispanics' success in college. College grades have some disadvantages, just as high school grades do. College grades may not reference similar levels of achievement across different subject-matter areas of study, and idiosyncrasies in course requirements also affect interpretation of grades earned. Furthermore, grades may not reflect the same levels of achievement across different institutions. Predictive validity studies typically deal with the latter limitation by being based only on single institutions; predictive validity studies, however, seldom deal with the other confounding factors indicated. Early college grades have a disadvantage in not spanning an extended period of college study; they are inadequate as a proxy variable for actual graduation and for progress in meeting significant academic requirements en route to graduation that are an integral part of coursework. Factors such as planning of course load, appropriate sequencing and selection of courses, and cultivation of contact with faculty and teaching assistants may be critical academic determinants of achievement in college.

Table 7, taken from Durán (1983), displays median correlations of high school grade-point average (labeled HSR) and college admissions test scores with early college grades for samples of Hispanic and white college students based on the studies referred to in note 2. The median correlations are based in part on an earlier survey of Breland (1979), but they also include new data from studies not previously reviewed by Breland in his population validity survey of studies involving blacks, Hispanics, and whites.

The median correlations displayed in table 7 indicate that there is less of a relation between college grades and predictor measures for Hispanics than for white non-Hispanics. The median correlations between high school grade-point average and college grade-point average indicate that high school grades did not predict college grades among Hispanics as well as they did among whites; this result was somewhat unexpected given Breland's (1979) earlier results, also shown in table 7. Data in table 7 also show that verbal college admissions test scores, mathematics college admissions test scores, and a composite of high school grades and admissions test scores all were less well related to college grades for Hispanics than for whites. These results are entirely consistent with Breland's earlier findings, which involved a smaller number of studies. While the total number of independent analyses on Hispanics that were reviewed is small, and while more research is needed, there appears to be enough evidence to suggest that the patterns of association that are reported are real.

Use of regression analysis to predict college grades from high school grades and admissions test scores is the most common procedure by which to evaluate how well grades can be predicted. Because of the theoretical connection between the R statistic and the results of a regression analysis, the entries in the bottom row of table 7 are reflective of how well high school grades and verbal and mathematics test scores predicted Hispanics' and whites' college grades in the regression analyses of the studies reviewed. The bottom-row entries indicate that combining information about high school grades and admissions test scores in ethnic specific regression equations leads to less accurate prediction of Hispanics' college grades. In terms of the college grade-point average variance accounted for, Hispanics' college grades were predicted 9 to 10 percent less accurately than were whites' grades.

One of the strengths of the regression analysis approach is that it allows analysis of whether Hispanics' grades would be systematically underpredicted or overpredicted had high school grade-point average and admissions test scores been weighed in the same fashion as was the case for whites at the same institutions. When this concern was investigated by Durán (1983), no consistent evidence was found that Hispanics' grades were primarily underpredicted versus overpredicted across studies reviewed. Patterns of overprediction or underprediction of Hispanics' college grades relative to whites' grades are idiosyncratic; they are very sensitive to the characteristics of institutions, to differences in the curriculum experiences of Hispanics versus non-Hispanics, and to the range of academic and personal characteristics of students.

Taken in toto, the results cited suggest that Hispanics' college grades are less well predicted than those of whites but that the reasons for this difference are not allied with a consistent bias in the direction of prediction. The most sensible interpretation is that heterogeneity among Hispanics and their characteristics, and heterogeneity in Hispanics' college experiences, moderates the relationship between high school grades and test scores with early college grades. This moderation ought to be less pronounced for white students. This hypothesis would suggest that we need to learn more about how personal and background characteristics of Hispanics interact with high school achievement admissions test performance, and college achievement in order to sort out the degree to which we can expect accurate prediction of grades. In addition, this hypothesis suggests

---

Table 7
Median Correlations Between College Predictor Measures and College Grades

| | Group | | |
| | Breland Review | | This Review[b] |
Predictor	White	Chicano	Hispanics[c]
High school record (HSR)	.37(32)[a]	.36(8)	.30(14)
Verbal test scores	.37(45)	.25(9)	.25(16)
Quantitative test scores	.33(45)	.17(9)	.23(16)
HSR and admissions test scores	.48(61)	.38(25)	.38(31)

[a]Number of independent analyses over studies is indicated in parentheses.
[b]Includes the same analyses in Breland (1979), plus additional results not cited in Breland but cited in new studies reviewed here. The review appears in Durán (1983).
[c]Hispanics in the 50 states and District of Columbia only.

that we ought to give more attention to alternative ways in which we can represent and assess Hispanic students' preparation for college and success in college. This added attention is necessary in order to develop information that can be used by college admissions staff in better evaluating the potential of Hispanic college candidates.

New Directions

The prediction of Hispanics' college achievement is influenced by the manner in which this question is framed. The most serious shortcoming in present procedures used to formulate this question is that they are unduly insensitive to the characteristics and educational experiences of Hispanic college candidates that may moderate prediction of their college achievement. In order to cope with the resulting inequities it is necessary to create a broader framework within which to conceptualize the problem of prediction. The problem may be broken into three parts:

- Deciding which kinds of information about Hispanic students and their precollege experiences are needed to improve prediction of college potential

- Deciding which kinds of information about Hispanic experiences in college and college environments best represent achievement or moderator variables for predicting achievement

- Deciding how to link information on precollege and college characteristics of Hispanics into prediction schemes for college achievement

In no small part, the attempt to derive an improved framework for prediction of Hispanics' college achievement is a sociopolitical one. This is so because the socioeconomic and educational characteristics of Hispanics are depressed relative to the nonminority population of the United States. The educational access problems faced by Hispanics in the United States have their roots in a larger historical and social arena that reflects the struggles that ethnic minority persons have faced in dealing with American life. These circumstances for Hispanics are distinctive from those of European ethnic immigrant groups, since Hispanics as a whole have a continuing and deep sociocultural and historical interaction with the rest of the Hispanic populaces of the American continents. The assimilation "problem" of Hispanics will not vanish as succeeding generations of Hispanics living in the United States become anglicized. Total assimilation will not occur in the foreseeable decades, since the population rise of Hispanics in the United States will continue to reflect immigration from Latin America of Hispanic persons aspiring to settle and live in the United States. This pattern of immigration in the future may be even more complex than it is now, and this may have unforeseen impacts on the education of Hispanics in the United States.

Our ability to comprehend what factors limit U.S. Hispanics' access to college, in the present as well as in the future, will need to be based on sound knowledge of the population characteristics of Hispanics and of the diversity of these characteristics. The fact that Hispanics differ among themselves and differ overall from nonminority U.S. persons in ways that have a significant relation to educational attainment means that the problem of predicting college aptitude may need to be approached in somewhat different ways across nonminority white and Hispanic populations. For example, in evaluating the information in admissions test scores of nonminority students, we need not worry about previous exposure to English and how this may affect the interpretation of admissions test scores. On the other hand, we need to take this factor into account in the case of Hispanics.

Nationally based educational-survey research over the past decade has begun to shed light on some significant experiential and background characteristics of Hispanics related to opportunity to learn prior to college. The results of such research are important as an empirical base by which to establish factors moderating Hispanics' preparation for college. National educational-survey data and descriptive data from college admissions testing programs are giving us the clear message that Hispanics' college preparation is not commensurate overall with the degree of college preparation of nonminority students. While we need to be sensitive to factors among Hispanics that moderate scholarly achievement and development of college aptitude prior to college, we must own up to the fact that many Hispanics are academically less prepared for college than nonminority students. Owning up to this fact should not be a passive matter. As we sharpen our understanding of what factors influence Hispanics' and other minority students' educational opportunity, we may be able to design high school and college institutional environments and academic interventions that will aid persons in better pursuing their chosen academic studies given their current academic aptitudes.

Improving Knowledge of Predictors of College Achievement

High school grades and college admissions test scores are likely to remain basic and important measures of college aptitude for the foreseeable future. Problems in the interpretation of such information primarily arise for Hispanics when these measures are low enough to be used as the basis for making a decision to exclude Hispanics from admissions consideration. We need to conduct research on procedures for guiding admissions staffs' interpretation of Hispanics' high school grade information and admissions test scores. One outcome of such research might be to develop a procedural manual for reviewing the characteristics of Hispanics excluded from admissions consideration because of high school grades and test scores. The objective of this manual, which might be computerized, would be systematically to review the background of Hispanic candidates in order to identify those persons whose academic credentials are possibly underestimated. For example, the following factors might be reviewed:

- Candidates' language background and English-language proficiency
- Candidates' exposure to schooling in Spanish and academic achievement in Spanish contexts
- High educational aspirations and high achievement motivation that are coupled with lower high school grades and admissions test scores than expected
- Higher-than-expected high school grades or admissions test scores given parents' educational background and income
- The presence of financial and other obligations to family during high school coupled with higher-than-expected high school grades and admissions test scores.

The foregoing list of suggestive factors all might be useful in identifying factors that could moderate the interpretation of candidates' high school achievement and admissions test scores. In addition, however, there might be another set of factors that reflect Hispanic students' academic aptitude in ways not reflected well by high school grades and admissions test scores. Such factors might include the following:

- Significant school and home or community activities involving use of academic and subject-matter skills related to schooling
- Frequency of voluntary participation in counseling programs and other programs exposing students to significant academic environments (e.g., visits to libraries, museums, science exhibits)
- Development of significant literacy skills in Spanish and functional utilization of these skills at advanced levels

The systematic availability of information such as has been described is problematic, but it could be realized in two ways. First, in college application materials, self-identified Hispanic students might be requested to fill out a computer-readable questionnaire touching on the topics mentioned. Other relevant information might be supplied in computer-readable data made available by testing programs; this information might come from student background questionnaires filled out by students when they take an admissions test. Second, to the extent feasible, admissions staff reviewing Hispanic students' letters of application or interview proceedings might quickly and easily code computer-readable forms indicating relevant information of the sort cited. The entire system would operate on readily available microcomputers at minimal expense.

The heart of the kind of system envisioned would be the computer algorithms that would suggest which students merited and did not merit further admissions consideration. The development of the appropriate questionnaire system and computerized admissions aid described would be a nontrivial, value-laden task that would need to be accomplished with extreme care. At present it is only possible to suggest that such a system could be developed and that if it were developed it might significantly help in making the admissions decision-making process more rational and valid for Hispanics. There are many conceptual questions that would need to be carefully thought through, and research would be needed to establish the validity of such a system.

Improving Knowledge about College Achievement

As discussed earlier in this paper, there are inherent limits in viewing college achievement in terms of early grades in college. This is not at all to say that early college grades are invalid measures of achievement; obviously, they are valid. It seems clear, however, that a more comprehensive picture of college achievement should draw on additional measures. Other academic measure areas such as the following might be included:

- Ability to graduate

- Advanced-level course performance

- Ability to accomplish significant course requirements and academic activities required in advancing toward graduation

- Academic-related accomplishments outside of course work and required activities that occur in college or community settings

Indices and measures for the foregoing sorts of accomplishments might not be as predictable from high school grades and admissions test scores as are first- and second-year college grades; this possibility, however, does not diminish their value as areas for assessing college achievement. This is so for Hispanics and other minority students because some of these students may need to grow academically in college at a steeper rate than will other nonminority students. Hence, Hispanics' and other minority students' patterns of accomplishment in college may show a sustained effort to accelerate development of academic skills that may not be reflected very well if concern is focused only on grades earned in the first two years of college. Because of this possibility, as an additional concern, it also would be unwise to suggest that speed factors, such as speed in completing a degree or speed in meeting degree objectives, should serve as valid measures of college achievement for all minority students.

Apart from a richer set of indices for academic achievement in college, there is an acute need for measures that reflect students' personal growth characteristics in college and institutional characteristics that affect educational opportunity. Factors such as the aforementioned will moderate students' opportunities to achieve in college. These are not at all trivial matters for Hispanic students, since their sociocultural characteristics, educational experiences, and early educational aspirations may vary so much from what is the norm for nonminority students. Institutional characteristics, such as services related to financial aid, study assistance, and counseling and the sociocultural climate of a college community may be very critical determinants of Hispanics' success in college. Moderating factors such as those mentioned may have more of an effect on some Hispanics' ability to achieve in college than academic credentials presented at the conclusion of high school.

At present we do not have an extensive base of research to inform us about the effect of personal and institutional moderator variables on Hispanic students' achievement in college. However, as reflected in the contributions to this volume, such a base is beginning to emerge. As mentioned in the final section, one of the exciting prospects of such research and other needed research is that it might help us go beyond merely improving prediction of Hispanics' success in college. The next steps would include interventions designed to promote development of Hispanics' college aptitude and success in college.

Improving Prediction of College Achievement

By its very nature, the topic of prediction of college achievement engenders concern for what will occur in the future as a result of what has occurred in the past. The issues discussed in the last two sections suggest that in order to improve prediction of Hispanics' college achievement, we need to extend the range of the kinds of information that we consider to be predictors of college aptitude and also our criterion measures of college achievement. In addition, we need to draw attention to factors that moderate the interpretation of college academic predictor measures and factors that moderate Hispanics' ability to demonstrate achievement in college. The goal of improving prediction of Hispanics' college achievement ought to be built on research findings that investigate connections between high–school–based predictors and moderator variables with college-based achievement measures and moderator variables. The problem of prediction as thus conceived is multivariate in nature. The approaches for investigation, however, could be either statistical research or case-study observational research.

Statistical research might use multivariate statistical methodology to investigate relationships between high–school–based and college-based measures. Such research would have a strong exploratory orientation because at present we do not know the strength of relationships among many of the variables involved, nor do we know the best measurement procedures to follow in operationalizing variables. It is almost certain to prove desirable to work with single institutions as a basic unit of study, though statistical metaanalysis techniques might be used to investigate trends across institutions. It is likely to emerge since students' achievement in college and admissions criteria are very much tied to the characteristics of particular institutional environments.

Case-study research appears to be very important, and perhaps it should be a prelude to highly quantitative research. The purpose and direction of case-study research would be to document carefully what is occurring to Hispanics on selective college campuses. Such field research needs to identify how Hispanics are treated and how they fare in the college admissions process, how Hispanics adjust to college life, and whether Hispanics are successful in college endeavors. Case-study research can be a rich resource for developing knowledge needed to operationalize significant variables for quantitatively oriented research such as that described earlier.

Design of Interventions

Recent research in the area of instructional psychology has begun to suggest that once we know a lot about factors that affect students' learning, we can then begin to explore ways in which education might be tailored to individuals with different learning characteristics and aptitudes (e.g., see Snow, 1982). At the forefront of the field there is now a belief that what we call "intelligence" itself may be increased by appropriate interventions based on cognitive-psychology research findings (see Detterman & Sternberg, 1982). At the present this emerging field has yet to contend with sociocultural and linguistic background factors, but the problems of addressing these additional factors are not insurmountable (see Durán, 1985). Snow (1982) suggests that current conceptions of college aptitude should not be narrow and that they should include allowances for motivational and personality variables that affect ability to learn. By opening up the range of factors we consider relevant to Hispanics' college aptitude, we are thus recognizing a richer field of influences on development of college aptitude. In the case of Hispanics, we may find that deliberate manipulation of experiences in high school or college would have a positive effect on their college admissions and college achievement. Predictive validity research of the sort that has been described might form the foundation for interventions we might design. Unlike attempts to influence admissions test scores by coaching, we might directly address the accelerated teaching of thinking and language skills required in college in a way that would be more sensitive and effective than the traditional curricula of high school or college.

Notes

1. In addition to the SAT, the Admissions Testing Program of the College Board currently administers thirteen separate achievement tests along with a written placement test known as the Test of Standard Written English. Hispanics' recent performance on these tests is not discussed in the present paper; the interested reader is referred to the publication *Profiles: College-Bound Seniors, 1983* (Ramist & Arbeiter, 1984). It should suffice to note that Hispanic subgroups performed lower on these tests than white non-Hispanics and that the pattern of differences was of similar magnitude as reported for SAT score differences.

2. The studies reviewed were as follows: D. S. Calkins & R. Whitworth, *Differential prediction of freshman grade point average for sex and two ethnic classifications at a southwestern university* (El Paso: University of Texas at El Paso, 1974; available as ERIC ED 102–199); N. Dittmar, *A comparative investigation of the predictive validity of admissions criteria for Anglos, Black, and Mexican-Americans,* unpublished doctoral dissertation, University of Texas at Austin, 1974; R. E. Goldman & B. Hewitt, "An investigation of test bias for Mexican-American college students," *Journal of Educational Measurement, 12,* no. 3 (Fall 1975), 187–196; R. Goldman & B. Hewitt, "Predicting the success of black, Chicano, oriental and white college students, *Journal of Educational Measurement, 13,* no. 2 (1976), 109–117; R. Goldman & M. Widawski, "An analysis of types of errors in the selection of minority college students," *Journal of Educational Measurement, 13,* no. 3 (1976), 185–200; R. Goldman & R. Richards, "The SAT prediction of grades for Mexican-American versus Anglo-American students of the University of California, Riverside," *Journal of Educational Measurement, 11,* no. 2 (1974), 129–135; R. Lowman & D. Spuck, "Predictors of college success for the disadvantaged Mexican-American," *Journal of College Student Personnel, 16,* (1975), 40–48; J. P. Mestre, "Predicting academic achievement among bilingual Hispanic college technical students," *Educational and Psychological Measurement, 41,* (1981), 1255–1264; C. Scott, *Longer-term predictive validity of college admission tests for Anglo, Black, and Mexican-American students* (Albuquerque, NM: New Mexico Department of Educational Administration, University of New Mexico, 1976); M. J. Vásquez, *Chicano and Anglo university women: Factors related to their performance, persistence and attrition,* unpublished doctoral dissertation, University of Texas at Austin, 1978; J. Warren, *Prediction of college achievement among Mexican-American Students in California,* College Board Research and Development Report (Princeton, NJ: Educational Testing Service, 1976).

References

Alderman, D. (1982). Language proficiency as a moderator variable in testing academic achievement. *Journal of Educational Psychology, 74*(4), 580–587.

American College Testing Program. (1980). *College student profiles: Norms for the ACT assessment.* 1980–81 ed. Iowa City, IA: ACT.

Breland, H. (1979). *Population validity and college entrance measures.* Research Monograph No. 8. New York: College Entrance Examination Board.

Brown, G. H., Rosen, N., Hill, S., & Olivas, M. A. (1980). *The condition of education for Hispanic Americans.* Washington, DC: National Center for Educational Statistics.

Buriel, R. (1983). Teacher-student interactions and their relationship to student achievement: A comparison of Mexican-American and Anglo-American children. *Journal of Educational Psychology, 75*(6), 889–897.

Detterman, D., & Sternberg, R. (Eds.). (1982). *How and how much can intelligence be increased.* Norwood, NJ: Ablex.

Durán, R. P. (1983). *Hispanics' education and background: Predictors of college achievement.* New York: College Entrance Examination Board.

Durán, R. P. (1985). Influences of language skills on bilingual problem solving. In S. Chipman, J. Sigel, & R. Claser (Eds.), *Thinking and learning skills: Vol. 2. Current research and open questions* (pp. 187–207). Hillsdale, NJ: Erlbaum.

Moll, R. *Playing the private college admissions game.* New York: Penguin Books. (1979).

Osterlind, S. (1983). *Test item bias.* Beverly Hills, CA: Sage.

Ramist, L., & Arbeiter, S. (1984). *Profits: College Bound Seniors,* 1983. New York: College Entrance Examination Board.

Snow, R. (1982). The training of intellectual aptitude. In D. Detterman & R. Sternberg (Eds.), *How much can intelligence be increased* (pp. 1–37). Norwood. NJ: Ablex.

Willingham, W. W., & Breland, H. M. (1982). *Personal qualities and college admissions.* New York: College Entrance Examination Board.

The Situation of Black Educational Researchers: Continuation of a Crisis

Henry T. Frierson, Jr.

The numbers and proportions of Blacks gaining doctorates and entering academe have continuously declined. This decline is seen in all fields including education, particularly educational research. Coupled with this downward trend is the fact that, psychologically, Black faculty often find themselves in work environments that are not fully supportive. Prejudice and discrimination remain as obstacles, and for many the lack of mentoring, at any level, is a reality. The situation for many Black faculty in education can be described best as a predicament. For black educational researchers and the nation, this situation has long been of crisis proportions, and it demands to be addressed directly, for it relates to the common good for American education. As never before, more involvement and more Black educational researchers are needed in the efforts to address the myriad problems that beset U.S. education. Related issues and recommendations are discussed in this article.

Educational Researcher, Vol. 19, No. 2, pp. 12–17

In the scheme of American education, educational research and development is a critical area and is thus critically associated with the education of African Americans. The implications of educational research are wide ranging, for studies conducted by educational researchers can affect all forms of education relative to Blacks and other Americans, and thus there is the need for more involvement of Black educational researchers. That point was discussed in an earlier *ER* article:

> In this country, educational R&D plays a crucial part in policymaking and program implementations within educational settings. The impact from R&D is often quite substantial, and the impact is often amplified in minority communities because the initial research may have often been conducted there. Because of the effects of the ensuing research-related developments, the involvement of minority researchers is essential. (Frierson, 1980, p. 5)

To date, neither the involvement nor the number of Black researchers has increased appreciably and, in fact, the need for involvement and an increase in numbers is more critical today. This demand is amplified by the existence of problems such as those pointed out in *A Nation at Risk* (National Commission on Excellence in Education, 1983), *One Third of a Nation* (American Council on Education and the Educational Commission of the States, 1988), *America's Shame America's Hope* (MDC, 1988), and *A Common Destiny: Blacks and American Society* (National Research Council, 1989a). Moreover, there is the increasing proportion of minority pupil enrollment in the schools. By the year 2000, minority groups will represent a majority of elementary and secondary schools' student populations in more than 50 major cities. These students will undoubtedly be the subjects in numerous (and possibly the majority of) future research studies. Thus, the need for more individuals in educational research and development who are sensitive to the needs of ethnic minorities and the disadvantaged is dearly urgent. Moreover, individuals are needed in educational research and development who are not only sensitive to the needs of minorities and the disadvantaged but also sincerely concerned with those groups' educational and social situations.

Black educational researchers, because of their experiences and backgrounds, are more inclined to be interested in addressing issues related to or affecting minorities and the disadvantaged. Unfortunately, since 1975 the number and percentage of black recipients of doctorates in education have declined, decreasing from 9.2% in 1975 to only 7.0% in 1986 (National Research Council, 1976, 1987). This is a foreboding trend concerning the production and contribution of Black faculty in fields related to educational research and development. As further indication of that downward trend, 691 Blacks received doctorate degrees in education in 1976, as compared with only 421 in 1986 (National Research Council, 1987). In 1985, the percentage of Black full-time faculty in all fields was only 4.0%, down from 4.4% in 1977 (U.S. Equal Employment Opportunity Commission, 1985). Further, half of all Black faculty are at Black colleges. Thus, the percentage of Black faculty at major doctorate-granting research universities in all fields, including education, is minuscule. Moreover, the American Council on Education (1988) reported that, between 1977 and 1983, the number of Black full-time faculty dropped from 19,674 to 18,827, while the number of White faculty increased 5% to 473,787. The American Council on Education also reported that, between 1979 and 1986, the number of Black recipients of doctorates dropped by 22%, from 1,056 to 820. In 1988, the National Research Council (1989b) reported that the number of Blacks receiving doctorates declined to 805. If this downward trend continues unabated, it portends an even dimmer future for Blacks in academia.

The number of Blacks with doctorates in education is small, and the number of those who are actually in research and development is significantly smaller. For example, of the 15,888 members of AERA, it is estimated that about 570 (less than 4%) are Black, and all of those individuals do not hold doctorates (membership information obtained from AERA). Thus, the simple numerical need for Blacks in educational research and development is just as critical as that observed for other fields. The social need, however, may be even greater.

A crucial question is why the visible participation of Blacks in research and development is so relatively low and why American education is missing out on this potential source that could significantly expand the horizon of educational research and development. The problems of insufficient and declining numbers have been presented, but there are other factors inherent to the academic community that suppress the participation and the subsequent production of Black educational researchers. Some factors involve the academic milieu at universities where research is a primary focus. At those institutions, Blacks may find themselves isolated with little or no professional support and the sense that there is little appreciation for their research interest, particularly if it centers around minority issues. Other militating factors involve racial discrimination and prejudice, although in forms far more subtle than in years past. Additionally, other factors are connected to the fact that relatively few Black doctorate holders have enjoyed solid protégé-mentor relationships. The results from the lack of such relationships could be long-lasting and have probably stifled the careers of many. These factors will be discussed, and recommendations to increase Black participation in educational research will be presented.

The Academic Milieu

Although the need for more Black faculty in educational research and development is critical, Blacks considering careers in the field should, however, be clearly aware of what they may face. For example, those individuals should be aware that with Black faculty numbers so small, Black faculty members are often judged solely by their White colleagues. Significantly, some of those colleagues will be the same individuals who will determine whether faculty are to be tenured and promoted. Moreover, Black faculty may often receive messages that their work focusing on or addressing issues that affect minorities warrants little scholarly respect. As a consequence, some Black faculty may feel pressured to compromise their research interests and to focus more on what their White colleagues may deem acceptable. Because of pressures to conform to values associated with mainstream research, they may thus find themselves in academic environments that, for them, are intellectually and professionally stifling.

Thus, many Blacks currently in educational research and development may find themselves physically and psychologically isolated and may experience feelings of alienation. Feelings of alienation exist because little professional support from colleagues is perceived. Further, they find that their research interests are generally dissimilar to those maintained by most of their White peers. Without appropriate support, such circumstances can adversely affect research and other academic productivity that is so closely tied to professional development and advancement.

Moore and Wagstaff (1974) pointed out that Blacks at predominantly White institutions are isolated socially from White colleagues. Possibly more important, because of their small numbers, Blacks are also isolated, socially and professionally, from their Black colleagues (Anderson, Frierson, & Lewis, 1979). As indicated earlier, Blacks constitute only about 2% of the faculty at predominantly White institutions. Harvey and Scott-Jones (1985) described the problems that Blacks confront when their numbers are small:

> When there is only one, or a very small number, of Black faculty members in a given institution, the burdens of institutional and individual racism weigh heavily. The psychological safety associated with numbers is not available to persons who labor in such situations. The usual protective network of sympathetic senior faculty also does not exist. Demands on Black faculty time and presence escalate. In the absence of a support group operating under the same circumstances, frustrations understandably mount. Black faculty members are subjected to the aggravating aspects of the academic milieu without enjoying some of its compensating benefits: contemplation, independence, and social and intellectual stimulation from colleagues sharing the same interests and outlook. (p. 70)

Black academicians also generally experience significant difficulty getting into the "network" (Roper, 1980). Thus they do not readily enjoy the, advantages that networking within the professional mainstream provides, such as the following: collaborating on or participating in funded research projects; increased opportunities for joint authorship on manuscripts of various types; increased opportunities for paid consulting; regular invitations to participate in symposia or panels at professional meetings; having one's name circulated for serious consideration for attractive professional positions; serving on editorial boards, major committees of professional organizations, major boards or commissions, and so forth. Consequently, Blacks often find themselves isolated not only in relation to their departments or institutions but from the entire academic community as well. For young Black academicians, this can be psychologically and professionally devastating. Further, although many Black faculty at predominantly White universities suffer from isolation and a lack of collegiality, at the same time inordinate demands are often placed on them by the need to be accessible to Black students, other Black faculty and staff, the community, and the frequent expectation to serve as minority spokespersons on many university committees or on university-related affairs in general. Those various circumstances point to the irony that often seems to occur when a Black faculty member voluntarily leaves one institution to take advantage of a better job opportunity at another, and the individuals at the first institution react as if the Black faculty member has betrayed them by leaving.

On another point, Scott (1981) argued the need for potential Black academicians to attend prominent research institutions where networks can be established with prominent faculty. But he also pointed out the structural constraints that exist. Hence, attending prominent institutions certainly does not guarantee Black academicians access to the "network." Moreover, in all likelihood, even while attending such institutions, they probably will not enjoy the type of protégé-mentor relationship that would fully prepare them for all the nuances associated with academia, nor will they likely be afforded meaningful introductions to various key members of the "network." Thus, although Blacks may attend a prominent research institution, they may well be denied entry to a network that would serve to rapidly advance their careers. Those and other situations serve to promote cynicism on the part of Black faculty that, in effect, can significantly reduce productivity and thus hamper professional development.

Prejudice and Discrimination

Black faculty at predominantly White universities may experience various forms of prejudice and discrimination. Menges and Exum (1983) discussed some of the problems related to negativism affecting Black academicians. They contended that institutions have failed to ensure equity for minority faculty. They further asserted that ambiguous standards for promotion can in effect shield both deliberate and unintentional bias, and, thus, subjectivity-based judgments that are related to attitude and personality are likely to occur. Menges and Exum suggested that although there is a lack of overt discrimination, Black faculty may be experiencing subtle and indirect forms of discrimination. These forms of discrimination may be an outgrowth of what Valverde (1980) termed dysfunctional attitudes toward minority researchers that are harbored by White researchers. Examples of how such discrimination is manifested are as follows: customarily excluding Black researchers from collaborating on potentially rewarding projects because of the unstated rationale that they would be unable to make worthwhile contributions to the project or they are just not needed; withholding from new Black faculty support and assistance that would be normally provided for any new faculty member, because of possible perceptions that the person is not really qualified and the accompanying resentment that the position was gained only because of affirmative action; unfavorable tenure and promotion decisions ostensibly based on the person's failure to meet prescribed criteria but more rooted in racial prejudice and discrimination; and smaller merit increases in salary that are often based on racial prejudice and discrimination rather than actual merit.

There has been evidence presented that Blacks at the same academic ranks as Whites, on average, earn lower salaries (National Advisory Committee on Black Higher Education and Black Colleges and Universities, 1978; Traynham & Green, 1977). Discrepancies still exist, for a recent study reported that although there has been a decline in the salary gap, Black faculty overall receive lower pay than the national average (Brown, 1988). Further, in actual job situations, Blacks find themselves overrepresented in the lower academic ranks and are thus more subject to job loss (Wilk, 1979). Moreover, it was reported that Blacks had the lowest faculty promotion and tenure rates when compared to Whites, Hispanics, and Asian-Americans (Brown).

As mentioned, the chances are greater that Blacks are more likely to lack professional support from colleagues. Because of perceptions associated with racism or prejudice, Black faculty often find that they are perceived to be not as qualified, despite their training, as their non-Black peers. Indeed, Black doctorate holders on faculties or employed as researchers in other professional capacities may find that their academic credentials may be viewed suspiciously with the rationalization that those degrees were received only because of their minority status. Under such situations, some Black faculty may be under severe pressure and believe that they must prove themselves worthy of the professional and academic status they have acquired. Moreover, some may be concerned themselves that they are viewed merely as "affirmative action hires." These factors may bring on additional stress if Black faculty feel that they must prove they belong. With the nonsupportive environments experienced by many Black academicians, such feelings may be difficult to overcome. This state of affairs may be especially problematic for young Blacks whose professional development consequently may be stifled.

Elmore and Blackburn (1983) suggested that Blacks in predominantly White higher education settings often pay a high psychic cost. The psychic costs may be in the form of self-doubt and reduced self-esteem, thus resulting in diminished professional productivity. A particular significance of Elmore and Blackburn's conclusions was that they were drawn from the perspectives of Black academicians who had attained creditable professional status and moreover had categorized themselves as being generally satisfied. If those individuals are paying high psychic costs, then what costs are unsatisfied Black academicians paying? There are probably a substantial number in the latter category. Even though those faculty may engage successfully in mainstream research, they often remain preoccupied with questions concerning whether their work is viewed as acceptable by their White colleagues.

Effects from the Lack of
Solid Protégé-Mentor Relationships

Mentoring is a system that provides individuals with support and protection during their graduate training and serves as an additional support source once they become academicians. The importance of mentoring in promoting professional success has been clearly acknowledged (Darrow, Klein, Levinson, & McKee, 1978; Rawlins & Rawlins, 1983; Vaughn, 1985). Mentors often play a considerable role in career development. Long (1978), for example, reported that individuals who had mentors are more productive in their careers, and Roche (1979) observed that they are promoted more quickly. Some universities have attempted to formally institute protégé-mentor relationships between junior and senior faculty.

Concerning mentoring for Black academicians, it appears that few have experienced the advantage of a protégé-mentor relationship. Blackwell (1983, 1984) reported that only one in eight Black doctorate recipients had the benefit of a true mentor during graduate school. Black doctoral recipients have had advisors at the dissertation stage, of course, but they have apparently had fewer opportunities to form protégé-mentor relationships with individuals well established in the academic community. Naïveté relative to academia is a price often paid for the lack of such relationships, and in many ways some continue to pay the price even after being in the field for a significant period of time.

Blackwell (1984) further reported that, whereas half of all White graduate students receive teaching assistantships, the proportion is only one fourth for Blacks. Further, whereas one third of all doctoral students receive research assistantships, only one fifth of underrepresented minority students have received the valuable experiences so often gained from such assistantships. For Blacks, it appears obvious that equal access to opportunities to professional careers in academe is far from reality as indicated by such discrepancies during the critical preprofessional phases.

Blackwell (1981, 1983, 1984) also reported that the most persistent and statistically significant predictor of enrollment and graduation of Black graduate students is the presence of Black faculty. This situation has "Catch-22" overtones. The obvious implications are that an increase in the presence of Black faculty is critical, but unless barriers are removed, conditions improved, and concerted actions taken, the production of Black faculty will continue to worsen.

Discussion

The presence of Black academicians involved in research and development is important for a number of reasons, but four critical reasons are as follows: (a) to advance scholarship in general, as well as to focus research on minorities and the disadvantaged; (b) to provide necessary support for Black and other minority colleagues; (c) to increase the number of Black scholars in the field; and (d) through research and development efforts, to have a significant effect on policy and programs that may enhance students' educational attainment and academic development.

As Black researchers are more likely to dutifully address issues and problems that acutely affect minorities and the disadvantaged, activities to promote and ensure the continued professional development of Black academicians are critical. Research by productive Black academicians may contribute significantly to the scholarly studies of such issues as the impact of test bias on minority students' standardized test performances, the use of differential admission criteria as factors for admission policies, the identification of critical variables for teaching children effectively, Afrocentric theory and its use to promote improved educational opportunities and academic achievement for Black students, examining the construct of cognitive style and its use in developing instructional procedures that are effective for Black children, varying perspectives in the examination of the validity of standardized tests in assessing academic potential, and the development and examination of intervention methods that enhance achievement.

With the country's need for future scientists, engineers, and others in highly technological fields being of critical proportions, it is vital that more Black and other underrepresented minority students have real educational opportunities that will allow them success in entering those fields. More Blacks involved in research and development and focusing on identifying variables that enhance and promote academic success in students can affect the chances of students' receiving substantially improved education.

Recommendations and Conclusion

Overall, the predicament of Black faculty in educational research and development is quite serious and, when the large picture is considered, probably moreso than is generally realized. One could argue that the same experiences cited can occur for White faculty, but the reasons often are based on race rather than on personality conflicts. Under such circumstances, there is little wonder why the number of Black academicians significantly involved in educational research is relatively low and cynicism exists. Given the current state, Black participation is likely to remain low unless vigorous action to address the problems is undertaken.

Despite the low numbers, however, Black faculty as a group can significantly affect their collective destiny to a large extent. Listed below are some major courses of actions that Black faculty can promote that can have the effect of increasing the number of Black faculty and enhancing professional development.

1. Overall, Black faculty should continue to support one another professionally and socioemotionally, but in a more proactive fashion. Professional networks should be further developed and expanded. Communication is the essential ingredient. Often, just the matter of "staying in touch" pays significant psychological and professional dividends.

2. Young Black faculty should be provided assistance in developing research projects in their areas of interest. Although the numbers are small, senior Black faculty who are involved in educational research and development should make sincere efforts to actively reach out to young Black faculty to offer assistance toward their research efforts. For example, this could be accomplished through invitations to participate in and collaborate on research projects; providing socioemotional support and encouragement; offering advice and suggestions; and being willing to read, react, or provide input for papers or research ideas. Additionally, young Black Ph.D.s should also be proactive in seeking assistance from experienced Black faculty.

3. Philosophically, Black faculty should expect to be received as full colleagues and to participate regularly in collaborative work with others in their department. Realistically, however, for most, that probably will not occur. New Black faculty should be aware of that possibility and thus prepare themselves for environments in which they will not be fully accepted as colleagues. Thus, new faculty should actively seek to communicate with experienced Black faculty at other institutions and even other departments or schools within their respective institutions to obtain advice, establish collaborative projects, and develop mentor protégé relationships that can be critical in the adjustments to academe.

4. In advancing scholarship, there should be active efforts to collaborate with others who, without regard to ethnicity, have similar research and professional interests.

5. New Ph.D.s should be encouraged to seriously consider postdoctorate fellowships, so that they can develop or expand their initial research and begin a publication track record that will give them a good start toward establishing a foundation that will facilitate professional promotions.

6. There should be active efforts to identify and encourage Black undergraduate students with potential for graduate school to give serious consideration to enrolling in doctoral programs. Those students should be provided with experiences and encouragement that will promote and reinforce the desire to enter graduate school and to embark on academic careers.

7. Black faculty should monitor Black doctoral students to ensure that they are receiving fair treatment and are making adequate progress in their programs. Black

faculty should see to it that Black graduate students have favorable chances of completing their graduate programs. (Although this is a responsibility of all faculty, with the critical need to increase the numbers of Black doctorates, it seems prudent that Black faculty see to it that Black students have equal chances for success.)

8. Black doctoral students should be encouraged to obtain as much research experience as possible. They should be provided the opportunity to immerse themselves in research. Black faculty can play a major role by making every effort to see that Black graduate students receive ample research experiences either by allowing the student to be involved with the faculty's research or urging other faculty to allow students to participate meaningfully in ongoing research projects.

9. Continuous and sincere efforts should be made toward exploring the development of cross-disciplinary collaborative projects with Black faculty in other disciplines to take advantage of strengths that interdisciplinary efforts often afford and mutually to expand individual scholarships.

10. Through their research efforts, Black faculty should aspire actively to become leaders in their fields.

All key individuals at predominantly White institutions who hire or seek to hire Black faculty should be conscious of the environment that will be presented to Black faculty, and there are steps that should be taken to ensure that the participation of Black faculty at those institutions will be worthwhile. Institutions that bring Black faculty to departments or schools where none are present or the numbers are negligible should acknowledge forthrightly the likelihood that those individuals are unlikely to be welcomed fully by their colleagues and hence will not likely be accorded the collegial amenities that most new faculty would expect. In other words, it is unrealistic for institutions to assume that Black faculty will be treated just as any other faculty member. In many academic situations, such assumptions are quite fallacious. Those facts should not be ignored. Listed below are some suggestions that institutions serious about attracting and retaining Black faculty should consider promoting.

1. The presence of racism in the institution should be acknowledged as a reality and should be addressed forthrightly when it is raised as an issue. In other words, when evidence of racism occurs, it should not be ignored, but the source should be identified and efforts should be made to reduce or eliminate the damage that is certain to be a result. Further, individuals of influence at predominantly White institutions should acknowledge the psychic costs that Black faculty often pay for being in those environments and thus suppress the attitude that Black faculty should feel fortunate that they are on those particular campuses.

2. Given the isolation that many Black faculty may experience, institutions should make every effort to ensure that Black faculty will have opportunities for professional growth and development.

3. Institutions hiring young Black faculty or bringing Black faculty into departments where they are likely to be isolated should make every effort to ensure that from the beginning, those faculty have support for scholarly activities that will promote their professional advancement. Support could be in the form of research assistants, funds for research, or active assistance in the securing of external funding. At institutions where research is emphasized, classroom teaching should be kept to a low level, there should be ample opportunities for research leaves, and young Black faculty should be encouraged strongly to take leaves for research and development purposes.

4. It was reported that less than 40% of Black doctoral students have teaching and research assistantships compared to more than 60% for White students (Educational Testing Service, 1988). Given this discrepancy and the fact that graduate research assistantships can be critical in the development of skills needed to advance success

in academe, institutions—with organizations such as AERA as advocates—should support a substantial increase in the number of research assistantships for Black doctoral students. This would ensure that those students will have increased opportunities to gain valuable research experiences. Institutions should make concerted efforts to gain resources to ensure that Black doctoral students have adequate support. Given the growing interest in the decline in the number of graduate students, particularly Black graduate students, stipends and other support should be sought from federal, state, and private sources. There seems to be evidence that funding agencies are becoming more receptive than what was obvious in the past.

5. Sincere efforts should be made to promote professional growth and development. Nonscholarship demands on Black faculty should be kept minimal, and those activities in which Black faculty are requested to participate should often have potential for promoting professional growth; for example, serving on or chairing panels or commissions that will bring about greater professional visibility.

6. Concerning tenure and promotion decisions, those involved in the decision-making process should be clearly aware of and should acknowledge the extra burden and demands often placed on Black faculty. The additional activities should be given credence and professional rewards should be granted accordingly.

7. At the undergraduate level, the development of early identification programs to orient Black undergraduate students to educational research should be attempted (Frierson, 1981). This could be done by involving the students in research projects to expose them to research methods and to develop and nurture their interest in research, and, importantly, to encourage them to pursue academic careers. Support for these programs could come from federal, state, and private sources. Institutions and organizations such as AERA could speak loudly to the need for such programs.

8. With the projected need for significantly more academicians, it is important that Black students be encouraged to enter educational research in numbers far greater than now. Students who enter graduate programs should be provided with support to succeed in the doctoral education phase and subsequently in the profession itself.

An academic career in educational research and development can be quite rewarding and, under equitable circumstances, very attractive to Blacks and other minorities. Despite the obstacles, Blacks should be encouraged to enter this potentially rewarding and fulfilling field. This is particularly significant given the increasing need for future academicians and the tremendous contributions that Black researchers can make. The continued loss of potential scholars is staggering, and the academic community will be remiss unless serious efforts are mounted not only to reverse the decline in Black doctorates, but also to increase substantially their production and the subsequent development of Black researchers. If not, the crisis will continue, and it will be to the detriment of the nation.

References

American Council on Education. (1988). *Minorities In higher education: Seventh annual status report 1988*. Washington, DC: Author.

American Council on Education and the Educational Commission of the States. (1988). *One third of a nation: Report of the commission on minority participation in education in American life*. Washington, DC: American Council on Education.

Anderson, W., Frierson, H. T., & Lewis, T. B. (1979). Black survival in White academe. *Journal of Negro Education, 48*, 92–102.

Blackwell, J. E. (1981). *Mainstreaming outsiders: The production of Black professionals*. Bayside, NY: General Hall.

Blackwell, J. E. (1983). *Networking and mentoring: A study of cross-generational experiences of Blacks in graduate and professional schools.* Atlanta, GA: Southern Educational Foundation.

Blackwell, J. E. (1984, October). *Increasing access and retention of minority students in graduate and professional schools.* Paper presented at the Educational Testing Service's Invitational Conference on Educational Standards, Testing, and Access, New York, NY.

Brown, S. V. (1988). *Increasing minority faculty: An elusive goal.* Princeton, NJ: Educational Testing Service.

Educational Testing Service. (1988). Minority students in higher education. *Focus,* No. 22. Princeton, NJ: Author.

Elmore, C. I., & Blackburn, R. T. (1983). Black and White faculty in research universities. *Journal of Higher Education, 54,* 1–15.

Frierson, H. T. (1980). Modifying the role and status of minorities in educational R&D: A much-needed undertaking. *Educational Researcher, 9*(9), 5–7.

Frierson, H. T. (1981). Minority participation in R&D: Developing an undergraduate feeder system. *Journal of Negro Education, 50,* 401–406.

Harvey, W. B., & Scott-Jones, D. (1985). We can't find any: The elusiveness of Black faculty members in American higher education. *Issues in Education, 3,* 68-76.

Levinson, D. J., Darrow, C. L., Klein, E. B., Levinson, M. H., & McKee, B. (1978). *The seasons of a man's life.* New York: Knopf.

Long, J. S. (1978). Productivity and academic positions in the scientific career. *American Sociological Review, 43,* 889–908.

MDC. (1988). *America's shame America's hope: Twelve million youth at risk.* Chapel Hill, NC: Author.

Menges, R. J., & Exum, W. H. (1983). Barriers to the progress of women and minority faculty. *Journal of Higher Education, 54,* 123–144.

Moore, W., & Wagstaff, L. (1974). *Black faculty in white colleges.* San Francisco: Jossey-Bass.

National Advisory Committee on Black Higher Education and Black Colleges and Universities. (1978). *Higher education equity: The crisis of appearance versus reality.* Washington, DC: Department of Health, Education and Welfare, Office of Education.

National Commission on Excellence in Education. (1983). *A nation at risk.* Washington, DC: Department of Education.

National Research Council. (1976). *Summary report 1975: Doctorate recipients from United States universities.* Washington, DC: National Academy Press.

National Research Council. (1987). *Summary report 1986: Doctorate recipients from United States universities.* Washington, DC: National Academy Press.

National Research Council. (1989a). *A common destiny: Blacks and American society.* Washington, DC: National Academy Press.

National Research Council. (1989b). *Summary report 1988: Doctorate recipients from United States universities.* Washington, DC: National Academy Press.

Rawlins, M. D., & Rawlins, L. (1983). Mentoring and networking for helping professionals. *Personnel and Guidance Journal, 62,* 116–118.

Roche, G. R. (1979). Much ado about mentors. *Harvard Business Review, 57,* 2–27.

Roper, D. (1980). The waning of the old boy network: Placement, publishing and faculty selection. *Improving College and University Teaching, 28,* 12–18.

Scott, R. R. (1981). Black faculty productivity and interpersonal academic contacts. *Journal of Negro Education, 50*, 224–236.

Traynham, E. C., & Green, G. (1977). Affirmative action programs and salary discrimination. *Negro Educational Review, 28*, 36–41.

U.S. Equal Employment Opportunity Commission. (1985). *Staff information, 1977 and 1984*. Washington, DC: U.S. Equal Employment Opportunity Commission.

Valverde, L. A. (1980). Development of ethnic researchers and the education of White researchers. *Educational Researcher, 9*(9), 16–20.

Vaughn, J. C. (1985). Minority students in graduate education. In B. L. R. Smith (Ed.), *The state of graduate education*. Washington, DC: Brookings Institution.

Wilk, A. S. (Ed.) (1979). *The hidden professorate: Credentialism, professionalism, and the tenure crisis*. Westport, CT: Greenwood.

Minority Student Access to, and Persistence and Performance in, College:
A Review of the Trends and Research Literature

Shirley L. Mow and Michael T. Nettles

Introduction

Minorities comprise a growing share of college and university undergraduate enrollments in the United States and an even larger proportion of the pool of potential students. For every 100 students attending American colleges and universities, approximately 78 are White, nine are Black, six are Hispanic, four are Asian American, one is American Indian, and two are foreign nationals. In 1986, minority students comprised 20.3 percent of the college population, compared with 17.5 percent 10 years earlier.

This chapter examines the enrollment, persistence and performance of undergraduate minority students. . . .

Undergraduate Enrollment Trends

Minority Enrollment, 1976–1986

Between 1976 and 1986 minority undergraduate enrollment increased by nearly a third, growing considerably more than total enrollment. The increase was primarily due to substantial enrollment growth among Asian and Hispanic Americans. Gains were relatively modest for American Indians and for Whites (16 and 8 percent respectively). For Blacks, however, enrollment increased less than 2.0 percent over the 10-year period. In fact, Black enrollment climbed sharply between 1976 and 1980 but declined steadily thereafter.

Because enrollments did not increase as much for Blacks and Whiles as for other groups, their shares of total enrollment decreased. In 1986, Blacks comprised 9.2 percent of the totals, down from 10.2 percent in 1976; White enrollment dropped from 81 percent to 77.8 percent in the same period. Asians and Hispanics, on the other hand, increased their shares of the total by approximately 2.0 percent each during the same period.

Already complex enough, the overall minority enrollment picture is further complicated by the fact that there are more than 3,200 undergraduate institutions across the nation, and they are of various types: public and private, two- and four-year, sectarian and nonsectarian. They have different admissions standards, persistence and graduation requirements, types of faculty, and academic programs. Thus, national trends do not reflect equally the challenges faced by different types of institutions or institutions located in different regions. The array of types of institutions, coupled with the ethnic diversity within minority groups, makes interpreting national trends difficult.

Growth of the General Minority Population

The growing proportion of undereducated minority students is cause for serious concern because minorities are rapidly increasing their share of the general U.S. population, and this trend is expected to continue over the next few decades (Hodgkinson, 1985; Pallas, Natriello, & McDill, 1989). Table 4 illustrates that, from 1980 to 1986, each of the non-White groups grew more rapidly (Blacks by 9.8 percent, all other races combined by 45.0 percent) than the population as a whole (6.4 percent). Data for the same period were not available for Hispanics (identified by the Bureau of the Census as individuals of Spanish origin, regardless of race), but data from 1982 and 1985 indicate that the Hispanic population grew faster (10.3 percent) in four years than either Whites or Blacks in six.

Even more important for the future of higher education are the changes in the 18- to 24-year-old cohort. While the total population in this age group declined 7.6 percent between 1980 and 1986, the Black population remained relatively stable, and other races grew by 29.3 percent (see Table 5). Between 1982 and 1985, Hispanics in this age group increased by 5.8 percent. Aggregate data of the type presented above are useful for understanding overall minority college participation, but these data provide no information about minority enrollment at various types of colleges and universities.

Table 4
U.S. Population Growth by Race 1980–86

	White	Black	Other Races	Hispanic*	Total
1980	195,086,000	26,803,000	5,172,000	—	227,061,000
1982	—	—	—	15,364,000	—
1985	—	—	—	16,940,000	—
1986	204,671,000	29,427,000	7,498.000	—	241,596,000
% Change	4.9%	9.8%	45.0%	10.3%	6.4%

Source: U.S. Department of Commerce Bureau of the Census. Current Population Reports Series P-25, No. 1000, Table A (1987).
Source: Current Population Reports Series P-20, No. 422. Table B-1 (1985).

Table 5
Population of 18- to 24-year-olds in the United States, 1980 and 1986

	White	Black	Other Races	Hispanic*	Total
1980	25,567,000	4,019,000	703,000	—	30,289,000
1982	—	—	—	2,273,872	—
1985	—	—	—	2,405,480	—
1986	23,108,000	3,956,000	909,000	—	27,973,000
% of Change	–9.6%	–1.6%	29.3%	5.8%	–7.6%

Source: U.S. Department of Commerce, Bureau of the Census. Current Population Reports Series P-25, No. 1000 (1987).
Source: Current Population Reports Series P-20, No. 422, Table B-1 (1985).

Distribution by Type of Institution

The lion's share of overall and particularly minority enrollment growth has occurred at two-year institutions. From 1976 to 1986, community college enrollments increased by 16.2 percent compared with 14 percent in all of higher education, and community colleges increased their share of the total college enrollment from 28 percent to more than 37 percent. Asian-American enrollment in two-year colleges climbed by more than 135 percent, and Hispanic enrollment by 64 percent. Overall, minority enrollment in community colleges went up 37.8 percent, more than double the increase in White enrollment in those institutions (American Council on Education, 1988).

Several studies underscore the fact that minority students are disproportionately concentrated in community colleges (American Council on Education, 1988; Arbeiter, 1986; Astin, 1982; Pelavin, in press; Richardson & Bender, 1987; Verdugo, 1986). In 1986–87, as Table 6 shows, larger percentages of Hispanics (56.3 percent) and American Indians (54.3 percent) attended public two-year institutions than Asian Americans (44.7 percent) and Blacks (40.6 percent). At the same time, only 36.9 percent of White students attended these institutions.

At four-year institutions, enrollments increased at less than half the rate of community colleges from 1976 to 1986. The overall growth at four-year institutions—10 percent—was due to significant increases in minority enrollment (28.4 percent), particularly among Asians (120 percent) and Hispanics (60 percent). American Indians gained by only 2.9 percent and Blacks, only 1.8 percent. White enrollment increased 5.7 percent (American Council on Education, 1988).

As Table 6 also shows, Whites were more likely than minority group members to attend four-year institutions, both public and private. Whites also were more likely to attend universities than four-year colleges. The significance here is that the larger public and private research universities have greater resources in important areas of educational expenditure and academic offerings than the two- and four-year public colleges in which minorities tend to be concentrated. Moreover, students who enter universities and four-year colleges are much more likely to earn the bachelor's degree than students who enter two-year colleges (Astin, 1982; Nettles, 1988a; Richardson & Bender, 1987).

Historically Black colleges and universities are major providers of higher education for Black students. Over the past decade, however, these institutions have experienced a great loss of Black enrollment to predominantly White institutions (Mingle, 1981; Nettles, 1988a; Thomas, McPartland, & Gottfredson, 1981; Thomas, Mingle, & McPartland, 1981). Today, historically Black institutions enroll only about 16 percent of the Blacks in higher education. Of these students, 86 percent are enrolled in undergraduate programs (American Council on Education, 1988; Brown, 1987; Thomas & Hill, 1987). Enrollment in Black institutions peaked in 1980 at 222,000 students; by 1986, the total had declined to 213,000, but it climbed slightly to 217,400 in 1987 (American Council on Education, 1988; Pelavin, in press). In the years just prior to 1980, enrollment growth at the Black institutions was due to increases in non-Black and nonresident-alien students and occurred primarily at four-year universities and colleges. As a result, the proportion of students from other races enrolled in these institutions rose from 12 percent in 1976 to 18 percent in 1982 (American Council on Education, 1988; Thomas & Hill, 1987).

Table 6
Percent Enrollment of Racial/Ethnic Groups by Type of Institution 1986–87

	Black	American Indian	Asian American	Hispanic	White	Nonresident Alien
2-Year Public	40.6	54.3	44.7	56.3	36.9	23.4
2-Year Private	3.7	3.9	.8	2.3	2.4	1.8
4-Year Public	39.2	34.3	41.4	31.2	42.3	42.9
4-Year Private	16.5	7.5	13.1	10.2	18.4	31.9
Total	100	100	100	100	100	100

Source: Unpublished data: National Center for Education Statistics, Integrated Postsecondary Education Data Systems (1986–87).

Geographical Distribution

In addition to being overrepresented in two-year institutions, minority students are also concentrated in colleges and universities in a small number of states, because minority population growth has been greater in some regions than in others. For example, three-fourths of the Hispanics in the U.S. reside in five states: Arizona, California. Florida, New Mexico, and Texas. Asian Americans live predominantly in the West and the Mid-Atlantic states, and one-third of the American Indian population resides on approximately 300 Indian lands (reservations, trusts, Alaskan native villages) across the nation (Fries, 1987). Compared with other minority groups, Blacks are more dispersed throughout the country, but they do reside predominantly in the South and in major urban centers, particularly in the East and Midwest.

These demographic facts are evident in the geographical distribution of minority enrollment in higher education, because minority students frequently enroll in public two- and four-year colleges that are close to home. In fact, proximity is an important factor among minorities, especially Hispanics and American Indians, in choosing a college (So, 1984). Because of lower income, as well as close family and community ties, minority students are frequently unable or reluctant to leave home to attend a distant college (Payán, Peterson, & Castille, 1984). For example, 50 percent of Hispanic undergraduates attend institutions in only two states, California and Texas. Fifty percent of Asian-American college students are also found in two states—California and Hawaii. (California alone accounts for 46 percent of them.) Black and American Indian students are more dispersed, but more than half of them attend institutions in a half-dozen states. For Blacks who live in the South, the greatest access to higher education is provided by historically Black institutions, while for those outside the South, community colleges provide the greatest access (Nettles, 1988c). On the other hand, American Indians gravitate to community colleges in the South and West, centers of American-Indian population.

In some states, minority students represent a substantial portion of the higher education enrollment. In others, minority students are barely visible.

Degree Attainment

Trends in minority degree attainment are somewhat parallel to enrollment trends. In 1987, the total of associate degrees awarded was 422,701, an increase of 5.8 percent over 1977 (see Table 7). All groups shared in the gain. Asian Americans had the greatest increase—69.8 percent—during the 10-year period; American Indians initially suffered a decline, then gained steadily for eight years; and Hispanics experienced uneven growth. Blacks had the least dramatic increase (6.3 percent). The number of associate degrees earned by Blacks peaked at 35,781 in 1981, then slid slowly downward until 1987. By comparison, White students experienced a 3.6 percent increase in associate degrees earned during this period. (National Center for Education Statistics, unpublished data, 1977, 1979, 1981, 1983, 1985, and 1987).

At the baccalaureate level, minorities made greater gains in the number of degrees earned during the same 10 years, and their gains outpaced those made by White students. The greatest increase was among Asian Americans (148.2 percent), growing from 13,610 degrees in 1977 to 33,784 in 1987; the next greatest increase was among Hispanics (68.7 percent), growing from 18,525 to 31,249 degrees. For each group, the gain in baccalaureates was more than double the gain in associate degrees during this period. In the same 10 years, the number of baccalaureates awarded to Whites increased by 12 percent, and those awarded to American Indians and Blacks increased by 50 percent and 20 percent, respectively.

The minority share of baccalaureate degrees increased, from 10.2 percent in 1977 to 13.1 percent in 1987. Furthermore, the share of class enrollment comprised by minority groups declined as they moved through college. Table 8 shows that Blacks, who made up 9.2 percent of total college enrollment in 1987, received only 8.2 percent of the associate degrees and 6.5 percent of the baccalaureates awarded that year. The drop was greatest for Hispanics, who comprised 6.6 percent of the enrollment but earned only 4.4 percent of the associate and 2.9 percent of the bachelor's degrees. By contrast, White students comprised 77.8 percent of the enrollment and received 82.9 percent of the associate and 84.2 percent of the bachelor's degrees.

Table 7
Percent Change in Undergraduate Degrees Awarded by Race/Ethnicity, 1977 to 1987

	White	Black	Hispanic	Asian American	American Indian	Total
Associate Degrees						
1977–79	–3.7	3	–2.6	9.8	–9.7	–2.6
1979–81	3.7	4.9	10.7	16.7	14.7	4.9
1981–83	3.0	–.2	7.6	17.5	5.2	3.1
1983–85	.0	–1.8	1.0	–1.8	8.9	–2.4
1985–87	.7	.3	–2.5	14.9	6.5	.5
1977–87						
% Change	3.6	6.3	14.1	69.8	26.4	5.8
Baccalaureate Degrees						
1977–79	–.8	2.6	7.6	12.3	2.5	.0
1979–81	.7	.8	8.9	22.2	4.7	1.8
1981–83	–1.4	–5.9	7.6	10.4	–5.8	–.8
1983–85	3.7	.8	10.3	22.6	26.2	4.4
1985–87	9.7	22.3	21.3	33.8	17.3	11.2
1977-87						
% Change	12.2	19.9	68.7	148.2	49.8	17.3

Source: Unpublished data: National Center for Education Statistics, Higher Education General Information Survey (1977, 1979, 1981, 1983, 1985, 1987).

Table 8
Percent of Undergraduate Enrollment, Associate Degrees Earned,
and Baccalaureate Degrees Earned by Race/Ethnicity, 1986–1987

	White	Black	Hispanic	Asian American	American Indian	Nonresident Alien
Percent of Undergraduate Enrollment	77.8%	9.2%	6.6%	3.7%	.7%	1.9%
Percent of Associate Degrees Earned	82.9%	8.2%	4.4%	2.7%	.7%	1.1%
Percent of Baccalaureate Degrees Earned	84.2%	6.5%	2.9%	3.2%	.5%	2.7%

Source: Unpublished data: National Center for Education Statistics, Higher Education General Information Survey (HEGIS) 1986–1987.

Major Fields of Study

Table 9 shows the distribution of bachelor's degrees earned in 1987 by race/ethnicity and field of study. Business was the most popular major among degree recipients, with about 20 percent of each racial/ethnic group earning degrees in that field. Except for this common interest in business, choice of field differed substantially among the various minority groups.

Blacks are becoming more similar to Whites in their choice of majors. Although increasing proportions of Blacks are receiving degrees in business, health sciences, and technical fields (Darling-Hammond, 1985), they continue to be underrepresented in these fields, and a substantial number—nearly one-third—of them continue to earn baccalaureate degrees in the social sciences, education, the arts, and the humanities. Nearly 37 percent of the Hispanic students also prefer to major in the arts, the humanities, education, and the social sciences. Among non-Asian minorities, Hispanics are more likely to earn degrees in engineering but equally unlikely to earn degrees in the biological sciences, computer science, and the physical sciences and mathematics. American Indian bachelor's degree recipients share a similar pattern in choosing their major fields.

Table 9
Percentage Distribution of Baccalaureate Degrees by Field of Study and Race/Ethnicity, 1986–87

	White	Black	Hispanic	Asian American	American Indian
Agriculture	1.7	.5	.9	.8	1.8
Architecture	.8	.4	1.1	1.1	.5
Arts & Humanities	15.6	12.3	14.6	11.8	13.2
Biological Sciences	3.4	2.7	3.9	7.6	2.9
Business	25.0	27.7	25.2	19.2	21.3
Computer Science	3.4	4.3	3.6	7.5	2.5
Education	9.0	6.2	7.4	3.6	9.4
Engineering	8.3	6.1	9.3	19.3	6.5
Health Science	7.7	11.2	7.1	5.5	10.0
Home Economics	1.9	2.6	1.9	1.6	3.9
Interdisciplinary Studies	1.5	1.5	1.7	1.8	2.0
Law	.17	.1	.15	.08	.04
Military Science	1.5	3.6	2.2	.5	1.5
Physical Sciences and Mathematics	3.3	2.4	2.2	5.7	2.5
Social Sciences	13.8	14.2	14.8	12.3	15.1
Trades	2.9	4.2	4.1	1.8	6.9
Total	100.0	100.0	100.0	100.0	100.0

Source: Unpublished data: National Center for Educational Statistics, Higher Education General Information Survey, (1986–87).

By contrast, Asian Americans as a group are the most likely to pursue baccalaureates in engineering, the biological sciences, computer science, and the physical sciences and mathematics. In fact, as bachelor's degree recipients, they are overrepresented in these fields. They are, however, severely underrepresented in education (1.3 percent of all degree recipients in education).

In general, non-Asian minority students pursuing baccalaureates avoid the biological sciences, computer science, and the physical sciences and mathematics. They are more likely to pursue degrees in the social sciences, the arts arid humanities, and education. However, the number of students receiving degrees in education has been declining since 1977 (U.S. Department of Education, *The Condition of Education*, 1988). Minority preference for these majors has serious implications because these fields have the lowest salaries and highest unemployment rates (Darling-Hammond, 1985; Nettles, 1988b). Thus, non-Asian minorities tend to select major fields that are not related to their high levels of professional aspiration.

Summary

Generally, minority groups other than Blacks have made some strides in higher education over the past decade; their college enrollments have increased significantly. For Blacks, overall enrollment declined, and the decline was particularly sharp among Black males. Enrollment gains among Black women did not make up for losses among men. Across all groups, women experienced greater growth in college enrollment than men. Asian-American women made the largest gains, Black women the smallest.

While greater numbers of minority students attend college today, their enrollment patterns contrast markedly with those of White students in terms of types of institutions and geographic distribution. Minority students, particularly Hispanics and American Indians, tend to enroll in community colleges, which rank at the bottom of the higher education hierarchy in terms of prestige and resources (Astin, 1982). Moreover, many of these institutions are predominantly minority (Nettles, 1988c) and are located in Black, Hispanic, Asian-American, and American-Indian population centers.

Both White and minority students are most likely to choose business as their field of study. Unlike Whites, however, non-Asian minority students continue to favor the social sciences, the arts and humanities, and education—fields with lower salaries and fewer employment opportunities. Blacks, Hispanics, and American Indians are severely underrepresented in the technical Fields and overrepresented in education and the arts and humanities.

Despite enrollment increases, most minority groups continue to be underrepresented in higher education relative to their share of the general population. Minority students also are more likely to drop out and, therefore, are even less adequately represented among degree recipients.

Data presented thus far provide general trends in the enrollment and degree attainment of various minority groups. However, these data do not reveal the diversity of these groups. For example, minorities have been typically classified as Blacks, Hispanics, Asian Americans, and American Indians, but within each of these groups, there are subpopulations. For example, the Hispanic population includes Mexican Americans, Puerto Ricans, Cubans, and "other Hispanics," mainly from Latin America (Clewell & Joy, 1988). More than 20 groups comprise Asian Americans (Hsia, 1988). Presently, Chinese, Filipinos, Japanese, and Koreans are the largest Asian-American groups in the U.S., but Cambodians, Laotians, Vietnamese, and others from Southeast Asia and the South Pacific islands are immigrating in increasing numbers. American Indians include Aleuts and Alaskans as well as the various tribes in the 48 contiguous states. Each tribe has its own government, language, religion, and customs (Tijerina & Biemer, 1987/88).

Not only do minority subpopulations differ with regard to socioeconomic status, educational achievement, and geographical concentration, they also vary greatly in language background and length of residence in the United States. Furthermore, the enrollment and graduation data presented to this point tell little about how well minority students perform in college and nothing about the factors related to their performance, persistence, and success. An examination of the barriers to participation and achievement—and of the probable reasons for them—is the focus of the next part.

. . .

Description of the Research Literature

This section describes the types of research on minority undergraduate students; a synthesis of the findings is presented later.

Attention to different minorities. Over the past two decades, most of the research on minority college students has focused on Black students entry, persistence, and performance. This is understandable, since Blacks comprise the largest minority population in the U.S. as well as in college enrollments, and because, with the obvious exception of Native Americans, they have the longest tradition of American citizenship among minority groups. In addition, Black student progress in higher education has been faltering over the past decade, prompting researchers to seek explanations.

With rapidly increasing numbers of Hispanic students, more attention is being devoted to understanding their college performance and persistence as well. By contrast, little attention has been devoted to American Indian students, because of their relatively small numbers in the population and among college students. There is little research on Asian Americans for the same reason—and also because their overrepresentation and overachievement in some areas of higher education mask the need for concern. The diversity among Asian Americans and the difficulties experienced by such recent immigrant groups as the Cambodians, Laotians, and Vietnamese are just beginning to surface, and the evidence suggests that these groups have very different educational profiles than the Chinese, Filipino, Japanese, and Korean immigrants who preceded them.

The scope of research methods. Research on minority students, although covering a broad range of topics, has involved reviews of transcripts and/or surveys of students conducted at single institutions, studies of multiple institutions and studies involving national representative samples. Good examples of such studies are the examination of factors related to Black and White student persistence at a major Southern state university (Bean and Hull, 1984); the study of the relationship between interracial experience and persistence among Black undergraduates at a predominantly White institution (Bennett, 1983); and the study relating alienation to attrition at a medium-sized, predominantly White, four-year university in the rural Midwest (Suen, 1983). These single-institution studies offer important insights that help explain the college experiences of minority students, and they may help the institutions address their own unique challenges. In addition, these studies open raise issues that should be addressed at other campuses. However, attempting to generalize on the basis of data from a single campus requires extreme caution because every institution and its community is unique.

Some researchers have gathered data from multiple institutions. For example, Allen (1985) surveyed Black students attending six predominantly White state-supported universities to identify factors related to Black students, college success. Nettles, Gosman, Thoeny, and Dandridge (1985) surveyed Black and White students at 30 colleges and universities in Southern and Mid-Atlantic states to compare and contrast their college performance and experiences. Other multi-institutional studies include Chacon, Cohen, and Strover (1986); Clewell and Ficklen (1986); Pennock-Román (in press); Peterson et al. (1978); Smith (1980): Tracey and Sedlacek (1987); and Tschechtelin (1981). While such studies lend themselves more readily to generalizations, there is a trade-off—they mask the unique characteristics of single institutions.

A growing number of studies of minority students use national databases that are either longitudinal (e.g., the National Longitudinal Study [NLS], High School and Beyond [HS&B], and Cooperative Institutional Research Program [CIRP]) or cross-sectional (e.g., the National Center for Education Statistics Higher Education General Information Services [HEGIS], now called the Integrated Postsecondary Education Data System [IPEDS]; Bureau of the Census's Current Population Survey [CPS]; and the College Board's Student Descriptive Questionnaire [SDQ]).

Thomas (1981b) used a subsample of the NLS database to examine the impact of standardized achievement test performance and family status on college entry of Blacks and Whites. Astin and Cross (1981) drew a sample of students from the CIRP database to compare background differences among Black students enrolled in predominantly White and predominantly Black institutions. Nielsen (1986) and Lee (1985) used the HS&B database to examine Hispanic and Black student access to college, while Pelavin, Kane, and Levine (in press) employed a varied of national databases (CPS, HEGIS/IPEDS, NLS, and HS&B) for their study of minority participation in higher education.

Research Methods

Descriptive and comparative studies. A large body of research on minority students is descriptive. These studies report rates of access, enrollment, attrition, and degree attainment among the various minority groups (American Council on Education, 1985, 1987; Arbeiter, 1986; Astin, 1975; Brown, 1987; Cope & Hannah, 1975; Darling-Hammond, 1985; Sedlacek & Webster, 1978; Thomas & McPartland, 1984). Generally, these studies (summarized in the preceding section) report what proportion of each minority group is entering, graduating from, and dropping out of college. Other descriptive studies present statistical results of survey data on student background and attitudes and institutional characteristics (Allen, 1988; Astin & Cross. 1981; Boyd. 1981; Clewell & Joy, 1987; Nettles, 1988b; Payán, Peterson, & Castille, 1984).

Another large body of research is comparative, seeking to identify and examine factors that explain differences in the performance and persistence of minority and White students. For example, Nettles and his colleagues (1986) compared the performance and experiences of Black and White students at 30 colleges in an effort to discern whether there were differences—and if so, to explain why. Most of the comparative studies examine differences between and among Black and White students (Thomas, 1981) or Hispanic and White students (Ballesteros, 1986; Durán, 1983).

There are also studies that examine differences within these groups. For example, Astin (1982) analyzed factors that influence college access and attainment among American Indians, Blacks, and two Hispanic subgroups— Chicanos and Puerto Ricans. Lee (1985) compared access to higher education among Blacks, Hispanics, and Whites of both low and high socioeconomic status (SES). There are very few studies, however, that compare differences among all of the sizable population groups or among the various ethnic groups within minority groups. Exceptions are Ramist and Arbeiter's (1986) descriptive profiles of Black, Hispanic, Asian-American, Native-American, and White college-bound high school seniors who take the SAT; Pennock-Román's (in press) study of language and test validity for Mexican-American. Puerto-Rican, and Cuban-American students; and Sue and Abe's (1988) examination of various predictors of academic performance for Chinese, Filipinos, Japanese, Koreans, and other Asian Americans.

Inferential studies. The research literature also includes studies that employ correlational methods or regression analyses to examine the relationships between minority college student characteristics and/or institutional factors (Nettles et al., 1986; Nettles & Johnson, 1987; Peng & Fetters, 1978). These methods were used by Astin (1982) to examine student characteristics (SES, high school grades, educational aspirations) and institutional characteristics (type, control, selectivity, financial aid) to college grade-point average, satisfaction, and persistence among Black, Mexican-American, Puerto Rican, Native-American, and White students. Cross and Astin (1981) also employed these techniques in their investigation of factors affecting Black student persistence.

Modeling. More recently, research has led to the development and use of predictive models to explain student performance and attrition. For example, Allen (1981) developed a causal model to investigate factors that influence Black student adjustments, achievements, and aspirations at a predominantly White university. Allen postulated that Black students, college satisfaction, academic performance, and occupational aspirations are influenced directly and indirectly by a series of variables (e.g., student background characteristics, high school experience, the college's perceived support of Black students). Bennett (1983) tested a theoretical causal model developed by Bean (1982) stipulating that precollege characteristics and experiences (e.g., high school grades, interracial interaction) influence the way students interact with their institutions, which in turn influences their attitudes toward the institution, and these attitudes in turn are related to retention and attrition.

Path analysis. The use of path analysis to conceptualize students' attrition process has also increased. This approach is very useful in examining the cumulative effects of students' backgrounds and experiences and institutional characteristics, and the relationship of these effects to educational outcomes. For example, Pascarella, Smart, Ethington, and Nettles (1987) used path analysis to examine how self-concept affects performance and achievement in high school, college, and careers. Hallmarks in this area of research are the models and theories developed by Spady (1971) and Tinto (1975) that take into consideration not only students' background characteristics but relationships between students and peers, and students and faculty, and the way these relationships affect student behavior and college experience. Numerous studies test Tinto's theories (Aitken, 1982; Pascarella, Smart, Ethington, & Nettles, 1987; Pascarella & Terenzini, 1980; Peng & Fetters, 1978; Terenzini & Pascarella, 1977) and attempt to adapt this model for explaining minority student attrition (Allen, 1985; Braddock, 1981).

College Access, Grades, Progress, and Retention of Minority Groups

Compared with their representation in the general U.S. population, Blacks, Hispanics, and American Indians are more underrepresented at each progressive transition point in higher education (American Council on Education, 1988; Astin, 1982; Brown, 1987; Darling-Hammond, 1985). This underrepresentation in higher education begins with their relatively low preparation and their low college-going rates, and the college-going rates have continued to change over time.

College enrollment. Studies examining college attendance report widely varying rates for minority students, but generally they show Black and Hispanic high school graduates attend college at lower rates than White and Asian-American high school graduates. Based on CPS data (1972–79), Astin (1982) estimated the college-going rates immediately after high school for Blacks and Chicanos were 39–41 percent and 38–40 percent, respectively, compared with 45–47 percent for Whites. Among Puerto Rican high school graduates, the rate was higher—about 50 percent.

Using the same database, but in more recent years, Darling-Hammond (1985) and Carnegie (1987) also showed lower college-going rates for Black and Hispanic high school graduates than for White graduates. According to Darling-Hammond, from 1975 to 1980, college-going rates dropped from 32 percent to 27 percent for Black graduates and from 35 percent to 30 percent for Hispanic graduates; for Whites, the rate remained stable, at about 32 percent, during the same period. The Carnegie study reported uniformly higher rates for 1984—30 percent for Blacks, 36 percent for Hispanics, and 38 percent for Whites—but a consistent pattern of college entrance among these three groups.

On the other hand, using the NLS database (1975–79). Santos (1986) found that after they graduate from high school, minority students—with the exception of Black males—are as likely as White graduates to attend college. Among high school graduates in this sample, 50 percent of Hispanic females and 51 percent of Hispanic males enrolled in college, as did 53 percent of Black females but only 40 percent of Black males. By comparison, the rates for White high school graduates were 51 percent for females and 50 percent for males. For all groups, these rates were somewhat higher than those cited in the other studies. Some researchers attribute the relatively high college-entrance rates among Hispanic and Black high school graduates to affirmative action (Peng & Fetters, 1978) and a creaming effect (Nielsen, 1986). (Creaming here describes the fact that minority students who graduate high school are the best among their group and therefore are likely to go on to college.)

Few studies provide college-going rates for Asian-American and American-Indian students. Two that have calculated rates for these groups used HS&B data. Peng (1985) found that Asian-American high school graduates attend college at higher rates (88 percent) and American Indian graduates at lower rates (42 percent) than Blacks (53 percent), Hispanics (48 percent), and Whites (62 percent). Pelavin, Kane, and Levine (in press) also estimated college attendance rates among Asian Americans (72 percent) to be higher than Blacks (35 percent), Hispanics (37 percent), and Whites (51 percent). It should be pointed out that the wide variations in college-enrollment figures for population subgroups from database to database raise significant questions about the quality and accuracy of those databases.

College grades and progression rates. While there is a paucity of research into differential rates of performance among minority and White college students, the research that has been conducted has centered on two performance indicators: students' grade-point averages and their progression rates. In the limited studies reported, the consensus is that Black and Hispanic college students have lower grade-point averages and progression rates than their White peers.

Although college grade-point average is considered to be the best available measure of academic learning, researchers may be reluctant to use it . Different types of institutions have varying criteria for grading, different types of students take different types of courses, and different instructors use different instructional and grading techniques. As an alternative (or confirming) measure, it is useful to look at students' tendency to follow prescribed progression patterns—becoming a sophomore in the second year, a junior in the third, a senior in the fourth, then graduating.

Studies using both measures. Nettles (1988b) examined differences in cumulative grade-point averages (GPA) and progression rates (as measured by credits earned per term of enrollment) of Black and White students attending 30 colleges and universities, six of which were private Black institutions and six public Black institutions. He found that Black and White students differed significantly on each of these indicators. On average, Whites successfully completed 15.3 credit hours per term and Blacks successfully completed 14.4; the GPA for Whites was higher than a B, compared with a GPA for Blacks between a B-minus and a C-plus.

Using the same database, Nettles (1988a) also found that average performance varied by type of institution attended. That is, students of the same race have different GPAs and progression rates at different types of institutions. Without controlling for abilities or background characteristics, Black students received higher grades and progressed through college at a faster pace when attending traditionally Black private universities. At four types of institutions—predominantly

White private universities, public research universities, and public regional four-year colleges; and predominantly Black public universities—Nettles found that, overall, White students had higher grades than their Black fellow students. Whites also had faster progression rates except at the Black public universities.

Comparing GPAs. Even fewer studies compare the college grades and progression rates of Hispanics, Asian Americans, and American Indians. Goldman and Hewitt (1976) investigated the significance of ethnicity, major, high school grades, and SAT scores in predicting college grades among Black, Asian-American, Chicano, and White undergraduates and compared their mean GPAs. At the University of California at Los Angeles, one of the institutions participating in the study, Blacks had a mean GPA of 2.52; Chicanos, 2.65; and Asian Americans, 2.81. By comparison, Whites had a mean GPA of 2.89.

Progression rates. Gosman, Nettles, Thoeny, and Dandridge (1982, 1983) found significant differences in the progression rates between Black and White student cohorts. At nearly all stages of their college careers, White students were much more likely to follow prescribed progression patterns than Black students were. Gosman and her colleagues (1983) found that, on average, 71.3 percent of the Whites who persisted to the fourth year graduated that year, and 91 percent of them graduated within five years. By comparison, 55.6 percent of the Black students who persisted lo the fourth year graduated that year, and 78.1 percent of them graduated within five years. Overall—that is, considering all students who began as freshmen in that class—42.8 percent of the White students graduated in four years and 56.1 percent within five years, while 29.4 percent of the Black students graduated in four years and 35.3 percent within five years.

Consistent findings resulted from a longitudinal study that tracked the academic careers of the 1970–72 freshman cohort at the City University of New York over a 13-year period to determine their graduation rates and time spent earning degrees (Lavin, Murtha, Kaufman, & Hyllegard, 1986). The study showed that Whites enrolled in the city's four-year institutions were more likely to earn baccalaureate degrees after five years than were Black or Hispanic students.

This freshman cohort entered the City University after its open admissions policy took effect. Those who entered with high school grades or class rank that would have met previous admission criteria are referred to in the study as regular students, and those who would not have met those criteria, as open admissions students. Among regular students, 65 percent of the Whites had graduated after five years, compared with 37 percent of the Blacks and 33 percent of the Hispanics. Among White open-admissions students, the five-year rate was 33 percent, compared with 16 percent for Blacks and 12 percent for Hispanics. Overall, minority students clearly took more time to earn degrees. Among senior college regular students, only 18 percent of the White students who earned degrees took more than five years to do so, compared with 42 percent of the Black students and 34 percent of the Hispanics.

Over the 13-year period, however, the gap in rates of degree attainment between White and minority students narrowed substantially. By the end of that period, 79 percent of the White regular students had earned their baccalaureates, compared with 64 percent of the Blacks and 50 percent of the Hispanics. Among open-admissions students, the 13-year degree-completion rates were 48 percent for Whites, 37 percent for Blacks, and 28 percent for Hispanics.

Similarly, in the city's community colleges, Black and Hispanic graduates were disproportionately more likely than White graduates to take more than three years to earn associate degrees. Among regular students, 48 percent of the Whites earned their associate degrees after three years, compared with 37 percent of the Blacks and 34 percent of the Hispanics. After nine years, however, 57 percent of those White students had received their associate degrees, compared with 53 percent of the Blacks and 45 percent of the Hispanics.

Retention. Retention is often used as a measure of college performance, but researchers define it in various ways. In many studies, retention is defined as the rate of graduation for a cohort of students within a specified time (e.g., the percent of a freshman cohort that graduates within four or five years), while other studies concentrate on enrollment after the freshman year.

Black, Hispanic, and American Indian students are consistently found to withdraw from college at higher rates and to attain baccalaureate degrees at appreciably lower rates than their White peers (American Council on Education, 1988; Ramist, 1981). Astin (1982) estimated retention rates to be significantly lower among Hispanics (31–42 percent) and American Indians (39 percent) than among Blacks (42–51 percent) and Whites (57–59 persons). To arrive at these estimates, Astin drew the percentages of entrants completing college from three sources: NLS data on the 1976 status of 1972 high school graduates who had entered college, CPS percentages of persons aged 25 to 29 who had completed four or more years of college, and CIRP surveys of 1971 freshmen followed up in 1980.

These rates are consistent with findings from an earlier Astin study (1975) based on longitudinal and multi-institutional data showing dropout rates among American Indians and Chicanos to be considerably higher than those among Blacks, Whites, and Asian Americans. Researchers commonly attribute the lower retention rates of Hispanics and American Indians to their high concentration in community colleges (Astin, 1982; Astin & Burciaga, 1981; Hilton & Schrader, 1987; Richardson & Bender, 1987).

The gap in retention rates between non-Asian minority groups and Whites increases over the college years, because more Black and Hispanic students withdraw from college after each of the first two years (American Council on Education, 1988; Brown, 1987). A study of NLS data by Hilton and Schrader (1987) confirmed these findings, as did a study by the American Council on Education (1988), regarding differences in retention rates for Black, Hispanic, and White students. Analysis of the NLS data showed that the proportion of Black students who entered four-year colleges (35 percent) was almost as large as the corresponding proportion of White students (38 percent), but that the proportions earning bachelor's degrees after seven years differed sharply— 18 percent of the Blacks to 27 percent of the Whites. Hilton and Schrader (1987) also found, consistent with other findings, that Hispanic students (32 percent) were more likely than Blacks (19 percent) or Whites (22 percent) to enter two-year institutions, and that a very small proportion of them (6 percent) transferred to four-year colleges and universities two years after graduating from high school. Consequently, a smaller proportion of Hispanic students (11 percent) than Black students (18 percent) received baccalaureate degrees.

In an investigation of college retention during the first three years after high school, Hilton (1982) noted that 52 percent of White students continued their education, compared with 44 percent of Black students. He found that the attrition rates for Blacks and Whites did not differ appreciably when calculated as percentages of those who entered college in the first year following high school (16.1 percent and 16.9 percent, respectively). When controlling for academic ability and SES, researchers have found that retention rates for Black students are either similar to or greater than those for White students (Kohen, Nertel, & Kamas, 1978; Lenning, Beal, & Sauer, 1980; Peng & Fetters, 1978; Ramist, 1981). These findings suggest that Black students' overall retention rates can be improved if institutions attract them immediately after they graduate from high school and if ways are found to compensate for differences in their preparation for college and their socioeconomic status.

Asian-American students show a high degree of persistence in college. They are more likely to persist at both two- and four-year institutions than Whites, Blacks, Hispanics, and American Indians. In an analysis of HS&B data, Peng (1985) revealed that about 86 percent of the Asian-American high school graduates who entered four-year colleges in 1980 were still enrolled a year and a half later, compared with 81 percent of the American Indians, 75 percent of the Whites. 71 percent of the Blacks, and 66 percent of the Hispanics who entered at the same time. At two-year colleges, retention rates for the same period were 70 percent for Asian Americans, 65 percent for Hispanics, 61 percent for Blacks, 61 percent for American Indians, and 57 percent for Whites. Significantly, Asian Americans (21 percent) also were more likely than Blacks (15 percent), Hispanics (11 percent), and Whites (16 percent) to transfer to four-year institutions.

For any group of students, retention rates vary from institution to institution. For example, at seven predominantly White universities located in four regions of the country, Smith (1980) found that, after freshman year, Black student retention rates ranged from 99 percent at a private Eastern university to 57 percent at private and public universities in the Midwest. These findings should be regarded with caution, however, because the populations sampled at the seven institutions were not comparable.

Summary

The literature clearly reveals several important findings regarding minority access, persistence, and performance. First, overall college-going rates for Blacks, Hispanics, and American Indians are lower than for Whites and Asian Americans, but the difference disappears when they are equally academically prepared to enter college. Second, non-Asian minority students have lower performance and persistence in college. Blacks are found to have lower retention rates, slower progression, and lower grades than Whites. Third, while Hispanics have lower retention rates than Blacks; their college grades may be somewhat higher; and their college-going rates are similar; and fourth, researchers consistently find that, unlike Blacks and Hispanics, Asian Americans have higher retention rates than Whites, but there is no general agreement on the retention rates of American Indians.

. . .

Research conducted during the last two decades has revealed numerous variables that are associated with minority student access, persistence, and performance. These include student academic and socioeconomic background characteristics, personality traits, institutional characteristics, and experiences while attending college. Figure 1 lists the various factors and a conceptual model that helps to explain the longitudinal process whereby these factors directly or indirectly affect student outcomes.

Most of the research on minorities has been devoted to Black students. Studies have revealed that Black students enter college at lower rates, are less likely to attend the best colleges and universities, perform at lower rates as measured by the grades, progress more slowly to degree completion, have lower quality experiences, and withdraw from college at higher rates than their White counterparts.

Precollege background factors, namely high school academic preparation, high school grades, and aptitude test scores are significantly related to Black students' access persistence and performance. Institutional characteristics (e.g. type, predominant race) have also been found to

---

Figure 1
Conceptual Model of Factors Related to Undergraduate Minority
Students' College Access, Experience, and Performance*

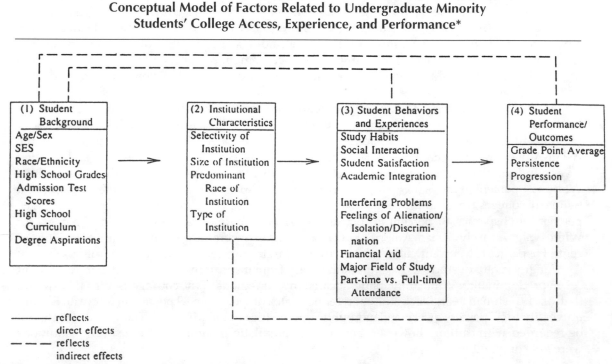

reflects direct effects
— — — reflects indirect effects

* Suggested definitions for the variables in this model are presented in Appendix A.

have significant influence upon Black students' grades and persistence in college. For instance Black students attending Black institutions tend to get higher grades than Black students at predominantly White institutions but attrition rates for Black students are higher at Black public universities than at all other types of four-year institutions. The research also shows that attitudinal factors such as educational aspirations and college experiences (e.g., frequency of interaction with faculty) are related to the success (e.g., grades and degree completion) of Blacks at predominantly White institutions: better extracurricular experiences lead to higher grades and retention. Moreover, these factors combined appear to be stronger predictors of Black students' performance and success than their precollege academic and SES background.

Substantially less is known about Hispanics in higher education. Like Blacks, they are less likely than Whites to go to college, and if they do, they take longer to earn degrees. In addition, Hispanics are more likely to withdraw from college. However, significant differences in rates of access persistence and performance are evident among the various Hispanic subgroups.

Although Hispanic students demonstrate higher educational aspirations than White students, they are less likely to have taken a college preparatory program or have solid grounding in academic subjects than Whites. The research presented in this literature review shows that high school academic background and SES are related to Hispanic student access and outcomes, but high school grades and admission test scores appear to be less predictive of access and outcomes for Hispanics than for Whites and Asian Americans. There are some important sex differences among Hispanic students: for example, among Mexican Americans, being a woman is found to be negatively related to college grades. The significance of the relationship of high school grades and test scores to college grades may be moderated by background factors in particular English language proficiency. Studies investigating the relationship of high school grades and SAT scores to Hispanic student performance and the effect of English language proficiency on that relationship account for a large segment of the research on Hispanic college students.

Hispanic students' lower rate of bachelor's degree attainment appears to be associated with their high concentration in community colleges. Community colleges are found to be negatively related to earning a bachelor's degree.

Numerous studies show Hispanic students have difficulty making the adjustment from high school to college, feel relatively high anxiety over finances, and experience isolation on campus. How these attitudes, behaviors, and experiences affect Hispanic students' persistence and performance has not been explored extensively in the research to date.

Compared with other minority groups, Asian Americans have higher rates of access, persistence, and performance (as measured by college grades). Asian Americans' relatively higher rate of college attendance and performance appear to be significantly related to their precollege academic background. They are more likely to have taken college preparatory curricula, to have completed more mathematics and science courses, and to have achieved relatively higher SAT scores than their peers in other minority groups. Although Asian Americans are more likely to have studied mathematics for four or more years in high school, they are also the least likely group to have studied English for four or more years.

On average, Asian Americans achieve higher scores on the SAT-math test than on the SAT-verbal test, illustrating their stronger ability in quantitative areas and reflecting their tendency to major in mathematics and sciences, subjects that involve relatively less verbal communication.

Among all groups, Asian Americans are the least likely to receive grant aid, and, along with American Indians, they are the least likely to take out loans to finance their college education.

From the research on minority students, we know the least about American Indians, and what we know is not very illuminating. American Indians are found to have higher dropout rates than Blacks and. Whites, possibly because they, like Hispanics, are more likely to attend two-year institutions. High school preparation appears to have an effect on their college persistence and performance. High school grades are significant predictors of college grades among American Indians, and the relationship is stronger than for Blacks and Hispanics. High school grades were also found to be strongly related to persistence for American Indians.

Like Hispanics, American Indians appear to have difficulty making the adjustment from high school to college. In addition, several studies show that they encounter difficulties in making cultural adjustments to predominantly White institutions. What these cultural difficulties are and how they relate to college success or failure are unclear.

Conclusions and Future Research Agenda

Research on minorities over the past two decades has provided valuable insights into their rates of participation, persistence, and performance. Researchers have also identified some important correlates of these outcomes. At the same time, however, the research literature on minority students is complex and ambiguous. The complexity relates to lack of agreement on definitions, variation in research methodology, and the absence of coherent theoretical models to guide the research. The effect of these inconsistencies is ambiguity in the results and findings.

With regard to definition, limited attention has been devoted in the research to classifying ethnic/racial groups and institutional types carefully. In addition, there have been inconsistencies in the way researchers categorize and define the vast array of independent and dependent variables used in their studies.

Inconsistencies are also apparent in the methods used in research on minority students. For example, inconsistent approaches to the sampling of minority populations are often employed to address similar questions. When analyzing one minority group, some researchers sample only the target minority population, and this prohibits any comparative analyses with other minority groups or with Whites. In addition, some studies focus attention on samples of special students (e.g., special admission students) and then attempt to generalize for an entire minority group or for all minority groups.

Another limitation of the current research on minority college students is the absence of a coherent theoretical framework that guides the research and helps explain the complex array of factors influencing minority students' college access, persistence, and performance.

In the future, researchers should carefully select, define, and describe the ethnic minority groups and subpopulation groups being studied. The research, as well as the applications using research results, would benefit from employing common definitions for input, process, and outcome variables. A suggested partial list of variables and definitions for research on minority students is presented in Figure 1. Careful attention also should be devoted to identifying and grouping institutions by type. Because colleges and universities and the students enrolled in them differ by type of governance, religious affiliation, predominant race, and geographical location, their environments may yield different types of college experiences and outcomes for minority students.

Research on the various minority groups would also be enhanced if the research community moves toward establishing databases for the various racial groups, ethnic subgroups, and various types of institutions. In addition, these databases should include information about the inputs, process, and outcome variables needed to study minority student achievement and related factors (see Figure 1). Existing databases do not include sufficient institutional characteristics and student attitudinal or behavior measures.

Finally, descriptive and correlational analyses using longitudinal theoretical models, such as the one represented in Figure 1, should be encouraged. The collection of literature abounds in descriptive studies that inform about the proportion of Blacks, Hispanics, and Native Americans attending, achieving, and leaving college. In order to understand why access, persistence, and performance are lower among these minority groups, empirical studies based on classical theories of college attendance, persistence, and performance, such as those developed by Tinto (1975), are preferable. Studies using Tinto's model have been particularly helpful in explaining the factors related to Black students' performance and persistence at predominantly White institutions. They should be expanded to studies of Hispanic, Asian-American, and Native-American students, and cross-cultural studies examining differences among and within the major racial groups are needed.

References and Bibliography

Abatso, Y. (1982). *Coping Strategies: Retaining Black Students in College:* Atlanta: Southern Education Foundation. (ED 235 741)

Adams, E. P., and Smith, B. S. (1987, Winter). Factors in student attrition among students at a historically Black university. *NASPA Journal* 24(3): 33–38.

Aitken, L. P., and Falk, D. R. (1983). A higher education study of Minnesota Chippewa tribal students. (ED 249 013)

Aitken, N. (1982). College student performance, satisfaction and retention: Specification and estimation of a structural model. *Journal of Higher Education* 53: 32–50.

Allen, W. R. (1981). Correlates of Black student adjustment, achievement, and aspirations at a predominantly White Southern university. In G. E. Thomas (ed.), *Black Students in Higher Education: Conditions and Experiences in the 1970s.* Westport, CT: Greenwood Press.

Allen, W. R. (1985). Black student, White campus: Structural, interpersonal and psychological correlates of success. *Journal of Negro Education,* 54(2): 134–147.

Allen, W. R. (May/June, 1987). Black colleges vs. White colleges. *Change,* Vol. 19: 28–34.

Allen, W. R. (1988, Summer). Improving Black student access and achievement in higher education. *The Review of Higher Education* 11(4): 403–416.

Allen, W. R. (1988). The education of Black students on White college campuses: What quality the experience? In M. T. Nettles (ed.), *Toward Black Undergraduate Student Equality in American Higher Education.* Westport, CT: Greenwood Press.

American Council on Education. (1986). *Minorities in Higher Education* (Fourth Annual Status Report). Washington, DC: American Council on Education. American Council on Education. (1986). *Minorities in Higher Education* (Fifth Annual Status Report). Washington, DC: American Council on Education.

Arbeiter, S. (1986, May) . *Minority Enrollment in Higher Education Institutions: A Chronological View.* New York: The College Board. Research and Development Update.

Astin, A. W. (1975). *Preventing Students from Dropping Out.* San Francisco: Jossey-Bass.

Astin, A. W. (1982). Minorities in American higher education. San Francisco: Jossey-Bass.

Astin. H. S., and Burciaga, C. P. (1981. November). *Chicanos in Higher Education: Progress and Attainment.* Los Angeles: Higher Education Research Institute.

Astin, H. S., and Cross, P. S. (1981). Black students in Black and White institutions. In G. Thomas (ed.), *Black Students in Higher Education: Conditions and Experiences in the 1970s.* Westport, CT: Greenwood Press.

Atkinson, D. R. (1987, November). Counseling Blacks: A review of relevant research. *Journal of College Student Personnel,* 28(6): 552–558.

Ballesteros. E. (1986). Do Hispanics receive an equal educational opportunity? The relationship of school outcomes, family background, and high school curriculum. In M. A. Olivas (ed.), *Latino College Students.* New York: Teachers College Press.

Beal, P. E., and Noel, L. (1979). *What Works in Student Retention.* Iowa City, IA, ACT program and Boulder, CO: National Center for Higher Education Management System.

Bean, J. P. (1980). Dropouts and turnover: The synthesis and test of a causal model of student attrition. *Research in Higher Education,* 12(2): 155–187.

Bean, J. P. (1982a). Conceptual models of student attrition: How theory can help the institutional researcher. In E. Pascarella (ed.), *Studying Student Attrition,* San Francisco: Jossey-Bass.

Bean, J. P. (1982b). Student attrition, intentions and confidence: Interaction effects in a path model. *Research in Higher Education*, 17: 291–320.

Bean, J. P., and Hull, D. F., Jr. (1984, April). The determinants of Black and White attrition at a major Southern state university. Paper presented at American Educational Research Association meeting, New Orleans.

Bennett. C. (1983). A study of interracial contact experience and attrition among Black undergraduates at a predominantly White university. Paper presented at American Educational Research Association meeting, Montreal.

Bennett, C., and Okinaka, A. (1984, April). Explanations of Black student attrition in predominantly White and predominantly Black universities. Paper presented at American Educational Research Association meeting, New Orleans.

Berryman, S. E. (1983). *Who Will Do Science?* New York: The Rockefeller Foundation.

Boyd, W. M., II. (1981). The forgotten side of the Black undergraduate: An assessment of academic achievements and aspirations during the 1970s. In G. E. Thomas. (ed.), *Black Students in Higher Education: Conditions and Experiences in the 1970s. Westport.* CT: Greenwood Press.

Braddock, F. H., II, and McPartland, J. M. (1988). Some cost and benefit considerations for Black college students attending predominantly White versus predominantly Black universities. In M. T. Nettles, (ed.), *Toward Black Undergraduate Student Equality in American Higher Education.* Westport, CT: Greenwood Press.

Braddock, J. H. (1981). Desegregation and Black students. *Urban Education,* 15(4): 403–418.

Braddock, J. H., and Dawkins, M. P. (1981). Predicting Black academic achievement in higher education. *Journal of Negro Education,* 50(3): 319–327.

Breland, H. *(1979). Population Validity and College Entrance Measures.* Research Monograph No. 8. New York: College Entrance Examination Board.

Brown, S. V. (1987). *Minorities in the Graduate Education Pipeline.* Princeton, NJ: Graduate Record Examinations Board and Educational Testing Service.

Burbach, H. J., and Thompson, M. A. (1971). Alienation among college freshmen: A comparison of Puerto Rican, Black, and White students. *Journal of College Student Personnel,* 12: 248–252.

Burbach, H. J., and Thompson, M. A. (1973). Note on alienation, race, and college attrition. *Psychological Reports,* 33: 273–274.

Carnegie Foundation for the Advancement of Teaching. (1987, May/June). Minority access: a question of equity. *Change,* 35–39.

Carnegie Foundation for the Advancement of Teaching. (1988, May/June). Hispanic students continue to be distinctive. *Change,* 20(3): 43–47.

Chacon, M., Cohen, E., and Strover, S. (1986). Chicanas and Chicanos: Barriers to progress in higher education. In M. A. Olivas (ed.), *Latino College Students,* New York: Teachers College Press.

Chase, C., and Johnson, J. J. (1977, May). Predicting college success with nontraditional data for inner-city students. *Journal of College Student Personnel,* 18(3): 210–214.

Cheatham, H. E., Shelton, T. O., and Ray, W. J. (1987, November). Race, sex, causal attribution, and help-seeking behavior. *Journal of College Student Personnel,* 28(6): 559–568.

Clewell, B. C., and Ficklen, M. F. (1986, June). *Improving Minority Retention in Higher Education: A Search for Effective Institutional Practices.* Princeton, NJ: Educational Testing Service.

Clewell, B. C., and Joy, M. F. (1988). *The National Hispanic Scholar Awards Program: A Descriptive Analysis of High-Achieving Hispanic Students* (Report No. 88–10). New York: College Entrance Examination Board.

Cohen, A. M. (1988, Summer). Degree achievement by minorities in community colleges. *The Review of Higher Education*, 11(4): 383–402.

Commission on Minority Participation in Education and American Life. (1988, May). *One-Third of a Nation*. Washington, DC: American Council on Education.

Cope, R., and Hannah, W. (1975). *Revolving College Doors: The Causes and Consequences of Dropping Out, Stepping Out, and Transferring*. New York: Wiley.

Cox, W. E., and Jobe, C. C. (1987/1988, Fall/Winter). Recruiting wars: Can higher education compete with the military? *Educational Record*, 68: 63–69.

Cross, P. S., and Astin, H. S. (1981). Factors affecting Black students' persistence in college. In G. Thomas (ed.), *Black Students in Higher Education: Conditions and Experiences in the 1970s*. Westport, CT: Greenwood Press.

Crosson, P. H. (1988, Summer). Four-year college and university environments for minority degree achievement. *Review of Higher Education*, 11(4): 365–382.

Darling-Hammond, L. (1985). *Equality and Excellence: The Educational Status of Black Americans*. New York: College Entrance Examination Board.

Dawkins, M. P., and Dawkins, R. L. (1980). Perceptions and experiences as correlates of academic performance among Blacks at a predominantly White university: A research note. *College and University*, 55(2): 171–180.

Dawkins, M. P., and Braddock, J. H. (1982, July/October). Explaining outcomes for Black students in higher education using national longitudinal data. *Negro Educational Review, Vol. XXXIII*, Nos. 3–4.

DiCesare, P. C., Sedlacek, W. E., and Brooks, G. C. (1972). Nonintellective correlates of Black student attrition. *Journal of College Student Personnel*, 13: 319–324.

Dunston, F. M. Review of literature: Black student retention in higher education institutions. (ED 228 912)

Durán, R. P., Enright, M. K., and Rock, D. A. (1985). *Language factors and Hispanic freshmen's student profile*. College Board Report No. 85-3. New York: College Entrance Examination Board.

Durán, R. P. (1983). *Hispanics' Education and Background: Predictors of College Achievement*. New York: College Entrance Examination Board.

Durán, R. P. (1989). Testing of linguistic minorities. In R. L. Linn (ed.), *Educational Measurement* (3rd Ed.) New York: Macmillan Co., 513–587.

Ekstrom, R. B., Goertz, M. E., Pollack, J. M., and Rock. D. A. (1986, Spring). Who drops out of high school, and why? Findings from a national study. *Teachers College Record*, 87 (3): 356–373.

El-Khawas, E. H., and Bisconti, A. (1974). *Five and Ten Years After College Entry: 1971 Follow-up of 1961 and 1966 College Freshmen*. Washington, DC: American Council on Education.

Estrada, L. F. (1988. May/June). Anticipating the demographic future: Dramatic changes are on the way. *Change*, 20(3): 14–19.

ETS Policy Information Center. (1989, March). *ETS Policy Notes*. I(2). Princeton, NJ: Educational Testing Service.

Fields, C. (1988, May/June). The Hispanic pipeline: Narrow, leaking and needing repair. *Change*, 2(3): 20–27.

Fleming, J. (1984). *Blacks in College*. San Francisco: Jossey-Bass.

Fries, J. E. (1987, March). *The American Indian in Higher Education 1975–76 to 1984–85*. National Center for Education Statistics. Washington, DC: U.S. Department of Education, Office of Educational Research and Improvement.

Gibbs, J. T. (ed.) (1988). *Young, Black, and Male in America: An Endangered Species*. Dover, MA: Auburn House Publishing Company.

Goldman, R., and Hewitt, B. (1976). Predicting the success of Black, Chicano, Oriental, and White college students. *Journal of Educational Measurement*, 13(2): 107–117.

Gosman, E. J:, Dandridge, B. A., Nettles, M. T., and Thoeny, A. R. (1983): Predicting student progression: The influence of race and other student and institutional characteristics on college student performance. *Research in Higher Education*, 18(2): 209–236.

Gosman, E. J., Nettles, M. T., Dandridge, B. A., and Thoeny, A. R. (1982). Student progression and attrition in college: does race make a difference? Paper presented at the annual meeting of the Association for the Study of Higher Education.

Graham, C., Baker, R. W., and Wapner, S . (1985). Prior interracial experience and Black student transition into predominantly White colleges. *Journal of Personality and Social Psychology*, 47(5): 1146–1154.

Gurin. P., and Epps, E. *Black Consciousness, Identity and Achievement: A Study of Students in Historically Black Colleges*. New York: John Wiley and Sons, Inc.

Guyette, S., and Heth, C. (1983). American Indian higher education: Needs and projections. Paper presented at the annual meeting of the American Educational Research Association, Montreal. (ED 232 810)

Hilton, T. L. (1982). *Persistence in Higher Education*. (College Board Report No. 825), New York: College Entrance Examination Board.

Hilton, T. L., and Schrader, W. B. (1987). *Pathways to Graduate School: An Empirical Study Based on National Longitudinal Data*. Princeton, NJ: Educational Testing Service.

Hodgkinson, H. I.. (1985). *All One System: Demographics of Education, Kindergarten Through Graduate School*. Washington, DC: The Institute for Educational Leadership, Inc.

Hsia, J. (1987–1988, Fall/Winter). Asian Americans fight the myth of the super student. *Educational Record*, 94–97.

Hsia, J. (1988). *Asian Americans in Higher Education and at Work*. Hillsdale, NJ: Lawrence Erlbaum Associates, Inc.

Hughes, M. S. (1987, November). Black students' participation in higher education. *Journal of College Student Personnel*, 28(6): 532–545.

Iffert. R. E. (1957). *Retention and Withdrawal of College Students*. (Bulletin 1958. #1). Washington, DC: U.S. Government Printing Office.

Iwai, S. I., and Churchill, W. D. (1982). College attrition and the financial support systems of students. *Research in Higher Education*. 17(2): 103–113.

Jordan-Cox. C. D. (1987, November). Psychosocial development of students in traditionally Black institutions. *Journal of College Student Personnel*. 28(6): 504–511.

Kennan. W. R., Cummings, H. W. and Lujan, P. D. (1980). A descriptive study of intercultural communication between Native American and Anglo-American college students. (ED 197 898)

Kohen. A. I., Nertel. G., and Kamas. C. (1978). Factors affecting individual persistence rates in undergraduate programs. *American Educational Research Journal*, 15: 233–252.

Lavin, D., Murtha, J., Kaufman, B. and Hyllegard, D. (1986). Long-term educational attainment in an open-access university system: effects of ethnicity, economic status, and college type. Paper presented at annual meeting of American Educational Research Association, San Francisco.

Lea, H. D., Sedlacek, W. E., and Stewart, S. S. (1979). Problems in retention research in higher education. *National Association of Student Personnel Administrators*, 17(1): 2–8.

Lee, V. (1985, May). *Access to Higher Education: The Experience of Blacks, Hispanics, and Low Socioeconomic Status Whites*. Division of Policy Analysis and Research Washington, DC: American Council on Education.

Lee, V. E.. and Ekstrom, R. B. (1987, Summer). Student access to guidance counseling in high school. *American Educational Research Journal*, 24(2): 287–310.

Lenning, O. T. (1982). Variable selection and measurement concerns. In E. T. Pascarella, (ed), *Studying Student Attrition*. San Francisco: Jossey-Bass.

Lenning, O. T., Beal, P. E., and Saver, K. (1980). *Attrition and Retention. Evidence for Action and Research*. Boulder, CO: National Center for Higher Education Management Systems.

Lewis. G. L. (1988). *Trends in Student Aid: 1980 to 1988*. New York: College Entrance Examination Board.

Linn, R. L. (ed.) (1989). *Educational Measurement* (3rd ed.). New York: Macmillan Co.

Madrazo-Peterson, R., and Rodriguez, M. (1978, May). Minority students' perception of a university environment. *Journal of College Student Personnel*. 259–263.

Mingle, J. R. (1981). The opening of White colleges and universities to Black students. In G. E. Thomas (ed.), *Black Students in Higher Education: Conditions and Experiences in the 1970s*. Westport, CT: Greenwood Press.

Morris, L. (1981). The role of testing in institutional selectivity and Black access to higher education. In G. E. Thomas (ed.), *Black Students in Higher Education: Conditions and Experiences in the 1970s*. Westport, CT: Greenwood Press.

Moten, C. H. (1978). Persistence of Indochinese refugee students enrolled in developmental studies. Ed.D. Practicum, Nova University. (ED 178 120)

Muñoz, D. G. (1986). Identifying areas of stress for Chicano undergraduates. In M. A. Olivas, (ed.), *Latino College Students*. New York: Teachers College Press.

Munro, B. (1981). Dropouts from higher education: Path analysis of a national sample. *American Educational Research Journal*, 18: 133–141.

Murdock, A. A. (1987, Autumn). It isn't just money: The effects of financial aid on persistence. *Review of Higher Education*, 11(1): 75–101.

Nettles, M. T. (1987). *Financial Aid and Minority Participation in Graduate Education*. Princeton, NJ: Graduate Record Examinations Board and Educational Testing Service.

Nettles, M. T. (1988a). Black and White performance at various types of universities. In M. T. Nettles (ed.), *Toward Black Undergraduate Student Equality in American Higher Education*. Westport, CT: Greenwood Press.

Nettles, M . T. (1988b). Factors related to Black and White students' college performance. In M. T. Nettles (ed.), *Toward Black Undergraduate Student Equality in American Higher Education*. Westport, CT: Greenwood Press.

Nettles, M. T. (1988c). Introduction: Contemporary barriers to Black student equality in higher education. In M. T. Nettles (ed.). *Toward Black Undergraduate Student Equality in American Higher Education*. Westport, CT: Greenwood Press.

Nettles. M. T. Precollegiate development of scientists and engineers. Unpublished paper.

Nettles. M. T., Gosman, E. J., Thoeny, A. R., and Dandridge, B. A. (1985). *Causes and Consequences of College Students' Performance—A Focus on Black and White Students' Attrition Rates, Profession and Grade-point Averages*. Nashville, TN: Tennessee Higher Education Commission.

Nettles, M. T., and Johnson, J. R. (1987, November). Race, sex, and other factors as determinants of college students' socialization. *Journal of College Student Personnel* 28(6): 512–524.

Nettles, M. T., Thoeny, A. R., and Gosman, E. J. (1986, May/June). Comparative and predictive analyses of Black and White students' college achievement and experiences. *Journal of Higher Education*, 57(3): 289–318.

Nielsen, F. (1986). Hispanics in high school and beyond. In M. A. Olivas (ed.), *Latino College Students*. New York: Teachers College Press.

Nielsen, F., and Fernandez, R. M . (1981). *Hispanic Students in American High Schools: Background Characteristics and Achievement*. National Opinion Research Center Washington, DC: U.S. Government Printing Office

Olivas, M. A. (1986). Financial aid for Hispanics: Access, ideology, and packaging policies. In M. A. Olivas (ed.), *Latino College Students*. New York: Teachers College Press.

Olivas, M. A. (1986). Introduction: Research on Latino college students: A theoretical framework and inquiry. In M. A. Olivas (ed.), Latino College Students. New York: Teachers College Press.

Orfield, G., and Paul, F. (1987/1988, Fall/Winter). Declines in minority access: a tale of five cities. *Educational Record*, 68: 57–62.

Ortiz, V. (1986). Generational status, family background and educational attainment among Hispanic youth and non-Hispanic White youth. In M. A. Olivas (ed.), *Latino College Students*. New York: Teachers College Press.

Pallas, A. M., Natriello, G., and McDill, E. D. (1989). The changing nature of the disadvantaged population: Current dimensions and future trends. *Educational Researcher*, 18(5): 16–22.

Pantages, T., and Creedon, C. (1978). Studies of college attrition: 1950-1975. *Review of Educational Research*, 48: 49–101.

Pascarella, E. T., and Terenzini, P. T. (1980). Predicting freshman persistence and voluntary dropout decisions from a theoretical model. *Journal of Higher Education*, 51: 60–75.

Pascarella, E. T. (1985). College environmental influence on learning and cognitive development: A critical review and synthesis. In J. C. Smart (ed.), *Higher Education: Handbook of Theory and Research*, (Vol. 1). New York: Agathon Press.

Pascarella, E. T. (1985). Racial differences in the factors influencing bachelor's degree completion: A nine-year follow-up. *Research in Higher Education*, 23(4): 351–373.

Pascarella, E. T., Smart, J. C., Ethington, C. A., and Nettles, M. T. (1987, Spring). The influence of college on self-concept: A consideration of race and gender differences. *American Educational Research Journal*, 24(1): 49–77.

Patton, W. S . (1972). An investigation of selected factors related to persistence of American-Indian students at two New Mexico universities. Unpublished doctoral dissertation, New Mexico State University.

Payán, R. M., Peterson, R. E., and Castille. N. A . (1984). *Access to College for Mexican Americans in the Southwest: Replication after 10 Years*. (Report No. 84-3). New York: College Entrance Examination Board.

Pearson, W. (1988). The role of colleges and universities in increasing Black representation in the scientific professions. In M. T. Nettles (ed.), *Toward Black Undergraduate Student Equality in American Higher Education*. Westport, CT: Greenwood Press.

Pelavin, S. H., Kane, M. B., and Levine, A. B. (in press). *Minority Participation in Higher Education*.

Peng, S. S. (1985). Enrollment pattern of Asian American students in postsecondary education. Paper presented at the Annual meeting of the American Educational Research Association, Chicago.

Peng, S. S., and Fetters, W. B. (1978). Variables involved in withdrawal during the first two years of college: Preliminary findings of the national longitudinal study of high school class of 1972. *American Educational Research Journal*, 15(3): 361–372.

Pennock-Román, M. (1986). Fairness in the use of tests for selective admissions of Hispanics. In M. A. Olivas (ed.). *Latino College Students*. New York: Teachers College Press.

Pennock-Román, M. (1988). *The Status of Research on the Scholastic Aptitude Test (SAT) and Hispanic Students in Postsecondary Education*. (ETS Research Report No. RR-88-36). Princeton, NJ: Educational Testing Service.

Pennock-Román, M. (in press). *Test Validity and Language Background: A Study of Hispanic American Students at Six Universities*. New York: College Entrance Examination Board.

Peterson, M. W., Blackburn, R. T., Gamson, Z. F., Arce, C. H., Davenport, R. W., and Mingle, J. R. (1978). *Black Students on White Campuses: The Impact of increased Black Enrollments*. Ann Arbor. MI: Institute for Social Research, University of Michigan.

Ramist, L. (1981). *College Student Attrition and Retention*. (College Board Report No. 81-1). New York: College Entrance Examination Board.

Ramist, L., and Arbeiter, S. (1986). *Profiles, College-bound Senior*. New York: College Entrance Examination Board.

Rendon, L. I., and Nora, A. (1987-1988, Fall/Winter). Hispanic students: Stopping the leaks in the pipeline. *Educational Record*, 79–85.

Richardson, R. C., Jr., and Bender, L. W. (1987). *Fostering Minority Access and Achievement in Higher Education: The Role of Urban Community Colleges and Universities*. San Francisco: Jossey-Bass.

Rootman, I. (1972, Summer). Voluntary withdrawal from a total adult socializing organization: a model. *Sociology of Education*, 45: 258–270.

Santos, R. (1986). Hispanic high school graduates: making choices. In M. A. Olivas (ed.), *Latino College Students*, New York: Teachers College Press.

Schmidt, D. K. (1972). Variables related to university student satisfaction. *Journal of College Student Personnel*, 233–238.

Sedlacek, W. E. (1987, November). Black students in White campuses: 20 years of research. *Journal of College Student Personnel*, 28(6): 484-495.

Sedlacek, W. E., and Webster, D. W. (1978, May). Admission and retention of minority students in large universities. *Journal of College Student Personnel*, 19(3): 242–248.

Smith, D. H. (1980). *Admission and Retention Problems of Black Students at Seven Predominantly White Universities*. Washington, DC: National Advisory Committee on Black Higher Education and Black Colleges and Universities.

Smith, D. G. (1988, September). The challenge of diversity: a question of involvement or alienation. (Unpublished.)

So, A. Y. (1984). The financing of college education by Hispanic parents. *Urban Education*, 19(2): 145–160.

Spady, W. (1971). Dropouts from higher education: Toward an empirical model. *Interchange*, 2: 38–62.

Stampen, J. O., and Fenske, R. H. (1988, Summer). The impact of financial aid on ethnic minorities. *Review of Higher Education*, 11 (4): 337–353.

Sue, G. W. (1977). Counseling the culturally different: a conceptual analysis. *Personnel and Guidance Journal*, 55(7): 422–425.

Sue, S., and Abe, J. (1988). *Predictors of Academic Achievement Among Asian American and White Students.* (College Board Report No. 88-11). New York: College Entrance Examination Board.

Suen, H. K. (1983, March). Alienation and attrition of Black college students on a predominantly White campus. *Journal of College Student Personnel,* 24(2): 117–121.

Suzuki, B. H. (1988, April). Asian Americans in higher education: impact of changing demographics and other social forces. Paper prepared for A National Symposium on the Changing Demographics of Higher Education. New York: The Ford Foundation.

Takeuchi, S. M. *Verbal Skills and the Asian American Student.* Boulder Co:, University of Colorado. (ED 097 395)

Terenzini, P., and Pascarella, E. (1977). Voluntary freshman attrition and patterns of social and academic integration in a university: a test of a conceptual model. *Research in Higher Education,* 6: 25–43.

Thomas, G. E. (1981a). *Black Students in Higher Education: Conditions and Experiences in the 1970s.* Westport, CT: Greenwood Press.

Thomas, G. E. (1981b). The effects of standardized achievement test performance and family status on Black-White college access. In G. E. Thomas (ed.), *Black Students in Higher Education: Conditions and Experiences in the 1970s.* Westport, CT: Greenwood Press.

Thomas, G. E., and Hill. S. (1987. November). Black institutions in U.S. higher education: Percent roles, contributions, future projections. *Journal of College Student Personnel,* 28(6): 496–503.

Thomas, G. E., Mingle, J. R., and McPartland, J. M. (1981). Recent trends in racial enrollment, segregation, and degree attainment in higher education. In G. E. Thomas (ed.), *Black Students in Higher Education: Conditions and Experiences in the 1970s.* Westport, CT: Greenwood Press.

Thomas, G. E., and McPartland, J. M. (1984). Have college desegregation policies threatened Black student enrollment in Black colleges? An empirical analysis. *Journal of Negro Education,* 53(4), 389–399.

Thomas, G. E., McPartland, J. M., and Gottfredson, D. C. (1981). Desegregation and Black students, higher education. In G. E. Thomas (ed.), *Black Students in Higher Education: Conditions and Experiences in the 1970s.* Westport, CT: Greenwood Press.

Thompson, D. C. (1978). Black college faculty and students: the nature of their interaction. In C. V. Willie and R. R. Edwards (eds.), *Black Colleges in America: Challenges Developments Survival.* New York: Teachers College Press.

Tijerina, K. H ., and Biemer, P. P. (1987/1988, Fall/Winter). The dance of Indian higher education: one step forward, two steps back. *Educational Record,* 68: 87–91.

Tinto, V. (1975). Dropouts from higher education: A theoretical synthesis of recent research. *Educational Research,* 45: 89–125.

Tinto, V. (1985). Rites of passage and the stages of institutional departure. Paper presented at the annual meeting of the American Educational Research Association, Chicago.

Tinto, V. (1987). *Leaving College: Rethinking the Causes and Cures of Student Attrition.* Chicago: University of Chicago Press.

Tracey. T. J., and Sedlacek, W. E. (1984). Noncognitive variables in predicting academic success by race. *Measurement and Evaluation in Guidance,* 16(4): 171–178.

Tracey, T. J., and Sedlacek, W. E. (1987, January). Prediction of college graduation using noncognitive variables by race. *Measurement and Evaluation in Counseling and Development,* pp. 177–184.

Tracey, T. J., and Sedlacek, W. E. (1985). The relationship of noncognitive variables to academic success: a longitudinal comparison by race. *Journal of College Student Personnel*, 26: 405–410.

Tracey, T. J., and Sedlacek, W. E., and Miars, R. D. (1983). Applying ridge regression to admissions data by race and sex. *College and University*, 58: 313-318.

Trent, W. (1985). Characteristics and patterns of Black two-year enrollment and degree attainment: a presentation to networks for the Ford Foundation Urban Community College Transfer and Opportunities Program, Chicago.

Tschechtelin, J. D. (1981). Black and White students in Maryland community colleges. In G. Thomas (ed.), *Black Students in Higher Education: Conditions and Experiences in the 1970s*. Westport, CT: Greenwood Press.

Tsuchida, N. (1983). A model for retention research on Asian/Pacific American students: A case study of the University of Minnesota. Paper presented at the annual conference of the National Association for Asian and Pacific American Education, site. (ED 234 115)

Verdugo, R. R. (1986). Educational stratification and Hispanics. In M. A. Olivas (ed.), *Latino College Students*. New York: Teachers College Press.

Warren, J. (1976). *Prediction of College Achievement Among Mexican American Students in California*. (College Board Research and Development Report). Princeton, NJ: Educational Testing Service.

Webster, D., Stockard, R. L., and Henson, J. W. (1981, Spring). Black student elite—Enrollment shifts in high achieving high socioeconomic status Black students from Black to White colleges during the 1970s. *College and University*, 283–291.

White, T. J., and Sedlacek. W. E. (1986). Noncognitive predictors. *Journal of College Admissions*, 3: 20–23.

Whittaker, D. (1986). Socio-psychological and background variables of Native Indian university students and persistence in a teacher preparation program. Paper presented at the American Education Research Association meeting, San Francisco. (ED 269 209)

Willie, C. V., and Edwards. R. R. (1978). *Black Colleges in America: Challenge, Development, Survival*. New York: Teachers College Press.

Wolfle, L. M. (1983). Postsecondary educational attainment among Whites and Blacks. Paper presented at the American Educational Research Association. Montreal. (ED 230 142)

Research on College Students:
Commonality, Difference, and Direction

Frances K. Stage

The study of college students is relatively old compared to such avenues of inquiry as environmental studies, computer science, or semiotics. Indeed, research on college student attrition has appeared in published form for at least sixty-five years (Minnesota University 1924). However, contemporary research on this familiar but elusive topic, compared with research conducted as recently as 1975, shows dramatic change. It is like comparing environmental studies with biology, computer science with logic, or semiotics with linguistics. Aside from a few authors who produced the landmark studies of the mid-seventies, such as Alexander Astin (1977), Kenneth Feldman and Theodore Newcomb (1973), research fifteen years ago, for the most part, seems limited in focus, direction, and method.

Commonality

The Tinto Model

For the last decade and a half, much of the college student research influenced by the Tinto model has focused on students from a sociological perspective. (I will not discuss the details of that model here. Both the Nora, Attinasi, and Matonak and the Cabrera, Stampen, and Hansen articles provide excellent summaries.) Most of that research has focused on students' overall success in college.

These years of research have resulted in a confidence about our knowledge that comes only with replication. Today few would question that students' commitment, academic integration, and social integration are crucial to their academic success. These constructs also served as common themes in the research reported here. All five studies employed measures of academic integration. Four demonstrated various operationalizations of social integration. Three incorporated some measure of students' commitment to a goal or to their institution.

Data Base Capabilities

The expansion of institutional and national data base capabilities has changed the administration of higher education. That expansion is also reflected in the work of the scholars published here. Two of the studies employed data collected for a national longitudinal data base. One of the studies used the transcript data, which today are typically encoded as part of an institution's tracking of students through college. Finally, two of the researchers employed their own resources to create data bases for analysis. While analysts of the largest data bases lost flexibility in the research questions they asked, they gained in generalizability of findings.

Quantitative Sophistication

In the past fifteen years, research on college students has moved from correlational and simple regression studies to sophisticated analyses for tracking longitudinal processes. Pascarella's and Terenzini's cutting-edge research through the late seventies explored a variety of techniques that set the standards for today's researchers.

Techniques employed included analysis of variance triangulated with interview data to track longitudinal development, path analysis, structural model analysis using LISREL, logistic regression, and path analysis with GEMINI.

Student Growth and Development

The mid-seventies also marked a stronger interest in psychologically based theories of college student development.

Difference

The Baxter Magolda study is particularly timely because of the current interest in assessing college outcomes. The recent interest in measuring value-added has been accompanied by a widespread dissatisfaction with our traditional measures of outcomes—standardized tests of verbal and quantitative skills. The article summarized research and the measurement of a college outcome that is more difficult to get at—students' cognitive development. Baxter Magolda's study explored gender differences and growth in epistemological development and compared, by gender and by developmental level, students' reflections on their first year in college.

The results raise an interesting question. How do reflections on environmental experiences differ for students who demonstrated positive changes in development in comparison with those who did not experience such growth? In general, men in this study described the classroom environment more positively than women. Men at all levels and both genders at higher levels of development reported more interaction with faculty. Did the men engage in more interaction, which then fostered their development, or did the men exhibit a higher level of development which was related to their becoming more involved with faculty?

A minor but interesting result of the study was that most of the students interviewed reported that they had never encountered discrepant information in their classes. Nevertheless, dissonance arising from discrepant information is thought to catalyze cognitive development (Piaget 1972). Such dissonance could be part of any college class. Could it be that, in our efforts to create an orderly, consistent, and "comfortable" classroom, we have removed some of the very challenges that feed intellectual growth?

The Nora, Attinasi, and Matonak study linked the post-positivistic and the naturalistic paradigms in persistence research while addressing a somewhat neglected population: academically underprepared community college students. The authors applied constructs that emerged from an ethnographic study of retention (Attinasi 1989) and tested their validity in the framework of the Tinto model. For the group of community college students studied, major elements of the Tinto model continued to be important. The authors found that on-campus pre-matriculation experiences and early college-going expectations were negatively related to persistence at the community college level. Perhaps students who had the "getting ready" experiences which typically occurred at four-year colleges transferred more quickly to those institutions, thus being recorded as dropouts from the community college

The Whiteley and Fenske study is an important marker in research on college-level mathematics and its societal effects as "gatekeeper" to both vocational and educational opportunity. The study brings together literatures on high school mathematics, women and minorities in mathematics, college mathematics, and changes in major to test a causal model of change from mathematics-based majors to nonmathematics-based majors over a four-year period.

One of the most positive aspects of this study was the technical detail with which it was crafted. The authors employed a standard institutional transcript data base to create interesting variables for the analysis. For example, they built the construct of college mathematics experience using measures of not only GPA in math, but also frustration ratio (failure rate), navigation (number of mathematics courses attempted but not successfully completed), and sequence (number of mathematics courses a student needed to take to meet the requirement of the major based on the first mathematics course taken). By separating students into meaningful subgroups according to levels of mathematics required by majors, the authors were able to tease out important differences.

Whiteley and Fenske successfully challenged the notion that high school mathematics exposure was a "critical filter" in the educational process. Students who had not taken highest-level mathematics in high school "recovered" by taking appropriate classes at the college level. College mathematics and academic experiences demonstrated significant effects over and above the effects of high school mathematics experiences on the final major.

The results suggest that, given the high failure rate of college students in mathematics courses through the calculus level, college math classes serve as a new "gatekeeper," again disproportionately screening out women and minorities. Clearly, a next step might be to explore models separately for men and women by minority and nonminority status. Gender and ethnicity had mixed effects on constructs representing college experiences across the three groups. Perhaps the "success pattern" would also differ for separate groups of students. By combining data for these three levels of majors, one might examine separate models for minority and majority males and females employing "with fourth-year high school mathematics" as a dummy variable.

Cabrera, Stampen, and Hansen made a significant methodological contribution to the study of persistence. They used the "High School and Beyond" data base, expanding the Tinto model by including an ability-to-pay measure, and then explored the moderating effects of that variable on persistence. In a twelve-step sequence, the authors tested a series of models for ability to explain persistence. Beginning with a simple model that included only ability-to-pay measures, they added student integration constructs, then added interaction terms created from those integration constructs, and finally factored in interaction terms created from ability to pay and integration constructs. Their analysis of the final model revealed several significant influences on persistence: significant others' influence, academic performance, social integration, socioeconomic status, interaction of faculty relationships with institutional prestige, and interaction of goal commitment with satisfaction of cost. Arguing persuasively against ordinary least-squares techniques or LISREL in such cases, they used logit analysis because of the skewed distribution of persistence as a variable.

This study prompts an interesting question. Can the moderating effects of ability to pay be further moderated by financial aid? In other words, does financial aid truly bring equity? If a student gets an aid package that fills the gap between his or her resources and the costs of college, does it erase the effects of socioeconomic status on persistence? If not, perhaps studies with variables like those included in the Nora, Attinasi, and Matonak study can begin to answer "why not?"

The Braxton, Brier, Herzog, and Pascarella study employed the Cooperative Institutional Research Program (CIRP) data base to identify important variables that influenced a student's decision to become an attorney. By examining separate causal models using path analysis, they explored the relative importance of the student's background characteristics, characteristics of the institution attended, and college experiences. They found gender differences in experience patterns leading to the ultimate outcome. Students' background characteristics exerted influence indirectly through college experience.

The authors' discussion of perspectives in the status attainment literature is particularly thought-provoking: The meritocratic perspective holds that performance and ability govern career attainment. An alternative perspective, conflict theory, maintains that educational systems perpetuate social inequity and that social origin is the principal determinant of individual status attainment. The researchers chose a unique perspective in selecting the sample for analysis. They included all students from the data base who enrolled in 1971 as first-time, full-time freshmen in a four-year institution, no matter what their career aspirations. If the authors had chosen to study only students who aspired to be attorneys, they would have been able to test the relative influences of background and achievement—in short, conflict theory. Because of the study's sample selection technique, it instead describes the broader process of becoming an attorney. Perhaps a new study will test the relative merits of conflict theory and meritocratic theory.

Direction

Like all good research, this set of papers suggests a number of new directions for subsequent study. Possible areas include: (1) further study of educational processes, (2) continued attention to methods of studying college students, (3) focus on behavior settings on the college campus, and (4) study of populations that are not mainstream.

Educational Processes

The articles that follow reflect the influence of Tinto's model. This model's power will no doubt continue to be seen in research that seeks to illuminate educational processes that both precede and follow the college years. The research presented in this issue of the *Review* provides new insights about the role of pre-college socialization in the educational process, the role of financial aid in the educational process, and the role of education in the status attainment process. As we learn more about the psychological aspects of student development, perhaps researchers will begin to use these nondemographic characteristics of students (developmental types or stages) as bases to describe varying patterns or processes of successful negotiation through educational systems (Stage 1989a).

Methods

The care in analysis demonstrated in the articles presented here will continue to be the standard for research on college students. I predict that as we model more and more complex educational systems, methodological sophistication and flexibility in analysis will come to be the norm rather than the exception. Increasingly, we will see a blend of qualitative and quantitative methods as we answer new questions and seek to triangulate research findings.

Behavior Settings

One of the most important behavior settings on campus, the college classroom, infrequently makes an appearance in our journals (Silverman 1987). The consistent importance of related variables—students' relationships with faculty and students' academic integration—and the studies presented here suggest the importance of paying attention to the individual college classroom. In the last two years, several writers (Conrad 1989; Menges 1988; Mentowski and Chickering 1987) have urged researchers to make our research more useful, including focus on studies of college classrooms.

Nonmainstream Populations

Still missing from most educational research is new data on nonmainstream college students. The Nora, Attinasi, and Matonak study, by focusing on academically underprepared community college students who are less likely to be white, middle-class, and upper-middle class, is the single example of such data in this set of studies. The data base employed in the Whiteley and Fenske study suggests the possibility of such a focus. However, simply employing gender, ethnicity, or first-generation status as variables in a regression equation does not enable us to identify "success patterns," which may differ for particular groups of students. Additionally, many campus populations may not be large enough nor easily identifiable within institutional data bases. Some of these students' experiences may have to be studied by employing qualitative research methods (Stage 1989b).

Conclusion

As a discussant for a research paper session at a recent meeting of the Association for the Study of Higher Education, Kenneth Feldman (1989) spoke about dissatisfaction and persistence. When the presenters and audience paused to catch the sage advice of a scholar who has provided much leadership in the study of college students, they were surprised. Instead of talking about persistence of college students, Feldman spoke of the persistence of the researchers whose papers he had read. The first had recently published a paper reporting counterintuitive results. His disquiet had resulted in the current paper with more finely honed variables and clearer results. The second researcher had refined an earlier ethnographic study with more interviews, varied settings, and the addition of a comparison group. The third researcher had written in an earlier paper of dissatisfaction with her model of student behavior. Her current research bore the fruits of that dissatisfaction, a more carefully selected sample, better conceptualization of variables, and results more useful to researchers and administrators.

In essence, Feldman's response had captured the roots of our research enterprise: dissatisfaction and persistence. As we inch along in understanding bits of the educational process, dissatisfaction is frequently our guide. The desire to know something that we are unable to discern from a review of others' work or from our own research creates dissatisfaction. Persistence in seeking answers to those questions guides the construction of the newest work.

A more general dissatisfaction with the content of our accumulating knowledge may also guide research of the future. As we conduct studies of access, achievement, and attainment, it becomes obvious that education is not the great equalizer. Our increasingly sophisticated models and techniques demonstrate more and more clearly that, lofty rhetoric to the contrary, family wealth and social status still exert a powerful influence on students' success in college.

Scholars who study college students continue to conduct analyses and build knowledge based on probabilities from the past. I encourage you to read the following articles as exemplars, not only of where our research has been, but where it might take us in the future. Instead of looking backward, perhaps we can now turn our attention toward the future. By taking a "critical theorist" perspective (Gage 1989), for example, we might ask research questions that can shape the society of the future to better serve those important stakeholders, college students. How might we moderate the powerfully negative effects of lack of privilege and low social status? Are there ways to "advantage" the disadvantaged? From this world view, we may find answers to questions that help us create rather than merely describe.

References

Astin, Alexander. *Four Critical Years: Effects of College on Beliefs, Attitude and Knowledge.* San Francisco: Jossey-Bass, 1977.

Attinasi, Louis C. "Getting In: Mexican Americans' Perceptions of University Attendance and the Implications for Freshman Year Persistence." *Journal of Higher Education 60* (May/June 1989): 247–77.

Conrad, Clifton F. "Meditations on the Ideology of Inquiry in Higher Education: Exposition, Critique, and Conjecture." *Review of Higher Education* 12 (Spring 1989): 199–220.

Feldman, Kenneth. "College Students: Choice and Success." Remarks for research paper session at the annual meeting of the Association for the Study of Higher Education, November 1989, Atlanta.

Feldman, Kenneth, and Theodore Newcomb. *The Impact of College on Students.* San Francisco: Jossey-Bass, 1973.

Gage, N. L. "The Paradigm Wars and Their Aftermath: A Historical Sketch of Research on Teaching Since 1989." *Educational Researcher* 18 (October 1989): 4–10.

Menges, Robert J. "Research on Teaching and Learning: The Relevant and the Redundant." *Review of Higher Education* 11 (Spring 1988): 259–68.

Mentowski, Marcia, and Arthur W. Chickering. "Linking Educators and Researchers in Setting a Research Agenda for Undergraduate Education." *Review of Higher Education* 11 (Winter 1987): 137–60.

Minnesota University. "Report of the Survey Commission VI: Student Mortality." *Bulletin of the University of Minnesota* 4 (1924): 27.

Piaget, Jean. "Intellectual Evolution from Adolescence to Adulthood." *Human Development* 15 (1972): 1–15.

Silverman, Robert J. "How We Know What We Know: A Study of Higher Education Journal Articles." *Review of Higher Education* 11 (Autumn 1987): 39–59.

Stage, Frances K. "Motivation, Academic and Social Integration, and the Early Dropout." *American Educational Research Journal* 26 (Winter 1989a): 385–402.

_____. "College Outcomes and Student Development: Filling the Gaps." *Review of Higher Education* 12 (Spring 1989b): 293–304.

Tinto, Vincent. "Dropout from Higher Education: A Theoretical Synthesis of Recent Research." *Review of Educational Research* 45 (Winter 1975): 89–125.

An Anthropological Analysis of Student Participation in College

WILLIAM G. TIERNEY

The fundamental factor that keeps Indians and non-Indians from communicating is that they are speaking about two entirely different perceptions of the world.

Vine Deloria, Jr., *The Metaphysics of Modern Existence*

In this article I take issue with Tinto's widely accepted theoretical model that views college participation as if it were a "rite of passage" where academic and social integration is essential for student persistence. First, I argue that Tinto has misinterpreted the anthropological notions of ritual, and in doing so he has created a theoretical construct with practical implications that hold potentially harmful consequences for racial and ethnic minorities. I critique the epistemological argument Tinto has articulated—that of social integration—from a cultural perspective informed by critical theory [11, 12, 13, 14, 36]. That is, I take a social constructionist view of reality and I operate from the perspective that the purpose of our theoretical models is not merely to describe the world, but to change it.

I then highlight the practical or "real world" implications of a social integrationist stance by deconstructing the discourse of two college administrators who were part of a two-year investigation pertaining to the college-going patterns of American Indian college students [36]. The administrators describe how they perceived Native American students' attendance at their institutions. The assumption here is that the ideas and discourse that speakers utilize influence the actions that occur on their campuses. And in large part, those actions and policies have been ineffectual in stemming the tide of minority student departure in general, and Native American leave-taking in particular. I conclude by suggesting that rather than think about student participation from a social integrationist perspective, an alternative model is to conceive of universities as multicultural entities where difference is highlighted and celebrated. Accordingly, if we want our colleges and universities to be multicultural, we need theoretical models different from those of the social integrationists, which in turn will call for different assumptions about reality and what must be done to engage college students.

A caveat is in order. This is an essay in the root sense of the word—a trial of some ideas. By taking issue with a theorist's notions or deconstructing the words of an individual one runs the risk of painting heroes and villains, of encasing one theory as morally wrong and another as politically correct. The argument here, however, is neither to canonize one discourse over another nor to accentuate the foibles of any administrator. Rather, the article seeks to provoke dialogue by taking issue with some of the most commonly held perceptions we currently have about college life, about students, and about how we think about cultural difference in order to develop more culturally responsive ways to engage minority students.

Perspectives on College Participation: Theory

Tinto's model and rituals of integration. Over the last twenty years a variety of researchers have sought to understand why some students leave college and others remain [1, 4, 28]. Indeed, one could argue that student departure has been the central focus of higher education research. In general, much of this research has tried to delineate different causal variables that might plausibly lead to the retention of students. The search for an understanding about why students leave college is not merely of theoretical interest; if a model may be built that explains student departure, then it may be possible for colleges to retain students. The successful retention of students offers at least three benefits: the student will be able to reap the rewards that a college degree affords, the college or university will be able to maintain the income that derives from the student's attendance, and society will be able to utilize the skills of students in becoming more productive. Clearly, it is to everyone's benefit to come to terms with why students leave college.

Such a concern is particularly germane in a discussion about minority student achievement. Researchers have long documented the underrepresentation of racial and ethnic minorities in academe. For the purpose of this article, we may add that American Indian involvement in postsecondary institutions is of particular concern. Although researchers differ about the precise percentages of Native Americans who attend college, everyone is in agreement about gross averages, and those averages highlight problems throughout the academic pipeline. If one hundred students are in ninth grade, about sixty of them will graduate from high school, and about twenty will enter academe. Of those twenty students, only about three will eventually receive a four-year degree [36].

Researchers have been able to discover that certain characteristics in a student's background help or deflect one's persistence in college. For example, we have learned that if a student's parents have gone to college, the student is more likely to attend and to graduate from college than a student whose parents did not go to a postsecondary institution. We know that an individual whose brothers or sisters have attended college is more likely to persist in college than the young man or woman whose siblings have not participated in college. We know that someone who has had an academic track in high school is more likely to attend a four-year college than someone who has pursued a vocational track.

We also have learned a great deal about gross characteristics that pertain to race and class. As noted, an individual who is white is more likely to go to college than someone who is African American or Native American. Someone whose parents earn over $40,000 a year is more likely to attend a four-year institution than someone whose parents are on welfare. Although each of these pieces of information may have helped researchers in predicting the success of students, such individualistic characteristics have stymied researchers in their search for a general causal model of student participation. In turn, minority student participation in academe has remained problematic.

Vincent Tinto has developed a theoretical model that takes into account the individualistic pieces of information such as those reported above, but he has done so in a manner that is comprehensive rather than particularistic [38, 39, 40]. That is, Tinto has sought to explain why students leave college by calling upon a framework that incorporates factors such as family income or student background. He has utilized such information not as ends in themselves but to develop a general theory of student participation, as opposed to an individualistic analysis of why one or another student is likely to attend and eventually graduate.

In doing so, Tinto has worked in the tradition of other researchers, such as Spady [28, 29], by asking two central questions: (1) what are those bonding mechanisms that integrate students into the life of the institution, and (2) how might postsecondary institutions and students be theoretically conceived? A significant number of researchers have accepted Tinto's basic formula and have returned to testing specific variables to see whether the model holds up under scrutiny when different characteristics are analyzed. As Stage has noted, "Today few would question that students' commitment, academic integration, and social integration are crucial to their academic success" [32, p. 250].

Following Spady, Tinto developed his model by calling upon the work of two prominent social theorists of the early twentieth century—Emile Durkheim and Arnold Van Gennep. Durkheim, considered by many to be the father of modern sociology, posited that the degree to which an individual was integrated into the fabric of societal institutions lessened the likelihood that someone experienced anomie. In turn, the less one experienced anomie, the less likely it was that the individual would commit suicide. Thus, by manipulating a variety of characteristics drawn from data about European countries, Durkheim showed how married Italian Catholics in tightly knit families in small towns, for example, were less likely to commit suicide than unmarried urban Protestant Englishmen [10].

Van Gennep was an anthropologist who studied tribal societies; in particular he investigated "rites de passage" [42]. Rites of passage in a particular culture were rituals designed to move individuals from one developmental stage to another. These rituals took place throughout an individual's life. The most obvious rites of passage in tribal societies occurred for young men and women when they were to assume the mantle of adulthood. Although the actual rituals differed dramatically from culture to culture both in act and duration, Van Gennep argued that all cultures had rituals that functioned in similar fashion. In effect, as a functionalist, Van Gennep believed that rituals were a crucial mechanism necessary to every tribal society. Without such rituals, the developmental patterns necessary for society's maintenance would be destroyed, and the culture would not survive.

Tinto has suggested that we ought to think of colleges in light of Durkheim's and Van Gennep's work. Following Durkheim, Tinto argues that to the degree participants are integrated into the institution's fabric, the greater likelihood exists that the individual will not develop a sense of anomie and will not commit "suicide" by leaving the institution. In effect, a college is an institution designed as a rite of passage that functions in much the same manner as ritualized institutions in other societies. Postsecondary institutions serve as functional vehicles for incorporating the young into society by way of their integration into the college or university.

Tinto is the first to acknowledge that his model is not perfect. Adult students, for example, may not necessarily fit the schema that he has outlined. Tinto also has been most vocal about redirecting how researchers think of college departure so that we no longer conceive of student leave-taking by using a pejorative term such as "dropping out," because the student may well return at another point in time. Nevertheless, Tinto's model also holds up well when one thinks of different populations. Traditionally aged students are more likely to graduate than nontraditionally aged populations. A residential institution that has an active social life is more likely to have a higher retention rate than urban commuter institutions. Full-time students have a greater likelihood of graduating from a four-year institution than do part-time students. On one level each of these facts gives credence to Tinto's formula: to the extent that institutions function as societal rites of passage and to the degree that individuals are bonded and integrated into the life of the institution, the more likely it is that students will persist and graduate.

Presently, most work has been in a similar vein; as noted, researchers have utilized different variables to test whether Tinto's model holds [7, 20]. Unfortunately, those individuals who have undertaken such studies implicitly have agreed with the epistemological foundations from which Tinto has worked. To his considerable credit, Tinto has developed a conceptual model that calls for investigation and analysis at the foundational level rather than simply at the causal level. Instead of merely accepting the scaffolding upon which he has built his theory, researchers need to interrogate the assumptions of that scaffolding. I turn now to one such possible interpretation and interrogation. A discussion of the foundations of social integration will highlight some essential dilemmas when considered from an anthropological perspective.

An anthropological analysis of Tinto's model. As I discuss Tinto's model, it is helpful to keep in mind racial and ethnic minorities such as American Indians who attend mainstream institutions. Social integrationists assert that all individuals—regardless of race, class or gender—must undergo a "rite of passage" in order to achieve full development in society. The assumption is that a uniform set of values and attitudes remain in an institution and that it is the individual's task to adapt to the system. The problems with such a view, however, are fourfold. Two problems pertain to (a) a misinterpretation of the cultural definition of ritual, and two problems concern (b) an overreliance on an integrative framework.

Culture and rituals. Consider the differences between Van Gennep's and Tinto's use of the term "ritual." When Van Gennep wrote about rites of passage, he spoke of rituals within a specific culture. The Maori of New Zealand or the Arunta of Australia had rituals that initiated the young into society. The Ndembu of Africa had puberty rites for girls and rituals of manhood for boys [41]. The same point, however, cannot be made of Tinto's rituals that occur in American colleges and universities. An American Indian who sets foot on a mainstream campus undergoes a disruptive cultural experience not because college is a rite of passage, but because the institution is culturally distinct from the Indian youth's own culture. When Van Gennep developed his functionalist theory, he never anticipated that it would be used to explain one culture's ritual to initiate a member of another culture.

The first problem, then, with social integrationist theory is that it borrows an anthropological term—ritual—yet extracts the term from its cultural foundations. One cannot speak of ritual without first considering the cultural contexts in which that ritual is embedded. In the case of American higher education, we find that colleges and universities reflect the culture of the dominant society. In America, that dominant culture is white.

To be sure, organizations such as traditionally black institutions or tribally controlled colleges exist in the United States, but of necessity these institutions also incorporate the dominant mores of American society simply by having to meet accreditation requirements, utilizing faculty who come from mainstream institutions, and the like [36]. Institutions such as tribal colleges are under perhaps the greatest pressure to conform, given the serious financial constraints in which they must operate; these institutions garner most of their income from a federal law which stipulates that they meet specified standards [21, 22]. To assume that colleges and universities do not reflect the culture of mainstream society is to overlook the crucial importance of the sociocultural contexts surrounding postsecondary organizations. Simply stated, higher education's institutions have histories and current contexts that help determine their ideology and culture. Up until very recently in American higher education, colleges and universities were designed to educate a clientele that was overwhelmingly composed of white males who came from the middle and upper classes.

Although critics may certainly argue with a cultural analysis of postsecondary institutions, one is hard pressed to do so while at the same time utilizing as a central concept the cultural idea of a rite of passage. In short, if social integrationists are to employ an anthropological term, such as a ritual, then of necessity they must take into account the cultures in which those rituals exist. If one does so with regard to Tinto's model, one finds that he has developed an analytic tool that is dysfunctional: individuals from one culture, such as Apache, are to undergo a ritual in another culture, such as Anglo.

A second conceptual problem with the utilization of a ritual in academe pertains to the assumption of one's leave-taking from such a ritual. In traditional cultures, rites of passage do not have notions such as "departure," "failure," or "dropout." Choice does not exist about whether to undergo the ritual; one simply partakes of it. As noted, Tinto has accurately pointed out that the use of a term such as "dropout" has negative connotations, and he has argued that one should instead use the term "departure," because it is value-neutral. He has assumed, however, that departure is normal. "It seems unlikely that we will be able to greatly reduce dropouts," he has noted [39, p. 695]. Along a similar line, he added:

> There is much to be said for a system of education that serves to distinguish between those with the competence or interest, motivation, and drive to finish given courses of study, and those who, for a variety of reasons, do not or simply will not seek to complete their programs [39, p. 695].

Although a term such as "departure" may well appear to be value-neutral to those who use the term, what social integrationists overlook is that concepts such as "departure" "dropout" or "failure" are all cultural constructs. Tinto assumes that for one reason or another, some students will choose not to participate in a rite of passage and other students will not complete the ritual. Yet when one considers rituals in traditional cultures, we find that an initiate neither chooses to participate nor to leave the ritual. The anthropologists George and Louise Spindler, are helpful in explaining how the Arunta of Australia conceive of initiation rituals:

Despite the onerous nature of the initiation, . . . all of the young initiates survive the ordeal and are dedicated to seeing that the next class of initiates gets the same treatment. All of the initiates succeed, none fail. . . . To fail would mean at least that one could not be an Arunta, and usually this must mean death as well, but not death at the hands of another, but social death. . . . The whole operation of the initiation school is managed to produce success. To fail to initiate the young successfully is unthinkable. The continuity of culture would be broken and the society would disintegrate. There are no dropouts [30, p. 10].

Nor are there "departers." To be sure, someone may die in a "rite of passage," but the essential point here is that in traditional societies individuals do not have the option to leave their group, as students do who attend a college or university. What Tinto again has failed to do is to investigate the cultural context of the anthropological term "ritual" and, in turn, how the language of student participation is a cultural construction. He has assumed that student departure is a universal concept rather than a cultural category developed by the society that utilizes the ritual. Dropouts exist in modern American schools and colleges; the term is absent from Arunta vocabulary as well as any number of other tribal societies. The language used to think and talk about students is a cultural construct. Failure exists in postsecondary institutions before students are admitted, enrolled, or take classes. Failure, or leave-taking, or departure, does not come in the door when students enter. Human discourse and action are cultural categories; to come to terms with these categories, one must investigate the categories themselves rather than assume that actions such as leaving college are natural and universal.

Individuals and integration. The third and fourth anthropological problems with Tinto's model pertain to the Durkheimian reliance on individuals and integration. Tinto has conceptualized college-going at the individualist level rather than a collective one. From a social integrationist perspective individuals attend college, become integrated or not, graduate or depart. Conformity is the norm, and it is the responsibility of the individual. Absent from this analysis is any discussion about the cultural formations of groups. Social integrationists assume that culture exists at a meta level—all cultures are similar and the institution merely reflects the culture of society. Indeed, Tinto's book *Leaving College* emphasizes the "roots of individual departure" and a "theory of individual departure." From an anthropological standpoint, to emphasize "individual" at the expense of the "group" or the "culture" is backwards. Indeed, Native American authors such as Badwound [3], Benally [5], McNeley [19], Padilla* and Pavel [24] and Wright and Tierney* [44] have effectively argued that the importance of tribal culture is crucial when thinking about the roots of student departure. Olneck has argued how critical this issue is with regard to minorities in general: "[We] must recognize the identities and claims of groups *as groups* and must facilitate, or at least symbolically represent and legitimate, collective identity" [23, p. 148]. Again, what is particularly odd with regard to Tinto's analysis is that he utilizes anthropological terms in an individualist manner.

Furthermore, Tinto never takes into account, or at least never explains to readers, that he is a "native" studying "native rituals." As a faculty member at a mainstream university, he describes processes in which he partakes. The point is not that a native observer's analysis is useless. To the contrary. Native perceptions of the world are essential to understanding that world, but one must necessarily accept that those understandings are provisional, subjective, and never complete. As Edmund Leach has observed, "to understand the word ritual we must take note of the user's background and prejudices" [17, p. 521]. Indeed, in our field of study Attinasi similarly has commented, "What are needed are naturalistic, descriptive studies guided by research perspectives that emphasize the insider's point of view" [2, p. 250].

The need to understand the user's "background and prejudices" reflects the anthropological belief that reality is socially constructed. Individuals and groups do not perceive reality in the same fashion. The researcher must come to terms not only with his or her own preconceived notions of reality and the phenomena under study but also with those of the individuals who partake in the ritual. Yet Tinto works from a positivist framework where law-like generalizations are possible and the implicit assumptions and beliefs of both the researcher and the researched are irrelevant. Again, one may reject a cultural model that assumes reality is socially constructed, but that cannot be done while at the same time one employs analytical tools that derive from those same cultural models.

Thus, an anthropological analysis of Tinto's model has two overarching concerns. On the one hand, rituals of transition have never been conceptualized as movements from one culture to another. Van Gennep never assumed that a Sioux youth underwent an initiation ritual in Navajo society. Yet Tinto's model assumes that same Sioux youth will undergo a rite of passage in Anglo society. On the other hand, a model of integration that never questions who is to be integrated and how it is to be done assumes an individualist stance of human nature and rejects differences based on categories such as class, race, and gender.

Such concerns bring into question Tinto's overall model; however, this discourse of integration is of particular importance when we consider college participation of underrepresented racial and ethnic groups. As Olneck has observed, the language of integration is "the voice of white middle-class education professionals speaking about 'problem' groups and about the solutions to the problems posed by diversity" [23, p. 163]. Although Tinto and other like-minded researchers should be applauded for their attempt to shift the burden of blame for dropouts away from the victims, essentially, models of integration have the effect of merely inserting minorities into a dominant cultural frame of reference that is transmitted within dominant cultural forms, leaving invisible cultural hierarchies intact [8].

I now turn to an example of how such implicit assumptions get played out at mainstream universities. The data derive from a two-year investigation of Native Americans on college campuses [36]. I undertook case studies at ten campuses and conducted slightly over two hundred interviews. The point of the following section is to analyze the discourse of two individuals in order to underscore how social integrationist notions get enacted.

Perspectives on College Participation: Practice

Defining the problem. At one university, the president commented on the problems Native Americans have in college by pointing out: "They have a terrible problem with acculturation. They grow up without competition, and when they come here to a university whose ethic is achievement and competition, it's tough." At a second institution a top administrator added, "The major problem is that they have a foot in each culture that draws them back to their roots. They are drawn back to their own culture, and it's a difficult transition to make. It's a real problem that's not easy for us to solve."

I offer these comments for two reasons. First, they are commonplace. I consistently heard similar kinds of observations from other individuals. Second, these comments logically accompany the social integrationist position. Following the recent deconstructionist work of Rhoades [25], Rhoades and Slaughter [26], Slaughter [27], and the content analysis of Bensimon [6], Goffman [15], Tannen [33] and Tierney [34], I will attempt here to deconstruct what these individuals have said by breaking apart their sentence structure so that we might contextualize more fully what the comments suggest. How one defines deconstructionism is notoriously contested; for the purposes of this analysis I call upon the work of Jonathan Culler. Culler notes, "Deconstruction emphasizes that discourse, meaning, and reading are historical through and through, produced in processes of contextualization, decontextualization, and recontextualization" [9, p. 129]. Essentially, following Derrida, Culler argues that one comes to "meaning" by interpreting the context in which statements are said, deconstructing those contexts and statements, and then "reconstructing" them. In doing so, a deconstructionist assumes that (1) final interpretation is never achieved, and (2) that reinterpretation is always necessary. Accordingly, I offer one possible interpretation of the speakers' comments.

The first speaker noted:

They have a terrible problem with acculturation.

The statement defined how the speaker perceived the situation. The group that has the "problem" are American Indians. The problem is acculturation, and it is not minor; it is a major problem which the speaker defined as "terrible."

The speaker made this point when asked a "grand tour" open-ended interview question [31], "Tell me about Native American participation on this campus." The speaker's comment presumably points out knowledge he had with regard to Native American recruitment and retention to postsecondary education in general, and to his campus in particular. Over ninety percent of those American Indian students who enter his university will not receive a degree from the institution. The nature of the problem, then, is that Native Americans need to become acculturated to the university in order to persist. Acculturation to the university presumably implies that the Indian student must learn the ways of the white world.

> They grow up without competition, and when they come here to a university whose ethic is achievement and competition, it's tough.

The speaker followed his first comment with a consistent line of reasoning. He offered a comparison; Native Americans do not compete, and the university is founded on competition. Indeed, a core "ethic" of the university appears to be "competition."

"Achievement" is in some way related to "competition." That is, the assumption of the speaker was that to achieve, one must necessarily compete. What one achieves, presumably, is a college degree. Again, drawing upon general and specific data, the speaker knew that Native Americans are not successful; they do not "achieve." The speaker also empathized with American Indians. He recognized the problems they face and pointed out that "it's tough." The speaker, then, assumed that he understood the problems the students face and that these problems are difficult.

The second speaker added:

> The major problem is that they have a foot in each culture that draws them back to their roots.

This speaker also pointed out that those who have the "problem" are Native Americans, and he believed the same problem existed as the first speaker pointed out. American Indians do not have both feet firmly planted in the university's soil. Their "roots" are in another culture. The problem, then, is that Native Americans have extensive roots, and until they cut those roots, they will not be successful. The speaker also thought that Indian students are involved in two cultures—an Indian culture and an Anglo culture, as experienced at the institution.

> They are drawn back to their own culture and it's a difficult transition to make.

The individual reiterated his first comment. The Indian culture has a serious pull; it "draws" students "back" rather than pushes them forward. To move from one's own culture to a mainstream university was seen as a "transition," and again, it is a "difficult" or terrible transition to make. To attend a mainstream institution requires that an individual move from one world to another—move from the Native American culture to the Anglo culture. Presumably, such movement propels students forward.

> It's a real problem that's not easy for us to solve.

The speaker concluded by objectifying American Indian students—they have become the problem—and the realization that the problem is a difficult one. The problem is also "real"; unlike some problems that mask other concerns, the speaker implied that he has been able to define the problem precisely. However, the problem is like a puzzle; the solution will not be easy.

The individuals who will solve the problem were identified as "us." Insofar as the speaker was a senior white male administrator at a mainstream university we can reasonably presume that the problem's solution lies in the hands of similar white male administrators. At a minimum, the answers will be found by "us"—university administrators—and not "them"—American Indian students.

Analyzing the discourse. The comments of both speakers reinforce the theoretical argument of the social integrationists. As Tinto has pointed out, college is a transition where a student leaves his or her past community. He stated:

College students are, after all, moving from one community or set of communities, most typically those of the family and local high school, to another, that of the college. Like other persons in the wider society, they too must separate themselves, to some degree, from past associations in order to make the transition to eventual incorporation in the life of the college [38 p. 94].

Thus, social integrationists have hypothesized that success in college is contingent upon an individual's ability to become academically and socially integrated into the life of the institution, a process that in part is predicated on the individual's ability to separate from previous communities. To utilize Tinto's Durkheimian formulation, the implicit assumption is that Native Americans will need to undergo a cultural suicide of sorts to avoid an intellectual suicide.

Because discourse is never fixed and determined, a number of alternative possibilities exists with regard to how one might see minority participation in academe. For example, rather than defining Native Americans as the ones who have the "problem," we might think of the institutions as having the "problem." Indeed, the "problem" might be defined not as a group's lack of "acculturation" but as an institution's inability to operate in a multicultural world. From a Native American perspective, a "problem" might be defined as the university's "ethic of achievement and competition" as opposed to an ethic of cooperation and willingness to work together.

Instead of implying that being "drawn back" to one's own culture is a shortcoming, one might accentuate that ripping one away from his or her native culture is detrimental and harmful. Rather than think of college as an abrupt transition from one world to another, we might try to conceptualize college life as reinforcing and incorporating what one has learned from one's extended family.

And, of course, regardless of how one defines a problem, it is possible to think of the "solution" lying not in the hands of the powerful but in the hands of those who are most centrally involved in the issue. Rather than objectify Native Americans as the problem, one might point out that institutional racism and the mindset of the powerful is the "real problem."

Discussion

My point in this article has been to highlight the conceptual inadequacy of current theories of student participation. I have concentrated on Tinto's research primarily because his work is the most widely accepted and sophisticated analysis we currently have. And as the statements from the college officials highlight, the theoretical formulations of social integrationists do get enacted in the words and actions of college administrators. My assumption here is that theory does inform practice and that many of the recent attempts by college officials pertaining to minority recruitment and retention have utilized researchers' findings in order to solve the "problem." However, the solutions have been inadequate precisely because we are asking the wrong questions.

From the argument advanced in this article, the challenge for researchers is twofold. First, we need to utilize different theoretical models rather than those that insist upon an integrative framework that assume an individualist stance. In effect, Tinto's use of culture as a framework has moved us in the right direction, but he has not gone far enough. Critical and feminist theories are but two examples of the kinds of models we might find useful as we reconceptualize student participation in academe. The recent work of Holland and Eisenhart [16] and others [35, 36, 43] are examples of how such theories may be usefully employed to analyze academe.

The second challenge relates to how decision makers might be able to utilize these more recent theoretical developments. The changes required are not just theoretical; as the examples from the administrators demonstrate, theoretical reconceptualizations also need to influence how individuals act. As McLaughlin has argued, "Many times, critical theorists' calls for transformative leadership and transformative intellectualism amount to obfuscating rhetoric which, in over-intellectualizing what is wrong with mainstream school practices without identifying what actually teachers and school administrators can do, simply add to the problem" [18]. Thus, we need to go further by not only delineating the scaffolding for critical or feminist theories and the like, but also by suggesting how we might employ such theoretical orientations in the daily operations of our institutions. We need to consider how institutionally sponsored interventions function within the variety of different contexts that exist for different issues, such as minority student retention.

I am arguing, then, for a radical reorientation of how we conceptualize and, hence, act in the organizational worlds of academe. The task of conceiving different theoretical horizons will enable us not only to offer alternative strategies for developing multicultural environments, but such horizons also will enable us to reconfigure the social conditions of power that give voice to some and silence others. In doing so, we will be moving away from a model of social integration and assimilation and toward a framework of emancipation and empowerment.

Note

*Not Native American.

References

1. Astin, A. *Four Critical Years: Effects of College on Beliefs, Altitudes, and Knowledge.* San Francisco: Jossey-Bass, 1977.

2. Attinasi, L. C., Jr. "Getting In: Mexican Americans' Perceptions of University Attendance and the Implications for Freshman Year Persistence." *Journal of Higher Education,* 60 (May/June 1989), 247–77.

3. Badwound, E. *Leadership and American Indian Values: The Tribal College Dilemma.* Ph.D. dissertation, The Pennsylvania State University, University Park, 1990.

4. Bean, J. P., and B. S. Metzner. "A Conceptual Model of Nontraditional Student Attrition." Paper presented at the annual meeting of the Association for the Study of Higher Education, Chicago, March 1985.

5. Benally, H. "Dine Philosophy of Learning." *Journal of Navajo Education,* 6 (1988), 10–13.

6. Bensimon, E. M. "A Feminist Reinterpretation of Presidents' Definitions of Leadership." *Peabody Journal of Education,* 66 (1989), 143–56.

7. Cabrera, A. F., O. J. Stampen, and W. L. Hansen. "Explaining the Effects of Ability to Pay on Persistence in College." *Review of Higher Education,* 13 (1990), 303–36.

8. Colon, A. "Race Relations on Campus: An Administrative Perspective. *The Racial Crisis in American Higher Education,* edited by P. G. Altbach and K. Lomotey. Albany, N.Y.: State University of New York Press, 1991.

9. Culler, J. *On Deconstruction: Theory and Criticism after Structuralism.* Ithaca, N.Y.: Cornell University Press, 1982.

10. Durkheim, E. *Suicide.* Trans. J. A. Spaulding and G. Simpson, Glencoe, N.J.: The Free Press, 1951.

11. Fay, B. *Critical Social Science.* Ithaca, N.Y.: Cornell University Press, 1987.

12. Foster, W. "The Administrator as a Transformative Intellectual." *Peabody Journal of Education,* 66 (1989), 5–18.

13. Giroux, H. "Border Pedagogy in the Age of Postmodernism." *Journal of Education,* 170 (1988), 162–81.

14. _____. "The Politics of Postmodernism." *Journal of Urban and Cultural Studies,* 1 (1990), 5–38.

15. Goffman, E. *Frame Analysis.* New York: Harper and Row, 1974.

16. Holland D. C., and M. A. Eisenhart. *Educated in Romance: Women, Achievement, and College Culture*. Chicago, Ill.: The University of Chicago Press, 1990.

17. Leach. E. *International Encyclopedia of the Social Sciences* (vols. 13–14). New York: Macmillan, 1968.

18. McLaughlin, D. "Power and the Politics of Knowledge: Transformative Leadership and Curriculum Development for Minority Language Learners." *Peabody Journal of Education*, 66 (1989), 41–60.

19. McNeley, J. P. "A Navajo Curriculum in the National Context." *Journal of Navajo Life* (1988), 125–36.

20. Nora, A., L. C. Attinasi, Jr., and A. Matonak. "Testing Qualitative Indicators of Precollege Factors in Tinto's Attrition Model: A Community College Student Population." *Review of Higher Education*, 13 (1990), 337–55.

21. Olivas, M. A. "Indian, Chicano, and Puerto Rican Colleges: Status and Issues." *Bilingual Review*, 9 (1982) 36–58.

22. _____. "The Tribally Controlled Community College Assistance Act of 1978: The Failure of Federal Indian Higher Education Policy." *American Indian Law Review*, 9 (1983), 219–51.

23. Olneck, M. R. "The Recurring Dream: Symbolism and Ideology in Intercultural and Multicultural Education." *American Journal of Education*, 98 (1990), 147–74.

24. Padilla, R. V., and M. Pavel. "The Role of Student Advising in Academic Integration." Paper presented at the annual meeting of the American Educational Research Association, San Francisco, March 1989.

25. Rhoades, G. "Calling on the Past: The Quest for the Collegiate Model." *Journal of Higher Education*, 61 (September/October 1990), 512–34.

26. Rhoades, G., and S. Slaughter. "The Public Interest and Professional Labor: Research Universities." In *Culture and Ideology in Higher Education: Advancing a Critical Agenda*, edited by W. G. Tierney, pp. 187–212. New York: Praeger, 1991.

27. Slaughter, S. "The 'Official' Ideology of Higher Education: Ironies and Inconsistencies." In *Culture and Ideology in Higher Education: Advancing a Critical Agenda*, edited by W. G. Tierney, pp. 59–86. New York: Praeger, 1991.

28. Spady, W. "Dropouts from Higher Education: An Interdisciplinary Review and Synthesis." *Interchange*, 1 (1970), 64–85.

29. _____. "Dropouts from Higher Education: Toward an Empirical Model. *Interchange*, 2 (1971), 38–62.

30. Spindler, G., and L. Spindler. "There Are No Dropouts among the Arunta and Hutterites." In *What Do Anthropologists Have to Say about Dropouts?*, edited by H. T. Trueba, G. Spindler, and L. Spindler, pp. 7–15. New York: The Falmer Press, 1989.

31. Spradley, J. P. *The Ethnographic Interview*. New York: Holt, Rinehart, and Winston, 1979.

32. Stage, F. K. "Research on College Students: Commonality, Difference and Direction." *Review of Higher Education*, 13 (1990), 249–58.

33. Tannen, D. *You Just Don't Understand*. New York: Morrow and Co., 1990.

34. Tierney, W. G. "Governance by Conversation: An Essay on the Structure, Function, and Communicative Codes of a Faculty Senate." *Human Organization*, 42 (1983), 172–77.

35. _____. *Curricular Landscapes, Democratic Vistas: Transformative Leadership in Higher Education*. New York: Praeger, 1989.

36. _____. *Official Encouragement, Institutional Discouragement: Minorities in Academe—The Native American Experience*. Norwood, N.J.: Ablex, 1992.

37. _____. "The College Experience of Native Americans: A Critical Analysis." In *Beyond Silenced Voices: Class, Race and Gender in United States Schools*, edited by L. Weis and M. Fine. Ithaca, N.Y.: SUNY Press, in press.

38. Tinto, V. "Dropout from Higher Education: A Theoretical Synthesis of Recent Research." *Review of Educational Research*, 45 (1975), 89–125.

39. _____. "Limits of Theory and Practice in Student Attrition." *Journal of Higher Education*, 53 (November/December 1982), 687–700.

40. _____ . *Leaving College: Rethinking the Causes and Cures of Student Attrition*. Chicago: The University of Chicago Press, 1987.

41. Turner, V. *The Ritual Process: Structure and Anti-Structure*. Ithaca, N.Y.: Cornell University Press, 1977.

42. Van Gennep, A. *The Rites of Passage*. Trans. M. Vizedon and G. Caffee, Chicago: University of Chicago Press, 1960.

43. Weis, L. *Between Two Worlds*. Boston: Routledge and Kegan Paul, 1985.

44. Wright, B., and W. G. Tierney. "American Indians in Higher Education: A History of Cultural Conflict." *Change*, 23 (March/April 1991), 11–18.